First Canadian Edition

Human Development

A Life-Span View

First Canadian Edition

Human Development

A Life-Span View

Robert V. Kail
Purdue University

John C. Cavanaugh
University of West Florida

Christine A. Ateah
University of Manitoba

THOMSON

NELSON

Australia   Canada   Mexico   Singapore   Spain   United Kingdom   United States

THOMSON

NELSON

**Human Development:
A Life-Span View
First Canadian Edition**

by Robert V. Kail, John C. Cavanaugh,
Christine A. Ateah

**Associate Vice-President,
Editorial Director:**
Evelyn Veitch

Publisher:
Joanna Cotton

Executive Marketing Manager:
Don Thompson

Developmental Editor:
Alwynn Pinard

Photo Researcher:
Cindy Howard

Permissions Coordinator:
Cindy Howard

Production Editor:
Tannys Williams

Copy Editor/Proofreader:
Wendy Thomas

Indexer:
Elizabeth Bell

Senior Production Coordinator:
Hedy Sellers

Creative Director:
Angela Cluer

Interior Design Modifications:
Roxanna Bennett

Cover Design:
Doris Chan

Cover Images:
From left to right:
Thomson Nelson
Klaus Lahnstein/Stone/Getty
Images
Julia Smith/The Image Bank/Getty
Images
Tim Flach/Stone/Getty Images

Compositors:
Zenaida Diores and
Courtney Hellam

Printer:
Transcontinental

**Library and Archives Canada
Cataloguing in Publication**

Kail, Robert V.
  Human development : a life-
span view / Robert Kail, John
Cavanaugh, Christine A. Ateah. —
1st Canadian ed.

Includes bibliographical references
and indexes.
ISBN 0-17-641494-0

1. Developmental psychology—
Textbooks. I. Cavanaugh, John C.
II. Ateah, Christine A. (Christine
Anne), 1956- III. Title.

BF713.K336 2005   155.2
C2005-900000-7

To Dea and Patrice
Robert V. Kail and John C. Cavanaugh

To Curwood, Jaymie, and Alexandra
Christine A. Ateah

BRIEF CONTENTS

CONTENTS

PART II
School-Age Children and Adolescents

CHAPTER 7

Off to School   232
PHYSICAL AND COGNITIVE DEVELOPMENT
IN MIDDLE CHILDHOOD

PREFACE

"To boldly go where no one has gone before" is a phrase familiar to millions of *Star Trek* fans around the world. The desire to explore the unknown to further our knowledge and understanding is a fundamental characteristic of being human. Boldly going into the unknown is also what each of us does in the course of our development. None of us has been where we are headed; indeed, in a real sense, we create our own destinies.

Just as all good starship captains rely on computer data banks and technical manuals to help guide them through the galaxy, *Human Development: A Life-Span View*, First Canadian Edition, serves as a resource to describe aspects of your past and point you toward your future. Human development is both the most fascinating and most complex science there is. Our text introduces you to the issues, forces, and outcomes that make us who we are.

Contemporary research and theory on human development consistently emphasize the multidisciplinary approach needed to describe and explain how people change (and how they stay the same) over time. Moreover, the great diversity of people requires an appreciation for individual differences in the course of development. *Human Development: A Life-Span View*, First Canadian Edition, incorporates both and aims to address two specific goals:

- To provide theoretical and empirical foundations that enable students to become educated and critical interpreters of developmental information.
- To provide a blend of basic and applied research, as well as controversial topics and emergent trends, to demonstrate connections between the laboratory and life and the dynamic science of human development.

ORGANIZATION

A MODIFIED CHRONOLOGICAL APPROACH The great debate among authors and instructors in the field of human development is whether to approach the study from a *chronological approach* (focusing on functioning at specific stages of the life span, such as infancy, adolescence, and middle adulthood), or from a *topical approach* (following a specific aspect of development, such as personality, throughout the life span). Both approaches have their merits. We have chosen a modified chronological approach that we believe combines the best aspects of both. The overall organization of the text is chronological: We trace development from conception through late life in sequential order, and dedicate several chapters to topical issues pertaining to particular points in the life span (such as infancy, early childhood, middle childhood, adolescence, young adulthood, middle adulthood, and late life).

But because the developmental continuity of topics such as social and cognitive development gets lost with narrowly defined, artificial age-stage divisions, we dedicate some chapters to tracing their development over larger segments of the life span. These chapters provide a much more coherent description of important developmental changes, emphasize the fact that development is not easily divided into "slices," and provide students with more understandable explications of developmental theories.

BALANCED COVERAGE OF THE ENTIRE LIFE SPAN   A primary difference between *Human Development: A Life-Span View*, First Canadian Edition, and similar texts is that this book provides a much richer and more complete description of adult development and aging. Following the introductory chapter, the remaining 16 chapters of the text are evenly divided between childhood, adolescence, adulthood, and aging. This even treatment reflects the rapid emergence of adult development and aging as a major emphasis in the science of human development, and a recognition that roughly three-fourths of most people's lives occurs beyond adolescence.

Reflecting our modified chronological approach, *Human Development: A Life-Span View*, First Canadian Edition, is divided into four main parts. After an introduction to the science of human development (Chapter 1), Part 1 includes a discussion of the biological foundations of life (Chapter 2) and development during infancy and early childhood (Chapters 3–6). Part 2 focuses on development during middle childhood and adolescence (Chapters 7–10). Part 3 (Chapters 11–14) focuses on young and middle adulthood. Part 4 examines late adulthood (Chapters 15 and 16), and concludes with a consideration of dying and bereavement (Chapter 17).

CONTENT AND APPROACH

BIOPSYCHOSOCIAL EMPHASIS   Our text provides comprehensive, up-to-date coverage of research and theory from conception to old age and death. We explicitly adopt the biopsychosocial framework as an organizing theme, describing it in depth in Chapter 1, and integrating it throughout the text—often in combination with other developmental theories.

AN ENGAGING PERSONAL STYLE   On several occasions, we communicate our personal involvement with the issues being discussed as illustrations of how human development plays itself out in people's lives.

Additionally, major sections of chapters open with a short vignette, helping to personalize a concept just before it is discussed. Other rich examples are integrated throughout the text narrative and are showcased in the *Real People* feature in nearly every chapter. Finally, we encourage students to find their own real-life examples of developmental issues through the *See for Yourself* features.

EMPHASIS ON INCLUSIVENESS   In content coverage, in the personalized examples used, and in the photo program, we emphasize diversity—within Canada and around the world—in ethnicity, gender, race, age, ability, and sexual orientation.

CHANGES IN THE FIRST CANADIAN EDITION

This edition has been revised from previous editions to reflect the Canadian context, such as the discussion of issues that are unique to our Aboriginal people, and inclusion of Canadian research, which helps us to understand our own experiences.

Of particular note are these content changes:

- **Reorganization of Part 1**. Part 1 has been reorganized to separate the discussions of infancy and early childhood regarding physical, cognitive, and socioemotional development (Chapters 3–5 in previous editions). Since the changes occurring in each of these developmental periods are numerous and extensive, they require full discussion. The First Canadian Edition therefore has discussed physical and cognitive development in infancy in Chapter 3, socioemotional development in infancy in Chapter 4, physical and cognitive development in early childhood in Chapter 5, and socioemotional development in early childhood in Chapter 6. This reorganization has resulted in an additional chapter from previous editions, allowing for improved and more detailed coverage of these age groups.

- **Inclusion of additional health promotion content**, particularly in Parts 1 and 2. Since age-related changes and health issues generally start in adulthood, health promotion activities are important to start during the early years. Good nutrition, physical activity, and safe sleeping practices for infants are examples of the practices discussed in the text.
- **Addition of Canadian context, data, and research study findings.** Canadian students will relate to examples and statistics that reflect their culture and experiences.
- **Updating of all additional resources** and inclusion of excellent Canadian website resources for assignments, further research, and interest.
- **Inclusion of new** *Healthy Living* **feature.** In a number of chapters, such as those dealing with childhood years, health promotion activities for that age group are summarized in a new feature entitled *Healthy Living*.
- **Enhanced discussion of physical changes.** The chapters have been reviewed and revised to ensure that a full discussion of physical as well as cognitive and psychosocial changes are addressed for each developmental group.
- **Exploration of current issues.** Controversial topics such as disciplinary practices for young children, euthanasia, and same-sex marriage are included and discussed within a Canadian context.

Specific improvements made throughout this new Canadian edition are detailed in the following list of changes by chapter.

Chapter 1: The Study of Human Development

- Inclusion of qualitative research as a type of research design for human development research
- Addition of ethical research guidelines within the Canadian context

Chapter 2: Foundations of Human Development

- Addition of a discussion on teratogens and congenital anomalies in Canada
- Addition of Canadian context of Fetal Alcohol Spectrum Disorder
- Inclusion of prenatal testing, such as the use of ultrasound and amniocentesis, in a Canadian context
- Inclusion of a brief discussion on the Genome Project and how this will affect future biological development
- Inclusion of Canadian studies on outcomes of low-birth-weight babies and infant mortality rates

Chapter 3: Tools for Exploring the World

- Updates with Canadian statistics and information on Sudden Infant Death Syndrome (SIDS) and Shaken Baby Syndrome (SBS)
- Inclusion of the Canadian Pediatric Society's and Health Canada's perspectives on breastfeeding and other aspects of infant nutrition
- Addition of Canadian research on pain in infants
- Discussion of the issue of assessing infant growth among different ethnic groups such as Aboriginal and Inuit infants

Chapter 4: Entering the Social World

- Addition of Canadian research and statistics on the topic of attachment in infants
- Updates of Canadian statistics regarding child care
- Inclusion of Canadian research on the effects of day care on child development
- Addition of more research on temperament and infant behaviour

Chapter 5: Growing and Learning in the Preschool Years

- Inclusion of updated growth charts
- Inclusion of Canadian research on handedness in children
- Expansion of discussion on the development of memory
- Expansion of Piaget discussion with inclusion of concept of reversibility
- Inclusion of additional discussion of and Canadian research on language development

Chapter 6: Interacting and the Work of Play

- Expansion of discussion of parenting types, strategies, effects on children, and disciplinary strategies and issues
- Inclusion of Canadian research on use of physical punishment and child abuse
- Addition of Canadian research in the area of empathy and prosocial behaviour

Chapter 7: Off to School

- Addition of discussion of physical growth and expected changes in middle childhood
- Updated discussion on intelligence testing, including tests used in Canada
- Inclusion of information on the Aboriginal Head Start Program in Canada
- Discussion of updated terminology, such as using "intellectual impairment" rather than "mental retardation"
- Inclusion of statistics on learning disabilities in Canada
- Replacement of previous *Spotlight on Research* with a Canadian study on learning disabilities and interventions
- Updated statistics on international comparisons of students' math skills (including Canadian statistics)
- Inclusion of a section on bilingual education as it relates to language and cognitive development (including Canadian research findings)

Chapter 8: Expanding Social Horizons

- Updates with Canadian statistics on adoption, divorce, and blended families as well as their effects on children
- Inclusion of Canadian research on effects of television on children
- Inclusion of Canadian research on peer relationships during middle childhood

Chapter 9: Rites of Passage

- New opening vignette focusing on how Clara Hughes, an outstanding Canadian athlete in two sports, developed her skills in adolescence
- Inclusion of Canada's guidelines for caloric needs in teens, and examination of issues of obesity
- Addition of Health Canada's position on the role of physical activity and good eating habits for teens
- Addition of Canadian statistics on sports participation, use of anabolic steroids, and accident and death rates

Chapter 10: Moving into the Adult Social World

- Updates with Canadian research on ethnic identity and self-esteem
- Updates with Canadian statistics on adolescent sexual behaviour, including sexual orientation, HIV/AIDS, and teen pregnancy

- Updates with Canadian statistics related to adolescent employment
- Updates with Canadian statistics on adolescent use of drugs, and depression and suicide rates
- Inclusion of a discussion of programs to prevent youth violence in Canada
- Inclusion of a *Current Controversies* discussion on the Canadian Youth Criminal Justice Act

Chapter 11: Becoming an Adult

- Updates with Canadian statistics and discussion regarding age of first marriage and parenthood
- Inclusion of Canadian examples for physical activity and accomplishment
- Updates with Canadian statistics on post-secondary education
- Updates with Canadian statistics on risky health behaviours in early adulthood, such as alcohol consumption and smoking, and leading causes of death

Chapter 12: Being with Others

- Inclusion of Canadian context and statistics on being single, living common-law, and marriage and divorce rates
- Updated discussion on the issue of same-sex rights and benefits, including the Canadian context
- Updated discussion on divorce and its reasons, as well as exploring other issues such as child support payments, based on Canadian research

Chapter 13: Work and Leisure

- Inclusion of Canadian context and updating of statistics on the issues of gender discrimination and sexual harassment
- Updated discussion of employment issues in Canada, such as job training, unemployment, parents working outside the home, day-care subsidies, mandatory retirement, and division of household duties

Chapter 14: Making It in Midlife

- Enhancement of the discussion of changes during menopause, including issues such as bone mass loss and recommended calcium intakes
- Clarification of the stages of the climacteric, perimenopause, menopause, and postmenopause
- Addition of description of expected physical changes, such as those to the cardiovascular system, vision, and hearing
- Inclusion of discussions on Health Canada's position on hormone replacement therapy and on the benefits of exercise
- Addition of Canadian research on the relationship between stress, coping, and psychological health
- Updates with Canadian statistics on caregiver stress, young people remaining at home, and grandparenting

Chapter 15: The Personal Context of Later Life

- Updates with Canadian statistics on demographics with regard to aging, projection of elderly population, average life expectancy, and differences in gender
- Inclusion of a discussion of gerontology as a specific discipline
- Increased discussion of physical changes expected with advanced age, such as loss of sensation and touch
- Inclusion of a discussion of cardiovascular disease with age, including differences in the Aboriginal population
- Updated *Current Controversies* feature to reflect Canadian statistics and programs for older drivers

⚏ Updates with Canadian material, research, and statistics on the issue of depression, dementia, and specifically Alzheimer disease

Chapter 16: Social Aspects of Later Life

⚏ Inclusion of a Canadian exemplar for the *Real People* section
⚏ Updates with Canadian statistics on retirees, activities, and agencies
⚏ Updates with Canadian statistics on relationships and marriage in later life, and nursing home and other living accommodations
⚏ Addition of guidelines for selecting a nursing home in Canada
⚏ Inclusion of a discussion on the issue of elder abuse in Canada
⚏ Discussion of health care and economic issues in Canada for individuals in late adulthood

Chapter 17: The Final Passage

⚏ Inclusion of Canadian guidelines for determining death
⚏ Enhanced life course approach to dying by including preschool, school age, and adolescent perspectives
⚏ Addition of Canadian material, including legal aspects and examples, for discussion of euthanasia and living wills
⚏ Updated discussion of end-of-life care in Canada, including related research and resources

SPECIAL FEATURES

Five special features are a significant reason that this textbook is unique. These features are woven seamlessly into the narrative, signalled by a distinct icon for each—not boxed off from the flow of the chapter. These features are

 Spotlight on Research, which emphasizes a fuller understanding of the science and scope of life-span development.

 Current Controversies, which highlights debates over social and developmental issues.

 Real People—Applying Human Development, which illustrates the everyday applications of life-span development issues.

 Forces in Action, which demonstrates how various biopsychosocial elements work to influence a particular aspect of development.

 Healthy Living, a new feature that discusses how age- and stage-related concepts and research presented in the chapter can be applied to the promotion of healthy living.

These features are described in the *How to Use This Book* section at the end of the Preface. Each one appears in nearly every chapter thereafter.

PEDAGOGICAL FEATURES

Among the most important aspects of *Human Development: A Life-Span View,* First Canadian Edition, is its exceptional integration of pedagogical features, designed to help students maximize their learning.

Integration of Photos, Art, Features, and Key Terms

Figures, tables, and photos are captioned and/or are described directly in the text narrative where they appear. Similarly, the five special features described earlier, which are normally set apart in boxes in other texts (boxes that students often skip!), are integrated directly into the narrative. Continuing with this integrative theme, definitions of key terms are provided in context within the chapter narrative. Key terms themselves are in bold and the definition sentences are in italics. This *unrivalled* integration is meant to help the student stay focused, providing a seamless presentation of human development across the life span.

Section-by-Section Pedagogy

Each major section (four or five per chapter) has been carefully crafted. The section opens with a set of learning objectives, a vignette, and a mini-table of contents for the section; typically includes one or more *Think About It* questions in the margin encouraging critical thinking; and ends with a set of questions called *Test Yourself* that reinforces key elements of the section. For easy assignment and to help readers visually organize the material, major units within each chapter are now numbered.

Chapter-by-Chapter Pedagogy

Each chapter opens with a table of contents and a brief *Introduction*. A *Putting It All Together* feature follows the chapter's final section to tie major chapter themes together (usually referring back to the individuals described in the section vignettes as well). It includes a bulleted, detailed *Summary* (broken down by section), followed by a list of *Key Terms* (with page references); *See for Yourself—Applying What You've Learned* (which suggests simple activities for students to explore human development on their own); and *Learn About It!* (which lists books and websites where students can learn more about human development).

In sum, we believe that our integrated pedagogical system will give the student all the tools she or he needs to comprehend the material and study for tests.

SUPPLEMENTARY MATERIALS

An extensive array of supplemental materials are available to accompany this text. These supplements are designed to make teaching and learning more effective. For more information on any of these resources, please contact your local sales representative or call Thomson Nelson Customer Support at 1-800-268-2222.

INSTRUCTOR RESOURCES

Available to qualified adopters. Please consult your local sales representative for details.

INSTRUCTOR'S MANUAL   The *Instructor's Manual* for the First Canadian Edition has been adapted to include a wealth of material, including Instructional Goals and Teaching Strategies, Chapter Outlines, Learning Objectives, Lecture

Expanders, Classroom Activities including Demonstrations and Role Plays, Writing Assignments, Student Projects, Questions to Stimulate Critical Thinking, Web Activities, InfoTrac® College Edition Articles and Activities, Video Recommendations, and Handouts. ISBN: 0-17-640745-6

TEST BANK   The revised and updated *Test Bank* for the First Canadian Edition includes over one hundred multiple-choice questions for each chapter. Each question includes the relevant learning objective and page reference, as well as classification (conceptual, factual, or applied), and level of difficulty. Additional questions from the book's website, where students can take interactive quizzes with instant feedback, are provided and flagged for the instructor's reference. ISBN: 0-17-640744-8

EXAMVIEW® COMPUTERIZED TEST BANK   Create, deliver, and customize tests (both print and online) in minutes with this easy-to-use assessment and tutorial system. *ExamView* offers both a Quick Test Wizard and an Online Test Wizard that guide you step-by-step through the process of creating tests, while its "what you see is what you get" capability allows you to see the test you are creating on the screen exactly as it will print or display online. You can build tests of up to 250 questions using up to 12 question types. Using *ExamView*'s complete word-processing capabilities, you can enter an unlimited number of new questions or edit existing questions. ISBN: 0-17-640743-X

MULTIMEDIA MANAGER   This one-stop lecture tool makes it easy to assemble, edit, publish, and present custom lectures. The *Multimedia Manager* brings together text-specific lecture outlines, art, video, and animations from the CD, the web, and an instructor's own material, culminating in a powerful, personalized, PowerPoint® presentation. ISBN: 0-17-640741-3

TRANSPARENCY ACETATES   One hundred full-colour illustrations of concepts presented in the text are available to qualifying adopters. ISBN: 0-17-640742-1

BOOK COMPANION WEBSITE   As users of this text, you and your students will have access to an extensive selection of additional online tools, quizzes, and activities available on the book's companion website (http://www.humandevelopment. nelson.com) in the Thomson Nelson Psychology Resource Centre. In addition, downloadable versions of the Instructor's Manual and PowerPoint® lecture outlines taken from the Multimedia Manager are also included in the password-protected portion of the site. (Please see *Student Resources* for a complete description.)

OBSERVING CHILDREN AND ADOLESCENTS VIDEO PACKAGE   More than just a video, this complete package offers 90 minutes of narrated observational footage that shows students the practical implications of what they study. The video features *Observational Modules* for six major phases of development: Prenatal Development, Birth, Infancy and Toddlerhood, Early Childhood, Middle Childhood, and Adolescence. An accompanying *Student Workbook with CD-ROM* offers interactive quizzing, critical thinking exercises, and applications. The *Instructor's Manual/Test Bank* provides suggestions for student projects, additional exercises, and ideas for integrating this package into your course. ISBN: 0-534-62273-9 (Video); 0-534-62272-0 (Student Workbook with CD-ROM); 0-534-62271-2 (Instructor's Manual/Test Bank)

CNN TODAY VIDEOS   Launch your lectures with riveting footage from CNN, the world's leading 24-hour global news television network. *CNN Today Videos*, a Thomson/Wadsworth exclusive, allow you to integrate the newsgathering and programming power of CNN into the classroom to show students the relevance of course topics to their everyday lives. Organized by topics covered in a typical course, these videos are divided into short segments—perfect for introducing key concepts.

CNN Today Videos for Child and Adolescent Development, Volume I.
ISBN: 0-534-36705-4

CNN Today Videos for Child and Adolescent Development, Volume II.
ISBN: 0-534-36937-5

CNN Today Videos for Child and Adolescent Development, Volume III.
ISBN: 0-534-51856-7

CNN Today Videos for Lifespan Development, Volume I.
ISBN: 0-534-52192-4

CNN Today Videos for Lifespan Development, Volume II.
ISBN: 0-534-52193-2

CNN Today Videos for Lifespan Development, Volume III.
ISBN: 0-534-55758-9

CNN Today Videos for Lifespan Development, Volume IV.
ISBN: 0-534-55817-8

STUDENT RESOURCES

STUDY GUIDE   The *Study Guide* for the First Canadian Edition provides detailed chapter outlines, learning objectives, key terms, true/false questions, multiple-choice questions, essay questions, and answer keys cross-referenced to appropriate pages of the text. ISBN: 0-17-640746-4

BOOK COMPANION WEBSITE   Users of this text have access to an extensive offering of online study and research tools, including pre- and post-test questions with personalized study plans, tutorial quizzes, Internet exercises, flashcards, and web links. Go to http://www.humandevelopment.nelson.com.

INFOTRAC® COLLEGE EDITION   Four months of FREE anywhere—anytime access to InfoTrac® College Edition, the online library, is automatically packaged with this book. The new and improved InfoTrac® College Edition puts cutting-edge research and the latest headlines at your students' fingertips, giving them access to an entire online library for the cost of one book! This fully searchable database offers more than 20 years' worth of full-text articles (more than 10 million) from almost 4,000 diverse sources, such as academic journals, newsletters, and up-to-the-minute periodicals.

LIFESPAN: A MULTIMEDIA INTRODUCTION TO HUMAN DEVELOPMENT CD-ROM   This student CD-ROM covers a semester's worth of content for the Life-Span Development course: prenatal development, infancy, childhood, adolescence, adulthood, aging, death, and dying. Features include interactive narrated concept overviews, explanatory photos and art, explanatory videos and animations, applications, email-based forms for applying theoretical concepts to real-world situations, interactive quizzing for each major subject area, interactive games for each major subject area for review of key terms and concepts, and web links for further research. ISBN: 0-534-54384-7

CASEBOOK FOR LIFE SPAN DEVELOPMENT   This new casebook—by Barbara M. Newman, University of Rhode Island; Philip R. Newman, University of Rhode Island; Laura Landry-Meyer, Bowling Green State University; and Brenda J. Lohman, Northwestern University—gives students an in-depth look at the forces that shape development. Each chapter of this casebook uses lively, contemporary case studies to illustrate developmental transitions and challenges at every period of life. The chapters follow a consistent presentation, which includes an overview of development issues, two or three case scenarios, followed by pedagogical prompts to consider a developmental analysis, a contextual analysis, and a psychosocial analysis. Chapters close with ideas for further research and study. The goal of the casebook is to stimulate critical thinking and the application of theory and research to authentic, real-world experiences. ISBN: 0-534-59767-X

ACKNOWLEDGMENTS

Many individuals were involved in revising this text to reflect the Canadian experience and be more meaningful for Canadian students. I would like to first thank Robert Kail and John Cavanaugh for writing such an excellent book; their accomplishment made the process of revision a great experience. I would also like to thank Alwynn Pinard, Developmental Editor, for her helpful guidance through the process of revision, Wendy Thomas for her expertise as copy editor, and Jamie Penner for her dedicated and excellent work as my research assistant.

I would also like to thank the many reviewers who generously gave their time and effort to help me sharpen my thinking about human development and, in so doing, shape the development of this text:

Darlene A. Brodeur, Acadia University
David Goldstein, University of Toronto
Lana-Lee Hardacre, Conestoga College
Scott R. Jones, University of Lethbridge
Jacqueline Kampman, University College of the Cariboo
Shauna Longmuir, Sir Sandford Fleming College
Keith Mauthe, Lethbridge Community College
Colleen McQuarrie, University of Prince Edward Island
Verna C. Pangman, University of Manitoba
Shawn Pentacost, Algonquin College
Verna C. Raab, Mount Royal College
Marty Whitney, Georgian College

Christine A. Ateah

How to Use This Book

Human Development is written with you, the student, in mind. In the next few pages, we describe several features of the book that will make life easier for you to learn. Please don't skip this material; it will save you time in the long run.

LEARNING AND STUDY AIDS

Each chapter in the text includes several distinctive features to help you learn the material and organize your studying.

- Each chapter opens with an overview of the main topics and a detailed outline.
- Each major section within a chapter begins with a mini-outline that lists the major subheadings of the section and a set of learning objectives. There is also a brief vignette introducing one of the topics to be covered in that section and providing an example of the developmental issues people face.
- When key terms are introduced in the text, they appear in **boldfaced italics**. The definition of the key term appears in *italics*. This should make key terms easy to find and learn.
- Data tables and photographs are integrated in the text where they are discussed, eliminating the need to search for them on other pages. This integration will help you tie the graphic material with the text. All tables and figures are numbered and referenced within the body of the text.
- Key developmental theories are introduced in Chapter 1 and are referred to throughout the text.
- Critical thinking questions appear in the margins. These *Think About It* questions are designed to help you make connections across sections within a chapter or across chapters.
- The end of each section includes a feature called *Test Yourself*, which will help you check your knowledge of the major ideas you just read about. The *Test Yourself* questions serve two purposes. First, they give you a chance to spot-check your understanding of the material. Second, at times the questions will relate the material you have just read to other facts, theories, or the biopsychosocial framework you read about earlier.

Text features that expand or highlight a specific topic are integrated with the rest of the material. This book includes the following five features, each identified by a distinctive icon.

Spotlight on Research elaborates a specific research study discussed in the text and provides more details on the design and methods used.

Current Controversies offers thought-provoking discussions about current issues affecting development.

Real People: Applying Human Development illustrates in a case study how an issue in human development is manifested in the life of a real person.

Forces in Action describes how the biopsychosocial framework is used to understand a particular issue in development.

 Healthy Living discusses how age- and stage-related concepts and research presented in the chapter can be applied to the promotion of healthy living.

The end of each chapter includes several special study tools:

- *Putting It All Together* returns to each vignette to reprise the major topics of the chapter.
- A *Summary* organized by major section headings provides a review of the key ideas in the chapter.
- *Key Terms* that appear in the chapter are listed with page references.
- *See for Yourself: Applying What You've Learned* provides ways for you to explore issues in human development on your own.
- *Learn More About It* draws the chapter to a close. It contains reading material and websites where you can find more information about human development.

We strongly encourage you to take advantage of these learning and study aids as you read the book. We have also left room in the margins for you to make notes to yourself on the material, so you can more easily integrate the text with your class and lecture material. When you are assigned a chapter, you may find it preferable to read it in more than one sitting. We suggest that you start by reading the introduction and notice how the chapter fits into the entire book. Then page through the chapter, reading the learning objectives, vignettes, mini-outlines, and major headings. Also read the italicized sentences and the boldfaced terms. Your goal is to first get a general overview of the entire chapter—a sense of what it's all about.

Now you're ready to begin reading. Go to the first major section and preview it again, reminding yourself of the topics covered. Then start to read. As you do, think about what you're reading. Every few paragraphs, stop briefly. Try to summarize, in your own words, the main ideas; ask yourself if the ideas describe your own experience or that of others you know; tell a friend about something interesting in the material. In other words, read actively—get involved in what you're reading.

Continue this pattern—reading, summarizing, thinking—until you finish the section. Then answer the *Test Yourself* questions to determine how well you've learned what you've read. If you've followed the read-summarize-think cycle as you worked your way through the section, you should be able to answer most of the questions.

The next time you sit down to read, start by reviewing the second major section. Then complete it with the read-summarize-think cycle. Repeat this procedure for all the major sections.

When you've finished the last major section, wait a day or two and then review each major section. Pay careful attention to the italicized sentences, the boldfaced terms, and the *Test Yourself* questions. Also, use the study aids at the end of the chapter to help you integrate the ideas in the chapters. Research consistently shows that you learn more effectively by having daily (or nearly daily) study sessions devoted both to reviewing familiar material *and* taking on a relatively small amount of new material.

TERMINOLOGY

Certain terms will be used to refer to different periods of the life span. Although you may already be familiar with the terms, we would like to clarify how they will be used in this text. The following terms will refer to a specific range of ages:

Newborn	birth to 1 month
Infant	1 month to 1 year
Toddler	1 year to 2 years
Preschooler	2 years to 6 years
School-age child	6 years to 12 years
Adolescent	12 years to 20 years
Young adult	20 years to 40 years
Middle-aged adult	40 years to 60 years
Young-old adult	60 years to 80 years
Old-old adult	80 years and beyond

Sometimes, for the sake of variety, we will use other terms that are less tied to specific ages, such as babies, youngsters, and older adults. However, you will be able to determine the specific ages from the context.

ORGANIZATION

Authors of textbooks on human development always face the problem of deciding how to organize the material into meaningful segments across the life span. This book is organized in four parts: Prenatal Development, Infancy, and Early Childhood; School-Age Children and Adolescents; Young and Middle Adulthood; and Later Adulthood. We believe this organization achieves two major goals. First, it divides the life span in ways that relate to the divisions encountered in everyday life. Second, it enables us to provide a more complete account of adulthood than other books do.

Part 1 covers prenatal development, infancy, and early childhood. Here we will see how genetic inheritance operates and how the prenatal environment affects a person's future development. During the first two years of life, the rate of change in both motor and perceptual arenas is amazing. How young children acquire language and begin to think about their world is as intriguing as it is rapid. Early childhood also marks the emergence of social relationships, as well as an understanding of gender roles and identity. By the end of this period, a child is reasonably proficient as a thinker, uses language in sophisticated ways, and is ready for the major transition into formal education.

Part 2 covers the years from elementary school through high school. In middle childhood and adolescence, the cognitive skills formed earlier in life evolve to adult-like levels in many areas. Family and peer relationships expand. During adolescence, there is increased attention to work, and sexuality emerges. The young person begins to learn how to face difficult issues in life. By the end of this period, a person is on the verge of legal adulthood. The typical individual uses logic and has been introduced to most of the issues that adults face.

Part 3 covers young adulthood and middle age. During this period, most people achieve their most advanced modes of thinking, achieve peak physical performance, form intimate relationships, start families of their own, begin and advance within their occupations, manage to balance many conflicting roles, and begin to confront aging. Over these years, many people go from breaking away from their families to having their children break away from them. Relationships with parents are redefined, and the pressures of being caught between the younger and older generations are felt. By the end of this period, most people have shifted focus from time since birth to time until death.

Part 4 covers the last decades of life. The biological, physical, cognitive, and social changes associated with aging become apparent. Although many changes reflect decline, many other aspects of old age represent positive elements: wisdom, retirement, friendships, and family relationships. We conclude this section, and the text, with a discussion of the end of life. Through our consideration of death, we will gain additional insights into the meaning of life and human development.

We hope the organization and learning features of the text are helpful to you—making it easier for you to learn about human development. After all, this book tells the story of people's lives, and understanding the story is what it's all about.

ABOUT THE AUTHORS

ROBERT V. KAIL

Robert V. Kail is Professor of Psychological Sciences at Purdue University. His undergraduate degree is from Ohio Wesleyan University and his Ph.D. is from the University of Michigan. Kail is editor of the *Journal of Experimental Child Psychology* and of *Advances in Child Development and Behavior*. He received the McCandless Young Scientist Award from the American Psychological Association, was named the Distinguished Sesquicentennial Alumnus in Psychology by Ohio Wesleyan University, and is a fellow of the American Psychological Society. Kail has also written *Children and Their Development*. His research focuses on cognitive development during childhood and adolescence. Away from the office, he enjoys working out and coaching his daughter's soccer team.

JOHN C. CAVANAUGH

John C. Cavanaugh is president of the University of West Florida. He received his undergraduate degree from the University of Delaware and his Ph.D. from the University of Notre Dame. Cavanaugh is a fellow of the American Psychological Association, the American Psychological Society, and the Gerontological Society of America, and has served as president of the Adult Development and Aging Division (Division 20) of the APA. Cavanaugh has also written (with Fredda Blanchard-Fields) *Adult Development and Aging*. His research interests in gerontology concern family caregiving as well as the role of beliefs in older adults' cognitive performance. For enjoyment he backpacks, writes poetry, and, while eating chocolate, ponders the relative administrative abilities of James T. Kirk, Jean-Luc Picard, Kathryn Janeway, Benjamin Sisko, and Jonathan Archer.

CHRISTINE A. ATEAH

Christine A. Ateah is an Associate Dean at the Faculty of Nursing, University of Manitoba, in Winnipeg. Her undergraduate and Ph.D. degrees are from the University of Manitoba and her Master of Education degree is from the University of Alberta. She has been a nurse educator for over two decades, and her clinical and research interests are in child and family health promotion, particularly in relation to parenting education and child abuse prevention. She has taught growth and development to undergraduate nursing students for over a decade and also enjoys working with graduate students in her area of expertise. Dr. Ateah has recently co-edited a book entitled *Within Our Reach: Preventing Abuse Across the Lifespan*. She enjoys spending time with her husband and daughters, especially while travelling or relaxing at the cottage, as well as in-line skating and watercolour painting.

First Canadian Edition

Human Development

A Life-Span View

Getty Images

CHAPTER 1

The Study of Human Development

You are about to begin an exciting personal journey. In this course, you will have the opportunity to ask some of the most basic questions there are: How did your life begin? How did you go from a single cell, about the size of the period at the end of a sentence in this text, to the fully grown, complex adult person you are today? Will you be the same or different by the time you reach late life? How do you influence other people's lives? How do they influence yours? How do the various roles you have throughout life—child, teenager, partner, spouse, parent, worker, grandparent—shape your development? How do we deal with our own and others' deaths?

*These are examples of the questions that create the scientific foundation of **human development**, the multidisciplinary study of how people change and how they remain the same over time.* Answering them requires us to draw on theories and research in the physical and social sciences, including biology, genetics, chemistry, medicine, nursing, psychology, sociology, demography, ethnography, economics, and anthropology. The science of human development reflects the complexity and uniqueness of each person and each person's experiences as well as commonalities and patterns across people. As a science, human development is firmly grounded in theory and research and seeks to understand human behaviour.

Before our journey begins, we need proper direction: a framework to organize theories and research, common issues and influences on development, and the methods developmentalists use to make discoveries. Let's begin.

1.1

Thinking About Development

LEARNING OBJECTIVES

▶ What fundamental issues of development have scholars addressed throughout history?

▶ What are the basic forces in the biopsychosocial framework? How does the timing of these forces make a difference in their impact?

Victor Ramos smiled broadly as he held his newborn grandson for the first time. So many thoughts rushed into his mind—What would Daniel experience growing up? Would the neighbourhood they live in prevent him from reaching his potential? Would the family genes for good health be passed on? How would Daniel's life growing up in Canada be different from Victor's own experiences in the Philippines?

Like many grandparents, Victor wonders what the future holds for his grandson. The questions he asks are interesting in their own right, but they are important for another reason: They bear on general issues of human development that have intrigued philosophers and scientists for centuries. In the next few pages, we introduce some of these issues, which surface when any aspect of development is being investigated.

RECURRING ISSUES IN HUMAN DEVELOPMENT

Three fundamental issues pervade modern research on human development: nature versus nurture, continuity versus discontinuity, and universal versus context-specific development. These issues cut across virtually all the topics in this book, so let's examine each one.

Nature Versus Nurture

Think for a minute about a particular characteristic that you and several people in your family have, such as intelligence, good looks, or a friendly, outgoing personality. Why is this trait so prevalent? Is it because you inherited the trait from your parents? Or is it because of where and how you and your parents were brought up?

*Answers to these questions illustrate different positions on the **nature-nurture issue**, which involves the degree to which genetic or hereditary influences (nature) and experiential or environmental influences (nurture) determine the kind of person you are.* Scientists once hoped to answer these questions by identifying either heredity or environment as the cause of a particular aspect of development. The goal was to be able to say, for example, that intelligence was due to heredity or that personality was due to experience. Today, however, we know that virtually no features of life-span development are due exclusively to either heredity or environment. Instead, development is always shaped by both: Nature and nurture are mutually interactive influences. For example, in Chapter 11 you will learn that one risk factor for cardiovascular disease is heredity, but that lifestyle factors such as diet and smoking play important roles in determining who has heart attacks.

As this example illustrates, a major aim of modern developmental science is to understand how heredity and environment jointly determine development. For Victor, it means his grandson's development will surely be shaped both by the genes he inherited and by the experiences he will have.

THINK ABOUT IT 💡

Think of some common, everyday behaviours, such as dancing or playing basketball with your friends. How do nature and nurture influence these behaviours?

Continuity Versus Discontinuity

Think of some ways in which you remain similar to how you were as a 5-year-old. Maybe you were outgoing and friendly at that age and remain outgoing and friendly today. Examples like these suggest a great deal of continuity in development, in that once a person begins down a particular developmental pathway—for example, toward friendliness or intelligence—he or she stays on that path throughout life. According to this view, if Daniel is a friendly and smart 5-year-old, he should be friendly and smart as a 25- and 75-year-old.

The other view is that development is not always continuous, but that people can change from one developmental path to another, perhaps several times in their lives. Consequently, Daniel might be smart and friendly at age 5, smart but shy at 25, and wise but aloof at 75!

The *continuity-discontinuity issue concerns whether a particular developmental phenomenon represents a smooth progression throughout the life span (continuity) or a series of abrupt shifts (discontinuity).* Throughout this book, you will find examples of both continuities and discontinuities. For example, in Chapter 4 you will see evidence of continuity: Infants who have satisfying emotional relationships with their parents typically become children with satisfying peer relationships. But in Chapter 16 you will see an instance of discontinuity: After spending most of adulthood trying to ensure the success of the next generation and to leave a legacy, older adults turn to evaluating their own lives, in search of closure and a sense that what they have done has been worthwhile.

Universal Versus Context-Specific Development

The *universal versus context-specific development issue concerns whether there is just one path of development or several.* In some cities in Brazil, 10- to 12-year-olds sell fruit and candy to pedestrians and passengers on buses. Although they have little formal education and often cannot identify the numbers on the money, they handle money proficiently (Saxe, 1988).

Life for Brazilian street vendors contrasts sharply with childhood in Canada, where 10- to 12-year-olds are formally taught at home or school to identify numbers and to perform the kinds of arithmetic needed to handle money. Can one theory explain development in both groups of children? Perhaps. Some theorists would argue that despite what look like differences in development, there is really only one fundamental developmental process for everyone. According to this view, differences in development are simply variations on a fundamental developmental process, in much the same way that cars as different as a Chevrolet, a Honda, and a Porsche are all products of fundamentally the same manufacturing process.

The opposing view is that differences among people may not be just variations on a theme. Advocates of this view argue that human development is inextricably intertwined with the context within which it occurs. A person's development is a product of complex interaction with the environment, and that interaction is *not* fundamentally the same in all environments.

Putting all three issues together, and using personality to illustrate, we can ask how heredity and environment interact to influence the development of personality, whether the development of personality is continuous or discontinuous, and whether personality develops in much the same way around the world. To answer these kinds of questions, we need to look at the forces that combine to shape human development.

BASIC FORCES IN HUMAN DEVELOPMENT: THE BIOPSYCHOSOCIAL FRAMEWORK

When trying to explain why people develop as they do, scientists usually consider four interactive forces:

■ **Biological forces** *include all genetic and health-related factors that affect development.*

■ **Psychological forces** *include all internal perceptual, cognitive, emotional, and personality factors that affect development.*

■ **Sociocultural forces** *include interpersonal, societal, cultural, and ethnic factors that affect development.*

■ **Life-cycle forces** *reflect differences in how the same event affects people of different ages.*

Each person is a product of a unique combination of these forces. No two individuals, even in the same family, experience these forces in the same way; even identical twins eventually have different friendship networks, partners, and occupations.

To see why each of these forces is important, think about whether a mother decides to breast-feed her infant. Her decision will be based on biological variables (e.g., amount of milk produced), her attitudes about the virtues of breast-feeding, the influences of other people (e.g., the father), and her cultural traditions about appropriate ways to feed infants. Additionally, her decision will reflect her age and stage of life. Only by focusing on all these forces can we have a complete view of the mother's decision.

FIGURE 1.1   Biopsychosocial Forces in Development

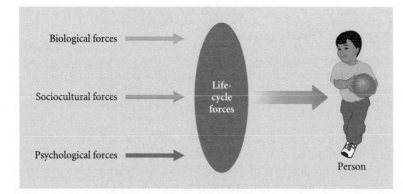

One useful way to organize the biological, psychological, and sociocultural forces on human development is with the **biopsychosocial framework.** *As you can see in* Figure 1.1, the biopsychosocial framework emphasizes that human development is more than any one of the basic forces considered alone. Rather, each force interacts with the others to make up development. Let's look at the different elements of the biopsychosocial model in more detail.

Biological Forces

Prenatal development, brain maturation, puberty, menopause, facial wrinkling, and change in cardiovascular functioning all illustrate biological forces. Many of these biological forces are determined by our genetic code and will be discussed in upcoming chapters. For example, looking at the children in the photo, you can see that they resemble their parents, which shows biological influences on development. But biological forces also include the effects of lifestyle factors, such as diet and exercise; these and other examples will also be explored throughout this text.

Collectively, biological forces can be viewed as providing the raw material necessary (in the case of genetics) and as setting the boundary conditions (in the case of one's general health) for development.

Psychological Forces

Psychological forces probably seem familiar because they are the ones used most often to describe the characteristics of a person. For example, think about how you describe yourself when you meet others. Most of us say that we have a nice personality and are intelligent, honest, self-confident, or something along those lines. Concepts like these reflect psychological forces.

In general, psychological forces are all the internal cognitive, emotional, personality, perceptual, spiritual, and related factors that influence behaviour. Psychological forces have received the most attention of the three main developmental forces. Much of what we discuss throughout the text reflects psychological forces. For example, we will see how the development of intelligence enables individuals to experience and think about their world in different ways. We'll also see how the emergence of self-esteem is related to the beliefs people have about their abilities, which in turn influence what they do.

Collectively, psychological factors provide the things we notice most about what makes people the way they are, as well as the interesting variations that make us individuals.

Sociocultural Forces

People develop in the world, not in a vacuum. To understand human development, we need to know how people and their environments interact and relate to each other. In other words, we need to view an individual's development as part of a much larger system, in which no part of the system can act without influencing all other aspects of the system. This larger system includes one's parents, children, and siblings as well as important individuals outside the family, such as friends, teachers, and co-workers. The system also includes institutions that influence development, such as schools, television, places of worship, and the workplace.

All these people and institutions fit together to form a person's culture— the knowledge, attitudes, and behaviour associated with a group of people. Culture can be linked to a particular country or people (e.g., French culture), to a specific point in time (e.g., popular culture of the 1990s), or to groups of individuals who maintain specific, identifiable cultural traditions (e.g., Indo-Canadians). Knowing the culture from which a person comes provides some general information about important influences that may appear throughout the life span.

Understanding the impact of culture is particularly important in Canada, one of the most diverse countries in the world. A large number of languages are spoken and the many customs people bring add to a growing richness that offers insights into the broad spectrum of human experience and attests to the diversity of the Canadian population.

Although the Canadian and American populations are changing rapidly, much of the research described in this text was conducted on individuals who have a middle-class socio-economic background and/or who are of European descent. Accordingly, we must be careful *not* to assume that findings from this group necessarily apply to people in other groups. You may feel frustrated at times, wondering whether results obtained with one group apply to other groups as well. Indeed, there is a great need for research on different cultural groups. Perhaps, as a result of taking this course, you will help fill this need by becoming a developmental researcher yourself.

Another practical problem that we face is how to describe each group, since appropriate terminology changes over time. For example, we use *European heritage* (instead of *Caucasian* or *white*) and *Aboriginal* (instead of *Indian* or *Native*).

These labels are not perfect. In some cases, they blur distinctions among ethnic groups. For example, the term *Aboriginal identity* is frequently used to refer to those persons with at least one Aboriginal origin, such as North American Indian, Metis, or Inuit (Statistics Canada, 2002a). However, their specific cultural backgrounds vary on several important dimensions, so we should not view them as being from a homogenous group. Similarly, the term *European* ignores differences between individuals of northern or southern European ancestry; the term *Asian* blurs variations among people whose heritage is, for example, Japanese, Chinese, or Korean. Whenever researchers have identified the subgroups in their research sample, we will use the more specific terms in describing results. When we use the more general terms, remember that conclusions may not apply to all subgroups within the more general term.

The Forces Interact

So far, we've described biological, psychological, and sociocultural forces in the biopsychosocial framework as if they were independent. But as we pointed out earlier in introducing the notion of the biopsychosocial framework, each shapes the others. Consider eating habits. Not too many years ago, a "red meat and potatoes" diet was common and was thought to be healthy. Subsequently, it became known that high-fat diets may lead to cardiovascular disease and some forms of cancer. Consequently, social pressures began to change what people eat; advertising campaigns were begun; and restaurants began to indicate which menu items were low in fat. Thus, the biological forces of fat in the diet were influenced by the social forces of the times, whether in support of or in opposition to having beef every evening. Finally, as consumers became more educated about diets and their effects on health, the psychological forces of thinking and reasoning also influenced their choice of diets.

This example illustrates that no aspect of human development can be fully understood by examining only one or two of the forces. All three must be considered in interaction. To understand the effects of genetic variation, we may need to examine some specific aspect of behaviour in a particular social context. To understand the effects of a sociocultural force such as poverty, we may need to look at how poverty affects people's health. In fact, we'll see later in this chapter that integration across the three major forces of the biopsychosocial framework is one criterion by which the adequacy of a developmental theory can be judged. Before we do that, however, we need to consider one more aspect of this framework: The point in life at which a specific combination of biological, psychological, and sociocultural forces operates matters a great deal.

FORCES IN ACTION

In Search of the Whole Person

The four forces of human development provide the best framework in which to understand human development. As we will see throughout this book, it is only when you consider the biological, psychological, sociocultural, and life-cycle forces together that you will have a full understanding of a person. Although this framework was first adopted in the field of gerontology (the study of older adults and aging), it is now the dominant framework for all of human development. ◗◗

Timing Is Everything: Life-Cycle Forces

Consider the following two situations. Jacqui, a 32-year-old woman, has been happily married for six years. She and her husband have a steady income. They decide to start a family, and a month later, Jacqui learns she is pregnant. Jenny, a 14-year-old girl, lives in the same neighbourhood as Jacqui. She has been sexually active for about six months but is not in a stable relationship. After missing her period, Jenny takes a pregnancy test and discovers that she is pregnant.

Although both Jacqui and Jenny became pregnant, the outcome of each pregnancy will certainly be affected by factors in each woman's situation such as her age, financial situation, and extent of her social support systems. The example illustrates life-cycle forces—the same event can have different effects, depending on when it happens in a person's life. In the scenarios with Jacqui and Jenny, the same event—pregnancy—produces happiness and eager anticipation for one woman but anxiety and concern for the other.

THINK ABOUT IT 💡

Getting a university degree is another event that has different effects based on when it happens in a person's life. Can you think of other events like these?

The influence of life-cycle forces can be depicted as a unified spiral consisting of biological, psychological, and sociocultural forces. (See Figure 1.2.) The spiral illustrates how a particular issue or event may recur, as indicated by the X's on the spiral, and how a person's accumulated experience, represented by the vertical arrow labelled "development," comes into play. For example, trust is an issue that is addressed throughout life (Erikson, 1982). From its beginnings as an infant's trust in parents, represented by the lower X on the spiral, it develops into progressively more complex forms of trust over the life span for friends and for lovers, as Jacqui can attest and Jenny will ultimately learn. Each time a person revisits trust issues, he or she builds on past experiences in light of intervening development. This accumulated experience means that the person will deal with trust in a new way and that trust is shown in different ways across the life span.

As noted in the Forces in Action feature above, by combining the four developmental forces, we can take a view of human development that encompasses the life span, appreciating the unique aspects of each phase of life. Indeed, the remainder of the book is based on this combination.

FIGURE 1.2   Life-Cycle Forces

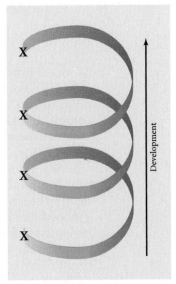

TEST YOURSELF

1. The nature-nurture issue involves the degree to which _____ and the environment influence human development.

2. Azar remarked that her 14-year-old son is incredibly shy and has been ever since he was a little baby. This illustrates the _____ of development.

3. _____ forces include genetic and health factors.

How does the biopsychosocial framework provide insight into the recurring issues of development (nature-nurture, continuity-discontinuity, universal–context-specific)?

Answers: (1) genetics, (2) continuity, (3) Biological

Developmental Theories

LEARNING OBJECTIVES

- How do psychodynamic theories account for development?
- What is the focus of learning theories of development?
- How do cognitive-developmental theories explain changes in thinking?
- What are the main points in the ecological and systems approach?
- What are the major tenets of life-span and life-cycle theories?

> **Developmental Theories**
>
> Psychodynamic Theory
>
> Learning Theory
>
> Cognitive-Developmental Theory
>
> The Ecological and Systems Approach
>
> Life-Span Perspective, Selective Optimization with Compensation, and Life Course Perspective
>
> The Big Picture

Marcus has just graduated from high school, first in his class. For his proud mother, Betty, this was a time to reflect on her son's past and ponder his future. Marcus has always been a happy, easy-going child—a joy to rear. And he's constantly been interested in learning. Betty wonders why he is so perpetually good-natured and so curious.

To answer Betty's questions about her son's growth, developmental researchers would provide a theory of his development. Unfortunately, for many people, the word *theory* means "boring." But that's not true. If you want to understand human development, theories are essential because they provide the "why's" for development. What is a theory? *In human development, a **theory** is an organized set of ideas that is designed to explain development.* For example, suppose friends of yours have a baby who cries often. You could imagine several explanations for her crying. Maybe the baby cries because she's hungry; maybe she cries to get her parents to hold her; maybe she cries because she's simply a cranky, unhappy baby. Each of these explanations is a very simple theory: It tries to explain why the baby cries so much. Of course, actual sophisticated theories in human development are much more complicated, but the purpose is the same—to explain behaviour and development. But do we really need them? Can't scientists simply study people and collect information? Check the Current Controversies feature for some insights.

CURRENT CONTROVERSIES

Who Needs Theories Anyway?

Many students wonder whether we really need theories of human development. Theories lead to predictions that we can test in research; in the process, the theory is supported or not. Think about the different explanations for the crying baby. Each one leads to unique predictions. If, for example, the baby is crying because she's hungry, we predict that feeding her more often should stop the crying. When results of research match the predictions, this supports the theory. When results differ from the predictions, this shows that the theory is incorrect and needs to be revised.

Perhaps now you see why theories are essential for human development research: They are the source for predictions for research, which often lead to changes in the theories. These revised theories then provide the basis for new predictions, which lead to new research, and the cycle continues.

Many theories guide research and thinking about human development. Just as lumber, bricks, pipes, and wires can be used to build an incredible variety of houses, the basic elements of the biopsychosocial framework have been assembled to form an incredible assortment of theories. Some theories attempt to explain a range of behaviours, whereas others focus on specific aspects. Additionally, some theories only consider development at

particular points in the life span, while others take a more holistic view. No modern theories of human development are truly comprehensive in attempting to cover all aspects of human behaviour throughout the life span (Cavanaugh, 1981), so we will draw upon many different theories throughout the book.

Some of these theories share many ideas and assumptions about human development but differ in their details. These theories are often grouped together to form a theoretical perspective. Table 1.1 lists five perspectives that guide contemporary thinking and research about development and describes the key aspects of each perspective. It also gives examples of theories, their main points, what aspects of the biopsychosocial framework they emphasize, and their position on the recurring developmental issues of nature-nurture, continuity-discontinuity, and universal versus context-specific development. In the next few pages, we'll introduce the five perspectives briefly. As we describe each of them, keep in mind that they were created to provide broad frameworks for understanding development and stimulating insightful research questions. And keep in mind that without them we would be unable to frame good questions about how people develop. So theories are essential after all.

TABLE 1.1		Theoretical Perspectives on Human Development		
Perspective	**Examples**	**Main Idea**	**Emphases in Biopsychosocial Framework**	**Positions on Developmental Issues**
Psychodynamic	Erikson's psychosocial theory	Personality develops through sequence of stages	Psychological, social, and life-cycle forces crucial; less emphasis on biological	Nature-nurture interaction, discontinuity, universal sequence but individual differences in rate
Learning	Behaviourism (Watson, Skinner)	Environment controls behaviour	In all theories, some emphasis on biological and psychological, major focus on social, little recognition of life cycle	In all theories, strongly nurture, continuity, and universal principles of learning
	Social learning theory (Bandura)	People learn through modelling and observing		
Cognitive	Piaget's theory (and extension) Kohlberg's moral reasoning theory	For Piaget and Kohlberg, thinking develops in a sequence of stages	For Piaget and Kohlberg, main emphasis on biological and social forces, less on psychological, little on life cycle	For Piaget and Kohlberg, strongly nature, discontinuity, individual differences in universal structures

TABLE 1.1 (CONTINUED)	Theoretical Perspectives on Human Development			
Perspective	**Examples**	**Main Idea**	**Emphases in Biopsychosocial Framework**	**Positions on Developmental Issues**
	Information-processing theory	Thought develops by increases in efficiency at handling information	Emphasis on biological and psychological, less on social and life cycle	Nature-nurture interaction, continuity, individual differences in universal structures
Ecological and Systems	Bronfenbrenner's theory	Developing person embedded in a series of interacting systems	Low emphasis on biological, psychological, and social, moderate on life cycle	Nature-nurture interaction, continuity, context-specific
	Competence-environmental press (Lawton and Nahemow)	Adaptation is optimal when ability and demands are in balance	Strong emphasis on the interactions of all four forces; cannot consider any in isolation	Nature-nurture interaction, continuity, context-specific
Life-Span, Selective Optimization with Compensation, and Life Course	Baltes' life-span perspective and selective optimization with compensation (SOC)	Development is multiply determined; optimization of goals	Strong emphasis on the interactions of all four forces; cannot consider any in isolation	Nature-nurture interaction, continuity, and discontinuity, context-specific
	Life course theory	Life course transitions decreasingly tied to age; increased continuity over time; specific life paths across domains are interdependent	Strong emphasis on psychological, sociocultural, life cycle; less on biological	Nature-nurture interaction, continuity, and discontinuity, context-specific

PSYCHODYNAMIC THEORY

Psychodynamic theories propose that human behaviour is largely governed by motives and drives that are internal and often unconscious. These hidden forces influence all aspects of our behaviour, thought, and personality, essentially shaping every part of our lives. Psychodynamic theories postulate that development occurs in a sequence of universal stages. This perspective underlies the oldest of the modern theories of human development, tracing its roots to Freud's work in the late 19th and early 20th centuries. His various theories of development included the idea that personality has several components that emerge over time. It also led to the development of the first comprehensive life-span view, Erik Erikson's psychosocial theory, which remains an important theoretical framework today.

Erikson's Theory

In Freud's view, development is largely complete by adolescence. In contrast, one of Freud's students, Erik Erikson (1902–1994), believed that development continues

throughout life. Erikson took the foundation laid by Freud and extended it through adulthood and into late life.

In his **psychosocial theory,** *Erikson proposed that personality development is determined by the interaction of an internal maturational plan and external societal demands.* He proposed that the life cycle is composed of eight stages and that the order of the stages is biologically fixed. The complete theory included the eight stages shown in Table 1.2. You can see that the name of each stage reflects the challenge people face at a particular age. For example, the challenge for young adults is to become involved in a loving relationship. Challenges are met through a combination of both inner psychological and outer social influences. When challenges are met successfully, people are well prepared to meet the challenge of the next stage.

TABLE 1.2		**The Eight Stages of Psychosocial Development in Erikson's Theory**
Psychosocial Stage	*Age*	*Challenge*
Basic trust vs. mistrust	Birth to 1 year	To develop a sense that the world is safe, a "good place"
Autonomy vs. shame and doubt	1 to 3 years	To realize that one is an independent person who can make decisions
Initiative vs. guilt	3 to 6 years	To develop the ability to try new things and to handle failure
Industry vs. inferiority	6 years to adolescence	To learn basic skills and to work with others
Identity vs. identity confusion	Adolescence	To develop a lasting, integrated sense of self
Intimacy vs. isolation	Young adulthood	To commit to another in a loving relationship
Generativity vs. stagnation	Middle adulthood	To contribute to younger people, through child rearing, child care, or other productive work
Integrity vs. despair	Late life	To view one's life as satisfactory and worth living

*The sequence of stages in Erikson's theory is based on the **epigenetic principle,** which means that each psychosocial strength has its own special time of ascendancy or period of particular importance.* The eight stages represent the order of this ascendancy. Because the stages extend across the whole life span, it takes a lifetime to acquire all the psychosocial strengths. Moreover, Erikson realizes that present and future behaviour must have its roots in the past, because later stages are built on the foundation laid in previous ones.

We examine each of Erikson's stages in more detail later in the book. In general, we can view them as a cycle that repeats (Logan, 1986): The first cycle goes from basic trust versus mistrust through identity versus identity confusion; the second cycle goes from intimacy versus isolation through integrity versus despair. In this view, the primary developmental progression is trust, achievement, wholeness. Throughout life, we first establish that we can trust others and ourselves, represented by basic trust versus mistrust in the first cycle. In the second cycle, we search for a person we can trust enough to establish a close relationship, represented by intimacy versus isolation. In achievement, we have a need to create something of our own, seen in the first cycle in the initiative versus guilt and industry versus inferiority stages, and in the second cycle in the generativity versus stagnation stage. Finally, we seek to answer the question of who we are, which in the first cycle is the identity versus identity confusion stage, and in the second cycle the integrity versus despair stage. From Erikson's perspective, there are only a few issues that face us in life, and we periodically return to them in order to reach higher resolutions of them. This return to certain key issues is a good example of the life-cycle forces we discussed earlier (page 9).

Whether we call them challenges, crises, or conflicts, the psychodynamic perspective emphasizes that the trek to adulthood is difficult because the path is strewn with obstacles. Outcomes of development reflect the manner and ease with which children surmount life's barriers. When children overcome early obstacles easily, they are better able to handle the later ones. A psychodynamic theorist would tell Betty that her son's cheerful disposition and his academic record suggest that he has handled life's early obstacles well, which is a good sign for his future development.

THINK ABOUT IT

How do Erikson's eight stages of psychosocial development relate to life experiences you or people you know have had?

LEARNING THEORY

In contrast to psychodynamic theory, learning theory concentrates on how learning influences a person's behaviour. This perspective emphasizes the role of experience, examining whether a person's behaviour is rewarded or punished. This perspective also emphasizes that people learn from watching others around them. Two influential theories in this perspective are behaviourism and social learning theory.

Behaviourism

At about the same time in the early 20th century that psychodynamic theory was attracting increased attention, John Watson (1878–1958) was among the first psychologists to champion the English philosopher John Locke's view that the infant's mind is a blank slate on which experience writes. Watson argued that learning determines what children will be. He assumed that, with the correct techniques, anything could be learned by almost anyone. In other words, in Watson's view, experience was just about all that mattered in determining the course of development.

Watson did little research to support his claims; B.F. Skinner (1904–1990) filled this gap. *Skinner studied operant conditioning, in which the consequences of a behaviour determine whether a behaviour is repeated in the future.* Skinner showed that two kinds of consequences were especially influential. *A reinforcement is a consequence that increases the future likelihood of the behaviour that it follows.* Positive reinforcement consists of giving a reward such as chocolate, gold stars, or paycheques to increase the likelihood of a previous behaviour. A father who wants to encourage his daughter to help with chores may reinforce her with praise, food treats, or money whenever she cleans her room. Negative reinforcement consists of rewarding people by taking away unpleasant things. The same father could use negative reinforcement by saying that whenever his daughter cleans her room she doesn't have to wash the dishes or fold laundry.

A *punishment* is a consequence that decreases the future likelihood of the behaviour that it follows. Punishment suppresses a behaviour by either adding something aversive or by withholding a pleasant event. Should the daughter fail to clean her room, the father may punish her by nagging (adding something aversive) or by not allowing her to watch television (withholding a pleasant event).

Skinner's research was done primarily with animals, but human development researchers soon showed that the principles of operant conditioning could be extended readily to people too (Baer & Wolf, 1968). Applied properly, reinforcement and punishment are indeed powerful influences on children, adolescents, and adults.

Social Learning Theory

Researchers discovered that people sometimes learn in ways that are not readily explained by operant conditioning. The most important of these is that people sometimes learn without reinforcement or punishment. *People learn much by simply watching those around them, which is known as imitation or observational learning.* Imitation is occurring when one toddler throws a toy after seeing a peer do so or when a school-age child offers to help an older adult carry groceries because she's seen her parents do the same.

Perhaps imitation makes you think of "monkey-see, monkey-do," in which people simply mimic what they see. Early investigators had this view too, but research quickly showed that this was wrong. People do not always imitate what they see around them. People are more likely to imitate if the person they see is popular, smart, or talented. They're also more likely to imitate when the behaviour they see is rewarded than when it is punished. Findings like these imply that imitation is more complex than sheer mimicry. People are not mechanically copying what they see and hear; instead, they look to others for information about appropriate behaviour. When popular, smart peers are reinforced for behaving in a particular way, it makes sense to imitate them.

Canadian-born Albert Bandura (1925 –) based his social cognitive theory on this more complex view of reward, punishment, and imitation. Bandura's theory is "cognitive" because he believes people actively try to understand what goes on in their world; the theory is "social" because, along with reinforcement and punishment, what other people do is an important source of information about the world.

Bandura also argues that experience gives people a sense of self-efficacy, which refers to people's beliefs about their own abilities and talents. Self-efficacy beliefs help to determine when people will imitate others. Children who see themselves as athletically untalented, for example, will not try to imitate Hayley Wickenheiser playing hockey despite the fact that she is obviously talented and popular. Thus, whether people will imitate others depends on who the other person is, whether that person's behaviour is rewarded, and the person's beliefs about his or her own talents.

Bandura's social cognitive theory is a far cry from Skinner's operant conditioning. The operant conditioned person who responds mechanically to reinforcement and punishment has been replaced by the social cognitive person who actively interprets these and other events. Nevertheless, Skinner, Bandura, and all learning theorists share the view that experience propels people along their developmental journeys. They would tell Betty that she can thank experience for making Marcus both happy and successful academically.

Archives of the History of American Psychology

COGNITIVE-DEVELOPMENTAL THEORY

Still another way to approach development is to focus on thought processes and the construction of knowledge. In cognitive-developmental theory, the key is how people think and how thinking changes over time. Two distinct approaches have developed. One approach postulates that thinking develops in a universal sequence of stages; Piaget's theory of cognitive development (and its recent extensions) and Kohlberg's theory of moral reasoning are two examples. The other approach proposes that people process information much like computers, becoming more efficient over much of the life span; information-processing theory is an example of this view.

Piaget's Theory

The cognitive-developmental perspective focuses on how children construct knowledge and how their constructions change over time. Jean Piaget (1896–1980), who was the most influential developmental psychologist of the 20th century, proposed the best known of these theories. Piaget believed children naturally try to make sense of their world. Throughout infancy, childhood, and adolescence, youngsters want to understand the workings of both the physical and the social world. For example, infants want to know about objects: "What happens when I push this toy off the table?" And they want to know about people: "Who is this person who feeds and cares for me?"

In their efforts to comprehend their world, Piaget argued that children act like scientists, creating theories about the physical and social worlds. Children try to weave all that they know about objects and people into a complete theory, and these theories are tested daily by experience because their theories lead them to expect certain things to happen. As with real scientific theories, when the predicted events do occur, a child's belief in her theory grows stronger. When the predicted events do not occur, the child must revise her theory. For example, an infant's theory of objects might include the idea that "toys pushed off the table fall to the floor." If the infant pushes some other object—a plate or an article of clothing—she will find that it, too, falls to the floor

Bettmann/Corbis/Magma

THINK ABOUT IT 💡

Try to use the basic ideas of operant conditioning (page 14) to explain how children create theories of the physical and social world.

and she can make the theory more general: "Objects pushed off the table fall to the floor."

Piaget also believed children begin to construct knowledge in new ways at a few critical points in development. When this happens, they revise their theories radically. These changes are so fundamental that the revised theory is, in many respects, a brand-new theory. Piaget claimed that these changes occurred three times in development: once at about age 2 years, a second time at about age 7, and a third time just before adolescence. These changes mean that children go through four distinct stages in cognitive development. Each stage represents a fundamental change in how children understand and organize their environment, and each stage is characterized by more sophisticated types of reasoning. For example, the sensorimotor stage begins at birth and lasts until about 2 years of age. As the name implies, sensorimotor thinking refers to an infant's constructing knowledge through sensory and motor skills. This stage and the three later stages are shown in Table 1.3.

TABLE 1.3	Piaget's Four Stages of Cognitive Development	
Stage	**Approximate Age**	**Characteristics**
Sensorimotor	Birth to 2 years	Infant's knowledge of the world is based on senses and motor skills. By the end of the period, uses mental representation.
Preoperational thought	2 to 6 years	Child learns how to use symbols such as words and numbers to represent aspects of the world but relates to the world only through his or her perspective.
Concrete operational thought	7 years to early adolescence	Child understands and applies logical operations to experiences provided they are focused on the here and now.
Formal operational thought	Adolescence and beyond	Adolescent or adult thinks abstractly, deals with hypothetical situations, and speculates about what may be possible.

Piaget's theory has had an enormous influence on how developmentalists and practitioners think about cognitive development. The theory has been applied in many ways—from the creation of discovery learning toys for children to the ways teachers plan lessons. However, his theory has also been criticized. Some say that Piaget underestimated the abilities of infants and young children. Also, the universality of his sequence of stages is not entirely supported by evidence from different cultures. More recently, Piaget's theory has been extended to include important cognitive changes in adulthood. We consider these issues in more detail in Chapters 3, 5, and 9.

Kohlberg's Theory

Because Piaget's theory attempts to tie together maturation and experience on the one hand and cognitive and social development on the other, it has inspired developmentalists with a wide variety of interests. One of the most influential of these was Lawrence Kohlberg, who built his theory of moral reasoning on the foundation of Piaget's theory of overall cognitive development.

As we'll see in detail in Chapter 9, Kohlberg described a sequence of fixed stages that reflect the different ways people think about moral dilemmas. Kohlberg's theory is an excellent example of how a general theory of development, Piaget's theory, can be focused to deal with the more circumscribed issue of moral reasoning. Kohlberg's stages correspond fairly well to Piaget's stages, but they involve levels of thinking beyond Piaget's final stage. In this respect, Kohlberg's theory constitutes an extension of Piaget's work.

Information-Processing Theory

Not all cognitive-developmental theorists view development as a sequence of stages. Information-processing theorists, for example, draw heavily on how computers work to explain thinking and how it develops through childhood and adolescence. *Just as computers consist of both hardware (disk drives, random-access memory, and central processing unit) and software (the programs we use),* **information-processing theory** *proposes that human cognition consists of mental hardware and mental software.* Mental hardware refers to cognitive structures, including different memories where information is stored. Mental software includes organized sets of cognitive processes that enable people to complete specific tasks, such as reading a sentence, playing a video game, or hitting a baseball. For example, an information-processing psychologist would say that, for the girl in the photo to do well on an exam, she must encode the information as she studies, store it in memory, then retrieve the necessary information during the test.

Photodisc

How do information-processing psychologists explain developmental changes in thinking? To answer this question, think about improvements in personal computers. Today's personal computers can accomplish much more than computers built just a few years ago. Why? Today's computers have better hardware (e.g., more memory and a faster central processing unit) and more sophisticated software that takes advantage of the better hardware. Like modern computers, older children and adolescents have better hardware and better software than younger children, who are more like last year's out-of-date model. For example, older children typically solve math word problems better than younger children because they have greater memory capacity to store the facts in the problem and because their methods for performing arithmetic operations are more efficient.

Some researchers also point to deterioration of the mental hardware, along with declines in the mental software, as explanations of cognitive aging. We will see in Chapter 14, for example, that normal aging brings with it significant changes in people's ability to process information.

For Piaget, Kohlberg, and information-processing theorists, children's thinking becomes more sophisticated as they develop. Piaget and Kohlberg explain this change as resulting from the more sophisticated knowledge that children construct from more sophisticated thinking; information-processing psychologists attribute it to more sophisticated mental hardware and mental software. None of these theorists would have much to say to Betty about Marcus's good nature. As to his academic success, Piaget and Kohlberg would explain that all children naturally want to understand their worlds; Marcus is simply unusually skilled in this regard. An information-processing psychologist would point to superior hardware and superior software as the keys to his academic success.

THE ECOLOGICAL AND SYSTEMS APPROACH

Most developmentalists agree that the environment is an important force in many aspects of development. However, only ecological theories have focused on the complexities of environments and their links to development. *In ecological theory, which gets its name from the branch of biology dealing with the relation of living things to their environment and to one another, human development is inseparable from the environmental contexts in which a person develops.* The ecological approach is broad; it proposes that all aspects of development are interconnected, much like the threads of a spider's web are intertwined. Interconnectedness means that no aspect of development can be isolated from others and understood independently. An ecological theorist would emphasize that, if we want to understand why adolescents behave as they do, we need to consider the many different systems that influence them, including parents, peers, teachers, television, the neighbourhood, and social policy.

We will consider two examples of the ecological and systems approach: Bronfenbrenner's theory and the competence–environmental press framework.

Bronfenbrenner's Theory

The best-known proponent of the ecological approach is Urie Bronfenbrenner (1979, 1989, 1995), who proposes that the developing person is embedded in a series of complex and interactive systems. Bronfenbrenner divides the environment into the four levels shown in Figure 1.3: the microsystem, the mesosystem, the exosystem, and the macrosystem. *At any point in life, the microsystem consists of the people and objects in an individual's immediate environment.* These are the people closest to a child, such as parents or siblings. Some children may have more than one microsystem; for example, a young child might have the microsystems of the family and of the day-care setting. As you can imagine, microsystems strongly influence development.

Microsystems themselves are connected to create the mesosystem. The mesosystem provides connections across microsystems, because what happens in one microsystem is likely to influence others. Perhaps you've found that if you have a stressful day at work or school you're often grouchy at home. This indicates that your mesosystem is alive and well; your microsystems of home and work are interconnected emotionally for you.

The exosystem refers to social settings that a person may not experience firsthand but that still influence development. For example, changes in government policy regarding welfare may mean that poor children have less opportunity for enriched preschool experiences. Although the influence of the exosystem is at least secondhand, its effects on the developing child can be quite strong.

The broadest environmental context is the **macrosystem,** *the subcultures and cultures in*

FIGURE 1.3   Bronfenbrenner's Ecological Theory

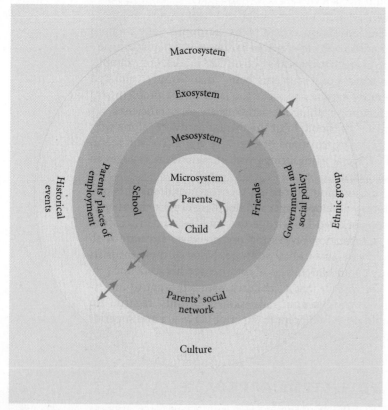

Adapted from *The Child: Development in a Social Context,* by Claire B. Kopp and Joanne B. Krakow, p. 648. Copyright © 1982 Addison-Wesley Publishing Co., Inc. Used with permission.

which the microsystem, mesosystem, and exosystem are embedded. A mother, her workplace, her child, and the child's school are part of a larger cultural setting, such as Asian Canadians living in Vancouver or Italian Canadians living in Toronto. Members of these cultural groups share a common identity, a common heritage, and common values. The macrosystem evolves over time; what is true about a particular culture today may or may not have been true in the past and may or may not be true in the future. Thus, each successive generation of children may develop in a unique macrosystem.

Competence–Environmental Press Theory

A second, less complex approach that also emphasizes the interaction of individuals with their environment is Lawton and Nahemow's (1973) competence–environmental press theory. As we will see in greater detail in Chapter 16, this theory was originally proposed to account for the ways in which older adults function in their environment. However, it can be used to understand how people of all ages deal with their environments.

Basically, according to the theory, how well people adapt depends on the match between their competence, or abilities, and the environmental press, or the demands put on them by the environment. This notion of "best match" or "best fit" leading to adaptation could be extended across the life span. For example, how well a child's social skills match her peer group's demands could account for whether she will be accepted by the peer group or not. As with Bronfenbrenner's theory, competence–environmental press theory emphasizes that in order to understand people's functioning, it is essential to understand the systems in which they live.

Ecological theorists would agree with learning theorists in telling Betty that the environment has been pivotal in her son's amiable disposition and his academic achievements. However, the ecological theorist would insist that environment means much more than the reinforcements, punishments, and observations that are central to learning theory. The ecological theorist would emphasize the different levels of environmental influence on Marcus. Betty's ability to balance home (microsystem) and work (mesosystem) so skilfully (which meant that she was usually in a good mood herself) contributed positively to Marcus's development as did Betty's membership in a cultural group (exosystem) that emphasized the value of doing well in school.

LIFE-SPAN PERSPECTIVE, SELECTIVE OPTIMIZATION WITH COMPENSATION, AND LIFE COURSE PERSPECTIVE

One criticism of most of the theories of human development we have considered thus far is that they pay little or no specific attention to the adult years of the life span. Historically, adulthood was downplayed due to the belief that it was a time when abilities had reached a plateau (rather than continuing to develop) and that adulthood was followed by inevitable decline in old age. However, the field of adult development and aging has evolved greatly since the late 1940s. As a result, new theoretical perspectives emphasize the importance of viewing human development as a lifelong process. These perspectives view development in terms of where a person has been and where he or she is heading.

Life-Span Perspective and Selective Optimization with Compensation

What would it be like to try to understand your best friend without knowing anything about his or her life? We cannot understand adults' experiences without appreciating their childhood and adolescence. Placing adults' lives in this broader context is what the life-span perspective does.

*According to the **life-span perspective,** human development is multiply determined and cannot be understood within the scope of a single framework.* Matilda Riley, the person most responsible for first developing the life-span perspective, insists that human development must be viewed from the biopsychosocial framework. The basic premises of the life-span perspective, in which aging is viewed in the context of the rest of the life span, are as follows (Riley, 1979):

- Aging is a lifelong process of growing up and growing old, beginning with conception and ending with death. No single period of a person's life (such as childhood, adolescence, or middle age) can be understood apart from its origins and its consequences. To understand a specific period, we must know what came before and what comes after.
- How one's life is played out is affected by social, environmental, and historical change. Thus, the experiences of one generation may not be the same as those of another.
- New patterns of development can cause social change. For example, the realization over the past few decades that the use of physical punishment with children has a number of negative developmental outcomes has resulted in the passage of laws in a number of countries outlawing parents' rights to use this form of punishment. Thus, not only does social change influence people's development, but patterns of development influence society.

Paul Baltes Courtesy of Paul Baltes/Center of Lifespan Psychology at the Max Planck Institute for Human Development

The life-span perspective divides human development into two phases: an early phase (childhood and adolescence) and a later phase (young adulthood, middle age, and old age). The early phase is characterized by rapid age-related increases in people's physical size and abilities. These changes also occur in the later phase, but more slowly; people's abilities continue to develop as they adapt to the environment (Baltes, Lindenberger, & Staudinger, 1998). When development is viewed from a life-span perspective, it is a complex phenomenon that cannot be understood from the vantage point of a single discipline. Understanding how people change requires input from many perspectives.

Paul Baltes and colleagues provide many of the main approaches to human development from a life-span perspective (Baltes, 1987; Baltes et al., 1998; Baltes, Staudinger, & Lindenberger, 1999). They identify four key features of the life-span perspective:

- *Multidirectionality:* Development involves both growth and decline; as people grow in one area they may lose in another and at different rates. For example, people's vocabulary ability tends to increase throughout life, but reaction time tends to slow down.
- *Plasticity:* One's capacity is not predetermined or carved in stone. Many skills can be learned or improved with practice, even in late life. For example, people can learn ways to help themselves remember information, which may help them deal with declines in memory ability with age. There are limits to the degree of potential improvement, though, as described in later chapters.
- *Historical context:* Each of us develops within a particular set of circumstances determined by the historical time in which we are born and the culture in which we grow up. For example, living in a middle-class suburb in the 1950s was very different from living in an isolated northern community in the 1990s.
- *Multiple causation:* How we develop results from biological, psychological, sociocultural, and life-cycle forces, which we considered earlier in this

chapter. For example, two children growing up in the same family will have different experiences if one has a developmental disability and one does not.

Based on these principles, Baltes and colleagues (1998) propose that life-span development consists of the dynamic interplay between growth, maintenance, and loss regulation. Different processes have different developmental trajectories. In their view, four factors are critical to understanding these differences across processes:

- There is an age-related reduction in the amount and quality of biologically based resources as people grow older.
- There is an age-related increase in the amount and quality of culture needed to generate continuously higher growth, usually resulting in a net slowing of growth as people mature and grow old.
- There is an age-related decline in the efficiency with which cultural resources are used.
- There is a lack of cultural support structures for growing old.

These four factors create the need to shift increasing resources to maintain function and deal with biologically related losses as we grow old, leaving fewer resources to be devoted to continued growth.

Taken together, the principles of the life-span perspective create a way to describe and explain the successful adaptation of people to the changes that occur with aging by proposing an interaction between three processes: selection, compensation, and optimization (Baltes, 1997; M. Baltes & Carstensen, 1999). Selection processes serve to choose goals, life domains, and life tasks; optimization and compensation concern maintaining or enhancing chosen goals. *The basic assumption of the **selective optimization with compensation (SOC)** model is that the three processes form a system of behavioural action that generates and regulates development and aging.*

As people mature and grow old, they select from a range of possibilities or opportunities. This selection occurs for two main reasons. *Elective selection* occurs when one chooses to reduce one's involvement to fewer domains as a result of new demands or tasks, such as when a college student drops out of some organizations due to the amount of work required in the courses she is taking that term. *Loss-based selection* occurs when this reduced involvement happens as a result of anticipated losses in personal or environmental resources, such as when an older person stops going to church because he can no longer drive. In either case, selection can involve the continuation of previous goals on a lesser scale, or the substitution of new goals, and may be proactive or reactive.

Compensation occurs when a person can no longer function well in a particular domain because the necessary behavioural skills have been lost or have fallen below the level necessary for adequate functioning. When a person compensates, she searches for an alternative way to accomplish the goal; for example, if one loses the ability to drive to work due to an injury, one might compensate by taking the bus. Sometimes, compensation requires learning a new skill; for example, an older adult who is experiencing short-term memory problems might compensate by learning to use a PDA device. Thus, compensation differs from selection in that the task or goal is maintained but other means are used to achieve it.

Optimization involves the minimization of losses and the maximization of gains. The main idea is to find the best match possible between one's resources (biological, psychological, and sociocultural) and one's desired goals. Given that people cannot achieve optimal outcomes in everything, development becomes a dynamic balancing process between selecting the right goals and compensating when possible to help maximize the odds of achieving them.

One can see the SOC model at work in many situations. For example, aging musicians may reduce the number of pieces they play (selection), rehearse them more often (optimization), and sing them in a lower key (compensation). This way, they can continue playing concerts later in life. Or a college athlete who excels at ice hockey and baseball may decide to concentrate on hockey (selection), work on training all year (optimization), and develop a wicked wrist shot to make up for a mediocre slap shot (compensation).

The life-span perspective and the SOC model have provided important approaches to the contemporary study of human development. The emphasis on the need for a multidisciplinary approach and recognition of many interactive forces will be developed throughout this text.

Life Course Perspective

If you ask an adult to describe his or her life, what you are likely to hear is a story that includes several key life transitions (e.g., going to school, getting a first job, getting married, having children). Such stories show how people move through their lives and experience unique interactions of the four forces of development.

The *life course perspective describes the ways in which various generations experience the biological, psychological, and sociocultural forces of development in their respective historical contexts.* Specifically, it lets researchers examine how historical time affects how people create their lives (Hagestad & Dannefer, 2001; Hareven, 1995; O'Rand & Campbell, 1999). A key feature of the life course perspective is the dynamic interplay between the individual and society. This interplay creates three major dimensions, all of which involve timing, which underlie the life course perspective:

- The individual timing of life events in relation to external historical events. This dimension addresses the question: How do people time and sequence their lives (e.g., getting a first job) in the context of changing historical conditions (e.g., economic good times or recession)?
- The synchronization of individual transitions with collective familial ones. This dimension addresses the question: How do people balance their own lives (e.g., work obligations) with those of their family (e.g., children's soccer games)?
- The impact of earlier life events, as shaped by historical events, on subsequent ones. This dimension addresses the question: How does experiencing an event earlier in life (e.g., a male turning 18 years old) at a particular point in history (e.g., when there is a military draft) affect one's subsequent life (e.g., choosing a particular career)?

Research from the life course perspective has clearly shown that major life transitions such as entering into a life partnership, childbearing, starting and ending a career, and completing one's education occur at many different ages across people and generations. These differences begin appearing after adolescence when people begin to have much more control over the course of their lives. Research has also shown that life transitions are more continuous and multidirectional than previously thought. For example, traditional models relegated education completion to early adulthood; current trends toward lifelong learning make this view obsolete. Finally, research shows that the various domains of people's lives are highly interdependent; for example, the decision to have a child is often made in the context of where one is in one's career and education.

The emphasis in the life course perspective on the interrelations between the individual and society through the emphasis on historical time has made it a dominant view in the social sciences. In particular, it is very useful in helping researchers understand how the various aspects of people's experiences (work, family, education) interact to create unique lives. Margaret Elder Hart, discussed in the Real People feature, is a good example of this.

REAL PEOPLE: APPLYING HUMAN DEVELOPMENT

Margaret Elder Hart

Dr. Margaret Elder Hart has lived through and was shaped by some of the most important historical events of the 20th century. She was born in 1907, before Canadian women had the right to vote and just a few years after the invention of the airplane, but lived in a time that saw space travel and men on the moon, as well as two world wars. She rose to prominence in her chosen profession of nursing and, convinced that education was important to advance her profession, attended Columbia University in New York and became one of the first doctorally prepared nurses in Canada. She has been the recipient of numerous awards, including an honorary Doctor of Laws degree by the University of Manitoba, where she had been the director of the School of Nursing from 1948 until 1972. At the age of 97 years, Dr. Hart continues to be interested in, and keeps up to date on, health care and nursing education issues. 47

Margaret Elder Hart University of Manitoba Imaging Services and Margaret Elder Hart

Overall, life-span and life-cycle theories have greatly enhanced the general body of developmental theory by drawing attention to the role of aging in the broader context of human development. These theories have played a major role in conceptualizing adulthood and have greatly influenced the research we consider in Chapters 11 through 16. Life-span and life course perspective theorists would tell Betty that Marcus will continue to develop throughout his adult years, and that this developmental journey will be influenced by biopsychosocial forces, including his own family.

THE BIG PICTURE

Each of the theories provides ways of explaining how the biological, psychological, sociocultural, and life-cycle forces create human development. But because no single theory provides a complete explanation of all aspects of development, we must rely on the biopsychosocial framework to help piece together an account based on many different theories. Throughout the remainder of this text, you will read about many theories that differ in focus and in scope. To help you understand them better, each theory will be introduced in the context of the issues that it addresses.

Because one of the criteria for a theory is that it be testable, developmentalists have adopted certain methods to help accomplish this. The next section provides an overview of the methods by which developmentalists conduct research and test their theories.

TEST YOURSELF

1. _____ organize knowledge in order to provide testable explanations of human behaviours and the ways in which they change over time.

2. The _____ perspective proposes that development is determined by the interaction of an internal maturational plan and external societal demands.

3. According to social cognitive theory, people learn from reinforcements, punishments, and through _____.

4. Piaget's theory, Kohlberg's theory, and _____ theory are examples of the cognitive-developmental perspective.

5. According to Bronfenbrenner, development occurs in the context of the _____, mesosystem, exosystem, and macrosystem.

6. A belief that human development is characterized by multidirectionality and plasticity is fundamental to the _____ perspective.

How are the psychodynamic perspective and Piaget's theory similar? How are they different?

Answers: (1) Theories, (2) psychosocial, (3) observing others, (4) information-processing, (5) microsystem, (6) life-span

1.3

Doing Developmental Research

LEARNING OBJECTIVES

▸ How do scientists measure topics of interest in studying children's development?

▸ What general research designs are used in human development research? What designs are unique to human development research?

▸ What ethical procedures must researchers follow?

Leah and Joan are both mothers of 10-year-old boys. Their sons have many friends, but the basis for the friendships is not obvious to the mothers. Leah believes "opposites attract"—children form friendships with peers who have complementary interests and abilities. Joan doubts this; her son seems to seek out other boys who are near clones of himself in their interests and abilities.

> **Doing Developmental Research**
>
> Measurement in Human Development Research
>
> General Designs for Research
>
> Designs for Studying Development
>
> Conducting Research Ethically
>
> Communicating Research Results
>
> Applying Research Results: Social Policy and Evidence-Based Practice

Suppose Leah and Joan know that you're taking a course in human development, so they ask you to settle their argument. Leah believes complementary children are more often friends, whereas Joan believes similar children are more often friends. You know that research could show whose ideas are supported under which circumstances, but how? In fact, human development researchers must make several important decisions as they prepare to study a topic. They need to decide how to measure the topic of interest; they must design their study; they must choose a method for studying development; and they must decide whether their plan respects the rights of the individuals who would participate in the research.

Human development researchers do not always stick to this sequence of steps. For example, often researchers will consider the rights of research participants as they make the other decisions, perhaps rejecting a measurement procedure because it violates the rights of participants. Nevertheless, for simplicity, we will use this sequence as we describe each of the steps in doing developmental research.

MEASUREMENT IN HUMAN DEVELOPMENT RESEARCH

Researchers usually begin by deciding how to measure the topic or behaviour of interest. For example, the first step in answering Leah and Joan's question about friendships would be to decide how to measure friendships.

Human development researchers typically use one of three approaches: observing systematically, using tasks to sample behaviour, and asking people for self-reports.

Systematic Observation

*As the name implies, **systematic observation** involves watching people and carefully recording what they do or say.* Two forms of systematic observation are common. *In **naturalistic observation**, people are observed as they behave spontaneously in some real-life situation.* Of course, researchers can't keep track of everything that someone does, so beforehand they must decide what variables to record. For example, researchers studying friendship might decide to observe children at the start of the first year in a middle school (chosen because many children will be making new friends at this time). They could decide to record where children sit in the lunchroom and to record who talks to whom.

Structured observations differ from naturalistic observations in that the researcher creates a setting that is particularly likely to elicit the behaviour of interest. Structured observations are particularly useful for studying behaviours that are difficult to observe naturally. Some phenomena occur rarely, such as emergencies. An investigator relying on natural observations to study people's responses to emergencies wouldn't make much progress with naturalistic observation because, by definition, emergencies don't occur at predetermined times and locations. However, using a structured observation, an investigator might stage an emergency—perhaps by simulating an accident with the cooperation of authorities—to observe other people's responses.

Other behaviours are difficult for researchers to observe because they occur in private settings, not public ones. For example, much interaction between friends takes place at home, where it would be difficult for investigators to observe unobtrusively. However, friends could be asked to come to the researcher's laboratory, which might be furnished to resemble a family room in a typical house. Friends would then be asked to perform some activity typical of friends, such as discussing a problem together or deciding what movie to see. The researchers would then observe their activity from another room, through a one-way mirror, or by videotaping them.

Structured observations are valuable in enabling researchers to observe behaviour(s) that would otherwise be difficult to study. However, investigators using this approach must be careful that the settings they create do not disturb the behaviour of interest. For example, observing friends as they discuss a problem in a mock family room has many artificial aspects to it: The friends are not in their own homes, they were told in general terms what to do, and they know they're being observed. Any or all of these factors may cause friends to behave differently than they would in the real world. This issue relates to the validity of the research. For example, are observations of friends in a mock family room telling us about friends' interactions as they occur naturally? If they are, then they represent a valid measure of people's behaviour. Investigators must take great care to document the validity of their measures.

Sampling Behaviour with Tasks

When investigators can't observe a behaviour directly, another popular alternative is to create tasks that are thought to sample the behaviour of interest. One task often used to measure older adults' memory is digit span: Adults listen as a sequence of digits is presented aloud. After the last digit is presented, they try to repeat the digits in order. Another example is shown in Figure 1.4. The child has been asked to look at the photographs and point to the face that looks happy. A child's answers on this sort of task are useful in determining his or her ability to recognize emotions.

FIGURE 1.4

This approach is popular with human development researchers primarily because it is so convenient. The main problem with this approach is validity: Does the task provide a realistic sample of the behaviour of interest? For example, asking children to judge emotions from photographs may not be valid because it underestimates what they do in real life. Can you think of reasons this might be the case? We mention several reasons on page 37.

Self-Reports

The last approach, self-reports, is a special case of using tasks to measure people's behaviour. *Self-reports are simply people's answers to questions about the topic of interest.* When questions are posed in written form, the self-report is a questionnaire; when questions are posed orally, the self-report is an interview. In either format, questions are created that probe different aspects of the topic of interest. For example, if you believe children are more often friends when they have interests in common, you might tell your research participants the following:

> Tom and Dave just met each other at school. Tom likes to read, plays the clarinet in the school orchestra, and is not interested in sports; Dave likes to watch videos on MTV, tinkers with his car, and is a star on the football team. Do you think Tom and Dave will become friends?

The participants would then decide, perhaps using a rating scale, whether the boys are likely to become friends.

Self-reports are useful because they can lead directly to information on the topic of interest. They are also relatively convenient, particularly when they can be administered to groups of participants. However, self-reports are not always valid measures of people's behaviour because answers are sometimes inaccurate. Why? When asked about past events, people may not remember them accurately. For example, an older adult asked about adolescent friends may not remember those friendships well. Sometimes people answer incorrectly due to response bias. For many questions, some responses are more socially acceptable than others. People are more likely to select socially acceptable answers than socially unacceptable ones. For example, many people would be reluctant to admit that they have no friends at all. As long as investigators keep these weaknesses in mind, self-report is a valuable tool for human development research.

THINK ABOUT IT

If you were studying middle-aged adults caring for their aging parents, what would be the advantages of systematic observation, sampling behaviour with tasks, and self-reports?

The three approaches to measurement are summarized in Table 1.4.

After researchers choose a method, they must show that it is both reliable and valid. *The **reliability** of a measure is the extent to which it provides a consistent index of a characteristic.* A measure of friendship, for example, is reliable to the extent that it gives a consistent estimate of a person's friendship network each time you administer it. All measures used in human development research must be shown to be reliable, or they cannot be used. *The **validity** of a measure refers to whether it really measures*

Method	Strength	Weakness
TABLE 1.4	**Measuring Behaviours of Interest in Human Development Research**	
Systematic observation		
Naturalistic observation	Captures people's behaviour in its natural setting	Difficult to use with behaviours that are rare or that typically occur in private settings
Structured observation	Can be used to study behaviours that are rare or that typically occur in private settings	May be invalid if structured setting distorts the behaviour
Sampling behaviour with tasks	Convenient—can be used to study most behaviours	May be invalid if the task does not sample behaviour as it occurs naturally
Self-reports	Convenient—can be used to study most behaviours	May be invalid because people answer incorrectly (due to either forgetting or response bias)

what researchers think it measures. For example, a measure of friendship is valid only if it can be shown to actually measure friendship (and not love, for example). Validity is often established by showing that the measure in question is closely related to another measure known to be valid. Because it is possible to have a measure that is reliable but not valid (e.g., a ruler is a reliable measure of length but not a valid measure of friendship), researchers must ensure that their measures are both reliable and valid.

Throughout this book, you'll see many studies using different methods. In addition, you'll often see that studies of the same topic or behaviour use different methods. That is, each of the approaches will be used in different studies. This can be particularly valuable: Because the approaches to measurement have different strengths and weaknesses, finding the same results regardless of the approach leads to particularly strong conclusions.

Representative Sampling

Valid measures also depend on the people who are tested. *Researchers are usually interested in broad groups of people called* **populations**. Examples of populations would be all Canadian 7-year-olds or all Ukrainian-Canadian grandparents. *Virtually all studies include only a* **sample** *of people, which is a subset of the population.* Researchers must take care that their sample really is representative of the population of interest. An unrepresentative sample can lead to invalid research. For example, what would you think of a study of older adults' friendships if you learned that the sample consisted entirely of adults who had no siblings? You would, quite correctly, decide that this sample is not representative of the population of older adults and question whether its results apply to adults with siblings.

As you read on, you'll soon discover that a lot of the research described was conducted with samples of middle-class European North American people. Are these samples representative of all people in Canada and/or the United States? Of all people in the world? Sometimes, but not always. Be careful *not* to assume that findings from this group necessarily apply to people in other groups. Additionally, some developmental issues have not been studied in all ethnic and racial groups.

In an effort to make samples more representative, funding agencies strongly encourage and may require that samples have representation of groups related to ethnicity, race, gender, age, etc., so that they more accurately reflect the reality of the diversity of our population. This may make it possible to obtain a broader view of developmental processes. Until we have representative samples in all developmental research, we cannot know whether a particular phenomenon applies only to the group studied or to people more generally. This is particularly relevant in Canada which, in 1971, became the first nation to make multiculturalism an official policy.

GENERAL DESIGNS FOR RESEARCH

Having selected a way to measure the topic or behaviour of interest, researchers next must embed this measure in a research design that yields useful, relevant results. Human development researchers rely on three primary designs in planning their work: qualitative, correlational, and experimental studies.

Qualitative Studies

In a **qualitative study,** *also known as systemic inquiry, researchers look at experiences and processes about which very little is known.* Whereas quantitative researchers use questionnaires or research scales to collect and measure responses for analysis, qualitative researchers collect data through in-depth interviews. The purpose of the interviews is to collect the description of the participant's own experience of the phenomena being studied, often called the "lived experience." For example, the experience of becoming a parent might be the focus of the study in which participants would be interviewed in relation to the meaning and dimensions of this experience for them. The data are the participants' verbal responses, which are usually tape-recorded, transcribed verbatim, and then qualitatively analyzed to generate new knowledge to contribute to the understanding of the phenomenon.

The specific steps of how a qualitative study is carried out and the types of questions asked may change during the course of a study based on the data collected and the interview process. Generally, qualitative studies have many fewer participants than quantitative studies. However, the in-depth interviews produce rich descriptions and responses that are meaningful to the participant and help researchers understand the phenomena of interest. The focus is not to understand what "causes" a phenomenon, but to seek understanding, i.e., either to describe the experience or to explain with theory development. Some researchers may incorporate both qualitative (meaningfulness) and quantitative (measurement) approaches in their design.

Correlational Studies

In a **correlational study,** *investigators look at relations between variables as they exist naturally in the world.* In the simplest possible correlational study, a researcher would measure two variables, then see how they are related. Imagine a researcher who wants to test the idea that smarter people have more friends. To test this claim, the researcher would measure two variables for each person in the sample. One would be the number of friends that the person has; the other would be the person's intelligence.

The results of a correlational study are usually measured by calculating a **correlation coefficient,** *abbreviated r, which expresses the strength and direction of a relation between two variables.* Correlations can range from -1.0 to 1.0 and reflect three different relations between intelligence and the number of friends:

- When $r = 0$, two variables are completely unrelated: People's intelligence is unrelated to the number of friends they have.
- When r is greater than 0, scores are related positively: People who are smart tend to have more friends than people who are not as smart. That is, *more* intelligence is associated with having *more* friends.
- When r is less than 0, scores are related, but inversely: People who are smart tend to have fewer friends than people who are not as smart. That is, *more* intelligence is associated with having *fewer* friends.

A researcher conducting a correlational study can determine whether the variables are related. However, this design doesn't address the question of cause and effect between the variables. For example, suppose a researcher finds that the correlation between intelligence and number of friends is .7. This would mean that people who are smarter have more friends than people who are not as smart. How would you interpret this correlation? Figure 1.5 shows that three interpretations are possible. Maybe being smart causes people to have more friends. Another interpretation is that having more friends causes people to be smarter. A third interpretation is that neither variable causes the other; instead, intelligence and number of friends are caused by a third variable that was not measured in the study. Perhaps parents who are warm and supportive tend to have children who grow up to both be smarter and have many friends. Any of these interpretations could be true. They cannot be distinguished in a correlational study. When investigators want to track down causes, they resort to a different design, an experimental study.

Experimental Studies

*An **experiment** is a systematic way of manipulating the key factor(s) that the investigator thinks causes a particular behaviour. The factor being manipulated is called the **independent variable**; the behaviour being observed is called the **dependent variable**.* In human development, an experiment requires that the investigator begin with one or more treatments, circumstances, or events (independent variables) that are thought to affect behaviour. People are then assigned randomly to conditions that differ in the treatment they are given; then an appropriate measure (the dependent variable) is taken of all participants to see whether the treatment or treatments had the expected effect. Because each person has an equal chance of being assigned to each treatment condition (the definition of random assignment), the groups should be the same except in the treatment they have received. Any differences between the groups can be attributed to the differential treatment people received in the experiment rather than to other factors.

Suppose, for example, that an investigator believes adolescents can learn more from a short story in a quiet room than in a room in which loud music is playing.

THINK ABOUT IT 💡

Describe a correlational study that would examine the impact of exercise on health in older adults. Now describe an experimental study to look at the same topic. What are the advantages of each design?

FIGURE 1.5

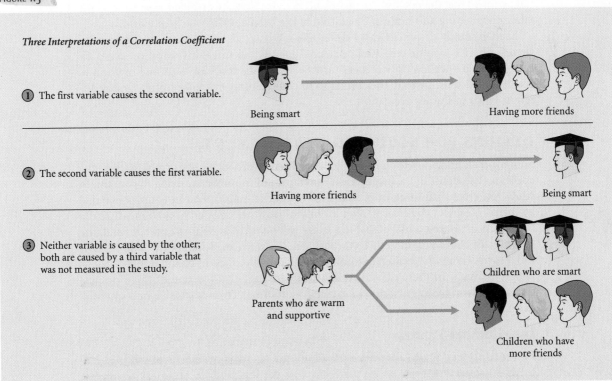

Three Interpretations of a Correlation Coefficient

① The first variable causes the second variable.

Being smart   Having more friends

② The second variable causes the first variable.

Having more friends   Being smart

③ Neither variable is caused by the other; both are caused by a third variable that was not measured in the study.

Parents who are warm and supportive

Children who are smart

Children who have more friends

FIGURE 1.6   **Example of Experimental Study**

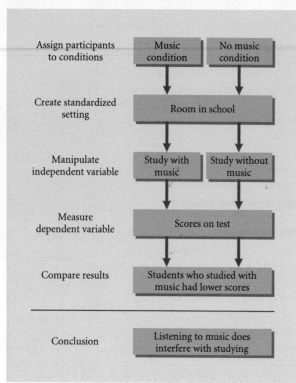

Figure 1.6 shows how we might test this hypothesis. Adolescents come to the testing site (perhaps a room in a school) where they read a brief story prepared specially for the study. Based on random assignment, individual adolescents read the story either while the room is quiet or while loud music is played. The loud music is always the same music, played at the same volume, for all adolescents in the loud-music condition. All the participants read the identical story under circumstances held as constant as possible except for the presence or absence of the music. They all get the same amount of time to read the story and are given the same test afterward. If scores on the test are, on average, better in the quiet condition than in the loud-music condition, the investigator may say with confidence that the music has an unfavourable effect on learning the story. Conclusions about cause and effect are possible in this example because the direct manipulation occurred under controlled conditions.

Human development researchers usually conduct experiments in laboratory-like settings because this allows full control over the variables that may influence the outcome of the research. A shortcoming of laboratory work is that the behaviour of interest is not studied in its natural setting. Consequently, there is always the potential problem that the results may be invalid because they are artificial—specific to the laboratory setting and not representative of the behaviour in the "real world."

Each research design used by developmentalists has both strengths and weaknesses. There is no one best method. Consequently, no single investigation can definitely settle a question. Researchers rarely rely on one study or even one method to reach conclusions. Instead, they prefer to find converging evidence from as many different kinds of studies as possible.

DESIGNS FOR STUDYING DEVELOPMENT

Sometimes human development research is directed at a single age group, such as the adolescent students in the example on the impact of music on studying. Or we might study retirement planning in 55-year-olds or marital satisfaction in couples married 25 years. In each of these cases, after an investigator has decided how to measure the behaviour of interest and whether the study will be correlational or experimental, the investigator could skip directly to the last step—determine whether the study is ethical. However, much research in human development concerns changes that occur as people develop. In these cases, investigators must also choose one of three designs that allow them to examine development: longitudinal, cross-sectional, or sequential designs.

Longitudinal Studies

*In a **longitudinal study**, the same individuals are observed or tested repeatedly at different points in their lives.* As the name implies, the longitudinal approach involves a lengthwise account of development and is the most direct way to watch growth occur. The longitudinal approach is well suited to studying almost any aspect of the course of development. More important, it is the only way to answer certain questions about the stability or instability of behaviour: Will characteristics such as aggression, dependency, or mistrust observed in infancy or early childhood persist into adulthood? How long will the beneficial effects of special academic training in the preschool years last? Will a regular exercise program begun in middle age have benefits in later life? Such questions can be explored only by testing people at one point in development and then retesting them later in their development.

The approach, however, has disadvantages that frequently offset its strengths. An obvious one is cost: The expense of merely keeping up with a large sample of individuals can be staggering. A related problem is the constancy of the sample over the course of the research. Experience has shown how difficult it is to maintain contact with people over several years (as long as several decades in some longitudinal studies!) in a highly mobile society. And even among those who do not move away, some lose interest and choose not to continue. These "dropouts" are often significantly different from their more research-minded peers, and this fact may also distort the outcome. For example, a group of older adults may seem to show intellectual stability late in life. What may have happened, however, is that those who found earlier testing most difficult quit the study and thereby raised the group average on the next round.

Even if the sample remains constant, though, if a study involves giving the same test many times, this may make subjects "test-wise." Improvement over time may be attributed to development when it actually stems from practice with a particular test. Changing the test from year to year solves the practice problem but raises the question of how to compare responses to different tests. Because of these challenges often associated with the longitudinal method, human development researchers often use cross-sectional studies instead.

An example of a longitudinal study is the Canadian Longitudinal Study of Children and Youth (NLSCY). The objectives of this study are to provide data on the prevalence of various biological, social, and economic characteristics and risk factors among children and youth. The NLSCY is following a representative sample of Canadian children from newborn to 25 years of age and data are collected every two years. The first year of data collection was 1994 and the sample included 22,831 children aged newborn to 11. Data are also collected from the many key people in children's lives, such as parents and teachers. Findings will help with the understanding of factors affecting child development and health-related outcomes in Canada and will be used to create policies and programs that promote the healthy development of children.

Cross-Sectional Studies

*In a **cross-sectional study**, developmental differences are identified by testing people of different ages in the study.* Development is charted by noting the differences between individuals of different ages at the same point in calendar time. The cross-sectional approach avoids almost all the problems associated with repeated testing; it avoids costly record keeping and sample loss as well. But cross-sectional research has its own weaknesses. Because people are tested at only one point in their development, we learn nothing about the continuity of development. Consequently, we cannot tell whether an aggressive 14-year-old remains aggressive at age 30 because the person would be tested at age 14 or age 30, but not at both ages.

*Cross-sectional studies are also affected by **cohort effects**, meaning that differences between age groups (cohorts) may result as easily from environmental events as from developmental processes.* In a typical simple cross-sectional study, we compare people from two age groups. If we find differences, we attribute them to the difference in age, but this needn't be the case. Why? The cross-sectional study assumes that when the older people were younger, they resembled the people in the younger age group. This isn't always true, and this fact rather than difference in age may be responsible for differences between the groups. An example of a cohort effect might come from a study measuring creativity in young and middle-aged adults. If the young adults were found to be more imaginative than middle-aged adults, should we conclude that imagination declines between these ages? Not necessarily. Perhaps a new curriculum to nourish creativity was introduced after the middle-aged adults completed school. Because the younger adults experienced the curriculum but the middle-aged adults did not, the difference between them is difficult to interpret.

When the two general research designs shown in Table 1.5 are combined with the two designs that are unique to development, four prototypic designs are possible: cross-sectional correlational studies, cross-sectional experimental studies, longitudinal-correlational studies, and longitudinal-experimental studies. You'll read about each of these designs in this book, although the two cross-sectional designs occur more frequently than the two longitudinal designs. Why? For most developmentalists, the ease of conducting cross-sectional studies more than compensates for their limitations. And, as demonstrated in the Spotlight on Research feature below, cross-sectional studies can point researchers in important directions to pursue with longitudinal studies.

TABLE 1.5   Designs Used in Human Development Research

Type of Design	Definition	Strengths	Weaknesses
General Designs			
Qualitative	Examine "the lived experience" through in-depth interviews.	Allow for rich descriptions and greater understanding.	Cannot determine cause, very time-consuming, and usually involve small samples.
Correlational	Observe variables as they exist in the world and determine their relations.	Behaviour is measured as it occurs naturally.	Cannot determine cause and effect.
Experimental	Manipulate independent variable and determine the effect on dependent variable.	Control of variables allows conclusions about cause and effect.	Work is often laboratory-based, which can be artificial.
Developmental Designs			
Longitudinal	One group of people is tested repeatedly as they develop.	Only way to chart an individual's development and look at the stability of behaviour over time.	Expensive, participants drop out, and repeated testing can distort performance.
Cross-sectional	People of different ages are tested at the same time.	Convenient—solves all problems associated with longitudinal studies.	Cannot study stability of behaviour; cohort effects complicate interpretation of differences between groups.
Sequential	Multiple groups of people are tested over time, based on either multiple longitudinal or cross-sectional designs.	Best way to address limitation of single longitudinal and cross-sectional designs.	Very expensive and time-consuming; may not completely solve limitations of longitudinal and cross-sectional designs.

SPOTLIGHT ON RESEARCH

Mapping Memory Across Adulthood

Who was the investigator and what was the aim of the study? As we will see in Chapters 11 and 14, memory changes across adulthood are very complex. Few studies, though, have examined several different types of memory simultaneously in adults of different ages. Denise Park and colleagues (2002) decided to study three main types: short-term memory, working memory, and long-term memory.

How did the investigator measure the topic of interest? Over three separate days, participants completed many tasks that measured the speed with which people process information, short-term memory, working memory, and long-term memory. Most of these were presented via computers, which automatically kept track of participants' performance.

Who were the participants in the study? A total of 345 adults, ranging in age from 20 to 92, participated. There were at least 48 people representing each decade of adulthood from the 20s through the 80s. All participants lived in or around Ann Arbor, Michigan. All participants had to be able to see a computer screen clearly, have at least a Grade 9 education level, and be able to provide their own transportation to the testing site.

What was the design of the study? The study used a cross-sectional design. Although this design provided a great deal of information about the pattern of age differences in the different types of memory, it did not provide information about whether these differences represent age changes.

Were there ethical concerns with the study? All the participants were provided information about the purpose of the study and the tests they would take. Each participant provided informed consent.

What were the results? The most important finding was that, beginning in the 20s, memory shows gradual age-related decline over the adult life span. The overall pattern for the major types of memory is shown in Figure 1.7. Note, though, that verbal knowledge shows the opposite pattern; until the 80s, it shows improvement across adulthood.

What did the investigators conclude? Although the aspects of memory examined by Park and colleagues showed similar age-related declines, this does not mean that they form a tightly organized whole. Each type of memory has distinctive aspects. However, the general downward age-related trends in memory ability are clear. Equally important, verbal knowledge operates in a very different manner. This shows that cognitive abilities may have separate developmental paths across the adult life span. We will examine why this might be the case in Chapters 11 and 14.

What converging evidence would strengthen these conclusions? The most important evidence that would strengthen Park and colleagues' study would be longitudinal data. Such data would provide insight into whether the age differences they found reflect real age changes, or whether cohort differences, for example, account for the pattern.

FIGURE 1.7   Memory Changes Across Adulthood

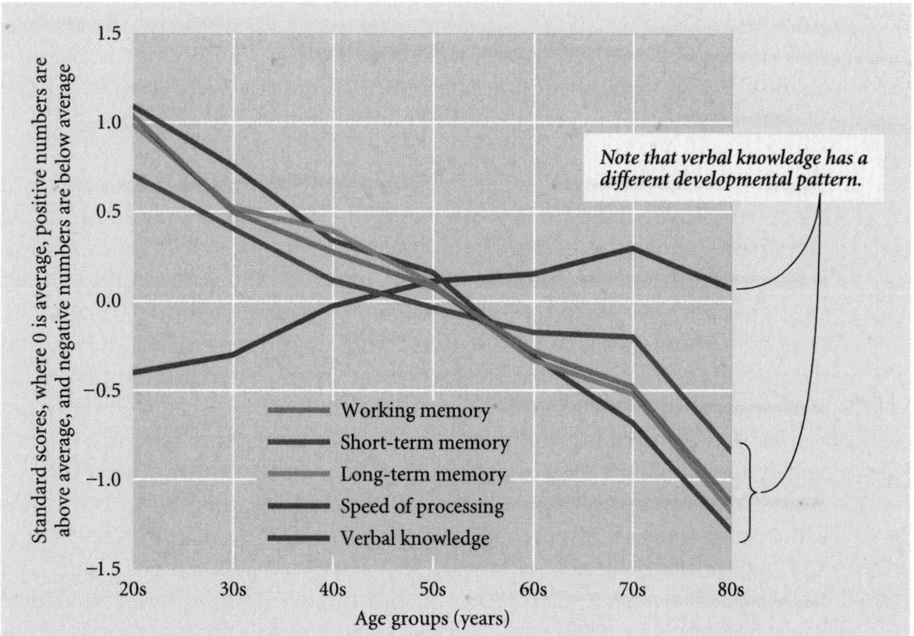

SOURCE: Park, Lantenschlager, Hedden, Davidson, Smith, & Smith (2002).

Sequential Studies

Some researchers who study human development and aging use another, more complex research approach, called a sequential design, which is based on cross-sectional and longitudinal designs. Basically, a sequential design begins with a simple cross-sectional or longitudinal design. At some regular interval, the researcher then adds additional cross-sectional or longitudinal designs, resulting in a sequence of these designs. For example, suppose a researcher wants to learn whether adults' memory ability changes with age. One way to do this would be to follow several groups of people of different ages over time, creating a sequence of longitudinal studies. The start would be a typical cross-sectional study in which 60- and 75-year-olds are tested. Then, every three years, the two groups would be retested, creating two separate longitudinal studies.

Although sequential designs are relatively rare because they are so expensive to conduct, they have several advantages. Most important, they help address most of the limitations described earlier concerning single cross-sectional and longitudinal studies. For example, sequential designs help isolate cohort effects, and they help determine whether age-related changes are due to participant dropout or to some other cause. We will encounter examples of sequential designs when we consider some of the large studies examining the normal processes of aging in Chapter 14.

CONDUCTING RESEARCH ETHICALLY

Choosing a good research design involves more than just selecting a particular method. Researchers must determine whether the methods they plan on using are ethical. That is, when designing a research study, investigators must do so in a way that does not violate the rights of people who participate in the study. To verify that every research project has these protections, investigators must present their proposed studies for formal review by a local panel of experts and community representatives prior to any data collection. Only with the approval of this panel can they begin their study. If the review panel objects to some aspects of the proposed study, the researcher must revise those aspects and present them anew for the panel's approval. Likewise, each time a component of a study is changed, the review panel must be informed and give its approval.

In Canada, the major government research funding bodies have developed the Tri-Council Policy Statement: Ethical Conduct for Research Involving Humans to ensure that only research that complies will receive funding. This policy is also utilized by many other agencies, including universities, when conducting research. The guiding ethical principals of the Tri-Council Policy Statement are as follows:

- *Respect for Human Dignity.* This is considered the "cardinal principle" of ethics in research and aspires to protect all interests of the person, including physical, psychological, and cultural integrity.
- *Respect for Free and Informed Consent.* In order for individuals and/or their legal guardians to make free and informed decisions about participation, careful attention must be paid to the dialogue, process, rights, duties, and requirements to facilitate the occurrence of free and informed consent.
- *Respect for Vulnerable Persons.* Those who have diminished competencies and/or decision-making abilities such as children or those who are institutionalized will likely require special procedures for their protection.
- *Respect for Privacy and Confidentiality.* Personal information is controlled with regard to its access, control, and dissemination to help protect mental and/or psychological integrity.
- *Respect for Justice and Inclusiveness.* Justice implies both fairness and equity. Regarding research, this means that the research review process should be fair and independent, and that the burden of participating in research and the benefits from advances in research be shared.

■ *Balancing Harms and Benefits.* There should be a favourable harms–benefit balance so that the foreseeable harms of the research process do not outweigh the anticipated benefits.

■ *Minimizing Harm.* There is a duty to avoid, prevent, or minimize any harm to individuals. This requires that the smallest number of participants and tests be used to ensure scientifically valid results.

■ *Maximizing Benefit.* Benefits of the research should be maximized so that they produce benefits for participants (if possible), others in society, and/or the advancement of knowledge. (Interagency Advisory Panel on Research Ethics, 1998)

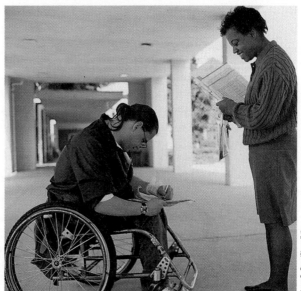

Conducting research ethically is an obligation of every investigator. If you conduct a project, even in connection with a course, you should submit your procedures for review. If you are a participant in someone else's project, make sure you are given appropriate and complete information, and read it thoroughly.

COMMUNICATING RESEARCH RESULTS

When the study is complete and the data analyzed, researchers will write a report of their work. This report describes, in great detail, what the researchers did and why, their results, and the meaning(s) behind their results. The researchers will submit the report to one of several scientific journals that specialize in human development research. Some of these are *Child Development, Developmental Psychology, Psychology and Aging,* and *Journal of Gerontology.* If the editor of the journal accepts the report, it will appear in the journal where other human development researchers can learn of the results.

These reports of research are the basis for virtually all the information we present in this book. As you read, you'll see names in parentheses, followed by a date, like this,

(Salthouse, 2000).

This indicates the person who did the research and the year in which it was published. By looking in the References at the end of the book, which are organized alphabetically by the first author's last name, you can find the title of the article and the journal where it was published.

Maybe all of these different steps in research seem tedious and involved to you. For a human development researcher, however, much of the fun of doing research is planning a study that no one has done before and that will provide useful information to other specialists. This is one of the most creative and challenging parts of human development research.

The Spotlight on Research features that appear in each chapter of this book are designed to convey both the creativity and the challenge of doing human development research. Each feature focuses on a specific study. Some are studies that have just appeared in the journals; others are classics that helped define a new area of investigation or provided definitive results in an existing area. In each of these features, we'll trace the decisions researchers made as they planned their study. We focus on the research question addressed, the design of the study, the measures used, ethical concerns, key findings, and the researchers' conclusions. Some of the studies provide examples of difficult decisions researchers must make in designing good research, as well as constraints on investigators examining development in real-world contexts. By reading these features, you'll see the ingenuity of researchers as they pursue questions of human development. You'll also see that any individual study has limitations; the way around these limits is to have converging evidence from different designs. We can have the most confidence when many studies—each using a unique combination of measurement methods and designs—all point to the same conclusion.

APPLYING RESEARCH RESULTS: SOCIAL POLICY AND EVIDENCE-BASED PRACTICE

One question many people have about research is whether any of it really matters. Actually, research on human development has a strong influence on policymakers and politicians. For example, every province in Canada, as well as many countries around the world, has laws against child abuse and child labour practices. Many countries have laws setting minimum ages for certain activities such as consuming alcohol. Some provinces are changing the way older drivers are screened when they renew their driver's licences.

At several points in the text, we will describe some of the most important connections between human development research and social policy. As you will see, these connections are broad ranging and include areas that you may even take for granted. For example, you may know that lead-based paint cannot be used any more in Canada or the United States. You may not know that it was the result of several research studies by developmentalists showing that infants and young children who were exposed to lead-based paint (and who sometimes ate paint chips as they flaked off) suffered brain damage and learning problems that led to the ban. Research on human development not only provides many insights into what makes people tick but can also provide ways to improve the quality of life.

Many professions, such as nursing and medicine, strive to incorporate research results into their everyday practice. This is commonly referred to as evidence-based practice (EBP). Rather than base diagnoses, responses, treatments, and care on intuition or usual practice, EBP incorporates the most up-to-date and best evidence from clinically based research, as well as the patient's perspective, in determining the best course of care. Consumers themselves have taken a greater role in their own decision-making and information seeking and it is important for practitioners and clients to work closely in this regard.

TEST YOURSELF

1. In _____, people are observed as they behave spontaneously in a real-life setting.

2. A _____ is a group of individuals thought to be representative of some larger population of interest.

3. The _____ variable is measured in an experiment to evaluate the impact of the variable that was manipulated.

4. Problems of longitudinal studies include the length of time to complete the work, loss of research participants over time, and _____.

5. Human development researchers must submit their plans for research to a review board that determines whether the research _____.

How could a longitudinal design be used to test Piaget's theory?

Answers: (1) naturalistic observation, (2) sample, (3) dependent, (4) influence of repeated testing on a person's performance, (5) preserves the rights of research participants

Problems with Using Photographs to Measure Understanding of Emotions

On page 26, we invited you to consider why asking children to judge emotions from photos may not be valid. Children's judgments of the emotions depicted in photographs may be less accurate than they would be in real life because (1) in real life, facial features are usually moving—not still as in the photographs—and movement may be one of the clues children naturally use to judge emotions; (2) in real life, facial expressions are often accompanied by sounds and children use both sight and sound to judge emotions; and (3) in real life, children most often judge facial expressions of people they know (parents, siblings, peers, teachers) and knowing the "usual" appearance of a face may help children judge emotions accurately.

FIGURE 1.4

PUTTING IT ALL TOGETHER

The opening section of this chapter introduced you to the terminology conventions used to communicate developmental research and theory effectively. We met Victor Ramos, whose reflections about his newborn grandson led us to the fundamental issues of nature versus nurture, continuity versus discontinuity, and universal versus context-specific development. This, in turn, prompted discussion of the four basic forces of development: biological, psychological, sociocultural, and life-cycle forces. Marcus and his mother, Betty, led us to several different theories about why people develop the way they do and how these theories connect to the three fundamental issues and the four basic forces of development. And we learned how Leah and Joan could rigorously determine why people form friendships with certain people and not with others.

The topics presented in this chapter form the foundation for all the information in the chapters that follow, so be sure you understand this material very well before you continue reading.

SUMMARY

1.1 Thinking About Development

Recurring Issues in Human Development

■ Three main issues are prominent in the study of human development. The nature-nurture issue involves the degree to which genetics and the environment influence human development. In general, theorists and researchers view nature and nurture as mutually interactive influences; development is always shaped by both. The continuity-discontinuity issue concerns whether the same explanations (continuity) or different explanations (discontinuity) must be used to explain changes in people over time. Continuity approaches emphasize quantitative change; discontinuity approaches emphasize qualitative change. In the issue of universal versus context-specific development, the question is whether development follows the same general path in all people or is fundamentally different, depending on the sociocultural context.

Basic Forces in Human Development: The Biopsychosocial Framework

■ Development is based on the combined impact of four primary forces. Biological forces include all genetic and health-related factors that affect development. Many of these biological forces are determined by our genetic code.
■ Psychological forces include all internal cognitive, emotional, perceptual, and personality factors that influence development. Collectively, psychological forces provide the things we notice most about people.
■ Sociocultural forces include interpersonal, societal, cultural, spiritual, and ethnic factors that affect development. Culture consists of the knowledge, attitudes, and behaviour associated with a group of people. Overall, sociocultural forces provide the context or backdrop for development.

- Life-cycle forces provide a context for understanding how people perceive their current situation and its effects on them.
- The biopsychosocial framework emphasizes that the four forces are mutually interactive; development cannot be understood by examining the forces in isolation. Furthermore, the same event can have different effects, depending on when it happens.

1.2 Developmental Theories

- Developmental theories organize knowledge so as to provide testable explanations of human behaviours and the ways in which they change over time. Current approaches to developmental theory focus on specific aspects of behaviour. At present, there is no single unified theory of human development.

Psychodynamic Theory

- Psychodynamic theories propose that behaviour is determined by unconscious motives. Erikson proposed a life-span theory of psychosocial development, consisting of eight universal stages, each characterized by a particular struggle.

Learning Theory

- Learning theory focuses on the development of observable behaviour. Operant conditioning is based on the notions of reinforcement, punishment, and environmental control of behaviour. Social learning theory proposes that people learn by observing others.

Cognitive-Developmental Theory

- Cognitive-developmental theory focuses on thought processes. Piaget proposed a four-stage universal sequence based on the notion that, throughout development, people create their own theories to explain how the world works. According to information-processing theory, people deal with information like a computer does; development consists of increased efficiency in handling information.

The Ecological and Systems Approach

- Bronfenbrenner proposed that development occurs in the context of several interconnected systems of increasing complexity. The competence–environmental press theory postulates that there is a "best fit" between a person's abilities and the demands placed on that person by the environment.

Life-Span Perspective, Selective Optimization with Compensation, and Life Course Perspective

- According to the life-span perspective, human development is characterized by multidirectionality, plasticity, historical context, and multiple causation. All four developmental forces are key.
- Selective optimization with compensation (SOC) refers to the developmental trends to focus one's efforts and abilities in successively fewer domains as

one ages and to acquire ways to compensate for normative losses.

- The life course perspective refers to understanding human development within the context of the historical time period in which a generation develops, which creates unique sets of experiences.

1.3 Doing Developmental Research

Measurement in Human Development Research

- Research typically begins by determining how to measure the topic of interest. Systematic observation involves recording people's behaviour as it takes place, either in a natural environment (naturalistic observation) or a structured setting (structured observation). Researchers sometimes create tasks to obtain samples of behaviour. In self-reports, people answer questions posed by the experimenter.
- Researchers must determine that their measures are reliable and valid; they must also obtain a sample representative of some larger population.

General Designs for Research

- In qualitative research designs, researchers use interviews to collect descriptions of the participants' own experiences. The in-depth interviews provide rich data to help in the understanding of the phenomena of interest.
- In correlational studies, investigators examine relations among variables as they occur naturally. This relation is often measured by a correlation coefficient, r, which can vary from -1 (strong inverse relation) to 0 (no relation) to +1 (strong positive relation). Correlational studies cannot determine cause and effect, so researchers do experimental studies in which an independent variable is manipulated and the impact of this manipulation on a dependent variable is recorded.
- Experimental studies allow conclusions about cause and effect, but the strict control of other variables that is required often makes the situation artificial.

Designs for Studying Development

- To study development, some researchers use a longitudinal design in which the same people are observed repeatedly as they grow. This approach provides evidence concerning actual patterns of individual growth but has several shortcomings as well: It is time-consuming, some people drop out of the project, and repeated testing can affect performance. An alternative, the cross-sectional design, involves testing people of different ages. This design avoids the problems of the longitudinal design but provides no information about individual growth. Also, what appear to be age differences may be cohort effects. Because neither design is problem-free, the best approach is to use both to provide converging evidence.

Conducting Research Ethically
- Planning research also involves selecting methods that preserve the rights of research participants. Experimenters must minimize the risks to potential research participants, describe the research so that potential participants can decide if they want to participate, avoid deception, and keep results anonymous or confidential.

Communicating Research Results
- Once research data are collected and analyzed, investigators publish the results in scientific outlets such as journals and books. Such results form the foundation of knowledge about human development.
- Evidence-based practice is the incorporation of the most relevant research in the practice setting incorporated by professions such as nursing and medicine.

KEY TERMS

human development (3)
nature-nurture issue (4)
continuity-discontinuity issue (5)
universal versus context-specific development issue (5)
biological forces (6)
psychological forces (6)
sociocultural forces (6)
life-cycle forces (6)
biopsychosocial framework (6)
theory (10)
psychodynamic theories (12)
psychosocial theory (12)
epigenetic principle (13)
operant conditioning (14)
reinforcement (14)
punishment (14)

imitation (observational learning) (14)
social cognitive theory (14)
self-efficacy (14)
information-processing theory (17)
ecological theory (18)
microsystem (18)
mesosystem (18)
exosystem (18)
macrosystem (18)
life-span perspective (20)
selective optimization with compensation (SOC) (21)
life course perspective (22)
systematic observation (25)
naturalistic observation (25)
structured observations (25)

self-reports (26)
reliability (26)
validity (26)
populations (27)
sample (27)
qualitative study (28)
correlational study (28)
correlation coefficient (28)
experiment (29)
independent variable (29)
dependent variable (29)
longitudinal study (30)
cross-sectional study (31)
cohort effects (31)
sequential design (31)

SEE FOR YOURSELF: APPLYING WHAT YOU'VE LEARNED

The terrorist attacks on the World Trade Center and the Pentagon on September 11, 2001, were a defining moment for Americans, Canadians, and others around the world. Prior to that attack, most North Americans gave little thought to their vulnerability; afterward, many people reevaluated their behaviour. For example, many people were reluctant or nervous to fly after the attacks, and others became afraid they would be victims of another attack.

Talk with several people of different ages about the effects on them of the September 11, 2001, attack. Ask them how safe they felt travelling, for example, before and after the attacks. Compare the responses, and see for yourself how their reactions differed; these differences illustrate life cycle for us.

LEARN MORE ABOUT IT

Readings

BALTES, P. B. (1987). Theoretical propositions of life-span developmental psychology: On the dynamics between growth and decline. *Developmental Psychology, 23*, 611–626. One of the classics in human development, this is an excellent overview of what it means to take a holistic view of life-span development. Written

by one of the leading proponents of this approach, the article is moderately difficult reading.

BALTES, P. B., REESE, H. W., & NESSELROADE, J. R. (1977). *Life-span developmental psychology: Introduction to research methods*. Pacific Grove, CA: Brooks/Cole. This is one of the classic texts on developmental research methods, and still one of the best. It's very readable and has an easily understood presentation of research designs and methods.

GARDINER, H. W., MUTTER, J. D., & KOSMITZKI, C. (1998). *Lives across cultures: Cross-cultural human development*. Boston: Allyn & Bacon. A readable introduction to how human development occurs in various world cultures. This book pulls together much of the available research.

 For additional readings, explore InfoTrac® College Edition, your online library. Go to http://www.infotrac.thomsonlearning.com.

Websites

http://www.cpa.ca
http://www.apa.org
http://www.psychologicalscience.org

The Canadian Psychological Association, American Psychological Association, and the American Psychological Society have numerous sources of information for researchers and consumers on their websites.

http://www.pre.ethics.gc.ca

This website includes the Tri-Council Policy Statement. These guidelines govern Canadian researchers who use human subjects.

http://www.cihr.ca

This website belongs to the Canadian Institutes of Health Research and describes the major health research programs funded by the Canadian government.

Website addresses are subject to change. The *Human Development* book companion website can be accessed for updated links.

The Human Development Book Companion Website

See http://www.humandevelopment.nelson.com for practice quiz questions, Internet links, updates, critical thinking exercises, discussion forums, and more.

PART 1

Prenatal Development, Infancy, and Early Childhood

© Stephen Marks, Inc./Getty Images

CHAPTER 2

Foundations of Human Development

HEREDITY, PRENATAL DEVELOPMENT, AND BIRTH

If you ask parents to name the most memorable experiences of their lives, many immediately mention the events associated with the birth of their children. From the initial exciting news that a woman is pregnant through birth nine months later, the entire experience of pregnancy and birth evokes awe and wonder.

The period before birth is the foundation for all human development and the focus of this chapter. Pregnancy begins when egg and sperm cells unite and exchange hereditary material. In the first section, you'll see how this exchange takes place and, in the process, learn about inherited factors that affect development. The second part of the chapter traces the events that transform sperm and egg into a living, breathing human being. You'll learn about the timetable that governs development before birth and, along the way, get answers to common questions about pregnancy. We'll also talk about some of the problems that can occur during development before birth. The last section of the chapter focuses on birth and the newborn baby. You'll find out how an expectant mother can prepare for birth and what labour and delivery are like.

2.1

In the Beginning: 23 Pairs of Chromosomes

LEARNING OBJECTIVES

- What are chromosomes and genes? How do they carry hereditary information from one generation to the next?
- What are common problems involving chromosomes and what are their consequences?
- How is children's heredity influenced by the environment in which they grow up?

Leslie and Glenn are excited at the thought of starting their own family. At the same time, they're nervous because Leslie's grandfather had sickle-cell disease and died when he was just 20 years old. Even though treatment for sickle-cell disease has improved since her grandfather's time, Leslie is scared that her baby may inherit the disease. Also, since she and Glenn are both of African descent, they know this makes them more prone to getting the disease and they wish someone could advise them on what the chances are that their children might inherit this disease.

What information do we need to know in order to understand the process of inheritance for this disease? For starters, we need to know more about sickle-cell disease. Red blood cells like the ones in the left photo carry oxygen and carbon dioxide to and from the body. When a person has sickle-cell disease, the red blood cells look like those in the right photo—they are long and curved like a sickle. These stiff, misshapen cells cannot pass through small capillaries, so oxygen cannot reach all parts of the body. The trapped sickle cells also block the way of white blood cells, which are the body's natural defence against bacteria. As a result, many people with sickle-cell disease—including Leslie's grandfather and many others of African or Caribbean descent, who are more prone to this painful disease than other groups—may get infections or other complications or have a decreased life expectancy.

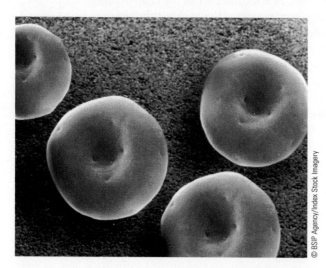

© BSIP Agency/Index Stock Imagery

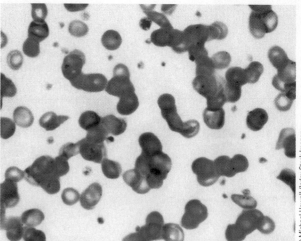

© Michael Howell/Index Stock Imagery

Sickle-cell disease is inherited and, because Leslie's grandfather had the disorder, it runs in her family, but Glenn is unaware of any history of the disease in his family. Will Leslie's baby inherit the disease? To answer this question, we need to examine the mechanisms of heredity.

MECHANISMS OF HEREDITY

At conception, egg and sperm unite to create a new organism that incorporates some characteristics of each parent. *Each egg and sperm cell has 23* **chromosomes,** *threadlike structures in the nucleus that contain genetic material.* When a sperm penetrates an egg, their chromosomes combine to produce 23 pairs of chromosomes. The photo shows all 46 chromosomes, organized in pairs ranging from the largest to the smallest. *The first 22 pairs of chromosomes are called* **autosomes.** *The 23rd pair determines the sex of the child, so these are known as the* **sex chromosomes.** When the 23rd pair consists of an X and a Y chromosome, the result is a boy; two X chromosomes produce a girl.

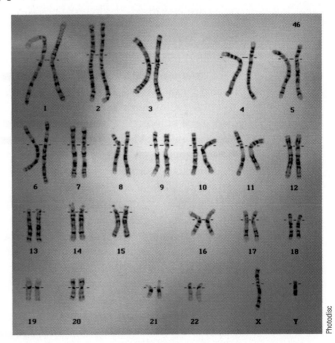

Each chromosome actually consists of one molecule of **deoxyribonucleic acid**—*DNA for short.* To understand the structure of DNA, imagine four different colours of beads placed on two strings. The strings complement each other precisely: Wherever a red bead appears on one string, a blue bead appears on the other; wherever a green bead appears on one string, a yellow one appears on the other. DNA is organized this way, except that the four colours of beads are actually four different chemical compounds—adenine, thymine, guanine, and cytosine. The strings, which are made up of phosphates and sugars, wrap around each other, creating the double helix shown in Figure 2.1.

The order in which the chemical compound "beads" appear is really a code that causes the cell to create specific amino acids, proteins, and enzymes—important biological building blocks. For example, three consecutive thymine "beads" make up the instruction to create the amino acid phenylalanine. *Each group of compounds that provides a specific set of biochemical instructions is a* **gene.** Thus, genes are the functional units of heredity, because they determine production of chemical substances that are, ultimately, the basis for all human characteristics and abilities.

Altogether, a child's 46 chromosomes include roughly 30,000 genes. Through biochemical instructions that are coded in DNA, genes regulate the development of all human characteristics and abilities. *The complete set of genes makes up a person's heredity and is known as the person's* **genotype.** *Genetic instructions, in conjunction with environmental influences, produce a* **phenotype,** *an individual's physical, behavioural, and psychological features.*

Photodisc

FIGURE 2.1   DNA Double Helix

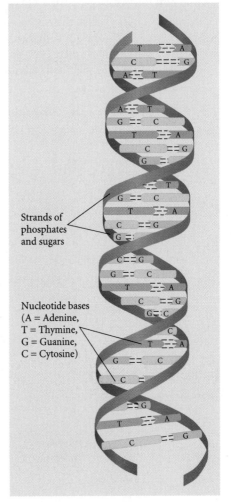

Strands of phosphates and sugars

Nucleotide bases (A = Adenine, T = Thymine, G = Guanine, C = Cytosine)

In the rest of this section, we'll see the ways in which the instructions contained in genes produce different phenotypes.

Single Gene Inheritance

How do genetic instructions produce the misshapen red blood cells of sickle-cell disease? *Genes come in different forms that are known as* **alleles.** In the case of red blood cells, for example, two alleles can be present on chromosome 11. One allele has instructions for normal red blood cells; another allele has instructions for sickle-shaped red blood cells. *The alleles in the pair of chromosomes are sometimes the same, which is known as being* **homozygous.** *The alleles sometimes differ, which is known as being* **heterozygous.** Leslie's baby would be homozygous if it had two alleles for normal cells *or* two alleles for sickle-shaped cells. The baby would be heterozygous by having one allele of each type.

How does a genotype produce a phenotype? With sickle-cell disease, for example, how do genotypes lead to specific kinds of blood cells? The answer is simple if a person is homozygous. When both alleles are the same—and therefore have chemical instructions for the same phenotype—that phenotype results. If Leslie's baby had an allele for normal red blood cells on both of its 11th chromosomes, the baby would be almost guaranteed to have normal cells. If, instead, the baby had two alleles for sickle-shaped cells, her baby would almost certainly suffer from the disease.

When a person is heterozygous, the process is more complex. *Often one allele is* **dominant,** *which means that its chemical instructions are followed and those of the other,* **recessive** *allele are ignored.* In sickle-cell disease, the allele for normal cells is dominant, and the allele for sickle-shaped cells is recessive. This is important information for Leslie: As long as either she or Glenn contributes the allele for normal red blood cells, their baby will not develop sickle-cell disease.

Figure 2.2 summarizes what we've learned regarding how sickle-cell disease is inherited where both parents carry the recessive allele. The letter *A* denotes the allele for normal blood cells and *a* denotes the allele for sickle-shaped cells. You can see that

FIGURE 2.2   **Example of Dominant and Recessive Alleles: Sickle-Cell Disease**

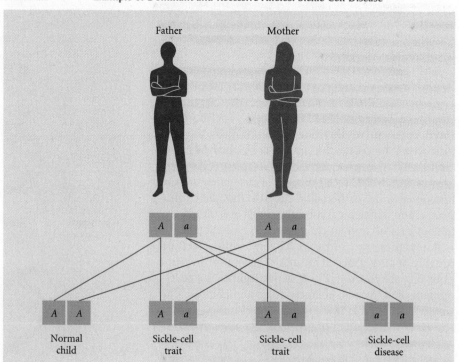

if both parents carry the recessive allele for sickle-cell disease, there is an equal (one in four or 25%) chance that the baby could either be normal or have the disease. Or alternatively, the baby could be affected in another way. *Sometimes one allele does not dominate another completely, a situation known as* **incomplete dominance.** In incomplete dominance, the phenotype that results often falls between the phenotype associated with either allele. This is the case for the genes that control red blood cells. *Individuals with one dominant and one recessive allele have* **sickle-cell trait:** *In most situations they have no problems but when they are seriously short of oxygen, they suffer a temporary, relatively mild form of disease.* Thus, sickle-cell trait is likely to appear when the person exercises vigorously or is at high altitudes (Sullivan, 1987). However, if only Leslie carries the affected allele and Glenn does not, which seems to be the case, there would be a 50% chance that the baby would inherit sickle-cell trait, but no chance of the baby inheriting the disease.

The simple genetic mechanism responsible for sickle-cell disease, involving a single gene pair, with one dominant allele and one recessive allele, is also responsible for numerous other common traits, as shown in Table 2.1.

TABLE 2.1 Some Common Phenotypes Associated with Single Pairs of Genes	
Dominant Phenotype	*Recessive Phenotype*
Curly hair	Straight hair
Normal hair	Pattern baldness (men)
Dark hair	Blond hair
Thick lips	Thin lips
Cheek dimples	No dimples
Normal hearing	Some types of deafness
Normal vision	Nearsightedness
Farsightedness	Normal vision
Normal colour vision	Red-green colour blindness
Type A blood	Type O blood
Type B blood	Type O blood
Rh-positive blood	Rh-negative blood

SOURCE: McKusick, 1995

In each of these instances, individuals with the recessive phenotype have two recessive alleles, one from each parent. Individuals with the dominant phenotype have at least one dominant allele.

You'll notice that the table includes many biological and medical phenotypes but lacks behavioural or psychological phenotypes. Behavioural and psychological characteristics can be inherited, but the genetic mechanism is usually more elaborate, as we'll see next.

Behavioural Genetics

Behavioural genetics is the branch of genetics that deals with inheritance of behavioural and psychological traits. Behavioural genetics is complex, in part because behavioural and psychological phenotypes are complex. Traits controlled by single genes are usually "either-or" phenotypes. A person either has dimpled cheeks or not; a person either has normal colour vision or red-green colour blindness; a person's blood either clots normally or it does not. In contrast, most important behavioural and psychological characteristics are *not* "either-or" cases. Instead, an entire range of different outcomes is possible. Take extroversion as an example. Imagine trying to classify 10 people that you know well as either extroverts or introverts. This would be easy for a few extremely outgoing individuals (extroverts) and a few intensely shy persons (introverts). Most are probably neither extroverts nor introverts, but "in between." The result is a distribution of individuals ranging from extreme introversion at one end to extreme extroversion at the other.

Many behavioural and psychological characteristics are distributed in this fashion, including intelligence and many aspects of personality. *When phenotypes reflect the combined activity of many separate genes, the pattern is known as **polygenic inheritance**.* Because so many genes are involved in polygenic inheritance, we usually cannot trace the effects of each gene. But we can use a hypothetical example to show how many genes work together to produce a behavioural phenotype that spans a continuum. Let's suppose that four pairs of genes contribute to extroversion, that the allele for extroversion is dominant, and that the total amount of extroversion is simply the sum of the dominant alleles. If we continue to use uppercase letters to represent dominant alleles and lowercase letters to represent the recessive allele, the four gene pairs would be Aa, Bb, Cc, and Dd.

These four pairs of genes produce 81 different genotypes and 9 distinct phenotypes. For example, a person with the genotype AABBCCDD has 8 alleles for extroversion (the proverbial party animal). A person with the genotype aabbccdd has no alleles (the proverbial wallflower). All other genotypes involve some combinations of dominant and recessive alleles, so these are associated with phenotypes representing intermediate levels of extroversion. In fact, Figure 2.3 shows that the most common outcome is for people to inherit exactly 4 dominant and 4 recessive alleles: 19 of the 81 genotypes produce this pattern (e.g., AABbccDd, aaBbcCDd). A few extreme cases (very outgoing or very shy), when coupled with many intermediate cases, produce the familiar bell-shaped distribution that characterizes many behavioural and psychological traits.

FIGURE 2.3

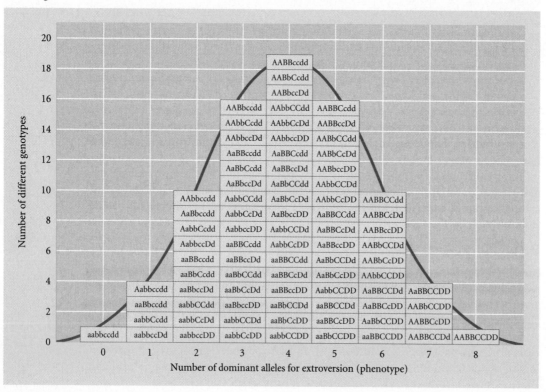

Number of different genotypes (y-axis) vs. Number of dominant alleles for extroversion (phenotype) (x-axis)

Remember, this example is completely hypothetical. Extroversion is *not* based on the combined influence of eight pairs of genes. However, the example shows how several genes working together *could* produce a continuum of phenotypes. Something like our example is probably involved in the inheritance of many human behavioural traits, except that many more pairs of genes are involved. Moreover, the environment also influences the phenotype.

If many behavioural phenotypes involve countless genes, how can we hope to unravel the influence of heredity? Twins and adopted children provide some important clues to the role of heredity.

Studying Twins and Adopted Children

Identical twins are called **monozygotic twins** *because they come from a single fertilized egg that splits in two.* Because identical twins come from the same fertilized egg, the same genes control their body structure, height, and facial features, which explains why identical twins like those in the photo look alike. *In contrast, fraternal or* **dizygotic twins** *come from two separate eggs fertilized by two separate sperm.* Genetically, fraternal twins are just like any other siblings—on average, about half their genes are the same. In twin studies, scientists compare identical and fraternal twins to measure the influence of heredity. If identical twins are more alike than are fraternal twins, this implicates heredity (Phelps, Davis, & Schartz, 1997).

A similar logic is used in adoption studies, in which adopted children are compared with their biological parents and their adoptive parents. The idea here is that biological parents provide their child's genes, but adoptive parents provide the child's environment. Consequently, if a behaviour has important genetic roots, then adopted children should behave more like their biological parents than their adoptive parents.

These and other methods are not foolproof. Maybe you thought of a potential flaw in twin studies: Parents and other people may treat monozygotic twins more similarly than they treat dizygotic twins. This would make monozygotic twins more similar than dizygotic twins in their experiences as well as in their genes. However, because each method has its unique pitfalls, when different methods converge on the same conclusion about the influence of heredity, we can be confident of that result. Throughout this book, you'll see many instances where twin studies and adoption studies have pointed to genetic influences on human development.

In addition, behaviour geneticists are moving beyond these methods (Dick & Rose, 2002; Plomin & Crabbe, 2000). Today, it is possible to isolate particular segments of DNA in human chromosomes. These segments then serve as markers for identifying specific alleles. The procedure is complicated, but the basic approach often begins by identifying people who differ in the behaviour or psychological trait of interest. For example, researchers might identify children who are outgoing and children who are shy. Or they might identify children who read well and children who read poorly. The children rub the inside of their mouth with a cotton swab, which yields cheek cells that contain DNA. The cells are analyzed in a lab and the DNA

markers for the two groups are compared. If the markers differ consistently, then the alleles near the marker probably contribute to the differences between the groups.

Techniques like these have the potential to identify the many different genes that contribute to complex behavioural and psychological traits. Of course, these new methods have limits. Some require very large samples of children, which can make rare disorders difficult to study in this way. Also, some require that an investigator have an idea, before even beginning the study, about which chromosomes to search and where. These can be major hurdles. But, when used with traditional methods of behaviour genetics (e.g., adoption studies), the new methods promise a much greater understanding of how genes influence behaviour and development (Plomin & Crabbe, 2000).

GENETIC DISORDERS

Some people are affected by heredity in a special way: They have genetic disorders that disrupt the usual pattern of development. Genetics can derail development in two ways. First, some disorders are inherited. Sickle-cell disease is one example of an inherited disorder. Second, sometimes eggs or sperm do not include the usual 23 chromosomes but have more or fewer chromosomes instead. In the next few pages, we'll see how inherited disorders and abnormal numbers of chromosomes can alter a person's development.

Inherited Disorders

You know that sickle-cell disease is a disorder that affects people who inherit two recessive alleles. *Another disorder that involves recessive alleles is **phenylketonuria** (**PKU**), a disorder in which babies are born lacking an important liver enzyme.* This enzyme converts phenylalanine—a protein found in dairy products, bread, diet soda, and fish—into amino acids that are required for normal body functioning. Without this enzyme, phenylalanine accumulates and produces poisons that harm the nervous system, resulting in mental delay (Diamond et al., 1997; Mange & Mange, 1990).

Most inherited disorders are like sickle-cell disease and PKU in that they are carried by recessive alleles. Relatively few serious disorders are caused by dominant alleles. Why? If the allele for the disorder is dominant, every person with at least one of these alleles would have the disorder. Individuals affected with these disorders typically do not live long enough to reproduce, so dominant alleles that produce fatal disorders soon vanish from the species. *An exception is **Huntington's disease**, a fatal disease characterized by progressive degeneration of the nervous system.* Huntington's disease is caused by a dominant allele found on chromosome 4. Individuals who inherit this disorder develop normally through childhood, adolescence, and young adulthood. However, during middle age, nerve cells begin to deteriorate, which produces symptoms such as muscle spasms, depression, and significant changes in personality (Shiwach, 1994). By this age, many adults with Huntington's disease have already reproduced, creating children who may well later display the disease themselves.

Abnormal Chromosomes

Sometimes individuals do not receive the normal complement of 46 chromosomes. If they are born with extra, missing, or damaged chromosomes, development is always disturbed. The most common chromosomal disorder is Down syndrome. Like the boy in the photo on page 51, people with Down syndrome have almond-shaped eyes and a fold over the eyelid. Their head, neck, and nose are usually smaller than normal. During the first several months of life, development of babies with Down syndrome seems to be normal. Thereafter, their mental and behavioural development begins to lag behind the average child's. For example, a child with Down syndrome might first sit up without help at about 1 year, walk at 2, and talk at 3, reaching each of these developmental milestones months or even years behind children without Down syndrome. By childhood, most aspects of cognitive and social development are seriously retarded (Cielinski et al., 1995; Rast & Meltzoff, 1995). Nevertheless, as you'll see in Chapter 7, many individuals with Down syndrome lead full, satisfying lives.

What causes Down syndrome? Individuals with Down syndrome typically have an extra 21st chromosome that is usually provided by the egg (Antonarakis et al., 1991). Why the mother provides two 21st chromosomes is unknown. Down syndrome occurs approximately once every 800 births (Wen et al., 2000). However, the odds that a woman will bear a child with Down syndrome increase markedly as she gets older. For a woman in her late 20s, the risk of giving birth to a baby with Down syndrome is about 1 in 1,000; for a woman in her early 40s, the risk is about 1 in 50. Why? A woman's eggs have been in her ovaries since her own prenatal development. Eggs may deteriorate over time as part

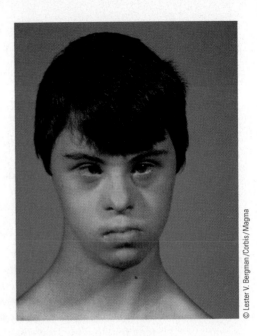

© Lester V. Bergman /Corbis /Magma

of aging or because an older woman has a longer history of exposure to hazards in the environment, such as X-rays, that may damage her eggs.

An extra autosome (as in Down syndrome), a missing autosome, or a damaged autosome always has far-reaching consequences for development because the autosomes contain huge amounts of genetic material. In fact, nearly half of all fertilized eggs abort spontaneously within two weeks, primarily because of abnormal autosomes. Thus, most eggs that cannot develop normally are removed naturally (Moore & Persaud, 1993).

Abnormal sex chromosomes can also disrupt development. Table 2.2 lists four of the more frequent disorders associated with atypical numbers of X and Y chromosomes. Keep in mind that "frequent" is a relative term; although these disorders are more frequent than PKU or Huntington's disease, the table shows that most are rare. Notice that there are no disorders consisting solely of Y chromosomes. The presence of an X chromosome appears to be necessary for life.

TABLE 2.2	Common Disorders Associated with the Sex Chromosomes		
Disorder	**Sex Chromosomes**	**Frequency**	**Characteristics**
Klinefelter's syndrome	XXY	1 in 500 male births	Tall, small testicles, sterile, below-normal intelligence, passive
XYY complement	XYY	1 in 1,000 male births	Tall, some cases apparently have below-normal intelligence
Turner's syndrome	X	1 in 2,500–5,000 female births	Short, limited development of secondary sex characteristics, problems perceiving spatial relations
XXX syndrome	XXX	1 in 500–1,200 female births	Normal stature but delayed motor and language development

SOURCE: Based on Bancroft et al., 1982; Downey et al., 1991; Linden et al., 1988; Plomin et al., 1990

Fortunately, most of us receive the correct number of chromosomes, and we do not inherit life-threatening illnesses. For most people, heredity reveals its power in creating a unique individual—a person unlike any other. Of course, heredity doesn't work alone. To fully understand how heredity influences development, we need to consider the environment, which we'll do next.

HEREDITY IS NOT DESTINY: GENES AND ENVIRONMENTS

Many people mistakenly view heredity as a set of phenotypes unfolding automatically from the genotypes that are set at conception. Nothing could be further from the truth. Although genotypes are fixed when the sperm fertilizes the egg, phenotypes are not. Instead, phenotypes depend on both the genotypes and the environment in which the person develops. In the next few pages, we'll look at other aspects of links between heredity and environment.

Paths from Genes to Behaviour

How does the information in strands of DNA end up influencing a person's behavioural and psychological development? The specific paths from genes to behaviour are largely uncharted, but some of their general properties are known. The most important is that genes never cause behaviour directly; instead, they influence behaviour indirectly, by making behaviours more or less likely. For example, there is no gene for dunking basketballs, but genes do regulate bone length. As a consequence, some people grow taller than others and they are therefore more capable of dunking. Similarly, there is no gene for alcoholism, but genes do regulate how the body breaks down alcohol that is consumed. Consequently, some people become nauseated because their bodies cannot break down alcohol and they are therefore less likely to become alcoholics. These examples show that genes for height and breaking down alcohol affect behaviour indirectly, by changing the odds that a person can dunk a basketball or become an alcoholic.

Another important property of gene behaviour paths is that the behavioural consequences of genetic instructions depend on environments. In a basketball-less world, the gene for height would still produce taller people, but they would no longer be more likely to dunk. In other words, to understand how heredity affects behaviour, we must consider the environment in which genetic instructions are carried out.

Reaction Range

If you read the fine print on a can of diet pop (and some other food products), you'll see the following warning:

"Phenylketonurics: contains phenylalanine."

Children with PKU are missing an enzyme needed to break down phenylalanine. When phenylalanine accumulates, it damages the nervous system. But why the warning on diet pop? Today Canadian hospitals routinely check for PKU at birth—with a blood test. Newborns who have the disease are immediately placed on a diet that limits intake of high-protein foods (e.g., meat, fish, dairy products), which tend to be high in phenylalanine, and mental retardation is avoided. Thus, an individual who has the genotype for PKU but is not exposed to phenylalanine has normal intelligence. PKU illustrates that development depends on heredity and environmental factors, in this case, diet.

In general, heredity and environment jointly determine the direction of development. Therefore, a genotype can lead to a range of phenotypes. *Reaction range refers to this fact that a genotype is manifested in reaction to the environment where development takes place.* Figure 2.4 illustrates this fact by showing how phenotypic intelligence might vary, depending on the environment. Look first at genotypic intelligence *A*, which has a small reaction range. This genotype leads to much the same phenotypic intelligence whether development takes place in an enriched environment filled with stimulation from

> **THINK ABOUT IT**
>
> How does the concept of reaction range help explain why nature and nurture are almost always involved in the developmental equation?

FIGURE 2.4   Reaction Range

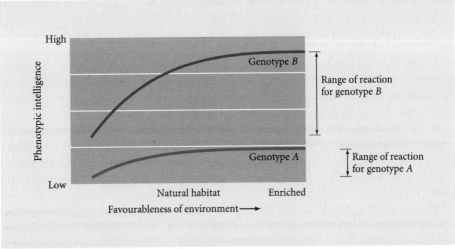

From "Genetic Aspects of Intelligent Behavior," by I.I. Gottesman. In N.R. Ellis (Ed.) *Handbook of Mental Deficiency*, p. 255. Copyright © 1963 Norman R. Ellis. Reprinted with permission.

parents, siblings, and books or in an impoverished environment that lacks all such stimulation. In contrast, genotype *B* has a larger reaction range: The enriched environment leads to a much greater phenotypic intelligence than the impoverished environment. Thus, a single genotype can lead to a range of phenotypes, depending on the quality of the rearing environment.

The conclusion to be drawn from the example is obvious: One genotype leads to quite different phenotypes, depending on the level of intellectual stimulation in the environment. Of course, what makes a "good" or "rich" environment is not the same for all facets of behavioural or psychological development. Throughout this book, you will see how specific kinds of environments influence very particular aspects of development (Wachs, 1983).

Changing Relations Between Nature and Nurture

How nature (genetics) and nurture (environment) work together partly depends on a person's age. Sandra Scarr (1992, 1993; Scarr & McCartney, 1983) describes three types of relations between heredity and environment. *In the first, a **passive gene-environment relation**, parents pass on genotypes to their children and provide much of the early environment for their young children.* For example, bright parents are likely to transmit genes that make for bright children. Bright parents are also likely to provide books, museum visits, and discussions that are intellectually stimulating. In this case, heredity and environment are positively related: Both foster brighter children. In both respects, children are passive recipients of heredity and environment. This passive type of relation is most common with infants and young children.

*In the second type of relation, an **evocative gene-environment relation**, different genotypes evoke different responses from the environment.* For example, children who are bright (due in part to their genes) may pay greater attention to their teachers and ask more questions and, in turn, receive greater positive attention in school than children who are not as bright. Or, children who are friendly and outgoing (again, due in part to their genes) may elicit more interactions with others (and, in particular, more satisfying interactions) than children who are not as friendly and outgoing. In the evocative relation, which is common in young children, a child's genotype evokes or prompts people to respond differently to the child.

*In the third type of relation, an **active gene-environment relation**, individuals actively seek environments related to their genetic makeup.* Children who are bright (due in part to heredity) may actively seek peers, adults, and activities that strengthen their intellectual development. Similarly, children like the ones in the photo on page 53, who are outgoing (due in part to heredity), seek the company of other people, particularly extroverts like themselves. *This process of deliberately seeking environments that fit one's heredity is called **niche-picking**.* Niche-picking is first seen in childhood and becomes more common as children get older and can control their environments. The children described in the Real People feature show niche-picking in action.

REAL PEOPLE: APPLYING HUMAN DEVELOPMENT

Ben and Matt Pick Their Niches

Ben and Matt Kail were born 25 months apart. Even as a young baby, Ben was always a "people person." He relished contact with other people and preferred play that involved others. From the beginning, Matt was different. He was more withdrawn and was quite happy to play alone. The first separation from parents was harder for Ben than for Matt, because Ben relished parental contact more. When they entered school, Ben enjoyed increasing the scope of his friendships; Matt liked all the different activities that were available and barely noticed the new faces. Though brothers, Ben and Matt are quite dissimilar in their sociability, a characteristic known to have important genetic components (Braungart et al., 1992).

As Ben and Matt have grown up (they're now young adults), they have consistently sought environments that fit their differing needs for social stimulation. Ben was involved in team sports and now enjoys working in the theatre. Matt took art and photography classes and now is happy when he's reading, drawing, or working at his computer. Ben and Matt have chosen very different niches, and their choices have been driven in part by the genes that regulate sociability.

The description of Ben and Matt illustrates that genes and environment rarely influence development alone. Instead, nature and nurture interact. Experiences determine which phenotypes emerge, and genotypes influence the nature of children's experiences. The story of Ben and Matt also makes it clear that, to understand how genes influence development, we need to look carefully at how environments work, which is our next topic.

The Nature of Nurture

Traditionally, psychologists have considered some environments as beneficial for children and others as detrimental. This view has been especially strong in regard to family environments. Some parenting practices were thought to be more effective than others, and parents who use these effective practices were believed to have children who were, on average, better off than children of parents who don't use these practices. This view leads to a simple prediction: Children within a family should be similar because they all receive the same type of effective (or ineffective) parenting. The effects of parenting on child development are well recognized. For example, in a Canadian study on risk factors for child development, the overall effect of positive parenting practices was found to reduce child problems in most areas (Landy & Tam, 1998). However, there will still be individual differences, and dozens of behavioural genetic studies show that, in reality, siblings are not very much alike in their cognitive and social development (Dunn & Plomin, 1990).

Does this mean that family environment is not important? No. *These findings point to the importance of nonshared environmental influences, the forces within a family that make children different from one another* (Deater-Deckard, 2000). The family environment is important but it usually affects each child in a unique way, which makes siblings differ. Each of the children in the photo is likely to have different experiences in daily family life. For example, parents may be more affectionate with one child than another or they may have higher expectations for school achievement for one child than another. All these contrasting parental influences tend to make siblings different, not alike (Turkheimer & Waldron, 2000). Family environments are vitally important and as we describe their influence throughout this book, you should also remember that families create multiple unique environments, one for each child.

Much of what we have said about genes, environment, and development is summarized in Figure 2.5 (Lytton, 2000). Parents are the source of children's genes and, at least for young children, the primary source of children's experiences. Children's genes also influence the experiences they have and the impact of those experiences on them.

FIGURE 2.5   Interplay of Genes, Environment, and Development

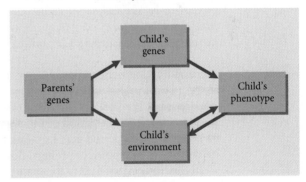

However, to capture the idea of nonshared environmental influences, we would need a separate diagram for each child, reflecting the fact that parents provide unique genes and a unique family environment for each of their offspring.

Most of this book explains the links between nature, nurture, and development. We can first see the interaction of nature and nurture during prenatal development, which we examine in the next section of this chapter.

TEST YOURSELF

1. The first 22 pairs of chromosomes are called _____.

2. _____ reflects the combined activity of a number of distinct genes.

3. Individuals with _____ have an extra 21st chromosome, usually inherited from the mother.

4. When a fertilized egg has defective autosomes, the usual result is that _____.

5. Children who inherit PKU can develop normal intelligence if _____.

6. The term _____ refers to the fact that the same genotype can be associated with many different phenotypes.

7. Nonshared environmental influences tend to make siblings _____.

How might niche-picking work in the domain of intelligence?

Answers: (1) autosomes, (2) Polygenic inheritance, (3) Down syndrome, (4) the fertilized egg is aborted spontaneously, (5) they have a special diet that is low in phenylalanine, (6) reaction range, (7) different from each other

From Conception to Birth

LEARNING OBJECTIVES

- What happens to a fertilized egg in the first two weeks after conception?
- When do body structures and internal organs emerge in prenatal development?
- When do body systems begin to function well enough to support life?

> **From Conception to Birth**
> Period of the Zygote (weeks 1–2)
> Period of the Embryo (weeks 3–8)
> Period of the Fetus (weeks 9–38)

Eun Jung has just learned that she is pregnant with her first child. Like many other parents-to-be, she and her husband, Kinam, are ecstatic. But they also soon realize how little they know about "what happens when" during pregnancy. Eun Jung is eager to visit her obstetrician to learn more about the normal timetable of events during pregnancy.

Prenatal development begins when a sperm successfully fertilizes an egg. *The many changes that transform the fertilized egg into a newborn human are known as* **prenatal development.** Prenatal development takes an average of 38 weeks, which are divided into three periods: the period of the zygote, the period of the embryo, and the period of the fetus. Each period gets its name from the scientific term used to describe the baby-to-be at that point in prenatal development.

In this section, we'll trace the major developments of each of these periods. As we do, you'll learn the answers to the "what happens when" question that intrigues Eun Jung.

PERIOD OF THE ZYGOTE (WEEKS 1–2)

The teaspoon or so of seminal fluid produced during a fertile male's ejaculation contains from 200 to 500 million sperm. Of the sperm released into the vagina, only a few hundred will actually complete the six- or seven-inch journey to the fallopian tubes. Here, an egg arrives monthly, hours after it is released by an ovary. If an egg is present, many sperm will simultaneously begin to burrow their way through the cluster of nurturing cells that surround the egg. Two sperm cells are doing just this in the photo. Their tails can be seen clearly, but one sperm has burrowed so deeply that the head is barely visible. When this or some other sperm finally penetrates the cellular wall of the egg, chemical changes occur in the wall immediately, blocking out all other sperm. Then the nuclei of the egg and sperm fuse and the two independent sets of 23 chromosomes are interchanged. The development of a new human being is under way!

For nearly all of history, sexual intercourse was the only way for egg and sperm to unite and begin the development that results in a human being. This is no longer the only way, as we see in the Current Controversies feature.

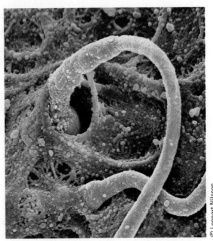

© Lennart Nilsson

CURRENT CONTROVERSIES

Conception in the 21st Century

More than 25 years ago, Louise Brown captured the world's attention as the first test-tube baby—conceived in a petri dish instead of in her mother's body. Today, this reproductive technology is no longer experimental. Many new techniques are available to couples who cannot conceive a child through sexual intercourse. *Perhaps the best known is **in vitro fertilization**, which involves mixing sperm and egg together in a petri dish and then placing several fertilized eggs in the mother's uterus, with the hope that they will become implanted in the uterine wall.* Other methods include injecting many sperm directly into the fallopian tubes or a single sperm directly into an egg.

The sperm and egg usually come from the prospective parents, but sometimes they are provided by donors. Typically, the fertilized eggs are placed in the uterus of the prospective mother, but sometimes they are placed in the uterus of a surrogate mother, who carries the baby to term. This means that a baby could have as many as five "parents": the man and woman who provided the sperm and egg; the surrogate mother who carried the baby; and the mother and father who will rear the baby.

For the many couples who have long yearned for a child, these techniques offer new hope. At the same time, they have led to much controversy because of some complex ethical issues associated with their use. One concerns the prospective parents' right to select particular egg and sperm cells; another involves who should be able to use this technology.

Pick your egg and sperm cells from a catalogue? Until recently, prospective parents have known nothing about egg and sperm donors. Today, however, they are sometimes able to select egg and sperm based on physical and psychological characteristics of the donors, including appearance and ethnicity. Some claim that such prospective parents have a right to be fully informed about the person who provides the genetic material for their baby. *Others argue that this amounts to **eugenics**, which is the effort to improve the human species by allowing only certain people to mate and pass along their genes to subsequent generations.*

Available to all? Most couples who use in vitro fertilization are in their 30s and 40s, but a number of older women have begun to use the technology. Many of these women cannot conceive naturally because they have gone through menopause and no longer ovulate. Some argue that it is unfair to a child to have parents who may not live until the child reaches adulthood. Others point out that people are living longer and that middle-aged (or older) adults make better parents. (We discuss this in more depth in Chapter 12.)

What do you think? Should prospective parents be allowed to browse a catalogue with photos and biographies of prospective donors? Should new reproductive technologies be available to all, regardless of age? ◙

*Whether by artificial means like those we've just described or by natural means, fertilization begins the period of the zygote, which takes its name from **zygote**, the technical term for the fertilized egg.* This period ends when the zygote implants itself in the wall of the uterus. During these two weeks, the zygote grows rapidly through cell division. Figure 2.6 traces the egg cell from the time it is released from the ovary until the zygote becomes implanted in the wall of the uterus. The zygote travels down the fallopian tube toward the uterus. Within hours, the zygote divides for the first time, then continues to do so every 12 hours. Occasionally, the zygote separates into two clusters that develop into identical twins. Fraternal twins, which are more common, are created when two eggs are released and each is fertilized by a different sperm cell.

FIGURE 2.6

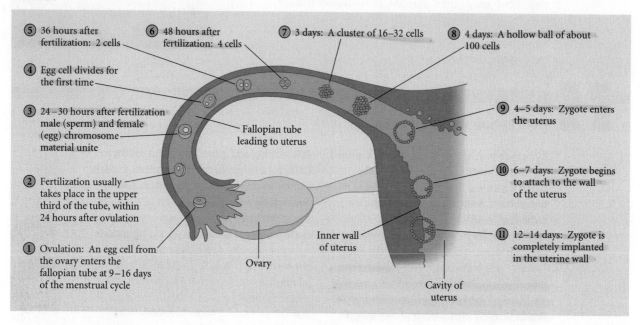

⑤ 36 hours after fertilization: 2 cells

⑥ 48 hours after fertilization: 4 cells

⑦ 3 days: A cluster of 16–32 cells

⑧ 4 days: A hollow ball of about 100 cells

④ Egg cell divides for the first time

③ 24–30 hours after fertilization male (sperm) and female (egg) chromosome material unite

Fallopian tube leading to uterus

⑨ 4–5 days: Zygote enters the uterus

② Fertilization usually takes place in the upper third of the tube, within 24 hours after ovulation

⑩ 6–7 days: Zygote begins to attach to the wall of the uterus

Inner wall of uterus

⑪ 12–14 days: Zygote is completely implanted in the uterine wall

① Ovulation: An egg cell from the ovary enters the fallopian tube at 9–16 days of the menstrual cycle

Ovary

Cavity of uterus

After about four days, the zygote includes about 100 cells and resembles a hollow ball. The inner part of the ball is destined to become the baby. The outer layer of cells will form a number of structures that provide a life-support system throughout prenatal development.

By the end of the first week, the zygote reaches the uterus. *The next step is **implantation,** in which the zygote burrows into the uterine wall and establishes connections with a woman's blood vessels.* Implantation takes about a week to complete and triggers hormonal changes that prevent menstruation, which is often the first sign letting the woman know that she has conceived.

The implanted zygote, shown in the photo, is less than a millimetre in diameter, yet its cells have already begun to differentiate. *A small cluster of cells near the centre of the zygote, the **germ disc,** will eventually develop into the baby.* The other cells are destined to become structures that support, nourish, and protect the developing organism. *For example, the layer of cells closest to the uterus will become the **placenta,** a structure through which nutrients and wastes are exchanged between the mother and the developing organism.*

Implantation and differentiation of cells mark the end of the period of the zygote. Comfortably settled in the shelter of the uterus, the zygote is well prepared for the remaining 36 weeks of the marvellous trek leading up to birth.

PERIOD OF THE EMBRYO (WEEKS 3–8)

*Once the zygote is completely embedded in the uterine wall, it is called an **embryo**.* This new period typically begins the third week after conception and lasts until the end of the eighth week. During the period of the embryo, body structures and internal organs develop. At the beginning of this period, three layers begin to form in the embryo. *The outer layer or **ectoderm** becomes hair, the outer layer of skin, and the nervous system; the middle layer or **mesoderm** forms muscles, bones, and the circulatory system; the inner layer or **endoderm** forms the digestive system and the lungs.*

One dramatic way to see these changes is to compare a three-week-old embryo with an eight-week-old embryo. The three-week-old embryo shown in the top photo is about 2 millimetres long. Specialization of cells is under way, but the organism looks more like a salamander than a human being. However, growth and specialization proceed so rapidly that an eight-week-old embryo—shown in the bottom photo—looks very different: You can see eyes, jaw, arms, and legs. The brain and the nervous system are developing rapidly, and the heart has been beating for nearly a month. Most of the organs found in a mature human are in place, in some form. (The sex organs are a notable exception.) Yet, being only an inch long and weighing a fraction of an ounce, the embryo is much too small for the mother to feel its presence.

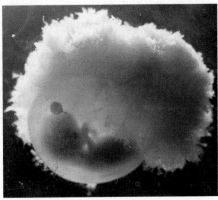

The embryo's environment is shown in Figure 2.7. *The embryo rests in a sac called the **amnion**, which is filled with **amniotic fluid** that cushions the embryo and maintains a constant temperature.* The embryo is linked to the mother via two structures. *The **umbilical cord** houses blood vessels that join the embryo to the placenta.* In the placenta, the blood vessels from the

FIGURE 2.7   Blood Flow in the Umbilical Cord

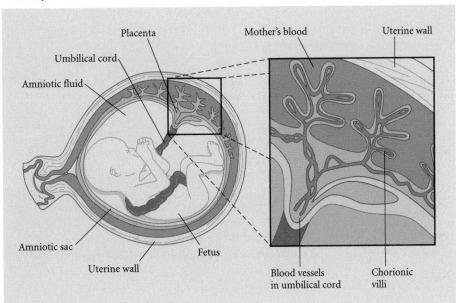

umbilical cord run close to the mother's blood vessels but aren't actually connected to them. The close proximity of the blood vessels allows nutrients, oxygen, vitamins, and waste products to be exchanged between mother and embryo.

With body structures and internal organs in place, the embryo has passed another major milestone in prenatal development. What's left is for these structures and organs to begin working properly. This is accomplished in the final period of prenatal development, as we'll see next.

PERIOD OF THE FETUS (WEEKS 9–38)

*The final and longest phase of prenatal development, the **period of the fetus**, begins at the ninth week (when cartilage begins to turn to bone) and ends at birth.* During this period, the baby-to-be becomes much larger and its bodily systems begin to work. The increase in size is remarkable. At the beginning of this period, the fetus weighs less than 30 grams. At about four months, the fetus weighs roughly 120 to 240 grams, which is large enough for the mother to feel its movements. In the last five months of pregnancy, the fetus will normally gain an additional 3.4 kilograms (approximately) before birth. Figure 2.8, which depicts the fetus at one-eighth of its actual size, shows these incredible increases in size.

During the fetal period, the finishing touches are placed on the many systems that are essential to human life, such as respiration, digestion, and vision. Some highlights of this period include the following:

- At four weeks after conception, a flat set of cells curls to form a tube. One end of the tube swells to form the brain; the rest forms the spinal cord. By the start of the fetal period, the brain has distinct structures and has begun to regulate body functions. *During the period of the fetus, all regions of the brain grow, particularly the **cerebral cortex**, the wrinkled surface of the brain that regulates many important human behaviours.*
- Near the end of the embryonic period, male embryos develop testes and female embryos develop ovaries. In the third month, the testes in a male fetus secrete a hormone that causes a set of cells to become a penis and scrotum; in a female fetus, this hormone is absent, so the same cells become a vagina and labia.

FIGURE 2.8   **Prenatal Development**

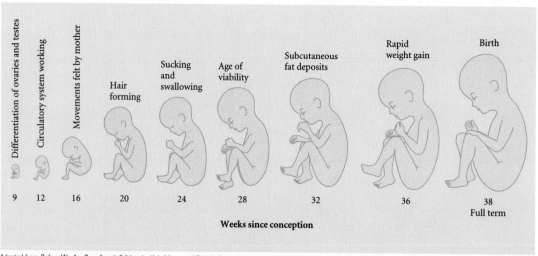

Adapted from *Before We Are Born*, Fourth Edition, by K. L. Moore and T. V. N. Persaud, p. 130. Copyright © 1993 W. B. Saunders. Reprinted with permission from Elsevier.

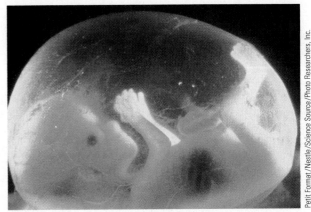

*In the fifth and sixth months after conception, eyebrows, eyelashes, and scalp hair emerge. The skin thickens and is covered with a thick greasy substance, **vernix**, that protects the fetus during its long immersion in amniotic fluid.*

*With these and other rapid changes, by 22 to 28 weeks most systems function well enough that a fetus born at this time has a chance to survive, which is why this age range is called the **age of viability**.* By this age, the fetus has a distinctly baby-like look, as you can see in the photo. However, babies born this early have trouble breathing because their lungs are not yet mature. Also they cannot regulate their body temperature very well because they lack the insulating layer of fat that appears in the eighth month after conception. With modern neonatal intensive care, infants born this early can survive, but they face other challenges, as we'll see later in this chapter.

The changes of the fetal period also mean that the fetus actually starts to behave (Joseph, 2000). The fetus responds to stimulation (Birnholz & Benacerraf, 1983; Kisilevsky & Low, 1998). For example, although we can't observe it directly, in the

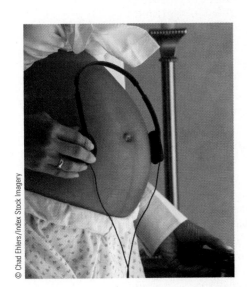

photo at the left the music played through the headphones probably causes the fetal heart rate to increase and may cause the fetus to move. Also, the fetus develops regular periods of activity: Most mothers report times when the fetus is moving and other times when the fetus is still. Some fetuses are more active than others and these differences may predict infants' behaviour: Higher levels of fetal activity have been linked with better regulatory processes (e.g., less distress to frustration) in later childhood (DiPietro et al., 2002).

Remarkably, newborns apparently can recognize some of the sounds they experience during prenatal development. DeCasper and Spence (1986) asked pregnant women to read aloud the famous Dr. Seuss story *The Cat in the Hat* twice a day for the last month and a half of pregnancy. As newborns, then, these babies had heard *The Cat in the Hat* more than 50 times! The newborns were then allowed to suck on a mechanical nipple connected to a tape recorder so that sucking could turn the tape on or off. Babies would suck to hear a tape of their mother reading *The Cat in the Hat* but not to hear her reading other stories. Evidently, newborns recognized the familiar, rhythmic quality of *The Cat in the Hat* from their prenatal story-times.

Findings like these tell us that the last few months of prenatal development leave the fetus remarkably well prepared for independent living as a newborn baby. Unfortunately, not all babies arrive well prepared; sometimes their prenatal development has been disrupted. In the next section, we'll see how prenatal development sometimes goes awry.

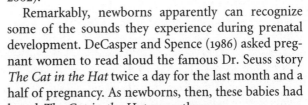

THINK ABOUT IT

Health care professionals often divide pregnancy into three three-month trimesters. How do these three trimesters correspond to the periods of the zygote, embryo, and fetus?

TEST YOURSELF

1. The period of the zygote ends
   _____.

2. Body structures and internal organs are created during the period of the
   _____.

3. _____ is called the age of viability because this is when most body systems function well enough to support life.

4. In the last few months of prenatal development, the fetus has regular periods of
   _____.

   A friend of yours says, "The environment starts to influence a child's development at birth." Do you agree? Why or why not?

Answers: (1) at two weeks after conception (when the zygote is completely implanted in the wall of the uterus), (2) embryo, (3) Between 22 and 28 weeks, (4) activity

---

2.3

Influences on Prenatal Development

LEARNING OBJECTIVES

▐ How is prenatal development influenced by a pregnant woman's age, her nutrition, and the stress she experiences while pregnant?

▐ How do diseases, drugs, and environmental hazards sometimes affect prenatal development?

▐ What are some general principles affecting the ways prenatal development can be harmed?

▐ How can prenatal development be monitored? Can abnormal prenatal development be corrected?

> **Influences on Prenatal Development**
>
> General Risk Factors
>
> Teratogens: Drugs, Diseases, and Environmental Hazards
>
> How Teratogens Influence Prenatal Development
>
> Prenatal Care

Chloe was two months pregnant at her first prenatal checkup. As her appointment drew near, she began a list of questions to ask her obstetrician. "I spend much of my workday at a computer. Is radiation from the monitor harmful to my baby?" "When my husband and I get home from work, we have a glass of wine to help unwind from the stress of the day. Is moderate drinking like this okay?" "I'm 38. I know older women give birth to babies with mental problems more often. Can I know if my baby will be affected this way?" Concern about whether a child will be born with an intellectual impairment is not uncommon for pregnant women in this age group.

Each of Chloe's questions concerns harm to her baby-to-be. She worries about the safety of her computer monitor, about her nightly glass of wine, and about her age. Chloe's concerns are well founded. Many factors influence the course of prenatal development, and they are the focus of this section. If you're sure you can answer *all* of Chloe's questions, skip this section and go directly to page 73. Otherwise, read on to learn about problems that sometimes arise in pregnancy.

GENERAL RISK FACTORS

As the name implies, general risk factors can have widespread effects on prenatal development. The most common types of risk factors are those associated with a pregnant woman's nutrition, stress level, age, and her exposure to teratogens.

Nutrition

The mother is the developing child's sole source of nutrition, so a balanced diet that includes foods from each of the four major food groups is vital. Current recommendations for weight gain during pregnancy range from 7 to 18 kilograms (15 to 40 lb.) depending on the woman's pre-pregnancy Body Mass Index (BMI), which is based on height and weight measurements (Health Canada, 1999c). According to this guideline, women whose pre-pregnant weight falls within the normal/healthy range should gain between 11.5 and 16 kilograms (25 and 35 lb.). Of this gain, about one-third reflects the weight of the baby, the placenta, and the fluid in the amniotic sac; another third comes from increases in a woman's fat stores; yet another third comes from the increased volume of blood and increases in the size of her breasts and uterus (Whitney & Hamilton, 1987).

Sheer amount of food is only part of the equation for a healthy pregnancy. *What a pregnant woman eats is also very important.* Proteins, vitamins, and minerals are essential for normal prenatal development. For example, folic acid, one of the B vitamins, is important for the baby's nervous system to develop properly (Shaw et al., 1995). *When mothers do not consume adequate amounts of folic acid, their babies are at risk for **spina bifida**, a disorder in which the embryo's neural tube does not close properly during the first month of pregnancy.* Since the neural tube develops into the brain and spinal cord, when it does not close properly, the result is permanent damage to the spinal cord and the nervous system. Many children with spina bifida need assistance with mobility such as braces or wheelchairs. Other prenatal problems have also been traced to inadequate proteins, vitamins, or minerals, so health care providers may recommend that pregnant women take nutrient supplements if nutrient intakes are insufficient.

When a pregnant woman does not provide adequate nourishment, the infant is likely to be born prematurely and to be underweight. Inadequate nourishment during the last few months of pregnancy can particularly affect the nervous system, because this is a time of rapid brain growth. Finally, babies who do not receive adequate nourishment are vulnerable to illness (Guttmacher & Kaiser, 1986).

Stress

Does a pregnant woman's mood affect the zygote, embryo, or fetus in her uterus? Is a woman who is happy during pregnancy more likely to give birth to a happy baby? Is a pregnant woman like the harried office worker in the photo more likely to give birth to an irritable baby? *These questions address the impact on prenatal development of chronic **stress,** which refers to a person's physical and psychological responses to threatening or challenging situations.* We can answer these questions with some certainty for nonhumans. When pregnant female animals experience constant stress—such as repeated electric shock or intense overcrowding—their offspring are often smaller than average and prone to other physical and behavioural problems (Schneider, 1992). In addition, stress seems to cause greater harm when experienced early in pregnancy (Schneider et al., 1999).

Determining the impact of stress on human pregnancy is more difficult because we must rely solely on correlational studies. (It would be unethical to do an experiment that assigned some pregnant women to a condition of extreme stress.) Studies typically show that women who report greater anxiety during pregnancy more often give birth early or have babies who weigh less than average (Copper et al., 1996; Paarlberg et al., 1995).

Michael Krasowitz/Getty Images

Increased stress can harm prenatal development in several ways. First, when a pregnant woman experiences stress, her body secretes hormones that reduce the flow of oxygen to the fetus while increasing its heart rate and activity level (Monk et al., 2000). Second, stress can weaken a pregnant woman's immune system, making her more susceptible to illness (Cohen & Williamson, 1991), which can, in turn, damage fetal development. Third, pregnant women under stress are more likely to smoke or drink alcohol and less likely to rest, exercise, and eat properly (Kolberg, 1999). All these behaviours endanger prenatal development.

We want to emphasize that the results described here apply to women who experience prolonged, extreme stress. Virtually all women sometimes become anxious or upset while pregnant. But occasional, relatively mild anxiety is not thought to have any harmful consequences for prenatal development.

Mother's Age

Traditionally, the 20s were thought to be the prime childbearing years. Teenage women as well as women who were 30 or older were considered less fit for the rigours of pregnancy. Is being a 20-something really important for a successful pregnancy? Let's answer this question separately for teenage and older women. Compared to women in their 20s, teenage women are more likely to have problems during pregnancy, labour, and delivery. This is largely because pregnant teenagers do not tend to get good prenatal care, usually because they are unaware of the need and do not seek it out. For example, it is recommended that pregnant adolescents should receive early nutritional care and that it be continued often and throughout the pregnancy since they may be at higher risk for insufficient nutritional intake (Health Canada, 1999c).

Nevertheless, even when a teenager receives adequate prenatal care and gives birth to a healthy baby, all is not rosy. Children of teenage mothers generally do less well in school and more often have behavioural problems (Fergusson & Woodward, 2000). The problems of teenage motherhood—incomplete education, poverty, and marital/relationship difficulties—affect the child's later development (Furstenberg, Brooks-Gunn, & Morgan, 1987).

Of course, not all teenage mothers and their infants follow this dismal life course. Some teenage mothers finish school, find good jobs, and have happy marriages/relationships; their children do well in school, academically and socially. However, teenage pregnancies with "happy endings" are definitely the exception; for most teenage mothers and their children, life is a struggle. Educating teenagers about the true consequences of teen pregnancy is crucial.

Are older women better suited for pregnancy? This is an important question because present-day Canadian women typically are waiting longer than ever to become pregnant. The proportion of women who are delaying childbirth into their later years has greatly increased in recent years (Health Canada, 2000c). Factors such as completing an education and beginning a career often delay childbearing.

Today we know that older women have more difficulty getting pregnant and are less likely to have successful pregnancies. Women in their 20s are twice as fertile as women in their 30s (Dunson, Colombo, & Baird, 2002); and beyond 35 years of age, the risks of miscarriage and stillbirth increase rapidly. Among 40- to 45-year-olds, for example, nearly half of all pregnancies result in miscarriage (Andersen et al., 2000). What's more, women in their 40s are more liable to give birth to babies with Down syndrome.

In general, then, prenatal development is most likely to proceed normally when women are between the ages of 20 and 35, are healthy and eat right, get good health care, and lead lives that are free of chronic stress. But even in these optimal cases prenatal development can be disrupted, as we'll see in the next section.

TERATOGENS: DRUGS, DISEASES, AND ENVIRONMENTAL HAZARDS

In the late 1950s, many pregnant women in Germany took the drug thalidomide, which was prescribed for treatment of nausea or "morning sickness" especially in the first trimester. Soon, however, came reports that many of these women were giving birth to babies with deformed arms, legs, hands, or fingers. *Thalidomide is a powerful teratogen, an agent that causes abnormal prenatal development.* Ultimately, more than 10,000 babies worldwide were harmed before thalidomide was withdrawn from the market (Kolberg, 1999).

Prompted by the thalidomide disaster, scientists began to study teratogens extensively. Today, we know a great deal about many teratogens that affect prenatal development. Most teratogens fall into one of three categories: drugs, diseases, and environmental hazards. Let's look at each.

Drugs

Thalidomide illustrates the harm that drugs can cause during prenatal development. Table 2.3 lists several other drugs that are known teratogens.

TABLE 2.3	Teratogenic Drugs and Their Consequences
Drug	*Potential Consequences*
Alcohol	Fetal alcohol syndrome, cognitive deficits, heart damage, delayed growth
Aspirin	Deficits in intelligence, attention, and motor skill
Caffeine	Lower birth weight, decreased muscle tone
Cocaine and heroin	Delayed growth, irritability in newborns
Marijuana	Lower birth weight, less motor control
Nicotine	Delayed growth, lower birth rate, possible cognitive impairments

Most of the drugs in the list are substances that are used routinely by some—alcohol, aspirin, caffeine, nicotine. Nevertheless, when consumed by pregnant women, they do present special dangers (Behnke & Eyler, 1993).

Cigarette smoking is typical of the potential harm from teratogenic drugs (Cornelius et al., 1995; Fried, O'Connell, & Watkinson, 1992). The nicotine in cigarette smoke constricts blood vessels and thus reduces the oxygen and nutrients that can reach the fetus over the placenta. Therefore, pregnant women who smoke are more likely to miscarry (abort the fetus spontaneously) and to bear children who are smaller than average at birth (Ernst, Moolchan, & Robinson, 2001). And, as children develop, they are more likely to show signs of impaired attention, language, and cognitive skills, along with behavioural problems (Brennan et al., 2002). Finally, even secondhand smoke harms the fetus: When pregnant women don't smoke but fathers do, babies tend to be smaller at birth (Friedman & Polifka, 1996). The message is clear and simple: Pregnant women shouldn't smoke and they should avoid others who do.

Alcohol also carries serious risk. *Prenatal exposure to alcoholic beverages can result in babies being born with Fetal Alcohol Syndrome (FAS), which is the leading cause of developmental disability in Canadian children. Fetal Alcohol Spectrum Disorders (FASD) is an umbrella term to describe the spectrum of disorders related to prenatal exposure to alcohol.* Children with FAS usually have learning or attention problems,

THINK ABOUT IT

A pregnant woman reluctant to give up her morning cup of coffee and nightly glass of wine says, "I drink so little coffee and wine that it couldn't possibly hurt my baby." What do you think?

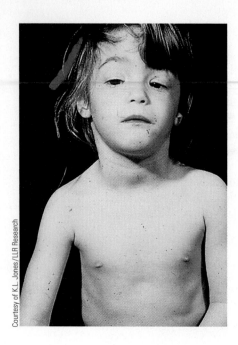

Courtesy of K.L. Jones / LLR Research

hyperactivity, below-average intelligence, and distinctive facial features. Like the child in the photo, children with FAS often have a small head, a thin upper lip, a short nose, and widely spaced eyes. Every day in Canada at least one child is born with FAS, and there is an estimated rate of 1 to 3 per 1,000 live births in industrialized countries (Health Canada Online); the rate is even higher in Canada's aboriginal communities (Square, 1997). FAS is a major birth defect with very serious consequences and yet it is 100% preventable.

No safe level of alcohol consumption has been identified due to difficulties in obtaining accurate rates of reported use and individual differences in metabolism. Since the effects of alcohol consumption can be so devastating, the government is increasing its funding for public awareness campaigns and education, and is putting more effort into early identification, diagnosis, and services related to the treatment of FAS and FAE.

It is impossible to offer guaranteed statements about any of the drugs listed in the table. For this reason, the best policy is for women to avoid all drugs throughout pregnancy.

Diseases

Sometimes women become ill while pregnant. Most diseases, such as colds and many strains of the flu, do not affect the fetus. However, several bacterial and viral infections can be quite harmful; five are listed in Table 2.4.

TABLE 2.4	Teratogenic Diseases and Their Consequences
Disease	**Potential Consequences**
AIDS	Frequent infections, neurological disorders, death
Cytomegalovirus	Deafness, blindness, abnormally small head, intellectual impairment
Genital herpes	Encephalitis, enlarged spleen, improper blood clotting
Rubella (German measles)	Intellectual impairment; damage to eyes, ears, and heart
Syphilis	Damage to the central nervous system, teeth, and bones

Some diseases pass from the mother through the placenta to attack the embryo or fetus directly. AIDS, cytomegalovirus, rubella, and syphilis are examples of diseases that are transmitted through the placenta. Other diseases attack during birth: The virus is present in the lining of the birth canal, and babies are infected as they pass through the canal. AIDS and genital herpes are two such diseases.

The only way to guarantee that these diseases will not harm prenatal development is for a woman to be sure that she does not contract the disease, before or during her pregnancy. Medicines that may help to treat a woman after she has become ill do not prevent the disease from damaging the fetus.

Environmental Hazards

As a by-product of life in an industrialized world, people are often exposed to toxins in foods they eat, fluids they drink, and air they breathe. Chemicals associated with industrial waste are the most common form of environmentally based teratogen. The quantity involved is usually minute; however, as was true for drugs, amounts that go unnoticed in an adult can cause serious damage to the fetus. Several environmental hazards that are known teratogens are listed in Table 2.5.

TABLE 2.5	Environmental Teratogens and Their Consequences
Hazard	**Potential Consequences**
Lead	Intellectual impairment
Mercury	Physical developmental delay, intellectual impairment, cerebral palsy
PCBs	Impaired memory and verbal skill
X-rays	Physical developmental delay, leukemia, intellectual impairment

You'll notice that although X-rays are included in the table, radiation associated with computer monitors or video display terminals (VDTs) is not. Several major studies have examined the impact of exposure to the electromagnetic fields generated by VDTs. For example, Schnorr and her colleagues (1991) compared the outcomes of pregnancies in telephone operators who worked at VDTs at least 25 hours weekly with operators who never used VDTs. For both groups of women, about 15% of their pregnancies ended in miscarriage. Further, other studies have not found links between exposure to VDTs and birth defects (Parazzini et al., 1993; Shaw, 2001). Evidently, VDTs can be used safely by pregnant women.

In the Spotlight on Research feature, we look at one of these environmental teratogens in detail.

SPOTLIGHT ON RESEARCH

Impact of Prenatal Exposure to PCBs on Cognitive Functioning

Who were the investigators, and what was the aim of the study? For many years, polychlorinated biphenyls (PCBs) were used in electrical transformers and paints, but the U.S. government banned them in the 1970s. Like many industrial by-products, they seeped into the waterways, where they contaminated fish and wildlife. The amount of PCBs in a typical contaminated fish does not affect adults, but Joseph Jacobson and Sandra Jacobson (1996) wanted to determine if this level of exposure was harmful to prenatal development. In particular, they knew from earlier work that substantial prenatal exposure to PCBs affected cognitive skills in infants and preschoolers; they hoped to determine if prenatal exposure similarly affected cognitive skills in school-age children.

How did the investigators measure the topic of interest? Jacobson and Jacobson needed to measure prenatal exposure to PCBs and cognitive skill. To measure prenatal exposure, they measured concentrations of PCBs in

(a) blood obtained from the umbilical cord and (b) breast milk of mothers who were breast-feeding. To measure cognitive skill, they used a standardized test of intelligence and a standardized test of reading comprehension.

Who were the children in the study? The sample included 212 children who were born in western Michigan in 1980–1981. This region was chosen because, at the time, Lake Michigan contained many contaminated salmon and lake trout.

What was the design of the study? The study was correlational because the investigators were interested in the relation that existed naturally between two variables: exposure to PCBs and cognitive skill. The study was longitudinal because children were tested several times: Their exposure to PCBs was measured immediately after birth, and their cognitive skill was measured at three ages: 7 months, 4 years, and 11 years.

Were there ethical concerns with the study? No. The children had been exposed to

PCBs naturally, prior to the start of the study. (Obviously, it would have been unethical for researchers to do an experiment that involved asking pregnant women to eat contaminated fish.) The investigators obtained permission from the parents for the children to participate.

What were the results? PCB exposure affected intelligence and reading comprehension. However, as you can see in Figure 2.9, lower levels of exposure to PCBs apparently had little effect on intelligence and reading comprehension. Only children with high levels of exposure to PCBs were affected.

What did the investigators conclude? Prenatal exposure to PCBs affects children's cognitive skills. Though children's scores were in the normal range, their reduced cognitive skills may create special hurdles in school.

What converging evidence would strengthen these conclusions? The results show that PCBs affect children's scores on standardized tests. More convincing would be longitudinal results showing that children exposed to PCBs were more likely to be diagnosed with a learning disability or language impairment, more likely to repeat a grade, or less likely to graduate from high school.

FIGURE 2.9

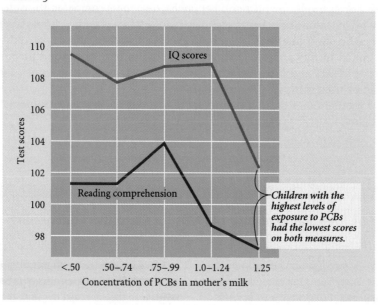

Environmental teratogens are treacherous because people are unaware of their presence in the environment. The women in the Jacobson and Jacobson (1996) study, for example, did not realize they were eating PCB-laden fish. This invisibility makes it more difficult for a pregnant woman to protect herself from environmental teratogens. The best advice is for a pregnant woman to be particularly careful of the foods she eats and the air she breathes. Be sure that all foods are cleaned thoroughly to rid them of insecticides. Avoid convenience foods, which often contain many chemical additives. Stay away from air that has been contaminated by household products such as cleansers, paint strippers, and fertilizers. Women in jobs such as housecleaning or hairdressing that require contact with potential teratogens should try to switch to less potent chemicals. For example, they should use baking soda instead of more chemically laden cleansers. And they should wear protective gloves, aprons, and masks to reduce their contact with potential teratogens. Finally, because environmental teratogens continue to increase, check with a health care provider to learn whether other materials should be avoided.

HOW TERATOGENS INFLUENCE PRENATAL DEVELOPMENT

By assembling all the evidence on the harm caused by drugs, diseases, and environmental hazards, scientists have identified five important general principles about how teratogens usually work (Hogge, 1990; Jacobson & Jacobson, 2000; Vorhees & Mollnow, 1987).

1. *The impact of a teratogen depends on the genotype of the organism.* A substance may be harmful to one species but not to another. To determine its safety, thalidomide was tested on pregnant rats and rabbits, and their offspring had normal limbs. Yet, when pregnant women took the same drug in comparable doses, many had children with deformed limbs. Moreover, some women who took thalidomide gave birth to babies with normal limbs while others, taking comparable doses of thalidomide at the same time in their pregnancies, gave birth to babies with deformed arms and legs. Apparently, heredity makes some individuals more susceptible than others to a teratogen.

2. *The impact of teratogens changes over the course of prenatal development.* The timing of exposure to a teratogen is very important. Teratogens typically have different effects in the three periods of prenatal development. Figure 2.10 shows how the consequences of teratogens differ for the periods of the zygote, embryo, and fetus. During the period of the zygote, exposure to teratogens usually results in spontaneous abortion of the fertilized egg. During the period of the embryo, exposure to teratogens produces major defects in bodily structure. For example, many women who took thalidomide during

FIGURE 2.10

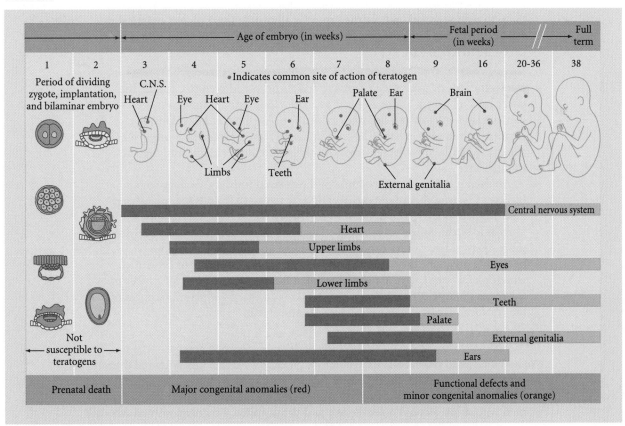

From *Before We Are Born*, Fourth Edition, by K. L. Moore and T. V. N. Persaud, p. 130. Copyright © 1993 W. B. Saunders. Reprinted with permission from Elsevier.

the period of the embryo had babies with ill-formed or missing limbs. Women who contract rubella during the period of the embryo have babies with heart defects. During the period of the fetus, exposure to teratogens produces either minor defects in bodily structure or causes body systems to function improperly. For example, heavy maternal alcohol consumption during this period has been found to result in the fetus developing fewer brain cells.

Even within the different periods of prenatal development, developing body parts and systems are more vulnerable at some times than others. The red shading in Figure 2.10 indicates a time of maximum vulnerability; orange shading indicates a time when the developing organism is less vulnerable. The heart, for example, is most sensitive to teratogens during the first half of the embryonic period. Exposure to teratogens before this time rarely produces heart damage; exposure after results in milder damage.

3. *Each teratogen affects a specific aspect (or aspects) of prenatal development.* Said another way, teratogens do not harm all body systems; instead, damage is selective. When women contract rubella, their babies often have problems with their eyes, ears, and heart, but they have normal limbs. When mothers consume PCB-contaminated fish, their babies typically have normal body parts and normal motor skills but below-average verbal and memory skills.

4. *The impact of teratogens depends on the dosage.* Just as a single drop of oil won't pollute a lake, small dosages of teratogens may not harm the fetus. In research on PCBs, for example, cognitive skills were affected only among children who had the greatest prenatal exposure to PCBs. In general, the greater the exposure, the greater the risk for damage (Adams, 1999).

An implication of this principle is that researchers should be able to determine safe levels for a teratogen. In reality, this is very difficult because sensitivity to teratogens will not be the same for all people (and it's not practical to establish separate safe amounts for each person). Hence, the safest rule is zero exposure to teratogens.

5. *Damage from teratogens is not always evident at birth but may appear later in life.* In the case of malformed limbs or babies born addicted to cocaine, the effects of a teratogen are obvious immediately. Sometimes, however, the damage from a teratogen becomes evident only as the child develops. For example, when women ate PCB-contaminated fish, their babies were normal at birth. Their below-average cognitive skills were not evident until several months later.

An even more dramatic example of the delayed impact of a teratogen involves the drug diethylstilbestrol (DES). Between 1947 and 1971, many pregnant women took DES to prevent miscarriages. Their babies were apparently normal at birth. However, as adults, daughters of women who took DES are more likely to have a rare cancer of the vagina and to have difficulties becoming pregnant themselves (Friedman & Polifka, 1996). Sons of women who took DES may have abnormal seminal fluid and are at risk for cancer of the testes (Sharpe & Skakkebaek, 1993). Here is a case in which the impact of the teratogen is not evident until decades after birth.

The Real World of Prenatal Risk

We have discussed risk factors individually, as if each were the only potential threat to prenatal development. In reality, many infants are exposed to multiple general risks and multiple teratogens (Giberson & Weinberg, 1992; Richardson, 1998). Pregnant women who drink alcohol often smoke and drink coffee. Pregnant women who are under stress often drink alcohol. Many of these same women may have poor nutrition. When all of the risks are combined, unfortunately, prenatal development will rarely be optimal (Schneider, Swan, & Fitzgerald, 1997).

From what we've said so far in this section, you may think that the developing child has little chance of escaping harm. But most babies *are* born in good health. Of course, a good policy for pregnant women is to avoid diseases, drugs, and environmental hazards that are known teratogens. This, coupled with thorough prenatal medical care and adequate nutrition, is the best recipe for normal prenatal development.

PRENATAL CARE

"I really don't care whether I have a boy or girl, just as long as it's healthy." Legions of parents worldwide have felt this way, but until recently, all they could do was hope for the best. Today, however, advances in technology mean that parents can have a much better idea whether their baby is developing normally.

Genetic Counselling

Often the first step in deciding whether a couple's baby is likely to be at risk is genetic counselling. A counsellor asks about family medical history and constructs a family tree for each parent to assess the odds that their child would inherit a disorder. If the family tree suggests that a parent is likely to be a carrier of the disorder, blood tests can determine the parent's genotype. With this information, a genetic counsellor then advises prospective parents about their choices. A couple might simply go ahead and attempt to conceive a child "naturally." Or they may decide to use sperm or eggs from other people. Yet another choice might be adoption.

Prenatal Assessment

After a woman is pregnant, how can we know whether prenatal development is progressing normally? Traditionally, obstetricians tracked the progress of prenatal development by feeling the size and position of the fetus through a woman's abdomen. This technique was not very precise and, of course, couldn't be done at all until the fetus was large enough to feel. Today, however, several new techniques have revolutionized our ability to monitor prenatal growth and development. *Ultrasound is a procedure in which sound waves are used to generate a picture of the fetus.* As shown in the photo, a tool about the size of a hair dryer is rubbed over the woman's abdomen; the image is shown on a nearby TV monitor. The pictures that are generated are hardly portrait quality; they are grainy and it takes an expert's eye to distinguish what's what. Nevertheless, parents are often thrilled to see their baby and to watch it move.

Ultrasound typically can be used as early as four or five weeks after conception; prior to this time the embryo is not large enough to generate an interpretable image. Ultrasound pictures are quite useful for determining the position of the fetus within the uterus and, at 16 to 20 weeks after conception, its sex. Ultrasound is also helpful in detecting twins or triplets. Finally, ultrasound is used to identify obvious physical deformities, such as abnormal growth of the head.

In pregnancies where a genetic disorder is suspected, two other techniques are particularly valuable because they provide a sample

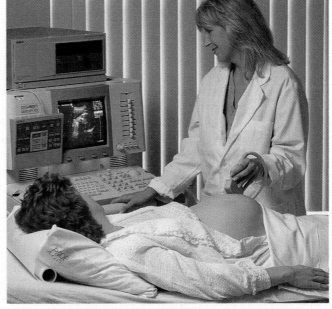

Richard Himelsen/Medichrome

of fetal cells that can be analyzed. *In **amniocentesis,** a needle is inserted through the mother's abdomen to obtain a sample of the amniotic fluid that surrounds the fetus.* As you can see in Figure 2.11a, ultrasound is used to guide the needle into the uterus. The fluid contains skin cells that can be grown in a laboratory dish and then analyzed to determine the genotype of the fetus.

FIGURE 2.11A

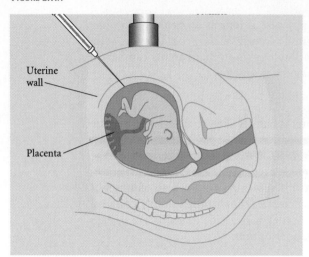

FIGURE 2.11B

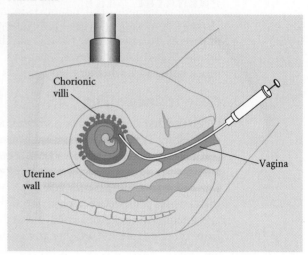

A drawback to amniocentesis is that although the amniotic fluid is extracted at about 16 weeks after conception, at least two weeks must pass for the individual cells to grow sufficiently to allow testing. *A procedure that can be used much earlier in pregnancy is **chorionic villus sampling,** in which a sample of tissue is obtained from part of the placenta.* As Figure 2.11b shows, a small tube is inserted through the vagina and into the uterus and is used to collect a small plug of cells from the placenta. This procedure can be performed eight or nine weeks after conception, and results are available within 24 hours.

With the samples obtained from either amniocentesis or chorionic villus sampling, roughly 200 different genetic disorders, including Down syndrome, can be detected. These procedures are virtually error-free but at a price: Miscarriages are slightly more likely after amniocentesis or chorionic villus sampling (Wilson, 2000). A woman must decide whether the information gained from amniocentesis or chorionic villus sampling justifies the slight risks of a possible miscarriage.

Fetal Medicine

Ultrasound, amniocentesis, and chorionic villus sampling have made it much easier to determine whether prenatal development is progressing normally. But what happens when it is not? Traditionally, a woman's options have been limited: She could continue the pregnancy or end it. However, the list of options is expanding. *A whole new field called **fetal medicine** is concerned with treating prenatal problems before birth.* One approach in fetal medicine is to treat disorders medically, by administering drugs or hormones to the fetus. In one case, ultrasound pictures showed a fetus with an enlarged thyroid gland that would have made delivery difficult. A hormone injected into the amniotic fluid caused the thyroid gland to shrink and resulted in a normal delivery (Davidson et al., 1991). In another case, amniocentesis revealed that a fetus had inherited a disorder in which the immune system did not work properly. This would leave a baby vulnerable to infection, so healthy immune cells were injected into the umbilical cord (Elmer-DeWitt, 1994).

THINK ABOUT IT

Imagine that you are 42 years old and pregnant. Would you want to have amniocentesis or chorionic villus sampling to determine the genotype of the fetus? Why or why not?

Another way to correct prenatal problems is fetal surgery. For example, more than 200 cases of spina bifida have been corrected with fetal surgery in the seventh or eighth month of pregnancy. Surgeons cut through the mother's abdominal wall to expose the fetus, then cut through the fetal abdominal wall; the spinal cord is repaired, and the fetus is returned to the uterus (Okie, 2000).

Fetal surgery has also been used to treat a disorder affecting identical twins in which one twin—the "donor"—pumps blood through its own and the other twin's circulatory system. The donor twin usually fails to grow; surgery corrects the problem by sealing off the unnecessary blood vessels between the twins (McCormick, 2000). Fetal surgery holds great promise, but it is still relatively experimental and not commonly undertaken.

Yet another approach is molecular medicine. With the completion of the main task of the Human Genome Project in 2003, which involved the identification of all the genes in human DNA, there have been remarkable impacts on biomedical research. Detailed genome maps have guided researchers in their quest for genes associated with many genetic conditions. The result may be further advances in treatments such as gene therapy and also focusing more on the fundamental causes of diseases and less on treating symptoms (Genome Programs of the U.S. Department of Energy Office of Science, 2003).

ANSWERS TO CHLOE'S QUESTIONS. Now you can return to Chloe's questions in the section-opening vignette (page 62) and answer them for her. If you're not certain, here are the pages in this chapter where the answers appear:

- About her computer monitor (page 67)
- About her nightly glass of wine (page 66)
- About giving birth to a baby with intellectual impairment (page 64)

TEST YOURSELF

1. General risk factors in pregnancy include a woman's _____, prolonged stress, age, and her exposure to teratogens.

2. _____ are some of the most dangerous teratogens because a pregnant woman is often unaware of their presence.

3. During the period of the zygote, exposure to a teratogen typically results in _____.

4. Two techniques used to determine whether a fetus has a hereditary disorder are amniocentesis and _____.

   Describe how the impact of teratogens on the fetus shows nature and nurture in action during prenatal development.

Answers: (1) nutrition, (2) Environmental hazards, (3) spontaneous abortion of the fertilized egg, (4) chorionic villus sampling

---

2.4

Labour and Delivery

LEARNING OBJECTIVES

- What are the different phases of labour and delivery?
- What are "natural" ways of coping with the pain of childbirth? Is childbirth at home safe?
- What are some complications that can occur during birth?

Labour and Delivery

Stages of Labour

Approaches to Childbirth

Birth Complications

Infant Mortality

Marlea is about to begin classes to prepare for her baby's birth. She is relieved that the classes are finally starting because this means the end of pregnancy is in sight. But all the talk she has heard about "breathing exercises" and "coaching" sounds pretty silly to her. Marlea would prefer to get a general anaesthetic for the delivery and wake up when everything is over.

As women like Marlea near the end of pregnancy, they find that sleeping and breathing become more difficult, that they tire more rapidly, that they become constipated, and that their legs and feet swell. Women look forward to birth, both to relieve their discomfort and, of course, to see their baby. In this section, you'll see the different steps involved in birth, review different approaches to childbirth, and look at problems that can arise. Along the way, we'll look at classes like those Marlea will take and the exercises that she'll learn.

STAGES OF LABOUR

"Labour" is an appropriate name for childbirth, which is the most intense, prolonged physical effort that humans experience. Labour is usually divided into the three stages shown in Figure 2.12.

FIGURE 2.12

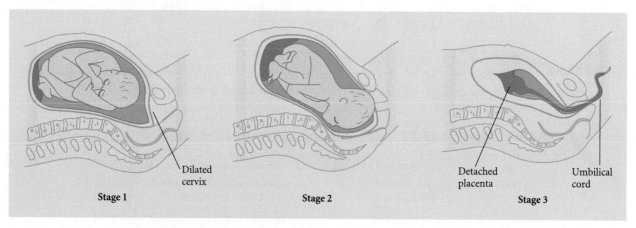

Dilated cervix

Detached placenta

Umbilical cord

Stage 1   Stage 2   Stage 3

- ▨ In Stage 1, which may last from 12 to 24 hours for a first birth, the uterus starts to contract. The first contractions are weak and irregular. Gradually, they become stronger and more rhythmic, enlarging the cervix (the opening from the uterus to the vagina) to approximately 10 centimetres.
- ▨ In Stage 2, the baby passes through the cervix and enters the vagina. The mother helps push the baby along by contracting muscles in her abdomen. *Soon the top of the baby's head appears, an event known as* **crowning**. Within about an hour, the baby is delivered.
- ▨ In Stage 3, which lasts only minutes, the mother pushes a few more times to expel the placenta (also called, appropriately, the *afterbirth*).

The times given for each of the stages are only approximations; the actual times vary greatly among women. For most women, labour with their second and subsequent children is much more rapid. Stage 1 may last 4 to 6 hours, and Stage 2 may be as brief as 20 minutes.

APPROACHES TO CHILDBIRTH

In the 1950s, women in labour were admitted to a hospital and administered a general anaesthetic. Fathers waited anxiously in a nearby room for news of the baby.

Since the 1960s, however, many people have tried more "natural" or prepared approaches to childbirth in which labour and delivery are seen as life events to be celebrated, not medical procedures to be endured. Prepared approaches to childbirth include many elements, but one of the fundamentals is the belief that birth is more likely to be problem-free and rewarding when mothers and fathers understand what's happening during pregnancy, labour, and delivery. Consequently, prepared childbirth means going to classes in which individuals learn basic facts about pregnancy and childbirth (not unlike the material presented in this chapter).

Childbirth classes also spend much time showing women how to handle the pain of childbirth. Natural methods of dealing with pain are emphasized over medication. Why? General anaesthesia (medication that causes a woman to lose consciousness) or local anaesthesia (medication that numbs the lower body) can prevent women from using their abdominal muscles to help push the baby through the birth canal. Without this pushing, obstetricians sometimes have to use mechanical devices to pull the baby through the birth canal, a practice that involves some risk to the baby (Johanson et al., 1993). Also, drugs that reduce the pain of childbirth cross the placenta and affect the baby. Consequently, when a woman receives large doses of pain-relieving medication, her baby is often withdrawn or irritable for days or even weeks (Brazelton, Nugent, & Lester, 1987; Ransjoe-Arvidson et al., 2001). These effects are temporary; nevertheless, they may give the new mother an inaccurate view of her new baby's personality. These problems make it important to minimize the use of pain-relieving drugs during birth.

Childbirth classes emphasize three related strategies to counter the pain of birth without drugs. One strategy is based on the fact that pain often feels greater when a person is tense. Consequently, pregnant women learn ways to relax during labour, such as deep-breathing techniques. A second approach involves visual imagery. Women are taught to imagine a reassuring, pleasant scene or experience. Whenever they begin to experience pain during labour, they focus intensely on this image instead of the pain. A third element is a supportive "coach." The father-to-be, a relative, or a close friend attends childbirth classes with the mother-to-be. The coach learns the techniques for coping with pain and practises them with the pregnant woman. During labour and delivery, the coach helps the woman to use these techniques and offers support and encouragement.

Although Marlea, the pregnant woman in the vignette, may have her doubts about these classes, research shows that they *are* useful (Hetherington, 1990). Although most mothers who attend childbirth classes use some medication to reduce the pain of labour, they typically use less than mothers who do not attend childbirth classes. Also, mothers and fathers who attend childbirth classes feel more positively about labour and birth when compared to mothers and fathers who have not attended classes.

Another element of the trend to natural childbirth is the idea that birth need not always take place in a hospital. The vast majority of babies in Canada are born in hospitals. However, home birth is a common practice in Europe. In the Netherlands, for example, about one-third of all births take place at home (Wiegers, van der Zee, & Keirse, 1998). Advocates note that home delivery is less expensive and that most women are more relaxed during labour in their homes. Advocates also point out that many women enjoy the greater control they have over labour and birth in a home delivery. A health care professional—often a nurse-midwife—is present in the home during labour and delivery.

For Canadians accustomed to hospital delivery, home delivery can seem like a risky proposition. Is home delivery safe? Yes, but with a very important catch. Birth problems are no more common in babies delivered at home than in babies delivered in a hospital, but only when the woman is healthy, her pregnancy has been problem-free, the labour and delivery are expected to be problem-free, and a trained health care professional assists with the delivery (Olsen, 1997). If there is *any* reason to believe that labour and delivery may encounter problems that require medical assistance, it is recommended that labour and delivery should take place in the hospital, not at home.

BIRTH COMPLICATIONS

Women who are healthy when they become pregnant usually have a normal pregnancy, labour, and delivery. When women are not healthy or don't receive adequate prenatal care, problems can surface during labour and delivery. (Of course, even healthy women can have problems, but not as often.) The more common birth complications are listed in Table 2.6.

TABLE 2.6	Common Birth Complications
Complication	**Features**
Cephalopelvic disproportion	The infant's head is larger than the pelvis, making it impossible for the baby to pass through the birth canal.
Irregular position	In shoulder presentation, the baby is lying crosswise in the uterus and the shoulder appears first; in breech presentation, the buttocks appear first.
Preeclampsia	A pregnant woman has high blood pressure, protein in her urine, and swelling in her extremities (due to fluid retention).
Prolapsed umbilical cord	The umbilical cord precedes the baby through the birth canal and is squeezed shut, cutting off oxygen to the baby.

Some of these complications, such as a prolapsed umbilical cord, are dangerous because they can disrupt the flow of blood through the umbilical cord. *If this flow of blood is disrupted, infants do not receive adequate oxygen, a condition known as* **hypoxia.** Hypoxia sometimes occurs during labour and delivery because the umbilical cord is pinched or squeezed shut, cutting off the flow of blood. Hypoxia is very serious because it can lead to intellectual impairment or death.

To guard against hypoxia, fetal heart rate is monitored during labour, either by ultrasound or with a tiny electrode that is passed through the vagina and attached to the scalp of the fetus. An abrupt change in heart rate can be a sign that the fetus is not receiving enough oxygen and will require further assessment to determine if the fetus is in distress.

When a fetus is in distress or when the fetus is in an irregular position or is too large to pass through the birth canal, a physician may decide to remove it from the mother's uterus surgically (Guillemin, 1993). *In a caesarean section, or C-section, an incision is made in the abdomen to remove the baby from the uterus.* A C-section is riskier for mothers than a vaginal delivery because of increased bleeding and greater danger of infection. A C-section poses little risk for babies, although activity is often briefly depressed from the anaesthesia that the mother receives before the operation. Mother-infant interactions are much the same for babies delivered vaginally or by planned or unplanned C-sections (Durik, Hyde, & Clark, 2000).

Birth complications are hazardous not just for a newborn's health—they have long-term effects too. Babies who experience many birth complications are at risk, for example, of aggressive behaviour (e.g., Kandel & Mednick, 1991). This is particularly true for newborns with birth complications who later experience family adversity, such as living in poverty (Arseneault et al., 2002). These outcomes underscore the importance of excellent health care throughout pregnancy and labour and the need for a supportive environment throughout childhood.

Problems also arise when babies are born too early or too small. Normally, a baby spends about 38 weeks developing before being born. *Babies born before the 36th week are called* **preterm** *or* **premature.** In the first year or so, premature infants often lag behind full-term infants in many facets of development. However, by 2 or 3 years of age, such differences have vanished, and most premature infants develop normally (Greenberg & Crnic, 1988).

Prospects are usually not as bright for babies who are "small for date." Though born after a normal-length pregnancy, these babies are much smaller than normal, usually because the mother's nutrition was inadequate or because of congenital infections (Allen, 1984). *Newborns who weigh 2,500 grams (5.5 pounds) or less are said to have **low birth weight**; newborns weighing less than 1,500 grams (3.3 pounds) are said to have **very low birth weight**; and those weighing less than 1,000 grams (2.2 pounds) are said to have **extremely low birth weight**.*

Babies with very or extremely low birth weight do not fare well. Many do not survive; those who live often lag behind in the development of intellectual and motor skills (Sykes et al., 1997; Ventura et al., 1994). The odds are better for newborns who weigh more than 1,500 grams. Most survive. Some will develop normally, but others will always lag behind. Why? The Forces in Action feature provides some clues.

THINK ABOUT IT
A friend of yours has just given birth six weeks prematurely. The baby is average size for a baby born prematurely and seems to be faring well, but your friend is concerned nonetheless. What could you say to reassure your friend?

FORCES IN ACTION

What Determines Life Outcomes for Low-Birth-Weight Babies?

Why do some low-birth-weight babies recover completely, but others do not? Biological forces are not the only factors determining whether low-birth-weight babies thrive. Sociocultural forces are critical: Low-birth-weight babies thrive *if* they receive excellent medical care and their home environment is supportive and stimulating. Unfortunately, not all low-birth-weight babies have optimal experiences. Many receive inadequate medical care because their families live in poverty. Others experience stress and disorder in their family life. For these low-birth-weight babies, development is usually delayed and sometimes permanently diminished.

The importance of a supportive environment for low-birth-weight babies is underscored by the results of a 30-year longitudinal study by Werner (1989, 1995) covering all children born on the Hawaiian island of Kauai in

1955. When low-birth-weight children grew up in stable homes—defined as the presence of two mentally healthy parents throughout childhood—they were indistinguishable from children born without birth complications. However, when low-birth-weight children experienced an unstable family environment—defined as experiencing divorce, parental alcoholism, or parental mental illness—they lagged behind their peers in intellectual and social development.

Thus, when biological and sociocultural forces are both harmful—low birth weight *plus* inadequate medical care or family stress—the prognosis for babies is grim. The message to parents of low-birth-weight newborns is clear: Do not despair, because excellent caregiving can compensate for all but the most severe birth problems (Werner, 1994; Werner & Smith, 1992). ◐

INFANT MORTALITY

Infant mortality is the number of infants out of 1,000 births who were born alive but die before their first birthday. This number has been used as the single most comprehensive measure of health in a society (Health Canada, 2000b). In 1999 the Canadian infant mortality rate was 5.3 deaths per 1,000 live births, compared to a rate of 7.1 for that same year in the United States (OECD Health Data, 2002). The infant mortality rates in most countries have dramatically improved over the past century due to better sanitation, nutrition, infant feeding, and maternal and child health care (Buehler et al., 1987). However there are also regional fluctuations in these rates within countries according to income and related standard of living differences.

Prenatal development is the foundation of all development and only with regular prenatal checkups can we know whether this foundation is being laid properly. Pregnant women and the children they carry *need* this care.

FIGURE 2.13   Infant Mortality Rate (per 1,000 Live Births), Selected OECD Countries, 1999

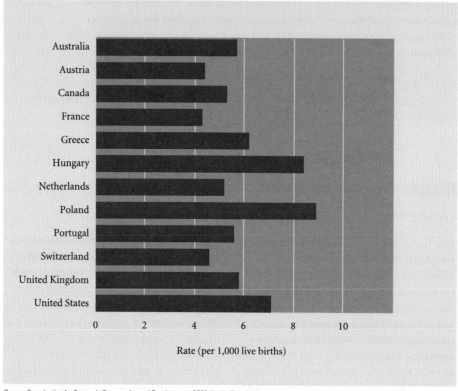

Rate (per 1,000 live births)

Source: Organisation for Economic Co-operation and Development, OECD Health Data 2002.

HEALTHY LIVING

What contributes to the best possible outcomes at birth?

We know so much about best health practices to improve the chances of having a healthy baby. If a pregnant woman asked you about healthy behaviours during pregnancy, what would you say? Pregnant women should be advised to seek prenatal care and learn all about the importance of good nutrition, rest, avoiding strenuous work, appropriate weight gain, use of supplements, and also about the risks of smoking, using alcohol and drugs, too much stress, and teratogens. In addition, many excellent resources for expectant parents are available, such as access to prenatal classes to guide them through the perinatal period with information on expected physical and psychological changes, impending signs of labour, coping methods for labour, and care of the newborn.

TEST YOURSELF

1. In the third stage of labour, the _____ is delivered.

2. Two problems with using anaesthesia during labour are that a woman can't use her abdominal muscles to help push the baby down the birth canal and _____.

3. Home delivery is safe when a pregnant woman is healthy, has had a problem-free pregnancy, expects to have a problem-free delivery, and _____.

4. When the supply of oxygen to the fetus is disrupted because the umbilical cord is squeezed shut, _____ results.

Do studies on the long-term effects of prematurity and low birth weight provide evidence for continuity in development or discontinuity? Why?

Answers: (1) placenta, (2) the pain-relieving medication crosses the placenta and affects the baby, (3) when trained health care professionals are present to deliver the baby, (4) hypoxia

PUTTING IT ALL TOGETHER

This chapter began with conception, covered 38 weeks of prenatal development, and ended with birth. You saw the mighty impact of genes that occurs at conception. Sometimes single genes influence development, as in the case of the sickle-cell disease that so frightens Leslie. More often, many genes work together to influence growth, with the outcome depending strongly on the impact of the environment. You learned that structures and processes unfold in a predictable sequence during prenatal development and this knowledge answered some of Eun Jung's questions about her pregnancy. You also learned how and why prenatal development sometimes goes awry and used this information to address Chloe's concerns about how her health and behaviour might affect her baby's develop-

ment. Finally, you looked at labour and delivery, including some of the advantages of a prepared childbirth such as Marlea plans to have.

This chapter, more than most of the others in this book, has emphasized the biological components of the biopsychosocial framework. Even here, however, biological forces do not operate in isolation but in interaction with the other elements of the framework. Prenatal development reflects biologically programmed events plus environmental influences on the fetus.

The development we have traced in this chapter serves as a prelude to the remainder of life-span human development. Each succeeding stage builds on the themes established in the prelude, as we'll see in the next chapter, which is devoted to infancy.

SUMMARY

2.1 In the Beginning: 23 Pairs of Chromosomes

Mechanisms of Heredity

■ At conception, the 23 chromosomes in the sperm merge with the 23 chromosomes in the egg. Each chromosome is one molecule of DNA; a section of DNA that provides specific biochemical instructions is called a gene.

■ All of a person's genes make up a genotype; the phenotype refers to the physical, behavioural, and psychological characteristics that develop when the genotype is exposed to a specific environment.

■ Different forms of the same gene are called alleles. A person who inherits the same allele on a pair of chromosomes is homozygous; in this case, the biochemical instructions on the allele are followed. A

person who inherits different alleles is heterozygous; in this case, the instructions of the dominant allele are followed whereas those of the recessive allele are ignored.

■ Behavioural and psychological phenotypes that reflect an underlying continuum (such as intelligence) often involve polygenic inheritance. In polygenic inheritance, the phenotype reflects the combined activity of many distinct genes. Polygenic inheritance is often examined by studying twins and adopted children.

Genetic Disorders

■ Most inherited disorders are carried by recessive alleles. Examples include sickle-cell disease, a serious blood disease, and phenylketonuria, in which toxins accumulate and cause mental retardation. Sometimes fertilized eggs do not have 46 chromosomes. Usually they are aborted spontaneously soon after conception. An exception is Down syndrome, in which individuals usually have an extra 21st chromosome. Individuals with Down syndrome have a distinctive appearance and are mentally retarded. Disorders of the sex chromosomes are more common because these chromosomes contain less genetic material than autosomes.

Heredity Is Not Destiny: Genes and Environments

- Genes never influence behaviour directly. Instead, they affect behaviour indirectly by increasing the odds that a child will behave in a particular way. Also, the impact of a gene on behaviour depends on the environment in which the genetic instructions are carried out.

- PKU does not lead to mental retardation when individuals with the disorder maintain a diet low in phenylalanine. This demonstrates the concept of reaction range; the same genotype can lead to different phenotypes. The outcome of heredity depends on the environment in which development occurs.

- In infants and young children, the gene-environment relation is passive: parents pass on genotypes to their children and provide much of their early environment. An evocative gene-environment relation increasingly occurs during development as the child's genotype evokes responses from the environment. In older children and adolescents, an active gene-environment relation is common: Individuals actively seek environments related to their genetic makeup.

- Family environments affect siblings differently, which is known as nonshared environmental influences. Parents provide a unique environment for each child in the family as well as providing a unique genotype for each child.

2.2 From Conception to Birth

Period of the Zygote (Weeks 1–2)

- The first period of prenatal development lasts two weeks. It begins when the egg is fertilized by the sperm in the fallopian tube and ends when the fertilized egg has implanted in the wall of the uterus. By the end of this period, cells have begun to differentiate.

Period of the Embryo (Weeks 3–8)

- The second period of prenatal development begins two weeks after conception and ends eight weeks after. This is a period of rapid growth in which most major body structures are created.

Period of the Fetus (Weeks 9–38)

- The third period of prenatal development begins eight weeks after conception and lasts until birth. The highlights of this period are a remarkable increase in the size of the fetus and changes in body systems that are necessary for life. By seven months, most body systems function well enough to support life.

2.3 Influences on Prenatal Development

General Risk Factors

- Parents' age can affect prenatal development. Teenagers often have problem pregnancies mainly because they rarely receive adequate prenatal care. Older women are more likely to have problem pregnancies. Prenatal development can also be harmed if a pregnant mother has inadequate nutrition or experiences considerable stress.

Teratogens: Drugs, Diseases, and Environmental Hazards

- Teratogens are agents that can cause abnormal prenatal development. Many drugs that adults take are teratogens. For most drugs, scientists have not established amounts that can be consumed safely. Several diseases are teratogens. Only by avoiding these diseases entirely can a pregnant woman escape their harmful consequences. Environmental teratogens are particularly dangerous because a pregnant woman may not know that these substances are present in the environment.

How Teratogens Influence Prenatal Development

- The impact of teratogens depends on the genotype of the organism, the period of prenatal development when the organism is exposed to the teratogen, and the amount of exposure. Sometimes the impact of a teratogen is not evident until later in life.

Prenatal Care

- Many techniques are used to track the progress of prenatal development, such as ultrasound, which uses sound waves to generate a picture of the fetus. This picture can be used to determine the position of the fetus, its sex, and whether there are gross physical deformities. When genetic disorders are suspected, amniocentesis and chorionic villus sampling may be used to determine the genotype of the fetus. Fetal medicine is a new field in which problems of prenatal development are corrected medically, with surgery, or using genetic engineering.

2.4 Labour and Delivery

Stages of Labour

- Labour consists of three stages. In Stage 1, the muscles of the uterus contract. The contractions, which are weak at first and gradually become stronger, cause the cervix to enlarge. In Stage 2, the baby moves through the birth canal. In Stage 3, the placenta is delivered.

Approaches to Childbirth

▪ Natural or prepared childbirth is based on the assumption that parents should understand what takes place during pregnancy and birth. In natural childbirth, pain-relieving medications are avoided because this medication prevents women from pushing during labour and because it affects the fetus. Instead, women learn to cope with pain through relaxation, imagery, and with the help of a supportive coach.

▪ Most Canadian babies are born in hospitals, but many European babies are born at home.

Birth Complications

▪ During labour and delivery, the flow of blood to the fetus can be disrupted because the umbilical cord is squeezed shut. This causes hypoxia, a lack of oxygen to the fetus, which puts the fetus at risk for mental disability. Some babies are born prematurely and others are small for date. Premature babies develop more slowly at first but catch up by 2 or 3 years of age. Small-for-date babies often do not fare well, particularly if they weigh less than 1,500 grams at birth and if their environment is stressful.

Infant Mortality

▪ Infant mortality is the number of deaths per 1,000 of live-born infants. Canada has one of the lowest rates of infant mortality in the world.

KEY TERMS

chromosomes (45)
autosomes (45)
sex chromosomes (45)
deoxyribonucleic acid (DNA) (45)
gene (45)
genotype (45)
phenotype (45)
alleles (46)
homozygous (46)
heterozygous (46)
dominant (46)
recessive (46)
incomplete dominance (47)
sickle-cell trait (47)
behavioural genetics (47)
polygenic inheritance (48)
monozygotic twins (49)
dizygotic twins (49)
phenylketonuria (PKU) (50)
Huntington's disease (50)
reaction range (52)
passive gene-environment relation (53)

evocative gene-environment relation (54)
active gene-environment relation (54)
niche-picking (54)
nonshared environmental influences (55)
prenatal development (56)
in vitro fertilization (57)
eugenics (57)
zygote (58)
implantation (58)
germ disc (58)
placenta (58)
embryo (59)
ectoderm (59)
mesoderm (59)
endoderm (59)
amnion (59)
amniotic fluid (59)
umbilical cord (59)
period of the fetus (60)
cerebral cortex (60)

vernix (61)
age of viability (61)
spina bifida (63)
stress (63)
teratogen (65)
Fetal Alcohol Syndrome (FAS) (65)
Fetal Alcohol Spectrum Disorders (FASD) (65)
ultrasound (71)
amniocentesis (72)
chorionic villus sampling (72)
fetal medicine (72)
crowning (74)
hypoxia (76)
caesarean section (C-section) (76)
preterm (premature) (76)
low birth weight (77)
very low birth weight (77)
extremely low birth weight (77)
infant mortality (77)

SEE FOR YOURSELF: APPLYING WHAT YOU'VE LEARNED

In this chapter we have further discussed how both heredity and environment (nature and nurture) influence a person's development. Although it is often debated among developmental scientists which influence is greater, it is generally understood that both aspects are important contributors to physical, psychological, and socioemotional development. To help illustrate the concept of heredity and environmental influences, consider how you are similar in some ways and dissimilar in others to your parents and siblings. Which of these similarities and differences would you consider to be primarily through "nature" and which through "nurture"? Are there some traits that seem to be equally influenced by both heredity and environment?

LEARN MORE ABOUT IT

Readings

ALDRIDGE, S. (1996). *The thread of life: The story of genes and genetic engineering.* Cambridge, NY: Cambridge University Press. The author, a chemist turned professional writer, first provides an excellent account of the structure and functioning of DNA. She also describes genetic engineering and shows how it may solve different genetic problems and may lead to the creation of new life forms.

BARRETT, J., & PITMAN, T. (1999). *Pregnancy and birth: The best evidence.* Toronto: Key Porter Books. This reference book covers all aspects of pregnancy such as prenatal care, prenatal development, labour, and delivery, and incorporates findings from related research.

HEALTH CANADA. (1999). *Nutrition for a healthy pregnancy: National guidelines for the childbearing years.* Ottawa: Minister of Public Works and Government Services Canada. This is an excellent resource that provides information and guidelines for nutrition during the childbearing years.

NILSSON, L., & HAMBERGER, L. (1990). *A child is born.* New York: Delacorte. This book is the source of many of the photos of prenatal development in this chapter. Nilsson developed a variety of techniques to photograph the fetus as it was developing; Hamberger provides an entertaining and informative text to accompany the photos.

PLOMIN, R. (1990). *Nature and nurture.* Pacific Grove, CA: Brooks/Cole. This brief book provides a very readable introduction to modern research on the role of genetics in human behaviour, written by one of the leading researchers in the field.

RIDLEY, M. (2000). *Genome: The autobiography of a species in 23 chapters.* New York: HarperCollins. The author describes progress in genetics research by telling fascinating stories about the impact of chromosomes on intelligence, language, cancer, and sex, to name just a few topics.

 For additional readings, explore InfoTrac® College Edition, your online library. Go to http://www.infotrac.thomsonlearning.com.

Websites

http://www.hc-sc.gc.ca

The Health Canada website provides links to an extensive number of resources on healthy pregnancy and prenatal development.

http://www.caringforkids.cps.ca

The website of the Canadian Paediatric Society contains information and guidelines on many topics related to children's health, including pregnancy and prenatal health.

http://www.canadian-health-network.ca

The Canadian Health Network website has been developed by Health Canada and major health care organizations across Canada and includes information on a wide variety of health topics including pregnancy.

http://www.noah-health.org

The website of the New York Online Access to Health (NOAH) provides a wealth of information about all aspects of pregnancy, including genetic factors.

http://www.doegenomes.org

The Human Genome Project, sponsored by involved U.S. government departments, presents this website with all the details on this amazing project, including its history, findings, and present and future implications.

Website addresses are subject to change. The *Human Development* book companion website can be accessed for updated links.

The Human Development Book Companion Website

See http://www.humandevelopment.nelson.com for practice quiz questions, Internet links, updates, critical thinking exercises, discussion forums, and more.

 Life-Span CD-ROM

For more information on the concepts covered in this chapter, go to Module 1: Prenatal Development, Birth, and the Newborn

- Prenatal Development
- Birth

Getty Images

CHAPTER 3

Tools for Exploring the World

PHYSICAL AND COGNITIVE DEVELOPMENT IN INFANCY

Think about what you were like two years ago. Whatever you were doing, you probably look, act, think, and feel in much the same way today as you did then. Two years in an adult's life usually doesn't result in profound changes. But two years makes a big difference early in life. The changes that occur over 24 months after birth are incredible. In less than two years, an infant is transformed from a seemingly helpless newborn into a talking, walking, havoc-wreaking toddler. No changes at any other point in the life span come close to the drama and excitement of these early years.

In this chapter, our tour of these two years begins with the newborn, then moves to physical growth—changes in the body and the brain. The third section of the chapter concerns motor skills. You'll discover how babies learn to walk and how they learn to use their hands to hold and then manipulate objects. In the fourth section, we'll examine changes in infants' sensory abilities that enable them to comprehend their world. In the remaining sections we'll examine how cognitive development proceeds and how language begins.

3.1

The Newborn

LEARNING OBJECTIVES

- How do reflexes help newborns interact with the world?
- How do we determine whether a baby is healthy and adjusting to life outside the uterus?
- What behavioural states are common among newborns?

Lisa and Steve, proud but exhausted parents, are astonished at how their lives revolve around 10-day-old Dan's eating and sleeping. Lisa feels as if she is feeding Dan around the clock. When Dan naps, Lisa thinks of many things she should do, but she usually naps as well because she is so tired. Steve wonders when Dan will start sleeping through the night, so that he and Lisa can get a good night's sleep themselves.

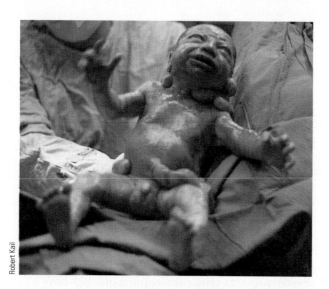

Robert Kail

Newborn babies, like Ben Kail shown in this photo when he was 20 seconds old, thrill their new parents, even though they may look quite different than parents expect. Like many newborns, he is covered with blood and vernix, a white-coloured "wax" that protected his skin during the many months of prenatal development. Ben's head is temporarily misshapen from its journey through the birth canal, he has a rounded abdomen, and he is rather bow-legged.

What can newborns like Dan and Ben do? We'll answer that question in this section and, as we do, you'll learn when Lisa and Steve can expect to resume a full night's sleep.

THE NEWBORN'S REFLEXES

Most newborns are well prepared to begin interacting with their world. *The newborn is endowed with a rich set of reflexes, unlearned responses that are triggered by a specific form of stimulation.* Table 3.1 shows the variety of reflexes commonly found in newborn babies.

You can see that some reflexes are designed to pave the way for newborns to get the nutrients that they need to grow: The rooting and sucking reflexes ensure that the newborn is well prepared to begin a new diet of life-sustaining milk. Others seem designed to protect the newborn from danger in the environment. The eye blink reflex, for example, helps newborns avoid unpleasant stimulation. Such reflexes, which have clear adaptive value, are called *survival reflexes.*

Other reflexes that are present yet not of such clear value are termed *primitive reflexes.* However, some may serve as the foundation for larger, voluntary patterns of motor activity. Motions such as the stepping reflex look like precursors to walking, so it probably won't surprise you to learn that babies who practise the stepping reflex often learn to walk earlier than those who don't practise this reflex (Zelazo, 1993).

Reflexes are also important because they can be a useful way to determine whether the newborn's nervous system is working properly. For example, infants who have problems with the lower part of the spine do not show the Babinski reflex. If these or

TABLE 3.1	Some Major Reflexes Found in Newborns	
Name	*Response*	*Significance*
Survival Instincts		
Blink	A baby's eyes close in response to bright light or loud noise	Protects the eyes
Rooting	When a baby's cheek is stroked, the baby turns head toward the stroking and opens mouth	Helps a baby find the nipple
Sucking	A baby sucks when an object is placed in mouth	Permits feeding
Primitive Instincts		
Babinski	A baby's toes fan out when the sole of the foot is stroked from heel to toe	Perhaps a remnant of evolution
Palmar	A baby grasps an object placed in the palm of hand	Precursor to voluntary grasping
Moro	A baby throws arms out and then inward (as if embracing) in response to loud noise or when head falls	May help a baby cling to mother
Stepping	A baby who is held upright by an adult and is then moved forward begins to step rhythmically	Precursor to voluntary walking

other reflexes are weak or missing altogether, a thorough physical and behavioural assessment is called for. Similarly, many of these reflexes normally vanish during infancy; if they linger, this too indicates the need for a thorough physical examination.

ASSESSING THE NEWBORN

Imagine that a mother has just asked you if her newborn baby is healthy. How would you decide? You would probably check to see whether the baby seems to be breathing and if her heart seems to be beating. In fact, breathing and heartbeat are two vital signs included in the Apgar score, which provides a quick, approximate assess-

Phanie/Firstlight.ca

ment of the newborn's status by focusing on the body systems needed to sustain life. The other vital signs are muscle tone, presence of reflexes such as coughing, and skin tone. Each of the five vital signs receives a score of 0, 1, or 2, with 2 being the optimal score. For example, a newborn whose muscles are completely limp receives a 0; a baby who shows strong movements of arms and legs receives a 2. The five scores are added together, with a score of 7 or more indicating a baby who is in good physical condition. A score of 4 to 6 means that the newborn needs special attention and care. A score of 3 or less signals a life-threatening situation that requires emergency medical care (Apgar, 1953).

For a comprehensive evaluation of the newborn's well-being, pediatricians and other child development specialists sometimes administer the Neonatal Behavioural Assessment Scale, or NBAS for short (Brazelton, 1984). This test evaluates a broad range of newborn abilities and behaviours that will help the infant adjust to life outside the uterus. The NBAS measures reflexes, hearing, vision, alertness, irritability, and consolability. The NBAS, along with a thorough physical examination, can determine whether the newborn is functioning normally. Scores from the NBAS can, for example, be used to diagnose disorders of the central nervous system (Brazelton et al., 1987).

SLEEPING AND WAKING STATES

Newborns spend most of each day alternating among four different states (St. James-Roberts & Plewis, 1996; Wolff, 1987):

Alert inactivity—*The baby is calm with eyes open and attentive; the baby seems to be deliberately inspecting the environment.*

Waking activity—*The baby's eyes are open but they seem unfocused; the arms or legs move in bursts of uncoordinated motion.*

Crying—*The baby cries vigorously, usually accompanied by agitated but uncoordinated motion.*

Sleeping—*The baby alternates from being still and breathing regularly to moving gently and breathing irregularly; eyes are closed throughout.*

Of these states, crying and sleeping have captured the attention of parents and researchers alike.

Crying

Newborns spend two to three hours each day crying or on the verge of crying. If you've not spent much time around newborns, you might think all crying is pretty much alike. In fact, scientists and parents can identify three distinctive types of cries (Holden, 1988). *A **basic cry** starts softly, then gradually becomes more intense and usually occurs when a baby is hungry or tired; an **angry cry** is a more intense version of a basic cry; and a **pain cry** begins with a sudden, long burst of crying, followed by a long pause, and gasping.* Thus, crying represents the newborn's first venture into interpersonal communication; by crying, babies tell their parents that they are hungry or tired, angry or hurt. By responding to these cries, parents are encouraging their newborn's efforts to communicate.

> **THINK ABOUT IT** 💡
>
> Newborns seem to be extremely well prepared to begin to interact with their environments. Which of the theories described in Chapter 1 predict such preparedness? Which do not?

Of course, parents are concerned when their baby cries. If they can't quiet a crying baby, their concern mounts and can easily give way to frustration and annoyance. For centuries, mothers have relied on a number of tricks for soothing their babies. Science hasn't contributed many new techniques, but it has told us which techniques work best and why. The first step should always be to determine why the baby began to cry. Is she hungry? Is her diaper wet? Addressing the needs that caused the crying will often quiet a baby. If crying persists, the best method is to lift the baby to the shoulder and rock or walk with her. This combination—being upright, restrained, and in physical contact with a person—helps calm babies. Also effective is swaddling—wrapping the baby tightly in a blanket—and then rocking it or taking it for a ride in a stroller. Here, too, the key seems to be the combination of bodily restraint and movement. A modern variation is to safely secure the infant in his car seat and go on a drive. This technique was used once as a last resort when Ben Kail was 10 days old and had been crying uncontrollably for more than an hour. After about the 12th time around the block, he finally fell asleep! Babies can also be soothed by giving them pacifiers; sucking apparently helps babies control their own level of arousal (Campos, 1989).

None of these techniques is foolproof. Some work well one day but not the next, and some seem to be better for one baby than for another. Sometimes you may need to combine techniques, such as holding a swaddled baby to your shoulder. If all these fail, just put the baby down. Every so often, just to make you wonder, a baby will stop crying spontaneously and go right to sleep!

Caring for an infant who won't stop crying can be extremely frustrating. Unfortunately, in some cases, extreme frustration has resulted in a preventable condition known as Shaken Baby Syndrome (SBS) where an infant or young child is shaken violently and severe brain injury or death has occurred. Most frequently this has occurred in infants less than one year of age and has been linked to a caregiver's response to an infant's behaviour such as crying. Since infants have proportionally large heads and weak neck muscles they are particularly susceptible to the effects of shaking. One of the preventive strategies that has been developed is to teach parents and other caregivers to seek help if baby's demands are causing anger or frustration and to remember "Never shake a baby!" (Canadian Paediatric Society, 2001).

Sleeping

Crying may get parents' attention, but sleep is what newborns do more than anything else. They sleep 16 to 18 hours daily. The problem for tired parents like the mom in the photo is that newborns sleep in naps taken round-the-clock. Newborns typically go through a cycle of wakefulness and sleep about every two hours. During the time when newborns are awake, they regularly move between the different waking states several times. Cycles of alert inactivity, waking activity, and crying are common.

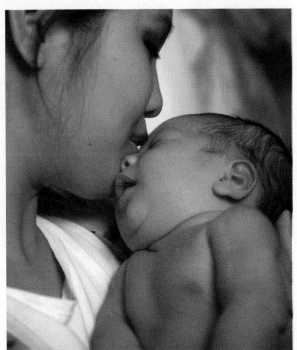

As babies grow older, the sleep-wake cycle gradually begins to correspond to the day-night cycle (St. James-Roberts & Plewis, 1996). Most babies begin sleeping through the night by about 3 or 4 months of age, a major milestone for bleary-eyed parents like Lisa and Steve.

Roughly half of newborns' sleep is irregular or **rapid-eye-movement (REM) sleep,** *a time when the body is quite active.* During REM sleep, newborns move their arms and legs, they may grimace, and their eyes may dart beneath their eyelids. Brain waves register fast activity, the heart beats more rapidly, and breathing is more rapid. *In* **regular (nonREM) sleep,** *breathing, heart rate, and brain activity are steady, and newborns lie quietly without the twitching associated with REM sleep.* REM sleep becomes less frequent as infants grow. By 4 months, only 40% of sleep is REM sleep. By the first birthday, REM sleep will drop to 25%, not far from the adult average of 20% (Halpern, MacLean, & Baumeister, 1995).

The function of REM sleep is still debated. Older children and adults dream during REM sleep, and brain waves during REM sleep resemble those of an alert, awake person. Consequently, many scientists believe REM sleep provides stimulation for the brain that fosters growth in the nervous system (Halpern et al., 1995; Roffwarg, Muzio, & Dement, 1966).

Sudden Infant Death Syndrome

For many parents of young babies, however, sleep is a cause of concern. *In* **Sudden Infant Death Syndrome (SIDS),** *a healthy baby dies suddenly, usually while sleeping, for no apparent reason.* In Canada, about three babies die of SIDS each week. The

FIGURE 3.1   Health Canada's "Back to Sleep" Campaign

Back to Sleep, Health Canada. Reproduced with the permission of the Minister of Public Works and Government Services Canada, 2004.

national SIDS rate is 0.5 per 1,000 live births and among Canada's Aboriginal population this rate is approximately three times higher (Canadian Perinatal Surveillance System, 1999).

Scientists don't know the exact causes of SIDS, but they do know several contributing factors. Infants are more vulnerable if their mother smoked during pregnancy and also if they are exposed to smoke in the household. SIDS is more likely to occur when a baby sleeps on its stomach (face down) than when it sleeps on its back (face up). In addition, overheating has been identified as a risk factor for SIDS, especially if the baby's head becomes covered.

Educational materials that are based on such findings have been developed jointly by Health Canada, the Canadian Foundation for the Study of Infant Deaths, the Canadian Institute of Child Health, and the Canadian Paediatric Society. In these materials parents are advised to put babies to sleep on their backs or sides on a firm mattress and to prevent overheating of infants with covers. In addition, breastfeeding is encouraged as it may give some protection against SIDS, and maintenance of a smoke-free environment is recommended. Since the start of the "Back to Sleep" campaign, which was widely publicized through brochures and posters like the one shown in Figure 3.1, far more infants are now sleeping on their backs and the incidence of SIDS has dropped (Canadian Perinatal Surveillance System, 1999).

TEST YOURSELF

1. Some reflexes help infants get necessary nutrients, other reflexes protect infants from danger, and still other reflexes _____.

2. The _____ is based on five vital functions and provides a quick indication of a newborn's physical health.

3. A baby lying calmly with its eyes open and focused is in a state of _____.

4. Newborns spend more time asleep than awake, and about half this time asleep is spent in _____, a time thought to foster growth in the central nervous system.

5. The campaign to reduce SIDS emphasizes that infants should _____.

Max, a father-to-be, says, "I'm sure I'll worry a lot about our baby, because babies are so helpless; they can't do anything." What might you say to Max to reassure him that, all things considered, newborns are quite talented?

Answers: (1) serve as the basis for later motor behaviours, (2) Apgar score, (3) alert inactivity, (4) REM sleep, (5) sleep on their backs

3.2

Physical Development

LEARNING OBJECTIVES

▸ How do height and weight change from birth to two years of age?

▸ What nutrients do developing infants need? How are they best provided?

▸ What are the consequences of malnutrition? How can it be treated?

▸ What are nerve cells, and how are they organized in the brain?

▸ How does the brain develop? When does it begin to function?

> **Physical Development**
> Growth of the Body
> The Emerging Nervous System

First-time parents Alexander and Anne are amazed at how quickly changes are occurring in their 13-month-old daughter Jaymie. In little more than a year she has gone from a seemingly helpless infant to one who learned to crawl just a few months later, then to one who could walk short distances on her own. Although Jaymie weighed less than average at birth, the nurse at the health clinic told Alexander and Anne that Jaymie has caught up to the normal range. She seems to enjoy eating the different kinds of foods given to her and although Alexander and Anne know that young children sometimes become picky eaters, they hope that Jaymie will continue with her healthy pattern of eating, growing, and developing.

For parents and children alike, physical growth is a topic of great interest and a source of pride. Parents marvel at the speed with which babies grow in height and weight; 2-year-olds proudly proclaim, "I bigger now!" In this section, we examine some of the basic features of physical growth and see how the brain develops.

GROWTH OF THE BODY

Growth is more rapid in infancy than during any other period after birth. Typically, infants double their birth weight by 3 months of age and triple it by their first birthday. If this rapid rate of growth continued throughout childhood, a typical 10-year-old boy would be nearly as long as an airliner and weigh almost as much (McCall, 1979).

The U.S. Centers for Disease Control and Prevention (CDC) developed new growth charts in 2000 for the first time since 1977 to more accurately reflect ethnic and economic diversities and account for differences in growth between breast-fed and formula-fed infants. These growth charts (see Figures 3.2a and 3.2b) are also used in Canada. Average heights and weights for young children are represented by the lines marked 50th percentile in the charts. An average girl weighs about 3.4 kilograms at birth, about 9.6 kilograms at 12 months, and about 12 kilograms at 24 months. If perfectly average, she would be 49 centimetres long at birth, grow to 74 centimetres at 12 months, and 86 centimetres at 24 months. Figures for an average boy are similar, but weights are slightly larger at 12 and 24 months.

These charts also highlight how much children of the same age vary in weight and height. The lines marked 90th percentile on the charts represent heights and weights for children who are larger than 90% of their peers; the lines marked 10th percentile represent heights and weights for children who are smaller than 90% of their peers. Any heights and weights between these lines are considered normal. At age one, for example, normal weights for boys range from about 8.6 kilograms to 12.4 kilograms. This means that an extremely light but normal boy weighs only about two-thirds as much as his extremely heavy but normal peer! Cultural differences can also make a difference. For example, the Canadian Paediatric Society (CPS) reports that Aboriginal

FIGURE 3.2A   Birth to 36 months: Girls   FIGURE 3.2B   Birth to 36 months: Boys

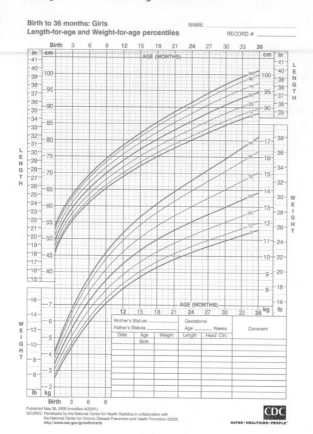

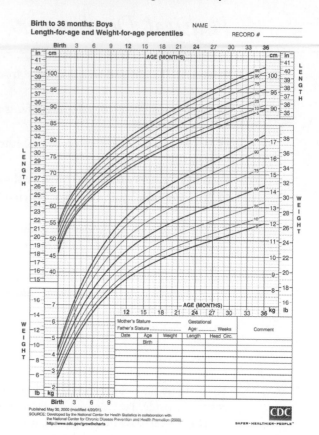

and Inuit infants may be of average length but heavier than Caucasian infants, but recommends that the standard growth charts should still be used. The CPS has concluded that a separate growth chart would not be applicable to all Aboriginal and Inuit children due to the individual variations in tribal and cultural areas.

The important message here is that average height and normal height are not one and the same. Many children are much taller or shorter than average but are still perfectly normal. This applies to all the age norms we mention in this book. Whenever we provide a typical or average age for a developmental milestone, remember that the normal range for passing the milestone is much wider.

Whether an infant is short or tall depends largely on heredity. Both parents contribute to their children's height. In fact, the correlation between the average of the two parents' heights and their child's height at 2 years of age is about .7 (Plomin, 1990). As a general rule, two tall parents will have tall offspring; two short parents will have short offspring; and one tall parent and one short parent will have offspring of medium height.

So far, we have emphasized the quantitative aspects of growth, such as height. This ignores an important fact: Infants are not simply scaled-down versions of adults. Figure 3.3 shows that compared to adolescents and adults, infants and young children look top-heavy because their heads and trunks are disproportionately large. A newborn's head is already 70% of its eventual size as an adult. *The sequence of growth occurs from the head downward, or cephalocaudal (head to caudal or tail region).* This means that the trunk starts to develop after the head and subsequently grows fastest during the infant's first year of life. As growth of the hips, legs, and feet catch up later in childhood, their bodies take on more adult proportions.

THINK ABOUT IT 💡

In Chapter 2, we explained how polygenic inheritance is often involved when phenotypes form a continuum. Height is such a phenotype. Propose a simple polygenic model to explain how height might be inherited.

FIGURE 3.3   Body Growth Proportions

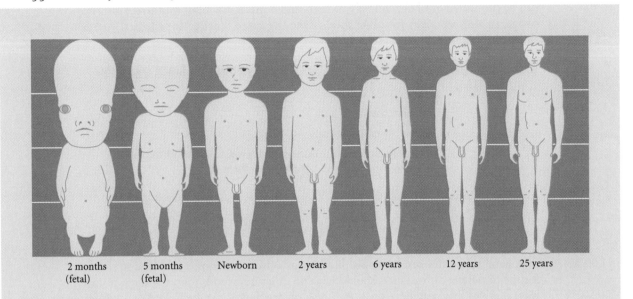

| 2 months (fetal) | 5 months (fetal) | Newborn | 2 years | 6 years | 12 years | 25 years |

SOURCE: Based on Eichorn, 1969.

Of course, as well as growing upward, children grow outward. *The pattern of this growth is **proximodistal** (from inward to outward).* Throughout infancy and early childhood this means that the trunk develops before the arms and legs, then the hands and feet, followed by the fingers and toes. This growth pattern is also reflected in their motor development as well, in that children will able to use their upper arms before their hands and fingers and their upper legs before their lower legs and toes. This pattern changes just before puberty when the hands and feet start to grow rapidly and are the first body parts to reach adult size.

Growth of this sort requires energy. Let's see how food and drink provide the fuel to grow.

"You Are What You Eat"—Nutrition and Growth

In a typical 2-month-old, roughly 40% of the body's energy is devoted to growth. Most of the remaining energy is used for basic bodily functions such as digestion and respiration. A much smaller portion is consumed in physical activity.

Because growth requires so much high energy, young babies must consume an enormous number of calories relative to their body weight. A typical 2-month-old, for example, should ingest about 100 to 120 calories for each kilogram of their body weight each day (Kalnins & Saab, 2001). An adult, by contrast, needs to consume less than half of that amount of calories for each kilogram of their body weight each day, depending on the person's level of activity.

Breast-feeding is the best way to ensure that babies get the nourishment they need. Human milk contains the proper amounts of carbohydrates, fats, protein, vitamins, and minerals for babies. Breast-feeding also has several other advantages compared to bottle-feeding (Shelov, 1993; Sullivan & Birch, 1990). First, breast-fed babies are ill less often because breast milk contains the mother's antibodies. Second, breast-fed babies are less prone to diarrhea and constipation. Third, breast-fed babies typically make the transition to solid foods more easily, apparently because they are accustomed to changes in the taste of breast milk that reflect a mother's diet. Fourth, breast milk cannot be contaminated, which is a significant problem in developing countries when formula is used to bottle-feed babies. Because of these many advantages, Health Canada, the Canadian Paediatric Society, and the Dietitians of Canada recommend that children be exclusively breast-fed for the first four months of life; the practice can be continued until the child is two years and beyond. At about four to six months of age, infants are ready for other foods. One suggested "menu" for the first year is shown in Table 3.2.

TABLE 3.2	Ages When Solid Foods Can Be Introduced into an Infant's Diet
Age (months)	Food
4–6	rice cereal, then other cereals
6–7	strained vegetables and fruits
7–9	meats and alternatives (e.g., pureed meat, egg yolk, tofu) and milk and milk products such as plain yogurt, or grated hard cheese
12	egg whites

SOURCE: Kalnins & Saab, 2001

A good rule is to introduce only one food at a time. A 7-month-old having cheese for the first time, for instance, should have no other new foods for a few days. In this way, allergies that may develop—skin rash or diarrhea—can be linked to a particular food, making it easier to prevent reoccurrences.

The many benefits of breast-feeding do not mean that bottle-feeding is harmful. Formula, when prepared in sanitary conditions, provides generally the same nutrients as human milk, but infants are more prone to develop allergies from formula, and formula does not protect infants from disease. A mother who cannot readily breast-feed can still enjoy the intimacy of feeding her baby, and other family members can participate in feeding. In fact, long-term longitudinal studies typically find that breast- and bottle-fed babies are similar in physical and psychological development (Fergusson, Horwood, & Shannon, 1987), so women in industrialized countries can choose either method and know that their babies' dietary needs will be met.

In developing nations, bottle-feeding is potentially disastrous. Often the only water available to prepare formula is contaminated; the result is that infants have chronic diarrhea, leading to dehydration and, sometimes, death. Or, in an effort to conserve valuable formula, parents may ignore instructions and use less formula than indicated in making milk; the resulting "weak" milk leads to malnutrition. For these reasons, the World Health Organization strongly advocates breast-feeding as the primary source of nutrition for infants and toddlers in developing nations.

David Young-Wolff /PhotoEdit

In later toddlerhood, many children become picky eaters. Like the little boy in the photo they may not always like new foods that are presented.

Experts (Canadian Paediatric Society, 2003, September; Leach, 1991) recommend several guidelines for encouraging children to be more open-minded about foods and how to deal with them when they aren't:

- When possible, allow children to pick among different healthy foods (e.g., milk or yogurt).
- Allow children to eat foods in any order they want.

- Serve food presented in an attractive and appealing way.
- Offer children new foods one at a time and in small amounts; encourage but don't force children to eat new foods.
- Don't force children to "clean their plates."
- Don't spend mealtimes talking about what the child is or is not eating; make mealtimes fun and relaxed.
- Never use food to reward or punish children.

By following these guidelines, mealtimes can be pleasant and children can receive the nutrition they need to grow.

Malnutrition

An adequate diet is only a dream to many of the world's children. *Worldwide, about one in three children under age 5 is* **malnourished,** *as indicated by being small for his or her age* (Grantham-McGregor, Ani, & Fernald, 2001). Many, like the children in the photo, are from third world countries. But malnutrition is regrettably common in industrialized countries too. In Canada approximately 15% (with regional variations) of children live in poverty (Statistics Canada, 2001b), a situation that has negative impacts on these children's nutritional intake and healthy development.

Malnourished children tend to develop less rapidly than their peers. Malnourishment is especially damaging during infancy because growth is ordinarily so rapid during these years. This is well illustrated by a longitudinal study conducted in Barbados in the West Indies (Galler & Ramsey, 1989; Galler, Ramsey, & Forde, 1986). Included were more than 100 children who were severely malnourished as infants, as well as 100 children whose family environments were similar but who had adequate nutrition as infants. The children who experienced malnutrition during infancy were indistinguishable from their peers physically—they were just as tall and weighed just as much. However, children with a history of infant malnutrition had much lower scores on intelligence tests. Also, many of the children who were malnourished during infancy had difficulty maintaining attention in school; they were easily distracted. Many similar studies

David Turnley/Corbis/Magma

suggest that malnourished youngsters tire easily, are more wary, and are often inattentive (Lozoff et al., 1998). In addition, malnutrition during rapid periods of growth may cause substantial and potentially irreversible damage to the brain (Morgane et al., 1993).

Malnutrition would seem to have a simple cure—an adequate diet. But as we see in the Forces in Action feature, the solution is more complex than you might expect.

FORCES IN ACTION

Fostering Development in Malnourished Children

Malnourished children are often listless and inactive (Ricciuti, 1993). They are unusually quiet and express little interest in what goes on around them. These behaviours *are* useful to children whose diet is inadequate because they conserve limited energy. Unfortunately, these behaviours may also deprive youngsters of experiences that would further their development. For example, when children are routinely unresponsive and lethargic, parents often come to believe their actions have little impact on the children. That is, when children do not respond to parents' efforts to stimulate their development, this discourages parents from providing additional stimulation in the future. Over time, parents tend to provide fewer experiences that foster their children's development. The result is a self-perpetuating cycle in which malnourished children are forsaken by parents who feel as if they can do little to contribute to their children's growth. A biological force (lethargy stemming from insufficient nourishment) causes a profound change in a sociocultural force (parental teaching), which, in turn, influences psychological development (children are less intelligent and less able to pay attention).

To break the vicious cycle, these children need more than an improved diet. Their parents must be taught how to foster their children's development and must be encouraged to do so. Programs that combine dietary supplements with parent training offer promise in treating malnutrition (Grantham-McGregor, Ani, & Fernald, 2001). Children in these programs often catch up with their peers in physical and intellectual growth, showing that the best way to reduce the effect of malnutrition on psychological forces is by addressing both biological and sociocultural forces (Super, Herrera, & Mora, 1990).

THE EMERGING NERVOUS SYSTEM

The physical changes we see as infants grow are impressive. Even more awe-inspiring are the changes we cannot see—those involving the brain and the nervous system. An infant's feelings of hunger or pain, its smiles or laughs, and its efforts to sit upright or to hold a rattle all reflect the functioning of the brain and the rest of the emerging nervous system.

How does the brain accomplish these many tasks? To begin to answer this question, we need to look at the organization of the brain. *The basic unit in the brain and the rest of the nervous system is the **neuron**, a cell that specializes in receiving and transmitting information.* Neurons have the basic elements shown in Figure 3.4. *The **cell body**, in the*

FIGURE 3.4   **Reaction Range**

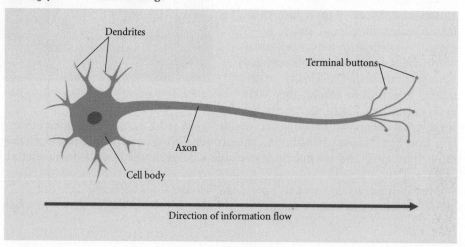

*centre of the cell, contains the basic biological machinery that keeps the neuron alive. The receiving end of the neuron, the **dendrite**, looks like a tree with its many branches.* This structure enables one neuron to receive input from thousands of other neurons (Morgan & Gibson, 1991). *The tubelike structure that emerges from the other side of the cell body, the **axon**, transmits information to other neurons. At the end of the axon are small knobs called **terminal buttons**, which release chemicals called **neurotransmitters.*** These neurotransmitters are the messengers that carry information to nearby neurons.

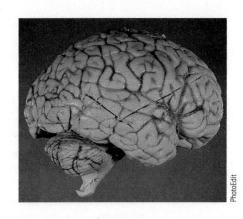

Take 50 billion to 100 billion neurons like these, and you have the beginnings of a human brain. An adult's brain, which weighs a little less than 1.4 kilograms (3 pounds) and would easily fit into your hands, is shown in the photo. The wrinkled surface of the brain is the cerebral cortex; made up of 10 billion neurons, the cortex regulates many of the functions we think of as distinctly human. *The cortex consists of left and right halves, called **hemispheres**, linked by a thick bundle of neurons called the **corpus callosum**.* The characteristics you value the most—your engaging personality, your "way with words," or your uncanny knack for "reading" others' emotions—are all controlled by specific regions in the cortex. *For example, your personality and your ability to make and carry out plans are largely centred in an area in the front of the cortex called (appropriately enough) the **frontal cortex**.* For most people, the ability to produce and understand language is mainly housed in neurons in the left hemisphere of the cortex. When you recognize that others are happy or sad, neurons in your right hemisphere are usually at work.

Now that we know a bit of the organization of the mature brain, let's look at how the brain grows and begins to function.

The Making of the Working Brain

At birth the brain is only about 25% the weight of an adult brain. However, you can see from Figure 3.5 that the brain grows

FIGURE 3.5   **Brain Development**

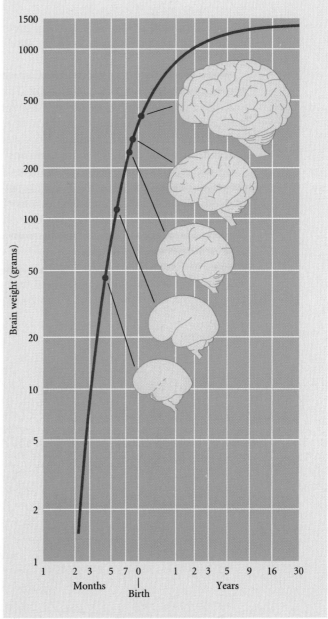

From *Normal and Abnormal Development of the Nervous System*, by R. J. Lemire, J. D. Loesser, R. W. Leech, and E. C. Alvord, Jr., p. 236. Copyright © J. B. Lippincott Company. Reprinted with permission.

rapidly during infancy and the preschool years. At 3 years of age, for example, the brain has achieved 80% of its ultimate weight. Brain weight doesn't tell us much, however, about the fascinating sequence of changes that take place to create a working brain. Instead, we need to move back to prenatal development.

Emerging Brain Structures

The beginnings of the brain can be traced to the period of the zygote. *At roughly three weeks after conception, a group of cells forms a flat structure known as the **neural plate.*** At four weeks, the neural plate folds to form a tube that ultimately becomes the brain and spinal cord. When the ends of the tube fuse shut, neurons are produced in one small region of the neural tube. Production of neurons begins about 10 weeks after conception, and by 28 weeks the developing brain has virtually all the neurons it will ever have. During these weeks, neurons form at the incredible rate of more than 4,000 per second (Kolb, 1989).

From the neuron-manufacturing site in the neural tube, neurons migrate to their final positions in the brain. The brain is built in stages, beginning with the innermost layers. Neurons in the deepest layer are positioned first, followed by neurons in the second layer, and so on. This layering process continues until all six layers of the mature brain are in place, which occurs about seven months after conception (Rakic, 1995).

*In the fourth month of prenatal development, axons begin to acquire **myelin**—the fatty wrap that speeds neural transmission.* This process continues throughout infancy and into childhood and adolescence (Casaer, 1993). Neurons that carry sensory information are the first to acquire myelin; neurons in the cortex are among the last. You can see the effect of more myelin in improved coordination and reaction times. The older the infant or child, the more rapid and coordinated are his or her reactions.

In the months after birth, the brain grows rapidly. Axons and dendrites grow longer, and, like a maturing tree, dendrites quickly sprout new limbs. As the number of dendrites increases, so does the number of synapses, reaching a peak at about the first birthday. This rapid neural growth is shown in Figure 3.6. *Soon after, synapses begin to disappear gradually, a phenomenon known as **synaptic pruning**.* Thus, beginning in infancy and continuing into early adolescence, the brain goes through its own version of "downsizing," weeding out unnecessary connections between neurons. This pruning depends on the activity of the neural circuits—synapses that are active are preserved, but those that aren't are eliminated (Webb, Monk, & Nelson, 2001).

FIGURE 3.6   Neural Growth

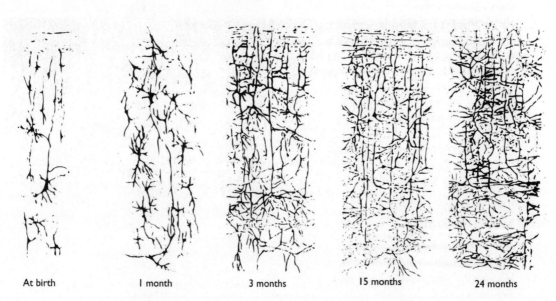

At birth   I month   3 months   I5 months   24 months

Structure and Function

Since the mature brain is specialized, with different psychological functions localized in particular regions, a natural question for developmental researchers is this: "How early in development does brain functioning become localized?" To answer this question, scientists have used many different methods to map functions onto particular brain regions.

Alexander Tsiaras/Stock Boston Inc.

- *Studies of children with brain damage:* Children who suffer brain injuries provide valuable insights into brain structure and function. If a region of the brain regulates a particular function (e.g., understanding speech), then damage to that region should impair the function.
- *Studies of electrical activity: Metal electrodes placed on an infant's scalp, as shown in the photo, produce an* **electroencephalogram (EEG)***, a pattern of brain waves.* If a region of the brain regulates a function, then the region should show distinctive EEG patterns while a child is using that function.
- *Studies using imaging techniques: One method,* **functional magnetic resonance imaging (F-MRI)***, uses magnetic fields to track the flow of blood in the brain.* In this method, shown in the photo below, the research participant's brain is literally wrapped in an incredibly powerful magnet that can track blood flow as participants perform different cognitive tasks (Casey, Giedd, & Thomas, 2000). *Another method,* **positron emission tomography (PET-scan)***, traces use of glucose in the brain.* If a region of the brain helps to regulate a function, then blood flow and use of glucose (a sugar that is a source of energy) should be higher in that region when a child is performing that function.

None of these methods is perfect; each has drawbacks. When studying children with brain injuries, for example, several areas of the brain may be damaged, making it difficult to link impaired functioning to a particular brain region. Most imaging techniques are used sparingly because they're very expensive, usually require participants to lie still for several minutes at a time, and, in the case of PET-scan, are potentially hazardous. (A PET-scan requires injecting children with a radioactive form of glucose, so it's more often used in clinical work to help diagnose suspected brain damage.)

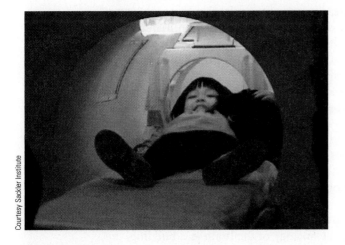

Courtesy Sackler Institute

Despite these limitations, the combined outcome of research using these different approaches indicates that many areas of the cortex begin to function in infancy. Early specialization of the frontal cortex is shown by the finding that damage to this region in infancy results in impaired decision-making and abnormal emotional responses (S.W. Anderson et al., 2001). Similarly, EEG studies how that a newborn infant's left hemisphere

THINK ABOUT IT

When you're trying to comprehend a difficult paragraph in a textbook, what part of your brain is probably particularly active?

generates more electrical activity in response to speech than the right hemisphere (Molfese & Burger-Judisch, 1991). Thus, by birth, the cortex of the left hemisphere is already specialized for language processing. And early in development the right hemisphere plays a role in nonverbal tasks, such as listening to music or integrating parts to form a whole (Stiles, 2000).

Of course, early specialization does not mean that the brain is functionally mature. Over the remainder of childhood and into adulthood, the brain continues to become more specialized. In Chapter 15, we'll see that some regions of the brain continue to develop into old age, whereas others are sometimes destroyed by diseases associated with aging.

Brain Plasticity

Neuroplasticity refers to the extent to which brain organization is flexible. How plastic is the human brain? Answers to this question reflect the familiar views on the nature-nurture issue (Nelson, 1999; Stiles, 2001). Some theorists believe that organization of brain function is predetermined genetically; it's simply in most children's genes that, for example, the left hemisphere will specialize in language processing. In this view, the brain is like a house—a structure that's specialized from the very beginning, with some rooms designed for cooking, others for sleeping, and others for bathing. Other theorists believe that few functions are rigidly assigned to specific brain sites at conception. Instead, experience helps determine the functional organization of the brain. In this view, the brain is more like an office building—an all-purpose structure with rooms designed to be used flexibly to meet the different business needs of the companies with offices in the building.

Research designed to test these views shows that the brain has some plasticity. For example, a young child who suffers brain damage in a car accident might have language skills impaired as a result of the location and type of injury. However, it is possible that within several months, complete recovery of language skills could occur if other neurons take over language-related processing from the damaged neurons. This recovery of function is not uncommon—particularly for young children—and shows the brain is plastic (Stiles, 2001).

However, the brain is not completely plastic—brains have a similar structure and similar mapping of functions on those structures. Visual cortex, for example, is almost always near the back of the brain. Sensory and motor cortex always run across the middle of the brain. But if a neuron's function is not specified at conception, how do different neurons take on different functions and in much the same pattern for most people? Researchers are trying to answer this question, and many details still need to be worked out. The answer probably lies in complex biochemical processes (Barinaga, 1997; Kunzig, 1998). You can get an idea of what's involved by imagining people arriving for a football game at a stadium where there are no reserved seats. As fans enter the stadium, they see others wearing their own school colours and move in that direction. Of course, not everyone does this. Some fans sit with friends from the other team. Some pick seats based on other factors (e.g., to avoid looking into the sun, to be close to the concession stand). In general, though, by game time, most fans have taken seats on their respective sides of the field.

In much the same way, as neurons are created and begin migrating through the layers of cortex, cellular biochemistry makes some paths more attractive than others. Yet, just as each fan can potentially sit anywhere because there are no reserved seats, an individual neuron can end up in many different locations because genetic instructions do not assign specific brain regions. Thus, the human brain is plastic—its organization and function can be affected by experience—but its development follows some general biochemical instructions that ensure most people end up with brains organized along similar lines.

Finally, it's important to emphasize the role of environmental stimulation in normal brain development. To return to the analogy of the brain as a building, the newborn's brain is perhaps best conceived as a partially finished, partially furnished house: a general organization is there, with preliminary neural pathways designed to perform certain functions. The left hemisphere no doubt has some language pathways and the frontal cortex has some emotion-related pathways. However, completing the typical organization of the mature brain requires input from the environment that stimulates other "general purpose" neurons to specialize. When infants hear speech, these experiences may stimulate other neurons in the brain to specialize in language processing. In this manner, experience is the catalyst that converts the partially furnished, partially finished newborn brain into a mature, specialized brain (Johnson, 2000; Webb et al., 2001).

TEST YOURSELF

1. Compared to older children and adults, an infant's head and trunk are _____.

2. Because of the high demands of growth, infants need _____ calories per kilogram than adults.

3. The most effective treatment for malnutrition is improved diet and _____.

4. The _____ is the part of the neuron that contains the basic machinery to keep the cell alive.

5. The frontal cortex is the seat of personality and regulates _____.

6. Human speech typically elicits the greatest electrical activity from the _____ of an infant's brain.

7. A good example of brain plasticity is that, although children with brain damage often have impaired cognitive processes, _____.

How does malnutrition illustrate the influence on development of life-cycle forces in the biopsychosocial framework?

Answers: (1) disproportionately large, (2) more, (3) parent training, (4) cell body, (5) goal-directed behaviour, (6) left hemisphere, (7) over time, they often regain their earlier skills

---

3·3
Moving and Grasping—Early Motor Skills

LEARNING OBJECTIVES

▪ What are the component skills involved in learning to walk? At what age do infants master them?

▪ How do infants learn to coordinate the use of their hands?

▪ How do maturation and experience influence mastery of motor skills?

Moving and Grasping—Early Motor Skills

Locomotion

Fine Motor Skills

Nancy is 14 months old and a world-class crawler. Using hands and knees, she can go just about anywhere she wants to. Nancy does not walk and seems uninterested in learning how. Nancy's dad wonders whether he should be doing something to help Nancy progress beyond crawling. Deep down, he worries that perhaps he was negligent in not providing more exercise for Nancy when she was younger.

Do you remember what it was like to learn typing, to play a musical instrument, or to play a sport? *Each of these activities involves* **motor skills**—*coordinated movements of the muscles and limbs.* Success demands that each movement be done in a precise way, in exactly the right sequence, and at exactly the right time. For example, to make a shot, a basketball player needs to remember to keep her elbows bent, to focus above the rim, and to follow through with her wrist.

These activities are demanding for adults, but think about similar challenges for infants. *Infants must learn to move about in the world: to locomote.* At first unable to move independently, infants soon learn to crawl, to stand, and to walk. Once the child can move through the environment upright, the arms and hands are free. To take advantage of this arrangement, the human hand has fully independent fingers (instead of a paw), with the thumb opposing the remaining four fingers. *Infants must learn the fine motor skills associated with grasping, holding, and manipulating objects.* In the case of feeding, for example, infants progress from being fed by others, to holding a bottle, to feeding themselves with their fingers, to eating with utensils.

Together, locomotion and fine motor skills give children access to an enormous variety of information about shapes, textures, and features in their environment. In this section, we'll see how locomotion and fine motor skills develop and, as we do, we'll see whether Nancy's dad should worry about her lack of interest in walking.

LOCOMOTION

Advances in posture and locomotion transform the infant in little more than a year. Figure 3.7 shows some of the important milestones in motor development and the age by which most infants have achieved them. By about 5 months of age, most babies will have rolled from back to front and will be able to sit upright with support. By 7 months, infants can sit alone, and by 10 months, they can creep. A typical 14-month-old is able to stand alone briefly and to walk with assistance. *This early, unsteady form of walking is called toddling, hence the term toddler.* Of course, not all children walk at exactly the same age. Some walk before their first birthday; others, like Nancy, the world-class crawler in the vignette, take their first steps as late as 18 or 19 months of age. By 24 months, most children can climb steps, walk backward, and kick a ball.

Researchers once thought these developmental milestones reflected maturation (e.g., McGraw, 1935). Walking, for example, emerged naturally when the necessary muscles and neural circuits matured. Today, however, locomotion—and in fact all of motor development—is viewed from a new perspective. *According to dynamic systems theory, motor development involves many distinct skills that are organized and reorganized over time to meet demands of specific tasks.* For example, walking includes maintaining balance, moving limbs, perceiving the environment, and having a reason to move. Only by understanding each of these skills and how they are combined to allow movement in a specific situation can we understand walking (Thelen & Smith, 1998).

Posture and Balance

The ability to maintain an upright posture is fundamental to walking. But upright posture is virtually impossible for newborns and young infants because of the shape of their body. An infant is top-heavy. Consequently, as soon as a young infant starts to lose her balance, she tumbles over. Only with growth of the legs and muscles can infants maintain an upright posture (Thelen, Ulrich, & Jensen, 1989).

Once infants can stand upright, they must continuously adjust their posture to avoid falling down. By a few months after birth, infants begin to use visual cues and an inner-ear mechanism to adjust their posture. To show the use of visual cues for balance, researchers had babies sit in a room with striped walls that moved. When adults sit in such a room, they perceive themselves as moving (not the walls) and adjust their posture accordingly; so do infants, which shows that they use vision to maintain upright posture (Bertenthal & Clifton, 1998). In addition, when 4-month-olds who are propped in a sitting position lose their balance, they try to keep their head upright. They do this even when blindfolded, which means they are using cues from their inner ear to maintain balance (Woollacott, Shumway-Cook, & Williams, 1989).

Balance is not, however, something that infants master just once. Instead, infants must relearn balancing for sitting, crawling, walking, and other postures. Why? The

FIGURE 3.7   **Motor Development Milestones**

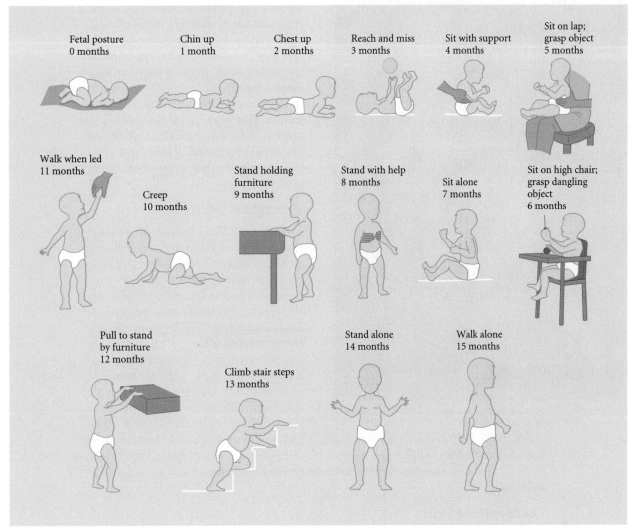

SOURCE: Based on Shirley, 1931, and Bayley, 1969.

body rotates around different points in each posture (e.g., the wrists for crawling versus the ankles for walking), and different muscle groups are used to generate compensating motions when infants begin to lose their balance. Consequently, it's hardly surprising that infants who easily maintain their balance while sitting topple over time after time when crawling. Infants must recalibrate the balance system as they take on each new posture, just as basketball players recalibrate their muscle movements when they move from dunking to shooting a three-pointer (Adolph, 2000, 2002).

Stepping

Another essential element of walking is moving the legs alternately, repeatedly transferring the weight of the body from one foot to the other. Children don't step spontaneously until approximately 10 months because they must be able to stand to step.

Can younger children step if they are held upright? Thelen and Ulrich (1991) devised a clever procedure to answer this question. Infants were placed on a treadmill and held upright by an adult. When the belt on the treadmill started to move, infants could respond one of several ways. They might simply let both legs be dragged rearward by the belt. Or they might let their legs be dragged briefly, then move them forward together in a hopping motion. Many 6- and 7-month-olds demonstrated the

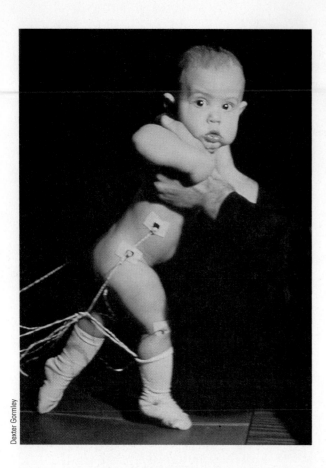

Dexter Gormley

mature pattern shown in the photo of alternating steps on each leg. Even more amazing, when the treadmill was equipped with separate belts for each leg that moved at different speeds, babies adjusted, stepping more rapidly on the faster belt.

Apparently, the alternate stepping motion that is essential for walking is evident long before infants walk alone. Walking unassisted is not possible, though, until other component skills are mastered.

Perceptual Factors

Many infants learn to walk in the relative security of flat, uncluttered floors at home. But they soon discover that the environment offers a variety of surfaces, some more conducive to walking than others. Infants use perceptual information to judge whether a surface is suitable for walking. When placed on a surface that gives way underfoot (e.g., a waterbed), they quickly judge it unsuitable for walking and resort to crawling (Gibson et al., 1987). And, when toddlers encounter a surface that slopes down steeply, few try to walk down, which would result in a fall. Instead, they slide or scoot backward (Adolph, 1997; Adolph, Eppler, & Gibson, 1993). Results like these show that infants use perceptual cues to decide whether a surface is safe for walking.

Coordinating Skills

Dynamic systems theory emphasizes that learning to walk demands orchestration of many individual skills. Each component skill must first be mastered alone and then integrated with the other skills (Werner, 1948). *That is, mastery of intricate motions requires both **differentiation**—mastery of component skills—and their **integration**—combining them in proper sequence into a coherent, working whole.* In the case of walking, not until 12 to 15 months of age have children mastered the component skills so that they can be coordinated to allow independent, unsupported walking.

Mastering individual skills and coordinating them well does not happen overnight. Instead, they take time and repeated practice. For example, when parents give their infants daily practice in sitting, their infants master sitting at a younger age. However, such practice has no effect on stepping, because different muscles and movements are involved (Zelazo et al., 1993). Similarly, when infants practise crawling on their bellies, this helps them crawl on hands and feet because many of the motions are the same (Adolph, Vereijken, & Denny, 1998). But when infants practise crawling on steep slopes, there is no transfer to walking on steep slopes because the motions differ (Adolph, 1997). Thus, experience can improve the rate of motor development, but the improvement is limited to the movements that were trained. In other words, just as daily practice kicking a soccer ball won't improve your golf game, infants who receive much practice in one motor skill usually don't improve in others.

These findings from laboratory research are not the only evidence that practice promotes motor development; cross-cultural research points to the same conclusion. Compared to infants growing up in Europe and North America, many infants from traditional African cultures reach the motor milestones shown in Figure 3.7 at an early age. For example, traditional African infants sit and walk at younger ages. Careful observations of these infants reveal two factors responsible for this early advantage in motor development. First, many common child care practices in traditional African societies have the unanticipated benefit of improving motor skill. For example, infants are commonly carried by their parents in the "piggyback" style shown in the photo, which helps develop muscles in the infants' trunk and legs. Second, mothers in traditional African cultures believe practice is essential for motor skills to develop normally and so they (or siblings) provide daily training sessions. For example, they may help children learn to sit by having them sit while propped up (Super, 1981). The combined effect of this unintentional and deliberate training is to provide additional opportunities for children to learn the elements of different motor skills. Not surprisingly, African infants with these opportunities learn to sit and walk earlier.

© Scott Smith /Index Stock Imagery

Beyond Walking

If you can recall the feeling of freedom that accompanied your first driver's licence, you can imagine how the world expands for infants and toddlers as they learn to move independently. The first tentative steps are soon followed by others that are more skilled. Most children learn to run a few months after they walk alone. Most 2-year-olds have a "hurried walk" instead of a true run; they move their legs stiffly (rather than bending them at the knees) and are not "airborne" as is the case when running.

THINK ABOUT IT 💡

How does learning to hop on one foot demonstrate differentiation and integration of motor skills?

FINE MOTOR SKILLS

A major accomplishment of infancy is skilled use of the hands (Bertenthal & Clifton, 1998). Newborns have little apparent control of their hands, but 1-year-olds are extraordinarily talented.

Reaching and Grasping

At about 4 months, infants can successfully reach for objects (Bertenthal & Clifton, 1998). These early reaches often look clumsy and for a good reason. When infants reach, they don't move their arm and hand directly and smoothly to the desired object (as older children and adults do). Instead, the infant's hand moves like a ship under the direction of an unskilled navigator—it moves a short distance, slows, then moves again in a slightly different direction, a process that's repeated until the hand finally contacts the object (McCarty &

Photodisc

Ashmead, 1999). As infants grow, their reaches have fewer movements, though they are still not as continuous and smooth as older children's and adults' reaches (Berthier, 1996).

Reaching requires that an infant move the hand to the location of a desired object. Grasping poses a different challenge; now the infant must coordinate movements of individual fingers to grab an object. Grasping, too, becomes more efficient during infancy. Most 4-month-olds just use their fingers to hold objects. Like the baby in the photo, they wrap an object tightly with their fingers alone. Not until 7 or 8 months do most infants use their thumbs to hold objects (Siddiqui, 1995). At about this same age, infants begin to position their hands to make it easier to grasp an object. If trying to grasp a long thin rod, for example, infants place their fingers perpendicular to the rod, which is the best position for grasping (Wentworth, Benson, & Haith, 2000). *This* **ulnar grasp** *is almost clawlike and permits very little manipulation.* In fact, infants need not see their hand to position it correctly: They position the hand just as accurately in reaching for a lighted object in a darkened room as when reaching in a lighted room (McCarty et al., 2001).

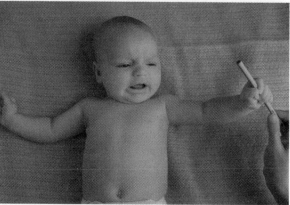

Infants' growing control of each hand is accompanied by greater coordination of the two hands. Although 4-month-olds use both hands, their motions are not coordinated; rather, each hand seems to have a mind of its own. Infants may hold a toy motionless in one hand while shaking a rattle in the other. At roughly 5 to 6 months of age, infants can coordinate the motions of their hands so that each hand performs different actions that serve a common goal. So a child might, for example, hold a toy animal in one hand and pet it with the other (Karniol, 1989).

These gradual changes in fine motor coordination are well illustrated by the ways

children feed themselves. Beginning at roughly 6 months of age, many infants experiment with "finger foods" such as sliced bananas and green beans. Infants can easily pick up such foods, but getting them into their mouths is another story. The hand grasping the food may be raised to the cheek, then moved to the edge of the lips, and finally shoved into the mouth. Mission accomplished, but only after many detours along the way! However, infants' eye-hand coordination improves rapidly, and foods varying in size, shape, and texture are soon placed directly in the mouth. The *pincer grasp* occurs when the thumb is used in opposition to the fingers, and once this ability has been achieved, usually by the end of the first year, their manipulative skills improve greatly.

At about the first birthday, many parents allow their children to try eating with a spoon. Youngsters first simply play with the spoon, dipping it in and out of a dish filled with food or sucking on an empty spoon. Soon they learn to fill the spoon with food and place it in their mouth, but the motions are awkward. For example, most 1-year-olds fill a spoon by first placing it directly over a dish. Then, they lower it until the bowl of the spoon is full. In contrast, 2-year-olds typically scoop food from a dish by rotating their wrist, which is the same motion that adults use.

Handedness

Are you right-handed or left-handed? If you're right-handed, you're in the majority. About 90% of the people worldwide prefer to use their right hand, although this figure varies somewhat from place to place, reflecting cultural influences. Most of the remaining 10% are left-handed; a relatively small percentage of people are truly ambidextrous.

When young babies reach for objects, they don't seem to prefer one hand over the other; they use their left and right hands interchangeably. They may shake a rattle with their left hand and, moments later, pick up blocks with their right. In one study, infants and toddlers were videotaped as they played with toys such as a pinwheel that could be manipulated with two hands (Cornwell, Harris, & Fitzgerald, 1991). The 9-month-olds used their left and right hands equally, but by 13 months, most grasped the toy with their right hand. Then they used their left hand to steady the toy while the right hand manipulated the object.

This early preference for one hand becomes stronger and more consistent during the toddler and preschool years. By age 2, a child's hand preference is clear; most children—about 90%—use their right hand in fine motor skills such as colouring, brushing teeth, or zipping a jacket. At this age, youngsters occasionally use their non-preferred hand for tasks.

TEST YOURSELF

1. According to _____, motor development involves many distinct skills that are organized and reorganized over time, depending on task demands.

2. When 4-month-olds tumble from a sitting position, they usually try to keep their head upright. This happens even when they are blindfolded, which means that the important cues to balance come from _____.

3. Skills important in learning to walk include maintaining upright posture and balance, stepping, and _____.

4. Akira uses both hands simultaneously, but not in a coordinated manner; each hand seems to be "doing its own thing." Akira is probably _____ months old.

5. Before the age of _____, children show no signs of handedness; they use their left and right hands interchangeably.

Describe how the mastery of a fine motor skill such as learning to use a spoon or a crayon illustrates the integration of biological, psychological, and sociocultural forces in the biopsychosocial framework.

Answers: (1) dynamic systems theory, (2) the inner ear, (3) using perceptual information, (4) 4, (5) 1 year

3.4

Coming to Know the World: Perception

LEARNING OBJECTIVES

- Are infants able to smell, to taste, and to experience pain?
- Can infants hear? How do they use sound to locate objects?
- How well can infants see? Can they see colour and depth?
- How do infants coordinate information between different sensory modalities, such as between vision and hearing?

Darla is mesmerized by her newborn daughter, Olivia. Darla loves holding Olivia, talking to her, and simply watching her. Darla is certain that Olivia is already getting to know her, coming to recognize her face and the sound of her voice. Darla's husband, Greg, thinks she is crazy: "Everyone knows that babies are born blind, and they probably can't hear much either." Darla doubts Greg and wishes someone could tell her the truth about Olivia's vision and hearing.

To answer Darla's questions, we need to define what it means for an infant to experience or sense the world. Humans have several kinds of sense organs, each of which is receptive to a different kind of physical energy. For example, the retina at the back of the eye is sensitive to some types of electromagnetic energy, and sight is the result. The eardrum detects changes in air pressure, and hearing is the result. Cells at the top of the nasal passage detect the passage of airborne molecules, and smell is the result. In each case, the sense organ translates the physical stimulus into nerve impulses that are sent to the brain. *The processes by which the brain receives, selects, modifies, and organizes these impulses is known as* **perception.** This is simply the first step in the complex process of accumulating information that eventually results in "knowing."

Darla's questions are really about her newborn daughter's perceptual skills. By the end of this section, you'll be able to answer her questions, because we're going to look at how infants use different senses to experience the world. We begin with smell and taste because they are among the most mature senses at birth.

Dion Ogust / The Image Works

SMELL AND TASTE

Newborns have a keen sense of smell. Infants respond positively to pleasant smells and negatively to unpleasant smells (Mennella & Beauchamp, 1997). They have a relaxed, contented-looking facial expression when they smell honey or chocolate but frown, grimace, or turn away when they smell rotten eggs or ammonia. Young babies can also recognize familiar odours. Newborns will look in the direction of a pad that is saturated with their own amniotic fluid (Schaal, Marlier, & Soussignan, 1998). They will also turn toward a pad saturated with the odour of their mother's breast or her perfume (Porter & Winberg, 1999).

Newborns also have a highly developed sense of taste. They readily differentiate salty, sour, bitter, and sweet tastes (Rostenstein & Oster, 1997). Most infants seem to have a "sweet tooth." They react to sweet substances by smiling, sucking, and licking their lips. In contrast, you can probably guess what the youngster in the photo has tasted! This grimace is typical when infants are fed bitter- or sour-tasting substances (Kaijura, Cowart, & Beauchamp, 1992). Infants are also sensitive to changes in the taste of breast milk that reflect a mother's diet. Infants will nurse more after their mother has consumed a sweet-tasting substance such as vanilla (Mennella & Beauchamp, 1996).

TOUCH AND PAIN

Newborns are sensitive to touch. As we saw earlier in this chapter, many areas of the newborn's body respond reflexively when touched. Touching an infant's cheek, mouth, hand, or foot produces reflexive movements, documenting that infants perceive touch.

If babies react to touch, does this mean they experience pain? This is difficult to answer because pain has such a subjective element to it. The same pain-eliciting stimulus that leads some adults to complain of mild discomfort causes others to report that they are in agony. Since infants cannot express their pain to us directly, we must use indirect evidence.

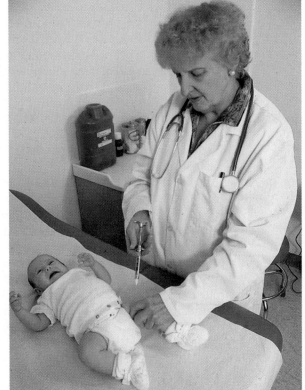

The infant's nervous system definitely is capable of transmitting pain: receptors for pain in the skin are just as plentiful in infants as they are in adults (Anand & Hickey, 1987). Furthermore, babies' behaviour in response to apparent pain-provoking stimuli also suggests that they experience pain (Buchholz et al., 1998). Look, for example, at the baby in the photo who is receiving an inoculation. She lowers her eyebrows, purses her lips, and, of course, opens her mouth to cry. Although we can't hear her, the sound of her cry is probably the unique pattern associated with pain. The pain cry begins suddenly, is high-pitched, and is not easily soothed. This baby is also agitated, moving her hands, arms, and legs (Craig et al., 1993; Goubet, Clifton, & Shah, 2001). Although for many years infants were denied pain medication because of inadequate understanding of their pain experience (Zisk, 2003), there is a much better understanding that even the youngest experience pain. In order to assist nurses to assess pain in infants, tools such as the Neotatal Infant Pain Scale (Lawrence et al., 1993) and the Premature Infant Pain Profile (Stevens et al. 1996) have been developed.

Perceptual skills are extraordinarily useful to newborns and young babies. Smell and touch help them recognize their mothers. Smell and taste make it much easier for them to learn to eat. Early development of smell, taste, and touch prepare newborns and young babies to learn about the world.

HEARING

Do you remember, from Chapter 2, the study in which mothers read *The Cat in the Hat* aloud late in pregnancy? This research showed that the fetus can hear at 7 or 8 months after conception. As you would expect from these results, newborns typically respond to sounds in their surroundings. If a parent is quiet but then coughs, an infant may startle, blink his eyes, and move his arms or legs. These responses may seem natural, but they do indeed indicate that infants are sensitive to sound.

Overall, adults can hear better than infants (Aslin, Jusczyk, & Pisoni, 1998). Adults can hear some very quiet sounds that infants can't. More interestingly, infants best hear sounds that have pitches in the range of human speech—neither very high- nor very low-pitched. Infants can differentiate speech sounds, such as vowels from consonant sounds, and by four and a half months they can recognize their own name (Jusczyk, 1995; Mandel, Jusczyk, & Pisoni, 1995).

In addition to carrying a message through words or music, sound can reveal much about its source. When we hear a person speak, the pitch of the speech can be used to judge the age and sex of the speaker; if the speech contains many relatively lower-pitched sounds, then the speaker is probably a man. The loudness of the speech tells us about the speaker's distance; if it can barely be heard, the speaker is far away. Also, differences in the time it takes sound to travel to the left and right ears tells us about the speaker's location; if the sounds arrive at exactly the same time, the speaker must be directly ahead or directly behind us.

Even infants can extract much of this information in sound. Young babies can distinguish sounds of different pitches; 6-month-olds do so nearly as accurately as adults (Spetner & Olsho, 1990). They are also able to differentiate speech sounds, such as different vowel and consonant sounds (a topic we examine in more detail later in this chapter).

Like adults, infants use sound to locate objects, looking toward the source of sound (Morrongiello, Fenwick, & Chance, 1990). Infants also use sound to decide whether objects are near or far. In one study (Clifton, Perris, & Bullinger, 1991), 7-month-olds were shown a rattle. Next, the experimenters darkened the room and shook the rattle, either 15 centimetres (6 inches) away from the infant or about 60 centimetres (2 feet) away. Infants would often reach for the rattle in the dark when it was 15 centimetres away but not when it was 60 centimetres away. These 7-month-olds were quite capable of using sound to estimate distance—in this case, distinguishing a toy they could reach from one they could not. Thus, by the middle of the first year, infants are responding to much of the information that is provided by sound.

SEEING

If you've ever watched infants, you've probably noticed that they spend much of their waking time looking around. Sometimes they seem to be generally scanning their environment, and sometimes they seem to be focusing on nearby objects. What do they see as a result? Perhaps their visual world is a sea of confusing grey blobs. Or maybe they see the world essentially as adults do. Actually, neither of these descriptions is entirely accurate, but the second is closer to the truth.

The various elements of the visual system—the eye, the optic nerve, and the brain—are relatively well developed at birth. Newborns respond to light and can track moving objects with their eyes. How well do infants see? *The clarity of vision, called* **visual acuity**, *is defined as the smallest pattern that can be distinguished dependably.* You've undoubtedly had your acuity measured, probably by being asked to read rows of progressively smaller letters or numbers from a chart. The same approach is used to assess newborns' acuity, adjusted to compensate for the fact that we can't use words to explain to infants what we'd like them to do. Most infants will look at patterned stimuli instead of plain, patternless stimuli (Snow, 1998). For example, if we were to show the two stimuli in Figures 3.8 and 3.9 to an infant, most babies would look longer at the striped pattern than at the grey pattern. As we make the lines narrower (along with the spaces between them), there comes a point at which the black and white stripes become so fine that they simply blend together and appear grey—just like the other pattern.

To estimate an infant's acuity, we pair the grey square with squares in which the widths of the stripes differ, as shown in the figures: When infants look at the two stimuli equally, this indicates that they are no longer able to distinguish the stripes of the patterned stimulus. By measuring the width of the stripes and their distance from an infant's eye, we can estimate acuity, with detection of thinner stripes indicating better acuity. Measurements of this sort indicate that newborns and 1-month-olds see at 6.1 metres (20 feet) what normal adults would see at 61 to 122 metres (200 to 400 feet). By the first birthday, infants' acuity is essentially the same as that of an adult with normal vision (Kellman & Banks, 1998).

FIGURE 3.8

FIGURE 3.9

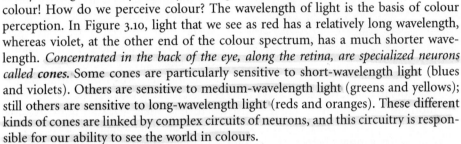

Colour

Not only do infants begin to see the world with greater acuity during the first year, they also begin to see it in colour! How do we perceive colour? The wavelength of light is the basis of colour perception. In Figure 3.10, light that we see as red has a relatively long wavelength, whereas violet, at the other end of the colour spectrum, has a much shorter wavelength. *Concentrated in the back of the eye, along the retina, are specialized neurons called cones.* Some cones are particularly sensitive to short-wavelength light (blues and violets). Others are sensitive to medium-wavelength light (greens and yellows); still others are sensitive to long-wavelength light (reds and oranges). These different kinds of cones are linked by complex circuits of neurons, and this circuitry is responsible for our ability to see the world in colours.

These circuits begin to function gradually in the first few months after birth (Adams, 1995). Apparently, newborns perceive few colours. However, 1-month-olds can differentiate blue from grey, which means that the short-wavelength circuit is functioning (Maurer & Adams, 1987). At this age, babies can also differentiate red from green, but not yellow from green or yellow from red. Apparently, the medium- and short-wavelength circuits are functioning (because infants discriminate between red and green) but not with complete fidelity (because they cannot distinguish yellow). However, 3- and 4-month-olds perceive colours in much the same way that adults do, despite the fact that their visual acuity is not yet fully developed (Adams & Courage, 1995; Dannemiller, 1998).

FIGURE 3.10   **Colour Wavelength**

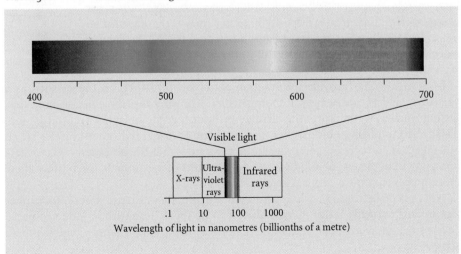

Depth

People see objects as having three dimensions: height, width, and depth. The retina of the eye is flat, so height and width can be represented directly on its two-dimensional surface. But the third dimension, depth, cannot be represented directly on this flat surface, so how do we perceive depth? We use perceptual processing to *infer* depth.

Depth perception tells us whether objects are near or far, which was the basis for some classic research by Eleanor Gibson and Richard Walk (1960) on the origins of

depth perception. *In their work, babies were placed on the glass-covered platform shown in the photo, a device known as the visual cliff.* On one side of the platform, a checkerboard pattern appeared directly under the glass; on the other side, the pattern appeared several feet below the glass. The result was that the first side looked shallow but the other looked deep, like a cliff.

Mothers stood on each side of the visual cliff and tried to coax their infants across the deep or the shallow side. Most babies willingly crawled to their mothers when they stood on the

shallow side. In contrast, almost every baby refused to cross the deep side, even when the mothers called them by name and tried to lure them with an attractive toy. Clearly, infants can perceive depth by the time they are old enough to crawl.

What about younger babies who cannot yet crawl? When babies as young as one and a half months are simply placed on the visual cliff, their hearts beat more slowly when they are placed on the deep side of the cliff. Heart rate often decelerates when people notice something interesting, so this would suggest that one-and-a-half-month-olds notice that the deep side is different. At 7 months, infants' heart rate accelerates, a sign of fear. Thus, although young babies can detect a difference between the shallow and the deep sides of the visual cliff, only older, crawling babies are actually afraid of the deep side (Campos et al., 1978).

How do infants infer depth? They rely upon many sources of information. *One is retinal disparity: When a person views an object, the retinal images in the left and the right eyes differ.* When objects are distant, the retinal images are nearly identical; when they are nearby, the images differ. Thus, greater disparity in retinal images signifies that an object is close. By 4 to 6 months of age, infants use retinal disparity as a depth cue, correctly inferring that objects are nearby when disparity is great (Kellman & Banks, 1998; Yonas & Owsley, 1987).

Motion can also provide information about depth. When an object such as a person or vehicle moves away, it looks smaller. Knowing that the object is not really getting smaller, we interpret the change to mean that the object is becoming more distant. Also, moving objects often pass in front of or behind other objects. When one object is partially obscured by another, we infer that the obscured object is farther away than the unobscured object. By 5 months of age, infants use both of these motion cues to deduce depth (Craton & Yonas, 1988).

Not only do infants use visual cues to judge depth, they also use sound. Remember that infants correctly judge quieter objects to be more distant than louder objects. Given such an assortment of cues, it is not surprising that infants gauge depth so accurately.

THINK ABOUT IT

Psychologists often refer to "perceptual-motor skills," which implies that the two are closely related. Based on what you've learned in this chapter, how might motor skills influence perception? How could perception influence motor skills?

Perceiving Objects

When you look at this pattern, what do you see? You probably recognize it as part of a human eyeball, even though all that's physically present in the photograph are many different coloured dots. In this case, perception actually creates an object from sensory stimulation. That is, our perceptual processes determine that certain features go together to form objects. This is particularly challenging because we often see only parts of objects—nearby objects often obscure parts of more distant objects. Nevertheless, in the photo we recognize that the orange is one object even though it is partially hidden by the glass.

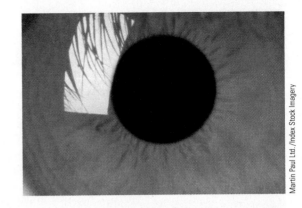

Perception of objects is limited in newborns but develops rapidly in the first few months after birth (S.P. Johnson, 2001). By 4 months, infants use a number of cues to determine which elements go together to form objects. One important cue is motion: Elements that move together are usually part of the same object (Kellman & Banks, 1998). For example, at the left of Figure 3.11a, a pencil appears to be moving back and forth behind a coloured square. If the square were removed, you would be surprised to see a pair of pencil stubs, as shown on the right side of the diagram. The common movement of the pencil's eraser and point lead us to believe that they're part of the same pencil.

Young infants, too, are surprised by demonstrations like this. If they see a display like the moving pencils, they will then look very briefly at a whole pencil, apparently because they expected it. In contrast, if after seeing the moving pencil they're shown the two pencil stubs, they look much longer, as if trying to figure out what happened (Eizenman & Bertenthal, 1998; Johnson & Aslin, 1995). Evidently, even very young babies use common motion to create objects from different parts.

FIGURE 3.11A

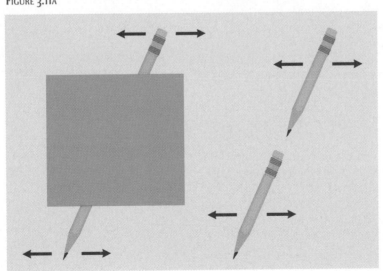

FIGURE 3.11B

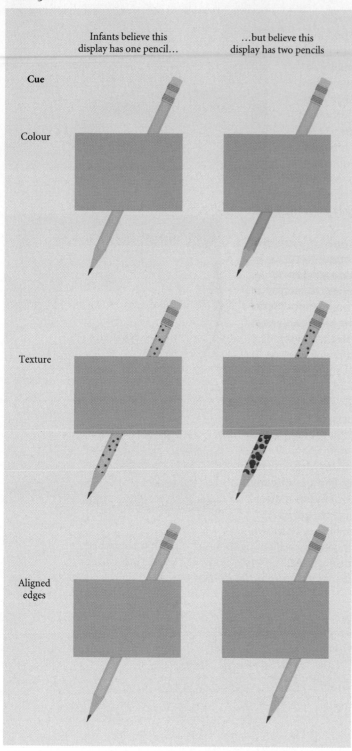

Infants believe this display has one pencil...   ...but believe this display has two pencils

Cue

Colour

Texture

Aligned edges

Motion is one clue to object unity, but infants use others too, including colour, texture, and aligned edges. As you can see in Figure 3.11b, infants more often group features together (i.e., believe they're part of the same object), when they're the same colour, have the same texture, and when their edges are aligned (S. P. Johnson, 2001).

One object that's particularly important for infants is the human face. Young babies readily look at faces. From Figure 3.11c, which shows a pattern of eye fixations, you can see that 1-month-olds look mostly at the outer edges of the face. Three-month-olds, however, focus almost entirely on the interior of the face, particularly the eyes and lips.

FIGURE 3.11C

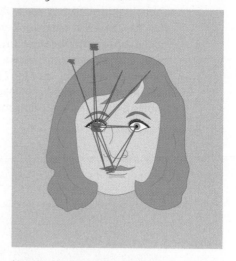

Adapted from Figure 3.21 on p. 201 from "Pattern Perception in Infancy," Chapter 3, pp. 133–234, by Philip Salapatek. In L.B. Cohen and P. Salapatek (Eds.), *Infant Perception: From Sensation to Cognition.* Copyright © 1975, with permission from Elsevier.

INTEGRATING SENSORY INFORMATION

So far, we have discussed infants' sensory systems separately. In reality, of course, most infant experiences are better described as "multimedia events." A nursing mother like the one in the photo provides visual and taste cues to her baby. A rattle stimulates vision, hearing, and touch. In fact, much stimulation is not specific to one sense but spans several senses. Temporal information, such as duration or tempo, can be seen or heard. For example, you can detect the rhythm of a person clapping by seeing the hands meet or by hearing the sound of hands striking. Similarly, the texture of a surface—whether it's rough or smooth—can be detected by sight or by feel.

Getty Images

Infants readily perceive many of these relations. For example, infants can recognize visually an object that they have only touched previously. Similarly, they can detect relations between information presented visually and auditorily. They know, for example, that an object moving into the distance looks smaller and is harder to hear (Bahrick & Lickliter, 2002). And they can link the temporal properties of visual and auditory stimulation, such as duration and rhythm (Lewkowicz, 2000).

Traditionally, coordinating information from different senses (e.g., vision with hearing, vision with touch) was thought to be a challenging task for infants. *More recently, however, some researchers have argued that the infant's sensory systems are particularly attuned to* **intersensory redundancy,** *that is, to information that is presented simultaneously to different sensory modes* (Bahrick & Lickliter, 2002). When we see and hear a person talking (visual + auditory), we focus on this information because it is presented to both senses, instead of paying attention to information available to only one sense, such as the colour of the person's hair or the sound of an unseen dog barking. The Spotlight on Research feature provides evidence of the importance of intersensory redundancy in infants' perception.

SPOTLIGHT ON RESEARCH

Infants Attend to Intersensory Redundancy

Who were the investigators, and what was the aim of the study? If infants are particularly attentive to information presented redundantly to several senses, they should be better able to notice when that information changes. In other words, if a person claps slowly at first but then quickly, infants should be able to detect this change more readily if they see and hear the clapping than if they can see or hear but not both. Testing this hypothesis was the aim of a study by Lorraine Bahrick and Robert Lickliter (2000).

How did the investigators measure the topic of interest? Bahrick and Lickliter wanted

to determine the conditions under which 5-month-olds could detect a change in a rhythmic pattern. Consequently, they included three different conditions, shown in Table 3.3.

In the condition of primary interest—audio + video—the infants watched a videotape in which they saw and heard a hammer striking a wooden surface. After several of these familiarization trials, test trials began: The hammer continued to strike the surface, but in a different rhythm, and the sound was turned off. The question was whether infants would look longer at the videotape during the test trials, indicating they had detected the

TABLE 3.3   Conditions in the Bahrick and Lickliter (2000) Study

Condition	Familiarization Trials		Test Trials	
	Visual	Auditory	Visual	Auditory
Audio + Video	Moving hammer striking a surface	Tapping sounds synchronized with video	Moving hammer striking a surface in a new rhythm	Silence
Video Only	Moving hammer striking a surface	Silence	Moving hammer striking a surface in a new rhythm	Silence
Audio Only	Still photo of hammer	Tapping sounds	Still photo of hammer	Tapping sounds in a new rhythm

change in rhythm. Performance in this condition was compared to performance in two other conditions: The video-only condition was exactly the same as the audio + video condition except no audio was presented during the familiarization or test trials. In the audio-only condition, the tapping sounds were exactly as in the audio + video condition, but the videotape depicted a motionless hammer throughout all trials.

Who were the children in the study? Each condition included eight 5-month-olds.

What was the design of the study? This study was experimental. The independent variable was the manner in which the information was presented: audio + video, video-only, and audio-only. The dependent variable was the change in infants' looking at the video on the test trials (following the change in rhythm). The study included only 5-month-olds, tested once, so it was not developmental.

Were there ethical concerns with the study? No. Most infants seemed to enjoy watching the videos.

What were the results? If infants detect the change in the rhythm, they should look more at the video following the change. If they do not detect the change, they should look about the same amount or less (reflecting growing boredom with what seems to be the same stimulus). Figure 3.12 shows that infants detected the change in rhythm only when auditory and visual information was redundant. Visual or auditory information alone was not enough for infants to detect the change.*

What did the investigators conclude? Bahrick and Lickliter (2000) concluded that "multimodal stimulation makes overlapping, temporally coordinated information available to the different senses. This 'redundancy' has a powerful impact on the deployment of attention" (p. 198).

What converging evidence would strengthen these conclusions? Bahrick and Lickliter could explore other instances of intersensory redundancy. That is, this study focused solely on rhythm, which is just one case of auditory and visual integration. Many other elements need to be explored (e.g., duration) and, of course, this effect needs to be shown for other combinations of senses (e.g., vision and touch, vision and taste).

FIGURE 3.12

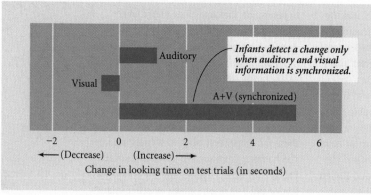

Infants detect a change only when auditory and visual information is synchronized.

Auditory

Visual

A+V (synchronized)

−2   0   2   4   6

← (Decrease)   (Increase) →

Change in looking time on test trials (in seconds)

*Perhaps you've thought of a problem with this procedure. Infants might look longer not because they notice a change in the pace of hammering but simply because the sound was turned off. To evaluate this possibility, Bahrick and Lickliter also included a condition in which the sound was turned off but the rhythm did not change. In this case, infants did not increase their looking. So, the change in rhythm, not the absence of sound, is the critical variable.

Integrating information from different senses is yet another variation on the theme that has dominated this section: Infants' sensory and perceptual skills are impressive. Darla's newborn daughter, from the opening vignette, can definitely smell, taste, and feel pain. She can distinguish sounds, and at about 7 months she will use sound to locate objects. Her vision is a little blurry now but will improve rapidly; in a few months, she'll see the full range of colours and perceive depth. In short, Darla's daughter, like most infants, is exceptionally well prepared to begin to make sense out of her environment.

HEALTHY LIVING

What are important practices to promote health in the first two years?

New parents undergo a major change in their lives that includes the responsibility for the health and well-being of their brand-new baby. They will need to learn about many important practices to provide the best chances of good health for their baby, including breast or formula feeding guidelines and introduction of solid foods; positioning baby on his/her back; keeping the home a non-smoking environment; proper use of infant car seats and cribs; careful supervision of the baby, especially when he/she puts objects in his/her mouth, learns to roll over, and begins to walk; immunization schedule; proper storage of dangerous materials; sunburn protection; healthy sleeping patterns; and dental care.

TEST YOURSELF

1. Infants respond negatively to substances that taste sour or _____.

2. Infants respond to _____ with a high-pitched cry that is hard to soothe.

3. If an infant seated in a completely darkened room hears the sound of her favourite rattle nearby, she will reach for it; this demonstrates _____.

4. At age _____, infants' acuity is like that of an adult with normal vision.

5. _____ are specialized neurons in the retina that are sensitive to colour.

6. The term _____ refers to the fact that images of an object in the left and right eyes differ for nearby objects.

7. When elements consistently move together, infants decide that they are

   _____.

8. Infants readily integrate information from different senses, and their sensory systems seem to be particularly attuned to

   _____.

   What features of infants' perceptual skill show the influence of nature? What features show the influence of nurture?

Answers: (1) bitter, (2) pain, (3) the use of sound to judge distances, (4) 1 year, (5) Cones, (6) retinal disparity, (7) part of the same object, (8) information presented redundantly to several senses

3.5

The Onset of Thinking

LEARNING OBJECTIVES

- What are the basic principles of cognitive development?
- What did Piaget describe as sensorimotor thinking?
- How do schemes become more advanced as infants progress through the six stages of sensorimotor thinking?
- According to Piaget, how do assimilation, accommodation, and equilibration provide the foundation for cognitive development throughout the life span?
- What are some of the shortcomings of Piaget's account of cognitive development?
- How does information-processing develop in infants?

Six-month-old Madison loves to play with her toys. It seems to her parents that overnight she went from merely holding her toys to purposefully shaking them to make noise. They are amazed that she seems to becoming more and more aware of her surroundings and seems to even have favourite toys. Her parents wonder how Madison learned so quickly which toys make noise and how to find those particular ones among all the others.

How does Madison learn to shake certain toys to make sounds and how to pick these toys from a group? Piaget's theory describes a type of thinking called sensorimotor thinking, which is broken down in stages that describe how infants learn about the world through experience and then incorporate what they learn by unintentional means into deliberate action. According to Piaget, this period of sensorimotor development occurs during the first two years of life and will be described in more detail in this section.

BASIC PRINCIPLES OF COGNITIVE DEVELOPMENT

According to Jean Piaget, the famous Swiss psychologist discussed in Chapter 1, children understand the world with **schemes,** *psychological structures that organize experience.* Schemes are mental categories of related events, objects, and knowledge. During infancy, most schemes are based on actions. That is, infants group objects based on the actions they can perform on them. For example, infants suck and grasp, and they use these actions to create categories of objects that can be sucked and objects that can be grasped.

Assimilation and Accommodation

Schemes change constantly, adapting to children's experiences. In fact, intellectual adaptation involves two processes working together: assimilation and accommodation. *Assimilation occurs when new experiences are readily incorporated into existing schemes.* Imagine a baby who has the familiar grasping scheme. Like the baby in the photograph on the next page, she will soon discover that the grasping scheme also works well on blocks, toy cars, and other small objects. Extending the existing grasping scheme to new objects illustrates assimilation. *Accommodation occurs when schemes are modified based on experience.* Soon the infant learns that some objects can only be lifted with two hands and that some can't be lifted at all. Changing the scheme so that it works for new objects (e.g., using two hands to grasp heavy objects) illustrates accommodation.

Assimilation and accommodation are often easier to understand when you remember Piaget's belief that infants, children, and adolescents create theories to try to understand events and objects around them. The infant whose theory is that objects can be lifted with one hand finds that her theory is confirmed when she tries to pick up small objects, but she's in for a surprise when she tries to pick up a heavy book. The unexpected result forces the infant, like a good scientist, to revise her theory to include this new finding.

Equilibration and Stages of Cognitive Development

Assimilation and accommodation are usually in balance, or equilibrium. Children find that many experiences are readily assimilated into their existing schemes but that they sometimes need to accommodate their schemes to adjust to new experiences. This balance between assimilation and accommodation is illustrated by the baby with the theory about lifting objects. Periodically, however, this balance is upset and a state of disequilibrium results. That is, children discover that their current schemes are not adequate because they are spending much time accommodating and much less time assimilating. *When disequilibrium occurs, children reorganize their schemes to return to a state of equilibrium, a process that Piaget called* **equilibration.** To restore the balance, current but now-outmoded ways of thinking are replaced by a qualitatively different, more advanced set of schemes.

One way to understand equilibration is to return to the metaphor of the child as a scientist. As we discussed in Chapter 1, good scientific theories readily explain some phenomena but usually must be revised to explain others. Children's theories enable them to understand many experiences by predicting—for example, what will happen ("It's morning, so it's time for breakfast") or who will do what ("Mom's gone to work, so Dad will take me to school")—but the theories must be modified when predictions go awry ("Dad thinks I'm old enough to walk to school, so he won't take me").

Sometimes scientists find that their theories contain critical flaws that can't be fixed simply by revising; instead, they must create a new theory that draws on the older theory but is fundamentally different. For example, when the astronomer Copernicus realized that the earth-centred theory of the solar system was fundamentally wrong, his new theory built on the assumption that the sun is the centre of the solar system. In much the same way, periodically children reach states in which their current theories seem to be wrong much of the time, so they abandon these theories in favour of more advanced ways of thinking about their physical and social worlds.

According to Piaget, these revolutionary changes in thought occur three times over the life span, at approximately 2, 7, and 11 years of age. This divides cognitive development into the following four stages:

TABLE 3.4

Period of Development	Age Range
Sensorimotor period	Infancy (0–2 years)
Preoperational period	Preschool and early elementary school years (2–7 years)
Concrete operational period	Middle and late elementary school years (7–11 years)
Formal operational period	Adolescence and adulthood (11 years and up)

The ages listed are only approximate. Some youngsters move through the periods more rapidly than others, depending on their ability and their experience. However, the only route to formal operations—the most sophisticated type of thought—is through the first three periods, in sequence. Sensorimotor thinking always gives rise to preoperational thinking; a child cannot "skip" preoperational thinking and move directly from the sensorimotor to the concrete operational period.

In the next few pages of this chapter, we consider Piaget's account of sensorimotor thinking, the period from birth to approximately 2 years of age. In subsequent chapters we will return to Piaget's theory to examine his account of preoperational, concrete, and formal operational thinking in preschool and school-age children, and adolescents.

SENSORIMOTOR THINKING

Piaget (1951, 1952, 1954) believed that the first two years of life form a distinct phase in human development. *The sensorimotor period, from birth to roughly 2 years of age, is the first of Piaget's four periods of cognitive development.* Piaget divided this period into six stages. All infants progress through the six stages in the same order, but they do so at different rates, so the ages we list here are only approximations.

1. *Exercising reflexes (roughly newborn to 1 month).* We know that newborns respond reflexively to many stimuli. As infants use these reflexes during the first month, they become much more coordinated. For example, just as major league baseball players swing a bat with greater power and strength than do Little Leaguers, 1-month-olds suck more strongly and steadily than do newborns. Reflexes like this one provide the foundation for much cognitive growth during infancy.

2. *Learning to adapt: Primary circular reactions (roughly 1 to 4 months).* During these months, reflexes become modified by experience. *The chief mechanism for change is the primary circular reaction, in which infants accidentally produce a pleasing event involving their own body and then try to re-create the event.* For example, an infant may inadvertently touch his lips with his thumb, thereby initiating sucking and the pleasing sensations associated with sucking. Later, the infant tries to re-create these sensations by guiding his thumb to his mouth. Sucking no longer occurs only when the mother places a nipple at the infant's mouth; instead, the infant has found a way to initiate sucking himself.

3. *Making interesting events (roughly 4 to 8 months).* Initially, primary circular reactions involve such reflexes as sucking or grasping. However, beginning in Stage 3, the infant begins to show greater interest in the world. Now objects are more often the focus of circular reactions. For example, the infant shown in the photo accidentally shook a new toy. Hearing the interesting noise, she grasped the toy anew, tried to shake it, and expressed great pleasure when the noise resumed. This sequence was repeated several times.

    Novel actions that are repeated with objects characterize the secondary circular reaction. They are significant because they represent an infant's first efforts to learn about objects in the environment, to explore their properties. No longer are infants grasping objects "mindlessly," simply because something is in contact with their hands. Instead, they are learning about the sights and sounds associated with the objects.

4. *Behaving intentionally: Separating means from ends (roughly 8 to 12 months).* This stage marks the onset of deliberate, intentional behaviour. For the first time, the means and the ends of activities are distinct.

Courtesy of Ingrid Crowther

For example, if a father places his hand in front of a toy, an infant will move the father's hand to be able to play with the toy. The "move the hand" scheme is the means to achieve the end of activating the "grasp the toy" scheme. Combining schemes in this way is the first solid evidence of deliberate, purposeful behaviour during infancy.

5. *Experimenting (roughly 12 to 18 months).* The infant at this stage is an active experimentalist. *An infant will repeat old schemes with novel objects—which Piaget called a **tertiary circular reaction**—as if trying to understand why different objects yield different outcomes.* A Stage 5 infant may deliberately shake a number of different objects, trying to discover which produce sounds and which do not. Or an infant may decide to drop different objects to see what happens. An infant in a crib discovers that stuffed animals land quietly, whereas harder toys often make a more satisfying "clunk" when they hit the ground.

    Tertiary circular reactions represent a significant extension of the intentional behaviour that emerged in Stage 4. Now babies repeat actions with different objects *solely* for the purpose of seeing what will happen.

6. *Using symbols (roughly 18 to 24 months).* By 18 months, most infants have begun to talk and gesture (the subject of the last section of this chapter). These actions are significant because they illustrate toddlers' emerging capacity to use symbols. Words and gestures are symbols that stand for something else: Waving and saying "bye-bye" are both ways to indicate that you're leaving. Pretend play, which we'll examine in more detail in Chapter 5, also shows a youngster's use of symbols. For example, a 20-month-old may move her hand back and forth in front of her mouth, pretending to brush her teeth. A summary of these stages is shown in Figure 3.13.

FIGURE 3.13   Substages During the Sensorimotor Stage of Development

Substage	Age (months)	Accomplishment	Example	
1	0–1	Reflexes become coordinated.	Sucking a nipple	
2	1–4	Primary circular reactions appear—an infant's first learned reactions to the world.	Thumb sucking	
3	4–8	Secondary circular reactions emerge, allowing infants to explore the world of objects.	Shaking a toy to hear a rattle	
4	8–12	Means–end sequencing of schemes is seen, marking the onset of intentional behaviour.	Moving an obstacle to reach a toy	
5	12–18	Tertiary circular reactions develop, allowing children to experiment.	Shaking different toys to hear the sounds they make	
6	18–24	Symbolic processing is revealed in language, gestures, and pretend play.	Eating pretend food with a pretend fork	

EVALUATING PIAGET'S THEORY

THINK ABOUT IT 🔎

Children with low birth weight often have delayed intellectual development (page 77). According to Piaget, what form might the delay take?

Researchers have questioned Piaget's studies of infants' understanding of objects (Goubet & Clifton, 1998; Munakata et al., 1997). According to Piaget, one of the milestones of infancy is the understanding that objects exist independently of oneself and one's actions. He claimed that 1- to 4-month-olds—who are in Stage 2 of the sensorimotor period—believe that objects no longer exist when they disappear from view (out of sight, out of mind). As astounding as this may seem, if you take a favourite toy from a 3-month-old and hide it under a cloth directly in front of her, she will not look for it. This is true even though the shape of the toy is clearly visible under the cloth and within reach!

Beginning at about 4 or 5 months, Piaget found that infants will search for objects. Understanding of objects is far from complete, because even older infants are sometimes unable to find hidden objects. If 9-month-olds see an object hidden under one container, then see it hidden under a second container, most of them routinely look for the toy under the first container. Piaget claimed that this showed 9-month-olds' fragmentary understanding of objects. Infants do not distinguish the object per se from the actions they used to locate it, such as lifting a particular container. Not until approximately 18 months of age do infants apparently have full understanding of the permanence of objects.

Investigators have since questioned Piaget's conclusions (Smith et al., 1999). Some fairly minor changes in procedures can affect 8- to 10-month-olds' success on the hidden object task. An infant is more likely to look under the correct container if, for example, the interval between hiding and looking is brief and if the containers are easily distinguished from each other. Therefore, infants who are unsuccessful on this task may be showing poor memory rather than inadequate understanding of the nature of objects (Marcovitch & Zelazo, 1999; Wellman, Cross, & Bartsch, 1986).

In addition, by devising some clever procedures, other investigators have shown that babies understand objects much earlier than Piaget claimed. Renée Baillargeon (1987, 1994), for example, assessed object permanence using the method shown in Figure 3.14. Infants first saw a silver screen that appeared to be rotating back and forth. When they were familiar with this display, one of two new displays was shown. In the *possible event*, a yellow box appeared in a position behind the screen, making it impossible for the screen to rotate as far back as it had previously. Instead, the screen rotated until it made contact with the box, then rotated forward. In the *impossible event*, the yellow box appeared, but the screen continued to rotate as before. The screen rotated back until it was flat, then rotated forward, again revealing the yellow

FIGURE 3.14   Assessing Object Permanence

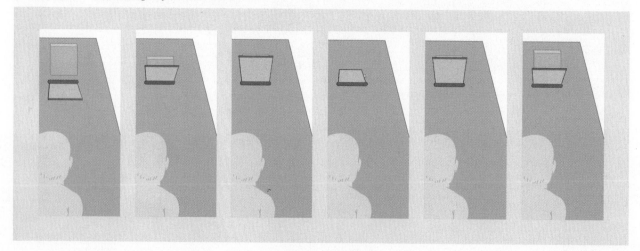

box. The illusion was possible because the box was mounted on a movable platform that allowed it to drop out of the way of the moving screen. However, from the infant's perspective, it appeared as if the box vanished behind the screen, only to reappear.

The disappearance and reappearance of the box violates the idea that objects exist permanently. Consequently, an infant who understands the permanence of objects should find the impossible event a truly novel stimulus and look at it longer than the possible event. Baillargeon found that four-and-a-half-month-olds consistently looked longer at the impossible event than the possible event. Infants apparently thought the impossible event was novel, just as we are surprised when an object vanishes from a magician's scarf.

Evidently, infants have some understanding of the permanence of objects at a much younger age than Piaget's theory would predict. Why the difference? Remember that Piaget usually based his assessments on tasks in which infants had to search for missing objects. Search requires locomotor skills—reaching and grasping, for example—and apparently it is these skills that are limited in younger infants, not their understanding that objects are permanent.

The contrary findings regarding infants' understanding of object permanence and conservation do not mean that Piaget's theory is fundamentally wrong. In some cases, the theory needs to be revised to include important constructs that Piaget overlooked.

EXTENDING PIAGET'S ACCOUNT: CHILDREN'S NAÏVE THEORIES

Piaget believed that children, like scientists, formulate theories about how the world works. Children's theories are usually called "naïve theories" because, unlike real scientific theories, they are not created by specialists and they are rarely evaluated by formal experimentation. In Piaget's view, children formulate a grand, comprehensive theory that attempts to explain an enormous variety of phenomena, including reasoning about objects, people, and morals, for example, within a common framework. More recent views cling to the idea of children as theorists but propose that children, like real scientists, develop specialized theories about much narrower areas. *For example, according to the **core knowledge hypothesis**, infants are born with rudimentary knowledge of the world; this knowledge is elaborated based on children's experiences* (Carey & Spelke, 1994). Some of the theories young children first develop concern physics, psychology, and biology. That is, young children rapidly develop theories that organize their knowledge about properties of objects, people, and living things (Wellman & Gelman, 1998).

Naïve Physics

As a scientific discipline, physics concerns matter (physical objects) and energy. In contrast, naïve physics refers to a person's understanding of objects and their properties. Examples would include understanding that an unsupported object falls and that tall objects are partially visible when placed behind shorter objects. For human development researchers, the goal is to discover when children are first aware of these kinds of object properties. The usual method to assess infants' knowledge is to show events that conform to physical laws as well as events that violate them (e.g., an object seems to "float" in air, with no visible means of support). If infants look longer or show greater surprise at the "impossible" events, this suggests they have an expectation about how objects are supposed to act.

Researchers have discovered that infants are aware of many important basic facts about objects. They know, for instance, that objects move along connected, continuous paths and that objects cannot move "through" other objects (Spelke, 1994; von Hofsten et al., 1998). Infants look longer at moving objects that violate these properties (e.g., a ball that somehow rolls "through" a solid wall) than moving objects that

FIGURE 3.15

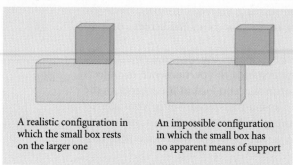

A realistic configuration in which the small box rests on the larger one

An impossible configuration in which the small box has no apparent means of support

are consistent with them, suggesting that infants are surprised when objects move in ways not predicted by their naïve theory of physics. By the middle of the first year, babies also understand that one object striking a second object will cause the latter to move (Kotovsky & Baillargeon, 1998; Spelke, 1994).

Later in the first year, if infants are shown the two situations depicted in Figure 3.15, they will look intently at the object that appears unsupported, apparently because it violates their expectations about what happens to unsupported objects (Baillargeon, 1998). And infants are surprised when a tall object is completely hidden when placed behind a shorter object, apparently because it violates their expectations about concealment (Hespos & Baillargeon, 2001).

These amazing demonstrations attest to the fact that the infant is indeed an accomplished naïve physicist. Of course, the infant's theories are far from complete; physical properties can be understood at many different levels (Hood, Carey, & Prasada, 2000). Using gravity as an example, infants can expect that unsupported objects will fall, elementary school children know that such objects fall due to gravity, and physics students know that the force of gravity equals the mass of an object times the acceleration caused by gravity. Obviously, infants do not understand objects at the level of physics students. However, the important point is that infants rapidly create a reasonably accurate theory of some basic properties of objects, a theory that helps them to expect that objects such as toys will act in predictable ways.

Naïve Biology

Fundamental to adults' naïve theories is the distinction between living and nonliving things. Adults know that living things, for example, are made of cells, inherit properties from parents, and move spontaneously. Adults' theories of living things begin in infancy, when youngsters first distinguish animate objects (e.g., people, insects, other animals) from inanimate objects (e.g., rocks, plants, furniture, tools). Motion is critical in early understanding of the difference between animate and inanimate objects. Infants and toddlers use motion to identify animate objects, and by 12 to 15 months they have determined that animate objects are self-propelled, can move in irregular paths, and act to achieve goals (Rakison & Poulin-Dubois, 2001).

INFORMATION PROCESSING DURING INFANCY

As discussed in Chapter 1, information processing is the view that human thinking is based on both mental hardware and mental software. According to psychologists, the combination of both kinds of software enables children to accomplish a specific task, and that as children develop, their software becomes more complex, powerful, and efficient. Attention is one of the first important cognitive processes that will be discussed.

Attention

Linda was only three days old and was often startled by the sounds of traffic outside her parents' apartment. Linda's parents worried that she might not get enough sleep. Yet, within a few days, traffic sounds no longer disturbed Linda; she slept blissfully. Why was a noise that had been so troubling no longer a problem? *The key is attention, a process that determines which sensory information receives additional cognitive processing.*

Linda's response was normal not only for infants but also for children and adolescents. *When presented with a strong or unfamiliar stimulus, an **orienting response** usually occurs: A person starts, fixes the eyes on the stimulus, and shows changes in heart rate and brain wave activity.* Collectively, these responses indicate that the infant has noticed the stimulus. Remember, too, that Linda soon ignored the sound of traffic. After repeated presentations of a stimulus, people recognize it as familiar and the orienting response gradually disappears. ***Habituation** is the diminished response to a stimulus as it becomes more familiar.*

The orienting response and habituation are both useful to infants. On the one hand, orienting makes the infant aware of potentially important or dangerous events in the environment. On the other hand, constantly responding to insignificant stimuli is wasteful, so habituation keeps infants from wasting too much energy on biologically nonsignificant events (Rovee-Collier, 1987).

Learning

An infant is always learning. For example, a 5-month-old learns that a new toy makes a noise every time she shakes it. Infants are born with many mechanisms that enable them to learn from experience. This learning can take many forms, including classical conditioning, operant conditioning, and imitation.

CLASSICAL CONDITIONING.

Some of the most famous experiments in psychology were conducted with dogs by the Russian physiologist, Ivan Pavlov. Dogs salivate when fed. Pavlov discovered that if something always happened just before feeding—for example, a bell sounded—dogs would begin to salivate to that event. *In **classical conditioning**, a neutral stimulus elicits a response that was originally produced by another stimulus.* In Pavlov's experiments, the bell was a neutral stimulus that did not naturally cause dogs to salivate. However, by repeatedly pairing the bell with food, the bell began to elicit salivation. Similarly, infants will suck reflexively when sugar water is placed in their mouth with a dropper; if a tone precedes the drops of sugar water, infants will suck when they hear the tone (Lipsitt, 1990).

Classical conditioning is important because it gives infants a sense of order in their environment. That is, through classical conditioning, infants learn that a stimulus is a signal for what will happen next. A youngster like the one in the photo may smile when she hears the family dog's collar because she knows the dog is coming to play with her. Or a toddler may smile when he hears water running in the bathroom because he realizes it's time for a bath.

Infants and toddlers are definitely capable of classical conditioning when the stimuli are associated with feeding or other pleasant events. It is much more difficult to demonstrate classical conditioning in infants and toddlers when the stimuli are aversive, such as loud noises or shock (Fitzgerald & Brackbill, 1976). Because adults care for very young children, learning about aversive stimulation is not a common biological problem for infants and toddlers (Rovee-Collier, 1987).

OPERANT CONDITIONING.

In classical conditioning, infants form expectations about what will happen in their environment. Operant conditioning focuses on the relation between the consequences of behaviour and the likelihood that the behaviour will reoccur. When a child's behaviour leads to pleasant consequences, the child will probably behave similarly in the future; when the child's behaviour leads to unpleasant consequences, the child will probably not repeat the behaviour. When a baby smiles, an adult may hug the baby in return; this pleasing consequence makes the baby more likely to smile in the future. When a baby grabs a family heirloom, an adult may become angry and shout at the baby; these unpleasant consequences make the baby less likely to grab the heirloom in the future.

IMITATION.   Older children, adolescents, and young adults learn much simply by watching others behave. Infants, too, are capable of imitation (Barr & Hayne, 1999). A 10-month-old may imitate an adult waving her finger back-and-forth or imitate another infant who knocks down a tower of blocks.

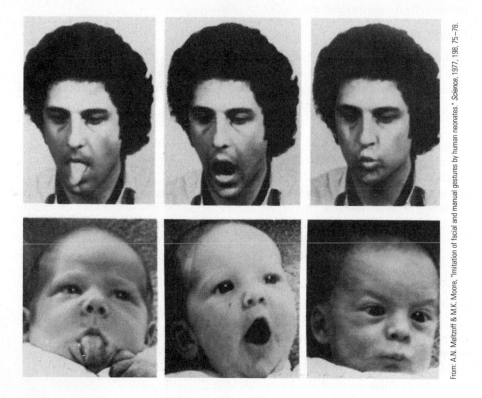

From: A.N. Meltzoff & M.K. Moore, "Imitation of facial and manual gestures by human neonates." *Science*, 1977, 198, 75—78.

Courtesy of Carolyn Rovee-Collier

More startling is the claim that even newborns imitate. As you can see in the photos above, Meltzoff and Moore (1989, 1994) found that 2- to 3-week-olds would stick out their tongue or open and close their mouth to match an adult's acts. This work is controversial because other researchers do not consistently obtain these results. In addition, because the newborns' behaviour is not novel—newborns are already capable of sticking out their tongues as well as opening and closing their mouths—some researchers do not consider this to be a "true" form of imitation (Anisfeld, 1991, 1996). This work may well represent an early, limited form of imitation; over the course of the first year of life, infants are able to imitate a rapidly expanding range of behaviour.

Memory

Young babies remember events for days or even weeks at a time. Some of the studies that opened our eyes to the infant's ability to remember used the method shown in the photo

(Rovee-Collier, 1997, 1999). A ribbon from a mobile is attached to a 2- or 3-month-old's leg; within a few minutes, the baby learns to kick to make the mobile move. When Rovee-Collier brought the mobile to the infants' homes several days or a few weeks later, babies would still kick to make the mobile move. If Rovee-Collier waited several weeks to return, most babies forgot that kicking moved the mobile. When that happened, Rovee-Collier gave them a reminder—she moved the mobile herself without attaching the ribbon to their foot. Then she would return the next day, hook up the apparatus, and the baby would kick to move the mobile.

Rovee-Collier's experiments show that three important features of memory exist as early as 2 and 3 months of age: (1) an event from the past is remembered, (2) over time, the event can no longer be recalled, and (3) a cue can serve to dredge up a memory that seems to have been forgotten.

From these humble origins, memory improves rapidly in older infants and toddlers (Rose, Feldman, & Jankowski, 2001). Youngsters can recall more of what they experience and remember it longer. When youngsters are shown novel actions with toys and later are asked to imitate what they saw, toddlers can remember more than infants and remember the actions for longer periods (Bauer, Burch, & Kleinknecht, 2002). For example, if shown how to make a rattle by first placing a wooden block inside a container, then putting a lid on the container, toddlers are more likely than infants to remember the necessary sequence of steps.

These improvements in memory can be traced, in part, to growth in the brain regions that support memory (Carver & Bauer, 2001; Nelson, 1997). On the one hand, the brain structures primarily responsible for the initial storage of information, including the hippocampus and amygdala, seem to develop very early—by 6 months after birth. On the other hand, the structure responsible for retrieving these stored memories, the frontal cortex, develops much later—into the second year. Development of memory over the first 2 years reflects growth in these two different brain regions.

Understanding Number

Powerful learning and memory skills enable infants to learn much about their worlds. This rapid growth is well illustrated by research on children's understanding of number. Basic number skills originate in infancy, long before babies learn names of numbers. Many babies experience daily variation in quantity. They play with two blocks and see that another baby has three; they watch as a father sorts laundry and finds two black socks but only one blue sock, and they eat one hot dog for lunch while an older brother eats three.

From these experiences, babies apparently come to appreciate that quantity or amount is one of the ways in which objects in the world can differ. That is, research suggests that 5-month-olds can distinguish two objects from three and, less often, three objects from four (Canfield & Smith, 1996; Wynn, 1996). Apparently, infants' perceptual processes enable them to distinguish differences in quantity. That is, just as colours (reds, blues) and shapes (triangles, squares) are basic perceptual properties, small quantities ("twoness" and "threeness") are too.

Strictly speaking, studies like these tell us that infants can distinguish one object from two objects and two objects from three objects. Of course, for older children and adults, these sets don't simply differ; one set has *more* objects than the other. *Ordinality refers to the fact that numbers can differ in magnitude; some values are greater than others.* Near the first birthday, infants can identify the larger set. If 10-month-olds watch an adult place two crackers in one container but three crackers in a second container, the infants usually reach for the container with more crackers (Feigenson, Carey, & Hauser, 2002), showing early sensitivity to the ordinal properties of sets. By 2 years of age, most youngsters know some number words and have begun to count, although usually their counting is full of mistakes. For example, they might count "1, 2, 6, 7" – skipping 3, 4, and 5.

TEST YOURSELF

1. Four-month old Tanya has forgotten that kicking moves a mobile. To remind her of the link between kicking and the mobile's movement, we could _____.

2. According to Piaget, the first two years of life form a distinct phase in human development called the _____ period.

3. During times of various sensory stimuli _____ is a process that determines which sensory information receives additional cognitive processing.

4. Piaget believed that children create _____ theories about how the world works, which allows them to under-

stand new experiences and predict future events.

5. A _____ is an event that infants try to repeat because it produces interesting outcomes with objects.

What forces in the biopsychosocial framework can you see in an infant's progress through the six stages of the sensorimotor period?

Answers: (1) let her view a moving mobile, (2) sensorimotor, (3) attention, (4) naïve, (5) secondary circular reaction

3.6

Language

LEARNING OBJECTIVES

☑ When do infants first hear and make speech sounds?

☑ When do children start to talk? Why?

> **Language**
>
> The Road to Speech
>
> First Words and Many More

Nabina is just a few weeks away from her first birthday. For the past month, she has seemed to understand much of her mother's speech. If her mom asks, "Where's Garfield?" (the family cat), Nabina scans the room and points toward Garfield. Yet Nabina's own speech is still gibberish—she "talks" constantly, but her mother can't understand a word of it. If Nabina apparently understands others' speech, why can't she speak herself?

An extraordinary human achievement occurs soon after the first birthday: Most children speak their first word, which is followed in the ensuing months by several hundred more. This marks the beginning of a child's ability to communicate orally with others. Through speech, youngsters impart their ideas, beliefs, and feelings to family, friends, and others.

Actually, the first spoken words represent the climax of a year's worth of language growth. To tell the story of language acquisition properly and explain Nabina's seemingly strange behaviour, we must begin with the months preceding the first words.

THE ROAD TO SPEECH

The photograph on page 129 depicts a common situation: a baby is upset and a concerned mother is trying to console it. The scene is overflowing with language-related information. The infant, not yet able to talk, is conveying its displeasure by one of the few means of communication available to it—crying. The mother, for her part, is using both verbal and nonverbal measures to cheer her baby, to send the message that the world is really not as bad as it may seem now.

The scene raises two questions about infants as nonspeaking creatures. First, can babies who are unable to speak understand any of the speech that is directed at them?

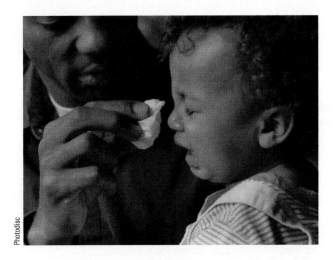

Photodisc

Second, how do infants progress from crying to more effective methods of oral communication, such as speech? Let's start by answering the first question.

Perceiving Speech

Even newborn infants hear remarkably well (pages 109–110). But can babies distinguish speech sounds? To answer this question, we first need to know more about the elements of speech. *The basic building blocks of language are phonemes, which are unique sounds that can be joined to create words.* Phonemes include consonant sounds, such as the sound of *t* in *toe* and *tap*, along with vowel sounds such as the sound of *e* in *get* and *bed*. Infants can distinguish many of these sounds, some of them as early as one month after birth (Aslin, Jusczyk, & Pisoni, 1998).

How do we know that infants can distinguish different vowels and consonants? Researchers have devised a number of clever techniques to determine if babies respond differently to distinct sounds. In one approach, a rubber nipple is connected to a tape recorder so that sucking turns on the tape and sound comes out of a loud-speaker. In just a few minutes, 1-month-olds learn the relation between their sucking and the sound: They suck rapidly to hear a tape that consists of nothing more than the sound of *p* as in *pin, pet,* and *pat* (pronounced "puh").

After a few more minutes, infants seemingly tire of this repetitive sound and suck less often, which represents the habituation phenomenon described on page 125. But, if the tape is changed to a different sound such as the sound of *b* in *bed, bat,* or *bird* (pronounced "buh"), babies begin sucking rapidly again. Evidently, they recognize that the sound of *b* is different from *p* because they suck more often to hear the new sound (Jusczyk, 1995).

THE IMPACT OF LANGUAGE EXPOSURE.   Not all languages use the same set of phonemes; a distinction that is important in one language may be ignored in another. For example, unlike English, French and Polish differentiate between nasal and nonnasal vowels. To hear the difference, say the word *rod*. Now repeat it, but holding your nose. The subtle difference between the two sounds illustrates a non-nasal vowel (the first version of *rod*) and a nasal one (the second).

Because an infant might be exposed to any of the world's languages, it would be adaptive for young infants to be able to perceive a wide range of phonemes. In fact, research shows that infants can distinguish phonemes that are not used in their native language. For example, Japanese does not distinguish the consonant sound of *r* in *rip* from the sound of *l* in *lip*, and Japanese adults trying to learn English have great dif-ficulty distinguishing these sounds. At about 6 months, infants in both Japanese- and English-speaking environments can distinguish them, but by 11 or 12 months, only infants in English-speaking environments can (Werker & Tees, 1999).

Newborns apparently are biologically capable of hearing the entire range of phonemes in all languages worldwide. But as babies grow and are more exposed to a particular language, they only notice the linguistic distinctions that are meaningful in their own language. Specialization in one language apparently comes at a cost; the potential to hear other language sounds easily is lost (Best, 1995).

IDENTIFYING WORDS.   Of course, hearing individual phonemes is only the first step in perceiving speech. One of the biggest challenges for infants is identifying recurring patterns of sounds—words. Imagine, for example, an infant overhearing this conversation between a parent and an older sibling:

Sibling:	Jerry got a new *bike.*
Parent:	Was his old *bike* broken?
Sibling:	No. He'd saved his allowance to buy a new mountain *bike.*

An infant listening to this conversation hears *bike* three times. Can the infant learn from this experience? Yes. When 7- to 8-month-olds hear a word repeatedly in different sentences, they later pay more attention to this word than to words they haven't heard previously. Evidently, 7- and 8-month-olds can listen to sentences and recognize the sound patterns that they hear repeatedly (Juscyzk & Aslin, 1995; Saffran, Aslin, & Newport, 1996). And, by 6 months, infants pay more attention to content words (e.g., nouns, verbs) than to function words (e.g., articles, prepositions), and they look at the correct parent when they hear "mommy" or "daddy" (Shi & Werker, 2001; Tincoff & Jusczyk, 1999).

In normal conversation, there are no silent gaps between words, so how do infants pick out words? Stress is one important clue. English contains many one-syllable words that are stressed and many two-syllable words that have a stressed syllable followed by an unstressed syllable (e.g., *dough'-nut, tooth'-paste, bas'-ket*). Infants pay more attention to stressed syllables than unstressed syllables, which is a good strategy for identifying the beginnings of words (Aslin, Saffran, & Newport, 1998; Mattys et al., 1999).

Of course, stress is not a foolproof sign. Many two-syllable words have stress on the second syllable (e.g., *gui-tar', sur-prise'*), so infants need other methods to identify words in speech. One method is statistical. Infants notice syllables that go together frequently (Jusczyk, 2002). For example, in a study by Aslin, Saffran, and Newport (1998), 8-month-olds heard the following sounds, which consisted of four three-syllable artificial words, said over and over in a random order.

pa bi ku go la tu da ro pi ti bu do da ro pi go la tu pa bi ku da ro pi . . .

We've underlined the words and inserted gaps between them so you can see them more easily, but in the study there were no breaks at all—just a steady flow of syllables for three minutes. Later, infants listened to these words less than to new words that were novel combinations of the same syllables. They had detected *pa bi ku, go la tu, da ro pi,* and *ti bu do* as familiar patterns and listened to them less than to words like *tu da ro,* a new word made up from syllables they'd already heard.

Yet another way that infants identify words is through their emerging knowledge of how sounds are used in their native language. For example, think about these two pairs of sounds: *s* followed by *t* and *s* followed by *d*. Both pairs of sounds are quite common at the end of one word and the beginning of the next: bu*s t*akes, ki*ss t*ook; thi*s d*og, pa*ss d*irectly. However, *s* and *t* occur frequently within a word (*st*op, li*st*, pe*st*, *st*ink) but *s* and *d* do not. Consequently, when *d* follows an *s,* it probably starts a new word. In fact, 9-month-olds follow rules like this one. When they hear novel words embedded in continuous speech, they're more likely to identify the novel word when the final sound in the preceding word occurs infrequently with the first sound of the novel word (Mattys & Jusczyk, 2001).

Thus, infants use many powerful tools to identify words in speech. Of course, they don't yet understand the meanings of these words; they just recognize a word as a distinct configuration of sounds.

Parents (and other adults) often help infants master language sounds by talking in a distinctive style. *In **infant-directed speech,** adults speak slowly and with exaggerated changes in pitch and loudness.* If you could hear the mother in the photo (page 131) talking to her baby, you would notice that she alternates between speaking softly and loudly and between high and low pitches and that her speech seems very expressive emotionally (Trainor, Austin, & Desjardins, 2000). (Infant-directed speech is also known as *motherese,* because this form of speaking was first noted in mothers, although it's now known that most caregivers talk this way to infants.)

Infant-directed speech may attract infants' attention more than adult-directed speech (Kaplan et al., 1995; Lewkowicz, 2000) because its slower pace and accentuated changes provide infants with more, and more salient, language clues. In addition, infant-directed speech includes especially good examples of vowels (Kuhl et al., 1997), which may help infants learn to distinguish these sounds.

Infant-directed speech, then, helps infants perceive the sounds that are fundamental to their language. But how do infants accomplish the next step, producing speech? We answer this question next.

Steps to Speech

As any new parent can testify, newborns and young babies make many sounds— they cry, burp, and sneeze. Language-based sounds don't appear immediately. *At two months, infants begin to produce vowel-like sounds, such as "ooooooo" or "ahhhhhh," a phenomenon known as cooing.* Sometimes infants become quite excited as they coo, perhaps reflecting the joy of simply playing with sounds.

After cooing comes **babbling,** *speechlike sound that has no meaning.* A typical 6-month-old might say "dah" or "bah," utterances that sound like a single syllable consisting of a consonant and a vowel. Over the next few months, babbling becomes more elaborate as babies apparently experiment with more complex speech sounds. Older infants sometimes repeat a sound as in "bahbahbah" and begin to combine different sounds, "dahmahbah" (Hoff, 2001).

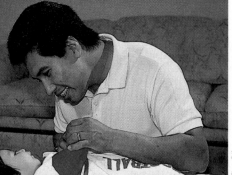

At roughly 8 to 11 months, infants' babbling sounds more like real speech because infants stress some syllables and vary the pitch of their speech (B. L. Davis et al., 2000). In English declarative sentences, for example, pitch first rises, then falls toward the end of the sentence. In questions, however, the pitch is level, then rises toward the end of the question. Older babies' babbling reflects these patterns: Babies who are brought up by English-speaking parents have both the declarative and question patterns of intonation in their babbling. *Babies exposed to a language with different patterns of* **intonation,** *such as Japanese or French, reflect their language's intonation in their babbling* (Levitt & Utman, 1992).

The appearance of intonation in babbling indicates a strong link between perception and production of speech: Infants' babbling is influenced by the characteristics of the speech that they hear. Beginning in the middle of the first year, infants try to reproduce the sounds of language that others use in trying to communicate with them (or, in the case of deaf infants with deaf parents, the signs that others use). Hearing *dog,* an infant may first say "dod," then "gog" before finally saying "dog" correctly. In the same way that beginning typists gradually link movements of their fingers with particular keys, through babbling infants learn to use their lips, tongue, and teeth to produce specific sounds, gradually making sounds that approximate real words (Poulson et al., 1991).

These developments in production of sound, coupled with the 1-year-old's advanced ability to perceive speech sounds, clearly set the stage for the infant's first true words.

THINK ABOUT IT

Compare and contrast the steps in learning to make speech sounds with the stages of Piaget's sensorimotor period.

FIRST WORDS AND MANY MORE

Remember that Nabina, the 1-year-old in the vignette, looks at the family cat when she hears its name. This phenomenon is common in 10- to 14-month-olds. They appear to understand what others say despite the fact that they have yet to speak. In response to "Where is the book?" children will go find the book. They grasp the question, even though their own speech is limited to advanced babbling (Fenson et al., 1994; Hoff-Ginsberg, 1997). Evidently, children have made the link between speech sounds and particular objects, even though they cannot yet manufacture the sounds themselves. As fluent adult speakers, we forget that speech is a motor skill requiring perfect timing and tremendous coordination.

A few months later, most youngsters utter their first words. Typically, these words have a structure borrowed from their advanced babbling, consisting of a consonant-vowel pair that may be repeated. *Mama* and *dada* are common examples of this type of construction. Other common words in early vocabularies denote animals, food, and toys (Caselli et al., 1995; Nelson, 1973). Also common are words that denote actions (e.g., *go*). By the age of 2, youngsters have a vocabulary of a few hundred words.; by 6, a typical child's vocabulary includes more than 10,000 words (Anglin, 1993). However, children differ markedly in the size of their vocabulary (Fenson et al., 1994). At 16 months, vocabularies typically range from as few as 10 words to as many as 150; at two and a half years, from 375 words to 650.

What's What? Fast Mapping of Words

Having the insight that a word can symbolize an object or action, the young talker now faces a formidable task. Matching a word with its exact referent is challenging because most words have many plausible but incorrect referents. To illustrate, imagine what's going through the mind of the child whose mother has just pointed to a flower and said, "Flower. This is a flower. See the flower." This all seems crystal clear to you and incredibly straightforward. But what might the child learn from this episode? Perhaps the correct referent for "flower." But a youngster could, just as reasonably, conclude that "flower" refers to a petal, to the colour of the flower, or to your actions in demonstrating the flower.

Surprisingly, though, most youngsters learn the proper meanings of simple words in just a few presentations. *Children's ability to connect new words to referents so rapidly that they cannot be considering all possible meanings for the new word is termed **fast mapping**.* How can young children learn new words so rapidly? Researchers believe many factors contribute to young children's rapid word learning (Hollich et al., 2000); one factor is joint attention, which will be discussed in this chapter, and other factors will be discussed in Chapter 5.

JOINT ATTENTION. Parents encourage word learning by carefully watching what interests their children. When toddlers touch or look at an object, parents often label it for them. When a youngster points to a banana, a parent may say, "Banana, that's a banana." Of course, to take advantage of this help, infants must be able to tell when parents are labelling instead of just conversing. In fact, when adults label an unfamiliar object, 18- to 20-month-olds assume that the label is the object's name *only* when adults show signs that they are referring to the object. For example, toddlers are more likely to learn the name of an object or action when adults look at the object or action while saying its name than when adults look elsewhere while labelling (Baldwin et al., 1996; Poulin-Dubois & Forbes, 2002). Thus, beginning in the toddler years, parents and children work together to create conditions that foster word learning: Parents label objects and youngsters rely on adults' behaviour to interpret the words they hear.

TABLE 3.5	Major Milestones of Language Development
Age	*Milestones*
Birth to 1 year	Babies hear phonemes; they begin to coo and then babble.
About the 1st birthday	Babies begin to talk and to gesture, showing they have begun to use symbols.
1–2 years	Vocabulary expands rapidly (due to fast mapping); referential and expressive language learning styles appear; two-word sentences emerge in telegraphic speech; turn-taking is evident in communication.

TEST YOURSELF

1. _____ are fundamental sounds used to create words.

2. Infants' mastery of language sounds may be fostered by _____, in which adults speak slowly and exaggerate changes in pitch and loudness.

3. Older infants' babbling often includes _____, a pattern of rising and falling pitch that distinguishes statements from questions.

Why do infants seem to prefer "motherese" and how does it help them produce speech sounds necessary for language development?

Answers: (1) Phonemes, (2) infant-directed speech, (3) intonation

PUTTING IT ALL TOGETHER

The first two years of life are remarkable. We saw that newborn babies are endowed with reflexes that prepare them well for life outside the uterus and that their behaviour is already well organized into a number of distinct states. We learned that physical growth is extraordinarily rapid but can be slowed when children are malnourished. Different regions of the infant's brain are already regulating distinct functions, such as goal-directed behaviour.

We also looked at improvements in motor skill. Infants gradually become more mobile during the first year. Most begin to walk soon after their first birthday, reflecting biological maturation and integration of the different component skills involved in walking.

Paralleling changes in locomotion are changes in fine motor skills. During the first year, infants become more skilled at grasping and manipulating objects.

We saw that infants are endowed with powerful perceptual skills. Even newborn babies can smell, taste, feel, hear, and see—in some cases with remarkable accuracy.

We learned that Piaget explained cognitive development in a progression through qualitatively different stages. The first two years form the sensorimotor period, which has as its climax the ability to use symbols. For example, infants like Nabina often understand words long before they have spoken.

SUMMARY

3.1 The Newborn

The Newborn's Reflexes

- Babies are born with a number of different reflexes. Some help them adjust to life outside the uterus, some help protect them from danger, and some serve as the basis for later voluntary motor behaviour.

Assessing the Newborn

- The Apgar measures five vital signs to determine a newborn baby's physical well-being. The Neonatal Behavioural Assessment Scale provides a comprehensive evaluation of a baby's behavioural and physical status.

Sleeping and Waking States

- Newborns spend their day in one of four states: alert inactivity, waking activity, crying, and sleeping. A newborn's crying includes a basic cry, an angry cry, and a pain cry. The best way to calm a crying baby is by putting it on the shoulder and rocking.

- Newborns spend approximately two-thirds of every day asleep and go through a complete sleep-wake cycle once every four hours. By three or four months, babies sleep through the night. Newborns spend about half their time asleep in REM sleep, an active form of sleep that may stimulate growth in the nervous system.

- Some healthy babies die from sudden infant death syndrome. Factors that contribute to SIDS are prematurity, low birth weight, and mothers' smoking. Also, babies are vulnerable to SIDS when they sleep on their stomach and when they are overheated. The goal of the Back to Sleep campaign is to prevent SIDS by encouraging parents to have infants sleep on their back.

3.2 Physical Development

Growth of the Body

- Physical growth is particularly rapid during infancy, but babies of the same age differ considerably in their heights and weights. Size at maturity is largely determined by heredity.

- The head and trunk develop before the legs. Consequently, infants and young children have disproportionately large heads and trunks.

- Infants must consume a large number of calories relative to their body weight, primarily because of the energy that is required for growth. Breastfeeding and bottle-feeding both provide babies with adequate nutrition.

- Malnutrition is a worldwide problem that is particularly harmful during infancy when growth is so rapid. Treating malnutrition adequately requires improving children's diet and training their parents to provide stimulating environments.

The Emerging Nervous System

- A nerve cell, called a *neuron,* includes a cell body, a dendrite, and an axon. The mature brain consists of billions of neurons, organized into nearly identical left and right hemispheres connected by the corpus callosum. The cerebral cortex regulates most of the functions we think of as distinctively human. The frontal cortex is associated with personality and goal-directed behaviour; the left hemisphere of the cortex with language; and the right hemisphere of the cortex with nonverbal processes such as perceiving music and regulating emotions.

- Brain structure begins in prenatal development when neurons form at an incredible rate. After birth, neurons in the central nervous system become wrapped in myelin, enabling them to transmit information more rapidly. Throughout childhood, unused synapses disappear gradually through a process of pruning.

- Methods used to investigate brain functioning in children include (a) studying children with brain damage, (b) recording electrical activity (the electroencephalogram or EEG), and (c) using imaging techniques. Research with these methods reveals that many regions of an infant's brain specialize early in life: the frontal cortex specializes in decision-making, the left hemisphere in language, and the right hemisphere in processing spatial information.

- The brain is moderately plastic. On the one hand, most brains are organized in much the same way. On the other hand, following brain injury, cognitive processes are sometimes transferred to undamaged neurons.

3.3 Moving and Grasping—Early Motor Skills

Locomotion

- Infants acquire a series of locomotor skills during their first year, culminating in walking a few months after the first birthday. Like most motor skills, learning to walk involves differentiation of individual skills, such as maintaining balance and using the legs alternately, and then integrating these skills into a coherent whole.

Fine Motor Skills

- Infants first use only one hand at a time, then both hands independently, then both hands in common actions and, finally, at about five months of age, both hands in different actions with a common purpose.

▥ Most people are right-handed, a preference that emerges after the first birthday. Handedness is determined by heredity but can also be influenced by cultural values.

3.4 Coming to Know the World: Perception

Smell and Taste

▥ Newborns are able to smell, and some can recognize their mother's odour; they also taste, preferring sweet substances and responding negatively to bitter and sour tastes.

Touch and Pain

▥ Infants respond to touch. They probably experience pain, because their responses to painful stimuli are similar to those of older children.

Hearing

▥ Babies can hear. More important, they can distinguish different sounds and use sound to locate objects in space.

Seeing

▥ A newborn's visual acuity is relatively poor, but 1-year-olds can see as well as an adult with normal vision. Colour vision develops as different sets of cones begin to function, a process that seems to be complete by 3 or 4 months of age. Infants perceive depth based on retinal disparity and cues from motion. They also use motion to recognize objects.

Integrating Sensory Information

▥ Infants coordinate information from different senses (e.g., sight and sound, sight and touch). Infants are particularly attentive to information presented redundantly to several senses.

3.5 The Onset of Thinking

Basic Principles of Cognitive Development

▥ In Piaget's view, children construct their own understanding of the world by creating schemes, categories of related events, objects, and knowledge. Infants' schemes are based on actions, but older children's and adolescents' schemes are based on functional, conceptual, and abstract properties.

▥ Schemes change constantly. In assimilation, experiences are readily incorporated into existing schemes. In accommodation, experiences cause schemes to be modified.

▥ When accommodation becomes much more common than assimilation, this is a sign that children's schemes are inadequate, so children reorganize them. This reorganization produces four different phases of mental development from infancy through adulthood.

Sensorimotor Thinking

▥ The first two years of life constitute Piaget's sensorimotor period, which is divided into six stages. As infants progress through the stages, schemes become more sophisticated. By 8 to 12 months, one scheme is used in the service of another; by 12 to 18 months, infants experiment with schemes; and by 18 to 24 months, infants engage in symbolic processing.

Evaluating Piaget's Theory

▥ One important contribution of Piaget's theory is the view that children actively try to understand their world. Another contribution is specifying conditions that foster cognitive development. However, the theory has been criticized because children's performance on tasks is sometimes better explained by ideas that are not part of his theory. Another shortcoming is that children's performance from one task to the next is not as consistent as the theory predicts it to be.

Extending Piaget's Account: Children's Naïve Theories

▥ In contrast to Piaget's idea that children create a comprehensive theory that integrates all their knowledge, the modern view is that children are specialists, generating naïve theories in particular domains, including physics and biology. Infants understand many properties of objects: they know how objects move, what happens when objects collide, and that objects fall when not supported.

▥ Infants understand the difference between animate and inanimate objects. As preschoolers, children know that, unlike inanimate objects, animate objects move themselves, grow, have distinct internal parts, resemble their parents, and repair through healing.

Information Processing During Infancy

▥ According to the information-processing view, cognitive development involves changes in mental hardware and in mental software.

▥ Infants use habituation to filter unimportant stimuli. Compared to older children, preschoolers are less able to pay attention to task-relevant information. Their attention can be improved by making irrelevant stimuli less noticeable.

▥ Infants are capable of many forms of learning, including classical conditioning, operant conditioning, and imitation.

▥ Infants can remember and can be reminded of events they seem to have forgotten.

3.6 Language

The Road to Speech

▪ Phonemes are the basic units of sound from which words are constructed. Infants can hear phonemes soon after birth. They can even hear phonemes that are not used in their native language, but this ability diminishes after the first birthday.

▪ Infant-directed speech is adults' speech to infants that is slower and has greater variation in pitch and loudness. Infants prefer infant-directed speech, perhaps because it gives them additional language clues.

▪ Newborns' communication is limited to crying, but at about three months of age babies coo. Babbling soon follows, consisting of a single syllable; over several months, infants' babbling comes to include longer syllables and intonation.

First Words and Many More

▪ After a brief period in which children appear to understand others' speech but do not speak themselves, most infants begin to speak around the first birthday. The first use of words is triggered by the realization that words are symbols.

KEY TERMS

reflexes (86)
survival reflexes (86)
primitive reflexes (86)
alert inactivity (88)
waking activity (88)
crying (88)
sleeping (88)
basic cry (88)
angry cry (88)
pain cry (88)
rapid-eye-movement (REM) sleep (89)
regular (nonREM) sleep (89)
sudden infant death syndrome (SIDS) (89)
cephalocaudal (92)
proximodistal (93)
malnourished (95)
neuron (96)
cell body (96)
dendrite (97)
axon (97)
terminal button (97)
neurotransmitter (97)

hemispheres (97)
corpus callosum (97)
frontal cortex (97)
neural plate (98)
myelin (98)
synaptic pruning (98)
electroencephalogram (EEG) (99)
functional magnetic resonance imaging (F-MRI) (99)
positron emission tomography (PET-scan) (99)
neuroplasticity (100)
motor skills (101)
locomote (102)
fine motor skills (102)
toddling (102)
toddler (102)
dynamic systems theory (102)
differentiation (104)
integration (104)
ulnar grasp (106)
pincer grasp (106)
perception (108)
visual acuity (110)

cones (111)
visual cliff (112)
retinal disparity (112)
intersensory redundancy (115)
scheme (118)
assimilation (118)
accommodation (118)
equilibration (119)
sensorimotor period (120)
primary circular reaction (120)
secondary circular reaction (120)
tertiary circular reaction (121)
core knowledge hypothesis (123)
attention (124)
orienting response (125)
habituation (125)
classical conditioning (125)
ordinality (127)
phonemes (129)
infant-directed speech (130)
cooing (131)
babbling (131)
intonation (131)
fast mapping (132)

SEE FOR YOURSELF: APPLYING WHAT YOU'VE LEARNED

Words can hardly capture the miracle of a newborn baby. If you have never seen a newborn, you need to see one. If possible, arrange a visit to someone you know who has a newborn. As you watch the baby, look for reflexive behaviour and changes in states. Watch while the baby sucks its fingers. Observe the baby when it is awake and alert, then note how long the baby stays this way. When alertness wanes, watch for the behaviours that replace it. Have you observed that newborns look and act differently from each other? Do all babies respond similarly to stimulation such as light and sound? When they're awake, some babies are more active than others. A recurring theme in this book is an appreciation of the wonderful variety and diversity found among human beings, and this is already evident in humans who are hours or days old. See for yourself!

LEARN MORE ABOUT IT

Readings

Aslin, R. N. (1987). Visual and auditory discrimination in infancy. In J. D. Osofsky (Ed.), *Handbook of infant development* (2nd ed.). New York: Wiley. This text is a comprehensive but technical account of research on infant perception.

Bartsch, K., & Wellman, H. M. (1995). *Children talk about the mind.* New York: Oxford. Wellman is one of the leading investigators of theory of mind and Bartsch is his student. In this book, they use actual samples of children's talk to show growth in children's understanding of the mind.

Brazelton, T. B. (1983). *Infants and mothers: Differences in development.* New York: Delta/Seymour Lawrence. In this classic book the author, a well-known pediatrician and creator of the Neonatal Behavioural Assessment Scale (NBAS), illustrates striking differences among babies by examining a few case studies in detail.

Kopp, C. (1993). *Baby steps: The "whys" of your child's behaviour in the first two years.* New York: Freeman. As the title indicates, this book is not about newborns only. However, we recommend it because the author begins with newborn babies and traces the changes that occur in physical, motor, mental, and socioemotional development.

Lamb, M.E., Bornstein, M.H., Teti, D.M. (2002). *Development in infancy: An introduction* (4th ed.). Mahwah, NJ: Erlbaum. The focus of this book is on the scientific progress that has been made in the study of infants.

Tanner, J. M. (1990). *Fetus into man: Physical growth from conception to maturity* (2nd ed.). Cambridge, MA: Harvard University Press. Tanner is a leading authority and presents a straightforward account of human growth.

 For additional readings, explore InfoTrac® College Edition, your online library. Go to http://www.infotrac.thomsonlearning.com.

Websites

http://www.cecw-cepb.ca

The Centre of Excellence for Children's Well-Being is a Health Canada website that is written by medical professionals and contains helpful information on specific stages of development as well as related health issues.

http://www.cps.ca

The Canadian Paediatric Society website covers all aspects of infant development for professionals and includes a helpful "caring for kids" link for parents.

http://kidshealth.org/

The Nemours Foundation maintains "Kidshealth," a site that has information about children's growth and nutrition.

Website addresses are subject to change. The *Human Development* book companion website can be accessed for updated links.

The Human Development Book Companion Website

See http://www.humandevelopment.nelson.com for practice quiz questions, Internet links, updates, critical thinking exercises, discussion forums, and more.

 ### Life-Span CD-ROM

For more information on the concepts covered in this chapter, go to Module 1: Prenatal Development, Birth, and the Newborn

• The Newborn

Module 2: Infancy and Toddlerhood

• Physical Growth and Motor Development

Getty Images

CHAPTER 4

Entering the Social World

SOCIOEMOTIONAL DEVELOPMENT IN INFANCY

In this chapter, we trace the origins of social relationships, beginning with the first social relationship—between an infant and a parent. You will also see how this relationship may be affected by the separation that comes when parents work outside the home.

Interactions with parents and others are often full of emotions—happiness, satisfaction, anger, and guilt, to name just a few. In the second section, you'll see how children express different emotions and how they recognize others' emotions.

4.1

Beginnings: Trust and Attachment

LEARNING OBJECTIVES

- What are Erikson's first two stages of psychosocial development?
- How do infants form emotional attachments to mother, father, and other significant people in their lives?
- What are the different varieties of attachment relationships, how do they arise, and what are their consequences?
- Is attachment jeopardized when parents of infants are employed outside of the home?

Kendra's son Alex is a happy, affectionate 18-month-old. Kendra so loves spending time with him that she is avoiding an important decision. She wants to return to her job as a loan officer at the local bank. Kendra knows a woman in the neighbourhood who has cared for some of her friends' children, and they all think she is a fantastic babysitter. But Kendra still has a nagging feeling that going back to work isn't a "motherly" thing to do—that being away during the day may hamper Alex's development.

Both developmental theorists and parents alike think the socioemotional relationship that develops between an infant and a parent (usually, but not necessarily, the mother) is special. This is a baby's first relationship, so theorists and parents believe it should be satisfying and trouble-free to set the stage for later relationships. In this section, we'll look at the steps involved in creating the baby's first emotional relationship. Along the way, you'll see how this relationship is affected by the separation that sometimes comes when a parent like Kendra works full-time.

ERIKSON'S STAGES OF EARLY PSYCHOSOCIAL DEVELOPMENT

Some of our keenest insights into the nature of psychosocial development come from a theory proposed by Erik Erikson (1982). We first encountered Erikson's theory in Chapter 1; recall that he describes development as a series of eight stages, each with a unique crisis for psychosocial growth. When a crisis is resolved successfully, an area of psychosocial strength is established. When the crisis is not resolved, that aspect of psychosocial development is stunted, which may limit the individual's ability to resolve future crises.

In Erikson's theory, infancy is represented by two stages, shown in Table 4.1. Let's take a closer look at each stage.

TABLE 4.1	Erikson's First Two Stages	
Age	*Crisis*	*Strength*
Infancy	Basic trust vs. mistrust	Hope
1–3 years	Autonomy vs. shame and doubt	Will

Basic Trust Versus Mistrust

Erikson argues that a sense of trust in oneself and others is the foundation of human development. Newborns leave the warmth and security of the uterus for an unfamiliar world. If parents respond to their infant's needs consistently, the infant comes to trust and feel secure in the world. Of course, the world is not always pleasant and can sometimes be dangerous. Parents may not always reach a falling baby in time, or they may accidentally feed an infant food that is too hot. Erikson sees value in these experiences, because infants learn mistrust. *With a proper balance of trust and mistrust, infants can acquire* **hope,** *which is an openness to new experience tempered by wariness that discomfort or danger may arise.*

Autonomy Versus Shame and Doubt

Between 1 and 3 years of age, children gradually come to understand that they can control their own actions. With this understanding, children strive for autonomy, for independence from others. However, autonomy is counteracted by doubt that the child can handle demanding situations and by shame that may result from failure. *A blend of autonomy, shame, and doubt gives rise to* **will,** *the knowledge that, within limits, youngsters can act on their world intentionally.*

One of the strengths of Erikson's theory is its ability to tie together important psychosocial developments across the entire life span. We will return to the remaining stages in later chapters. For now, let's concentrate on the first of Erikson's crises—the establishment of trust in the world—and look at the formation of bonds between infants and parents.

THE GROWTH OF ATTACHMENT

Sigmund Freud was the first modern theorist to emphasize the importance of the infant's emotional ties to the mother. Today, however, the dominant view of early human relationships is that of John Bowlby (1969). *His work originated in* **ethology,** *a branch of biology concerned with the adaptive behaviours of different species. Bowlby believed that children who form an* **attachment** *to an adult—that is, an enduring socioemotional relationship—are more likely to survive.* This person is usually the mother but need not be; the key is a strong emotional relationship with a responsive, caring person. Attachments also form with fathers, grandparents, and others. In the following section on attachment, reference is usually made to the infant's relationship with the mother, although clearly the primary caregiver for the infant could be the father or another adult.

Bowlby argued that evolutionary pressure favours behaviours likely to elicit caregiving from an adult, such as clinging, sucking, crying, and smiling. That is, over the course of human evolution, these behaviours have become a standard part of the human infant's biological heritage. Together with adults' responses, they create an interactive system that leads to the formation of attachment relationships.

Let's look at some of the steps in the formation of such attachments.

Steps Toward Attachment

The attachment relationship develops gradually over the first several months after birth, reflecting the baby's growing cognitive skill (described in Chapter 3). The first step is for the infant to learn the difference between people and other objects. Typically, in the first few months, babies begin to respond differently to people and to objects—for example, smiling more and vocalizing more to people. This suggests that they have begun to identify members of the social world.

During these months, mother and infant begin to synchronize their interactions (Nwokah & Fogel, 1993). Remember from Chapter 3 that young babies' behaviour goes through cycles. Infants move from a state in which they are alert and attentive to a state in which they are distressed and inattentive. Caregivers begin to recognize these states of behaviour and adjust their own behaviour accordingly. A mother who notices that her baby is awake and alert begins to smile at her baby and talk to it. These interactions often continue until the baby's state changes, which prompts the mother to stop. By 3 months of age, if the baby is

> **THINK ABOUT IT**
>
> Based on Piaget's description of infancy (pages 120–121), what cognitive skills might be important prerequisites for the formation of an attachment relationship?

alert and the mother does not interact but just stares silently, the baby becomes at least moderately distressed, looking away from her and sometimes crying (Toda & Fogel, 1993).

Thus, interactions between mothers and infants gradually become well coordinated. When vocalizing, mothers and infants alternate more smoothly between speaking and listening (Jaffe et al., 2001). And they begin to calibrate their behaviours so that they are both "on" at the same time (Gable & Isabella, 1992). These interactions provide the foundation for more sophisticated communication and foster the infant's trust that the mother will respond predictably and reassuringly.

By approximately 6 or 7 months, most infants have singled out the attachment figure—usually the mother—as a special individual (Thompson, 1998). An infant smiles at the mother and clings to her more than to other people. The attachment figure has emerged as the infant's stable socioemotional base. For example, a

7-month-old like the one in the photograph may explore a novel environment but periodically look toward the mother, as if seeking reassurance that all is well. Such behaviour suggests that the infant trusts and has confidence in the mother, and it indicates that the attachment relationship has been established.

After infants become attached to their mother, they rapidly develop attachment relationships with other people, including their father, siblings, and grandparents (Schaffer & Emerson, 1964). Let's look at the nature of infants' relationships with their fathers.

Father-Infant Relationships

In North America, attachment typically first develops between infants and their mothers because mothers are most often the primary caregivers. However, most babies soon become attached to their fathers too (Belsky, 1996; Parke, 1995).

Although infants usually become attached to both parents, they interact with them differently. Fathers tend to spend much more time playing with their babies than they do taking care of them. In many countries around the world "playmate" is the customary role for fathers (Roopnarine, 1992). Fathers even play with infants differently than mothers do. Rough-and-tumble, physical play is the norm for fathers, whereas mothers spend more time reading and talking to babies, showing them toys, and playing games like pat-a-cake (Parke, 1990). These differences in interaction style remain even when fathers care for their infants full-time while mothers are employed full-time outside the home (Lamb & Oppenheim, 1989).

Given the opportunity to play with mothers or fathers, infants more often choose their fathers. However, when infants are distressed, mothers are preferred (Field, 1990). Thus, although most infants become attached to both parents, mothers and fathers typically have distinctive roles in their children's early social development.

Forms of Attachment

Thanks to biology, virtually all infants behave in ways that elicit caregiving from adults, and, because of this behaviour, attachment almost always develops between infant and caregiver by 8 or 9 months of age. However, attachment can take many forms, and environmental factors help determine the quality of attachment between infants and caregivers. Mary Ainsworth, who was raised in Canada and received her university education at the University of Toronto, pioneered the study of attachment relationships using a procedure that has come to be known as the Strange Situation

(1978, 1993). You can see in Table 4.2 that the Strange Situation involves a series of episodes, each about three minutes long. The mother and infant enter an unfamiliar room filled with interesting toys. The mother leaves briefly, then mother and baby are reunited. Meanwhile, the experimenter observes the baby, recording its response to both separation and reunion.

TABLE 4.2	Sequence of Events in the Strange Situation

Step	Action
1	Observer shows the experimental room to mother and infant, then leaves the room.
2	Infant is allowed to explore the playroom for three minutes; mother watches but does not participate.
3	A stranger enters the room and remains silent for one minute, then talks to the baby for a minute, then approaches the baby. Mother leaves unobtrusively.
4	The stranger does not play with the baby but attempts to comfort the baby as necessary.
5	After three minutes, the mother returns, greets, and consoles the baby.
6	When the baby has returned to play, the mother leaves again, this time saying "bye-bye" as she leaves.
7	Stranger attempts to calm and play with the baby.
8	After three minutes, the mother returns, and the stranger leaves.

Based on how the infant reacts to separation from, and reunion with, the mother, Ainsworth and other researchers have discovered four primary types of attachment relationships (Ainsworth, 1993; Main & Cassidy, 1988). One is a secure attachment, and three are different types of insecure attachment (avoidant, resistant, and disorganized):

- **Secure attachment:** *The baby may or may not cry when the mother leaves, but when she returns, the baby wants to be with her and if the baby is crying, it stops.* Babies in this group seem to be saying, "I missed you terribly, I'm delighted to see you, but now that all is well, I'll get back to what I was doing." Approximately two-thirds of infants in normative samples have this form of attachment (van IJzendoorn et al., 1992).

- **Avoidant attachment:** *The baby is not upset when the mother leaves and, when she returns, may ignore her by looking or turning away.* Infants with an avoidant attachment look as if they're saying, "You left me again. I always have to take care of myself!" Approximately 20% of infants in normative samples have this form of attachment (van IJzendorn et al., 1992), which is one of the three forms of insecure attachment.

© Laura Dwight

- **Resistant attachment:** *The baby is upset when the mother leaves and remains upset or even angry when she returns, and is difficult to console.* Like the baby in the photo, these babies seem to be telling the mother, "Why do you do this? I need you desperately and yet you just leave me without warning. I get so angry when you're like this." Approximately 14% of babies in normative samples have this form of attachment (van IJzendoorn et al., 1992), which is another form of insecure attachment.

⬛ *Disorganized (disoriented) attachment: The baby seems confused when the mother leaves and when she returns, as if not really understanding what's happening.* The baby often behaves in contradictory ways, such as nearing the mother when she returns but not looking at her, as if wondering, "What's happening? I want you to be here, but you left and now you're back. I don't get what's going on!" It is estimated that 15% of babies from normative backgrounds have this type of attachment relationship, the last of the three kinds of insecure attachment (van IJzendoorn et al., 1992).

More than 30 years later, the Strange Situation remains an important tool for studying attachment. But some scientists have criticized its emphasis on separation and reunion as the primary means for assessing quality of attachment; they suggest that what is considered an appropriate response to separation may not be the same in all cultures (Rothbaum et al., 2000). Consequently, investigators now use other methods to complement the Strange Situation. One of them, the Attachment Q-Set, can be used with young children as well as infants and toddlers. In this method, trained observers watch mothers and children interact at home; then the observer rates the interaction on many attachment-related behaviours (e.g., "Child greets mother with a big smile when she enters the room"). The ratings are totalled to provide a measure of the security of the child's attachment.

Cross-cultural studies from around the world indicate that the majority of infants were classified as securely attached. Whether measured with the Strange Situation or the Attachment Q-Set, secure attachments are the most common throughout the world as you can see in Figure 4.1 (van IJzendoorn & Kroonenberg, 1988; van IJzendoorn & Sagi, 1998). This is fortunate because, as you'll see, a secure attachment provides a solid basis for subsequent social development.

Infants typically form the same type of attachment relationships with both parents (Fox, Kimmerly, & Schafer, 1991). An infant who is securely attached to its mother is usually securely attached to its father too. In addition, when an infant is securely attached, the infant's siblings are likely to be securely attached too, especially when they're the same sex (van IJzendoorn et al., 2000). However, you shouldn't conclude that security of attachment is etched in stone in infancy. Attachment security can and does change, particularly when changes in family circumstances (e.g., birth of a sibling, divorce) produce a change in the quality of care a child receives (Sagi et al., 2002; Thompson, 2000).

FIGURE 4.1   **Secure Attachment**

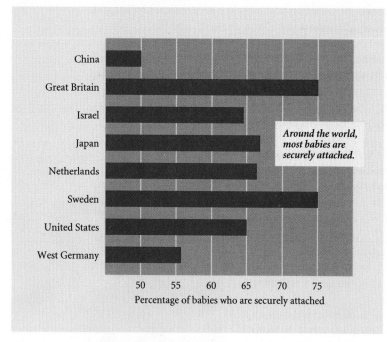

Consequences of Attachment

Erikson and other theorists (e.g., Waters & Cummings, 2000) believe that infant-parent attachment, the first social relationship, lays the foundation for all of the infant's later social relationships. In this view, infants who experience the trust and compassion of a secure attachment should develop into preschool children who interact confidently and successfully with their peers. In contrast, infants who do not experience a successful, satisfying first relationship should be more prone to problems in their social interactions as preschoolers.

Many findings are consistent with these predictions. For example, children with secure attachment relationships have higher-quality friendships and fewer conflicts in their friendships than children with insecure attachment relationships (Lieberman, Doyle, & Markiewicz, 1999). And school-age children are less likely to have behaviour problems if they have secure attachment relationships and more likely to have behaviour problems if they have insecure attachment relationships (Carlson, 1998; Moss et al., 1998).

However, the most compelling evidence comes from a meta-analysis of 63 studies that examined possible links between parent–child attachment and children's peer relations (Schneider, Atkinson, & Tardif, 2001). As predicted, children with secure attachments tended to have better relations with their peers and, in particular, had higher-quality friendships. And, although some theorists (Thompson, 1998) have argued that an insecure attachment is particularly detrimental to peer relations in children who are exposed to other risk factors (e.g., they have a history of maltreatment, their parents have a psychiatric disorder), the positive relation between attachment and peer relations was evident in children from high- and low-risk groups.

The conclusion seems inescapable: Secure attachment serves as the prototype for later successful social interactions. That is, a secure attachment evidently promotes trust and confidence in other humans, which leads to more skilled social interactions later in childhood (Thompson, 1998).

Of course, attachment is only the first of many steps along the long road of social development. Infants with insecure attachments are not forever damned, but this initial misstep *can* interfere with their social development. Consequently, we need to look at the conditions that determine the quality of attachment, which is the topic of the Forces in Action feature.

FORCES IN ACTION

What Determines Quality of Attachment?

The answer to this question begins with biological forces. Remember, infants' biological heritage includes behaviours such as clinging and smiling, which are designed to elicit caregiving from adults. Along with their appearance, such behaviours make it clear that babies are dependent on others, which prods adults to care for them.

Once caregiving is under way, the quality of attachment reflects the quality of interaction between parents and their babies (DeWolff & van IJzendoorn, 1997). A secure attachment is most likely when parents respond to their infants predictably and appropriately. For example, Fabio always notices when his son Sasha smiles or talks. When Sasha cries, gestures, or tries to communicate in other ways, Fabio attempts to understand Sasha's intent and respond appropriately. Behaviours like Fabio's evidently help convey to babies that social interactions are pre-

dictable and satisfying (Pederson et al., 1998). Apparently, they instil in infants the trust and confidence that is the hallmark of secure attachment.

Of course, not all caregivers react to babies in a reliable and proper manner. Some respond intermittently or only after the infant has cried long and hard. When these caregivers finally do respond, they are sometimes annoyed by the infant's demands and may misinterpret the baby's intent. Over time, these babies tend to see social relationships as erratic and often frustrating. Such conditions do little to foster trust and confidence.

Why does predictable and responsive parenting promote secure attachment relationships? To answer this question, think about your own friendships and romantic relationships. These relationships are usually most satisfying when we believe we can trust the other person and depend on him or her in times of need. The same formula seems to hold for infants. *Infants develop an internal working model, a set of expectations about parents' availability and responsivity.* When parents are dependable and caring, babies come to trust them, knowing they can be relied on for comfort in times of stress. That is, babies develop an internal working model in which they believe that the parent is concerned about their needs and will try to meet them (Bretherton, 1992, 1995).

Many research findings attest to the importance of a caregiver's sensitivity for quality of attachment. For example, in a study conducted in Israel, infants were less likely to develop secure attachment when they slept in dormitories with other children under age 12, where they received inconsistent (if any) attention when they became upset overnight (Sagi et al., 1994). And, in a study conducted in the Netherlands, infants were more likely to form a secure attachment when their mother had three months of training that emphasized monitoring an infant's signals and responding appropriately and promptly (van den Boom, 1994, 1995). Thus, secure attachment is most likely when parents are sensitive and responsive.

Another factor contributing to the quality of attachment is temperament. Babies with difficult temperaments are somewhat less likely to form secure attachment relationships (Goldsmith & Harman, 1994; Seifer et al.,

1996). That is, babies who fuss often and are difficult to console are more prone to insecure attachment. This may be particularly likely when a difficult, emotional infant has a mother whose personality is rigid and traditional rather than accepting and flexible (Mangelsdorf et al., 1990). Rigid mothers do not adjust well to the often erratic demands of their difficult babies; instead, they want the baby to adjust to them. This means that rigid mothers less often provide the responsive, sensitive care that leads to secure attachment.

Fortunately, even brief training for mothers of newborns can help them respond to their babies more effectively (Wendland-Carro, Piccinini, & Millar, 1999). Mothers can be taught how to interact more sensitively, affectionately, and responsively, paving the way for secure attachment and the lifelong benefits associated with a positive internal working model of interpersonal relationships.

The formation of attachment illustrates well the combined influence of the different components of the biopsychosocial framework. Many infant behaviours that elicit caregiving in adults—smiling and crying, for example—are biological in origin. When the caregiver is responsive to the infant (a sociocultural force), then a secure attachment forms in which the infant trusts caregivers and knows that they can be relied on in stressful situations (psychological force).

ATTACHMENT, WORK, AND ALTERNATIVE CAREGIVING

Since the 1970s, more women in the workforce and more single-parent households have made child care a fact of life for many Canadian families. Today, approximately 1.4 million of Canada's children are cared for by child care services. Parents generally have two options for such care: They may choose privately arranged care within their own home, or in the homes of other caregivers such as relatives, friends, or babysitters, or their children may attend more formal programs such as day-care centres (Stafford, 2002).

Parents and policymakers alike have been concerned about the impact of such care on children generally, and, specifically, its impact on attachment. Is there, for example, a maximum amount of time per week that infants should spend in care outside the home? Is there a minimum age below which infants should not be placed in care outside the home? To answer these questions, a comprehensive study of early child care was initiated in the United States by the National Institute of Child Health and Human Development (NICHD), which was created in 1962 to study children's physical, emotional, and cognitive development. Planning for the Early Child Care Study began in 1989, and by 1991 the study was under way. Researchers recruited 1,364 mothers and their newborns from 12 U.S. cities. Both mothers and children have been tested repeatedly (and testing continues in this ongoing study).

Bob Daemmrich /Stock Boston Inc.

From the outset, one of the concerns was the impact of early child care on mother–infant attachment. In fact, the results so far show no overall effects of child care experience on mother–infant attachment, for either 15- or 36-month-olds (NICHD Early Child Care Research Network, 1997, 2001). In other words, a secure mother–infant attachment was just as likely, regardless of the quality of child care, the amount of time the child spent in care, the age when the child began care, how frequently the parents changed child care arrangements, and the type of child care (e.g., child care centre or in the home with a nonrelative).

However, when the effects of child care were considered along with characteristics of mothers, an important pattern was detected: At 15 and 36 months, insecure attachments were more common when less sensitive mothering was combined with low quality or large amounts of child care (NICHD Early Child Care Research Network, 1997, 2001). As the investigators put it: "Poor quality, unstable, or more than minimal amounts of child care apparently added to the risks already inherent in poor mothering, so that the combined effects were worse than those of low maternal sensitivity and responsiveness alone" (1997, p. 877). These conclusions are particularly convincing because the same pattern of results was found in Israel in a large-scale study of child care and attachment that was modelled after the NICHD Early Child Care Study (Sagi et al., 2002).

These results provide clear guidelines for parents like Kendra, the mother in the vignette. They can enrol their infants and toddlers in high-quality day-care programs with no fear of harmful consequences. As long as the quality is good, other factors (e.g., the type of child care or the amount of time the child spends in child care) typically do not affect the mother–child attachment relationship. Regarding the effect of day care on child development in general, Palacio-Quentin (2000), a Canadian researcher who analyzed close to 200 studies that examined this issue, concluded that attending high-quality day care has a positive effect on all aspects of child development. These aspects include intellectual and language development as well as emotional and social development. And, although the quality of day care had the greatest impact on development, day-care centres appear to offer better conditions to promote such development than family day-care facilities.

The results of such research on child care are reassuring for parents, who often have misgivings about their infants and toddlers spending so much time in the care of others. Nevertheless, they raise another, equally important question: What are the features of high-quality child care? That is, what should parents look for when trying to find care for their children? In general, high-quality child care has the following features (Burchinal et al., 2000; Lamb, 1999; Rosenthal & Vandell, 1996):

- a low ratio of children to caregivers;
- a well-trained, experienced staff;
- low staff turnover;
- ample opportunities for educational and social stimulation; and
- effective communication between parents and day-care workers concerning the general aims and routine functioning of the day-care program.

Collectively, these variables do *not* guarantee that a child will receive high-quality care. Sensitive, responsive caregiving—the same behaviour that promotes secure attachment relationships—is the real key to high-quality child care. Centres that have

> **THINK ABOUT IT**
>
> Imagine that your best friend is the mother of a 3-month-old. Your friend is about to return to her job as a social worker, but she's afraid that she'll harm her baby by going back to work. What could you say to reassure her?

Boulton-Wilson/Jeroboam

well-trained, experienced staff caring for a relatively small number of children are more likely to provide good care, but the only way to know the quality of care with certainty is to see for yourself (Lamb, 1999).

Fortunately, employers have begun to realize that convenient, high-quality child care makes for a better employee. In Kirkland, Quebec, for example, Pfizer Canada constructed an additional building to house a day-care centre that provides services for employees and residents of the neighbouring community. Businesses are realizing that the availability of high-quality child care helps attract and retain a skilled labour force.

With effort, organization, and help from the community and business, full-time employment and high-quality caregiving *can* be compatible. We will return to this issue in Chapter 13, from the perspective of the parents. For now, the Real People feature provides one example of a father who stays home to care for his daughter while her mother works full-time.

REAL PEOPLE: APPLYING HUMAN DEVELOPMENT
Lois, Bill, and Sarah

Lois, 46, and Bill, 61, had been married nearly four years when Lois gave birth to Sarah. Lois, a kindergarten teacher, returned to work full-time four months after Sarah was born. Bill, who had been half-heartedly pursuing a Ph.D. in education, became a full-time househusband. Bill does the cooking and takes care of Sarah during the day. Lois comes home from school at noon so that the family can eat lunch together, and she is home from work by four in the afternoon. Once a week, Bill takes Sarah to a parent–infant play program. The other parents, all mothers in their 20s or 30s, first assumed that Bill was Sarah's grandfather and

had trouble relating to him as an older father. Soon, however, he was an accepted member of the group. On the weekends, Lois's and Bill's grown children from previous marriages often visit and enjoy caring for and playing with Sarah. By all accounts, Sarah looks to be a healthy, happy, outgoing 9-month-old. Is this arrangement nontraditional? Clearly. Is it effective for Sarah, Lois, and Bill? Definitely. Sarah receives the nurturing care that she needs, Lois goes to work assured that Sarah is in Bill's knowing and caring hands, and Bill relishes being the primary caregiver.

TEST YOURSELF

1. _____ proposed that maturational and social factors come together to pose eight unique challenges for psychosocial growth during the life span.

2. Infants must balance trust and mistrust to achieve _____, an openness to new experience that is coupled with awareness of possible danger.

3. By approximately _____ months of age, most infants have identified a special individual—usually but not always the mother—as the attachment figure.

4. Joan, a 12-month-old, was separated from her mother for about 15 minutes. When they were reunited, Joan would not let her mother pick her up. When her mother approached, Joan would look the other way or toddle to another part of the room. This behaviour suggests that Joan has a(n) _____ attachment relationship.

5. The single most important factor in fostering a secure attachment relationship is _____.

6. An insecure attachment relationship is likely when an infant receives poor-quality child care and _____.

Most research on attachment has relied on Ainsworth's Strange Situation. What are some of the assets of this method? What are some potential problems?

Answers: (1) Erik Erikson, (2) hope, (3) 6 or 7, (4) avoidant insecure, (5) responding consistently and appropriately, (6) insensitive, unresponsive mothering

4.2

Emerging Emotions

LEARNING OBJECTIVES

- At what ages do children begin to express basic emotions?
- What are complex emotions and when do they develop?
- When do children begin to understand other people's emotions? How do they use this information to guide their own behaviour?

> **Emerging Emotions**
> Experiencing and Expressing Emotions
> Recognizing and Using Others' Emotions
> Regulating Emotions
> Temperament

Nicole is ecstatic that she is finally going to see her 7-month-old nephew, Claude. She rushes into the house, and seeing Claude playing on the floor with blocks, sweeps him up in a big hug. After a brief, puzzled look, Claude bursts into angry tears and begins thrashing his arms and legs, as if saying to Nicole, "Who are you? What do you want? Put me down! Now!" Nicole quickly hands Claude to his mother, who is surprised by her baby's outburst and even more surprised that he continues to sob while she rocks him.

This vignette illustrates three common emotions. Nicole's initial joy, Claude's anger, and his mother's surprise are familiar to all of us. In this section, we look at when children first express emotions, how children come to understand emotions in others, and, finally, how children regulate their emotions. As we do, we'll learn why Claude reacted to Nicole as he did and how Nicole could have prevented Claude's outburst.

EXPERIENCING AND EXPRESSING EMOTIONS

The three emotions from the vignette—joy, anger, and fear—are considered "basic emotions," as are interest, disgust, distress, sadness, and surprise (Draghi-Lorenz, Reddy, & Costall, 2001). *Basic emotions are experienced by people worldwide and consist of three elements: a subjective feeling, a physiological change, and an overt behaviour* (Izard, 1991). For example, suppose you wake to the sound of a thunderstorm and then discover your roommate has left for class with your umbrella. Subjectively, you might feel ready to explode with anger; physiologically, your heart would beat faster; and behaviourally, you would probably be scowling.

Measuring Emotions

How can we determine when infants first experience basic emotions? Overt behaviours such as facial expression provide important clues. To see for yourself, look at the photos of young babies. Which one is angry? Which are the sad and happy babies? The

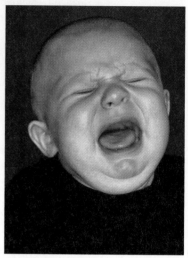

facial expressions are so revealing that no doubt you guessed the babies are, in order, sad, happy, and angry. But do these distinctive facial expressions mean the infants are actually experiencing these emotions? Not necessarily. Facial expressions are only one component of emotion—the behavioural manifestation. Emotion also involves physiological responses and subjective feelings. Of course, infants can't express their feelings to us verbally, so we don't know much about their subjective experiences. But at least some of the physiological responses that accompany facial expressions are the same in infants and adults. For example, when infants and adults smile—which suggests they're happy—the left frontal cortex of the brain tends to have more electrical activity than the right frontal cortex (Fox, Kimmerly, & Schafer, 1991).

Research has revealed several other reasons to believe facial expressions are an accurate barometer of an infant's emotional state:

- Infants (and adults) worldwide express basic emotions in much the same way (Izard, 1991). For example, the boy in the photo shows the universal signs of fear. His eyes are open wide, his eyebrows are raised, and his mouth is relaxed but slightly open. The universality of emotional expression suggests that humans are biologically programmed to express basic emotions in a specific way.

- By 5 to 6 months, infants' facial expressions change predictably and meaningfully in response to events. When a happy mother greets her baby, the baby usually smiles in return; when a tired, distracted mother picks up her baby roughly, the baby usually frowns at her (Izard et al., 1995; Weinberg & Tronick, 1994).

- When adults are really happy or amused, they smile differently than when they smile to greet an acquaintance or to hide hurt feelings. In "joyful" smiles, the muscles around the eyes contract, which lifts the cheeks. Similarly, infants smile at both moms and other interesting objects, but are more likely to raise their cheeks during smiling when looking at mom (Messinger, 2002). The close parallel between the

details of infants' and adults' smiles suggests that smiling has the same meaning, emotionally, for infants and adults.

Collectively, these findings make it reasonable to assume that facial expressions reflect an infant's underlying emotional state.

Development of Basic Emotions

Using facial expressions and other overt behaviours, scientists have traced the growth of basic emotions in infants. According to one influential theory (Lewis, 2000), newborns experience only two general emotions: pleasure and distress. Rapidly, though, more discrete emotions emerge, and by 8 or 9 months of age, infants are thought to experience all basic emotions. For example, joy emerges at about 2 or 3 months. *At this age, social smiles first appear: Infants smile when they see another human face.* Sometimes social smiling is accompanied by cooing, the early form of vocalization described in Section 3.6 (Sroufe & Waters, 1976). Smiling and cooing seem to be the infant's way of expressing pleasure at seeing another person. Sadness is also observed at about this age: Infants look sad, for example, when their mothers stop playing with them (Lewis, 2000).

Anger typically emerges between 4 and 6 months. Infants will become angry, for example, if a favourite food or toy is taken away (Sternberg & Campos, 1990). Reflecting their growing understanding of goal-directed behaviour (see Section 3.2), infants also become angry when their attempts to achieve a goal are frustrated. For example, if a parent restrains an infant trying to pick up a toy, the guaranteed result is a very angry baby.

Like anger, fear emerges later in the first year. *At about 6 months, infants become wary in the presence of an unfamiliar adult, a reaction known as stranger wariness.* When a stranger approaches, a 6-month-old typically looks away and begins to fuss (Mangelsdorf, Shapiro, & Marzolf, 1995). The baby in the photo is showing the signs of stranger wariness. The grandmother has picked him up without giving him a chance to warm up to her, and the outcome is as predictable as it was with Claude, the baby boy in the vignette who was frightened by his aunt: he cries, looks frightened, and reaches with arms outstretched in the direction of someone familiar.

How wary an infant feels around strangers depends on a number of factors (Thompson & Limber, 1991). First, infants tend to be less fearful of strangers when the environment is familiar and more fearful when it is not. Many parents know this firsthand from travelling with their infants: Enter a friend's house for the first time and the baby clings tightly to its mother. Second, the amount of anxiety depends on the stranger's behaviour. Instead of rushing to greet or pick up the baby, as Nicole did in the vignette, a stranger should talk with other adults and, in a while, perhaps offer the baby a toy (Mangelsdorf, 1992). Handled this way, many infants will soon be curious about the stranger instead of afraid.

Robert Kail

Wariness of strangers is adaptive because it emerges at the same time that children begin to master creeping and crawling (described in Section 3.3). Like Curious George, the monkey in a famous series of children's books, babies are inquisitive and want to use their new locomotor skills to explore the world. Being wary of strangers provides a natural restraint against the tendency to wander away from familiar caregivers. However, as youngsters learn to interpret facial expressions and recognize when a person is friendly, their wariness of strangers declines.

THINK ABOUT IT

How might an infant's ability to express emotions relate to the formation of attachment? To his temperamental characteristics?

Emergence of Complex Emotions

In addition to basic emotions such as joy and anger, people feel complex emotions such as pride, guilt, and embarrassment. Most scientists (e.g., Lewis, 2000) believe that complex emotions don't surface until 18 to 24 months of age because they depend on the child having some understanding of the self, which typically occurs between 15 and 18 months. Children feel guilty or embarrassed, for example, when they've done something they know they shouldn't have done: A child who breaks a toy is thinking, "You told me to be careful. But I wasn't!" Similarly, children feel pride when they accomplish a challenging task for the first time. Thus, children's growing understanding of themselves helps them to experience complex emotions like pride and guilt (Lewis, 2000).

THINK ABOUT IT

Explain how the different forces in the biopsychosocial framework contribute to the development of basic and complex emotions.

Cultural Differences in Emotional Expression

Children worldwide express many of the same basic and complex emotions. However, cultures differ in the extent to which emotional expression is encouraged (Hess & Kirouac, 2000). In many Asian countries, for example, outward displays of emotion are discouraged in favour of emotional restraint. Consistent with these differences, in one study (Camras et al., 1998) European American 11-month-olds cried and smiled more often than Chinese 11-month-olds. In another study (Zahn-Waxler et al., 1996), U.S. preschoolers were more likely than Japanese preschoolers to express anger in interpersonal conflicts.

And cultures differ in the events that trigger emotions, particularly complex emotions. Situations that evoke pride in one culture may evoke embarrassment or shame in another. For example, North American elementary school children often show pride at personal achievement, such as getting the highest grade on a test or coming in first place. In contrast, Asian elementary school children are embarrassed by a public display of individual achievement but show great pride when their entire class is honoured for an achievement (Stevenson & Stigler, 1992).

Thus, culture can influence when and how much children express emotion. Of course, expressing emotion is only part of the developmental story. Children must also learn to recognize others' emotions, which is our next topic.

RECOGNIZING AND USING OTHERS' EMOTIONS

Imagine you need to borrow $20 from your roommate when she returns from class. Shortly, she storms into your apartment, slams the door, and throws her backpack on the floor. Immediately, you change your plans, realizing that now is hardly a good time to ask for a loan. This example reminds us that we often need to recognize others' emotions and sometimes change our behaviour as a consequence.

When can infants first identify emotions in others? Perhaps as early as 4 months and definitely by 6 months infants begin to distinguish facial expressions associated with different emotions. They can, for example, distinguish a happy, smiling face from a sad, frowning face (Ludemann, 1991; Montague & Walker-Andrews, 2001). Of course, infants might be able to distinguish an angry face from a happy one but not know the emotional significance of the two faces. How can we tell whether infants understand the emotions expressed in a face? The best evidence is that infants often match their own emotions to other people's emotions. When happy mothers smile and talk in a pleasant voice, infants express happiness themselves. If mothers are angry or sad, infants become distressed too (Haviland & Lelwica, 1987; Montague & Walker-Andrews, 2001).

Also like adults, infants use others' emotions to direct their behaviour. *Infants in an unfamiliar or ambiguous environment often look at their mother or father, as if searching for cues to help them interpret the situation, a phenomenon known as social*

FIGURE 4.2

referencing. Social referencing is illustrated in Figure 4.2. If a parent looks afraid when shown a novel object, 12-month-olds are less likely to play with the toy than if a parent looks happy (Repacholi, 1998). Furthermore, infants can use parents' facial expressions or their vocal expressions alone to decide whether they want to explore an unfamiliar object (Mumme, Fernald, & Herrera, 1996). And infants' use of parents' cues is precise. If two unfamiliar toys are shown to a parent who expresses disgust at one toy but not the other, 12-month-olds will avoid the toy that elicited the disgust but not the other toy (Moses et al., 2001). Thus, social referencing shows that infants are remarkably skilled in using their parents' emotions to help them direct their own behaviour.

REGULATING EMOTIONS

Think back to a time when you were *really* angry at a good friend. Did you shout at the friend? Did you try to discuss matters calmly? Or did you simply ignore the situation altogether? Shouting is a direct expression of anger, but calm conversation and overlooking a situation are purposeful attempts to regulate emotion. People often regulate emotions; for example, we routinely try to suppress fear (because we know there's no real need to be afraid of the dark), anger (because we don't want to let a friend know just how upset we are), and joy (because we don't want to seem like we're gloating over our good fortune).

Child development researchers have studied two aspects of emotion regulation: its origins and its links to social competence. Emotion regulation clearly begins in infancy. By 4 to 6 months, infants use simple strategies to regulate their emotions (Buss & Goldsmith, 1998; Mangelsdorf et al., 1995). When something frightens or confuses an infant—for example, a stranger or a mother who suddenly stops responding—he or she often looks away (just as older children and even adults often turn away or close their eyes to block out disturbing stimuli). Frightened infants also move closer to a parent, another effective way of helping to control their fear (Parritz, 1996).

TEMPERAMENT

So far, we've talked as if all babies are alike. But if you've seen a number of babies together, you know this isn't true. Perhaps you've seen some babies who are quiet most of the time alongside others who cried often and impatiently. Maybe you've known infants who responded warmly to strangers next to others who seemed shy. *These characteristics of infants indicate a consistent style or pattern to an infant's behaviour and, collectively, they define an infant's* **temperament***.*

According to one important theory, proposed by Buss and Plomin (1984), temperament includes three primary dimensions: emotionality, activity, and sociability.

■ *Emotionality refers to the strength of the infant's emotional response to a situation, the ease with which that response is triggered, and the ease with which the infant can be returned to a nonemotional state.* At one extreme are infants whose emotional responses are strong, easily triggered, and not easily calmed; at the other are infants whose responses are subdued, relatively difficult to elicit, and soothed readily.

■ *Activity refers to the tempo and vigour of a child's activity.* Active infants are always busy, like to explore their environment, and enjoy vigorous play. Inactive infants have a more controlled behavioural tempo and are more likely to enjoy quiet play.

■ *Sociability refers to a preference for being with other people.* Some infants relish contact with others, seek their attention, and prefer play that involves other people. Other infants, like the girl in the photo, enjoy solitude and are quite content to play alone with toys.

Robert Kail

Thomas and Chess (1984), in their research on child temperament, studied nine behaviours in children, namely activity level, rhythmicity, approach or withdrawal, adaptability, threshold of responsiveness, intensity of reaction, quality of mood, distractibility, and attention span and persistence. Their research led them to theorize that while all children show some of these behaviours at times, about 60% of children fall into one of three groups. In brief, these are the easy child, who is often in a good mood and easily adaptable to new situations; the difficult child, who is slow to adapt to change and may have tantrums or cry loudly when frustrated; and the slow-to-warm child, who shows negative responses when initially exposed to new situations but who slowly comes to accept them with further exposure.

Although not all developmentalists agree on the dimensions of temperament (Goldsmith et al., 1987), it is clear that temperament consists of a handful of biologically based dimensions. Some temperament characteristics are more common in some cultures than in others. Asian babies tend to be less emotional than European-American babies. For instance, Asian babies cry less often and less intensely than European-American babies (Kagan et al., 1994; Lewis, Ramsay, & Kawakami, 1993). However, an important aspect to consider is how infant temperament is affected by cultural differences in caregiving.

Hereditary and Environmental Contributions to Temperament

Most theories agree that temperament reflects both heredity and experience. The influence of heredity is shown in twin studies: Identical twins are more alike in most aspects of temperament than fraternal twins. For example, Goldsmith, Buss, and Lemery (1997) found that the correlation for identical twins' activity level was .72 but the correlation for fraternal twins was only .38. In other words, if one identical twin is temperamentally active, the other usually is too. Goldsmith et al. (1997) also found that identical twins were more alike than fraternal twins on social fearfulness (shyness), persistence, and proneness to anger.

Recently, scientists looking for links between genes and temperament came up with a surprising finding: Infants and toddlers who are upset by novel stimulation (and who often become shy preschoolers) have narrower faces than youngsters who respond calmly to novel stimulation (Arcus & Kagan, 1995). This observation is provocative because the brain and the facial skeleton originate in the same set of cells in prenatal development. Thus, one fascinating hypothesis is that genes influence levels of hormones that affect both facial growth and temperament.

The environment also contributes to children's temperament. Positive emotionality—youngsters who laugh often, seem to be generally happy, and often express pleasure—seems to reflect environmental influences (Goldsmith et al., 1997). Conversely, infants more often develop intense, difficult temperaments when mothers are abrupt in dealing with them and lack confidence (Belsky, Fish, & Isabella, 1991).

There's no question that heredity and experience cause babies' temperaments to differ, but how stable is temperament? We'll find out in the next section.

THINK ABOUT IT

How would a learning theorist explain why children have different temperaments?

Stability of Temperament

Do calm, easygoing babies grow up to be calm, easygoing children, adolescents, and adults? Are difficult, irritable infants destined to grow up to be cranky, whiny children? The first answers to these questions came from the Fels Longitudinal Project, a study of many aspects of physical and psychological development from infancy. Although not a study of temperament per se, Jerome Kagan and his collaborators (Kagan, 1989; Kagan & Moss, 1962) found that fearful preschoolers in the Fels Project tended to be inhibited as older children and adolescents.

Spurred by findings like this one, later investigators attempted to learn more about the stability of temperament. Their research shows that temperament is somewhat stable during the infant and toddler years. Newborns who cry under moderate stress tend, as 5-month-olds, to cry when they are placed in stressful situations (Stifter & Fox, 1990). And, as we mentioned previously, infants who are frightened or upset by novel stimulation tend to be inhibited and less sociable as preschoolers (Kagan, Snidman, & Arcus, 1998).

Thus, evidence suggests that temperament is at least somewhat stable throughout infancy and the toddler years (Lemery et al., 1999). Of course, the links are not perfect. Sam, an emotional 1-year-old, is more likely to be emotional as a 12-year-old than Dave, an unemotional 1-year-old. However, it's not a "sure thing" that Sam will still be emotional as a 12-year-old. Instead, think of temperament as a predisposition. Some infants are naturally predisposed to be sociable, emotional, or active; others *can* act in these ways too, but only if the behaviours are nurtured by parents and others.

Though temperament is only moderately stable during infancy and toddlerhood, it can still shape development in important ways. For example, an infant's temperament may determine the experiences that parents provide. Parents may read more to quiet babies but play more physical games with their active babies. These different experiences, driven by the infants' temperaments, contribute to each infant's development, despite the fact that the infants' temperaments may change over the years. Although infants have many features in common, temperament characteristics remind us that each baby also seems to have its own unique personality from the very start.

Photodisc

TEST YOURSELF

1. Basic emotions include a subjective feeling, a physiological change, and _____ .

2. Newborns experience two general emotions: pleasure and _____ .

3. The first detectable form of fear is _____, which emerges at about 6 months.

4. Wariness of strangers is adaptive because it emerges at about the same time that _____ .

5. Complex emotions, such as guilt and shame, emerge later than basic emotions because _____ .

6. In social referencing, infants use a parent's facial expression _____ .

7. Infants often control fear by looking away from a frightening event or by _____ .

8. One prominent theory proposes three dimensions of temperament, including emotionality, _____, and sociability.

Most theories of cognitive development, such as Piaget's and the information-processing approach, don't explicitly consider emotion. How might emotions affect thinking? How could these theories include emotions?

Answers: (1) an overt behaviour, (2) distress, (3) wariness of strangers, (4) infants master creeping and crawling, (5) complex emotions require understanding of the self, (6) to direct their own behaviour (e.g., deciding if an unfamiliar situation is safe or frightening), (7) moving closer to a parent, (8) activity

4.3

Becoming Self-Aware

LEARNING OBJECTIVES

▣ When do children begin to realize that they exist?

▣ What are toddlers' self-concepts like?

> **Becoming Self-Aware**
> Origins of Self-Concept

When Ximena brushes her teeth, she puts her 20-month-old son, Christof, in an infant seat facing the bathroom mirror. She's been doing this for months, and Christof always seems to enjoy looking at the images in the mirror. Lately, he seems to pay special attention to his own reflection. Ximena thinks that sometimes Christof deliberately frowns or laughs just to see what he looks like. Is this possible, Ximena wonders, or is her imagination simply running wild?

As infants' physical, motor, and perceptual skills grow, they learn more and more of the world around them. As part of this learning, infants and toddlers begin to realize that they exist independently of other people and objects in the environment and that their existence continues over time. In this section, you'll see how infants start to become self-aware and learn what Christof knows about himself.

ORIGINS OF SELF-CONCEPT

When do children begin to understand that they exist? Measuring the onset of this awareness is not easy. Obviously, we can't simply ask a 2-year-old, "So, tell me, when did you first realize you existed and weren't just part of the furniture?" A less direct approach is needed, and the photograph at the top of page 157 shows one route many investigators have taken. Like Christof, the 9-month-old in the photograph is smiling at the face he sees in the mirror. Babies at this age sometimes touch the face in the mirror or wave at it, but none of their behaviours indicate that they recognize themselves in the mirror. Instead, babies act as if the face in the mirror is simply a very interesting stimulus.

PT Santana/Getty Images

How would we know that infants recognize themselves in a mirror? One clever approach is to have mothers place a red mark on their infant's nose; they do this surreptitiously, while wiping the baby's face. Then the infant is returned to the mirror. Many 1-year-olds touch the red mark on the mirror, showing that they notice the mark on the face in the mirror. By 15 months, however, an important change occurs: babies see the red mark in the mirror, then reach up and touch their own noses. By age 2, virtually all children do this (Bullock & Lütkenhaus, 1990; Lewis & Brooks-Gunn, 1979). When these older children notice the red mark in the mirror, they understand that the funny-looking nose in the mirror is their own!

We don't need to rely solely on the mirror task to know that self-awareness emerges between 18 and 24 months. During this same period, toddlers look more at photographs of themselves than at photos of other children. They also refer to themselves by name or with a personal pronoun, such as "I" or "me," and sometimes they know their age and their gender. These changes suggest that self-awareness is well established in most children by age 2 (Lewis, 1987).

TEST YOURSELF

1. The most likely reason that babies would smile at their own image in a mirror is because _____.

2. Apparently children are first self-aware at age 2 because this is when they first recognize themselves in the mirror and in photographs and when they first use _____.

Often babies smile at each other and we think it's because they know they are meeting someone their own age. What do you think is a more reasonable explanation?

Answers: (1) it's an interesting stimulus, but they do not recognize themselves, (2) personal pronouns such as "I," and "we"

4·4

Interacting with Others

LEARNING OBJECTIVES

▸ When do young children first begin to play with each other? How does play change during infancy?

▸ What determines whether children help one another?

> **Interacting with Others**
> The Joys of Play
> Helping Others

Best friends Alexandra and Maxine place their baby girls on the floor beside each other on a blanket with some soft toys. Although the babies are both only around 5 months of age, their moms are hoping that the girls will become best friends like they are. The babies seem generally oblivious to each other but react with smiles and movement to their own mothers. Why don't the babies seem to connect with each other for social interaction?

Infants' initial interactions are with parents, but soon they begin to interact with other people, notably their peers. In this section, we'll trace the beginnings and development of these interactions.

THE JOYS OF PLAY

If you watch two 5-month-olds together, like the ones described above, hoping to see some social interaction, you'll be disappointed. The infants will look at each other, but you won't observe anything that qualifies as an interaction. However, at about 6 months, the first signs of peer interactions appear: Now an infant may point to or smile at another infant (Hartup, 1983).

Soon after the first birthday, children begin **parallel play,** *in which each youngster plays alone but maintains a keen interest in what another is doing.* For example, each of the toddlers in the photograph has his own toys, but each is watching the other play too. Exchanges between youngsters become more common. When one toddler talks or smiles, the other usually responds (Howes, Unger, & Seidner, 1990).

Beginning at roughly 15 to 18 months, toddlers no longer simply watch one another at play. *Instead, they engage in similar activities and talk or smile at one another, illustrating* **simple social play.** Play has now become truly interactive. For example, youngsters now offer toys to one another (Howes & Matheson, 1992).

Toward the second birthday, **cooperative play** *is observed: Now a distinct theme organizes children's play, and they take on special roles based on the theme.* They may play "hide-and-seek" and alternate the roles of hider and finder, or they may have a tea party and take turns being the host and the guest (Parten, 1932).

The nature of young children's play changes dramatically in a few years (Howes & Matheson, 1992). In a typical day-care centre, 1- and 2-year-olds spend most of their time in parallel play whereas in older children cooperative play is the norm.

HELPING OTHERS

Prosocial behaviour is any behaviour that benefits another person. Cooperation is one form of prosocial behaviour. Of course, cooperation often "works" because individuals gain more than they would by not cooperating. *In contrast,* **altruism** *is behaviour that is driven by feelings of responsibility toward other people, such as helping and sharing, in which individuals do not benefit directly from their actions.* If two youngsters pool their funds to buy a candy bar to share, this is cooperative behaviour. If one youngster gives half of her lunch to a peer who forgot his own, this is altruism.

Rudimentary acts of altruism can be seen by 18 months of age. When toddlers see other people who are obviously hurt or upset, they will, like the toddler in the photograph, appear concerned, try to comfort the person who is in pain (by hugging or patting), and try to determine why the person is upset (Zahn-Waxler et al., 1992). Apparently, at this early age, they recognize some of the qualities of states of distress. During the preschool years, children gradually begin to understand others' needs and learn appropriate altruistic responses (Farver & Branstetter, 1994).

TEST YOURSELF

1. Toddlers who are 12 to 15 months old often engage in _____ play, in which they play separately but look at one another and sometimes communicate verbally.

2. A behaviour that benefits another person is referred to as _____.

3. At about age 2 years children's play starts to consist of them taking on special roles based on a theme, referred to as _____ play.

Even though toddlers may not engage in each other's play, why do you think they are so interested in what the other is doing?

Answers: (1) parallel, (2) prosocial, (3) cooperative

PUTTING IT ALL TOGETHER

Interactions with other people are so important throughout life. Having completed this chapter, you now know that these interactions start early in life. In the first part of this chapter, we saw that responsive caregiving often leads to the formation of a secure attachment between infant and parent. When infants who have had secure attachments grow up, they tend to interact more successfully with other people. Infants who spend much time in early alternative child care also form secure attachments unless the child care is low quality and the mother is unresponsive. Children like Alex, Kendra's 18-month-old, are not harmed by

time spent in early alternative child care as long as the care is of high quality and mothers remain responsive and sensitive.

We showed that infants like Claude can express basic emotions such as happiness and anger. By age 2, children experience complex emotions such as guilt. Babies use others' emotions to guide their behaviour, and this skill improves as children grow cognitively.

We also traced how children's social relations expand from parents to peers.

Even babies start to interact and toddlers learn to play with each other.

SUMMARY

4.1 Beginnings: Trust and Attachment

Erikson's Stages of Early Psychosocial Development

- In Erikson's theory of psychosocial development, individuals face certain psychosocial crises at different phases in development. The crisis of infancy is to establish a balance between trust and mistrust of the world, producing hope; between 1 and 3 years of age, youngsters must blend autonomy and shame to produce will; and between 3 and 5 years of age, initiative and guilt must be balanced to achieve purpose.

The Growth of Attachment

- Attachment is an enduring socioemotional relationship between infant and parent. For both adults and infants, many of the behaviours that contribute to the formation of attachment are biologically programmed. Attachment develops gradually over the first year of life; by about 6 or 7 months, infants have identified an attachment figure, typically the mother. In the ensuing months, infants often become attached to other family members.

- Research with the Strange Situation, in which infant and mother are separated briefly, reveals four primary forms of attachment. Most common is a secure attachment, in which infants have complete trust in the mother. Less common are three types of attachment relationships in which this trust is lacking. In avoidant relationships, infants deal with the lack of trust by ignoring the mother; in resistant relationships, infants often seem angry with her; in disorganized relationships, infants do not appear to understand the mother's absence.

▪ Children who have had secure attachment relationships during infancy often interact with their peers more readily and more skilfully. Secure attachment is most likely to occur when mothers respond sensitively and consistently to their infant's needs.

Attachment, Work, and Alternative Caregiving

▪ Many Canadian children are cared for at home by a father or other relative, in a day-care provider's home, or in a day-care centre. Infants and young children are not harmed by such care as long as the care is of high quality and parents remain responsive to their children.

4.2 Emerging Emotions

Experiencing and Expressing Emotions

▪ Scientists often use infants' facial expressions to judge when different emotional states emerge in development. Basic emotions, which include joy, anger, and fear, emerge in the first year. Fear first appears in infancy as stranger wariness. Complex emotions have an evaluative component and include guilt, embarrassment, and pride. They appear between 18 and 24 months and require more sophisticated cognitive skills than basic emotions such as happiness and fear. Cultures differ in the rules for expressing emotions and the situations that elicit particular emotions.

Recognizing and Using Others' Emotions

▪ By 6 months, infants have begun to recognize the emotions associated with different facial expressions. They use this information to help them evaluate unfamiliar situations. Beyond infancy, children understand the rules for displaying emotions appropriately.

Regulating Emotions

▪ Infants use simple strategies to regulate emotions such as fear. As children grow, they become better skilled at regulating their emotions. Children who do not regulate emotions well tend to have problems interacting with others.

Temperament

▪ Temperament refers to a consistent style or pattern to an infant's behaviour. Dimensions of temperament include emotionality, activity, and sociability. Temperament is influenced by both heredity and environment and is a reasonably stable characteristic of infants and young children.

4.3 Becoming Self-Aware

Origins of Self-Concept

▪ Beginning at about 15 months, infants begin to recognize themselves in the mirror, which is one of the first signs of self-recognition. They also begin to prefer to look at pictures of themselves, begin to refer to themselves by name (or use personal pronouns), and sometimes know their age and gender. Evidently, by 2 years, most children are self-aware.

4.4 Interacting with Others

The Joys of Play

▪ Even infants notice and respond to one another, but the first real interactions, at about 12 to 15 months, take the form of parallel play, in which toddlers play alone while watching each other. A few months later, simple social play emerges, in which toddlers engage in similar activities and interact with one another. At about 2 years of age, cooperative play organized around a theme becomes common.

Helping Others

▪ Acts of altruism can be seen as early as 18 months of age, when toddlers begin to show empathy and concern.

KEY TERMS

hope (141)
will (141)
ethology (141)
attachment (141)
secure attachment (143)
avoidant attachment (143)
resistant attachment (143)

disorganized (disoriented) attachment (143)
internal working model (146)
basic emotions (149)
social smiles (151)
stranger wariness (151)
social referencing (152)
temperament (153)

emotionality (154)
activity (154)
sociability (154)
parallel play (158)
simple social play (158)
cooperative play (158)
prosocial behaviour (158)
altruism (158)

SEE FOR YOURSELF: APPLYING WHAT YOU'VE LEARNED

As discussed in this chapter there is some evidence that at least some aspects of temperament are stable during life starting in infancy. To see if you can find any evidence for or against this theory, informally ask some friends or relatives about their or their children's personality development. You may want to ask parents of teenagers if they think that their children's personalities are similar to how they were as babies, or ask individuals themselves if they feel they have changed their personalities as they have become older. Ask senior citizens or those who have known them since they were children the same question. Consider your own personality and that of your siblings and other family members and friends whom you have known since they were very young and consider if they have personality traits that have persisted. Think about the different personality types that may emerge from a single household. Can you understand the argument some developmentalists have that "nature" has more influence than "nuture" in personality development?

LEARN MORE ABOUT IT

Readings

BRAZELTON, T. B., & CRAMER, R. (1990). *The earliest relationship*. Reading, MA: Addison-Wesley. This book, written by a well-known pediatrician and his colleague, illustrates the drama of attachment through lively case studies.

ERIKSON, E.H. (1982). *The life cycle completed: A review*. New York: Norton. Erikson summarizes his theory.

 For additional readings, explore InfoTrac® College Edition, your online library. Go to http://www.infotrac.thomsonlearning.com.

Websites

http://www.cpa.ca

The Canadian Psychological Association has numerous sources of information on psychosocial aspects of development.

http://www.apa.org/pubinfo/altruism.html

The American Psychological Association includes information on its website about why children care for others and includes tips for parents who want to encourage their children to be more altruistic.

http://www.hc-sc.gc.ca/hppb/mentalhealth/mhp/pub/fc/index.html

This Health Canada website provides information and resources on the importance of first connections for infants.

Website addresses are subject to change. The *Human Development* book companion website can be accessed for updated links.

The Human Development Book Companion Website

See http://www.humandevelopment.nelson.com for practice quiz questions, Internet links, updates, critical thinking exercises, discussion forums, and more.

 Life-Span CD-ROM

For more information on the concepts covered in this chapter, go to

Module 2: Infancy and Toddlerhood

• Emotional and Social Development

Comstock

CHAPTER 5

Growing and Learning in the Preschool Years

PHYSICAL AND COGNITIVE DEVELOPMENT IN EARLY CHILDHOOD

The first section of this chapter describes the physical development and changes in preschoolers as well as their nutritional needs. In the second section we'll discuss motor development of the large and small muscles, allowing for greater control in physical and fine motor activities in young children.

The next two sections of the chapter concern alternative accounts of cognitive development. One account, the information-processing perspective, traces children's emerging cognitive skills in many specific domains, among them memory skills. The other, Lev Vygotsky's theory, emphasizes the cultural origins of cognitive development and explains why children sometimes talk to themselves as they play or work.

Throughout development, children express their thoughts in oral and written language. In the last section of this chapter, you'll see how children master the sounds, words, and grammar of their native language.

5.1

Physical Development: Growth and Change

LEARNING OBJECTIVES

- How do height and weight change from 2 to 5 years of age?
- What nutritional needs and issues are there for preschool children?
- How do sleeping patterns change?

Lindsay is 3 years old and is generally a happy and active child. Lately her parents have become worried because the only thing she seems to want to eat are grilled cheese sandwiches and apple juice. Also, she now refuses to take her afternoon nap. Her parents wonder if her behaviour is cause for concern. It seemed like just yesterday she was willing to give different foods a try and always seemed to enjoy naptime.

The preschool years are a time when children are moving from being dependent on others to anticipate and meet all their needs to being able to express themselves and their preferences. Their physical, motor, and cognitive skills make great advances during these exciting and fun years.

GROWTH OF THE BODY

In early childhood, growth slows down considerably from the infancy stage. The average child gains approximately 2.5 kilograms in weight and grows five to seven centimetres per year between the ages of 3 and 5 years. These increases are variable and are affected by cultural, genetic, and environmental factors, such as nutritional intake. In addition, body shape changes to a proportion seen in older children and adults, a change from the rather top-heavy toddler. These changes, along with arm and leg growth, allow children in this age group to advance in both gross and fine motor skills.

NUTRITIONAL NEEDS AND ISSUES

Since growth slows during the preschool years, children need less to eat. This is also a time when many children become picky eaters. Preschool children may start to find foods "yucky" that they once ate willingly. As a toddler, Laura Kail loved green beans. When she reached age 2, she decided that green beans were awful and adamantly refused to eat them. Though such finickiness can be annoying, it may actually be adaptive for increasingly independent preschoolers. Because toddlers don't know what is safe to eat and what isn't, eating only familiar foods protects them from potential harm (Birch & Fisher, 1995).

Parents should not be overly concerned about this finicky period. Although some children do eat less than before (measured by calories per kilogram), virtually all picky eaters get adequate food for growth. Nevertheless, picky eaters can make mealtime miserable for all. As discussed in Chapter 3, parents should encourage children to try different foods but give them lots of choices between healthy foods. In addition, parents should understand this is a normal stage for children, and they may refuse to eat foods they used to eat and/or they may want to eat only a few select food items at mealtimes.

SLEEP FOR TODDLERS AND PRESCHOOLERS

By the toddler and preschool years, sleep routines are well established. Most 2-year-olds spend about 13 hours sleeping, compared to just under 11 hours for 6-year-olds. At about age 4, most youngsters give up their afternoon nap and sleep longer at nighttime to compensate. This can be a challenging time for parents and caregivers who use the child's naptime as an opportunity to complete some work or to relax.

Following an active day, most preschool children drift off to sleep easily. However, most children will have an occasional night when bedtime is a struggle. Furthermore, for 20 to 30% of preschool children, bedtime struggles occur nightly (Lozoff, Wolf, & Davis, 1985). More often than not, these bedtime problems reflect the absence of a regular bedtime routine that's followed consistently. The key to a pleasant bedtime is to establish a nighttime routine that helps children "wind down" from busy daytime activities. This routine should start at about the same time every night ("It's time to get ready for bed . . .") and end at about the same time (when the parent leaves the child and the child tries to fall asleep). This nighttime routine may be anywhere from 15 to 45 minutes long, depending on the child. Also, as children get older, parents can expect their children to perform more of these tasks independently. A 2-year-old will need help all along the way, but a 5-year-old can do many of these tasks alone. But remember to follow the routine consistently; this way children know that each step is getting them closer to bedtime and falling asleep.

TEST YOURSELF

1. In early childhood, physical growth _____ considerably compared to the first two years of life.

2. The body shape changes in early childhood from top heavy to proportions closer to older children and adults help with _____ development.

3. Growth changes during preschool years usually mean that children need to eat _____ than previously, based on calories per kilogram.

4. Parents should encourage a bedtime _____ for young children to decrease the likelihood of bedtime problems.

Many children go through periods when they are very particular about foods they eat. What are some positive aspects of this behaviour?

Answers: (1) decreases, (2) motor, (3) less, (4) routine

5.2

Gross and Fine Motor Skills

LEARNING OBJECTIVES

- How do gross motor skills change from 2 to 5 years of age?
- What fine motor skills are developing during this period?

Gross and Fine Motor Skills
Beyond Walking
Fine Motor Skills

At 5 years old, Conye loves to play baseball with his mom and older brother. Although he usually misses when he tries to hit the ball, he is getting better. His brother is amazed that his catching has improved so much over the past month. Also, although Conye would throw the ball with either hand when he was younger, lately he will throw with only his right hand.

In this section we'll discuss the large (gross motor) and small muscle (fine motor) development that occurs during the preschool years. Also, we will consider what determines whether a person is right- or left-handed.

BEYOND WALKING

By 5 or 6 years, children run easily, quickly changing directions or speed. Hopping also shows young children's growing skill. A typical 2- or 3-year-old will hop a few times on one foot, typically keeping the upper body very stiff; by 5 or 6, children can hop long distances on one foot or alternate hopping first on one foot a few times, then on the other.

With their advanced motor skills, older preschoolers delight in unstructured play. They enjoy swinging, climbing over jungle gyms, and balancing on a beam. Some learn to ride a tricycle or to swim.

FINE MOTOR SKILLS

As preschoolers, children become much more dexterous, able to make many precise and delicate movements with their hands and fingers. Greater fine motor skill means that preschool children can begin to care for themselves. No longer must they rely primarily on parents to feed and clothe them; instead, they become increasingly skilled at feeding and dressing themselves. A 2- or 3-year-old, for example, can put on some simple clothing and use zippers but not buttons; by 3 or 4 years, children can fasten buttons and take off their clothes; like the child in the photo, most 5-year-olds can dress and undress themselves, except for tying shoes, which children typically master at about age 6.

Joel Gordon

Greater fine motor coordination also leads to improvements in preschool children's printing and drawing. Given a crayon or marker, 2-year-olds will scribble, expressing delight in the simple lines that are created just by moving a crayon or marker across paper. By 4 or 5 years of age, children use their drawings to depict recognizable objects.

All these actions illustrate the principles of differentiation and integration that were introduced in our discussion of locomotion. Complex acts involve many constituent movements. Each must be performed correctly and in the proper sequence. Development involves first mastering the separate elements and then assembling them into a smoothly functioning whole.

HANDEDNESS

By age 5 children typically use their nonpreferred hand only when the preferred hand is busy doing something else. By the time children are ready to enter kindergarten, handedness is well established and very difficult to reverse (McManus et al., 1988).

What determines whether children become left- or right-handed? Heredity plays a role (Corballis, 1997). Parents who are both right-handed tend to have right-handed children. Children who are left-handed generally have a parent or grandparent who was also left-handed. Regarding motor function, since the right side of the brain controls the left side of the body and vice versa, it is generally believed that handedness is associated with dominance of the opposite side of the brain. *This implies that handedness may be associated with other aspects of brain specialization such as **lateralization**, where certain cognitive functions are located on one side of the brain more than the other, but research is mixed regarding these effects.* Because emotions are believed to be primarily regulated by the left side of the brain, Canadian researchers Mueller, Grove, & Thompson (1993) were interested in the relationship between anxiety with test writing and handedness but found no correlation between the two. This suggests that the implications of hemispheric dominance are not fully understood.

Experience also contributes to handedness. Modern industrial cultures favour right-handedness. School desks, scissors, and can openers, for example, are designed for right-handed people and can be used by left-handers only with difficulty.

Sometimes cultural values influence handedness. The Islam religion dictates that the left hand is unclean, and so forbids its use in eating and greeting others. And, traditionally in China, writing with the left hand was a cultural taboo; however, when children of Chinese parents grow up elsewhere, left-handers like the youngster in the photo are more common (Harris, 1983). In the past, elementary school teachers urged left-handed children to use their right hand. As this practice has diminished in the last 50 years, the percentage of left-handed children has risen steadily (Levy, 1976). Thus, handedness seems to have both hereditary and environmental influences.

Mary-Kate Denney/PhotoEdit

HEALTHY LIVING

What practices can promote health during the preschool years?

During the preschool years children become increasingly independent in their mobility and ability to learn and express themselves. However, they still require close supervision in activities because they may become too distracted to follow rules, such as not running into the street. However, they can begin to understand simple rules and should be taught safety rules related to topics such as traffic, fire, sharp objects, stranger awareness, and good touch/bad touch. Parents should be aware of where their children are at all times. A regular regime of dental care and regular physical checkups will help determine if a

child's growth and development are proceeding normally and in a healthful fashion. Parents should encourage good nutrition and activity habits as well as healthy sleep routines and patterns. Disciplinary strategies should be non-physical and directed at teaching self-control and empathy; they should include fair and logical consequences for misbehaviour. Children should be frequently informed and reminded of the rules for expected behaviour. Consequences for misbehaviour should always be presented in a manner that preserves a child's dignity and self-esteem.

TEST YOURSELF

1. By the end of the preschool years, most children can dress and undress themselves due to _____ skill development.

2. By age 5 children typically use their _____ hand unless their other hand is busy doing something else.

3. When certain cognitive functions are located on one side of the brain more than the other this is called

_____.

4. Although preschool children seem to be becoming so much more independent they still need close _____ because they can be easily distracted.

What effect do you think it might have on a child who is demonstrating left-handed preference when parents and/or teachers try to encourage right-handed writing?

Answers: (1) fine motor, (2) preferred, (3) lateralization, (4) supervision

5.3

Cognitive Development: Piaget's Account

LEARNING OBJECTIVES

☑ According to Piaget, how do assimilation, accommodation, and equilibration provide the foundation for cognitive development throughout the life span?

☑ What are some of the shortcomings of Piaget's account of cognitive development?

Three-year-old Jamila loves talking to her grandmother ("Gram") on the telephone. Sometimes these conversations are not very successful because Gram asks questions and Jamila replies by nodding her head "yes" or "no." Jamila's dad has explained that Gram (and others on the phone) can't see her nodding—that she needs to say "yes" or "no." But Jamila invariably returns to head-nodding. Her dad can't see why such a bright and talkative child doesn't realize that nodding is meaningless over the phone.

Why does Jamila insist on nodding her head when she's talking on the phone? This behaviour is quite typical according to psychologist Jean Piaget, some of whose ideas were presented in Chapter 3. Piaget believed that children's thinking progresses through four qualitatively different stages. In this section, we'll examine Piaget's account of thinking during the preschool years and consider some of the strengths and weaknesses of the theory.

Recall from Chapter 3 that Piaget believed that children understand the world with schemes—psychological structures that organize experience. In the preschool years schemes are based primarily on functional or conceptual relationships, not action as in infancy. For example, preschoolers learn that forks, knives, and spoons form a functional category of "things I use to eat." Or they learn that dogs, cats, and goldfish form a conceptual category of "pets."

Like preschoolers, older children and adolescents have schemes based on functional and conceptual schemes. But they also have schemes that are based on increasingly abstract properties. For example, an adolescent might put fascism, racism, and sexism in a category of "ideologies I despise."

Thus, schemes of related objects, events, and ideas are present throughout development. But as children develop, their rules for creating schemes shift from physical activity to functional, conceptual, and, later, abstract properties of objects, events, and ideas.

As you will recall from Chapter 3, intellectual adaptation involves two processes working together: assimilation and accommodation.

Assimilation and accommodation are often easier to understand when you remember Piaget's belief that infants, children, and adolescents create theories to try to understand events and objects around them.

PREOPERATIONAL THINKING

Once young children have crossed into preoperational thinking—which always follows sensorimotor thinking—the magical power of symbols is available to them. Of course, mastering this power is a lifelong process; the preschool child's efforts are tentative and sometimes incorrect (DeLoache, 1995). Piaget identified a number of characteristic shortcomings in preschoolers' fledgling symbolic skills. Let's look at three.

Egocentrism

Preoperational children typically believe others see the world—both literally and figuratively—exactly as they do. *Egocentrism is difficulty in seeing the world from another's outlook.* When youngsters stubbornly cling to their own way, they are not simply being contrary. Pre-operational children simply do not comprehend that other people differ in their ideas, convictions, and emotions.

One of Piaget's famous experiments, the three-mountains problem, demonstrates preoperational children's egocentrism (Piaget & Inhelder, 1956, chap. 8). Youngsters were seated at a table like the one shown in Figure 5.1. When preoperational children were asked to choose the photograph that corresponded to another person's view of the mountains, they usually picked the photograph that showed their own view of the mountains, not the other person's. Preoperational youngsters evidently suppose that the mountains are seen the same way by all; they presume that theirs is

FIGURE 5.1   Preoperational Egocentrism

the only view, not one of many conceivable views. According to Piaget, only concrete operational children fully understand that all people do not experience an event in exactly the same way.

Recall that 3-year-old Jamila (from the vignette) nods her head during phone conversations with her grandmother. This, too, reflects preoperational egocentrism. Jamila assumes that because she is aware that her head is moving up and down (or side-to-side) her grandmother must be aware of it too. In the Real People feature, we see yet another manifestation of this egocentrism.

REAL PEOPLE: APPLYING HUMAN DEVELOPMENT

Cathleen, Egocentrism, and Animism

Because of their egocentrism, preoperational youngsters often attribute their own thoughts and feelings to others. *They may even credit inanimate objects with life and lifelike properties, a phenomenon known as animism* (Piaget, 1929). A three-and-a-half-year-old we know, Cathleen, illustrated this in a conversation we had with her recently on a dreary, rainy day when she was forced to stay indoors.

CATHLEEN: Mr. Sun is very sad today.
US: Why?
CATHLEEN: Because it's cloudy. He can't shine. And he can't see me!

US: That's too bad.
CATHLEEN: Trike [tricycle] is sad too.
US: Why is that?
CATHLEEN: Because I can't ride him. And because he's all alone in the garage, where it's dark.

Caught up in her egocentrism, preoperational Cathleen believes objects like the sun and her tricycle think and feel as she does. That is, because she has thoughts and feelings, she believes other people and inanimate objects have them too. ⏘

Centration

A second characteristic of preoperational thinking is that children seem to have the psychological equivalent of tunnel vision: They often concentrate on one aspect of a problem but totally ignore other equally relevant aspects. *Centration is Piaget's term for this narrowly focused thought that characterizes preoperational youngsters.*

Piaget demonstrated centration in his experiments involving conservation. In the conservation experiments, Piaget wanted to determine when children realize that important characteristics of objects (or sets of objects) stay the same despite changes in their physical appearance, known as *reversibility*. Some tasks that Piaget used to study conservation are shown in Figure 5.2. Each begins with identical objects (or sets of objects). Then one of the objects (or sets) is transformed, and children are asked if the objects are the same with regard to some important feature.

FIGURE 5.2   Conservation Experiments

Type of conservation	Starting configuration	Transformation	Final configuration
Liquid quantity	 Is there the same amount of water in each glass?	Pour water from one glass into a shorter, wider glass.	 Now is there the same amount of water in each glass, or does one glass have more?
Number	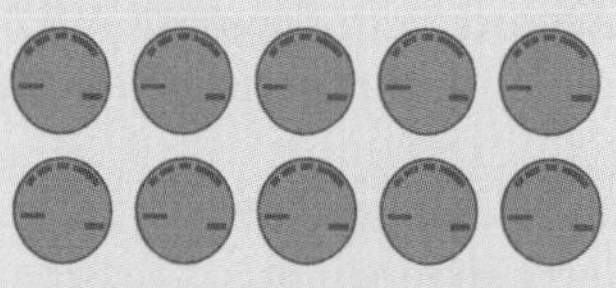 Are there the same number of pennies in each row?	Stretch out the top row of pennies, push together the bottom row.	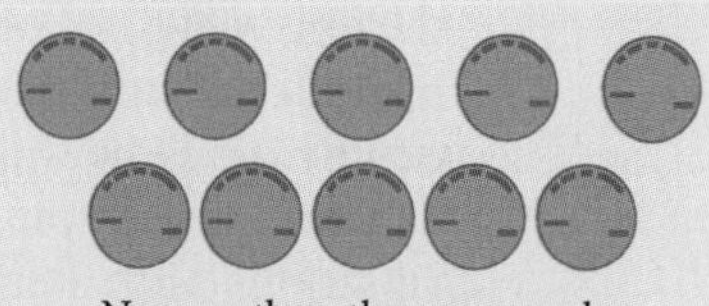 Now are there the same number of pennies in each row, or does one row have more?
Length	 Are these sticks the same length?	Move one stick to the left and the other to the right.	 Now are the sticks the same length, or is one longer?
Mass	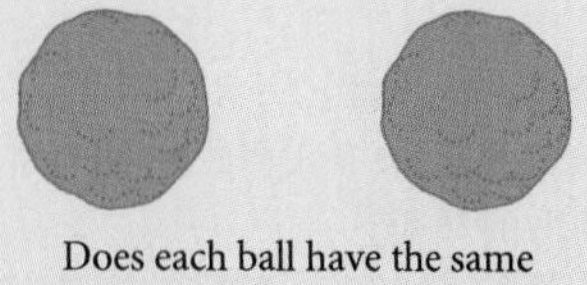 Does each ball have the same amount of clay?	Roll one ball so that it looks like a sausage.	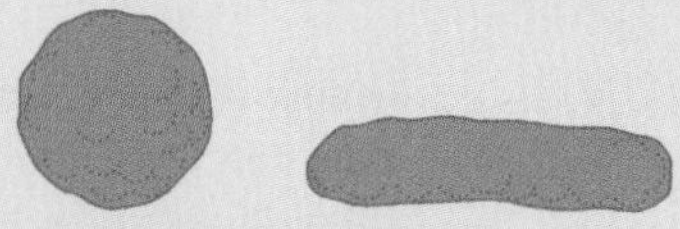 Now does each piece have the same amount of clay, or does one have more?
Area	 Does each cow have the same amount of grass to eat?	Spread out the squares in one field.	 Now does each cow have the same amount to eat, or does one cow have more?

A typical conservation problem, involving conservation of liquid quantity, is shown in the photo. Children are shown identical beakers filled with the same amount of juice. After children agree that the two beakers have the same amount of juice, the juice is poured from one beaker into a taller, thinner beaker. The juice looks different in the tall, thin beaker—it rises higher—but of course the amount is unchanged. Nevertheless, preoperational children claim that the tall, thin beaker has more juice than the original beaker. (And, if the juice is poured into a wider beaker, they believe it has less.)

What is happening here? According to Piaget, preoperational children centre on the level of the juice in the beaker. If the juice is higher after it is poured, preoperational children believe there must be more juice now than before. Because preoperational thinking is centred, these youngsters ignore the fact that the change in the level of the juice is always accompanied by a change in the diameter of the beaker.

In other conservation problems, preoperational children also tend to focus on only one aspect of the problem. In conservation of number, for example, preoperational children concentrate on the fact that, after the transformation, one row of objects is now longer than the other. In conservation of length, preoperational children concentrate on the fact that, after the transformation, the end of one stick is farther to the right than the end of the other. Preoperational children's centred thinking means that they overlook other parts of the problem that would tell them the quantity is unchanged.

Appearance as Reality

A final feature of preoperational thinking is that preschool children believe an object's appearance tells what the object is really like. For instance, many a 3-year-old has watched with quiet fascination as an older brother or sister put on a ghoulish costume only to erupt in frightened tears when this sibling put on scary makeup. For the youngster in the photo, the scary made-up face is reality, not just something that looks frightening but really isn't.

Confusion between appearance and reality is not limited to costumes and masks. It is a general characteristic of preoperational thinking. Consider the following cases where appearances and reality conflict:

- A boy is angry because a friend is being mean but smiles because he's afraid the friend will leave if he reveals his anger.
- A glass of milk looks brown when seen through sunglasses.
- A piece of hard rubber looks like food (e.g., like a piece of pizza).

Older children and adults know that the boy looks happy, the milk looks brown, and the object looks like food but that the boy is really angry, the milk is really white, and the object is really rubber. Preoperational children, however, confuse appearance and reality, thinking the boy is happy, the milk is brown, and the piece of rubber is edible.

Distinguishing appearance and reality is particularly difficult for children in the early years of preoperational thinking. This difficulty is evident in research on children's use of scale models, which are objects that also symbolize some much larger object. A model of a house, for example, can be an interesting object in its own right as well as a representation of an actual house. The ability to use scale models develops early in the preoperational period. If young children watch an adult hide a toy in a full-size room, then try to find the toy in a scale model of the room that contains all the principal features of the full-scale room (e.g., carpet, window, furniture), 3-year-olds find the hidden toy readily but two-and-a-half-year-olds do not (DeLoache, 1995).

Why is this task so easy for 3-year-olds and so difficult for two-and-a-half-year-olds? Judy DeLoache believes that two-and-a-half-year-olds' "attention to a scale model as an interesting and attractive object makes it difficult for them to simultaneously think about its relation to something else" (DeLoache, Miller, & Rosengren, 1997, p. 308). In other words, for young children the appearance of the object *is* reality and, consequently, they find it hard to think about the model as a symbol of something else (i.e., the full-size room).

If this argument is correct, two-and-a-half-year-olds should be more successful using the model if they don't have to think of it as a symbol for the full-size room. DeLoache tested this hypothesis in the study described in the Spotlight on Research feature. (This is one of our favourite studies of all time, for reasons that will soon be obvious.)

SPOTLIGHT ON RESEARCH

Finding Toys in a Shrunken Room

Who were the investigators and what was the aim of the study? Judy DeLoache, Kevin Miller, and Karl Rosengren (1997) believed that two-and-a-half-year-olds could not find the toy in the model because it was difficult for them to think of the model as an object *and* as a symbol of the full-size room. To test this argument, they created a condition designed to eliminate the need for children to think of the model as an object and as a symbol. Children were told that a machine could shrink the full-size room. In this case, the model is no longer a symbol of the full-size room; it *is* the room, just shrunken. Consequently, DeLoache and her colleagues expected two-and-a-half-year-olds to find the hidden toy because they believed the model was the full-size room shrunk to miniature size.

How did the investigators measure the topic of interest? Some children were tested with the usual procedures: hiding the toy in the full-size room and asking children to find it in the scale model. Other children were tested in the new condition designed to help them find the toy. Children were shown the oscillo-

scope shown in the photograph, which was described as a shrinking machine. They saw a toy doll—"Terry the Troll"—placed in front of the oscilloscope; then the experimenter and child left the room briefly while a tape recorder played sounds that were described as sounds "the machine makes when it's shrinking something." When experimenter and child returned, Terry had shrunk from eight inches to two inches. Next, Terry was hidden in the full-size room, the experimenter aimed the "shrinking machine" at the full-size room, then experimenter and child left the room. While the tape recorder played shrinking sounds, research assistants quickly removed everything from the full-size room and substituted the model. Experimenter and child returned and the child was asked to find Terry. This procedure was repeated so that children searched for Terry on four separate trials.

Who were the children in the study? DeLoache and her colleagues tested 32 children whose average age was two and a half years.

What was the design of the study? The study was experimental. The independent

Judy Deloache

What were the results? The top part of Figure 5.3 shows the percentage of trials in which children found the toy. Children rarely found the toy in the standard condition, but they did frequently in the "shrinking machine" condition. The bottom part of the graph shows the percentage of children who found Terry on at least three of the four trials. No children in the standard condition were this accurate, but most children in the "shrinking machine" condition were.

What did the investigators conclude? When two-and-a-half-year-olds must think of the model as an object *and* as a symbol, they find this very difficult and, consequently, cannot find the hidden toy, even though the model is an exact replica of the full-size room. When children need only think of the model as the original room, but much smaller, they readily find the toy.

variable was the presence or absence of the shrinking machine. The dependent variable was the percentage of trials on which the children found Terry.

Were there ethical concerns with the study? For children tested with the "shrinking machine," the study involved deception. Parents were fully informed about the shrinking machine before they gave consent, and parents were present throughout the experiment. Immediately after the experiment, children were told that the machine could not really shrink objects. They were shown the model, the full-size room, and both small and large versions of Terry. The deception seemed warranted, and no child seemed upset when told what really happened.

What converging evidence would strengthen these conclusions? Because the changes observed by DeLoache and her colleagues appeared across a fairly narrow age range, this would be an ideal opportunity to conduct a microgenetic study. The goal would be to show, for individual children, the age at which they understand the model is a symbol of something else. Additional useful evidence would be to compare the results with other situations in which an object also serves a symbolic function (e.g., children's understanding that a map is a colourful piece of paper as well as symbol of a much larger physical space).

FIGURE 5.3

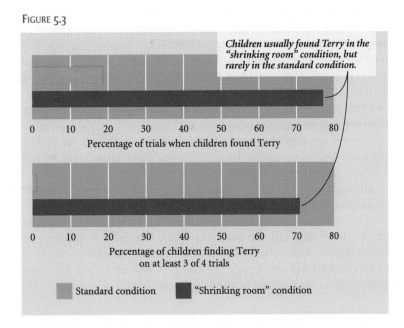

Children usually found Terry in the "shrinking room" condition, but rarely in the standard condition.

Percentage of trials when children found Terry

Percentage of children finding Terry
on at least 3 of 4 trials

Standard condition   "Shrinking room" condition

THINK ABOUT IT 🔎

How might the different features of preoperational thought affect children's interactions with peers?

The appearance of an interesting object that beckons "come play with me" is reality for two-and-a-half-year-olds; they cannot "see through" the model to realize that in this task the model really is a symbol for something else (DeLoache, 2000). Difficulty in distinguishing appearance and reality is a deep-seated characteristic of preoperational thinking (especially in the early years of this stage), as are egocentrism and centration.

These defining characteristics of preoperational thought are summarized in Table 5.1.

TABLE 5.1	Characteristics of Preoperational Thinking	
Characteristic	Definition	Example
Egocentrism	Child believes all people see the world as he or she does.	A child gestures during a telephone conversation, not realizing that the listener cannot see the gestures.
Centration	Child focuses on one aspect of a problem or situation but ignores other relevant aspects.	In conservation of liquid quantity, child pays attention to the height of the liquid in the beaker but ignores the diameter of the beaker.
Appearance as reality	Child assumes that an object really is what it appears to be.	Child believes that a person smiling at another person is really happy even though the other person is being mean.

EVALUATING PIAGET'S THEORY

Because Piaget's theory is so comprehensive, it has stimulated much research. Much of this work supports Piaget's view that children actively try to understand the world around them and organize their knowledge and that cognitive development includes major qualitative changes (Brainerd, 1996; Flavell, 1996).

One important contribution of Piaget's theory is that many teachers and parents have found it a rich source of ideas about ways to foster children's development. In fact, the theory has several straightforward implications for teaching practices that promote cognitive growth:

- Cognitive growth occurs as children construct their own understanding of the world, so the teacher's role is to create environments where children can discover for themselves how the world works. A teacher shouldn't simply try to tell children how addition and subtraction are complementary but instead should provide children with materials that enable them to discover the complementarity themselves.
- Children profit from experience only when they can interpret this experience with their current cognitive structures. It follows, then, that the best teaching experiences are slightly ahead of the child's current level of thinking. As a youngster begins to master basic addition, don't jump right to subtraction but go to slightly more difficult addition problems.
- Cognitive growth can be particularly rapid when children discover inconsistencies and errors in their own thinking. Teachers should therefore encourage children to look at the consistency of their thinking but then let children take the lead in sorting out the inconsistencies. If a child is making mistakes in borrowing on subtraction problems, a teacher shouldn't correct the error directly but should encourage the child to look at a large number of these errors to discover what he or she is doing wrong.

Despite these important contributions of Piaget's theory, some aspects of his theory have been challenged. Let's look at some of the criticisms that have been raised.

Alternative Explanations of Performance

As we have seen, Piaget explained cognitive development by using constructs like accommodation, assimilation, and schemes. However, subsequent researchers have found that children's performance on Piaget's tasks is often better explained by other theoretical constructs. For example, preoperational children's performance on the conservation task appears to reflect, at least in part, their growing sensitivity to the nuances of language rather than purely their lack of reversibility. The phrasing of the questions concerning the amount of water turns out to be critical (Winer, Craig, & Weinbaum, 1992). Remember that, in this procedure, youngsters are twice asked if the amount of water in the two beakers is the same—once before the water is poured and once after. In everyday conversation, a question is usually repeated like this because the answer was wrong the first time. Or it may be repeated because the answer was correct at first but something has changed so that it is now wrong. Both of these rules about questions would lead young children who had answered yes to the first question to wonder whether they were wrong and perhaps say no the second time. In fact, when the procedure is changed (e.g., by asking the question only once), preschoolers are more likely to answer correctly. Thus, children's performance on conservation problems is based partly on language development, not just the concepts that Piaget included in his theory.

Consistency in Performance

In Piaget's view, each stage of intellectual development consists of a unified set of mental structures that pervades children's thinking. For example, preoperational thinking should leave its mark on all of a child's activities. On conservation and three-mountains tasks, a 4-year-old should always respond in a preoperational way: He should claim that the water is not the same after pouring and believe that the other person sees the mountains as he does. In fact, research reveals some consistency in performance on various tasks, but exceptions are common too (Siegler, 1981). A youngster may be advanced on the conservation task, perfectly average on the three-mountains task, and somewhat delayed on other Piagetian tasks. This variability is not readily incorporated into Piaget's view of uniform stages that should leave the same characteristic imprint in all domains.

These criticisms do not mean that Piaget's theory is invalid or should be ignored. As noted earlier, it remains the most complete account of cognitive development. However, in recent years, researchers have attempted to round out our understanding of cognitive development, using other theoretical perspectives such as the information-processing approach that is examined later in this chapter.

EXTENDING PIAGET'S ACCOUNT: CHILDREN'S NAÏVE THEORIES

Piaget believed that children, like scientists, formulate theories about how the world works, but that children's theories are usually called "naïve theories." We examined some aspects of children's naïve theories in Chapter 3; in the next few pages, we'll continue this discussion.

Naïve Biology

By the preschool years, children's naïve theories of biology have come to include many of the specific properties associated with living things (Wellman & Gelman, 1998). Many 4-year-olds' theories of biology include the following elements:

- *Movement:* Children understand that animals can move themselves but inanimate objects can be moved only by other objects or by people. Shown an animal and a toy hopping across a table in exactly the same manner, preschoolers claim that only the animal can move itself (Gelman & Gottfried, 1996).

■ *Growth:* Children understand that, from their first appearance, animals get bigger and physically more complex but that inanimate objects do not change in this way. They believe, for example, that sea otters and termites become larger as time goes by but that teakettles and teddy bears do not (Rosengren et al., 1991).

■ *Internal parts:* Children know that the insides of animate objects contain different materials than the insides of inanimate objects. Preschool children judge that blood and bones are more likely to be inside an animate object but that cotton and metal are more likely to be inside an inanimate object (Simons & Keil, 1995).

■ *Inheritance:* Children realize that only living things have offspring that resemble their parents. Asked to explain why a dog is pink, preschoolers believe that some biological characteristic of the parents probably made the dog pink; asked to explain why a can is pink, preschoolers rely on mechanical causes (e.g., a worker used a machine), not biological ones (Springer & Keil, 1991; Weissman & Kalish, 1999).

■ *Healing:* Children understand that, when injured, animate things heal by regrowth whereas inanimate things must be fixed by humans. Preschoolers know that hair will grow back when cut from a child's head but must be repaired by a person when cut from a doll's head (Backschedier, Shatz, & Gelman, 1993).

Findings like these make it clear that preschoolers' naïve theories of biology are complex. Of course, their theories aren't complete; they don't know, for instance, that genes are the biological basis for inheritance (Springer & Keil, 1991). And preschoolers' theories include some misconceptions; they believe, for example, that adopted children will physically resemble their adoptive parents (Solomon et al., 1996).

Armed with their expanding theories of physics, biology, and (from Chapter 3) psychology, toddlers and preschoolers are well prepared to make sense of their world and to understand new experiences.

The next two sections of the chapter concern alternative accounts of cognitive development. One account, the information-processing perspective, traces children's emerging cognitive skills in many specific domains, among them memory skills. The other, Lev Vygotsky's theory, emphasizes the cultural origins of cognitive development and explains why children sometimes talk to themselves as they play or work.

Throughout development, children express their thoughts in oral and written language. In the last section of this chapter, you'll see how children master the sounds, words, and grammar of their native language.

TEST YOURSELF

1. According to Piaget, _____ are psychological structures that organize experience.

2. Preschoolers are often _____, meaning that they are unable to take another person's viewpoint.

3. Preoperational children sometimes attribute thoughts and feelings to inanimate objects. This is called

_____.

4. One criticism of Piaget's theory is that children's performance on tasks like con-

servation and object performance is

_____.

5. Most 4-year-olds know that living things move, _____, have internal parts, resemble their parents, and heal when injured.

What forces in the biopsychosocial framework can you see in a young child's progress through the preoperational period?

Answers: (1) schemes, (2) egocentric, (3) animism, (4) better explained by ideas that are not part of Piaget's theory, (5) grow.

Information Processing During Early Childhood

LEARNING OBJECTIVES

☑ What is the basis of the information-processing approach?

☑ How well do young children pay attention?

☑ Do preschool children have good memories?

☑ What are the shortcomings of preschoolers' eyewitness testimony? What can we do to make it more reliable?

☑ How do preschoolers count?

One afternoon, 4-year-old Cheryl came home sobbing and reported that Mr. Johnson, a neighbour and long-time family friend, had touched her "private parts." Her mother was shocked. She had always believed Mr. Johnson to be an honest, decent man, which made her wonder if it could have really happened. Yet Mr. Johnson had sometimes seemed a bit peculiar, so her daughter's claim did raise her suspicions.

Today, many developmentalists borrow from computer science to formulate their ideas about human thinking and how it develops (Kail & Bisanz, 1992; Plunkett, 1996). As you recall from Chapter 1, this approach is called information processing. In this section, we'll see what information processing has revealed about young children's thinking.

GENERAL PRINCIPLES OF INFORMATION PROCESSING

In Chapter 1, we explained that, in the information-processing view, human thinking is based on both mental hardware and mental software. *The term* ***mental hardware*** *refers to mental and neural structures that are built in and that allow the mind to operate. The term* ***mental software*** *refers to mental programs that are the basis for performing particular tasks.* According to information-processing psychologists, the combination of mental hardware and mental software enables children to accomplish a specific task. Information-processing psychologists claim that, as children develop, their mental software becomes more complex, more powerful, and more efficient.

In the next few pages, we'll look at the development of many important cognitive processes in young children, beginning with attention.

ATTENTION

It may seem that preschool children have very short attention spans. Although preschool children gradually learn how to focus their attention, when compared to older children and adults, they are often not very attentive (Ruff, Capozzoli, & Weissberg, 1998). Preschoolers are easily distracted by extraneous information. However, we can help children to pay attention better. One straightforward approach is to make relevant information stand out. For example, closing a classroom door may not eliminate competing sounds and smells entirely, but it does make them less noticeable. When preschoolers are working at a table or desk, we can remove other objects that are not necessary for the task. Another useful tack, particularly for young children, is to remind them to pay attention to relevant information and ignore the rest.

LEARNING BY IMITATION

Children, adolescents, and young adults learn much simply by watching others behave. As discussed earlier in this text, social learning theory stresses the role of observation and imitation. For example, children learn new sports moves by watching pro athletes, they learn how to pursue romantic relationships by watching TV, and they learn how to play new computer games by watching peers.

MEMORY

Recognition is the ability to recognize something previously encountered (e.g., identify one's own toothbrush), and **recall** *is the ability to replicate something from one's memory (e.g., describe how to brush teeth).* Both are part of the development of memory. Young children find recognition easier than recall, which is true for all ages, but both abilities tend to improve over time.

Nelson (1993) distinguishes between three types of memory in childhood: generic, episodic, and autobiographical memory. *Generic memory starts at about age 2 years and it results in the production of a script, which is an outline of a repeated event, such as nap time at day care, and helps in the recall of what to expect.* **Episodic memory** *is the awareness that a specific event has occurred, but in young children this memory will last for only up to a few months unless it is repeated a number of times and subsequently transferred to generic memory.*

Autobiographical memory refers to people's memory of the significant events and experiences of their own lives which are long lasting. You can see your own autobiographical memory by answering these questions:

Who was your teacher in Grade 4?
Where (and with whom!) was your first kiss?
Was your high school graduation indoors or outdoors?

In answering these questions, you searched memory, just as you would search memory to answer questions such as "What is the capital of Manitoba?" and "Who invented the sewing machine?" However, answers to questions about Manitoba and sewing machines are based on general knowledge that you have experienced personally; answers to questions about *your* Grade 4 teacher, *your* first kiss, and *your* high school graduation are based on knowledge unique to your own life. Autobiographical memory is important because it helps people construct a personal life history. In addition, autobiographical memory enables people to relate their experiences to others, creating socially shared memories (Conway & Pleydell-Pearce, 2000; Nelson, 1993).

Autobiographical memory originates in the preschool years, when parents encourage children to think about the past by talking with them about recent events (Hudson, 2001). Picking up a 3-year-old from day care, a parent may ask, "What did you play?" "What did you have for snack?" In questions like these, parents usually focus on *who, what, where, when,* and *why.* In this way, they teach their children the important features of events and how events are organized. Children's autobiographical memories are richer when parents talk about past events in detail and encourage their children to participate in these conversations. In contrast, when parents' talk is limited to direct questions that can be answered "yes" or "no," children's autobiographical memories are less extensive (Farrant & Reese, 2000).

Research on children's autobiographical memory has played a central role in cases of suspected child abuse. When abuse is suspected, the victim is usually the sole witness. To prosecute the alleged abuser, the child's testimony is needed. But can preschoolers accurately recall these events? We'll try to answer this question in the Current Controversies feature.

UNDERSTANDING NUMBERS AND COUNTING

By preschool age children begin to have a mastery of the concept of numbers and counting. Gelman and Meck (1986) charted preschoolers' understanding of counting. They simply placed several objects in front of a child and asked, "How

CURRENT CONTROVERSIES

Preschoolers on the Witness Stand

Remember Cheryl, the 4-year-old who claimed that a neighbour had touched her "private parts"? Regrettably, episodes like this one are not uncommon in our society today. When abuse is suspected, the victim is usually the sole eyewitness. Can preschool children like Cheryl provide reliable testimony?

Answering this question is not as easy as it might seem. One obstacle to accurate testimony is that young children are often interviewed repeatedly during legal proceedings, which can cause them to confuse what actually happened with what others suggest may have happened. When, as in the situation in the photo, the questioner is an adult in a position of authority, children can believe that what is suggested by the adult actually happened (Ceci & Bruck, 1995, 1998; Lampinen & Smith, 1995). They may tell a convincing tale about "what really happened" simply because adults have led them to believe things must have happened that way. Although enforcement officials and child protection workers believe they can usually tell if children are telling the truth, young children's storytelling can be so convincing that professionals often cannot distinguish true and false reports (Gordon, Baker-Ward, & Ornstein, 2001). Maybe you doubt that interviewers routinely ask the leading or suggestive questions that are the seeds of false memories. But analyses of videotapes of actual interviews reveal that trained investigators may ask children leading questions and make suggestive comments (Lamb, Sternberg, & Esplin, 2000).

Peers can also influence children's memories. When some children in a class experience an event (e.g., a class field trip, a special class visitor), they often talk about the event with classmates who weren't there; later, these absent classmates readily describe what happened and often insist they were actually there (Principe & Ceci, 2002).

Young children can provide reliable testimony. Here are guidelines recommended for improving the reliability of child witnesses (Ceci & Bruck, 1995, 1998; Gordon et al., 2001):

- Warn children that interviewers may sometimes suggest things that didn't happen.
- Interviewers' questions should evaluate alternative explanations of what happened and who was involved.
- Children should not be questioned repeatedly on a single issue.

Following these guidelines can foster the conditions under which preschoolers (and older children too) are more likely to provide accurate testimony. And, based on these guidelines, Cheryl's report is definitely plausible as it was spontaneous rather than elicited by repeated questioning.

Tony Freeman/PhotoEdit

many?" By analyzing children's answers to many of these questions, Gelman and Meck discovered that by age three most children have mastered three basic principles of counting, at least when it comes to counting up to five objects.

- *One-to-one principle: There must be one and only one number name for each object that is counted.* A child who counts three objects as "1, 2, a" understands this principle because the number of number words matches the number of objects to be counted.
- *Stable-order principle: Number names must be counted in the same order.* A child who counts in the same sequence—for example, consistently counting four objects as "1, 2, 4, 5"—shows understanding of this principle.
- *Cardinality principle: The last number name differs from the previous ones in a counting sequence by denoting the number of objects.* Typically, 3-year-olds reveal their understanding of this principle by repeating the last number name, often with emphasis: "1, 2, 4, 8 . . . EIGHT!"

During the preschool years, children master these basic principles and apply them to ever-larger sets of objects. By age 5, most youngsters apply these counting principles to as many as nine objects. Of course, children's understanding of these principles does not mean that they always count accurately. To the contrary, children can apply all these principles consistently while counting incorrectly. They must master the conventional sequence of the number names and the counting principles to learn to count accurately.

Learning the number names beyond 9 is easier because the counting words can be generated based on rules for combining decade number names (20, 30, 40) with unit names (1, 2, 3, 4). And later, similar rules are used for hundreds, thousands, and so on. By age 4, most youngsters know the numbers to 20 and some can count to 99. Usually, they stop counting at a number ending in 9 (29, 59), apparently because they don't know the next decade name (Siegler & Robinson, 1982).

Learning to count beyond 10 is more complicated in English than in other languages. For example, *eleven* and *twelve* are completely irregular names, following no rules. Also, the remaining "teen" number names differ from the 20s, 30s, and the rest in that the decade number name comes after the unit (thir-*teen,* four-*teen*) rather than before (*twenty*-three, *thirty*-four). Also, some decade names only loosely correspond to the unit names on which they are based: twenty, thirty, and fifty resemble two, three, and five but are not the same.

In contrast, the Chinese, Japanese, and Korean number systems are almost perfectly regular. *Eleven* and *twelve* are expressed as *ten-one* and *ten-two.* There are no special names for the decades: *Two-ten* and *two-ten-one* are names for 20 and 21. These simplified number names help explain why youngsters growing up in Asian countries count more accurately than U.S. preschool children of the same age (Miller et al., 1995). Furthermore, the direct correspondence between the number names and the base-ten system makes it easier for Asian youngsters like the girl in the photo to learn base-ten concepts (Miura et al., 1988).

Thus far we have not considered the impact of the social context on children's thinking. In the next section, we'll examine a theory developed by Vygotsky, who believed that cognitive development has its roots in social interactions.

Alan Oddie/PhotoEdit

TEST YOURSELF

1. One way to improve preschool children's attention is to make irrelevant stimuli _____.

2. Preschoolers' testimony is more likely to be reliable if interviewers test alternative hypotheses and avoid repeated questioning, and if we warn the children that _____.

3. When a child who is counting a set of objects repeats the last number, usually with emphasis, this indicates the child's understanding of the _____ principle of counting.

Think back to the changes in attention and memory we've described in this section. Were the changes all quantitative in nature, or were some qualitative, like those emphasized by Piaget?

Answers: (1) less noticeable, (2) interviewers may try to trick them, (3) cardinality

5·5

Mind and Culture: Vygotsky's Theory

LEARNING OBJECTIVES

☑ What is the zone of proximal development? How does it help explain how children accomplish more when they collaborate with others?

☑ What is a particularly effective way of teaching youngsters new tasks?

☑ When and why do children talk to themselves as they solve problems?

> **Mind and Culture: Vygotsky's Theory**
>
> The Zone of Proximal Development
>
> Scaffolding
>
> Private Speech

Victoria, a 4-year-old, enjoys solving jigsaw puzzles, colouring, and building towers with blocks. While busy with these activities, she often talks to herself. For example, once as she was colouring a picture, she said, "Where's the red crayon? Stay inside the lines. Colour the blocks blue." These remarks were not directed at anyone else; after all, Victoria was alone. Why did she say these things? What purpose did they serve?

Human development is often referred to as a journey that takes people along many different paths. For Piaget and for information-processing psychologists, children make the journey alone. Other people (and culture in general) certainly influence the direction that children take, but fundamentally the child is a solitary adventurer-explorer, boldly forging ahead. Lev Vygotsky (1896–1934), a Russian psychologist, proposed a very different account. He believed development is an apprenticeship, in which children advance when they collaborate with others who are more skilled. According to Vygotsky (1934/1986), children rarely make much headway on the developmental path when they walk alone; they progress when they walk hand in hand with an expert partner.

Vygotsky died of tuberculosis at the age of 37, so he never had the opportunity to develop his theory fully. He did not provide a complete theory of cognitive development throughout childhood and adolescence (as Piaget did), nor did he give definitive accounts of cognitive change in specific domains (as information-processing theorists do). However, many of his ideas are influential, largely because they fill in some gaps in the Piagetian and information-processing accounts. In the next few pages, we'll look at three of Vygotsky's most important contributions—the zone of proximal development, scaffolding, and private speech—and discover why Victoria talks to herself.

THE ZONE OF PROXIMAL DEVELOPMENT

Four-year-old Ian and his father, shown in the photo, often solve puzzles together. Although Ian does most of the work, his father encourages him, sometimes finds a piece that he needs, or shows Ian how to put parts together. When Ian tries to assemble the same puzzles by himself, he can rarely complete them. *The difference between what Ian can do with assistance and what he does alone defines his zone of proximal development.* That is, the zone is the area between the level of performance a child can achieve when working independently and a higher level of performance that is possible when working under the guidance or direction of more skilled adults

or peers (Wertsch & Tulviste, 1992). For example, elementary school children are often asked to solve arithmetic story problems. Many youngsters have trouble with these problems, often because they simply don't know where to begin. By structuring the task for them—"First decide what you're supposed to figure out, then decide what information you're told in the problem"— teachers can help children accomplish what they cannot do by themselves. Thus, just as training wheels help children learn to ride a bike by allowing them to concentrate on certain aspects of bicycling, collaborators help children perform more effectively by providing structure, hints, and reminders.

David Young-Wolff/PhotoEdit

The idea of a zone of proximal development follows naturally from Vygotsky's basic premise: Cognition develops first in a social setting and only gradually comes under the child's independent control. What factors aid this shift? This leads us to the second of Vygotsky's key contributions.

SCAFFOLDING

Have you ever had the good fortune to work with a master teacher, one who seemed to know exactly when to say something to help you over an obstacle but otherwise let you work uninterrupted? *Scaffolding is a style in which teachers gauge the amount of assistance they offer to match the learner's needs.* Early in learning a new task, children know little, so teachers give much direct instruction about how to do all the different elements of a task. As the children catch on, teachers need to provide much less direct instruction; they are more likely to be giving reminders.

Worldwide, parents attempt to scaffold their children's learning, but not always using the same methods. Rogoff and her colleagues (1993) observed mothers in four countries—Guatemala, India, Turkey, and the United States—as they showed their toddlers how to operate a novel toy. In all cultures, most mothers attempted to scaffold their children's learning, either by dividing a difficult task into easier subtasks or by doing parts of the task themselves, particularly the more complicated parts. However, mothers in different cultures accomplish scaffolding in different ways. Mothers in Turkey and the United States relied primarily on verbal instruction. Mothers in India and Guatemala used verbal instruction, but they also used touches (e.g., nudging a child's elbow) or gaze (e.g., winking or staring) to guide their youngsters. Evidently, parents worldwide try to simplify learning tasks for their children, but they use different methods.

The defining characteristic of scaffolding—giving help but not more than is needed—clearly promotes learning (Plumert & Nichols-Whitehead, 1996). Youngsters do not learn readily when they are constantly told what to do or when they are simply left to struggle through a problem unaided. However, when teachers collaborate with them, allowing children to take on more and more of a task as they master its different elements, they learn more effectively (Murphy & Messer, 2000). Scaffolding is an important technique for transferring skills from others to the child, both in formal settings like schools and in informal settings like the home or playground.

PRIVATE SPEECH

Remember Victoria, the 4-year-old in the vignette who talked to herself as she coloured? *Her behaviour demonstrates* **private speech:** *comments that are not intended for others but are designed to help children regulate their own behaviour* (Vygotsky, 1934/1986). Thus, Victoria's remarks are simply an effort to help her colour the picture.

Vygotsky viewed private speech as an intermediate step toward self-regulation of cognitive skills. At first, children's behaviour is regulated by speech from other people that is directed toward them. When youngsters like the girl in the photo first try to control their own behaviour and thoughts, without others present, they instruct themselves by speaking aloud. Private speech seems to be children's way of guiding themselves, of making sure they do all the required steps in solving a problem. Finally, as children gain ever-greater skill, private speech becomes *inner speech,* which was Vygotsky's term for thought (Behrend, Rosengren, & Perlmutter, 1992).

If private speech functions in this way, can you imagine when a child would be most likely to use it? We should see children using private speech more often on difficult tasks than on easy tasks, because children are most likely to need extra guidance on harder tasks. Also, children should be more likely to use private speech after a mistake than after a correct response. These predictions are generally supported by research (Berk, 1992), which suggests the power of language in helping children learn to control their own behaviour and thinking.

Eric A. Wessman/Stock Boston Inc.

Thus, Vygotsky's work has characterized cognitive development not as a solitary undertaking but as a collaboration between expert and novice. His work reminds us of the importance of language, which we'll examine in detail in the last section of this chapter.

THINK ABOUT IT

Vygotsky emphasized cognitive development as collaboration. How could such collaboration be included in Piaget's theory? In information-processing theory?

TEST YOURSELF

1. The _____ is the difference between the level of performance youngsters can achieve with assistance and the level they can achieve alone.

2. The term _____ refers to a style in which teachers adjust their assistance to match a child's needs.

3. According to Vygotsky, _____ is an intermediate step between speech from others and inner speech.

Compare the role of sociocultural influences in Piaget's theory, the information-processing approach, and Vygotsky's theory.

Answers: (1) Theories, (2) psychosocial, (3) observing others, (4) information-processing, (5) microsystem, (6) life-span

5.6

Language

LEARNING OBJECTIVES

■ How do youngsters learn the meanings of words?

■ How do young children progress from two-word speech to more complex sentences?

■ How well do youngsters communicate?

Three-year-old Connie loves it when her parents read to her and ask her questions about the stories they read. Connie's parents notice that she seems to be learning new words every day and they are constantly surprised when she uses new words seemingly without knowing she's using them for the first time.

There is great progress in language development during the preschool years. Young children learn to use new words and put them together in conversation. Once they learn new words they like to use them often and love learning new names and labels. In this section we will discuss language and communication development during the amazing preschool years.

LANGUAGE DEVELOPMENT AND LEARNING TO COMMUNICATE IDEAS

You will recall from Chapter 3 that joint attention occurs when parents encourage word learning by labelling objects that interest their children. Although joint attention helps children to learn words, it is not required: Children learn new words that are used in ongoing conversation and when they overhear others use novel words (Akhtar, Jipson, & Callanan, 2001). And when speakers appear unfamiliar with a novel person or object, 4- and 5-year-olds are less likely to learn new words, as if they doubt that speakers know what they're talking about (Birch & Bloom, 2002; Sabbagh & Baldwin, 2001).

Constraints on Word Names

Joint attention simplifies word learning for children, but the problem still remains: How does a young child know that banana refers to the object that she's touching, as opposed to her activity (touching), or to the object's colour? Many researchers believe young children follow several simple rules that limit their conclusions about what labels mean.

A study by Au and Glusman (1990) identified one of the rules young children use. Au and Glusman presented preschoolers with a stuffed animal with pink horns that otherwise resembled a monkey and called it a *mido. Mido* was then repeated several times, always referring to the monkeylike stuffed animal with pink horns. Later, these youngsters were asked to find a *theri* in a set of stuffed animals that included several *mido.* Never having heard of a *theri,* what did the children do? They never picked a *mido;* instead, they selected other stuffed animals. Knowing that *mido* referred to monkeylike animals with pink horns, evidently they decided that *theri* had to refer to one of the other stuffed animals.

Apparently children were following this simple but effective rule for learning new words:

■ If an unfamiliar word is heard in the presence of objects that already have names and objects that don't, the word refers to one of the objects that doesn't have a name.

Researchers have discovered several other simple rules that help children match words with the correct referent (Hoff, 2001; Woodward & Markman, 1998):

- A name refers to a whole object, not its parts or its relation to other objects, and refers not just to this particular object but to all objects of the same type. For example, when a grandparent points to a stuffed animal on a shelf and says "dinosaur," children conclude that *dinosaur* refers to the entire dinosaur, not just its ears or nose, not to the fact that the dinosaur is on a shelf, and not to this specific dinosaur but to all dinosaurlike objects.

- If an object already has a name and another name is presented, the new name denotes a subcategory of the original name. If the child who knows the meaning of *dinosaur* sees a brother point to another dinosaur and hears the brother say "T-rex," the child will conclude that *T-rex* is a special type of dinosaur.

- Given many similar category members, a word applied consistently to only one of them is a proper noun. If a child who knows *dinosaur* sees that one of a group of dinosaurs is always called "Dino," the child will conclude that *Dino* is the name of that dinosaur.

Rules like these make it possible for children to learn words rapidly because they reduce the number of possible referents. The child in the photo follows these rules to decide that *flower* refers to the entire object, not its parts or the action of pointing to it.

Sentence Cues

Children hear many unfamiliar words embedded in sentences containing words they already know. The other words and the overall sentence structure can be helpful clues to a word's meaning. For example, when a parent describes an event using familiar words but an unfamiliar verb, children often infer that the verb refers to the action performed by the subject of the sentence (Fisher, 1996; Woodward & Markman, 1998). When youngsters watching a man juggle apples hear "The man is juggling," they will infer that *juggling* refers to the man's actions with the apples because they already know *man* and *apple* and because *-ing* refers to ongoing actions.

As another example of how sentence context aids word learning, look at the blocks in Figure 5.4 and point to "the boz block." You probably pointed to the middle block. Why? In English, adjectives usually precede the nouns they modify, so you inferred that *boz* is an adjective describing *block*. Since *the* before *boz* implies that only one block is *boz*, you picked the middle one, having decided that *boz* means "winged."

FIGURE 5.4

Toddlers, too, use sentence cues like these to judge word meanings. Hearing "This is a Zav," a young child will interpret *zav* as a category name, but hearing "This is Zav" (without the *a*), they interpret *zav* as a proper name (Hall, Lee, & Belanger, 2001).

Cognitive Factors

The naming explosion coincides with a time of rapid cognitive growth, and children's increased cognitive skill helps them to learn new words. As children's thinking becomes more sophisticated and, in particular, as they start to have goals and intentions, language becomes a means to express those goals and to achieve them. Thus, intention provides children with an important motive to learn language—to help achieve their goals (Bloom & Tinker, 2001). In addition, young children's improving attentional and perceptual skills also promote word learning. Many objects with the same name have a common shape (e.g., balls are round, pencils are slender rods), and children's growing ability to detect perceptual similarities enables them to extend new words to novel instances of objects (Smith et al., 2000).

Naming Errors

Of course, these rules for learning new words are not perfect; initial mappings of words onto meanings are often only partially correct (Hoff & Naigles, 2002). *A common mistake is **underextension**, defining a word too narrowly.* Using *car* to refer only to the family car and *ball* to a favourite toy ball are examples of underextension. *Between one and three years of age, children sometimes make the opposite error, **overextension**, defining a word too broadly.* Children may use *car* to also refer to buses and trucks or use *doggie* to refer to all four-legged animals.

The overextension error occurs more frequently when children are producing words than when they are comprehending words. Jason may say "doggie" to refer to a goat but nevertheless correctly point to a picture of a goat when asked. Because overextension is more common in word production, it may actually reflect another fast mapping rule that children follow: "If you can't remember the name for an object, say the name of a related object" (Naigles & Gelman, 1995).

Both underextension and overextension disappear gradually as youngsters refine meanings for words as they have more exposure to language.

ENCOURAGING LANGUAGE GROWTH

How can parents and other adults help children learn words? For children to expand their vocabularies, they need to hear others speak. Not surprisingly, then, children learn words more rapidly if their parents speak to them frequently (Huttenlocher et al., 1991; Roberts, Burchinal, & Durham, 1999). Of course, sheer quantity of parental speech is not all that matters. Parents can foster word learning by naming objects that are the focus of a child's attention (Dunham, Dunham, & Curwin, 1993). Parents can name different products on store shelves as they point to them. During a walk, parents can label the objects—birds, plants, vehicles—that the child sees. In addition, children learn more words when their parents' speech is rich in different words and is grammatically sophisticated (Hoff & Naigles, 2002), and when parents respond promptly and appropriately to their children's talk (Tamis-Lemonda & Bornstein, 2002).

Parents can also help children learn words by reading books with them. Reading together is fun for parents and children alike and provides opportunities for children to learn new words. However, the way that parents read makes a difference. When parents carefully describe pictures as they read, preschoolers' vocabularies increase (Reese & Cox, 1999). Asking children questions during reading also helps (Sénéchal, Thomas, & Monker, 1995). When an adult reads a sentence (e.g., Arthur is angling), then asks a question (e.g., What is Arthur doing?), a child must match the new word (*angling*) with the pictured activity (*fishing*) and say the word aloud. When parents read without questioning, children can ignore words they don't understand. Questioning forces children to identify meanings of new words and practise saying them.

Watching television can help word learning, under some circumstances. For example, preschool children who frequently view *Sesame Street* often have larger vocabularies by the time they enter kindergarten than do preschoolers who watch

Sesame Street less often (Rice et al., 1990). Other kinds of television programs—notably cartoons—do not have this positive influence.

What accounts for the difference? The key to success is encouraging children to become actively involved in language-related activities. Video segments like the one shown in the photo encourage youngsters to name objects, to sing, and to count. Apparently, the fundamental principle is much the same for television and parents: Children expand their vocabularies when they have experiences that engage and challenge their emerging language talents.

© 1994 Don Perdue/Children's Television Workshop

SPEAKING IN SENTENCES: GRAMMATICAL DEVELOPMENT

Within months after children say their first words, they begin to form simple two-word sentences. Such sentences are based on "formulas" that children figure out from their own experiences (Braine, 1976; Radford, 1995). Armed with a few formulas, children can express an enormous variety of ideas:

TABLE 5.2

Formula	Example
actor + action	Mommy sleep, Timmy run
action + object	gimme cookie, throw ball
possessor + possession	Kimmy pail, Maya shovel

Each child develops a unique repertoire of formulas, reflecting his or her own experiences. However, the formulas listed here are commonly used by children growing up in many different countries around the world.

From Two Words to Complex Sentences

Children rapidly move beyond two-word sentences, first doing so by linking two-word statements together: "Rachel kick" and "Kick ball" become "Rachel kick ball." Even longer sentences soon follow; sentences with 10 or more words are common in 3-year-olds' speech. For example, at one and a half years, Laura Kail would say,

"Gimme juice" or "Bye-bye Ben." As a two-and-a-half-year-old, she had progressed to "When I finish my ice cream, I'll take a shower, okay?" and "Don't turn the light out—I can't see better!"

Children's two- and three-word sentences often fall short of adults' standards of grammar. Youngsters will say, "He eating" rather than "He is eating," or "two cat" rather than "two cats." *This sort of speech is called* **telegraphic** *because, like telegrams of days gone by, children's speech includes only words directly relevant to meaning, and nothing more. The missing elements,* **grammatical morphemes,** *are words or endings of words (such as* -ing, -ed, or -s*) that make a sentence grammatical.* During the preschool years, children gradually acquire the grammatical morphemes, first mastering those that express simple relations such as *-ing,* which is used to denote that the action expressed by the verb is ongoing. More complex forms, such as appropriate use of the various forms of the verb *to be,* are mastered later (Peters, 1995).

Children's use of grammatical morphemes is based on their growing knowledge of grammatical rules, not simply memory for individual words. This was first demonstrated in a landmark study by Berko (1958) in which preschoolers were shown pictures of nonsense objects like the one in Figure 5.5. The experimenter labelled it, saying, "This is a wug." Then youngsters were shown pictures of two of the objects, and the experimenter said, "These are two...." Most children spontaneously said "wugs." Because both the singular and plural forms of this word were novel for these youngsters, they could have generated the correct plural form only by applying the familiar rule of adding *-s.*

Children growing up in homes where English is spoken face the problem that their native tongue is highly irregular, with many exceptions to the rules. *Sometimes children apply rules to words that are exceptions to the rule, errors called* **overregularizations.** With plurals, for example, youngsters may incorrectly add an *-s* instead of using an irregular plural—two "mans" instead of two "men." With the past tense, children may add *-ed* instead of using an irregular past tense: "I goed home" instead of "I went home" (Marcus et al., 1992; Mervis & Johnson, 1991).

FIGURE 5.5

This is a wug.

Now there is another one.
There are two of them.
There are two _____.

Source: Berko, 1958.

These examples give some insight into the complexities of mastering the grammatical rules of one's language. Not only must children learn an extensive set of specific rules, but they must also absorb, on a case-by-case basis, all the exceptions. Despite the magnitude of this task, most children have mastered the basics of their native tongue by the time they enter school. How do they do it? As we see in the Forces in Action feature, biological, psychological, and sociocultural forces all contribute.

FORCES IN ACTION

How Children Learn Grammar

Mastery of grammar depends on biological, sociocultural, and psychological forces. On the biological side, the linguist Noam Chomsky claimed that the brain is "prewired" for learning grammar. That is, children are born with neural circuits to help them infer grammatical rules (Atkinson, 1992).

Sociocultural influences are important too. Parents fine-tune their speech to include examples of the forms their children are learning (Hoff-Ginsberg, 1990). For example, when preschoolers first experiment with pronouns like *you, I,* and *they,* parents use many examples of these pronouns in their own speech. Thus, parents make it easier for children to unearth new grammatical rules by providing additional relevant speech.

Psychological forces are also fundamental. Children actively try to make sense out of language (Bloom, 1991; Braine, 1992). They formulate tentative grammatical rules, then look for feedback to evaluate them. For example, when a child's speech is incorrect or incomplete, parents rephrase or elaborate it. If a child says, "Sara eat cookie," a parent may reply, "Yes, Sara is eating a cookie." The parent's reply captures the meaning of the child's remark but demonstrates correct grammatical forms (Bohannon et al., 1996). When a child's remark is well formed, parents simply continue the conversation. By rephrasing their child's speech or continuing the conversation, parents give children feedback about their tentative rules.

The key players in grammatical development are thus a specialized brain (biological force), a rich language environment (sociocultural force), and a child actively seeking to identify rules in speech (psychological force). Combined, they direct children down the trail that leads to the mastery of grammar. ⧑

COMMUNICATING WITH OTHERS

Imagining these two preschoolers arguing is an excellent way to learn what is needed for effective communication. Both youngsters probably try to speak at the same time; their remarks may be rambling or incoherent; and they neglect to listen to each other altogether. These actions reveal three key elements needed for effective oral communication (Grice, 1975):

Susan Johns/Photo Researchers, Inc.

⧑ People should take turns, alternating as speaker and listener.
⧑ When speaking, remarks should be clear to the listener, from his or her own perspective.
⧑ When listening, pay attention and let the speaker know if his or her remarks don't make sense.

Complete mastery of these elements is a lifelong pursuit. After all, even adults often miscommunicate with one another, violating each of these prescriptions in the process. However, youngsters grasp many of the basics of communication early in life. By three years of age, children have progressed to the point that if a listener fails to reply promptly, the child will often repeat his or her remarks to elicit a response and keep the conversation moving (Garvey & Berninger, 1981).

Speaking Effectively

The meaning of a message should be clear. However, clarity can only be judged with regard to the listener's age, the topic of conversation, and the setting of the conversation. For example, think about the simple request, "Please hand me the Phillips screwdriver." This message may be clear to older listeners who are familiar with variants of screwdrivers, but it is vague to younger listeners to whom all screwdrivers are alike. Of course, if the toolbox is filled with Phillips screwdrivers of assorted sizes, the message is ambiguous even to a knowledgeable listener.

Consistently constructing clear messages is a fine art, which we would hardly expect young children to have mastered. By the preschool years, however, youngsters

THINK ABOUT IT

Compare Piaget's theory, Vygotsky's theory, and the information-processing approach in their emphasis on the role of language in cognitive development.

have made their initial attempts to calibrate messages, adjusting them to match the listener and the context. For example, preschool children give more elaborate messages to listeners who lack critical information and less elaborate messages to listeners who have this information (Nadig & Sedivy, 2002; O'Neill, 1996). For example, a child describing where to find a toy will give more detailed directions to a listener whose eyes were covered when the toy was hidden. And, if listeners appear to misunderstand, 2- and 3-year-olds will clarify their messages (Shwe & Markman, 1997). These findings show that preschoolers are already sensitive to the importance of the listener's skill and understanding in formulating a clear message.

Listening Well

Sometimes messages are vague or confusing; in such situations, a listener needs to ask the speaker to clarify the message. Preschoolers do not always realize when a message is ambiguous. Told to find "the red toy," they may promptly select the red ball from a pile that includes a red toy car, a red block, and a red toy hammer. Instead of asking the speaker to refer to a specific red toy, preschool listeners often assume they know which toy the speaker had in mind (Beal & Belgrad, 1990). During the elementary school years, youngsters gradually master the many elements involved in determining whether another person's message is consistent and clear (Ackerman, 1993).

Improvement in communication skill is yet another astonishing accomplishment in language during the first five years of life; these changes for the ages 3 to 5 years are summarized as follows:

- Vocabulary continues to expand.
- Grammatical morphemes are added.
- Children begin to adjust speech to listeners, but listeners often ignore problems in the messages they receive.

By the time children are ready to enter kindergarten, they use language with remarkable proficiency and are able to communicate with growing skill.

TEST YOURSELF

1. Youngsters with a(n) _____ style have early vocabularies dominated by words that are names, and use language primarily as an intellectual tool.

2. In _____, a young child's meaning of a word is broader than an adult's meaning.

3. Noam Chomsky, a noted linguist, emphasized the role of _____ in children's acquisition of grammar.

4. When talking to listeners who lack critical information, preschoolers _____.

According to Piaget's theory, preschoolers are egocentric. How should this egocentrism influence their ability to communicate? Are the findings we have described on children's communication skills consistent with Piaget's view?

Answers (1) referential, (2) overextension, (3) biological mechanisms, (4) provide more elaborate messages

PUTTING IT ALL TOGETHER

The preschool years mark the transition from a toddler who routinely depends on others to an independent 5-year-old ready to begin the long process of schooling. Piaget explained this transition in terms of a progression through qualitatively different stages. The years 2 to 7 form the preoperational period, when children begin to explore the power of symbolic thought. Their thinking has limits, however, including the egocentrism that explains Jamila's head-nodding during phone conversations.

We also looked at the information-processing approach, in which cognitive development is described in terms of both general and task-specific processes. We saw that the basic skills of attention and memory improve considerably during the preschool years. However, there are imperfections in children's memory, so preschoolers like Cheryl (the child involved in an alleged case of abuse) do not always provide reliable testimony.

Next, we examined Vygotsky's view of cognitive development—that is, as an apprenticeship in which children progress when collaborating with others who are more knowledgeable than they. We learned that children like Victoria talk to themselves during a transition period in which the control of cognitive processes is transferred from others to self.

In the last section, we saw that preschoolers master the sounds, meanings, and grammar of their native language. However, effective use of language to communicate is much slower to develop, continuing throughout the life span.

As a result of this growing intellectual and linguistic power, children are able to have more elaborate interactions and relationships with others, as we'll see in Chapter 6.

SUMMARY

5.1 Physical Development: Growth and Change

Growth of the Body

- During preschool years children gain approximately 2.5 kilograms per year and grow five to seven centimetres in height per year. Their shapes change from top-heavy toddlers to more even proportions.

Nutritional Needs and Issues

- Preschoolers often become fussy eaters. Parents should not be overly concerned since this is a normal stage and virtually all picky eaters get adequate food for growth.

Sleep for Toddlers and Preschoolers

- Sleeping patterns change along with activity levels, and night hours of sleep average 11 to 13 during preschool years. During this time period, the daytime nap is dropped.

5.2 Gross and Fine Motor Skills

Beyond Walking

- By 5 or 6 years, children run easily, quickly changing directions or speed, and hop. They enjoy unstructured play and may learn to ride a tricycle.

Fine Motor Skills

- Children become much more dexterous, able to make many precise and delicate movements with their hands and fingers, which allows them to begin to take care of themselves.

- A 2- or 3-year-old, for example, can put on some simple clothing and use zippers but not buttons; by 3 or 4 years, children can fasten buttons and take off their clothes; most 5-year-olds can dress and undress themselves, except for tying shoes, which children typically master at about age 6.
- By 4 or 5 years of age, children use their drawings to depict recognizable objects.

Handedness

- By age 5 children typically use their nonpreferred hand only when the preferred hand is busy doing something else, and by the time children are ready to enter kindergarten, handedness is well-established.

5.3 Cognitive Development: Piaget's Account

Preoperational Thinking

- From 2 to 7 years of age, children are in Piaget's preoperational period. Although now capable of using symbols, their thinking is limited by egocentrism, the inability to see the world from another's point of view. Preoperational children are also centred in their thinking and sometimes confuse appearance with reality.

Evaluating Piaget's Theory

- One important contribution of Piaget's theory is the view that children actively try to understand their world. Another contribution is specifying conditions that foster cognitive development.

However, the theory has been criticized because children's performance on tasks is sometimes better explained by ideas that are not part of his theory. Another shortcoming is that children's performance from one task to the next is not as consistent as the theory predicts it to be.

Extending Piaget's Account: Children's Naïve Theories

- In contrast to Piaget's idea that children create a comprehensive theory that integrates all their knowledge, the modern view is that children are specialists, generating naïve theories in particular domains, including physics and biology. Infants understand many properties of objects: they know how objects move, what happens when objects collide, and that objects fall when not supported.

- Infants understand the difference between animate and inanimate objects. As preschoolers, children know that, unlike inanimate objects, animate objects move themselves, grow, have distinct internal parts, resemble their parents, and repair through healing.

5.4 Information Processing During Early Childhood

General Principles of Information Processing

- According to the information-processing view, cognitive development involves changes in mental hardware and in mental software.

Attention

- Compared to older children, preschoolers are less able to pay attention to task-relevant information. Their attention can be improved by making irrelevant stimuli less noticeable.

Learning by Imitation

- Young children, just like older children and adults, learn a lot simply by observation and imitation, or social learning.

Memory

- Preschool children can remember events they experienced more than one year previously. Autobiographical memory emerges in the preschool years, in part due to parents' questioning children about past events.

- Preschoolers sometimes testify in cases of child abuse. When they are questioned repeatedly, preschoolers often have difficulty distinguishing what they experienced from what others may suggest they have experienced. Inaccuracies of this sort can be minimized by following certain guidelines when interviewing children, such as warning them that interviewers may try to trick them.

Understanding Numbers and Counting

- By 3 years of age, children can count small sets of objects and in so doing adhere to the one-to-one, stable-order, and cardinality principles.

- Learning to count larger numbers involves learning rules about unit and decade names. This learning is more difficult for English-speaking children compared to children from Asian countries because names for numbers are irregular in English.

5.5 Mind and Culture: Vygotsky's Theory

The Zone of Proximal Development

- Vygotsky believed that cognition develops first in a social setting and only gradually comes under the child's independent control. The difference between what children can do with assistance and what they can do alone constitutes the zone of proximal development.

Scaffolding

- Control of cognitive skills is most readily transferred to the child through scaffolding, a teaching style in which teachers let children take on more and more of a task as they master its different components. Scaffolding is common worldwide, but the specific techniques for scaffolding children's learning vary from one cultural setting to the next.

Private Speech

- Children often talk to themselves, particularly when the task is difficult or after they have made a mistake. Such private speech is one way children regulate their behaviour, and it represents an intermediate step in the transfer of control of thinking from others to the self.

5.6 Language

Language Development and Learning to Communicate Ideas

- Some youngsters use a referential style that emphasizes words as names and that views language as an intellectual tool. Other children use an expressive style that emphasizes phrases and that views language as a social tool.

- Most children learn the meanings of words much too rapidly for them to consider all plausible meanings systematically. Instead, children use certain rules to determine the probable meanings of new words. The rules do not always yield the correct meaning. An underextension is a child's meaning that is narrower than an adult's meaning; an overextension is a child's meaning that is broader.

- Children's vocabulary is stimulated by experience. Both parents and television can foster the growth of vocabulary. The key ingredient is to actively involve children in language-related activities.

Speaking in Sentences: Grammatical Development

- Soon after children begin to speak, they create two-word sentences that are derived from their own experiences. Moving from two-word to more complex sentences involves adding grammatical morphemes. Children first master grammatical morphemes that express simple relations, then those that denote complex relations. Mastery of grammatical morphemes involves learning rules as well as exceptions to the rules.

■ Some linguists claim that grammar is too complex for children to learn solely from their experience; instead, the brain must be prewired for the task. However, language experience is important. Parents' speech is a model for their children. Children try to infer grammatical rules from speech that they hear;

parents give children feedback concerning these tentative rules.

Communicating with Others

■ By 3 years of age, children spontaneously take turns and prompt one another to take their turn.

■ Preschool children adjust their speech in a rudimentary fashion to fit the listener's needs. However, preschoolers are unlikely to identify ambiguities in another's speech; instead, they are likely to assume they knew what the speaker meant.

KEY TERMS

lateralization (166)
egocentrism (168)
animism (169)
centration (170)
reversibility (170)
mental hardware (177)
mental software (177)
recognition (178)

recall (178)
generic memory (178)
episodic memory (178)
autobiographical memory (178)
one-to-one principle (180)
stable-order principle (180)
cardinality principle (180)
zone of proximal development (182)

scaffolding (182)
private speech (183)
underextension (186)
overextension (186)
telegraphic speech (188)
grammatical morpheme (188)
overregularization (188)

SEE FOR YOURSELF: APPLYING WHAT YOU'VE LEARNED

The best way to see some of the developmental changes that Piaget described is to test some children with the same tasks Piaget used. The conservation task shown on page 171 is good because it's simple to set up and children usually enjoy it. First ask a 3- or 4-year-old to confirm that the containers have the same amount of liquid. Then, pour the liquid from one container into a third, different-shaped container. Now ask the child if the quantities are still the same and have the child explain his or her answer.

Test the child on some appearance-reality tasks. Find rubber "play food" and ask what the objects "look like" and what they "really and truly are." Have the child look at a glass of water through sunglasses and ask what the water looks like and what it really and truly is. Just like the youngsters that Piaget tested, the child will probably claim that the amount of liquid changes when you pour it into a different container, that the rubber is really and truly food, and that the water is really and truly brown. See for yourself!

LEARN MORE ABOUT IT

Readings

CECI, S. J., & BRUCK, M. (1995). *Jeopardy in the courtroom: A scientific analysis of children's testimony.* Washington, D.C.: American Psychological Association. In this book written by leading experts on the proper use of children as witnesses, the authors describe how best to ensure that interviews with child witnesses are conducted sensitively and professionally.

FLAVELL, J. H., MILLER, P. H., & MILLER, S. A. (2002). *Cognitive development* (4th ed.). Englewood Cliffs, NJ: Prentice Hall. This book, written by a trio of leading

researchers, describes cognitive development during infancy and the preschool years. Piaget's and Vygotsky's theories are presented, as is the information-processing perspective. This is probably the best general purpose reference book on cognitive development for undergraduates.

GARVEY, C. (1984). *Children's talk.* Cambridge, MA: Harvard University Press. This engaging book shows how children use language socially and also as an intellectual tool. It is filled with many entertaining examples of children's talk.

Kᴀɪʟ, R. (1990). *The development of memory in children* (3rd ed.). New York: Freeman. This book describes memory in infants and toddlers, as well as in older children and adolescents. Much research is discussed, but in a straightforward, easy-to-read style.

Sɪᴇɢʟᴇʀ, R.S. (1998). *Children's thinking* (3rd ed.). Englewood Cliffs, NJ: Prentice Hall. The author is a leading proponent of the information-processing approach to cognitive development, and this book reflects that orientation. He discusses Piaget's theory and language, but the best coverage is given to information-processing topics such as memory, problem solving, and academic skills.

 For additional readings, explore InfoTrac® College Edition, your online library. Go to http://www.infotrac.thomsonlearning.com.

Websites

http://www.hc-sc.gc.ca

Health Canada's website provides links to an extensive number of resources on healthy living for children.

http://www.caringforkids.cps.ca

The website of the Canadian Pediatric Society contains information and guidelines on many topics related to children's health.

http://www.piaget.org

The Jean Piaget Society maintains a website that includes biographical information about Piaget, suggested readings on Piaget's life and theory, and articles about cognitive development.

http://www.caslpa.ca/

The Canadian Association of Speech Language Pathologists and Audiologists represents some 4,200 speech, language, and hearing professionals across Canada. This site includes a wide range of resources including publications, online access to their journal, fact sheets, etc.

Website addresses are subject to change. The *Human Development* book companion website can be accessed for updated links.

The Human Development Book Companion Website

See http://www.humandevelopment.nelson.com for practice quiz questions, Internet links, updates, critical thinking exercises, discussion forums, and more.

Life-Span CD-ROM

For more information on the concepts covered in this chapter, go to

Module 3: Early and Middle Childhood

- Cognitive Development
- Language Development

Arthur Tilley/Getty Images

CHAPTER 6

Interacting and the Work of Play

SOCIOEMOTIONAL DEVELOPMENT IN EARLY CHILDHOOD

If you're a fan of the NBC TV show *Friends,* these lyrics are probably familiar: "I'll be there for you, when the rain starts to pour, I'll be there for you, like I've been there before, I'll be there for you, 'cause you're there for me too . . ." Friends *are* important but they're only one of the many ways we humans relate to each other. Friends, lovers, spouses, parents and children, co-workers, and teammates are different types of social relationships that make our lives both interesting and satisfying.

In this chapter, we first trace the development of social relationships, starting with relationships between child and parent and the critical role that parents play. Interactions with parents and others are often full of emotions—happiness, satisfaction, anger, and guilt, to name just a few. The development of independence during the preschool years is traced and you'll see how children express different emotions and how they recognize others' emotions.

The development of young children's self-awareness will be explored and the concept of "theory of mind." You'll learn how children's social horizons expand beyond parents to include peers. Then you'll discover some factors that determine whether children cooperate and whether they help others in distress.

As children's interactions with others become more wide-ranging, they begin to learn about the social roles they are expected to play. Among the first social roles children learn are those associated with gender—how society expects boys and girls to behave. In the final section of the chapter, you'll learn how children become aware of gender roles.

6.1

Parenting

LEARNING OBJECTIVES

▪ What are the primary dimensions of parenting? How do they affect children's development?

▪ What factors contribute to child abuse?

Val and Louise are discussing strategies that they use with their young children during mealtime. Val believes that young children should not be allowed to leave the table until everyone else is finished eating, and if her son Stevie leaves the table before that time she gives him a time-out. Louise says that as long as her daughter Molly eats something at mealtime she doesn't mind if she leaves the table once she's done as it makes for a more relaxing mealtime for her and her husband. They know that other parents have different approaches and wonder which is the best.

This vignette illustrates what we all know from personal experience—parents go about child rearing in different ways. We'll study these different approaches in this chapter and learn how Stevie and Molly are likely to be affected by their mothers' style of parenting. First we'll look at dimensions and styles of parenting.

DIMENSIONS AND STYLES OF PARENTING

Parenting can be described in terms of general dimensions that are like personality traits in that they represent stable aspects of parental behaviour—aspects that hold across different situations (Holden & Miller, 1999). Research consistently reveals two general dimensions of parental behaviour. One is the degree of warmth and responsiveness parents show their children; the other is the amount of control parents exert over their children.

Let's look first at warmth and responsiveness. At one end of the spectrum are parents who are openly warm and affectionate with their children. They are involved with them, respond to their emotional needs, and spend considerable time with them. At the other end of the spectrum are parents who are relatively uninvolved with their children and sometimes are even hostile toward them. These parents often seem more focused on their own needs and interests than on their children's. Warm parents enjoy hearing their children describe the day's activities; uninvolved or hostile parents aren't interested, considering it a waste of their time. Warm parents see when their children are upset and try to comfort them; uninvolved or hostile parents pay little attention to their children's emotional states and invest little effort comforting them when they're upset.

As you might expect, children benefit from warm and responsive parenting (Pettit, Bates, & Dodge, 1997). When parents are warm toward them, children typically feel secure and happy, and they're better behaved. In contrast, when parents are uninvolved or hostile, their children are often anxious and less controlled. And children often have low self-esteem when their parents are uninvolved (Rothbaum & Weisz, 1994).

A second general dimension of parental behaviour concerns the control parents exercise over their children's behaviour. At one end of this spectrum are controlling, demanding parents. These parents virtually run their children's lives. Overcontrol is shown by parents who are insistent on having all the details regarding where their teenagers are and what they are doing and are inflexible with rules. At the other end of the spectrum are parents who make few demands and rarely exert control. Their children are free to do almost anything without fear of parental reproach. Parents who undercontrol don't seem to care where their teenagers are or what they are doing.

Neither of these extremes is desirable. Overcontrol deprives children of the opportunity to meet behavioural standards on their own, which is the ultimate goal of socialization. When parents direct every aspect of preschoolers' lives, their children never learn to make decisions for themselves. Undercontrol fails children because it doesn't teach them cultural standards for behaviour. When parents allow preschoolers to do whatever they want, their children don't believe they are accountable for their behaviour, which is definitely not true in the long run.

Parents need to strike a balance, maintaining adequate control while still allowing children freedom to make some decisions for themselves. This is often easier said than done, but a good starting point is setting standards that are appropriate for the child's age, then showing the child how to meet them, and, finally, rewarding the child for complying (Powers & Roberts, 1995; Rotto & Kratochwill, 1994). Suppose a mother wants her preschooler to fold and put away her socks. This is a reasonable request because the child is physically capable of this simple task and she knows where the socks should be stored. Like the mother in the photo, she should show her daughter how to complete the task, and then praise her when she does it.

© Jean Hangarter/Index Stock Imagery

Once standards are set, they should be enforced consistently. For example, the mother should require that her daughter always fold and put away her socks, not just occasionally. When parents enforce rules erratically, children come to see rules as optional instead of obligatory, and they try to avoid complying with them (Conger, Patterson, & Ge, 1995).

Effective control is also based on good communication. Parents should explain why they've set standards and why they reward or punish as they do. If a mother wants her son to clean his room, she should explain that a messy room is unsafe, makes it difficult to find toys that he wants, and makes it difficult for cleaning. Parents can also encourage children to ask questions if they don't understand or disagree with standards. If the son feels that his mother's standards for orderliness are so high that it's impossible to play in his room, he should feel free to raise the issue with his mother without fear of making her angry.

A balanced approach to control—based on age-appropriate standards, consistency, and communication—avoids the problems associated with overcontrol because the expectations more likely reflect the child's level of maturity and they are open to discussion. A balanced approach also avoids the problems of undercontrol because standards are set and parents expect children to meet those standards consistently.

> **THINK ABOUT IT**
>
> How would a social learning theorist explain the importance of consistency and communication in effective parental control? Would an information-processing theorist's explanation be similar?

Cultural Differences in Warmth and Control

Control and warmth are universal aspects of parents' behaviour, but views about the "proper" amounts of each vary with particular cultures. European North Americans generally want their children to be happy and self-reliant individuals, and they believe these goals can best be achieved when parents are warm and exert moderate control (Goodnow, 1992; Spence, 1985). In many Asian and Latin American countries, however, individualism is less important than cooperation and collaboration (Okagaki & Sternberg, 1993). In China, for example, Confucian principles dictate that parents are always right and that emotional restraint is the key to family harmony

(Chao, 1994). In fact, consistent with their cultural values, mothers and fathers in China are more likely to emphasize parental control and less likely to express affection (Lin & Fu, 1990).

Parenting Styles

Combining the dimensions of warmth and control produces four prototypic styles of parenting, as shown in Figure 6.1 (Baumrind, 1975, 1991).

■ *Authoritarian parenting combines high control with little warmth.* These parents lay down the rules and expect them to be followed without discussion. Hard work, respect, and obedience are what authoritarian parents wish to cultivate in their children. There is little give-and-take between parent and child because authoritarian parents do not consider children's needs or wishes.

■ *Authoritative parenting* combines a fair degree of parental control with being warm and responsive to children. Authoritative parents explain rules and encourage discussion.

■ *Indulgent-permissive parenting offers warmth and caring but little parental control.* These parents generally accept their children's behaviour and punish them infrequently.

■ *Indifferent-uninvolved parenting provides neither warmth nor control.* Indifferent-uninvolved parents provide for their children's basic physical and emotional needs but little else. They try to minimize the amount of time spent with their children and avoid becoming emotionally involved with them.

FIGURE 6.1   Parenting Styles

		Parental control	
		High	Low
Parental involvement	High	Authoritative	Indulgent-permissive
	Low	Authoritarian	Indifferent-uninvolved

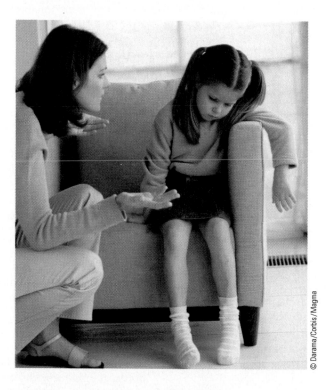

© Darama/Corbis/Magma

Of these four styles, children are usually best served by the combination of warmth and control that is the hallmark of authoritative parenting (Baumrind, 1991; Maccoby & Martin, 1983). Children with authoritative parents tend to be responsible, self-reliant, and friendly. In contrast, children with authoritarian parents typically have lower self-esteem and are less skilled socially. Children with indulgent-permissive parents are often impulsive and easily frustrated. Children with indifferent-uninvolved parents have low self-esteem and are impulsive, aggressive, and moody.

As important as these different dimensions and styles are for understanding parenting, there is more to effective child rearing, as we'll see in the next section.

Parental Behaviour

Dimensions and styles are general characterizations of how parents typically behave. If, for example, we describe a parent as warm or controlling, you immediately have a sense of that parent's usual style in dealing with his or her children. Nevertheless, the price for such a broad description is that it tells us little about how parents behave in specific situations and how these parental behaviours influence children's development. Put another way, what specific behaviours can parents use to influence their children? Researchers who study parents name three: direct instruction, modelling, and feedback.

DIRECT INSTRUCTION.   Parents often tell their children what to do. But simply playing the role of drill sergeant in ordering children around—"Clean your room!" "Turn off the TV!"—is not very effective. *A better approach is direct instruction, which involves telling a child what to do, when, and why.* Instead of just shouting "Share your candy with your brother!" a parent should explain when and why it's important to share with a sibling.

In addition, just as coaches help athletes master sports skills, parents can help their youngsters master social and emotional skills. Parents can explain links between emotions and behaviour—"Catlin is sad because you broke her crayon" (Gottman, Katz, & Hooven, 1996). They can also teach how to deal with difficult social situations—"When you ask Lindsey if she can sleep over, do it privately so you won't hurt Kaycee's or Hannah's feelings" (Mize & Pettit, 1997). In general, children who get this sort of parental "coaching" tend to be more socially skilled and, not surprisingly, get along better with their peers.

Direct instruction and coaching are particularly powerful when paired with modelling. Urging children to act in a particular way, such as sharing with others, is more compelling when children also see others sharing. In the next section, we'll see how children learn by observing others.

LEARNING BY OBSERVING.   Applying what we learned from social learning theory, children can learn a great deal from parents simply by watching them. The parents' modelling and the youngsters' observational learning thus lead to imitation, so children's behaviour resembles the behaviour they observe. *Observational learning can also produce counterimitation, learning what should not be done.* If an older sibling kicks a friend and parents punish the older sibling, the younger child may learn not to kick others.

So far, we've seen that parents influence their children's development by direct instruction and by acting as models that children can observe. In the next section, we'll see how parents use feedback to affect children's behaviour.

FEEDBACK.   By giving feedback to their children, parents indicate whether a behaviour is appropriate and should continue or is inappropriate and should stop. Feedback comes in two general forms. *Reinforcement* is any action that increases the likelihood of the response that it follows. Parents may use praise to reinforce a child's studying or give a reward for completing household chores. *Punishment* is any action that discourages the reoccurrence of the response that it follows. Parents may forbid children to watch television when they get poor grades in school or make children go to bed early for neglecting household chores.

Of course, parents have been rewarding and punishing their children for centuries, so what do psychologists know that parents don't know already? In fact, researchers have made some surprising discoveries concerning the nature of reward and punishment. *Parents often unwittingly reinforce the very behaviours they want to discourage, a situation called the **negative reinforcement trap*** (Patterson, 1980). The negative reinforcement trap occurs in three steps, most often between a mother and her son. In the first step, the mother tells her son to do something he doesn't want to do. She might tell him to clean his room, to come inside while he's outdoors playing with friends, or to study instead of watching television. In the next step, the son responds with some behaviour that most parents find intolerable: he argues, complains, or whines—not just briefly, but for an extended period of time. In the last step, the mother gives in—saying that the son needn't do as she told him initially—simply to get the son to stop the behaviour that is so intolerable.

The feedback to the son is that arguing (or complaining or whining) works; the mother rewards that behaviour by withdrawing the request the son did not like. We usually think a behaviour is strengthened when it is followed by the presentation of something that is valued, but a behaviour is also strengthened when it is followed by removing something that is disliked.

As for punishment, research (Parke, 1977) shows that punishment works best when

- administered directly after the undesired behaviour occurs, not hours later.
- an undesired behaviour *always* leads to punishment, not usually or occasionally.
- accompanied by an explanation of why the child was punished and how punishment can be avoided in the future.
- the child has a warm, affectionate relationship with the person administering the punishment.

At the same time, research reveals some serious drawbacks to punishment, sometimes referred to as consequences. One is that punishment is primarily suppressive: Punished responses are stopped, but only temporarily if children do not learn new behaviours to replace those that were punished. For example, denying TV to brothers who are fighting stops the undesirable behaviour, but fighting is likely to recur unless the boys learn new ways of solving their disputes.

A second drawback is that punishment can have undesirable side effects. Children become upset as they are being punished, which makes it unlikely that they will understand the feedback punishment is meant to convey. A child denied TV for misbehaving may become angry over the punishment itself and ignore why he's being punished.

Physical punishment in particular has been found to have negative developmental outcomes and risks associated with its use. For example, when children are punished physically, they often imitate this behaviour with peers and younger siblings (Whitehurst & Vasta, 1977). In a review of research studies conducted on how physical or corporal punishment affects children, Gershoff (2002) found that although physical punishment was associated with immediate compliance, most of the childhood outcomes were negative, such as increased aggression, delinquent and antisocial behaviour, decreased quality of parent–child relationship, and perhaps most concerning, physical child abuse. Since physical punishment generally occurs in situations where a parent feels anger and frustration, loss of control can occur and small children in particular are therefore vulnerable to injury. In the Canadian Incidence Study of Reported Child Abuse and Neglect (Trocmé et al., 2001), it is reported that over two-thirds of substantiated cases of physical abuse was as a result of inappropriate punishment.

Children need clear guidelines, expectations, and consequences for misbehaviour and the consequences of misbehaviour should be applied so as not to instil shame, negative guilt, or a loss of trust. The Canadian Paediatric Society (CPS, 2004) recommends that spanking and all other forms of physical punishment should be discouraged. In its position statement on effective discipline for children, the CPS has recommended the following guidelines:

- Reinforce desirable behaviour. Praise positive behaviour and "catch children being good."
- Avoid nagging and making threats without consequences.
- Apply rules consistently.
- Ignore unimportant and irrelevant behaviour.
- Set reasonable and consistent limits. Consequences need to be realistic.
- State acceptable and appropriate behaviour that is attainable.

- ▸ Prioritize rules. Give top priority to safety, then to correcting behaviour that harms people and property, and then to behaviour such as whining, temper tantrums, and interrupting. Concentrate on two or three rules first.
- ▸ Know and accept age-appropriate behaviour.
- ▸ Allow for the child's temperament and individuality. A strong-willed child needs to be raised differently from the so-called compliant child.

Parents can influence children by direct instruction, by modelling behaviour that they value and not modelling what they don't want their children to learn, by giving feedback, and through the parenting styles that we examined at the beginning of this section. Now we'll switch perspectives and see how children affect their parents' behaviour.

Children's Contributions: Reciprocal Influence

Children begin at birth to influence the way their parents treat them. That is, parents behave differently depending on a child's specific behaviour (Kochanska, 1993).

To illustrate the reciprocal influence of parents and children, imagine two children with different temperaments as they respond to a parent's authoritative style. The first child has an "easy" temperament and readily complies with parental requests and responds well to family discussions about parental expectations. These parent–child relations are a textbook example of successful authoritative parenting. But suppose the second child has a "difficult" temperament and complies reluctantly and sometimes not at all. Over time, the parent becomes more controlling and less affectionate. The child in turn complies even less in the future, leading the parent to adopt an authoritarian parenting style (Bates et al., 1998).

As this example illustrates, parenting behaviours and styles often evolve as a consequence of the child's behaviour. With a young child who is eager to please adults and is less active, a parent may discover a modest amount of control is adequate. But for a child who is not as eager to please and is very active, a parent may need to be more controlling and directive (Dumas, LaFreniere, & Serketich, 1995; Hastings & Rubin, 1999). Influence is reciprocal; children's behaviour helps determine how parents treat them and the resulting parental behaviour influences children's behaviour, which in turn causes parents to again change their behaviour (Stice & Barrera, 1995).

As time goes by, these reciprocal influences lead many families to adopt routine ways of interacting with each other. Some families end up functioning smoothly: Parents and children cooperate, anticipate each other's needs, and are generally happy. Unfortunately, other families end up troubled: Disagreements are common, parents spend much time trying unsuccessfully to control their defiant children, and everyone is often angry and upset (Belsky, Woodworth, & Crnic, 1996; Kochanska, 1997).

Over the long term, such troubled families do not fare well, so it's important that these negative reciprocal influences be nipped in the bud (Carrere & Gottman, 1999; Christensen & Heavey, 1999). When parents recognize the problem early on, they can modify their own behaviour. For example, they can try to be less controlling, which sometimes causes children to be less defiant. We are *not* suggesting that parents allow children to do as they please. Instead, parents should decide aspects of children's lives where they need less control and relinquish it.

Parents should also discuss expectations for appropriate behaviour with their preschoolers. Such discussions may seem odd for children so young, but phrased properly these conversations can help parents and children to better understand one another. And, just as important, they help to establish a style for dealing with family issues that will serve everyone well as the children grow.

Of course, many parents find it hard to view family functioning objectively because they are, after all, an integral part of that family. And parents often lack the expertise needed to change their children's behaviour. In these circumstances, a family therapist can provide invaluable assistance, identifying the obstacles to successful family functioning and suggesting ways to eliminate them.

PARENT–CHILD RELATIONSHIPS GONE AWRY: CHILD ABUSE

The first time 5-year-old Max came to preschool with bruises on his face, he told his teacher that he had fallen down the basement steps. When Max had similar bruises a few weeks later, his teacher spoke with the director of the preschool, who contacted local authorities. It turned out that Max's mother hit him with a belt for even minor misconduct; for serious transgressions, she beat Max and made him sleep alone in the basement.

Unfortunately, cases like Max's occur far too often. Maltreatment comes in many forms (Cicchetti, Toth, & Maughan, 2000):

- *Physical abuse*, involving assault that leads to injuries including cuts, welts, bruises, and broken bones
- *Sexual abuse*, involving fondling, intercourse, or other sexual behaviours
- *Psychological abuse*, involving ridicule, rejection, or humiliation
- *Neglect*, in which children do not receive adequate food, clothing, or medical care

The frequency of child maltreatment is difficult to estimate because so many cases go unreported. According to the Canadian Incidence Study of Reported Child Abuse and Neglect (Trocmé et al., 2001), in 1998 there were an estimated 22 investigations of child maltreatment for every 1,000 children and close to half were substantiated. Of these, approximately 40% were due to neglect, 31% were due to physical abuse, 19% were due to emotional maltreatment, and 10% were due to sexual abuse.

Who Are the Abusing Parents?

Parents who abuse their children were once thought to be severely disturbed or deranged. Today, we know that the vast majority of abusing parents cannot be distinguished from other parents by standard psychiatric criteria (Wolfe, 1985). In fact, modern accounts of child abuse no longer look to a single or even a small number of causes. Instead, a host of factors combine to place some children at risk for abuse and to protect others; the number and combination of factors determine whether the child is a likely target for abuse (Cicchetti et al., 2000). Let's look at three of the most important factors: those associated with the cultural context, those associated with parents, and those associated with children themselves.

The most general category of contributing factors are those dealing with cultural values and the social conditions in which parents rear their children. As discussed earlier, most physical child abuse is as a result of physical punishment use with children. In 1979 Sweden became the first country to legally ban the use of physical punishment for children, and since that time 10 more countries have followed with similar laws. Although there have been recent legal challenges and attempts in Canada to do likewise, currently caregivers who use physical punishment with children are protected from legal sanctions, as long as the force used is "reasonable" and for the purposes of correction. However, in 2004 the Supreme Court of Canada determined that the following types of physical responses with children would be deemed unreasonable: (1) using objects for the punishment, (2) slaps or blows to the head, (3) physical punishment with children under the age of 2 years and over the age of 12 years, (4) physical punishment carried out by a caregiver who is angry or frustrated, and (5) actions that are degrading, inhuman, or harmful (cited in Ateah, Durrant & Mirwaldt, 2004). Therefore, although the risks of physical punishment for children are acknowledged, efforts to decrease this type of punishment will continue to focus on parent and caregiver education and awareness of its risks and alternatives.

What kinds of social conditions seem to foster maltreatment? Poverty is one. Maltreatment is more common among children living in poverty in part because lack of money increases the stress of daily life (Coulton et al., 1995). When parents are worrying about whether they can buy groceries or pay rent, it appears that they are more likely to punish their children physically instead of making the extra effort to reason with them.

Social isolation is a second force. Abuse is more likely when families are socially isolated from other relatives or neighbours. When a family like the one in the photo lives in relative isolation, it deprives the children of adults who could protect them and deprives parents of social support that would help them better deal with life's stresses (Garbarino & Kostelny, 1992).

Cultural factors clearly contribute to child abuse, but they are only part of the puzzle. Although maltreatment is more common among families living in poverty, it does not occur in a majority of these families, and it does occur in middle- and upper-class families too. Consequently, we need to look for additional factors to explain why abuse occurs in some families but not in others.

Researchers have identified several important factors that increase the odds a parent will abuse his or her children (Cicchetti et al., 2000). First, parents who maltreat their children often were maltreated themselves, which may lead them to believe that abuse is simply a normal part of childhood. Second, parents who mistreat their children often use ineffective parenting techniques and have such unrealistic expectations that their children can never meet them. In addition, studies have shown that most cases of physical abuse have been as a result of a disciplinary response to a misbehaviour (e.g., Kadushin & Martin, 1981). Third, in families where abuse occurs, the couple's interactions are often unpredictable, unsupportive, and unsatisfying, for both husbands and wives. Thus, mistreatment of children is simply one symptom of family dysfunction.

© Allen Russell /Index Stock Imagery

To place the last few pieces in the puzzle, we must look at the abused children themselves. Infants and preschoolers are more often abused than older children, probably because they are less able to regulate aversive behaviours that may elicit abuse (Belsky, 1993). As discussed in Chapter 3, Shaken Baby Syndrome occurs when a caregiver shakes a baby, usually due to excessive crying. Because younger children are more likely to cry or whine excessively—behaviours that irritate all parents sooner or later—they are more likely to be the targets of parent anger, frustration, and possibly abuse.

However, any single factor will usually not result in abuse. Maltreatment becomes a possibility due to a number of circumstances, such as when cultures condone physical punishment and when parents lack effective knowledge and skills for dealing with expected child behaviours.

Effects of Abuse on Children

You probably aren't surprised to learn that the prognosis for youngsters like Max is not very good. Some, of course, suffer permanent physical damage. Even when there is no lasting physical damage, the children's social and emotional development is often disrupted. They tend to have poor relationships with peers, often because they are too aggressive (Bolger & Patterson, 2001). Their cognitive development and academic performance are also disturbed. Abused youngsters tend to get lower grades in school, score lower on standardized achievement tests, and be retained in a grade rather than promoted. Also, school-related behaviour problems, such as being disruptive in class, are common, in part because maltreated children don't regulate their emotions well (Maughan & Cicchetti, 2002; Shonk & Cicchetti, 2001).

Adults who were abused as children often experience emotional problems such as depression or anxiety, are more prone to think about or attempt suicide, and are more likely to abuse spouses and their own children (Malinosky-Rummell & Hansen, 1993). In short, when children are maltreated, virtually all aspects of their development are affected, and these effects do not vanish with time.

Preventing Abuse and Maltreatment

The complexity of child abuse dashes any hopes for a simple solution. Because maltreatment is more apt to occur when several contributing factors are present, eradicating child maltreatment requires many different approaches.

Although physical punishment has become a lot less socially acceptable over the last number of years in Canada, many parents still believe that physical punishment is a normal part of parenting. An estimated 71% to 75% of Canadian parents have used physical punishment with their children (Durrant, 1993–94; Durrant, Rose-Krasnor & Broberg, 1997). In a Canadian study on parental use of physical punishment with children, Ateah and Durrant (in press) found that the strongest predictor of physical punishment was a positive attitude toward its use. In addition, this study found that anger and the parent's assessment that the child's misbehaviour was both serious and purposeful also predicted physical punishment use with their children. Therefore, in order to decrease the use of physical punishment parents need to learn the risks involved in its use, normal and expected child behaviours, and effective non-physical and age-appropriate disciplinary strategies.

It would be naïve to expect all these changes to occur overnight. However, by focusing on some of the more manageable factors, the risk of maltreatment can be reduced. Social supports help. When parents know they can turn to other helpful adults for advice and reassurance, they better manage the stresses of child rearing that might otherwise lead to abuse. And families can be taught more effective ways of coping with situations that might otherwise trigger abuse (Wicks-Nelson & Israel, 1991).

Providing social supports and teaching effective parenting are typically done when maltreatment and abuse have already occurred. Of course, preventing maltreatment in the first place is more desirable and more cost-effective. For prevention, one useful tool is familiar—early childhood intervention programs. That is, maltreatment and abuse can be cut in half when families participate for two or more years in intervention programs that include preschool education along with family support activities aimed at encouraging parents to become more involved in their children's education (Reynolds & Robertson, 2003). When parents participate in these programs, they become more committed to their children's education. This leads their children to be more successful in school, reducing a source of stress and enhancing parents' confidence in their child-rearing skills, reducing the risks of maltreatment in the process.

Finally, we need to remember that most parents who have mistreated their children deserve compassion and help. In most cases, parents and children are attached to each other; maltreatment is a consequence of ignorance and burden, not malice.

TEST YOURSELF

1. A(n) _____ parental style combines high control with low involvement.

2. Children who have low self-esteem and are impulsive, aggressive, and moody often have parents who rely on a(n) _____ style.

3. Parental behaviours that influence children include direct instruction, modelling (learning through observation), and _____.

4. Children are more likely to be abused when they are younger because they are _____.

How can child abuse be explained in terms of the biological, psychological, and sociocultural forces in the biopsychosocial framework?

Answers: (1) authoritarian, (2) indifferent-uninvolved, (3) feedback (reward and punishment), (4) less able to regulate their own behaviour

6.2

Independence and Emotions

LEARNING OBJECTIVES

- What stage of Erikson's theory of psychosocial development applies to preschool children?
- How do emotions develop during the preschool years?

> **Independence and Emotions**
> Erikson's Stages of Psychosocial Development
> Regulating Emotions

ERIKSON'S STAGES OF PSYCHOSOCIAL DEVELOPMENT

You will recall that one of the strengths of Erikson's theory is its ability to tie together important psychosocial developments across the entire life span. In Erikson's theory the preschool years are represented by the stage of Initiative versus Guilt.

Initiative Versus Guilt

Most parents have their 3- and 4-year-olds take some responsibility for themselves (by dressing themselves, for example). Youngsters also begin to identify with adults and their parents; they begin to understand the opportunities that are available in their culture. Play begins to have purpose as children explore adult roles, such as mother, father, teacher, athlete, or writer. Youngsters start to explore the environment on their own, ask innumerable questions about the world, and imagine possibilities for themselves. These activities help even very young children develop a sense of purpose.

This initiative is moderated by guilt as children realize that their initiative may place them in conflict with others; they cannot pursue their ambitions with abandon. *Purpose is achieved with a balance between individual initiative and a willingness to cooperate with others.* A child must come to terms with wanting to do something with the possibility that it may be met with disapproval. It is in this context that they deal with their emerging emotions and sense of self.

Emotional Development in Preschool Children

As children grow, they continue to experience basic and complex emotions, but different situations or events elicit these emotions. In the case of complex emotions, cognitive growth means that elementary school children experience shame and guilt in situations they would not have when younger (Reimer, 1996). For example, unlike preschool children, many school-age children would be ashamed if they neglected to defend a classmate who had been wrongly accused of a theft. Pride is another emotion that is directed toward the self and is generally thought to develop around the age of 3 when self-awareness has increased.

Fear can be elicited in different ways, depending on a child's age. Many preschool children are afraid of the dark and of imaginary creatures. These fears typically diminish during the elementary school years as children grow cognitively and better understand the difference between appearance and reality (see Section 8.2). Replacing these fears are concerns about school, health, and personal harm (Silverman, La Greca, & Wasserstein, 1995). Such worries are common and not cause for concern in most children. In some youngsters, however, they become so extreme that they overwhelm the child (Chorpita & Barlow, 1998). For example, a 7-year-old's worries about school would not be unusual unless her concern grew to the point that she refused to go to school.

Recognizing and Using Others' Emotions

As children's cognitive skills continue to grow in childhood, they become more adept at identifying others' emotions and more adept at modifying their behaviour accordingly (Boone & Cunningham, 1998; Dunn, Brown, & Maguire, 1995). Children learn that sometimes they should conceal their emotions (Jones, Abbey, & Cumberland, 1998). And they begin to understand why people feel as they do and how emotions can influence a person's behaviour. Preschool children, for example, understand that an angry child is more likely to hurt someone than a happy child (Russell & Paris, 1994).

What experiences contribute to children's understanding of emotions? Not surprisingly, children learn about emotions when parents talk about feelings, explaining how they differ and the situations that elicit them (Brown & Dunn, 1992; Cervantes & Callanan, 1998). Also, a positive, rewarding relationship with parents and siblings is related to children's understanding of emotions (Brown & Dunn, 1992; Laible & Thompson, 1998). The nature of this connection is still a mystery. One possibility is that within positive parent–child and sibling relationships, people express a fuller range of emotions (and do so more often) and are more willing to talk about why they feel as they do, providing children with more opportunities to learn about emotions.

REGULATING EMOTIONS

As we learned in Chapter 4, emotion regulation clearly begins in infancy. Older children and adolescents encounter a wider range of emotional situations, so it's fortunate they develop a number of related new ways to regulate emotion (Eisenberg & Morris, 2002):

- Children begin to regulate their own emotions and rely less on others to do this for them. A fearful child no longer runs to a parent but instead devises her own methods for dealing with fear (e.g., "I know the thunderstorm won't last long, and I'm safe inside the house").
- Children more often rely on mental strategies to regulate emotions. For example, a child might reduce his disappointment at not receiving a much-expected gift by telling himself that he didn't really want the gift in the first place.
- Children more accurately match the strategies for regulating emotion with the particular setting. For example, when faced with emotional situations that are unavoidable (e.g., a child must go to the dentist to have a cavity filled), children adjust to the situation (e.g., thinking of the positive consequences of treating the tooth) instead of trying to avoid the situation.

Collectively, these age-related trends give children tools for regulating emotions. Nevertheless, not all children regulate their emotions well, and those who don't tend to have problems interacting with peers and have adjustment problems (Eisenberg & Morris, 2002; Lengua, 2002). When children can't control their anger, worry, or sadness, they often have difficulty resolving the conflicts that inevitably surface in peer relationships (Fabes et al., 1999). For example, faced with a dispute over what game to play, children's unregulated anger interferes with finding a mutually satisfying solution. Thus, ineffective regulation of emotions leads to more frequent conflicts with peers, and, consequently, less satisfying peer relationships and less adaptive adjustment to school (Eisenberg et al., 2001).

TEST YOURSELF

1. According to Erikson, the activities of preschoolers help them to develop a sense of _____.

2. Social development of preschool children includes striving to try new things but sometimes experiencing _____ when met with disapproval.

3. Preschool children become more adept at observing others' _____ and moderating their behaviour accordingly.

4. Complex emotions, such as guilt and shame, emerge later than basic emotions because _____.

5. Children who have difficulty moderating their emotional responses may develop _____ problems.

What are some common activities by preschool children that demonstrate their developing sense of purpose?

Answers: (1) purpose, (2) guilt, (3) emotions, (4) complex emotions require understanding of the self, (5) adjustment

---

6.3

Self-Awareness During Preschool Years

LEARNING OBJECTIVES

☑ What are preschoolers' self-concepts like?

☑ When do preschool children begin to acquire a theory of mind?

> **Self-Awareness During Preschool Years**
> Self-Concept in Early Childhood
> Theory of Mind

Four-year-old Ling tells her uncle that she is hungry and asks him if he is too, and if he would like a cookie. Her uncle is surprised to hear Ling be so considerate of someone else's feelings. He wonders, "When do children start to think about how others might be feeling in a situation in comparison to themselves?"

In this section we will consider how preschoolers' self-concepts continue to develop. In addition, we will discuss theory of mind—the developing understanding of the link between one's mind and behaviour.

SELF-CONCEPT IN EARLY CHILDHOOD

As children's understanding of the mind becomes more elaborate, they begin to acquire a self-concept. That is, once children fully understand that they exist, they begin to wonder who they are. They want to define themselves.

Some insights into the first phases of self-concept come from Levine (1983), who studied 20- to 28-month-olds. This is an age when children are just beginning to become self-aware. Children were tested on several measures of self-awareness, including the mirror recognition task described earlier. They were also observed as they interacted with an unfamiliar peer in a playroom filled with toys. The key finding was that children who are self-aware are much more likely to say "Mine!" while playing with toys than children who are not yet self-aware. Maybe you're thinking that these self-aware children were being confrontational in saying "Mine," as in "This car is mine and don't even think about taking it." But they weren't. Actually, self-aware children are more likely to say positive things during their interactions with peers. Levine argued that "claiming toys was not simply a negative or aggressive behaviour, but appeared to be an important part of the child's definition of himself within his social world" (p. 547). In other words, the girl on the left in the photograph saying "Mine!" is not trying to deny the doll to the other girl; she is simply saying that playing with toy dolls is part of who she is.

Throughout the preschool years, possessions continue to be one of the ways in which children define themselves. Preschoolers are also likely to mention physical characteristics ("I have blue eyes"), their preferences ("I like spaghetti"), and their competencies ("I can count to 50"). What these features have in common is a focus on a child's characteristics that are observable and concrete (Damon & Hart, 1988).

As children enter school, their self-concepts become even more elaborate (Harter, 1994), changes that we'll explore in Chapter 8.

THEORY OF MIND

As youngsters gain more insights into themselves as thinking beings, they begin to realize that people have thoughts, beliefs, and intentions. They also understand that thoughts, beliefs, and intentions often cause people to behave as they do. *Collectively, ideas about connections between thoughts, beliefs, intentions, and behaviour form a **theory of mind**, an intuitive understanding of the link between mind and behaviour.*

One of the leading researchers on theory of mind, Henry Wellman (1992, 1993), believes that children's theory of mind moves through three phases during the preschool years. In the earliest phase, 2-year-olds are aware of desires and often speak of their wants and likes, as in "Lemme see" or "I wanna sit." And they often link their desires to their behaviour, such as "I happy there more cookies" (Wellman, 1993). Thus, by age 2, children understand that people have desires and that desires can cause behaviour.

By about age 3, children clearly distinguish the mental world from the physical world. For example, if told about a girl who has a cookie and another who is thinking about a cookie, 3-year-olds know that only the first girl can see, touch, and eat her cookie (Harris et al., 1991). And most 3-year-olds use "mental verbs" like "think," "believe," "remember," and "forget," which suggests that they have a beginning understanding of different mental states (Bartsch & Wellman, 1995). Although 3-year-olds talk about thoughts and beliefs, they nevertheless emphasize desires when trying to explain why people act as they do.

Not until 4 years of age do mental states really take centre stage in children's understanding of their and others' actions. That is, by age 4, children understand that behaviour is often based on a person's beliefs about events and situations, even when those beliefs are wrong. This developmental transformation is particularly evident when children are tested on false-belief tasks like the one shown in Figure 6.2. In all

FIGURE 6.2

This is Sally. Sally has a basket.

This is Anne. Anne has a box.

Sally has a ball.

She puts the ball in her basket.

Sally goes out for a walk.

Anne takes the ball from the basket and puts it into the box.

Now Sally comes back. She wants to play with her ball. Where will she look for her ball?

false-belief tasks, a situation is set up so that the child being tested has accurate information but someone else does not. For example, in the story in the figure, the child being tested knows the ball is really in the box, but Sally, the girl in the story, believes the ball is still in the basket. Remarkably, although 4-year-olds correctly say that Sally will look for the ball in the basket (acting on her false belief), most 3-year-olds claim that she will look for the ball in the box. The 4-year-olds understand that Sally's behaviour is based on her beliefs, despite the fact that her beliefs are incorrect (Frye, 1993).

This basic developmental progression is remarkably robust. Wellman, Cross, and Watson (2001) conducted a meta-analysis of approximately 175 studies in which more than 4,000 young children were tested on false-belief tasks. Before three and a half years, children typically make the false-belief error: Attributing their own knowledge of the ball's location to Sally, they say she will search in the correct location. Yet six short months later, children now understand that Sally's false belief will cause her to look for the ball in the box. This rapid developmental transition from incorrect to correct performance is unaffected by many procedural variables (e.g., whether Sally is a doll, a picture, a person in a videotape, or a real person) and is much the same whether the children are from Europe, North America, Africa, or Asia.

Thus, this pattern signifies a fundamental change in children's understanding of the centrality of beliefs in a person's thinking about the world. By age 4, children "realize that people not only have thoughts and beliefs, but also that thoughts and beliefs are crucial to explaining why people do things; that is, actors' pursuits of their desires are inevitably shaped by their beliefs about the world" (Bartsch & Wellman, 1995, p. 144).

Preschoolers understand false belief at a younger age if they have older siblings (Ruffman et al., 1998). During play, older brothers and sisters often talk with their younger siblings about internal states—who is happy or sad and why—and these conversations may help youngsters to see the link between beliefs and behaviour.

You can see preschool children's growing understanding of false belief in the Real People feature on page 212.

Preschool children's growing knowledge of the mind is not an isolated accomplishment. This understanding is simply part of profound cognitive growth that occurs during the preschool years as discussed in the previous chapter.

THINK ABOUT IT

Suppose you believe that a theory of mind develops faster when preschoolers spend much time with other children. What sort of correlational study would you devise to test this hypothesis? How could you do an experimental study to test the same hypothesis?

REAL PEOPLE: APPLYING HUMAN DEVELOPMENT

"Seeing Is Believing . . ." for 3-Year-Olds

Preschoolers gradually recognize that people's behaviour is sometimes guided by mistaken beliefs. We once witnessed an episode at a day-care centre that documented this growing understanding. After lunch, Karen, a 2-year-old, saw ketchup on the floor and squealed, "Blood, blood!" Lonna, a 3-year-old, said in a disgusted tone, "It's not blood—it's ketchup." Then, Shenan, a 4-year-old, interjected, "Yeah, but Karen *thought* it was blood." A similar incident took place a few weeks later, on the day after Halloween. This time Lonna put on a monster mask and scared Karen. When Karen began to cry, Lonna said, "Oh stop. It's just a mask." Shenan broke in again, saying, "You know it's just a mask. But she *thinks* it's a monster." In both cases, only Shenan understood that Karen's behaviour was based on her beliefs (that the ketchup is blood and that the monster is real), even though her beliefs were false.

TEST YOURSELF

1. During the preschool years, children's self-concepts emphasize _____, physical characteristics, preferences, and competencies.

2. Unlike 4-year-olds, most 3-year-olds don't understand that other people's behaviour is sometimes based on _____.

During the preschool years, children acquire more sophisticated understanding of the mind. Do you think this change occurs in much the same way in all cultures, or does it vary from one culture to another?

Answers: (1) possessions, (2) false beliefs

6.4

Interacting with Others

LEARNING OBJECTIVES

- When do youngsters first begin to play with each other? How does play change during the preschool years?
- What determines whether preschool children cooperate with one another?
- What determines whether children help one another? What experiences make children more inclined to help?

> **Interacting with Others**
>
> Preschool Play
>
> Learning to Cooperate
>
> Helping Others

Six-year-old James got his finger trapped in the VCR when he tried to remove a tape. While he cried and cried, his 3-year-old brother, Doug, and his 2-year-old sister, Casey, watched but did not help. Later, when their mother had soothed James and concluded that his finger was not injured, she worried about her younger children's reactions. In the face of their brother's obvious distress, why did Doug and Casey do nothing?

Infants' initial interactions are with parents, but soon they begin to interact with other people, notably their peers. In this section, we'll trace the development of these interactions and learn why children like Doug and Casey don't always help others.

PRESCHOOL PLAY

The nature of young children's play changes dramatically in a few years (Howes & Matheson, 1992). Whereas 1- and 2-year-olds spend most of their time in parallel play, among 3- and 4-year-olds, parallel play is much less common, and cooperative play is the norm.

Make-Believe

As we learned in Chapter 4, children starting about the age of 2 usually begin to participate in cooperative play such as "hide and go seek" like the children in the picture. During the preschool years, cooperative play often takes the form of make-believe. Preschoolers have telephone conversations with imaginary partners or pretend to drink imaginary juice. In the early phases of make-believe, children rely on realistic props to support their play. While pretending to drink, younger preschoolers use a real cup; while pretending to drive a car, they use a toy steering wheel. In the later phases of make-believe, children no longer need realistic props; instead, they can imagine that a block is the cup, or that a paper plate is the steering wheel. Of course, this gradual movement toward more abstract make-believe is possible because of cognitive growth that occurs during the preschool years (Harris & Kavanaugh, 1993).

© Tony Freeman /PhotoEdit

As you might suspect, make-believe reflects the values important in a child's culture. This influence is apparent in the results of research by Farver and Shin (1997), who studied European-American and Korean-American preschoolers. The Korean-American children came from families who had recently immigrated to the United States and who still stressed the importance of traditional Korean values, such as emphasis on the family and favouring harmony over conflict. The two groups of children differed in the themes common during make-believe. Adventure and fantasy were common themes for European-American youngsters, but family roles and everyday activities were common for the Korean-American youngsters. In addition, the groups differed in their style of play during make-believe.

European-American children were more assertive in their make-believe and more likely to disagree with their play partner's ideas about pretending ("*I* want to be the king; *you* be the mom!"). In contrast, Korean-American children were more polite and more likely to strive for harmony in their play ("Could I *please* be king?"). Thus cultural values influence both the form and the content of make-believe.

Make-believe play is entertaining for children, and it also seems to promote cognitive development (Berk, 1994). Children who spend much time in make-believe play tend to be more advanced in their language, memory, and reasoning. They also tend to be more sophisticated in their understanding of other people's thoughts, beliefs, and feelings (Howe, Petrakos, & Rinaldi, 1998; Youngblade & Dunn, 1995).

THINK ABOUT IT

How might Jean Piaget have explained the emergence of make-believe during the preschool years? How would Erik Erikson explain it?

Another benefit of make-believe is that it allows children to explore topics that frighten them. Children who are afraid of the dark may reassure a doll who is also afraid of the dark. By explaining to the doll why she need not be afraid, children come to understand and regulate their own fear of darkness. Or children may pretend that a doll has misbehaved and must be punished, which allows them to experience the parent's anger and the doll's guilt. With make-believe, children explore other emotions as well, including joy and affection (Gottman, 1986).

For many preschool children, make-believe play involves imaginary companions. These children can easily describe their imaginary playmates, mentioning their sex and age as well as the colour of their hair and eyes. Imaginary companions were once thought to be fairly rare and a sign of possible developmental problems. But more recent research shows that nearly two-thirds of all preschoolers report imaginary companions (Taylor, Cartwright, & Carlson, 1993). Moreover, the presence of an imaginary companion is associated with many *positive* social characteristics: Preschoolers with imaginary companions tend to be more sociable and have more real friends than preschoolers without imaginary companions. Furthermore, vivid fantasy play with imaginary companions does *not* mean that the distinction between fantasy and reality is blurred: Children with imaginary companions can distinguish fantasy from reality just as readily as youngsters who do not have imaginary companions (Taylor et al., 1993).

Solitary Play

At times throughout the preschool years, many children prefer to play alone. Should parents be worried? Usually, no. Solitary play comes in many forms and most are normal—even healthy. Spending free playtime alone colouring, solving puzzles, or assembling Legos is not a sign of maladjustment. Many youngsters enjoy solitary activities and, at other times, choose very social play.

However, some forms of solitary play *are* signs that children are uneasy interacting with others (Coplan et al., 1994; Harrist et al., 1997). One type of unhealthy solitary play is wandering aimlessly. Sometimes children go from one preschool activity centre to the next, as if trying to decide what to do. But really they just keep wandering, never settling in to play with others or for constructive solitary play. Another unhealthy type of solitary play is hovering: A child stands nearby peers who are playing, watching them play, but not participating. Over time, these behaviours do not bode well for youngsters, so it's best for these youngsters to see a professional who can help them overcome their reticence in social situations (Ladd, 1998).

Gender Differences in Play

Between 2 and 3 years of age, the situation shown in the photo becomes more and more common; most youngsters begin to prefer playing with peers of their own sex. This preference increases during childhood, reaching a peak in preadolescence (Hartup, 1983). This tendency for boys to play with boys and girls with girls has several distinctive features (Maccoby, 1990):

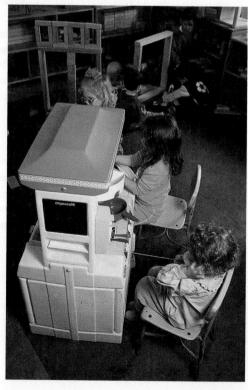

Mary Kate Denney/PhotoEdit

■ In some cultures, adults select playmates for children. However, in cultures where children choose playmates, boys select boys as playmates and girls select girls.

- Children spontaneously select same-sex playmates. Adult pressure ("James, why don't you play with John, not Amy") is not necessary.
- Children resist parents' efforts to get them to play with members of the opposite sex. Girls are often unhappy when parents encourage them to play with boys, and boys are often unhappy when parents urge them to play with girls.
- Children's reluctance to play with members of the opposite sex is not restricted to gender-typed games, such as playing house or playing with cars. Boys and girls prefer same-sex playmates even in gender-neutral activities such as playing tag or doing puzzles.

Why do boys and girls seem so attracted to same-sex play partners? Eleanor Maccoby (1988, 1990) believes two factors are critical. First, boys specifically prefer rough-and-tumble play and generally are more competitive and dominating in their interactions. Girls' play is not as rough and is less competitive, so Maccoby argues that boys' style of play may be aversive to girls.

Second, when girls and boys play together, girls do not readily influence boys. Girls' interactions with one another are typically enabling—their actions and remarks tend to support others and sustain the interaction. In contrast, boy's interactions are often constricting—one partner tries to emerge as the victor by threatening or contradicting the other, by exaggerating, and so on. When these styles are brought together, girls find their enabling style is ineffective with boys. The same subtle overtures that work with other girls have no impact on boys. Boys ignore girls' polite suggestions about what to do and ignore girls' efforts to resolve conflicts with discussion.

Whatever the exact cause, the preference to play with same-sex peers that emerges in the preschool years is a constant throughout the life span (Moller, Hymel, & Rubin, 1992). As we shall see in Chapters 8, 10, and 12, time spent at leisure (and later, at work) is commonly segregated by sex during adolescence and adulthood.

Parental Influence

Parents get involved in their preschool children's play in several ways (Isley et al., 1999). Sometimes they take the role of playmate (and many parents deserve an Oscar for their performances). They use the opportunity to scaffold their children's play, often raising it to more sophisticated levels (Tamis-LeMonda & Bornstein, 1996). For example, if a toddler is stacking toy plates, a parent might help the child stack the plates (play at the same level) or might pretend to wash each plate (play at a more advanced level). When parents demonstrate more advanced forms of play, their children often play at the more advanced levels later (Bornstein et al., 1995).

Another parental role during preschoolers' play is mediator. Preschoolers often disagree, argue, and sometimes fight. As shown in the photo, children play more cooperatively and longer when parents are present to help iron out conflicts (Mize, Pettit, & Brown, 1995; Parke & Bahvnagri, 1989). When young children can't agree on what to play, a parent can negotiate a mutually acceptable activity. When both youngsters want to play with the same toy, a parent can arrange for them to share. Here, too, parents scaffold their preschoolers' play, smoothing the interaction by providing some of the social skills that preschoolers lack.

Michael Newman/PhotoEdit

Yet another parental role is coach. Preschool children often encounter social problems that, although minor from an adult's perspective, seem overwhelming to the child. For example, a child might be colouring when another child approaches and demands the crayon the child is using. Parents can help their preschoolers understand and handle such problems. When parents coach—and when their advice is constructive—their children tend to be skilled socially and less aggressive (Mize & Pettit, 1997).

THINK ABOUT IT 💡

Suppose friends of yours ask you how their preschool daughter could get along well with peers. What advice would you give them?

Parents also influence the success of their children's peer interactions in a much less direct manner. Children's relationships with peers are most successful when, as infants, they had a secure attachment relationship with their mother (Ladd & Le Sieur, 1995; Lieberman, Doyle, & Markiewicz, 1999).

Why does quality of attachment predict the success of children's peer relationships? One view is that a child's relationship with his or her parents is the internal working model for all future social relationships. When the parent–child relationship is of high quality and emotionally satisfying, children are encouraged to form relationships with other people. Another possibility is that a secure attachment relationship with the mother makes an infant feel more confident about exploring the environment, which, in turn, provides more opportunities to interact with peers. These two views are not mutually exclusive; both may contribute to the relative ease with which securely attached children interact with their peers (Hartup, 1992b).

LEARNING TO COOPERATE

Play is built on the implicit and sometimes explicit agreement that all players will adhere to certain rules for the common benefit. Hide-and-seek, for example, is no fun when one child only wants to hide and refuses to take a turn as the seeker. Of course, although cooperation may be the ideal, children do not always play together well; conflicts and arguments are common.

What are some factors that determine whether children cooperate? Age is one. Older children are less egocentric, and knowing that others view things differently helps reduce conflicts. Also, preschoolers' growing communicative and social skills make it easier for them to cooperate (Lourenco, 1993).

Cooperation is also influenced by other factors. Children are more likely to cooperate if they see peers who are cooperative and can observe, firsthand, that cooperation works. Children who observe successful cooperation more often cooperate when given the opportunity (Liebert, Sprafkin, & Poulos, 1975).

Children's eagerness to cooperate is strongly influenced by the response to their cooperative overtures (Brady, Newcomb, & Hartup, 1983). When children try to cooperate but their peers do not go along, the incentive to cooperate vanishes rapidly;

© Frank Siteman

instead, youngsters look after their own interests. In contrast, when one child's cooperative gesture leads to another youngster's cooperative response, children see for themselves the beauty of working together, and, as shown in the photo, cooperation flourishes.

Piecing these findings together, we see why long-lasting cooperation is so fragile. Cooperation works only when all participants agree to cooperate; a few people—or perhaps even just one person—who fail to go along can undermine all the benefits of cooperation. Young children in particular need to be directed by their parents into practical cooperative relationships so that they can directly experience the benefits associated with greater cooperation (Parke & Bahvnagri, 1989).

Some cultures go to greater lengths than others to encourage cooperation. In North America, the rights of the individual are emphasized, and self-reliance is encouraged. Other cultures, such as China, place a premium on what is good for all; people are seen as being strongly interdependent. Reflecting these cultural differences, Chinese children tend to be substantially more cooperative than North American children (Domino, 1992). For example, in one study (Orlick, Zhou, & Partington, 1990), investigators recorded the frequency of cooperation among kindergartners in Beijing, China, and those in Ottawa. In the Canadian kindergartens, 22% of the interactions were cooperative, which meant that children supported or helped a peer. In the Chinese kindergartens, 85% of the interactions were cooperative.

What should we make of this difference? Evidently, young children *can* be cooperative if they view such behaviour as mutually beneficial and if their culture expects them to cooperate. The See for Yourself feature at the end of the chapter describes how you can determine whether youngsters living near you are cooperative.

HELPING OTHERS

As we discussed in Chapter 4, rudimentary acts of altruism can be seen by 18 months of age. During the preschool years, children gradually begin to understand others' needs and learn appropriate altruistic responses (Farver & Branstetter, 1994). Let's look at some specific skills that set the stage for altruistic behaviours.

Skills Underlying Altruistic Behaviour

Remember from Chapter 5 that preschool children are often egocentric, so they may not see the need for altruistic behaviour. For example, young children might not share candy with a younger sibling because they cannot imagine how unhappy the sibling is without the candy. In contrast, school-age children, who can more easily take another person's perspective, would perceive the unhappiness and would be more inclined to share. In fact, research consistently indicates that altruistic behaviour is related to perspective-taking skill. Canadian researchers Roberts and Strayer (1996) found that youngsters who understand others' thoughts and feelings share better with others and help them more often.

© David Turnley/Corbis/Magma

Related to perspective-taking is empathy, which is the actual experiencing of another's feelings. Children who deeply feel another individual's fear, disappointment, sorrow, or loneliness are more inclined to help than children who do not feel those emotions (Carlo et al., 1996). In other words, youngsters like the boy in the photo, who is obviously distressed by what he is seeing, are most likely to help if they can. The Spotlight on Research feature describes a study that investigated this link between empathy and prosocial behaviour.

SPOTLIGHT ON RESEARCH

Are Empathic Children More Likely to Help?

What was the aim of the study and who were the investigators? A common idea in many theories of helping is that children (and adults) who "feel" another person's discomfort or distress should be more likely to help that person. That is, children and adults who are more empathic are thought to be more likely to help. Paul Miller and his colleagues Nancy Eisenberg, Richard Fabes, and Rita Shell (1996) tested this claim by measuring children's emotional responding and their tendency to help.

How did the investigators measure the topic of interest? Miller and his colleagues prepared brief films in which children appeared to hurt themselves when they fell. After watching the films, the children in the study were asked how they felt. Children responded by pointing to a happy, sad, sorry, or neutral face. Next, they were asked if they felt a little bit this way, kind of, or very much this way. Next, children were told that the child in the film was in the hospital and that the experimenter wanted to send that child some crayons. However, the crayons were loose in a large box and needed to be put into smaller boxes before they could be sent to the hospitalized child. The children were shown some toys and told that they could help sort the crayons or they could play with the toys. Thus, the measures were the type and intensity of the child's emotional response to the films and the number of crayons that they sorted.

Who were the children in the study? The researchers tested 74 5- and 6-year-old boys and girls.

What was the design of the study? This study was correlational because the investigators looked at the relations that existed naturally between helping (as measured by the number of crayons sorted) and the emotions

that children experienced while watching the film. The study included only 5- and 6-year-olds, so it was neither longitudinal nor cross-sectional.

Were there ethical concerns with the study? No. The emotional episodes depicted in the films were fairly mild and similar to what children might experience in their own lives.

What were the results? Figure 6.3 shows the correlations between children's emotions and their helping. Helping was greatest when children said they were sad after watching the film and least when they said they were happy after the film. Neutral or sorry emotional responses were unrelated to helping.

What did the investigators conclude? As predicted, children who are saddened by another person's discomfort are most likely to help that person. Children who are happy (perhaps because they think it is funny to see others make mistakes, such as falling down) are unlikely to help.

What converging evidence would strengthen these conclusions? One interesting extension of this study would be to obtain different kinds of measures of helping and emotional responding. For example, parents might be asked to report on their children's emotional responding and teachers could rate their students' willingness to help. Doing this research in a cross-sectional study would also be useful in revealing whether the relation between helping and emotional responding changes as children grow. ▄

FIGURE 6.3

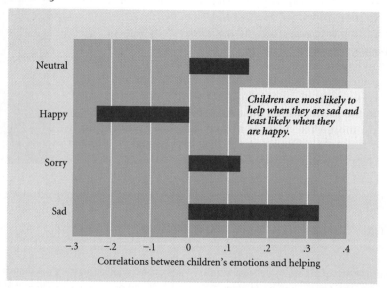

Children are most likely to help when they are sad and least likely when they are happy.

Correlations between children's emotions and helping

Of course, responding empathically does not guarantee that children will act altruistically. Some caring children who would like to help others may not be able to do so. An older brother might want to share candy with a younger sibling but will not because a parent forbids it. Sometimes children may not help because they lack the time or believe that others will help. It is necessary to consider the context in which behaviour occurs, as this helps determine whether a child will act altruistically. A number of contextual features are known to influence children's altruism.

- *Feelings of responsibility.* Children act altruistically when they feel responsible for the person in need. Children may help siblings and friends more often than strangers, for example, simply because they feel a direct responsibility for people they know well (Costin & Jones, 1992).
- *Feelings of competence.* Children act altruistically when they feel they have the skills to help the person in need. Suppose, for example, that a preschooler is growing more and more upset because she can't figure out how to work a computer game; a peer who knows little about computer games is not likely to come to the young girl's aid because the peer doesn't know what to do to help. If the peer tries to help, he or she could end up looking foolish (Peterson, 1983).
- *Mood.* Children act altruistically when they are happy or feeling successful but not when they are sad or feeling as if they have failed. A preschool child who has just spent an exciting morning as the "leader" in nursery school is more inclined to share treats with siblings than is a preschooler who was punished by the teacher (Moore, Underwood, & Rosenhan, 1973).
- *Costs of altruism.* Children act altruistically when such actions entail few or modest sacrifices. A preschool child who was given a snack that she doesn't particularly like is more inclined to share it with others than one who was given her very favorite food (Eisenberg & Shell, 1986).

So when are children most likely to help? When they feel responsible for the person in need, have the needed skills, are happy, and believe they will give up little by helping. When are children least likely to help? When they feel neither responsible nor capable of helping, are in a bad mood, and believe helping will entail a large personal sacrifice.

With these guidelines in mind, can you explain why Doug and Casey, the children in the opening vignette, watched idly as their older brother cried? The last two factors—mood and costs—are not likely to be involved. However, the first two factors may explain the failure of Doug and Casey to help their older brother. Our explanation appears on page 220, just before Test Yourself.

THINK ABOUT IT

Suppose some kindergarten children want to raise money for a gift for one of their classmates who is ill. Based on the information presented here, what advice can you give the children as they plan their fundraising?

Socialization of Altruism

Contextual factors clearly play an important role in children's altruism. However, children also differ from one another in their feelings of obligation to other humans. Some youngsters are more inclined to help regardless of the setting. Why do some children feel a stronger obligation to help than others?

One factor that has been linked to children's altruism is parents' disciplinary style. Altruistic children typically have parents who emphasize reasoning when disciplining their children. This approach often emphasizes the rights and needs of others as well as the impact of a child's misbehaviour on others (Hoffman, 1988, 1994). For example, in the following dialogue, the father tries to make his daughter see how her actions upset her friend.

FATHER: Why did you take the crayons away from Annie?

DAUGHTER: Because I wanted them.

FATHER: How do you think that made her feel? Do you think she was happy or sad?

DAUGHTER: I dunno.

FATHER: I think you know.

DAUGHTER: Okay. She was sad.

FATHER: Would you like it if I took the crayons away from you? How would *you* feel?

DAUGHTER: I'd be mad. And sad too.

FATHER: Well, that's how Annie felt, and that's why you shouldn't just grab things away from someone. It makes them angry and unhappy. Ask first, and if they say no, then you mustn't take them.

Repeated exposure to reasoning during discipline apparently strengthens children's general feelings of responsibility toward other people (Krevans & Gibbs, 1996).

Parents also influence their children's altruism by their own altruistic behaviour. When parents express warmth and concern for other people, this increases their children's feelings of empathy (Eisenberg et al., 1991). Parents who behave altruistically— by being helpful to others and being responsive to them—have children who help, share, and are less critical of others (Bryant & Crockenberg, 1980). Thus, by serving as good models of altruistic behaviour, parents foster their children's altruism.

A third way to influence children's altruism is by praising them for it. By frequently making remarks such as "It really makes me happy that you helped Matt tie his shoes," parents encourage their children's altruism. *Particularly effective is dispositional praise, in which parents link the child's altruistic behaviour to an underlying altruistic disposition.* For example, a parent might say, "Thanks for helping me make breakfast; I knew I could count on you because you are such a helpful person." When children hear remarks like this repeatedly, their self-concept apparently changes to include these characteristics. Children begin to believe they really are helpful (or nice or friendly). With these characteristics as important elements of their self-concept, children (like the one in the photo) are more likely to behave altruistically when others are in need (Mills & Grusec, 1989).

Thus, parents can foster altruism in their youngsters by using reasoning to discipline them, behaving altruistically themselves, and praising the children's altruistic acts. Also, contextual factors play a role, and altruism requires perspective-taking and empathy. Combining these ingredients, we can give a general account of children's altruistic behaviour. As children get older, their perspective-taking and empathic skills develop, which enables them to see and feel another's needs. Nonetheless, children are never invariably altruistic (or, fortunately, invariably nonaltruistic), because particular contexts affect altruistic behaviour too.

Postscript: Why Didn't Doug and Casey Help?

Here are our explanations. First, neither Doug nor Casey may have felt sufficiently responsible to help, because (a) with two children who could help, each child's feeling of individual responsibility is reduced, and (b) younger children are less likely to feel responsible for an older sibling. Second, it's our guess that neither child has had many opportunities to use the VCR. In fact, it's likely that they both have been strongly discouraged from even touching it. Consequently, they don't feel very competent to help, because neither knows how it works or what they should do to help James remove his finger.

TEST YOURSELF

1. One of the advantages of _____ play is that children can explore topics that frighten them.

2. When girls interact, conflicts are typically resolved through _____; boys more often resort to intimidation.

3. Compared to young children in North America, youngsters in China are _____ cooperative.

4. _____ is the ability to understand and feel another person's emotions.

5. Contextual influences on prosocial behaviour include feelings of responsibility, feelings of competence, _____, and

the costs associated with behaving prosocially.

6. Parents can foster altruism in their children by using reasoning to discipline them, behaving altruistically themselves, and _____.

How might children's temperament influence the development of their play with peers?

Answers: (1) make-believe, (2) discussion and compromise, (3) more, (4) Empathy, (5) mood, (6) praising their children for altruistic behaviour

---

6.5

Gender Roles and Gender Identity

LEARNING OBJECTIVES

- What are our stereotypes about males and females? How well do they correspond to actual differences between boys and girls?

- When do young children understand that gender is fixed? How does this understanding influence their learning about roles for girls and boys?

- How are gender roles changing? What further changes might the future hold?

Gender Roles and Gender Identity

Images of Men and Women: Facts and Fantasy

Gender Typing

Evolving Gender Roles

Meda and Frank are in their early 50s. Though not married, they have lived together since the early 1970s, when both were active in political protests. Their daughter, Hope, is now 6 years old. True to their countercultural roots, both Meda and Frank want their daughter to pick activities, friends, and, ultimately, a career based on her interests and abilities, not on her gender. Both are now astonished that Hope seems to be totally indistinguishable from other 6-year-olds reared by parents with conventional outlooks. Hope's close friends are all girls, and they often play "house" or play with dolls. What seems to be going wrong with Meda and Frank's plans for a "gender-neutral" girl?

Family and well-wishers are always eager to know the gender of a newborn. Why are people so interested in a baby's gender? The answer is that being a "boy" or "girl" is not simply a biological distinction. Instead, these terms are associated with distinct social roles. *Like a role in a play, a **social role** is a set of cultural guidelines as to how a person should behave, particularly with other people.* The roles associated with gender are among the first that children learn, starting in infancy. Youngsters rapidly learn about the behaviours that are assigned to males and females in their culture. At the same time, they begin to identify with one of these groups. As they do, they take on an identity as a boy or girl.

In this section, you'll learn about the "female role" and the "male role" in North America today, and you'll also discover why Meda and Frank are having so much trouble rearing a gender-neutral girl.

IMAGES OF MEN AND WOMEN: FACTS AND FANTASY

*All cultures have **gender stereotypes**—beliefs and images about males and females that may or may not be true.* For example, many men and women believe that males are rational, active, independent, competitive, and aggressive. At the same time, many men and women claim that females are emotional, passive, dependent, sensitive, and gentle (Best, 2001; Lueptow, Garovich-Szabo, & Lueptow, 2001; Lutz & Ruble, 1995).

Based on gender stereotypes, we expect males and females to act and feel in particular ways, and we respond to their behaviour differently, depending on their gender (Smith & Mackie, 2000). For example, if you saw the toddler in the photo, you would probably assume that she was a girl, based on her taste in toys. Furthermore, your assumption would lead you to believe (a) that she plays more quietly and (b) that she is more readily frightened than if you had assumed the child to be a boy (Stern & Karraker, 1989). Once we assume the child is a girl, our gender stereotypes lead to a whole host of inferences about behaviour and personality.

By the time children are ready to enter elementary school, they are well on their way to learning gender stereotypes. For example, 5-year-olds believe that boys are strong and dominant and that girls are emotional and gentle (Best et al., 1977; Etaugh & Liss, 1992).

Beyond the preschool years, children learn more about stereotypes, but they also have greater flexibility when it comes to gender stereotypes (Serbin, Powlishta, & Gulko, 1993). They understand that it is often acceptable for children to deviate from gender stereotypes—a girl can be ambitious and a boy can be gentle (Levy, Taylor, & Gelman, 1995).

Of course, these are only people's *beliefs* about differences between males and females, and many of them are false. Research reveals that males and females often *do not* differ in the ways specified by cultural stereotypes. What are the bona fide differences between males and females? In addition to the obvious anatomical differences, males are typically larger and stronger than females throughout most of the life span. Beginning in infancy, boys are more active than girls (Eaton & Enns, 1986). In contrast, girls have a lower mortality rate and are less susceptible to stress and disease (Zaslow & Hayes, 1986).

When it comes to social roles, activities for males tend to be more strenuous, involve more cooperation with others, and often require travel. Activities for females are usually less demanding physically, more solitary, and take place closer to home. This division of roles is much the same worldwide (Whiting & Edwards, 1988).

The extent of gender differences in the intellectual and psychosocial arenas remains uncertain. Research suggests differences between males and females in several areas:

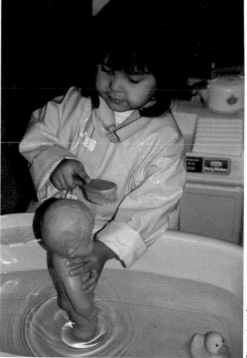

Courtesy Ingrid Crowther

FIGURE 6.4   Manipulating Visual Information

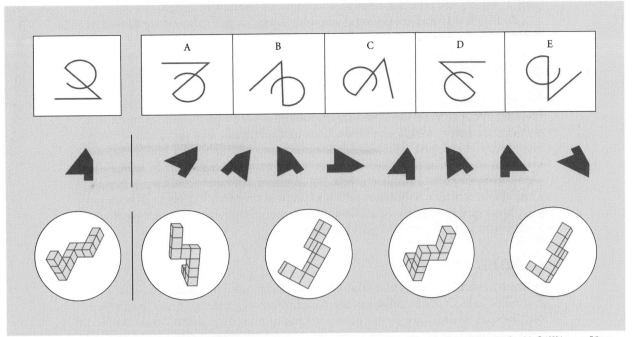

SOURCE: From "Process Analysis of Spatial Aptitude," by J. W. Pellegrino and R. V. Kail. In R. J. Sternberg (Ed.) *Advances in the Psychology of Human Intelligence, Vol. 1*, p. 316. Copyright © 1982 Lawrence Erlbaum Associates, Inc. Reprinted with permission.

- *Verbal ability.* During the toddler years, girls have larger vocabularies than boys (Feldman et al., 2000). During elementary school and high school, girls read, write, and spell better than boys, and more boys have reading and other language-related problems such as stuttering (Halpern, 2000).

- *Mathematics.* Boys tend to get higher grades on math achievement tests, but girls often get better grades in math courses (Beller & Gafni, 1996; Kimball, 1989).

- *Spatial ability.* On problems like those in Figure 6.4, which measure the ability to manipulate visual information mentally, you must decide which figures are rotated variants of the standard shown at the left. Males typically respond more rapidly and accurately than females (Govier & Salisbury, 2000; Voyer, Voyer, & Bryden, 1995).

- *Social influence.* Girls are more likely than boys to comply with the directions of adults (Maccoby & Jacklin, 1974). Girls and women are also more readily influenced by others in a variety of situations, particularly when they are under group pressure (Becker, 1986; Eagly, Karau, & Makhijani, 1995). However, these gender differences may stem from the fact that females value group harmony more than males do and thus seem to give in to others (Miller, Danaher, & Forbes, 1986; Strough & Berg, 2000). For instance, at a meeting to plan a school function, girls are just as likely as boys to recognize the flaws in a bad idea, but girls are more willing to go along simply because they don't want the group to start arguing.

- *Aggression.* In virtually all cultures that have been studied, males are more physically aggressive, particularly when aggression is not provoked by others (Bettencourt & Miller, 1996; Knight, Fabes, & Higgins, 1996). This difference begins as early as the preschool years and remains throughout the life span (Sanson et al., 1993). *In contrast, girls are more likely to resort to relational aggression in which they try to hurt others by damaging their relationships with peers.* They may call children names, make fun of them, spread rumours about them, or pointedly ignore them (Crick & Grotpeter, 1995).

Preschoolers become more aggressive after watching TV with high-action content and especially with violent content (Josephson, 1995).

■ *Emotional sensitivity.* Girls are better able to express their emotions and interpret others' emotions (Hall & Halberstadt, 1981; Weinberg et al., 1999). For example, throughout infancy and childhood, girls identify facial expressions (e.g., happy face versus a sad face) more accurately than boys do (McClure, 2000).

In most other intellectual and social domains, boys and girls are similar. When thinking about areas in which sex differences have been found, keep in mind that gender differences often depend on a person's experiences and social class (Casey, 1996; Serbin et al., 1993). Also, gender differences may fluctuate over time, reflecting historical change in the contexts of childhood for boys and girls. Finally, each result just described refers to a difference in the *average* performance of boys and girls. These differences tend to be small, which means that they do not apply to all boys and girls. Many girls have greater spatial ability than many boys; many boys are more susceptible to social influence than are some girls.

GENDER TYPING

Folklore holds that parents and other adults—teachers and television characters, for example—directly shape children's behaviour toward the roles associated with their sex. Boys are rewarded for boyish behaviour and punished for girlish behaviour. The folklore even has a theoretical basis. According to social learning theorists like Albert Bandura (1977, 1986) and Walter Mischel (1970), children learn gender roles in much the same way they learn other social behaviours, through reinforcement and observational learning. Parents and others thus shape appropriate gender roles in children, and children learn what their culture considers appropriate behaviour for males and females by simply watching how adults and peers act.

How well does research support social learning theory? The best answer to this question comes from an extensive analysis of 172 studies involving 27,836 children showing that parents tend to treat sons and daughters similarly (Lytton & Romney, 1991). Parents interact equally with sons and daughters, are equally warm to both, and encourage both sons and daughters to achieve and be independent. But there are some important exceptions to the general rule of comparable treatment:

> **THINK ABOUT IT** 💡
>
> The women's liberation movement became a powerful social force in North America during the 1960s. Describe how you might do research to determine whether the movement has changed the gender roles that children learn.

■ In behaviour related to gender roles, parents respond differently to sons and daughters (Lytton & Romney, 1991). Activities such as playing with dolls, dressing up, or helping an adult are more often encouraged in daughters than in sons; rough-and-tumble play and playing with blocks are more encouraged in sons than in daughters.

■ Mothers often talk differently to sons and daughters: They tend to use more supportive statements and more commands with their daughters (Leaper, Anderson, & Sanders, 1998).

■ Parents assign sons and daughters different household chores. Daughters tend to be assigned stereotypically female chores such as washing dishes or housecleaning, whereas sons are assigned stereotypically male chores such as taking out the garbage or mowing the lawn (McHale et al., 1990).

Fathers are more likely than mothers to treat sons and daughters differently. More than mothers, fathers often encourage gender-related play. Fathers punish their sons more, but they accept dependence in their daughters (Snow, Jacklin, & Maccoby, 1983). A father, for example, may urge his frightened young son to jump off the diving board ("Be a man!") but not insist that his daughter do so ("That's okay, honey").

Apparently mothers are more likely to respond based on their knowledge of the needs of individual children, but fathers respond based on gender stereotypes. A mother responds to her son knowing that he's smart but unsure of himself; a father may respond based on what he thinks boys generally should be like.

Peers are also influential. Preschoolers are critical of peers who engage in cross-gender play (Langlois & Downs, 1980). This is particularly true of boys who like feminine toys or who play at feminine activities. A boy who plays with dolls and a girl like the one in the photo who plays with trucks may both be ignored, teased, or ridiculed by their peers, but the boy more harshly than the girl (Levy et al., 1995). Once children learn rules about gender-typical play, they often harshly punish peers who violate those rules.

Peers influence gender roles in another way too. We've seen that by 2 and 3 years of age, children most often play with same-sex peers (Martin & Fabes, 2001). This early segregation of playmates based on a child's sex means that boys learn primarily from boys and girls from girls. This helps solidify a youngster's emerging sense of membership in a particular gender group and sharpens the contrast between their own gender and the other gender.

© Scholastic Studio 10/Index Stock Imagery

Thus, through encouraging words, critical looks, and other forms of praise and punishment, other people influence boys and girls to behave differently (Jacobs & Eccles, 1992). However, children learn more than simply the specific behaviours associated with their gender. *A child gradually begins to identify with one group and to develop a gender identity—a sense of the self as a male or a female.*

Gender Identity

If you were to listen to a typical conversation between two preschoolers, you might hear something like this:

MARIA: When I grow up, I'm going to be a singer.

JENNA: When I grow up, I'm going to be a daddy.

MARIA: No, you can't be a papa—you'll be a mommy.

JENNA: No, I wanna be a daddy.

MARIA: You can't be a daddy. Only boys can be daddies and you're a girl!

Obviously, Maria's understanding of gender is more developed than Jenna's. How can we explain these differences? According to Lawrence Kohlberg (1966; Kohlberg & Ullian, 1974), children gradually develop a basic understanding that they are of either the female or the male sex. Gender then serves to organize many perceptions, attitudes, values, and behaviours. Full understanding of gender is said to develop gradually in three steps:

 *Gender labelling: By age 2 or 3, children understand that they are either boys or girls, and label themselves accordingly.*

▨ *Gender stability: During the preschool years, children begin to understand that gender is stable: Boys become men and girls become women.* However, children in this stage believe that a girl who wears her hair like a boy will become a boy and a boy who plays with dolls will become a girl (Fagot, 1985).

▨ *Gender constancy: Between 4 and 7 years, most children understand that maleness and femaleness do not change over situations or according to personal wishes.* They understand that a child's sex is unaffected by the clothing a child wears or the toys a child likes. Jenna and Maria both know that they're girls, but Maria has developed a greater sense of gender stability and gender constancy.

In Kohlberg's theory, only children who understand gender stability should have extensive knowledge of gender-stereotyped activities (Newman, Cooper, & Ruble, 1995). That is, not until children understand that gender is stable do they begin to learn about activities that are appropriate for their gender and those that are not. This pattern is found in research. For example, Martin and Little (1990) measured preschool children's understanding of gender and their knowledge of gender-typed activities (e.g., that girls play with dolls and that boys play with airplanes). The youngest children in their study—three-and-a-half- to 4-year-olds—did not understand gender stability, and they knew little of gender-stereotyped activities. By age 4, children understood gender stability but still knew little of gender-stereotyped activities. By four and a half years, many children understood gender stability *and* knew gender-typical and gender-atypical activities. Importantly, there were no children who lacked gender stability but knew about gender-stereotyped activities, a combination that is impossible according Kohlberg's theory.

Kohlberg's theory specifies when children should begin to learn about gender-appropriate behaviour and activities (once they understand gender stability) but not *how* such learning takes place. A theory proposed by Martin and Halverson (1987) addresses how children learn about gender. *In gender-schema theory, children first decide if an object, activity, or behaviour is female or male, then use this information to decide whether they should learn more about the object, activity, or behaviour.* That is, as you can see in Figure 6.5, once children know their gender, they pay attention primarily to experiences and events that are gender appropriate (Martin & Halverson, 1987). For example, a preschool boy who sees a group of girls playing in sand will decide that playing in sand is for girls and, because he is a boy, playing in sand is not for him. Seeing a group of older boys playing football, he will decide that football is for boys and, because he is a boy, football is acceptable and he should learn more about it.

FIGURE 6.5   Children's Sex Typing and Stereotyping

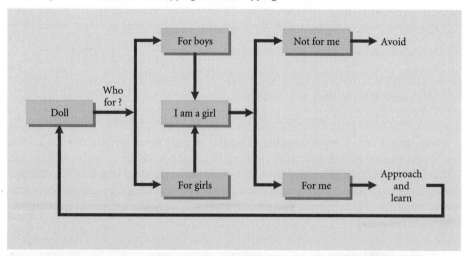

SOURCE: From "A Schematic Processing Model of Sex Typing and Stereotyping in Children," by C. L. Martin and C. F. Halverson, 1981, *Child Development, 52*, p. 1121. Copyright © 1981 Society for Research in Child Development, Inc. Reprinted with permission.

According to gender-schema theory, after children understand gender, it's as if they see the world through special glasses that allow only gender-typical activities to be in focus (Liben & Signorella, 1993). When children understand gender, their taste in TV programs begins to shift along gender-specific lines (Luecke-Aleksa et al., 1995). In addition, they begin to use gender labels to evaluate toys and activities. Shown an unfamiliar toy and told that children of a specific gender *really* like this toy, children like the toy much more if others of their gender do too (Martin, Eisenbud, & Rose, 1995).

EVOLVING GENDER ROLES

Gender roles are not etched in stone; they change with the times. In North America, the range of acceptable roles for girls and boys and women and men has never been greater than today. For example, some fathers like the man in the photo stay home to be primary caregivers for children, and some mothers work full-time as sole support for the family. What is the impact of these changes on gender roles? Some insights come from the results of the Family Lifestyles Project (Weisner & Wilson-Mitchell, 1990). This research has examined families in which the adults were members of the counterculture of the 1960s and 1970s. Some of the families are deeply committed to living their own lives and to rearing their children without traditional gender stereotypes. In these families, men and women share the household, financial, and child care tasks.

The results of this project show that parents like Meda and Frank, from the opening vignette, can influence some aspects of gender stereotyping more readily than others. On the one hand, children in these families tend to have same-sex friends and to like gender-typed activities: The boys enjoy physical play, and the girls

© Denise Marcotte/Stock Boston Inc.

enjoy drawing and reading. On the other hand, the children have few stereotypes concerning occupations: They agree that girls can drive trucks and that boys can be secretaries. They also have fewer gender-typed attitudes about the use of objects. They claim that boys and girls are equally likely to use an iron, a shovel, a hammer and nails, and a needle and thread.

Apparently, some features of gender roles and identities are more readily influenced by experience than others. For most of our history as a species, *Homo sapiens* have existed in small groups of families, hunting animals and gathering vegetation. Women have given birth to the children and cared for them. Over the course of human history, it has been adaptive for women to be caring and nurturing because this increases the odds of a secure attachment and, ultimately, the survival of the infant. Men's responsibilities have included protecting the family unit from predators and hunting with other males, roles for which physical strength and aggressiveness are crucial.

Circumstances of life at the start of the 21st century are, of course, substantially different. Men can rear children, and women can generate income to purchase food for the family. The range of acceptable roles for girls and boys and women and men has never been wider. At the same time, the cultural changes of the past few decades cannot erase hundreds of thousands of years of evolutionary history (Kenrick, 1987). Consequently, we should not be surprised to find that boys and girls often differ in their styles of play, that girls tend to be more supportive of one another in their interactions, and that boys are usually more aggressive.

TEST YOURSELF

1. _____ are beliefs and images about males and females that may or may not be true.

2. Research on intellectual functioning and social behaviour has revealed sex differences in verbal ability, mathematics, _____, social influence, aggression, and emotional sensitivity.

3. _____ may be particularly influential in teaching gender roles, because they more often treat sons and daughters differently.

4. According to Kohlberg's theory, understanding of gender includes gender labelling, gender stability, and _____.

5. Children studied in the Family Lifestyles Project, whose parents were members of the counterculture of the 1960s and 1970s, had traditional gender-related views toward friends and _____.

How do the different forces in the biopsychosocial framework contribute to the development of gender roles?

Answers: (1) Gender stereotypes, (2) spatial ability, (3) Fathers, (4) gender constancy, (5) preferred activities

PUTTING IT ALL TOGETHER

Having completed this chapter, you now know that interactions with others start early in life. The psychosocial task identified by Erikson is initiative versus guilt, where young children learn to balance their desire to act with the reaction of others. As children grow, they continue to experience basic and complex emotions, but different situations or events elicit these emotions. In the case of complex emotions, cognitive growth means that children in early childhood experience shame and guilt in situations they would not have when younger.

We traced how children's social relations expand from parents to peers. Play rapidly becomes more complex over the preschool years. Toddlers may begin to show concern for others. However, as children grow older, whether they actually help others depends on perspective-taking and empathic skills, the context in which help is required, and styles of parental discipline. For example, in the vignette, Doug and Casey did not help their older brother because they did not feel great responsibility to help and because they did not feel capable of helping.

As children's social horizons continue to expand, they soon learn that they are expected to play certain roles in society based on their gender. By the end of the preschool years, most children know that gender is fixed, and they begin to use this knowledge to select activities and objects that are appropriate for them. These choices are influenced by parents' values and expectations, but some aspects of gender roles are easier to change than others. For example, Meda and Frank, the parents in the vignette, will probably find it easier to modify their daughter's career goals than to modify her style of play.

Of course, despite the rapid and sometimes dramatic change we've witnessed in this chapter, social and interpersonal development is far from complete by the end of the preschool years. Much additional change takes place in school-age children and adolescents, as we'll see in Chapter 8.

SUMMARY

6.1 Parenting

Dimensions and Styles of Parenting

■ One key factor in parent–child relationships is the degree of warmth that parents express. Children clearly benefit from warm, caring parents. A second factor is control, which is complicated because neither too much nor too little control is desirable. Effective parental control involves setting appro-priate standards, enforcing them, and trying to anticipate conflicts.

■ Taking into account both warmth and control, four prototypic parental styles emerge: (a) Authoritarian parents are controlling but uninvolved; (b) authoritative parents are fairly controlling but are also responsive to their children; (c) indulgent-permissive parents are loving but exert little control; and (d) indifferent-uninvolved parents are neither warm nor controlling. Authoritative parenting seems best for children with regard to both cognitive and social development.

- 🔟 Parents influence development by direct instruction and coaching. In addition, parents serve as models for their children, who sometimes imitate parents' behaviour directly. Parents also use feedback to influence children's behaviour. Sometimes parents fall into the negative reinforcement trap, inadvertently reinforcing behaviours that they want to discourage. Punishment is effective when it is prompt, consistent, accompanied by an explanation, and delivered by a person with whom the child has a warm relationship. Punishment has limited value because it suppresses behaviours but does not eliminate them, and it often has side effects.

- 🔟 Parenting is influenced by characteristics of children themselves. A child's temperament will influence how a parent tries to exert control over the child.

6.2 Independence and Emotions

Erikson's Stages of Psychosocial Development

- 🔟 In Erikson's theory of psychosocial development, between 3 and 5 years of age, initiative and guilt must be balanced to achieve purpose.

- 🔟 Preschool children continue to experience basic and complex emotions, but are affected by different situations than in the first two years.

- 🔟 As children's cognitive skills continue to develop, they become more adept at identifying others' emotions and modifying their behaviour accordingly.

Regulating Emotions

- 🔟 Children who do not regulate emotions well tend to have problems interacting with others.

6.3 Self-Awareness During Preschool Years

Self-Concept in Early Childhood

- 🔟 Once young children fully understand that they exist, they begin to wonder who they are and they want to define themselves.

Theory of Mind

- 🔟 Young children begin to realize that other people have thoughts, beliefs, and intentions that affect how they behave.

6.4 Interacting with Others

Preschool Play

- 🔟 At about 2 years of age, cooperative play organized around a theme becomes common. Make-believe play is also common; in addition to being fun, it allows children to examine frightening topics.

Learning to Cooperate

- 🔟 Cooperation becomes more common as children get older. Children cooperate more readily if they

are shown that cooperation is effective and if peers respond to their cooperation with further cooperation. Cooperation is also influenced by societal values; it is more common in cultures that prize cooperation more highly than competition.

Helping Others

- 🔟 Prosocial behaviours, such as helping or sharing, are more common in children who understand (perspective-taking) and experience (empathy) another's feelings.

- 🔟 Prosocial behaviour is more likely when children feel responsible for the person in distress. Also, children help more often when they believe they have the skills needed, when they are feeling happy or successful, and when the perceived costs of helping are small.

- 🔟 Parents can foster prosocial behaviour in their children by using reasoning during discipline, by serving as good models of prosocial behaviour, and by praising their children for prosocial acts.

6.5 Gender Roles and Gender Identity

Images of Men and Women: Facts and Fantasy

- 🔟 Gender stereotypes are beliefs about males and females that are often used to make inferences about a person, simply based on his or her gender. Studies of gender differences reveal that girls have greater verbal skill and get better grades in math courses but boys have greater spatial skill and get higher scores on math achievement tests. Girls are better able to interpret emotions and are more prone to social influence, but boys are more aggressive. These differences vary based on a number of factors, including the historical period.

Gender Typing

- 🔟 Parents treat sons and daughters similarly, except in gender-typed activities. Fathers may be particularly important in gender typing because they are more likely to treat sons and daughters differently.

- 🔟 In Kohlberg's theory, children gradually learn that gender is stable over time and cannot be changed according to personal wishes. Once children understand gender stability, they begin to learn gender-typical behaviour. According to gender-schema theory, children learn about gender by paying attention to behaviours of members of their own sex and ignoring behaviours of members of the other sex.

Evolving Gender Roles

- 🔟 Gender roles are changing. However, studies of nontraditional families indicate that some components of gender stereotypes are more readily changed than others.

KEY TERMS

authoritarian parenting (200)
authoritative parenting (200)
indulgent-permissive parenting
    (200)
indifferent-uninvolved parenting
    (200)
direct instruction (201)

counterimitation (201)
negative reinforcement trap (201)
purpose (207)
theory of mind (210)
empathy (217)
dispositional praise (220)
social role (221)

gender stereotypes (222)
relational aggression (223)
gender identity (225)
gender labelling (225)
gender stability (226)
gender constancy (226)
gender-schema theory (226)

SEE FOR YOURSELF: APPLYING WHAT YOU'VE LEARNED

You may not be convinced that youngsters growing up in Canada are especially uncooperative. To see for yourself, arrange to spend an hour observing young children. You could go to a neighbourhood playground, but parents are often present to regulate youngsters' behaviour. A better choice would be a nursery school or day-care centre. Your university may have a facility where you could, with permission, observe children from behind a one-way mirror. Record all occurrences of cooperative behaviour, defined as sharing, helping, or being physically affectionate with another child. Also record each instance of conflict behaviour, defined as inconsiderate, aggressive, or destructive behaviour.

If the facility where you make your observations is typical of those in North America, you can expect to see about 5 to 7 instances of cooperative behaviour in one hour, but 15 to 30 cases of conflict behaviour! If you should have the good fortune to travel to China and repeat your observations, you would observe 35 to 40 instances of cooperative behaviour in that same hour, compared to perhaps 5 to 10 cases of conflict behaviour. At least compared to their Chinese counterparts, North American preschoolers are much less considerate of their peers!

LEARN MORE ABOUT IT

Readings

BRAZELTON, T. B., & CRAMER, R. (1990). *The earliest relationship.* Reading, MA: Addison-Wesley. This book, written by a well-known pediatrician and his colleague, illustrates the drama of attachment through lively case studies.

ERIKSON, E.H. (1982). *The life cycle completed: A review.* New York: Norton. Erikson summarizes his theory.

GOLOMBOK, S., & FIVUSH, R. (1994). *Gender development.* New York: Cambridge University Press. The authors provide a comprehensive overview of how and why boys and girls develop differently. Their approach is balanced and emphasizes the interactive influence of biological, psychological, and sociocultural forces on gender development.

 For additional readings, explore InfoTrac® College Edition, your online library. Go to http://www.infotrac.thomsonlearning.com.

Websites

http://www.todaysparent.com/
This Canadian website of *Today's Parent* offers tips on how to deal with the different problems—large and small—that come up in rearing children.

http://www.hcsc.gc.ca/hppb/familyviolence/index.html
The website of the National Clearinghouse on Family Violence through Health Canada provides information on all aspects of family violence including child abuse.

http://www.cpa.ca
The Canadian Psychological Association's website provides information and links to information related to psychosocial development of children.

Website addresses are subject to change. The *Human Development* book companion website can be accessed for updated links.

The Human Development Book Companion Website

See http://www.humandevelopment.nelson.com for practice quiz questions, Internet links, updates, critical thinking exercises, discussion forums, and more.

 Life-Span CD-ROM

For more information on the concepts covered in this chapter, go to:

Module 3: Early and Middle Childhood
    • Emotional and Social Development

PART 2

School-Age Children and Adolescents

Getty Images

CHAPTER 7

Off to School

PHYSICAL AND COGNITIVE DEVELOPMENT IN MIDDLE CHILDHOOD

Every fall in Canada, most 5-year-olds trot off to kindergarten, starting an educational journey that lasts 13 or more years. During the middle childhood years there is steady growth in height and weight and developing brain functions. The first section of this chapter describes these physical changes that can be expected in middle childhood. Many children can read only a few words and know little math at the start of middle childhood but by the end, most can read complete books and many have learned algebra and geometry. This mastery of complex academic skills is possible because of profound changes in children's thinking, changes described in the second section of this chapter.

For most Canadian schoolchildren, intelligence and aptitude tests are a common part of their educational travels. In the third section of this chapter, you'll see what tests measure and why some children get lower scores on tests. In the fourth section, you'll discover how tests are often used to identify schoolchildren with atypical or special needs.

Next we look at the way students learn to read, write, and do math. We conclude with a look at the variety of educational experiences available in Canada. In this section, you'll discover some of the educational practices that seem to foster students' learning.

7.1

Physical Development in Middle Childhood

LEARNING OBJECTIVES

- What are the growth patterns that can be expected during this development stage?
- How do gross and fine motor skills continue to develop?

Irene watches her 10-year-old daughter Zoe run across the backyard. Could it be that the newest pair of jeans is looking short in the legs already? Irene recalls that a few months ago Zoe seemed to be hungry all the time, which was quite unusual for her. Irene feels she can practically watch Zoe get taller and she wonders when her growth will slow down.

Many physical changes and developments occur during middle childhood. One just has to look at the physical differences between 6- and 12-year-olds to see this is true. Let's begin this section by discussing the expected physical development during the school years.

PHYSICAL GROWTH

Although the middle childhood years are discussed as one developmental period, there is a great difference between the look and abilities of a child between the ages of 6 and 12 years. During this development period children grow an average of five to seven centimetres and gain an average of three kilograms per year. Of course, gender, cultural, environmental, and genetic variations can be expected. Slow but steady growth is seen, and density development in long bones and more muscle development occur. Girls generally have a growth spurt at 10 years while boys may not have such a spurt for another three years. During this time parents will likely notice an increase in appetite as more calories are needed for these changes.

GROSS AND FINE MOTOR SKILLS DEVELOPMENT

Developing gross and fine motor skills during this period allows for riding a bicycle and playing sports with increasing speed and agility. Fine motor skill development allows for cursive writing, ability to learn a musical instrument, and increased competence in art and fine control activities such as crafts.

The amount of sleep required is variable depending on the child's energy expenditure, but adequate rest is important for optimum functioning. The amount needed may range from 10 hours a night at the beginning of the school years to a more adult requirement of eight hours near the end of this developmental period. The incredible cognitive changes in development that also influence physical abilities and coordination will be discussed in the next section.

HEALTHY LIVING

What are important activities to promote health during middle childhood?

During middle childhood, children should have regular screening tests for vision and hearing as well as physical and dental examinations. Although children are generally healthy during this development period, it's important to reinforce safety concerns, particularly when they are related to motor vehicles, playgrounds, bicycle riding, skateboarding, inline skating, and other sport activities. In the older part of this age group, issues such as drug and alcohol use, peer pressure, personal safety, and sex education should be discussed with children at home and in school settings. Parents should oversee computer and Internet use, and children should be taught about personal safety as it applies to the Internet, as well as in public. Children will still need encouragement to eat healthy foods, take regular exercise, and develop good sleep habits. Although disciplinary issues generally decline during this period, there may be more disagreements over household chores and curfews. Parents should continue to provide children with the guidelines they need to help keep them safe. Encourage children to participate in developing family rules so that expectations and consequences are clear and agreed on. Because children compare themselves to others constantly, it's important to preserve their self-esteem for good mental health development. Children need encouragement and unconditional love and support, no matter what their abilities and achievements.

TEST YOURSELF

1. During middle childhood, children grow an average of _____ centimetres and gain an average of 3 kilograms per year.

2. Girls generally have a growth spurt at _____ years of age, while boys may not for another three years.

3. _____ development during this stage of development allows for such activities as cursive writing and the ability to learn a musical instrument.

4. It is important for parents to help school-age children preserve their _____ with encouragement and unconditional love to facilitate healthy mental development, since children of this age compare themselves to others frequently.

How do you think the differences in school-age children's physical growth patterns can affect their self-esteem?

Answers: (1) 5 to 7, (2) 10, (3) Fine motor skill, (4) self-esteem

---

7.2

Cognitive Development

LEARNING OBJECTIVES

- What are the distinguishing characteristics of thought during Piaget's concrete-operational and formal-operational stages?
- What are some of the limitations of Piaget's account of thinking during the formal-operational stage?
- How do children use strategies to improve learning and remembering?
- What is the role of monitoring in successful learning and remembering?

Cognitive Development

More Sophisticated Thinking: Piaget's Version

Information-Processing Strategies for Learning and Remembering

Adrian, a sixth-grader who is starting middle school, just took his first social studies test—and failed. He is shocked because he'd always got A's and B's in elementary school. Adrian realizes that glancing through the textbook chapter once before a test is probably not going to work in middle school, but he's not sure what else he should be doing.

You're about one-third of the way through the book and deserve a break. Try this joke.

> Mr. Jones went into a restaurant and ordered a whole pizza for dinner. When the waiter asked if he wanted it cut into six or eight pieces, Mr. Jones said: "Oh, you'd better make it six! I could never eat eight!" (McGhee, 1976, p. 422)

Okay, this is not such a great joke (to put it mildly). However, many 6- to 8-year-olds think it's hilarious. To understand why children find this joke so funny and to learn more about the skills that will save Adrian's social studies grade, we need to learn more about cognitive development. Let's start with Piaget's theory, then look at information-processing accounts.

MORE SOPHISTICATED THINKING: PIAGET'S VERSION

You probably remember Jean Piaget from Chapters 1, 3, and 5. Piaget believed that thought develops in a sequence of stages. The first two stages, sensorimotor and preoperational thinking, characterize infancy and the preschool years. In the next few pages, we describe the remaining two stages, the concrete-operational and formal-operational, which apply to school-age children and adolescents.

The Concrete-Operational Period

Let's start by reviewing three important limits of preoperational thinking described in Chapter 5:

- Preschoolers are egocentric, believing that others see the world as they do.
- Preschoolers sometimes confuse appearances with reality.
- Preschoolers are unable to reverse their thinking.

None of these limits applies to children in the concrete-operational stage, which extends from approximately 7 to 11 years. Egocentrism wanes gradually. Why? As youngsters have more experiences with friends and siblings who assert their own perspectives on the world, children realize that theirs is not the only view (LeMare & Rubin, 1987). The understanding that events can be interpreted in different ways leads to the realization that appearances can be deceiving. *Also, thought can be reversed, because school-age children have acquired **mental operations**, which are actions that can be performed on objects or ideas and that consistently yield a result.* Recall from Chapter 5 that on the conservation task concrete-operational children realize that the amount of liquid is the same after it has been poured into a different beaker, pointing out that the pouring can always be reversed.

Now you can understand why 7-year-olds laugh at the joke about cutting a pizza into six pieces instead of eight. Think of a joke as a puzzle in which the aim is to determine why a particular remark is funny or incongruous. Generally, people like jokes that are neither too simple nor too complex to figure out. Jokes are best when understanding the punch line involves an intermediate level of difficulty (Brodzinsky & Rightmyer, 1980). For children just entering the concrete-operational stage, knowing that the amount of pizza is the same whether it is cut into six or eight pieces taps their newly acquired understanding of conservation, so they laugh (McGhee, 1976).

In discussing the concrete-operational period, we have emphasized the advantages to children of mental operations. At the same time, as the name implies, concrete-operational thinking is limited to the tangible and real, to the here and now. The

THINK ABOUT IT 💡

Piaget, Freud, and Erikson each propose unique stages for ages 7 to 11 years. How similar are the stages they propose? How do they differ?

concrete-operational youngster takes "an earthbound, concrete, practical-minded sort of problem-solving approach" (Flavell, 1985, p. 98). Thinking abstractly and hypothetically is beyond the ability of concrete-operational children; these skills are acquired in the formal-operational period, as you'll see in the next section.

The Formal-Operational Period

With the onset of the formal-operational period, which extends from roughly age 11 into adulthood, children and adolescents expand beyond thinking about only the concrete and the real. Instead, they apply psychological operations to abstract entities too; they are able to think hypothetically and reason abstractly (Bond, 1995).

To illustrate these differences, let's look at problem solving, where formal-operational adolescents often take a very different approach from concrete-operational children. In one of Piaget's experiments (Inhelder & Piaget, 1958), children and adolescents were presented with several flasks, each containing what appeared to be the same clear liquid. They were told that one combination of the clear liquids would produce a blue liquid; they were asked to determine the necessary combination. A typical concrete-operational youngster, like the ones in the photo, plunges right in, mixing liquids from different flasks in a haphazard way. In contrast, formal-operational adolescents understand that setting up the problem in abstract terms is

the key. The problem is not really about pouring liquids but about combining different elements until all possible combinations have been tested. So a teenager might mix liquid from the first flask with liquids from each of the other flasks. If none of those combinations produces a blue liquid, the teenager would conclude that the liquid in the first flask is not an essential part of the mixture. The next step would be to mix the liquid in the second flask with each of the remaining liquids. A formal-operational thinker would continue in this manner until he or she finds the critical pair that produces the blue liquid. For adolescents, the problem is not one of concrete acts of pouring and mixing. Instead, they understand that it involves identifying possible combinations and then evaluating each one.

Richard Hutchings/Photo Researchers, Inc.

*Adolescents' more sophisticated thinking is also shown in their ability to make appropriate conclusions from facts, what is known as **deductive reasoning**.* Suppose we tell a person the following two statements:

1. If you hit a glass with a hammer, the glass will break.

2. You hit the glass with a hammer.

The correct conclusion, of course, is "The glass will break"—a conclusion that formal-operational adolescents do reach. Concrete-operational youngsters sometimes reach this conclusion too—but based on their experience, not because the conclusion is logically necessary. To see the difference, imagine that the two statements are now

1. If you hit a glass with a feather, the glass will break.

2. You hit the glass with a feather.

The conclusion "the glass will break" follows from these two statements just as logically as it did from the first pair. In this instance, however, the conclusion is contrary to fact—it goes against what experience tells us is really true. Concrete-operational 10-year-olds resist reaching conclusions that are contrary to known facts, whereas formal-operational 15-year-olds reach them much of the time (Markovits & Vachon, 1989). Formal-operational teenagers understand that these problems are about abstractions that need not correspond to real-world relations. In contrast, concrete-operational youngsters reach conclusions based on their knowledge of the world.

Comments on Piaget's View

As mentioned in Chapters 3 and 5, although Piaget provides our single most comprehensive theory of cognitive development, his account of mental development during the early years has some shortcomings. The same is true of his description of formal-operational thinking. Let's look at two questionable aspects.

1. *Formal-operational thinking as a capability.* Simply because adolescents have attained the formal-operational stage does not mean that they always reason at this level. Adolescents (and adults) often fail to reason logically, even when they are capable of doing so and when it would be beneficial to them (Klaczynski & Narasimham, 1998). For example, adolescents typically show more sophisticated reasoning when the problems are relevant to them personally than when they are not (Ward & Overton, 1990). And, as you'll see in Chapter 9, adolescents' thinking is sometimes egocentric and irrational. Consequently, Piaget's account of formal operations is really a description of how adolescents can think, not how they always or even usually think.

2. *Formal operations as an end point.* Cognitive development is complete by age 12 or 13 in Piaget's theory. After adolescents have attained the formal-operational level, their thinking is said to remain the same qualitatively. Of course, people continue to acquire more knowledge and skills, but the fundamental processes of thinking do not change, according to Piaget. Many theorists have criticized this aspect of the theory and have proposed further developmental changes in thinking during late adolescence and adulthood (Moshman, 1998), which we'll discuss in Chapter 11.

Because of these limits to Piaget's theory, we need to look at other approaches to complete our account of mental development during childhood and adolescence. In the next few pages, we'll focus on the information-processing approach we examined in earlier chapters.

INFORMATION-PROCESSING STRATEGIES FOR LEARNING AND REMEMBERING

Once one of us had just written four pages for this book when the unthinkable happened: A power failure knocked out the computer, and all those words were lost. If only the text had been saved to the hard drive . . . but it hadn't.

This tale of woe sets the stage for a main issue of the information-processing approach. As you'll recall, information-processing psychologists believe cognitive development proceeds by increases in the efficiency with which children process information.

One of the key issues in this approach is the means by which children store information in permanent memory and retrieve it when needed later. *That is, according to* *information-processing psychologists, most human thought takes place in **working memory**, where a relatively small number of thoughts and ideas can be stored briefly.* As you read these sentences, for example, the information is stored in working memory. However, as you read additional sentences, they displace the contents of sentences you read earlier. *For you to learn this information, it must be transferred to **long-term memory**, a permanent storehouse of knowledge that has unlimited capacity.* If information you read is not transferred to long-term memory, it is lost, just as our words vanished from the computer's memory when the power failed.

Memory Strategies

How do you try to learn the information in this or your other textbooks? If you're like the student in the photo, you probably use some combination of highlighting key sentences, outlining chapters, taking notes, writing summaries, and testing yourself. These are all effective learning strategies that make it easier for you to store text information in long-term memory.

Children begin to use simple strategies fairly early. For example, 7- or 8-year-olds use rehearsal, a strategy of repetitively naming information that is to be remembered. As they get older, children learn other memory strategies, and they also learn when it is best to use them. That is, children and adolescents begin to identify the unique characteristics of different memory problems and figure out which memory strategies are most appropriate. For example, when reading a textbook or watching a television newscast, the aim is to remember the main points, not the individual words or sentences. Rehearsal is ineffective here. However, outlining or writing a summary works well in these instances because such strategies identify the main points *and* group them (Kail, 1990).

Thus, successful learning and remembering involves identifying the goals of memory problems and choosing suitable strategies (Pierce & Lange, 2000; Schneider & Bjorklund, 1998). As you might expect, younger children sometimes misjudge the objectives of a memory task and therefore choose an inappropriate strategy (Lovett & Pillow, 1996; McGilly & Siegler, 1990). Or they may understand the memory task but not pick the best strategy. These skills improve gradually during childhood and adolescence, but even high school students do not always use effective learning strategies when they should (Kuhn, 2000; Lovett & Pillow, 1996).

These developmental changes can be seen in research in which children and adolescents are taught two memory strategies. One is effective for the material to be learned, but the other is not. The children then have an opportunity to use each strategy. Later, when asked to learn more of the same material, 11- and 12-year-olds usually opt for the more effective strategy. Younger children, in contrast, use either strategy indiscriminately, apparently not understanding that only one is well suited for the material (McGivern et al., 1990).

THINK ABOUT IT

Which elements of the biopsychosocial framework are emphasized in the information-processing approach to cognitive development?

Monitoring

Learning is most likely to occur when students evaluate their progress toward the goal of the memory task. That is, they need to monitor the effectiveness of the strategy they have chosen. Is the strategy working? If not, students should begin anew, reanalyzing the memory task to select a better approach. If the strategy *is* working, they should determine the portion of the material that they have not yet mastered and concentrate their efforts there.

Monitoring skills improve gradually with age. For example, elementary school children can accurately identify material that they have not yet learned, but they do not consistently focus their study efforts on this material (Kail, 1990).

Figure 7.1 summarizes all these events and the sequence in which they should occur. Beginning by analyzing a task to determine the goals, people select an appropriate strategy, then monitor its usefulness until the task is completed. Throughout childhood and adolescence, individuals gradually become more competent in each of these skills, as well as more adept at coordinating them.

Perhaps this has a familiar ring to it. It should, for the chart simply summarizes an important set of study skills. Analyzing, strategizing, and monitoring are key elements of productive studying. The study goals change when you move from this book to a science or English course, but the basic sequence still holds. Studying should always begin with a clear understanding of what goal you are trying to achieve, because this sets the stage for all the events that follow. Too often, we see students like Adrian—the student in the vignette—who just read text material, without any clear idea of what they should be getting out of it. Instead, students should be active readers (Adams, Treiman, & Pressley, 1998). Always study with a plan. Start by skimming the text to become familiar with the material. Before you read more carefully, try to anticipate some of the topics the author will cover in detail. When you reach natural breaks in the material, try to summarize what you've read and think of questions a teacher might ask about the material. Finally, when you don't understand something in the text, stop and determine the source of your confusion. Perhaps you don't know a word's meaning. Maybe you skipped or misunderstood an earlier section of the material. By reading actively, using strategies like these, you'll be much more likely to understand and remember what you've read (Adams et al., 1998; Brown et al., 1996).

FIGURE 7.1   Monitoring Effectiveness of Learning

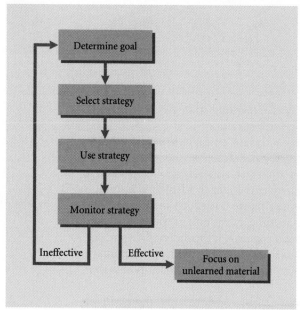

TEST YOURSELF

1. During Piaget's _____, children are first able to represent objects mentally in different ways and to perform mental operations.

2. Hypothetical and deductive reasoning are characteristic of children in Piaget's _____ stage.

3. Piaget's account of formal operations has been criticized because adolescents'

reasoning is often less sophisticated than the theory predicts and because

_____.

4. Children and adolescents often select a memory strategy after they have

_____.

5. The term _____ refers to periodic evaluation of a strategy to determine whether it is working.

Formal-operational adolescents are able to reason abstractly. How might this ability help them use the study skills in Figure 7.1 more effectively?

Answers: (1) concrete-operational stage, (2) formal-operational, (3) the formal-operational stage is portrayed as the final stage of intellectual development, (4) determined the goal of the memory task, (5) monitoring

7.3

Aptitudes for School

LEARNING OBJECTIVES

- What is the nature of intelligence?
- Why were intelligence tests first developed? What are their features?
- How well do intelligence tests work?
- How do heredity and environment influence intelligence?
- How and why do test scores vary for different racial and ethnic groups?

Aptitudes for School
Theories of Intelligence
Binet and the Development of Intelligence Testing
Do Tests Work?
Hereditary and Environmental Factors
The Impact of Ethnicity and Social Class

Max is 12 years old and has a moderate intellectual impairment. That is, he performs most tasks at the level of a non-intellectually impaired 5- or 6-year-old. For example, he can't do many of Piaget's conservation tasks and he reads very slowly and with much effort. Nevertheless, if Max hears a song on the radio, he can immediately sit down at the piano and play the melody flawlessly, despite having had no musical training. Everyone who sees Max do this is astonished. How can a person who is otherwise so limited intellectually perform such an amazing feat?

Before you read further, how would you define intelligence? If you're typical, your definition probably includes the ability to reason logically, connect ideas, and solve real problems. You might mention verbal ability, meaning the ability to speak clearly and articulately. You might also mention social competence, referring, for example, to an interest in the world at large and an ability to admit when you make a mistake (Sternberg & Kaufman, 1998).

As you'll see in this section, many of these ideas about intelligence are included in psychological theories of intelligence. We'll begin by considering the theories of intelligence, where we'll get some insights into Max's uncanny musical skill. Next, you'll see how intelligence tests were devised initially to assess individual differences in intellectual ability. Then we'll look at a simple question: "How well do modern tests work?" Finally, we'll examine how race, ethnicity, social class, gender, environment, and heredity influence intelligence.

THEORIES OF INTELLIGENCE

Psychometricians are psychologists who specialize in measuring psychological characteristics such as intelligence and personality. When psychometricians want to research a particular question, they usually begin by administering a large number of tests to many individuals. Then they look for patterns in performance across the different tests. The basic logic underlying this technique is similar to the logic a jungle hunter uses to decide whether some dark blobs in a river are three separate rotting logs or a single alligator (Cattell, 1965). If the blobs move together, the hunter decides they are part of the same structure, an alligator. If they do not move together, they are three different structures, three logs. Similarly, if changes in performance on one test are accompanied by changes in performance on a second test—that is, they move together—one could assume that the tests are measuring the same attribute or factor.

Suppose, for example, that you believe there is such a thing as general intelligence. That is, you believe some people are smart regardless of the situation, task, or problem, whereas others are not so smart. According to this view, children's performance should be very consistent across tasks. Smart children should always receive high scores, and the less smart youngsters should always get lower scores. As early as 1904, Charles Spearman reported findings supporting the idea that a general factor for intelligence, or *g*, is responsible for performance on all mental tests.

Other researchers, however, have found that intelligence consists of distinct abilities. For example, Thurstone and Thurstone (1941) analyzed performance on a wide range of tasks and identified seven distinct patterns, each reflecting a unique ability: perceptual speed, word comprehension, word fluency, space, number, memory, and induction. Thurstone and Thurstone also acknowledged a general factor that operated in all tasks, but they emphasized that the specific factors were more useful in assessing and understanding intellectual ability.

The Hierarchical View of Intelligence

These conflicting findings have led many psychometric theorists to propose hierarchical theories of intelligence that include both general and specific components. John Carroll (1993), for example, proposed the hierarchical theory with three levels that's shown in Figure 7.2. At the top of the hierarchy is *g*, general intelligence. In the level underneath *g* are eight broad categories of intellectual skill, ranging from fluid intelligence to processing speed. Each of the abilities in the second level is further divided into the skills listed in the third and most specific level. Crystallized intelli-

FIGURE 7.2   Hierarchical Theory of Intelligence

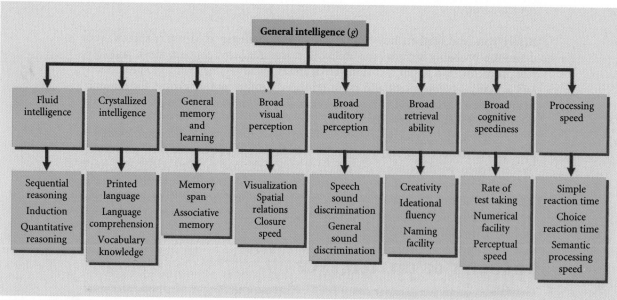

SOURCE: Carroll, 1993.

gence, for example, includes understanding printed language, comprehending language, and knowing vocabulary.

Carroll's hierarchical theory is, in essence, a compromise between the two views of intelligence—general versus distinct abilities. But some critics find it unsatisfactory because it ignores the research and theory on cognitive development. They believe we need to look beyond the psychometric approach to understand intelligence. In the remainder of this section, then, we'll look at two newer theories that have gained a following.

Gardner's Theory of Multiple Intelligences

Only recently have developmental psychologists viewed intelligence from the perspective of Piaget's theory and information-processing psychology. These new theories present a much broader theory of intelligence and how it develops. Among the most ambitious is Howard Gardner's (1983, 1999, 2002) theory of multiple intelligences. Rather than using test scores as the basis for his theory, Gardner draws on research in child development, studies of brain-damaged persons, and studies of exceptionally talented people. Using these criteria, Gardner identified seven distinct intelligences when he first proposed the theory in 1983. In subsequent work, Gardner (1999, 2002) has identified two additional intelligences; the complete list is shown in Table 7.1.

TABLE 7.1	Nine Intelligences in Gardner's Theory of Multiple Intelligences
Type of Intelligence	**Definition**
Linguistic	Knowing the meanings of words, having the ability to use words to understand new ideas, and using language to convey ideas to others
Logical-mathematical	Understanding relations that exist among objects, actions, and ideas, as well as the logical or mathematical operations that can be performed on them
Spatial	Perceiving objects accurately and imagining in the "mind's eye" the appearance of an object before and after it has been transformed
Musical	Comprehending and producing sounds varying in pitch, rhythm, and emotional tone
Bodily-kinesthetic	Using one's body in highly differentiated ways, as dancers, craftspeople, and athletes do
Interpersonal	Identifying different feelings, moods, motivations, and intentions in others
Intrapersonal	Understanding one's emotions and knowing one's strengths and weaknesses
Naturalistic	Recognizing and distinguishing among members of a group (species) and describing relations between such groups
Existential	Considering "ultimate" issues, such as the purpose of life and the nature of death

From *Intelligence Reframed: Multiple Perspectives for the 21st Century* by Howard Gardner. Copyright © 1999 by Howard Gardner. Reprinted by permission of Basic Books, a member of Perseus, L.L.C.

The first three intelligences in this list—linguistic intelligence, logical-mathematical intelligence, and spatial intelligence—are included in psychometric theories of intelligence. The last six intelligences are not: Musical, bodily-kinesthetic, interpersonal, intrapersonal, naturalistic, and existential intelligences are unique to Gardner's theory. According to Gardner, a gifted athlete, a talented dancer, and a sensitive, caring child are showing intelligence just as is the child who writes well or is skilled at math.

How did Gardner arrive at these nine distinct intelligences? First, each has a unique developmental history. Linguistic intelligence, for example, develops much earlier than the others. Second, each intelligence is regulated by distinct regions of the brain, as shown in studies of brain-damaged persons. Spatial intelligence, for example, is regulated by particular regions in the brain's right hemisphere. Third, each has special cases of talented individuals. *Musical intelligence is often shown by savants, individuals with intellectual impairment who are extremely talented in one domain* (Miller, 1999). Max, the 12-year-old in the section-opening vignette, is a savant whose special talent is music. Some savants can play a tune correctly after a single hearing and without ever having had formal musical training (Shuter-Dyson, 1982).

Prompted by Gardner's theory, researchers have begun to look at nontraditional aspects of intelligence. *For example, one aspect of interpersonal intelligence is **social cognitive flexibility**, which refers to a person's skill in solving social problems with relevant social knowledge.* Jones and Day (1997) studied social cognitive flexibility by presenting different social scenarios to adolescents. In one scenario, a man and a woman walk past each other; the woman says, "Hello" but the man ignores her. Following each scenario, adolescents were asked a series of questions about what happened in the scenario. Some adolescents were much better at understanding that each scenario might have many different interpretations (e.g., "The man ignored the woman because he's very shy." "The man was lost in thought and didn't see her.") and that a person's interpretation of the scenario would cause him or her to act differently.

Adolescents who understood the different interpretations of the scenarios were not more skilled in solving verbal or logical reasoning problems. But they were more competent socially (e.g., could deal more effectively with peers) and were less likely to have social problems (e.g., be shy or anxious). Thus, as Gardner's theory predicts, acting skilfully in social situations is an element of intelligence that is distinct from the linguistic and logical-mathematical intelligences of psychometric theories.

The theory of multiple intelligences has important implications for education. Gardner (1993, 1995) believes schools should foster all intelligences, not just the traditional linguistic and logical-mathematical intelligences. Teachers should capitalize on the strongest intelligences of individual children. Some students may best understand unfamiliar cultures, for example, by studying their dance, whereas other students may understand these cultures by studying their music.

These guidelines do not mean that teachers should gear instruction solely to a child's strongest intelligence, pigeon-holing youngsters as "numerical learners" or "spatial learners." Instead, whether the topic is the signing of the Canadian Constitution or Shakespeare's *Hamlet,* instruction should try to engage as many different intelligences as possible (Gardner, 1999, 2002). The typical result is a much richer understanding of the topic by all students.

Some schools have enthusiastically embraced Gardner's ideas (Gardner, 1993). Are these schools better? Educators in schools using the theory think so; they claim that their students have higher test scores and better discipline and that their parents are more involved (Project Zero, 1999). Although these findings are encouraging, they need to be supported by research that evaluates children's learning and achievement, not educators' opinions. In the meantime, there is no doubt that Gardner's work has helped liberate researchers from narrow psychometric-based views of intelligence. A comparably broad but different view of intelligence comes from another new theory that we'll look at in the next section.

Sternberg's Triarchic Theory

Robert Sternberg's (1977) early work included a theory of how adults solve problems on intelligence tests. *He later elaborated this theory into what he called the **triarchic theory** because it includes three parts or subtheories* (Sternberg, 1985).

*According to the **componential subtheory**, intelligence depends on basic cognitive processes called **components**.* A component is simply Sternberg's term for the different information-processing skills described earlier in this chapter, such as monitoring. Whether the task is solving an item on an intelligence test, reading a newspaper, or understanding a conversation, components must be selected and organized in the proper sequence to complete the task successfully. In this subtheory, intelligence reflects more efficient organization and use of components.

The triarchic theory includes two other subtheories. *According to the* ***experiential*** ***subtheory, intelligence is revealed in both novel and familiar tasks.*** For novel tasks, intelligence is associated with the ability to apply existing knowledge to a new situation. At the start of a new school year, for example, readily adjusting to new tasks is a sign of intelligence. Bright children learning multiplication readily draw on relevant math knowledge to grasp what's involved in multiplication.

For familiar tasks, intelligence is associated with automatic processing. Completing a task automatically means using few mental resources (i.e., less working memory capacity). At the end of a school year, performing now-familiar school tasks automatically rather than with effort is a sign of intelligence. Bright children now solve multiplication problems automatically, without thinking about the intermediate steps.

According to the ***contextual subtheory,*** *intelligent behaviour involves skilfully adapting to an environment.* That is, intelligence is always partly defined by the demands of an environment or cultural context. What is intelligent for children growing up in cities in North America may not be intelligent for children growing up

Michele Burgess/Stock Boston Inc.

in the Sahara desert, the Australian outback, or on a remote island in the Pacific Ocean. Moreover, what is intelligent at home may not be intelligent in the neighbourhood. For example, in Brazil, many elementary-school-age boys like the one in the photo sell candy and fruit to bus passengers and pedestrians. These children often cannot identify the numbers on paper money, yet they know how to purchase their goods from wholesale stores, make change for customers, and keep track of their sales (Saxe, 1988).

If the Brazilian vendors were given the tests that measure intelligence in North American students, they would fare poorly. Does this mean they are less intelligent than North American children? Of course not. The skills that are important to North American conceptions of intelligence and assessed on our intelligence tests are less valued in these other cultures and so are not cultivated in the young. Each culture defines what it means to be intelligent, and the specialized computing skills of vendors are just as intelligent in their cultural settings as verbal skills are in North American culture (Sternberg & Kaufman, 1998).

Sternberg's theory also underscores the dangers of comparing test scores of different cultural, ethnic, or racial groups. Comparisons are usually invalid because the test items are not equally relevant in different cultures. In addition, most test items are not equally novel in different cultures. A vocabulary test, for example, is useful in assessing intelligence in cultures where formal education is essential to skilled adaptations (because skilled use of language is important for success in schools). In cultures where schooling is not a key to success, a vocabulary test would not provide useful information because it would be irrelevant to cultural goals and much too novel.

As with Gardner's theory, researchers are still evaluating Sternberg's theory. And theorists are still debating the question of what intelligence is. However it is defined, the fact is that individuals differ substantially in intellectual ability, and numerous tests have been devised to measure these differences. We'll examine the construction, properties, and limitations of these tests in the next section.

BINET AND THE DEVELOPMENT OF INTELLIGENCE TESTING

To understand the history of intelligence testing we must review history. Let's look at the United States at the beginning of the 20th century. At that time, American schools faced a crisis. Between 1890 and 1915, school enrolment nearly doubled nationally due to an influx of immigrants and reforms that restricted child labour and emphasized education (Chapman, 1988). With the increased enrolment, teachers were confronted by ever-greater numbers of students who did not learn as readily as the "select few" students who had populated their classes previously. How to deal with "feeble-minded" children was one of the pressing issues of the day for American educators.

These problems were not unique to the United States. In 1904, the Minister of Public Instruction in France asked two noted psychologists of the day, Alfred Binet and Theophile Simon, to formulate a way to recognize children who would be unable to learn in school without special instruction. Binet and Simon's approach was to select simple tasks that French children of different ages ought to be able to do, such as naming colours, counting backward, and remembering numbers in order. Based on preliminary testing, Binet and Simon identified problems that normal 3-year-olds could solve, that normal 4-year-olds could solve, and so on. *Children's mental age (MA) referred to the difficulty of the problems they could solve correctly.* A child who solved problems that the average 7-year-old could solve would have an MA of 7.

Binet and Simon used mental age to distinguish "bright" from "dull" children. A "bright" child would have the MA of an older child—for example, a 6-year-old with an MA of 9. A "dull" child would have the MA of a younger child—for example, a 6-year-old with an MA of 4. Binet and Simon confirmed that "bright" children identified using their test did better in school than "dull" children. Voilà—the first objective measure of intelligence!

THINK ABOUT IT

If Jean Piaget were to create an intelligence test, how would it differ from the type of test Binet created?

The Stanford-Binet

Lewis Terman, of Stanford University, revised Binet and Simon's test substantially and published a version known as the Stanford-Binet in 1916. *Terman described performance as an intelligence quotient (IQ), which was simply the ratio of mental age to chronological age (CA), multiplied by 100:*

$$IQ = MA/CA \times 100$$

At any age, children who are perfectly average have an IQ of 100, because their mental age equals their chronological age. Furthermore, roughly two-thirds of children taking a test will have IQ scores between 85 and 115. The IQ score can also be used to compare intelligence in children of different ages. A 4-year-old girl with an MA of 5 has an IQ of 125 (5/4 × 100), just like that of an 8-year-old boy with an MA of 10 (10/8 × 100).

IQ scores are no longer computed in this manner. Instead, children's IQ scores are determined by comparing their test performance to that of others their age. When children perform at the average for their age, their IQ is 100. Children who perform above the average have IQs greater than 100; children who perform below the average have IQs less than 100. Nevertheless, the concept of IQ as the ratio of MA to CA helped to popularize the Stanford-Binet test.

By the 1920s, the Stanford-Binet had been joined by many other intelligence tests. Educators greeted these new devices enthusiastically, for they seemed to offer an efficient and objective way to assess a student's chances of succeeding in school (Chapman, 1988).

At this point, you're probably wondering why we've spent so much time discussing a test that is more than 85 years old. The reason is that the Stanford-Binet has more than historical value; it remains a popular test. The Stanford-Binet, last revised in 2003, along with the Wechsler Intelligence Scale for Children-III (WISC-III) and the Kaufman Assessment Battery for Children (K-ABC) are the primary individualized tests of intelligence in use today.

DO TESTS WORK?

To answer this question, two separate issues are important. First, we need to know whether a test is reliable, which means that it yields scores that are consistent. Reliability is often measured by administering similar forms of a test on two occasions. On a reliable test, a person will have similar scores on both occasions. In fact, modern intelligence tests are quite reliable. If a child takes an intelligence test and then retakes it days or a few weeks later, the two scores are usually quite similar (Wechsler, 1991).

What do these scores *mean*? Are they really measuring intelligence? These questions raise the issue of validity, which refers to the extent to which a test really measures what it claims to measure. Validity is usually assessed by determining the relation between test scores and other, independent measures of the construct that the test is thought to measure. For example, to measure the validity of a test of extroversion, we would first have children take the test. Then we would observe these same youngsters in some social setting, such as during a school recess, and record who is outgoing and who is shy. The test would be valid if scores correlated highly with our independent observations of extroverted behaviour.

How can this approach be extended to intelligence tests? Ideally, we would administer the intelligence tests and then correlate the scores with other, independent estimates of intelligence. Therein lies the problem. There are no other independent ways to estimate intelligence; the only way to measure intelligence is with tests. Consequently, many follow Binet's lead and obtain measures of performance in school, such as grades or teachers' ratings of their students. The correlations between these measures and scores on intelligence tests typically fall somewhere between .4 and .6 (Neisser et al., 1996). For example, the correlation between scores on the WISC-III and grade point average is .47 (Wechsler, 1991). That is, children with high scores on the WISC-III tend to get better grades. However, the correlation is far from perfect, which means that some youngsters with high test scores do not excel in school, whereas others with low scores get good grades. In general, however, tests do a reasonable job of predicting school success.

Not only are intelligence tests reasonable predictors of performance in school, they also predict performance in the workplace, particularly for more complex jobs (Gottfredson, 1997; Schmidt & Hunter, 1998). Workers with higher IQ scores tend to be more successful in their on-the-job training and, following training, more successful in their actual work performance. If, for example, two teenagers have summer jobs running tests in a biology lab, the smarter of the two will probably learn the procedures more rapidly and, once learned, conduct them more accurately.

Increasing Validity with Dynamic Testing

Traditional tests of intelligence such as the Stanford-Binet and the WISC-III measure knowledge and skills that a child has accumulated up to the time of testing. These tests do *not* directly measure a child's potential for future learning; instead, the usual assumption is that children who have learned more in the past will probably learn more in the future. Critics argue that tests would be more valid if they directly assessed a child's potential for future learning.

Dynamic testing measures a child's learning potential by having the child learn something new in the presence of the examiner and with the examiner's help. Thus, dynamic testing is interactive and measures new achievement rather than past achievement. It is based on Vygotsky's ideas of the zone of proximal development and scaffolding (page 182). Learning potential can be estimated by the amount of material the child learns during interaction with the examiner and from the amount of help the child needs to learn the new material (Grigorenko & Sternberg, 1998; Sternberg & Grigorenko, 2002a).

To understand the difference between traditional, static methods of intelligence testing and new, dynamic approaches, imagine a group of children attending a week-long soccer camp. On the first day, all children are tested on a range of soccer skills and receive a score that indicates their overall level of soccer skill. If this score were shown to predict later success in soccer, such as number of goals scored in a season, this would be a valid static measure of soccer skill. To make this a dynamic measure of soccer skill, children would spend all week at camp being instructed in new skills. At the end of the week, the test of soccer skills would be re-administered. The amount of the child's improvement over the week would measure learning potential, with greater improvement indicating greater learning potential.

Dynamic testing is a recent innovation and is still being evaluated. Preliminary research does indicate, however, that static and dynamic testing both provide useful and independent information. If the aim is to predict future levels of a child's skill, it is valuable to know a child's current level of skill (static testing) as well as the child's potential to acquire greater skill (dynamic testing). By combining both forms of testing, we achieve a more comprehensive view of a child's talents than by relying on either method alone (Day et al., 1997).

HEREDITARY AND ENVIRONMENTAL FACTORS

Joanna, a 7-year-old girl, was administered the WISC-III and obtained a score of 112. Ted, a 7-year-old boy, took the same test and received a score of 92. What accounts for the 20-point difference in these youngsters' scores? Heredity and experience both matter.

Some of the evidence for hereditary factors is shown in Figure 7.3. If genes influence intelligence, then siblings' test scores should become more alike as siblings become more similar genetically (Plomin & Petrill, 1997). In other words, since identical twins are identical genetically, they typically have virtually identical test scores, which would be a correlation of 1. Fraternal twins have about 50% of their genes in common, just like nontwins of the same biological parents. Consequently, their test scores should be (a) less similar than scores for identical twins, (b) as similar as other siblings who have the same biological parents, and (c) more similar than scores of children and their adopted siblings. You can see in the graph that each of these predictions is supported.

Heredity also influences patterns of developmental change in IQ scores (Wilson, 1983). Patterns of developmental change in IQ are more alike for identical twins than for fraternal twins. If one identical twin gets higher IQ scores with age, the other twin almost certainly will too. In contrast, if one fraternal twin gets higher scores with age, the other twin may not necessarily show the same pattern. Thus, identical twins are not only more alike in overall IQ but in developmental change in IQ as well.

Studies of adopted children suggest that the impact of heredity increases during childhood and adolescence: If heredity helps determine IQ, then children's IQs should be more like their biological parents' IQs than their adoptive parents' IQs. In fact, these correlations were computed in the Colorado Adoption Project (Plomin et al., 1997), which included adopted children as well as their biological and

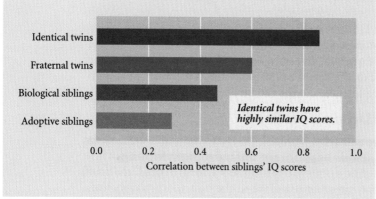

FIGURE 7.3   Correlation Between Siblings' IQ Scores

Identical twins have highly similar IQ scores.

Correlation between siblings' IQ scores

SOURCE: Based on data in Bouchard and McGue, 1981.

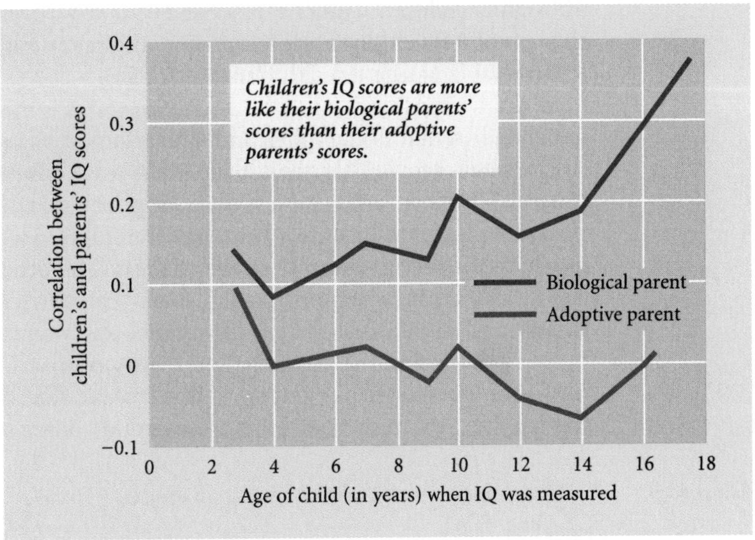

adoptive parents. Biological parents' IQ was measured before the child was born; adoptive parents' IQ was measured before the child's first birthday; children's IQs were tested repeatedly in childhood and adolescence. The results, shown in Figure 7.4, are clear. At every age, the correlation between children's IQ and their biological parents' IQ (shown by the blue line) is greater than the correlation between children's IQ and their adoptive

FIGURE 7.4   Correlation Between Children's and Parents' IQ Scores

Children's IQ scores are more like their biological parents' scores than their adoptive parents' scores.

parents' IQ (shown by the red line). In fact, children's IQ scores are essentially unrelated to their adoptive parents' IQs.

Notice, too, that the relation between children's IQs and their biological parents' IQs actually gets *stronger* as children get older. In other words, as adopted children get older, their test scores increasingly resemble their biological parents' scores. These results are evidence for the greater impact of heredity on IQ as a child grows.

Do these results mean that heredity is the sole determiner of intelligence? No. Three areas of research show the importance of environment on intelligence. The first is research on characteristics of families and homes. If intelligence were solely due to heredity, environment should have little or no impact on children's intelligence. But we know that many characteristics of parents' behaviour and home environments are related to children's intelligence. For example, children with high test scores tend to come from homes that are well organized and have plenty of appropriate play materials (Bradley et al., 1989).

The impact of the environment on intelligence is also implicated by research on historical change in IQ scores. During most of the 20th century, IQ test scores rose dramatically (Flynn, 1998). For example, scores on the WISC increased by nearly 10 points over a 25-year-period (Flynn, 1999). Heredity cannot account for such a rapid increase over a few decades (a mere fraction of a second in genetic time). Consequently, the rise must reflect the impact of some aspect of the environment. The change might reflect smaller, better-educated families with more leisure time (Dickens & Flynn, 2001). Or it might be due to movies, television, and more recently, the computer and Internet, providing children with an incredible wealth of virtual experience (Greenfield, 1998). Although the exact cause remains a mystery, the increase per se shows the impact of changing environmental conditions on intelligence.

Intervention programs that prepare economically disadvantaged children for school also demonstrate the importance of a stimulating environment for intelligence. When children grow up in never-ending poverty, the cycle is predictable and tragic: Youngsters have few of the intellectual skills to succeed in school, so they fail; lacking an education, they find minimal jobs (if they can work at all), guaranteeing that their children, too, are destined to grow up in poverty.

The Aboriginal Head Start (AHS) program is an early childhood intervention program for Canadian First Nations, Inuit, and Metis children from both urban and northern communities. The purpose of the program is to help pre-school-age children become successful in school by giving them the opportunity to develop the necessary attitudes, capabilities and confidence (Health Canada, 2002b). However, currently the program is able to accommodate only a small percentage of the eligible Aboriginal children living off reserve. Feedback shows that there is improvement in all areas of AHS children's development, and many children are learning in their own Aboriginal language (Health Canada, 2002b).

In the United States, one of the success stories is the Carolina Abecedarian Project designed by Frances Campbell and Craig Ramey (1994; Campbell et al., 2001; Ramey & Campbell, 1991). This project included 111 children; most were born to African-American mothers who had less than a high school education, an average IQ score of 85, and typically no income. About half the children were assigned to a control group in which they received no special attention. The others attended a special day-care facility daily from 4 months until 5 years. The curriculum emphasized mental, linguistic, and social development for infants, and prereading skills for preschoolers.

Every few years, the children were assessed on a battery of tests. The results for IQ scores are shown in Figure 7.5. You can see that during the period of the intervention (i.e., the preschool years), the groups differ substantially: Youngsters in the treatment group have above-average IQ scores and those in the control group have below-average scores. For the remaining 15 years, scores for both groups decline slowly, but the children who participated in the special preschool programs always have higher scores, even as young adults. Intervention had a similar benefit on students' reading and math achievement.

FIGURE 7.5   Effectiveness of the Carolina Abecedarian Project

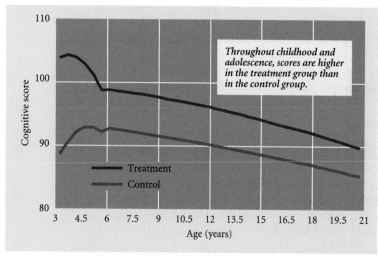

Throughout childhood and adolescence, scores are higher in the treatment group than in the control group.

Thus, intervention works. Of course, massive intervention over eight years is expensive. But so are the economic consequences of poverty, unemployment, and their by-products. Programs like the Abecedarian Project show that the repetitive cycle of school failure and education can be broken. And, in the process, they show that intelligence is fostered by a stimulating and responsive environment.

THE IMPACT OF CULTURE AND SOCIAL CLASS

On many intelligence tests, children from economically advantaged homes tend to have higher test scores than children from economically disadvantaged homes. Some differences in intelligence tests between cultures also reflect the differences in socioeconomic status. When children from comparable socioeconomic status are compared, group differences in IQ test scores for different cultural groups are reduced but not eliminated (Brooks-Gunn, Klebanov, & Duncan, 1996). Let's look at three explanations for this difference.

A Role for Genetics?

On pages 248–249, you learned that heredity helps determine a child's intelligence: Smart parents tend to beget smart children. Does this also mean that group differences in IQ scores reflect genetic differences? No. Most researchers agree that there is no evidence that some ethnic groups have more "smart genes" than others. Instead, they believe the environment is largely responsible for these differences (Neisser et al., 1996).

A popular analogy (Lewontin, 1976) demonstrates the thinking here. Imagine two kinds of corn: Each kind produces both short and tall plants, and height is known to be due to heredity. If one kind of corn grows in good soil—plenty of water and nutrients—the mature plants will reach their genetically determined heights; some short, some tall. If the other kind of corn grows in poor soil, few of the plants will reach their full height and overall the plants of this kind will be much shorter. Thus, even though height is quite heritable for each type of corn, the difference in height between the two groups is due solely to the quality of the environment.

The same conclusion applies to ethnic groups. Differences within ethnic groups are partly due to heredity, but differences between groups apparently reflect environmental influences. Two potential influences have been studied, and we'll look at these next.

Experience with Test Contents

Some critics contend that differences in test scores reflect bias in the tests themselves. They argue that test items reflect the cultural heritage of the test creators, most of whom are from economically advantaged European backgrounds, and so tests are biased against economically disadvantaged children from other groups. They point to test items like this one:

> A conductor is to an orchestra as a teacher is to what?
> book   school   class eraser

Children whose background includes exposure to orchestras are more likely to answer this question correctly than children who lack this exposure.

The problem of bias has led to the development of culture-fair intelligence tests, which include test items based on experiences common to many cultures. An example is Raven's Progressive Matrices, which consists solely of items like the one shown in Figure 7.6. Examinees are asked to select the piece that would complete the design correctly (6, in this case).

Culture-fair tests predict achievement in school but do not eliminate group differences in test scores (Anastasi, 1988; Herrnstein & Murray, 1994). Why? Culture can influence a child's familiarity with the entire testing situation, not simply familiarity with particular items.

FIGURE 7.6

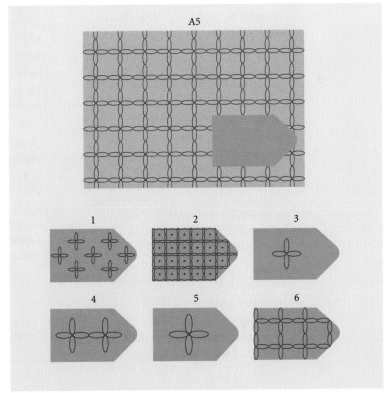

Test-Taking Skills

The impact of experience and cultural values can extend beyond particular items to a child's familiarity with the entire testing situation. Tests underestimate a child's intelligence if, for example, the child's culture encourages children to solve problems in collaboration with others and discourages them from excelling as individuals. Moreover, because they are wary of questions posed by unfamiliar adults, many economically disadvantaged children often answer test questions by saying, "I don't know." Obviously, this strategy guarantees an artificially low test score. When these children are given extra time to feel at ease with the examiner, they respond less often with "I don't know" and their test scores improve considerably (Zigler & Finn-Stevenson, 1992).

Interpreting Test Scores

If all tests reflect cultural influences, at least to some degree, how should we interpret test scores? Remember that tests assess successful adaptation to a particular cultural context. Most intelligence tests predict success in a school environment, which usually espouses middle-class values. Regardless of ethnic group, a child with a high test score has the intellectual skills needed for academic work based on middle-class values. A child with a low test score apparently lacks those skills. Does a low score mean that that child is destined to fail in school? No. Helping that child learn the skills necessary for academic work will produce an improvement in school performance.

By focusing on groups of people, it's easy to overlook the fact that individuals within these groups differ in intelligence. The average difference in IQ scores between various ethnic groups is relatively small compared to the entire range of scores for these groups. You can easily find youngsters with high IQ scores from all ethnic groups, just as you can find youngsters with low IQ scores from all groups. And, in the next section, we'll look at children at the extremes of ability.

TEST YOURSELF

1. If some children consistently have high scores on different intelligence tests while other children consistently have lower scores on the same tests, this would support the view that intelligence

   _____.

2. According to _____ theories, intelligence includes both general intelligence as well as more specific abilities, such as verbal and spatial skill.

3. Gardner's theory of multiple intelligences includes linguistic, logical-mathematical, and spatial intelligences, which are included in psychometric theories, as well as musical, _____, interpersonal, intrapersonal, naturalistic, and existential intelligences, which are ignored in psychometric theories.

4. Based on Gardner's view of intelligence, teachers should _____.

5. According to Sternberg's _____ subtheory, intelligence refers to adapting to an environment to achieve goals.

6. Modern intelligence tests are typically validated by _____.

7. As adopted children get older, their IQ scores increasingly resemble the IQ scores of their _____ parents.

8. Evidence for the impact of environment on intelligence comes from studies of children's homes, from historical change in IQ scores, and from _____.

9. The problem of cultural bias on intelligence tests led to the development of

   _____.

Compare and contrast the major perspectives on intelligence in terms of the extent to which they make connections between different aspects of development. That is, to what extent does each perspective emphasize cognitive processes versus integrating physical, cognitive, social, and emotional development?

Answers: (1) consists of a general factor, 8, (2) hierarchical theories, (3) bodily kinesthetic, (4) teach in a manner that engages as many different intelligences as possible, (5) contextual, (6) showing that test scores correlate with school grades, (7) biological, (8) intervention studies, (9) culture-fair intelligence tests

7.4

Special Children, Special Needs

LEARNING OBJECTIVES

▪ What are the characteristics of gifted and creative children?

▪ What are the different forms of intellectual impairment?

▪ What is a learning disability?

▪ What are the distinguishing features of hyperactivity?

Sanjit, a second-grader, has taken two separate intelligence tests, and both times he had above-average scores. His parents took him to an ophthalmologist, who determined that his vision is 20-30 — nothing wrong with his eyes. Nevertheless, Sanjit absolutely cannot read. Letters and words are mysterious to him. What is wrong?

Throughout history, societies have recognized children with unusual abilities and talents. Today, we know much about the extremes of human skill. Let's begin with a glimpse at gifted and creative children.

GIFTED AND CREATIVE CHILDREN

In many respects the boy in the photo, Bernie, is an ordinary middle-class 12-year-old: He is the goalie on his soccer team, takes piano lessons on Saturday mornings, sings in his church youth choir, and likes to go inline skating. However, when it comes to intelligence and academic prowess, Bernie leaves the ranks of the ordinary—he's gifted. He received a score of 175 on an intelligence test and is taking a university-level calculus course.

Traditionally, giftedness was defined by scores on intelligence tests: a score of 130 or greater was the criterion for being gifted. Today, however, definitions of giftedness are broader and include exceptional talent in an assortment of areas, such as art, music, creative writing, and dance (Robinson & Clinkenbeard, 1998; Winner, 2000).

Exceptional talent—whether defined solely by IQ scores or more broadly—seems to have several prerequisites (Feldman & Goldsmith, 1991; Rathunde & Csikszentmihalyi, 1993):

Firstlight.ca

▪ The child's love for the subject and overwhelming desire to master it

▪ Instruction, beginning at an early age, with inspiring and talented teachers

▪ Support and help from parents, who are committed to promoting their child's talent

The message here is that exceptional talent must be nurtured. Without encouragement and support from stimulating and challenging mentors, a youngster's talents will wither, not flourish. Talented children need a curriculum that is challenging and complex; they need teachers who know how to foster talent; and they need like-minded peers who stimulate their interests (Feldhusen, 1996).

What of the stereotype that gifted children are emotionally troubled and unable to get along with their peers? Bernie doesn't seem to fit this stereotype and, in fact, research discredits the stereotype of gifted people as distressed and socially inept. Actually, gifted youngsters tend to be more mature than their peers and to have fewer emotional problems (Luthar, Zigler, & Goldstein, 1992).

Creativity

What is creativity and how does it differ from intelligence? *Intelligence is often associated with* **convergent thinking,** *which means using the information provided to determine a standard, correct answer. In contrast, creativity is often linked to* **divergent thinking,** *in which the aim is not a single correct answer (often there isn't one) but instead to think in novel and unusual directions* (Callahan, 2000).

Divergent thinking is often measured by asking children to produce a large number of ideas in response to some specific stimulus (Kogan, 1983). Children might be asked to name different uses for a common object, such as a coat hanger. Or they might be shown a page filled with circles and asked to draw as many different pictures as they can, as shown in Figure 7.7. Both the number of responses and their originality are used to measure creativity.

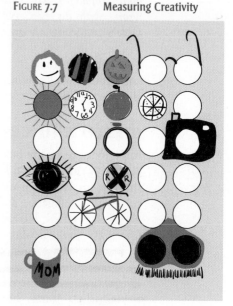

FIGURE 7.7   Measuring Creativity

Creativity, like giftedness, must be cultivated. Youngsters are more likely to be creative when their home and school environments value nonconformity and encourage children to be curious. When schools, for example, emphasize mastery of factual material and discourage self-expression and exploration, creativity usually suffers (Thomas & Berk, 1981). In contrast, creativity can be enhanced by experiences that stimulate children to be flexible in their thinking and to explore alternatives (Starko, 1988).

Gifted and creative children represent one extreme of human ability. Who is at the other extreme?—youngsters with intellectual impairment due to development disability, the topic of the next section.

CHILDREN WITH INTELLECTUAL IMPAIRMENT

"Little David" was the oldest of four children. He learned to sit days before his first birthday, he began to walk at 2, and said his first words as a 3-year-old. At 5 years of age, David's development was far behind that of his age-mates. Many years ago David would have been called "feebleminded" or "mentally defective" and he may be diagnosed with mental retardation. In fact, David had Down syndrome, which we first described in Chapter 2 (see pages 50–51). David had an extra 21st chromosome; as a consequence of this extra gene, David experienced mental or intellectual development that is delayed or impaired.

In Canada the preferred terms for mental retardation are developmental disability (Bradley, Thompson, & Bryson, 2002) or **intellectual impairment.** *These terms refer to substantially below-average intelligence and problems adapting to an environment that emerge before the age of 18.* A Canadian study reported that the overall prevalence for developmental disability is estimated to be about 7 out of 1,000 children, and was close to equally divided between mild disability (IQ between 50 and 75) and severe disability (IQ below 50) (Bradley et al., 2002).

THINK ABOUT IT

How might our definitions of giftedness and intellectual impairment differ if they were based on Robert Sternberg's triarchic theory?

Types of Intellectual Impairment

Your image of a child with intellectual impairment may be someone with Down syndrome, like the child in the photograph on page 51. In reality, individuals with intellectual impairment are just as varied as are people without such impairment. How should we describe this variety? One approach is to distinguish the causes of intellectual impairment (Baumeister & Baumeister, 1995). *Some cases can be traced to a specific biological or physical problem which would then be determined to be **organic intellectual impairment**.* Down syndrome is the most common organic form of intellectual impairment. Other forms of organic intellectual impairment can be linked to the teratogens described in Chapter 2. Other types of intellectual impairment apparently do not involve biological damage. *Familial intellectual impairment simply represents the lower end of the normal distribution of intelligence.*

In Canadian schools, children with mild intellectual impairment are usually included in mainstream classes, possibly receiving a modified program and remedial help (Bradley et al., 2002). Children with severe disabilities generally require special supports and services and may participate in residential programs.

LEARNING DISABILITIES

For some children with normal intelligence, learning is a struggle. *The Learning Disabilities Association of Canada (LDAC, 2002) has defined **learning disabilities** as a "number of disorders which may affect the acquisition, organization, retention, understanding or use of verbal or nonverbal information."* These disorders are considered separately from intellectual impairments since they occur in individuals with at least average abilities for thinking and reasoning. One or more of the following areas may be affected: oral language, reading, written language, or mathematics. Such disorders are lifelong, although their expression may vary over a lifetime depending on an individual need for specific skills and the supportive interventions provided (LDAC, 2002).

In Canada, estimates of learning disorders range from 10 to 12% of the population (LDAC, 2001). The variety of learning disabilities complicates the task for teachers and researchers because it suggests that each type of learning disability may have its own cause and treatment (Lyon, 1996). Take reading, the most common area of learning disability, as an example. Many children with a reading disability have problems in phonological awareness, which refers to understanding and using the sounds in written and oral language. For a reading-disabled child like Sanjit (in the vignette) or the boy in the photograph, all vowels sound alike. Thus *pin* sounds like *pen,* which sounds like *pan.* These youngsters benefit from explicit, extensive instruction on the connections between letters and their sounds (Lyon, 1996). Each province and territory determines the policies and practices for specialized education and supports. However, provinces and territories do have similarities in their services, such as the use of individual education plans, while differences are primarily in relation to the teacher training requirements and definitions of exceptionalities as well as the funding models for such programs (Dworet & Bennett, 2002).

The Spotlight on Research feature looks at a successful training program.

© Richard Orton /Index Stock Imagery

SPOTLIGHT ON RESEARCH

Improving Reading Skill in Children with a Reading Disability

Who were the investigators and what was the aim of the study? Most reading experts agree that, compared to children who read normally, children with a reading disability have difficulty translating print into sound. Experts also agree that the aim of treatment should be to improve such translation skills. Where experts disagree is in the best way to achieve this aim. Some emphasize exercises in which children manipulate sounds and letters in syllables (e.g., "Which one is 'ook'?" "Which is 'koo'?"). Other experts emphasize articulatory awareness in which children learn the positions of their mouth and tongue as they make different vowel and consonant sounds. Barbara Wise, Jerry Ring, and Richard Olson (1999) wanted to compare the effects of these two approaches in improving reading in children with reading disabilities.

How did the investigators measure the topic of interest? Children in the study were assigned to one of four conditions. Some were in a control group that received no special treatment. Others were in a sound manipulation condition, an articulatory awareness condition, or a condition that included both sound manipulation and articulatory awareness. The training included exercises like those just mentioned and lasted six months. All children were tested on a large battery of reading-related tests before and after training. For simplicity, we're going to focus on just one outcome measure: children's ability to read individual words accurately.

Who were the children in the study? Wise and her colleagues tested 122 children with reading disabilities from Grades 2 to 5. About one-fourth of the children were assigned to each of the four conditions.

What was the design of the study? The study was experimental. The independent variable was the condition to which the child was assigned; the dependent variable was the number of words children read accurately. The study was also longitudinal: Students were tested in October and again in May of the same school year.

Were there ethical concerns with the study? No. Parental permission was obtained for all children who participated. You may question the ethics of denying treatment to one-fourth of the children (those in the control group). However, all these children were promised treatment in the following school year, and this was deemed an acceptable risk by the review panel at the University of Colorado where the study was conducted.

What were the results? As we mentioned, the children were administered a large battery of tasks. On some of the tasks, the training groups differed. For example, children who had sound manipulation training were more accurate on phoneme deletion tasks (e.g., "Say 'pran' without the 'r'?"). But the most important result is shown in Figure 7.8: In actual reading, the various training methods were equally effective. That is, measuring the increase in reading skill from before training to

FIGURE 7.8   Training to Improve Reading Scores

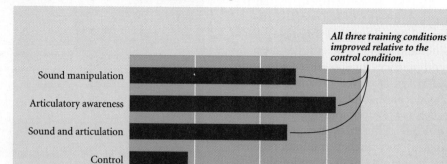

All three training conditions improved relative to the control condition.

Percentage increase in reading scores from pretest to posttest after training, all three groups improved 12 to 15% compared to 4% for the control group.

What did the investigators conclude? Children with reading disabilities must learn about language sounds, but apparently there is no single best method. Consequently, teachers can be successful with either method and can alter their approach based on their own background and their students' strengths.

What converging evidence would strengthen these conclusions? Two types of findings would complement the results of this study. First, it would be useful to include a group of children who read normally as another way to assess the effectiveness of training (i.e., after training, are children with a reading disability reading normally?). Second, it would be important to test these children in subsequent years to determine if the training has long-lasting benefits.

The findings in the Spotlight on Research feature are good news for children with learning disabilities. The key to helping these children is to move beyond the generic label "learning disability" to pinpoint specific cognitive and academic deficits that hamper an individual child's performance in school (e.g., for children with a reading disability, processing language sounds). Then instruction can be specifically tailored to improve the child's skills (Moats & Lyon, 1993).

This is much easier said than done because diagnosing learning disabilities remains so difficult. Some children have both reading and language disabilities; others have reading and arithmetic disabilities; still others have a learning disability and another problem, attention-deficit hyperactivity disorder, which we discuss next.

ATTENTION-DEFICIT HYPERACTIVITY DISORDER

Let's begin with a case study of Stuart, an 8-year-old.

> [His] mother reported that Stuart was overly active as an infant and toddler. His teachers found him difficult to control once he started school. He is described as extremely impulsive and distractible, moving tirelessly from one activity to the next. . . . His teacher reports that he is immature and restless, responds best in a structured, one-on-one situation, but is considered the class pest because he is continually annoying the other children and is disobedient. (Rapaport & Ismond, 1990, p. 120)

For many years, children like Stuart, who were restless and impulsive, were said to have "hyperactive child syndrome" (Barkley, 1996). In the 1960s and 1970s, researchers realized that these children often also had difficulty paying attention. By the 1980s, the disorder had been renamed attention-deficit hyperactivity disorder (ADHD).

Roughly 3 to 5% of children have ADHD, with boys being affected two to four times as often as girls (Offord et al., 1987; Scahill, 2000). Three symptoms are at the heart of ADHD (Rapport, 1995):

- *Overactivity.* Children with ADHD are unusually energetic, fidgety, and unable to keep still, especially in situations where they need to limit their activity, such as school classrooms.
- *Inattention.* Youngsters with ADHD do not pay attention in class and seem unable to concentrate on schoolwork; instead, they skip from one task to another.
- *Impulsivity.* Children with ADHD often act before thinking; they may run into a street before looking for traffic or interrupt others who are already speaking.

© Tony Freeman /PhotoEdit

Not all children with ADHD show all these symptoms to the same degree. Some, like the boy in the photograph, may be primarily hyperactive and impulsive. Others may be primarily inattentive and show fewer signs of hyperactivity and impulsivity; their disorder is often described simply as attention-deficit disorder (Barkley, 1990). Children with ADHD often have problems with conduct and academic performance. Like Stuart, many hyperactive children are aggressive, which can negatively affect peer relationships (Barkley, 1990; McGee, Williams, & Feehan, 1992). Although youngsters with ADHD usually have normal intelligence, their scores on reading, spelling, and arithmetic achievement tests are often below average (Pennington, Groisser, & Welsh, 1993).

Many myths surround ADHD. Some concern causes. At one time or another, TV, food allergies, sugar, and poor home life have all been proposed as causes of ADHD, but research does not consistently support any of these (e.g., Wolraich et al., 1994). Instead, ADHD has biological roots and a hereditary component (Edelbrock et al., 1995). Another myth is that most children "grow out of" ADHD in adolescence or young adulthood. More than half the children who are diagnosed with ADHD will have problems related to overactivity, inattention, and impulsivity as adolescents and young adults. Few of these young adults complete college, and some will have work- and family-related problems (Fischer et al., 1993; Rapport, 1995).

Because ADHD affects academic and social success throughout childhood and adolescence, researchers have worked hard to find effective treatments. The Forces in Action feature traces these efforts and reveals what we know about the best ways to treat children with ADHD.

FORCES IN ACTION

Treating ADHD

By the mid-1980s, it was clear that ADHD could be treated. For example, children with ADHD often respond well to stimulant drugs such as Ritalin. It may seem odd that stimulants are given to children who are already overactive, but these drugs stimulate the parts of the brain that normally inhibit hyperactive and impulsive behaviour. Thus, stimulants actually have a calming influence for many youngsters with ADHD, allowing them to focus their attention (Aman, Roberts, & Pennington, 1998).

Drug therapy was not the only approach; psychosocial treatments also worked and were designed to improve children's cognitive and social skills and often included home-based intervention and intensive summer programs (Richters et al., 1995). For example, children can be taught to remind themselves to read instructions before starting assignments.

And they can be reinforced by others for inhibiting impulsive and hyperactive behaviour (Barkley, 1994).

These treatments were well known by the late 1980s, yet many researchers were troubled by large gaps in our understanding. One gap concerned the long-term success of treatment. Most studies had measured the impact of weeks or months of treatment; virtually nothing was known about the effectiveness of treatment over longer periods. Another gap concerned the most effective combination of treatments and whether this was the same for all children. That is, is medication plus psychosocial treatment the best for all children and for all facets of children's development (i.e., academic and social)?

Prompted by these concerns, in the early 1990s the National Institute of Mental

Health in the United States initiated the Multimodal Treatment Study of Children with ADHD—the MTA for short (Richters et al., 1995). The MTA involves 18 scientists who are experts on ADHD and nearly 600 elementary school children with ADHD. The children were assigned to different treatment modes, and the impact of treatment is measured in several different domains of the children's development.

The MTA is ongoing, but initial results show that medical treatment alone is the best way to treat hyperactivity per se. However, for a variety of other measures, including academic and social skills as well as parent–child relations, medication plus psychosocial treat-ment is slightly more effective than medication treatment alone. The MTA also makes it clear that medication is effective only when dosage is monitored carefully, with regular follow-up visits to a health care professional, and there is regular communication with schools regarding children's functioning (Jensen et al., 2001).

Thus, effective treatment of ADHD addresses the biological, psychological, and sociocultural contributions to the disorder. Such comprehensive treatment enables children with ADHD to become more attentive and to improve their schoolwork (Carlson et al., 1992).)

TEST YOURSELF

1. A problem with defining giftedness solely in terms of IQ scores is that _____.

2. Creativity is associated with _____ thinking, in which the goal is to think in novel and unusual directions.

3. Cases of _____ intellectual impairment can be linked to specific biological or physical problems.

4. Individuals with _____ intellectual impairment often go to school, have jobs, and marry.

5. The most common forms of learning disability are _____.

6. Key symptoms of attention-deficit hyperactivity disorder are overactivity, _____, and impulsivity.

7. The results of the MTA show that the best way to treat the full spectrum of symptoms of ADHD is through stimulant drugs combined with _____.

How might Jean Piaget have explained differences in intellectual functioning between children with intellectual impairment and children without intellectual impairment? How might an information-processing psychologist explain these differences?

Answers: (1) it excludes talents in areas such as art, music, and dance, (2) divergent, (3) organic, (4) mild or educable, (5) reading and other language-related disabilities, (6) inattentiveness, (7) psychosocial treatment that improves children's cognitive and social skills

---

7.5

Academic Skills

LEARNING OBJECTIVES

- What are the components of skilled reading?
- As children develop, how does their writing improve?
- When do children understand and use quantitative skills?

Angelique is a fifth grader who absolutely loves to read. When Angelique was a preschooler, her parents read Dr. Seuss stories to her,

Academic Skills
Reading
Writing
Math Skills

and now she has progressed to the point where she can read (and understand!) 400-page novels intended for teens. Her parents marvel at this accomplishment and wish they better understood the skills that were involved so they could help Angelique's younger brother learn to read as well as his sister does.

Reading is indeed a complex task and learning to read well is a wonderful accomplishment. Much the same can be said for writing and arithmetic. We'll examine each of these academic skills in this section. As we do, you'll learn about the skills that underlie Angelique's mastery of reading.

READING

Try reading the following sentence:

Sumisu-san wa nawa o naifu de kirimashita.

You probably didn't make much headway, did you? (Unless you know Japanese.) Now try this one:

Snore secretary green plastic sleep trucks.

These are English words and you probably read them quite easily, but did you get anything more out of this sentence than the one in Japanese? These examples show two important processes involved in skilled reading. ***Word recognition is the process of identifying a unique pattern of letters.*** Unless you know Japanese, your word recognition was not successful in the first sentence. You did not know that *nawa* means *rope* or that *kirimashita* is the past tense of the English verb *cut*. What's more, because you could not recognize individual words, you had no idea of the meaning of the sentence. ***Comprehension is the process of extracting meaning from a sequence of words.*** In the second sentence, your word recognition was perfect, but comprehension was still impossible because the words were presented in a random sequence. These examples remind us just how difficult learning to read can be.

In the next few pages, we'll look at some of the skills children must acquire to learn to read and to read well. We'll start with prereading skills, then move to word recognition and comprehension.

Foundations of Reading Skill

English words are made up of individual letters, so children need to know their letters before they can learn to read. Consequently, it's not surprising that knowledge of letter names is consistently one of the best predictors of success in learning to read; that is, youngsters who know most of their letters learn to read more easily than their peers who don't know their letters (Treiman, 2000).

A second essential skill is phonological awareness, which can be measured by presenting several words—*fun, pin, bun, gun*—then asking the child to pick the word that didn't rhyme with the others. Another way is to ask children to say the first, last, or middle sound of a word: "What's the first sound in *cat*?" These measures have been used in dozens of studies and the outcome is always the same: Phonological awareness is strongly related to success in learning to read (Hulme et al., 2002). That is, children who can readily distinguish language sounds learn to read more readily than children who do not.

As children get older, phonological skill continues to be an excellent predictor of reading ability (Wagner et al., 1999). Furthermore, phonological skills are not only important in learning to read in alphabet-based languages such as English; they are also important for children learning to read in nonalphabet-based languages such as Chinese (McBride-Chang & Kail, 2002).

If phonological skills are so essential, how can we help children master them? Reading to children is one approach that's fun for children and parents alike. When parents read stories to their children, they learn many language-related skills that prepare them for reading (Sénéchal & LeFevre, 2002).

Recognizing Words

The first step in actual reading is identifying individual words. One way to do this is to say the sounds associated with each letter and then blend the sounds to produce a recognizable word. Such "sounding out" is a common technique among beginning readers. Older children sometimes sound out words, but only when they are unfamiliar, which points to another common way of recognizing words (Coltheart et al., 1993). Words are recognized through direct retrieval from long-term memory: As the individual letters in a word are identified, long-term memory is searched to see if there is a matching sequence of letters. Knowing that the letters are, in sequence, *c-a-t*, long-term memory is searched for a match and the child recognizes the word as *cat*.

So far, word recognition may seem like a one-way street where readers first recognize letters and then recognize words. In reality, readers constantly use context to help them recognize letters and words. For example, readers typically recognize *t* faster in *cast* than in *asct*. That is, readers recognize letters faster when they appear in words than in nonwords. How do the nearby letters in *cast* help readers to recognize the *t*? As children recognize the first letters in the word as *c*, *a*, and *s*, the possibilities for the last letter become more limited. Because English only includes four 4-letter words that start with *cas* (well, five if you include *Cass*), the last letter can only be *e*, *h*, *k*, or *t*. In contrast, there are no 4-letter words (in English) that begin with *acs*, so all 26 letters must be checked, which takes more time than just checking 4 letters. In this way, a reader's knowledge of words simplifies the task of recognizing letters, which in turn makes it easier to recognize words (Seidenberg & McClelland, 1989).

Readers also use the sentence context to speed word recognition. Read these two sentences:

> The last word in this sentence is cat.
> The little girl's pet dog chased the cat.

Most readers recognize cat more rapidly in the second sentence. The reason is that the first seven words put severe limits on the last word: It must be something "chaseable," and because the "chaser" is a *dog, cat* is a very likely candidate. In contrast, the first seven words in the first sentence put no limits on the last word; virtually any word could end the sentence. Beginning and skilled readers both use sentence context like this to help them recognize words (Archer & Bryant, 2001; Kim & Goetz, 1994).

As you can imagine, most beginning readers, like the child in the photo, rely more heavily on "sounding out" because they know fewer words. As they gain more reading experience, they are more likely to be able to retrieve a word directly from long-term memory. You might be tempted to summarize this as "Beginning readers sound out and more advanced readers retrieve directly." Don't! From their very first efforts to read, most children use direct retrieval for a few words. From that point on, the general strategy is to try retrieval first and, if that fails, sound out the word or ask a more skilled reader for help (Booth, Perfetti, & MacWhinney, 1999; Siegler, 1986). For example, when shown a sentence like this,

> Mark saw the fat cat run,

© Joel Gordon

a beginning reader might say, "Mark s-s-s. . . ah-h. . . wuh . . . saw the fat cat er-r-r. . . uh-h-h . . n-n-n . . . run." Familiar words like *Mark, the, fat,* and *cat* are retrieved rapidly but the unfamiliar ones are slowly sounded out. With more experience, fewer words are sounded out and more are retrieved (Siegler, 1986). That is, by sounding out novel words, children store information about words in long-term memory that is required for direct retrieval (Cunningham et al., 2002; Share, 1999). Of course, all readers sometimes fall back on sounding out when they confront unfamiliar words. Try reading this sentence:

> The rock star rode to the concert in a palanquin.

You may well need to do some sounding out, then consult a dictionary (or look in the paragraph before Test Yourself) for the correct meaning.

Comprehension

Once individual words are recognized, reading begins to have a lot in common with understanding speech. That is, the means by which people understand a sequence of words is much the same whether the source of words is printed text or speech or, for that matter, Braille or sign language (Crowder & Wagner, 1992). *In all of these cases, children derive meaning by combining words to form* **propositions** *or ideas and then combining propositions.* For example, as you read

> The tall boy rode his bike,

you spontaneously derive a number of propositions, including "There is a boy," "The boy is tall," and "The boy was riding." If this sentence were part of a larger body of text, you would derive propositions for each sentence, then link the propositions together to derive meaning for the passage as a whole (Perfetti & Curtis, 1986).

As children gain more reading experience, they better comprehend what they read. Several factors contribute to this improved comprehension (Siegler, 1998):

- *Working memory capacity increases, which means that older and better readers can store more of a sentence in memory as they try to identify the propositions it contains* (De Beni & Palladino, 2000; Nation et al., 1999): This extra capacity is handy when readers move from sentences like "Kevin hit the ball" to "In the bottom of the ninth, with the bases loaded and the Cardinals down 7–4, Kevin put a line drive into the left-field bleachers, his fourth home run of the Series."
- *Children acquire more general knowledge of their physical, social, and psychological worlds, which allows them to understand more of what they read* (Ferreol-Barbey, Piolat, & Roussey, 2000; Graesser, Singer, & Trabasso, 1994): For example, even if a 6-year-old could recognize all the words in the longer sentence about Kevin's home run, the child would not fully comprehend the meaning of the passage because he or she lacks the necessary knowledge of baseball.
- *With experience, children use more appropriate reading strategies:* The goal of reading and the nature of the text dictate how you read. When reading a novel, for example, do you often skip sentences (or perhaps paragraphs or entire pages) to get to "the good parts"? This approach makes sense for pleasure reading but not for reading textbooks or recipes or how-to manuals. Reading a textbook requires attention to both the overall organization and the relation of details to that organization. Older, more experienced readers are better able to select a reading strategy that suits the material being read (Brown et al., 1996; Cain, 1999).
- *With experience, children better monitor their comprehension:* When readers don't grasp the meaning of a passage because it is difficult or confusing, they read it again (Baker, 1994). Try this sentence (adapted from Carpenter & Daneman, 1981): "The Midwest State Fishing Contest would draw fishermen from all around the region, including some of the best bass guitarists in Michigan." When you first encountered "bass guitarists" you probably inter-

preted "bass" as a fish. This didn't make much sense, so you reread the phrase to determine that "bass" refers to a type of guitar. Older readers are better able to realize that their understanding is not complete and take corrective action.

Thus, several factors contribute to improved comprehension as children get older. And greater comprehension, along with improved word recognition skills, explains why children like Angelique are able to read ever-more complex texts as they grow.

THINK ABOUT IT

Reading and speaking are both important elements of literacy. How is learning to read like learning to speak? How do they differ?

WRITING

Though few of us end up being a Carol Shields, a Margaret Atwood, or a Mordecai Richler, most adults do write, both at home and at work. The basics of good writing are remarkably straightforward (Williams, 1997), but writing skill develops very gradually during childhood, adolescence, and young adulthood. Research indicates that a number of factors contribute to improved writing as children develop (Adams et al., 1998; Siegler, 1998).

Greater Knowledge and Access to Knowledge About Topics

Writing is about telling "something" to others. With age, children have more to tell as they gain more knowledge about the world and incorporate this knowledge in their writing (Benton et al., 1995). For example, asked to write about a mayoral election, 8-year-olds are apt to describe it as much like a popularity contest; 12-year-olds more often describe it in terms of political issues. Of course, students are sometimes asked to write about topics quite unfamiliar to them. In this case, older children's and adolescents' writing is usually better because they are more adept at finding useful reference material and incorporating it in their writing.

Greater Understanding of How to Organize Writing

One difficult aspect of writing is organization, arranging all the necessary information in a manner that readers find clear and interesting. In fact, children and young adolescents organize their writing differently than do older adolescents and adults (Bereiter & Scardamalia, 1987). *Young writers often use a knowledge telling strategy, writing down information on the topic as they retrieve it from memory.* For example, asked to write about the day's events at school, a second grader wrote:

> It is a rainy day. We hope the sun will shine. We got new spelling books.
> We had our pictures taken. We sang Happy Birthday to Barbara.
> (Waters, 1980, p. 155)

The story has no obvious structure. The first two sentences are about the weather but the last three deal with completely independent topics. Apparently, the writer simply described each event as it came to mind.

Toward the end of the elementary school years, children begin to use a knowledge transforming strategy, deciding what information to include and how best to organize it for the point they wish to convey to their reader. This approach involves considering the purpose of writing (e.g., to inform, to persuade, to entertain) and the information needed to achieve this purpose. It also involves considering the needs, interests, and knowledge of the anticipated audience.

Asked to describe the day's events, older children's writing can take many forms, depending on the purpose and audience. An essay written to entertain peers about humorous events at school would differ from one written to convince parents about problems in schoolwork. And both of these essays would differ from one written to inform an exchange student about a typical day at school. In other words, although a child's knowledge telling strategy gets words on paper, the more mature knowledge transforming strategy produces a more cohesive text for the reader.

Greater Ease in Dealing with the Mechanical Requirements of Writing

Compared to speaking, writing is more difficult because we need to worry about spelling, punctuation, and actually forming the letters. These many mechanical aspects of writing can be a burden for all writers, but particularly for young writers. For example, when youngsters like the one in the photo are absorbed by the task of printing letters correctly, the quality of their writing usually suffers (Graham, Harris, & Fink, 2000; Jones & Christensen, 1999). As children master printed and cursive letters, they can pay more attention to other aspects of writing. Similarly, correct

spelling and good sentence structure are particularly hard for younger writers; as they learn to spell and to generate clear sentences, they write more easily and more effectively (Graham et al., 1997; McCutchen et al., 1994).

Greater Skill in Revising

Few authors get it down right the first time. Instead, they revise and revise, then revise some more. Unfortunately, young writers often don't revise at all—the first draft is usually the final draft. To make matters worse, when young writers revise, the changes do not necessarily improve their writing (Fitzgerald, 1987).

Effective revising requires being able to detect problems and to know how to correct them (Baker & Brown, 1994; Beal, 1996). As children develop, they're better able to find problems and to know how to correct them, particularly when the topic is familiar to them (Chanquoy, 2001; McCutchen, Francis, & Kerr, 1997).

Considering all the factors involved, it's quite clear why good writing is so long in developing. Many different skills are involved and each is complicated in its own right. Mastering them collectively is a huge challenge, one that spans all of childhood, adolescence, and adulthood. Much the same could be said for mastering quantitative skills, as we'll see in the next section.

MATH SKILLS

In Chapter 5 we saw that preschoolers understand many of the principles underlying counting, even if they sometimes stumble over the mechanics of counting. By kindergarten, children have mastered counting, and they use this skill as the starting point for learning to add. For instance, suppose you ask a kindergartner to solve the following problem: "John had four oranges. Then Mary gave him two more oranges. How many oranges does John have now?" Like the child in the photo, many 6-year-old children solve the problem by counting. They first count out four fingers on one hand, then count out two more on the other. Finally, they count all six fingers on both hands. To subtract, they do the same procedure in reverse (Siegler & Jenkins, 1989; Siegler & Shrager, 1984).

Youngsters soon abandon this approach for a slightly more efficient method. Instead of counting the fingers on the first hand, they simultaneously extend the number of fingers on the first hand corresponding to the larger of the two numbers to be added. Next, they count out the smaller number, with fingers on the second hand. Finally, they count all of the fingers to determine the sum (Groen & Resnick, 1977).

After children begin to receive formal arithmetic instruction in Grade 1, addition problems are less often solved by counting aloud or by counting fingers. Instead, children add and subtract by counting mentally. That is, children act as if they are counting silently, beginning with the larger number, and adding on. By age 8 or 9, children have learned the addition tables so well that sums of the single-digit integers (from 0 to 9) are facts that are simply retrieved from memory (Ashcraft, 1982).

These counting strategies do not occur in a rigid developmental sequence. Individual children use many or all of these strategies, depending on the problem. Children usually begin by trying to retrieve an answer from memory. If they are not reasonably confident that the retrieved answer is correct, then they resort to counting aloud or on fingers (Siegler, 1988). Retrieval is most likely for problems with small addends (e.g., 1 + 2, 2 + 4) because these problems are presented frequently in text-books and by teachers. Consequently, the sum is highly associated with the problem, which makes the child confident that the retrieved answer is correct. In contrast, problems with larger addends, such as 9 + 8, are presented less often. The result is a weaker link between the addends and the sum and, consequently, a greater chance that children will need to determine an answer by counting.

Of course, arithmetic skills continue to improve as children move through elementary school. They become more proficient in addition and subtraction, learn multiplication and division, and move on to the more sophisticated mathematical concepts involved in algebra, geometry, trigonometry, and calculus.

THINK ABOUT IT

What information-processing skills may contribute to growth in children's arithmetic skills?

Comparing Canadian Students with Students in Other Countries

When compared to students worldwide in math skills, Canadian students hold their own. For example, Figure 7.9 shows the results of the Third International Mathematics and Science Study (National Center for Education Statistics, 1997), which compares math and science achievement of students in 41 countries. Although the very best Canadian students perform only at the level of average students in Asian countries such as Singapore and Korea, Canadian students did as well as or better than students from 31 other countries who participated (McConaghy, 1998). It is interesting to note that the cultural differences in math achievement hold for both math operations and math problem solving (Stevenson & Lee, 1990).

FIGURE 7.9   Comparing Math Scores

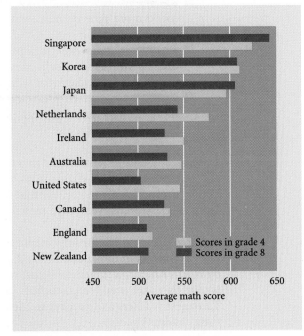

SOURCE: Based on data from the Third International Math and Science Study, 1997.

REAL PEOPLE: APPLYING HUMAN DEVELOPMENT

Shin-ying Loves School

Shin-ying is an 11-year-old attending school in Taipei, the largest city in Taiwan. Like most fifth graders, Shin-ying is in school from 8 a.m. until 4 p.m. daily. Most evenings, she spends two to three hours doing homework. This academic routine is gruelling by standards in Canada, where fifth graders typically spend six to seven hours in school each day and less than an hour doing homework. We asked Shin-ying what she thought of school and schoolwork. Her answers surprised us.

US: Why do you go to school?
SHIN-YING: I like what we study.
US: Any other reasons?
SHIN-YING: The things that I learn in school are useful.

US: What about homework? Why do you do it?
SHIN-YING: My teacher and my parents think it's important. And I like doing it.
US: Do you think you would do nearly as well in school if you didn't work so hard?
SHIN-YING: Oh no. The best students are always the ones who work the hardest.

Schoolwork is the focal point of Shin-ying's life. Although many North American schoolchildren are unhappy when schoolwork intrudes on time for play and television, Shin-ying is enthusiastic about school and school-related activities. ▣

What contributes to cultural differences in math skills? The Real People feature has some answers.

Shin-ying is not unusual among Chinese elementary school students. Many of her comments exemplify those from a comprehensive comparison of students in Japan, Taiwan, and the United States (Stevenson & Lee, 1990):

- ▣ *Time in school and how it is used.* By Grade 5, students in Japan and Taiwan spend 50% more time in school than U.S. students, and more of this time is devoted to academic activities than in the United States.
- ▣ *Time spent in homework and attitudes toward it.* Students in Taiwan and Japan spend more time on homework and value homework more than American students.
- ▣ *Parents' attitudes.* American parents are more often satisfied with their children's performance in school; in contrast, Japanese and Taiwanese parents set much higher standards for their children.
- ▣ *Parents' beliefs about effort and ability.* Japanese and Taiwanese parents believe more strongly than American parents that effort, not native ability, is the key factor in school success.

Thus, students in Japan and Taiwan excel because they spend more time both in and out of school on academic tasks. Furthermore, their parents (and teachers) set loftier scholastic goals and believe that students can attain these goals with hard work. Japanese classrooms even post a motto describing ideal students: *gambaru kodomo*—they who strive the hardest.

Parents underscore the importance of schoolwork in many ways to their children. For example, even though homes and apartments in Japan and China are very small by North American standards, Asian youngsters typically have a desk in a quiet area where they can study undisturbed (Stevenson & Lee, 1990). For Japanese and Taiwanese teachers and parents, academic excellence is paramount, and it shows in their children's success.

What can be learned from Japanese and Taiwanese educational systems? From their experiences with Asian students, teachers, and schools, Stevenson and Stigler (1992) suggest several ways schools could be improved:

- Give teachers more free time to prepare lessons and correct students' work.
- Improve teachers' training by allowing them to work closely with older, more experienced teachers.
- Organize instruction around sound principles of learning such as providing multiple examples of concepts and giving students adequate opportunities to practise newly acquired skills.
- Set higher standards for children, who need to spend more time and effort in school-related activities to achieve those standards.

Changing teaching practices and attitudes toward achievement would begin to reduce the gap between North American students and students in other industrialized countries, particularly Asian countries. Ignoring the problem will mean an increasingly undereducated workforce and citizenry in a more complex world—an alarming prospect for the 21st century.

DEFINITION ON PAGE 262: A palanquin is a covered couch resting on two horizontal poles carried by four people, one at each end of the poles.

TEST YOURSELF

1. Important prereading skills include knowing letters and the _____.

2. Beginning readers typically recognize words by sounding them out; with greater experience, readers are more likely able to _____.

3. Older and more experienced readers understand more of what they read because the capacity of working memory increases, they have more general knowledge of the world, _____, and they are more likely to use appropriate reading strategies.

4. Children typically use a _____ to organize their writing.

5. Children revise best when revising other children's writing and when _____.

6. The simplest way of solving addition problems is to _____; the most advanced way is to retrieve sums from long-term memory.

Imagine two children just entering Grade 1. One has mastered prereading skills, can sound out many words, and recognizes a rapidly growing set of words. The second child knows most of the letters of the alphabet but knows only a handful of letter-sound correspondences. How are these differences in reading skills likely to lead to different experiences in Grade 1?

Answers: (1) sounds associated with each letter, (2) retrieve words from long-term memory, (3) they monitor their comprehension more effectively, (4) knowledge telling strategy, (5) the topic is familiar to them, (6) count on one's fingers

7.6

Learning in School

LEARNING OBJECTIVES

- How effectively do schools educate their students?
- What are the hallmarks of effective schools and effective teachers?
- What happens in bilingual education?

Learning in School
Effective Schools, Effective Teachers
Bilingual and Second Language Education

EFFECTIVE SCHOOLS, EFFECTIVE TEACHERS

Because education is under provincial jurisdiction, provinces, school divisions, and individual schools differ on many dimensions, including their emphasis on academic goals and the involvement of parents. Teachers, too, differ in many ways, such as how they run their classrooms and how they teach. These and other variables affect student achievement, as you'll see in the next few pages. Let's begin with school-based influences.

School-Based Influences on Student Achievement

Researchers (Good & Brophy, 1994; Stevenson & Stigler, 1992; Walberg, 1995) have identified a number of characteristics of schools where students typically succeed rather than fail:

- *Staff and students alike understand that academic excellence is the primary goal of the school and of every student in the school.* The school day emphasizes instruction (not simply filling time from 8:30 to 3:30 with nonacademic activities), and students are recognized publicly for their academic accomplishments.
- *The school climate is safe and nuturing.* Students know that they can devote their energy to learning (instead of worrying about being harmed in school) and that the staff truly cares that they succeed.
- *Parents are involved.* In some cases, this may be through formal arrangements, such as parent-teacher organizations. Or it may be informal. Parents may spend some time each week in school grading papers or, like the dad in the photo, tutoring a child. Such involvement signals both teachers and students that parents are committed to students' success.
- *Progress of students, teachers, and programs is monitored.* The only way to know whether schools are succeeding is by measuring performance. Students, teachers, and programs need to be evaluated regularly, using objective measures that reflect academic goals.

© Myrleen Ferguson Cate/PhotoEdit

In schools where these guidelines are followed regularly, students usually succeed. In schools where these guidelines are ignored, students more often fail.

Some educators argue that schools should take greater advantage of technology—primarily computers—to improve instruction. Opponents believe computers remove the all-important human factor from learning. The Current Controversies feature examines this issue.

CURRENT CONTROVERSIES

Computers in the Classroom

New technologies soon find their way into the classroom. Computers are no exception; virtually all Canadian public schools include com-

puters to aid instruction. A primary function of computers in the schools is as a tutor (Lepper & Gurtner, 1989). Children use computers to learn reading, spelling, arithmetic, science, and social studies. Computers allow instruction to be individualized and interactive. Students proceed at their own pace, receiving feedback and help when necessary.

Computers are also valuable as a medium for experiential learning (Lepper & Gurtner, 1989). Simulation programs allow students to explore the world in ways that would be impossible or dangerous otherwise. Students can change the law of gravity or see what happens to a city when no taxes are imposed.

Finally, the computer is a multipurpose tool that can help students achieve traditional academic goals (Steelman, 1994). A graphics program enables artistically untalented students to produce beautiful illustrations. A word processing program relieves much of the drudgery associated with revising, thereby encouraging better writing.

Not all parents and teachers are enthusiastic about computers in classrooms. Some critics fear that computers eliminate an important human element in learning. Many worry that computers isolate students from each other and from the teacher and make learning a solitary activity. In reality, students interact with each other more when computers are introduced into the classroom, not less (Pozzi, Healy, & Hoyles, 1993). As the photo shows, students often cluster around one student as he or she works, and they often consult the class "expert" on a particular program. Teachers, freed from many of the drill-type tasks that now occupy the school day, can turn their attention to other aspects of instruction. ▨

Photodisc

Of course, on a daily basis, individual teachers have the most potential for impact. Let's see how teachers can influence their students' achievement.

Teacher-Based Influences

Take a moment to recall your teachers in elementary school, junior high, and high school. Some you probably remember fondly, for they were enthusiastic and innovative, and they made learning fun. You may remember others with bitterness. They seemed to have lost their love of teaching and children, making class unpleasant for everyone. Your experiences tell you that some teachers are better than others, but what is it that makes an effective teacher? Personality and enthusiasm are *not* the key elements. Although you may enjoy warm and eager teachers, research (Good & Brophy, 1994; Stevenson & Stigler, 1992; Walberg, 1995) has revealed that several other factors are critical when it comes to students' achievement. Students tend to learn the most when teachers

▨ *Manage the classroom effectively so they can devote most of their time to instruction.* When teachers spend a lot of time disciplining students, or when students do not move smoothly from one class activity to the next, instructional time is wasted, and students are apt to learn less.

- ▪ *Believe they are responsible for their students' learning and that their students will learn when taught well.* When students don't understand a new topic, these teachers may repeat the original instruction (in case the student missed something) or create new instructions (in case the student heard everything but just didn't "get it"). These teachers keep plugging away because they feel at fault if students don't learn.

- ▪ *Emphasize mastery of topics.* Teachers should introduce a topic, then give students many opportunities to understand, practise, and apply the topic. Just as you'd find it hard to go directly from driver's ed to driving a race car, students more often achieve when they grasp a new topic thoroughly, then gradually move on to other, more advanced topics.

- ▪ *Teach actively.* They don't just talk or give students an endless stream of worksheets. Instead, they demonstrate topics concretely or have hands-on demonstrations for students. They also have students participate in class activities and encourage students to interact, generating ideas and solving problems together.

- ▪ *Pay careful attention to pacing.* They present material slowly enough so that students can understand a new concept, but not so slowly that students get bored.

- ▪ *Value tutoring.* They work with students individually or in small groups, so they can gear their instruction to each student's level and check each student's understanding. They also encourage peer tutoring, in which, as shown in the photo, more capable students tutor less capable students. Children who are tutored by peers *do* learn, and so do the tutors, evidently because teaching helps tutors to organize their knowledge.

- ▪ *Teach children techniques for monitoring and managing their own learning.* Students are more likely to achieve when they are taught how to recognize the aims of school tasks and know effective strategies for achieving those aims (like those described on pages 238–240).

When teachers rely on most of the guidelines for effective teaching most of the time, their students generally learn the material and enjoy doing so. When teachers rely on few of them, their students often fail, or, at the very least, find learning difficult and school tedious (Good & Brophy, 1994; Stevenson & Stigler, 1992; Walberg, 1995).

BILINGUAL AND SECOND LANGUAGE EDUCATION

Since Canada has two official languages and many citizens who speak other languages, many parents choose to educate their children formally or informally in two (or more) languages. The most common type of formal second language education is the French immersion program, which strives to have students competent in both French and English. Proponents of French immersion programs promote their role in preparing young Canadians with the "knowledge, skills, attitudes and mobility needed to meet the challenges of the global, knowledge-based society" and believe such programs can lead to the "richness of bilingual and bicultural thinking" (Manitoba Education, Training and Youth, 2002). French immersion programming is offered in every part of Canada, and there are generally three entry levels of immersion programs, early (kindergarten or Grade 1), middle (Grade 4), or late (Grade 7), but there are variations throughout the country. The amount of time per day when French is the language of instruction (and therefore immersion) is 100% in kindergarten, 75 to 80% in Grades 1 to 6, and 50 to 80% in Grades 7 to Senior 4 (Manitoba Education, Training and Youth, 2002).

Canadian researchers Bialystok, Majumder, and Martin (2003) identified that most published studies have reported that bilingual children have an advantage regarding word and syntactic awareness, although they did not find any clear or consistent effect of bilingualism on phonological awareness in their study. It has been reported that French immersion students' oral French is better than their written French (Romney, Romney, & Menzies, 1995). However, the supporters of this program strongly emphasize its immediate and far-reaching benefits.

> **THINK ABOUT IT**
>
> Are some of the ways to promote students' learning more appropriate for students in Piaget's concrete-operational stage? Are some better for students in the formal-operational stage?

TEST YOURSELF

1. In schools where students usually succeed, academic excellence is a priority, the school is safe and nurturing, progress of students and teachers is monitored, and _____.

2. Effective teachers manage classrooms well, believe they are responsible for their students' learning, _____, teach actively, pay attention to pacing, value

tutoring, and show children how to monitor their own learning.

Many schools use computers to help students learn to read and to learn math facts. What characteristics of "effective teachers" would apply to computers?

Answers: (1) parents are involved, (2) emphasize mastery of topics

PUTTING IT ALL TOGETHER

We began the chapter by examining the physical changes that occur during the school years and cognitive development. At about the same time that children begin school, they enter Piaget's period of concrete operations. As they grow, their thinking moves beyond the concrete to the abstract. Like Adrian, they gradually pick up the study strategies that are essential for school achievement.

Next, we traced the origins of intelligence testing and examined how tests are used today. Test scores predict school achievement because they tap the knowledge and skills that are prerequisites for school success. Low test scores indicate that the student probably lacks the skills needed for school success.

We also examined one of the reasons educating children is such a challenge: Contemporary schools serve a wide range of youngsters, including gifted children, children with intellectual impairment, and children with learning disabilities like Sanjit. The aim is for all children to be educated to their fullest potential, but we still don't know how best to accommodate all students in today's schools. Research has revealed several school- and teacher-related factors that enhance students' achievement.

SUMMARY

7.1 Physical Development in Middle Childhood

Physical Growth

- During this development period children grow an average of five to seven centimetres and gain an average of three kilograms per year. Of course gender, cultural, environmental, and genetic variations can be expected.

Gross and Fine Motor Skills Development

- Developing gross and fine motor skills during this period allow for riding a bicycle and playing sports with increasing speed and agility. Fine motor skill development allows for cursive writing, ability to learn a musical instrument, increased competence in art and fine control activities such as crafts.

7.2 Cognitive Development

More Sophisticated Thinking: Piaget's Version

- In progressing to Piaget's stage of concrete operations, children become less egocentric, rarely confuse appearances with reality, and are able to reverse their thinking. They now solve perspective-taking, conservation, and class-inclusion problems correctly. Thinking at this stage is limited to the concrete and the real.

- With the onset of formal-operational thinking, adolescents can think hypothetically and reason abstractly. In deductive reasoning, they understand that conclusions are based on logic, not on experience.

- Critics of Piaget's account of formal-operational thinking point to two shortcomings. First, in everyday thinking, adolescents' reasoning is often less sophisticated than would be expected of formal-operational thinkers. Second, Piaget assumed that after the formal-operational stage is reached, thinking never again changes qualitatively.

Information-Processing Strategies for Learning and Remembering

- Rehearsal and other memory strategies are used to transfer information from working memory, a temporary store of information, to long-term memory, a permanent store of knowledge. Children begin to rehearse at about age 7 or 8 and take up other strategies as they get older.

- Effective use of strategies for learning and remembering begins with an analysis of the goals of any learning task. It also includes monitoring one's performance to determine whether the strategy is working. Collectively, these processes make up an important group of study skills.

7.3 Aptitudes for School

Theories of Intelligence

- Psychometric approaches to intelligence include theories that describe intelligence as a general factor as well as theories that include specific factors. Hierarchical theories include both general intelligence as well as various specific skills, such as verbal and spatial ability.

- Gardner's theory of multiple intelligences proposes nine distinct intelligences. Three are found in psychometric theories (linguistic, logical-mathematical, and spatial intelligence), but six are new (musical, bodily-kinesthetic, interpersonal, intrapersonal, naturalistic, and existential intelligence). Gardner's theory has stimulated research on nontraditional forms of intelligence, such as social cognitive flexibility. The theory also has implications for education, suggesting, for example, that schools should adjust teaching to each child's unique intellectual strengths.

- Robert Sternberg's triarchic theory includes (a) the contextual subtheory, which specifies that intelligent behaviour must always be considered in relation to the individual's culture; (b) the experiential subtheory, which specifies that intelligence is associated with the familiarity of the task; and (c) the componential subtheory, which specifies that intelligent behaviour involves organizing basic cognitive processes into an efficient strategy for completing a task.

Binet and the Development of Intelligence Testing

- Binet created the first intelligence test to identify students who would have difficulty in school. Using this work, Terman created the Stanford-Binet in 1916; it remains an important intelligence test. The Stanford-Binet introduced the concept of the intelligence quotient (IQ): MA/CA $\times$ 100.

Do Tests Work?

- Intelligence tests are reasonably valid measures of achievement in school. They also predict people's performance in the workplace. Dynamic tests are designed to improve validity by measuring children's potential for future learning.

Hereditary and Environmental Factors

- Evidence for the impact of heredity on IQ comes from the findings that (a) siblings' IQ scores become more alike as siblings become more similar genetically, and (b) adopted children's IQ scores are more like their biological parents' test scores than their adoptive parents' scores.

- Evidence for the impact of the environment comes from several sources: (a) children who live in responsive, well-organized home environments tend to have higher IQ scores; (b) IQ scores increased in the 20th century; and (c) IQ scores increase when children participate in intervention programs.

The Impact of Culture and Social Class

- Ethnic groups differ in their average scores on IQ tests. This difference is not due to genetics or to familiarity with specific test items but rather to children's familiarity and comfort with the testing situation. Nevertheless, IQ scores remain valid predictors of school success because middle-class experience is often a prerequisite for school success.

7.4 Special Children, Special Needs

Gifted and Creative Children

- Traditionally, gifted children have been those with high scores on IQ tests. Modern definitions of giftedness have been broadened to include exceptional talent in, for example, the arts. However defined, giftedness must be nurtured by parents and teachers alike. Contrary to folklore, gifted children are socially mature and emotionally stable.

- Creativity is associated with divergent thinking, in which the aim is to think in novel and unusual directions. Tests of divergent thinking can predict which children are most likely to be creative. Creativity can be fostered by experiences that encourage children to think flexibly and to explore alternatives.

Children with Intellectual Impairment

- Individuals with intellectual impairment have IQ scores of 75 or lower and deficits in adaptive behaviour. Organic intellectual impairment, which is severe but relatively infrequent, can be linked to specific biological or physical causes; familial intellectual impairment, which is less severe but more common, reflects the lower end of the normal distribution of intelligence.

Learning Disabilities

- Children with a learning disability have normal intelligence but have difficulty mastering specific academic subjects. The most common is reading disability, which often can be traced to inadequate understanding and use of language sounds.

Attention-Deficit Hyperactivity Disorder

- Children with ADHD are distinguished by being overactive, inattentive, and impulsive. They often have conduct problems and do poorly in school. They can be taught more effective ways of regulating their behaviour and attention and may be also be treated with stimulant medication.

7.5 Academic Skills

Reading

- Reading includes a number of component skills. Prereading skills include knowing letters and the sounds associated with them. Word recognition is the process of identifying a word. Beginning readers more often accomplish this by sounding out words; advanced readers more often retrieve a word from long-term memory. Comprehension, the act of extracting meaning from text, improves with age due to several factors: working memory capacity increases, readers gain more world knowledge, and readers are better able to monitor what they read and to match their reading strategies to the goals of the reading task.

Writing

- As children develop, their writing improves, reflecting several factors: They know more about the world, so have more to say; they use more effective ways of organizing their writing; they master the mechanics (e.g., handwriting, spelling) of writing; and they become more skilled at revising their writing.

Math Skills

- Children first add and subtract by counting but then use more effective strategies such as retrieving addition facts directly from memory. In international tests of mathematics, Canadian students did as well as or better than students from 31 other countries.

7.6 Learning in School

Effective Schools, Effective Teachers

- Students are most likely to achieve when their school emphasizes academic excellence, has a safe and nurturing environment, monitors pupils' and teachers' progress, and encourages parents to be involved.

Students achieve at higher levels when their teachers manage classrooms effectively, take responsibility for their students' learning, teach mastery of material, pace material well, value tutoring, and show children how to monitor their own learning.

Bilingual and Second Language Education

Many Canadian children complete at least part of their education in a second language. Research findings indicate that bilingual children have an advantage regarding word and syntactic awareness.

KEY TERMS

mental operations (236)
deductive reasoning (237)
working memory (239)
long-term memory (239)
psychometricians (241)
savants (244)
social cognitive flexibility (244)
triarchic theory (244)
componential subtheory (244)
components (244)

experiential subtheory (245)
contextual subtheory (245)
mental age (MA) (246)
intelligence quotient (IQ) (246)
dynamic testing (247)
culture-fair intelligence tests (251)
convergent thinking (254)
divergent thinking (254)
intellectual impairment (254)
organic intellectual impairment (255)

familial intellectual impairment (255)
learning disability (255)
word recognition (260)
comprehension (260)
propositions (262)
knowledge telling strategy (263)
knowledge transforming strategy (263)

SEE FOR YOURSELF: APPLYING WHAT YOU'VE LEARNED

The best way to understand the differences between good and bad teaching is to visit some actual school classrooms. Try to visit three or four rooms in at least two different schools. (You can usually arrange this by speaking with the school's principal.) Take along the principles of good teaching listed on pages 269–270. Start by watching how the teachers and children

interact. Then, decide how much the teacher relies on each of the principles. If possible, ask the teacher about teaching philosophies and practices. You'll probably see that most teachers use some but not all of these principles. And you'll also see that, in today's classroom, consistently following all the principles is very challenging. See for yourself!

LEARN MORE ABOUT IT

Readings

BARKLEY, R. A. (1995). *Taking charge of ADHD: The complete, authoritative guide for parents.* New York: Guilford. Written by one of the leading experts on ADHD, this book clearly describes what research has revealed about the nature of ADHD. The book also provides a wealth of practical information for parents and teachers on many topics, such as the effects of medications and how to improve children's performance in the classroom.

FLAVELL, J. H., MILLER, P. H., & MILLER, S. A. (2003). *Cognitive development* (4th ed.). Englewood Cliffs, NJ: Prentice Hall. We recommended this book in Chapter 5 as a good source of information about cognitive development in young children, but it also covers the development of thinking in school-age children and adolescents.

GARDNER, H. (1993). *Creating minds.* New York: Basic Books. The author describes the lives of extraordinarily

creative persons such as Einstein and Picasso in order to understand the conditions that foster creativity.

 For additional readings, explore InfoTrac® College Edition, your online library. Go to http://www.infotrac.thomsonlearning.com.

Websites

http://www.schoolnet.ca/home/e

This Canadian website was developed for school use with thousands of learning resources, and a daily information news service on the world of e-learning.

http://www.skeptic.com/03.3.fm-sternberg-interview.html

The website of *Skeptic* magazine includes an interview with Robert Sternberg in which Sternberg talks about his triarchic theory, the influence of heredity and environment on intelligence, and Gardner's model of multiple intelligences.

http://www.nagc.org/

The website of the National Association for Gifted Children contains information for parents of gifted children and links to related sites.

http://www.cec.sped.org/ab/

This is the website of the Council for Exceptional Children (CEC), which is the largest international professional organization dedicated to improving educational outcomes for individuals with exceptionalities, students with disabilities, and/or the gifted. Includes a link to the Canadian branch of this organization.

http://www.ldac-taac.ca/

This is the website for The Learning Disabilities Association of Canada (LDAC), which is a national, non-profit voluntary association. The mission of the LDAC is to be the national voice for persons with learning disabilities and those who support them.

Website addresses are subject to change. The *Human Development* book companion website can be accessed for updated links.

The Human Development Book Companion Website

See http://www.humandevelopment.nelson.com for practice quiz questions, Internet links, updates, critical thinking exercises, discussion forums, and more.

 Life-Span CD-ROM

For more information on the concepts covered in this chapter, go to

Module 3: Early and Middle Childhood

- Cognitive Development

© Staffan Widstrand /Corbis /Magma

CHAPTER 8

Expanding Social Horizons

SOCIOEMOTIONAL DEVELOPMENT IN MIDDLE CHILDHOOD

Although you've never had a course called Culture 101, your knowledge of your culture is deep. Like all human beings, you have been learning since birth to live in your culture. *Teaching children the values, roles, and behaviours of their culture—socialization—is a major goal of all peoples.* In most cultures, the task of socialization falls initially to parents. In the first section of this chapter, we'll continue our look at the important influence of the family on this process.

Other powerful forces also contribute to socialization. In the second section, you'll discover how peers become influential, through both individual friendships and social groups. Next, you'll learn how the media—particularly television—contribute to socialization as well.

As children become socialized, they begin to understand more about other people. We'll examine this growing understanding in the last section of the chapter.

8.1

Family Relationships

LEARNING OBJECTIVES

▨ What determines how siblings get along? How do first-born, later-born, and only children differ?

▨ How do divorce and remarriage affect children?

Tanya and Sheila each have two children in Grades 2 and 4. Tanya lives with her husband in a mid-sized city two blocks from where she herself grew up and where her mother still lives. She works part-time as a teaching assistant and has joined an informal parenting network at their church. Sheila recently moved to the neighbourhood from a small rural area. She is recently divorced and is currently looking for work to support herself and her two children. She doesn't know many people in the area and her parents live in another province.

This vignette provides an example of how different family experiences and influences can be. It is well accepted that parents have a very important role to play in child rearing. However, parents themselves are key components of a broader family system. In this section we'll look at families and relationships.

THE FAMILY AS A SYSTEM

In Chapter 6 we looked at the role of parents and the different styles of parenting. A simple-minded view of child rearing is that parents' actions are all that really matter. That is, through their behaviour, parents directly and indirectly determine their children's development. This view of parents as "all powerful" was part of early psychological theories (e.g., Watson, 1925) and is held even today by some first-time parents. But most theorists now view families from an ecological perspective (described in Chapter 1). That is, families form a system of interacting elements—parents and children influence one another (Parke & Buriel, 1998).

In the systems view, parents still influence their children, both directly (for example, by encouraging them to study hard) and indirectly (for example, by being generous and kind to others). However, the influence is no longer exclusively from parents to children but is mutual: Children influence their parents too. By their behaviours, attitudes, and interests, children affect how their parents behave toward them. When children resist discipline, for example, parents may become less willing to reason and more inclined to use force (Ritchie, 1999).

Even more subtle influences become apparent when families are viewed as systems of interacting elements. For example, fathers' behaviours can affect mother-child relationships—a demanding husband may leave his wife with little time, energy, or interest in helping her daughter with her homework. Or, when siblings argue constantly, parents may become preoccupied with avoiding problems rather than encouraging their children's development.

These many examples show that narrowly focusing on parents' impact on children misses the complexities of family life. But there is even more to the systems view. The family itself is embedded in other social systems, such as neighbourhoods and religious institutions (Parke & Buriel, 1998). These other institutions can affect family dynamics. Sometimes they simplify child rearing, as when neighbours are trusted friends and can help care for each other's children. Sometimes, however, they complicate child rearing. Grandparents who live nearby and visit constantly can create friction within the family. At times, the impact of the larger systems is indirect, as when work schedules cause a parent to be away from home or when schools must eliminate programs that benefit children. Figure 8.1 summarizes the numerous interactive influences that exist in a systems view of families.

FIGURE 8.1   Systems View of Family

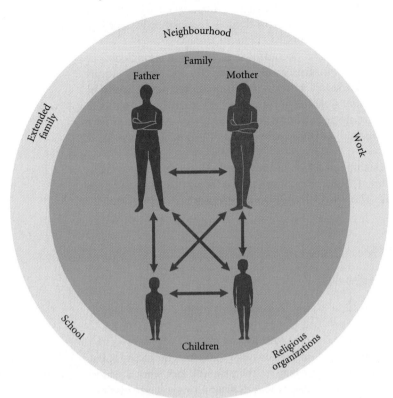

A reciprocal parent-child relationship is central to human development, but other relationships within the family are also influential. For many children, relationships with siblings are very important, as we'll see in the next few pages.

SIBLINGS

For most of a year, all first-born children are only children. Some children remain "onlies" forever, but most get brothers and sisters. Some first-borns are joined by many siblings in rapid succession; others are simply joined by a single brother or sister. As the family acquires these new members, parent-child relationships become more complex. Parents can no longer focus on a single child but must adjust to the needs of several children. Just as important, siblings influence each other's development.

From the very beginning, sibling relationships are complicated. On the one hand, most expectant parents are excited by the prospect of another child, and their enthusiasm is contagious. Their children, too, eagerly await the arrival of the newest family member. On the other hand, the birth of a sibling is often distressing for older children, who may become withdrawn or return to more childish behaviour because of the changes that occur in their lives, particularly the need to share parental attention and affection (Gottlieb & Mendelson, 1990). However, distress can be avoided if parents remain responsive to their older children's needs (Howe & Ross, 1990). In fact, one of the benefits of a sibling's birth is that fathers become more involved with their older children (Stewart et al., 1987).

Many older siblings enjoy helping their parents take care of newborns. Older children play with the baby, console it, feed it, or change its diapers. In middle-class Western families, such caregiving often occurs in the context of play, with parents nearby. But in some cultures children—particularly girls like the one in the photo—play an important role in providing care for their younger siblings (Zukow-Goldring, 2002). As the infant grows, interactions between siblings become more frequent and more complicated. For example, toddlers tend to talk more to parents than to older siblings. But by the time the younger sibling is 4 years old, the situation is reversed; now young siblings talk more to older siblings than to

their mother (Brown & Dunn, 1992). Older siblings become a source of care and comfort for younger siblings when they are distressed or upset (Garner, Jones, & Palmer, 1994). And older siblings serve as teachers for their younger siblings, teaching them to play games or how to cook simple foods (Maynard, 2002).

As time goes by, some siblings grow close, becoming best friends in ways that non-siblings can never be. Other siblings constantly argue, compete, and overall simply do not get along with each other. The basic pattern of sibling interaction seems to be established early in development and remains fairly stable. Siblings who get along as preschoolers often continue to get along as young adolescents, whereas siblings who quarrel as preschoolers often quarrel as young adolescents (Dunn, Slomkowski, & Beardsall, 1994).

Why are some sibling relationships so filled with love and respect and others dominated by jealousy and resentment? Put more simply, what factors contribute to the quality of sibling relationships? The Forces in Action feature has the answers.

FORCES IN ACTION

When Do Siblings Get Along?

Biological, psychological, and sociocultural forces all help determine how well siblings get along. Among the biological forces are the child's sex and temperament. Sibling relations are more likely to be warm and harmonious between siblings of the same sex than between siblings of the opposite sex (Dunn & Kendrick, 1981) and when neither sibling is temperamentally emotional (Brody, Stoneman, & McCoy, 1994). Age is also important: Sibling relationships generally improve as the younger child approaches adolescence because siblings begin to perceive one another as equals (Buhrmester & Furman, 1990).

Parents contribute to the quality of sibling relationships, both directly and indirectly (Brody, 1998). The direct influence stems from parents' treatment. Siblings more often get along when they believe their parents have no "favourites" but treat all siblings fairly (Kowal & Kramer, 1997). When parents lavishly praise one child's accomplishments while ignoring another's, children notice the difference and their sibling relationship suffers.

This doesn't mean parents must treat all their children the same. Children understand that parents should treat their kids differently—based on their age or personal needs. Only when differential treatment is not justi-

fied do sibling relationships deteriorate (Kowal & Kramer, 1997).

The indirect influence of parents on sibling relationships stems from the quality of the parents' relationship with each other. A warm, harmonious relationship between parents fosters positive sibling relationships; conflict between parents is associated with conflict between siblings (Erel, Margolin, & John, 1998; Volling & Belsky, 1992). When parents don't get along, they no longer treat their children the same, leading to conflict among siblings (Brody et al., 1994).

A biopsychosocial perspective on sibling relationships makes it clear that, in their pursuit of family harmony (otherwise known as peace and quiet), parents can influence some of the factors affecting sibling relationships but not others. Parents *can* help reduce friction between siblings by being equally affectionate, responsive, and caring to all of their children and by caring for one another. At the same time, parents must realize that some dissension is natural in families, especially those with young boys and girls. Children's different interests lead to conflicts that youngsters cannot resolve because their social skills are limited.

Adopted Children

It is estimated that 1.2% of Canadian children under the age of 12 are adopted (Vanier Institute of the Family, 2000). Numbers of adoptions have decreased over the last few decades, and most adoptions involve adults who are already related to the child either as a stepparent or a relative such as a grandparent or aunt (Ambert, 2002). Since adoption agencies have in the past given preference to prospective adoptive parents with a stable financial situation, adoptive couples continue to be of higher socioeconomic status than other parents on average (Ambert, 2002).

Although it was thought at one time that adopted children were likely to have more problems in a number of areas, when compared to children living with biological parents, adopted children are quite similar in temperament, mother-infant attachment, and cognitive development (Brodzinsky & Pinderhughes, 2002).

It has been found that the extent of problems that do develop hinges on the child's age when adopted and the quality of care provide prior to adoption (Brodzinsky & Pinderhughes, 2002; Gunnar et al., 2000). Perhaps the best way to summarize this research is that adoption per se is not a fundamental developmental challenge for most children, but quality of life before adoption certainly places some adopted children at risk. It's important to remember that most adopted children fare quite well.

Impact of Birth Order

First-born children are often "guinea pigs" for parents, who have lots of enthusiasm but little practical experience rearing children. Parents typically have high expectations for their first-borns (Furman, 1995). They are both more affectionate and more punitive toward them. As more children arrive, most parents become more adept at their roles, having learned "the tricks of the trade" from earlier children. With later-born children, parents have more realistic expectations and are more relaxed in their discipline (Baskett, 1985).

The different approaches parents use with their first- and later-born children help explain differences commonly observed between these children. First-born children generally have higher scores on intelligence tests and are more likely to continue with post-secondary education. They are also more willing to conform to parents' and adults' requests. In contrast, perhaps because later-born children are less concerned about pleasing parents and adults, they are more popular with their peers and more innovative (Eaton, Chipperfield, & Singbeil, 1989).

What about only children? According to conventional wisdom, parents like the ones in the photo dote on "onlies," who therefore become selfish and egotistical. Is the folklore correct? In a comprehensive analysis of more than 100 studies, only children were not worse off than other children on any measure. In fact, only children were found to succeed more often in school and to have higher levels of intelligence, leadership, autonomy, and maturity (Falbo & Polit, 1986).

This general pattern is not limited to only children in North America. In China, only children are common because of governmental efforts to limit population growth. There, too, comparisons between only and non–only children often find no differences; when differences are found, the advantage usually goes to the only child (Jiao, Ji, & Jing, 1996; Yang et al., 1995). Thus, contrary to the popular stereotype, only children are not "spoiled brats." Instead, only children are, for the most part, much like children who grow up with siblings.

Whether North American children grow up with siblings or as onlies, they are more likely than children in other countries to have their family relationships disrupted by divorce. What is the impact of divorce on children and adolescents?

DIVORCE AND REMARRIAGE

In 2000 the Canadian divorce rate was 38% (Statistics Canada, 2002d). In addition, the rate of separation is reportedly even higher in common-law unions (Statistics Canada, 2003, May). According to all theories of child development, divorce and separation are distressing for children because they involve conflict between parents and, usually, separation from one of them. (Of course, divorce is also distressing to parents, as we describe in Chapter 12.) But what aspects of children's development are most affected by divorce? Are these effects long-lasting or are at least some of them temporary? To begin to answer these questions, let's start with a profile of life after divorce.

Family Life After Divorce

After divorce, children usually live with their mothers. In Canada in 2000 custody was awarded to the mother in 54% of cases, to the father in 9% of cases, and jointly in 37% of cases (Statistics Canada, 2002d). Although fathers are more likely to get custody today than in previous generations, this arrangement is still rare. Not much is known about family life in homes headed by single fathers, so the description on the next few pages is based on research done on children living with their mothers.

One of the most comprehensive portraits of family life after divorce comes from the Virginia Longitudinal Study of Divorce and Remarriage conducted by Mavis Hetherington and her colleagues (1988, 1989; Hetherington & Kelly, 2002). The Virginia study traced the lives of families for several years after divorce along with a comparison sample of families with parents who had not divorced. In the first few months after divorce, mothers were often less affectionate toward their children. They also accepted less mature behaviour from their children than they would have before the divorce but, at the same time, had a harder time controlling their children than before. Apparently, both mothers and children showed the distress of a major change in life circumstances: Children regressed to less mature forms of behaviour, and mothers were less able to parent effectively. Fathers, too, were less able to control their children, but this was probably because they were often extremely indulgent with them.

Two years after the divorce, mother–child relationships had improved, particularly for daughters. Mothers were more affectionate. They were more likely to expect age-appropriate behaviour from their children and to discipline their children effectively. Fathers also demanded more mature behaviour of their children, but fathers had often become relatively uninvolved with their children.

Six years after divorce, the children in the study were adolescents. Family life continued to improve for mothers with daughters; many mothers and daughters grew extremely close. In contrast, family life was often problematic for mothers with sons. Mothers and sons were frequently in conflict. Neither was very happy with the other or with the overall quality of family life. Of course, conflict between mothers and adolescent sons is common when parents are married, but it is more intense with single moms, perhaps because adolescent sons are more willing to confront their mothers concerning standards for their behaviour.

Results like these from the Virginia study underscore that divorce changes family life for parents and children alike (Parke & Buriel, 1998). Next, we'll look at the effects of these changes on children's development.

> **THINK ABOUT IT**
>
> Based on the description provided here, what kinds of parental styles did mothers and fathers tend to use following divorce?

Impact of Divorce on Children

Do the disruptions, conflict, and stress associated with divorce affect children? Of course they do. Having answered this easy question, however, a host of more difficult questions remain: Are all aspects of children's lives affected equally by divorce? How does divorce influence development? Why is divorce more stressful for some children than others?

WHAT ASPECTS OF CHILDREN'S LIVES ARE AFFECTED BY DIVORCE?

By 2000, nearly 200 studies on divorce had been conducted, involving tens of thousands of preschool through college-age children. Amato (2001; Amato & Keith, 1991) conducted comprehensive meta-analyses of this research. The outcome? In school achievement, conduct, adjustment, self-concept, and parent-child relations, children whose parents had divorced fared poorly compared to children from intact families. However, the effects of divorce dropped from the 1970s to the 1980s, perhaps because as divorce became more frequent it became more familiar and less frightening. The effects of divorce increased again in the 1990s, perhaps reflecting a widening gap in income between single- and two-parent families (Amato, 2001).

When children of divorced parents become adults, the effects of divorce persist. As adults, children of divorce are more likely to become teenage parents and to become divorced themselves. Also, they report less satisfaction with life and are more likely to become depressed (Furstenberg & Teitler, 1994; Hetherington & Kelly, 2002). For example, in one study (Chase-Lansdale, Cherlin, & Kiernan, 1995), 11% of children of divorce had serious emotional problems as adults compared to 8% of children from intact families. The difference is small—11% versus 8%—but divorce does increase the risk of emotional disorders in adulthood.

Life for children after divorce is *not* all gloom and doom. Children adjust to their new circumstances (Chase-Lansdale & Hetherington, 1990). However, certain factors can ease the transition. Children adjust to divorce more readily if their divorced parents cooperate with each other, especially on disciplinary matters (Hetherington, 1989). *In joint custody, both parents retain legal custody of the children.* Children benefit from joint custody if their parents get along (Bauserman, 2002).

Of course, many parents do not get along after a divorce, which eliminates joint custody as an option. Traditionally, mothers have been awarded custody, but in recent years fathers more often have been given custody, especially of sons. This practice coincides with findings that children often adjust better when they live with same-sex parents: Boys often fare better with fathers and girls fare better with mothers (Goodman, Emery, & Haugaard, 1998). One reason boys are often better off with their fathers is that boys are likely to become involved in negative reinforcement traps (described on page 201) with their mothers. Another explanation is that both boys and girls may forge stronger emotional relationships with same-sex parents than with other-sex parents (Zimiles & Lee, 1991).

HOW DOES DIVORCE INFLUENCE DEVELOPMENT?

Divorce usually results in several changes to family life that affect children (Amato & Keith, 1991). First, the absence of one parent means that children lose a role model, a source of parental help and emotional support, and a supervisor. For instance, a single parent may have to choose between helping one child complete an important paper and watching another child perform in a school play. She can't do both, and one child will miss out.

Second, single-parent families experience economic hardship, which creates stress and often means that activities once taken for granted are no longer available (Goodman et al., 1998). A family may no longer be able to afford books for pleasure reading, music lessons, or other activities that promote child development. Moreover, when a single parent worries about having enough money for food and rent, she has less energy and effort to devote to parenting.

Third, conflict between parents is extremely distressing to children and adolescents (Fincham, 1998), particularly for children who are emotionally insecure (Davies & Cummings, 1998). In fact, many of the problems ascribed to divorce are really caused by marital conflict occurring before the divorce (Erel & Burman, 1995; Shaw, Winslow, & Flanagan, 1999). Children whose parents are married but fight constantly often show many of the same effects associated with divorce (Katz & Woodin, 2002).

WHICH CHILDREN ARE MOST AFFECTED BY DIVORCE? WHY? Some children are more affected by divorce than others. Amato and Keith's (1991) analysis, for example, showed that although the overall impact of divorce is the same for boys and girls, divorce is more harmful when it occurs during childhood and adolescence than during the preschool or college years. Also, children who are temperamentally more emotional tend to be more affected by divorce (Lengua et al., 1999).

Some children suffer more from divorce because of their tendency to interpret events negatively. Suppose, for example, that a father forgets to take a child on a promised outing. One child might believe that an emergency prevented the father from taking the child. A second child might believe that the father hadn't really wanted to spend time with the child in the first place and will never make similar plans again. Children like the second child, who tend to interpret life events negatively, are more likely to have behavioural problems following divorce (Mazur et al., 1999).

Finally, when children actively cope with problems brought on by divorce—either by trying to solve them or by trying to make them feel less threatening—they gain confidence in their ability to control future events in their lives. This confidence acts as a buffer against anxiety or depression, which can be triggered when children feel that problems brought on by divorce are insurmountable (Sandler et al., 2000).

Just as children can reduce the harm of divorce by being active problem solvers, parents can reduce divorce-related stress and help children adjust to their new life circumstances. Parents should explain together to children why they are divorcing and what their children can expect to happen to them. They should reassure children that they will always love them and always be their parents; parents must back up these words with actions by remaining involved in their children's lives despite the increased difficulty of doing so. Finally, parents must expect that their children will sometimes be angry or sad about the divorce, and they should encourage children to discuss these feelings with them.

To help children deal with divorce, parents should *not* compete with each other for their children's love and attention; children adjust to divorce best when they maintain good relationships with both parents. Parents should neither take out their anger with each other on their children nor criticize their ex-spouse in front of the children. Finally, parents should not ask children to mediate disputes; parents should work out problems without putting the children in the middle.

Following all these rules all the time is not easy. After all, divorce is stressful and painful for adults too. But parents owe it to their children to try to follow most of these rules most of the time to minimize the disruptive effects of their divorce on their children's development.

Blended Families

Following divorce, most children live in a single-parent household. In Canada an estimate in 2001 was that 20% of children aged 11 and younger were either born into a single parent household or had experienced their parents' divorce or separation (Government of Canada, 2002). However, most who divorce eventually remarry, and the number of children in Canada whose parents have separated, divorced, and then found new partners has been increasing. *The resulting unit, consisting of a biological parent, stepparent, and children is known as a **blended family**.* Because mothers are more often granted custody of children, the most common form of blended family is a mother, her children, and a stepfather. School-age boys typically benefit from the presence of a stepfather, particularly when he is warm and involved. School-age girls, however, do not adjust readily to their mother's remarriage, apparently because it disrupts the intimate relationship they have established with her. Nevertheless, as boys and girls leave the elementary school years and enter adolescence, both benefit from the presence of a caring stepfather (Hetherington, 1993).

Jack Hollingsworth/Photodisc

The best strategy for stepfathers is to be interested in their new stepchildren but avoid encroaching on established relationships. Newly remarried mothers must be careful that their enthusiasm for their new spouse does not come at the expense of time and affection for their children. And both parents and children need to have realistic expectations. The blended family can be successful, but it takes effort because of the complicated relationships, conflicting loyalties, and jealousies that usually exist (S. W. Anderson et al., 1999).

Over time, children adjust to the blended family. If the marriage is happy, most children profit from the presence of two caring adults. Unfortunately, second marriages are slightly more likely than first marriages to end in divorce, so many children relive the trauma. As you can imagine, another divorce—and possibly another remarriage—severely disrupts children's development, accentuating the problems that followed the initial divorce (Capaldi & Patterson, 1991).

TEST YOURSELF

1. According to the systems approach, the family consists of interacting elements that influence each other, and the family itself is _____.

2. With later-born children, parents often have more realistic expectations and are _____.

3. Among the effects of divorce on children are inadequate supervision of children,

conflict between parents, and _____.

How can an individual's culture, extended family, workplace, religious activities, and neighbourhood affect the type of parent they become?

Answers: (1) embedded in other social systems, such as neighbourhoods, (2) more relaxed in their discipline, (3) economic hardship

8.2

Peers

LEARNING OBJECTIVES

- What are the benefits of friendship?
- What are the important features of groups of children and adolescents? How do these groups influence individuals?
- Why are some children more popular than others? What are the causes and consequences of being rejected?

Peers
Friendships
Groups
Popularity and Rejection

Only 36 hours had passed since the campers arrived at Crab Orchard Summer Camp. Nevertheless, groups had already formed spontaneously based on the campers' main interests: arts and crafts, hiking, and swimming. Within each group, leaders and followers had already emerged. This happens every year, but the staff is always astonished at how quickly a "social network" emerges at camp.

The groups that form at summer camps—as well as in schools and neighbourhoods—represent one of the more complex forms of peer relationships: Many children are involved and there are many relationships. We'll examine these kinds of interactions later in this section. Let's start by looking at a simpler social relationship, friendship.

FRIENDSHIPS

As you saw in Chapters 4 and 6, peer interactions begin in late infancy and become more frequent and more influential as children grow. How do peer interactions lead to friendships? According to an influential early theory proposed by Harry Stack Sullivan (1953), the development of interpersonal relationships follows a stagelike sequence. Between 4 and 8 years of age, children single out specific peers as playmates and companions. However, the relationships are usually short-lived and the interactions often superficial. At about age 8 or 9, Sullivan proposed, more advanced cognitive development means that children begin to have their first real friendships, which are characterized by intimacy and reciprocity. Friends care for each other, and the relationship has mutual give-and-take.

More recent research provides support for some of Sullivan's ideas. By 4 or 5 years of age, many youngsters will claim to have a "best friend." If you ask them how they can tell that a child is their best friend, their comments will probably resemble those of 5-year-old Kara.

Interviewer: *Why* is Heidi your best friend?

Kara: Because she plays with me. And she's nice to me.

Interviewer: Are there any other reasons?

Kara: Yeah, she lets me play with her dolls.

Of course, older children and adolescents also have best friends, but they describe them differently. Comments by 12-year-old Shauna are typical:

Interviewer: Why is Leah your best friend?

Shauna: She helps me. And we think alike. My mom says we're like twins!

Interviewer: What else tells you that she's your best friend?

Shauna: Because I can tell her stuff—special stuff, like secrets—and I know she won't tell anybody else.

Interviewer: Anything else?

Shauna: Yeah. If we fight, later we always tell each other we're sorry.

As Sullivan proposed, Kara's description of her friendship emphasizes Heidi's role as a playmate. In contrast, Shauna's account of her friendship with Leah emphasizes trust and intimacy.

Older children and adolescents also emphasize loyalty in their friendships. They believe friends should defend one another and that friends should not deceive or abandon one another (Newcomb & Bagwell, 1995). The emphasis on loyalty in adolescent friendships apparently goes hand in hand with the emphasis on intimacy. If a friend is disloyal, adolescents are afraid they may be humiliated because their intimate thoughts and feelings will become known to a much broader circle of people (Berndt & Perry, 1990).

Intimacy is more common in friendships among girls, who are more likely than boys to have one exclusive "best friend." Because intimacy is at the core of their friendships, girls are also more likely to be concerned about the faithfulness of their friends and to worry about possible rejection by them (Buhrmester & Furman, 1987).

The emergence of intimacy in adolescent friendships means that friends also come to be seen as sources of social and emotional support. Levitt, Guacci-Franco, and Levitt (1993) asked children aged 7, 10, and 14 years of various ethnic backgrounds to whom they would turn when they need help or are bothered by something. For all ethnic groups, 7- and 10- year-olds relied on close family members—parents, siblings, and grandparents—as primary sources of support, but not friends. However, 14-year-olds relied on close family members less often and said they would turn to friends instead. Because adolescent friends share intimate thoughts and feelings, they can provide support during emotional or stressful periods (Denton & Zarbatany, 1996).

Who Are Friends?

Like the girls in the photo, most friends are alike in age, gender, and race (Hartup, 1992a). Because friends are supposed to treat each other as equals, friendships are rare between an older, more experienced child and a younger, less experienced child. Because children typically play with same-sex peers, boys and girls rarely become friends.

Of course, not only are friends usually alike in age, sex, and race but they are also drawn together because they have similar attitudes toward school, recreation, and the future (Newcomb & Bagwell, 1995). Tom, who enjoys school, likes to read, and plans to go to Harvard, will probably not befriend Barry, who thinks school is stupid, listens to his disc player constantly, and plans to quit high school to become a rock star (Haselager et al., 1998). As time passes, friends become more similar in their attitudes and values (Kandel, 1978).

Although children's friendships are overwhelmingly with members of their own sex, a few children have friendships with opposite-sex children. Who are these children and why do they have opposite-sex friendships? Boys and girls are equally likely to have opposite-sex friendships. The important factor in understanding these children is whether they have same- *and* opposite-sex friends or *only* opposite-sex friends. Children with same- and opposite-sex friendships tend to be very well adjusted whereas children with only opposite-sex friendships tend to be unpopular, less competent academically and socially, and have lower self-esteem. Apparently, children with both same- and opposite-sex friends are so socially skilled and popular that both boys and girls are eager to be their friends. In contrast, children with only opposite-sex friendships are socially unskilled, unpopular youngsters who are rejected by their same-sex peers and form friendships with opposite-sex children as a last resort (Kovacs, Parker, & Hoffman, 1996).

Quality and Consequences of Friendships

If you think back to your childhood friendships, you probably remember some that were long-lasting and satisfying as well as others that rapidly wore thin and soon

© Elan Sun Star/Index Stock Imagery

dissolved. What accounts for these differences in the quality and longevity of friendships? Sometimes friendships are brief because children have the skills to create friendships—they know funny stories, they kid around, they know good gossip—but lack the skills to sustain them—they can't keep secrets, or they're too bossy (Jiao, 1999; Parker & Seal, 1996). Sometimes friendships end because children are unwilling to compromise or negotiate when conflicts arise (Fonzi et al., 1997; Rose & Asher, 1999). And sometimes friendships end when children discover that their needs and interests aren't as similar as they thought initially (Gavin & Furman, 1996).

Considering that friendships disintegrate for many reasons, you're probably reminded that truly good friends are to be treasured. In fact, researchers consistently find that children benefit from having good friends (Berndt & Murphy, 2002). Compared to children who lack friends, children with good friends have higher self-esteem, are less likely to be lonely and depressed, and more often act prosocially—sharing and cooperating with others (Hartup & Stevens, 1999; Ladd, 1998). Children with good friends cope better with life stresses, such as the transition from elementary school to middle school or junior high (Berndt & Keefe, 1995) and they're less likely to be victimized by peers (Hodges et al., 1999). The benefits of friendship are also long-lasting; children who have friends have greater self-worth as young adults (Bagwell, Newcomb, & Bukowski, 1998).

Thus, friends are not simply special playmates and companions; they are important resources. Children learn from their friends and can turn to them for support in times of stress. Friendships are one important way in which peers influence children's development. Peers also influence development through groups, the topic of the next section.

GROUPS

At the summer camp in the vignette, new campers always form groups based on common interests. Groups are just as prevalent in schools. "Jocks," "skaters," "punks," and "geeks," you may remember these or similar terms referring to groups of older children and adolescents. During late childhood and early adolescence, the peer group becomes the focal point of social relationships for youth (Rubin, Bukowski, & Parker, 1998). *The starting point is often a **clique**—a small group of children or adolescents who are friends and tend to be similar in age, sex, race, and attitudes.* Members of a clique spend time together and often dress, talk, and act alike. *Several cliques that have similar values and attitudes sometimes become part of a larger group called a **crowd**, known by a label such as "jocks" or "geeks."*

Some crowds have more status than others. For example, students in many high schools say that the "jocks" are the most prestigious crowd, whereas the "geeks" may be among the least prestigious. Self-esteem in older children and adolescents often reflects the status of their crowd. During the school years, young people from high-status crowds tend to have greater self-esteem than those from low-status crowds (Brown & Lohr, 1987).

Why do some students join one group rather than another? Parenting style is part of the answer. A study by Brown and his colleagues (1993) examined the impact of three parental practices on students' membership in particular crowds. The investigators measured the extent to which parents emphasized academic achievement, monitored their children's out-of-school activities, and involved their children in joint decision-making. They found that types of parenting practices affected groups that students joined. What seems to happen is that when parents use the practices associated with authoritative parenting—control coupled with warmth—their children become involved with crowds that endorse adult standards of behaviour. However, when parents' style is uninvolved or indulgent, their children are less likely to identify with adult standards of behaviour. In fact, they become involved with crowds who disavow these standards.

Group Structure

Groups—be they in school, at a summer camp as in the vignette, or elsewhere—typically have a well-defined structure. *Often groups have a **dominance hierarchy**, headed by a leader to whom all other members of the group defer.* Other members know their position in the hierarchy. They yield to members who are above them in the hierarchy and assert themselves over members who are below them. A dominance hierarchy is useful in reducing conflict within groups because every member knows his or her place.

What determines where members stand in the hierarchy? In children, especially boys, physical power is often the basis for the dominance hierarchy. The leader is usually the member who is the most intimidating physically (Pettit et al., 1990). Among girls and older boys, hierarchies are often based on individual traits that relate to the group's main function. At Crab Orchard Summer Camp, for example, the leaders are most often the children with the greatest camping experience. Among Girl Scouts, girls chosen to be patrol leaders tend to be bright and goal-oriented and to have new ideas (Edwards, 1994). These characteristics are appropriate, because the primary function of patrols is to help plan activities for an entire troop of Girl Scouts or Girl Guides. Thus, this type of group structure is effective; the people with the most useful skills have the greatest influence (Rubin, Bukowski, & Parker, 1998).

THINK ABOUT IT

Chapter 6 described important differences in the ways boys and girls interact with same-sex peers. How might these differences help explain why boys' and girls' dominance hierarchies differ?

Peer Pressure

Groups establish norms—standards of behaviour that apply to all group members. Groups may pressure members to conform to these norms. Such "peer pressure" is often characterized as an irresistible, harmful force. The stereotype is that teenagers exert enormous pressure on each other to behave antisocially. In reality, peer pressure is neither all-powerful nor always evil. For example, most high school students *resist* peer pressure to behave in ways that are clearly antisocial, such as stealing (Brown, Lohr, & McClenahan, 1986). Peer pressure can be positive too, such as urging peers to participate in school or community activities.

Peer pressure is most powerful when the standards for appropriate behaviour are not clear-cut. Tastes in music and clothing, for example, are completely subjective; consequently, youth conform to peer group guidelines, as you can see in the all-too-familiar sight shown in the photo on page 290—girls wearing very similar "in" clothing.

Similarly, standards concerning smoking, drinking, and using drugs are often fuzzy. Drinking is a good case in point. Parents and groups like OSAID (Ontario Students Against Impaired Driving) may discourage teens from drinking, yet our North American culture is filled with youthful models who drink, seem to enjoy it,

Brand X Pictures

and suffer no apparent ill effects. To the contrary, they seem to enjoy life even more. With such contradictory messages, it is not surprising that youths look to their peers for answers (Urberg, Değirmencioğlu, & Pilgrim, 1997). Consequently, some youths *will* drink (or smoke, use drugs, have sex) to conform to *their* group's norms; others will abstain, again, reflecting their group's norms.

Even when standards are fuzzy, not all teenagers are equally susceptible to peer influence (Vitaro et al., 1997). Adolescents are less likely to be influenced by peer pressure when their parents use an authoritative style and are more likely to be influenced when their parents are not authoritative (Mounts & Steinberg, 1995).

POPULARITY AND REJECTION

Eileen is, without question, the most popular child in her Grade 4 class. Most of the other youngsters like to play with her and want to sit near her at lunch or on the school bus. Whenever the class must vote to pick a child for something special—to be class representative to the student council, to recite the class poem on Remembrance Day, or to lead the classroom to the lunchroom—Eileen invariably wins.

Jay is not as fortunate as Eileen. In fact, he is the least popular child in the class. His presence is obviously unwanted in any situation. When he sits down at the lunch table, other kids move away. When he tries to join a game of tag, the others quit. Students in the class detest Jay as much as they like Eileen.

Popular and rejected children like Eileen and Jay are common. In fact, studies of popularity (Rubin, Bukowski, & Parker, 1998) reveal that most children in elementary school classrooms can be placed, fairly consistently, in one of five categories:

- *Popular children* are liked by many classmates.
- *Rejected children* are disliked by many classmates.
- *Controversial children* are both liked and disliked by classmates.
- *Average children* are liked and disliked by some classmates, but without the intensity found for popular, rejected, or controversial children.
- *Neglected children* are ignored by classmates.

What determines who's hot and who's not? Why is a child popular, rejected, controversial, or neglected? Smarter and physically attractive children are more often popular (Johnstone, Frame, & Bouman, 1992). However, the most important ingredient in popularity is social skill. Popular children are better at initiating social interactions with other children (Rubin, Bukowski, & Parker, 1998). They are more skilful at communicating and better at integrating themselves into an ongoing conversation or play session. Popular children also seem relatively gifted in assessing and monitoring their own social impact in various situations and in tailoring their responses to the requirements of each new social situation (Crick & Dodge, 1994; Wentzel & Asher, 1995). For example, Wentzel and Erdley (1993) asked Grades 6 and 7 children to evaluate their peers' prosocial behaviour, antisocial behaviour, and popularity. Popular youngsters were more likely than unpopular children to share, cooperate, and help; popular children were also less likely to start fights and break rules.

Why do some children fail in their efforts to be popular and end up in one of the other categories—rejected, controversial, average, or neglected? We know the most about rejected children, who tend to be socially unskilled (Harrist et al., 1997). Many rejected children are aggressive. When children are too bossy or tease others too much, their peers quickly shun them (Rubin, Chen, & Hymel, 1993). Other rejected children are withdrawn and timid (Volling et al., 1993). When children act "like babies," their peers start to avoid them.

Being well liked seems straightforward: Be pleasant and friendly, not obnoxious. Share, cooperate, and help instead of being disruptive. These results hold for children in many areas of the world, including Canada, the U.S., Europe, Israel, and China. Sometimes, however, popular children have other characteristics unique to their cultural setting. In Israel, for example, popular children are more likely to be assertive and direct (Krispin, Sternberg, & Lamb, 1992). In China, popular children are more likely to be shy (Chen, Rubin, & Li, 1995). Evidently, good social skills are at the core of popularity in most countries, but other features are important, reflecting culturally specific values.

THINK ABOUT IT
Effective parents and popular children have many characteristics in common. What are they?

Consequences of Rejection

No one enjoys being rejected. For children, repeated peer rejection in childhood can have serious long-term consequences, including dropping out of school, committing juvenile offences, and suffering from psychopathology (Bagwell et al., 1998; Rubin, Bukowski, & Parker, 1998). The Spotlight on Research describes one study that shows some of the long-term effects of popularity and rejection.

SPOTLIGHT ON RESEARCH

Long-Term Consequences of Popularity and Rejection

Who were the investigators and what was the aim of the study? Is the outcome of development the same for popular and unpopular children? Or do popularity and rejection steer children down different developmental paths? Patricia Morison and Ann Masten (1991) wanted to answer these questions.

How did the investigators measure the topic of interest? Morison and Masten identified popular and rejected children by asking students in Grades 3 to 6 to nominate classmates for roles in an imaginary class play.

Popular children were identified as those who were frequently nominated for roles like "a good leader," "everyone likes to be with," and "has many friends." Rejected children were those frequently nominated for roles like "picks on other kids," "too bossy," and "teases other children too much." Seven years later, children and their parents completed questionnaires measuring academic achievement, social skill, and self-worth.

Who were the children in the study? Initially, 207 children in Grades 3 to 6 were tested, and 183 of them completed the questionnaires seven years later.

What was the design of the study? This study was correlational because Morison and Masten were interested in the relation that existed naturally between two sets of variables: popularity and rejection at the first testing and academic achievement, social skill, and self-worth at the second. The study was longitudinal because children were tested twice, once in Grades 3 to 6 and again seven years later.

Were there ethical concerns with the study? No. The general purpose of the study was explained and then parents and children consented to participate.

What were the results? Figure 8.2 shows correlations between popularity and rejection in Grades 3 to 6, and academic achievement, social skill, and self-worth measured seven years later. Children popular in Grades 3 to 6 were doing well in school, were socially skilled,

and had high self-esteem. In contrast, children who were most rejected in Grades 3 to 6 were not doing well in school and had low self-esteem.

What did the investigators conclude? Popular children fit in with groups instead of making groups adjust to them. When conflicts arise, popular children try to understand the problem and provide solutions. Over time, popular children's prosocial skill pays dividends; unfortunately, rejected children's lack of skill has a price as well.

What converging evidence would strengthen these conclusions? One useful step would be to continue the longitudinal study to examine the consequences of rejection later in adolescence. Another important addition would be to replace the questionnaires used to measure social skill with observations of actual social skills in a natural setting.

FIGURE 8.2   **Effects of Popularity**

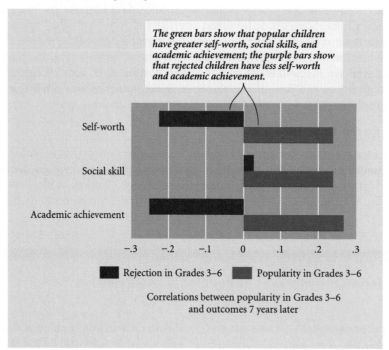

SOURCE: Based on data from Morison and Masten, 1991.

Causes of Rejection

Peer rejection can be traced, at least in part, to the influences of parents (Ladd & Le Sieur, 1995; Pettit & Mize, 1993). As expected from Bandura's social cognitive theory, children see how their parents respond in different social situations and often imitate these responses later. Parents who are friendly and cooperative with others demonstrate effective social skills for their youngsters. Parents who are belligerent and combative demonstrate tactics that are much less effective. In particular, when parents typically respond to interpersonal conflict with intimidation or aggression, their children may imitate them, hampering the development of their social skills and making them less popular in the long run (Keane, Brown, & Crenshaw, 1990).

Parents also contribute to their children's social skill and popularity through their disciplinary practices. Inconsistent discipline—punishing a child for misbehaving one day and ignoring the same behaviour the next—is associated with antisocial, aggressive behaviour, paving the way for rejection. Consistent punishment that does not rely on power assertion but is tied to parental love and affection is more likely to promote social skill and, in the process, popularity (Dekovic & Janssens, 1992; Rubin, Stewart, & Chen, 1995).

Thus, the origins of rejection are clear. Socially awkward, aggressive children are often rejected because they rely on an aggressive interpersonal style, which can be traced to parenting. The implication is that by teaching youngsters (and their parents) more effective ways of interacting with others, we can make rejection less likely. With improved social skills, rejected children would not need to resort to antisocial behaviours that peers deplore. Training of this sort *does* work. Rejected children can learn skills that lead to peer acceptance and thereby avoid the long-term harm associated with being rejected (LaGreca, 1993; Mize & Ladd, 1990).

© Benelux Press/Index Stock Imagery

Bullying

Another form of distress that some children experience that may or may not be seen in conjunction with rejection behaviours is bullying. In fact, rejecting behaviours may in themselves be viewed as a form of bullying. Bullying has been defined as a type of aggressive behaviour in which one child uses power in an aggressive manner, causing a victim distress through physical and/or verbal means (Pepler et al., 1993). The effects of bullying can be mild to extreme, can affect the daily lives of children, and can affect the social, psychological, and emotional status of individuals right into adulthood.

One study (O'Connell et al., 1997) examined the prevalence of bullying and victimization among 4,743 Canadian elementary and middle school children and found these experiences were not uncommon. Almost a third (29.5%) of children reported bullying others at least once or twice during the term, and over a third (38%) of children reported being bullied at least once or twice during the term. There were no gender differences in either bullying or victimization. These researchers concluded that bullying is a pervasive problem that may require intervention by parents and teachers because of the long-term effects on children, whether as victims, bullies, or witnesses (O'Connell et al., 1997).

TEST YOURSELF

1. Friends are usually similar in age, sex, race, and _____.

2. Children with friends have higher self-esteem, are less likely to be lonely, and _____ than children without friends.

3. As a group forms, a _____ typically emerges, with the leader at the top.

4. Peer pressure is most powerful when _____.

5. Popular children are usually _____.

6. Rejected youngsters are more likely to drop out of school, to commit juvenile offences, and _____.

How could developmental change in the nature of friendship be explained in terms of Piaget's stages of intellectual development, discussed in Chapters 3 and 5?

Answers: (1) interests, (2) more often act prosocially (sharing and cooperating), (3) dominance hierarchy, (4) standards for appropriate behaviour are vague, (5) socially skilled, (6) to suffer from psychopathology

8.3

Television: Window on the World or Negative Influence?

LEARNING OBJECTIVES

- What is the impact of watching television on children's attitudes and behaviour?
- How does TV viewing influence children's cognitive development?
- Does TV viewing per se affect children?

> **Television: Window on the World or Negative Influence?**
> Influence on Attitudes and Social Behaviour
> Influences on Cognition
> Criticisms of TV

Every day, 7-year-old Robert follows the same routine when he gets home from school: He watches one action-adventure cartoon after another until it's time for dinner. Robert's mother is disturbed by her son's constant TV viewing, particularly because of the amount of violence in the shows he likes. Her husband tells her to stop worrying: "Let him watch what he wants to. It won't hurt him, and besides, it keeps him out of our hair."

A typical North American child and adolescent spends much more time watching TV than interacting with his parents or in school. A U.S. study indicates that a high school graduate has watched 20,000 hours of TV (Nielson, 1990)—the equivalent of two full years of watching TV 24 hours daily! No wonder social scientists and laypeople alike have come to see TV as an important contributor to the socialization of North American children.

Of course, not all children watch the same amount of TV. For most youngsters, however, viewing time increases gradually during the preschool and elementary school years, reaching a peak at about 11 or 12 years of age. Boys watch more TV than girls. Also, children with lower IQs watch more than those with higher IQs; children from lower-income families watch more TV than children from higher-income families (Huston & Wright, 1998).

It is hard to imagine that such massive viewing of TV would have no effect on children's behaviour. After all, 30-second TV ads are designed to influence children's preferences in toys, cereals, and hamburgers, so the programs themselves ought to have even more impact.

INFLUENCE ON ATTITUDES AND SOCIAL BEHAVIOUR

Ever since television became a common fixture in North American homes in the 1950s, citizens have been concerned about violence on TV. For good reason: Children's cartoons typically have one violent act every three minutes. (The term *violence* here refers to use of physical force against another person.) The average North American youngster will see several thousand murders on TV before reaching adolescence (Waters, 1993).

Photodisc

What is the impact of this steady diet of televised mayhem and violence? According to Bandura's (1986) social cognitive theory, described in Chapter 1, children learn by observing others; they watch others and often imitate what they see. Applied to TV, this theory predicts more aggressive behaviour from children who watch violent TV. This prediction was supported by laboratory studies conducted in the 1960s (Bandura, Ross, & Ross, 1963). Children watched specially created TV programs in which an adult behaved violently toward a plastic "Bobo" doll; the adult kicked and hit the doll with a plastic hammer. When children were given the opportunity to play with the doll, those who had seen the TV program were much more likely to behave aggressively toward the doll than were children who had not seen the program.

Critics noted many limitations in this and other early studies and doubted that viewing TV violence in more realistic settings would have such pronounced effects on children (Klapper, 1968). Consequently, scientists began to study the impact of viewing actual TV violence on children's behaviour. The results of this research showed a consistent result: Frequent exposure to TV violence causes children to be more aggressive (Huston & Wright, 1998).

One of the most compelling studies examined the impact of children's TV viewing at age 8 on criminal activity at age 30 (Huesmann & Miller, 1994). Figure 8.3 shows quite clearly that 8-year-olds exposed to large doses of TV violence had the most extensive criminal records as 30-year-olds. The link was found for both males and females, although females' level of criminal activity was much lower overall.

More recent studies (e.g., Johnson et al., 2002) confirm the long-term impact of TV on aggression and violence, particularly for boys, even when confounding variables such as parents' education and family income are controlled. What's more, playing violent video games seems to lead to violence in much the same way that watching violent TV does (Anderson & Bushman, 2001). Children and adolescents who play violent video games frequently tend to be more aggressive and less altruistic. In a comprehensive review of the effects of television violence on different ages, Canadian researcher Wendy Josephson (1995) concludes that middle childhood is considered an especially important period to understand these effects due to the fact

FIGURE 8.3   Effects of TV on Boys

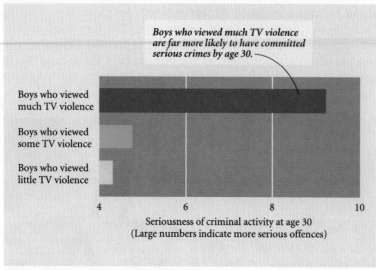

SOURCE: Based on data in Huesmann and Miller, 1994.

that there is so much TV watched during this period. In addition, between the ages of 10 and 12 years is when long-term interests are developed and behaviour patterns are formed (Winick & Winick, 1979).

Thus, children like Robert who frequently view TV violence learn to resort to aggression in their interactions with others. Of course, violence is only one part of what children see on TV. Let's examine other ways in which TV is an important influence on children as they develop.

Stereotypes

TV is said to provide a "window on the world." Unfortunately, the view on prime time TV is distorted, particularly when it comes to minorities, women, and the elderly. Members of minority groups appear very infrequently in prime time (Huston & Wright, 1998). In contrast, educational programs for children often include minority characters and often depict them in positions of authority (Williams & Cox, 1995).

The situation is much the same for women and the elderly. Their portrayal on prime time TV bears little resemblance to reality. No more than one-third of all TV roles are for women. When women are shown on TV, they are often passive and emotional. Most are not employed; those who have jobs are often in stereotypical female careers such as teachers or secretaries (Huston & Wright, 1998). Also, the land of television evidently has a fountain of youth, because older Americans are grossly underrepresented. Although a growing portion of the North American population is 60 or older, less than 5% of the characters in prime time TV are that age. Ironically, older adults on TV are usually men, despite the fact that women far outnumber men at this point in the life span (Gerbner, 1993).

Surprisingly, we know relatively little about the effects of these stereotyped portrayals on children's attitudes toward minorities or the elderly. However, the impact of the stereotyped presentation of males and females is clear. As you can imagine, children who watch TV frequently end up with more stereotyped views of males and females. For example, Kimball (1986) studied sex-role stereotypes in a small Canadian town located in a valley that could not receive TV programs until a transmitter was installed nearby. Two years later, views of personality traits, behaviours,

THINK ABOUT IT

Some skeptics remark that TV programming is simply a reflection of society at large, so children are learning nothing—good or bad— that they wouldn't learn from their culture sooner or later. Do you agree?

FIGURE 8.4   Effects of TV on Children's Stereotyping

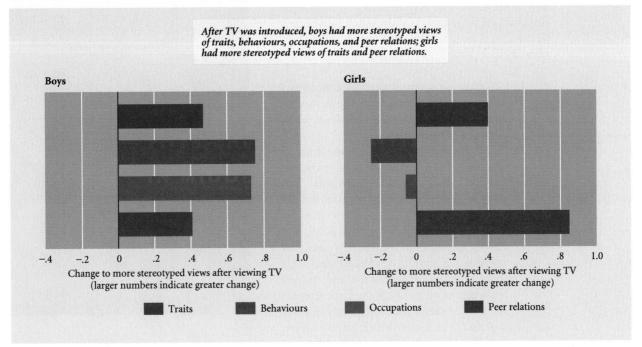

After TV was introduced, boys had more stereotyped views of traits, behaviours, occupations, and peer relations; girls had more stereotyped views of traits and peer relations.

SOURCE: Based on data in Kimball, 1986.

occupations, and peer relations were measured in the town's children. Figure 8.4 shows that boys' and girls' views on these issues became more stereotyped after TV was introduced. For example, after the introduction of TV, girls had more stereotyped views of peer relations. They believed that boasting and swearing were characteristic of boys but that sharing and helping were characteristic of girls. The boys in the town acquired more stereotyped views of occupations, believing that girls could be teachers and cooks, whereas boys could be physicians and judges.

Findings like these indicate that TV viewing causes children to adopt many of the stereotypes that dominate television programming (Signorielli & Lears, 1992). For many children and adolescents, TV's slanted depiction of the world *becomes* reality.

Consumer Behaviour

Sugary cereals, hamburgers and French fries, snack foods, expensive toys—these products are the focus of a phenomenal amount of TV advertising directed toward children. A typical youngster may see more than 50 commercials a day! As early as 3 years of age, children distinguish commercials from programs. However, preschool children often believe commercials are simply a different form of entertainment— one designed to inform viewers. Not until 8 or 9 years of age do most children understand the persuasive intent of commercials. At the same time that children grasp the aim of commercials, they begin to realize that commercials are not always truthful (Liebert & Sprafkin, 1988).

Commercials are effective sales tools with children. Children grow to like many of the products advertised on TV. Like the youngster in the photograph on page 298, they may urge parents to buy products they have seen on television. In one study (Greenberg, Fazel, & Weber, 1986), more than 75% of the children reported that they had asked their parents to buy a product they had seen advertised on TV. More often than not, parents purchased the product for them!

This selling power of TV commercials has long concerned advocates for children, because so many ads focus on children's foods that have little nutritional value and that are associated with problems such as obesity and tooth decay. The responsibility to determine the kinds of programs children watch falls largely to parents. Here are some ways for parents to regulate their children's TV viewing:

- Children need absolute rules concerning the amount of TV and the types of programs they can watch. These rules must be enforced consistently!
- Children shouldn't fall into the trap of "I'm bored, so I'll watch TV." Children should be encouraged to know what they want to watch *before* they turn on the TV set.
- Adults should watch TV with children and discuss the programs. Parents can, for example, express their disapproval of a character's use of aggression and suggest other means of resolving conflicts. Parents can also point to the stereotypes that are depicted. The aim is for children to learn that TV's account of the world is often inaccurate and to encourage the children to watch TV critically. (What may happen, of course, is that they can't stand the parent's constant chatter and stop watching altogether!)
- Parents need to be good TV viewers themselves. The first two tips listed here apply to viewers of all ages! When a child is present, parents shouldn't watch violent programs or others that are inappropriate for the young. And parents should throw away the remote control so that they, too, will watch TV deliberately and selectively, not mindlessly flip between channels.

Prosocial Behaviour

TV is clearly a potent influence on children's aggression and on the stereotypes they form. Can this power be put to more prosocial goals? Can TV viewing help children learn to be more generous, to be more cooperative, and to have greater self-control? Yes, according to early laboratory studies. In these experiments, children were more likely to act prosocially after they watched brief films in which a peer acted prosocially. For example, children were more likely to share or more likely to resist the temptation to take from others when they had seen a filmed peer sharing or resisting temptation (Liebert & Sprafkin, 1988).

Research with actual TV programs leads to the same conclusion. Youngsters who watch TV shows that emphasize prosocial behaviour, such as *Mister Rogers' Neighborhood,* are more likely to behave prosocially (Huston & Wright, 1998). In fact, the impact of viewing prosocial TV programs is much greater than the impact of viewing televised violence (Hearold, 1986). Boys, in particular, benefit from viewing prosocial TV, perhaps because they are usually much less skilled prosocially than girls are.

Although research indicates that prosocial behaviour *can* be influenced by TV watching, two important factors restrict the actual prosocial impact of TV viewing. First, prosocial behaviours are portrayed on TV programs far less frequently than aggressive behaviours; opportunities to learn prosocial behaviours from television are limited. Second, in the real world of TV watching, the relatively small number of prosocial programs must compete with other kinds of television programs, as well as other activities, for children's time.

THINK ABOUT IT

Would all developmental theories predict that *merely* watching prosocial behaviour on TV is enough to lead children to behave prosocially themselves?

Children simply may not watch the few prosocial programs that are televised. Clearly, we are far from harnessing the power of television for prosocial uses.

INFLUENCES ON COGNITION

You undoubtedly know Big Bird, Kermit the Frog, Cookie Monster, Oscar the Grouch, and their friends, for they are the cast of *Sesame Street,* one of the longest-running shows in TV history. First appearing in 1969, *Sesame Street* has helped educate generations of preschoolers. Today, mothers and fathers who watched *Sesame Street* as preschoolers are watching with their own youngsters.

Produced by Children's Television Workshop, the goal of *Sesame Street* was to use the power of video and animation to foster skills like recognizing letters and numbers, counting, and vocabulary in preschool children. Evaluations conducted in the early years of *Sesame Street* showed that the program achieved its goals—preschoolers who watched *Sesame Street* regularly were more proficient at the targeted academic skills than were children who watched less often. And frequent viewers adjusted to school more readily, according to teachers' ratings (Bogatz & Ball, 1972).

Studies have confirmed these benefits. Wright and Huston (1995), for example, found that preschoolers who watch *Sesame Street* frequently have larger vocabularies and better math and prereading skills, and are better prepared for school than preschoolers who watch infrequently. Importantly, these gains were the same for children of different ethnic backgrounds and children from lower-class and middle-class homes.

Building on the success of *Sesame Street,* Children's Television Workshop developed a number of other successful programs. *Electric Company* was designed to teach reading skills, *3-2-1 Contact* has a science and technology focus, and *Square One TV* aims at mathematics (Liebert & Sprafkin, 1988). More recent programs have included *Reading Rainbow, Ghostwriter, Where in the World Is Carmen Sandiego?* and *Bill Nye Science Guy.* These programs have not been evaluated to the same extent as *Sesame Street.* However, the typical finding is that children who watch these sorts of programs frequently improve their academic skills and develop more positive attitudes as well (Huston & Wright, 1998).

Programs like these leave little doubt that TV's socializing influence need not be limited to learning aggression and stereotypes. Children *can* learn academic skills and useful social skills if parents insist that their youngsters be good viewers and if they insist that TV improve the quality and variety of programs available for children and adolescents.

CRITICISMS OF TV

Television has its critics. Although they concede that some TV programs help children learn, they also argue that the medium itself—independent of the contents of programs—has several harmful effects on viewers, particularly children (Huston & Wright, 1998). One common criticism is that because TV programs consist of many brief segments presented in rapid succession, children who watch a lot of TV develop short attention spans and have difficulty concentrating in school. Another concern heard frequently is that because TV provides ready-made, simple-to-interpret images, children who watch a lot of TV become passive, lazy thinkers and become less creative.

In fact, as stated, neither criticism is consistently supported by research (Huston & Wright, 1998). The first criticism—TV watching reduces attention—is the easiest to dismiss. Research repeatedly shows that increased TV viewing does not lead to reduced attention, greater impulsivity, reduced task persistence, or increased activity levels. The contents of TV programs can influence these dimensions of children's behaviour—children who watch impulsive models behave more impulsively themselves—but TV per se does not harm children's ability to pay attention.

As for the criticism that TV viewing fosters lazy thinking and stifles creativity, the evidence is mixed. Many studies find no link between amount of TV viewing and creativity (Anderson et al., 2001). Some find a negative relation; as children watch more TV, they tend to get lower scores on tests of creativity (Valkenburg & van der Voort, 1994, 1995). Researchers don't know why the negative effects aren't found more consistently, although one idea is that the effects depend on what programs children watch, not simply the amount of TV watched.

In general, then, although the contents of TV programs can clearly influence children (positively or negatively, depending on what children watch), there is no strong evidence that TV watching per se has harmful effects on children.

TEST YOURSELF

1. When children watch a lot of TV violence, they often become _____.

2. Preschool children believe commercials _____.

3. Youngsters who watch *Sesame Street* frequently improve their academic skills and, according to their teachers, _____.

4. Contrary to popular criticisms, frequent TV-viewing is not consistently related to reduced attention or to _____.

Use the difference between divergent and convergent thinking, explained in Chapter 5, to describe the impact of TV viewing on children.

Answers: (1) more aggressive, (2) represent a different, informative type of program but do not understand the intent to persuade, (3) adjust to school more readily, (4) reduced creativity

8.4

Understanding Others

LEARNING OBJECTIVES

■ As children develop, how do they describe others differently?

■ How does understanding of others' thinking change as children develop?

■ When do children develop prejudice toward others?

Understanding Others
Describing Others
Understanding What Others Think
Prejudice

When 12-year-old Ian agreed to baby-sit his 5-year-old brother, Kyle, their mother reminded Ian to keep Kyle out of the basement because Kyle's birthday presents were there, unwrapped. But as soon as their mother left, Kyle wanted to go to the basement to ride his tricycle. When Ian told him no, Kyle burst into angry tears and shouted, "I'm gonna tell Mom that you were mean to me!" Ian wished he could explain to Kyle but he knew that would just cause more trouble!

As children spend more time with other people, they begin to understand them better. In this vignette, for example, Ian realizes why Kyle is angry and he knows that if he gives in to Kyle now, his mother will be angry when she returns. Children's growing understanding of others is the focus of this section. We begin by looking at how children describe others, then examine their understanding of how others think. Finally, we'll also see how children's recognition of different social groups can lead to prejudices.

DESCRIBING OTHERS

As children develop, more sophisticated cognitive processes cause self-descriptions to become richer, more abstract, and more psychological. These same changes occur in children's descriptions of others. Children begin by describing other people by concrete features, such as behaviour, and progress to describing them by abstract traits (Barenboim, 1981; Livesley & Bromley, 1973). The Real People feature shows this progression in one child.

REAL PEOPLE: APPLYING HUMAN DEVELOPMENT

Tell Me About a Girl That You Like a Lot

Every few years, Tamsen was asked to describe a girl that she liked a lot. Each time, she described a different girl. More important, the contents of her descriptions changed, focusing less on behaviour and emphasizing psychological properties. Let's start with the description she gave as a 7-year-old:

> Vanessa is short. She has black hair and brown eyes. She uses a wheelchair because she can't walk. She's in my class. She has dolls just like mine. She likes to sing and read.

Tamsen's description of Vanessa is probably not too different from the way she would have described herself. The emphasis is on concrete characteristics, such as Vanessa's appearance, possessions, and preferences. Contrast this with the following description, which Tamsen gave as a 10-year-old:

> Cindy lives in my apartment. She is a very good reader and is also good at math and science. She's nice to everyone in our class. And she's very funny. Sometimes her jokes make me laugh so-o-o hard! She takes piano lessons and likes to play soccer.

Tamsen's account still includes concrete features, such as where Cindy lives and what she likes to do. However, psychological traits are also evident: Tamsen describes Cindy as nice and funny. By age 10, children move beyond the purely concrete and observable in describing others. During adolescence, descriptions become even more complex, as you can see in the following, from Tamsen as a 16-year-old:

> Jeannie is very understanding. Whenever anyone at school is upset, she's there to give a helping hand. Yet in private Jeannie can be so sarcastic. She can say some really nasty things about people. But I know she'd never say that stuff if she thought people would hear it because she wouldn't want to hurt their feelings.

This description is more abstract: Tamsen now focuses on psychological traits like understanding and concern for others' feelings. It's also more integrated: Tamsen tries to explain how Jeannie can be both understanding and sarcastic. 〽️

Each of Tamsen's three descriptions is very typical. As a 7-year-old, she emphasized concrete characteristics; as a 10-year-old, she began to include psychological traits; and as a 16-year-old, she tried to integrate traits to form a cohesive account.

The progression in how children perceive others was illustrated vividly in a classic study by Livesley and Bromley (1973). They interviewed 320 7- to 15-year-olds attending school in Merseyside, England (near Liverpool, home of the Beatles). All participants were asked to describe eight people they knew: two boys, two girls, two men, and two women. The examiner told the participants, "I want you to describe what sort of person they are. I want you to tell me what you think about them and what they are like" (p. 97).

The participants at different ages typically produced descriptions much like Tamsen's at different ages. Livesley and Bromley then categorized the contents of the descriptions. Some of their results appear in Figure 8.5. Descriptions referring to appearances or possessions become less common as children grow older, as do descriptions giving general information, such as the person's age, gender, religion, or school. In contrast, descriptions of personality traits (e.g., "friendly" or "conceited") increased between 8 and 14 years of age. Thus, children's descriptions of others begin with the concrete and later become more conceptual.

FIGURE 8.5   Children's Progression in Describing People

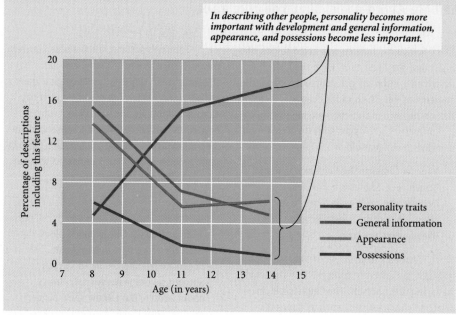

SOURCE: Based on data from Livesley and Bromley, 1973.

By the time they enter school, children use the information in their descriptions to predict others' future behaviour (Heyman & Gelman, 1999; Yuill & Pearson, 1998). To illustrate, suppose kindergarten children are told that Alissa did something nice (e.g., helped another child finish a difficult puzzle), but Celeste did something mean (e.g., scribbled in another child's favourite book). Kindergarten children will judge that, in the future, Alissa is more likely than Celeste to help a child who is hurt, to give money to a needy child, and to hope that an elaborate art project turns out well for the child who created it. Thus, descriptions of others are useful, even for young children, because they allow children to predict how others will behave in the future.

UNDERSTANDING WHAT OTHERS THINK

One trademark of the preschooler's thinking is difficulty in seeing the world from another's view. Piaget's term for this is egocentrism, and it is a defining characteristic of his preoperational stage of development. As children move beyond the preschool years, though, they realize that others see the world differently, both literally and figuratively. For example, in the vignette, Ian knows why his little brother Kyle is angry—Kyle thinks Ian is being bossy and mean—and Ian understands that Kyle doesn't know there is a good reason why he can't go to the basement.

Sophisticated understanding of how others think is achieved gradually throughout childhood and adolescence. Robert Selman (1980, 1981) proposed a theory of how understanding others' thinking—perspective-taking, for short—occurs. Selman's theory is based on two of Piaget's key assumptions, namely, that understanding of others occurs in stages and that movement from one stage to the next is based on cognitive development.

Selman (1980) based his theory on children's responses to social dilemmas like this one:

> Holly is an 8-year-old girl who likes to climb trees. She is the best tree climber in the neighborhood. One day while climbing down from a tall tree she falls off the bottom branch but does not hurt herself. Her father sees her fall. He is upset and asks her to promise not to climb trees anymore. Holly promises.
>
> Later that day, Holly and her friends meet Sean. Sean's kitten is caught up in a tree and cannot get down. Something has to be done right away or the kitten may fall. Holly is the only one who climbs well enough to reach the kitten and get it down, but she remembers her promise to her father. (Selman & Byrne, 1974, p. 805)

This dilemma is typical in that it includes several people who don't share the same knowledge about the events taking place. After hearing the story, children and adolescents were asked questions to investigate their ability to take on each character's view and predict what would happen to Holly.

Selman found that answers to dilemmas like this became more sophisticated as children developed. In fact, he proposed the five different stages of perspective-taking shown in Table 8.1.

TABLE 8.1		Selman's Stages of Perspective-Taking
Stage	**Approximate Ages**	**Description**
Undifferentiated	3–6 years	Children know that self and others can have different thoughts and feelings but often confuse the two.
Social-informational	4–9 years	Children know that perspectives differ because people have access to different information.
Self-reflective	7–12 years	Children can step into another's shoes and view themselves as others do. They know that others can do the same.
Third-person	10–15 years	Children can step outside of the immediate situation to see how they and another person are viewed by a third person.
Societal	14 years to adult	Adolescents realize that a third person's perspective is influenced by broader personal, social, and cultural contexts.

The first stage is called undifferentiated because children in this stage get confused about "who thinks what." A child in this stage might reply, "Holly's father will be happy because he likes kittens." This answer confuses Holly's feelings with her father's and ignores Holly's promise. Children in the social-informational stage might say, "If Holly's father knew why she climbed the tree, he probably wouldn't be angry." This answer indicates that the child understands that the father's response depends on whether he knows the reason for Holly's behaviour.

In the self-reflective stage, a child might say, "Holly's father would understand that she thought saving the kitten's life was really important, so he wouldn't be mad. He'd probably be proud." This comment

THINK ABOUT IT

How do Selman's stages of perspective-taking correspond to Piaget's and Erikson's stages?

shows Holly's father stepping into Holly's shoes, the defining characteristic of the self-reflective stage.

At the next level, the third-person stage, a child might respond, "Holly remembers the promise, but she doesn't think her father will be angry when she explains that she wouldn't have climbed the tree except to save the kitten's life. Her father might wish that Holly had asked an adult for help, but he'd also understand why it was important to Holly to save the kitten." This child simultaneously considers both Holly's and her father's perspectives on the dilemma. That is, in answering, the child has stepped outside the immediate situation to take the perspective of a neutral third party who can look at both Holly's and her father's views.

At the most advanced level, the societal stage, an adolescent might reply, "Holly and her father both know that she almost always obeys him. So, they'd both know that if she disobeyed him to climb the tree, there would have to be an awfully good reason. So, they'd talk about it." This child's answer, like the previous one, considers Holly's and her father's perspectives simultaneously. The difference is that this comment puts the issue in the broader context of the history of their father–daughter relationship.

As predicted by Selman's theory, research shows that as children develop, their reasoning moves through each stage, in sequence. In addition, regardless of age, children at more advanced cognitive levels tend to be at more advanced stages in perspective-taking (Gurucharri & Selman, 1982; Krebs & Gillmore, 1982).

Other support for Selman's theory comes from studies of the connections between perspective-taking and social behaviour. In the photo, the children with the soccer ball apparently recognized that the girl on the sidelines wanted to play, so they're inviting her to join the game. Children who can anticipate what others are thinking should get along better with their peers, and research indicates that they do. For example, children with good perspective-taking skills are typically well liked by their peers (LeMare & Rubin, 1987). Of course, mere understanding does not guarantee good social behaviour; sometimes children who understand what another child is thinking take advantage of that child. But, in general, greater understanding of others seems to promote positive interactions with others.

PREJUDICE

As children learn more about others, they discover that people belong to different social groups, based on variables such as gender, ethnicity, and social class. By the preschool years, most children can distinguish males from females and can identify people from different ethnic groups (Aboud, 1993). *Once children learn their membership in a specific group, they typically show* **prejudice,** *a negative view of others based on their membership in a specific group.* Actually, in young children prejudice is not so much a negative view of others as it is an enhanced view of one's own group. That is, preschool and kindergarten children attribute many positive traits such as being friendly and smart to their own group and few negative traits such as being mean (Bigler, Jones, & Lobliner, 1997; Black-Gutman & Hickson, 1996).

As children move into the elementary school years, prejudice usually declines somewhat (Powlishta et al., 1994). Cognitive development explains the decline. Preschool and kindergarten children usually view people in social groups as much more homogeneous than they really are. People from other groups are seen as all alike and, typically, not as good as people from the child's own group. As children grow, they begin to understand that people in social groups are heterogeneous—they know that individual Chinese Canadians, girls, and tall children, for example, are not all alike. And they have learned that people from different groups may be more alike than people from the same group. As children realize that social groups consist of all kinds of different people, prejudice lessens.

During early adolescence, prejudice often increases again. This resurgence apparently reflects two different processes (Black-Gutman & Hickson, 1996; Teichman, 2001). One is experiential: Exposed to prejudices of those around them, children and adolescents internalize some of these views. A second process concerns adolescents' identity. In the search for identity (described on pages 346–349), adolescents' preferences for their own group often intensify. Thus, greater prejudice in older children and adolescents reflects both a more positive view of their own group as well as a more negative view of other groups.

Identifying *how* children form actual prejudices is challenging because ethical concerns limit us to correlational studies. (Obviously, we could not do an experiment in which some children are deliberately exposed to biased information about actual groups of children.) Consequently, to study the processes underlying prejudice, researchers sometimes conduct experiments in which children are temporarily assigned to different groups.

To illustrate this approach, many researchers believe social status contributes to prejudice: Children are more likely to develop strong preferences for their group when it has high status. In experimentation designed to test this prediction (Bigler, Brown, & Markell, 2001; Brown & Bigler, 2002), children attending a summer school program were assigned to wear either a blue or yellow T-shirt. To increase the status of children wearing yellow shirts, children were told that in the previous summer students wearing yellow shirts were smarter, better leaders, and better athletes. Throughout the four-week program, teachers mentioned T-shirt colour frequently (e.g., had children sit with others wearing the same colour of shirt) but did *not* favour one group over the other. Nevertheless, at the end of the program, children wearing yellow shirts viewed themselves much more positively than they viewed children wearing blue shirts; in contrast, children wearing blue shirts (low status) had no biases. Thus, high status breeds a preference for one's own group (Nesdale & Flesser, 2001).

What can parents, teachers, and other adults do to rid children of prejudice? One way is to encourage friendly and constructive contacts between children from different groups (Ramsey, 1995). Adults can create situations in which children from different groups work together toward common goals. In school, this might be a class project, as shown in the photo. In sports, it might be mastering a new skill.

From experiences like these, children and adolescents discover for themselves that a person's membership in a social group tells us very little about that person. They learn, instead, that all children are different, each a unique mix of experiences, skills, and values.

TEST YOURSELF

1. When adolescents describe others, they usually _____.

2. In the most advanced stage of Selman's theory, adolescents _____.

3. Prejudice declines some as children get older because _____.

How might an information-processing theorist describe the stages of Selman's perspective-taking theory?

Answers: (1) try to provide a cohesive, integrated account, (2) provide a third person's perspective on situations and recognize the influence of context on this perspective, (3) with cognitive development children realize that social groups are heterogeneous

PUTTING IT ALL TOGETHER

In this chapter, we've examined some of the many forces that contribute to socialization. Parents, peers, and TV emerged as mighty shapers of children's development. We saw that groups like those at Crab Orchard Summer Camp are an important element of social life among older children and adolescents and that their impact is greatest when behavioural standards are not clear. We saw that TV's influence is tremendous. It can cause children like Robert to rely on aggression to resolve interpersonal conflict, and it can give them a stereotyped view of the world. Finally, we learned that children's descriptions and understanding of others become more complex with age, so

that young adolescents like Ian are often fully aware of what others are thinking. And we saw that prejudice declines with age, especially when children interact with peers from other groups.

Thus, parents, siblings, peers, and television define much of the sociocultural context of development for North American children, and their impact is considerable. Through the combined power of parents, siblings, peers, and television, children acquire the beliefs and behaviours of their culture. Full, adult membership in their culture is not far away. Only adolescence remains, and that topic will be examined in Chapters 9 and 10.

SUMMARY

8.1 Family Relationships

The Family as a System

■ According to the systems approach, the family consists of interacting elements—parents and children influence each other. The family itself is influenced by other social systems, such as neighbourhoods and religious organizations.

Siblings

■ The birth of a sibling can be stressful for children, particularly when the children are still young and when parents ignore their needs. Siblings get along better when they are of the same sex, believe that parents treat them similarly, enter adolescence, and have parents who get along well.

■ Adopted children are similar to children living with biological parents in many respects, although these results depend strongly on the child's age when adopted and the quality of care prior to adoption.

■ Parents have higher expectations for first-born children, which explains why such children are more

intelligent and more likely to go to college. Later-born children are more popular and more innovative. Contradicting the folklore, only children are almost never worse off than children with siblings. In some respects (such as intelligence, achievement, and autonomy), they are often better off.

Divorce and Remarriage

■ In the months after a divorce, a mother's parenting is often less effective and her children behave immaturely.

■ Divorce can harm children in a number of areas, ranging from school achievement to adjustment. The impact of divorce stems from less supervision of children following divorce, economic hardship, and conflict between parents. Children often benefit when parents have joint custody following divorce, or when they live with the same-sex parent.

8.2 Peers

Friendships

- Friendships among preschoolers are based on common interests and getting along well. As children grow, loyalty, trust, and intimacy become more important features in their friendships. Friends are usually similar in age, sex, race, and attitudes. Children with friends are more skilled socially and better adjusted.

Groups

- Older children and adolescents often form cliques—small groups of like-minded individuals—that become part of a crowd. Some crowds have higher status than others, and members of higher-status crowds often have higher self-esteem than members of lower-status crowds.

- Common to most groups is a dominance hierarchy, a well-defined structure with a leader at the top. Physical power often determines the dominance hierarchy, particularly among boys. However, with older children and adolescents, dominance hierarchies are more often based on skills that are important to the group.

- Peer pressure is neither totally powerful nor totally evil. In fact, groups influence individuals primarily in areas where standards of behaviour are unclear, such as tastes in music or clothing, or concerning drinking, drug use, and sex.

Popularity and Rejection

- Popular children are socially skilled. They often share, cooperate, and help others. They are unlikely to behave in antisocial ways, such as starting a fight.

- Some children are rejected by their peers, typically because they are too aggressive or withdrawn. Such children are often unsuccessful in school and have behavioural problems. The aggressive style of some rejected children can be linked to parents who are belligerent or combative and who are inconsistent in their discipline.

8.3 Television: Window on the World or Negative Influence?

Influence on Attitudes and Social Behaviour

- Children's social behaviours and attitudes are influenced by what they see on TV. Youngsters who fre-

quently watch televised violence become more aggressive, whereas those who watch prosocial TV become more socially skilled. Children who watch TV frequently may adopt TV's distorted view of women, minorities, and older people.

Influences on Cognition

- TV programs designed to foster children's cognitive skills, such as *Sesame Street* and *Ghostwriter*, are effective. Children frequently improve their academic skills and often adjust more readily to school.

Criticisms of TV

- Many popular criticisms about TV as a medium are not consistently supported by research. TV watching per se does not shorten children's attention span nor does it consistently lead to reduced creativity.

8.4 Understanding Others

Describing Others

- Children's descriptions of others change in much the same way that children's descriptions of themselves change. During the early elementary school years, descriptions emphasize concrete characteristics. In the late elementary school years, they emphasize personality traits. In adolescence, they emphasize providing an integrated picture of others.

Understanding What Others Think

- According to Selman's theory, children's understanding of how others think progresses through five stages. In the first, the undifferentiated stage, children often confuse their own and another's view. In the last, the societal stage, adolescents can take a third person's perspective and know that this perspective is influenced by context.

Prejudice

- Prejudice emerges in the preschool years soon after children recognize different social groups. Prejudice declines during childhood as children's cognitive growth helps them understand that social groups are heterogeneous, not homogeneous. However, older children and adolescents still show prejudice, which is best reduced by additional exposure to individuals from other social groups.

KEY TERMS

socialization (277)
joint custody (283)
blended family (284)

clique (288)
crowd (288)
dominance hierarchy (289)

prejudice (304)

SEE FOR YOURSELF: APPLYING WHAT YOU'VE LEARNED

Most middle and high school students know the different crowds in their school and the status of each. The number of crowds varies, as do their names, but beginning in middle school the existence of crowds is a basic fact of children's social life.

To learn more about crowds, try to talk individually to four or five students from the same middle school. You could begin by describing one of the crowds from your own school days. Then ask each student to name the different crowds in his or her school. Ask each student to describe the defining characteristics of people in each crowd. Finally, ask each student which crowd has the highest status in school and which has the lowest.

When you've interviewed all the students, compare their answers. Do the students agree about the number and types of crowds in their school? Do they agree on the status of each? Next, compare your results with those of other students in your class. Are the results similar in different schools? Can you find any relation between the types of crowds and characteristics of the school (e.g., rural versus urban)? See for yourself!

LEARN MORE ABOUT IT

Readings

CANTOR, J. (1998). *Mommy, I'm scared: How TV and movies frighten children and what we can do to protect them.* New York: Harvest Books. The author shows some of the consequences of violent programs and movies on children, gives some age-related guidelines for what kind of material is likely to scare children, and describes ways to comfort frightened children. An excellent resource for parents.

DUNN, J. (1993). *Young children's close relationships.* Newbury Park, CA: Sage. A leading expert provides a straightforward and entertaining account of children's social relationships.

MCCLANAHAN, S., & SANDEFUR, G. (1996). *Growing up with a single parent: What hurts, what helps.* Cambridge, MA: Harvard University Press. The authors describe many disadvantages for children growing up in a single-parent family. Then they recommend changes in government policies for assisting single-parent families.

 For additional readings, explore InfoTrac® College Edition, your online library. Go to http://www.infotrac.thomsonlearning.com.

Websites

http:// www.eric.ed.gov

The Education Resources Information Center (ERIC) maintains a website that facilitates access to documents related to education. This comprehensive educational database is used frequently by Canadian students.

http://www.ncbi.org

The National Coalition Building Institute maintains this website, which describes methods to eliminate prejudice and discrimination.

http://www.cps.ca

The Canadian Paediatric Society website has excellent information for parents and professionals, including a number of position statements.

Website addresses are subject to change. The *Human Development* book companion website can be accessed for updated links.

The Human Development Book Companion Website

See http://www.humandevelopment.nelson.com for practice quiz questions, Internet links, updates, critical thinking exercises, discussion forums, and more.

 Life-Span CD-ROM

For more information on the concepts covered in this chapter, go to

Module 3: Early and Middle Childhood
  • Emotional and Social Development

Module 4: Adolescence
  • Emotional and Social Development

Mike King/Corbis/Magma

CHAPTER 9

Rites of Passage

PHYSICAL AND COGNITIVE DEVELOPMENT IN ADOLESCENCE

At age 16, Clara Hughes earned a silver medal at the Canadian National Speed Skating Championships and was named Manitoba Junior Athlete of the Year. About the same time Clara also discovered cycling, and at 17 years old, she participated in the Western Canada Games. She has won medals at the Pan Am Games and World Cycling Championships, and holds numerous national championship titles. Clara also stayed committed to skating and won two gold medals at the National Junior Speed Skating Championships at the age of 19, while setting national junior records. Since these remarkable feats in her adolescent years, Clara has gone on to compete in three Pan Am Games, two Commonwealth Games, and both the summer and winter Olympic games. In fact, Clara made history by becoming the first Canadian to earn medals in both the summer and winter Olympics!

Clara's steady march to the top of her sports over her adolescent years is a remarkable feat. Yet in a less dramatic and less public way, these years are times of profound changes for *all* adolescents. In this chapter, we'll examine physical and cognitive development in adolescence. We'll begin by describing the important features of physical growth in the teenage years. Then we'll consider some of the necessary ingredients for healthy growth in adolescence. Next, we'll examine the nature of information processing during adolescence. Finally, we'll examine how adolescents reason about moral issues.

9.1

Physical Changes

LEARNING OBJECTIVES

■ What physical changes occur in adolescence that mark the transition to a mature young adult?

■ What factors cause the physical changes associated with puberty?

■ How do physical changes affect adolescents' psychological development?

Physical Changes
Signs of Physical Maturation
Mechanisms of Maturation
Psychological Impact of Puberty

Pete just celebrated his 15th birthday, but, as far as he is concerned, there is no reason to celebrate. Although most of his friends have grown about 15 centimetres in the past year or so and have more genital development, Pete looks just as he did when he was 10 years old. He is embarrassed by his appearance, particularly in the locker room, where he looks like a boy among men. "Won't I ever change?" he wonders.

The appearance of body hair, the emergence of breasts, and the enlargement of the penis and testicles are all signs that the child is gone and the adolescent is here. Many adolescents take great satisfaction in these signs of maturity. Others, like Pete, worry through their teenage years as they wait for the physical signs of adolescence.

In this section, we'll begin by describing the normal pattern of physical changes that take place in adolescence and look at the mechanisms responsible for them. Then we'll discover the impact of these physical changes on adolescents' psychological functioning. As we do, we'll learn about the possible effects of Pete's maturing later than his peers.

SIGNS OF PHYSICAL MATURATION

Puberty denotes two general types of physical changes that mark the transition from childhood to young adulthood. The first are bodily changes, including a dramatic increase in height and weight, as well as changes in the body's fat and muscle content. The second concerns sexual maturation, including change in the reproductive organs and the appearance of secondary sexual characteristics, such as facial and body hair and the growth of the breasts.

Physical Growth

When it comes to physical growth, the elementary school years represent the calm before the adolescent storm. As Figure 9.1 shows, in an average year, a typical 6- to 10-year-old girl or boy gains about 2.3 to 3.2 kilograms (5 to 7 pounds) and grows 5 to 7.5 centimetres (2 to 3 inches). In contrast, during the peak of the adolescent growth spurt, a girl may gain as much as 9 kilograms (20 pounds) in a year and a boy 11.4 kilograms (25 pounds) (Tanner, 1970).

THINK ABOUT IT 🔎

Compare and contrast the events of puberty for boys and girls.

The figure also shows that girls typically begin their growth spurt about two years before boys do. That is, girls typically start their growth spurt at about age 11, reach their peak rate of growth at about 12, and achieve their mature stature at about age 15. In contrast, boys start their growth spurt at 13, hit peak growth at 14, and reach mature stature at 17. This two-year difference in the growth spurt can lead to awkward social interactions between 11- and 12-year-old boys and girls because, as the photo on page 313 shows, girls are often taller and much more mature-looking than boys of the same age.

Body parts don't all mature at the same rate. Instead, the head, hands, and feet usually begin to grow first, followed by growth in the arms and legs. The trunk and shoulders are the last to grow (Tanner, 1990). The result of these differing growth

FIGURE 9.1   Adolescent Growth Spurt

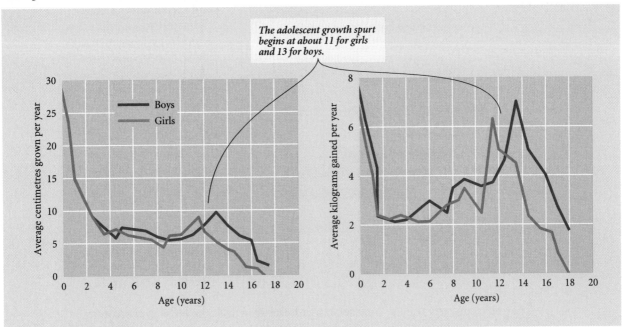

The adolescent growth spurt begins at about 11 for girls and 13 for boys.

rates is that an adolescent's body sometimes seems to be out of proportion—teens have a head and hands that are too big for the rest of their body. Fortunately, these imbalances don't last long as the later developing parts catch up.

During the growth spurt, bones become longer (which, of course, is why adolescents grow taller) and denser. Bone growth is accompanied by several other changes that differ for boys and girls. Muscle fibres become thicker and denser during adolescence, producing substantial increases in strength. However, muscle growth is much more pronounced in boys than in girls (Smoll & Schutz, 1990). Body fat also increases during adolescence, but much more rapidly in girls than in boys. Finally, heart and lung capacity increases more in adolescent boys than in adolescent girls. Together, these changes help to explain why the typical adolescent boy is stronger, is quicker, and has greater endurance than the typical adolescent girl.

Sexual Maturation

Not only do adolescents become taller and heavier, they also become mature sexually. *Sexual maturation includes change in* **primary sex characteristics,** *which refers to organs that are directly involved in reproduction.* These include the ovaries, uterus, and vagina in girls and the scrotum, testes, and penis in boys. *Sexual maturation also includes changes in* **secondary sex characteristics,** *which are physical signs of maturity that are not linked directly to the reproductive organs.* These include the growth of breasts and the widening of the pelvis in girls, the appearance of facial hair and the broadening of shoulders in boys, and the appearance of body hair and changes in voice and skin in both boys and girls.

FIGURE 9.2   Average Timing of Pubertal Changes in North American Youth

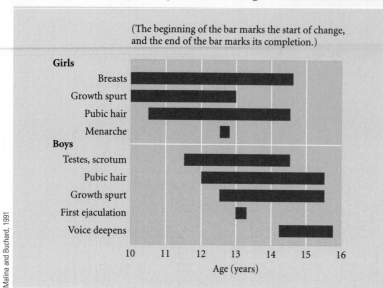

(The beginning of the bar marks the start of change, and the end of the bar marks its completion.)

Malina and Buchard, 1991

Changes in primary and secondary sexual characteristics occur in a predictable sequence for both boys and girls. Figure 9.2 shows these changes and the ages when they typically occur. For girls, puberty begins with growth of the breasts and the growth spurt, followed by the appearance of pubic hair. *Menarche, the onset of menstruation, typically occurs at about age 13.* Early menstrual cycles are usually irregular and without ovulation.

For boys, puberty usually commences with the growth of the testes and scrotum, followed by the appearance of pubic hair, the start of the growth spurt, and growth of the penis. *At about age 13, most boys reach* **spermarche,** *the first spontaneous ejaculation of sperm-laden fluid.* Initial ejaculations often contain relatively few sperm; only months or sometimes years later are there sufficient sperm to fertilize an egg (Chilman, 1983).

MECHANISMS OF MATURATION

What causes the many physical changes that occur during puberty? The hypothalamus, located in the middle of the base of the brain, sends hormones to the pituitary gland, triggering the release of growth hormone. In addition, the pituitary regulates pubertal changes by signalling other glands to secrete hormones. During the early elementary school years—long before there are any outward signs of puberty—the pituitary signals the adrenal glands to release androgens, initiating the biochemical changes that will produce body hair. A few years later, in girls the pituitary signals the ovaries to release estrogen, which causes the breasts to enlarge, the female genitals to mature, and fat to accumulate. In boys the pituitary signals the testes to release the androgen testosterone, which causes the male genitals to mature and muscle mass to increase.

Although estrogen is often described as a "female hormone" and androgen as a "male hormone," estrogen and androgen are present in both boys and girls. As we've seen, in girls the adrenal glands secrete androgens. The amount is very small compared to that secreted by boys' testes but is enough to influence the emergence of body hair. In boys, the testes secrete very small amounts of estrogen, which explains why some boys' breasts enlarge, temporarily, early in adolescence.

The timing of pubertal events is regulated, in part, by genetics. For example, a daughter's age at menarche is related to her mother's age at menarche (Graber, Brooks-Gunn, & Warren, 1995). However, these genetic forces are strongly influenced by the environment, particularly an adolescent's nutrition and health. In general, puberty occurs earlier in adolescents who are well nourished and healthy than in adolescents who are not. For example, puberty occurs earlier in girls who are heavier and taller but later in girls who are afflicted with chronic illnesses or who receive inadequate nutrition (St. George, Williams, & Silva, 1994).

Two other findings underscore the importance of nutrition and health in the onset of puberty. Cross-cultural comparisons reveal that menarche occurs earlier in areas of the world where nutrition and health care are adequate. For example, menarche occurs an average of two to three years earlier in Western European and North American countries than in African countries. And, within regions, socioeconomic status matters. Girls from affluent homes are more likely to receive adequate nutrition and health care and, consequently, they reach menarche earlier (Steinberg, 1999).

Historical data point to the same conclusion concerning the importance of nutrition and health care. In many industrialized countries around the world, the average age of menarche has declined steadily over the past 150 years. For example, in Europe the average age of menarche was 17 in 1840 compared to about 13 today. This drop reflects improvements in nutrition and better health care over this period. In these countries, age of menarche is no longer dropping, which suggests that with adequate nutrition the genetic lower limit for menarche is, on average, about 13 years.

What may surprise you is that the social environment also influences the onset of puberty, at least for girls. Menarche occurs at younger ages in girls who experience much family conflict (Belsky, Steinberg, & Draper, 1991; Moffit et al., 1992). For example, Ellis and Garber (2000) found that girls entered puberty at a younger age when their mothers' romantic relationships were stressful and when their mothers had remarried or had a boyfriend. The underlying nature of these links is not known, although repeated exposure to stress may affect the hormones that trigger menstruation (Graber et al., 1995).

PSYCHOLOGICAL IMPACT OF PUBERTY

Of course, teenagers are well aware of the changes taking place in their bodies. Not surprisingly, some of these changes affect adolescents' psychological development.

Body Image

Compared to children and adults, adolescents are much more concerned about their overall appearance. Like the girl in the photo, many teenagers look in the mirror regularly, checking for signs of additional physical change. Generally, girls worry more about appearance and are more likely to be dissatisfied with their appearance (Brooks-Gunn & Paikoff, 1993; Unger & Crawford, 1996). In contrast, boys are concerned about their appearance in early adolescence but become more pleased over the course of adolescence as pubertal change takes place (Gross, 1984).

Response to Menarche and Spermarche

Fortunately, most adolescent girls today know about menstruation well before they experience it—usually from discussions with their mothers. Being prepared, their responses are usually fairly mild. Most girls are moderately pleased at this new sign of maturity but moderately irritated by the inconvenience of menstruation (Brooks-Gunn & Ruble, 1982). Girls usually tell their mothers about menarche right away, and after two or three menstrual periods they tell their friends too (Brooks-Gunn & Ruble, 1982).

Menarche is usually a private occasion for adolescents living in industrialized countries, but it is often celebrated in traditional cultures. For example, the Western Apache, who live in the southwest portion of the United States, traditionally have a spectacular ceremony to celebrate a girl's menarche (Basso, 1970). After a girl's first

© Bill Gillette/Stock Boston Inc.

period, a group of older adults decide when the ceremony will be held and select a sponsor—a woman of good character and wealth (she helps to pay for the ceremony) who is unrelated to the initiate. On the day before the ceremony, the sponsor serves a large feast for the girl and her family; at the end of the ceremony, the family reciprocates, symbolizing that the sponsor is now a member of their family.

The ceremony itself begins at sunrise and lasts a few hours. As shown in the photo, the initiate dresses in ceremonial attire. The ceremony includes eight distinct phases in which the initiate dances or chants, sometimes accompanied by her sponsor or a medicine man. The intent of these actions is to transform the girl into "Changing Woman," a heroic figure in Apache myth. With this transformation comes longevity and perpetual strength. The ceremony is a signal to all in the community that the initiate is now an adult. And it tells the initiate herself that her community now has adult-like expectations for her.

In contrast to menarche, much less is known about boys' reactions to spermarche. Most boys know about spontaneous ejaculations beforehand, and they get their information by reading, not by asking parents (Gaddis & Brooks-Gunn, 1985). When boys are prepared for spermarche, they feel more positively about it. Nevertheless, boys rarely tell parents or friends about this new development (Stein & Reiser, 1994).

> Can you think of other ceremonies similar to the Apache celebration for menarche—but perhaps not as elaborate—that take place to celebrate other milestones of adolescent development?

Moodiness

Adolescents are often thought to be extraordinarily moody—moving from joy to sadness to irritation to anger over the course of a morning or afternoon. And the source of teenage moodiness is often presumed to be the influx of hormones associated with puberty—"hormones running wild." In fact, the evidence indicates that adolescents are moodier than children and adults but not primarily due to hormones (Steinberg, 1999). Scientists often find that rapid increases in hormone levels are associated with greater irritability and greater impulsivity, but the relation tends to be small and is found primarily in early adolescence (Buchanan, Eccles, & Becker, 1992).

If hormones are not responsible, what causes teenage moodiness? Some insights come from an elaborate study in which teenagers carried electronic pagers for a week (Csikszentmihalyi & Larson, 1984). When paged by researchers, the adolescents briefly described what they were doing and how they felt. The record of a typical adolescent is shown in Figure 9.3. His mood shifts frequently from positive to negative, sometimes several times in a single day. For this boy, like most of the adolescents in the study, mood shifts were associated with changes in activities and social settings. Teens are more likely to report being in a good mood when with friends or when engaged in recreational activities; they tend to report being in a bad mood when in adult-regulated settings such as school classrooms or at a part-time job. Because adolescents often change activities and social settings many times in a single day, they appear to be moodier than adults.

Rate of Maturation

Although puberty begins at age 10 in the average girl and at age 12 in the average boy, for many children puberty begins months or even years before or after these norms. An early-maturing boy might begin puberty at age 11, whereas a late-maturing boy

FIGURE 9.3   The Week of Gregory Stone

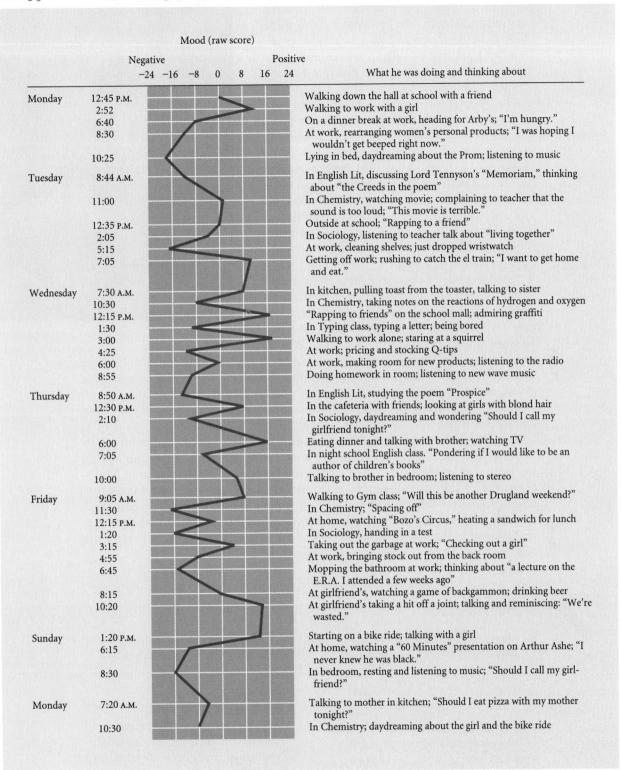

Mood (raw score)

		Negative				Positive			What he was doing and thinking about

Monday — 12:45 P.M. — Walking down the hall at school with a friend
2:52 — Walking to work with a girl
6:40 — On a dinner break at work, heading for Arby's; "I'm hungry."
8:30 — At work, rearranging women's personal products; "I was hoping I wouldn't get beeped right now."
10:25 — Lying in bed, daydreaming about the Prom; listening to music

Tuesday — 8:44 A.M. — In English Lit, discussing Lord Tennyson's "Memoriam," thinking about "the Creeds in the poem"
11:00 — In Chemistry, watching movie; complaining to teacher that the sound is too loud; "This movie is terrible."
12:35 P.M. — Outside at school; "Rapping to a friend"
2:05 — In Sociology, listening to teacher talk about "living together"
5:15 — At work, cleaning shelves; just dropped wristwatch
7:05 — Getting off work; rushing to catch the el train; "I want to get home and eat."

Wednesday — 7:30 A.M. — In kitchen, pulling toast from the toaster, talking to sister
10:30 — In Chemistry, taking notes on the reactions of hydrogen and oxygen
12:15 P.M. — "Rapping to friends" on the school mall; admiring graffiti
1:30 — In Typing class, typing a letter; being bored
3:00 — Walking to work alone; staring at a squirrel
4:25 — At work; pricing and stocking Q-tips
6:00 — At work, making room for new products; listening to the radio
8:55 — Doing homework in room; listening to new wave music

Thursday — 8:50 A.M. — In English Lit, studying the poem "Prospice"
12:30 P.M. — In the cafeteria with friends; looking at girls with blond hair
2:10 — In Sociology, daydreaming and wondering "Should I call my girlfriend tonight?"
6:00 — Eating dinner and talking with brother; watching TV
7:05 — In night school English class. "Pondering if I would like to be an author of children's books"
10:00 — Talking to brother in bedroom; listening to stereo

Friday — 9:05 A.M. — Walking to Gym class; "Will this be another Drugland weekend?"
11:30 — In Chemistry; "Spacing off"
12:15 P.M. — At home, watching "Bozo's Circus," heating a sandwich for lunch
1:20 — In Sociology, handing in a test
3:15 — Taking out the garbage at work; "Checking out a girl"
4:55 — At work, bringing stock out from the back room
6:45 — Mopping the bathroom at work; thinking about "a lecture on the E.R.A. I attended a few weeks ago"
8:15 — At girlfriend's, watching a game of backgammon; drinking beer
10:20 — At girlfriend's taking a hit off a joint; talking and reminiscing: "We're wasted."

Sunday — 1:20 P.M. — Starting on a bike ride; talking with a girl
6:15 — At home, watching a "60 Minutes" presentation on Arthur Ashe; "I never knew he was black."
8:30 — In bedroom, resting and listening to music; "Should I call my girlfriend?"

Monday — 7:20 A.M. — Talking to mother in kitchen; "Should I eat pizza with my mother tonight?"
10:30 — In Chemistry; daydreaming about the girl and the bike ride

might start at 15 or 16. An early-maturing girl might start puberty at 9, a late-maturing girl at 14 or 15.

Maturing early or late has psychological consequences that differ for boys and girls. Several longitudinal studies show that early maturation benefits boys but, most often, not girls. Boys who mature early tend to be more independent and self-confident. They're also more popular with peers. In contrast, girls who mature early often lack self-confidence, are less popular, are more likely to be depressed and have behaviour problems, and are more likely to smoke and drink (Dick et al., 2000; Ge, Conger, & Elder, 2001; Stice, Presnell, & Bearman, 2001).

The differing consequences of early maturation on boys and girls is shown in the results of an extensive longitudinal study of adolescents growing up in Milwaukee during the 1970s (Simmons & Blyth, 1987). The early-maturing boys in this study dated more often and had more positive feelings about their physical development and athletic abilities. The early-maturing girls had more negative feelings about their physical development, received poorer grades, and were more often in trouble in school.

Why does rate of maturation have these consequences? Early maturation may benefit boys because others perceive them as more mature and may be more willing to give them adultlike responsibilities. Late-maturing boys, like Pete in the vignette at the beginning of this section, are often frustrated because others treat them like little boys instead of like young men. Early maturation may hamper girls' development by leading them to associate with older adolescents who apparently encourage them to engage in age-inappropriate activities, such as drinking, smoking, and sex, for which they are ill-prepared (Ge, Conger, & Elder, 1996).

By young adulthood, many of the effects associated with rate of maturation vanish. When Pete, for example, finally matures, others will treat him like an adult and the few extra years of being treated like a child will not be harmful. But for some adolescents, particularly early-maturing girls, rate of maturation can have long-lasting effects. A girl who matures early and is pressured into sex and becomes pregnant ends up with a different life course than a girl who matures later and is better prepared to resist pressures for sex. Thus, sometimes rate of maturation can lead to events that pick the path that development follows throughout life.

TEST YOURSELF

1. Puberty refers to changes in height and weight, to changes in the body's fat and muscle content, and to _____.

2. Girls tend to have their growth spurts about _____ earlier than boys.

3. During adolescent physical growth, boys have greater muscle growth than girls, acquire less _____, and have greater increases in heart and lung capacity.

4. Primary sex characteristics are organs directly related to reproduction whereas secondary sex characteristics are _____.

5. During puberty, the ovaries secrete estrogen, which causes the breasts to enlarge, the genitals to mature, and _____.

6. We know that nutrition and health determine the timing of puberty because puberty is earlier in girls who are taller and heavier, in regions of the world where nutrition and health care are adequate, and _____.

7. Adolescents are moodier than children and adults, primarily because _____.

8. Early maturation tends to benefit boys because _____.

At first blush, the onset of puberty would seem to be due entirely to biology. In fact, the child's environment influences the onset of puberty. Summarize the ways biology and experience interact to trigger the onset of puberty.

Answers: (1) sexual maturation, (2) two years, (3) fat, (4) physical signs of maturity not linked directly to reproductive organs, such as the appearance of body hair, (5) fat to accumulate, (6) today, compared to earlier in history, (7) they change activities and social settings frequently and their mood tracks these changes, (8) others treat them as more mature and are more willing to give them adultlike responsibilities.

9.2

Health

LEARNING OBJECTIVES

- What are the elements of a healthy diet for adolescents? Why do some adolescents suffer from eating disorders?
- Do adolescents get enough exercise? What are the pros and cons of participating in sports in high school?
- What are common obstacles to healthy growth in adolescence?

> **Health**
>
> Nutrition
>
> Physical Fitness
>
> Threats to Adolescent Well-Being

Dana had just started Grade 7 and was overjoyed that he could try out for the junior high football team. He'd always excelled in sports and was usually the star when he played football on the playground or in gym class. But this was Dana's first opportunity to play on an actual team—with a real helmet, jersey, pads, and everything—and he was thrilled! Dana's dad played football in high school and thought Dana could benefit from the experience. His mom wasn't so sure—she was afraid he'd be hurt and be crippled for the rest of his life.

Adolescence is a time of transition when it comes to health. On the one hand, teens are much less affected by the minor illnesses that would have kept them at home in bed as children. On the other hand, teens are at much greater risk for harm because of their own unhealthy and risky behaviours. In this section, we'll look at some of the factors essential to adolescent health and see whether Dana's mother should be worried about sports-related injuries. We'll start with nutrition.

© Spencer Grant/PhotoEdit

NUTRITION

The physical growth associated with puberty means that the body has special nutritional needs. According to the Dieticians of Canada (2004), a typical teenage girl between the ages of 13 and 15 should consume about 2,200 calories per day and about 2,100 calories between the ages of 16 and 19; a typical boy should consume about 2,800 calories between the ages of 13 and 15 and about 3,200 calories between the ages of 16 and 18. (The exact levels depend on a number of factors, including body composition, growth rate, and activity level.) Teenagers also need calcium for bone growth and iron to make extra hemoglobin, the matter in red blood cells that carries oxygen. Boys need additional hemoglobin because of their increased muscle mass; girls need hemoglobin to replace that lost during menstruation.

Unfortunately, although many teenagers consume enough calories each day, too much of their intake consists of fast food rather than well-balanced meals. The result of too many meals like the one shown in the photo (page 319)—burgers, French fries, and a shake—is that teens may get inadequate iron or calcium and far too much sodium and fat. With inadequate iron, teens are often listless and moody; with inadequate calcium, bones may not develop fully, placing the person at risk later in life for osteoporosis.

Obesity

In part because of a diet high in fast foods, many North American children and adolescents are overweight. *The technical definition for overweight is based on the **body mass index (BMI)**, which is an adjusted ratio of weight to height.* A BMI greater than 25 (very heavy for height) is considered as overweight, and a BMI greater than 30 is considered as obese. As part of an international trend, Canadian children and youth appear to be getting heavier, although the picture is not clear since there is not a systematic way to monitor the prevalence of obese and overweight children. The Canadian Community Health Survey (Health Canada, 2000/2001) found that 5% of adolescents were considered obese, and 17% of 12- to 18-year-old males and 10% of 12- to 19-year-old females were considered overweight.

Like the boy in the photo, overweight youngsters are often unpopular and have low self-esteem (Braet, Mervielde, & Vandereycken, 1997). Furthermore, they are at risk for many medical problems, including high blood pressure and diabetes throughout life because the vast majority of overweight children and adolescents become overweight adults (Serdula et al., 1993). Subsequently, overweight adults face an increased risk of diabetes, heart disease, and other health problems.

Heredity plays an important role in juvenile obesity. In adoption studies, children's and adolescents' weight is related to the weight of their biological parents, not to the weight of their adoptive parents (Stunkard et al., 1986). Genes may influence obesity

© M. Douglas / The Image Works

by influencing a person's activity level. In other words, being genetically more prone to inactivity makes it more difficult to burn off calories and easier to gain weight. *Heredity may also help set the **basal metabolic rate**, the speed at which the body consumes calories.* Children and adolescents with a slower basal metabolic rate burn off calories less rapidly, making it easier for them to gain weight (Epstein & Cluss, 1986).

One's environment is also influential. Television advertising, for example, encourages youths to eat tasty but fattening foods. Parents play a role too. They may inadvertently encourage obesity by emphasizing external eating signals rather than internal ones. Thus, obese children and adolescents may overeat because they rely on external cues (e.g., a tempting candy bar shown on TV) and disregard internal cues to stop (Birch, 1991).

Obese youth *can* lose weight. The most effective programs have several features in common (Epstein et al., 1995; Foreyt & Goodrick, 1995; Israel et al., 1994):

- The focus of the program is to change obese children's eating habits, encourage them to become more active, and discourage sedentary behaviour.
- As part of the treatment, children learn to monitor their eating, exercise, and sedentary behaviour. Goals are established in each area and rewards are earned when the goals are met.
- Parents are trained to help children set realistic goals and to use behavioural principles to help children meet these goals. Parents also monitor their own lifestyle to be sure they aren't accidentally fostering their child's obesity.

When programs incorporate these features, obese children do lose weight. However, even after losing weight, many of these children remain overweight. Consequently, it is best to avoid overweight and obesity in the first place; Health Canada (2003g) emphasizes the role of increased physical activity and good eating habits in preventing overweight and obesity.

Fast food is not the only risky diet common among adolescents. Many teenage girls worry about their weight and are attracted to the "lose 10 pounds in 2 weeks!" diets advertised on TV and in teen magazines. Many of these diets are flatly unhealthy—they deprive youth of the many substances necessary for growth. Similarly, for philosophical or health reasons, many adolescents decide to eliminate meat from their diets. Vegetarian diets can be healthy for teens, but only when adolescents do more than eliminate meat. That is, vegetarians need to adjust the rest of their diet to ensure that they have adequate sources of protein, calcium, and iron.

Yet another food-related problem common in adolescence are two similar eating disorders: anorexia and bulimia.

Anorexia and Bulimia

When Amber turned 15, she began dieting compulsively. In a few months, she had withered away to a mere 40 kilograms (90 pounds) and had to be hospitalized. Amber suffered from an eating disorder. ***Anorexia nervosa is a disorder marked by a persistent refusal to eat and an irrational fear of being overweight.*** Individuals with anorexia nervosa have a grossly distorted image of their own body. Like the girl in the photo, they claim to be overweight despite being painfully thin (Wilson, Hefferman, & Black, 1996).

Anorexia is a very serious disorder, often leading to heart damage. Without treatment, as many as 15% of adolescents with anorexia die (Wicks-Nelson & Israel, 1991). A related eating disorder is bulimia nervosa. ***Individuals with bulimia nervosa alternate between binge eating—periods when they eat uncontrollably—and purging through self-induced vomiting or with laxatives.*** The frequency of binge eating varies remarkably among people with bulimia nervosa, from a few times a week to more than 30 times. What's common to all is the feeling that they cannot stop eating (Mizes, 1995).

Anorexia and bulimia are alike in many respects. Both disorders primarily affect females and emerge in adolescence (Tyrka, Graber, & Brooks-Gunn, 2000), and both disorders have their origins in cultural ideals of the female body. In many industrialized cultures and certainly in Canada

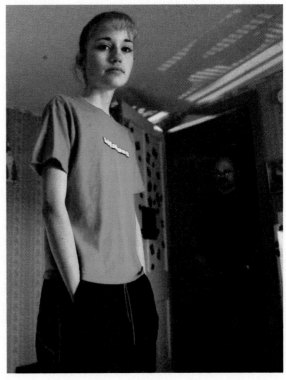

THINK ABOUT IT

Describe how obesity, anorexia, and bulimia are influenced by heredity and environment.

and the United States, the ideal female body is tall and slender. As girls enter adolescence (and as they begin to date), these cultural norms become particularly influential. Also, during adolescence girls experience a "fat spurt," gaining about 11 kilograms (25 pounds)—most of it fat. Though this pattern of growth is normal, many girls internalize the "thin-body" ideal; they become dissatisfied with their appearance and begin to diet. Most diets fail, leading girls to be even more unhappy with their appearance and leading some to the drastic dieting (sometimes accompanied by binge eating) that characterizes eating disorders (Stice, 2001).

Why would adolescents resort to drastic dieting or binging and purging? The Forces in Action feature has the answer.

FORCES IN ACTION

What Causes Anorexia and Bulimia?

Biological, psychological, and sociocultural influences all contribute to eating disorders. In many industrialized cultures, the ideal female body is tall and slender. These cultural norms become particularly salient during adolescence, when girls typically experience a "fat spurt" in which they gain a significant amount of weight. Although this pattern is normal, some girls see themselves as overweight and begin to diet. Faced with a culture that values being thin (sociocultural influence) and a change in her body (biological influence), the adolescent girl believes she is fat (psychological force) and tries to lose weight.

The elements of the biopsychosocial framework foster eating disorders in other ways. Family dynamics—including psychological and sociocultural forces—are important. Eating disorders are more likely with autocratic parents who give daughters little freedom. As girls enter adolescence and seek greater autonomy, they discover that their weight is something they can control. In dieting or binging, they can assert their autonomy (Swarr & Richards, 1996).

Cultural emphasis on thinness and a regimented home life contribute to eating disorders, but there is also a biological factor. Twin and family studies point to an inherited predisposition for anorexia and bulimia, perhaps in the form of a personality that tends to be rigid and anxious (Strober, 1995).

Summarizing all these influences, who is most susceptible to eating disorders? The disorder is most likely to develop in girls who inherit the predisposition (biological force), who internalize cultural ideals of thinness (psychological force), and whose parents grant them little independence (sociocultural force).

PHYSICAL FITNESS

Being physically active promotes mental and physical health, both during adolescence and throughout adulthood. Individuals who regularly engage in physical activity reduce their risk for obesity, cancer, heart disease, diabetes, and psychological disorders including depression and anxiety. "Regular activity" typically means exercising for 30 minutes, at least three times a week, at a pace that keeps an adolescent's heart rate at about 140 beats per minute. Running, vigorous walking, swimming, aerobic dancing, biking, and cross-country skiing are all examples of activities that can provide this level of intensity.

Unfortunately, all the evidence indicates that most adolescents rarely get enough exercise. For example, in one study the researchers (Kann et al., 1995) asked high school students whether they had exercised at least three times for 20 minutes during the past week at a level that made them sweat and breathe hard. In Grade 9, about 75% of boys and 65% of girls said they had; by Grade 12, these figures had dropped to

65% for boys and 40% for girls. Part of the problem here is that, for many high school students, physical education classes provide the only regular opportunity for exercise, yet a minority of high school students are enrolled in physical education, and most who are enrolled do not attend daily.

Many teenagers get exercise by participating in physical activities outside of school such as organized sports. Canadian studies have found that of children in Grades 6 to 10, although a half to three-quarters of girls and three-quarters of boys participated in vigorous activities at least twice a week, overall the percentage of young Canadians who are active at that level has decreased by approximately 10% between 1990 and 1998 (Health Canada, 2003g). According to the 1998–99 National Population Health Survey (NPHS) of Canadian youths aged 12 to 19, 84% may not have been active enough for optimal growth and development based on international guidelines. Further, girls are significantly less active than boys; youths living in higher income families tend to be most likely to be physically active. In Canada, the amount of physical education available in schools has been steadily declining, presumably due to a greater emphasis on scholastics. Physical education has become optional in most secondary schools. However, a number of efforts have been undertaken to increase the amount of physical activities in schools as educators recognize the preventive health benefits offered.

AP/World Wide Photos

Participating in sports has many benefits for youth. In addition to improved physical fitness, sports can enhance participants' self-esteem and can help them learn initiative (Larson, 2000; Whitehead & Corbin, 1997). Athletes can also learn about teamwork and competitiveness. At the same time, there are some potential costs. Boys are most likely to be injured while playing hockey or basketball; girls are most likely to be injured while playing basketball or soccer. Injuries due to basketball peaked for males at age 14 and for females at age 13. The most common types of injuries were sprains and strains (49%) and fractures (25%), and the most common sites of injury were fingers (37%) and ankles (23%) (Canadian Hospitals Injury Reporting and Prevention Program, 1994). Dana's mom can rest easy; the odds are Dana won't be injured, and if he is, it won't be serious.

A serious issue, though, is the use of illegal drugs to improve performance. Some athletes use anabolic steroids, drugs that are chemically similar to the male hormone testosterone, to increase muscle size and strength and to promote more rapid recovery from injury. Health Canada reports that most steroid users are male and are involved in a regular physical activity or a fitness club or weight training program. Young men sometimes believe that steroids will help them look better and are motivated to use these drugs to get immediate results and to be admired by others. Young steroid users reportedly are influenced by professional body builders, magazines, comic heroes, advertising, music videos, role models, peer pressure, and peer expectations.

THINK ABOUT IT

Many teenagers do not eat well-balanced meals, and many do not get enough exercise. What would you do to improve teenagers' dietary and exercise habits?

The use of steroids for this purpose is disturbing because they can damage the liver, reproductive system, skeleton, and cardiovascular system (increasing blood pressure and cholesterol levels); in addition, use of anabolic steroids is associated with mood swings, aggression, and depression. Parents, coaches, and health professionals need to be sure that high school athletes are aware of the dangers of steroids and should encourage youths to meet their athletic goals without drug use.

THREATS TO ADOLESCENT WELL-BEING

Every year, approximately one Canadian adolescent out of 2,000 between the ages of 15 and 19 dies. Relatively few die from disease; instead, they are killed in accidents, typically involving automobiles (Statistics Canada, 2001c). Sadly, many of these deaths are completely preventable. Deaths in automobile accidents are frequently linked to driving too fast, drinking alcohol, and not wearing seat belts.

Adolescent deaths from accidents can be explained, in part, because adolescents take risks that adults often find unacceptable (Nell, 2002). Teens like the boy in the photo take unnecessary risks while riding skateboards, scooters, or bicycles. They drive cars recklessly, engage in unprotected sex, and sometimes use illegal and dangerous drugs (we'll discuss this more in Chapter 10). Although it is tempting to call such behaviour "stupid" or "irrational," research suggests that adolescents and adults often make decisions similarly, even though the outcome of that decision-making process sometimes differs for adolescents and adults (Fischhoff & Quadrel, 1995). Specifically, adolescents and adults typically determine

© Dennis MacDonald/PhotoEdit

- the alternative courses of action available,
- the consequences of each action, and
- the desirability and likelihood of these consequences.

Then they integrate this information to make a decision.

To see this decision-making in action, consider a teen deciding whether to drive home from a party with friends who have been drinking alcohol. She decides that she has two alternatives: (1) try to find a ride with people who haven't been drinking but whom she doesn't know well, or (2) ask her parents to come get her. Her analysis might run something like this:

If I go home with my friends, I won't upset them (+) but I might be in an accident (—). If I go home with other people, I'll definitely make my friends mad (—) but will probably make it home safely (+). If I call my parents, I'll definitely upset my friends (—), probably annoy other people at the party (—) but I'll get home safely (+).

This basic analysis is sound and not much different from what an adult might do. The difference comes in the adolescent's weighting of the desirability of different consequences. Adolescents are likely to place greater emphasis on the social consequences of their decisions, such as upsetting their friends, and less emphasis on the health consequences, such as getting home safely (Steinberg, 1999). And, as we saw in Chapter 8, they're particularly likely to consider these social consequences when the standards for appropriate behaviour are not clear, as is often the case when it comes to drinking or having sex.

TEST YOURSELF

1. An adolescent's diet should contain adequate calories, _____, and iron.

2. A vegetarian diet can be healthy for teens, but only when adolescents _____.

3. Individuals with _____ alternate between binge eating and purging.

4. Teenage girls are more prone to anorexia when their parents _____.

5. Regular physical activity helps to promote _____ and physical health.

6. Some teenage athletes use anabolic steroids to increase muscular strength and to _____.

7. More teenagers die from _____ than any other single cause.

8. Because they place greater emphasis on the _____ consequences of their actions, adolescents make what adults think are risky decisions.

How does adolescent risk-taking illustrate the idea that individuals help to shape their own development?

Answers: (1) calcium, (2) adjust the rest of their diet so they consume adequate protein, calcium, and iron, (3) bulimia nervosa, (4) are autocratic and leave them little sense of self-control, (5) mental health, (6) promote more rapid recovery from an injury, (7) automobile accidents, (8) social

---

9.3

Information Processing During Adolescence

LEARNING OBJECTIVES

▨ How does information processing become more efficient during adolescence?

▨ Why is adolescent thinking sometimes not as sophisticated as it could be?

> **Information Processing During Adolescence**
>
> How Does Information Processing Improve in Adolescence?
>
> Limits on Information Processing

Calvin, a 14-year-old boy, was an enigma to his mother, Crystal. On the one hand, Calvin's growing reasoning skills impressed and sometimes even surprised her. He not only readily grasped technical discussions of her medical work, but he was becoming adept at finding loopholes in her explanations of why he wasn't allowed to do some things with his friends. On the other hand, sometimes Calvin was a real teenage "space cadet." Simple problem solving stumped him, or he made silly mistakes and got the wrong answer. Calvin didn't correspond to Crystal's image of the formal operational thinker that she remembered from her university child-development class.

According to information-processing theories, many important cognitive processes reach mature levels of functioning during adolescence. We'll look at some of these processes in the first part of this section. Of course, that doesn't mean that adolescents' thinking is always flawless; it's not, and in this section we'll see why adolescents like Crystal's son don't always think in the sophisticated manner predicted by theories of cognitive development.

HOW DOES INFORMATION PROCESSING IMPROVE IN ADOLESCENCE?

For information-processing theorists, adolescence does not represent a distinct, qualitatively different stage of cognitive development. Instead, adolescence is considered to be a transition period between the rapidly changing cognitive processes of childhood and the mature cognitive processes of young adulthood. Cognitive changes do take place in adolescence, but they are small compared to those seen in childhood. Adolescence is a time when cognitive processes are "tweaked" to adult levels. These changes take place in several different elements of information processing.

Working Memory and Processing Speed

Working memory is the site of ongoing cognitive processing, and processing speed is the speed with which individuals complete basic cognitive processes. Both achieve adultlike levels during adolescence. Adolescents' working memory has about the same capacity as adults' working memory, which means teenagers are better able to store information needed for ongoing cognitive processes. In addition, Figure 9.4 illustrates change in processing speed, exemplified in this case by performance on a simple response-time task in which individuals press a button as rapidly as possible in response to a visual stimulus. Simple response time declines steadily during childhood—from about one-third of a second at age 8 to one-quarter of a second at age 12—but changes little thereafter. This pattern of change is not specific to simple response time but is, instead, found for a wide range of cognitive tasks: Adolescents generally process information just about as quickly as young adults (Kail, 1991). Changes in working memory and processing speed mean that, compared to children, adolescents process information very efficiently.

FIGURE 9.4   Simple Response Time

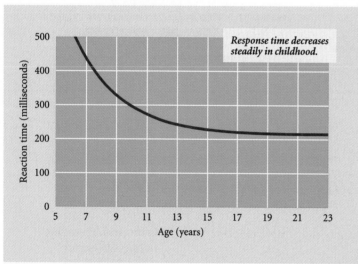

Response time decreases steadily in childhood.

Content Knowledge

As children move into adolescence, they acquire adultlike levels of knowledge and understanding in many domains. Children, for example, may enjoy baseball or computers, but as adolescents they acquire true expertise. For example, like the parent and child in the photo on page 327, top, many parents turn to their teens for help learning how to navigate the Internet. This increased knowledge is useful for its own sake, but it also has the indirect effect of allowing adolescents to learn, understand, and remember more of new experiences (Schneider & Bjorklund, 1998; Schneider & Pressley, 1997). Imagine two junior high students—one a hockey expert, the other not—watching a hockey game. Compared to the novice, the adolescent expert would understand many of the nuances of the game and, later, remember many more features of the game.

Strategies and Metacognitive Skill

Adolescents become much better skilled at identifying strategies appropriate for a specific task, then monitoring the chosen strategy to verify that it is working (Schneider & Pressley, 1997). For example, like the teen in the photo below, adolescents are more likely to outline and highlight information in a text. They are more likely to make lists of material they don't know well and should study more. And they more often embed these activities in a master study plan (e.g., a list of assignments, quizzes, and tests for a two-week period). All these activities help adolescents learn more effectively and remember more accurately (Schneider & Pressley, 1997; Thomas et al., 1993).

These changing features of information processing are summarized in Table 9.1.

THINK ABOUT IT

Adolescents typically are introduced to the study of complex topics such as philosophy and experimental science. Explain how their maturing cognitive skills contribute to the study of these and other subject areas.

TABLE 9.1	Information Processing During Adolescence
Feature	**State in Adolescence**
Working memory and processing speed	Adolescents have adultlike working memory capacity and processing speed, allowing them to process information efficiently.
Content knowledge	Adolescents' greater knowledge of the world facilitates understanding and memory of new experiences.
Strategies and metacognition	Adolescents are better able to identify task-appropriate strategies and to monitor the effectiveness of those strategies.

Change in each of these elements of information processing occurs gradually. When combined, they contribute to the steady progress to mature thinking that is the destination of adolescent cognitive development.

LIMITS ON INFORMATION PROCESSING

Adolescents' improved information processing affords them much greater cognitive power. Of course, adolescents may not always use their skills effectively. Sometimes they resort to simpler, less mature ways of thinking because such thinking takes less effort—it's easier. And, as we'll see in the Spotlight on Research feature, sometimes adolescents' beliefs interfere with effective thinking.

SPOTLIGHT ON RESEARCH

Beliefs Can Interfere with Effective Reasoning

Who were the investigators and what was the aim of the study? People's beliefs sometimes interfere with their ability to think clearly. When evidence is inconsistent with their beliefs, people may dismiss the evidence as being irrelevant or try to reinterpret the evidence to make it consistent with their beliefs. Paul Klaczynski and Gayathri Narasimham (1998) wanted to determine whether children and adolescents would show such biases in their scientific reasoning.

How did the investigators measure the topic of interest? The experiment was conducted in two sessions. In one session, participants completed a number of questionnaires, including one in which they indicated their religious preference. In a second session, participants read brief descriptions of hypothetical research studies that involved members of different religious groups. The studies were tailored so that each participant read about some studies that presented results depicting the participant's religion positively, some that presented results depicting the participant's religion negatively, and some that did not involve the participant's own religion. For example, if the participant was Lutheran, one study might conclude that Lutherans make better parents (favourable outcome), a second might conclude that Lutherans are less creative than Catholics (unfavourable outcome), and a third might conclude that Baptists handle stress more effectively than Mormons (neutral outcome). After reading about each hypothetical study, participants rated how well the study was conducted on a 9-point scale ranging from 1, extremely poorly conducted, to 9, extremely

well conducted. (In fact, each hypothetical study had a serious flaw, so there was reason to be critical of the results.)

Who were the children in the study? Klaczynski and Narasimham tested 41 10-year-olds, 42 13-year-olds, and 41 16-year-olds. The sample included approximately the same number of boys and girls at each age.

What was the design of the study? This study was experimental because Klaczynski and Narasimham included two independent variables: the age of the participant and the nature of the outcome in the results of the hypothetical study (favourable, unfavourable, neutral). The dependent variable was the participant's rating of the validity of the results (i.e., how well the study had been conducted). The study was cross-sectional because 10-, 13-, and 16-year-olds were all tested at approximately the same time.

Were there ethical concerns with the study? No. As soon as the participants had completed the second session, they were told that the studies they had read were completely hypothetical.

What were the results? The results are shown in Figure 9.5, which shows the average ratings for the three types of studies separately for the three age groups. The same pattern is evident at each age. Relative to studies that had neutral outcomes, children and adolescents believed that studies with favourable outcomes were conducted better and that studies with unfavourable outcomes were conducted worse. In other words, participants were quick to find flaws in studies when the results were inconsistent with their beliefs but overlooked similar flaws when the results were consistent with their beliefs. This pattern is particularly strong for the 10-year-olds, but was also found for the 13- and 16-year-olds.

What did the investigators conclude? Klaczynski and Narasimham believe adolescents use their scientific reasoning skills selectively, raising their standards to dismiss findings that threaten their beliefs and lowering them to admit findings compatible with their beliefs. Such biased reasoning can be traced to two factors. One concerns self-esteem. When outcomes favour groups to which a person belongs, self-esteem is enhanced. Consequently, people overlook flaws in studies that produce results favourable to their group. The children and adolescents who participated in this study may have ignored flaws in studies that were critical about their own religious group because accepting the evidence would have reduced their own self-esteem. A second factor concerns people's naïve theories of the world (like those described in Chapter 4). Such theories are often created over long periods of time, and individuals come to believe them to be self-evident and true. Consequently, a person's naïve theories are protected by adjusting standards depending on the fit of the results with the person's theory. That is, children and adolescents may have ignored flaws in studies that were critical about their own religious group because accepting the flaws would force them to revise a well-developed and well-believed naïve theory about their religious group.

What converging evidence would strengthen these conclusions? An obvious way to bolster these results would be to show that they are not specific to religious beliefs but, instead, extend to other types of beliefs. For example, they might study political beliefs (although this would be difficult with the younger participants in the study). The prediction is that adolescents who, for example, identified themselves with the Conservative party would be less likely to detect flaws in studies that portrayed Conservatives positively. ▨

FIGURE 9.5

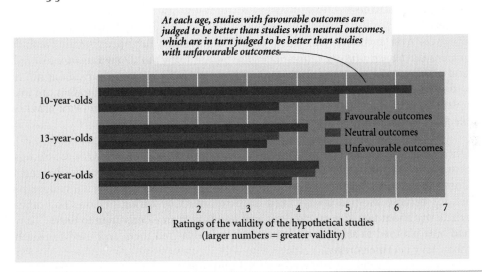

At each age, studies with favourable outcomes are judged to be better than studies with neutral outcomes, which are in turn judged to be better than studies with unfavourable outcomes.

The Spotlight on Research feature tells us that Crystal, the mother in the opening vignette, should not be so perplexed by her son's seemingly erratic thinking: Adolescents (and adults, for that matter) do not always use the most powerful levels of thinking they possess. The information-processing account of intellectual functioning in adolescence is really a description of how children and adolescents *can* think, not how they always or even usually think.

TEST YOURSELF

1. According to information-processing theorists, adolescence is a time of important changes in working memory, processing speed, _____, strategies, and metacognition.

2. Information-processing theorists view adolescence as a time of _____.

3. When evidence is inconsistent with their beliefs, adolescents often _____.

The information-processing account of cognitive change in adolescence emphasizes working memory, knowledge, and strategies. How might each of these factors be influenced by nature? By nurture?

Answers: (1) content knowledge, (2) gradual cognitive change, (3) ignore or dismiss the evidence

9.4

Reasoning About Moral Issues

LEARNING OBJECTIVES

☑ How do adolescents reason about moral issues?

☑ Is moral reasoning similar in all cultures?

☑ How do concern for justice and caring for other people contribute to moral reasoning?

☑ What factors help promote more sophisticated reasoning about moral issues?

Reasoning About Moral Issues

Kohlberg's Theory

Cultural Differences in Moral Reasoning

Beyond Kohlberg's Theory

Promoting Moral Reasoning

Drew, the least popular boy in Grade 8, had been wrongly accused of stealing a sixth grader's CD player. Min-shen, another eighth grader, knew that Drew was innocent but said nothing to the school principal for fear of what his friends would say about siding with Drew. A few days later, when Min-shen's father heard about the incident, he was upset that his son apparently had so little "moral fibre." Why hadn't Min-shen acted in the face of an injustice?

One day the local paper had two articles about youths from the area. One article was about a 15-year-old girl who was badly burned while saving her younger brothers from a fire in their apartment. Her mother said she wasn't surprised by her daughter's actions because she had always been an extraordinarily caring person. The other article was about two 17-year-old boys who had beaten an elderly man to death. They had only planned to steal his wallet, but when he insulted them and tried to punch them, they became enraged.

Reading articles like these, you can't help but question why some teenagers (and adults, as well) act in ways that earn our deepest respect and admiration, whereas others earn our utter contempt as well as our pity. And, at a more mundane level, we wonder why Min-shen didn't tell the principal the truth about the stolen CD player. In this section, we'll start our exploration of moral reasoning with an influential theory proposed by Lawrence Kohlberg.

KOHLBERG'S THEORY

Some of the world's great novels are based on moral dilemmas. Victor Hugo's *Les Misérables*, for example, begins with the protagonist, Jean Valjean, stealing a loaf of bread to feed his sister's starving child. You could probably think of many reasons Valjean should have stolen the bread as well as arguments why he shouldn't have stolen the bread. Lawrence Kohlberg (1969) created stories like this one in which decisions are difficult because every alternative involves some undesirable consequences. In fact, there is no "correct" answer—that's why the stories are referred to as moral "dilemmas." Kohlberg was primarily interested in the reasoning used to justify a decision—Why should Jean Valjean steal the bread? Why should he not steal the bread?—not the decision itself.

Kohlberg's best-known moral dilemma is about Heinz, whose wife is dying:

> In Europe, a woman was near death from cancer. One drug might save her, a form of radium that a druggist in the same town had recently discovered. The druggist was charging $2,000, ten times what the drug cost him to make. The sick woman's husband, Heinz, went to everyone he knew to borrow the money, but he could only get together about half of what it cost. He told the druggist that his wife was dying and asked him to sell it cheaper or let him pay later. But the druggist said, "No." The husband got desperate and broke into the man's store to steal the drug for his wife. (p. 379)

Thus, Heinz and Jean Valjean both face moral dilemmas in which the various alternative courses of action have both desirable and undesirable features.

Kohlberg analyzed children's, adolescents', and adults' responses to a large number of dilemmas and identified three levels of moral reasoning, each divided into two stages. Across the six stages, the basis for moral reasoning shifts. In the earliest stages, moral reasoning is based on external forces, such as the promise of reward or the threat of punishment. At the most advanced levels, moral reasoning is based on a personal, internal moral code and is unaffected by others' views or society's expectations. Let's take a closer look.

Kohlberg's three levels of moral reasoning are preconventional, conventional, and postconventional. Each level is further subdivided into two substages. *At the preconventional level, moral reasoning is based on external forces.* For most children, many adolescents, and some adults, moral reasoning is controlled almost exclusively by rewards and punishments. *Individuals in Stage 1 moral reasoning assume an **obedience orientation,** which means believing that authority figures know what is right and wrong.* Consequently, Stage 1 individuals do what authorities say is right to avoid being punished. At this stage, one might argue that Heinz shouldn't steal the drug because an authority figure (e.g., parent or police officer) said he shouldn't do it. Alternatively, one might argue that he should steal the drug because he would get into trouble if he let his wife die.

*In Stage 2 of the preconventional level, people adopt an **instrumental orientation,** in which they look out for their own needs.* Stage 2 individuals are nice to others because they expect the favour to be returned in the future. Someone at this stage could justify stealing the drug because Heinz's wife might do something nice for Heinz in return. Or they might argue that Heinz shouldn't steal the drug because it will create more problems for him if his wife remains bedridden and he is burdened with caring for her.

*At the **conventional level,** adolescents and adults look to society's norms for moral guidance.* In other words, people's moral reasoning is largely determined by others' expectations of them. *In Stage 3, adolescents' and adults' moral reasoning is based on **interpersonal norms.*** The aim is to win the approval of other people by behaving as "good boys" and "good girls" would. Stage 3 individuals might argue that Heinz shouldn't steal the drug because he must keep his reputation as an honest man, or that no one would think negatively of him for trying to save his wife's life.

*Stage 4 of the conventional level focuses on **social system morality.*** Here, adolescents and adults believe that social roles, expectations, and laws exist to maintain order within society and to promote the good of all people. Stage 4 individuals might reason that Heinz shouldn't steal the drug, even though his wife might die, because it

CP Picture Archive/Fred Chartrand

is illegal and no one is above the law. Alternatively, they might claim that he should steal it to live up to his marriage vow of protecting his wife, even though he will face negative consequences for his theft. Politicians, like the one in the photo, who emphasize "law and order" appeal to people who reason at this stage.

*At the **postconventional level**, moral reasoning is based on a personal moral code.* The emphasis is no longer on external forces like punishment, reward, or social roles. *In Stage 5, people base their moral reasoning on a **social contract**.* Adults agree that members of social groups adhere to a social contract because a common set of expectations and laws benefits all group members. However, if these expectations and laws no longer promote the welfare of individuals, they become invalid. Consequently, Stage 5 individuals might reason that Heinz should steal the drug because social rules about property rights no longer benefit individuals' welfare. They could alternatively argue that he shouldn't steal it because it would create social anarchy.

*Finally, in Stage 6 of the postconventional level, **universal ethical principles** dominate moral reasoning.* Abstract principles such as justice, compassion, and equality form the basis of a personal code that may sometimes conflict with society's expectations and laws. Stage 6 individuals might argue that Heinz should steal the drug because saving a life takes precedence over everything, including the law. Or they might claim that Heinz's wife has a right to die and that he should not force his views on her by stealing and administering the drug.

Putting the stages together, the entire sequence of moral development looks like this:

PRECONVENTIONAL LEVEL: PUNISHMENT AND REWARD

Stage 1: Obedience to authority

Stage 2: Nice behaviour in exchange for future favours

CONVENTIONAL LEVEL: SOCIAL NORMS

Stage 3: Live up to others' expectations

Stage 4: Follow rules to maintain social order

POSTCONVENTIONAL LEVEL: MORAL CODES

Stage 5: Adhere to a social contract when it is valid

Stage 6: Personal moral system based on abstract principles

The developmental sequence described by Kohlberg usually takes many years to unfold. But on occasion we may see the process occur much more dramatically, such as when individuals undergo a major transformation in their moral motivation. One noteworthy example of such a transformation was depicted in Steven Spielberg's Oscar-winning movie *Schindler's List,* and it is described in the Real People feature.

REAL PEOPLE: APPLYING HUMAN DEVELOPMENT

Schindler's List

The outbreak of war typically provides numerous opportunities for shrewd business-people to profit from the increased demand for manufactured goods. The outbreak of World War II in Europe in 1939 was no exception. Oskar Schindler, shown in the photograph, was one such entrepreneur who made a great deal of money working for the Germans after they conquered Poland. His flamboyant demeanour brought him to the attention of the local German commanders, for whom Schindler did favours. Motivated at first strictly by the potential for personal profit, he opened a factory in which he employed Jews as slave labour with few, if any, qualms.

E. Baitel/P. Landmann/Getty Images

Schindler's company was quite successful. But as the war continued, official German policy toward Jews changed to one of extermination. Jewish citizens in Poland and other countries were rounded up and shipped to concentration camps or summarily executed. Schindler was deeply disturbed by this, and his attitudes began to change. His employees suggested that he give the Germans a list of workers essential to the factory's continued operation. The list provided protection, as the plant's products were used in the war effort. This, of course, also kept the profits rolling in. But Schindler's motivation gradually underwent a profound transformation as well. No longer driven by profit, he went to great lengths to preserve life, at no small danger to

himself. He created cover stories to support his claims that certain employees were essential, and he went to Auschwitz to rescue employees who were sent there by mistake.

Oskar Schindler's list saved many lives. Profits were made (and helped provide the perfect cover), but he employed Jews in his factory primarily to save them from the gas chamber. Schindler may have begun the war at Kohlberg's preconventional level—where he was motivated solely by personal profit—but he ultimately moved to the postconventional level—where he was motivated by the higher principle of saving lives. And it is at the postconventional level that heroes are made.

Support for Kohlberg's Theory

Kohlberg proposed that his stages form an invariant sequence. That is, individuals move through the six stages in the order listed and in only that order. If his stage theory is right, then level of moral reasoning should be strongly associated with age and level of cognitive development. Older and more advanced thinkers should, on the average, be more advanced in their moral development, and indeed they usually are (Stewart & Pascual-Leone, 1992).

For example, Figure 9.6 shows developmental change in the percentage of individuals who reason at Kohlberg's different stages. Stages 1 and 2 are common among children and young adolescents but not among older adolescents and adults. Stages 3 and 4 are common among older adolescents and adults. The figure also shows that most individuals do not progress to the final stages. Most adults' moral reasoning is at Stages 3 and 4.

FIGURE 9.6   Kohlberg's Stages of Moral Reasoning: Age Differences

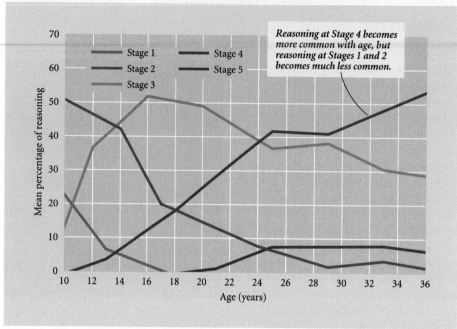

Support for Kohlberg's invariant sequence of stages also comes from longitudinal studies measuring individuals' level of reasoning over several years. Individuals do progress through each stage in sequence, and virtually no individuals skip any stages (Colby et al., 1983). Longitudinal studies also show that, over time, individuals become more advanced in their level of moral reasoning or remain at the same level. They do not regress to a lower level (Walker & Taylor, 1991).

Additional support for Kohlberg's theory comes from research on the link between moral reasoning and moral behaviour. In general, level of moral reasoning should be linked to moral behaviour. Remember that less advanced moral reasoning reflects the influence of external forces such as rewards and social norms, whereas more advanced reasoning is based on a personal moral code. Therefore, individuals at the preconventional and conventional levels would act morally when external forces demand, but otherwise they may not. In contrast, individuals at the postconventional level, where reasoning is based on personal principles, should be compelled to moral action even when external forces may not favour it.

Let's return to the example in the vignette. Suppose you know that one of the least popular students has been wrongly accused of stealing a CD player, and you know that some friends in your group are actually responsible. What would you do? Speaking out on behalf of the unpopular student is unlikely to lead to reward. Furthermore, there are strong social norms against "squealing" on friends. So if you are in the preconventional or conventional level of moral reasoning, like Min-shen, you would probably let the unpopular student be punished unfairly. But if you are at the postconventional level and see the situation in terms of principles of justice and fairness, you would be more likely to identify the real perpetrators despite the price to be paid in rejection by the group.

Many researchers report findings that support the hypothesized link between moral reasoning and moral action. In one study (Gibbs et al., 1986), high school teachers were asked to judge whether their students would defend their principles in difficult situations, or if they

THINK ABOUT IT

Research shows that people sometimes do not reason at the most advanced levels of which they are capable; instead they revert to simpler, less-mature levels. Might this happen in the realm of moral reasoning too? What factors might make it more likely for a person's moral reasoning to revert temporarily to a less sophisticated level?

would act morally only when it was fashionable or handy. High school students who were judged by their teachers to have greater moral courage tended to be more advanced in Kohlberg's stages than students who were judged less courageous. That is, students like those in the photograph who protest social issues tend to have higher moral reasoning scores. The converse is also true: delinquent adolescents, whose actions are more likely to be morally offensive, tend to have lower moral reasoning scores than nondelinquent adolescents (Chandler & Moran, 1990). That is, delinquent adolescents are more likely to emphasize punishment and reward in their moral reasoning, not social norms and personal moral codes.

On another point of Kohlberg's theory, support is mixed. Kohlberg claimed his sequence of stages is universal: All people in all cultures progress through the six-stage sequence. Some research shows that children and adolescents in cultures worldwide reason about moral dilemmas at Stages 2 or 3, just like North American children and adolescents. But as we'll see in the next section, beyond the earliest stages, moral reasoning in other cultures is often not described well by Kohlberg's theory (Turiel & Neff, 2000).

CULTURAL DIFFERENCES IN MORAL REASONING

Many critics note that Kohlberg's emphasis on individual rights and justice reflects traditional North American culture and Judeo-Christian theology. Not all cultures and religions share this emphasis; consequently, moral reasoning might be based on different values in other cultures (Carlo et al., 1996; Keller et al., 1998).

The Hindu religion, for example, emphasizes duty and responsibility to others, not individual rights and justice (Simpson, 1974). Accordingly, children and adults reared with traditional Hindu beliefs might emphasize caring for others in their moral reasoning more than individuals brought up in the Judeo-Christian tradition do.

Miller and Bersoff (1992) tested the hypothesis that cultural differences affect moral reasoning by constructing dilemmas with both justice- and care-based solutions. For example:

> Ben planned to travel to San Francisco in order to attend the wedding of
> his best friend. He needed to catch the very next train if he was to be on

time for the ceremony, as he had to deliver the wedding rings. However, Ben's wallet was stolen in the train station. He lost all of his money as well as his ticket to San Francisco.

Ben approached several officials as well as passengers . . . and asked them to loan him money to buy a new ticket. But, because he was a stranger, no one was willing to lend him the money he needed.

While Ben . . . was trying to decide what to do next, a well-dressed man sitting next to him walked away. . . . Ben noticed that the man had left his coat unattended. Sticking out of the man's coat pocket was a train ticket to San Francisco. . . . He also saw that the man had more than enough money in his coat pocket to buy another train ticket. (p. 545)

One solution emphasized individual rights and justice:

Ben should not take the ticket from the man's coat pocket even though it means not getting to San Francisco in time to deliver the wedding rings to his best friend. (p. 545)

The other solution placed a priority on caring for others:

Ben should go to San Francisco to deliver the wedding rings to his best friend even if it means taking the train ticket from the other man's coat pocket. (p. 545)

When children and adults living in the United States responded to dilemmas like this one about Ben, a slight majority selected the justice-based alternative. In contrast, when Hindu children and adults living in India responded to the same dilemmas, the overwhelming majority selected the care-based alternative.

Clearly, moral reasoning reflects the culture in which a person is reared. The judgments by Indian children and adults reflect their culture's emphasis on caring for other people. The bases of moral reasoning are not universal as Kohlberg claimed; instead, they reflect cultural values.

BEYOND KOHLBERG'S THEORY

Kohlberg's theory obviously is not the final word on moral development. Much about his theory seems valid, but research findings indicate that Kohlberg's theory applies primarily to cultures with Western philosophical and religious traditions. In the next few pages, we describe some work that helps complete our picture of moral reasoning.

Gilligan's Ethic of Caring

Researcher Carol Gilligan (1982; Gilligan & Attanucci, 1988) questions how applicable Kohlberg's theory is even within the Western tradition. Gilligan argues that Kohlberg's emphasis on justice applies more to men than to women, whose reasoning about moral issues is often rooted in concern for others. Gilligan (1982) writes, "The moral imperative that emerges repeatedly in interviews with women is an injunction to care, a responsibility to discern and alleviate the real and recognizable trouble of this world" (p. 100).

Gilligan proposes a developmental progression in which individuals gain greater understanding of caring and responsibility. In the first stage, children are preoccupied with their own needs. In the second stage, people care for others, particularly those who are less able to care for themselves, such as infants and the aged. The third stage unites caring for others and for oneself by emphasizing caring in all human relationships and by denouncing exploitation and violence between people. For example, consider the teen in the photo who is helping at a homeless shelter. She does so not because she believes the homeless are needy but because she believes, first, that all humans should care for each other, and, second, that many people are in the shelter because they've been exploited.

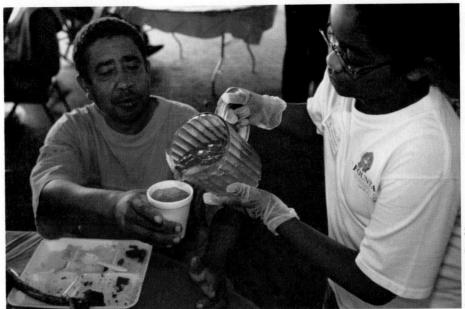

Like Kohlberg, Gilligan also believes moral reasoning becomes qualitatively more sophisticated as individuals develop, progressing through a number of distinct stages. However, Gilligan emphasizes care (helping people in need) instead of justice (treating people fairly).

What does research tell us about the importance of justice and care in moral reasoning? Do females and males differ in the bases of their moral reasoning? The best answer to these questions comes from a comprehensive meta-analysis conducted by Jaffee and Hyde (2000) that included 113 studies with more than 12,000 participants. Overall, boys and men tended to get slightly higher scores on problems that emphasized justice, whereas girls and women tended to get slightly higher scores on problems that emphasized caring. But the differences are small and do not indicate that moral reasoning is predominated by a concern with care for females and a concern with justice for males. Instead, girls and boys as well as men and women reason about moral issues similarly (Walker, 1995); both often think about moral issues in terms of care and interpersonal relationships.

Eisenberg's Levels of Prosocial Reasoning

Nancy Eisenberg (1982; Eisenberg et al., 1995) argues that Kohlberg's theory is flawed because the dilemmas are unrealistic. They involve breaking a law or disobeying a person in authority. In real life, says Eisenberg, most children's moral dilemmas involve choosing between self-interest and helping others. For example, in one of Eisenberg's moral dilemmas, a child walking to a party comes upon a child injured from a fall. The first child must decide whether to continue to the party or help the second child and miss the party.

Like Kohlberg, Eisenberg focuses on how children explain their choices. *Most preschool and many elementary school children have a **hedonistic orientation:** They pursue their own pleasure.* These children do not help the injured child because they would miss the party. Or they might help because they expect that the injured child would return the favour in the future. In either case, self-interest is the basis of their decision.

*Some preschool and many elementary school children have a **needs-oriented orientation:** They are concerned about others' needs and want to help.* Children at this stage have learned a simple rule: to help others. They often explain their desire to help as a straightforward, "He needs my help." Their desire to help is not based on imagining how the injured child feels or on a personal moral code.

SW Productions/Photodisc

*Many elementary school children and adolescents have a **stereotyped approval-focused orientation**, behaving as they think society expects "good people" to behave.* The helpful teen in the photo would explain her behaviour by saying that the person she's helping will like her more because she's helping.

*Finally, some children and many adolescents develop an **empathic orientation**; they consider the injured child's perspective and how their own actions will make them feel.* An adolescent with this orientation might say, "He'd be in pain, so I'd feel bad if I didn't help."

The same kinds of evidence that support Kohlberg's theory support Eisenberg's. For example, longitudinal studies indicate that children in many countries move through Eisenberg's different orientations in sequence (Eisenberg, 1986; Eisenberg et al., 1995). Moreover, children who reason at more advanced levels are more likely to actually help others than children who reason at less advanced levels (Miller et al., 1996).

Eisenberg's theory is like Kohlberg's in emphasizing that moral development involves a developmental shift away from self-centred thinking to social norms and moral principles. Her theory is like Gilligan's in emphasizing that caring for others is an important element in everyday moral reasoning.

PROMOTING MORAL REASONING

Whether it is based on justice or care, most cultures and most parents want to encourage adolescents to think carefully about moral issues. What can be done to help adolescents develop more mature forms of moral reasoning? Sometimes simply being exposed to more advanced moral reasoning is sufficient to promote developmental change (Walker, 1980). Adolescents may notice, for example, that older friends do not wait to be rewarded to help others. Or a teenager may notice that respected peers take courageous positions regardless of the social consequences. Such experiences apparently cause adolescents to reevaluate their reasoning on moral issues and propel them toward more sophisticated thinking.

© Bob Daemmrich/Stock Boston Inc.

Kohlberg himself wasn't content to simply chart how moral reasoning changed with age. He also wanted to devise ways to foster sophisticated moral reasoning. Kohlberg discovered that discussion can be particularly effective in revealing shortcomings in moral reasoning. When people, like the adolescents in the photo, reason about moral issues with others whose reasoning is at a higher level, the usual result is that individuals reasoning at lower levels improve (Berkowitz & Gibbs, 1985). This is particularly true when the conversational partner with the more sophisticated reasoning makes an effort to understand the other's view by requesting clarification or paraphrasing what the other child is saying (Walker, Hennig, & Krettenauer, 2000). Imagine, for example, two 13-year-olds discussing the Heinz dilemma. Suppose one takes the position that Heinz should not steal the drug because he might get caught—reasoning at the preconventional level. The other argues that Heinz should steal the drug because a husband should do anything to save his wife's life—reasoning at the conventional level. During conversations of this sort, individuals at the preconventional level usually adopt the logic of the children arguing at the higher conventional level.

To foster discussion and expose students to more advanced moral thinking, Kohlberg and his colleagues set up "Just Communities," special groups of students and teachers within public high schools (Higgins, 1991; Power, Higgins, & Kohlberg, 1989). Teachers and students met weekly to plan school activities and discuss school policies. Decisions were reached democratically with teachers and students alike, each having one vote. However, during discussions, teachers acted as facilitators, encouraging students to consider the moral consequences of different courses of action. Students who participated in Just Communities tended to be more advanced in their moral thinking (Higgins, 1991; Power et al., 1989).

Research findings such as these send an important message to parents: Discussion is probably the best way for parents to help their children think about moral issues in more mature terms (Walker & Taylor, 1991). Research consistently shows that mature moral reasoning comes about when adolescents are free to express their opinions on moral issues to their parents, who are, in turn, expressing their own opinions and, consequently, exposing their adolescent children to more mature moral reasoning (Hoffman, 1988, 1994).

TEST YOURSELF

1. Kohlberg's theory includes the preconventional, conventional, and _____ levels.

2. For children and adolescents in the preconventional level, moral reasoning is strongly influenced by _____.

3. Supporting Kohlberg's theory are findings that level of moral reasoning is associated with age, that people progress through the stages in the predicted sequence, and that _____.

4. Gilligan's view of morality emphasizes _____ instead of justice.

5. Eisenberg's theory of prosocial reasoning is like Kohlberg's theory in claiming that moral reasoning involves a shift away

from self-centred thinking; her theory is like Gilligan's in _____.

6. In Just Communities, teachers encourage students to _____.

7. If parents wish to foster their children's moral development, they should _____ with them.

How similar is Piaget's stage of formal operational thought to Kohlberg's stage of conventional moral reasoning?

Answers: (1) postconventional, (2) reward or punishment, (3) more advanced moral reasoning is associated with moral action, (4) caring for others, (5) its emphasis on caring for others as an important feature in moral reasoning, (6) consider the moral consequences of their decisions, (7) discuss moral issues

PUTTING IT ALL TOGETHER

Teenagers are "nearly" adults, and throughout this chapter we've seen many of the factors that contribute to this remarkable push toward maturity. We began with the physical changes associated with puberty. These outward signs of looming adulthood come early in adolescence for some youth but for others, like Pete, they come much later. Next we looked at adolescent health, where we learned of the importance of adequate nutrition and exercise but discovered that many teenagers receive inadequate nutrition and do not exercise regularly. We discovered that for adolescents like Dana who participate in sports, dangerous injuries are uncommon.

From health we moved to information processing, which improves gradually during the teenage years because of increased working memory and processing speed, greater content knowledge, and more efficient strategies. Adolescents like Crystal's son Calvin do not always think as effectively as they could, sometimes because their beliefs interfere with effective cognition.

We ended the chapter by examining moral reasoning. As children and adolescents develop, their moral reasoning is more likely to be guided by moral principles than by rewards and punishments, but adolescents' moral thinking is often based on their desire to win others' approval, which explains why Min-shen did not tell the school principal who really stole the CD player.

SUMMARY

9.1 Physical Changes

Signs of Physical Maturation

▪ Puberty includes bodily changes in height and weight as well as sexual maturation. Girls typically begin the growth spurt earlier than boys, who acquire more muscle, less fat, and greater heart and lung capacity. Sexual maturation, which includes primary and secondary sex characteristics, occurs in predictable sequences for boys and girls.

Mechanisms of Maturation

▪ Pubertal changes take place when the pituitary gland signals the adrenal gland, ovaries, and testes to secrete hormones that initiate physical changes. The timing of puberty is influenced strongly by health and nutrition. In addition, the timing of puberty is influenced by the social environment, coming earlier when girls experience family conflict or depression.

Psychological Impact of Puberty

▪ Pubertal changes affect adolescents' psychological functioning. Teens, particularly girls, become particularly concerned about their appearance. When forewarned, adolescents respond positively to menarche and spermarche. Adolescents are moodier than children and adults, primarily because their moods shift in response to frequent changes in activities and social setting. Early maturation tends to be harmful to girls but beneficial to boys.

9.2 Health

Nutrition

▪ For proper growth, teenagers need to consume adequate calories, calcium, and iron. Unfortunately, many teenagers do not eat properly and do not receive adequate nutrition.

▪ Anorexia and bulimia are eating disorders that typically affect adolescent girls who have an irrational fear of being overweight. Several factors contribute to these disorders, including cultural standards of thinness, a need for independence within an autocratic family, and heredity.

Physical Fitness

▪ Individuals who work out at least three times weekly often have improved physical and mental health. Unfortunately, many high school students do not get enough exercise.

▪ Most Canadian boys and girls participate in sports. The benefits of participating in sports include improved physical fitness, enhanced self-esteem, and understanding about teamwork. The potential costs include injury and abuse of performance-enhancing drugs.

Threats to Adolescent Well-Being

▪ Accidents involving automobiles are the most common cause of death in Canadian teenagers. Many of these deaths could be prevented if, for example, adolescents did not drive recklessly (e.g., too fast and without wearing seat belts). Adolescents and adults often make decisions similarly, considering the alternatives available, the consequences of each alternative, and the desirability and likelihood of these consequences. The outcomes of decision-making sometimes differ because adolescents are more likely to emphasize the social consequences of actions.

9.3 Information Processing During Adolescence

How Does Information Processing Improve in Adolescence?

- According to information-processing theorists, adolescence is a time of gradual cognitive change. Working memory and processing speed achieve adultlike levels; content knowledge increases to expertlike levels in some domains; and strategies and metacognitive skills become much more sophisticated.

Limits on Information Processing

- Adolescents do not always think as effectively as they can. Sometimes they resort to simpler, less mature levels of thinking, and sometimes their beliefs blind them to more sophisticated forms of thought.

9.4 Reasoning About Moral Issues

Kohlberg's Theory

- Kohlberg proposed that moral reasoning includes preconventional, conventional, and postconventional levels. Moral reasoning is first based on rewards and punishments and, much later, on a personal moral code. As predicted by Kohlberg's theory, people progress through the stages in sequence and do not regress, and morally advanced reasoning is associated with more frequent moral behaviour. However, few people attain the most advanced levels, and cultures differ in the bases of moral reasoning.

Cultural Differences in Moral Reasoning

- Not all cultures emphasize justice in moral reasoning. The Hindu religion emphasizes duty and responsibility to others, and, consistent with these beliefs, Hindu children and adults emphasize caring for other people in their moral reasoning.

Beyond Kohlberg's Theory

- Gilligan proposed that females' moral reasoning is based on caring and responsibility for others, not justice. Research does not support consistent sex differences in moral reasoning but has found that males and females both consider caring as well as justice in their moral judgments, depending on the situation. According to Eisenberg, reasoning about prosocial dilemmas shifts gradually from a self-interested, hedonistic orientation to concern for others based on empathy.

Promoting Moral Reasoning

- Many factors can promote more sophisticated moral reasoning, including (a) noticing that one's current thinking is inadequate (is contradictory or does not lead to clear actions), (b) observing others reason at more advanced levels, and (c) discussing moral issues with peers, teachers, and parents.

KEY TERMS

puberty (312)
primary sex characteristics (313)
secondary sex characteristics (313)
menarche (314)
spermarche (314)
body mass index (BMI) (320)
basal metabolism rate (320)
anorexia nervosa (321)

bulimia nervosa (321)
preconventional level (331)
obedience orientation (331)
instrumental orientation (331)
conventional level (331)
interpersonal norms (331)
social system morality (331)
postconventional level (332)

social contract (332)
universal ethical principles (332)
hedonistic orientation (337)
needs-oriented orientation (337)
approval-focused orientation (338)
empathic orientation (338)

SEE FOR YOURSELF: APPLYING WHAT YOU'VE LEARNED

Most young adults remember well the onset of puberty and their feelings at the time. Ask several of your friends—men and women—when puberty began for them and how they knew. Then ask them for some of the positive experiences associated with puberty as well as some of the negative experiences. You should find that the timing of puberty is very important: Men who matured early will report many more positive experiences than men who matured late. The opposite pattern should hold for women. See for yourself!

LEARN MORE ABOUT IT

Readings

COOPER, K. (1992). *Kid fitness.* New York: Random House. The originator of the concept of aerobic fitness describes a program of diet and exercise developed just for children and adolescents.

GIBBS, J.C. (2003). *Moral development and reality: Beyond the theories of Kohlberg and Hoffman.* Thousand Oaks, CA: Sage. This book examines current theory and thinking in cognitive-emotional development.

HAYWARD, C. (ed.) (2003). *Gender differences at puberty.* New York: Cambridge University Press. This book focuses on gender differences in development and summarizes the latest research on the area.

 For additional readings, explore InfoTrac® College Edition, your online library. Go to http://www.infotrac.thomsonlearning.com.

Websites

http://www.anred.com/

Anorexia Nervosa and Related Eating Disorders, Inc. maintains a website that describes different eating disorders, their causes, and treatments.

http://www.cflri.ca

The Canadian Fitness and Lifestyle Research Institute, which sponsors this website, is a national research agency dedicated to advising, educating, and informing Canadians and professions on the importance of activity for healthy lives.

http://www.hc-sc.gc.ca/english/for_you/youth.html

Health Canada's website includes a link specific to youth and adolescence on various topics such as alcohol and drugs, body image, depression, family issues, health, sexuality, risky behaviours, and violence.

Website addresses are subject to change. The *Human Development* book companion website can be accessed for updated links.

The Human Development Book Companion Website

See http://www.humandevelopment.nelson.com for practice quiz questions, Internet links, updates, critical thinking exercises, discussion forums, and more.

 Life-Span CD-ROM

For more information on the concepts covered in this chapter, go to

Module 4: Adolescence

- Physical Development
- Cognitive Development
- Emotional and Social Development

© David Pollack /Corbis / Magma

CHAPTER 10

Moving into the Adult Social World

SOCIOEMOTIONAL DEVELOPMENT IN ADOLESCENCE

You probably have vivid memories of your teenage years. Remember the exhilarating moments—high school graduation, your first paycheque from a part-time job, and your first feelings of love and sexuality? There were, of course, painful times—your first day on the job when you couldn't do anything right, not knowing what to say on a date with a person you desperately wanted to impress, and countless arguments with your parents. Feelings of pride and accomplishment accompanied by feelings of embarrassment and bewilderment are common for individuals on the threshold of adulthood.

Adolescence represents the transition from childhood to adulthood and is a time when individuals grapple with their identity; many have their first experiences with love and sex; and some enter the world of work. In the first three sections of this chapter, we investigate these challenging developmental issues. Then we look at the special obstacles adolescents sometimes encounter that make this transition difficult to handle.

10.1

Identity and Self-Esteem

LEARNING OBJECTIVES

▧ How do adolescents achieve an identity?

▧ What is an ethnic identity? What are the stages in acquiring an ethnic identity?

▧ How does self-esteem change in adolescence?

▧ What influences adolescents' self-esteem?

▧ How do parent-child relationships change in adolescence?

Identity and Self-Esteem

The Search for Identity

Ethnic Identity

Self-Esteem in Adolescence

Influences on Adolescents' Self-Esteem

The Myth of Storm and Stress

Bernadette was born in Seoul of Korean parents but was adopted by a Dutch couple in Ontario when she was 3 months old. Growing up, she considered herself a Canadian. In high school, however, Bernadette realized that others saw her as an Asian Canadian, an identity about which she had never given much thought. She began to wonder, "Who am I really? Canadian? Dutch Canadian? Asian Canadian?"

Like Bernadette, do you sometimes wonder who you are? Self-concept refers to the attitudes, behaviours, and values that make a person unique. In adolescence, self-concept takes on special significance as adolescents struggle to achieve an identity that will enable them to participate in the adult world. Through self-reflection, youths search for an identity to integrate the many different, and sometimes conflicting, elements of the self. In this section, we'll learn more about the adolescent search for identity. Along the way, we'll also learn more about Bernadette's struggle to learn who she is.

THE SEARCH FOR IDENTITY

Erik Erikson's (1968) account of identity formation has been particularly influential in our understanding of adolescence. Erikson argued that adolescents face a crisis between identity and role confusion. This crisis involves balancing the desire to try out many possible selves and the need to select a single self. Adolescents who achieve a sense of identity are well prepared to face the next developmental challenge—establishing intimate, sharing relationships with others. However, Erikson believed that teenagers who are confused about their identity can never experience intimacy in any human relationship. Instead, throughout their lives, they remain isolated and respond to others stereotypically.

How do adolescents achieve an identity? They use the hypothetical reasoning skills of the formal operational stage to experiment with different selves to learn more about possible identities (Nurmi, Poole, & Kalakoski, 1996). Adolescents' advanced cognitive skills enable them to imagine themselves in different roles.

Much of the testing and experimentation is career oriented. Some adolescents, like the ones shown in the photo on page 347, may envision themselves as rock stars; others may imagine being professional athletes, nurses, lawyers, or best-selling novelists. Other testing is romantically oriented. Teens may fall in love and imagine living with the loved one. Still other exploration involves religious and political beliefs (King, Elder, & Whitbeck, 1997; Yates & Youniss, 1996). Teens give different identities a trial run just as you might test-drive different cars before selecting one. By fantasizing about their future, adolescents begin to discover who they will be. As adolescents strive to achieve an identity, they often progress through the different phases or statuses listed in Table 10.1 (Marcia, 1980, 1991).

Unlike Piaget's stages, these four phases do not necessarily occur in sequence. Most young adolescents are in a state of diffusion or foreclosure. The common element in these phases is that teens are not exploring alternative identities. They are

© Lawrence Manning/Corbis/Magma

TABLE 10.1		Marcia's Four Different Identity Statuses
Status	**Definition**	**Example**
Diffusion	The person is overwhelmed by the task of achieving an identity and does little to accomplish the task.	Larry hates the idea of deciding what to do with his future, so he spends most of his free time playing video games.
Foreclosure	The person has a status determined by adults rather than from personal exploration.	For as long as she can remember, Sakura's parents have told her that she should be a lawyer and join the family law firm. She plans to take courses in university that can help get her into law, though she's never given the matter much thought.
Moratorium	The person is examining different alternatives but has yet to find one that's satisfactory.	Brad enjoys almost all his high school classes. Some days he thinks it would be fun to be a chemist, some days he wants to be a novelist, and some days he'd like to be an elementary school teacher. He thinks it's a little weird to change his mind so often, but he also enjoys thinking about different jobs.
Achievement	The person has explored alternatives and has deliberately chosen a specific identity.	Throughout elementary school, Efrat wanted to play women's professional hockey as a career. During Grades 9 and 10, she took a computing course and everything finally "clicked"—she'd found her niche. She knew that she wanted to study computer science in university.

avoiding the crisis altogether or have resolved it by taking on an identity suggested by parents or other adults. However, as individuals move beyond adolescence and into young adulthood, they have more opportunity to explore alternative identities, and so diffusion and foreclosure become less common, and as Figure 10.1 shows, achievement and moratorium become more common (Meilman, 1979).

Typically, young people do not reach the achievement status for all aspects of identity at the same time (Dellas & Jernigan, 1990; Kroger & Green, 1996). Some adolescents may reach the achievement status for occupations before achieving it for religion and politics. Others reach the achievement status for religion before other domains. Evidently, few youths achieve a sense of identity all at once; instead, the crisis of identity is first resolved in some areas and then in others.

FIGURE 10.1   Age Difference in Identity Statuses

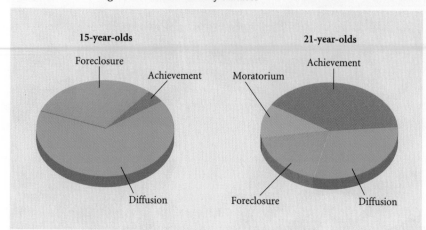

When the achievement status is attained, the period of active experimentation ends and individuals have a well-defined sense of self. However, during adulthood, an individual's identity is sometimes reworked in response to new life challenges and circumstances. Consequently, individuals may return to the moratorium status for a period, only to reemerge later with a changed identity. In fact, adults may go through these changes several times, creating "MAMA" cycles in which they alternate between the *m*oratorium and *a*chievement statuses as they explore new alternatives in response to personal and family crises (Marcia, 1991). For example, a man like the one in the photo who has placed career above all else but finds himself unemployed may reorganize his life around family and become the primary caregiver of his children.

During the search for identity, adolescents reveal a number of characteristic ways of thinking. They are often very self-oriented. *The self-absorption that marks the teenage search for identity is referred to as **adolescent egocentrism*** (Elkind, 1978). Unlike preschoolers, adolescents know that others have different perspectives on the world. Adolescents are simply *much* more interested in their own feelings and experiences than in anyone else's experiences. In addition, as they search for an identity, many adolescents wrongly believe they are the focus of others' thinking. A teen like the one in the photo who spills food on herself may imagine that all her friends are thinking only about the stain on her blouse and how sloppy she is. *Many adolescents feel that they are, in effect, actors whose performance is watched constantly by their peers, a phenomenon known as the **imaginary audience**.*

Adolescent self-absorption is also demonstrated by the **personal fable**, teenagers' tendency to believe that their experiences and feelings are *unique—that no one has ever felt or thought as they do.* Whether the excitement of first love, the despair of a broken relationship, or the confusion of planning for the future, adolescents often believe they are the first to experience these feelings and that no one else could possibly understand the power of their emotions (Elkind & Bowen, 1979). *Adolescents' belief in their uniqueness also contributes to an* **illusion of invulnerability**—*the belief that misfortune only happens to others.* They think they can have sex without becoming pregnant and that they can drive recklessly without being in an auto accident. Those misfortunes only happen to other people.

These characteristics of adolescents' thinking are summarized in Table 10.2.

TABLE 10.2	**Characteristics of Adolescents' Thinking**	
Feature	*Definition*	*Example*
Adolescent egocentrism	*Adolescents are overly concerned with their own thoughts and feelings.*	When Levi's grandmother died unexpectedly, Levi was preoccupied with how the funeral would affect his weekend plans and ignored how upset his mother was by her own mother's death.
Imaginary audience	*Adolescents believe others are watching them constantly.*	Tom had to ride his bike to football practice because his dad wouldn't let him have the car; he was sure that all his car-driving friends would see and make fun of him.
Personal fable	*Adolescents believe their experiences and feelings are unique.*	When Rosa's boyfriend decided to date another girl, Rosa cried and cried. She couldn't believe how sad she was, and she was sure her mom had never felt this way.
Illusion of invulnerability	*Adolescents think that misfortune only happens to others.*	Kumares and his girlfriend had been having sex for about six months. Although she thought it would be a good idea to use birth control, he thought it was unnecessary. There was no way his girlfriend would get pregnant.

As adolescents make progress toward achieving an identity, adolescent egocentrism, imaginary audiences, personal fables, and the illusion of invulnerability become less common. What circumstances help adolescents achieve identity? Parents are influential (Marcia, 1980). When parents encourage discussion and recognize children's autonomy, their children are more likely to reach the achievement status. Apparently these youths feel encouraged to undertake the personal experimentation that leads to identity. In contrast, when parents set rules with little justification and enforce them without explanation, children are more likely to remain in the foreclosure status. These teens are discouraged from experimenting personally; instead, their parents simply tell them what identity to adopt. Overall, adolescents are most likely to establish a well-defined identity in a family atmosphere where parents encourage their children to explore alternatives on their own but do not pressure or provide explicit direction (Harter, 1990, 1999).

> **THINK ABOUT IT**
>
> Although Piaget's theory of cognitive development was not concerned with identity formation, how might his theory explain why identity is a central issue in adolescence?

ETHNIC IDENTITY

Canada is one of the most ethnically diverse countries in the world. Approximately 44% of people living in Canada reported origins other than British, French, or Canadian, and the ethnic mix of each province is unique (Canadian Heritage Multiculturalism, 1998). *Individuals typically develop an* **ethnic identity:** *They feel a part of their ethnic group and learn the special customs and traditions of their group's culture and heritage* (Phinney, 1996).

Achieving an ethnic identity seems to occur in three phases. Initially, adolescents have not examined their ethnic roots and may not yet view ethnicity as an important personal issue.

In the second phase, adolescents begin to explore the personal impact of their ethnic heritage. Part of this phase involves learning cultural traditions; for example, like the girl in the photo, many adolescents learn to prepare ethnic food.

In the third phase, individuals achieve a distinct ethnic self-concept. To see if you understand the differences between these stages of ethnic identity, reread the vignette on page 346 about Bernadette, the Dutch Asian-Canadian high school student, then decide which stage applies to her. The answer appears on page 354 just before Test Yourself.

Older adolescents are more likely than younger ones to have achieved an ethnic identity because they are more likely to have had opportunities to explore their cultural heritage (Phinney & Chavira, 1992). Also, as is the case with overall identity, adolescents are most likely to achieve an ethnic self-concept when their parents encourage them to explore alternatives instead of pressuring them to adopt a particular ethnic identity (Rosenthal & Feldman, 1992).

Ethnic identity poses a special challenge for immigrant adolescents. Unlike native-born ethnic children who have exposure to mainstream and ethnic culture from a young age, from the time immigrant adolescents enter a new country, they face the task of negotiating a culture largely unfamiliar to them. And many immigrant adolescents have already established a strong identity with their native land. Consequently, it's not surprising that immigrant adolescents do not immediately identify with their new culture. For example, in one study (Birman & Trickett, 2001), Jewish adolescents who had fled the former Soviet Union report that, although they acted like most American teenagers (e.g., they ate American food, spent time with native-born American teens), they still "felt Russian" despite having lived in the United States for nearly 10 years.

Do adolescents benefit from a strong ethnic identity? Yes. Adolescents who have achieved an ethnic identity tend to have higher self-esteem and find their interactions with family and friends more satisfying (Roberts et al., 1999). In addition, many investigators have found that adolescents with a strong ethnic identity do better in school than adolescents whose ethnic identities are weaker (Stalikas & Gavaki, 1995; Taylor et al., 1994).

Some individuals achieve a well-defined ethnic self-concept and, at the same time, identify strongly with the mainstream culture. In Canada, for example, many Chinese Canadians embrace both Chinese and Canadian cultures; in England, many Indians identify with both Indian and British cultures. For other individuals, the cost of strong ethnic identification is a weakened tie to mainstream culture (Phinney, 1990). A Canadian study on the development of ethnic identity in children of Chinese immigrants highlighted the importance of the acculturation process, which involves changes in values and behaviours based on another culture, and revealed the many different strategies that young people take in developing their identity. A number of young people who participated felt that they would become "more Canadian" after spending more time in their new country, with responses such as "I feel I am gradually becoming a Canadian" and "I am a Taiwanese right now. In the future I feel I am Canadian" (Tsang et al., 2003).

We shouldn't be too surprised that identifying with mainstream culture weakens ethnic identity in some groups but not others (Berry, 1993). Even within any particular group, the nature and consequences of ethnic identity may change over successive generations (Cuellar et al., 1997). As successive generations become more acculturated to mainstream culture, they may identify less strongly with ethnic culture. Thus parents may maintain strong feelings of ethnic identity that their children don't share (Phinney, Ong, & Madden, 2000).

> **THINK ABOUT IT**
>
> What factors in the biopsychosocial framework are shown by adolescents who develop an ethnic identity?

SELF-ESTEEM IN ADOLESCENCE

Self-esteem is usually very high in preschool children but declines gradually during the early elementary school years as children compare themselves to others. By the later elementary school years, self-esteem has usually stabilized—it neither increases nor decreases in these years (Harter, Whitesell, & Kowalski, 1992). Evidently, children learn their place in the "pecking order" of different domains and adjust their self-esteem accordingly. However, self-esteem sometimes drops when children move from elementary school to middle school or junior high (Twenge & Campbell, 2001). Apparently, when students from different elementary schools enter the same middle school or junior high, they know where they stand compared to their old elementary school classmates but not compared to students from other elementary schools. Thus peer comparisons begin anew, and self-esteem often suffers temporarily. But as a new school becomes familiar and students gradually adjust to the new pecking order, self-esteem again increases.

There is more to developmental change in self-esteem, however. The pattern of change also depends on the specific domain and the child's sex, as you'll see in the Spotlight on Research feature.

SPOTLIGHT ON RESEARCH

Developmental Change in Self-Esteem in Different Domains

Who were the investigators, and what was the aim of the study? The developmental change we see in global self-esteem need not hold for all domains. Specific domains (e.g., academic, behaviour) might change in different ways as children develop. In addition, developmental change in self-esteem in specific domains might differ for boys and girls. To study these issues, David Cole and his colleagues (2001) examined developmental change in five domains of self-esteem between Grades 3 and 11.

How did the investigators measure the topic of interest? The investigators assessed self-perception in five domains—academic, sports, social, appearance, and behaviour. Examples of the test items they used include "very good at schoolwork" (academic), "popular with others" (social), "better than others at sports" (sports), "happy with the way they look" (appearance), and "act as supposed to" (behaviour). Each domain was assessed with five different items.

Who were the children in the study? The study began in the fall of 1993 with 435 third graders and 420 sixth graders attending public schools in a medium-sized U.S. city. The sample included approximately equal numbers of boys and girls. The children completed the test items every fall and spring for a five-year period. Thus the younger participants were in Grade 8 when the study ended and the older participants were in Grade 11.

What was the design of the study? This study was correlational because Cole and his colleagues were interested in the relations that existed naturally between children's self-perception and their age and sex. The study was longitudinal-sequential because children in the two groups (those in Grades 3 and 6 at the start of the study) were tested repeatedly over a five-year period.

Were there ethical concerns with the study? No. The investigators obtained permission from the parents for the children to participate.

FIGURE 10.2

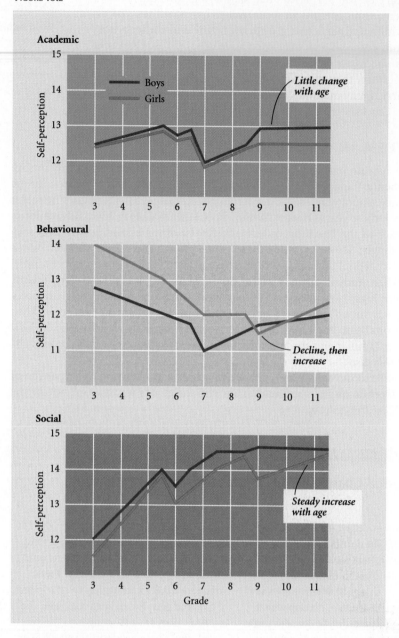

What were the results? Average levels of self-esteem are shown in Figure 10.2. For simplicity, we've only shown the results for three domains: academic, behaviour, and social. Let's look at three aspects of these findings. First, let's compare the outcomes for boys and girls. Their self-perceptions were similar for the academic and social domains, but in the behaviour domain girls have greater self-esteem than boys in the elementary school years but not during middle school and high school. Next, let's examine developmental change in different domains: academic self-perception changes little with age, social self-perception increases substantially, and behavioural self-perception declines during the elementary school years but increases somewhat in middle school and high school. Finally, let's consider the impact of school transitions on children's self-perceptions. These students entered middle school in Grade 7 and high school in Grade 9. You can see that the middle school transition affects children's self-perceptions in the academic domain more than in the social and behavioural domains.

What did the investigators conclude? Each of the three results leads to a straightforward conclusion. Let's review them in order.

First, boys' and girls' self-perceptions are similar in some domains but not others. Second, the nature of developmental change in self-perception depends on the domain. Third, school transitions do affect self-perceptions, more so in some domains than others.

What converging evidence would strengthen these conclusions? One limitation of the study concerns the sample. The results may be specific to children and adolescents growing up in the Midwestern United States, where the study was conducted. Testing samples from other populations would strengthen the authors' conclusions.

These changes in overall level of self-esteem are accompanied by another important change: Self-esteem becomes more differentiated as children enter adolescence (Boivin, Vitaro, & Gagnon, 1992). Youths are able to evaluate themselves in more domains as they develop, and their evaluations in each domain are increasingly independent. That is, children's ratings of self-esteem are often consistent across different dimensions of self-esteem but adolescents' ratings more often vary from one domain to another.

As children progress through elementary school and enter junior high or middle school, their academic self-concepts become particularly well defined (Byrne & Gavin, 1996; Marsh & Yeung, 1997). As students accumulate successes and failures in school, they form beliefs about their ability in different content areas (e.g., English, math, science), and these beliefs contribute to their overall academic self-concept. A teen who believes she is skilled at English and math but not so skilled in science will probably have a positive academic self-concept overall. But a teen who believes he is untalented in most academic areas will have a negative academic self-concept.

Not only does self-esteem vary with age, it varies across settings. To show this variation, Harter, Waters, and Whitesell (1998) and their colleagues created test items so they could assess self-worth in the context of specific relationships. For example, they included an item "some kids like the kind of person they are when they are around _____" and the blank was filled with either *parents, teachers, male class mates,* or *female classmates.* In this manner, adolescents were asked to describe their self-worth in the context of different relationships. The important finding was that most adolescents clearly distinguish self-worth across these settings. Adolescents who judge themselves positively in the context of adults, for example, might value themselves less positively in the context of classmates. Or adolescents who feel negative about themselves at home may feel positive about themselves in relationships outside the home.

INFLUENCES ON ADOLESCENTS' SELF-ESTEEM

What factors contribute to adolescents' self-esteem? Parents matter. Children and adolescents are more likely to view themselves positively when their parents are affectionate toward them and involved with them (Lord, Eccles, & McCarthy, 1994). Around the world, children have higher self-esteem when families live in harmony and parents nurture their children (Scott, Scott, & McCabe, 1991). A father who routinely helps his daughter with her homework and gladly takes her to piano lessons is saying to her, "You are important to me."

In a Canadian study, adolescents with higher scores on self-esteem were found to be more likely to have good relationships with their parents, to be well-adjusted and successful at school, and to feel happy and healthy. In addition, they were less likely to feel helpless or depressed, have negative moods, feel lonely or left out, or be victims of bullying (Health Canada, 2002e).

Parents' discipline also is related to self-esteem. Youths with high self-esteem generally have parents who aren't afraid to set rules but are also willing to discuss rules and discipline with their children (Coopersmith, 1967). Parents who fail to set rules are, in effect, telling their children that they don't care—they don't value them enough to go to the trouble of creating rules and enforcing them. In much the same way, parents who refuse to discuss discipline with their children are saying, "Your opinions don't matter to me." Not surprisingly, when youths internalize these messages, the result is lower overall self-worth.

Adolescents spend much of their lives in school, so it's not surprising that experiences there also contribute to self-esteem. In general, self-esteem is greater when students work hard in school, get along with their peers, and avoid disciplinary problems. In addition, self-esteem is greater when students participate in extracurricular activities, such as music, student council, sports, and clubs. Finally, students' self-esteem is enhanced when the overall climate of the school is nurturing—when students believe teachers care about them and listen to them. Grades matter too, but good grades affect students' self-esteem in specific disciplines—in math or English— not their overall self-esteem (Hoge, Smit, & Hanson, 1990; Marsh & Yeung, 1997).

THE MYTH OF STORM AND STRESS

Novelists and filmmakers commonly portray adolescence as a time of storm and stress—a period in which parent-child relationships deteriorate in the face of a combative, argumentative youth. Although this view may make for best-selling novels and hit movies, in reality, the rebellious teen is largely a myth. Think about the following conclusions derived from research findings (Steinberg, 1990). Most adolescents

- Admire and love their parents
- Rely on their parents for advice
- Embrace many of their parents' values
- Feel loved by their parents

Not exactly the image of the rebel, is it? Of course, parent-child relations *do* change during adolescence. As teens become more independent, their relationships with their parents become more egalitarian. Parents must adjust to their children's growing sense of autonomy by treating them more like equals (Laursen & Collins, 1994). This growing independence means that teens spend less time with their parents, are less affectionate toward them, and argue more often with them about matters of style, taste, and freedom. And teenagers are more likely to enjoy spending some time alone (Larson, 1997; Wolfson & Carskadon, 1998).

Thus, adolescence is definitely an interesting and challenging time for youths and their parents, as both parties deal with challenges brought on by an evolving parent-child relationship in which the "child" is nearly a fully independent young adult (Steinberg, 1990). However, it is not inherently tempestuous as the myth of "storm and stress" would lead us to believe.

ANSWER TO QUESTION ABOUT BERNADETTE'S ETHNIC IDENTITY.

Bernadette, the Dutch-Asian-Canadian high school student, doesn't know how to integrate the Korean heritage of her biological parents with the Dutch-Canadian culture in which she was reared. This would put her in the second phase of acquiring an ethnic identity. On the one hand, she is examining her ethnic roots, which means she's progressed beyond the initial stages. On the other hand, she has not yet integrated her Asian and European roots, and so has not reached the third and final phase.

TEST YOURSELF

1. According to Erikson, adolescents face a crisis between identity and _____.

2. The _____ status would describe an adolescent who has attained an identity based almost entirely on her parents' advice and urging.

3. A person who has simply put off searching for an identity because it seems too confusing and too overwhelming is in the _____ status.

4. _____ refers to the fact that adolescents sometimes believe that their lives are a performance, with their peers watching them constantly.

5. Adolescents are most likely to achieve an identity when parents encourage them _____.

6. In the second phase of achieving an ethnic identity, adolescents _____.

7. When individuals have a strong ethnic identity, their identification with mainstream culture _____.

8. Self-esteem often drops when students enter middle school or junior high school because young adolescents _____.

Your local newspaper has just printed a feature describing all the "storm and stress" that typifies adolescence. Write a letter to the editor in which you set the record straight.

Answers: (1) role confusion, (2) foreclosure, (3) diffusion, (4) imaginary audience, (5) to explore alternative identities but do not pressure them or provide direction, (6) start to explore the personal impact of their ethnic roots, (7) is sometimes strong and sometimes weak, depending on specific circumstances, (8) no longer know where they stand among their peers, so they must establish a new "pecking order."

10.2

Romantic Relationships and Sexuality

LEARNING OBJECTIVES

▪ What function does dating serve?

▪ Why are some adolescents sexually active? Why do so few use contraceptives?

▪ What determines an adolescent's sexual orientation?

▪ What circumstances make date rape especially likely?

> **Romantic Relationships and Sexuality**
>
> Dating
>
> Sexual Behaviour
>
> Sexual Orientation
>
> Date Rape

For six months, 15-year-old Gretchen has been dating Jeff, a 17-year-old. She thinks she is truly in love for the first time, and she often imagines being married to Jeff. They have had sex a few times, each time without contraception. It sometimes crosses Gretchen's mind that if she gets pregnant she could move into her own apartment and begin a family.

The fires of romantic relationships have long warmed the hearts of North American adolescents. Often, as with Jeff and Gretchen, romance leads to sex. In this section, we'll explore adolescent dating and sexual behaviour. As we do, you'll better understand Gretchen's reasons for having unprotected sex with Jeff.

DATING

The social landscape adds a distinctive landmark in adolescence—romantic relationships. Children's social interactions are almost exclusively with their own sex; in contrast, adolescents spend 5 to 10 hours each week interacting with members of the other sex and an equal amount of time thinking about them. The first step toward

Photodisc

romantic relationships usually consists of activities involving mixed groups of boys and girls; typical would be the group of boys and girls in the photo spending time at a mall. The next step would involve several pairs of boys and girls going out together as a group; ultimately, relationships involve well-defined couples (Furman, 2002). For younger adolescents, romantic relationships offer companionship like that provided by a best friend and an outlet for sexual exploration. For older adolescents, trust and support become important features of romantic relationships (Shulman & Kipnis, 2001).

As you might suspect, cultural factors strongly influence dating patterns. For example, parents from some cultures tend to encourage independence in their teenagers more than others, who might emphasize family ties and loyalty to parents. Since dating is a sign of independence and usually results in less time spent with family, parents from some cultures may not allow their teenagers to date until an older age and date less frequently (Xiaohe & Whyte, 1990).

SEXUAL BEHAVIOUR

We've already seen that sexual exploration is an important feature of romantic relationships for younger adolescents. In a survey of Canadian adolescents, 40% of males and 46% of females in Grade 11 reported having have had intercourse at least once (Health Canada, 2002e). Why are some adolescents sexually active? Parents are influential: Adolescents are less likely to have sex when they feel close to their parents, when parents monitor their teenagers' activities, and when parents' values discourage sex (Miller, Benson, & Galbraith, 2001). Peers matter too. Adolescents are more likely to have sex when their peers approve and when they believe their peers are also having sex (Brown & Theobald, 1999).

Although a large percentage of boys and girls have sex at some point during adolescence, sexual activity has very different meanings for boys and girls (Brooks-Gunn & Paikoff, 1993). Girls tend to describe their first sexual partner as "someone they love," but boys describe their first partner as a "casual date." Girls report stronger feelings of love for their first sexual partner than for a later partner, but boys don't. Girls have mixed feelings after their first sexual experience—fear and guilt mixed with happiness and excitement—boys'

THINK ABOUT IT

According to the "storm and stress" view of adolescence, sexual behaviour would be one way for adolescents to rebel against their parents. Does research on adolescent sexuality support this prediction?

feelings are more uniformly positive. Finally, when describing their sexual experiences to peers, girls' peers typically express some disapproval but boys' peers typically do not. In short, for boys, sexual behaviour is viewed as recreational and self-oriented; for girls, sexual behaviour is viewed as romantic and is interpreted through their capacity to form intimate interpersonal relationships (Steinberg, 1999).

Sexually Transmitted Diseases

Adolescent sexual activity is cause for concern because a number of diseases are transmitted from one person to another through sexual intercourse. For example, herpes and genital warts are two common viral infections. Other diseases, including chlamydia, syphilis, and gonorrhea, are caused by bacteria. Although these diseases can have serious complications if left untreated, they are usually cured readily with penicillin. In contrast, the prognosis is bleak for individuals who contract the human immunodeficiency virus (HIV), which typically leads to acquired immunodeficiency syndrome (AIDS). In persons with AIDS, the immune system is no longer able to protect the body from infections, and they often die from one of these infections.

Youths and young adults—those in their 20s—account for roughly 3.4% of all AIDS cases in Canada (Health Canada, 2003c). Many factors make adolescents especially susceptible to AIDS. Teenagers and young adults are more likely than older adults to engage in unprotected sex and to use intravenous drugs—common pathways for the transmission of AIDS.

Teenage Pregnancy and Contraception

Adolescents' sexual behaviour is a cause for concern because approximately 4 in 100 Canadian adolescent girls become pregnant each year and about half of them give birth (Statistics Canada, 2000b). In addition, the Aboriginal and Inuit teenage pregnancy rate is up to four times the national rate (Health Canada, 1999b).

Teenage mothers and their children usually face bleak futures. If this is the case, why do so many teens become pregnant? The answer is simple—few sexually active teenagers use birth control. And those who do often use ineffective methods, such as withdrawal, or practise contraception inconsistently (Besharov & Gardiner, 1997; Kirby, 2002b).

Adolescents' infrequent use of contraceptives can be traced to several factors (Adler, 1994; Gordon, 1996):

- *Ignorance:* Many adolescents are seriously misinformed about the facts of conception. For example, many do not know when conception is most likely to occur during the menstrual cycle.
- *Illusion of invulnerability:* Too many adolescents deny reality. They believe they are invincible—"It couldn't happen to me"—only others become pregnant.
- *Lack of motivation:* For some adolescent girls, becoming pregnant is appealing. Like Gretchen in the vignette, they think having a child is a way to break away from parents, gain status as an independent-living adult, and have "someone to love them."
- *Lack of access:* Some teenagers do not know where to obtain contraceptives and others are embarrassed to buy them. Still others don't know how to use contraceptives.

THINK ABOUT IT 💡

Suppose you had to convince a group of 15-year-olds about the hazards of adolescent sex and teenage pregnancy. What would you say?

What's the best way to reduce adolescent sexual behaviour and teen pregnancy? Programs that focus primarily on abstinence receive lots of headlines, but they are not consistently effective; some versions may work, but many do not (Kirby, 2002a). In contrast, comprehensive sex education programs *are* effective (Kirby, 2002b). These programs teach the biological aspects of sex and emphasize responsible sexual behaviour or abstaining from premarital sex altogether. They also include discussions of the pressures to become involved sexually and ways to respond to this pressure. A key element is that in role-playing sessions students practise strategies for refusing to have sex. Youths who participate in programs like these are less likely to have intercourse; when they do have intercourse, they are more likely to use contraceptives (Kirby, 2002b).

SEXUAL ORIENTATION

For most adolescents, dating and romance involve members of the opposite sex. However, as part of the search to establish an identity, many adolescents wonder, at least in passing, if they are homosexual. For most adolescents, these experiences are simply a part of the larger process of role experimentation common to adolescence. However, like the teens in the photo, the adolescent search for self-definition leads a number of teenage boys and girls to identify themselves as gay in their sexual orientation.

H. Vincent DeWitt/Stock Boston Inc.

According to a survey of Canadian youths that was designed to determine the sexual behaviour of adolescents, less than 3% of the students in Grades 9 and 11 reported a same-sex orientation. The report suggests that this may be an underestimate due to adolescents not being fully aware of their sexual orientation or not being comfortable in disclosing same-sex orientation (Health Canada, 2002a). Although this identification usually occurs in midadolescence, it is not until young adulthood that most gay individuals express their sexual orientation publicly (D'Augelli, 1996).

Why do gay adolescents wait so long—three to five years—before declaring their sexual orientation? Many believe, correctly, that their peers are not likely to support them (Newman & Muzzonigro, 1993). For example, in one American survey, only 40% of 15- to 19-year-old boys agreed that they could befriend a gay person (Marsiglio, 1993). Adolescents who said that they could not befriend a gay peer were most often younger, identified themselves as religious fundamentalists, and had parents who were less educated.

The roots of sexual orientation are poorly understood. Scientists have, however, discredited several theories of sexual orientation. Research (Bell, Weinberg, & Hammersmith, 1981; Golombok & Tasker, 1996; Patterson, 1992) shows that each of the following statements is *false:*

- Sons become gay when raised by a domineering mother and a weak father.
- Girls become lesbians when their father is their primary role model.
- Children raised by gay or lesbian parents usually adopt their parents' sexual orientation.
- Gay and lesbian adults were, as children, seduced by an older person of their sex.

If all these ideas are false, what determines a person's sexual orientation? The exact factors probably differ from one person to the next, but many scientists today believe that biology plays an important role (Lalumière, Blanchard, & Zucker, 2000). Some evidence suggests that heredity and hormones influence sexual orientation (Bailey, Dunne, & Martin, 2000). Another idea is based on the finding that men are more often gay when they have older brothers, and this effect gets stronger with each additional older brother. The explanation given for this effect is that a pregnant woman's immune system responds to some biochemical feature of a male fetus. The response is weak at first but increases with each successive male, ultimately affecting brain development in later-born sons (Blanchard, 1997; Blanchard et al., 1998).

Yet another intriguing idea—one that applies to males and females—is that genes and hormones don't produce sexual orientation per se but lead to temperaments that affect children's preference for same- and other-sex activities (Bem, 1996). Children who do not enjoy gender-typical activities come to see themselves as different and thus ultimately acquire a different gender identity.

Though the origins of sexual orientation may not be obvious, it is clear that gay and lesbian individuals face many special challenges. Their family and peer relationships are often disrupted. They are often attacked, both verbally and physically. Given these problems, it's not surprising that gay and lesbian youths often experience mental health problems such as anxiety and depression (D'Augelli, 1996; Hershberger & D'Augelli, 1995; Rotheram-Borus et al., 1995).

In recent years, social changes have helped gay and lesbian youths respond more effectively to these unique challenges. The "official" stigma associated with being gay or lesbian was removed in 1973 when the American Psychological Association and the American Psychiatric Association declared that homosexuality was not a psychological disorder. Other helpful changes include more (and more visible) gay role models and more numerous centres in cities for gay and lesbian youths. These resources are making it easier for gay and lesbian youths to understand their sexual orientation and to cope with the many other demands of adolescence.

DATE RAPE

Shelly reported that her date removed her clothes when she was drunk and had sex with her without her consent. *Like Shelly, many adolescent and young women are forced to have sexual intercourse by males they know, a situation known as **date rape** or **acquaintance rape*** (Ogletree, 1993). Traditional sex-role socialization helps to set the stage for sexual coercion. Males learn that an intense sexual drive is a sign of masculinity. Females learn that being sexually attractive is one way to gain a male's attention. However, "good girls" are expected to be uninterested in sex and to resist attempts for sex. Both males and females learn these expectations; consequently, males often assume that a female says "no" because she is supposed to say "no," not because she really means it (Muehlenhard, 1988). Unless, and sometimes even if, a woman's communications are crystal clear—"STOP!! I don't want to do this!"—an adolescent or young adult male will often assume, incorrectly and egocentrically, that her interest in sex matches his own (Kowalski, 1992).

A number of circumstances increase the possibility that adolescent and young adult males will misinterpret or ignore a female's verbal or nonverbal communications regarding sexual intent. For example, heavy drinking usually impairs a female's ability to send a clear message and makes males less able and less inclined to interpret such messages (Gross et al., 2001). Similarly, when a female dresses provocatively, males assume she is interested in sex and may ignore what she says (Cassidy & Hurrell, 1995). Yet another factor is a couple's sexual history. If a couple has had sex previously, the male may tend to dismiss his partner's protests, interpreting them as fleeting feelings that can be overcome easily (Shotland & Goodstein, 1992).

Most programs designed to prevent date rape emphasize the importance of communication. Date rape workshops represent another approach (Feltey, Ainslie, & Geib, 1991). Most focus on educating participants about the many myths that surround date rape, such as "When women say 'no' they really mean 'yes'" and "Intimate touching means that intercourse is inevitable." They also emphasize the need for females to be clear and consistent in expressing their intent. And males are told to be sure they know (not just assume) a female's intentions concerning sex and that they respect those intentions. Workshops that include these kinds of elements are effective in changing attitudes toward date rape (Holcomb et al., 2002; Shultz, Scherman, & Marshall, 2000).

Here are some guidelines often presented at such workshops; you may find them useful (Allgeier & Allgeier, 1995):

1. Know your own sexual policies. Decide when sexual intimacy is acceptable for *you.*

2. Communicate these policies openly and clearly.

3. Avoid being alone with a person until you have communicated these policies and believe you can trust the person.

4. Avoid using alcohol or other drugs when you are with a person with whom you do not wish to become sexually intimate.

5. If someone tries to force you to have sex, make your objections known: Talk first, but struggle and scream if necessary.

TEST YOURSELF

1. For younger adolescents, romantic relationships offer companionship and _____.

2. Boys more often view sexual behaviour as _____ but girls view sex as romantic.

3. When parents approve of sex, their adolescent children are _____.

4. Adolescents and young adults are at particular risk for contracting AIDS because they _____ and use intravenous drugs.

5. Adolescents often fail to use contraception, due to ignorance, the illusion of invulnerability, lack of motivation, and _____.

6. Not until _____ do most gay individuals express their sexual orientation publicly.

7. _____ apparently plays a key role in determining sexual orientation.

8. Date rape is more likely if either partner has been drinking and if the couple _____.

Sexually active teenagers typically do not use contraceptives. How do the reasons for this failure show connections between cognitive, social, and emotional development?

Answers: (1) an outlet for sexual exploration, (2) recreational, (3) more likely to be active sexually, (4) engage in unprotected sex, (5) lack of access to contraceptives, (6) young adulthood, (7) Biology, (8) has had sex previously

10.3

The World of Work

LEARNING OBJECTIVES

- How do adolescents select an occupation?
- What is the impact of part-time employment on adolescents?

The World of Work
Career Development
Part-Time Employment

When 15-year-old Aaron announced that he wanted an after-school job at the local supermarket, his mother was delighted, believing he would learn much from the experience. Five months later, she has her doubts. Aaron has lost interest in school, and they argue constantly about how he spends his money.

"What do you want to be when you grow up?" Children are often asked this question in fun. Beginning in adolescence, however, it takes on special significance because work is such an important element of the adult life that is looming on the horizon. A job—be it as a bricklayer, reporter, or child care worker—helps define who we are. In this section, we'll see how adolescents begin to think about possible occupations. We'll also look at adolescents' first exposure to the world of work, which usually comes about with part-time jobs after school or on weekends. As we do, we'll see if Aaron's changed behaviour is typical of teens who work part-time.

CAREER DEVELOPMENT

Faced with the challenge of selecting a career, many adolescents are uncertain about what they see themselves doing in the future. Choosing a career is difficult, in part because it involves determining the kinds of jobs that will be available in the future. Predicting the future is difficult, but currently in Canada approximately 75% of all jobs are in service industries such as education, health care, and banking. The remaining 25% of jobs are associated with the production of goods (Statistics Canada, 2003b).

How do adolescents begin the long process of selecting an occupation that will both match their interests and have the potential to give them a fulfilling career? Theories of vocational choice describe this process. According to a theory proposed by Donald Super (1976, 1980), identity is a primary force in an adolescent's choice of a career. *At about age 13 or 14, adolescents use their emerging identities as a source of ideas about careers, a process called **crystallization**.* Teenagers use their ideas about their own talents and interests to limit potential career prospects. A teenager who is extroverted and sociable may decide that working with people would be the career for him. Another who excels in math and science may decide she'd like to teach math. Decisions are provisional, and adolescents experiment with hypothetical careers, trying to envision what each might be like.

At about age 18, adolescents extend the activities associated with crystallization and enter a new phase. *During **specification**, individuals further limit their career possibilities by learning more about specific lines of work and starting to obtain the training required for a specific job.* Our extroverted teenager who wants to work with people may decide that a career in sales would be a good match for his abilities and interests. The teen who likes math may have learned more about careers and decided she'd like to be an accountant. Some teens, like the young man in the photo, may begin an apprenticeship as a way to learn a trade.

The end of the teenage years or the early 20s marks the beginning of the third phase. *During **implementation**, individuals enter the workforce and learn firsthand about jobs.* This is a time of learning about responsibility and productivity, of learning to get along with co-workers, and of altering one's lifestyle to accommodate work. This period is often unstable; individuals may change jobs frequently as they adjust to the reality of life in the workplace.

In the Real People feature, you can see these three phases in one young woman's career development.

Mark Richards/PhotoEdit

REAL PEOPLE: APPLYING HUMAN DEVELOPMENT

"The Life of Lynne," A Drama in Three Acts

Act 1: Crystallization. Throughout high school, Lynne was active in a number of organizations. She enjoyed being busy and liked the constant contact with people. Lynne was often nominated for office, and more often than not, she asked to be treasurer. Not that she was greedy or had her hand in the till; she simply found it satisfying to keep the financial records in order. By the end of Grade 11, Lynne decided that she wanted to study business at university, a decision that fit with her good grades in English and math.

Act 2: Specification. Lynne was accepted into the business school of a large university. She decided that accounting fit her skills and temperament, so this became her major. During the summers, she worked as a cashier at Zellers. This helped to pay for university and gave her experience in the world of retail sales.

Act 3: Implementation. A few months after graduation, Lynne was offered a junior accounting position with Wal-Mart. Her job required that she work Tuesday through Friday auditing Wal-Mart stores in several nearby cities. Lynne liked the pay, the company car, the pay, the feeling of independence, and the pay. However, having to hit the road every morning by 7:30 a.m. was a jolt to someone used to rising casually at 10 a.m. Also, Lynne often found it awkward to deal with store managers, many of whom were twice her age and very intimidating. She was coming to the conclusion that there was much more to a successful career as an accountant than simply having the numbers add up correctly. ◗

The "Life of Lynne" illustrates the progressive refinement that takes place in a person's career development. An initial interest in math and finance led to a degree in business, which led to a job as an accountant. However, one other aspect of Lynne's life sheds more light on Super's theory. After 18 months on the job, Lynne's accounting group merged with another; this would have required Lynne to move to another province, so she quit. After six months looking for another accounting job, Lynne gave up and began to study to become a real estate agent. The moral? Economic conditions and opportunities also shape career development. Changing times can force individuals to take new, often unexpected career paths.

Career Interests and Development

Super's (1976, 1980) work helps to explain how self-concept and career aspirations develop hand in hand, but it does not explain why particular individuals are attracted to one line of work rather than another. Explaining the match between people and occupations has been the aim of a theory devised by John Holland (1985, 1987, 1996). According to Holland's theory, people find work fulfilling when the important features of a job or profession fit the worker's interests. Holland identified six Themes, broad areas of interest, that are relevant to the world of work. Each one is best suited to a specific set of occupations, as indicated in the right-hand column of

Rod Morata/Stone

TABLE 10.3	Holland's Theory—Six General Occupational Themes	
Theme	**Description**	**Some Potential Careers**
Realistic	Individuals enjoy physical labour and working with their hands, and they like to solve concrete problems.	mechanic, truck driver, construction worker
Investigative	Individuals are task oriented and enjoy thinking about abstract relations.	scientist, technical writer
Social	Individuals are skilled verbally and interpersonally, and they enjoy solving problems using these skills.	teacher, counsellor, social worker
Conventional	Individuals have verbal and quantitative skills that they like to apply to structured, well-defined tasks assigned to them by others.	bank teller, payroll clerk, traffic manager
Enterprising	Individuals enjoy using their verbal skills in positions of power, status, and leadership.	business executive, television producer, real estate agent
Artistic	Individuals enjoy expressing themselves through unstructured tasks.	poet, musician, actor

Table 10.3. Most people do not match any one Theme exactly. Instead, their work-related interests are a blend of the six Themes.

This model is useful in describing the career preferences of adolescents (Day, Rounds & Swaney, 1998). When people have jobs that match their interests, research shows that in the short run they are more productive employees and in the long run they have more stable career paths (Holland, 1996). For example, an enterprising youth like the one in the photo on page 362 is likely to be successful in business where she will enjoy positions of power in which she can use her verbal skills.

Combining Holland's work-related interest Themes with Super's theory of career development gives us a very comprehensive picture of vocational growth. On the one hand, Super's theory explains the developmental progression by which individuals translate general interests into a specific career; on the other hand, Holland's theory explains what makes a good match between specific interests and specific careers.

Of course, trying to match interests to occupations can be difficult. Fortunately, several assessments can be used to describe a person's work-related interests and the jobs for which he or she is best suited. In the Strong Interest Inventory® assessment, for example, people express their liking of different occupations, school subjects, activities, and types of people (e.g., very old people, people who live dangerously). These answers are compared to the responses obtained from a normative sample of individuals from different occupations. The result is a profile, a portion of which is shown in Figure 10.3 on page 364.

You can see that each of Holland's six Themes—called "General Occupational Themes" on the Strong Interest Inventory® assessment—is listed. Under each heading are black and shaded bars that show typical responses of women and men. The dot shows where the person's responses fall compared to other people of the person's own gender. You can see that this woman has less interest than the average female on the Enterprising Theme (right column) yet has more interest than the average female on the Investigative Theme (left column). This woman displays average interest on the Realistic, Artistic, Social, and Conventional Themes. Of the six General Occupational Themes, this person's interests seem to correspond best with the Investigative Theme in Holland's theory.

By looking at the Basic Interest Scales listed under the Artistic General Occupational Theme, we can get an even more precise idea of this woman's interests. Compared to the average female, this woman shows high interest in music/dramatics while showing only average interest in art, applied arts, and writing. Her interest in culinary arts is below average. Based on interests, a musical or theatrical career could be possible areas of pursuit for this woman.

FIGURE 10.3

GENERAL OCCUPATIONAL THEMES

BASIC INTEREST SCALES

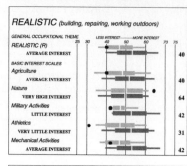

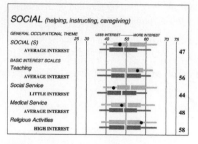

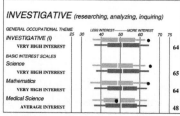

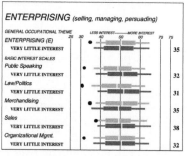

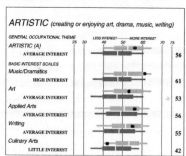

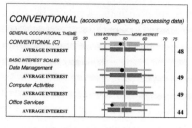

Looking at the remaining General Occupational Themes will serve as a reminder that when comparing overall Basic Interest Scales with General Occupational Themes, it is possible that some anomalies may arise. For instance, although this woman's interest in the Social General Occupational Theme is only average overall, she shows a high interest in religious activities and may wish to pursue this area for potential career possibilities.

If you are still undecided about a career, we encourage you to visit your university's counselling centre and arrange to take an assessment like the Strong Interest Inventory® assessment. The results will help you to focus on careers that would match your interests and help you to choose a post-secondary path that would lead to those careers.

Even if you are fairly certain of your vocational plans, you might take one of these assessments anyway. As we saw with Lynne, career development does not end with the first job. People continually refine their career aspirations over the life span, and these assessment results might be useful later in your life.

THINK ABOUT IT 💡

How do the General Occupational Themes in Holland's theory relate to the different types of intelligence proposed by Howard Gardner, described in Chapter 6?

PART-TIME EMPLOYMENT

The teen in the top photo is engaged in a North American adolescent ritual—the part-time job. Today, a substantial majority of high school seniors work part-time. Approximately 62% of Canadian Grade 12 students work at a part-time job. Most of these jobs are in sales and service occupations such as cashiers, restaurant servers, babysitters and as retail salespersons (Statistics Canada, 2003b).

Most adults praise teens for working, believing that early exposure to the work-place teaches adolescents self-discipline, self-confidence, and important job skills (Snedeker, 1992). For most adolescents, however, the reality is very different. Part-time work can actually be harmful, for several reasons:

1. *School performance suffers.* When students work more than approximately 15 hours per week, they devote less time to homework and are more apt to cut classes. Not surprisingly, their grades are lower than those of their peers who work less or not at all (Steinberg, Fegley, & Dornbusch, 1993). Why should 15 hours of work be so detrimental to school performance? A 15-hour work schedule usually means four three-hour shifts after school and another three-hour shift on the weekend. This would seem to leave ample opportunity to study, but only if students use their time effectively. In fact, many high school students apparently do not have the fore-sight and discipline necessary to consistently meet the combined demands of work and school. Like the girl in the bottom photo, many teens have great difficulty balancing work, study, and sleep.

2. *Mental health and behavioural problems.* Adolescents who work long hours—more than 15 or 20 hours a week—are more likely to experience anxiety and depression, and their self-esteem often suffers. Many adolescents find themselves in jobs that are repetitive and boring but stressful, and such conditions undermine self-esteem and breed anxiety.

    Extensive part-time work frequently leads to substance abuse, including cigarettes, alcohol, marijuana, and cocaine (Mortimer et al., 1996; Valois et al., 1999). Extensive work is also associated with more frequent problem behaviour, including violence toward others, trouble with police, and arguments with parents (Bachman & Schulenberg, 1993).

    Why employment is associated with all these problems is not clear. Perhaps employed adolescents turn to drugs to help them cope with the anxiety and depression brought on by work. Arguments with parents may become more common because anxious, depressed adolescents are more prone to argue or because wage-earning adolescents may believe that their freedom should match their income. Whatever the exact mechanism, extensive part-time work is clearly detrimental to the mental health of most adolescents.

3. *Misleading affluence.* Adults sometimes argue that work is good for teenagers because it teaches them "the value of a dollar." Here, too, reality is at odds

with the adage. The typical teenage pattern is to "earn and spend." Working adolescents spend most of their earnings on themselves—to buy clothing, snack food, or cosmetics, and to pay for entertainment. Few working teens set aside much of their income for future goals, such as a college education, or use it to contribute to their family's expenses (Shanahan et al., 1996a). Because parents customarily pay for many of the essential expenses associated with truly independent living—rent, utilities, and groceries, for example— working adolescents often have a vastly higher percentage of their income available for discretionary spending than working adults. Thus, for many teens, the part-time work experience provides unrealistic expectations about how income can be allocated (Bachman, 1983).

The message that emerges repeatedly from research on part-time employment is hardly encouraging. Like Aaron, the teenage boy in the vignette, adolescents who work long hours at part-time jobs do not benefit from the experience. To the contrary, they do worse in school, are more likely to have behavioural problems, and learn how to spend money rather than how to manage it. These effects are similar for adolescents from different ethnic groups (Steinberg & Dornbusch, 1991) and are comparable for boys and girls (Bachman & Schulenberg, 1993).

Does this mean that teenagers who are still in school should never work part-time? Not necessarily. Part-time employment can be a good experience, depending on the circumstances. One key is the number of hours of work. Although the exact number of hours varies, of course, from one student to the next, most students could easily work 5 hours weekly without harm, and many could work 10 hours weekly. Another key is the type of job. When adolescents have jobs that allow them to use their skills (e.g., bookkeeping, computing, or typing) and acquire new ones, self-esteem is enhanced, and they learn from their work experience (Mortimer, Harley, & Staff, 2002). Yet another factor is how teens spend their earnings. When they save their money or use it to pay for clothes and school expenses, their parent-child relationships often improve (Shanahan et al., 1996b).

By these criteria, who is likely to show the harmful effects of part-time work? A teen who spends 30 hours a week bagging groceries and spends most of it on CDs or videos. And who is likely to benefit from part-time work? A teen who likes to tinker with cars and spends Saturdays working in a repair shop and sets aside some of his earnings for college.

Finally, summer jobs typically do not involve conflict between work and school. Consequently, many of the harmful effects associated with part-time employment during the school year do not hold for summer employment. In fact, such employment sometimes enhances adolescents' self-esteem, especially when they save part of their income for future plans (Marsh, 1991).

> **THINK ABOUT IT**
>
> Think back to your own high school years and those of your friends. Can you think of students (including yourself!) who showed harmful effects from part-time work? Can you think of people who benefited from part-time work?

TEST YOURSELF

1. During the _____ phase of vocational choice, adolescents learn more about specific lines of work and begin training.

2. Individuals with high interest in the _____ General Occupational Theme are best suited for a career as a teacher or counsellor.

3. Adolescents who work extensively at part-time jobs during the school year often get lower grades, have behaviour problems, and _____.

4. Part-time employment during the school year can be beneficial if adolescents limit the number of hours that they work and _____.

Based on the description of Lynne's career, how would you describe continuity of vocational development during adolescence and young adulthood?

Answers: (1) specification, (2) Social, (3) experience mis- leading affluence, (4) hold jobs that allow them to use and develop skills

10.4

The Dark Side

LEARNING OBJECTIVES

- Why do teenagers drink?
- What leads some adolescents to become depressed? How can depression be treated?
- What are the causes of juvenile delinquency?

James was an excellent student and a starter on his high school cross-country team. He was looking forward to going to grad with Pam, his long-time girlfriend, and then going to university with her in the fall. Then, without a hint that anything was wrong in their relationship, Pam dropped James and moved in with the drummer of a local rock band. James was stunned and miserable. Without Pam, life meant so little. Cross-country and university seemed pointless. Some days James wondered if he should just kill himself to make the pain go away.

Some young people do not adapt well to the new demands and responsibilities of adolescence and respond in ways that are unhealthy. In this section, we look at three problems, often interrelated, that create the "three D's" of adolescent development: drugs, depression, and delinquency. As we look at these problems, you'll understand why James feels so miserable without Pam.

DRUG USE

Throughout history, people have used substances that alter their behaviour, thoughts, or emotions. Today drugs used most commonly by Canadian youths include alcohol, tobacco, and cannabis (which includes marijuana, hash, and hash oil). Other substances used include hallucinogens, inhalants, stimulants, barbiturates, cocaine, and heroin. The use of most of these substances was declining steadily until the early 1990s and since then there has been a steady increase in the use of these drugs. The most commonly used substance by youths is alcohol with about two-thirds of all high school students reporting having consumed it in the past year (Statistics Canada, 2001j).

Teenage Drinking

Why do so many adolescents drink alcohol? There are a number of reasons (Fields, 1992):

- *Experimentation:* something new to try
- *Relaxation:* a means to reduce tension
- *Escape:* to avoid a harsh or unpleasant real world
- *Feelings of exhilaration:* to increase self-confidence, usually by reducing one's inhibitions

Of course, these reasons don't apply to all teenagers. Some never drink. Others experiment briefly with drinking, then decide it is not for them, and others may drink heavily. What determines whether an adolescent joins the majority who drink? Many factors contribute (Petraitis, Flay, & Miller, 1995). Parents are instrumental in determining adolescents' drinking. When drinking is an important part of parents' social lives—for example, stopping at a bar after work or inviting friends over for a drink—adolescents apparently learn that drinking is a pleasant activity and are more likely themselves to drink. In contrast, when parents don't drink at all or limit their drinking to small quantities of alcohol to complement meals, their adolescent

children are less likely to drink (Andrews, Hops, & Duncan, 1997; Kline, Canter, & Robin, 1987).

Not surprisingly, peers are influential. As the photo shows, many adolescents drink because their peers do and exert pressure on them to join the group (Dielman et al., 1992).

Finally, like adults, many adolescents drink to cope with stress. Teens who report frequent life stresses—problems with parents, with interpersonal relationships, or at school—are more likely to drink and to drink more often (Rhodes & Jason, 1990; Windle & Windle, 1996).

Because teenage drinking has so many causes, no single approach is likely to eliminate alcohol abuse. Adolescents who drink to reduce their tension can profit from therapy designed to teach them more effective means of coping with stress. School-based programs that are interactive—featuring student-led discussion—can be effective in teaching the facts about drinking and strategies for resisting peer pressure to drink (Baker, 1988; Tobler & Stratton, 1997).

Teenage Smoking

Many youths experiment with cigarette smoking at some point in their teenage years. Among those teenagers between the ages of 15 and 17 who report themselves to be smokers, most had tried smoking by age 14 (Health Canada, 2002d). As was true for teenage drinking, parents and peers are influential in determining whether youths smoke. When parents smoke, their teenage children are more likely to smoke too (Chassin et al., 2000). But the parent-child relationship also contributes: Teens are less likely to smoke when they experience the supportive parenting associated with authoritative parenting (Adamczyk-Robinette, Fletcher, & Wright, 2002). Like parents, peer influences can be direct and indirect. Teenagers more often smoke when their friends do. However, a more subtle influence of peers on teen smoking comes from informal school norms. When most students in a school think it's okay to smoke—even though many of them do not themselves smoke—teens are more likely to start smoking (Kumar et al., 2002; Rose et al., 1999). Smoking rates for Canadian teens have begun to fall; in 2002 22% of teens aged 15 to 19 reported that they smoked, down from 28% in 1999.

The dangers of cigarette smoking for adults are well known. Many teenagers (particularly those who smoke) are convinced that cigarette smoking is harmless for healthy adolescents, but they're absolutely wrong: Smoking can interfere with the growth of the lungs, and when teens smoke they more often have a variety of health problems such as respiratory illnesses. What's more, smoking is often the fateful first step on the path to abuse of more powerful substances, including alcohol, marijuana, and cocaine (Chen et al., 2002).

Faced with these many harmful consequences of teenage smoking, health care professionals and human development researchers have worked hard to create effective programs to discourage adolescents from smoking. In fact, just as comprehensive school-based programs can reduce teenage sex, such programs are effective in reducing teenage smoking (USDHHS, 2000). Such programs typically include these common features:

⚡ The school has a no-smoking policy for all students, staff, and school visitors.

■ The program provides information about short- and long-term health and social consequences of smoking and provides students with effective ways to respond to peer pressure to smoke.

■ The program goes beyond the school to involve parents and the community.

These programs can reduce teenage smoking by more than one-third, but they have been implemented in only a handful of schools. By encouraging more schools to provide comprehensive antismoking programs, we could vastly reduce the number of teens who start to smoke.

DEPRESSION

At some time in your life, you have probably had the blues—days when you had little energy or enthusiasm for activities that you usually enjoy. You wanted to be alone, and you may have doubted your abilities. These feelings are perfectly normal, can usually be explained as reactions to specific events, and vanish in a matter of hours or days. For example, after an exciting vacation with family and friends, you may be depressed at the thought of returning to school to start new and difficult courses. Yet your mood improves as you renew friendships and become involved in activities on campus.

Now imagine experiencing these same symptoms continuously for weeks or months. Also suppose that you lost your appetite, slept poorly, and were unable to concentrate. *Pervasive feelings of sadness, irritability, and low self-esteem characterize an individual with depression.* Nearly 10% of Canadian females aged 12 to 19 years were at high risk of having had an episode of major depression compared to 3.4% of males the same age (Statistics Canada, 2003g).

Research reveals that unhappiness, anger, and irritation often dominate the lives of depressed adolescents. They believe that family members, friends, and classmates are not friendly to them (Cole & Jordan, 1995). Depressed adolescents wish to be left alone much more often than do nondepressed adolescents (Larson et al., 1990). Rather than being satisfying and rewarding, life is empty and joyless for depressed adolescents.

For some adolescents, depression is triggered by a life event that results in fewer positive reinforcements. The loss of a friend, for example, would deprive a teenager of many rewarding experiences and interactions, making the teen feel sad. Feeling lethargic and melancholy like the girl in the photo, the adolescent withdraws from social interaction and thereby misses further opportunities for rewarding experiences. This situation can degenerate rapidly into a vicious circle in which the depressed adolescent becomes progressively more depressed and more likely to avoid interactions that might be rewarding (Lewinsohn & Gotlib, 1995).

Depression often begins with a situation in which an adolescent feels helpless to control the outcome. Think back to James, the adolescent in the vignette at the beginning of this section. His girlfriend had been the centre of his life. When she left him unexpectedly, he felt helpless to control his own destiny. Similarly, an athlete may play poorly in the championship game because of illness, or a high school senior may get a lower score on a test due to a family crisis the night before taking the test. In each case, the adolescent could do nothing to avoid an undesirable result. Most teens recognize that such feelings of helplessness are specific to the particular situation. *In* **learned helplessness,** *however, adolescents and adults generalize these feelings of helplessness and believe that they are always at the mercy of external events, with no ability to control their own destiny.* Such feelings of learned helplessness often give rise to depression (Peterson, Maier, & Seligman, 1993).

Experiences like these do not lead all adolescents to become depressed. Some adolescents seem more vulnerable to depression than others, which has led scientists to look for biological factors. Studies of twins and adopted children indicate that heredity definitely plays a part in depression. The exact biochemical mechanism seems to involve neurotransmitters (Sevy, Mendlewicz, & Mendelbaum, 1995). *Some depressed adolescents have reduced levels of* **norepinephrine** *and* **serotonin,** *neurotransmitters that help regulate brain centres that enable people to experience pleasure.* Some adolescents may feel depressed because lower levels of neurotransmitters make it difficult for them to experience happiness, joy, and other pleasurable emotions (Peterson, 1996).

Treating Depression

It is essential to treat depression; otherwise, depressed adolescents are prone to more serious problems. Two general approaches are commonly used in treating depression (Kazdin, 1990). One is to administer antidepressant drugs designed to correct the imbalance in neurotransmitters. The other approach is psychotherapy. Many different forms are available (Lewinsohn & Gotlib, 1995; Sacco & Beck, 1995), but the most effective teach social skills—so that adolescents can have rewarding social interactions—and how to restructure their interpretation of events—so that they can recognize situations where they can exert control over their lives (Hollon, Thase, & Markowitz, 2002).

Preventing Teen Suicides

Suicide is the second-most frequent cause of death (after motor vehicle accidents) among Canadian adolescents. The suicide rate increases with age in youth and is more common in males than females. The rate of suicide is 1 in 100,000 for 10- to 14-year-olds, 10 in 100,000 for 15- to 19-year-olds, and 14 in 100,000 for 20- to 24-year-olds. Aboriginal adolescents have a suicide rate of approximately five to six times non-Aboriginal adolescents (Health Canada, 2000a).

Depression is one frequent precursor of suicide; substance abuse is another (Rich, Sherman, & Fowler, 1990; Summerville, Kaslow, & Doepke, 1996). Few suicides are truly spontaneous; in most cases, there are warning signals (Atwater, 1992). Here are some common signs:

- Threats of suicide
- Preoccupation with death
- Change in eating or sleeping habits
- Loss of interest in activities that were once important
- Marked changes in personality
- Persistent feelings of gloom and helplessness
- Giving away valued possessions

If someone you know shows these signs, *don't ignore them,* hoping that they aren't for real. Instead, ask if he or she is planning on hurting him- or herself. Be calm and supportive and, if the person appears to have made preparations to commit suicide, don't leave him or her alone. Stay with the person until other friends or relatives can come. More important: *insist* that the adolescent seek professional help. Therapy is essential to treat the feelings of depression and hopelessness that give rise to thoughts of suicide (Garland & Zigler, 1993).

DELINQUENCY

Skipping school. Shoplifting. Selling drugs. Murder. *When adolescents commit acts like these, which are illegal as well as destructive toward themselves or others, this represents juvenile delinquency.* Although delinquency applies to such a broad range of activities, it is frequently broken down into property-related (e.g., stealing, damaging property) and violent (e.g., causing injury, carrying a weapon, threatening) delinquent acts. Canadian police reports demonstrate that the majority of youths involved and charged with such activities are males, by a ratio of 3:1 compared to females.

Causes of Delinquency

Why is delinquent behaviour so common among adolescents? To answer this question, Moffitt (1993) has shown it's important to distinguish two kinds of delinquent behaviour. *Life-course persistent antisocial behaviour refers to antisocial behaviour that emerges at an early age and continues throughout life.* These individuals may start with hitting at 3 years, then progress to shoplifting at age 12, and then to car theft at 16. Perhaps only 5% of youths fit this pattern of antisocial behaviour, but they account for most of the criminal activity.

A second form of delinquent behaviour described by Moffitt (1993) is far more common. *Adolescent-limited antisocial behaviour refers to youths who engage in relatively minor criminal acts yet aren't consistently antisocial.* These youths may become involved in petty crimes, such as shoplifting or using drugs, but may be careful to follow all school rules. And, as the name implies, their antisocial behaviour is short-lived, usually vanishing in late adolescence or early adulthood.

Why do so many teens have this brief bout of delinquent activity? Remember, part of the struggle of adolescence is to acquire adult status. Youths with life-course persistent antisocial behaviour are often high-status models. These youths seem to be relatively independent (free of parental influence), they have desirable possessions like cars and expensive clothes, and they're often sexually experienced. These are attractive features, so many youths apparently imitate the criminal activity that supports this adultlike lifestyle. However, as adolescence ends, the same desirable outcomes can be reached through more prosocial means and the potential costs of antisocial behaviour increase, so most youths rapidly abandon this antisocial behaviour. Thus, adolescence-limited antisocial behaviour can be understood as one way for adolescents to achieve adultlike status and privileges (Moffitt, 1993).

Explaining life-course persistent antisocial behaviour is more complex. Researchers have identified several forces that contribute to this type of delinquent behaviour.

1. *Socioeconomic status.* Adolescent crime occurs in all social strata but is more frequent among adolescents from lower-income families. This relation may reflect a number of factors. First, crime is more common in economically disadvantaged neighbourhoods, so adult criminal models are readily available to children. Second, adolescents from lower-income families often experience little success in school and usually have little invested in the outcome of their academic efforts; criminal activity is an arena in which they can excel and gain the recognition of their peers. This is supported by Canadian data from the 1998/1999 National Longitudinal Survey of Children and Youth that demonstrates that as the level of school commitment increases, the likelihood of involvement in property-related delinquent behaviour decreases for both males and females. Third, the constant stress of life on the brink of economic disaster can reduce the effectiveness of parenting in lower-income homes (Patterson, DeVaryshe, & Ramsey, 1989).

2. *Family processes.* Delinquent behaviour is often related to inadequate parental supervision. Adolescents who are unsupervised (because, for example, their parents are at work) are much more likely to become involved in delinquent acts. Parents may also contribute to delinquent behaviour if their discipline is inconsistent and if their marital relationship is marked by constant conflict (Patterson, 1995). When family life is riddled with stress, arguments, and threats, a gang like the one shown in the photo represents an appealing makeshift family for some adolescents.

3. *Self-control.* As most children develop, they become more capable of regulating their own behaviour. They become better able to inhibit impulsive tendencies, to delay gratification, and to consider the impact of their behaviour on others (Rotenberg & Mayer, 1990). That is, they learn to rise above the immediate pressures of a situation, to avoid giving in to impulses, and to think about the consequences of their actions. Delinquent youths do not follow the usual developmental pattern. Instead, they are much more inclined to act impulsively, and they often are unable or unwilling to postpone pleasure (Patterson, 1995). Seeing a fancy new CD player or a car, delinquent youths are tempted to steal it, simply so that they can have it *right now*. When others inadvertently get in their way, delinquent adolescents often respond without regard to the nature of the other person's acts or intentions.

4. *Biological forces.* The aggressive and impulsive behaviour that is a common part of antisocial behaviour has biological roots. Some antisocial youths apparently inherit a predisposition to behave aggressively and impulsively (Carey, 1996). This is *not* an "antisocial gene." Instead, individuals who are genetically predisposed to aggression and impulsivity will be more sensitive to experiences that foster antisocial behaviour than will individuals who are not genetically predisposed in this way.

Treatment and Prevention

Given the wide-ranging causes of delinquency, it would be naïve to expect a single or simple cure. Instead, delinquency must be attacked along several fronts simultaneously:

- Delinquent adolescents can be taught effective techniques for self-control.
- Parents of delinquent youth can be taught the importance of supervising and monitoring their children's behaviour and the necessity for consistent discipline.
- Families of delinquents can learn to function more effectively as a unit, with special emphasis on better means of resolving conflict.
- Schools can develop programs that motivate delinquent youth to become invested in their school performance.

THINK ABOUT IT

A letter to the editor of your local paper claims "juvenile delinquents should be thrown in jail because they're born as 'bad apples' and will always be that way." Write a reply that states the facts correctly.

■ Communities can improve economic conditions in neighbourhoods where delinquency reigns.

Programs that include many of these strategies have met with success; adolescents who participate are less likely to be arrested again. The programs thereby address a major problem affecting not only adolescent development but all of North American society (Alexander et al., 1989; Dryfoos, 1990).

An effective intervention program for preventing delinquency is the Earlscourt Under 12 Outreach Project (ORP). This is the only program in Canada specifically designed to deal with these children. Long-term studies indicate it has a 52% success rate in deterring juvenile court appearances. The program is funded by the Ontario Ministry of Community and Social Services and operates in conjunction with the Toronto Police Service. It is a multifaceted intervention for boys under 12 years of age who have already been involved with the police. Treatment components may also be offered intermittently through adolescence. The program involves the parents, providing classes where they learn behaviour management strategies, and the boys attend classes where they learn through discussion, modelling, and role-playing how to stop and think before they act during difficult situations. In addition, the boys are encouraged to apologize to their victim, usually by writing an apology letter or engaging in some form of community service. Other components of the program that may be added as needed on an individual basis are individual family sessions, home-based tutoring, or school advocacy and consultation (Day, 1998).

In the Current Controversies feature, we describe a very different approach to dealing with adolescent crime.

CURRENT CONTROVERSIES

When Young Offenders Commit Serious Crimes, Should They Be Tried As Adults?

Traditionally, when adolescents under 18 commit crimes, the case is handled in the juvenile justice system. The minimum age for charging a child with an offence in Canada is 12, and the maximum age is 17. The Youth Criminal Justice Act, which came into effect in 2003, attempts to meet the needs of society and the young offender by placing emphasis on the treatment and rehabilitation of the young person. Most adolescents do not go to court as law enforcement agencies and justice committees have considerable discretionary powers, and extrajudicial measures may consist of such steps as restitution or meeting the victim. The court system continues to be used for serious or violent crime but rather than transferring these children to adult court, youth court judges have authority to impose adult sentences. However, the emphasis is on treatment and rehabilitation for young offenders.

Because young offenders are committing more serious crimes, many law enforcement and legal authorities believe young offenders should be tried as adults. Advocates of this position argue for lowering the minimum age for mandatory transfer of a case to adult courts, increasing the range of offences that must be tried in adult court, and giving prosecutors more authority to file cases with young offenders in adult criminal court. Critics argue that treating young offenders as adults ignores the fact that juveniles are less able than adults to understand the nature and consequences of committing a crime. Also, they argue, punishments appropriate for adults are inappropriate for juveniles (Steinberg & Cauffman, 2001).

What do you think? Should we lower the age at which juveniles are tried as adults? Based on the theories of development we have discussed, what guidelines would you propose in deciding when a juvenile should be tried as an adult? ■

TEST YOURSELF

1. The reasons teenagers drink include relaxation, escape, a desire for feelings of exhilaration, and _____.

2. Teens are less likely to drink when their parents drink _____.

3. Peers influence teenage smoking indirectly by _____.

4. Depression has been linked to life events that produce fewer positive reinforcements, situations in which teenagers feel helpless, and _____.

5. Treatments for depression include drugs that correct imbalances in neurotransmit-

ters and therapy that emphasizes _____.

6. The factors that contribute to juvenile delinquency include low family income, _____, and inadequate self-control.

Describe potential biological and environmental contributions to delinquency.

Answers: (1) experimentation, (2) in small amounts to complement meals, (3) establishing informal school norms in which smoking is approved, (4) an imbalance in neurotransmitters, (5) the development of social skills, (6) disrupted family processes

PUTTING IT ALL TOGETHER

In the voyage from the land of childhood to the land of adulthood, the choppy waters of adolescence must be navigated. Most teens complete the journey successfully, becoming adults who will someday watch their own children make the same trip. The spreading of wings that characterizes adolescence is evident in all its splendour and aggravation in this chapter.

We began by looking at the struggle to achieve an identity. Adolescents and young adults often experiment with different roles in their efforts to realize an identity. When parents support this experimentation, the search for identity is more likely to succeed. For example, Bernadette came to realize that she is uniquely blessed with roots in three different cultures; she loves elements of each, and she is forging a novel Dutch-Asian-Canadian identity.

Our next stop was romance and sex. Interest in sex mounts in the teenage years, and many adolescents become sexually active. Like Gretchen, many teenagers have unprotected sex, which can lead to pregnancy and sexually transmitted diseases.

From romance and sex we moved to the world of work. We saw that selecting a career involves matching interests and aptitudes with specific occupations, then determining the skills and education needed for the chosen line of work. Aaron's experiences in part-time work are typical. Adolescents rarely balance school and heavy part-time work effectively.

We ended the chapter by looking at the dark side of adolescence. Some young people do not handle adolescent difficulties well, leading to use of illegal drugs, depression (like James, the cross-country runner in the throes of first love), and delinquency.

SUMMARY

10.1 Identity and Self-Esteem

The Search for Identity

■ The task for adolescents is to find an identity. This search typically involves four statuses. Diffusion and foreclosure are more common in early adolescence; moratorium and achievement are more common in late adolescence and young adulthood.

■ As they seek identity, adolescents often believe that others are always watching them and that no one else has felt as they do.

■ Adolescents are more likely to achieve an identity when parents encourage discussion and recognize their autonomy; they are least likely to achieve an identity when parents set rules and enforce them without explanation.

Ethnic Identity

■ Adolescents from ethnic groups often progress through three phases in acquiring an ethnic identity: initial disinterest, exploration, and identity achievement. Achieving an ethnic identity usually results in higher self-esteem but is not consistently related to the strength of one's identification with mainstream culture.

Self-Esteem in Adolescence

Social comparisons begin anew when children move from elementary school to middle or junior high school, and, consequently, self-esteem usually declines somewhat during this transition. However, self-esteem begins to rise in middle and late adolescence as teenagers see themselves acquiring more adult skills and responsibilities.

Influences on Adolescents' Self-Esteem

Adolescents have higher self-esteem when their parents are affectionate toward them and involved with them, and when parents set rules for their children. School contributes too; adolescents have more self-esteem when they work hard in school, get along with their peers, avoid disciplinary problems, participate in extracurricular activities, and attend a school where the overall climate is nurturing.

The Myth of Storm and Stress

The parent-child relationship becomes more egalitarian during the adolescent years, reflecting adolescents' growing independence. Contrary to myth, adolescence is not usually a period of storm and stress. Most adolescents love their parents, feel loved by them, rely on them for advice, and adopt their values.

10.2 Romantic Relationships and Sexuality

Dating

Boys and girls begin to date in midadolescence. Dating often begins with the meeting of same-sex groups and progresses to well-defined couples. For younger adolescents, dating is for both companionship and sexual exploration; for older adolescents, it is a source of trust and support.

Sexual Behaviour

By the end of adolescence, many Canadian boys and girls have had sexual intercourse, which boys view as recreational but girls see as romantic. Adolescents are more likely to be sexually active if they believe that their parents and peers approve of sex. Sexually transmitted diseases and pregnancy are two common consequences of adolescent sexual behaviour because sexually active adolescents use contraceptives infrequently.

Sexual Orientation

A small percentage of adolescents are attracted to members of their own sex. Sexual orientation probably has its roots in biology. Gay and lesbian youths may face many special challenges that can contribute to their risk of experiencing emotional or mental health issues.

Date Rape

Adolescent and young adult females are sometimes forced into sex against their will, typically because males misinterpret or disregard females' intentions. Sexual coercion is particularly likely when either partner has been drinking alcohol or when the couple has had sex previously. Date rape workshops strive to improve communication between males and females.

10.3 The World of Work

Career Development

In his theory of vocational choice, Super proposes three phases of vocational development during adolescence and young adulthood: crystallization, in which basic interests are identified; specification, in which jobs associated with interests are identified; and implementation, which marks entry into the workforce.

Holland identified six Themes: Realistic, Investigative, Social, Conventional, Enterprising, and Artistic. Each is uniquely suited to certain jobs. People are happier when their interests fit their job and less happy when they do not.

Part-Time Employment

Most adolescents in Canada have part-time jobs. Employed adolescents save relatively little of their income. Instead, they spend it on clothing, food, and their entertainment, which can give misleading expectations about how to allocate income.

Part-time employment can be beneficial if adolescents work relatively few hours, if the work allows them to use existing skills or acquire new ones, and if teens save some of their earnings. Summer employment, which does not conflict with the demands of school, can also be beneficial.

10.4 The Dark Side

Drug Use

Today many adolescents drink alcohol regularly. Adolescents are attracted to alcohol and other drugs by their need for experimentation, for relaxation, for escape, and for feelings of exhilaration. The primary factors that influence whether adolescents drink are encouragements from others (parents and peers) and stress. Similarly, teenage smoking is also influenced by parents and peers.

Depression

Depressed adolescents have little enthusiasm for life, believe that others are unfriendly, and wish to be left alone. Depression can be triggered by an event that deprives them of rewarding experiences, by an event in which they feel unable to control their own destiny, or by an imbalance in neuro-transmitters. Treating depression relies on medications that correct the levels of neurotransmitters and on therapy designed to improve social skills and restructure adolescents' interpretation of life events.

Delinquency

Many young people engage in antisocial behaviour briefly during adolescence. Life-course persistent antisocial behaviour has been linked to low income, family processes, lack of self-control, and heredity. Efforts to reduce adolescent criminal activity must address all these variables.

KEY TERMS

diffusion (347)
foreclosure (347)
moratorium (347)
achievement (347)
adolescent egocentrism (348)
imaginary audience (348)
personal fable (348)
illusion of invulnerability (349)

ethnic identity (349)
date (acquaintance) rape (359)
crystallization (361)
specification (361)
implementation (361)
depression (369)
learned helplessness (370)
norepinephrine (370)

serotonin (370)
juvenile delinquency (371)
life-course persistent antisocial behaviour (371)
adolescent-limited antisocial behaviour (371)

SEE FOR YOURSELF: APPLYING WHAT YOU'VE LEARNED

In recent years, post-secondary institutions in Canada have taken a more visible and vigorous stance against sexual assault and date rape. Many now offer a range of programs and services designed to prevent sexual assault and to assist those who are victims of it. Most universities have an office—usually associated with student services—dealing with women's issues. These offices offer educational programs as well as counselling and confidential advice to women with problems. Some campuses sponsor sexual assault awareness days that include workshops, films, and plays planned to promote greater understanding of the issues associated with sexual assault. On some campuses, female self-defence programs are offered. In these programs, which are often run by campus police, women are taught ways to reduce the risk of sexual assault and ways to defend themselves if they are attacked.

Find out which of these programs and services are available to women on your campus. If it's difficult to learn how your university deals with issues related to sexual assault and date rape, think about how you could make this information more available. And if some of these services and activities are not available, think about how you could urge your college to provide them. See for yourself!

LEARN MORE ABOUT IT

Readings

BARRON, C. L. (2000). *Giving youth a voice: A basis for rethinking adolescent violence.* Halifax: Fernwood. This book examines the issue of traditional approaches and understanding of youth violence and offers new insights into how young offenders understand and explain their reality.

GALLO, D. R. (Ed.) (1997). *No easy answers: Short stories about teenagers making tough choices.* New York: Basic Books. This readable collection of short stories shows youths dealing with common problems of adolescence, including peer pressure, substance abuse, and teen pregnancy.

OSTER, G. D., & MONTGOMERY, S. S. (1994). *Helping your depressed teenager: A guide for parents and caregivers.* New York: Wiley. The authors use many case studies to describe depression, its causes, and its treatment.

STEINBERG, L. D., & LEVINE, A. (1997). *You and your adolescent.* New York: HarperPerennial. This outstanding book has a number of useful guidelines to help parents recognize when their teenager has a problem that may require professional help.

 For additional readings, explore InfoTrac® College Edition, your online library. Go to http://www.infotrac.thomsonlearning.com.

Websites

http://www.noah-health.org

The New York Online Access to Health has a website that discusses many sexually transmitted diseases, including why they are harmful, how they can be prevented, and how they can be treated.

http://www.hc-sc.gc.ca/english/for_you/youth.html

The Health Canada website includes a link specific to youth and adolescence. It is kept up to date and includes information on a variety of topics such as alcohol and drug use, body image, depression, family issues, behaviour problems, and emotional health.

http://www.childdevelop.ca

This is the website of the Child Development Institute, a Canadian institute formed in April 2004 through the merger of The Crèche Child and Family Centre and Earlscourt Child and Family Centre. The website provides a wealth of information on programs and research in child development, parenting, childhood aggression, children in conflict with the law, early childhood disorders, and child abuse.

http://www.focusas.com/

The Focus Adolescent website offers a directory of links to family help in Canada and the U.S. It is current and offers a wide selection of resources and information on teen and family issues.

Website addresses are subject to change. The *Human Development* book companion website can be accessed for updated links.

The Human Development Book Companion Website

See http://www.humandevelopment.nelson.com for practice quiz questions, Internet links, updates, critical thinking exercises, discussion forums, and more.

 ### Life-Span CD-ROM

For more information on the concepts covered in this chapter, go to

Module 4: Adolescence

- Emotional and Social Development

PART 3

Young and Middle Adulthood

Eyewire

CHAPTER 11

Becoming an Adult

PHYSICAL AND COGNITIVE DEVELOPMENT

There comes a time in life when we turn away from our childhood and aspire to being adults. In some societies, the transition to adulthood is abrupt and dramatic, marked by clear rites of passage. In Western society, it is fuzzier; the only apparent marker may be a birthday ritual. We may even ask "real" adults what it's like to be one. Adulthood is marked in numerous ways, some of which we explore in the first section.

Without question, young adulthood is the peak of physical processes and health. It is also a time when people who acquired unhealthy habits earlier in life may decide to adopt a better lifestyle. Young adulthood also marks the peak of some cognitive abilities, and the continued development of others.

On a more personal level, young adulthood is a time when we make plans and dream of what lies ahead. It is a time when we think about what life as an adult will be like. But above all, young adulthood is a time when we lay the foundation for the developmental changes we will experience during the rest of our lives. For these reasons, young adulthood is a very important time in our lives. We will consider these issues as we examine young adulthood in this chapter.

11.1

When Does Adulthood Begin?

LEARNING OBJECTIVES

⚊ What role transitions mark entry into adulthood in Western societies? How do non-Western cultures mark the transition to adulthood?

⚊ How does going to college or university fit in the transition to adulthood?

⚊ What psychological criteria mark the transition to adulthood?

⚊ What aspects of early young adulthood make it a separate developmental stage?

Jake woke up with the worst headache he ever remembered having. "If this is adulthood, they can keep it," he muttered to himself. Like many young adults in Canada, Jake spent his "becoming an adult" birthday celebrating at a bar. But the phone call from his mother that woke him in the first place reminds him that he isn't an adult in every way; she called to see if he needs money.

Imagine that you are Jake. Think for a minute about the first time you felt like an adult. When was it? What was the context? Who were you with? How did you feel? Now think about yourself between the ages of 18 and 22. Is this the period when you completed transition to adulthood? Why or why not?

Even though becoming an adult is one of our most important life transitions, it is difficult to pin down exactly when it occurs in Western societies. Birthday celebrations marking the achievement of a certain age are helpful but do not signal a clean break with youth and full acceptance as an adult. Certainly, Jake may feel like an adult because he can purchase alcohol legally, but he may not feel that way in other respects, such as supporting himself financially.

In this section, we examine some of the ways societies mark the transition to adulthood, and we'll see that the criteria vary widely from culture to culture.

ROLE TRANSITIONS MARKING ADULTHOOD

One cool spring evening, a group of former high school classmates got together to catch up on what had been going on in their lives. The conversation eventually turned to the topic of growing up and becoming adults. Joyce looked older than her 20 years. Her 5-year-old son was playing quietly on the floor. Next to Joyce sat Sheree, an art major. She wore the latest stylish clothes, purchased at the store where she works part-time. The third young woman, Marcia, looked a bit tired from her long day as an intern at Deloitte & Touche, one of the world's major accounting firms. Joyce spoke first. "I had Jimmy when I was 15. I thought it would make me grown-up and give me someone who would love me. But it gave me grown-up bills and no job. I still can't afford my own place, so I live with my mom." Sheree declared, "It's like, sure I'm an adult. I can do whatever I want, whenever I want. It's like, I don't have to answer to anybody, okay?" Marcia had a different view: "As for me, I don't think I'll *really* be an adult until I complete my education, can support myself, and get married."

Are these young people adults? Yes and no. As we will see, it depends on how you define adulthood.

Role Transitions in Western Cultures

The most widely used criteria for deciding whether a person has reached adulthood are **role transitions,** *which involve assuming new responsibilities and duties.* A number of role transitions serve as key markers for attaining adulthood: completing education, beginning full-time employment, establishing an independent household, getting married, and becoming a parent (Hogan & Astone, 1986).

Interestingly, the age at which people tend to experience these marker events varies over time. Such changes are examples of cohort effects, described in Chapter 1. For example, the average age of completion of school has been increasing; in addition, the proportion of people continuing their education past high school has increased from only a small percentage of the population to 62% of high school graduates aged 18 to 24 (Statistics Canada, 2002e). In contrast, the average age of first marriage and of parenthood has been increasing. The age of first marriage in Canada in 2001 for women was 28 and for males was 30 (Statistics Canada, 2001g). Such complexities make it difficult to use any one event as the marker for becoming an adult. Like the three women we encountered earlier, people experience some marker events but not others, further complicating the issue. Such is not the case in all cultures, however.

Cross-Cultural Evidence of Role Transitions

Non-Western cultures tend to be clearer about when a person becomes an adult. In these cultures, marriage is the most important determinant of adult status (Schlegel & Barry, 1991). The Indian family in the photograph is representative of this view.

Many non-Western cultures also have a well-defined set of requirements that boys must meet to become men (Gilmore, 1990). These requirements typically focus on three key features: being able to provide, protect, and impregnate. In contrast, most cultures rely on menarche as the primary, and usually the only, marker of adulthood for girls (Gilmore, 1990).

Rituals marking initiation into adulthood, often among the most important ones in a culture, are termed **rites of passage.** Rites of passage may involve highly elaborate steps that take days or weeks, or they may be compressed into a few minutes. Initiates are usually dressed in apparel reserved for the ritual to denote their special position. Traces of these rites remain in Western culture; consider, for example, the ritual attire for graduations or weddings. Tribal rituals marking the transition to adulthood tend to be public and may involve pain or mutilation. Because rites change little

© Patrick Ward/Stock Boston Inc.

over the years, they provide continuity throughout the life span (Keith, 1990); older adults lead young people through the same rites they themselves experienced years earlier. Western counterparts are much less formalized and diffuse; indeed, you may be hard pressed to think of any. However, a father buying his son his first razor or a mother helping her daughter with her first menstrual period may be as close as we get in the larger society. Certain ethnic groups maintain more formal rites, such as bar and bat mitzvahs. Through rites of passage, cultures the world over maintain contact and social continuity across the generations.

GOING TO UNIVERSITY OR COLLEGE

One of the most common markers of adulthood in Canada is completing one's education. As discussed previously, for 62% of high school graduates aged 18 to 24, this means going to university, college, or some other form of post-secondary education (Statistics Canada, 2002e), which serves as a catalyst for intellectual and personal growth

THINK ABOUT IT

Why do Western cultures lack clear-cut transitions to adulthood?

Joe Sohm / The Image Works

(Kitchener & King, 1989; Perry, 1970). We examine some of these cognitive changes later in this chapter.

Many students attending university or college are no longer attending directly from high school, which may be a positive influence on their post-secondary school experience. Overall, returning adult students like the woman in the photograph tend to be problem-solvers, self-directed, and pragmatic, and they have relevant life experiences they can integrate with their coursework (Harringer, 1994). They tend to be more highly motivated, more involved in studying and learning, more likely to use critical thinking in their learning, and more likely to interact with faculty. Why these differences exist is related to the kinds of changes in thinking that occur in adulthood, which we explore in detail in Section 11.3.

One group of Canadians experiencing the post-secondary education "rite of passage" in greater numbers is people with disabilities. All Canadians have an equal right to be protected from discrimination and have the opportunity to continue their education, and most colleges and universities have a disability services department to assist students with disabilities by providing resources. The National Educational Association of Disabled Students also notes that it is becoming more widely recognized that people with disabilities are under-represented in the workplace. One of the most effective ways to address this under-representation is to be sure people with disabilities can participate in post-secondary education. There is a strong correlation between educational attainment and employment rates among persons with disabilities (Statistics Canada, 2001i).

PSYCHOLOGICAL VIEWS

From a psychological perspective, becoming an adult means interacting with the world in a fundamentally different way. Cognitively, young adults think in different ways than adolescents (King & Kitchener, 1994). Behaviourally, a major difference between adolescence and adulthood is the significant drop in the frequency of reckless behaviour such as driving at high speed, having sex without contraception, or committing antisocial acts like vandalism (Arnett & Taber, 1994). From this perspective, young adults maintain a higher degree of self-control and compliance with social conventions (Hart, 1992).

On the psychosocial front, young adulthood marks the transition from concern with identity (see Section 11.4) to concern with autonomy and intimacy, which we explore here and in Chapter 12. Becoming independent from one's parents entails being able to fend for oneself, but it does not imply a complete severing of the relationship. On the contrary, adult children usually establish a rewarding relationship with their parents, as we will see in Chapter 14.

Establishing Intimacy

According to Erikson, the major task for young adults is dealing with the psychosocial conflict of intimacy versus isolation. This is the sixth step in Erikson's theory of psychosocial development, the basic tenets of which are summarized in Chapter 1. Once a person's identity had been established, Erikson (1982) believed he or she was ready to create a shared identity with another, the key ingredient for intimacy. Without a clear sense of identity, Erikson argued, young adults would be afraid of committing to a long-term relationship or might become overly dependent on the partner for his or her identity.

Several studies support this view (Matula et al., 1992). For example, Whitbourne and Tesch (1985) interviewed college seniors and 24- to 27-year-old alumni to ascertain their levels of identity formation and intimacy. Interestingly, the researchers found that identity formation continues into young adulthood; more alumni than seniors were classified as being in the moratorium or achievement stages of identity formation (see Section 10.1 for discussion of these levels). Additionally, more alumni than seniors had begun developing intimate relationships. Most important, those alumni who had well-formed identities were more likely than those who did not to be capable of true intimacy, which is exactly what Erikson predicted.

However, some research shows different results. For example, Berliner (2000) also found that identity formation correlated with intimacy in adults aged 35 to 45. But this relationship held even for those people who demonstrated diffusion, the lowest level of identity formation, which Erikson argued should not be the case. Consequently, the extent to which successful resolution of identity is necessary for the successful development of intimacy is still unresolved.

Another key question is whether the relation between identity and intimacy holds equally for men and women. The results of this research are also equivocal. Apparently, most men and career-oriented women resolve identity issues before intimacy issues (Dyk & Adams, 1990; Patterson, Sochting, & Marcia, 1992). These individuals complete their education and make initial career choices before becoming involved in a committed relationship.

Women show a different pattern. Some women resolve intimacy issues before identity issues by marrying and rearing children, and only after their children have grown and moved away do they deal with the question of their own identity. Still other women deal with both identity and intimacy issues simultaneously—for example, by entering into relationships that allow them to develop identities based on caring for others (Dyk & Adams, 1990).

Thus, this part of Erikson's theory is most applicable in the cases of men and career-oriented women. But many women confront and resolve the issues of identity and intimacy in young adulthood in reverse order or even simultaneously.

THINK ABOUT IT

Why do you think it mattered to Erikson whether identity issues are resolved before intimacy issues?

SO WHEN DO PEOPLE BECOME ADULTS?

Increasingly, researchers and writers are arguing that the years between 18 and 25 may reflect a distinct life stage. Apter (2001) coined the term "thresholders" to describe the fact that these young adults are no longer adolescents but are not yet full-fledged adults either. Economic and social realities now mean that greater numbers of post post-secondary students expect to live with their parents again for some period of time after graduation.

The perspectives considered in this section do not provide any definitive answers to the question of when people become adults. All we can say is that the transition depends on culture and a number of psychological factors. In cultures without clearly defined rites of passage, defining oneself as an adult rests on one's perception of whether personally relevant key criteria have been met. In North American society, this can be very complicated when success comes at a young age. Is Britney Spears, discussed in the Real People feature, an adult?

REAL PEOPLE: APPLYING HUMAN DEVELOPMENT

Britney Spears's Transition to Adulthood

Britney Spears is a huge international star and one of the most successful young recording artists of today. Only 17 when her debut album was released, she worked hard to maintain her image as a wholesome teen. However, the sales from the album quickly made her a multimillionaire and a worldwide celebrity. Clearly, she had achieved financial independence.

By 2002, Britney had three extremely successful albums, numerous lucrative contracts including a major product endorsement for Pepsi, and many awards. Her heavily publicized relationships indicated that she was beginning to deal with Erikson's stage of intimacy versus isolation. During this period, a key issue was a need to change her image from teen idol to adult female pop star.

One way Britney tried to emphasize the change was through her dress, which became more revealing as shown in the photographs comparing her look early in her career with one from 2002. One of her now famous routines during this period had her take off a more modest costume to reveal a more risqué one. Does this change represent an effective way of indicating that Britney is an adult? What do you think? 🌐

CP Picture Archive/Kevin Frayer

CP Picture Archive/Anthony Harvey

TEST YOURSELF

1. The most widely used criteria for deciding whether a person has reached adulthood are _____.

2. Rituals marking initiation into adulthood are called _____.

3. Behaviourally, a major difference between adolescence and adulthood is a significant drop in the frequency of _____.

4. Research indicates that Erikson's idea of resolving identity followed by intimacy best describes men and _____.

Why are formal rites of passage important? What has Western society lost by eliminating them? What have we gained?

Answers: (1) role transitions, (2) rites of passage, (3) reckless behaviour, (4) career-oriented women

11.2

Physical Development and Health

LEARNING OBJECTIVES

▶ In what respects are young adults at their physical peak?

▶ How healthy are young adults in general?

▶ How do smoking, drinking alcohol, and nutrition affect young adults' health?

▶ How does young adults' health differ as a function of socio-economic status, gender, and ethnicity?

Physical Development and Health

Growth, Strength, and Physical Functioning

Health Status

Lifestyle Factors

Social, Gender, and Ethnic Issues in Health

Tyler is a 25-year-old who started smoking cigarettes in high school to be popular. Tyler wants to quit, but he knows it will be difficult. He has also heard that it doesn't really matter if he quits or not because his health will never recover. Tyler wonders whether it is worthwhile to try.

Tyler is at the peak of his physical functioning. Most young adults are in the best physical shape of their lives. Indeed, the early 20s are the best years for strenuous work, trouble-free reproduction, and peak athletic performance. These achievements reflect a physical system at its peak. But people's physical functioning is affected by several health-related behaviours, including smoking.

GROWTH, STRENGTH, AND PHYSICAL FUNCTIONING

As a young adult, you're as tall as you will ever be (Whitbourne, 1999). Height remains stable through middle adulthood, declining somewhat in old age (as described in Chapter 15). Although men have more muscle mass and tend to be stronger than women, physical strength in both sexes peaks during the late 20s and early 30s, declining slowly throughout the rest of life (Whitbourne, 1996). Coordination and dexterity peak around the same time (Whitbourne, 1996). Because of these trends, few professional athletes remain at the top of their sport in their mid-30s. Indeed, individuals such as Lui Passaglia, a kicker who played for the Canadian Football Leagues' BC Lions for 25 years until he was 46, and Mark Messier, in his 40s still playing hockey with the New York Rangers, are famous partly because they are exceptions. Most sports stars are in their 20s.

Sensory acuity is also at its peak in the early 20s (Fozard & Gordon-Salant, 2001). Visual acuity remains high until middle age, when people tend to become farsighted and require glasses for reading. Hearing begins to decline somewhat by the late 20s, especially for high-pitched tones. By old age, this hearing loss may affect one's ability to understand speech. People's ability to smell, taste, feel pain and changes in temperature, and maintain balance remain largely unchanged until late life.

HEALTH STATUS

How is your overall health? If you are a young adult, chances are that you will say that your health is good or better. Relatively speaking, young adults get many fewer colds and respiratory infections than they did when they were children. Indeed, only about 1% of young adults are limited in their ability to function because of a health-related condition.

Because of the overall healthy status of Canadian young adults, death from disease, especially during the early 20s, is less likely than accidental death. So what are the leading causes of death among young adults in the Canada? Between the ages of 20 and 39, accidents are the leading cause of death, followed by suicide and then cancer (Statistics Canada, 2001e).

There are important gender and ethnic differences in these statistics (Statistics Canada, 2001d). Death by injury is the cause of over half the deaths of males between the ages of 20 and 39 compared to a third of females in the same age group. Within Canada, specific population groups have a higher risk of injury. For example, Aboriginal people experience three times the injury death rate of Canadians as a whole.

LIFESTYLE FACTORS

The young adults in the photograph illustrate something you should *not* do if you are trying to maintain good health—smoking. Lifestyle factors such as smoking, drinking, and eating poorly negatively affect health. We return to this theme in Chapter 14, where we examine additional aspects of health promotion, especially concerning cardiovascular disease and exercise.

© Colin Young-Wolff/PhotoEdit

Smoking

Smoking is the single biggest contributor to health problems, a fact known for decades. In Canada, roughly 45,000 people die each year due to tobacco use, and the average smoker will die about eight years earlier than a non-smoker (Health Canada, 2004d). Health care costs in Canada related to smoking amount to approximately $2.67 billion a year (Canadian Centre on Substance Abuse, 1999).

The risks of smoking are many. Of deaths associated with smoking, approximately 39% are cancer related, another 39% are due to cardiovascular disease, and the remainder are due to respiratory disease (Health Canada, 2000b). As noted in Chapter 2, nicotine in cigarettes is a potent teratogen; smoking during pregnancy is associated with stillbirth, low birth weight, and perinatal death.

Nonsmokers who breathe smoke in the environment around them—often called second-hand smoke—are also at considerably higher risk for smoking-related diseases; current Canadian estimates predict that every year 300 adult nonsmokers will die from lung cancer and 700 adult nonsmokers will die from coronary heart disease (Health Canada, 2004c). Children also experience negative health effects from environmental smoke such as an increased risk of SIDS, the likelihood of developing asthma and damage to lungs, and becoming smokers themselves. For these reasons, many cities and communities have passed legislation banning smoking in public buildings, and smoking is banned entirely on airline flights within North America and on many international flights. Still, second-hand smoke remains a major problem; although only 3 in 10 people report being exposed to second-hand smoke, 9 in 10 people have detectable levels from a previous three-day period in their blood (Health Canada, 2004c).

Tyler, the young man in the vignette, is typical of people who want to stop smoking. Most people who try to stop smoking begin the process in young adulthood. Although some smokers who want to quit find formal programs helpful, more than 90% of those who stop do so on their own. But as Tyler suspects, quitting is not easy; 70 to 80% of those who try to quit relapse at least once (Cohen et al., 1989). For most people, success is attained only after a long period of stopping and relapsing.

Regardless of how it happens, quitting smoking has enormous health benefits for all types of smokers; factors such as gender and how long or heavily a smoker smoked aren't related to the health benefits of quitting (Health Canada, 2004d). Even those who have developed a smoke-related illness can benefit. For example, quitting smoking after having a heart attack can decreased the chances of having another heart attack by 50%. Within two weeks to three months of quitting smoking, lung function improves up to 30%, within 10 years of quitting the risk of dying from lung cancer is cut in half, and after 15 years of quitting the risk of dying of a heart attack is the same as someone who has never smoked (Health Canada, 2004e). In sum, the evidence is clear: If you don't smoke, don't start. If you do, it's not too late to stop.

Drinking Alcohol

If you are between the ages of 25 and 44, chances are you drink occasionally, as it is estimated that approximately half of women and three-quarters of men in this age category consider themselves to be regular drinkers, defined as at least one drink each month (Statistics Canada, 1999b). Regular drinkers who are male also reported higher average weekly alcohol consumption and drinking more frequently than females.

For the majority of people, drinking alcohol poses no serious health problems as long as they do not drink and drive. In fact, numerous studies show that for people like those in the photograph who drink no more than two glasses of wine per day, alcohol consumption may be beneficial. For example, light drinkers (one glass of beer or wine per day) have a lower risk of stroke than either abstainers or heavy drinkers, even after controlling for hypertension, smoking, and medication (Ebersole & Hess, 1998).

*One type of drinking that is particularly troublesome among young adults, especially university and college students, is **binge drinking**, defined as consuming five or more drinks on one occasion, twelve or more times a year* (Statistics Canada, 2003h). Binge drinking has been the focus of several efforts to reduce the number of university and college students who binge. As discussed in the Current Controversies feature, efforts are being directed at the problem.

CURRENT CONTROVERSIES

Binge Drinking on Campus

A widely held notion about university and college life is that it is a time when young adults "cut loose" and enjoy all available social activities. For many students, this involves drinking alcohol. Indeed, to many students, university parties and drinking alcohol are virtually synonymous.

Unfortunately, drinking among university and college students often goes beyond moderate intake. According to a Canadian survey of 7,800 undergraduate students at 16 Canadian universities, 87% of the students acknowledged drinking alcohol over the previous 12-month period (averaging 6.5 drinks a week). However, nearly two-thirds reported drinking five or more drinks on one occasion during a previous four-month period and about a third drank eight or more drinks at one sitting (Gliksman et al, 2003).

Which students are most likely to binge drink? Canadian findings indicate that heavy drinking by undergraduate students was associated with students who lived in residence, had a low academic orientation, and had a high recreation orientation (Gliksman et al., 2003). Other research shows that binge-drinking students are more likely to have observed family members binge drinking at home, meaning that they have been socialized into this drinking pattern (Gomez, 2000). Men are sometimes shown to binge drink more than women, such as in Sardinia (DiGrande et al., 2000), but in other studies, such as one in Britain, women sometimes have higher rates (Pickard et al., 2000). Research indicates that students binge drink for several reasons, including insecure attachment to parents and impaired ability to express emotion (Camlibel, 2000) and stressful life events during late adolescence (Aseltine & Gore, 2000). Incoming students who believe drinking is part of the social experience of college are more likely to be binge drinkers; males are particularly likely to show this pattern (Read et al., 2002).

Binge drinking is extremely dangerous. Coma and death are only two of its numerous ill effects. Other negative consequences associated with these experiences with alcohol are missed classes, bad behaviour, unplanned sexual activity, and driving after consuming alcohol. Also important, but often overlooked, are second-hand drinking effects, those negative drinking-related consequences experienced by others. For example, a nondrinker may be insulted, assaulted, or have to care for an ill binge drinker, which may in turn have important academic consequences for these students. These negative social outcomes need to be viewed as part of the overall problem posed by binge drinking (Vicary & Karshin, 2002).

Many colleges and universities are developing programs to respond to this growing problem. The key is to change the culture of universities and colleges from one strongly supportive of binge drinking to one in which binge drinking is something popular people do not do. Whether programs now in place actually lower the rate of binge drinking remains to be seen. However, one thing is certain—binge drinking must be dealt with. But it will not be easy. ▨

THINK ABOUT IT 💡

What would be some specific strategies to reduce binge drinking on your campus?

*Alcoholism is viewed by most experts as a form of **addiction**, which means that alcoholics demonstrate physical dependence on alcohol and experience withdrawal symptoms when they do not drink.* According to the Canadian Community Health Survey (Statistics Canada, 2002b), 2.6% of Canadians are considered alcohol-dependent. This figure represents 3.8% of men and 1.3% of women. Dependence occurs when a drug, such as alcohol, becomes so incorporated into the functioning of the body's cells that the drug becomes necessary for normal functioning (Mayo Clinic, 2001). Alcohol addiction occurs over time as drinking alcohol alters the balance of some chemicals in the brain, causing a strong desire for more alcohol. These chemicals include gamma-aminobutyric acid (GABA), which inhibits impulsiveness; glutamate, which excites the nervous system; norepinephrine, which is released in response to stress; and dopamine, serotonin, and opioid peptides, which are responsible for pleasurable feelings. Excessive, long-term drinking can deplete or increase the levels of some of these chemicals, causing the body to crave alcohol to restore good feelings or to avoid negative feelings. Additionally, other factors come into play, including genetics; high stress, anxiety, or emotional pain; close friends or partners who drink excessively; and sociocultural factors that glorify alcohol.

The most widely known treatment option is Alcoholics Anonymous, founded in the United States in the state of Ohio, in 1935 by two recovering alcoholics. Other treatment approaches include inpatient and outpatient programs at treatment centres, behaviour modification, cognitive behavioural therapy, aversion therapy, motivational enhancement therapy, and acupuncture (Mayo Clinic, 2001). Typically, the goal of these programs is abstinence. Unfortunately, we know very little about the long-term success of the various programs.

Nutrition

How many times did your parents tell you to eat your vegetables? Or perhaps they said, "You are what you eat." Most people have disagreements with parents about food while growing up, but as adults they later realize that those lima beans and other despised foods really are healthful.

Experts agree that nutrition directly affects one's mental, emotional, and physical functioning. For example, diet has been linked to cancer, cardiovascular disease, diabetes, anemia, and digestive disorders. Nutritional requirements and eating habits change across the life span. *This change is due mainly to differences in metabolism, or how much energy the body needs.* Body metabolism and the digestive process slow down with age (Rowe & Kahn, 1998).

In general the same nutritional guidelines hold for younger, middle-aged, and older adults, with a few modifications (Rowe & Kahn, 1998). Because of slowing metabolic rates with age, older adults need fewer calories than younger adults, who in turn need more carbohydrates. Older adults are also at higher risk for dehydration, so they should drink more water. Older adults also need more protein.

Did you ever worry as you were eating a triple-dip cone of premium ice cream that you really should be eating fat-free frozen yogurt instead? If so, you, like the couple in the photograph eating a healthy dinner, are among the people who have taken to heart (literally) the link between diet and cardiovascular disease. It's generally accepted that foods high in saturated fat (such as ice cream) should be replaced with foods low in fat (such as fat-free frozen yogurt).

The main goal of these recommendations is to lower the level of cholesterol in your body because high cholesterol is one risk factor for cardiovascular disease. There is an important difference between two different types of cholesterol, which are defined by their effect on blood flow. Lipoproteins are fatty chemicals attached to proteins carried in the blood. *Low-density lipoproteins (LDLs) cause fatty deposits to accumulate in arteries, impeding blood flow, whereas high-density lipoproteins (HDLs) help keep arteries clear and break down LDLs.* It is not so much the overall cholesterol number but the ratio of LDLs to HDLs that matters most in cholesterol screening. High levels of LDLs are a risk factor in cardiovascular disease, and high levels of HDLs are considered a protective factor. Reducing LDL levels is effective in diminishing the risk of cardiovascular disease in adults of all ages (Löwik et al., 1991). HDL levels can be raised through exercise and a high-fibre diet. Weight control is also an important component.

Obesity is a growing health problem related to diet. One good way to assess your own status is to compute your body mass index. *Body mass index (BMI) is a ratio of body weight and height and is related to total body fat.* You can compute BMI as follows:

$$BMI = w/h^2$$

Where: w = weight in kilograms (or weight in pounds divided by 2.2)
H = height in metres (or inches divided by 39.37)

Health Canada (2003a) defines healthy weight as having a BMI less than 25. BMI is related to the risk of serious medical conditions and mortality: the higher one's BMI, the higher one's risk. In particular, you may want to lower your BMI if it's above 25. As indicated in Table 11.1, many health problems are associated with overweight and obesity. But be careful—lowering your BMI too much may not be healthy either. Very low BMIs may indicate malnutrition, which is also related to increased health problems (Health Canada, 2003a).

TABLE 11.1

Health Problems Associated with Overweight and Obesity	*Health Problems Associated with Underweight**
Type 2 diabetes	Undernutrition
Dyslipidemia	Osteoporosis
Insulin resistance	Infertility
Gallbladder disease	Impaired immunocompetence
Obstructive sleep apnea and respiratory problems	
Cardiovascular disease (e.g., coronary heart disease and ischemic stroke)	
Hypertension	
Osteoarthritis	
Some types of cancer (breast, endometrial, colon, prostate, and kidney)	
Psychosocial problems	
Functional limitations	
Impaired fertility	

*Underweight may be an indication of an eating disorder or underlying illness

Source: Health Canada, 2003, *Canadian Guidelines for Body Weight Classification*. Reproduced with permission from the Minister of Public Works and Government Services Canada, 2004.

SOCIAL, GENDER, AND ETHNIC ISSUES IN HEALTH

We have indicated that although most young adults are very healthy there are important individual differences. Let's see what they are.

Social Factors

Two important social predictors of health are socioeconomic status and education, with higher levels of education and income associated with improved health status (Statistics Canada, 1998b). Does education *cause* good health? Not exactly. Higher educational level is associated with higher income, as well as more awareness of dietary and lifestyle influences on health. Thus, more highly educated people are in a better position to afford health care and to know about the kinds of foods and lifestyle that affect health.

Gender

Are men or women healthier? This question is difficult to answer, primarily because women were not routinely included in many major studies of health until the 1990s (Kolata, 1990). For example, most of the longitudinal data about risk factors for cardiovascular disease comes from studies of men. We do know that women live longer than men, for reasons discussed in Chapter 15. Women also use health services more often because they tend to pay more attention to changes in their bodies (Ebersole & Hess, 1998).

Aboriginal Population Health

In Canada, poor health conditions exist for the Aboriginal population compared to the non-Aboriginal population. Many factors contribute to the overall poorer health status of the Aboriginal population. As noted, poverty is associated with inadequate health care and higher mortality throughout life. The 1996 unemployment rate was almost three times higher for Aboriginal people than the Canadian rate in general, and 44% of the Aboriginal population was below Statistics Canada's low income cut-off, compared to 20% of the total Canadian population (Health Canada, 1999d).

Aboriginal people make up the largest population subgroup that is most likely to become homeless in Canada. Risk factors for homelessness include high unemployment, welfare dependency, poverty, substance abuse, physical and mental health problems, and domestic and sexual abuse, and these conditions tend to be more common in Aboriginal communities. Further, Aboriginal people sometimes face racism and discrimination in the housing market. Many live in poor housing and severely depressed conditions on reserves and in remote communities, leading some of them to migrate to urban areas in search of jobs, education, and better housing.

Health experts maintain that inadequate housing can be associated with a long list of health problems. Although the situation for Aboriginals is improving in all regions of the country, Aboriginal people in non-reserve areas lived in more crowded housing conditions than any other group of Canadians. In 2001, 7% of the total Canadian non-reserve population who are non-Aboriginals lived in crowded conditions, compared with 17% of Aboriginal people in non-reserve areas (Statistics Canada, 2001a).

Another issue for Aboriginal people is a predisposition to certain diseases, such as diabetes. Rates of diabetes are considerably higher for the Aboriginal population than for the total Canadian population. The erosion of the traditional ways of life among some Aboriginal people has resulted in the reduction or elimination of the need to fish, hunt, or trap in order to survive, resulting in a more sedentary lifestyle (Health Canada, 1999d). Additionally, in 2001, 45% of the Aboriginal population aged 15 and over reported having one or more chronic conditions, that is, a health condition that had been diagnosed by a health care professional and had lasted, or was expected to last, at least six months (Statistics Canada, 2001a).

CP Picture Archive/Andrew Vaughan

Furthermore, the 2001 Aboriginal Peoples Survey showed that Aboriginal people often have poor access to health care professionals, especially Aboriginal people living in northern Canada. Despite improvements in many areas, Aboriginal and Inuit people continue to be in poorer health than the general Canadian population. This discrepancy is, in part, due to the widespread inequities the Aboriginal population faces in opportunities for attaining and maintaining good health, notably in socio-economic conditions (Health Canada, 1999d).

TEST YOURSELF

1. In young adulthood, most people reach their maximum _____.

2. Sensory acuity peaks during the _____.

3. During the early 20s, death from disease is _____.

4. Young adult _____ are the most likely to die.

5. _____ is the biggest contributor to health problems.

6. Alcoholism is viewed by most experts as a form of _____.

7. The two most important social influences on health are education and _____.

8. In Canada, the poorest health conditions exist for _____.

How could you design a health care system that provides strong incentives for healthy lifestyles during young adulthood?

Answers: (1) height, (2) 20s, (3) rare, (4) men, (5) Smoking, (6) addiction, (7) socioeconomic status, (8) Aboriginal peoples

---

11.3

Cognitive Development

LEARNING OBJECTIVES

- What is intelligence in adulthood?
- What types of abilities have been identified? How do they change?
- What is postformal thought? How does it differ from formal operations?
- How do stereotypes influence thinking?

Susan, a 33-year-old woman recently laid off from her job as a secretary, slides into her seat on her first day of her university classes. She is clearly nervous. "I'm worried that I won't be able to compete with these younger students, that I may not be smart enough," she sighs. "Guess we'll find out soon enough, though, huh?"

Many returning adult students like Susan worry that they may not be "smart enough" to keep up with 18- or 19-year-olds. Are these fears realistic? In this section, we examine the evidence concerning intellectual performance in adulthood. We will see how the answer to this question depends on the types of intellectual skills being used.

HOW SHOULD WE VIEW INTELLIGENCE IN ADULTS?

We interrupt this section for a brief exercise. Take a sheet of paper and write down all the abilities that you think reflect intelligence in adults. When you have finished, read further to see how your perceptions match research results.

Cognitive Development

How Should We View Intelligence in Adults?

What Happens to Intelligence in Adulthood?

Going Beyond Formal Operations: Thinking in Adulthood

The Role of Stereotypes in Thinking

It's a safe bet that you listed more than one ability as reflecting adults' intelligence. You are not alone. *Most theories of intelligence are* **multidimensional**—*that is, they identify several types of intellectual abilities.* As discussed in Chapter 7, there is disagreement about the number and types of abilities, but virtually everyone agrees that no single generic type of intelligence is responsible for all the different kinds of mental activities we perform.

Sternberg (1985) emphasized multidimensionality in his triarchic theory of intelligence (discussed in Chapter 7). Based on the life-span perspective (described in Chapter 1), Baltes and colleagues introduced three other concepts as vital to intellectual development in adults: multidirectionality, interindividual variability, and plasticity (Baltes, 1997; Baltes et al., 1998, 1999; Schaie, 1995). Let's look at each of these concepts in turn.

Over time, the various abilities underlying adults' intelligence show **multidirectionality:** *Some aspects of intelligence improve and other aspects decline during adulthood. Closely related to this is* **interindividual variability:** *These patterns of change also vary from one person to another.* In the next two sections, we will see evidence for both multidirectionality and interindividual variability when we examine developmental trends for specific sets of intellectual abilities.

Finally, people's abilities reflect **plasticity:** *They are not fixed but can be modified under the right conditions at just about any point in adulthood.* Because most research on plasticity has focused on older adults, we return to this topic in Chapter 15.

Baltes and colleagues emphasize that intelligence has many components, and these components show varying development in different abilities and different people. Let's turn our attention to the evidence that supports this theoretical view.

WHAT HAPPENS TO INTELLIGENCE IN ADULTHOOD?

Given that intelligence in adults is a complex, multifaceted construct, how might we study adult intelligence? Two common ways involve formal testing and assessing practical problem-solving skills. Formal testing such as the session shown in the photograph typically assesses primary or secondary abilities and involves tests from which we can compute overall IQ scores like those discussed in Chapter 7. Tests involving practical problems assess people's ability to use intelligence in everyday situations. So what happens in each type of ability?

Primary Abilities

From our previous discussion, we know that intelligence consists of many different skills and abilities. *Since the 1930s, researchers have agreed that intellectual abilities can be studied as groups of related skills (such as memory or spatial ability) organized into hypothetical constructs called* **primary mental abilities.** Roughly 25 primary mental abilities have been identified (Horn, 1982). Because it is difficult to study all the primary mental abilities, researchers have focused on five representative ones:

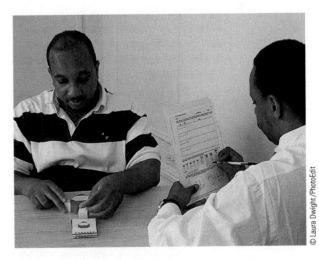

- *Number*—the basic skills underlying our mathematical reasoning
- *Word fluency*—how easily we produce verbal descriptions of things
- *Verbal meaning*—our vocabulary ability
- *Inductive reasoning*—our ability to extrapolate from particular facts to general concepts

■ *Spatial orientation*—our ability to reason in the three-dimensional world in which we live

Do these primary abilities show change in adulthood? One answer is examined in the Spotlight on Research feature.

SPOTLIGHT ON RESEARCH

The Seattle Longitudinal Study

Who was the investigator and what was the aim of the study? In the 1950s, little information was available concerning longitudinal changes in adults' intellectual abilities. What little there was showed a developmental pattern quite different from the picture of across-the-board decline obtained in cross-sectional studies. To provide a more thorough picture of intellectual change, K. Warner Schaie began the Seattle Longitudinal Study in 1956.

How did the investigator measure the topic of interest? Schaie used standardized tests of primary mental abilities to assess a wide range of abilities such as logical reasoning and spatial ability.

Who were the participants in the study? Over the course of the study, more than 5,000 individuals were tested at seven testing cycles (1956, 1963, 1970, 1977, 1984, 1991, and 1998). The participants were representative of the upper 75% of the socioeconomic spectrum and were recruited through a very large health maintenance organization in Seattle. Extensions of the study include longitudinal data on second-generation family members and on the grandchildren of some of the original participants.

What was the design of the study? To provide a thorough view of intellectual change over time, Schaie invented a new type of research design—the sequential design (see Chapter 1). Participants were tested every seven years. Like most longitudinal studies, Schaie's sequential study encountered selectivity effects—that is, people who return over the years for retesting tend to do better initially than those who fail to return. However, an advantage of Schaie's sequential design is that by bringing in new groups of participants, he was able to estimate the importance of selection effects, a major improvement over previous research.

Were there ethical concerns with the study? The most serious issue in any study in which participants are followed over time is confidentiality. Because people's names must be retained for future contact, the researchers were very careful about keeping personal information secure.

What were the results? Among the many important findings from the study are differential changes in abilities over time and cohort effects. As you can see in Figure 11.1, scores on tests of primary mental abilities improve gradually until the late 30s or early 40s. Small declines begin in the 50s, increase as people age into their 60s, and become increasingly large in the 70s (Schaie, 1994).

Cohort differences were also found. Figure 11.2 shows that on some skills, such as inductive reasoning ability, but not others, more recently born younger and middle-aged cohorts performed better than cohorts born earlier. An example of the latter is that older cohorts outperformed younger ones on number skills (Schaie, 1994). These cohort effects probably reflect differences in educational experiences; younger groups' education emphasized figuring things out on one's own, whereas older groups' education emphasized rote learning. Additionally, older groups did not have calculators or computers, so they had to do mathematical problems by hand.

Schaie uncovered many individual differences as well; some people showed developmental patterns closely approximating the overall trends, but others showed unusual patterns. For example, some individuals showed steady declines in most abilities beginning in their 40s and 50s, others showed declines in some abilities but not others, but some people showed little change in most abilities over a 14-year period. Such individual variation in developmental patterns means that average trends, like those depicted in the figures, must be interpreted cautiously; they reflect group averages and do not represent the patterns shown by each person in the group.

FIGURE 11.1

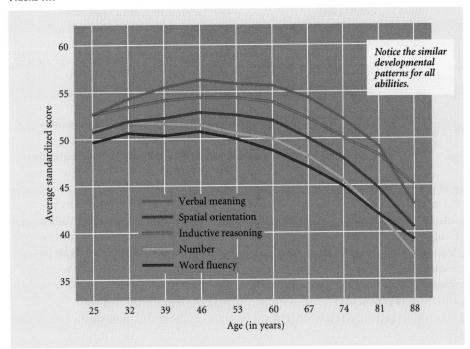

Notice the similar developmental patterns for all abilities.

From "The Course of Adult Intellectual Development" by K. W. Shaie, 1994, *American Psychologist, 49*, 304–313. Copyright © 1994 by the American Psychological Association. Reprinted with permission of the author.

FIGURE 11.2

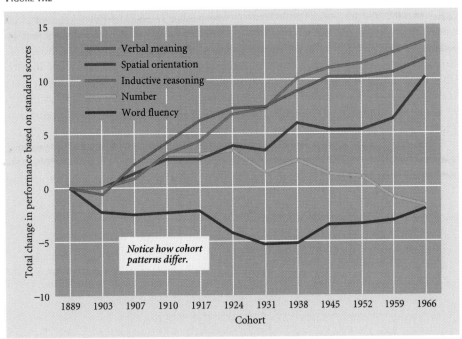

Notice how cohort patterns differ.

From "The Course of Adult Intellectual Development" by K. W. Shaie, 1994, *American Psychologist, 49*, 304–313. Copyright © 1994 by the American Psychological Association. Reprinted with permission of the author.

Another key finding is that how intellectual abilities are organized in people does not change over time (Schaie et al., 1998). This finding is important because it means that the tests, which presuppose a particular organizational structure of intellectual abilities, can be used across different ages.

Additionally, Schaie (1994) identified several variables that appear to reduce the risk of cognitive decline in old age:

■ Absence of cardiovascular and other chronic diseases

- Living in favourable environmental conditions (such as good housing)
- Remaining cognitively active through reading and lifelong learning
- Having a flexible personality style in middle age
- Being married to a person with high cognitive status
- Being satisfied with one's life achievements in middle age

What did the investigator conclude? Three points are clear. First, intellectual development during adulthood is marked by a gradual levelling off of gains, followed by a period of relative stability, and then a time of gradual decline in most abilities. Second, these trends vary from one cohort to another. Third, individual patterns of change vary considerably from person to person.

Overall, Schaie's findings indicate that intellectual development in adulthood is influenced by a wide variety of health, environmental, personality, and relationship factors. By attending to these influences throughout adulthood, we can at least stack the deck in favour of maintaining good intellectual functioning in late life.

What converging evidence would strengthen these conclusions? Although Schaie's study is one of the most comprehensive ever conducted, it is limited. Studying people who live in different locations around the world would provide evidence as to whether the results are limited geographically. Additional cross-cultural evidence comparing people with different economic backgrounds and differing access to health care would also provide insight into the effects of these variables on intellectual development.

Secondary Mental Abilities

Rather than focusing separately on specific primary abilities, some researchers argue that it makes more sense to study a half dozen or so broader skills, termed secondary mental abilities, that subsume and organize the primary abilities. Figure 11.3 shows how performance data, primary mental abilities, and secondary mental abilities relate to each other. Notice that as you move up to secondary mental abilities you are moving away from the data. Two secondary mental abilities have received a great deal of attention in adult developmental research: fluid intelligence and crystallized intelligence (Horn, 1982).

Fluid intelligence consists of the abilities that make you a flexible and adaptive thinker, that allow you to make inferences, and that enable you to understand the relations among concepts. It includes the abilities you need to understand and respond to

FIGURE 11.3   **Mental Abilities**

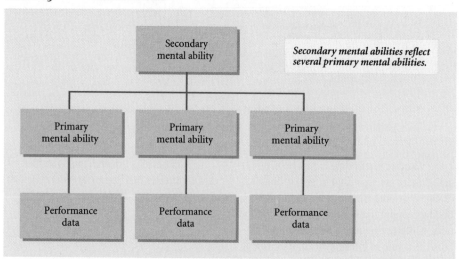

any situation, but especially new ones: inductive reasoning, integration, abstract thinking, and the like (Horn, 1982). An example of a question that taps fluid abilities is the following:

What letter comes next in the series d f i m r x e?*

Other typical ways of testing fluid intelligence include mazes, puzzles, and relations among shapes. Most of the time, these tests are timed, and higher scores are associated with faster solutions.

Crystallized intelligence is the knowledge you have acquired through life experience and education in a particular culture. Crystallized intelligence includes your breadth of knowledge, comprehension of communication, judgment, and sophistication with information (Horn, 1982). Your ability to remember historical facts, definitions of words, knowledge of literature, and sports trivia information are some examples. Many popular television game shows (such as *Who Wants to Be a Millionaire?*, *Jeopardy*, and *Wheel of Fortune*) are based on contestants' accumulated crystallized intelligence.

Even though crystallized intelligence involves cultural knowledge, it is based partly on the quality of a person's underlying fluid intelligence (Horn, 1982; Horn & Hofer, 1992). For example, the breadth of your vocabulary depends to some extent on how quickly you are able to make connections between new words you read and information already known, which is a component of fluid intelligence.

Developmentally, fluid and crystallized intelligence follow two very different paths, as you can see in Figure 11.4. Notice that fluid intelligence declines throughout adulthood, whereas crystallized intelligence improves. Although we do not yet fully understand why fluid intelligence declines, it may be related to underlying changes in the brain from the accumulated effects of disease, injury, and aging or from lack of practice (Horn & Hofer, 1992). In contrast, the increase in crystallized intelligence (at least until late life) indicates that people continue adding knowledge every day.

FIGURE 11.4   Development of Fluid and Crystallized Intelligence

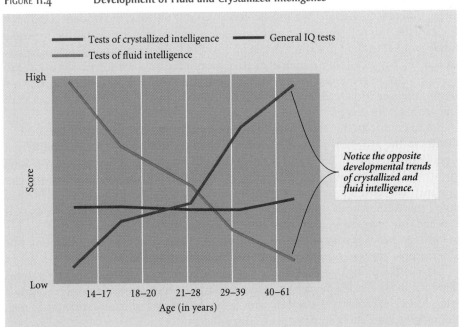

SOURCE: From "Organization of Data on Life-Span Development of Human Abilities" by J. L. Horn. In L. R. Goulet and P. B. Baltes (Eds.), *Life-Span Developmental Psychology: Research and Theory*, p. 463. Copyright © 1970 Academic Press.

*The next letter is *m*. The rule is to increase the difference between adjacent letters in the series by one each time *and* use a continuous circle of the alphabet for counting. Thus, *f* is two letters from *d*, *i* is three letters from *f*, and *e* is seven letters from *x*.

What do these different developmental trends imply? First, they indicate that although learning continues through adulthood, it becomes more difficult the older one gets. Consider what happens when Michael, age 17, and Marge, age 50, learn a second language. Although Marge's verbal skills in her native language (a component of crystallized intelligence) are probably better than Michael's, his probable superiority in the fluid abilities necessary to learn another language will usually make it easier for him to do so.

Second, these developmental trends point out once again that intellectual development varies a great deal from one set of skills to another. Beyond the differences in overall trends, differences in individuals' fluid and crystallized intelligence also vary. Whereas individual differences in fluid intelligence remain relatively uniform over time, individual differences in crystallized intelligence increase with age, largely because maintaining crystallized intelligence depends on being in situations that require its use (Horn, 1982; Horn & Hofer, 1992). For example, few adults get much practice in solving complex letter series tasks like the one on page 399. But because people can improve their vocabulary skills by reading, and because people differ considerably in how much they read, differences are likely to emerge. In short, crystallized intelligence provides a rich knowledge base to draw on when material is somewhat familiar, whereas fluid intelligence provides the power to deal with learning in novel situations.

GOING BEYOND FORMAL OPERATIONS: THINKING IN ADULTHOOD

Suppose you are faced with the following dilemma:

> You are a member of your institution's student judicial board and are currently hearing a case involving plagiarism. The student handbook indicates that plagiarism is a serious offence that results in expulsion. The student accused of plagiarizing a paper admits copying but says that she has never been told that she needed to use a formal citation and quotation marks. Do you vote to expel the student?

When this and similar problems are presented to adolescents and adults, interesting differences emerge. Adolescents tend to point out that the student handbook is clear, the student ignored it, and conclude that the student should be expelled. Adolescents thus tend to approach the problem in formal-operational terms, as discussed in Chapter 7. They reason deductively from the information given to come to a single solution grounded in their own experience. Formal-operational thinkers are certain that such solutions are right because they are based on their own experience and are logically driven.

But many adults are reluctant to draw any conclusions based on the limited information in the problem, especially when the problem can be interpreted in different ways (Sinnott, 1998). They point out that there is much about the student we don't know: Has she ever been taught the proper procedure for using sources? Was the faculty member clear about what plagiarism is? From this perspective, the problem is much more ambiguous. Adults may eventually decide that the student is (or is not) expelled, but they do so only after considering aspects of the situation that go well beyond the information given in the problem. Such thinking shows a recognition that other people's experiences may be quite different from one's own.

Clearly, the thought process these adults use is different from formal operations (Sinnott, 1998). Unlike formal-operational thinking, this approach involves considering situational constraints and circumstances, realizing that reality sometimes constrains solutions, and knowing that feelings matter.

Perry (1970) first uncovered adults' different thinking and traced its development. He found that 18-year-old first-year students tend to rely heavily on the expertise of authority figures to determine which ways of thinking are right and which are wrong.

For these students, thinking is tightly tied to logic, as Piaget had argued, and the only legitimate answers are ones that are logically derived.

Perceptions change over the next few years. Students go through a phase in which they are much less sure of which answers are right—or whether there are any right answers at all. However, by the time they are ready to graduate, students are fairly adept at examining different sides of an issue and have developed commitments to particular viewpoints. They recognize that they are the source of their own authority, that they must take a position on an issue, and that other people may hold different positions from theirs but be equally committed. During the college years, then, individuals become able to understand many perspectives on an issue, choose one, and still acknowledge the right of others to hold differing views. Perry concluded that this kind of thinking is very different from formal operations and represents another level of cognitive development.

Based on several additional longitudinal studies and numerous cross-sectional investigations, researchers have concluded that this type of thinking represents a qualitative change beyond formal operations (King & Kitchener, 1994; Kitchener & King, 1989; Kramer et al., 1991; Sinnott, 1998). *Postformal thought is characterized by a recognition that truth (the correct answer) may vary from situation to situation, that solutions must be realistic to be reasonable, that ambiguity and contradiction are the rule rather than the exception, and that emotion and subjective factors usually play a role in thinking.* In general, the research evidence indicates that postformal thinking has its origins in young adulthood (Sinnott, 1998).

Several research-based descriptions of the development of thinking in adulthood have been offered. *One of the best is the description of the development of reflective judgment, a way in which adults reason through dilemmas involving current affairs, religion, science, personal relationships, and the like.* Based on more than a decade of longitudinal and cross-sectional research, Kitchener and King (1989; King & Kitchener, 1994) refined descriptions and identified a systematic progression of reflective judgment in young adulthood, which is described in Table 11.2 on page 402.

The first three stages in the model represent prereflective thought. People in these stages typically do not acknowledge and may not even perceive that knowledge is uncertain. Consequently, they do not understand that some problems exist for which there is not a clearly and absolutely correct answer. For example, Martina's pressuring of her instructor for the "right" theory to explain human development reflects this stage. She is also likely to hold firm positions on controversial issues, but she does so without acknowledging other people's ability to reach a different, but nevertheless equally logical, position.

About halfway through the developmental progression, Martina thinks very differently. In Stages 4 and 5, she is likely to say that nothing can be known for certain and to change her conclusions based on the situation and the evidence. At this point, she argues that knowledge is quite subjective. She is also less persuasive with her positions on controversial issues: "Each person is entitled to his or her own view; I cannot force my opinions on anyone else." Kitchener and King refer to thinking in these stages as quasi-reflective thinking.

As Martina continues her development into Stages 6 and 7, she begins to show true reflective judgment, understanding that people construct knowledge using evidence and argument after very careful analysis of the problem or situation. She once again holds very firm convictions, but she reaches them only after careful consideration of several points of view. Martina also realizes that she has to continually reevaluate her beliefs in view of new evidence.

How does a person like Martina move from prereflective judgment to reflective judgment? Is the progression a gradual one or one involving qualitative shifts? Kitchener and Fischer (1990) argue that the progression involves both, depending on which aspect of development one emphasizes. Their view is based on the distinction between optimal level and skill acquisition aspects of development. *The optimal level of development is the highest level of information-processing capacity that a person is capable of doing.* The optimal level increases with age and is marked by abrupt changes ("growth spurts") followed by periods of stability. Each spurt represents the emergence of a new developmental level (stage) of thinking; the period of stability reflects the time needed to become proficient at using the newly acquired skills. *Skill acquisition is the gradual, somewhat haphazard process by which people learn new abilities.* People progress through many small steps in acquiring skills before they are ready for the next growth spurt.

TABLE 11.2	Description of the Stages of Reflective Judgment
Stage 1	
View of knowledge Knowledge is assumed to exist absolutely and concretely. It can be obtained with absolute certainty through direct observation.	
Concept of justification Beliefs need no justification because there is assumed to be an absolute correspondence between what is believed and what is true. There are no alternatives.	
Stage 2	
View of knowledge Knowledge is absolutely certain, or certain but not immediately available. Knowledge can be obtained via direct observation or via authorities.	
Concept of justification Beliefs are justified via authority, such as a teacher or parent, or are unexamined and unjustified. Most issues are assumed to have a right answer, so there is little or no conflict in making decisions about disputed issues.	
Stage 3	
View of knowledge Knowledge is assumed to be absolutely certain or temporarily uncertain. In areas of temporary uncertainty, we can know only via intuition and bias until absolute knowledge is obtained.	
Concept of justification In areas in which answers exist, beliefs are justified via authorities. In areas in which answers do not exist, because there is no rational way to justify beliefs, they are justified arationally or intuitively.	
Stage 4	
View of knowledge Knowledge is uncertain and idiosyncratic because situational variables (for example, incorrect reporting of data, data lost over time) dictate that we cannot know with certainty. Therefore, we can only know our own beliefs about the world.	
Concept of justification Beliefs often are justified by reference to evidence but still are based on idiosyncratic reasons, such as choosing evidence that fits an established belief.	
Stage 5	
View of knowledge Knowledge is contextual and subjective. Because what is known is known via perceptual filters, we cannot know directly. We may know only interpretations of the material world.	
Concept of justification Beliefs are justified within a particular context via the rules of inquiry for that context. Justifications are assumed to be context-specific or are balanced against each other, delaying conclusions.	
Stage 6	
View of knowledge Knowledge is personally constructed via evaluations of evidence, opinions of others, and so forth across contexts. Thus we may know our own and other's personal constructions of issues.	
Concept of justification Beliefs are justified by comparing evidence and opinion on different sides of an issue or across contexts and by constructing solutions that are evaluated by personal criteria, such as one's personal values or the pragmatic need for action.	
Stage 7	
View of knowledge Knowledge is constructed via the process of reasonable inquiry into generalizable conjectures about the material world or solutions for the problem at hand, such as what is most probable based on the current evidence or how far it is along the continuum of how things seem to be.	
Concept of justification Beliefs are justified probabilistically via evidence and argument or as the most complete or compelling understanding of an issue.	

SOURCE: Adapted from King, P. M., & Kitchener, K. S. (1994). *Developing reflective judgment: Understanding and promoting intellectual growth and critical thinking in adolescents and adults.* Copyright © 1994. This material is used by permission of John Wiley & Sons, Inc.

One's optimal level indicates the highest stage a person has achieved in cognitive development but probably does not indicate the level he or she will use most of the time (King & Kitchener, 1994). Why is this the case? Mostly it is because the environment does not provide the supports necessary for high-level performance, especially for issues concerning knowledge. Consequently, if pushed and if given the necessary supports, people demonstrate a level of thinking and performance far higher than they typically show on a daily basis. This discrepancy may explain why fewer people are found at each more complex level of thinking who consistently use it.

The reflective judgment model is not the only way to describe the development of thinking in adulthood. Other researchers describe similar trends. For example, Kramer (1989; Kramer et al., 1991) reported a developmental process involving three stages: absolutist, relativistic, and dialectical. Absolutist thinking involves firmly believing that there is only one correct solution to a problem and that personal experience is the basis for all truth. People aged 18 to 22 tend to think this way. Relativistic thinking involves realizing that there are many sides to an issue and that correct actions or solutions depend on circumstances. Adults in their late 20s through early middle age use this style most. One potential danger with relativistic thinking is that it can lead to a cynical approach to life: "I'll do my thing and you do yours." Because relativistic thinkers tend to reason things out on a case-by-case basis, they are unlikely to be committed to any one position for long. The final stage, dialectical thinking, solves this problem. Dialectical thinkers see the merits in different viewpoints but are able to synthesize them into a workable solution to which they are strongly committed (Kramer & Kahlbaugh, 1994; Sinnott, 1994a, 1994b; Sinnott, 1998).

Although the various approaches to postformal thinking differ in some details, they all agree that some, but not all, adults progress from believing in one and only one right way of thinking and acting to accepting the fact that there are many solutions, each potentially equally acceptable (or equally flawed). This progression is important; it allows for the integration of emotion with thought in dealing with practical, everyday problems, as we will see next.

Integrating Emotion and Logic in Life Problems

One theme in descriptions of postformal thinking is the movement from thinking "I'm right because I've experienced it" to thinking "I'm not so sure who's right because your experience is different from mine." Problem situations that had seemed pretty straightforward now appear much more complicated; the "right thing to do" is much tougher to figure out.

Differences in thinking styles have major implications for dealing with life problems. For example, couples who are able to understand and synthesize each other's point of view are much more likely to resolve conflicts; couples not able to do so are more likely to feel resentful, drift apart, or even break up (Kramer, 1989; Kramer et al., 1991).

Besides an increasing understanding that there is more than one "right" answer, Labouvie-Vief (1997; Labouvie-Vief & Diehl, 2000) argues that adult thinking is characterized by the integration of emotion with logic. Beginning in young adulthood and continuing through middle age, people gradually shift from an orientation emphasizing conformity and context-free principles to one emphasizing change and context-dependent principles. As they age, adults tend to make decisions and analyze problems not so much on logical grounds but rather on pragmatic and emotional grounds. Rules and norms are not viewed as absolute but as relative. Mature thinkers realize that thinking is an inherently social enterprise that demands making compromises with other people and tolerating contradiction and ambiguity. Such shifts mean that one's sense of self also undergoes a fundamental change (Magai, 2001).

A good example of this developmental shift would be the differences between the way late adolescents and young adults view an emotionally charged issue such as

THINK ABOUT IT

Why are formal operations inadequate for integrating emotion and thought?

cheating on one's partner compared to the views of middle-aged adults. The younger people may view such behaviour as completely inexcusable with the inescapable outcome being the end of the relationship. Middle-aged adults may take contextual factors into consideration and consider everyone's feelings. Researchers might argue that this is because the topic is too emotionally charged for adolescents to deal with intellectually, whereas adults are better able to incorporate emotion into their thinking. But is this interpretation reasonable?

It appears to be. In a now classic study, high school students, college students, and middle-aged adults were given three dilemmas to resolve (Blanchard-Fields, 1986). One dilemma had low emotional involvement, involving conflicting accounts of a war between two fictitious countries, North and South Livia, written by a partisan from each country. The other two dilemmas had high emotional involvement. In one, parents and their adolescent son disagreed about going to visit the grandparents (the son did not want to go). In the other, a man and a woman had to resolve an unintentional pregnancy (the man was antiabortion, the woman was prochoice).

The results are shown in Figure 11.5. You should note two important findings. First, there were clear developmental trends in reasoning level, with the middle-aged adults best able to integrate emotion into thinking. Second, the high school and college students were equivalent on the fictitious war dilemma, but the young adult students more readily integrated emotion and thought on the visit and pregnancy dilemmas. These results support the kinds of developmental shifts suggested by Labouvie-Vief. To continue the earlier example, dealing with a cheating partner may require the integration of thought and emotion, which is done better by middle-aged adults.

FIGURE 11.5   Measuring Reasoning Levels

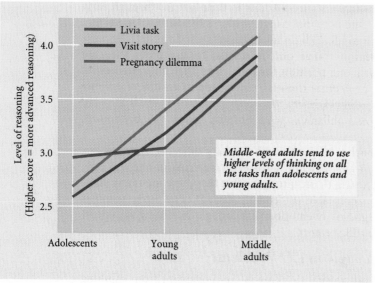

Middle-aged adults tend to use higher levels of thinking on all the tasks than adolescents and young adults.

SOURCE: From "Reasoning on Social Dilemmas Varying in Emotional Saliency: An Adult Developmental Study," by F. Blanchard-Fields, 1986, *Psychology and Aging, 1*, 325–333. Copyright © 1986 by the American Psychological Association. Reprinted with permission of the author.

The mounting evidence of continued cognitive development in adulthood paints a more positive view of adulthood than that of Piaget, who focused only on logical thinking. The integration of emotion with logic that happens in adulthood provides the basis for decision-making in the very personal and sometimes difficult arenas of love and work, which we examine in detail in Chapters 12 and 13, respectively. In the present context, it sets the stage for envisioning one's future life, a topic we take up later in this chapter.

THE ROLE OF STEREOTYPES IN THINKING

Thus far, we have concentrated on the developmental course of thinking in adulthood. One powerful influence on the use of these intellectual powers is revealed in how social knowledge structures and social beliefs guide behaviour. What are social knowledge structures and social beliefs? They are defined by how we represent and interpret the behaviour of others in a social situation (Fiske, 1993). They come in many different forms. For example, we have scripted knowledge structures regarding everyday activities such as what people should do when they go to the doctor's office or a restaurant. We also have stereotypes of groups of people and how we feel they will act in certain situations. Finally, we have been socialized to adhere to and believe in social rules, or how to behave in specific social situations such as how a husband should act toward his wife.

One important type of social knowledge structure is stereotypes. *Stereotypes are a special type of social knowledge structure or social belief that represents organized prior knowledge about a group of people that affects how we interpret new information* (Hilton & von Hippel, 1996). In other words, stereotypes help us process information when we are engaged in social interactions. We use our stereotypes to size up people when we first meet them. They help us understand why people behave the way they do and guide us in our behaviour toward other people. Remember that stereotypes are not inherently negative in their effect. But too many times they are applied in ways that underestimate the potential of the person we are observing.

Social psychologists suggest that stereotypes are automatically activated because they become overlearned and thus spontaneously activated when you encounter a member or members of a stereotyped group, such as older adults (Devine, 1989; Greenwald, McGhee, & Schwaartz, 1998). *The activation of strong stereotypes is not only automatic but also nonconscious, making it more likely that they will influence your behaviour without you being aware of it, an effect called* **implicit stereotyping**. The effects of such implicit stereotyping are illustrated in a clever study conducted by Bargh and colleagues (1996). They demonstrated that if you subliminally (out of conscious awareness) prime young people with the image of an older adult, the young people's behaviour is influenced in an age-related manner. In this case, the implicitly primed young adults walked down the hall more slowly after the experiment than young adults who were not primed with the older adult image. This is a powerful demonstration of how our unconscious stereotypes of aging can guide our behaviour.

In another study, Perdue and Gurtman (1990) also presented stimuli subliminally to participants. They found that the subliminal presentation of the word *old* increased the speed of a subsequent decision that a word presented on a computer screen (such as *ugly*) was a negative word. When these participants were subliminally presented with the word *young*, their decision time to indicate that a word such as *pretty* was a positive word was much quicker. In other words, when we are unconsciously presented with the word *old* it activates a negative evaluation and makes it easier and quicker to evaluate a negative word, such as *ugly*. Both the Bargh et al. (1996) and Perdue and Gurtman (1990) experiments demonstrate that the activation of our negative stereotypes about aging affects our behaviour without our being aware of it.

Implicit Social Beliefs

Stereotypes are only one of many types of belief systems that differ in content across age groups and also influence behaviour. There are three important considerations in understanding age differences in social belief systems (Blanchard-Fields & Hertzog, 2000). First, we must examine the specific content of social beliefs (i.e., the particular beliefs and knowledge people have about "rules," norms, and patterns of social behaviour). Second, we must consider the strength of these beliefs to know under what conditions they may influence behaviour. Third, we need to know the likelihood that these beliefs will be activated automatically when they are violated or questioned. If these three aspects of the belief system are understood, it is possible to explain when and why age differences occur in social judgments. In other words, middle-aged and older adults may hold different beliefs than other age groups (e.g., different "rules" for appropriate social behaviour during dating). Furthermore, how strongly people hold these beliefs may vary as a function of how particular generations were socialized. For example, although many adults of all ages may believe couples should not live together before marriage, older generations may be more adamant and rigid about this belief.

A good portion of the research literature focuses on age differences in the content of attitudes, beliefs, and values. However, evidence of age differences in the content of social beliefs does not completely account for age differences in how and when such beliefs are activated and how they influence behaviour.

Social cognition researchers argue that individual differences in the strength of social representations of rules, beliefs, and attitudes are linked to specific situations (Mischel & Shoda, 1995). Such representations can be both cognitive (how we conceptualize the situation) and emotional (how we react to the situation). When one encounters a specific situation, the person's belief system triggers an emotional reaction and related goals tied to the content of that situation. This in turn drives social judgments. Consider the belief that couples should not live together before marriage. If you were socialized from childhood to believe in this "rule," you would evaluate anyone violating that rule negatively. For example, suppose you were told about a man named Allen who put pressure on Joan to live with him before they were married, and they subsequently broke up. You may have a negative emotional response and blame Allen for the breakup of the relationship because he was lobbying for cohabitation.

A study exploring social beliefs found age differences in the types of social rules and evaluations evoked in different types of situations (Blanchard-Fields, 1996, 1999). For example, when subjects considered a husband who chooses to work long hours instead of spending more time with his wife and children, the social evaluation "marriage is more important than a career" tended to increase in importance with age. As can be seen in Figure 11.6, this was particularly evident from age 24 to age 65. The figure also shows that the social rule "the marriage was already in trouble" was also produced and has an inverted *U*-shaped relationship. In other words, adults around age 35 to 55 years produced this social evaluation the most.

These findings may relate to how the oldest generation was socialized with respect to the social rules of marriage. Your grandparents' generation probably was socialized very differently from your generation with regard to what's considered appropriate behaviour by husbands and wives. Thus, these findings may reflect cohort differences. Alternatively, viewing marriage as more important than one's career may relate to the particular life stage and life circumstances different age groups confront. During midcareer and mid–child-rearing stages, making a living and proving one-

FIGURE 11.6   Age Differences in Social Beliefs

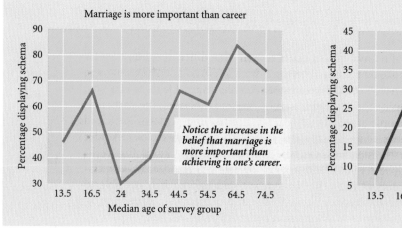

Marriage is more important than career

Notice the increase in the belief that marriage is more important than achieving in one's career.

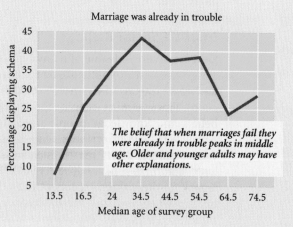

Marriage was already in trouble

The belief that when marriages fail they were already in trouble peaks in middle age. Older and younger adults may have other explanations.

self in a career may take precedence. In contrast, during the retirement and empty nest phase, the importance of a marital relationship may reemerge. On the other hand, the middle-aged group may not have relied on social rules to guide their thinking about the problem situation and focused more on the marital conflict itself. This could possibly reflect the 1960s focus on communicating feelings. These are only a few examples of sociocultural experiential factors that may influence different social beliefs.

For a situation involving a young couple who eloped despite the objections of their parents, the social rules "parents should have talked, not provoked the young couple" and "they were too young" also showed an inverted *U*-shaped relationship with age. In other words, middle-aged people endorsed these rules, whereas younger and older people did not. On the other hand, the social rule "you can't stop true love" showed a *U*-shaped relationship with age. In other words, younger and older age groups endorsed this rule, whereas people in middle adulthood did not. It may be that in middle adulthood, between ages 30 and 45, people are not focusing on issues of true love. This makes sense because they are in the stage of life where the pragmatics of building a career are important. They also emphasized the pragmatics of age (e.g., being too young) as an important factor in marriage decisions.

One possible explanation for these findings is that cohort effects or generational differences (as we discussed in Chapter 1) influenced whether strong family social rules would be activated. For example, older women adopted the social rule "marriage is more important than career" much more than men of their same generation and more than women and men of younger generations. The fact that older women endorsed this social rule more strongly than the other age groups is a good example of how emotionally laden values are evoked in these situations.

TEST YOURSELF

1. Most modern theories of intelligence are _____ because they identify many domains of intellectual abilities.

2. Number, verbal fluency, and spatial orientation are some of the _____ mental abilities.

3. _____ reflects knowledge that you have acquired through life experience and education in a particular culture.

4. Kitchener and King describe a kind of postformal thinking called _____.

5. _____ are a special type of social knowledge structure or social belief that represent organized prior knowledge about a group of people that affects how we interpret new information.

Many young adult university students seemingly get more confused about what they want to major in and less certain about what they know as they progress through university. From a cognitive-developmental approach, why does this happen?

Answers: (1) multidimensional, (2) primary, (3) Crystallized intelligence, (4) reflective judgment, (5) Stereotypes

11.4

Who Do You Want to Be? Personality in Young Adulthood

LEARNING OBJECTIVES

- What is the life-span construct? How do adults create scenarios and life stories?
- What are possible selves? Do they show differences during adulthood?
- What are personal control beliefs?
- How does self-concept come to take adult form? What is its developmental course through adulthood?

Felicia is a 19-year-old student. She expects her study of early childhood education to be difficult but rewarding. She figures that along the way she will meet a great guy, whom she will marry soon after graduation. They will have two children before she turns 30. Felicia sees herself getting a good job teaching preschool children and some day owning her own day-care centre.

In earlier chapters, we saw how children and adolescents deal with the question "What do you want to be when you grow up?" As a young adult, Felicia has arrived at the "grown-up" part and is experimenting with some idealistic answers to the question. Are Felicia's answers typical of most young adults?

In this section, we examine how the search for identity in adolescence meets the cognitive, social, and personal reality of adulthood. In particular, we will see how people create life scenarios and life stories, possible selves, self-concept, and personal control beliefs. Let's begin by considering how Felicia and the rest of us construct images of our adult lives.

CREATING SCENARIOS AND LIFE STORIES

Figuring out what (and who) you want to be as an adult takes lots of thought, hard work, and time. *Based on personal experience and input from other people, young adults create a **life-span construct** that represents a unified sense of the past, present, and future.* Several factors influence the development of a life-span construct; identity, values, and society are only a few. Together they not only shape the creation of the life-span construct, they influence the way it is played out (Whitbourne, 1987). The life-span construct represents a link between Erikson's notion of identity, which is a major focus during adolescence, and our adult view of ourselves.

*The first way the life-span construct is manifested is through the **scenario**, which consists of expectations about the future.* The scenario takes aspects of a person's identity that are particularly important now and projects them into a plan for the future. For example, you may find yourself thinking about the day you will graduate and be able to apply all the knowledge and skills you have learned. In short, a scenario is a game plan for how your life will play out in the future.

Felicia, an early childhood education student, has a fairly typical scenario in Western-industrialized countries. She plans on completing a degree, marrying after graduation, and having two children by age 30. *Tagging future events with a particular time or age by which they are to be completed creates a **social clock.*** This personal timetable gives people a way to track progress through adulthood. They use biological markers of time (such as menopause), social aspects of time (such as getting married), and historical time (such as the turn of the century) (Hagestad & Neugarten, 1985).

Felicia will use her scenario to evaluate her progress toward her personal goals. With each new event, she will check where she is against where her scenario says she should be. If she is ahead of her plan, she may be proud of having made it. If she is lagging behind, she may chastise herself for being slow. But if she criticizes herself too much, she may change her scenario altogether. For example, if she does not go to university, she may decide to change her career goals entirely: Instead of owning her own day-care centre, she may aim to be a manager in a department store.

*As people begin to achieve some of the goals in their scenarios, they create the second aspect of the life-span construct, the **life story**, which is a personal narrative that organizes past events into a coherent sequence.* Our life story becomes our autobiography as we move through adulthood.

According to research, what we remember about the events that make up our life is not evenly distributed across the life span (Fitzgerald, 1999), a point we will examine in more detail in Chapter 16. Some researchers (e.g., Rubin, Rahhal, & Poon, 1998) argue that people simply remember things from young adulthood best, but other views have been offered. For example, Fitzgerald (1999) believes late adolescence and young adulthood are times of intense psychological activity related to the self that favours the creation of autobiographical memories. In either case, it is the novelty of the event that appears to make the difference; that probably explains why events that happen during the transition to post-secondary education are remembered better than events later in one's career (Pillemer et al., 1996).

How does one's scenario or life story, as created through autobiographical memory, affect one's identity? As shown in Figure 11.7, Whitbourne (1986) believes we use assimilation and accommodation to create our own identities in much the same way Piaget said we create our knowledge. As the figure shows, there is continuous feedback between identity (what we believe to be true about ourselves based on our collection of memories) and experience (what we encounter in our daily lives); this explains why we may evaluate ourselves positively at one time yet appear defensive and self-protective at another. This assimilation-accommodation process results in a developmental progression in which people show increasingly mature identity with age (Whitbourne & VanManen, 1996). Chapter 13 discusses how this process results in changes in middle age, and Chapter 15 examines how it relates to integrity in late life.

FIGURE 11.7   **Assimilation–Accommodation Process**

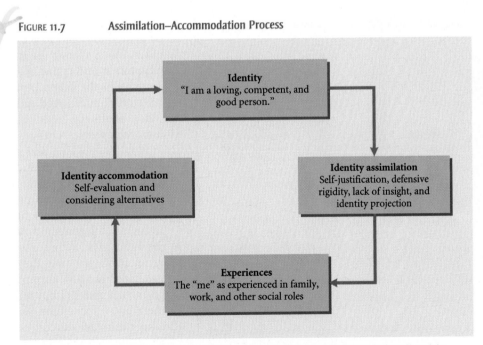

SOURCE: From *The Me I Know: A Study of Adult Identity,* by S. K. Whitbourne. Copyright © 1986 Springer-Verlag Publishing. Reprinted with permission.

POSSIBLE SELVES

Creating a scenario presupposes that adults have the ability to project themselves into the future and to speculate about what they might be like (Markus & Nurius, 1986). How do we do this? *Projecting ourselves into the future involves creating **possible selves** that represent what we could become, what we would like to become, and what we are afraid of becoming.*

What you could or would like to become reflects personal goals or values; you may envision yourself as a good parent, as rich and famous with thousands of adoring fans, or as in good physical condition. What you are afraid of becoming is usually reflected in specific fears—of being alone, of having little meaning in your life, or of being a certifiable couch potato. Possible selves are the embodiment of life's goals (Hooker, 1999). They are changeable and provide support for the view that development is personally guided, dynamic, and sensitive to context.

Whether age differences appear in possible selves is a complicated issue. For one thing, possible selves exist in fewer domains the older people get, but older adults show more behaviours to support their possible selves than do younger adults (Hooker, 1999). Possible selves in young adulthood and middle age map more directly onto age-graded developmental tasks (such as getting married and starting a career) than do possible selves in later life.

Keeping these complications in mind, let's see how possible selves differ across age. In one approach, researchers asked people to describe their hoped-for and feared possible selves (Cross & Markus, 1991). The subjects were mostly middle-class men and women, ranging in age from 18 to 86. Their responses were grouped into categories (such as family, personal, material). Age differences depended on the type of possible self examined. In terms of hoped-for selves, 18- to 24-year-olds list family concerns most often (such as marrying the right person). In contrast, 25- to 39-year-olds list family concerns last; their main concerns are personal issues such as being a more caring or loving person. By age 40 to 59, family issues reemerge as primary, but the focus is on different issues (such as being the kind of parent who can "let go" of the children). For 60- to 86-year-olds, personal issues are again the most important, involving such things as remaining active and healthy.

Health becomes increasingly important as a feared self across adulthood (Hooker, 1999). As you can see in Figure 11.8, about 33% of college students and young adults do not have health as an aspect of their possible selves compared to about 10% of older adults. We will see in Chapters 14 and 15 that this increase in the salience of health for middle-aged and older adults is based in important physical changes.

How do possible selves relate to one's goals in life? Smith (2001) examined this question by examining college students' ratings of 10 current life goals and 24 life outcomes. When students perceived that they had failed at their current goals, they also did not see themselves succeeding on longer-term life outcomes. Segal and colleagues (2001)

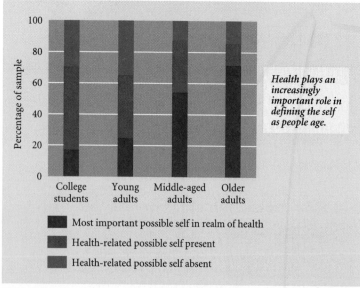

FIGURE 11.8   **Importance of Health Over Adulthood**

Health plays an increasingly important role in defining the self as people age.

■ Most important possible self in realm of health
■ Health-related possible self present
■ Health-related possible self absent

SOURCE: Reprinted from Hooker, K. (1999). Possible Selves in Adulthood: Incorporating Teleonomic Relevance into Studies of the Self. In T. M. Hess & F. Blanchard-Fields (Eds.), *Social Cognition and Aging*, p. 107, with permission from Elsevier.

found significant gender differences among male and female college first-year students in the relation between possible selves and one's personal future. Women were more likely to predict career choice, marriage, children, divorce, and death of a spouse than were men. Women also demonstrated more psychological complexity and a better awareness of the implications of their role choices and conflicts.

Taken together, the research on possible selves enables us to examine the creation of scenarios and life stories systematically. It also helps us understand how adults organize their self-perceptions into a coherent whole and create personal goals for the future.

SELF-CONCEPT

Once one has constructed a scenario or life story, a key task for adults is to incorporate these into a coherent sense of self. This integration process also entails a reconsideration of the self-perceptions first formed in adolescence (see Chapter 10). The changes that occur in self-concept during young adulthood as a result of these processes can best be understood as the outcome of a developmental process integrating self-concept with thinking (Kegan, 1982).

Does the self-concept created through this interactive process undergo further change with age? The answer is, apparently not. In one of the few longitudinal studies of self-concept, researchers first surveyed a group of men about their self-concept when they were first-year college students, and then followed them for 14 years (Mortimer, Finch, & Kumka, 1982). The results raise important issues concerning the stability of self-concept and the importance of self-perceptions and life events. Over the 14-year period, the men showed little change in self-concept as a group. The basic components of self-concept remained stable, despite some fluctuations in specific variables. For example, well-being and competence declined during college but increased after graduation. A man's degree of confidence as a college senior is related to his later evaluation of life events—this may even be a self-fulfilling prophecy. The researchers suggest that these men may actively seek and create experiences that fit their perceptions of competence.

This explanation is supported by longitudinal research on gifted women, whose high self-confidence in early adulthood is mirrored as high life satisfaction during their 60s (Sears & Barbee, 1978). These findings also provide additional support for Whitbourne's (1986) model (see page 409) as they demonstrate that identity colours the way people interpret and experience events, which in turn shapes the future directions of their identity.

> **THINK ABOUT IT**
>
> How might the development of self-concept be related to cognitive development?

Ethnic aspects of adults' self-concept also undergo development during young adulthood. For example, Collins (2000) studied this process in biracial Japanese-American young adults. Collins found that these adults often select their own social and geographic settings to maximize the opportunities for change. In these settings they took advantage of new acquaintances and mentors, resulting in new behaviours and roles. These elements led to some confusion in participants' biracial identity, but all of them eventually asserted new and positive aspects of their biracial identity.

PERSONAL CONTROL BELIEFS

As you were reading about young adults creating scenarios, life stories, and self-concepts (and perhaps reflecting on your own), you may have thought about the degree to which you feel that you are in control of your life. Such beliefs are becoming an important element of theories about how adults create their lives (Antonucci, 2001). *Personal control beliefs reflect the degree to which you believe your performance in a situation depends on something you do.* For example, suppose you don't get a job you think you should have gotten. Was it your fault? Or was it because the company was

too shortsighted to recognize your true talent? Which of these options you select provides insight into a general tendency? Do you generally believe that outcomes depend on the things you do? Or are they due to factors outside of yourself, such as luck or the power of others?

A high sense of personal control implies a belief that performance is up to you, whereas a low sense of personal control implies that your performance is under the influence of forces other than your own. Personal control has become an extremely important idea in a wide variety of settings because of the way it guides behaviour (Brandtstädter, 1999; Soederberg Miller & Lachman, 1999). Successful leaders such as Prime Minister Paul Martin, shown here, need to exude a high sense of personal control to demonstrate that they are in charge.

Personal control is a very important concept that can be applied broadly to several domains such as social networks and health (Antonucci, 2001). For example, personal control beliefs are not only important in personality development, but also (as we will see in Chapter 15) in memory performance in late life. Research indicates that people experience four types of personal control (Tiffany & Tiffany, 1996): control from within oneself, control over oneself, control over the environment, and control from the environment.

Despite its importance, we do not have a clear picture of the developmental course of personal control beliefs. Evidence from both cross-sectional studies and longitudinal studies (Lang & Heckhausen, 2001) is contradictory. Some data indicate that younger adults are less likely to hold internal control beliefs (i.e., believe they are in control of outcomes) than are older adults. Other research finds the opposite.

The contradiction may derive from the complex nature of personal control beliefs (Lachman, 1985). These beliefs vary depending on which domain, such as intelligence or health, is being assessed. Indeed, other research shows that perceived control over one's development declines with age, whereas perceived control over marital happiness increases (Brandtstädter, 1989). Additionally, younger adults are more satisfied when attributing success in attaining a goal to their own efforts whereas older adults are more satisfied when they attribute such success to their ability (Lang & Heckhausen, 2001).

Clearly, people of all ages and cultures try to influence their environment irrespective of whether they believe they will be successful. Schulz and Heckhausen (1999) pulled together the various perspectives on control beliefs and proposed a life-span model to describe this striving that distinguishes between primary and secondary control. *Primary control* is behaviour aimed at affecting the individual's external world; working a second job to increase one's earnings is an example. One's ability to influence the environment is heavily influenced by biological factors (e.g., stamina to work two jobs), so it changes over time, from very low during early childhood to high during middle age, to very low again in very late life. *Secondary control* is behaviour or cognition aimed at affecting the individual's internal world; believing that one is capable of success even when faced with challenges is an example. The developmental patterns of both are shown in Figure 11.9.

The figure also shows that people of all ages strive to control their environment, but how they do this changes. Note that for the first half of life, primary and secondary control operate in parallel. During midlife, primary control begins to decline but secondary control does not. Thus, the desire for control does not change; whether we can actually affect our environment or whether we need to think about things differently is what differs with age.

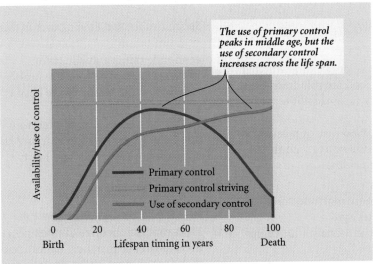

FIGURE 11.9   Using Primary Control

The use of primary control peaks in middle age, but the use of secondary control increases across the life span.

Primary control
Primary control striving
Use of secondary control

Availability/use of control

0   20   40   60   80   100
Birth   Lifespan timing in years   Death

SOURCE: Adapted from R. Schulz and J. Heckhausen (1996). A Lifespan Model of Successful Aging. *American Psychologist, 51,* 702–714. Copyright © 1996 by the American Psychological Association. Adapted by permission.

TEST YOURSELF

1. A _____ is a unified sense of a person's past, present, and future.

2. A personal narrative that organizes past events into a coherent sequence is a _____.

3. Representations of what we could become, what we would like to be, and what we are afraid of becoming are our _____.

4. The organized, coherent, integrated pattern of self-perceptions that includes the notions of self-esteem and self-image is called the _____.

5. _____ reflect the degree to which a person's performance in a situation is believed to be under his or her control.

How might people's scenarios, life stories, and other aspects of personality vary as a function of cognitive-developmental level and self-definition as an adult?

Answers: (1) life-span construct, (2) life story, (3) possible selves, (4) self-concept, (5) Personal control beliefs

PUTTING IT ALL TOGETHER

In this chapter, we have seen how people make the transition from adolescence to adulthood. For many people like Jake, the transition is fuzzy, having more to do with arbitrary legal issues than anything else. In some cultures, though, there are clear, formalized rites of passage that make it much easier to pinpoint the beginning of adulthood. Young adults are fine physical specimens, reaching their peak in most areas of functioning. It is a time when people like Tyler think about abandoning unhealthy habits acquired earlier in life in favour of healthier lifestyles. People like Susan decide to return to university to further their education. Indeed, young adulthood is a time when intellectual growth continues in some areas but decline begins in others. Young adults also tend to dream about their future like Felicia does, mapping out their lives in detail.

All in all, young adulthood is an exciting time of life. In many respects, life will never be this good, at least physically, ever again. New avenues are opened, and adult responsibilities are undertaken. The most important of these responsibilities are the topics for the next two chapters: love and work.

SUMMARY

11.1 When Does Adulthood Begin?

Role Transitions Marking Adulthood

▥ The most widely used criteria for deciding whether a person has reached adulthood are role transitions, which involve assuming new responsibilities and duties.

▥ Some societies use rituals, called rites of passage, to mark this transition clearly. However, such rituals are largely absent in Western culture.

Going to University or College

▥ Older students tend to be more motivated and have many other positive characteristics.

▥ University and college serve as a catalyst for cognitive development.

Psychological Views

▥ Adolescents and adults differ in their abilities to acquire knowledge and to apply knowledge and skills.

▥ A second major difference is a drop in the rate of participation in reckless behaviour.

So When Do People Become Adults?

▥ In cultures without clearly defined rites of passage, people become adults when they fully feel like adults.

11.2 Physical Development and Health

Growth, Strength, and Physical Functioning

▥ Young adulthood is the time when certain physical abilities peak: strength, muscle development, coordination, dexterity, and sensory acuity. Most of these abilities begin to decline in middle age.

Health Status

▥ Young adults are also at the peak of health. Death from disease is relatively rare, especially during their 20s. Accidents are the leading cause of death.

Lifestyle Factors

▥ Smoking is the single biggest contributor to health problems. It is related to half of all cancers and is a primary cause of respiratory and cardiovascular disease. Although it is difficult, quitting smoking has many health benefits.

▥ For most people, drinking alcohol poses few health risks. Several treatment approaches are available for alcoholics.

▥ Nutritional needs change somewhat during adulthood, mostly due to changes in metabolism. Some nutrient needs, such as carbohydrates, change. The ratio of LDLs to HDLs in serum cholesterol, which can be controlled through diet in most people, is an important risk factor in cardiovascular disease.

Social, Gender, and Ethnic Issues in Health

▥ Two important social factors in health are socioeconomic status and education.

▥ Whether women or men are healthier is difficult to answer because women have been excluded from much health research.

▥ Higher education is associated with better health due to better access to health care and more knowledge about proper diet and lifestyle.

11.3 Cognitive Development

How Should We View Intelligence in Adults?

▥ Most modern theories of intelligence are multidimensional. For instance, Baltes's research shows that development varies among individuals and across different categories of abilities.

What Happens to Intelligence in Adulthood?

▥ Intellectual abilities can be studied as groups of related skills called primary mental abilities. These abilities develop differently and change in succeeding cohorts. More recent cohorts perform better on some skills, such as inductive reasoning, but older cohorts perform better on number skills.

▥ Fluid intelligence consists of abilities that make people flexible and adaptive thinkers. Fluid abilities generally decline during adulthood.

▥ Crystallized intelligence reflects knowledge that people acquire through life experience and education in a particular culture. Crystallized abilities improve until late life.

Going Beyond Formal Operations: Thinking in Adulthood

▥ Postformal thought is characterized by a recognition that truth may vary from one situation to another, that solutions must be realistic, that ambiguity and contradiction are the rule, and that emotion and subjectivity play a role in thinking. One example of postformal thought is reflective judgment.

The Role of Stereotypes in Thinking

▥ Stereotypes are a special type of social knowledge structure or social belief that represent organized prior knowledge about a group of people that affects how we interpret new information. Activating stereotypes can have a powerful effect on cognitive processing.

11.4 Who Do You Want to Be? Personality in Young Adulthood

Creating Scenarios and Life Stories

▥ Young adults create a life-span construct that represents a unified sense of the past, present, and future. This is manifested in two ways: through a scenario that maps the future based on a social clock, and in the life story, which creates an autobiography.

Possible Selves

■ People create possible selves by projecting themselves into the future and thinking about what they would like to become, what they could become, and what they are afraid of becoming.

■ Age differences in these projections depend on the dimension examined. In hoped-for selves, 18- to 24-year-olds and 40- to 59-year-olds report family issues as most important, whereas 25- to 39-year-olds and older adults consider personal issues to be

most important. However, all groups include physical aspects as part of their most feared selves.

Self-Concept

■ Self-concept in adulthood is believed to develop in stages that integrate Piagetian and postformal thinking with emotional development. Self-concept appears to be relatively stable during adulthood.

Personal Control Beliefs

■ Personal control is an important concept with broad applicability. However, the developmental trends are complex because personal control beliefs vary considerably from one domain to another.

KEY TERMS

role transitions (382)
rites of passage (383)
intimacy versus isolation (384)
binge drinking (389)
addiction (390)
metabolism (391)
low-density lipoproteins (LDLs) (391)
high-density lipoproteins (HDLs) (391)
body mass index (BMI) (391)

multidimensional (395)
multidirectionality (395)
interindividual variability (395)
plasticity (395)
primary mental abilities (395)
secondary mental abilities (398)
fluid intelligence (398)
crystallized intelligence (399)
postformal thought (401)
reflective judgment (401)
optimal level of development (401)

skill acquisition (402)
stereotypes (405)
implicit stereotyping (405)
life-span construct (408)
scenario (408)
social clock (408)
life story (409)
possible selves (410)
personal control beliefs (411)

SEE FOR YOURSELF: APPLYING WHAT YOU'VE LEARNED

How do people think through the future and create scenarios? Here's an exercise for you. First, over the next few days write your own scenario. Imagine what your future will be like (or what you thought it would be like). Will you get married? When? To what kind of person? Will you have children? A career? How far will you advance? What will you be known for? Will you coach your child's sports team? Run for the school board?

When you've finished your scenario, talk to your friends and ask them the same kinds of questions. Are there similarities and differences between their responses and yours? Ask them where they got their ideas about the future. Bring the results of your explorations into class for discussion and comparison. Have you and your classmates identified common themes that people see in their future? See for yourself!

LEARN MORE ABOUT IT

Readings

DAVEY, J. D., & DAVEY, L. D. (2001). *The conscience of the campus: Case studies in moral reasoning among today's college students.* Westport, CT: Praeger. Discusses how college students deal with contemporary moral issues such as race, poverty, sex, educational funding, and constitutional rights.

FURSTENBERG Jr., FRANK F. (Ed.) (2002). *Early Adulthood in Cross-National Perspective.* Thousand Oaks, CA: Sage. Discusses the phases of early adulthood development and includes cross-national perspectives and comparisons.

ROBBINS, A., & WILNER, A. (2001). *Quarterlife crisis: The unique challenges of life in your twenties.* New York:

Putnam. An intriguing book written by two people in their 20s.

SCHAIE, K. W. (1996). *Intellectual development in adulthood: The Seattle longitudinal study.* New York: Cambridge University Press. This is an excellent summary of the history and findings of the most extensive study of intellectual development across adulthood.

SINNOTT, J. D. (1998). *The development of logic in adulthood: Postformal thought and its applications.* New York: Plenum. This book provides both a history of research on postformal thinking and Sinnott's own ideas.

 For additional readings, explore InfoTrac® College Edition, your online library. Go to http://www.infotrac.thomsonlearning.com.

Websites

http://www.hc-sc.gc.ca/hecs-sesc/tobacco/index.html

Health Canada promotes the "Go smokefree!" program. This associated website includes information on smoking, including research, policy, legislation, youth, and quitting.

http://www.ccsa.ca

This is the website for Canada's national substance abuse prevention agency and features the latest Canadian and international research, statistics, and publications on various aspects of addiction, its treatment, and policy.

http://www.bacchus.ca/cyaid_conference.html

The Student Life Education Company is a non-profit organization dedicated to saving the lives of Canadian students. The website provides information on alcohol-related issues, particularly in the post-secondary population.

Website addresses are subject to change. The *Human Development* book companion website can be accessed for updated links.

The Human Development Book Companion Website

See http://www. humandevelopment.nelson.com for practice quiz questions, Internet links, updates, critical thinking exercises, discussion forums, and more.

 ### Life-Span CD-ROM

For more information on the concepts covered in this chapter, go to

Module 5: Early and Middle Adulthood

- Physical Development
- Cognitive Development

Getty Images

CHAPTER 12

Being with Others

FORMING RELATIONSHIPS IN YOUNG AND MIDDLE ADULTHOOD

Imagine yourself years from now. Your children are grown and have children and grandchildren of their own. In honour of your 80th birthday, they have all come together, along with your friends, to celebrate. Their present to you is an assemblage of hundreds of photographs and dozens of home videos. As you look at them, you realize how lucky you've been to have so many wonderful people in your life. Your relationships have made your adult life fun and worthwhile. As you watch the videos and look at the pictures, you wonder what it must be like to go through life totally alone. You think of all the wonderful experiences you would have missed in early and middle adulthood—never knowing what friendship is all about, never being in love, never dreaming about children and becoming a parent. That is what we'll explore in this chapter—the ways in which we share our lives with others. First, we consider what makes good friendships and love relationships. Because these relationships form the basis of our lifestyles, we examine these next. In the third section, we consider what it is like to be a parent. Finally, we see what happens when marriages end. Throughout this chapter, the emphasis is on aspects of relationships that nearly everyone experiences during young adulthood and middle age. In Chapter 14, we examine aspects of relationships specific to middle-aged adults; in Chapter 16, we will do the same for relationships in later life.

12.1

Relationships

LEARNING OBJECTIVES

- What types of friendships do adults have? How do adult friendships develop?
- What is love? How does it begin? How does it develop through adulthood?
- What is the nature of violence in some relationships?

Jamal and Deb, both 25, have been madly in love since they met at a party about a month ago. They spend as much time together as possible and pledge that they will stay together forever. Deb finds herself daydreaming about Jamal at work and can't wait to go over to his apartment. She wants to move in, but her co-workers tell her to slow down.

You know what Jamal and Deb are going through. Each of us wants to be wanted by someone else. What would your life be like if you had no one to share it with? There would be no one to go shopping or cruising with, no one to talk to on the phone, no one to cuddle close to while watching the sunset at a mountain lake. Although there are times when being alone is desirable, for the most part we are social creatures. We need people. Without friends and lovers, life would be pretty lonely.

In the next sections, we explore both life-enhancing and life-diminishing relationships. We consider friendships, what happens when love enters the picture, and how people find mates. Unfortunately, some relationships turn violent; we'll also examine the factors underlying aggressive behaviours between partners.

FRIENDSHIPS

What is an adult friend? Someone who is there when you need to share? Someone not afraid to tell you the truth? Someone to have fun with? Friends, of course, are all of these and more.

Friends are very different from family and represent a point of contrast (de Vries, 1996). Friendships are predominantly based on feelings and grounded in reciprocity and choice. Friendships are different from love relationships in that they are less emotionally intense and involve less sexual energy or contact (Rose & Zand, 2000). Our friends help us develop self-esteem, self-awareness, and self-respect. They also help us become socialized into new roles throughout adulthood.

Friendship in Adulthood

From a developmental perspective, adult friendships can be viewed as having identifiable stages (Levinger, 1980, 1983): Acquaintanceship, Buildup, Continuation, Deterioration, and Ending. This ABCDE model describes not only the stages of friendships but also the processes by which they change. For example, whether the friendship between the two women in the photograph on page 421 will develop from Acquaintanceship to Buildup depends on where the individuals fall on several dimensions, such as the basis of the attraction, what each person knows about the other, how good the communication is between the partners, the perceived importance of the friendship, and so on. Although many friendships reach the Deterioration stage, whether a friendship ultimately ends depends importantly on the availability of alternative relationships. If new potential friends appear, old friendships end; if not, they may continue even though they may not be considered important by either person.

People tend to have more friends and acquaintances during young adulthood than at any subsequent period (Sherman et al., 2000). Friendships are important throughout adulthood, in part because a person's life satisfaction is strongly related to the quantity and quality of contacts with friends. College students who have strong friendship networks adjust better to stressful life events (Brissette, Scheier, & Carver, 2002) and play a major role in determining how much we enjoy life.

Researchers have uncovered three broad themes that underlie adult friendships (de Vries, 1996):

- The most frequently mentioned dimension represents the *affective* or emotional basis of friendship. This dimension refers to self-disclosure and expressions of intimacy, appreciation, affection, and support, all of which are based on trust, loyalty, and commitment.
- A second theme reflects the *shared or communal* nature of friendship, in which friends participate in or support activities of mutual interest.
- The third dimension represents *sociability and compatibility*; our friends keep us entertained and are sources of amusement, fun, and recreation.

These three dimensions are found in friendships among adults of all ages (de Vries, 1996).

FIGURE 12.1   Importance of Sibling Relationships

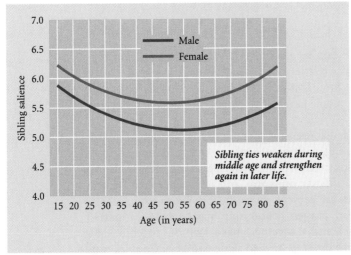

Schmeeckle, M., Giarusso, R., and Wang, Q. (1998, November). When being a brother or sister is important to one's identity: Life stage and gender differences. Paper presented at the annual meeting of the Gerontological Society, Philadelphia.

One special type of friendship exists with one's siblings. Although little research has focused on the development and maintenance of sibling friendships across adulthood, we know that the importance of these relationships varies with age. As you can see in Figure 12.1, women place more importance on sibling ties across adulthood than do men; however, for both the strength of these ties is greatest in adolescence and late life (Schmeeckle, Giarusso, & Wang, 1998). We will consider sibling relationships in more detail in Chapter 16.

Gender Differences in Friendships

Men's and women's friendships tend to differ in adulthood, reflecting continuity in the learned behaviours from childhood (Fehr, 1996; Sherman et al., 2000). Women tend to base their friendships on more intimate and emotional sharing and use friendship as a means to confide in others. For women, getting together with friends often takes the form of getting together to discuss personal matters. Confiding in others is a basis of women's friendships. In contrast, men tend to base friendships on shared activities or interests. They are more likely to go bowling or fishing or to talk sports with their friends. For men, confiding in others is inconsistent with the need to compete; this may be one reason men are reluctant to do so (Cutrona, 1996). Rather, competition often is a part of men's friendships as evidenced in basketball games with friends. However, the competition usually is set up so that the social interaction is the most important element, not who wins or loses (Rawlins, 1992). Men's friendships usually are less intimate than women's, no matter how one defines intimacy (Fehr, 1996).

Women tend to have more close relationships than do men. Although you may think this puts women at an advantage, research shows that this is not always the case. Sometimes, friends can get on people's nerves or make high demands. When these things happen, women tend to be less happy even when they have lots of friends (Antonucci, Akiyama, & Lansford, 1998).

Why are women's friendships typically more intimate than men's? Compared to men, women have much more experience with such intimate sharing from early childhood, and they are more comfortable with vulnerability. Social pressure on men to be brave and strong may actually inhibit their ability to form close friendships (Rawlins, 1992).

LOVE RELATIONSHIPS

Love is one of those things everybody feels but nobody can define completely. (Test yourself: Can you explain fully what you mean when you look at someone special and say, "I love you"?) One way researchers have tried to understand love is to think about what components are essential. In an interesting series of studies, Sternberg (1986) found that love has three basic components: (1) *passion*, an intense physiological desire for someone; (2) *intimacy*, the feeling that one can share all one's thoughts and actions with another; and (3) *commitment*, the willingness to stay with a person through good and bad times. Ideally, a true love relationship has all three components. As we will see next, the balance among these components often shifts as time passes.

Love Through Adulthood

The different combinations of love can be used to understand how relationships develop (Sternberg, 1986). Early in any relationship, passion is usually high, but intimacy and commitment tend to be low. This is infatuation: an intense, physically based relationship in which the two people have a high risk of misunderstanding and jealousy.

But infatuation is short-lived. Whereas even the smallest touch is enough to incite intense lustful feelings in the beginning, with time it takes more and more effort to get the same level of feeling. As passion fades, a relationship either acquires emotional intimacy or it is likely to end. Trust, honesty, openness, and acceptance must be part of any strong relationship; when they are present, romantic love develops.

Given more time, people who work at their relationship may become committed to each other. They spend much of their time together, make decisions together, care for each other, share possessions, and develop ways to settle conflicts. Couples usually show outward signs of commitment, such as wearing a lover's ring, having children together, or simply sharing the mundane details of daily life from making toast at breakfast to before-bed rituals.

Falling in Love

Everybody wants to be loved by somebody, but actually having it happen is fraught with difficulties. In his book *The Prophet*, Kahlil Gibran (1923) points out that love is two-sided: Just as it can give you great ecstasy, so can it cause you great pain. Yet most of us are willing to take the risk.

As you may have experienced, taking the risk is fun (at times) and difficult (at other times). Making a connection can be ritualized, as when people use pickup lines in a bar, or it can happen almost by accident, as when two people literally run into each other in a crowded corridor. The question that confronts us is "How do people fall in love?" Do birds of a feather flock together? Or do opposites attract?

*The best explanation of the process is the theory of **assortative mating**, which states that people find partners based on their similarity to each other.* Assortative mating occurs along many dimensions, including religious beliefs, physical traits, age, socioeconomic status, intelligence, and political ideology among others (Sher, 1996). Such nonrandom mating occurs most often in Western societies, which allow people to have more control over their own dating and pairing behaviours. But does where people meet influence the likelihood that they "click" on particular dimensions and whether they form a couple?

Kalmijn and Flap (2001) found that it did. *Using data from more than 1,500 couples, they found that meeting at school promoted most forms of **homogamy**, or the degree to which people are similar.* Meeting through other methods (being from the same neighbourhood or through family networks) did not promote most forms of homogamy other than religious. Not surprisingly, the pool of available people to meet is strongly shaped by the opportunities available, which in turn constrain the type of people one is likely to meet.

Once people have met someone compatible, what happens next? Some researchers believe couples progress in stages. According to Murstein's (1987) classic theory, people apply three filters, representing discrete stages, when they meet someone:

Stimulus: Do the person's physical appearance, social class, and manners match your own?

Values: Do the person's values regarding sex, religion, politics, and so on match your own?

Role: Do the person's ideas about the relationship, communication style, gender roles, and so on match your own?

If the answer to all three filters is "yes," then you are likely to form a couple.

An important aspect in understanding how adults form couples relates to the attachments they made to adults in infancy and childhood as described in Chapter 6 (Hazan & Shaver, 1994). Researchers have shown that each of us tends to re-create in our partnership relationships the kind of attachments we had as children to key adults (e.g., Hazan & Shaver, 1994; Kobak, 1994; Main, 1996). For example, Hazan and Shaver (1987, 1990) found that adults who get close to people fairly easily (*secure style*) had the strongest relationships as children; those who are lonely had trouble forming close relationships (*avoidant style*) as children. Similarity in attachment styles is an important element for assortative mating (Collins & Read, 1990).

> **THINK ABOUT IT** 💡
>
> What are the effects of increasing interactions among cultures on mate selection?

It also turns out that whether the couple in the photograph find each other physically attractive is more important in love relationships than most people realize. Certainly, physical attractiveness acts as an initial filter, as described earlier. In a study of nearly 2,000 Spanish respondents, physical attractiveness was important in sporadic relationships, but it also influenced the way people fell in love and was linked to feelings and thoughts associated with love (intimacy, passion, commitment) and to satisfaction with the relationship (Sangrador & Yela, 2000).

© Myrleen F. Cate/PhotoEdit

How do these couple-forming behaviours compare cross-culturally? In an extraordinary study, Buss and a large team of researchers (1990) identified the effects of culture and gender on heterosexual mate preferences in 37 cultures worldwide. This research is described in the Spotlight on Research feature. What characteristics predict mate selection? Read on and find out.

SPOTLIGHT ON RESEARCH

The Mating Game Around the World

Who were the investigators and what was the aim of the study? Culture and gender may play major roles in determining who is desirable as a mate in various locations around the world. To conduct the most thorough study of this topic ever, David Buss assembled a large international team of researchers.

How did the investigators measure the topic of interest? The researchers asked participants to complete questionnaires concerning important factors in choosing a mate, such as rating desired characteristics of potential mates, and preferences concerning potential mates, such as ranking characteristics of potential mates from highest to lowest.

Who were the participants in the study? A total of 9,474 adults from 33 countries, on 6 continents and 5 islands, took part in the study. Such large and diverse samples are unusual in developmental research.

What was the design of the study? Data for this cross-sectional, nonexperimental study were gathered by research teams in each country. In some cases, the survey items had to be modified to reflect the local culture. For example, many couples in Sweden, Finland, and Norway never get married, opting instead simply to live together. In Nigeria, items had to reflect the possibility of multiple wives due to the practice of polygyny. Data collection in South Africa was described as "a rather frightening experience" due to the difficulty in collecting data from both white and Zulu samples in the midst of civil unrest. Finally, in some cases data were never received because of government interference or the lack of official approval to conduct the study. Such problems highlight the difficulty in doing cross-cultural research and the need to take local culture into account in designing research instruments.

Were there ethical concerns with the study? Because the study involved volunteers, there were no ethical concerns. However, ensuring that all participants' rights were protected was a challenge because of the number of countries and cultures involved.

What were the results? Men and women in each culture displayed unique orderings of their preferences concerning the ideal characteristics of a mate. When all of the orderings and preferences were compared, the two main dimensions shown in Figure 12.2 emerged. As you look at the figure, the closer two or more countries are, the more similar men and women in them were in ranking desirable qualities in a mate.

In the first main dimension (represented in the figure by the horizontal axis), the characteristics of a desirable mate changed because of cultural values—that is, whether the respondents' country has more traditional values or Western-industrial values. In traditional cultures, men place a high value on a woman's chastity, desire for home and children, and being a good cook and housekeeper; women place a high value on a man's ambition and industry, being a good financial prospect, and holding favourable social status. Countries such as China, India, Iran, and Nigeria represent the traditional end of this dimension. In contrast, people in Western-industrial cultures value these qualities to a much lesser extent. Countries such as the Netherlands, Great Britain, Finland, and Sweden represent this end of the dimension.

The second main dimension (the vertical axis) reflects the relative importance of education, intelligence, and social refinement as opposed to a pleasing disposition in choosing a mate. As you can see in the figure, people in Spain, Colombia, and Greece highly value education, intelligence, and social refinement; in contrast, people in Indonesia place a greater emphasis on having a pleasing disposition. Note that this dimension emphasizes the same traits for both men and women.

Chastity proved to be the characteristic showing the most variability across cultures,

FIGURE 12.2

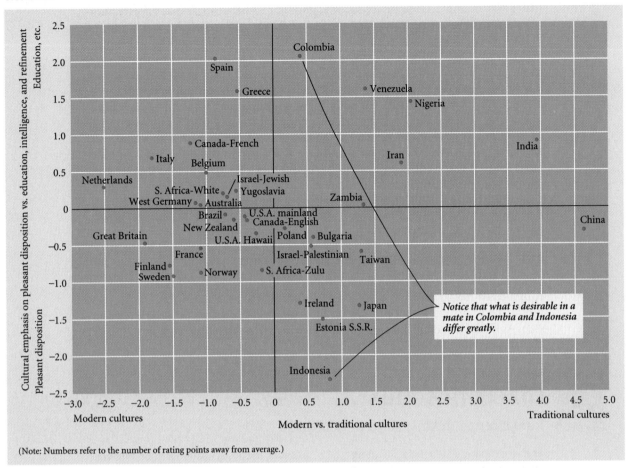

(Note: Numbers refer to the number of rating points away from average.)

SOURCE: From "International Preferences in Selecting Mates: A Study of 37 Cultures," by D. M. Buss, et al., 1990, *Journal of Cross-Cultural Psychology, 21,* 5–47. Copyright © 1990 by Sage Publications, Inc. Reprinted by permission of Sage Publications, Inc.

being highly desired in some cultures but mattering little in others. Interestingly, in their respective search for mates, men around the world value physical attractiveness in women, whereas women around the world look for men capable of being good providers. But men and women around the world agree that love and mutual attraction are most important, and nearly all cultures rate dependability, emotional stability, kindness, and understanding as important factors. Attraction, it seems, has some characteristics that transcend culture.

What have the investigators concluded? Overall, Buss and his colleagues concluded that mate selection is a complex process no matter where you live. However, each culture has a describable set of high-priority traits that men and women look for in the perfect mate.

The study also shows that socialization within a culture plays a key role in being attractive to the opposite sex; characteristics that are highly desirable in one culture may not be so desirable in another.

What converging evidence would strengthen these conclusions? Although this is one of the best designed among large cross-cultural studies, there are several additional lines of evidence that would help bolster the conclusions. Most important, representative samples from the countries under study would provide more accurate insights into people's mate selection. Additionally, paying attention to ethnic variations within a country rather than treating all respondents from a country as reflecting one group would also be an improvement.

The power of culture in shaping mate selection choices must not be underestimated. For example, despite decades of sociopolitical change in China, research indicates that the same status hierarchy norms govern assortative mating in urban China despite the socialist transformation in the 1950s, the Cultural Revolution in the 1960s, and the economic reforms in the 1990s (Xu, Ji, & Tung, 2000). Clearly, cultural norms are sometimes very resistant to change. Arranged marriages are a major way that some cultures ensure an appropriate match on key dimensions. For example, loyalty of the individual to the family is a very important value in India; consequently, many marriages are carefully arranged to avoid selecting inappropriate mates. Data show that this approach appears to work; among urban professionals polled in one study, 81% said their marriage had been arranged and 94% of them rated their marriage as "very successful" (Lakshmanan, 1997). Similarly, Islamic societies use matchmaking as a way to preserve family consistency and continuity and to ensure that couples follow the prohibition on premarital relationships between men and women (Adler, 2001). Matchmaking in these societies occurs through both family connections and personal advertisements in newspapers.

The Developmental Forces and Relationships

From our discussion and your experience, you know that finding a relationship is a complicated matter. Many things must work just right: timing, meeting the right person, luck, and effort are but a few of the things that shape the course of a relationship. As discussed in the Forces in Action feature, all the developmental forces affect the creation and maintenance of relationships.

FORCES IN ACTION

Influences on Relationships in Adulthood

As is clear from the ABCDE and Sternberg models, adult relationships are complex. Who chooses whom, and whether the feelings will be mutual, results from the interaction of developmental forces described in the biopsychosocial model presented in Chapter 1. Biologically, it turns out that there are two distinct stages, attraction and attachment (Liebowitz, 1983), which reflect fundamentally different neurochemical processes (Fisher, 1994). Attraction is associated with neurochemicals related to amphetamines, which account for the exhilaration of falling in love. Attachment, which some people might call long-term commitment and tranquillity, is reflected neurochemically in substances related to morphine, a powerful narcotic. (Love really does do a number on your brain!)

Psychologically, as we saw in Chapter 10, an important developmental issue is intimacy;

according to Erikson, mature relationships are impossible without it. Additionally, the kinds of relationships you saw and experienced as a child (and whether they involved violence) affect how you define and act in relationships you develop as an adult. Sociocultural forces shape the characteristics you find desirable in a mate and determine whether you are likely to encounter resistance from your family when you have made your choice. Life-cycle forces matter too; different aspects of love are more or less important, depending on your stage in life.

In short, to understand adult relationships, we must take the forces of the biopsychosocial model into account. Relying too heavily on one or two of the forces provides an incomplete description of why people are successful (or not) in finding a partner or a friend.

Unfortunately, the developmental forces do not influence only good relationships. As we will see next, sometimes relationships turn violent.

THE DARK SIDE OF RELATIONSHIPS: VIOLENCE

Up to this point, we have been considering relationships that are healthy and positive. Sadly, this is not always the case. *Sometimes relationships become violent; one person becomes aggressive toward the partner, creating an* **abusive relationship**. Such relationships have received increasing attention over the past few decades. Indeed, some authors believe, under some circumstances, that abusive relationships can be used as an explanation for one's behaviour (Walker, 1984). *For example,* **battered woman syndrome** *occurs when a woman believes she cannot leave the abusive situation and may even go so far as to kill her abuser.*

What kind of aggressive behaviours occur in abusive relationships? What causes such abuse? Researchers are beginning to find answers to these and related questions. Based on a decade of research on abusive partners, O'Leary (1993) argues that there is a continuum of aggressive behaviours toward a spouse, which progresses as follows: verbally aggressive behaviours, physically aggressive behaviours, severe physically aggressive behaviours, and murder of the partner. The causes of the abuse also vary with the type of abusive behaviour being expressed. O'Leary's continuum is shown in Figure 12.3.

FIGURE 12.3   Continuum of Aggressive Behaviour Toward a Spouse

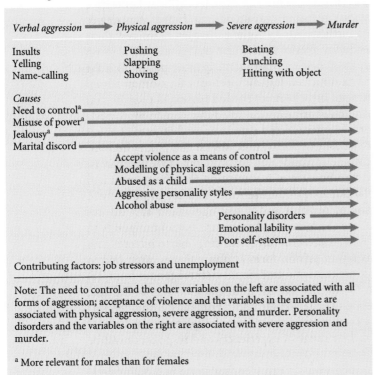

Note: The need to control and the other variables on the left are associated with all forms of aggression; acceptance of violence and the variables in the middle are associated with physical aggression, severe aggression, and murder. Personality disorders and the variables on the right are associated with severe aggression and murder.

[a] More relevant for males than for females

SOURCE: From "Through a Psychological Lens: Personality Traits, Personality Disorders, and Levels of Violence" by K. D. O'Leary. In R. J. Gelles and D. R. Loeske (Eds.), *Current Controversies on Family Violence*, pp. 7–30. Copyright © 1993 by Sage Publications, Inc. Reprinted by permission of Sage Publications, Inc.

Two points about the continuum are interesting. First, there may be fundamental differences in the types of aggression that go beyond level of severity. Canadian findings indicate that men were more likely than women to report being slapped (57% versus 40%), having something thrown at them (56% versus 40%), or being kicked, bitten, or hit (51% versus 33%), whereas women were more than twice as likely as men to report being beaten or having a knife or gun used against them and five times more likely to report being choked. In addition, 38% of women feared for their life compared to 7% of men (Statistics Canada, 2000a).

The second interesting point, depicted in the figure, is that the suspected underlying causes of aggressive behaviours differ as the type of aggressive behaviours change (O'Leary, 1993). As can be seen, the number of suspected causes of aggressive behaviour increases as the level of aggression increases. Thus, the causes of aggressive behaviour become more complex as the level of aggression worsens. Such differences in cause imply that the approaches to treating abusers should vary with the nature of the aggressive behaviour (O'Leary, 1993). Situational factors that contribute to all levels of aggression are alcoholism, job stressors, and unemployment; the presence of these factors increases the likelihood that violence will occur in the relationship (O'Leary, 1993).

M. P. Johnson (2001, 1995; Johnson & Ferraro, 2000) goes even further in making a very important distinction in the types of violence that occur in relationships, distinguishing between common couple violence and patriarchal terrorism. *Common couple violence refers to violence that occurs occasionally and that can be instigated by either partner. Patriarchal terrorism refers to women who are victims of systematic violence from men.* Data supporting this distinction clearly show that women are not as violent as men in relationships (e.g., M. P. Johnson, 2001). Additional research has uncovered different patterns within common couple violence that range from aggressive to abusive (Olson, 2000).

Gender differences in some of the underlying causes of aggressive behaviour in relationships have been reported (O'Leary, 1993). Most important, the triad of need to control, misuse of power, and jealousy are more pertinent causes for men than for women. For example, men are more likely than women to act aggressively because they want to make sure their partner knows "who the boss is" and who makes the rules.

Culture is also an important contextual factor. For example, cultures that emphasize honour and portray females as passive, nurturing supporters of men's activities, along with beliefs that emphasize loyalty and sacrifice for the family, may contribute to tolerating abuse. Vandello (2000) reported two studies of Latino Americans, southern Anglo Americans, and northern Anglo Americans that examined these ideas. Latino Americans and southern Anglo Americans placed more value on honour. These groups rated a woman in an abusive relationship more positively if she stayed with the man, and they communicated less disapproval of a woman whom they witnessed being shoved and restrained if she portrayed herself as contrite and self-blaming than did northern Anglo Americans, who rated the woman more positively if she left the man. Additionally, international data indicate that rates of abuse are higher in cultures that emphasize female purity, male status, and family honour. For example, a common cause of women's murders in Arab countries are brothers or other male relatives killing the victim because of a perception that the woman had violated the family's honour (Kulwicki, 2002). Chinese Americans are more likely to define domestic violence in terms of physical and sexual aggression and do not include psychological forms of abuse (Yick, 2000). And South Asian immigrants to the United States report the use of social isolation (e.g., not being able to interact with family, friends, or co-workers) as a very painful form of abuse that is often tied to being financially dependent on the husband and traditional cultural gender roles (M. Abraham, 2000). In a discussion of violence against immigrant women in Canada, Migliardi, Blum, and Heinomen (2004) cite similar issues but caution that "immigrant women" do not constitute a homogenous group even though they may have all been born outside of Canada and their range of experiences and responses must be acknowledged.

Many university and college students report experiencing abuse in a dating relationship. Although there is a wide range of rates of physical assault in dating relationships reported in different studies, there is some consensus that the prevalence rate is approximately 30% (Legge et al., 2004). These authors summarize a number of factors that have been linked with relationship violence, either for perpetrators or victims: low self-esteem, insecure attachment, approval of violence and belief in its effectiveness, alcohol use, and poor problem-solving or communication skills (p. 63).

Alarmed at the seriousness of abuse, many communities have established shelters for battered women and their children, like the one in the photograph on page 429, and programs that treat abusive men. In Canada, the first shelters for women opened in 1973, and they have become the primary resource for protecting women from violent partners (Tutty & Rothery, 2002). However, much remains to be done to protect women and their children from the fear and the reality of continued abuse.

© A. Ramey/PhotoEdit

TEST YOURSELF

1. Friendships based on intimacy and emotional sharing are more characteristic of _____.

2. Competition is a major part of most friendships among _____.

3. Love relationships in which intimacy and passion are present but commitment is not are termed _____.

4. Chastity is an important quality that men look for in a potential female mate in _____ cultures.

5. Aggressive behaviour that is based on abuse of power, jealousy, or the need to control is more likely to be displayed by _____.

Why is intimacy (discussed in Chapter 10) a necessary prerequisite for adult relationships according to Erikson? What aspects of relationships discussed here support (and refute) this view?

Answers: (1) women, (2) men, (3) romantic love, (4) traditional, (5) men

12.2

Lifestyles

LEARNING OBJECTIVES

■ Why do some people decide not to marry, and what are these people like?

■ What are the characteristics of cohabiting people?

■ What are gay and lesbian relationships like?

■ What is marriage like through the course of adulthood?

Lifestyles
Singlehood
Cohabitation
Gay and Lesbian Couples
Marriage

Kevin and Beth are on cloud nine. They got married one month ago and have recently returned from their honeymoon. Everyone who sees them can tell that they love each other a lot. They are highly compatible and have much in common, sharing most of their leisure activities. Kevin and Beth wonder what lies ahead in their marriage.

Developing relationships is only part of the picture in understanding how adults live their lives with other people. Putting relationships like Kevin and Beth's in context is important for us to understand how relationships come into existence and how they change over time. In the following sections, we explore relationship lifestyles: singlehood, cohabitation, gay and lesbian couples, and marriage.

SINGLEHOOD

When Audrey graduated from university with a degree in accounting, she took a job at a consulting firm. For the first several years in her job, she spent more time travelling than she did at home. During this time, she had a series of love relationships, but none resulted in commitment even though she had marriage as a goal. By the time she was in her mid-30s, Audrey had decided that she no longer wanted to get married. "I'm now a partner in my firm, I enjoy travelling, and I'm pretty flexible about moving if something better comes along," she stated to her friend Michele. "But I do miss being with someone to share my day or to just hang around with."

During early adulthood, most men and women are single, like Audrey, defined as not living with an intimate partner. Estimates are that approximately 85% of Canadian men and 73% of Canadian women between ages 20 and 24 are unmarried, with increasing numbers deciding to stay that way (Statistics Canada, 2001f).

Audrey's experience is common among women who ultimately decide not to marry (Dalton, 1992). Many women and men focus on establishing their careers rather than marriage or relationships. Others report that they simply did not meet "the right person" or prefer singlehood (Lamanna & Riedmann, 2003). However, the pressure to marry is especially strong for women; frequent questions such as "Any good prospects yet?" may leave women feeling conspicuous or left out as many of their friends marry. Research indicates that single women have unresolved or unrecognized ambivalences about being single (Lewis & Moon, 1997). Such feelings result from being aware of the advantages and disadvantages of being single and ambivalence about the reasons they are single.

Men tend to remain single longer in young adulthood because they tend to marry at a later age than women (Statistics Canada, 2001f). Fewer men than women remain unmarried throughout adulthood, largely because men find partners more easily as they select from a larger age range of unmarried women.

An important distinction is between adults who are temporarily single (i.e., those who are single only until they find a suitable marriage partner) and those who choose to remain single. Results from an in-depth interview study with never-married women in their 30s revealed three distinct groups: Some suffer with acute distress about being single and long to be married with children; others describe a volatile emotional situation; and others say that they are quite happy with a healthy self-image and high quality of life (Cole, 2000). For most singles, the decision to never marry is a gradual one. Still, a key question is what marks the decision to remain single? For some, it is reaching a milestone birthday (e.g., 30) and still being single, although the particular age that reflects this varies a great deal (Davies, 2000). For many middle-aged single women, it is purchasing a house that marks the decision:

> I always thought you got married, you bought a house. Well, I bought a house and I'm not married. . . . I've laid down roots. . . . You're sort of saying, "Okay, this is it." And it makes you feel more settled. (Davies, 2000, p. 12)

For most, though, the transition to permanent singlehood is a gradual one they drift into by circumstance rather than a lifestyle they choose. For example, having to care for parents or other family members may conflict with personal goals related to marriage, family, education, or career (Connidis, 2001).

In general, singles recognize the pluses and minuses in their lifestyles. They enjoy the freedom and flexibility but also feel loneliness, dissatisfaction with dating, limited social life in a couple-oriented society, and less sense of security (Chasteen, 1994). Gender differences are evident between single men and women. Single men have higher mortality rates and higher incidence of alcoholism, suicide, and mental health problems (Whitbourne, 1996). However, single women experience more problems overall than single men (Lamanna & Riedmann, 2003). Because they tend to live alone, single women are more likely than their married counterparts to be mugged, raped, or burglarized and to encounter problems when travelling. Single women are also more likely to be asked to perform extra functions at work because they are perceived as having no other duties to perform. Despite the challenges, though, most singles who choose to stay that way are content with their lives.

COHABITATION

Being unmarried does not necessarily mean living alone. *People in committed, intimate, sexual relationships may decide that living together in a common law arrangement or* **cohabitation,** *provides a way to share daily life.* Cohabitation is becoming an increasingly popular lifestyle choice in Canada, as well as in the United States, Europe, Australia, and elsewhere. In the last decade of the 20th century the number of legally married couples in Canada increased by less than 1% compared to the number of couples in a common law relationship, which increased by 26% (The Vanier Institute of the Family, 2000).

Couples cohabit for a number of reasons including as a trial period before marriage, awaiting a divorce before remarriage, seeking a partner after being widowed, or as the preferred relationship arrangement (The Vanier Institute of the Family, 2000).

In most European, South American, and Caribbean countries cohabitation is a common alternative to marriage. For example, cohabitation is extremely common in the Netherlands, Norway, and Sweden, where this lifestyle is part of the culture; 99% of married couples in Sweden lived together before they married and nearly one in four couples are not legally married. Couples living together there are just as devoted to each other as are married couples and believe that such relationships are grounded in love and commitment to each other (Kaslow, Hansson, & Lundblad, 1994). Decisions to marry in these countries are typically made to legalize the relationship after children are born, whereas North Americans marry to confirm their love and commitment to each other.

In contrast, cohabitation rates are lower in Africa and Asia. For example, in China, cohabitation is largely limited to rural villages where couples below the legal age for marriage live together (Neft & Levine, 1997).

Interestingly, having cohabitated does not seem to make Canadian or American marriages any better; in fact, it may do more harm than good, resulting in marriages that are less happy with a higher risk of divorce (Hall & Zhao, 1995). Other research indicates that transitioning to marriage from cohabitation does not lessen depression, and concern about getting approval from friends increases distress for cohabitors who marry (Marcussen, 2001). Why is this the case? Part of the answer may be that cohabiting couples tend to be less conventional and less religious, and come from lower socioeconomic backgrounds, which may put them at higher risk for divorce (DeMaris & Rao, 1992). Part of the reason may also be that marrying after already having lived with someone represents much less of a change in the relationship than when a couple marries who have not been cohabiting; such couples lack the newly wedded bliss seen in couples who have not cohabited (Thomson & Colella, 1992).

Data indicate that the negative relation between cohabiting and marital stability may be weakening somewhat (McCrae, 1997). Why would this be the case? Much of the previous data comes from a time when cohabitation was viewed as unconventional. As cohabitation becomes more common, and perhaps the majority pattern, this negative link is likely to grow progressively weaker (McCrae, 1997). Additionally,

> **THINK ABOUT IT**
>
> Why might there be large differences in cohabitation rates among countries?

many countries are now extending the same rights and benefits to cohabiting couples as they do to married couples. For instance, Canada extends insurance benefits, Argentina provides pension rights to cohabiting partners, and Australia has laws governing the disposition of property when cohabiting couples sever their relationship (Neft & Levine, 1997).

GAY AND LESBIAN COUPLES

What is it like to be in a gay or lesbian relationship? One woman shares her experience in the Real People feature.

REAL PEOPLE: APPLYING HUMAN DEVELOPMENT

Maggie O'Carroll's Story

I am a 35-year-old woman who believes that each person is here with a purpose to fulfil in his or her lifetime. "Add your light to the sum of light" are words I live by in my teaching career, my personal life with friends and family, and living in general. I do not believe that our creator makes mistakes, although at times I am very discouraged by the level of hatred that is evident in the world against many groups, but against homosexuals in particular.

For me, being a lesbian is the most natural state of being. I do not think of it as a mishap of genetics, a result of an unhappy or traumatic childhood, or an unnatural tendency. From the time I was a child I had a definite and strong sense of my sexual identity. However, I am aware of the homophobia that is present at all levels of my own life and in the community. That is where my sense of self and living in the world collide.

Society does not value diversity. We, as a people, do not look to people who are different and acknowledge the strength it takes to live in this society. Being gay in a homophobic, heterosexist society is a burden that manifests itself in many forms, such as through alcohol and drug abuse rates that are much higher than in the heterosexual community. The lack of acknowledgment of gay people's partners by family members, co-workers, and society at large is a stamp of nonexistence and invisibility. How can we build a life with a partner and then not share that person with society?

I consider myself a fortunate gay person in that I have a supportive family. Of the five children in my family, two of us are gay. My parents are supportive and love our partners. My siblings vary in their attitudes. One sister invited me and my partner to her wedding. Nine years later, my other sister refused to do that. Her discomfort over my sexual orientation meant that I spent a special event without my partner at my side. However, my straight brother was allowed to bring a date. It was very hurtful and hard to forgive.

In the larger community, I have been surprised by the blatant hatred I have experienced. I have demeaning comments aimed at me. The home I live in has been defaced with obscenities. But on a more positive note, I have never been more strongly certain of who I am. I am indebted to those who have supported me over the years with love and enlightenment, knowing that who I am is not a mistake. As I age, it becomes clearer to me that I am meant to share the message that our differences are to be appreciated and respected.

Less is known about the developmental course of gay and lesbian relationships than heterosexual relationships, largely because they were almost never the focus of research. To date, gay and lesbian relationships have been studied most often in comparison to married heterosexual couples. Like heterosexuals, gay and lesbian couples must deal with issues related to effective communication, power, and household responsibilities.

For the most part, the relationships of gay and lesbian couples like the one in the photograph show similar stressors to those of heterosexual couples: Conflicts tend to be about finances, lack of equality in the relationship, possessiveness, personal flaws, dissatisfaction over the sexual relationship, and physical absence due to work or education commitments (Kurdek, 1995a, 1995b). However, heterosexual couples are more likely to argue over personal values, social and political issues, and relationships with in-laws, whereas gay and lesbian couples reported more distrust, especially regarding former lovers (Kurdek, 1995a, 1995b). Most gay and lesbian couples are in dual-worker relationships, much like the majority of married couples. Thus, they are likely to share household chores.

Gender differences are more important than differences in sexual orientation (Huston & Schwartz, 1995). Gay men, like heterosexual men, tend to separate love and sex and have more short-term relationships; both lesbian and heterosexual women are more likely to connect sex and emotional intimacy in fewer, longer-lasting relationships. Men in any type of relationship tend to want more power if they earn more money. Women in any type of relationship are likely to be more egalitarian and to view money as a way to maintain independence from one's partner.

Gay and lesbian couples often report less support from family members than do either married or cohabiting couples (Benokraitis, 1999). The more that one's family holds traditional ethnic or religious values, the less likely it is that the family will provide support. At a societal level, the legal recognition for gay and lesbian relationships in Canada has made some advancement. In 2000 an Act of Parliament formally extended benefits and obligations related to income tax and pension plan qualifications to all couples, both same and opposite sex, as long as they have been cohabiting in a conjugal relationship for at least one year (Government of Canada, 2000). In 2003, the Ontario Appeals court determined that the definition of marriage was too restrictive and changed Ontario's definition of marriage from that of a union between a man and woman to a union of two people. Ontario became the first province to legalize gay and lesbian marriages, but other provinces have also started to recognize same-sex marriages. The differing laws and practices across Canada are likely to result in the Supreme Court of Canada being asked to consider if the current federal definition of marriage, that of an opposite-sex union, is constitutional (Department of Justice Canada, 2004).

MARRIAGE

Most adults want their love relationships to result in marriage. However, Canadians are in less of a hurry to achieve this goal; the median age at first marriage for adults in Canada has been rising over the years. Between 1986 and 2001, the median age for first marriage rose three years for both men and women, from roughly age 27 to 30 for men, and from roughly age 25 to 28 for women (Statistics Canada, 2001f). Let's explore age and other factors that keep marriages going strong over time.

What Factors Help Marriages Succeed?

One reason age is important has to do with the couple's level of psychosocial development. Erikson (1982) points out that intimacy, the task of young adulthood, is difficult to achieve unless one has developed a strong sense of identity, the task of adolescence (see Chapter 10). Because many adolescents are still trying to decide who they are, teenage newlyweds may initially find themselves compatible but soon grow apart as they mature. Additional complicating factors, such as pregnancy and unemployment, also stack the deck against successful teenage marriages.

A second important predictor of successful marriage is homogamy, or similarity of values and interests. As we saw in relation to choosing a mate, the extent that the partners share similar values, goals, attitudes, socioeconomic status, and ethnic background increases the likelihood that their relationship will succeed.

A third factor in predicting marital success is a feeling that the relationship is equal. *According to exchange theory, marriage is based on each partner contributing something to the relationship that the other would be hard-pressed to provide.* Satisfying and happy marriages result when both partners perceive that there is a fair exchange, or equity, in all the dimensions of the relationship. Problems achieving such equity can arise because of the competing demands of work and family, an issue we will take up again in Chapter 13.

Do Married Couples Stay Happy?

Take a look at the couple in the photograph. They certainly look as though they are deeply in love with each other. Few sights are happier than a couple on their wedding day. Newlyweds, like Kevin and Beth in the vignette, are at the peak of marital bliss. But will this happiness be sustained?

The beliefs people bring into a marriage influence how satisfied they will be as the marriage develops. As you might suspect, couples' feelings change over time. Like any relationship, marriage has its peaks and valleys. Much research has been conducted on marital satisfaction across adulthood. As illustrated in Figure 12.4, research shows that for most couples overall marital satisfaction is highest at the beginning of the marriage, falls until the children begin leaving home, and rises again in later life (Miller, Hemesath, & Nelson, 1997). However, for some couples, satisfaction never rebounds and remains low; in essence, they have become emotionally divorced.

Overall, marital satisfaction ebbs and flows over time. The pattern of a particular marriage over the years is determined by the nature of the dependence of each spouse on the other. When dependence is mutual and about equal, the marriage is strong and close. When the dependence of one partner is much higher than that of the other, however, the marriage is likely to be characterized by stress and conflict. Changes in individual lives over adulthood shift the balance of dependence from one partner to the other; for example, one partner may go back to school, become ill, or lose status. Learning how to deal with these changes is the secret to long and happy marriages.

The fact that marital satisfaction has a general downward trend but varies widely across couples led Karney and Bradbury (1995) to propose a vulnerability–stress–adaptation model of marriage. This model sees marital quality as a dynamic process resulting from the couples' ability to handle stressful events in the context of their particular vulnerabilities and resources. For example, as couples' ability to

FIGURE 12.4   Changes in Marital Satisfaction

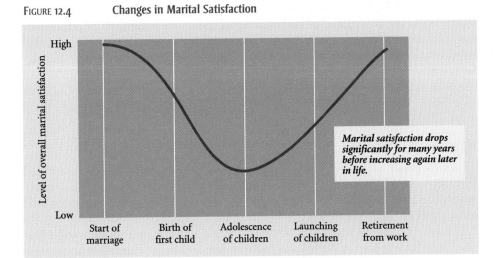

Marital satisfaction drops significantly for many years before increasing again later in life.

adapt to stressful situations gets better over time, the quality of the marriage probably will improve.

The Early Years

Marriages are most intense in their early days. When husbands and wives share many activities and are open to new experiences together, bliss results (Olson & McCubbin, 1983). When the marriage is troubled, the intensity of the early phase creates considerable unhappiness (Swenson, Eskew, & Kohlhepp, 1981).

Early in a marriage, the couple must learn to adjust to the different perceptions and expectations each person has for the other. Many wives tend to be more concerned than their husbands with keeping close ties with their friends. Women are also more likely to identify problems in the marriage and want to talk about them (Peplau & Gordon, 1985). The couple must also learn to handle confrontation. Indeed, learning effective strategies for resolving conflict is an essential component of a strong marriage, as these strategies provide ways for couples to discuss their problems maturely.

Less-educated couples experience greater dissatisfaction with their marriages, as do couples who do not pool their financial resources (Kurdek, 1991a). This occurs because less-educated couples face many additional stressors (e.g., higher rates of unemployment, lower financial security), and the failure to pool resources may reflect a lack of trust in the partner.

As couples settle into a routine, marital satisfaction tends to decline (Lamanna & Riedmann, 2003). Research shows that the primary reason for this drop for most couples is the birth of children (Carstensen et al., 1996). Indeed, for most couples having children means strong pressures to engage in traditional gender-role behaviours for mothers and fathers (Carstensen et al., 1996). Parenthood also means having substantially less time to devote to the marriage. Taking care of children is hard work, requiring energy that used to be spent on keeping the marriage alive and well (Acock & Demo, 1994; Noller & Fitzpatrick, 1993). Most couples are ecstatic over having their first child, a tangible product of their love for each other. But soon the reality of child care sets in, with 2:00 a.m. feedings, diaper changing, and the like, not to mention the long-term financial obligations that will continue at least until the child becomes an adult.

THINK ABOUT IT

What types of interventions would help keep married couples happier?

However, using the birth of a child as the explanation of the drop in marital satisfaction is much too simplistic (Clements & Markman, 1996). In fact, child-free couples also experience a decline in marital satisfaction. It appears that a decline in overall marital satisfaction over time is a common developmental phenomenon, even for couples who choose to be child-free (Clements & Markman, 1996). Additionally, couples who are child-free because of infertility face the stress associated with the inability to have children, which lowers their marital satisfaction (Matthews & Matthews, 1986). Longitudinal research indicates that disillusionment, as demonstrated by a decline in feeling in love, in demonstrations of affection, and in the feeling that one's spouse is responsive, as well as an increase in feelings of ambivalence, is a key predictor of marital dissatisfaction (Huston et al., 2001).

Marriage at Midlife

For most couples marital satisfaction improves after the children leave, a state called the *empty nest,* which we will examine in more detail in Chapter 14. The departure of children usually gives middle-aged couples a chance to relax and spend more time with each other (Rosenberg, 1993).

For some middle-aged couples, however, marital satisfaction continues to be low. They may have grown apart but continue to live together, a situation sometimes referred to as *married singles* (Lamanna & Riedmann, 2003). In essence, they have become emotionally divorced and essentially live more as housemates than as a married couple; for these couples, spending more time together is not a welcome change. Because the physical appearance of one's partner is a contributor to marital satisfaction, particularly for men, age-related changes in appearance may contribute to further deterioration of the relationship (Margolin & White, 1987).

Older Couples

As we will discuss in more detail in Chapter 16, marital satisfaction is fairly high in older couples (Miller et al., 1997). However, satisfaction in long-term marriages—that is, marriages of 40 years or more—is a complex issue. In general, however, marital satisfaction among older couples increases shortly after retirement but then decreases with health problems and advancing age (Miller et al., 1997). The level of satisfaction in these marriages appears to be unrelated to the amount of past or present sexual interest or sexual activity, but it is positively related to the degree of interaction with friends (Bullock & Dunn, 1988). Indeed, many older couples have simply developed detached, contented styles (Connidis, 2001; Lamanna & Riedmann, 2003).

Keeping Marriages Happy

Although no two marriages are exactly the same, couples must be flexible and adaptable. Couples who have been happily married for many years show an ability to roll with the punches and to adapt to changing circumstances in the relationship. For example, a serious problem experienced by one spouse may not be detrimental to the relationship and may even make the bond stronger. Likewise, couples' expectations about marriage change over time, gradually becoming more congruent (Weishaus & Field, 1988). In contrast, the physical illness of one spouse almost invariably affects marital quality negatively, even after other factors such as work stress, education, and income are considered (Wickrama et al., 1997).

How well couples communicate their thoughts, actions, and feelings to each other largely determines the level of conflict couples experience, and, by extension, how happy they are likely to be over the long term (Notarius, 1996). And increasing demands from work and family put enormous pressures on a marriage (Rogers & Amato, 1997). It takes a great deal of love, humour, and perseverance to stay happily married a long time. But it *can* be done, providing couples work at seven key things (Donatelle & Davis, 1997; Enright, Gassin, & Wu, 1992; Knapp & Taylor, 1994):

- Make time for your relationship.
- Express your love to your spouse.

- Be there in times of need.
- Communicate constructively and positively about problems in the relationship.
- Be interested in your spouse's life.
- Confide in your spouse.
- Forgive minor offences, and try to understand major ones.

TEST YOURSELF

1. A difficulty for many single people is that other people may expect them to _____.

2. In Canada, many young adults view cohabitation as a _____ marriage.

3. Gay and lesbian relationships are similar to _____.

4. According to _____, marriage is based on each partner contributing some-

thing to the relationship that the other would be hard-pressed to provide.

5. For most couples, marital satisfaction _____ after the birth of the first child.

What sociocultural forces affect decisions to marry rather than to cohabit indefinitely?

Answers: (1) marry, (2) step toward, (3) marriages, (4) exchange theory, (5) decreases

12.3

The Family Life Cycle

LEARNING OBJECTIVES

- Why do people have children?
- What is it like to be a parent? What differences are there in different types of parenting?

The Family Life Cycle
Deciding Whether to Have Children
The Parental Role

Bob, 32, and Denise, 33, just had their first child, Matthew, after several years of trying. They've heard that having children in their 30s can have advantages, but Bob and Denise wonder whether people are just saying that to be nice to them. They are also concerned about the financial obligations they are likely to face.

"When are you going to start a family?" is a question young couples like Bob and Denise are asked frequently. Most couples want children because they believe they will bring great joy, which they often do. But once the child is born, adults may feel inadequate because children don't come with instructions. Young adults may be surprised when the reality of being totally responsible for another person hits them. Experienced middle-aged parents often smile knowingly to themselves.

Frightening as it might be, the birth of a child transforms a couple (or a single parent) into a family. *Although the most common form of family in Western societies is the **nuclear family**, consisting only of parent(s) and child(ren), the most common form around the world is the **extended family**, in which grandparents and other relatives live with parents and children.* Because we have discussed families from the child's perspective in earlier chapters, here we focus on families from the parents' point of view.

DECIDING WHETHER TO HAVE CHILDREN

One of the biggest decisions couples have to make is whether to have children. This decision is more complicated than most people think. A couple must weigh the many

FIGURE 12.5   Deciding to Have Children

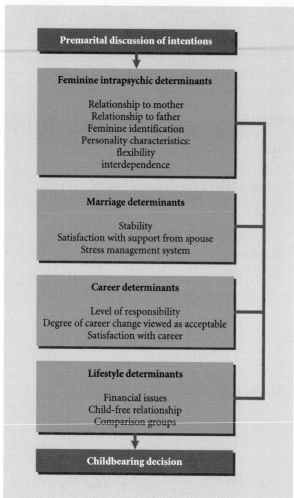

Premarital discussion of intentions

Feminine intrapsychic determinants

Relationship to mother
Relationship to father
Feminine identification
Personality characteristics:
flexibility
interdependence

Marriage determinants

Stability
Satisfaction with support from spouse
Stress management system

Career determinants

Level of responsibility
Degree of career change viewed as acceptable
Satisfaction with career

Lifestyle determinants

Financial issues
Child-free relationship
Comparison groups

Childbearing decision

SOURCE: From *Career, Women, and Childbearing: A Psychological Analysis of the Decision Process,* by C. Wilk. Copyright © 1986 Van Nostrand Reinhold. Reprinted with permission.

benefits of child rearing, such as personal satisfaction, fulfilling personal needs, continuing the family line, and companionship, with the many drawbacks, including expense and lifestyle changes. What influences the decision process? Psychological and marital factors are always important, and career and lifestyle factors matter when the prospective mother works outside the home (Benokraitis, 1999). As you can see in Figure 12.5, these four factors are interconnected.

Whether the pregnancy is planned or not, a couple's first pregnancy is a milestone event with both benefits and costs (Benokraitis, 1999). Having a child raises many important matters for consideration, such as relationships with one's own parents, marital stability, career satisfaction, and financial issues. Parents largely agree that children add affection, improve family ties, and give parents a feeling of immortality and a sense of accomplishment. Most parents willingly sacrifice a great deal for their children and hope that they grow up to be happy and successful.

Nevertheless, finances are of great concern to most couples because children are expensive. How expensive? Based on the goods and services needed to maintain physical and social well-being of a child, the projected cost of raising a child to age 18 in Manitoba is approximately $167,000 (Manitoba Agriculture and Food, 2004). Post-secondary education expenses would be additional. No wonder couples are concerned.

For many reasons, such as personal choice, financial instability, and infertility, an increasing number of couples are child-free. In some respects, these couples have several advantages over those who choose to have children (Benokraitis, 1999): higher marital satisfaction, more freedom, and a higher standard of living. But the larger society does not tend to view being child-free as something positive, providing that being child-free is by choice and not due to infertility (Lampman & Dowling-Guyer, 1995). Couples who are child-free by choice face social criticism as being self-indulgent and less loving by the larger child-oriented society (Arenofsky, 1993) and may run the risk of feeling more lonely in old age (Connidis, 2001).

THE PARENTAL ROLE

Today, Canadian couples have fewer children and have their first child later than in the past. The number of births to women aged 30 to 34 increased by 115% over the last quarter century, whereas the number of births to women under the age of 25 have substantially decreased over this time period (The Vanier Institute of the Family, 2000). Delaying the birth of one's first child like the couple in the photograph on page 439 did has important benefits from both the mother's and the father's perspective.

Older mothers, like Denise in the vignette, are more at ease being parents, spend more time with their babies, and are more affectionate and sensitive to them (Ragozin et al., 1982). The age of the father also makes a difference in how fathers interact with their children. Remember Bob, the 32-year-old first-time father in the vignette? Compared to men who become fathers in their 20s, men like Bob who become fathers in their 30s are generally more invested in their paternal role and spend up to three times as much time in caring for their preschool children as younger fathers do (Cooney et al., 1993). However, men who become fathers in their 30s are also more likely to feel ambivalent and resentful about time lost to their careers (Cooney et al., 1993).

Photodisc

Parenting skills do not come naturally; they must be acquired. Having a child changes all aspects of couples' lives. As we have seen, children place a great deal of stress on a relationship. Both motherhood and fatherhood require major commitment and cooperation. Parenting is full of rewards, but it also takes a great deal of work. Caring for young children is demanding. It may create disagreements over division of labour, especially if both parents are employed outside the home (see Chapters 4 and 13). Even when mothers are employed outside the home (and more than 70% of women with children under age 18 are), they still perform most of the child-rearing tasks. Pleck (1997) estimated that men spend only 44% as much time raising their children as women do.

In general, parents manage to deal with the many challenges of child rearing reasonably well. They learn how to compromise when necessary, and when to apply firm but fair discipline. Given the choice, most parents do not regret their decision to have children.

Single Parents

The number of single parents in Canada, most of whom are women, has been increasing rapidly. The number of babies born to non-married women tripled between 1975 and 1996 (The Vanier Institute of the Family, 2000). High divorce rates, changing fertility rates, and the desire of many single adults to have or adopt children account for the increase in single parenthood.

Two main questions arise concerning single parents: How are children affected when only one adult is responsible for child care? How do single parents meet their own needs for emotional support and intimacy?

Many divorced single parents report complex feelings such as frustration, failure, guilt, and a need to be overindulgent (Lamanna & Riedmann, 2003). Frustration usually results from a lack of companionship and from loneliness, as many social activities are typically reserved for couples. Feelings of guilt may lead to attempts to make up for the child's lack of a father or mother. Some single parents make the mistakes of trying to be peers to their children, using inconsistent discipline, or, if they are the noncustodial parent, of spoiling their children with lots of monetary or material goods.

Single parents, regardless of gender, face considerable obstacles. Financially, they are usually much less well-off than their married counterparts. Integrating the roles of work and parenthood are difficult enough for two persons; for the single parent, the hardships are compounded. Financially, single mothers are hardest hit.

One particular concern for many divorced single parents is dating. Several common questions asked by single parents involve dating: "How do I become available again?" "How will my children react?" "How do I cope with my own sexual needs?" Initiating a new relationship is not difficult for many single parents, especially those who are younger themselves or have older children (Montgomery et al., 1992). Some single parents with younger children, though, may be hesitant to date. Other divorced women with young children may rush into remarriage to provide their children with a father figure (Montgomery et al., 1992).

Alternative Forms of Parenting

Not all parents raise their own biological children. In fact, roughly one-third of North American couples like the one in the photograph become stepparents or foster or adoptive parents some time during their lives.

To be sure, the parenting issues we have discussed thus far are just as important in these situations as when people raise their own biological children. However, some special problems arise as well.

A big issue for foster parents, adoptive parents, and stepparents is how strongly the child will bond with them. Although infants less than 1 year old will probably bond well, children who are old enough to have formed attachments with their biological parents may have competing loyalties. For example, some stepchildren remain strongly attached to the noncustodial parent and actively resist attempts to integrate them into the new family ("My real mother wouldn't make me do that"), or they may exhibit behavioural problems. Children in blended families also tend not to have as good mental health as children in nondivorced families (Cherlin & Furstenberg, 1994). Stepparents must often deal with continued visitation by the noncustodial parent, which may exacerbate any difficulties. These problems are a major reason second marriages are at high risk for dissolution.

Still, many stepparents and stepchildren ultimately develop good relationships with each other. Stepparents must be sensitive to the relationship between the stepchild and his or her biological, noncustodial parent. Allowing stepchildren to develop the rela-

tionship with the stepparent at their own pace also helps. What style of stepparenting ultimately develops is influenced by the expectations of the stepparent, stepchild, spouse, and nonresidential parent (Erera-Weatherley, 1996).

Adoptive parents like those in the photograph also contend with attachment to birth parents, but in different ways. Even if they don't remember them, adopted children may wish to locate and meet their birth parents. Wanting to know one's origins is understandable, but such searches can strain the relationship between these children and their adoptive parents, who may interpret these actions as a form of rejection (Rosenberg, 1992).

Foster parents tend to have the most tenuous relationship with their children because the bond can be broken for any number of reasons having nothing to do with the quality of the care being provided. For example, a court may award custody back to the birth parents, or another couple may legally adopt the child. Dealing with attachment is difficult; foster parents want to provide secure homes, but they may not have the children long enough to establish continuity. Furthermore, because many children in foster care have been unable to form attachments at all, they are less likely to form ones that will inevitably be broken. Thus, foster parents must be willing to tolerate considerable ambiguity in the relationship and have few expectations about the future.

Finally, many gay men and lesbian women also want to be parents. Some have biological children themselves, whereas others choose adoption or foster parenting. Although gay men and lesbian women make good parents, they often experience resistance to having children. Actually, research indicates that children reared by gay or lesbian parents do not experience any more problems than children reared by heterosexual parents. Substantial evidence exists that children raised by gay or lesbian parents do not develop sexual identity or any other problems any more than children raised by heterosexual parents (Flaks et al., 1995; Patterson, 1992). For example, research evidence indicates that roughly 90% of sons (aged 17 or older) of gay fathers are heterosexual (Bailey et al., 1995).

Additional evidence shows that children raised by gay men may even have some advantages over children raised by heterosexual men. Gay men are often especially concerned about being good and nurturing fathers, and they try hard to raise their children with nonsexist, egalitarian attitudes (Flaks et al., 1995). Children of lesbian couples and heterosexual couples are equally adjusted behaviourally, show equivalent cognitive development, and have similar behaviours in school. Indeed, one study found that the only difference between such couples was that lesbian couples exhibit more awareness of parenting skills than do heterosexual couples (Flaks et al., 1995).

These data will not make the controversy go away, as much of it is based on long-held beliefs and prejudices. Admittedly, the data comparing children raised by different types of parents are inadequate; for example, there is very little information about children raised by lesbian women. Only when societal attitudes toward gay men and lesbians become more accepting will there be greater acceptance of their right to be parents like anyone else.

TEST YOURSELF

1. The series of relatively predictable changes that families experience is called
   _____.

2. Major influences on the decision to have children are marital factors, career factors, lifestyle factors, and _____.

3. A new father who is invested in his parental role, but who may also feel ambivalent about time lost to his career, is probably over age _____.

4. A major issue for foster parents, adoptive parents, and stepparents is
   _____.

What difference do you think it would make to view children as a financial asset (i.e., a source of income) as opposed to a financial burden (i.e., mainly an expense)? Which of these do you think characterizes most Western societies? Can you think of an example of the other type?

Answers: (1) the family life cycle, (2) psychological factors, (3) 30, (4) how strongly the child will bond with them

12.4

Divorce and Remarriage

LEARNING OBJECTIVES

- Who gets divorced? How does divorce affect parental relationships with children?
- What are remarriages like? How are they similar to and different from first marriages?

Frank and Marilyn, both in their late 40s, thought their marriage would last forever. They weren't so lucky; they just got divorced. Although two of their children are married, their youngest daughter is still in university. The financial pressures Marilyn feels now that she's on her own are beginning to take their toll. She wonders whether her financial situation is similar to that of other recently divorced women.

Despite what Frank and Marilyn pledged on their wedding day, their marriage did not last until death parted them; they dissolved their marriage through divorce. But even though divorce is stressful and difficult, thousands of people each year also choose to try again. Most enter their second (or third or fourth) marriage with renewed expectations of success. Are these new dreams realistic? As we'll see, it depends on many things; among the most important is whether children are involved.

DIVORCE

Most couples enter marriage with the idea that their relationship will be permanent. Unfortunately, fewer and fewer couples experience this permanence. Rather than growing together, couples grow apart.

Who Gets Divorced and Why?

FIGURE 12.6   Divorce Rates

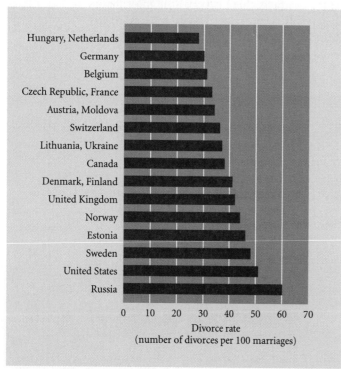

Divorce rate
(number of divorces per 100 marriages)

SOURCE: U.S. Census Bureau, 2001b.

As you can see in Figure 12.6, divorce rates vary according to country, and in Canada about 38% of couples divorce. Divorce rates in nearly every developed country have increased significantly over the past several decades (Lester, 1996).

Major factors are the changes in laws and social norms reflected in the reasons people give for divorcing. With the passing of Canada's Divorce Act in 1968 to include "no-fault" divorce and changing expectations about marriage, reasons for divorce have shifted over the years. Some reasons now cited include communication problems, unhappiness, and incompatibility (Cleek & Pearson, 1985). Men and women typically agree on the reasons for divorce from most frequently cited to least:

REASONS MEN GIVE	REASONS WOMEN GIVE
Communication problems	Communication problems
Basic unhappiness	Basic unhappiness
Incompatibility	Incompatibility
Sexual problems	Emotional abuse
Financial problems	Financial problems
Emotional abuse	Sexual problems
Women's liberation	Alcohol abuse by spouse
In-laws	Infidelity by spouse
Infidelity by spouse	Physical abuse
Alcohol abuse by self	In-laws

Couples now expect to find partners who will help them grow personally and provide much more than just financial support, a sexual partner, and children. Such expectations have paradoxically lowered the quality of marriages in recent generations (Rogers & Amato, 1997). In many other cultures, such expectations are rare or contrary to traditional values.

Why people divorce is certainly complex. As shown in Figure 12.7, macro-level social issues, demographic variables, and interpersonal problems all factor into the decision to divorce (Lamanna & Riedmann, 2003).

Effects of Divorce on the Couple

Although the changes in attitudes toward divorce have eased the social trauma associated with it, divorce still takes a high toll on the psyche of the couple. Both partners in a failed marriage feel deeply disappointed, misunderstood, and rejected (Brodie, 1999). Unlike the situation when one's spouse dies, divorce often means that the person's ex-spouse is present to provide a reminder of the failure. As a result, divorced people are typically unhappy in general, at least for a while. Indeed, divorced people of all ages are less likely than married, never-married, and widowed people to say that they are "very happy" with their lives (Kurdek, 1991b; Lee, Seccombe, & Shehan, 1991). Even 10 years afterward, many divorced people still report feeling angry, lonely, disappointed, abandoned, and betrayed (Wallerstein & Blakeslee, 1989).

Divorced people sometimes find the transition very difficult; researchers refer to these problems as "divorce hangover" (Walther, 1991). Divorce hangover reflects divorced partners' inability to let go, develop new friendships, or reorient themselves as single parents. Indeed, ex-spouses who are preoccupied with thoughts of their former partner, and who have high feelings of hostility toward

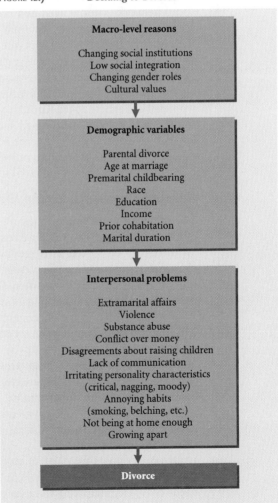

FIGURE 12.7   Deciding to Divorce

Macro-level reasons

Changing social institutions
Low social integration
Changing gender roles
Cultural values

Demographic variables

Parental divorce
Age at marriage
Premarital childbearing
Race
Education
Income
Prior cohabitation
Marital duration

Interpersonal problems

Extramarital affairs
Violence
Substance abuse
Conflict over money
Disagreements about raising children
Lack of communication
Irritating personality characteristics
(critical, nagging, moody)
Annoying habits
(smoking, belching, etc.)
Not being at home enough
Growing apart

Divorce

SOURCE: Benokraitis, N. *Marriages and Families: Changes, Choices, and Constraints*, 4/e, © 2002, p. 401. Reprinted with permission of Pearson Education, Inc., Upper Saddle River, New Jersey.

him or her, have significantly poorer emotional well-being than ex-spouses who are not preoccupied or who have feelings of friendship toward the former partner (Masheter, 1997). It appears that low preoccupation is the key to healthy postdivorce relationships, and it may be an indicator of the extent to which ex-spouses are able to move on with their lives.

THINK ABOUT IT 💡

Given the serious impact of divorce, what changes in mate selection might lower the divorce rate?

Gender differences are also found. Men report being shocked by the breakup, especially if the wife filed for divorce (Arendell, 1995). Men are more likely to be blamed for the problems that led to the divorce, to accept the blame, to move out, and to thereby find their social life disrupted. Women are affected differently (Ross, 1995). For example, divorced mothers have fewer prospects for potential remarriage, and they find it more difficult to establish new friendship networks if they have custody of the children (Albeck & Kaydar, 2002). Women are at a serious financial disadvantage, largely because they usually have custody of the children, are typically paid less than men, and are likely to have inadequate child support from their ex-husbands (Gallagher, 1996; Kurz, 1995). Marilyn, the recently divorced middle-aged woman we met in the vignette, probably has a difficult road ahead as she tries to meet her own expenses as well as help pay her daughter's university tuition.

Divorce in middle age or later has some special characteristics. In general, the trauma is greater for these individuals because of the long period of investment in each other's emotional and practical lives (Uhlenberg, Cooney, & Boyd, 1990). Longtime friends may turn away or take sides, causing additional disruption to the social network. Middle-aged and older women are at a significant disadvantage for remarriage—an especially traumatic situation for women who obtained much of their identity from their roles as wife and mother. Support groups help people adjust; for men this works best in large groups and for women it works best when the group provides emotional support (Oygard & Hardeng, 2001).

We must not overlook the financial problems faced by middle-aged divorced women (Gallagher, 1996; Kurz, 1995). These problems are especially keen for the middle-aged divorcee who may have spent years as a homemaker and has few marketable job skills. For her, divorce presents an especially difficult financial hardship, especially if she has children in university or college and the father provides little support (Lamanna & Riedmann, 2003).

Relationships with Young Children

The difficulty in adjusting to divorce often depends on whether young children are involved. Deciding who will have custody of the children often triggers the problems. Women may be forced to agree to lower alimony or child support payments in exchange for custody. Consequently, men are sometimes encouraged to wage an all-out battle for custody even when they do not want it, simply to gain bargaining power over their financial obligations (Winner, 1996).

Like the woman in the photograph on page 445, most divorced mothers of young children end up being the primary custodial parent. For many of them, the price they pay for custody is very high; at the same time as their parental responsibilities are increasing, their financial resources are decreasing significantly (Gallagher, 1996; Kurz, 1995). Child care is expensive, and most divorced fathers contribute less than before the separation. Furthermore, in Canada, many noncustodial parents do not make their child support payments; to address this problem, all provinces have enforcement programs to assist recipients to obtain the support they were awarded (Statistics Canada, 2001/2002).

Divorced fathers pay a psychological price (Nicholls & Pike, 2002). One reason why fathers may no longer remain active in their children's lives is that children's needs change; anticipating these changes requires frequent contact, which poses difficulty for many men. Additionally, even when child support payments are made,

© Michael Newman /PhotoEdit

noncustodial fathers find it difficult to develop good relationships with their children, often because their ex-wives express their anger by limiting contact with the children. The unfortunate result is that many divorced fathers become peripheral in their children's lives, often through no fault of their own (Seltzer, 1991).

It is possible to overcome the problems between divorced people who have young children. Some former couples are able to get over their anger and cooperate with each other (Masheter, 1991). Adjustment is easier if both remarry or neither does. Interestingly, it is easier for a new husband to accept his wife's friendly relationship with her former husband than it is for a new wife to accept her husband's friendly relationship with his ex-wife (Masheter, 1991).

Relationships with Adult Children

We saw in Chapter 6 that young children can be seriously affected by their parents' divorce. But what happens when the parents of adult children divorce? Are adult children affected too? It certainly looks that way. Young adults whose parents divorce experience a great deal of emotional vulnerability and stress (Cooney & Uhlenberg, 1990). One young man put it this way:

> The difficult thing was that it was a time where, you know [you're] making the transition from high school to college . . . your high school friends are dispersed . . . they're all over the place. . . . It's normally a very difficult transition [college], new atmosphere, new workload, meeting new people. You've got to start deciding what you want to do, you've got to sort of start getting more independent, and so forth. And then, at the same time you find out about a divorce. You know, it's just that much more adjustment you have to make. (Cooney et al., 1986, p. 473)

Anger, conflicting loyalties, and worry about the parents' future are common reactions. Relationships with parents may be irreparably harmed. Even many years later, divorced fathers are less likely than mothers to experience positive relationships with their adult children. Fathers also do not believe they will be able to rely on their children for support in times of need (Cooney & Uhlenberg, 1990). In contrast, adult daughters' relationships with their mothers are much more resilient; they may even intensify after the divorce (Cooney et al., 1986).

REMARRIAGE

The trauma of divorce does not deter people from beginning new relationships, which often lead to another marriage. Approximately 75% of men and 65% of women in Canada remarry after divorce (The Vanier Institute of the Family, 2000). Research indicates that there are few differences between first marriages and remarriages (Ganong & Coleman, 1994). However, controlling for the number of years married, remarriages after a divorce have an approximately 10% higher rate of dissolution.

Although women are more likely to initiate a divorce, they are less likely to remarry (Buckle, Gallup, & Rodd, 1996) unless they are poor (Schmiege, Richards, & Zvonkovic, 2001). For Canadian women between the ages of 25 and 35, the probability of marriage is 66% and closer to 80% among men. The probability between the ages of 35 and 50 for women is 48% compared to 61% for men (The Vanier Institute of the Family, 2000). However, women in general tend to benefit more from remarriage than do men, particularly if they have children (Ozawa & Yoon, 2002). Divorced men without children tend to marry women who have never been married; divorced men with children tend to marry divorced women (Buckle et al., 1996). Results from a Canadian study indicate that men with higher educational attainment are more likely to remarry than their female counterparts (Wu, 1994). This appears to be because women with higher educational and socioeconomic status have less to gain from remarriage because they are economically independent. They also have a smaller pool of potential mates as they are less likely than men to marry someone from a lower socioeconomic or educational status.

Like the couple in the photograph, adapting to new relationships in remarriage is different for men and women (Hobart, 1988). For remarried men, the preeminent relationship is with his new wife; other relationships, especially those with his children from his first marriage, take a back seat. For remarried women, the relationship with a new husband remains more marginal than the relationship with the children from the first marriage.

TEST YOURSELF

1. Following divorce, most women suffer disproportionately in the _____ domain compared to most men.

2. On average, within two years after a divorce, _____ fathers remain central in their children's lives.

3. Even many years later, divorced _____ may not experience positive relationships with their adult children.

Despite greatly increased divorce rates over the past few decades, the rate of marriage has not changed very much. Why do you think this is?

Answers: (1) financial, (2) few, (3) fathers

PUTTING IT ALL TOGETHER

In this chapter, we have seen how people find and develop adult relationships. We considered the important role that friendships play in adulthood. Some relationships, like Jamal and Deb's, turn into love. Although the romantic love they feel won't last forever, their love may evolve so that the relationship can last. Although young love like Jamal and Deb's gets played out the world over, what people look for in a mate varies in different cultures. Turning a love relationship into newly wedded bliss, as Kevin and Beth did, is very common; it's still true that the vast majority of people get married at some point in their lives. If Kevin and Beth have children, their newfound happiness is likely to fade a bit, but as long as they maintain their commitment to each other, their marriage will probably last. Frank and Marilyn's divorce has had fairly typical results: Marilyn is having trouble making financial ends meet. Because Bob and Denise were in their 30s when their first child was born, they will likely be better suited and better prepared for parenthood than many younger parents.

Throughout the chapter, we saw that human relationships are complex. Although there are similarities around the world in how people find mates, culture plays a large part in helping people find the person who will say, "I am for you." Maintaining a strong relationship takes a great deal of work, and there are many pressures that can divert partners' attention from each other.

SUMMARY

12.1 Relationships

Friendships

■ People tend to have more friendships during young adulthood than during any other period. Friendships are especially important for maintaining life satisfaction throughout adulthood.

■ Men tend to have fewer close friendships and to base them on shared activities, such as sports. Women tend to have more close friendships and to base them on intimate and emotional sharing. Gender differences in same-gender friendship patterns may explain the difficulties men and women have forming cross-gender friendships.

Love Relationships

■ Although styles of love change with age, the priorities within relationships do not. Men tend to be more romantic earlier in relationships than women, who tend to be cautious pragmatists.

■ Selecting a mate works best when there are shared values, goals, and interests. There are cross-cultural differences with regard to the specific aspects of these that are considered most important.

The Dark Side of Relationships: Violence

■ Levels of aggressive behaviour range from verbal aggression to physical aggression to murdering one's partner. The causes of aggressive behaviours become more complex as the level of aggression increases. People remain in abusive relationships for many reasons, including low self-esteem.

12.2 Lifestyles

Singlehood

■ Most adults decide by age 30 whether they plan on getting married. Never-married adults often develop a strong network of close friends. Dealing with other people's expectations that they should marry is often difficult for single people.

Cohabitation

■ Young adults usually cohabit as a step toward marriage, and adults of all ages may also cohabit for financial reasons. Overall, more similarities than differences exist between cohabiting and married couples.

Gay and Lesbian Couples

■ Gay and lesbian relationships are similar to marriages with regard to relationship issues. Lesbian couples tend to be more egalitarian and are more likely to remain together than gay couples. Frequency of sexual expression differs in gay, lesbian, and heterosexual couples.

Marriage

■ The most important factors in creating stable marriages are creating a stable sense of identity as a foundation for intimacy, similarity of values and interests, effective communication, and the contribution of unique skills by each partner.

■ For couples with children, marital satisfaction tends to decline until the children leave home, although individual differences are apparent, especially in long-term marriages. Most long-term marriages are happy.

12.3 The Family Life Cycle

Deciding Whether to Have Children

- Although having children is stressful and very expensive, most people do it anyway. However, the number of child-free couples is increasing.

The Parental Role

- The timing of parenthood is important in how involved parents are in their families as opposed to their careers.
- Single parents are faced with many problems, especially if they are women and are divorced. The main problem is significantly reduced financial resources.
- A major issue for adoptive parents, foster parents, and stepparents is how strongly the child will bond with them. Each of these relationships has some special characteristics.
- Gay and lesbian parents also face numerous obstacles, but they usually prove to be good parents.

12.4 Divorce and Remarriage

Divorce

- Currently, Canadian divorce rates are about 38%. Recovery from divorce is different for men and women. Men tend to have a tougher time in the short run, but women clearly have a harder time in the long run, often for financial reasons. Difficulties between divorced partners usually involve visitation and child support. Disruptions also occur in divorced parents' relationships with their children, whether the children are young or are adults themselves.

Remarriage

- Most divorced couples remarry. Second marriages are especially vulnerable to stress if spouses must adjust to having stepchildren. Remarriage in middle age and beyond tends to be happy.

KEY TERMS

assortative mating (423)
homogamy (423)
abusive relationship (427)
battered woman syndrome (427)

common couple violence (428)
patriarchal terrorism (428)
cohabitation (431)
exchange theory (434)

nuclear family (437)
extended family (437)

SEE FOR YOURSELF: APPLYING WHAT YOU'VE LEARNED

One of the most overlooked effects of divorce is how it changes the relationships between parents and their adult children. Indeed, most of the research conducted on the effects of divorce on children focuses on school-age children and ignores those over the age of 18. This emphasis ignores the importance of life-cycle forces in the biopsychosocial model (see Chapter 1). Being an adult child of divorced parents creates problems that are different from those experienced by young children of divorce.

Adult children of divorced parents form two subgroups: those whose parents divorced when they were young, and those whose parents divorced when they were 18 or older. An interesting question is whether these subgroups differ in their experiences. You be the judge and find out. While you're at it, you may gain important insights into developmental research and the importance of life-cycle influences in the biopsychosocial model.

Ask your classmates, friends, co-workers, and family members. Locate one person from each of the two subgroups, and interview them about their experiences. Find out what they thought (and still think) about their parents' divorce, what their relationships with them are like now, and how having divorced parents influences their own love relationships. Collate and tabulate your results, then compare them to those in this section. Do they agree? See for yourself!

LEARN MORE ABOUT IT

Readings

Boss, P. G., Doherty, W.J., Larossa, R., Schumm, W. R., & Steinmetz, S. K. (Eds.). (1993). *Sourcebook of family theories and methods.* New York: Plenum. This superb resource book covers all major theories and methods used in family and relationship research.

Prather, H., & Prather, G. (1990). *Notes to each other.* New York: Bantam. This collection of reflections on making relationships work, staying happy, and parenting makes easy reading.

TANNEN, D. (2001). *I only say this because I love you: How the way we talk can make or break family relationships throughout our lives.* New York: Random House. This highly readable and intriguing book discusses the different communication styles people use.

VANZETTI, N., & DUCK, S. (1996). *A lifetime of relationships.* Pacific Grove: Brooks/Cole. A very readable summary of the research literature on different types of relationships across the life span.

WALSH, F. (Ed.) (2003). *Normal family processes: Growing diversity and complexity* 3rd ed. New York: The Guilford Press. This book updates and expands what is known about well-functioning families as family life and societies become more complex and diverse.

 For additional readings, explore InfoTrac® College Edition, your online library. Go to http://www.infotrac.thomsonlearning.com.

Websites

http://familyconflict.freeyellow.com/

The website of the National Child and Family Advocacy of Canada offers general information about children and families, the Family Assistance and Parent Support Program, and research studies and links to other networks.

http://www.hc-sc.gc.ca/hppb.familyviolence/

The National Clearinghouse on Family Violence (NCFV) is a national resource centre for all Canadians seeking information about violence within the family.

http://www.vifamily.ca/

The Vanier Institute of the Family is a national charitable organization dedicated to promoting the well-being of Canadian families by creating awareness of and providing leadership on the importance and strengths of families in Canada.

Website addresses are subject to change. The *Human Development* book companion website can be accessed for updated links.

The Human Development Book Companion Website

See http://www.humandevelopment.nelson.com for practice quiz questions, Internet links, updates, critical thinking exercises, discussion forums, and more.

 Life-Span CD-ROM

For more information on the concepts covered in this chapter, go to

Module 5: Early and Middle Adulthood
- Emotional and Social Development

Getty Images

CHAPTER 13

Work and Leisure

OCCUPATIONAL AND LIFESTYLE ISSUES IN YOUNG AND MIDDLE ADULTHOOD

Work—it seems as though that's all we do sometimes. From the small chores children do to putting in 12-hour days at the office, we are taught that working is a natural part of life. For some, work *is* life. In this chapter, we explore the world of work first by considering how people choose occupations and develop in them. After that, we examine how women and minorities contend with barriers to their occupational selection and development. Dealing with occupational transitions is considered in the third section. How to balance work and family obligations is a difficult issue for many people; this is discussed in the fourth section. Finally, we will see how people spend their time away from work in leisure activities.

As in Chapter 12, our focus in this chapter is on issues faced by both young and middle-aged adults. No longer is it the case that only young adults have to deal with occupational selection issues. It is increasingly common for middle-aged people to have to confront the issues of occupational selection all over again as their industry changes or their company downsizes. Similarly, the other topics we consider apply to both younger and middle-aged adults.

13.1

Occupational Selection and Development

LEARNING OBJECTIVES

- How do people view work? How do occupational priorities vary with age?
- How do people choose their occupations?
- What factors influence occupational development?
- What is the relation between job satisfaction and age?

Monique, a 28-year-old college student taking communications, wonders about careers. Should she enter the broadcast field as a behind-the-scenes producer, or would she be better suited as a public relations spokesperson? She thinks her outgoing personality is a factor she should consider. Should she become a broadcast producer?

Choosing one's work is serious business. Like Monique, we try to select a field in which we are trained and that is also appealing. Work colours much of what we do in life. You may be taking this course as part of your preparation for work. People make friends at work and arrange personal activities around work schedules. Parents often choose child care centres on the basis of their proximity to their place of employment.

In this section, we explore what work means to adults and then examine occupational development. Finally, we will see how satisfaction with one's job changes during adulthood.

THE MEANING OF WORK

Did you ever stop to think about why we fight the commuting crowds like the people in the photograph are doing? Studs Terkel, the author of the fascinating book *Working* (1974), writes that work is "a search for daily meaning as well as daily bread,

Photodisc

for recognition as well as cash, for astonishment rather than torpor; in short, for a sort of life rather than a Monday through Friday sort of dying" (p. xiii). Kahlil Gibran (1923), in his mystical book *The Prophet*, put it this way: "Work is love made visible" (p. 28).

For some of us, work is a source of prestige, social recognition, and a sense of worth. For others, the excitement, creativity, and the opportunity to give something of themselves make work meaningful. But for most, the main purpose of work is to earn a living. This is not to imply, of course, that money is the only reward in a job; friendships, the chance to exercise power, and feeling useful are also important. The meaning most of us derive from working includes both the money that can be exchanged for life's necessities (and maybe a few luxuries too) and the possibility of personal growth.

The kind of occupation one has appears to have no effect on people's need to derive meaning from work. Even when their occupation consists of highly repetitive work (Isaksen, 2000) or is in a declining industry experiencing a high number of layoffs (Dorton, 2001), people find great personal meaning in what they do. The specific meanings people get from their work vary with the type of occupation and are influenced by socialization (Chetro-Szivos, 2001).

What meanings do people derive from their work? Lips-Wiersma (2000) sought answers to this question by interviewing people in depth about the meanings they derive from work and whether and how these meanings determine work behaviour. Despite wide diversity of backgrounds in the participants in her study, Lips-Wiersma found four common meanings: developing and becoming self, union with others, expressing self, and serving others. To the extent that these meanings can all be achieved, people experience the workplace as a place of personal fulfilment. These meanings also provide a framework for understanding occupational transitions as opportunities people may use to find better balance among the four main meanings.

Given the various meanings people derive from work, occupation is clearly a key element of a person's sense of identity (Whitbourne, 1996). This can be readily observed when adults introduce themselves socially. When asked to tell something about themselves, you've probably noticed that people usually provide information about what they do for a living. Occupation affects your life in a host of ways, often influencing where you live, what friends you make, and even what clothes you wear. In short, the impact of work cuts across all aspects of life. Work, then, is a major social role and influence on adult life. Occupation is an important anchor that complements the other major role of adulthood—love relationships.

As we will see, occupation is part of human development. Young children, in their pretend play, are in the midst of the social preparation for work. Adults are always asking them, "What do you want to be when you grow up?" School curricula, especially in high school and college, are geared toward preparing people for particular occupations. Young adult college students have formulated perspectives on the meanings they believe they will get from work. Hance (2000) organized these beliefs into three main categories: working to achieve social influence, working to achieve personal fulfilment, and working due to economic reality. These categories reflect fairly well the actual meanings working adults report.

OCCUPATIONAL DEVELOPMENT

For most of us, getting a job is not enough; we would also like to move up the ladder. Promotion is a measure of how well one is doing in one's career. How quickly occupational advancement occurs (or does not) may lead to such labels as "fast-tracker" or "dead-ender." Bernard Lord, who at the age of 33 became the youngest elected premier of New Brunswick in 1999, is an example of a fast-tracker. People who want to advance learn quickly how long to stay at one level and how to seize opportunities as they occur, while others experience the frustration of remaining in the same job, with no chance for promotion.

How a person advances in a career seems to depend on professional socialization, which includes several factors besides those that are important in choosing an occupation. Among these are expectations, support from co-workers, priorities, and job satisfaction. Before we consider these aspects, let's look at a general scheme of occupational development.

Super's Theory

Over four decades, Super (1957, 1980) developed a theory of occupational development based on self-concept, first introduced in Chapter 10 (see Section 10.3). He proposed a progression through five distinct stages during adulthood, resulting from changes in individuals' self-concept and adaptation to an occupational role: implementation, establishment, maintenance, deceleration, and retirement. (See Figure 13.1.) *People are located along a continuum of vocational maturity through their working years; the more congruent their occupational behaviours are with what is expected of them at different ages, the more vocationally mature they are.* The initial two phases of Super's theory, crystallization and specification, occur primarily during adolescence, and the first adulthood phase has its origins then as well. Each of the stages in adulthood has distinctive characteristics:

FIGURE 13.1   Continuum of Vocational Maturity

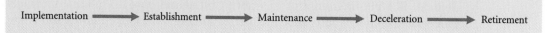

Implementation ⟶ Establishment ⟶ Maintenance ⟶ Deceleration ⟶ Retirement

- The *implementation* stage begins in late adolescence or the early 20s when people take a series of temporary jobs to learn firsthand about work roles and to try out some possible career choices. Summer internships, which many students use to gain experience, are one example.
- The *establishment* stage begins with selecting a specific occupation during young adulthood. It continues as the person advances up the career ladder in the same occupation. Taking a position in a law firm and working one's way up to partner or beginning as a sales clerk in a store in a mall and moving up to store manager are two examples.
- The *maintenance* stage is a transition phase during middle age as workers begin to reduce the amount of time they spend fulfilling work roles. Some middle-aged adults increase the time they spend volunteering as coaches for children's sports teams or for their church. Other middle-aged adults spend more time with their families.
- The *deceleration* stage begins as workers begin planning in earnest for their upcoming retirement and separating themselves from their work. Sitting down with a financial planner to review one's retirement savings and starting a hobby that one plans to do after retirement are examples.
- The *retirement* stage begins when people stop working full-time. Ideally, people are then able to implement the plans they made in the previous stage.

In Super's framework, people's occupations evolve in response to changes in their self-concept (Salomone, 1996). Consequently, this is a developmental process that reflects and explains important life changes. This developmental process complements Holland's ideas from Chapter 10. Investigative and enterprising types are likely to come from more affluent families in which the parents tend not to be in investigative or enterprising occupations. Interestingly, initial occupational goals are not as important for social types as for the other two; social types appeared more flexible in eventual occupational choice.

THINK ABOUT IT

What biological, psychological, sociocultural, and life-cycle forces influence the progression of one's career?

However, a shortcoming of Super's theory is that the progression assumes that once people choose an occupation they stay in it for the rest of their working lives. Although this may have been true for many employees in the past, it is not the case for most North American workers today (Cascio, 1995). The downsizing of public and private organizations since the late 1980s has all but eliminated the notion of lifetime job security with a particular employer. It remains to be seen whether new developmental stages will be found to underlie the new occupational reality.

Nevertheless, a longitudinal study of 7,649 individuals born in the United Kingdom showed that occupational aspirations at age 16 predicted actual occupational attainments in science, health professions, or engineering at age 33 (Schoon, 2001). Adult occupational attainment was also related to belief in one's own ability, mathematical test performance, several personality characteristics, sociocultural background, and gender. These results point to the importance of viewing occupational development as a true developmental process, as Super claimed, as well as the importance of personal characteristics, as Holland claimed.

Occupational Expectations

Individuals form opinions about what work in a particular occupation will be like based on what they learn in school and from their parents, peers, other adults, and the media. People have expectations regarding what they want to become and when they hope to get there. Levinson and his colleagues (1978) built these expectations into their theory of adult male development, which was later extended to women (Levinson & Levinson, 1996). Based on findings from the original longitudinal study begun in the 1940s on men attending an elite private college, Levinson and his colleagues (1978) found considerable similarity among the participants in major life tasks during adulthood. *Forming a **dream**, with one's career playing a prominent role, is one of the young adult's chief tasks.*

Throughout adulthood, people continue to refine and update their occupational expectations. This usually involves trying to achieve the dream, monitoring progress toward it, and changing or even abandoning it as necessary. For some, modifying the dream comes as a result of realizing that interests have changed or that the dream was not a good fit. In other cases, failure leads to changing the dream—for example, dropping a business major because one is failing economics courses. Other causes are age, racial, or sexual discrimination; lack of opportunity; obsolescence of skills; and changing interests. In some cases, one's initial occupational choice may simply have been unrealistic. Some goal modification is essential from time to time, but it usually surprises us to realize that we could have been wrong about what seemed to be a logical choice in the past. As Marie, a 38-year-old advertising manager, put it, "I really thought I wanted to be a pilot; the travel sounded really interesting. But it just wasn't what I expected."

Research supports these personal experiences. Rindfuss, Cooksey, and Sutterlin (1999) examined the stability of occupational expectations during the first seven years after high school and their correspondence with occupations held at age 30. They found much instability in occupational expectations during the late teens and early 20s. Even when occupational expectations are measured as late as age 25, fewer than half of the men and women studied actually achieved their expectations. When they do not achieve their expectations, work roles at age 30 differed by gender. Men tend to move into higher managerial occupations whereas women tend to move down or leave the labour force.

Perhaps the rudest jolt for most of us first comes during the transition from school to the real

© Zefa Visual Media - Germany/Index Stock Imagery

world (Rindfuss et al., 1999). Reality shock sets in, and things never seem to happen the way we expect. Reality shock befalls everyone, from the young worker in the photograph on page 455 to the accountant who learns that the financial forecast that took days to prepare may simply end up in a file cabinet (or, worse yet, in the wastebasket). The visionary aspects of the dream may not disappear altogether, but a good dose of reality goes a long way toward bringing a person down to earth. Such feedback comes to play an increasingly important role in a person's occupational development and self-concept. For example, the woman who thought she would receive the same rewards as her male counterparts for comparable work is likely to become increasingly angry and disillusioned when her successes result in smaller raises and fewer promotions.

The Role of Mentors

Imagine how hard it would be to figure out everything you needed to know in a new job with no support from the people around you. Entering an occupation involves more than the relatively short formal training a person receives. Indeed, much of the most critical information is not taught in training seminars. Instead, most people are shown the ropes by co-workers. In many cases, an older, more experienced person makes a specific effort to do this, taking on the role of *mentor*. Although mentors by no means provide the only source of guidance in the workplace, they have been studied fairly closely.

A mentor is part teacher, part sponsor, part model, and part counsellor (Heimann & Pittenger, 1996). The mentor helps a young worker avoid trouble ("Be careful what you say around Harry"). He or she also provides invaluable information about the unwritten rules that govern day-to-day activities in the workplace (not working too fast on the assembly line, wearing the right clothes, and so on; Levinson et al., 1978; Levinson & Levinson, 1996). As part of the relationship, a mentor makes sure his or her protégé is noticed and receives credit for good work from supervisors. Thus, occupational success often depends on the quality of the mentor-protégé relationship. The mentor fulfils two main functions: improving the protégé's chances for advancement and promoting his or her psychological and social well-being (Kram, 1980, 1985).

Kram (1985) also theorized that the mentor relationship develops through four phases: initiation (mentors and protégés begin the relationship), cultivation (mentors work with protégés), separation (protégés and mentors spend less time together), and redefinition (the mentor-protégé relationship either ends or is transformed into a different type of relationship). Research supports this developmental process, as well as the benefits of having a mentor (Chao, 1997). Clearly, protégés get tangible benefits from having a mentor.

What do mentors get from the relationship? In Chapter 1, we saw that the ideas in Erikson's (1982) theory included important aspects of adulthood related to work. Helping a younger employee learn the job is one way to fulfil aspects of Erikson's phase of generativity. As we will see in more detail in Chapter 14, generativity reflects middle-aged adults' need to ensure the continuity of society through activities such as socialization or having children. In work settings, generativity is most often expressed through mentoring. In particular, the mentor ensures that there is some continuity in the corporation or profession by passing on the knowledge and experience he or she has gained over the years. Being a mentor helps middle-aged people fulfil their need to ensure the continuity of society and accomplish or produce something worthwhile (Erikson, 1982).

Some authors suggest that women have a greater need for mentors than men. For example, Blake-Beard (2001) points out that although women have achieved virtual parity with men in entering most organizations, within five to six years their careers begin to lag behind those of their male counterparts. When paired with mentors, women have higher expectations about career advancement opportunities (Baugh,

Lankau, & Scandura, 1996). Female lawyers with mentors earn more, are promoted more often, are treated more fairly, and are integrated better in the firm than women without mentors (Wallace, 2001). However, women seem to have a more difficult time finding adequate mentors; some evidence suggests that only one-third of professional women find mentors as young adults (Kittrell, 1998). One reason is that there are relatively few female role models, such as the woman in the photo, who could serve a mentoring function, especially in upper-level management. Although many young women report that they would feel comfortable with a male mentor (Olian et al., 1988), researchers note that male mentor–female protégé relationships may involve conflict and tension resulting from possible sexual overtones, even when there has been no overtly sexual behaviour on anyone's part (Kram, 1985). Although female lawyer protégés with male mentors may earn more than those with female mentors, those mentored by women report more career satisfaction, more intent to continue practising law, more achievement of professional expectations, and less work-family conflict (Wallace, 2001).

Comstock

Despite the evidence that having a mentor can have many positive effects on one's occupational development, there is an important caveat: Having a poor mentor is worse than having no mentor at all (Ragins, Cotton, & Miller, 2000). A mentoring program is only as good as the mentor. Consequently, prospective protégés must choose a mentor carefully, and mentorship programs need to select motivated and skilled individuals who are provided with extensive training.

JOB SATISFACTION

What does it mean to be satisfied with one's job or occupation? In a general sense *job satisfaction is the positive feeling that results from an appraisal of one's work.* In general, job satisfaction tends to increase gradually with age (Sterns & Gray, 1999). Why is this the case? There are several reasons.

First, self-selection factors suggest that people who truly like their jobs may tend to stay in them, whereas people who do not may tend to leave (Hom & Kinicki, 2001). This connection is explored in more detail in the Spotlight on Research feature. To the extent that this is the case, age differences in job satisfaction may simply reflect the fact that with sufficient time, many people eventually find a job in which they are reasonably happy.

SPOTLIGHT ON RESEARCH

The Connection Between Job Satisfaction and Employee Turnover

Who were the investigators and what was the aim of the study? Hom and Kinicki (2001) tested a model of how employee dissatisfac-

tion results in the decision to leave one's job. Researchers since the 1970s have been studying the various steps between people's attitudes toward their jobs and their ultimate decision to quit. Despite decades of work, the causal mechanisms underlying the dissatisfaction-quit process have yet to be specified clearly. Hom and Kinicki wanted to learn whether avoiding certain jobs, inter-role conflict, and employment conditions also affect people's decisions to quit.

How did the investigators measure the topic of interest? The researchers used a set of questions for most of the variables of interest. In addition, they used the following scales. Satisfaction with work hours, team, and duties were measured with 5-point scales. Inter-role conflict reported the extent to which jobs interfered with community and personal activities and was measured on a 4-point scale. Participants rated the extent to which job-seeking would produce stress, alternative jobs, personal costs, impact on personal and work time, and job interference on 5-point scales. Respondents also indicated how often during the last three months they had used methods to prepare or to look for jobs on a 4-point scale.

Who were the participants in the study? Hom and Kinicki used data from a national survey of 438 managers, salespersons, and auto mechanics conducted in the spring of 1997. The average age of the sample was 31.4 years, 62% were married, and 91% were European Americans.

What was the design of the study? The study used a cross-sectional design for the administration of the survey.

Were there ethical concerns with the study? Because the study involved voluntary completion of a survey, there were no ethical concerns.

What were the results? Hom and Kinicki's findings supported a complex model shown in Figure 13.2 that provides an explanatory framework for why people leave their jobs. Several aspects of the model are important. First, conflict between work and other aspects of a person's life (inter-role conflict) affect job satisfaction and thoughts about leaving the job (withdrawal cognitions). These in turn affect whether the person thinks things might be better elsewhere (withdrawal's expected utility), which in turn affects whether the person actually begins a job search. Actually resigning (turnover) results from a combination of thinking about leaving, finding a better alternative (compared alternatives), and the actual unemployment rate.

What have the investigators concluded? The most important finding from the study is the importance of inter-role conflict between work and other aspects of a person's life. Prior to this study, few researchers included this concept in studies of employee turnover. The importance of inter-role conflict means that

FIGURE 13.2

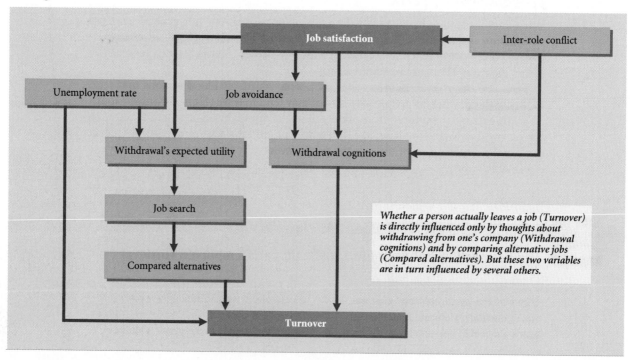

Whether a person actually leaves a job (Turnover) is directly influenced only by thoughts about withdrawing from one's company (Withdrawal cognitions) and by comparing alternative jobs (Compared alternatives). But these two variables are in turn influenced by several others.

employers need to pay more attention to the balance people need between their work roles and their other roles.

What converging evidence would strengthen these conclusions? Hom and Kinicki's study examined only a few job types. It will be important to test their model with other occupational classifications. Also, it will be important to study a more diverse group of employees. The present study had overrepresentation by European Americans compared with the actual labour force in the United States. ▨

Second, the relationship between worker age and job satisfaction is complex. Satisfaction does not increase in all areas and job types with age. Middle-aged workers are more satisfied with the intrinsic personal aspects of their jobs, such as perceived control and self-efficacy, than they are with the extrinsic aspects, such as pay (Glickman, 2001; Mirabella, 2001). White-collar professionals show an increase in job satisfaction, whereas those in blue-collar positions do not (Sterns, Marsh, & McDaniel, 1994).

Third, increases in job satisfaction may not result from age alone but rather from the degree to which there is a good fit between the worker and the job (Holland, 1985). Middle-aged workers have had more time to find a job that they like or may have resigned themselves to the fact that things are unlikely to improve, resulting in a better congruence between worker desires and job attributes (Glickman, 2001). Middle-aged workers also may have revised their expectations over the years to better reflect the actual state of affairs.

Fourth, as workers get older, they make work less of a focus in their lives, partly because they have achieved occupational success. Consequently, it takes less to keep them satisfied.

Fifth, the type of job and the degree of family responsibilities at different career stages may influence the relationship between age and job satisfaction (Engle et al., 1994). This suggests that the accumulation of experience, changing context, and the stage of one's career development may contribute to the increase in job satisfaction.

Finally, job satisfaction may be cyclical. That is, it may show periodic fluctuations that are not related to age per se but rather to changes people intentionally make in their occupations (Shirom & Mazeh, 1988). The idea is that job satisfaction increases over time because people change jobs or responsibilities on a regular basis, thereby keeping their occupation interesting and challenging.

Alienation and Burnout

No job is perfect; there is always something about it that is not as good as it could be. Perhaps the hours are not optimal, the pay is lower than one would like, or the boss does not have a pleasant personality. For most workers, such negatives are merely annoyances. But for others, like the air traffic controller in the photograph, extremely stressful situations on the job may result in deeply rooted unhappiness with work: alienation and burnout.

*When workers feel that what they are doing is meaningless and that their efforts are devalued, or when they do not see the connection between what they do and the final product, a sense of **alienation** is likely to result.* Studs Terkel's (1974) classic study in which he interviewed

several alienated workers found that all of them expressed the feeling that they were nameless, faceless cogs in a large machine. He reported that employees are most likely to feel alienated when they perform routine, repetitive actions such as those on an assembly line, jobs that are most likely to be replaced by technology. But other workers can become alienated too. White-collar managers and executives do not have the same level of job security that they once had. Consequently, their feelings toward their employers have become more negative in many cases (Roth, 1991).

What makes employees become alienated? R. Abraham (2000) found that the personality trait of cynicism was the strongest predictor of organizational cynicism and alienation, which resulted in job dissatisfaction.

How can employers avoid alienating workers? Research indicates that it is helpful to involve employees in the decision-making process, create flexible work schedules, and institute employee development and enhancement programs (Roth, 1991). Indeed, many organizations have instituted new practices such as total quality management (TQM) partly as a way to address worker alienation. TQM and related approaches make a concerted effort to get employees involved in the operation and administration of their plant or office. Such programs work: Absenteeism drops and the quality of work improves in organizations that implement them (Offermann & Growing, 1990).

Sometimes the pace and pressure of the occupation becomes more than a person can bear, resulting in **burnout**, *a depletion of a person's energy and motivation, the loss of occupational idealism, and the feeling that one is being exploited.* Burnout is a stress syndrome, characterized by emotional exhaustion, depersonalization, and diminished personal accomplishment (Cordes & Dougherty, 1993). Burnout is most common among people in the helping professions, such as teaching, social work, health care (Bozikas et al., 2000), and occupational therapy (Bird, 2001), as well as the military (Harrington et al., 2001). For example, nurses in intensive care units like the one in the photograph have high levels of burnout from stress (Iskra et al., 1996). People in these professions must constantly deal with other people's complex problems, usually under difficult time constraints. Dealing with these pressures every day, along with bureaucratic paperwork, may become too much for the worker to bear. Ideals are abandoned, frustration builds, and disillusionment and exhaustion set in. In short, the worker is burned out. The situation is exacerbated when people must work long shifts in stressful jobs (Iskra et al., 1996). Burnout also tends to increase with age and years on the job, and increases the likelihood that the person will leave a job (Stanton-Rich, Iso-Ahola, & Seppo, 1998).

The best defences against burnout appear to be practising stress-reduction techniques, lowering people's expectations of themselves, and enhancing communication within organizations. Providing longer rest periods between shifts in highly stressful jobs may help (Iskra et al., 1996). No one in the helping professions can resolve all problems perfectly; lowering expectations of what can be realistically accomplished will help workers deal with real-world constraints. Similarly, improving communication among different sections of organizations to keep workers informed of the outcome of their efforts gives them a sense that what they do matters in the long run. Finally, research also suggests that lack of support from one's co-workers may cause depersonalization; improving such support through teamwork can

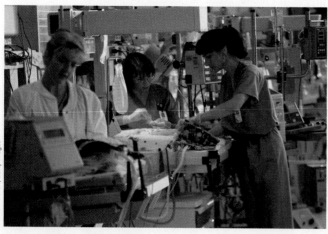

Stewart Cohen /Getty Images

be an effective intervention (Corrigan et al., 1994; Greenglass, Burke, & Konarski, 1998).

In short, making workers feel that they are important to the organization by involving them in decisions, keeping expectations realistic, ensuring good communication, and promoting teamwork help employees avoid alienation and burnout. As organizations adopt different management styles, perhaps these goals can be achieved.

TEST YOURSELF

1. Compared with workers a few decades ago, workers today are more concerned with individual freedom, personal growth, and _____.

2. Holland's theory deals with the relationship between occupation and _____.

3. Throughout their working years, Super believes people are located along a continuum of _____.

4. The role of a mentor is part teacher, part sponsor, part model, and part _____.

5. Recent research has shown that job satisfaction does not increase consistently as a person ages; rather, satisfaction may be _____.

6. Two negative aspects of job satisfaction are alienation and _____.

Why do you think middle-aged workers are more satisfied with the personal aspects of their jobs, such as perceived control and self-efficacy, than they are with the extrinsic aspects, such as pay?

Answers: (1) cooperation, (2) personality, (3) vocational maturity, (4) counsellor, (5) cyclical, (6) burnout

13.2

Gender, Ethnicity, and Discrimination Issues

LEARNING OBJECTIVES

▶ How do women's and men's occupational expectations differ? How are people viewed when they enter occupations that are not traditional for their gender?

▶ What factors are related to women's occupational development?

▶ What factors affect ethnic minority workers' occupational experiences and occupational development?

▶ What types of bias and discrimination hinder the occupational development of women and ethnic minority workers?

> **Gender, Ethnicity, and Discrimination Issues**
> Gender Differences in Occupational Selection
> Women and Occupational Development
> Ethnicity and Occupational Development
> Bias and Discrimination

Janice, a 35-year-old manager at a business consulting firm, is concerned because her career is not progressing as rapidly as she had hoped. Janice works hard and has received excellent performance ratings every year. But she has noticed that there are very few women in upper management positions in her company. Janice wonders when she will be promoted.

Occupational choice and development are not equally available to all, as Janice is experiencing. Gender, ethnicity, and age may create barriers to achieving one's occupational goals. Although they're in similar occupations, the men and women depicted in the photograph on page 462 come from different backgrounds. Each received somewhat different socialization as children and adolescents, which made it easier or harder for them to set their sights on a career in the health professions. Bias and discrimination also create barriers to occupational success. In this section, we'll get a better appreciation for the personal and structural barriers that exist for many people.

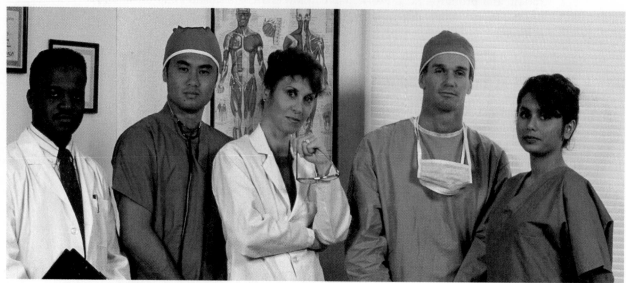

© Tom McCarthy/PhotoEdit

GENDER DIFFERENCES IN OCCUPATIONAL SELECTION

Approximately 57% of Canadian women are employed outside the home (Statistics Canada, 2003j), and this number is expected to increase. Therefore, although it is still the case that many occupational opportunities are more available to men than to women (Lyness & Thompson, 1997), it is important that women be exposed to the same occupational socialization opportunities as men.

Traditional and Nontraditional Occupations

In the past, women employed outside the home tended to enter traditional, female-dominated occupations such as secretarial, teaching, and social work jobs. This was due mainly to their socialization into these occupational tracks. However, as more women enter the workforce and as new opportunities are opened for women, a growing number work in occupations that traditionally have been male-dominated, such as construction and engineering. Research in this area has focused on three issues: selection of nontraditional occupations, characteristics of women in nontraditional occupations, and perceptions of nontraditional occupations (Swanson, 1992).

Why some women end up in nontraditional occupations appears to be related to personal feelings and experiences as well as expectations about the occupation (Brooks & Betz, 1990). Concerning personal experiences, women who attend single-sex high schools and who have both brothers and sisters end up in the least traditional occupations, apparently because they have been exposed to more options and fewer gender-role stereotypes (Rubenfeld & Gilroy, 1991).

Despite the efforts to counteract gender stereotyping of occupations, women who choose nontraditional occupations may still be viewed with disapproval by their peers of either sex, even though they have high job satisfaction themselves (Brabeck & Weisgerber, 1989; Pfost & Fiore, 1990). This finding holds up in cross-cultural research as well. In a study conducted in India, both women and men gave higher "respectability" ratings to males than to females in the same occupation (Kanekar, Kolsawalla, & Nazareth, 1989). People even make inferences about working condi-

THINK ABOUT IT

What changes in children's school and other socialization experiences will encourage girls to prepare for the same range of occupational skills as boys?

tions based on their perception of an occupation as traditionally masculine or feminine. Scozzaro and Subich (1990) report that occupations such as a secretarial job are perceived as offering nice working conditions, whereas male-dominated occupations are perceived as offering good pay and promotion potential. Worst of all, people are less likely to perceive incidents of sexual coercion as harassing when a woman is in a nontraditional occupation (Burgess & Borgida, 1997).

Taken together, these studies show that we still have a long way to go before people can choose any occupation they want without having to contend with gender-related stereotypes. Although differences in opportunities for women in traditional and nontraditional occupations are narrowing, key differences remain. Finally, little research has examined differences between males in traditional and nontraditional occupations (Swanson, 1992). This lack of data is troubling, for it prevents our answering important questions such as why men choose traditional or nontraditional occupations, and why some men still perpetuate gender stereotypes about particular occupations.

WOMEN AND OCCUPATIONAL DEVELOPMENT

If you were to guess what the young woman in the photograph who has just graduated from university will be doing occupationally 10 years from now, what would you say? Would you guess that she will be strongly committed to her occupation? Will she have abandoned it for other things?

Studies of women MBAs with children have identified a number of family and workplace issues that influence whether they stay or leave their occupations (Rosin & Korabik, 1990, 1991). Family obligations, such as child care, appear to be most important for mothers working part-time. For these women, adequate child care arrangements or having the flexibility to be at home when children get out of school often make the difference between being able to accept a job or remaining at home. In contrast, mothers who have made the decision to work full-time have resolved the problem of child care.

Photodisc

The most important workplace issues for these women are gender-related. Unsupportive or insensitive work environments, organizational politics, and the lack of occupational development opportunities appear most important for women working full-time (Silverstein, 2001). In particular, women professionals leave their jobs for two sets of reasons. First, although women professionals need to work interdependently with others to grow professionally, develop personally, and achieve satisfaction in their work, the corporations in which they work are felt to hold contrary values. Corporations more highly value masculine values of working, rewarding individuality, self-sufficiency, and individual contributions, and emphasize tangible outputs, competitiveness, and rationality rather than valuing relationships, interdependence, and collaboration that women seek. Second, women feel disconnected from the workplace. They feel disconnected from their colleagues, clients, and co-workers, derive less meaning from work, and feel alienated from themselves. By mid-career, they had concluded that to achieve satisfaction, growth, and development at work, and to be rewarded for the relational skills they considered essential for success, they needed to leave corporate life. Clearly, women are focusing on issues that create barriers to their occupational development and personal satisfaction and are looking for ways around the barriers.

Such barriers are a major reason women's workforce participation is discontinuous. Because they cannot find affordable and dependable child care, or freely choose to take on this responsibility, many women stay home while their children are young. Discontinuous participation makes it difficult to maintain an upward trajectory in one's career through promotion, and to maintain skills. Some women make this choice willingly; however, many find themselves forced into it.

ETHNICITY AND OCCUPATIONAL DEVELOPMENT

What factors are related to occupational selection and development for people from ethnic minorities? Unfortunately, not much research has been conducted from a developmental perspective. Rather, most researchers have focused on the limited opportunities ethnic minorities have and the structural barriers, such as discrimination, that they face. Most of the developmental research to date focuses on occupational selection issues and variables that foster occupational development. Three topics have received the most focus: nontraditional occupations, vocational identity, and issues pertaining to occupational aspirations.

In the United States, African-American women and European-American women were found to not differ in their plans to enter nontraditional occupations (Murrell, Frieze, & Frost, 1991). However, African-American women who choose nontraditional occupations tend to plan for more formal education than necessary to achieve their goal. This may actually make them overqualified for the jobs they get; for example, a woman with a university degree may be working in a job that does not require that level of education.

Vocational identity is the degree to which one views one's occupation as a key element of identity. Research shows that vocational identity varies with both ethnicity and gender. American researchers found that compared to European-American women and Latino men, African-American and European-American men have higher vocational identity when they graduate from college (Steward & Krieshok, 1991). Lower vocational identity means that people define themselves primarily by aspects of their lives other than work. Research on occupational development of ethnic minority workers is clear on one point: Whether an organization is responsive to the needs of ethnic minorities like the woman in the photograph makes a big difference for employees.

BIAS AND DISCRIMINATION

Since the 1960s, organizations in North America have been sensitized to the issues of bias and discrimination in the workplace. Hiring, promotion, and termination procedures have come under close scrutiny in numerous court cases, resulting in judicial rulings governing these processes.

Gender Bias and the Glass Ceiling

Even though the majority of women work outside the home, women in high-status jobs are unusual (Mitchell, 2000). In 1993 Kim Campbell became the first female to be the prime minister of Canada (photograph on left), and in 1999 Beverley McLaughlin was the first woman appointed Chief Justice of the Supreme Court of Canada (photograph on right). However, these accomplishments are exceptional because, as Janice noticed in the vignette, few women also serve in the highest ranks of major corporations, and women are substantially outnumbered at the senior faculty level of most universities and colleges. In Canada in 1999, 44% of companies had no female corporate officers, and of those who did, only 27% had numerous female corporate officers (Wirth, 2001).

Why are there so few women at the highest ranks? *The most important reason is sex discrimination, denying a job to someone solely on the basis of whether the person is a man or a woman.* Lovoy (2001) points out that sexual discrimination is pervasive in the workplace. Despite some progress over the past two decades, sex discrimination is still common; women are being kept out of high-status jobs by the men at the top (Lyness & Thompson, 1997; Shaiko, 1996; Yamagata et al., 1997).

*Women themselves refer to a **glass ceiling**, the level to which they may rise in a company but beyond which they may not go.* The greatest barrier facing women is at the boundary between lower-tier and upper-tier job grades (Morrison et al., 1992). Women like Janice tend to move to the top of the lower tier and remain there, whereas men are more readily promoted to the upper tier, even when other factors, such as personal attributes and qualifications and job performance, are controlled (Lovoy, 2001).

What can be done to begin eliminating the glass ceiling? Mitchell (2000) suggests that companies must begin to value the competencies women develop, such as being more democratic and interpersonally oriented than men, and to assist men in feeling more comfortable with their female colleagues. Mentoring is also an important aspect. Lovoy (2001) adds that companies must be more proactive in promoting diversity, provide better and more detailed feedback about performance and where employees stand regarding promotion, and establish ombuds offices that help women deal with difficulties on the job.

Besides discrimination in hiring and promotion, women are also subject to pay discrimination. According to Statistics Canada (2001h), in 1997 women earned on average about 80% of the average male hourly wage. However, among full-time workers during that same time period, women earned approximately 73% of annual earnings that males earned.

Several solutions to this problem have been promoted. *One of these is* **comparable worth:** *equalizing pay in occupations that are determined to be equivalent in importance but differ in the gender distribution of the people doing the jobs.* Determining which male-dominated occupations should be considered equivalent to which female-dominated occupations for pay purposes can be difficult and controversial. One way to do this is with gender-neutral job evaluations, which examine all positions within an organization to establish fair-pay policies (Castro, 1997).

Sexual Harassment

Suppose you have been working very hard on a paper for a course and think that you've done a good job. When indeed you receive an "A" for the paper, you are elated. When you discuss your paper (and your excitement) with your instructor, you receive a big hug. How do you feel? What if this situation involved a project at work and the hug came from your boss? Your co-worker? What if it were a kiss on your lips instead of a hug?

Whether such behaviour is acceptable or not has become a major topic of debate in North America over the past few decades. Although sexual harassment of women has been documented for centuries, only more recently has it received much attention from researchers (Sbraga & O'Donohue, 2000). Sexual harassment is not only a North America phenomenon; sad to say, it occurs around the world (Luo, 1996).

Research on sexual harassment focuses on situations in which there is a power differential between two people, most often involving men with more power over women (Berdahl, Magley, & Waldo, 1996). Such situations exist in the workplace and in academic settings (Zappert, 1996). However, peer-to-peer harassment also occurs, such as among classmates in academic settings (Ivy & Hamlet, 1996). Under the Canada Labour Code, every employee is entitled to employment free of sexual harassment. Canadian employers must make every reasonable effort to ensure that no employee is subjected to sexual harassment and, in consultation with employees, must issue a policy on sexual harassment.

How many people have been sexually harassed? It has been reported that 56% of Canadian working women experienced sexual harassment during the prior year although the lifetime rate was reportedly 77% (Crocker & Kalemba, 1999). The most common types of incidents reported by the women surveyed were staring, jokes or comments about women in general, or jokes about themselves specifically. The least common types of harassment incidents reported were physical or attempted physical force, threats, or bribery. Women reported being upset by all forms of sexual harassment (Crocker & Kalemba, 1999).

What kinds of effects does being sexually harassed have? Research evidence shows clear, negative emotional, mental health, and job-related outcomes (Schneider et al., 1997). Establishing the degree of problems is difficult, though, because many women try to minimize or hide their reactions or feelings (Tang & McCollum, 1996). It is becoming evident, though, that one does not have to experience the worst kinds of sexual harassment to be affected. Even low-level but frequent experience of sexual harassment can have significant negative consequences for women (Schneider et al., 1997).

Sexual harassment also has numerous ripple effects throughout a company (Piotrkowski, cited in Murray, 1998). For example, men in all ethnic backgrounds who work in companies that have cases of sexual harassment, but who are not harassers themselves, report less satisfaction with their jobs. Productivity at such companies also declines, as does general worker morale.

Of course, the crux of the matter is what constitutes harassment, which is discussed in the Current Controversies feature. Although research indicates that men can also be subjected to sexual harassment (Sbraga & O'Donohue, 2000), most of the emphasis has been on women's experiences.

CURRENT CONTROVERSIES

Is It Sexual Harassment?

What would have to be going on in the situation depicted in the photograph for you to say that it is sexual harassment? Defining sexual harassment turns out to be much more difficult than many people think. Sure, the most egregious forms (such as requiring a woman to have sex in exchange for a promotion or a grade) are easy. Where it gets more difficult are in the "grey areas" such as brief touches and comments.

Sbraga and O'Donohue (2000) review 30 years of writing in psychology and law concerning the definition of sexual harassment. They point out that definitions disagree whether a power differential must be present for the behaviours to be called sexual harassment, whether a specific location must be identified, whether the behaviour must be perceived as harassment by the victim, whether men can be the objects of harassment, whether sexist behaviour is included under the guise of sexual harassment, and whether the behaviours are considered to be harassment apart from any negative consequences they create. Based on considerable research, Fitzgerald and colleagues (1997) proposed three major categories of sexual harassment:

- *Sexual coercion:* an attempt to force sexual compliance in exchange for workplace (or educational) benefits or threats of punishment. It is the least frequently reported type.
- *Unwanted sexual attention:* sexual conduct in the workplace or school that can be either verbal or nonverbal and that is unwanted by the victim and creates an intimidating, hostile, or offensive environment. Common examples include repeated requests for a date and risqué comments about clothing.
- *Gender harassment:* sexist remarks or behaviour based on stereotypes of the sexes, including making sexist jokes, displaying nude photographs, and making comments about another's body. This is the most common form, with up to 70% of women reporting experiencing gender harassment (Sbraga & O'Donohue, 2000).

In general, women are more likely to view such behaviours as offensive than are men (Rotundo, Nguyen, & Sackett, 2001). Specifically, women perceive a broader range of social-sexual behaviour as harassing.

When specific behaviours are examined, touching the cheek of a person of the opposite sex sends particularly strong relational and

Photodisc

emotional messages (e.g., flirtation and attraction), and is rated as the most inappropriate and sexually harassing of types of touch (Lee & Guerrero, 2001). Putting one's arm around another's waist is also seen as highly inappropriate and harassing. Shaking hands is viewed as the least offensive form of touch.

Most companies now have training programs to try to eliminate sexual harassment. If designed well, they can be effective in reducing the number of complaints (Sbraga & O'Donohue, 2000). However, it is unlikely that sexual harassment will disappear in the near future. Only through considerable socialization and education can we hope to eliminate it eventually.

What can be done to provide people with safe work and learning environments, free from sexual harassment? Training in gender awareness is a common approach that often works (Tang & McCollum, 1996). And clearly differentiating between workplace romance and sexual harassment is another essential element (Pierce & Aguinis, 1997).

Age Discrimination

Another structural barrier to occupational development is age discrimination, which involves denying a job or promotion to someone solely on the basis of age. Individuals in mid- and later life are potential victims of discrimination based on negative characterizing of their specific age group or a general view of "old" versus "young." Under the Canadian Human Rights Act, it is against the law for employers to discriminate on the basis of age.

THINK ABOUT IT

What are the key biological, psychological, sociocultural, and life-cycle factors that should inform training programs concerning sexual harassment?

Dennis Wise/Getty Images

Employment prospects for middle-aged people around the world are lower than for their younger counterparts. For example, age discrimination toward those over age 45 is common in Germany (Frerichs & Naegele, 1997), Britain (Ginn & Arber, 1996), and Hong Kong (Chiu et al., 2001), resulting in longer periods of unemployment, early retirement, or negative attitudes. Such practices may save companies money in the short run, but the loss of expertise and knowledge comes at a high price. Indeed, global corporations are beginning to realize that retraining and integrating middle-aged workers is a better strategy (Frerichs & Naegele, 1997).

Age discrimination may occur in several ways, but it is not typically demonstrated by professional human resources staff (Kager, 2000). Age discrimination usually happens prior to or after interaction with human resources staff. For example, employers can make certain types of physical or mental performance a job requirement and argue that older workers cannot meet the standard prior to an interview. Or they can attempt to get rid of older workers by using retirement incentives. Supervisors' stereotyped beliefs sometimes factor in performance evaluations for raises or promotions or in decisions about which employees are eligible for additional training (Chiu et al., 2001).

TEST YOURSELF

1. Women who choose nontraditional occupations are viewed _____ by their peers.

2. Among the reasons women in well-paid occupations leave, _____ are most important for part-time workers.

3. Ethnic minority workers are more satisfied with and committed to organizations that are responsive and provide _____.

4. Three barriers to women's occupational development are sex discrimination, the glass ceiling, and _____.

What steps need to be taken to eliminate gender, ethnic, and age bias in the workplace?

Answers: (1) negatively, (2) family obligations, (3) positive work environments, (4) pay discrimination

13.3

Occupational Transitions

LEARNING OBJECTIVES

▪ Why do people change occupations?

▪ Is worrying about potential job loss a major source of stress?

▪ How does the timing of job loss affect the amount of stress experienced?

> **Occupational Transitions**
> Retraining Workers
> Occupational Insecurity
> Coping with Unemployment

Fred has 32 years of service with an automobile manufacturer. Over the years, more and more assembly-line jobs have been eliminated by robots and other technology, and the export of manufacturing jobs to other countries. Although Fred has been assured by his boss that his job is safe, he isn't so sure. He worries that he could be laid off at any time.

In the past, people like Fred commonly chose an occupation during young adulthood and stayed in it throughout their working years. Today, however, not many people take a job with the expectation that it will last a lifetime. Changing jobs is almost taken for granted; the average North American will change jobs between 5 and 10 times during adulthood (Toffler, 1970). Some authors view occupational changes as positive; Havighurst (1982), for example, strongly advocates such flexibility. According to his view, building change into the occupational life cycle may help to avoid disillusionment with one's initial choice. Changing occupations may be one way to guarantee challenging and satisfying work, and it may be the best option for those in a position to exercise it (Shirom & Mazeh, 1988). The case of Alistair, told in the Real People feature, exemplifies many of these aspects of occupational change.

REAL PEOPLE: APPLYING HUMAN DEVELOPMENT

Changing Occupations to Find Satisfying Work

From the time he was in university, Alistair knew he wanted to be an accountant. His only question was whether it would be in a large public accounting firm or in a private corporation. After much consideration (and several job offers), he chose to work for a major global corporation. Alistair rose through the ranks, and all seemed well. He eventually was in charge of the Far East division of the international tax unit, which allowed him to travel to interesting and exotic places.

However, Alistair's company, like many others, went through several rounds of downsizing. Although his job was extremely secure, Alistair saw his staff reduced considerably. These cuts led to many long hours and much more job stress. So, after 17 years with the company, Alistair decided that even though the pay was good, the hours and the stress were not worth it. He left and began working for a start-up biotechnology firm. At first, conditions were much better. But soon the long hours and stress started in again. This time, he quit with no new job. He needed time to think and reset his priorities.

After much careful thought, he decided that what he really wanted was to work in a nonprofit organization. Eventually, he ended up with a large foundation that funds minority businesses and other community-based companies.

The change for Alistair has been very successful. Although he makes less money than he did in the private sector, he is much happier and less stressed. And for him, this is worth it all.

Several factors have been identified as important in determining who will remain in an occupation and who will change. Some factors—such as whether the person likes the occupation—lead to self-initiated occupation changes such as Alistair experienced. For example, people who really like their occupation, like those in the photograph, may seek additional training or accept overtime assignments in hope of acquiring new skills that will enable them to get better jobs. Others will use the training to become more marketable. However, other factors, such as obsolete skills and economic trends, cause forced occupational changes. For example, continued improvement of robots has caused some auto industry workers to lose their jobs; corporations send jobs overseas to increase profits; and economic recessions usually result in large-scale layoffs. But even forced occupational changes can have benefits. As we will see in Chapter 14, for instance, many adults go to university or college. Some are taking advantage of educational benefits offered as part of a separation

Zephyr Picture, Inc. /Index Stock Imagery

package. Others are pursuing educational opportunities to obtain new skills; still others are looking to advance in their careers.

In this section, we explore the positive and negative aspects of occupational transitions. First we examine the retraining of mid-career and older workers. The increased use of technology, corporate downsizing, and an aging workforce have focused attention on the need to keep older workers' skills current. Later, we will examine occupational insecurity and the effects of job loss.

RETRAINING WORKERS

When you are hired for a specific job, you are selected because your employer believes you offer the best fit between abilities you already have and those needed to perform the job. As most people can attest, though, the skills needed to perform a job usually change over time. Such changes may be due to the introduction of new technology, additional responsibilities, or promotion.

Unless a person's skills are kept up to date, the outcome is likely to be either job loss or career plateauing (Froman, 1994). *Career plateauing occurs when there is a lack of promotional opportunity in the organization or when a person decides not to seek advancement.* Research in Canada shows that feeling that one's career has plateaued results in less organizational commitment and a greater tendency to leave (Lemire, Saba, & Gagnon, 1999).

In cases of job loss or career plateauing, retraining or upgrading may be an appropriate response. Over half of Canadian employees (55%) received at least one job training session, consisting of either or both in-classroom instruction and on-the-job training (Statistics Canada, 2003e). One objective of these courses is to improve technical skills, such as new computer skills. For mid-career or older employees, retraining might focus on how to advance in one's occupation or how to find new career opportunities—for example, through résumé preparation and career counselling. Additional research indicates that companies can take several specific steps to address the problems associated with career plateauing (Lemire et al., 1999; Rotondo & Perrewe, 2000). For example, positive activities such as expanding job assignments, mentoring, clearly defined career paths, and new projects or teams result in more positive attitudes and higher perceived performance among career plateaued employees.

Many corporations, as well as community and technical colleges, offer retraining programs in a variety of fields. Organizations that promote employee development typically promote in-house courses to improve employee skills. Or they may offer tuition reimbursement programs for individuals who successfully complete courses at colleges or universities.

The retraining of mid-career and older workers highlights the need for lifelong learning (Sinnott, 1994b). If corporations are to meet the challenges of a global economy, it is imperative that they include retraining in their employee development programs. Such programs will help improve people's chances of advancement in their chosen occupations, and they will also assist people in making successful transitions from one occupation to another.

OCCUPATIONAL INSECURITY

Changing economic conditions in North America over the past few decades (such as the move toward a global economy), as well as changing demographics, have forced many people out of their jobs. Heavy manufacturing and support businesses (such as the steel, oil, and automotive industries) and farming were the hardest hit during the 1970s and 1980s. But no one is immune. Indeed, the corporate takeover frenzy of the 1980s and the recession of the early 1990s put many middle- and upper-level corporate executives out of work in all kinds of businesses.

THINK ABOUT IT ♀

How do recent changes in job security affect the occupational socialization that children and adolescents receive?

As a result of these trends, many people feel insecure about their jobs. Like Fred, the autoworker in the vignette, many worried workers have numerous years of dedicated service to a corporation. Unfortunately, people who worry about their jobs tend to have poorer mental health (Roskies & Louis-Guerin, 1990). For example, anxiety about one's job may result in negative attitudes about one's employer or even work in general, which in turn may result in diminished desire to be successful. Whether there is any actual basis for people's feelings of job insecurity may not matter; sometimes what people think is true about their work situation is more important than what is actually the case. If people believe they are at risk of losing their jobs, their mental health and behaviour are often affected negatively even when the risk is very low (Roskies & Louis-Guerin, 1990).

COPING WITH UNEMPLOYMENT

What does it feel like to lose one's job after many years of dedicated service? One man put it this way.

> After becoming used to living like a human being, then losing your job, working six days a week just to make the house payment for two years before selling it at a loss, then losing your wife because of all the hardships that were not your fault, then looking endlessly for a decent job only to find jobs for [minimum wage so that I] can't afford an apartment or any place to live so having to live out of a van for the past two-and-one-half years, *how should one feel?* Please, I'm a hard worker and did a good job. I always go to work—check my record! I want to be normal again, like a real human being with a house instead of a van. (Leana & Feldman, 1992, p. 51)

As this man states so poignantly, losing one's job can have enormous personal impact (Creed, Bloxsome, & Johnston, 2001; Ebberwein, 2001; Waters & Moore, 2001).

Unemployed people commonly experience declines in physical health and self-esteem, alcohol abuse, depression, anxiety, and suicide (Viinamaki, Koskela, & Niskanen, 1996). Men and women generally experience similar levels of distress following the loss of a job (Leana & Feldman, 1992; Vosler & Page-Adams, 1996). However, these effects vary with age and gender. Middle-aged men are more vulnerable to negative effects than older or younger men, largely because they have greater financial responsibilities than the other two groups, but women report a sharper decline in health (Kulik, 2001a).

Life-cycle factors are also important in understanding the reaction to job loss. Leana and Feldman (1992) write that workers in their 50s who lose their jobs are not always highly distressed. Some may have been planning to retire in the near future, others may be hired back as consultants, and still others see it as an opportunity to try something new. If they want to become re-employed, middle-aged people spend more hours per week searching for jobs than do younger adults (Kulik, 2001a).

Unemployment rates for many ethnic minority groups in Canada are higher than Canada's overall employment rate (Statistics Canada, 2001h). As far as is known, however, the nature of the distress resulting from job loss is the same regardless of ethnicity. Research also offers some advice for adults who are trying to manage occupational transitions (Ebberwein, 2001):

THINK ABOUT IT ♀

What are some of the broader effects of unemployment on an individual's personal and family life?

- ▮ Approach job loss with a healthy sense of urgency.
- ▮ Consider your next career move and what you must do to achieve it, even if there are no prospects for it in sight.
- ▮ Admit and react to change as soon as you realize it is there.

- Be cautious of stop-gap employment.
- Identify a realistic goal and list the steps you must take to achieve it.

These steps may not guarantee that you will find a new job quickly, but they will help create a better sense that you are in control.

TEST YOURSELF

1. One response to the pressures of a global economy and an aging workforce is to provide _____.

2. Two factors that could cause involuntary occupational change are economic trends and _____.

3. Fear of job loss is often a more important determinant of stress than _____.

4. The age group that is most at risk for negative effects of job loss is _____.

It is likely that the trend toward several careers in a lifetime will continue and become the norm. What implications will this have for theories of career development in the future?

Answers: (1) worker retraining, (2) obsolete skills, (3) actual likelihood of job loss, (4) middle-aged adults

13·4

Work and Family

LEARNING OBJECTIVES

- What are the issues faced by employed people who care for dependents?
- How do partners view the division of household chores? What is work-family conflict? How does it affect couples' lives?

> **Work and Family**
> The Dependent Care Dilemma
> Juggling Multiple Roles

Jennifer, a 38-year-old sales clerk at a department store, feels that her husband, Bill, doesn't do his share of the housework or child care. Bill says that real men don't do house-work and that he's really tired when he comes home from work. Jennifer thinks this isn't fair, especially because she works as many hours outside the home as her husband.

One of the most difficult challenges facing adults like Jennifer is trying to balance the demands of occupation with the demands of family. Over the past few decades, the rapid increase in the number of families in which both parents are employed has fun-

damentally changed how we view the relation between work and family. As the photograph shows, this can even mean taking a young child to work as a way to deal with the pushes and pulls of being an employed parent. In nearly 70% of two-parent Canadian households today, both adults work outside the home (Statistics Canada, 1996a). The main reason? Families need the dual income to pay the bills and maintain a moderate standard of living.

As we will see, dual-earner couples with children experience both benefits and costs from this arrangement. The stresses of living in this arrangement are substantial—and gender differences are clear, especially in the division of household chores.

THE DEPENDENT CARE DILEMMA

Many employed adults must also provide care for dependent children or parents. As we will see, the issues they face are complex.

Employed Caregivers Revisited

Many mothers have no option but to return to work after the birth of a child. In fact, approximately 63% of mothers with children under the age of 3 years work for pay (Statistics Canada, 2003i). The number of mothers in the workforce with children of any age is even higher. The overall number of mothers in the workforce with children under age 16 has increased dramatically from 39% in 1976 to 72% in 2003 (Statistics Canada, 2003i).

Some women, though, grapple with the decision of whether they want to return to work. Surveys of mothers with preschool children reveal that the motivation for returning to work tends to be related to financial need and how attached mothers are to their work. For example, in one survey of Australian mothers, those with high work attachment were more likely to cite intrinsic personal achievement reasons for returning. Those with low work attachment cited pressing financial needs. Those with moderate work attachment were divided between intrinsic and financial reasons (Cotton, Anthill, & Cunningham, 1989). Those who can afford to give up careers and stay home also must deal with changes in identity (Milford, 1997).

Giving up a career means that those aspects of one's identity that came from work must be redefined to come from being a stay-at-home mother. Mothers also worry about conflicts between work and family roles. For some women, returning to work part-time may offer a compromise. Although switching from full-time to part-time work may seem appealing, what matters more is whether mothers were working hours that are close to what they consider ideal and accommodating to their family's needs (Kim, 2000). Perceptions of ideal working hours differ as a function of gender and life-cycle stage regarding children, as shown in Figure 13.3.

FIGURE 13.3   Perception of Ideal Working Hours

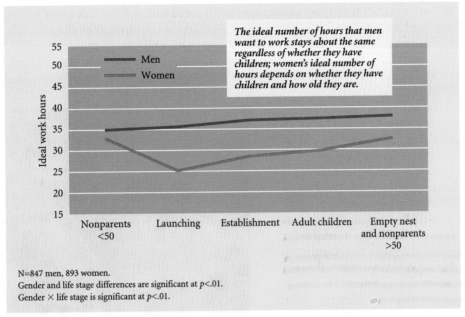

The ideal number of hours that men want to work stays about the same regardless of whether they have children; women's ideal number of hours depends on whether they have children and how old they are.

N=847 men, 893 women.
Gender and life stage differences are significant at $p<.01$.
Gender $\times$ life stage is significant at $p<.01$.

SOURCE: Cornell Couples and Careers Study, 1998.

An increasing and often overlooked group of employed caregivers are those caring for a parent or partner. Because most of these women are middle-aged, we will consider their situation in more detail in Chapter 14. Whether assistance is needed for one's children or parent, key factors in selecting an appropriate care site are quality of care, price, and hours of availability (Metropolitan Area Agency on Aging, 1998; Vandell, Pierce, & Stright, 1997). Depending on one's economic situation, it may not be possible to find affordable quality care that is available when needed. In such cases, there may be no option but to drop out of the workforce or enlist the help of friends and family.

Dependent Care and Effects on Workers

Workers who care for dependents face tough choices. Especially when both partners are employed, dependent care is the central organizing aspect of the couple's lives (Hertz, 1997).

Being responsible for dependent care has significant negative effects, especially for women. For example, when they are responsible for caring for an older parent, women report missing more meetings and being absent from work more often (Gignac, Kelloway, & Gottlieb, 1996). Such women also report higher levels of stress (Jenkins, 1997). Likewise, parents often exhibit poor quality of life and report higher stress and trouble coping with it (Galinsky, Bond, & Friedman, 1996).

How can these negative effects be lessened? For example, when women's partners provide good support and women have average or high control over their jobs, employed mothers are significantly less distressed than employed nonmothers (Roxburgh, 1997) and mothers without support (Rwampororo, 2001). When support and job control are lacking, though, employed mothers are significantly more distressed than employed nonmothers. Clearly, having partner support and being in a job that allows one to have control over such things as one's schedule is key. What employers provide is also important, as we see next.

THINK ABOUT IT

How do the effects of dependent care on mothers relate to the debate of whether children should be placed in day care?

Dependent Care and Employer Responses

Employed parents with small children are confronted with the difficult act of leaving their children in the care of others. Most industrialized countries, including Canada, provide some level of subsidization for the costs of child care, and a number of institutions have child care available at the workplace. Does providing a child care centre make a difference in an employee's feelings about work, absenteeism, and productivity?

Courtesy of Ingrid Crowther

The answer is that there is no simple answer. Just making a child care centre like the one in the photograph available to employees does not necessarily reduce parents' work-family conflict or their absenteeism (Goff, Mount, & Jamison, 1990). A "family-friendly" company must also pay attention to the attitudes of their employees and make sure that the company provides broad-based support (Allen, 2001; Grandey, 2001). The keys are how supervisors act and the number and type of benefits the company provides. When the organization adopts a justice approach in which supervisors are sympathetic and supportive regarding family issues and child care, and the organization provides benefits that employees consider important, employees report less work-family conflict, have lower absenteeism, and report higher job satisfaction.

Research on specific working conditions and benefits that help caregivers perform optimally on the job points to several consistent conclusions. To the extent that employers provide better job security, autonomy, lower productivity demands, supervisor support, and flexible schedules, caregivers fare better (Aryee & Luk, 1996; Frone & Yardley, 1996; Galinsky et al., 1996). Job applicants tend to perceive an organization more positively if it provides flexible work schedules and dependent care and nonwork-life assistance (Casper, 2000).

Many companies and institutions provide the option of parental leave in addition to the maternity or paternity benefits that are provided by the government. Parental leave affects each parent differently. For example, a large-scale study in Sweden showed that fathers who take parental leave are more likely to continue their involvement in child care and to reduce their work involvement. Regardless of fathers' participation, however, mothers still retain primary responsibility for child care and stay less involved in and receive fewer rewards in the labour market (Haas, 1990; Schwartz, 1992).

JUGGLING MULTIPLE ROLES

When both members of a heterosexual couple with dependents are employed, who cleans the house, cooks the meals, and takes care of the children when they are ill? This question gets to the heart of the dilemma of modern, dual-earner couples: How are household chores divided? How are work and family role conflicts handled?

Dividing Household Chores

Despite much media attention and claims of increased sharing in the duties, women still perform the lion's share of housework, regardless of employment status. In

Canadian homes women spend, on average, 4.3 hours on household work and 2.4 hours on primary child care each day, compared to men who spend, on average, 2.8 hours on household work and 1.8 hours on primary child care each day (Statistics Canada, 1998a). This unequal division of labour causes the many arguments and the most unhappiness for dual-earner couples. This is the case with Jennifer and Bill, the couple in the vignette; Jennifer does most of the housework.

A great deal of evidence indicates that since the 1970s women have reduced the amount of time they spend on housework, especially when they are employed, and that men have increased the amount of time they spend on such tasks (Swanson, 1992). The increased participation of men in these tasks is not all that it seems, however. American research indicates that most of the increase is on weekends, with specific tasks that they agree to perform, and it is largely unrelated to women's employment status (Zick & McCullough, 1991).

Men and women view the division of labour in very different terms. Men are often most satisfied with an equitable division of labour based on the number of hours spent, especially if the amount of time needed to perform household tasks is relatively small. Women are often most satisfied when men are willing to perform women's traditional chores (Benin & Agostinelli, 1988).

International data comparing the United States, Sweden, and the Netherlands indicates that even women who are employed outside the home do much more of the household chores than men in all three countries (Gjerdingen et al., 2000). Not surprisingly, such heavy workloads contribute to poorer health, lower marital satisfaction, and less career advancement. Findings from research in Israel show differences in the amount of gender inequality when women are employed part-time versus full-time; inequality in the division of household chores is greater when women are employed part-time (Stier & Lewin-Epstein, 2000).

In sum, the available evidence from heterosexual couples indicates that women still perform more household tasks than men but that the difference varies with ethnic groups. The discrepancy is greatest when the male endorses traditional masculine gender roles and is less when the male endorses more feminine or androgynous gender roles (Gunter & Gunter, 1990).

Work-Family Conflict

When people have both occupations and children, they must figure out how to balance the demands of each. People agonize over how to be at their daughter's ball game at the same time they have to be at an important business meeting. *These competing demands cause* **work-family conflict,** *which is the feeling of being pulled in multiple directions by incompatible demands from one's job and one's family.* Dual-earner couples must find a balance between their occupational and family roles. With the majority of married couples with children comprising dual-earner households, how to divide the household chores and how to care for the children have become increasingly important.

Many people believe that work and family roles influence each other in such families. When things go badly at work, family suffers; and when there are troubles at home, work suffers. However, this appears not to be the case all the time (Aryee & Luk, 1996). Whether work influences family or vice versa is a complex function of support resources, type of job, and a host of other factors (Frone, Russell, & Barnes, 1996; Matthews, Conger, & Wickrama, 1996; Stephens & Sommer, 1996). One key, but often overlooked factor is whether the work schedules of both partners mesh (Jacobs & Gerson, 2001).

Of course, it is important that the partners negotiate agreeable arrangements of household and child care tasks, but (as noted earlier) truly equitable divisions of labour are clearly the exception. Most households with heterosexual dual-worker couples still operate under a gender-segregated system: There are traditional chores for men and women. All of these tasks are important and must be performed to keep homes safe, clean, and sanitary. These tasks also take time.

So how and when will things change? An important step would be to talk about these issues with your partner. Keep communication lines open all the time, and let your partner know if something is bothering you. Teaching your children that men and women are equally responsible for household chores will also help end the problem. Only by creating true gender equality, without differentiating among household tasks, will the unfair division of labour be ended.

Research provides some evidence of how to deal with work-family conflict successfully. Women in one study were clear in their commitment to their careers, marriage, and children, and they successfully combined them without high levels of distress (Guelzow, Bird, & Koball, 1991). How did they do it? Contrary to popular belief, the age of the children was not a factor in stress level. However, the *number* of children was important, as stress increases greatly with each additional child, irrespective of their ages. Guilt was also not an issue for these women. In the same study, men reported sharing more of the child care tasks as a way of dealing with multiple role pressures. Additionally, stress is lower for men who have a flexible work schedule that allows them to care for sick children and other family matters. Together, these findings are encouraging; they indicate that more heterosexual dual-earner couples are learning how to balance work and family.

THINK ABOUT IT

How does the issue of dependent care relate to the level of work-family stress felt by women?

This study also indicates the importance of taking a life-stage approach (see Chapter 1) to work-family conflict (Blanchard-Fields, Baldi, & Constantin, in preparation). For example, several studies find that the highest conflict between the competing demands of work and family occurs during the peak parenting years when there are at least two preschool children in the home. Inter-role conflict diminishes in later life stages, especially when the quality of the marriage is high. Overall, it is important to note that perception of the quality of one's roles is a key indicator of whether one will experience work-family stress (Reid & Hardy, 1999).

Dual-earner couples often have difficulty finding time for each other, especially if both work long hours. The amount of time together is not necessarily the most important issue; as long as the time is spent in shared activities such as eating, playing, and conversing, couples tend to be happy (Jacobs & Gerson, 2001). Especially when both partners are employed, getting all the schedules to work together smoothly can be a major challenge.

Cross-cultural data show that burnout from work and parenting is more likely to affect women. A study of dual-earner married couples in Singapore showed that wives are more likely to suffer from burnout than husbands; wives' burnout resulted from both work and nonwork stress, whereas husbands' burnout resulted only from work stress (Aryee, 1993). Japanese career women's job satisfaction declines and turnover becomes more likely to the extent they have high work-family conflict (Honda-Howard & Homma, 2001). Research comparing sources of work-family conflict in the United States and China reveals that work demand does not differ, indicating that work pressure is a significant source of work-family conflict in both countries (Yang et al., 2000).

So exactly what effects do family matters have on work performance and vice versa? Evidence suggests that our work-family conflict is a major source of stress in couples' lives. In general, women feel the work-to-family spillover to a greater extent than men, but both men and women feel the pressure (Gutek, Searle, & Klepa, 1991).

TEST YOURSELF

1. Parents report lower work-family conflict and have lower absenteeism when supervisors are sympathetic and supportive regarding _____.

2. Research indicates that _____ increases greatly for working women with each additional child.

What should organizations do to help ease work-family conflict?

Answers: (1) family issues and child care, (2) stress

13.5

Time to Relax: Leisure Activities

LEARNING OBJECTIVES

■ What activities are leisure activities? How do people choose among them?

■ What changes in leisure activities occur with age?

■ What do people derive from leisure activities?

> **Time to Relax: Leisure Activities**
>
> Types of Leisure Activities
>
> Developmental Changes in Leisure
>
> Consequences of Leisure Activities

Claude is a 55-year-old electrician who has enjoyed outdoor activities his whole life. From the time he was a boy, he has fished and water-skied on the West Coast. Although he doesn't compete in slalom races any more, Claude still skis regularly, and he participates in fishing competitions every chance he gets.

Adults do not work every waking moment of their lives. As each of us knows, we need to relax sometimes and engage in leisure activities. Intuitively, leisure consists of activities not associated with work. *More formally, researchers define* **leisure** *as discretionary activity that includes simple relaxation, activities for enjoyment, creative pursuits, and sensual transcendence* (Gordon, Gaitz, & Scott, 1976). However, men and women differ in their views of leisure, as do people in different ethnic groups (Henderson, 1990). For example, one study of African-American women revealed that they view leisure as both freedom from the constraint of needing to work and as a form of self-expression (Allen & Chin-sang, 1990).

TYPES OF LEISURE ACTIVITIES

Leisure can include virtually any activity. To organize the options, researchers have classified leisure activities into four categories: cultural—such as attending sporting events, concerts, church services, and meetings; physical—such as basketball, hiking, aerobics, and gardening; social—such as visiting friends and going to parties; and solitary—including reading, listening to music, and watching television (Glamser & Hayslip, 1985). Leisure activities can also be considered in relation to the degree of cognitive, emotional, or physical involvement; backpackers like those in the photograph on page 480 would have high activity in all three areas.

An alternative approach to classifying leisure activities involves the classic distinction between preoccupations and interests (Rapoport & Rapoport, 1975). Preoccupations are much like daydreaming. Sometimes, preoccupations become more focused and are converted to interests. Interests are ideas and feelings about things you would like to do, are curious about, or are attracted to. Jogging, surfing the web, fishing, and painting are some examples of interests.

Rapoport and Rapoport's distinction draws attention to a key truth about leisure: Any specific activity has different meaning and value, depending on the individual involved. For example, cooking a gourmet meal is an interest, or a leisure activity, for many people. For professional chefs, however, it is work and thus is not leisure at all.

Given the wide range of options, how do people pick their leisure activities? Apparently, each of us has a leisure repertoire, a personal library of intrinsically motivated activities that we do regularly (Mobily, Lemke, & Gisin, 1991). The activities in our repertoire are determined by two things: perceived competence (how good we think we are at the activity compared to other people our age) and psychological comfort (how well we meet our personal goals for performance). Other factors are important as well: income, interest, health, abilities, transportation, education, and social characteristics. For example, some leisure activities, such as downhill skiing, are relatively expensive and require transportation and reasonably good health and physical coordination for maximum enjoyment. In contrast, reading requires minimal finances (if one uses a public library) and is far less physically demanding. Women in all ethnic groups tend to participate less in leisure activities that involve physical activity (Eyler et al., 2002).

The use of computer technology in leisure activities has increased dramatically (Bryce, 2001). Most usage involves either electronic mail or the World Wide Web for such activities as keeping in touch with family and friends, pursuing hobbies, and lifelong learning. Adults of all ages use computers for leisure, but this trend is growing especially quickly among middle-aged and older adults.

DEVELOPMENTAL CHANGES IN LEISURE

Cross-sectional studies report age differences in leisure activities. Young adults participate in a greater range of activities than middle-aged adults. Furthermore, young adults tend to prefer intense leisure activities, such as scuba diving and hang gliding. In contrast, middle-aged adults focus more on home- and family-oriented activities. In later middle age, they spend less of their leisure time in strenuous physical activities and more in sedentary activities such as reading and watching television. People of all ages report feelings of freedom during leisure activities (Larson, Gillman, & Richards, 1997).

Longitudinal studies of changes in individuals' leisure activities over time show considerable stability over reasonably long periods (Cutler & Hendricks, 1990).

Claude, the 55-year-old in the vignette who likes to fish and ski, is a good example of this overall trend. As Claude demonstrates, frequent participation in leisure activities during childhood tends to continue into adulthood. Similar findings hold for the pre- and post-retirement years. Apparently, one's preferences for certain types of leisure activities are established early in life; they tend to change over the life span primarily in how physically intense they are.

CONSEQUENCES OF LEISURE ACTIVITIES

What do people like the woman in the photograph gain from participating in leisure activities? Researchers have long known that involvement in leisure activities is related to well-being (Kelly, Steinkamp, & Kelly, 1987). Research shows that participating in leisure activities helps promote better mental health in women (Ponde & Santana, 2000) and, as discussed in the Forces in Action feature, buffers the effects of stress and negative life events.

FORCES IN ACTION

How Do You Spell Relief?

You have probably felt the real benefits of leisure activities yourself—the really relaxing feeling you have after a week at your favourite beach, the way your mind gets cleared after a few days in Jasper National Park looking at nature, or the reconnection you get with yourself and your family after spending time together doing something fun. Perhaps without realizing it, you have experienced the outcomes researchers have investigated concerning leisure.

Studies show that leisure activities provide an excellent forum for the interaction of biological, psychological, and sociocultural forces (Kleiber, Hutchinson, & Williams, 2002).

Leisure activities are a good way to deal with stress, which as we have seen has significant biological effects. This is especially true for unforeseen negative events (Janoff-Bulman & Berger, 2000). Psychologically, leisure activities have been well documented as one of the primary coping mechanisms people use (Iwasaki & Mannell, 2000; Kleiber et al., 2002). How people cope using leisure varies across cultures depending on the various types of leisure activities that are permissible and available. Likewise, leisure activities vary across social class; basketball is one activity that cuts across class because it is inexpensive, whereas downhill skiing is more associated with people who can afford to get to ski resorts and pay the fees.

How do leisure activities provide protection against stress? Kleiber and colleagues (2002) offer four ways leisure activities serve as a buffer against negative life events:

- Leisure activities distract us from negative life events.
- Leisure activities generate optimism about the future because they are pleasant.
- Leisure activities connect us to our personal past by allowing us to participate in the same activities over much of our lives.

- Leisure activities can be used as vehicles for personal transformation.

Whether the negative life events we experience are personal, such as the loss of a loved one, or societal, such as a terrorist attack, leisure activities are a common and effective way to deal with them. They truly represent the confluence of biopsychosocial forces, and they are effective at any point in the life cycle.

Participating with others in leisure activities may also strengthen feelings of attachment to one's partner, friends, and family (Carnelley & Ruscher, 2000). Adults use leisure as a way to explore interpersonal relationships or to seek social approval. In fact, some research suggests that marital satisfaction is helped more when couples spend some leisure time with others than if they spend it just as a couple (Shebilske, 2000).

But what if leisure activities are pursued very seriously? In some cases, people create leisure-family conflict by engaging in leisure activities to extremes (Goff, Fick, & Opplinger, 1997). Only when there is support from others for such extreme involvement are problems avoided (Goff et al., 1997). As in most things, moderation in leisure activities is probably best.

THINK ABOUT IT

What can employers do to address the post-vacation workload problem?

You have probably heard the saying that "no vacation goes unpunished." It appears to be true. Workers report that the high levels of post-vacation workload eliminate most of the positive effects of vacation (Strauss-Blasche, Ekmekcioglu, & Marktl, 2002). Restful vacations do not prevent declines in mood or in sleep due to one's post-vacation workload.

One often overlooked outcome of leisure activity is social acceptance. For persons with disabilities, this is a particularly important consideration (Devine & Lashua, 2002). There is a positive connection between frequency of leisure activities and social acceptance, friendship development, and acceptance of differences. These findings highlight the importance of designing inclusive leisure activity programs.

TEST YOURSELF

1. Preoccupations are conscious mental absorptions, whereas interests are _____.

2. Compared to younger adults, middle-aged and older adults prefer leisure activities that are more family- and home-centred and _____.

3. Being involved in leisure activities is related to _____.

How are choices of leisure activities related to physical, cognitive, and social development?

Answers: (1) focused preoccupations, (2) less physically intense, (3) well-being

PUTTING IT ALL TOGETHER

Sigmund Freud once said that the two most important aspects of adulthood are love and work. In this chapter, we have seen how pervasive work is in our lives and how it is affected by many things. The occupation Monique ultimately chooses is partly influenced by talents or skills she may have inherited from her parents, the kind of environment in which she grew up, and the match between her personality style and her occupational skills.

We saw that occupational development is not an inevitable outcome of hard work. Unfortunately, the world of work also reflects the biases, prejudices, and discrimination people face in the world at large. Janice found that being a woman and a member of an ethnic minority may make it difficult to achieve the levels of advancement in her career that she truly deserves.

Work spills over into our personal lives too. Fred and others like him worry about job security, and this sometimes affects home life. Although retraining may be an option, it may not alleviate all the concerns. Dual-earner couples are forced to think about how to divide household tasks to maintain balance. Jennifer and her husband are struggling with this issue; too often, women perform most of the chores at home.

But a life that is all work and no play is dull. Just as children need a certain amount of play for their development, adults like Claude find playful outlets through leisure activities. Such activities may be as quiet as reading a book or as daring as skydiving, but being able to do something besides work gives these activities value.

SUMMARY

13.1 Occupational Selection and Development

The Meaning of Work

- Although most people work for money, other reasons are highly variable. Occupational priorities have changed over time; younger workers' expectations from their occupations are now lower, and their emphasis on personal growth potential is higher.

Occupational Development

- Super's developmental view of occupations is based on self-concept and adaptation to an occupational role. Super describes five stages in adulthood: implementation, establishment, maintenance, deceleration, and retirement.
- Reality shock is the realization that one's expectations about an occupation are different from the reality one experiences. Reality shock is common among young workers.
- A mentor is a co-worker who teaches a new employee the unwritten rules and fosters occupational development. Mentor-protégé relationships develop over time, through stages, like other relationships.

Job Satisfaction

- Older workers report higher job satisfaction than younger workers, but this may be partly due to self-selection; unhappy workers may quit. Other reasons include intrinsic satisfaction, good fit, lower importance of work, finding nonwork diversions, and life-cycle factors.

- Alienation and burnout are important considerations in understanding job satisfaction. Both involve significant stress for workers.

13.2 Gender, Ethnicity, and Discrimination Issues

Gender Differences in Occupational Selection

- Women who choose nontraditional occupations may still be viewed with disapproval by their peers of either sex, even though they have high job satisfaction themselves.

Women and Occupational Development

- Women leave well-paid occupations for many reasons, including family obligations and workplace environment. Women who continue to work full-time have adequate child care and look for ways to further their occupational development.

Ethnicity and Occupational Development

- Vocational identity and vocational goals vary in different ethnic groups. Whether an organization is sensitive to ethnicity issues is a strong predictor of satisfaction among ethnic minority employees.

Bias and Discrimination

- Sex discrimination remains the chief barrier to women's occupational development. In many cases, this operates as a glass ceiling. Pay inequity is also a problem; women are often paid less than men in similar jobs.
- Sexual harassment is a problem in the workplace.
- Denying employment to anyone because of age is age discrimination.

13.3 Occupational Transitions

Retraining Workers

■ To adapt to the effects of a global economy and an aging workforce, many corporations are providing retraining opportunities for workers. Retraining is especially important in cases of outdated skills and career plateauing.

Occupational Insecurity

■ Important reasons people change occupations include personality, obsolescence, and economic trends. Occupational insecurity is a growing problem. Fear that one may lose one's job is a better predictor of anxiety than the actual likelihood of job loss.

Coping with Unemployment

■ Job loss is a traumatic event that can affect every aspect of a person's life. Degree of financial distress and the extent of attachment to the job are the best predictors of distress.

13.4 Work and Family

The Dependent Care Dilemma

■ Whether a woman returns to work after having a child depends largely on how attached she is to her work. Simply providing child care on-site does not always result in higher job satisfaction. The more

important factor is the degree to which supervisors are sympathetic.

Juggling Multiple Roles

■ Although women have reduced the amount of time they spend on household tasks over the past two decades, they still do most of the work.

■ Flexible work schedules and number of children are important factors in role conflict. Recent evidence shows that work stress has a much bigger impact on family life than family stress has on work performance. Some women pay a high personal price for having careers.

13.5 Time to Relax: Leisure Activities

Types of Leisure Activities

■ Preoccupations can become more focused as interests, which can lead to the selection of particular leisure activities. People develop a repertoire of preferred leisure activities.

Developmental Changes in Leisure

■ As people grow older, they tend to engage in leisure activities that are less strenuous and more family-oriented. Leisure preferences in adulthood reflect those earlier in life.

Consequences of Leisure Activities

■ Leisure activities enhance well-being and can benefit all aspects of people's lives.

KEY TERMS

vocational maturity (454)
dream (455)
job satisfaction (457)
alienation (459)

burnout (460)
sex discrimination (465)
glass ceiling (465)
comparable worth (466)

age discrimination (468)
career plateauing (471)
work-family conflict (477)
leisure (479)

SEE FOR YOURSELF: APPLYING WHAT YOU'VE LEARNED

Before reading about the research findings on the types of things people do for fun, try to find out as much about them as possible on your own. Here's an easy way. Ask several of your friends, as well as adults of different ages, what their current favourite leisure activities are. Ask your parents, their friends, your grandparents, your adult children if you have any, and

so on to get a good cross-section of ages. Once you have a list of current favourites, ask them what their favourites were 10 years ago. Now compare the lists and see for yourself; which activities changed and which did not? Compare your results to the research described in the text, and discuss the similarities and differences in class.

LEARN MORE ABOUT IT

Readings

BOLLES, R. N. (2001). *The 2002 what color is your parachute: A practical manual for job-hunters and career changers*. Berkeley, CA: Ten Speed Press. This popular reference is a valuable resource for people in search of careers. It is regularly updated.

BOLTON, M. K. (2000). *The third shift: Managing hard choices in our careers, homes, and lives as women*. San Francisco: Jossey-Bass. Discusses the decisions that factor into women's decisions to have careers and families based on a longitudinal study.

COLTRANE, S. (1996). *Family man: Fatherhood, housework, and gender equity*. New York: Oxford University Press. Examines men's family roles from a scholarly, research-based approach.

DUXBURY, L. E., HIGGINS, C., & COGHILL, D. (2003). *Voices of Canadians: Seeking work-life balance*. Hull, Quebec: Human Resources Development Canada, Labour. This report is a compilation based on the comments of 10,000 Canadian workers dealing with the stress of balancing home and work.

SBRAGA, T. P., & O'DONOHUE, W. (2000). Sexual harassment. *Annual Review of Sex Research, 11*, 258–285. A superb review of the history of sexual harassment writings in the psychology and legal literatures.

VANNOY, D., & DUBECK, P. (1998). *Challenges for work and family in the twenty-first century*. New York: Aldine & Gruyter. Explores issues and changes in family life, especially the stresses of inter-role conflict.

WILLIAMS, M. E., STALCUP, B., & SWISHER, K. (Eds.). (1998). *Working women: Opposing viewpoints*. San Diego, CA: Greenhaven Press. Essays from scholars and journalists on both sides of work-family issues.

 For additional readings, explore InfoTrac® College Edition, your online library. Go to http://www.infotrac.thomsonlearning.com.

Websites

http://www.monster.com

Monster.com provides a broad range of services for people looking for a job and employers looking for potential employees. They also provide help with creating a résumé, salary data, and information about companies.

http://www.hrsdc.gc.ca/en/home.shtml

The Government of Canada - Human Resources and Skills Development Canada website is current, comprehensive, and user-friendly. This government department is responsible for providing Canadians with the tools they need to thrive and prosper in the workplace and community.

http://www.swc-cfc.gc.ca/

The website of Status of Women Canada (SWC) is an informational link to the federal government department that promotes gender equality and the full participation of women in the economic, social, cultural, and political life of the country. SWC focuses its work in three areas: improving women's economic autonomy and well-being, eliminating systemic violence against women and children, and advancing women's human rights.

http://www.vifamily.ca

The Vanier Institute of the Family website is a current and comprehensive resource related to Canadian families, based on research from Statistics Canada.

Website addresses are subject to change. The *Human Development* book companion website can be accessed for updated links.

The Human Development Book Companion Website

See http://www.humandevelopment.nelson.com for practice quiz questions, Internet links, updates, critical thinking exercises, discussion forums, and more.

 ### Life-Span CD-ROM

For more information on the concepts covered in this chapter, go to

Module 5: Early and Middle Adulthood

• Emotional and Social Development

Module 6: Late Adulthood

• Emotional and Social Development

Getty Images

CHAPTER 14

Making It in Midlife

THE UNIQUE CHALLENGES OF MIDDLE ADULTHOOD

There's an old saying that life begins at 40. That's good news for middle-aged adults. As we will see, they face many stressful events, but they also leave many of the pressures of young adulthood behind. In many respects, middle age is the prime of life: People's health is generally good and their earnings at their peak.

Of course, during middle age people typically get wrinkles, grey hair, and a bulging waistline. But middle-aged adults also achieve new heights in cognitive development, change their behaviour if they choose, develop adult relationships with their children, and ease into grandparenthood. Along the way, they must deal with stress, changes in the way they learn, and the challenges of dealing with their aging parents.

Some of these issues are based more on stereotypes than on hard evidence. Which is which? You will know by the end of the chapter.

14.1

Physical Changes and Health

LEARNING OBJECTIVES

- How does appearance change in middle age?
- How do bone and joint problems affect women and men in middle age?
- What reproductive changes occur in men and women in middle age?
- What is stress? How does it affect physical and psychological health?
- What benefits are there to exercise?

> **Physical Changes and Health**
> Changes in Appearance
> Changes in Bones and Joints
> Sensory Changes
> Reproductive Changes
> Stress and Health
> Exercise

By all accounts, Sean is extremely successful. Among other things, he became the head of a moderate-sized manufacturing firm by the time he was 43. Sean has always considered himself to be a rising young star in the company. Then one day he found more than the usual number of hairs in his brush. "Oh no!" he exclaimed. "I can't be going bald! What will people think?" What does Sean think about these changes?

The reality of middle age generally strikes early one morning in the bathroom mirror. Standing there, staring through half-awake eyes, you see *it*. One solitary grey hair, or one tiny wrinkle at the corner of your eye, or, like Sean, some excess hairs falling out, and you worry that your youth is gone, your life is over, and you will soon be acting the way your parents did when they totally embarrassed you in your younger days. Middle-aged people become concerned that they are over the hill, sometimes going to great lengths to prove that they are still vibrant.

Crossing the boundary to middle age in North America is typically associated with turning 40 (or the big four-oh, as many people term it). This event is frequently marked with a special party as shown in the photograph. Often the party has an "over the hill" motif. Such events are society's attempt at creating a rite of passage between youth and maturity.

As people move into middle age, they begin experiencing some of the physical changes associated with aging. In this section, we focus on the ones most obvious in middle-aged adults: appearance, reproductive capacity, and stress and coping. In Chapter 15, we will consider changes that may begin in middle age but are usually not apparent until later in life, such as slower reaction time and sensory changes. A critical factor in setting the stage for healthy aging is living a healthy lifestyle in young adulthood and middle age. Eating a healthy diet and exercising regularly across adulthood can help reduce the chances of chronic disease later in life (Leventhal et al., 2002).

Romilly Lockyer/Image Bank

CHANGES IN APPEARANCE

On that fateful day when the hard truth stares at you in the bathroom mirror (as for the person in the photograph on page 489), it probably doesn't matter to you that getting wrinkles and grey hair is universal and inevitable. Wrinkles are caused by changes in the structure of the skin and its connective and supporting tissues, as well as the cumulative effects of damage from exposure to sunlight and smoking cigarettes (Whitbourne, 1996). It may not make you feel better to know that grey hair is perfectly natural and caused by a normal cessation of pigment production in hair follicles (Kenney, 1982). Male pattern baldness, a genetic trait in which hair is lost progressively begin-

ning with the top of the head, often begins to appear in middle age (Whitbourne, 1996). No, the scientific evidence that these changes occur to many people isn't what matters most. What matters is that these changes are affecting *you*.

To make matters worse, you may have also noticed that your clothes aren't fitting properly, even though you watch what you eat. You remember a time not very long ago when you could eat whatever you wanted; now it seems that as soon as you look at food you put on weight. Your perceptions are correct; most people gain weight between their early 30s and mid-50s, producing the infamous "middle-aged bulge" as metabolism slows down (Whitbourne, 1996).

People's reactions to these changes in appearance vary. Sean wonders how people will react to him now that he's balding. Some people rush out to purchase hair colouring and wrinkle cream. Others just take it as another stage in life. You've probably experienced several different reactions yourself. There is a wide range of individual differences, especially between men and women and across cultures.

CHANGES IN BONES AND JOINTS

Another physical change is loss of bone mass, a potentially serious problem. Bone mass peaks in one's 20s, and then declines with age (Weldon, 1997). Loss of bone mass makes bones weaker and more brittle, thereby making them easier to break. Because there is less bone mass, bones also take longer to heal in middle-aged and older adults. *If the loss of bone mass is severe, the disease* **osteoporosis** *results; as you can see in Figure 14.1, bones become porous like honeycombs and extremely easy to break.* In severe cases, osteoporosis can cause spinal vertebrae to collapse, causing the person to stoop and to become shorter as shown in Figure 14.2 (Masi & Bilezikian, 1997; Weldon, 1997). Osteoporosis is the leading cause of broken bones in older women (Ebersole & Hess, 1998). Although the severe

FIGURE 14.1   Loss of Bone Mass in Osteoporosis

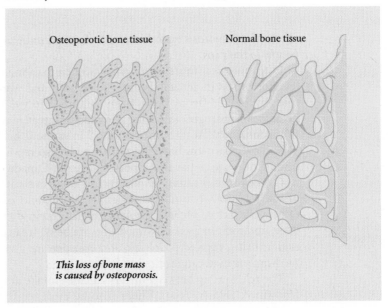

Osteoporotic bone tissue   Normal bone tissue

This loss of bone mass is caused by osteoporosis.

FIGURE 14.2   Compression of Vertebrae Due to Osteoporosis

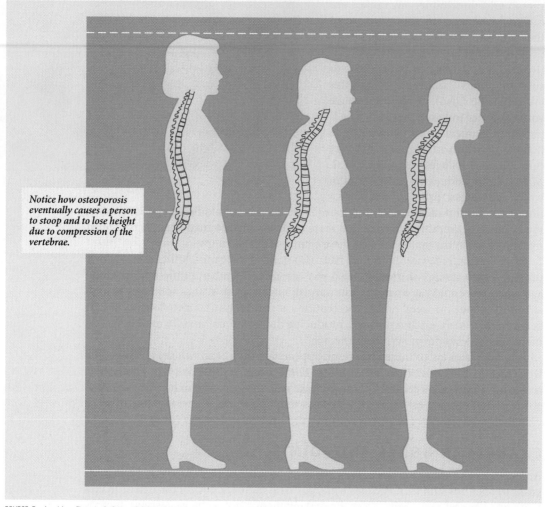

Notice how osteoporosis eventually causes a person to stoop and to lose height due to compression of the vertebrae.

SOURCE: Reprinted from Ebersole, P., & Hess, P. (1998). *Toward healthy aging* (5th ed., p. 395), with permission from Elsevier Science.

effects of osteoporosis typically are not observed until later life, this disease can occur in people in their 50s.

Osteoporosis is more common in women than men, largely because women have less bone mass in general, because some girls and women do not consume enough calcium to build strong bones from childhood to young adulthood, and because the decrease in estrogen following menopause greatly accelerates bone loss (Masi & Bilezikian, 1997). According to a Canadian women's health study 46% of women aged 50 and over have low bone mass. The study also reports that 16% of women and 7% of men over age 50 have osteoporosis (Health Canada, 2003i).

Osteoporosis is caused in part by low bone mass at skeletal maturity, deficiencies of calcium and vitamin D, estrogen depletion, and lack of weight-bearing exercise. Other risk factors include smoking, high-protein diets, and excessive alcohol, caffeine, and sodium intake. Women who are being treated for asthma, cancer, rheumatoid arthritis, thyroid problems, and epilepsy are also at increased risk because the medications used can lead to loss of bone mass.

The relationship between dietary calcium intake and osteoporosis is controversial (Aldwin & Gilmer, 1999). There is some evidence that calcium supplements after menopause may slow the rate of bone loss and delay the onset of osteoporosis, but benefits appear to be greater when the supplements are provided before menopause (Plosker & McTavish, 1996). The reasons estrogen depletion affects bone loss are not fully understood, mainly because the effects must be indirect because there are no estrogen receptors in bone tissue. Although estrogen replacement therapy may slow bone loss, this approach must be used cautiously because of potential side effects (Kawas et al., 1997). (We explore hormone replacement therapy in detail later in the chapter when we consider reproductive changes in women.) Additionally, estrogen therapy must be continued indefinitely because bone loss speeds up as soon as the therapy is stopped.

Data showing that vitamin D metabolism plays a causative role in osteoporosis are clear; however, whether supplementary dietary vitamin D retards bone loss is less certain. Some research shows that vitamin D administered after menopause slows bone loss, whereas other research does not (Dawson Hughes, 1996). To reduce the risk of osteoporosis dietary, drug, and activity approaches are recommended. People should eat foods high in calcium (such as milk, cheese, and yoghurt), reduce alcohol intake, drink caffeine moderately, and take calcium supplements if necessary. Recommended calcium intakes for men and women of various ages are shown in Table 14.1. Some evidence supports the view that oral ingestion of magnesium, zinc, vitamin K, and special forms of fluoride may also be effective. There is also some evidence that regular exercise is beneficial, but results vary depending on the type and intensity of the regimen. The best results come from a regular regimen of moderate aerobic exercise.

TABLE 14.1	Recommended Calcium Intakes
Children and young adults	**Amount (mg/day)**
1-8 years	500 to 800
9-18 years	1300
Adult women and men	
19-50	1000
51 - >70	1200
Pregnant and Lactating Women	
<18 years	1300
19-50	1000

Source: Food and Nutrition Board Canada, 1997.

You may have heard some of the claims about using human growth hormone to treat various problems related to changes in the muscles and bones. Some researchers have found positive effects of human growth hormone in studies of normal aging (Welle et al., 1996). But most studies have failed to support the advertised benefits (Taaffe et al., 1996) and some have found harmful side effects such as increased risk of breast cancer (Dorgan et al., 1997).

Many middle-aged adults complain of aching joints. They have good reason. Beginning in the 20s, the protective cartilage in joints shows signs of deterioration, such as thinning and becoming cracked and frayed. *Over time the bones underneath the cartilage become damaged, which can result in* **osteoarthritis,** *a disease marked by gradual onset and progression of pain and disability, with minor signs of inflammation* (Ettinger, 1995). The disease usually becomes noticeable in late middle age or early old age, and it is especially common in people whose joints are subjected to routine overuse and abuse, such as athletes and manual labourers. Thus, osteoarthritis is a wear-and-tear disease. Pain typically is worse when the joint is used, but skin redness, heat, and swelling are minimal or absent. Osteoarthritis usually affects the hands, spine, hips, and knees, sparing the wrists, elbows, shoulders, and ankles. Effective management approaches consist mainly of certain steroids and anti-inflammatory drugs, rest and nonstressful exercises that focus on range of motion, diet, and a variety of homeopathic remedies.

A second form of arthritis is **rheumatoid arthritis,** *a more destructive disease of the joints that also develops slowly and typically affects different joints and causes different types of pain than osteoarthritis* (Ettinger, 1995). Most often, a pattern of morning stiffness and aching develops in the fingers, wrists, and ankles on both sides of the body. Joints appear swollen. The typical therapy for rheumatoid arthritis consists of aspirin or other nonsteroidal anti-inflammatory drugs. Rest and passive range-of-motion exercises are also helpful. Contrary to popular belief, rheumatoid arthritis is not contagious, hereditary, or self-induced by any known diet, habit, job, or exposure. Interestingly, the symptoms often come and go in repeating patterns.

SENSORY CHANGES

Most people, once they are in their 40s, are likely to notice some changes in their vision, especially when reading small print. These changes become more pronounced as we age; they will be discussed in more detail in Chapter 15. Essentially, due to a decreased ability of the muscles around the lens to adjust and focus, *presbyopia,* or the difficulty in seeing close objects clearly, occurs, necessitating either corrective lenses or longer arms. It's not uncommon for individuals to obtain their first pair of reading glasses during this period and to require brighter light for reading. In addition, the length of time our eyes need to change focus from near to far (or vice versa) increases (Fozard & Gordon-Salant, 2001).

Hearing loss, one of the most common age-related changes, may also start during mid-life (Whitbourne, 1999). Presbycusis, a reduced ability to hear high-pitched sounds, is the result of specific age-related changes in the inner ear (detailed in Chapter 15) as well as exposure to the cumulative effects of noise. Although hearing loss will occur for both sexes, it is greater for men than women on average (see Figure 15.5).

REPRODUCTIVE CHANGES

Besides changes in the way we look, middle age brings transitions in our reproductive systems. These changes differ dramatically for women and men. Even in the context of these changes, though, middle-aged adults continue to have active sex lives. In fact, 73% of men and 69% of women between the ages of 40 and 49, and 67% of men and 48% of women between 50 and 59 have sex at least several times a month (Michael et al., 1994). The declines in frequency of sexual activity with age reflect complex biopsychosocial factors, including physiological changes, the stresses of everyday life, and negative social stereotypes about sex and growing older (Michael et al., 1994).

The Climacteric and Menopause

For women, middle age brings a major biological change: the loss of the ability to bear children through natural means. *This process, termed the* **climacteric,** *usually begins in the 40s and is usually complete by the late 50s.* The length of time it takes for all of the reproductive changes to occur differs considerably from woman to woman; for some it takes only a year or two, but others may experience more gradual changes for a decade. The most important change during the climacteric is a dramatic drop in the production of estrogen, the primary female hormone (Whitbourne, 1999).

During the climacteric, menstruation becomes irregular and eventually stops; this specific change is termed **menopause.** Although some women stop menstruating between their late 30s and early 40s, and others may still be having regular periods in their mid-50s, most women have their last period in their early 50s. However, ovulation may continue for a year or two after the last period; thus, women who do not want to risk pregnancy should continue to use contraceptives for this length of time. *The time from when the first symptoms of menopause start until menopause occurs is termed **perimenopause**, a process which may take months or years. The time following completion of menopause is termed **postmenopause**.*

Researchers have identified two primary sets of symptoms associated with the climacteric and menopause (DeAngelis, 1997). *Estrogen-related symptoms include hot flashes, night sweats, vaginal dryness, and frequent urination, which are due to the rapid drop in estrogen. **Somatic symptoms** include difficulty sleeping, headaches, rapid heartbeat, and stiffness or soreness in the joints, neck, or shoulders.*

Women's genital organs undergo progressive change after menopause (Whitbourne, 1999). The vaginal walls shrink and become thinner, the size of the vagina decreases, vaginal lubrication is reduced and delayed, and some shrinkage of the external genitalia occurs. These changes may have important effects on sexual activity, such as an increased possibility of painful intercourse. Use of water-soluble vaginal lubricant or prescription estrogen vaginal cream may help alleviate symptoms. However, maintaining an active sex life throughout adulthood lowers the degree to which problems are encountered.

Despite the physical changes, there is no physiological reason most women cannot continue sexual activity and enjoy it well into old age. Whether this happens depends more on the availability of a suitable partner than on a woman's desire for sexual relations. This is especially true for older women. The AARP *Modern Maturity* sexuality study (AARP, 1999) found that older married women were far more likely to have an active sex life than unmarried women. The primary reason for the decline in women's sexual activity with age is the lack of a partner, not a lack of physical ability or desire (AARP, 1999).

Recent advances in reproductive technology have enabled women who have undergone the climacteric to have children. As discussed in the Current Controversies feature, such births force us to rethink the meaning of the climacteric.

CURRENT CONTROVERSIES

Having Babies After Menopause

Reproductive technology such as fertility drugs and in vitro fertilization (see Chapter 2) has made it possible for postmenopausal women to have children. Indeed, in 1997 Rosanno Dalla Corta, a 63-year-old woman from Viterbo, Italy, gave birth to a baby conceived through in vitro fertilization. Scientists have thus fundamentally changed the rules of reproduction. Even though a woman has gone through the climacteric, she can still have children. Technology can make her pregnant, if she so chooses and if she has access to the proper medical centres.

What does this do to our understanding of human reproduction? It changes the whole notion of menopause representing an absolute end to childbearing. Some of the women who have given birth after menopause have done so because their daughters were unable to

have children; they consider this act another way to show their parental love. Others view it as a way to equalize reproductive potential in middle age between men and women, as men remain fertile throughout adulthood.

Clearly, these are complicated issues that currently affect a very small number of women. But as reproductive technology continues to advance faster than our ability to think through the issues, we will be confronted with increasingly complex ethical questions (Lindlaw, 1997). Should children be born to older parents? Might not there be some advantage, considering the life experience such parents would have, compared to young parents? Are such births merely selfish acts? Are they a viable alternative way for younger adults to have a family? What dangers are there to older pregnant women? How do you feel about it?

Treating Symptoms of Menopause

The decline in estrogen that women experience after menopause is related to increased risk of osteoporosis, cardiovascular disease, stress urinary incontinence, weight gain, and memory loss (Lichtman, 1996; Mayo Clinic, 2000b; Sherwin, 1997). In the case of cardiovascular disease, before they turn 50, women are three times less likely to have heart attacks than men. Ten years after menopause, when women are about 60, their risks equal that of men.

*Due to these increased risks, and the estrogen-related symptoms women experience, many physicians and researchers advocate the use of **hormone replacement therapy (HRT)**, in which women take low doses of estrogen, which is often combined with progestin.* HRT is controversial and has been the focus of many research studies (Krauss, 2002; Sagraves, 2001). There appear to be both benefits and risks with HRT.

THINK ABOUT IT

Why does sexual desire remain largely unchanged despite the biological changes that are occurring?

It has been well documented for decades that HRT reduces the estrogen-related symptoms described earlier. More recent evidence indicates that HRT also reduces the risk of osteoporosis (Sagraves, 2001). Although there is a belief that HRT reduces the risk of cardiovascular disease, evidence is mixed. Some studies find no evidence that HRT protects against cardiovascular disease (Krauss, 2002; Welty, 2001). Other research shows that HRT may lower the level of low-density lipoproteins (LDL, or so-called bad cholesterol) and raise high-density lipoproteins (HDL, or so-called good cholesterol) in some women (Skegg, 2001). Results also indicate that HRT helps maintain short- and long-term memory (Sherwin, 1997), although other research shows no effect of HRT on reasoning (Bertrand, Lachman, & Tun, 2000). There are suggestive data that HRT may have a role in helping prevent Alzheimer's disease (Henderson, 1997; Simpkins et al., 1997).

Despite these benefits, HRT can have drawbacks. The primary concerns are increased risk of endometrial cancer (cancer in the lining of the uterus) and breast cancer, especially after being on HRT for 10 or more years (Lichtman, 1996; Sagraves, 2001). Fortunately, the risk of endometrial cancer is greatly reduced when HRT is based on a lower dosage of estrogen combined with progestin (Mahvani & Sood, 2001). A comprehensive review of research from 1975 to 2000 concerning breast cancer and HRT revealed no increase in risk in breast cancer from using HRT (Bush, Whiteman, & Flaws, 2001). A new medication, selective estrogen receptor modulators (SERMs), is a group of "designer estrogens" that have the beneficial effects of estrogen but no increased risks for either cancer or uterine bleeding; however, they may cause hot flashes and increase the risk for blood clots and gallstones (Mayo Clinic, 2000b).

Health Canada continues to monitor the benefits and risks associated with HRT. Combined estrogen and progestin are not recommended to be used as long-term therapy because the health risks in women over the age of 65 have been found to outweigh the benefits (Health Canada, 2004a).

Alternative approaches to addressing both estrogen-related and somatic symptoms are gaining in popularity (Soffa, 1996). Herbal remedies, especially those rich in phytoestrogens (such as soybeans, chickpeas, and other legumes), used effectively in Asian cultures, may be one reason Asian-American women report fewer symptoms of menopause (DeAngelis, 1997).

Reproductive Changes in Men

Unlike women, men do not have a physiological (and cultural) event to mark reproductive changes. Men do not experience a complete loss of the ability to have children. However, men do experience a normative decline in the quantity of sperm (Lewis, 1995). Sperm production declines by approximately 30% between ages 25 and 60 (Whitbourne, 1996). However, even at age 80 a man is still half as fertile as he was at age 25 and is quite capable of fathering a child.

With increasing age the prostate gland enlarges, becomes stiffer, and may obstruct the urinary tract. Prostate cancer becomes a real threat during middle age. The Canadian Cancer Society (2004) recommends that once men reach the age of 50 they should discuss with their doctor testing for prostate cancer by using a blood test to check for Prostate Specific Antigen (PSA) and digital rectal examinations (DRE). In addition, men who may be at higher risk due to family history of cancer or men of African ancestry may want to consider screening at an earlier age. Although prostate cancer is not caused by enlargement (indeed, the cause is unknown), enlargement may be misdiagnosed as cancer unless more careful diagnostic tests are performed (Calciano et al., 1995), and therefore routine DREs are seen as controversial because of the possibility of "false positive" results.

The majority of men show a gradual reduction in testosterone levels after the mid-20s (Whitbourne, 1996). However, some men who experience an abnormally rapid decline in testosterone production during their late 60s report symptoms similar to those experienced by some menopausal women, such as hot flashes, chills, rapid heart rate, and nervousness (Mayo Clinic, 2000a). Some physicians label this drop *andropause* and consider it a male parallel to menopause. When testosterone levels decline significantly, some men opt for testosterone replacement therapy (TRT). Long-term benefits and risks of TRT have not been studied in detail.

Men experience some physiological changes in sexual performance. By old age, men report less perceived demand to ejaculate, a need for longer time and more stimulation to achieve erection and orgasm, and a much longer resolution phase during which erection is impossible (Saxon & Etten, 1994). Older men also report more frequent failures to achieve orgasm and loss of erection during intercourse (AARP, 1999). However, the advent of the drug Viagra in 1998, which helps men achieve and maintain an erection, has provided a medical treatment for erectile dysfunction.

As with women, as long as men enjoy sex and have a willing partner, sexual activity is a lifelong option. As for women, the most important ingredient of sexual intimacy for men is a strong relationship with a partner (AARP, 1999).

STRESS AND HEALTH

There's no doubt about it—life is full of stress. Look at the man in the photograph and think for a moment about all the things that bother you, such as exams, jobs, relationships, and finances. For most people, this list lengthens quickly. But, you may wonder, isn't this true for people of all ages? Is stress more important in middle age?

Although stress affects people of all ages, it is during middle age that the effects of both short- and long-term stress become most apparent. In part, this is because it takes time for stress disorders to manifest themselves, and in part it is due to the gradual loss of physical capacity, as the normal changes accompanying aging begin to take their toll. As we will see, psychological factors play a major role as well.

You may think that stress affects health mainly in people who hold certain types of jobs, such as air traffic controllers, high-level business executives, and textbook authors. In fact, business executives actually have *fewer* stress-related health problems than waitresses, construction workers, secretaries, laboratory technicians, machine operators, farm workers, and painters (McEwen, 1998; Smith et al., 1978). What do all of these truly high-stress jobs have in common? These workers have little direct control over their jobs.

Although we understand some important workplace factors related to stress, our knowledge is largely based on research examining middle-aged men. Unfortunately, the relation of stress to age, gender, and ethnic status remains to be researched. Canadian women reported more stress than did men but for both sexes stress levels were higher among the less educated, less affluent, and previously married (Statistics Canada, 2004). Part of the reason that middle-aged adults feel stress may be due to the number of pressures in their lives: children may be in university or college, the job has high demands, the mortgage payment and other bills always need paying, the marriage needs some attention, the in-laws would like to visit, and on it goes.

What Is Stress?

Think about the last time you felt stressed. What was it about the situation that made you feel stressed? How did you feel? *The answers to questions like these provide a way to understand the dominant framework used to study stress, the **stress and coping paradigm**.* Because the stress and coping paradigm emphasizes the transactions between a person and the environment, it fits well with the biopsychosocial framework. An example of a transactional model of stress is shown in Figure 14.3.

Physiologically, stress refers to a number of specific changes in the body (e.g., increased heart rate, sweaty palms, hormone secretion; McEwen, 1998). In the short run, stress can be beneficial and may even enable you to perform at your peak. In the long run, though, a high physical toll and even death may result (McEwen, 1998).

FIGURE 14.3   Transactional Model of Stress

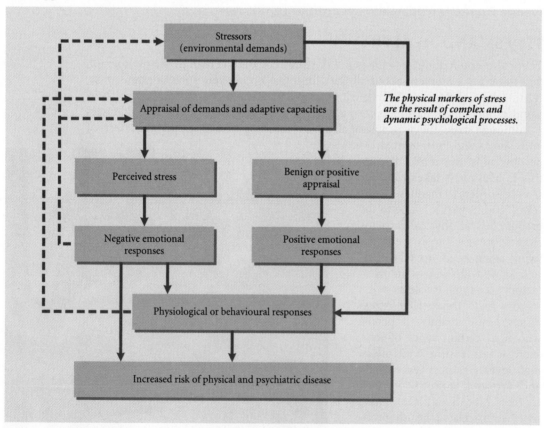

SOURCE: From *Measuring stress: A guide for health and social scientists,* edited by Sheldon Cohen, Kessler, and Gordon, copyright © 1995 by Oxford University Press, Inc. Used by permission of Oxford University Press, Inc.

Whether you report feeling stressed depends on how you interpret a situation or an event (Lazarus & Folkman, 1984). What the situation or event is, or what you do to deal with it, does not matter. *Stress results when you **appraise** a situation or event as taxing or exceeding your personal, social, or other resources and endangering your well-being. It is the day-to-day **hassles,** or the things that upset and annoy us, that prove to be particularly stressful.*

Interestingly, culture plays an important role in how people perceive stress (Laungani, 2001). These differences are grounded in the values people hold. For example, what constitutes stressors varies a great deal between Eastern societies such as India and Western societies such as England. Indians tend to believe that much of life is determined, whereas the British tend to emphasize personal choice and free will. Consequently, frustrations that Britons may feel when free will is thwarted may not be perceived as stressful by those from India. These differences point out the importance of understanding a culture when studying a concept such as stress.

Coping is any attempt to deal with stress. People cope in several different ways (Ishler et al., 1998). Sometimes people cope by trying to solve the problem at hand; for example, you may cope with a messy roommate by moving out. At other times, people focus on how they feel about the situation and deal with things on an emotional level; feeling sad after breaking up with your partner would be one way of coping with the stress of being alone. Sometimes people cope by simply redefining the event as not stressful—saying that it was no big deal that you failed to get the job you wanted would be an example of this approach. Still others focus on religious or spiritual approaches, perhaps asking God for help.

People appraise different types of situations or events as stressful at different times during adulthood. For example, the pressures from work and raising a family are typically greater for younger and middle-aged adults than for older adults. However, stressors due to chronic disease are often more important to older adults than to their younger counterparts. Similarly, the same kind of event may be appraised differently at different ages. For example, uncertainty about one's job security may be less stressful in young adulthood, when one might get another job more easily, than in middle age, when alternative job prospects might diminish. From a biopsychosocial perspective, such life-cycle factors must be taken into account when considering what kinds of stress adults of different ages are experiencing.

> **THINK ABOUT IT**
>
> How might life experience and cognitive developmental level influence the appraisal of and coping with stress?

How Are Stress and Coping Related to Physical Health?

A great deal of research has been conducted over the years examining links between stress and physical health. Being under chronic stress suppresses the immune system, resulting in increased susceptibility to viral infections, increases risk of atherosclerosis and hypertension, and impaired memory and cognition (Davis, McKay, & Eshelman, 2000). However, these effects depend on the kind of event (Cohen & Hebert, 1996). Experiencing negative events results in lower immune function (Stone et al., 1994). Likewise, experiencing positive events seems to improve immune functioning (Stone et al., 1994). Although the links between stress and immune system functioning are becoming well established, it remains to be seen whether stress-reduction techniques can reverse the effects of negative events (Cohen & Hebert, 1996).

Many specific diseases and conditions are caused or exacerbated by stress (WebMD, 2000). Stress serves as a major trigger for angina, causes arrhythmias, causes blood to become stickier (making it more likely to cause a clot in an artery), raises cholesterol, reduces estrogen in women, increases production of certain proteins that damage cells, causes sudden increases in blood pressure, increases the risk of irritable bowel syndrome, causes weight fluctuations, is associated with the development of insulin resistance (a primary factor in diabetes), causes tension headaches, causes sexual dysfunction and infertility, and results in poorer memory and cognitive performance. Clearly, chronic stress is harmful to one's health!

Surprisingly, little research has been conducted testing whether successful coping strategies reverses these health effects of stress. At best, we can only surmise that if stress causes these health problems then effective coping strategies may prevent them.

How Are Stress and Coping Related to Behaviour and Psychological Health?

Probably the best-known connection between stress and behaviour involves the link with cardiovascular disease. Due mostly to the pioneering work of Friedman and Rosenman (1974), we know that two behaviour patterns differ dramatically with regard to the risk of cardiovascular disease. *People who demonstrate a **Type A behaviour pattern** tend to be intensely competitive, angry, hostile, restless, aggressive, and impatient. In contrast, people who show a **Type B behaviour pattern** tend to be just the opposite.* Type A individuals are at least twice as likely as Type B people to develop cardiovascular disease, even when other risk factors such as smoking and hypertension are taken into account. In fact, Type A behaviour is a more important predictor than body weight, alcohol intake, or activity level (Zmuda et al., 1997).

How do these behaviour types relate to *recovery* from a heart attack? Although it is relatively rare, Type B people sometimes do have heart attacks. Who recovers better, Type A people or Type B people?

The answer may surprise you. In a classic study, Ragland and Brand (1988) conducted a 22-year longitudinal follow-up of the original Friedman and Rosenman study and discovered that Type A people recover from a heart attack better than Type B people. Why? Some of the characteristics of being Type A may help motivate people to stick to diet and exercise regimens after heart attacks and to have a more positive attitude toward recovery (Ivancevich & Matteson, 1988). Indeed, although the anger and hostility components of Type A behaviour increase the risk for cardiovascular disease, the other components appear to aid the recovery process (Ivancevich & Matteson, 1988). In contrast, the laid-back approach to life of Type B people may work against them during recovery.

Although experiencing stress is not directly related to psychopathology, it is associated with other psychological processes. For example, chronic stress related to financial pressures and fear of crime promotes social isolation and distrust of others in some adults (Krause, 1991). Thus, although stress does not directly cause psychopathology, it does influence how people behave. For example, the stress many people experienced after the terrorist attacks of September 11, 2001, resulted in higher levels of anxiety experienced through nightmares, flashbacks, insomnia, traumatic grief, emotional numbing, and avoidance (LeDoux & Gorman, 2001).

Data examining ethnic group differences highlight the importance of self-esteem. For example, a U.S. study of Latin-American professionals showed that self-esteem predicted overall stress, marital stress, family-cultural conflict, and occupational-economic stress (Arellano, 2001). Additionally, results indicated that emotion-focused coping reflects Western concepts and that other traditional approaches to coping do not capture the dynamic process of coping that these women showed. Mexican immigrant farm workers who reported high levels of stress due to cultural pressures also reported lower levels of self-esteem and higher levels of symptoms of depression (Hovey & Magana, 2000). Cross-cultural research in Hong Kong indicates that with increased age the effects of stress on one's well-being is reduced (Siu et al., 2001). This could be a result of people learning how to cope better as they gain experience in dealing with stress.

Another way to lessen the effects of stress is to disclose and discuss one's health problems (Pennebaker, 1999). For example, women who disclosed the fact that they have breast cancer, which was a source of considerable stress in their lives, had more optimism and lower reported levels of stress than women who did not disclose their disease (Henderson et al., 2002). How people disclose such information matters. Pennebaker and Graybeal (2001) showed that particular patterns of word use can be analyzed by a computer to predict health and personality style. Such analyses may prove useful to physicians and clinicians in providing guidance to individuals who need help in discussing stressful situations.

EXERCISE

Ever since the time of Hippocrates, physicians and researchers have known that exercise significantly slows the aging process. Indeed, evidence suggests that a program of regular exercise, in conjunction with the healthy lifestyles we discussed in Chapter 11, can slow the physiological aging process (Whitbourne, 1999). Being sedentary is hazardous to your health.

Adults benefit from **aerobic exercise**, *which places moderate stress on the heart by maintaining a pulse rate between 60 and 90% of the person's maximum heart rate.* You can calculate your maximum heart rate by subtracting your age from 220. Thus, if you are 40 years old, your target range would be 108–162 beats per minute. The minimum time necessary for aerobic exercise to be of benefit depends on its intensity; at low heart rates, sessions may need to last an hour, whereas at high heart rates, 15 minutes may suffice. Examples of aerobic exercise include jogging, step aerobics, swimming, and cross-country skiing.

What happens when a person exercises (besides becoming tired and sweaty)? According to Health Canada (2003e), endurance activities help heart, lungs, and the circulatory system, which gives more energy. Activities that involve flexibility help a person move more easily, help relax the muscles, and keep joints mobile. Strength activities help muscles and bones remain strong, improve posture, and help prevent diseases such as osteoporosis and colon cancer. Psychological benefits include reduced anxiety and stress and improved confidence and self-esteem (Health Canada, 2003e).

The best way to gain the benefits of aerobic exercise is to maintain physical fitness throughout the life span, beginning at least in middle age like the people in the photograph. According to Canada's Physical Activity Guide it is recommended that people accumulate a half to a full hour of moderate physical activity each day. One suggestion to getting started is to climb stairs whenever possible, as the person's physical condition allows. It is important before starting a physical activity program that your health be assessed by a physician. A study of nearly 17,000 middle-aged and older men found that those who exercised moderately (walked 14 kilometres per week or cycled for six to eight hours per week) had a 21 to 50% lower risk of dying in the next year than men who did not exercise, whereas men who exercised strenuously (walked 32 kilometres per week or cycled more than 15 hours per week) had a significantly

Ryan McVay/Getty Images

higher risk of dying than men who exercised moderately. Third, the reasons people exercise change during adulthood. Younger adults tend to exercise to improve their physical appearance, whereas middle-aged and older adults are more concerned with physical and psychological health (Trujillo, Walsh, & Brougham, 1991).

TEST YOURSELF

1. Severe bone loss may result in the disease
_____.

2. The cessation of menstruation is termed
_____.

3. Reduction of fertility in men usually
occurs _____.

4. The stress and _____ paradigm
defines stress on the basis of the person's
appraisal of a situation as taxing his or
her well-being.

5. Research indicates that Type
_____ individuals have a better
chance of recovering from a heart attack
than Type _____ individuals.

The media are full of advertisements for
anti-aging creams, diets, and exercise
plans. Based on what you have read in
this section, how would you evaluate
these ads?

Answers: (1) osteoporosis, (2) menopause, (3) gradually, (4) coping, (5) A, B

14.2

Cognitive Development

LEARNING OBJECTIVES

▶ How does practical intelligence develop in adulthood? What
are the developmental trends of exercised and unexercised
abilities?

▶ How does a person become an expert?

▶ What is meant by lifelong learning? What differences are there
between adults and young people in how they learn?

Cognitive Development
Practical Intelligence
Becoming an Expert
Lifelong Learning

*Kesha, a 54-year-old social worker, is widely regarded as the resident expert when it
comes to working the system of human services. Her co-workers look up to her for her
ability to get several agencies to cooperate, which they do not do normally, and to keep
clients coming in for routine matters and follow-up visits. Kesha claims there is nothing
magical about it—it's just her experience that makes the difference.*

Compared to the rapid cognitive growth of childhood, or the controversies about
post-formal cognition in young adulthood, cognitive development in middle age is
relatively quiet. For the most part, the trends in intellectual development discussed in
Chapter 11 are continued and solidified. The hallmark of cognitive development in
middle age involves developing higher levels of expertise, such as Kesha shows, and
flexibility in solving practical problems, such as dealing with complex forms like the
tax form shown in Figure 14.4. We will also see how important it is to continue
learning throughout adulthood.

PRACTICAL INTELLIGENCE

Take a moment to think about the following problems (Denney, 1989, 1990; Denney,
Pearce, & Palmer, 1982).

▶ A middle-aged woman is frying chicken in her home when, all of a sudden, a
grease fire breaks out on top of the stove. Flames begin to shoot up. What
should she do?

▶ A man finds that the heater in his apartment is not working. He asks his landlord to send someone out to fix it, and the landlord agrees. But after a week

FIGURE 14.4   Income Tax and Benefit Return

Canada Customs and Revenue Agency. Reproduced with permission of the Minister of Public Works and Government Services Canada, 2004.

of cold weather and several calls to the landlord, the heater is still not fixed. What should the man do?

These practical problems are different from the examples of measures of fluid and crystallized intelligence in Chapter 11. These problems are more realistic; they reflect real-world situations that people routinely face. One criticism of traditional measures of intelligence is that they do not assess the kinds of skills adults actually use in everyday life (Diehl, 1998). Most people spend more time at tasks such as managing their personal finances, dealing with uncooperative people, and juggling busy schedules than they do solving esoteric mazes.

The shortcomings of traditional approaches to testing adults' intelligence led to different ways of viewing intelligence that differentiate academic (or traditional) intelligence from other skills (Sternberg & Grigorenko, 2000b). *The broad range of skills related to how individuals shape, select, or adapt to their physical and social environments is termed **practical intelligence**.* The examples at the beginning of this section illustrate how practical intelligence is measured. Such real-life problems differ in three main ways from traditional tests (Diehl, 1998): People are more motivated to solve them; personal experience is more relevant; and they have more than one correct answer. Research evidence supports the view that practical intelligence is distinct from general cognitive ability (Taub et al., 2001).

Denney's Theory

Denney (1982) postulated that performance on tests of practical intelligence depends on two different components whose developmental trends are shown in Figure 14.5. *The bottom red line represents **unexercised ability**, the level of performance a person exhibits without practice or training.* Unexercised abilities are those that are not used very often, are not well developed, or are called upon to handle new situations. For example, when you are presented with a problem you have never seen before, the cognitive skills you bring to bear are your unexercised abilities. Unexercised abilities reflect the lower limit to your ability to perform cognitive problems. Notice that performance on traditional laboratory tasks, such as those included in many intelligence tests, closely approximates unexercised ability.

*The green line represents **optimally exercised ability**, the level of performance a normal, healthy adult demonstrates under the best conditions of training or practice.* Optimally exercised abilities are those you use the most, or ones you have practised the most. Problems that tap these abilities are typically performed accurately and more quickly than those that test unexercised abilities, as you can see by comparing the orange line with the purple line in the figure. Optimally exercised abilities, then, reflect areas in which you have greater expertise.

FIGURE 14.5   Tests of Practical Intelligence

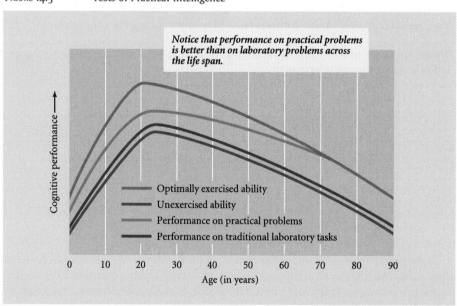

Notice that performance on practical problems is better than on laboratory problems across the life span.

Optimally exercised ability
Unexercised ability
Performance on practical problems
Performance on traditional laboratory tasks

SOURCE: From "Aging and Cognitive Changes," by N. W. Denney. In B. B. Wolman (Ed.), *Handbook of Developmental Psychology*, p. 821. Copyright © 1982. Reprinted by permission of Prentice Hall, Inc., Upper Saddle River: NJ.

Whether a specific ability is unexercised or optimally exercised varies from individual to individual; for example, one person may have little training in computer programming, whereas the leader of a programming team at Microsoft would be highly skilled. Thus, how an ability is classified depends on the person's experience and expertise; it is not a property of the skill in question. This is an important distinction, as it means that interventions such as additional practice or education could shape the developmental trajectory of a particular ability.

The developmental course of unexercised and optimally exercised abilities is the same: They increase until young adulthood, plateau through middle age, and decline thereafter. As shown in the figure, the difference between performance on practical problems and optimally exercised ability is hypothesized to close rapidly during middle age. But do the data support Denney's speculations?

When people's answers to practical problems are evaluated by how likely their answers are to be effective, practical intelligence does not appear to decline appreciably until late life (Heidrich & Denney, 1994). Diehl (1998) and Allaire and Marsiske (1999) showed that practical intelligence is related to psychometric intelligence; to the extent that everyday problems reflect well-structured challenges in daily life, how well people deal with them is related to traditional psychometric abilities.

Applications of Practical Intelligence

Practical intelligence and post-formal thinking across adulthood have been linked (Blanchard-Fields, Janke, & Camp, 1995). Specifically, the extent to which a practical problem evokes an emotional reaction, in conjunction with experience and one's preferred mode of thinking, determines whether one will use a cognitive analysis (thinking one's way through the problem), a problem-focused action (tackling the problem head-on by doing something about it), passive-dependent behaviour (withdrawing from the situation), or avoidant thinking and denial (attempting to manage the meaning of the problem). For late middle-aged adults, highly emotional problems are associated most with passive-dependent and avoidant-denial approaches. Interestingly, though, problems that deal more with instrumental issues such as consumer questions and home management are dealt with differently (Blanchard-Fields, Chen, & Norris, 1997). Middle-aged adults use problem-focused strategies more frequently in dealing with instrumental problems than do adolescents or young adults. Clearly, we cannot characterize problem solving in middle age in any one way.

Other research has shown connections between practical intelligence and the Russians' ability to deal with rapid change (Grigorenko & Sternberg, 2001), and leaders' ability to convince people that their vision is where people need to go (Sternberg, 2002). Practical intelligence has also emerged as an important approach in assessing adults' competence in performing everyday tasks. The Observed Tasks of Daily Living (OTDL) test assesses food preparation, medication intake, and telephone use, three key skills necessary for independent living (Diehl, Willis, & Schaie, 1995). The OTDL is a useful tool in determining whether adults are capable of living on their own. We will learn more about this issue in Chapter 16 when we consider the topic of frail older adults.

THINK ABOUT IT 💡

How are cognitive analysis, problem-focused action, passive-dependent behaviour, and avoidant thinking and denial related to coping with stress?

When we combine the research on practical intelligence with the research on the components or mechanics of intelligence discussed in Chapter 11, we have a more complete description of cognition in adulthood. Most important, we have a better understanding of how adult intelligence reflects the four developmental forces, as discussed in the Forces in Action feature.

FORCES IN ACTION

The Mechanics and Pragmatics of Intelligence

The two-component model of life-span intelligence (Baltes et al., 1998, 1999) is grounded in the dynamic interplay between biological, sociocultural, psychological, and life-cycle forces. However, as Baltes points out, these forces differentially influence the mechanics and pragmatics of intelligence. Whereas the mechanics of intelligence is more directly an expression of the neurophysiological architecture of the mind, the pragmatics of intelligence is associated more with the bodies of knowledge that are available from and mediated through one's culture (Baltes et al., 1998).

This is illustrated in the left portion of Figure 14.6. The mechanics of intelligence in later life is more associated with the fundamental organization of the central nervous system (i.e., biological forces). Thus, it is more closely linked with a gradual loss of brain efficiency with age (Horn & Hofer, 1992).

On the other hand, the pragmatics of intelligence is more closely associated with psychological and sociocultural forces. At the psychological level, knowledge structures change as a function of the accumulated acquisition of knowledge over time. At the sociocultural level, knowledge structures are also influenced by how we are socialized given the particular historical period in which we are raised. Overall, these knowledge structures influence the way we implement our professional skills, solve everyday problems, and conduct the business of life (Baltes et al., 1998; Staudinger, 1999).

Finally, as the right portion of the figure suggests, different weightings of the forces of intelligence lead to specific predictions about the developmental pathway they take across the adult life span. Given that biological and genetic forces govern the mechanics more, there is a downward trajectory with age. However, given that the pragmatics of intelligence is governed more by environmental and cultural factors, there is an upward trajectory that is maintained across the adult life span.

FIGURE 14.6

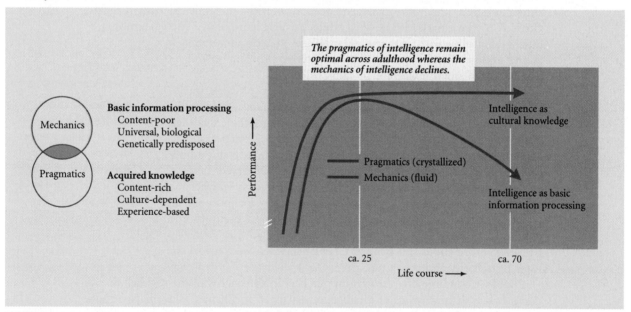

SOURCE: Baltes, P. B., Staudinger, U. M., and Lindenberger, U. (1999). *Lifespan psychology: Theory and application to intellectual functioning.* Reprinted with permission from the *Annual Review of Psychology.* Volume 50, 471–507, © 1999 by Annual Reviews, www.AnnualReviews.org.

BECOMING AN EXPERT

One day, John Cavanaugh was driving along when his car suddenly began coughing and sputtering. As deftly as possible, he pulled over to the side of the road, turned off the engine, opened the hood, and proceeded to look inside. It was hopeless; to him, it looked like a jumble of unknown parts. After the car was towed to a garage, a middle-aged mechanic set about fixing it. Within a few minutes, the car was running like new. How?

We saw in Chapter 11 that aspects of intelligence grounded in experience (crystallized intelligence) tend to improve throughout most of adulthood. Some developmentalists have gone so far as to claim that each of us becomes an expert at something that is important to us, such as our work, interpersonal relationships, cooking, sports, or auto repair (Dixon, Kramer, & Baltes, 1985). In this sense, an expert (like the mechanic, or Kesha, the social worker in the vignette) is someone who is much better at a task than people who have not put much effort into it (such as John Cavanaugh, with regard to auto repair). We tend to become selective experts in some areas while remaining rank amateurs or novices at others.

What makes experts like Kesha, whom we met in the vignette, better than novices? Most important, experts have built up a wealth of knowledge about alternative ways of solving problems or making decisions. These enable them to bypass steps needed by novices (Ericsson & Smith, 1991). Experts don't always follow the rules as novices do; they are more flexible, creative, and curious and have superior strategies for accomplishing a task (Charness & Bosman, 1990). Even though their raw speed may be slower because they spend more time planning, experts' ability to skip steps puts them at a decided advantage. In a way, this represents "the triumph of knowledge over reasoning" (Charness & Bosman, 1990).

Research evidence indicates that expert performance tends to peak in middle age and drop off slightly after that (Charness & Bosman, 1990). However, the declines in expert performance are not nearly as great as they are for the abilities of information processing, memory, and fluid intelligence that underlie expertise. Thus, it appears that knowledge based on experience is an important component of expertise.

THINK ABOUT IT

Can expertise be taught? Why or why not?

But why are expertise and information processing, memory, and fluid intelligence not strongly related? After all, we saw in Chapter 11 that the latter abilities underlie good cognitive performance. Rybash, Hoyer, and Roodin (1986) proposed a process called *encapsulation* as the answer. *Their notion is that the processes of thinking (information processing, memory, fluid intelligence) become connected or encapsulated to the products of thinking (expertise).* This process of encapsulation allows expertise to compensate for declines in underlying abilities, perhaps by making thinking more efficient (Hoyer & Rybash, 1994).

Let's consider how encapsulation might work with auto mechanics. As a rule, people who become auto mechanics are taught to think as if they were playing a game of Twenty Questions, in which the optimal strategy is to ask a question such that the answer eliminates half of the remaining possibilities. In the beginning, the mechanic learns the thinking strategy and the content knowledge about automobiles separately. But as the person's experience with repairing automobiles increases, the thinking strategy and content knowledge merge; instead of having to go through a Twenty Questions approach, the expert mechanic just "knows" how to proceed. This cognitive-developmental pattern in adults is very different from the one that occurs in children (Hoyer & Rybash, 1994). In the adult's case, development is directed toward mastery and adaptive competency in specific domains, whereas during childhood it is more uniform across content domains.

One of the outcomes of encapsulation appears to be a decrease in the ability to explain how one arrives at a particular answer (Hoyer & Rybash, 1994). It appears that the increased efficiency that comes through merging the process with the product of thinking comes at the cost of being able to explain to others what one is doing. This could be why some instructors have a difficult time explaining the various steps involved in solving a problem to novice students but have an easier time explaining it to graduate students who have more background and experience.

We will return to the topic of expertise in Chapter 15 when we discuss wisdom, which some believe to be the outcome of becoming an expert in living.

LIFELONG LEARNING

What do all of the people in the photographs have in common? They work in occupations in which information and technology change rapidly. To keep up with these changes, many organizations and professions now emphasize the importance of learning how to learn rather than learning specific content that may become outdated in a couple of years. For most people, a college education will probably not be the last educational experience they have in their careers. Workers in many professions, such as medicine, nursing, social work, psychology, and teaching, are now required to obtain continuing education credits to stay current in their fields. Online learning has made lifelong learning more accessible to professionals and interested adults alike (Fretz, 2001; Ranwez, Leidig, & Crampes, 2000).

The need for lifelong learning is obvious on most university campuses. You have probably seen middle-aged adults in your classes (or you may be one yourself). The story of one middle-aged student is presented in the Real People feature. Many post-secondary educators are including experiential elements in courses as a response to the need for real-world connections.

Lifelong learning takes place in settings other than university or college campuses too. Many organizations offer workshops for their employees on a wide range of topics, from specific job-related topics to leisure-time activities. Additionally, many channels on cable television offer educational programming, and online courses, computer networks, and bulletin boards are available for educational exchanges. Only a few generations ago, a high school education was the ticket to a lifetime of secure employment. Today, lifelong learning is rapidly becoming the norm.

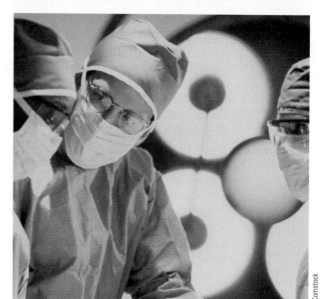

Lifelong learning is gaining acceptance as the best way to approach the need for continuing education and for retraining displaced workers. But should lifelong learning be approached as merely an extension of earlier educational experiences? Knowles (1984) argues that teaching aimed at children and youths differs from

REAL PEOPLE: APPLYING HUMAN DEVELOPMENT

University at Midlife

Patrice worked for a savings and loan company for 15 years, rising to the level of Vice President for Savings and Investment. Her achievement was even more remarkable because she had only a high school education. But when she wanted to change jobs, she ran into a cruel reality. Without a degree, she had little chance of getting another executive-level position, even with her 15 years of experience. So, at age 37, Patrice decided to quit her job and attend university.

Overcoming her fear that she couldn't compete with young adults was hard at first. Her reasons for being in school were much different from those of her younger classmates: Patrice was there for her self-esteem more than to please someone else. She found that

her life experience was an advantage; many students eventually looked up to her for her insights. Her study skills were different. She found it hard to learn information by rote memorization; instead, she emphasized how information fit together. Although grades were somewhat important to her, learning was her primary goal. She enjoyed seeing how she could apply knowledge learned in one class to another one, and professors expressed delight at having her in class.

After five and a half years, Patrice graduated with a degree in accounting. She distinguished herself by being on the dean's list every term, which really made her feel good about what she had accomplished. ▨

---

teaching aimed at adults. Adult learners differ from their younger counterparts in several ways:

- ▨ Adults have a higher need to know why they should learn something before undertaking it.
- ▨ Adults enter a learning situation with more and different experience on which to build.
- ▨ Adults are most willing to learn those things they believe are necessary to deal with real-world problems rather than abstract, hypothetical situations.
- ▨ Most adults are more motivated to learn by internal factors (such as self-esteem or personal satisfaction) than by external factors (such as a job promotion or pay raise).

Lifelong learning is becoming increasingly important, but educators need to keep in mind that learning styles change as people age.

TEST YOURSELF

1. The skills and knowledge necessary for people to function in everyday life make up _____.

2. The difference between performance on practical problems and optimally exercised ability is hypothesized to _____ during middle age.

3. Even though they may be slower in raw speed, experts are at a distinct advantage over novices because they _____.

4. The way in which the process of thinking becomes connected to the products of thinking is termed _____.

5. Due to rapidly changing technology and information, many educators now support the concept of _____.

Based on the cognitive-developmental changes described in this section, what types of jobs would be done best by middle-aged adults?

Answers: (1) practical intelligence, (2) narrow, (3) can skip steps, (4) encapsulation, (5) lifelong learning

14.3

Personality

LEARNING OBJECTIVES

▪ What is the five-factor model? What evidence is there for stability in personality traits?

▪ What changes occur in people's priorities and personal concerns? How does a person achieve generativity? How is midlife best described?

Jim showed all the signs. He divorced his wife of nearly 20 years to enter into a relationship with a woman 15 years younger, sold his ordinary-looking midsize sedan for a red sports car, and began working out regularly at the health club after years of being a couch potato. Jim claims he hasn't felt this good in years; he is happy to be making this change in middle age. All of Jim's friends agree: This is a clear case of midlife crisis. Or is it?

The topic of personality development in middle age immerses us in one of the hottest debates in theory and research in adult development and aging. Take Jim's case. *Many people believe strongly that middle age brings with it a normative crisis called the* **midlife crisis.** There would appear to be lots of evidence to support this view based on case studies like Jim's. But is everything as it seems? We'll find out in this section.

Unlike most of the other topics we have covered in this chapter, research on personality in middle-aged adults is grounded in several competing theories, like the psychoanalytic approach we encountered in Chapter 1. Another difference is that much of the research we will consider is longitudinal research, which was also discussed in Chapter 1.

First, we examine the evidence that personality traits remain fairly stable in adulthood. This position makes the claim that what you are like in young adulthood predicts pretty well what you will be like the rest of your life. Second, we consider the evidence that people's priorities and personal concerns change throughout adulthood, requiring adults to reassess themselves from time to time. This alternative position claims that change is the rule during adulthood.

At no other point in the life span is the debate about stability versus change as heated as it is concerning personality in middle age. In this section, we consider the evidence for both positions.

STABILITY IS THE RULE: THE FIVE-FACTOR MODEL

One of the most important advances in research on adult development and aging in the past few decades has been the emergence of a personality theory aimed specifically at describing adults. Due mostly to the efforts of Paul Costa Jr. and Robert McCrae (1997), we are able to describe adults' personality traits using five dimensions: neuroticism, extraversion, openness to experience, agreeableness, and conscientiousness. These dimensions are strongly grounded in cross-sectional, longitudinal, and sequential research. First, though, let's take a closer look at each dimension.

▪ Neuroticism. *People who are high on the* **neuroticism** *dimension tend to be anxious, hostile, self-conscious, depressed, impulsive, and vulnerable.* They may show violent or negative emotions that interfere with their ability to get along with others or to handle problems in everyday life. People who are low on this dimension tend to be calm, even-tempered, self-content, comfortable, unemotional, and hardy.

▪ Extraversion. *Individuals who are high on the* **extraversion** *dimension thrive on social interaction, like to talk, take charge easily, readily express their opinions* *and feelings, like to keep busy, have boundless energy, and prefer stimulating and challenging environments.* Such people tend to enjoy people-oriented jobs, such as social work and sales, and they often have humanitarian goals. People who are low on this dimension tend to be reserved, quiet, passive, sober, and emotionally unreactive.

▥ Openness to experience. *Being high on the openness to experience dimension tends to mean a vivid imagination and dream life, appreciation of art, and a strong desire to try anything once.* These individuals tend to be naturally curious about things and to make decisions based on situational factors rather than absolute rules. People who are readily open to new experiences place a relatively low emphasis on personal economic gain. They tend to choose jobs such as the ministry or counselling, which offer diversity of experience rather than high pay. People who are low on this dimension tend to be down-to-earth, uncreative, conventional, uncurious, and conservative.

▥ Agreeableness. *Scoring high on the agreeableness dimension is associated with being accepting, willingness to work with others, and caring.* Interestingly, people who score low on this dimension (i.e., demonstrate high levels of *antagonism*) show many of the characteristics of the Type A behaviour pattern discussed earlier in this chapter. They tend to be ruthless, suspicious, stingy, antagonistic, critical, and irritable.

▥ Conscientiousness. *People who show high levels of conscientiousness tend to be hard-working, ambitious, energetic, scrupulous, and persevering.* Such people have a strong desire to make something of themselves. People at the opposite end of this scale tend to be negligent, lazy, disorganized, late, aimless, and nonpersistent.

What's the Evidence for Trait Stability?

Costa and McCrae, as well as other researchers, have examined whether their dimensions of personality remain stable through adulthood. In one study (Costa, McCrae, & Arenberg, 1980), more than 100 men were tested three times, with each of the follow-up tests about six years apart. Even over a 12-year span, the personality trait dimensions examined remained very stable.

Was this finding a fluke? Apparently not. Other researchers find similar stability over eight-year spans (Siegler, George, & Okun, 1979) and even 30-year spans (Leon et al., 1979). Even spouses' ratings of their partner's personality traits showed no systematic changes over a six-year period (Costa & McCrae, 1988). Thus, it looks like people's personality traits change little over very long periods of time.

Although the five-factor model enjoys great popularity and appears to have much supporting evidence, it is not perfect. Some writers have argued that the findings of stability are due to statistical artifacts and that more carefully designed research is needed (Alwin, 1994; Block, 1995). Others point out that the five-factor model does not explain human behaviour, ignores the sociocultural context in which development occurs, and reduces a person to scores on five dimensions anchored by terms that are assumed to be both meaningful and opposite (McAdams, 1992). Some data also indicate that certain personality traits (self-confidence, cognitive commitment, outgoingness, and dependability) show some change over a 30- to 40-year period (Jones & Meredith, 1996). Women tend to show some change in middle adulthood in response to specific changes in social roles (Labouvie-Vief & Diehl, 1999; Van Manen & Whitbourne, 1997).

Even acknowledging the problems, though, evidence for overall stability in personality traits across adulthood is a very important finding, especially considering the many life situations that do change (e.g., getting married, changing jobs, having children leave home). One way to view this evidence is that the traits

THINK ABOUT IT 🔍

Does very long-term stability in traits support the idea that some aspects of personality are genetic? Why or why not?

described by Costa and McCrae only provide the building blocks of one's personality (McAdams, 1992). In this view, the raw material on which personality is built remains relatively constant. But, as we will see next and again in Chapter 15, what a person chooses to do with these building blocks, and the behaviours based on them, may not be as consistent.

CHANGE IS THE RULE: CHANGING PRIORITIES IN MIDLIFE

Joyce, a 52-year-old preschool teacher, thought carefully about what she thinks is important in life. "I definitely feel differently about what I want to accomplish. When I was younger, I wanted to advance and be a great teacher. Now, although I still want to be good, I'm more concerned with providing help to the new teachers around here. I've got lots of on-the-job experience that I can pass along."

Joyce is not alone. Despite the evidence that personality traits remain stable during adulthood, many middle-aged people report that their personal priorities change during middle age. In general, they report that they are increasingly concerned with helping younger people achieve rather than with getting ahead themselves. *In his psychosocial theory, Erikson argued that this shift in priorities reflects* **generativity,** *or being productive by helping others to ensure the continuation of society by guiding the next generation.*

Achieving generativity can be very enriching. It is grounded in the successful resolution of the previous six phases of Erikson's theory (see Chapter 1). There are many avenues for generativity, such as parenting (Pratt et al., 2001), mentoring (Lucas, 2000; see Chapter 12), volunteering, foster grandparent programs, and many other activities. Sources of generativity do not vary across ethnic groups (Ellen, 2000).

Some adults do not achieve generativity. Instead, they become bored, self-indulgent, and unable to contribute to the continuation of society. *Erikson referred to this state as* **stagnation,** *in which people are unable to deal with the needs of their children or to provide mentoring to younger adults.*

What Are Generative People Like?

In order to describe generativity so that we can recognize it in someone, several researchers have constructed various research-based descriptions of it (Washko, 2001). One of the best is McAdams's model (McAdams, 2001; McAdams, Hart, & Maruna, 1998), shown in Figure 14.7. This multidimensional model shows how generativity results from the complex interconnections among societal and inner forces, which create a concern for the next generation and a belief in the goodness of the human enterprise, leading to generative commitment, which produces generative actions. A person derives personal meaning from being generative by constructing a life story, or narration, which helps create the person's identity (Whitbourne, 1996; see Chapter 11).

The components of McAdams's model relate differently to personality traits. For example, generative *concern* relates to life satisfaction and overall happiness, whereas generative *action* does not (de St. Aubin & McAdams, 1995). New grandparents may derive much satisfaction from their grandchildren and are greatly concerned with their well-being but have little desire to engage in the daily hassles of caring for them on a regular basis. Women who exhibit high generativity tend to have prosocial personality traits, are personally invested in being a parent, express generative attitudes at work, and exhibit caring behaviours toward others outside their immediate families (Peterson & Klohnen, 1995), as well as show high well-being in their role as a spouse (MacDermid, De Haan, & Heilbrun, 1996). These results have led to the creation of positive and negative generativity indices that reliably identify differences between generative and nongenerative individuals (Himsel et al., 1997).

The growing evidence on generativity indicates that the personal concerns and priorities of middle-aged adults are different from those of younger adults. But is this

FIGURE 14.7   **McAdams's Model of Generativity**

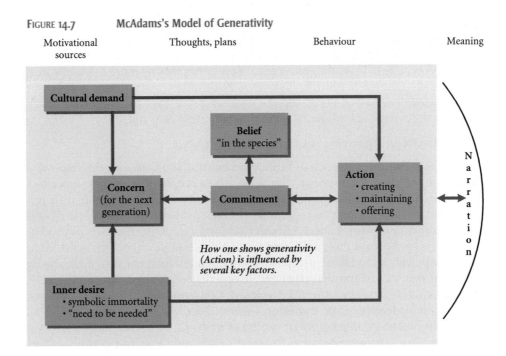

view supported in other aspects of personality? Let's consider gender-role identity as an example.

Does Gender-Role Identity Converge?

People's beliefs about the appropriate characteristics for men and women reflect shared cultural beliefs and stereotypes of "masculinity" and "femininity" (Williams & Best, 1990).

As we know, the five-factor model makes a strong case for the stability of personality traits throughout adulthood. In contrast, we have seen that people's priorities and personal concerns change during adulthood. Does stability or change describe what happens to gender-role identity?

Beginning with Jung (1960/1933), several researchers and theorists argue for a "crossover effect" of gender identity during middle age. Specifically, Jung (1960/1933) proposed that certain aspects of personality are suppressed in adolescence and young adulthood, only to reemerge during middle age. For example, Jung believed women initially suppress their masculine aspects and men initially suppress their feminine aspects; each discovers these suppressed aspects and develops them in midlife, with the goal of achieving a balance between one's masculine and feminine characteristics. For example, during midlife women may place increased emphasis on achievement and accomplishment, and men may place more emphasis on familial and nurturant concerns (Parker & Aldwin, 1997). Women also report more identity certainty and confident power in midlife than in young adulthood (Stewart, Ostrove, & Helson, 2001).

Overall, the data on actual changes in people's gender-role identity are mixed. Some studies find a tendency for middle-aged and older adults to endorse similar self-descriptions concerning gender-role identity. For example, some research indicates that both men and women describe themselves as more nurturing, intimate, and tender with increasing age (Gutmann, 1987; Sinnott, 1986), trends that are related to generativity. Other studies show decreasing endorsement of traditional feminine traits in both men and women, but stable endorsements of masculine traits (Parker & Aldwin, 1997). Collectively, the data indicate that men and women are most different in their gender-role identities in late adolescence and young adulthood but become increasingly similar in midlife and old age (Huyck, 1990).

Increasing similarity in self-descriptions does not guarantee increased similarity in the way men and women behave. For example, older men often indicate a willingness to develop close relationships, but few actually do because they lack the necessary skills (Turner, 1982). Thus, the convergence may be happening more internally than behaviourally (Parker & Aldwin, 1997; Troll & Bengtson, 1982). Does gender-role identity converge? At this point, the statistical evidence appears to indicate that it does, but the behavioural evidence appears to indicate it does not.

Life Transition Theories and the Midlife Crisis

We have seen that theorists such as Erikson believe that adults face several important challenges and that by struggling with these issues people develop new aspects of themselves. Erikson's notion that people experience fundamental changes in their priorities and personal concerns was grounded in the possibility that middle adulthood includes other important changes. Indeed, Carl Jung, one of the founders of psychoanalytic theory, believed that adults may experience a midlife crisis. This belief led to the development of several theories postulating that adulthood consists of alternating periods of stability and transition that people experience in a fixed sequence.

Levinson and colleagues (1978; Levinson & Levinson, 1996), Gould (1978), and Vaillant (1977) developed life transition theories based on longitudinal studies of fairly exclusive and nonrepresentative groups of adults (in some cases only men) over several decades. Data were gathered mainly through interviews and personal reflections of the participants. These approaches led to a popularization of "midlife crisis" so that most people thought that people like Jim, the recently divorced guy with the red sports car in the vignette, was typical. Indeed, few people in North America would have difficulty providing an example, as most people believe that a midlife crisis is inevitable. In part, this belief is fostered by descriptions of personality development in adulthood that have appeared in the popular press.

Despite the popularity of these theories, some of which were turned into bestselling books, the evidence for universal age-related stages is based on far fewer and much more selective samples than are the data from the personality trait research or research on generativity. For several decades the bulk of the research evidence fails to support the idea that most adults experience difficulty at the level of a crisis in midlife. Research involving women and men, using a variety of methods such as interviews and personality tests, shows that unexpected events (such as divorce or job transfers) are much more likely to create stress than are normative midlife events (such as menopause or becoming a grandparent). In fact, it may be the case that those who do experience a crisis are those who are suffering from general problems of psychopathology (Labouvie-Vief & Diehl, 1999). Reanalysis and extension of Costa and McCrae's data, specifically looking for evidence of a midlife crisis, revealed only a handful of men who fit the classic profile, and even then the crisis came anywhere between the ages of 30 and 60 (Rosenberg, Rosenberg, & Farrell, 1999). There may be universal stresses during midlife, but there is no set way of dealing with them (Rosenberg et al., 1999).

Is there a midlife crisis? The evidence indicates that for most people, midlife is no more or no less traumatic than any other period. Even investigators who believed strongly in the existence of a midlife crisis when they began their research admitted that they could find no support for it despite extensive testing and interviewing (Rosenberg et al., 1999). Thus, Jim's behaviour may have an explanation, but it's not because he's going through a universal midlife crisis.

Despite the lack of evidence for a universal midlife crisis, as we saw in our consideration of generativity, there is substantial evidence that people do experience some sort of fundamental change in themselves at some point during adulthood. Thus, it may well be that most adults pass through transitions at some point; when those transitions will occur, though, is largely unpredictable. Perhaps a better way to view midlife is as a time that presents unique challenges and issues that must be negotiated (Bumpass & Aquilino, 1995).

If midlife is not characterized by a crisis but does present unique challenges and issues, how do people negotiate it successfully? *The secret seems to be **ego resilience,** a powerful personality resource that enables people to handle midlife changes.* Longitudinal data from two samples indicate that people who enter middle age with high ego resilience are more likely to experience it as an opportunity for change and growth, whereas people with low ego resilience are more likely to experience it as a time of stagnation or decline (Klohnen, Vandewater, & Young, 1996). Individual differences in the timing of such experiences and how people deal with midlife are very large, which probably accounts for the failure to find a universal midlife crisis (Klohnen et al., 1996). Ego resilience may also be the resource that could account for the two outcomes (generativity and stagnation) of Erikson's view of midlife.

In sum, perhaps the best way to view the life transitions associated with middle age is through the words of a 52-year-old woman (Klohnen et al., 1996):

> Middle age.... The time when you realize you've moved to the caretaker, senior responsibility role.... A time of discomfort because you watch the generation before you, whom you have loved and respected and counted on for emotional back-up, for advice ... become more dependent on you and then die. Your children grow up, move out, try their wings . . . ; indeed, they attempt to teach you the "truths" they've discovered about life. . . . It's time to make some new choices—groups, friends, activities need not be so child related anymore.

TEST YOURSELF

1. The _____ dimension in the five-factor theory of personality includes anxiety, hostility, and impulsiveness.

2. According to Erikson, an increasing concern with helping younger people achieve is termed _____.

3. According to McAdams, the meaning one derives from being generative happens through the process of _____.

4. Statistical evidence indicates that gender-role identity _____ in middle age.

5. Research indicates that _____ is a key personality factor in predicting who will negotiate midlife successfully.

How can you reconcile the data from trait research, which indicate little change, with the data from other research, which show substantial change in personality in adulthood?

Answers: (1) neuroticism, (2) generativity, (3) narration, (4) converges, (5) ego resilience

14.4

Family Dynamics and Middle Age

LEARNING OBJECTIVES

▪ How does the relationship between middle-aged parents and their young adult children change?

▪ How do middle-aged adults deal with their aging parents?

▪ What styles of grandparenthood do middle-aged adults experience? How do grandchildren and grandparents interact?

> **Family Dynamics and Middle Age**
>
> Letting Go: Middle-Aged Adults and Their Children
>
> Giving Back: Middle-Aged Adults and Their Aging Parents
>
> Grandparenthood

Esther is facing a major milestone. Her youngest child, Megan, is about to leave home. But instead of feeling depressed, as she thought she would, Esther feels almost elated at the prospect. She and Bill are finally free of the day-to-day parenting duties of the past 30 years. Esther is looking forward to getting to know her husband again. She wonders whether there is something wrong with her for being excited that her daughter is moving away.

People like Esther connect generations. Family ties across the generations in a family like the one shown in the photograph provide the context for socialization and for continuity in the family's identity. At the centre agewise are members of the middle-aged generation, like Esther, who serve as the links between their aging parents and their own maturing children (Hareven & Adams, 1996). *Middle-aged mothers (more than fathers) tend to take on this role of **kinkeeper**, the person who gathers family members together for celebrations and keeps them in touch with each other.*

Think about the major issues confronting a typical middle-aged couple: maintaining a good marriage, parenting responsibilities, children who are becoming adults themselves, job pressures, and concern about aging parents, just to name a few. Middle-aged adults truly have quite a lot to deal with every day (Hamill & Goldberg, 1997). *Indeed, middle-aged adults are sometimes referred to as the **sandwich generation;** they are caught between the competing demands of two generations (their parents and their children).* Being in the sandwich generation means different things for women and men. When middle-aged women assess how well they are dealing with the midlife transition, their most pressing issues relate more to their adolescent children than to their aging parents; for middle-aged men, it is the other way around (Hamill & Goldberg, 1997).

Corbis/Magma

In this section, we first examine the dynamics of middle-aged parents and their maturing children and discover whether Esther's feelings are typical. Next, we consider the issues facing middle-aged adults and their aging parents. Later, we consider what happens when people become grandparents.

LETTING GO: MIDDLE-AGED ADULTS AND THEIR CHILDREN

Being a parent has a rather strange side, when you think about it. After creating children out of love, parents spend considerable time, effort, and money preparing them to become independent and leave. For most parents, the leaving (and sometimes returning) occurs during midlife.

Becoming Friends and the Empty Nest

At some time during middle age, most parents experience two positive developments with regard to their children. Suddenly their children see them in a new light, and the children leave home.

After the strain of raising adolescents, parents generally appreciate the transformation that occurs when their children head into young adulthood. In general, parent–child relationships improve when children become young adults (Troll & Fingerman, 1996).

The difference can be dramatic, as in the case of Deb, a middle-aged mother. "When Sacha was 15, she acted as if I was the dumbest person on the planet. But now that she's 21, she acts as if I got smart all of a sudden. I like being around her. She's a great kid, and we're really becoming friends."

A key factor in making this transition as smoothly as possible is the extent to which parents foster and approve of their children's attempts at being independent. Most parents are like Esther, the mother in the vignette, and manage the transition to an empty nest successfully (Lewis & Lin, 1996). That's not to say that parents are heartless. When children leave home, emotional bonds are disrupted. Parents feel the change, although differently; women who define themselves more in the context of a relationship tend to report more distress and negative mood (Hobdy, 2000). But only about 25% of mothers and fathers report being very sad and unhappy when the last child leaves home (Lewis & Lin, 1996).

Stewart Cohen/Taxi

Still, parents provide considerable financial help (such as paying tuition) when possible. Most help in other ways ranging from the mundane (such as making the washer and dryer available to their university-age children) to the extraordinary (providing the down payment for their child's house). Adult children and their parents generally believe that they have strong, positive relationships and that they can count on each other for help when necessary (Connidis, 2001).

When children leave, parents are able to better ascertain how their children turned out. As discussed in the Spotlight on Research feature, this issue is rather complex.

SPOTLIGHT ON RESEARCH

How Do You Think Your Children Turned Out?

Who was the investigator and what was the aim of the study? Carol Ryff and colleagues (1994) believed that parents' assessment of their children's accomplishments is an important part of the parents' midlife evaluation of themselves. Moreover, because parents are the major influence on children (see Chapters 4 and 8), the stakes for this self-evaluation are high; how one's child turns out is a powerful statement about one's success or failure as a parent (Ryff et al., 1994). Ryff and colleagues decided to see how these issues actually play out in parents' and children's lives.

How did the investigators measure the topic of interest? Ryff and colleagues asked

parents to rate their child's adjustment and educational and occupational attainment, to compare the child to others of that age, and to rate their psychological well-being.

Who were the participants in the study? Ryff and colleagues selected a random sample of 114 middle-aged mothers and 101 middle-aged fathers, all from different middle-class families in the Midwest United States, who had at least one child aged 21 or over. With these characteristics, the sample was not representative of the population at large.

What was the design of the study? The study was a cross-sectional examination of parents' ratings of their children's achievements.

Were there ethical concerns with the study? Because the study used volunteers who completed surveys containing no questions about sensitive topics, there were no ethical concerns.

What were the results? As you can see in Figure 14.8, mothers and fathers have many hopes and dreams for their children. Happiness and educational success were the most common responses, followed by career success. There were no statistically significant differences between mothers' and fathers' responses.

The data also showed that the parents' views of their children's personal and social adjustment correlated closely with measures of the parents' own well-being. Parents' sense of self-acceptance, purpose in life, and environmental mastery were strongly related to how well they thought their children were adjusted. Similar, but somewhat weaker, relations were found between children's accomplishments and parental well-being. Again, no differences between mothers and fathers were found.

Parents were also asked how well they thought their children were doing compared to themselves when they were the same age. These data were intriguing. Parents who thought their children were better adjusted (i.e., more self-confident, happy, and interpersonally skilled) than they themselves were in early adulthood reported low levels of well-being. Why? Shouldn't parents be pleased that their children are well adjusted? Ryff and col-

leagues suggest that this finding, though seemingly counterintuitive, is really understandable with regard to social comparison. That is, people suffer negative consequences (such as having lower self-esteem) when they perceive other people as doing better than they are (Suls & Wills, 1991). Even though parents by and large want their children to be happy, they may have difficulty accepting it if they turn out to be *too* happy.

In contrast, parents who rated their children as having attained better educational and occupational levels felt more positive about themselves compared to parents who rated their children lower on these dimensions. In this case, parents may feel that they have fulfilled the commonly held goal of helping the next generation do better than they did.

What did the investigators conclude? Ryff and colleagues showed that midlife parents' self-evaluations of their own well-being are clearly related to their perceptions of how their children turned out. Thus, their supposition that how children turn out is strongly connected with middle-aged parents' sense of self was supported.

What converging evidence would strengthen these conclusions? The findings would be strengthened with longitudinal data, which would be able to track parents' feelings over time. Additionally, a representative sample is essential for the results to be generalizable to the population at large. 🔊

FIGURE 14.8

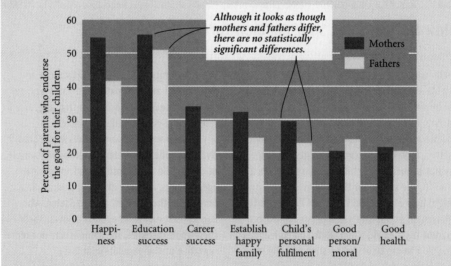

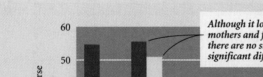

Although it looks as though mothers and fathers differ, there are no statistically significant differences.

© Tony Freeman/PhotoEdit

Photodisc

When Children Come Back

Parents' satisfaction with the empty nest is sometimes short-lived. The father in the photograph isn't alone. In Canada the percentage of young adults in their 20s and early 30s living with their parents has been increasing steadily since the 1980s; it is estimated that 23% of young women aged 20 to 34 and 33% of young men in that age range are living at their parental home (Statistics Canada, 1999a).

Why do so many young adult children continue to live with their parents or move back after having previously moved out? There are several factors that influence this decision. One possibility is the increasing numbers of young people attending colleges and universities, a trend that tends to extend their adolescence and dependence on their parents. Also, with economic downturns, young people tend to experience higher rates of unemployment than more experienced older workers, and moving back home may be a response to unemployment. The fact that young people delay first marriage also affects the rate at which they move out. Finally, there can also be a cultural component to living at home, since these rates are greater for some ethnic and immigrant groups than others (Statistics Canada, 1999a).

GIVING BACK: MIDDLE-AGED ADULTS AND THEIR AGING PARENTS

No matter how old you may be, being someone's child is a role that people still play well into adulthood and, sometimes, into their 60s and 70s. How do middle-aged adults relate to their parents?

What happens when their parents become frail? How do middle-aged adults like the woman in the photograph deal with the need to care for their parents?

Caring for Aging Parents

Most middle-aged adults have parents who are in reasonably good health. For a growing number of people, however, being a middle-aged child of aging parents involves providing some level of care. The job of caring for older parents usually falls to a daughter or a daughter-in-law (Stephens & Franks, 1999). Even after ruling out all other demographic characteristics of adult child caregivers and their care recipients, daughters are more than three times as likely to provide care as sons (Stephens et al., 2001). This gender difference is also found in other cultures. For example, in Japan, even though the oldest son is responsible for parental care, it is his wife who actually does the day-to-day caregiving (Morioka, 1998).

It has been projected that the number of employees in Canada who are caring for elders will increase in the next decade due to the aging of the baby boomers (Duxbury et al., 2003). In some situations, older parents must move in with one of their children. Such moves usually occur after decades of both generations living independently. This history of independent living sets the stage for adjustment difficulties following the move; both lifestyles must be accommodated. Most of the time, adult children provide care for their mothers, who may in turn have provided care for their husbands before they died. (Spousal caregiving is discussed in Chapter 16.) In other situations, adult daughters must try to manage care from a distance. As we will see later, irrespective of the location of care, women are under considerable stress from the pressures of caregiving.

Caring for one's parent presents a dilemma (Wolfson et al., 1993). *Most adult children feel a sense of responsibility, termed* **filial obligation,** *to care for their parent if necessary.* For example, adult child caregivers sometimes express the feeling that they "owe it to Mom or Dad" to care for them; after all, their parent provided for them for many years, and now the shoe is on the other foot (Myers & Cavanaugh, 1995). This appears to be universal; adult children provided care when needed to their parents in all Western and non-Western cultures studied (Hareven & Adams, 1996). Viewed from a global perspective, all but a small percentage of care to older adults is provided by adult children and other family members (Hareven & Adams, 1996; Pavalko & Artis, 1997).

Caring for an older parent is not easy. It usually doesn't happen by choice; each party would just as soon live apart. The potential for conflict over daily routines and lifestyles is high. Indeed, one major source of conflict between middle-aged daughters and their older mothers is differences in perceived need for care, with middle-aged daughters believing that their mothers need care more than the mothers believe they do (Fingerman, 1996).

Caregiving Stress

Caregiving is also a major source of stress. Adult children and other family caregivers are especially vulnerable to stress from two main sources (Pearlin et al., 1990):

- Adult children may have trouble coping with declines in their parents' functioning, especially those involving cognitive abilities and problematic behaviour, and with the work overload, burnout, and loss of the previous relationship with a parent.
- When the caregiving situation is perceived as confining, or seriously infringes on the adult child's other responsibilities (spouse, parent, employee, etc.), the situation is likely to be perceived negatively, which may lead to family or job conflicts, economic problems, loss of self-identity, and decreased competence.

Caring for a parent entails psychological costs. Even the most devoted adult child caregiver feels depressed, resentful, angry, and guilty at times (Halpern, 1987). Many middle-aged caregivers are pressed financially, as they may still be paying child care or tuition expenses and trying to save adequately for their own retirement.

The stresses of caring for one's parent are especially difficult for women. Looking at the life course, caring for a parent typically coincides with women's peak employment years of 35 to 64 (Moen, Robinson, & Fields, 1994). Longitudinal research clearly shows that employment status has no effect on women's decisions to become caregivers (many have little choice) but that becoming a caregiver makes it likely that women will reduce employment hours or stop working (Pavalko & Artis, 1997). When you consider that most women caring for parents are also mothers, wives, and employees, it should come as no surprise that stress from these other roles exacerbates the effects of stress due to caregiving (Stephens & Townsend, 1997).

What aspects of women's roles reduce the stress of caregiving? Having a secure attachment style to one's parent appears to buffer some aspects of stress (Crispi, Schiaffino, & Berman, 1997). Additionally, the rewards one gains as an employee, but not those from being a wife or mother, also seem to buffer the experience of caregiving stress (Stephens & Townsend, 1997).

From the parent's perspective, things aren't always rosy either. Independence and autonomy are important traditional values in some ethnic groups, and their loss is not taken lightly. Older adults in these groups are more likely to express the desire to pay a professional for assistance rather than ask a family member for help; they may find it demeaning to live with their children (Hamon & Blieszner, 1990). Most move in only as a last resort. As many as two-thirds of older adults who receive help with daily activities feel negatively about the help they receive (Newsom, 1999).

Determining whether older parents are satisfied with the help their children provide is a complex issue (Newsom, 1999). Based on a critical review of the research, Newsom (1999) proposes a model of how certain aspects of care can produce negative perceptions of care directly or by affecting the interactions between caregiver and care recipient. It is clear from this model, shown in Figure 14.9, that even under the best circumstances there is no guarantee that the help adult children provide their

THINK ABOUT IT

Why does parental caregiving fall mainly to women?

FIGURE 14.9 Older Parents' Satisfaction with Help Provided by Children

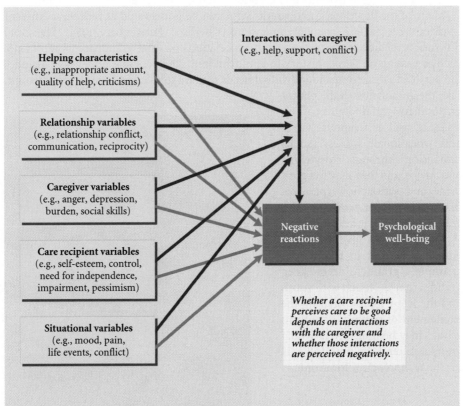

SOURCE: From Newsom, J. T. (1999). Another side to caregiving: Negative reactions to being helped. *Current Directions in Psychological Science, 8,* 185. Reprinted by permission of Blackwell Scientific Publications, Ltd.

parents will be well received. Misunderstandings can occur, and the frustration caregivers feel can be translated directly into negative interactions.

In sum, taking care of one's aging parents is a difficult task. Despite the numerous challenges and risks of negative psychological and financial outcomes, many caregivers nevertheless experience positive outcomes.

GRANDPARENTHOOD

Becoming a grandparent takes some help. Being a parent yourself, of course, is a prerequisite. But it is your children's decisions and actions that determine whether you will experience the transition to grandparenthood, making this role different from most others we experience throughout life (Stephens & Clark, 1996). Most people become grandparents in their 40s and 50s (Thomas, 1992), though some are older or perhaps as young as their late 20s or early 30s (Kivnick, 1982). In most cases, grandparents are quite likely to still be employed and to have living parents themselves. Thus, although being a grandparent may be an exciting time, it is often only one part of their busy lives (Stephens & Clark, 1996).

How Do Grandparents Interact with Grandchildren?

Keisha, an 8-year-old girl, smiled brightly when asked to describe her grandparents. "Nana Mary gives me chocolate ice cream, and that's my favourite! Poppa Bill sometimes takes care of me when Mom and Dad go out, and plays ball with me." Kyle, a 14-year-old, had a different view. "My grandparents generally tell me stories of what life was like back when they were young."

As Keisha's and Kyle's experiences show, grandparents have many different ways of interacting with their grandchildren. Categorizing these styles has been attempted over the years (e.g., Neugarten & Weinstein, 1964), but none has been overly successful because grandparents use different styles with different grandchildren and styles change as grandparents and grandchildren age (Stephens & Clark, 1996).

Many of the functions grandparents serve can be understood as reflecting different levels of the social and personal dimensions (Cherlin & Furstenberg, 1986). The social dimension includes societal needs and expectations of what grandparents are to do, such as passing on family history to grandchildren. The personal dimension includes the personal satisfaction and individual needs that are fulfilled by being a grandparent.

Like the grandfather in the photograph, many grandparents pass on skills, as well as religious, social, and vocational values (social dimension) through storytelling and advice, and they may feel great pride and satisfaction (personal dimension) from working with grandchildren on joint projects.

Grandchildren give grandparents a great deal in return. For example, grandchildren keep grandparents in touch with youth and the latest trends. Sharing the excitement of surfing the web in school may be one way in which grandchildren keep grandparents on the technological forefront.

Being a Grandparent Is Meaningful

Does being a grandparent matter to people? You bet it does, at least to the vast majority of grandparents. Kivnick (1982, 1985) identified five dimensions of meaning that grandparents often assign to their roles. *For some, grandparenting is the most important thing in their lives, termed* **centrality**. *For others, meaning comes from being seen as wise (***valued elder***), from spoiling grandchildren (***indulgence***), from recalling the relationship they had with their own grandparents (***reinvolvement with personal past***), or from taking pride in the fact that they will be followed by not one but two generations (***immortality through clan***).*

THINK ABOUT IT 💡

How is being a grandparent related to generativity?

Most grandparents derive several different meanings, regardless of the style of their relationship with the grandchildren (Miller & Cavanaugh, 1990). Similar findings are reported when overall satisfaction with being a grandparent is examined; no matter what their style is, grandparents find their role meaningful (Thomas, Bence, & Meyer, 1988).

Grandchildren also highly value their relationships with grandparents (Kennedy, 1991). Grandparents are valued as role models, and for their personalities, the activities they share, and the attention they show to grandchildren. Grandchildren also note that when their grandparents are frail, helping their grandparents is a way for them to act on their altruistic beliefs (Kennedy, 1991).

Multigenerational Households

In Canada, the arrangement of grandparents living with their children and grandchildren tends to occur more often among the immigrant population, especially Asian-Canadian families. Aboriginal families are also more likely to have grandparents and grandchildren sharing a home (Statistics Canada, 2003a). While there are many benefits to these kinds of arrangements, some families may also experience a clash in values between grandparents' traditional values and those of their children and grandchildren.

When Grandparents Care for Grandchildren

Grandparenthood today is tougher than it used to be. Families are more mobile, which means that grandparents are more often separated from their grandchildren by geographical distance. Grandparents are more likely to have independent lives, apart from their children and grandchildren. What being a grandparent entails in the 21st century is more ambiguous than it once was (Stephens & Clark, 1996).

Perhaps the biggest change for grandparents is the increasing number who serve as custodial parents for their grandchildren (Waldrop & Weber, 2001). At last estimate, 82,995 Canadian children, representing 1.2% of all children under the age of 18 years, lived in a household with at least one grandparent and no parent in residence (Statistics Canada, 1996b) but this figure is generally considered an underestimate. Such situations usually occur when parents are addicted, are incarcerated, or are unable to raise their children for some other reason (Cox, 2000; Hayslip & Goldberg-Glen, 2000), or because of discipline or behaviour problems exhibited by the grandchild (Giarusso et al., 2000). The grandparents' lack of legal guardianship also poses problems and challenges, for example, in dealing with schools and obtaining records.

Raising grandchildren is not easy. Rates of problem behaviour, hyperactivity, and learning problems in the children are high and negatively affect the grandparent–grandchild relationship (Hayslip et al., 1998). Even custodial grandparents raising grandchildren without these problems report more stress and role disruption than noncustodial grandparents (Emick & Hayslip, 1999). And custodial grandmothers who are employed report that they arrive late, miss work, must leave work suddenly, or leave early to tend to the grandchild's needs (Pruchno, 1999). Taking on the responsibility for young children again in their lives affects grandparents' social lives as well. In a Canadian study on grandparents caring for grandchildren, one participant commented, "Friends disappear because you can no longer do anything at the drop of a hat, you have to get a sitter before you leave the house or you have to take the children with you. You just don't have anything in common with them anymore" (Inwood, 2002). But most custodial grandparents consider their situation better for their grandchild than any other alternative and report surprisingly few negative effects on their marriages.

TEST YOURSELF

1. The term _____ refers to middle-aged adults who have both living parents and children of their own.

2. The people who gather the family together for celebrations and keep family members in touch are called _____.

3. Most caregiving for aging parents is provided by _____.

4. The sense of personal responsibility to care for one's parents is called _____.

5. The _____ meaning of grandparenthood refers to the desire to be an esteemed and wise resource to grandchildren.

   If you were to create a guide to families for middle-aged adults, what would your most important pieces of advice be? Why did you select these?

Answers: (1) sandwich generation, (2) kinkeepers, (3) daughters and daughters-in-law, (4) filial obligation, (5) valued elder

PUTTING IT ALL TOGETHER

Is it any wonder that middle age gets bad press? There's a lot to face: signs of biological aging, children leaving, cognitive abilities changing, and parents dying. But middle age also has much going for it from many people's perspective: generally good relationships with children, grandparenthood, and accumulated experience. We saw how middle age is partly a continuation of previous developmental trends (e.g., in aspects of cognitive development and personality) and partly a time of new challenges (such as getting used to physical changes and dealing with different generations in the family).

We learned that Sean, the man who reacted negatively to losing his hair, is pretty typical of many middle-aged people confronting the first signs of aging. Kesha's expertise in social work is also typical of middle-aged adults, many of whom become experts in one area or another. We saw that Jim's behaviour is not a reflection of a universal midlife crisis. Esther's joy and relief when her youngest daughter moved out is the reaction of most middle-aged parents who acquire an empty nest (at least until their adult children decide to move back).

Middle age has many positive aspects—relatively good health, the best financial security most people ever have, stable relationships with partners, good relations with children, expertise in some area, and the prospect of rewarding relationships with grandchildren. It has its challenges too. Getting used to physical aging can be hard, as is caring for an aging parent. But for many people, on balance, these are the best years of their lives.

SUMMARY

14.1 Physical Changes and Health

Changes in Appearance

- Some of the signs of aging appearing in middle age include wrinkles, grey hair, and weight gain.

Changes in Bones and Joints

- An important change, especially in women, is loss of bone mass, which in severe form may result in the disease osteoporosis.

- Osteoarthritis generally becomes noticeable in late middle or early old age. Rheumatoid arthritis is a more common form affecting fingers, wrists, and ankles.

Sensory Changes

- Vision and hearing changes commonly begin in middle age.

Reproductive Changes

- The climacteric (loss of the ability to bear children by natural means) and menopause (cessation of menstruation) occur in the 40s and 50s and constitute a major change in reproductive ability in women. Most women do not have severe physical symptoms associated with the hormonal changes.
- Reproductive changes in men are much less dramatic; even older men are usually still fertile. Physical changes do affect sexual response.

Stress and Health

- In the stress and coping paradigm, stress results from a person's appraisal of an event as taxing his or her resources. Daily hassles are viewed as the primary source of stress.
- The types of situations people appraise as stressful change throughout adulthood. Family and career issues are more important for young and middle-aged adults; health issues are more important for older adults.
- Type A behaviour pattern is characterized by intense competitiveness, anger, hostility, restlessness, aggression, and impatience. It is linked with a person's first heart attack and with cardiovascular disease. Type B behaviour pattern is the opposite of Type A; it is associated with lower risk of first heart attack, but the prognosis after an attack is poorer. Following an initial heart attack, Type A behaviour pattern individuals have a higher recovery rate.
- Whereas stress is unrelated to serious psychopathology, it is related to social isolation and distrust.

Exercise

- Regular exercise has numerous benefits, especially to cardiovascular health and fitness. The best results are obtained through a moderate exercise program maintained throughout adulthood.

14.2 Cognitive Development

Practical Intelligence

- Research on practical intelligence reveals differences between optimally exercised ability and unexercised ability. This gap closes during middle adulthood. Practical intelligence appears not to decline appreciably until late life.

Becoming an Expert

- People tend to become experts in some areas and not in others. Experts tend to think in more flexible ways than novices and are able to skip steps in solving problems. Expert performance tends to peak in middle age.

Lifelong Learning

- Adults learn differently than children and youth. Older students need practical connections and a rationale for learning and are more motivated by internal factors.

14.3 Personality

Stability Is the Rule: The Five-Factor Model

- The five-factor model postulates five dimensions of personality: neuroticism, extraversion, openness to experience, agreeableness, and conscientiousness. Several longitudinal studies indicate that personality traits show long-term stability.

Change Is the Rule: Changing Priorities at Midlife

- Erikson believed that middle-aged adults become more concerned with doing for others and passing social values and skills to the next generation—a set of behaviours and beliefs he labelled *generativity*. Those who do not achieve generativity are thought to experience stagnation.
- For the most part, there is little support for theories based on the premise that all adults go through predictable life stages at specific points in time. Individuals may face similar stresses, but transitions may occur at any time in adulthood. Research indicates that not everyone experiences a crisis at midlife.
- There is some evidence that gender-role identity converges in middle age to the extent that men and women are more likely to endorse similar self-descriptions. However, these similar descriptions do not necessarily translate into similar behaviour.

14.4 Family Dynamics and Middle Age

- Middle-aged mothers tend to adopt the role of kin-keepers to keep family traditions alive and as a way to link generations.
- Middle age is sometimes referred to as the sandwich generation.

Letting Go: Middle-Aged Adults and Their Children

- Parent–child relations improve dramatically when children emerge from adolescence. Most parents look forward to having an empty nest. Difficulties emerge to the extent that raising children has been a primary source of personal identity for parents. However, once children have left home, parents still provide considerable support.
- Children move back home primarily for financial or child-rearing reasons. Neither parents nor children generally choose this arrangement.

Giving Back: Middle-Aged Adults and Their Aging Parents

- Middle-aged children contact their parents fairly frequently and use the visits to strengthen the relationship.
- Caring for aging parents usually falls to a daughter or daughter-in-law. Caregiving creates a stressful situation due to conflicting feelings and roles. The potential for conflict is high, as is financial pressure.
- Caregiving stress is usually greater in women, who must deal with multiple roles. Older parents are often dissatisfied with the situation as well.

Grandparenthood

- Becoming a grandparent means assuming new roles. Styles of interaction vary across grandchildren and with the age of the grandchild. Also relevant are the social and personal dimensions of grandparenting.
- Grandparents derive several different types of meaning regardless of style: centrality, valued elder, indulgence, reinvolvement with personal past, and immortality through clan. Most children and young adults report positive relationships with grandparents, and young adults feel a responsibility to care for them if necessary.
- In an increasingly mobile society, grandparents are more frequently assuming a distant relationship with their grandchildren. An increasing number of grandparents serve as the custodial parent. These arrangements are typically stressful.

KEY TERMS

osteoporosis (489)
osteoarthritis (491)
rheumatoid arthritis (492)
climacteric (492)
menopause (492)
perimenopause (493)
postmenopause (493)
estrogen-related symptoms (493)
somatic symptoms (493)
hormone replacement therapy (HRT) (494)
stress and coping paradigm (496)
appraise (497)
hassles (497)

coping (497)
Type A behaviour pattern (498)
Type B behaviour pattern (498)
aerobic exercise (499)
practical intelligence (502)
unexercised ability (502)
optimally exercised ability (502)
processes of thinking (505)
encapsulated (505)
products of thinking (505)
midlife crisis (508)
neuroticism (508)
extraversion (508)
openness to experience (509)

agreeableness (509)
conscientiousness (509)
generativity (510)
stagnation (510)
ego resilience (513)
kinkeeper (514)
sandwich generation (514)
filial obligation (518)
centrality (521)
valued elder (521)
indulgence (521)
reinvolvement with personal past (521)
immortality through clan (521)

SEE FOR YOURSELF: APPLYING WHAT YOU'VE LEARNED

How do people deal with the signs of physical aging? Find out for yourself by doing the following exercises.

1. Look through popular fashion magazines such as *Vogue, Cosmopolitan, GQ,* and *Elle,* and watch television programs. Pay attention to advertisements and articles dealing with wrinkles, hair, and weight. How many give the message that these natural signs of aging are acceptable? Do you detect a difference between messages aimed at men and at women?

2. Talk to men and women you know who are over 40. Ask them how they feel about the physical changes they are experiencing. Do you detect any gender differences?

3. Talk to someone from a culture other than your own. Find out how people in other cultures view the physical changes associated with aging. Are the changes that accompany aging viewed the same way around the world?

   These exercises should provide you with some insights into how people and corporations (through their advertisements) view the physical changes that occur in middle age. Compare your findings with other students' results and discuss any gender differences you have uncovered. Do people ignore these changes? See for yourself!

LEARN MORE ABOUT IT

Readings

ARP, D. H., ARP, C. S, STANLEY, S. M., MARKMAN, H. J., & BLUMBERG, S. L. (2000). *Fighting for your empty nest marriage: Reinventing your relationship when the kids leave home.* San Francisco: Jossey-Bass. A research-based guide for married couples to help them get through a difficult period for most marriages.

ESTES, C. P. (1992). *Women who run with the wolves.* New York: Ballantine Books. Femininity is discussed from a Jungian point of view, as revealed through story and myth.

MCADAMS, D. P., & DE ST. AUBIN, E. (Eds.). (1998). *Generativity and adult development: How and why do we care for the next generation?* Washington, DC: American Psychological Association. Excellent collection of articles about generativity and how people put Erikson's concept into practice.

ROOTS, C. R. (1998). *The sandwich generation: Adult children caring for aging parents.* New York: Garland. A good summary of research findings concerning caring for aging parents.

TAN, A. (1989). *The Joy Luck Club.* New York: Putnam. This novel explores the bond among four Chinese-American women and their adult daughters.

WESTHEIMER, R., & KAPLAN, S. (2000). *Grandparenthood.* New York: Routledge. Provides a research-based but practical overview of the major issues in grandparenthood.

 For additional readings, explore InfoTrac® College Edition, your online library. Go to http://www.infotrac.thomsonlearning.com.

Websites

http://www.hc-sc.gc.ca
http://www.mayoclinic.com

The Health Canada and Mayo Clinic websites are excellent resources for information on health. These sites are also worthwhile for general medical information on most specific conditions, such as menopause, and treatments.

http://www.cwhn.ca

The Canadian Women's Health Network provides helpful information, resources, and strategies to improve women's health. Many relevant topics are included such as menopause.

http://www.osteoporosis.ca

The Osteoporosis Society of Canada aims to educate, empower, and support individuals and communities in the prevention and treatment of osteoporosis.

http://www.clickintocaregivers.com/

This interactive website is designed to assist Canadian caregiving families and includes links to additional helpful resources.

http://www.cangrands.com

This website welcomes all grandparents and family members who are raising grandchildren or extended family members. Resources and helpful links are provided.

http://www.vifamily.ca/library/cft/grandparenthood.html

Devoted to grandparenthood issues and resources, this website is part of the main website of The Vanier Institute of the Family.

Website addresses are subject to change. The *Human Development* book companion website can be accessed for updated links.

The Human Development Book Companion Website

See http://www.humandevelopment.com for practice quiz questions, Internet links, updates, critical thinking exercises, discussion forums, and more.

 ### Life-Span CD-ROM

For more information on the concepts covered in this chapter, go to

Module 5: Early and Middle Adulthood
- Physical Development
- Cognitive Development
- Emotional and Social Development

PART 4

Late Adulthood

Getty Images

Getty Images

CHAPTER 15

The Personal Context of Later Life

PHYSICAL, COGNITIVE, AND MENTAL HEALTH ISSUES

STOP! Before you read this chapter, do the following exercise. Take out a piece of paper and write down all the adjectives you can think of that describe aging and older adults, as well as all of the "facts" about aging that you know.

Now that you have your list, look over it carefully. Are most of your descriptors positive or negative? Do you have lots of "facts" written down, or just a few? Most people's lists contain at least some words and phrases that reflect images of older adults as portrayed by the media. Many of the media's images are stereotypes of aging that are only loosely based on reality. For example, people over age 60 are almost never pictured in ads for perfume (Elizabeth Taylor is a notable exception), but they are shown in ads for wrinkle treatment products.

In this chapter, our journey through old age begins. Our emphasis in this chapter is on physical and cognitive changes. To begin, we consider the key physical changes and health issues confronting older adults. Changes in cognitive abilities, as well as interventions to help remediate the changes are discussed next. Finally, some well-known mental health issues are considered, including depression, anxiety disorders, and Alzheimer disease.

15.1

What Are Older Adults Like?

LEARNING OBJECTIVES

▪ What are the characteristics of older adults in the population?

▪ How long will most people live? What factors influence this?

▪ What is meant by the Third Age and the Fourth Age?

Justine is an 87-year-old Aboriginal woman who comes from a family of long-lived individuals. She has never been to a physician in her entire life, and she has never really been seriously ill. Because she feels healthy and has more living that she wants to do, Justine figures that she'll live for several more years.

What is it like to be old? Do you want your own late life to be described by the words and phrases you wrote at the beginning of the chapter? Do you look forward to becoming old, or are you afraid of what may lie ahead?

Most of us probably want to be like Justine and enjoy a long, healthy life. Growing old is not something we think about very much until we have to. It's as if we go to bed one night middle-aged and wake up the next day feeling old. But we can take comfort in knowing that when that day comes we will have plenty of company.

THE DEMOGRAPHICS OF AGING

Did you ever stop to think about how many older adults you see in your daily life? Did you ever wonder whether your great-grandparents had the same experience? There have never been as many older adults alive as there are now. The proportion of older adults in the population of industrialized countries increased tremendously in the 20th century, due mainly to better health care and to lowering women's mortality rate during childbirth. This trend will continue well into the 21st century.

People who study population trends, called **demographers,** *use a graphic technique called a* **population pyramid** *to illustrate these changes.* Figure 15.1 shows population pyramids for both developed and developing countries. Let's consider developed countries first (they're designated by the colour blue in the figure). Notice the shape of the population pyramid in 1950, shown in the first panel of the figure. In the middle of the 20th century, there were fewer people over age 60 than under age 60, so the figure tapers toward the top. Compare that to projections for 2030 (when the last of the baby boomers reach 65)—a dramatic change will occur in that the number of people over 65 will equal or outnumber those in other age groups.

These changes also occur in developing countries, shown in the lighter colour. Notice that the graphs for both 1950 and 1990 look like pyramids because there are so many fewer older adults than younger people. But by 2030 the number of older adults in developing countries will also have increased dramatically, changing the shape of the figure.

In Canada, seniors (aged 65 years and older) represent the fastest growing population group (Health Canada, 2003d). The rapid increase in the number of older adults will bring profound changes to everyone's lives. In the first half of the 21st century, older adults will be a major marketing target, and they will wield considerable political and economic power. The sheer number of older adults will place enormous pressure on pension systems, health care, and other human services. The costs will be borne by a relatively small number of taxpaying workers in the cohorts behind them.

The increasing strain on social service systems will be intensified because the most rapidly growing segment of the Canadian population is the group of people over age 85. Approximately 1 in 10 Canadian seniors is over the age of 85 years compared to

THINK ABOUT IT

How will the demographic changes in the first 30 years of the 21st century affect the need for retraining workers?

FIGURE 15.1   Population Pyramids for Developed and Developing Countries

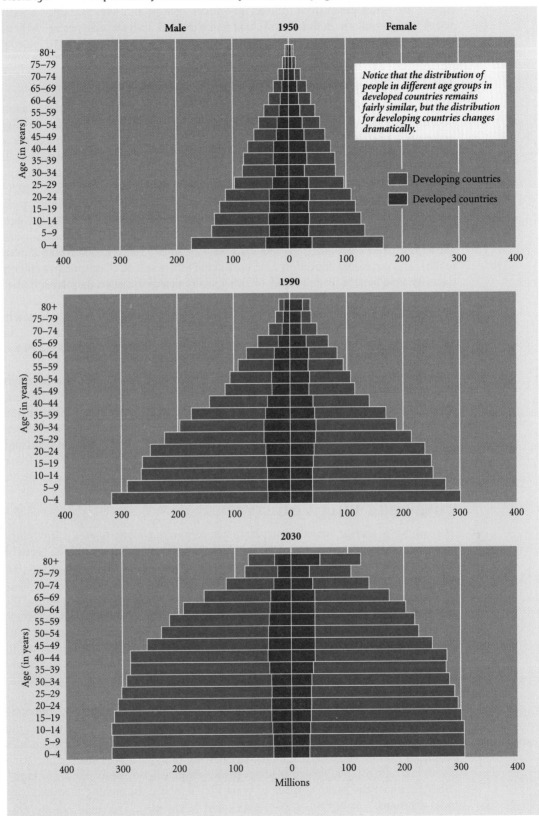

SOURCE: United Nations, 1999, and U.S. Census Bureau, 2000.

1 in 20 in the 1920s. Further, Statistics Canada projects that in 2051 there will be almost five times the current number of seniors aged 85 and over (Health Canada, 2003d). As we will see in this chapter and in Chapter 16, individuals over age 85 generally need more assistance with daily living than do people under 85, placing increasing strain on the health care system.

The Diversity of Older Adults

Older adults are not all alike, any more than are people at other ages. Older women outnumber older men in Canada for reasons we will explore later. Seniors currently make up a relatively small portion of the Aboriginal population in Canada, for a variety of reasons, including a higher than average rate of chronic diseases and overall deficient health care and living conditions. However, the numbers of Aboriginal seniors are expected to triple between by 2016 (Health Canada, 1998).

Because more Canadians are receiving post-secondary education than in the past, older adults in the future will be better educated too. It is estimated that in the last part of the 20th century, only about 25% of Canadian seniors had attended high school, 8% had a university degree, and 16% had other post-secondary training (Statistics Canada, 1996b). The increasing education of seniors in the future will be a very positive change since better-educated people tend to live longer, mostly because they have higher incomes, a factor that is positively associated with overall health outcomes.

Internationally, the number of older adults is also growing rapidly, especially among developing countries. To a large extent, these rapid increases are due to improved health care in these countries. Such increases will change the face of the population as more people live to old age.

Economically powerful countries around the world such as Japan are trying to cope with increased numbers of older adults that strain the country's resources. Indeed, the rate of growth of older adults in Japan is the highest in the industrialized world; by 2025 there will be twice as many adults over age 65 as there will be children (WuDunn, 1997). The economic impact will include much higher pension costs and very substantial increases in health care costs, which will have to be borne by far fewer workers (WuDunn, 1997).

HOW LONG WILL YOU LIVE?

*The number of years a person can expect to live, termed **longevity,** is jointly determined by genetic and environmental factors.* Researchers distinguish between three types of longevity: average life expectancy, useful life expectancy, and maximum life expectancy.

Average life expectancy (or median life expectancy) is the age at which half of the people born in a particular year will have died. As you can see in Figure 15.2, average life expectancy for people in Canada increased steadily during the 20th century. This increase was due mainly to significant declines in infant mortality and the number of women dying during childbirth, elimination of major diseases such as smallpox and polio, and improvements in medical technology that prolong the lives of people with chronic disease.

Useful life expectancy is the number of years that a person is free from debilitating chronic disease and impairment. Ideally, useful life expectancy exactly matches the actual length of a person's life. However, medical technology sometimes enables people to live for years even though they may be unable to perform routine daily tasks. Accordingly, people are placing greater emphasis on useful life expectancy, rather than just the sheer number of years they may live, in making medical treatment decisions.

Maximum life expectancy is the oldest age to which any person lives. Currently, scientists estimate that the maximum limit for humans is around 120 years, mostly because the heart and other key organ systems are limited in how long they can last without replacement (Hayflick, 1998).

FIGURE 15.2   Average Life Expectancy in Canada

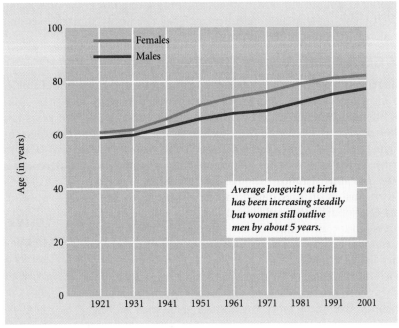

SOURCE: Statistics Canada, 2004.

Genetic and Environmental Factors in Life Expectancy

We have known for a long time that a good way to increase one's chances of a long life is to come from a family with a history of long-lived individuals (Hayflick, 1998). Researchers have suspected that this is due in large part to genetic factors. The Human Genome Project research and its spin-offs in microbiology and behaviour genetics have produced some astounding results in discovering genetic linkages to disease and aging (Bergeman, 1997). Some attempts are even being made to treat genetic diseases by implanting "corrected" genes in people in the hope that the good genes will reproduce and eventually wipe out the defective genes.

Payoffs from such research are already helping us understand how increasing numbers of people are living to 100 or older. For example, Perls (1995) showed that genetic factors play a major role in determining how well older people cope with disease. The oldest-old are hardy because they have a high threshold for disease and show slower rates of disease progression than their peers who develop chronic diseases at younger ages and die earlier.

Although heredity is a major determinant of longevity, environmental factors also affect the life span (Bergeman, 1997; Hayflick, 1998). Some environmental factors are more obvious; diseases, toxins, lifestyle, and social class are among the most important. Diseases, such as cardiovascular disease and Alzheimer disease, and lifestyle issues, such as smoking and exercise, receive a great deal of attention from researchers. Environmental toxins, encountered mainly as air and water pollution, are a continuing problem. For example, toxins in fish, bacteria and cancer-causing chemicals in drinking water, and airborne pollutants are major agents in shortening longevity.

How environmental factors influence average life expectancy changes over time. For example, acquired immunodeficiency syndrome (AIDS) became a factor in longevity during the 1980s and continues to kill millions of people around the world. In contrast, the life expectancy impact of cardiovascular diseases is lessening somewhat as the rates of those diseases decline.

The sad part about most environmental factors is that people are responsible for them. Continuing to pollute our environment and failing to address the underlying causes of poverty have undeniable consequences: They needlessly shorten lives and dramatically increase the cost of health care.

Ethnic and Gender Differences in Life Expectancy

There are differences in life expectancy related to ethnicity and gender. For example, in 2000 the life expectancy of Aboriginal women was five years less than non-Aboriginal women and the life expectancy of Aboriginal men was seven years less than non-Aboriginal men. Even with these disheartening statistics, the life expectancies of Aboriginal men and women have increased by 10 years from the 1970s (Health Canada, 2003h). In the United States, the complexity of ethnic group differences is evident in the fact that Latinos' average life expectancy exceeds European-Americans' at all ages despite access problems to health care for many (National Center for Health Statistics, 2001). As indicated, there are gender differences in life expectancy. In Canada in 2001 the life expectancy was 82.2 years for women and 77.1 years for men (Statistics Canada, 2003d).

> **THINK ABOUT IT**
>
> How do ethnic and gender differences in life expectancy relate to biological, psychological, sociocultural, and life-cycle factors?

A visit to a seniors' centre or to a nursing home can easily lead to the question "Where are all the very old men?" Women's average longevity is about five years more on average than men at birth (Statistics Canada, 2003d). These differences are fairly typical of most industrialized countries but not of developing countries. Indeed, the female advantage in average longevity became apparent only in the early 20th century (Hayflick, 1996). Why? Until then, so many women died in childbirth that their average longevity as a group was reduced to that of men. Death in childbirth still partially explains the lack of a female advantage in developing countries today; however, part of the difference in some countries also results from infanticide of baby girls. Socioeconomic factors such as access to health care, work and educational opportunities, and athletics also help account for the emergence of the female advantage in industrialized countries (Hayflick, 1998).

Many ideas have been offered to explain the significant advantage women have over men in average longevity in industrialized countries (Hayflick, 1996). Overall, men's rates of dying from the top 15 causes of death are significantly higher than women's at nearly every age, and men are also more susceptible to infectious diseases. These differences have led some to speculate that perhaps there is no fundamental biological difference in longevity but rather a much greater susceptibility in men of contracting certain fatal diseases (Hayflick, 1996).

Other researchers disagree; they argue that there are potential biological explanations. These include the fact that women have two X chromosomes, compared with one in men; men have a higher metabolic rate; women have a higher brain-to-body weight ratio; and women have lower testosterone levels. However, none of these explanations has sufficient scientific support to explain why most women in industrialized countries can expect, on average, to outlive most men (Hayflick, 1996).

Despite their longer average longevity, women do not have all the advantages. Interestingly, older men who survive beyond age 90 are the hardiest segment of their birth cohort in performance on cognitive tests (Perls, 1995). Between ages 65 and 89, women score higher on cognitive tests; beyond age 90, men do much better.

International Differences in Life Expectancy

Countries around the world differ dramatically in how long their populations live on average. As you can see from Figure 15.3, the current range extends from 38 years in Sierra Leone in Africa to 80 years in Japan. Such a wide divergence in life expectancy reflects vast discrepancies in genetic, sociocultural and economic conditions, health care, disease, and the like across industrialized and developing nations.

FIGURE 15.3   Life Expectancy at Birth

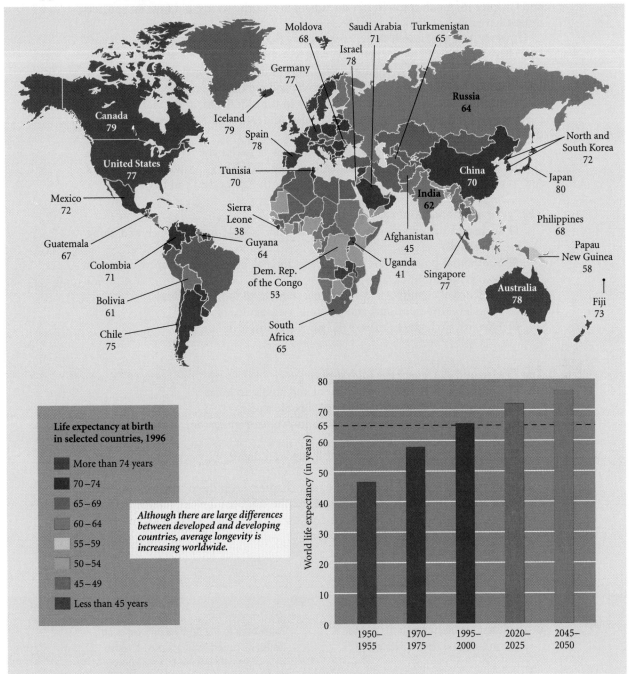

Life expectancy at birth in selected countries, 1996

- More than 74 years
- 70–74
- 65–69
- 60–64
- 55–59
- 50–54
- 45–49
- Less than 45 years

Although there are large differences between developed and developing countries, average longevity is increasing worldwide.

SOURCE: U.N. Population Division Database, 1996 Revision.

THE THIRD-FOURTH AGE DISTINCTION

The second half of the 20th century was exciting for gerontology. The development of the science of the study of older adults led to cultural, medical, and economic advances for older adults (e.g., longer average longevity, increased quality of life) that in turn resulted in fundamental, positive changes in how older people are viewed in society. Gerontology has become a specialty in a number of fields such as medicine, nursing, and psychology. Gerontologists and policymakers became optimistic that old age was a time of potential growth rather than decline. This combination of factors is termed the Third Age (Baltes & Smith, 2002). As we will see in this chapter and Chapter 16, much research has documented that the young-old (age 60–80) do indeed have much to look forward to.

However, recent research shows conclusively that the oldest-old (over age 80) typically have a much different experience, which is referred to as the Fourth Age (Baltes & Smith, 2002). The oldest-old are at the limits of their functional capacity, and few interventions have been successful to date. We will see that the rates of diseases such as cancer and dementia increase dramatically in the oldest-old, and other aspects of psychological functioning (e.g., memory) also undergo significant and fairly rapid decline.

Baltes and Smith (2002) view the differences between the Third Age and the Fourth Age as important for research and social policy. They characterize the Third Age as the "good news" about aging, and the Fourth Age as the "bad news":

The "good news": the third age (young-old)
- Increased life expectancy, with more older people living longer and aging successfully
- Substantial potential for physical and mental fitness, with improvement in each generation
- Evidence of cognitive and emotional reserves in the aging mind
- High levels of emotional and personal well-being
- Effective strategies to master the gains and losses of later life

The "bad news": the fourth age (oldest-old)
- Sizable losses in cognitive potential and ability to learn
- Increases in the negative effects of chronic stress
- High prevalence of dementia (50% in people over age 90), frailty, and multiple chronic conditions
- Problems with quality of life and dying with dignity

As you proceed through this and the next chapter, keep the distinction between the Third and the Fourth Ages in mind. Note the different developmental patterns shown by the young-old and oldest-old. In Chapter 16, we will consider some of the social policy implications of this distinction.

TEST YOURSELF

1. The fastest-growing segment of the population in Canada is people over age _____.

2. The age at which half of the people born in a particular year have died is called _____.

3. The Fourth Age refers to the _____-old.

Think back to the lifestyle influences on health discussed in Chapter 13. If most people actually followed very healthy lifestyles, what do you think would happen to average life expectancy?

Answers: (1) 85, (2) average life expectancy, (3) oldest

15.2

Physical Changes and Health

LEARNING OBJECTIVES

☑ What are the major biological theories of aging?

☑ What physiological changes normally occur in later life?

☑ What are the principal health issues for older adults?

Frank is an 80-year-old man who has been physically active his whole life. He still enjoys sailing, long-distance biking, and cross-country skiing. Although he considers himself to be in excellent shape, he has noticed that his endurance has decreased, and his hearing isn't quite as sharp as it used to be. Frank wonders: Can he do something to stop these declines, or are they an inevitable part of growing older?

If your family has kept photograph albums over many years, you are able to see how your grandparents or great-grandparents changed over the years. Some of the more visible differences are changes in the colour and amount of hair and the addition of wrinkles, but many other physical changes are harder to see. In this section, we consider some of these, as well as a few things that adults can do to improve their health. As noted in Chapter 14, many aging changes begin during middle age but typically do not affect people in their daily lives until later in life, as Frank is discovering. But first, we will ask a basic question: Why do people grow old in the first place?

BIOLOGICAL THEORIES OF AGING

Why does everyone who lives long enough grow old and eventually die? To date, there is no one definitive answer, but several complementary biological theories, taken together, provide some insights (Cristofalo et al., 1999).

There are four major groups of biological theories of aging. *Wear-and-tear theory suggests that the body, much like any machine, gradually deteriorates and finally wears out.* This theory explains some diseases, such as osteoarthritis, rather well. Years of use of the joints causes the protective cartilage lining to deteriorate, resulting in pain and stiffness. However, wear-and-tear theory does not explain most other aspects of aging very well (Hayflick, 1998).

Cellular theories explain aging by focusing on processes that occur within individual cells, which may lead to the buildup of harmful substances or the deterioration of cells over a lifetime.

A second family of ideas points to causes of aging at the cellular level. One notion focuses on the number of times cells can divide, which presumably places limits on the life span of a complex organism. Cells grown in laboratory culture dishes undergo only a fixed number of divisions before dying, with the number of possible divisions dropping depending on the age of the donor organism; this phenomenon is called the Hayflick limit, after its discoverer, Leonard Hayflick (Hayflick, 1996). For example, cells from human fetal tissue are capable of 40 to 60 divisions; cells from a human adult are capable of only about 20. What causes cells to limit their number of divisions? *Evidence suggests that the tips of the chromosomes, called* **telomeres,** *play a major role* (Cristofalo et al., 1999; Mera, 1998). An enzyme called *telomerase* is needed in DNA replication to fully replicate the telomeres. But telomerase normally is not present in cells, so with each replication the telomeres become shorter. Eventually, the chromosomes become unstable and cannot replicate because the telomeres become too short (Hayflick, 1998). Some researchers believe cancer cells proliferate so quickly in some cases because they can activate telomerase, meaning that the cancer cells may become functionally immortal and take over the organ system (Mera, 1998).

Other cellular theories stress the destructive effects that certain substances have on cellular functioning. *For example, some theorists believe that **free radicals**—chemicals produced randomly during normal cell metabolism, which bond easily to other substances inside cells—cause cellular damage that impairs functioning.* Aging is caused by the cumulative effects of free radicals over the life span. Free radicals may play a role in some diseases, such as atherosclerosis and cancer. The formation of free radicals can be prevented by substances called antioxidants. Although there is growing evidence that taking antioxidants, such as vitamins A, C, and E, postpones the appearance of some age-related diseases, there is little evidence that taking antioxidants increases average longevity (Cristofalo et al., 1999). *Another cellular theory focuses on **cross-linking**, in which some proteins interact randomly with certain body tissues, such as muscles and arteries.* The result of cross-linking is that normal, elastic tissue becomes stiffer, so that muscles and arteries are less flexible over time. The results in some cases can be serious; for example, stiffening in the heart muscle forces the heart to work harder, which may increase the risk of heart attacks. Although we know that these substances accumulate, there is little evidence that cross-linking causes all aspects of aging (Hayflick, 1998).

Metabolic theories focus on aspects of the body's metabolism to explain why people age. Two important processes in this approach are caloric intake and stress. There is some evidence that people who limit the number of calories they eat in an otherwise well-balanced diet can expect longer life expectancy and lower rates of disease. For example, Okinawans, who eat only 60% of the normal Japanese diet, have 40 times as many centenarians per capita, and their incidence of cardiovascular disease, diabetes, and cancer is half that of the rest of Japan (Monczunski, 1991). It remains to be seen whether the type of diet (e.g., low fat) or the number of calories per se is the secret. Another variant of metabolic theory suggests that the hormonal regulatory system's ability to adapt to stress declines (Finch & Seeman, 1999). Much research shows that younger adults can tolerate higher levels of physical stress than can older adults (Whitbourne, 1999). It is possible that death occurs because the body can no longer adapt to stress (Hayflick, 1998).

*Finally, **programmed cell death theories** suggest that aging is genetically programmed.* This possibility seems more likely as the explosion of knowledge about human genetics continues to unlock the secrets of our genetic code. Even when cell death appears random, researchers now believe that such losses may be part of a master genetic program (Bergeman, 1997; Cristofalo et al., 1999; Hayflick, 1998).

Programmed cell death appears to be a function of physiological processes, the innate ability of cells to self-destruct, and the ability of dying cells to trigger key processes in other cells. At present, we do not know how this self-destruct program is activated, nor do we understand how it works. However, understanding programmed cell death may be the key to understanding how genes and physiological processes interact with psychological and sociocultural forces to produce aging (Bergeman, 1997).

THINK ABOUT IT 💡

What would be the psychological and sociocultural effects of discovering a single, comprehensive biological theory of aging?

It is possible that the other explanations we have considered in this section and the changes we examine throughout this text are the result of a genetic program. For example, there is evidence that osteoarthritis (Charles, 1998), changes in brain cells (Martin, 1998), Alzheimer disease (Woodruff-Pak & Papka, 1999), certain types of memory (Johansson et al., 1999), and personality (Bouchard, 1997) have key genetic underpinnings. As genetics research continues, it is likely that we will have some exciting answers to the question "Why do we age?"

PHYSIOLOGICAL CHANGES

Growing older brings with it several inevitable physiological changes. Like Frank, whom we met in the vignette, older adults find that their endurance has declined, relative to what it was 20 or 30 years earlier, and that their hearing has declined. In this section, we consider some of the most important physiological changes that occur in neurons, the cardiovascular and respiratory systems, the motor system, and the sensory systems. We also consider general health issues such as sleep, nutrition, and cancer. Throughout this discussion, you should keep in mind that, although the changes we will consider happen to everyone, the rate and the amount of change varies a great deal across people.

Changes in the Neurons

The most important normative changes with age involve structural changes in the neurons, the basic cells in the brain, and in communication among neurons (Whitbourne, 1996). Recall the basic structures of the neuron we encountered in Chapter 3 and shown again here in Figure 15.4. Two structures in neurons are most important in understanding aging: the dendrites, which pick up information from other neurons, and the axon, which transmits information inside a neuron from the dendrites to the terminal branches. Each of the changes we consider impairs the neurons' ability to transmit information, which ultimately affects how well the person functions (Vinters, 2001). Three structural changes are most important in normal aging: neurofibrillary tangles, dendritic changes, and neuritic plaques.

FIGURE 15.4

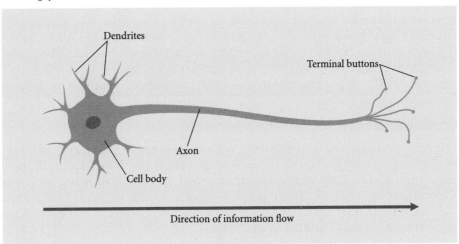

Direction of information flow

*For reasons that are not understood, fibres that compose the axon sometimes become twisted together to form spiral-shaped masses called **neurofibrillary tangles.*** These tangles interfere with the neuron's ability to transmit information down the axon. Some degree of tangling occurs normally with age, but large numbers of neurofibrillary tangles are associated with Alzheimer disease (Vinters, 2001).

Changes in the dendrites are more complicated. Some dendrites shrivel up and die, making it more difficult for neurons to communicate with each other (Vinters, 2001). However, some dendrites continue to grow (Curcio, Buell, & Coleman, 1982). This may help explain why older adults continue to improve in some areas, as we will discover later in this chapter. Why some dendrites degenerate and others do not is poorly understood; it may reflect the existence of two different families of neurons.

*Damaged and dying neurons sometimes collect around a core of protein and produce **neuritic plaques.*** It is likely that plaques interfere with normal functioning of healthy neurons. Although large numbers of plaques are associated with dementia (e.g., Alzheimer disease), researchers have not established an "allowable number" of plaques that indicate a healthy aging brain (Vinters, 2001).

Because neurons do not physically touch each other, they must communicate via chemicals called neurotransmitters. With age, the levels of these neurotransmitters decline (Whitbourne, 1999). These declines are believed to be responsible for numerous age-related behavioural changes, including those in memory and sleep, and perhaps in afflictions such as Parkinson's disease.

These changes in neurons are a normal part of aging. However, when these changes occur at a much greater rate, they cause considerable problems and are associated with Alzheimer or related diseases, conditions we discuss in more detail later in the chapter. This point is important, as it means that serious behavioural changes such as very severe memory impairment are not a result of normative changes in the brain; rather, they are indicators of disease.

We are learning a great deal about the relations between changes in the brain and changes in behaviour through technological advances in noninvasive imaging and in assessing psychological functioning (Albert & Killiany, 2001). On the brain imaging front, two types of techniques are used:

- *Structural imaging* provides highly detailed images of anatomical features in the brain. The most commonly used are X-rays, computerized tomography (CT scans), and magnetic resonance imaging (MRI).
- *Functional imaging* provides an indication of brain activity but not high anatomical detail. The most commonly used are single photon emission computerized tomography (SPECT), positron emission tomography (PET), and functional magnetic resonance imaging (fMRI).

These noninvasive imaging techniques coupled with sensitive tests of cognitive processing have shown quite convincingly that age-related changes in the brain are, at least in part, responsible for the age-related declines in cognition we will consider later (Albert & Killiany, 2001). Why these declines occur has yet to be discovered, although fMRI, the newest technique, offers considerable promise in helping researchers unlock this mystery.

Cardiovascular and Respiratory Systems

The incidence of cardiovascular diseases, such as heart attack, stroke, and hypertension increases with age (Health Canada, 2003f). However, the overall death rates from these diseases have been declining in recent decades, mainly because fewer adults smoke cigarettes and many people have reduced the amount of fat in their diets. In Canada, the death rate for all cardiovascular diseases decreased by 56% between 1969 and 1999 (Health Canada, 2003f).

Normative changes in the cardiovascular system that contribute to disease begin by young adulthood. Fat deposits are found in and around the heart and in the arteries (Whitbourne, 1999). Eventually, the amount of blood that the heart can pump per minute will decline roughly 30%. The amount of muscle tissue in the heart also declines, due to its replacement by connective tissue. There is also a general stiffening of the arteries, due to calcification. These changes appear irrespective of lifestyle, but they occur more slowly in people who exercise, eat low-fat diets, and manage to lower stress effectively (see Chapter 13). In persons who do not have hypertension, blood pressure changes little over adulthood (Pearson et al., 1997).

As people grow older, their chances of having a stroke increase. *Strokes, or cerebral vascular accidents, are caused by interruptions in the blood flow in the brain due to a blockage or to a hemorrhage in a cerebral artery.* Blockages of arteries may be caused by clots or by deposits of fatty substances due to the disease atherosclerosis. Hemorrhages are caused by ruptures of the artery. *Older adults often experience transient ischemic attacks (TIAs), which involve an interruption in blood flow to the brain and are often early warning signs of stroke.* A single, large cerebral vascular accident may produce serious cognitive impairment, such as the loss of the ability to speak, or physical problems, such as the inability to move an arm. The nature and severity of the impairment in functioning a person experiences is usually determined by the specific area of the brain affected. Recovery from a single stroke depends on many factors, including the extent and type of the loss, the ability of other areas in the brain to assume the functions that were lost, and personal motivation.

Numerous small cerebral vascular accidents can result in a disease termed **vascular dementia.** Unlike Alzheimer disease, another form of dementia discussed later in this chapter, vascular dementia can have a sudden onset and may or may not progress gradually. Moreover, individuals' symptom patterns vary a great deal, depending on which specific areas of the brain are damaged. In some cases, vascular dementia has a much faster course than Alzheimer disease, resulting in death an average of two to three years after onset; in others, the disease may progress much more slowly with idiosyncratic symptom patterns (Qualls, 1999).

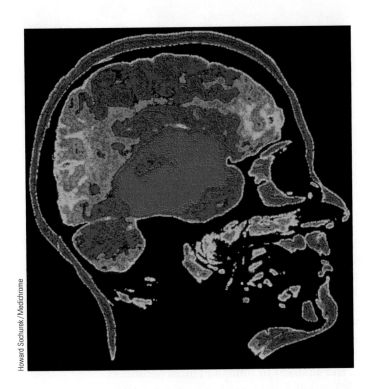

Howard Sochurek / Medichrome

Single cerebral vascular accidents and vascular dementia are diagnosed similarly. Evidence of damage may be obtained from diagnostic structural imaging (e.g., CT or MRI), which provides pictures like the one shown here. This damage is then confirmed by neuropsychological tests. Known risk factors for both conditions include hypertension and a family history of the disorders.

The maximum amount of air in one breath drops 40% from age 25 to age 85, due mostly to stiffening of the rib cage and air passages with age, and destruction of the air sacs in the lungs from pollution and smoking (Whitbourne, 1999). This decline is the main cause of shortness of breath after physical exertion in later life. Because of the cumulative effects of breathing polluted air over a lifetime, it is hard to say how much of these changes are strictly age-related. *The most common form of incapacitating respiratory disease among older adults is* **chronic obstructive pulmonary disease (COPD).** COPD can be an extremely debilitating condition, resulting in depression, anxiety, and the need to be continually connected to oxygen (Frazer, Leicht, & Baker, 1996). Emphysema is the most common form of COPD; although most cases of emphysema are due to smoking, some forms are genetic. Asthma is another common type of COPD.

Parkinson's Disease

Parkinson's disease is known primarily for its characteristic motor symptoms: very slow walking, difficulty getting into and out of chairs, and a slow hand tremor. These problems are caused by a deterioration of neurons in the midbrain that produce the neurotransmitter dopamine. Pope John Paul II, former boxing champion Muhammad Ali, and Canadian-born actor Michael J. Fox (shown in the photograph on page 542) all have Parkinson's disease.

Symptoms are treated effectively with the drug L-dopa, which raises the functional level of dopamine in the brain (Youngjohn & Crook, 1996), or a catechol-O-methyltransferase (COMT) inhibitor (e.g., Tasmar), which makes L-dopa more effective (Henkel, 1998). Research indicates that a device that acts like a brain pacemaker by regulating brain activity may prove effective in eliminating the tremors and shaking (www.medtronic.com/neuro/parkinsons/presentation/pages/news-release.pdf).

For reasons we do not yet understand, roughly 30 to 50% of the time Parkinson's disease also involves severe cognitive impairment, with additional brain changes similar to Alzheimer disease (Youngjohn et al., 1992). It remains to be seen whether this form of Parkinson's disease actually represents a separate disease.

AP/World Wide Photos

Sensory Changes

Two major kinds of age-related structural changes occur in the eye. One is a decrease in the amount of light that passes through the eye, resulting in the need for more light to do tasks such as reading. As you might suspect, this change is one reason older adults do not see as well in the dark, which may account in part for their reluctance to go places at night. One possible logical response to the need for more light would be to increase illumination levels in general. However, this solution does not work in all situations because we also become increasingly sensitive to glare (Whitbourne, 1999). Additionally, our ability to adjust to changes in illumination, called adaptation, declines. Going from outside into a darkened movie theatre involves dark adaptation; going back outside involves light adaptation. Research indicates that the time it takes for both types of adaptation increases with age (Fozard & Gordon-Salant, 2001). These changes are especially important for older drivers, who have more difficulty seeing after being confronted with the headlights of an oncoming car.

The other key structural changes involve the lens. As we grow older, the lens becomes more yellow, causing poorer colour discrimination in the green–blue–violet end of the spectrum, and its ability to adjust and focus declines as the muscles around it stiffen (Fozard & Gordon-Salant, 2001). *This is what causes presbyopia, the difficulty in seeing close objects clearly, necessitating either longer arms or corrective lenses.* To complicate matters further, the time our eyes need to change focus from near to far (or vice versa) increases (Fozard & Gordon-Salant, 2001). This also poses a major problem in driving. Because drivers are constantly changing their focus from the instrument panel to other autos and to signs on the highway, older drivers may miss important information because of their slower refocusing time.

Besides these normative structural changes, some people experience diseases caused by abnormal structural changes. First, opaque spots called cataracts may develop on the lens, which limits the amount of light transmitted. Cataracts often are treated by surgical removal and use of corrective lenses. Second, the fluid in the eye may not drain properly, causing very high pressure; this condition, called glaucoma, can cause internal damage and loss of vision. Glaucoma is a fairly common disease in middle and late adulthood and is usually treated with eye drops.

The second major family of changes in vision result from changes in the retina. The retina lines approximately two-thirds of the interior of the eye. The specialized receptor cells in vision, the rods and the cones, are contained in the retina. They are most densely packed toward the rear and especially at the focal point of vision, a region called the macula. At the centre of the macula is the fovea, where incoming light is focused for maximum acuity, as when one is reading. With increasing age the probability of degeneration of the macula increases (Fozard & Gordon-Salant, 2001). Macular degeneration involves the progressive and irreversible destruction of receptors from any of a number of causes. This disease results in the loss of the ability to see details; for example, reading is extremely difficult, and television often is reduced to a blur. Macular degeneration is the leading cause of functional blindness in older adults.

A second age-related retinal disease is a by-product of diabetes. Diabetes is accompanied by accelerated aging of the arteries, with blindness being one of the more serious side effects. Diabetic retinopathy, as this condition is called, can involve fluid retention in the macula, detachment of the retina, hemorrhage, and aneurysms (Fozard & Gordon-Salant, 2001). Because it takes many years to develop, diabetic retinopathy is more common among people who developed diabetes early in life.

The combined effects of the structural changes in the eye create two other types of changes. First, the ability to see detail and to discriminate different visual patterns, called acuity, declines steadily between ages 20 and 60, with a more rapid decline thereafter. Loss of acuity is especially noticeable at low light levels (Fozard & Gordon-Salant, 2001).

Experiencing hearing loss is one of the most common normative changes with age (Whitbourne, 1999), as Frank, the man we met in the vignette, is noticing. A visit to any housing complex for older adults will easily verify this point; you will quickly notice that television sets and radios are turned up fairly loudly in most of the apartments. Yet you don't have to be old to experience significant hearing problems. When it became difficult to hear what was being said to him, former U.S. President Bill Clinton obtained two hearing aids. He was 51 years old at the time, and he attributed his hearing loss to too many high school bands and rock concerts when he was young. His situation is far from unique. Loud noise is the enemy of hearing at any age. You probably have seen people who work in noisy environments wearing protective gear on their ears so that they are not exposed to loud noise over extended periods of time.

But you can do serious damage to your hearing with short exposure too; in 1988, San Francisco punk rock bassist Kathy Peck was performing at the Oakland Coliseum and played so loudly that she had ringing in her ears for three days and suffered permanent hearing loss. As a result, she founded Hearing Education and Awareness for Rockers (HEAR) shortly thereafter to educate musicians about the need to protect their ears (Soulsman, 1999). HEAR has picked up momentum ever since; in 1998 they distributed 60,000 pairs of free ear plugs to musicians and fans of the Lollapalooza Tour. You don't need to be at a concert to damage your hearing either. Using headphones, especially at high volume, can cause the same serious damage and should be avoided. It is especially easy to cause hearing loss with headphones if you wear them while exercising, for example; the increased blood flow to the ear during exercise makes hearing receptors more vulnerable to damage.

The cumulative effects of noise and normative age-related changes create the most common age-related hearing problem: reduced sensitivity to high-pitched tones, called **presbycusis,** *which occurs earlier and more severely than the loss of sensitivity to low-pitched tones.* Research indicates that by the late 70s, roughly half of older adults have presbycusis. Men typically have greater loss than women, but this may be because of differential exposure to noisy environments. Hearing loss usually is gradual at first but accelerates during the 40s, a pattern seen clearly in Figure 15.5.

Presbycusis results from four types of changes in the inner ear (Fozard & Gordon-Salant, 2001): sensory, consisting of atrophy and degeneration of receptor cells; neural, consisting of a loss of neurons in the auditory pathway in the brain; metabolic, consisting of a diminished supply of nutrients to the cells in the receptor area; and mechanical, consisting of atrophy and stiffening of the vibrating structures in the receptor area. Knowing the cause of a person's presbycusis is important because the different causes have different implications for other aspects of hearing. Sensory presbycusis has little effect on other hearing abilities. Neural presbycusis seriously affects the ability to understand speech. Metabolic presbycusis produces severe loss of sensitivity to all pitches. Finally, mechanical presbycusis also produces loss across all pitches, but the loss is greatest for high pitches.

FIGURE 15.5   Hearing Loss in Adulthood

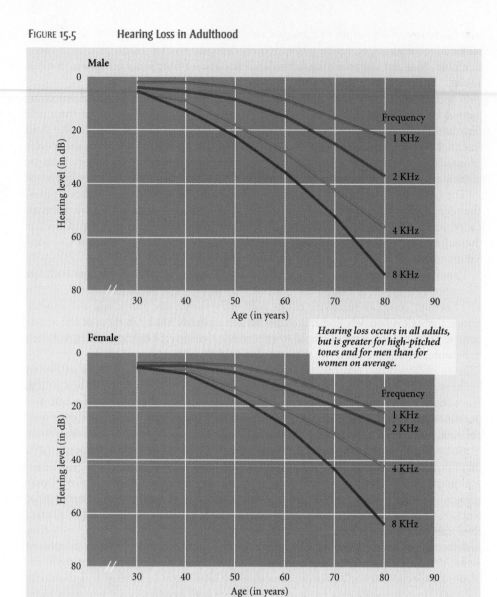

SOURCE: Ordy, J. M., Brizzee, K. R., Beavers, T., and Medart, P. (1979). Age differences in the functional and structural organization of the auditory system in man. In J. M. Ordy and K. R. Brizzee (Eds.), *Sensory systems and communication in the elderly*. Reprinted by permission of Lippincott, Williams and Wilkins.

Because hearing plays a major role in social communication, its progressive loss could have an equally important effect on social adjustment. Loss of hearing in later life can cause numerous adverse emotional reactions, such as loss of independence, social isolation, irritation, paranoia, and depression. Much research indicates hearing loss per se does not cause social maladjustment or emotional disturbance. However, friends and relatives of an older person with hearing loss often attribute emotional changes to hearing loss, which strains the quality of interpersonal relationships (Whitbourne, 1996). Thus, hearing loss may not directly affect older adults' self-concept or emotions, but it may negatively affect how they feel about interpersonal communication. By understanding hearing loss problems and ways to overcome them, those without hearing loss can play a large part in minimizing the effects of hearing loss on the older people in their lives.

Fortunately, many people with hearing loss can be helped through two types of amplification systems and cochlear implants, described in Table 15.1. Analog hearing aids are the most common and least expensive, but they provide the lowest-quality

TABLE 15.1

Type of Device	How It Works
Analog hearing aid	Although there are various styles, the basic design is always the same. A mould is placed in the outer ear to pick up sound and send it through tubes to a microphone. The microphone sends the sound to an amplifier. The amplifier enhances the sound and sends it to the receiver. The receiver sends the amplified sound to the ear.
Digital hearing aid	These are similar to analog hearing aids, but digital aids use directional microphones to control the flow of sound. Compression technology allows the sound to be increased or decreased as it rises and falls naturally in the room. Microchips allow hearing aids to be programmed for different hearing situations. This technology also uses multiple channels to deliver sound with varying amplification characteristics.
Cochlear implant	The main difference between hearing aids and cochlear implants is that implants do not make the sound louder. Rather, the implant is a series of components. A microphone, usually mounted behind the ear on the scalp, picks up sound. The sound is digitized by microchips and turned into coded signals, which are broadcast via FM radio signals to electrodes that have been inserted into the inner ear during surgery. The electrodes stimulate the auditory nerve fibres directly.

sound. Digital hearing aids include microchips that can be programmed for different hearing situations. Cochlear implants do not amplify sound; rather, a microphone transmits sound to a receiver, which stimulates auditory nerve fibres directly. Although technology continues to improve, none of these devices can duplicate our original equipment, so be kind to your ears. Although using a hearing aid reduces one's self-perceived hearing handicap, it does not by itself improve one's social interactions (Tesch-Römer, 1997). One's level of social skills is equally as important as hearing in improving interactions.

The sense of taste remains largely intact in older adults, as does pain sensitivity (Whitbourne, 1999). However, substantial declines in smell occur after age 70 in many people (Murphy, 1986), which may contribute to the perception of some loss of sense of taste or that food sometimes tastes more bland than in the past. Large declines in the sense of smell are characteristic of Alzheimer disease (Youngjohn & Crook, 1996). These changes can be dangerous; for example, very old adults often have difficulty detecting the substance added to natural gas to make leaks noticeable, which can prove fatal.

Changes in balance make older people increasingly likely to fall. Indeed, the fear of falling and getting injured is a real concern for many older adults and can affect their willingness to engage in certain types of activities (Lachman et al., 1998).

The ability to perceive temperature change, or thermal sensitivity, especially in the extremities decreases during the aging process. Stevens and Choo (1998) found that there was a profound deterioration of thermal sensitivity in the extremities, particularly the feet, which may start in middle age but is more pronounced in the elderly. These researchers propose that this may be due to chronic decreased circulation to the peripheral areas and therefore decreased oxygenation of those thermal receptors. Older adults may be more prone to burns or frostbite since they may not be able to sense the extremes in temperature in order to prevent damage from occurring.

The sensory changes people experience have important implications for their everyday lives (Whitbourne, 1996). Some, such as difficulty reading things close up, are minor annoyances that are easily corrected (by wearing reading glasses). Extra precautions may have to be taken to prevent burns by testing the water temperature with a thermometer before placing feet in the water, or wearing extra gloves to prevent frostbite. Others are more serious and less easily addressed. For example, the ability to drive a car is affected by changes in vision and in hearing.

Because sensory changes may also lead to accidents around the home, it is important to design a safer environment that takes these changes into account. Many accidents can be prevented by maintaining health through prevention and conditioning. But making some relatively simple environmental changes also helps. For example, falls are the most common cause of accidental serious injury and death among older adults. Here are some steps that can help reduce the potential for falls:

- Illuminate stairways and provide light switches at both the top and the bottom of the stairs.
- Avoid high-gloss floor finishes, due to glare and their tendency to be slippery when wet.
- Provide nightlights or bedside remote-control light switches.
- Be sure that both sides of stairways have sturdy handrails.
- Tack down carpeting on stairs, or use nonskid treads.
- Remove throw or area rugs that tend to slide on the floor.
- Arrange furniture and other objects so that they are not obstacles.
- Use grab bars on bathroom walls and nonskid mats or strips in bathtubs.
- Keep outdoor steps and walkways in good repair.

HEALTH ISSUES

In Chapter 14, we examined how lifestyle factors can lower the risk of many chronic diseases. The importance of health promotion does not diminish with increasing age. As we will see, lifestyle factors influence sleep, nutrition, and cancer.

Sleep

Older adults have more trouble sleeping than do younger adults (Bootzin et al., 1996). Compared to younger adults, older adults report that it takes roughly twice as long to fall asleep, that they get less sleep on an average night, and that they feel more negative effects following a night with little sleep. Some of these problems are due to physical disorders, medication side effects, and the effects of caffeine, nicotine, and stress (Bootzin et al., 1996). *Sleep problems can disrupt a person's* **circadian rhythm,** *or sleep-wake cycle.* Circadian rhythm disruptions can cause problems with attention and memory. Research shows that interventions such as properly timed exposure to bright light is effective in correcting circadian rhythm sleep disorders (Terman, 1994).

Nutrition

Under normal circumstances, older adults do not need any vitamin or mineral supplements as long as they are eating a well-balanced diet (Bortz & Bortz, 1996). Even though body metabolism declines with age, older adults need to consume the same amounts of proteins and carbohydrates as young adults because of changes in how readily the body extracts the nutrients from these substances. Because they are typically in poor health, residents of nursing homes are prone to weight loss and may have various nutritional deficiencies, such as vitamin B_{12} and folic acid, unless closely monitored (Wallace & Schwartz, 1994).

Cancer

One of the most important health promotion steps people can take is cancer screening. In many cases, screening procedures involve little more than tests performed in a physician's office (e.g., screening for colon cancer), at home (breast self-exams), blood tests (screening for prostate cancer), or X-rays (mammograms).

Why is cancer screening so important? As you can see in Figure 15.6, the risk of getting cancer increases markedly with age (Frazer et al., 1996). Why this happens is not fully understood. Unhealthy lifestyles (smoking

> **THINK ABOUT IT**
>
> How might fear of falling and osteoporosis (see Chapter 14) be linked?

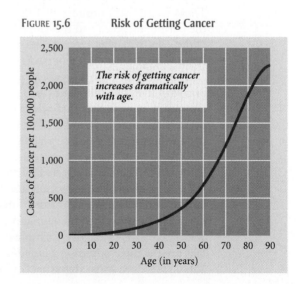

FIGURE 15.6   Risk of Getting Cancer

The risk of getting cancer increases dramatically with age.

and poor diet), genetics, and exposure to cancer-causing chemicals certainly are important, but they do not fully explain the age-related increase in risk (Frazer et al., 1996). Early detection of cancer even in older adults is essential to maximize the odds of surviving (Segal, 1996). As our knowledge of the genetic underpinnings of some forms of cancer continues to increase, early detection and lifestyle changes will be increasingly important.

TEST YOURSELF

1. The biological theory of aging that includes the factors of free radicals and cross-linking is _____.

2. Damaged and dying neurons that collect around a core of protein produce _____.

3. The risk of getting cancer _____ markedly with age.

In this section, we have concentrated on the biological forces in development. Think about the other forces (psychological, social, and life-cycle), and list some reasons scientists have yet to propose a purely biological theory that accounts for all aspects of aging.

Answers: (1) cellular theory, (2) neuritic plaques, (3) increases

15.3

Cognitive Processes

LEARNING OBJECTIVES

☑ What changes occur in attention and reaction time as people age? How do these changes relate to everyday life?

☑ What changes occur in memory with age? What can be done to remediate these changes?

☑ What is wisdom, and how is it related to age?

Cognitive Processes

Information Processing

Memory

Creativity and Wisdom

Anne is a 75-year-old widow who feels that she does not remember recent events, such as whether she took her medicine, as well as she used to, but she has no trouble remembering things from her 20s. Anne wonders if this is normal, or whether she should be worried.

Anne, like many older people, takes medications for arthritis, allergies, and high blood pressure. However, each drug has its own pattern; some are taken only with meals, others are taken every eight hours, and still others are taken twice daily. Keeping these regimens straight is important to avoid potentially dangerous interactions and side effects, and older people thus face the problem of remembering to take each medication at the proper time.

Such situations place a heavy demand on cognitive resources, such as attention and memory. In this section, we examine age-related changes in these and other cognitive processes, such as reaction time, intelligence, and wisdom.

INFORMATION PROCESSING

In Chapter 1 we saw that one theoretical framework for studying cognition is information-processing theory. This framework provides a way to identify and study the basic mechanisms by which people take in, store, and remember information. We have already seen in Chapters 5 and 7 that information-processing theory has guided much research on cognition in childhood and adolescence. This approach has also been important to investigators examining age-related differences in basic processes such as attention and reaction time (Stine-Morrow & Soederberg Miller, 1999).

Attention

Researchers view attention as having three major components: selection, vigilance, and control (Parasuraman, 1998). Taken together, these components comprise the processes that enable people to perform a variety of functions.

We are constantly bombarded with stimulation to all of our senses, which we must somehow sort out. For example, when talking with someone at a party, we have to focus on what that person is saying and filter out all other noise. *Selective attention involves the selection of relevant information and inhibition of irrelevant information.* Older adults tend to perform more poorly than younger adults on most selective attention tasks (McDowd & Shaw, 2000). However, age differences are minimized when the task involves simple searches for target information or when people are given sufficient practice.

Vigilance, also called sustained attention, involves the maintenance of attention over time. Listening for one's name to be called at a take-out restaurant, watching for the traffic light to change, and monitoring a screen connected to security cameras are all examples of vigilance tasks. Whether vigilance ability declines with age is uncertain (Rogers & Fisk, 2001). To the extent that memory demands are minimized, practice on the task is provided, and visual defects are corrected, age differences are minimized.

*People's abilities to focus, switch, and divide attention are referred to as **attentional control**.* Results concerning age differences in attentional control are mixed (Rogers & Fisk, 2001). If older adults are told where to focus their attention, if a cue is provided to help them shift attention, or if the task is simple, then they perform about as well as younger adults. But if the rate at which attention must be shifted is fast or if the task is complex, older adults do more poorly.

In sum, whether there is an age-related difference in attention depends on many factors, such as task complexity, visual ability, and other cognitive factors. It also turns out that aerobic exercise can improve performance on attention tasks (Kramer et al., 2001). What is clear is that there is no simple description of developmental changes in attentional abilities (Rogers & Fisk, 2001).

Psychomotor Speed

You are driving home from a friend's house when all of a sudden a car pulls out of a driveway right into your path. You must hit the brakes as fast as possible or you will have an accident. How quickly can you move your foot from the accelerator to the brake?

*This real-life situation is an example of **psychomotor speed**, the speed with which a person can make a specific response.* Psychomotor speed (also called reaction time) is one of the most studied phenomena of aging, and hundreds of studies all point to the same conclusion: People slow down as they get older. In fact, the slowing-with-age finding is so well documented that many researchers accept it as the only universal behavioural change in aging yet discovered (Salthouse, 2000). Data suggest, however, that the rate at which cognitive processes slow down from young adulthood to late life varies a great deal depending on the task (Madden, 2001; Stine-Morrow & Soederberg Miller, 1999).

The most important reason reaction times slow down is that older adults take longer to decide that they need to respond, especially when the situation involves ambiguous information (Salthouse, 2000). Even when the information presented indicates that a response will definitely be needed, there is an orderly slowing of responding with age. As the uncertainty of whether a response is needed increases, older adults get differentially slower; the difference between them and middle-aged adults increases as the uncertainty level increases.

Although response slowing is inevitable, the amount of the decline can be reduced if older adults are allowed to practise making quick responses or if they are experienced in the task. In a classic study, Salthouse (1984) showed that although older secretaries' reaction times (measured by how fast they could tap their finger) were slower than those of younger secretaries, their computed typing speed was no slower than that of their younger counterparts. Why? Typing speed is calculated on the basis of words typed corrected for errors; because older typists are more accurate, their final speeds were just as good as those of younger secretaries, whose work tended to include more errors. Also, older secretaries are better at anticipating what letters come next (Kail & Salthouse, 1994).

Because psychomotor slowing is a universal phenomenon, many researchers have argued that it may explain a great deal of the age differences in cognition (e.g., Salthouse, 2000). Indeed, psychomotor slowing is a very good predictor of cognitive performance, but there's a catch. The prediction is best when the task requires little effort (Park et al., 1996). When the task requires more effort and is more difficult, then working memory (which we consider later) is a better predictor of performance (Park et al., 1996). Also, older adults who are physically fit do not show as much slowing (Bunce, 2001).

Psychomotor slowing with age has also sparked considerable controversy concerning whether older adults should be allowed to drive. As discussed in the Current Controversies feature, knowledge about sensory and cognitive changes has resulted in research on this issue and the development of screening tests.

> **THINK ABOUT IT**
>
> What are some of the practical consequences of psychomotor slowing?

CURRENT CONTROVERSIES

Information Processing in Everyday Life: Older Drivers

Several bits of information we have considered so far coalesce around a controversial issue: whether older drivers should be screened more closely before their driver's licences are renewed. This is a sensitive topic. For many people, the automobile is their only reliable means of transportation, and a means of remaining independent. However, age-related changes in vision, hearing, attention, and reaction time do affect people's competence as drivers. Moreover, the number of older adults is rapidly increasing.

Transport Canada (2001) reports that over the 10-year period between 1988 and 1998, although the casualty-producing collision rate overall decreased, involvement of drivers aged 65 years and older increased by 12%. Some argue that this is due to older drivers' age-related decline in key sensory, attentional, and psychomotor abilities (Bowles, 2001).

Experts agree that decisions about whether "at-risk" drivers should be allowed to continue driving must be based on performance measures rather than age or medical diagnosis alone. Since the mid-1980s, researchers such as Karlene Ball and others have been working to develop these measures. Their work resulted in the *Useful Field of View (UFOV)* measure, which is the area from which one can extract visual information in a single glance without turning one's head or moving one's eyes (Ball & Owsley, 1993). The UFOV test simulates driving in that it demands quick pro-

cessing of information, simultaneous monitoring of central and peripheral stimuli, and the extraction of relevant target stimuli from irrelevant background information while performing a task. A reduction in the UFOV is directly related to the odds of being in automobile accidents (Ball et al., 1993). Indeed, in an analysis of 364 crashes involving older adults, 220 occurred at intersections and were caused by inattention (e.g., not seeing an on-coming car), exactly as would be predicted by a decline in UFOV (Ball et al., 1993). Importantly, driving performance improves after training in how to expand one's UFOV; for example, people reduce the number of dangerous manoeuvres made while driving (Ball, 1997).

Should there be mandatory testing of older drivers? The data clearly indicate that the answer should be yes. What form this testing should take, however, will spark increasing debate over the next few decades. In Canada, only Ontario has a mandatory driver's test and traffic safety workshop when seniors who are licensed drivers reach the age of 80 and every two years thereafter, although most provinces and territories require a mandatory medical exam for drivers of certain ages, e.g., 75 years (Bess, 1999). However, the Canada Safety Council has developed the 55 Alive Driver Refresher Course for Canadians aged 55 years and older who wish to improve their driving skills. ◙

Working Memory

One evening while you are watching television, you suddenly remember that your partner's birthday is a week from tomorrow. You decide that a nice romantic dinner would be just the thing, so you open the phone book, look up the number for a special restaurant, go over to the phone, and make the call. Remembering the number long enough to dial it successfully requires good working memory. Working memory involves the processes and structures that hold information in the mind and simultaneously use it to solve a problem, make a decision, perform some function, or learn new information.

Working memory is an umbrella term for many similar short-term holding and computational processes relating to a wide range of cognitive skills and knowledge domains (Zacks, Hasher, & Li, 2000). Working memory has a relatively small capacity. Because working memory deals with information that is being used right at the moment, it acts as a kind of mental scratchpad or blackboard. Unless we take some action to keep the information active (perhaps by rehearsal), or pass it along to long-term storage, the page we are using will get filled up quickly; in order to handle more information, some of the old information must be discarded.

Working memory generally declines with age (Zacks et al., 2000), and several researchers use it to explain age-related differences in cognitive performance on tasks that are difficult and demand considerable effort and resources (Park et al., 1996). Taken together, working memory and psychomotor speed provide a powerful set of explanatory constructs in predicting cognitive performance (Salthouse, 2000).

MEMORY

"Memory is power" (Johnson-Laird, 1988, p. 41). Indeed it is, when you think of the importance of remembering tasks, faces, lists, instructions, and our personal past and identity. Perhaps that is why people put such a premium on maintaining a good memory in old age; many older adults use their ability to remember to judge whether their mind is intact. Poor memory is often viewed as an inevitable part of aging. Many people like Anne, the woman in the vignette, believe that forgetting a loaf of bread at the store when one is 25 is not a big deal, but forgetting it when one is 65 is cause for alarm—a sign of Alzheimer disease or some other malady. In this section, we sort out the myth and the reality of memory changes with age.

What Changes?

The study of memory aging generally focuses on two types of memory: **explicit memory,** *the deliberate and conscious remembering of information that is learned and remembered at a specific time, and* **implicit memory,** *the unconscious remembering of information learned at some earlier time. Explicit memory is further divided into* **episodic memory,** *the general class of memory having to do with the conscious recollection of information from a specific time or event, and* **semantic memory,** *the general class of memory concerning the remembering of meanings of words or concepts not tied to a specific time or event.*

The results from hundreds of studies point to several conclusions (Bäckman, Small, & Wahlin, 2001). Older adults tend to perform worse than younger adults on tests of episodic memory recall in that they omit more information, include more intrusions, and repeat more previously recalled items. These age differences are large; for example, more than 80% of a sample of adults in their 20s will do better than adults in their 70s (Verhaeghen & Salthouse, 1997). These differences are not reliably lowered by providing slower presentation or by giving cues or reminders during recall. On recognition tests, age differences are smaller but are not eliminated (Zacks et al., 2000). Older adults also tend to be less efficient at spontaneously using memory strategies to help themselves remember (Dunlosky & Hertzog, 2001).

In contrast, age differences on semantic memory tasks are typically absent (Bäckman et al., 2001). However, one area in which older adults have difficulty is in word-finding, such as coming up with the right word based on a definition and having more tip-of-the-tongue experiences. Similarly, age differences are typically absent on tests of implicit memory (Fleischman & Gabrieli, 1998).

A final area of memory research concerns autobiographical memory, memory for events that occur during one's life. An interesting phenomenon arises when the distribution of highly memorable autobiographical events across the lifespan is examined. As you can see in Figure 15.7, for both younger and older adults vivid memories experienced between ages 10 and 30 are reported more often than those occurring after age 30 (Fitzgerald, 1999). This same pattern holds when people are asked to name Academy Award winners, news stories, and teams that played in the World Series (Rubin, Rahhal, & Poon, 1998). It is possible that this earlier period of life has greater importance in defining oneself and thus helps people organize their memories (Fitzgerald, 1999).

FIGURE 15.7   Memories of Life Events

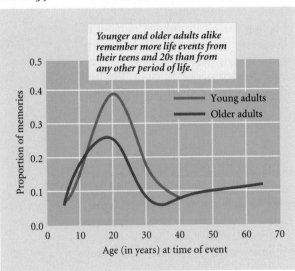

Younger and older adults alike remember more life events from their teens and 20s than from any other period of life.

SOURCE: Reprinted from Fitzgerald, J. (1999). Autobiographical memory and social cognition. In T. M. Hess & F. Blanchard-Fields (Eds.), *Social cognition and aging* (p. 161) with permission from Elsevier.

In sum, contrary to social stereotypes of a broad-based decline in memory ability with age, research shows that the facts are more complex. Whether memory declines with age depends on the type of memory. But social stereotypes are powerful, as we will see next.

The Impact of Beliefs About Memory Aging

Regardless of the results from research, there is widespread belief that memory inevitably declines. This is significant because research shows that what adults believe about their memory ability is related to how well they perform (Cavanaugh, 1996). This relation is seen in how much effort people exert trying to remember, how well people predict they will perform, and what strategies people use. For example, people who believe their memory is good work harder at remembering than people who believe their memory is poor. Moreover, these beliefs are also related to the assumptions people make about the degree to which memory (or other cognitive abilities) is "supposed" to change (Cavanaugh, Feldman, & Hertzog, 1998). For example, if you think memory is supposed to get much worse as you get older, then your estimate of how much your memory has declined will be much greater than an estimate by someone who thinks memory should decline only a little with age.

Although some changes in memory are normal, research on memory beliefs shows that people can essentially convince themselves that these changes are much worse and more pervasive than they really are (Cavanaugh et al., 1998). It may even be the case that altering your central beliefs about memory aging may help you develop compensatory strategies that lower the magnitude of these changes, or at least help compensate for them (Cavanaugh, 2000).

Still, one's beliefs about memory are influenced by changes in basic information processing, such as working memory (Hertzog & Hultsch, 2000). Although beliefs are important, they must also be realistic about normative change.

When Is Memory Change Abnormal?

Many older adults believe that their forgetfulness is indicative of something much worse. Because people are concerned that memory failures may reflect disease, identifying true cases of memory-impairing disease is extremely important. Differentiating normal and abnormal memory changes is usually accomplished through a wide array of tests that are grounded in the various developmental patterns discussed earlier. Such testing focuses on measuring performance and identifying declines in aspects of memory that typically do not change, such as tertiary memory (Edelstein & Kalish, 1999).

Even if a decline is identified in an aspect of memory that is cause for concern, it does not automatically follow that there is a serious problem. A first step is to find out whether the memory problem is interfering with everyday functioning. When the memory problem does interfere with functioning, such as not remembering how to get home or your spouse's name, it is appropriate to suspect a serious, abnormal underlying reason.

Once a serious problem is suspected, the next step is to obtain a thorough examination (Edelstein & Kalish, 1999). This should include a complete physical and neurological examination and a complete battery of neuropsychological tests. These may help identify the nature and extent of the underlying problem and provide information about what steps, if any, can be taken to alleviate the difficulties.

The most important point to keep in mind is that there is no magic number of times that a person must forget something before it becomes a matter for concern. Indeed, many memory-impairing diseases progress slowly, and poor memory performance may only be noticed gradually over an extended period of time. The best course is to have the person examined; only with complete and thorough testing can these concerns be checked appropriately.

Remediating Memory Problems

Remember Anne, the person in the vignette who had to remember when to take several different medications? In the face of normal age-related declines, how can her problem be solved?

Support programs can be designed for people to help them remember. Sometimes, people like Anne who are experiencing normal age-related memory changes need extra help because of the high memory demands they face. At other times, people need help because the memory changes they are experiencing are greater than normal.

Camp and colleagues (1993; Camp, 2001) developed the E-I-E-I-O framework to handle both situations. The E-I-E-I-O framework combines two types of memory: explicit and implicit. The framework also includes two types of memory aids. *External aids are memory aids that rely on environmental resources, such as notebooks or calendars. Internal aids are memory aids that rely on mental processes, such as imagery.* The "aha" experience that comes with suddenly remembering something (as in, "Oh, I remember!) is the O that follows these E's and I's. As you can see in Table 15.2, the E-I-E-I-O framework allows different types of memory to be combined with different types of memory aids to provide a broad range of intervention options to help people remember.

TABLE 15.2

Type of memory	Type of memory aid	
	External	**Internal**
Explicit	Appointment book	Mental imagery
	Grocery list	Rote rehearsal
Implicit	Colour-coded maps	Spaced retrieval
	Sandpaper letters	Conditioning

You are probably most familiar with the explicit-external and explicit-internal types of memory aids. Explicit-internal aids like rehearsal help people remember phone numbers. Explicit-external aids are used when information needs to be better organized and remembered, such as taking notes during a visit to the physician (McGuire & Codding, 1998). Implicit-internal aids represent nearly effortless learning, such as the association between the colour of the particular wing of the apartment building one lives in and the fact that one's residence is there. Implicit-external aids such as icons representing time of day and the number of pills to take help older adults remember their medication (Morrow et al., 1998).

THINK ABOUT IT

How might people's beliefs about memory be important elements of memory training programs?

In general, explicit-external interventions are the most frequently used to remediate the kinds of memory problems older adults face, probably because they are easy to use and widely available (Camp, 2001). For example, virtually everyone owns an address book, and small notepads are sold in hundreds of stores. Explicit-external interventions have other important applications too. The medication problem is best solved with an explicit-external intervention: a pillbox that is divided into compartments corresponding to days of the week and different times of the day. Research shows that this type of pillbox is the easiest to load and results in the fewest errors (Park, Morrell, & Shifren, 1999). Memory interventions like this can help older adults maintain their independence.

Nursing homes often use explicit-external interventions, such as bulletin boards with the date and weather conditions, or activities charts to help residents keep in touch with current events and to assist those who have dementia. Reality Orientation (RO), as it is frequently referred to, consists of presenting orientation information (such as time, place, and person) to provide residents with an improved understanding of their surroundings, a practice that may improve their sense of control and self-esteem. When the effectiveness of these programs was studied, there was evidence that RO has benefits related to both cognition and behaviour for those suffering from dementia. However, a continued program is necessary to continue its benefits (Spector, Orrell, Davis, & Woods, 2004).

CREATIVITY AND WISDOM

Creativity

What makes a person creative? Is it exceptional productivity? David Foster has written numerous musical pieces, Diego Rivera painted hundreds of pictures, and Thomas Edison had 1,093 patents (still the record for one person). But Gregor Mendel had only seven scientific papers, yet he endures as a major figure in the history of genetics. Lao Tzu is remembered mostly for the enduring *Tao Te Ching*. Does creativity mean having a career marked by precocity and longevity? Wolfgang Goethe wrote poetry as a teenager, a best-selling novel in his 20s, popular plays in his 30s and 40s, Part I of *Faust* at 59, and Part II at 83. But others are "early bloomers" and decline thereafter, whereas still others are relatively unproductive early and are "late bloomers."

Researchers define creativity in adults as the ability to produce work that is novel, high in demand, and task appropriate (Sternberg & Lubart, 2001). Creative output, measured by the number of creative ideas a person has or the major contributions a person makes, varies across adult life span and across disciplines (Simonton, 1997; Sternberg & Lubart, 2001). When considered as a function of age, the overall number of creative ideas a person has tends to increase through one's 20s, plateaus in one's 30s, and declines thereafter, as shown in Figure 15.8. However, the decline does *not* mean that people stop being creative at all; rather, it means that creative people keep producing creative ideas, but fewer of them than they did when they were younger (Dixon & Hultsch, 1999). When translated into a mathematical equation,

FIGURE 15.8   Productivity in Adulthood

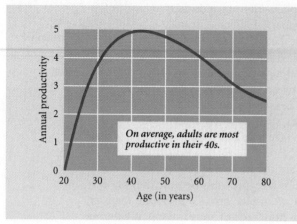

On average, adults are most productive in their 40s.

FIGURE 15.9   Contributing in Adulthood

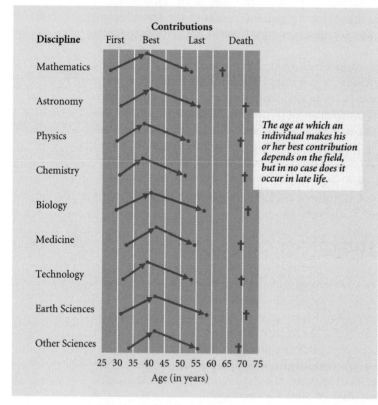

The age at which an individual makes his or her best contribution depends on the field, but in no case does it occur in late life.

Figure 15.8 can be used to predict the creative output of a specific individual (e.g., David Foster) or a group of similar people (e.g., music composers). In both cases, the figure accurately describes the level of creative output. Thus, creative output peaks in early to middle adulthood, and declines thereafter.

What does the trend look like if one compares different disciplines, such as mathematics, biology, and earth sciences? One way to examine this is to compare three points in a career: the age at the time of the first major contribution, most important contribution, and the last important contribution (Simonton, 1997). As you can see in Figure 15.9, the overall shape of the curve in several scientific disciplines is the same as in Figure 15.8, with a rise, a peak, and a decline with increasing age. The average age at which the people studied died is shown by small crosses. Notice that the specific ages for the three contributions depends on the discipline. For example, mathematics has the youngest age of first major contribution, and earth sciences tends to have the oldest age at last important contribution.

Taken together, Simonton's (1997) analysis provides the most powerful model available to explain individual differences in creative output across adulthood. The trend is clear. Across a variety of disciplines, creative output tends to peak during late young adulthood to early middle age and decline thereafter. This pattern may help explain why senior researchers include many younger scholars in their work. The senior scholar can provide the overall context, while the younger researchers may provide a continuous flow of innovative ideas (Dixon & Hultsch, 1999).

Wisdom

For thousands of years, cultures around the world have greatly admired people who were wise. Tales of wise people, usually older adults, have been passed down from generation to generation to teach lessons about important matters of life and love (Chinen, 1989). What is it about these truths that makes someone who knows them wise?

From a psychological perspective, wisdom has been viewed from three main perspectives (Sternberg & Lubart, 2001): the orchestration of mind and virtue, involving the ability to solve difficult real-world problems; post-formal thinking (see Chapter 11); and action-oriented knowledge acquired without direct help from others that enables people to achieve goals they value. A growing body of research has been examining these aspects.

Based on years of research using in-depth think-aloud interviews with young, middle-aged, and older adults about normal and unusual problems that people face, Baltes and Staudinger (1993, 2000) describe four characteristics of wisdom:

- Wisdom deals with important or difficult matters of life and the human condition.
- Wisdom is truly "superior" knowledge, judgment, and advice.
- Wisdom is knowledge with extraordinary scope, depth, and balance, applicable to specific situations.
- Wisdom, when used, is well intended and combines mind and virtue (character).

The researchers used this framework to discover that people who are wise are experts in the basic issues in life (Baltes & Staudinger, 2000). Wise people know a great deal about how to conduct life, how to interpret life events, and what life means.

Research studies indicate that contrary to what many people expect, there is no association between age and wisdom (Baltes & Staudinger, 2000; De Andrade, 2000; Hartman, 2001). As is depicted in Baltes and Staudinger's (2000) model (Figure 15.10), whether a person is wise depends on whether he or she has extensive life experience with the type of problem given and has the requisite cognitive abilities and personality.

Research based on cognitive developmental changes in adulthood, such as those discussed in Chapter 11, has uncovered other aspects in the growth of wisdom. According to several investigators, a wise person is one who is able to integrate thinking, feeling, and acting into a coherent approach to a problem (Kramer, 1990;

FIGURE 15.10   **Wisdom Related Performance**

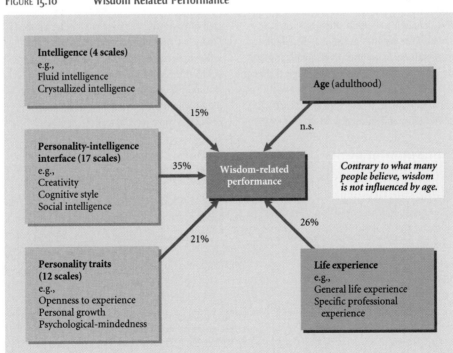

Orwoll & Perlmutter, 1990). This research implies that empathy and compassion are important characteristics of wise people (Wink & Helson, 1997). They are able to overcome automatic responses so as to show concern for core human experiences and values (Pascual-Leone, 1990). Thus, wise people are able to see through situations and get to the heart of the matter rather than being caught in the superficial aspects (Wink & Helson, 1997).

So what specific factors help one become wise? Baltes (1993) identified three factors: (a) *general personal conditions,* such as mental ability; (b) *specific expertise conditions,* such as mentoring or practice; and (c) *facilitative life contexts,* such as education or leadership experience. Other researchers point to additional criteria. For example, Kramer (1990) argues that the *integration of affect and cognition* that occurs during adulthood results in the ability to act wisely. Personal growth during adulthood, reflecting Erikson's concepts of generativity and integrity, helps foster the process as well. All of these factors take time. Thus, although growing old is no guarantee of wisdom, it does provide the time that, if used well, creates a supportive context for it. As discussed in the Forces in Action feature, all cognitive changes in later life are the result of complex processes.

FORCES IN ACTION

Cognitive Changes in Later Life

Normal aging brings decline in several abilities, whereas others remain largely intact or even improve. Why is there such variation in developmental trends? The interactive model shown in Figure 15.11 provides some insights.

Biological forces (e.g., the brain, genetics, health, and disease) operate to reduce the efficiency of basic information-processing abilities. Additionally, psychological forces from the differential use of cognitive abilities and the sociocultural forces from lower cognitive demands in certain situations can help account for declines in some areas. Similar explanations of abilities that remain constant or improve can be made. Physiological changes in the brain do not affect all areas equally; psychological forces create greater practice with some skills; and sociocultural pressures to maintain contact with the world mean that some skills, such as in areas of expertise, continue to operate well.

Life-cycle forces are also important in understanding cognitive changes in later life. The same cognitive event often has very different meanings, depending on where in life people are. For example, not being efficient at remembering grocery items without a list may be only mildly annoying and easily dismissed in young adulthood but may be viewed as a sign of cognitive slippage by an older adult. Such changes in interpretation even of apparently universal events, such as forgetting something at the grocery store, become more common as people reach late life and worry about whether they may be getting Alzheimer disease, a topic we will explore next.

FIGURE 15.11

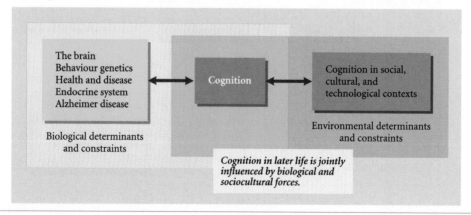

TEST YOURSELF

1. As long as the competing tasks in a test of divided attention are easy, older adults perform _____ younger adults.

2. Compared to age differences in free recall performance, age differences in recognition memory performance are _____.

3. Three factors that help a person become wise are general personal conditions, special expertise conditions, and _____.

How would the view that wisdom involves life experience fit into the discussion of expertise in Chapter 14?

Answers: (1) as well as, (2) smaller, (3) facilitative life contexts

---

15.4

Mental Health and Intervention

LEARNING OBJECTIVES

- ⊞ How does depression in older adults differ from depression in younger adults? How is it diagnosed and treated?
- ⊞ How are anxiety disorders treated in older adults?
- ⊞ What is Alzheimer disease? How is it diagnosed and managed? What causes it?

> **Mental Health and Intervention**
> Depression
> Anxiety Disorders
> Dementia: Alzheimer Disease

Nora is an 86-year-old widow living alone. Over the past few months, her friends have noticed that she has lost weight, looks tired, and has not been her normally cheerful self. Nora says that she feels down "now and then" but that she is fine otherwise. But Nora's friends think something may be wrong.

Suppose Nora is a friend of yours. How would you deal with this situation? How would you decide whether her behaviour is normal? What would you do to find out?

Every day, families turn to mental health professionals for help in dealing with psychological problems their aging relatives are having. Unfortunately, myths interfere with appropriate mental health diagnoses and interventions for older adults. For example, many people mistakenly believe that nearly all older adults are either depressed, demented, or both. When they observe older adults behaving in these ways, they take no action because they believe nothing can be done.

In this section, we will see that such beliefs are wrong. Only a minority of older adults have mental health problems, and most such problems respond to therapy. Sometimes these problems manifest themselves differently in younger and older adults, so we need to know what to look for. Accurate diagnosis is essential. Let's examine some of the most commonly occurring and widely known disorders: depression, anxiety disorders, and Alzheimer disease.

DEPRESSION

Most people feel down or sad from time to time, perhaps in reaction to a problem at work or in one's relationships. But does this mean that most people are depressed? How is depression diagnosed? Are there age differences in the symptoms examined in diagnosis? How is depression treated?

First of all, let's dispense with a myth. Contrary to the popular belief that most older adults are depressed, the rate of severe depression *declines* from young adulthood to old age (Qualls, 1999). According to Statistics Canada (2002c), the incidence of depression peaked among those aged 20 to 24 years (9.6%), and the lowest rate (3.2%) was among those aged 65 years and older. For those people who do experience depression, let's examine its diagnosis and treatment.

How Is Depression Diagnosed in Older Adults?

Depression in later life is usually diagnosed on the basis of two clusters of symptoms that must be present for at least two weeks: feelings and physical changes. *As with younger people, the most prominent symptom of depression in older adults is feeling sad or down, termed **dysphoria**.* But whereas younger

people are likely to label these feelings directly as "feeling depressed," older adults like the man in the photograph may refer to them as "feeling helpless" or in terms of physical health such as "feeling tired" (Wolfe, Morrow, & Fredrickson, 1996). Older adults are also more likely than younger people to appear apathetic and expressionless, to confine themselves to bed, to neglect themselves, and to make derogatory statements about themselves. Nora, the woman in the vignette, shows some of these behaviours.

The second cluster of symptoms includes physical changes such as loss of appetite, insomnia, and trouble breathing (Whitbourne, 2000). In young people, these symptoms usually indicate an underlying psychological problem. But in older adults, they may simply reflect normal age-related changes. Thus, older adults' physical symptoms of depression must be evaluated very carefully (Qualls, 1999). This would be true in Nora's case.

An important step in diagnosis is ruling out other possible causes of the symptoms. For example, other physical health problems, neurological disorders, medication side effects, metabolic conditions, and substance abuse can all cause behaviours that resemble depression (Qualls, 1999). For many minorities, immigration status and degree of acculturation and assimilation are key factors to consider (Black, Markides, & Miller, 1998). An important criterion to be established is that the symptoms interfere with daily life; clinical depression involves significant impairment of daily living (Edelstein & Kalish, 1999; Qualls, 1999).

What Causes Depression?

There are two main schools of thought about the causes of depression. One focuses on biological and physiological processes, particularly on imbalances in specific neurotransmitters (see Chapter 9). Because most neurotransmitter levels decline with age, some researchers believe that depression in later life is likely to be a biochemical problem (Whitbourne, 2000). The general view that depression has a biochemical basis underlies current approaches to drug therapies, which are discussed a bit later.

The second view focuses on psychosocial factors, such as loss and internal belief systems. Although several types of loss have been associated with depression, including loss of a spouse, a job, or good health, it is how a person interprets a loss, rather than the event itself, that causes depression (Gaylord & Zung, 1987). *In this approach, **internal belief systems**, or what one tells oneself about why certain things are happening, are emphasized as the cause of depression.* For example, experiencing an unpredictable and uncontrollable event such as the death of a spouse may cause depression because you believe the event happened to you because you are a bad person (Beck, 1967). People who are depressed tend to believe they are personally responsible for all the bad things that happen to them, that things are unlikely to get better, and that their whole life is a shambles.

Gatz (2000) takes a comprehensive view that depression depends on the balance between biological dispositions, stress, and protective factors. Developmentally, biological factors become more important with age, whereas stress factors diminish. Better protective factors, such as coping skills, with age may help explain why the rate of depression decreases across the adult life span.

How Is Depression Treated in Older Adults?

Regardless how severe depression is, people benefit from treatment, often through a combination of medication and psychotherapy (Qualls, 1999; Wolfe et al., 1996). Medications work by altering the balance of specific neurotransmitters in the brain. *For very severe cases of depression, medications such as heterocyclic antidepressants (HCAs), monoamine oxidase (MAO) inhibitors, or selective serotonin reuptake inhibitors (SSRIs) can be administered.* Although they are widely prescribed, HCAs cannot be used if the person is also taking medications to control hypertension or has certain metabolic conditions. MAO inhibitors cause very dangerous and potentially fatal interactions with foods containing tyramine or dopamine, such as cheddar cheese, wine, and chicken liver. Consequently, MAO inhibitors are usually used only as a last resort. Selective serotonin reuptake inhibitors (SSRIs) gained wide popularity beginning in the late 1980s because they have the lowest overall side effects of any antidepressant. SSRIs work by boosting the level of serotonin, which is a neurotransmitter involved in regulating moods. One of the SSRIs, Prozac, has been the subject of controversy, as it has been linked in a small number of cases with the serious side effect of high levels of agitation. Other SSRIs, such as Zoloft and Serzone, appear to have fewer adverse reactions.

Psychotherapy is a popular approach to treating depression, based on the idea that focusing on the psychological aspects of depression is helpful. Two forms of psychotherapy have been shown to be effective with older adults. *The basic idea in behaviour therapy is that depressed people experience too few rewards or reinforcements from their environment.* Thus, the goal of behaviour therapy is to increase the good things that happen and minimize the negative things (Lewinsohn, 1975). Often, this is accomplished by having people increase their activities; simply by doing more, the likelihood that something nice will happen is increased. Additionally, behaviour therapy seeks to get people to reduce the negative things that happen by learning how to avoid them. The net increase in positive events and net decrease in negative events comes about through practice and homework assignments during the course of therapy, such as going out more or joining a club to meet new people.

A second effective approach is cognitive therapy, which is based on the idea that maladaptive beliefs or cognitions about oneself are responsible for depression. From this perspective, a depressed person views him- or herself as unworthy and inadequate, the world as insensitive and ungratifying, and the future as bleak and unpromising (Beck et al., 1979). In a cognitive therapy session, the person is taught how to recognize these thoughts and to reevaluate the self, the world, and the future more realistically, resulting in a change in the underlying beliefs.

The most important fact to keep in mind about depression is that it *is* treatable. Thus, if an older person behaves in ways that indicate depression, it is a good idea to have him or her examined by a mental health professional. Even if it turns out not to be depression, another underlying and possibly treatable condition may be uncovered.

ANXIETY DISORDERS

Imagine you are about to give a speech to an audience of several hundred people. During the last few minutes before you begin, you start to feel nervous, your heart begins to pound, your mouth gets very dry, and your palms get sweaty. These feelings, common even to veteran speakers, are similar to those experienced more frequently by people with anxiety disorders.

Anxiety disorders include problems such as feelings of severe anxiety for no apparent reason, phobias with regard to specific things or places, and obsessive-compulsive disorders, in which thoughts or actions are repeatedly performed (Fisher & Noll, 1996; Qualls, 1999). Although anxiety disorders occur in adults of all ages, they are particularly common in older adults due to loss of health, relocation stress, isolation, fear of losing independence, and many other reasons. Anxiety disorders are diagnosed more frequently in women than men (Cohen, 1990). The reasons for this gender difference are unknown.

Anxiety disorders can be treated with medication and psychotherapy (Fisher & Noll, 1996). The most commonly used medications are benzodiazepine (e.g., Valium and Librium), SSRIs (Paxil, among others), buspirone, and beta-blockers. Though moderately effective, these drugs must be monitored very carefully in older adults because the amount needed to treat the disorder is very low and the potential for side effects is great. For older adults, the clear treatment of choice is psychotherapy, especially relaxation therapy (Fisher & Noll, 1996). Relaxation therapy is highly effective, is easily learned, and presents a technique that is useful in many situations (e.g., falling asleep at night).

To this point, we have focused on psychopathologies that can be treated effectively. In the next section, we consider Alzheimer disease, which at present cannot be treated effectively over the long run, progressively worsening until the person dies.

DEMENTIA: ALZHEIMER DISEASE

*Arguably the most serious condition associated with aging is **dementia**, a family of diseases involving serious impairment of behavioural and cognitive functioning.* Of these disorders, Alzheimer disease is the most common. One case is presented in the Real People feature.

REAL PEOPLE: APPLYING HUMAN DEVELOPMENT

What's the Matter with Mary?

Mary lived by herself for 30 years after her husband died. For all but the last five years or so, she managed very well. Little by little, though, family members and friends began noticing that Mary wasn't behaving quite right. For example, her memory had slipped badly, she sounded confused sometimes, and her moods changed without warning. Her appearance deteriorated. Some of her friends attributed these changes to the fact that Mary was in her 80s.

However, when Mary started forgetting where she lived, her family and friends knew that something serious was wrong. Her family ultimately realized that Mary could no longer care for herself, and they moved her to an assisted-living facility. Mary's memory continued to decline; she started forgetting the names of her children and grandchildren. When she started to wander at night, Mary was transferred to a nursing home. Her physical abilities declined further, and she lost the ability to feed herself. Toward the end of her life, Mary could not eat solid food and had to be force-fed. Mary died from Alzheimer disease after 15 years of slow decline.

Alzheimer disease causes people to change from thinking, communicative human beings to confused, bedridden victims unable to recognize their family members and close friends. As a result, the *fear* of Alzheimer disease among healthy older adults is a significant problem beyond the actual disease (Youngjohn & Crook, 1996).

Throughout North America, millions of people are afflicted with Alzheimer disease, including such well-known individuals as former U.S. President Ronald Reagan;

the disease cuts across ethnic, racial, and socioeconomic groups. The incidence of Alzheimer disease increases with age. Canadian estimates are from extremely low rates in those younger than 65 years to roughly 26% of the people aged 85 and older, with women having a higher incidence (Health Canada - National Advisory Council on Aging, 2003). As the number of older adults increases rapidly over the next several decades, the number of cases is expected to increase substantially.

What Are the Symptoms of Alzheimer Disease?

The key symptoms of Alzheimer disease are gradual declines in memory, learning, attention, and judgment; confusion as to time and place; difficulties in communicating and finding the right words; decline in personal hygiene and self-care skills; inappropriate social behaviour; and changes in personality. These classic symptoms may be vague and only occur occasionally in the beginning, but as the disease progresses, they become much more pronounced and are exhibited much more regularly (Youngjohn & Crook, 1996). Wandering away from home and not being able to remember how to return increases. Paranoid and other accusatory behaviours develop. Spouses become strangers. Patients may not even recognize themselves in a mirror; they wonder who is looking back at them. *In its advanced stages, Alzheimer disease often causes* **incontinence** *(the loss of bladder or bowel control) and total loss of mobility.* Like the man in the photograph, victims eventually become completely dependent

© Alan Oddie/PhotoEdit

on others for care. At this point many caregivers seek facilities such as adult day-care centres and other sources of help, such as family and friends, to provide a safe environment for the Alzheimer patient while the primary caregiver is at work or doing basic errands.

The rate of deterioration in Alzheimer disease varies widely from one patient to another, although progression usually is faster when onset occurs earlier in adulthood (Wilson et al., 2000). Thus, it is difficult to generalize about the level of a person's impairment based solely on how long ago the diagnosis was made. Likewise, it is very difficult to predict how long a specific patient will survive, which only adds to the stress experienced by the caregiver (Cavanaugh & Nocera, 1994).

THINK ABOUT IT

How do the memory problems in Alzheimer disease differ from those in normal aging?

How Is Alzheimer Disease Diagnosed?

Given that the behavioural symptoms of Alzheimer disease eventually become quite obvious, one would assume that diagnosis would be straightforward. Quite the contrary. In fact, absolute certainty that a person has Alzheimer disease cannot even be achieved while the individual is still alive. Definitive diagnosis must be based on an autopsy of the brain after death, because the defining criteria for diagnosing Alzheimer disease involve documenting large numbers of structural changes in neurons that can only be observed under a microscope after brain tissue has been removed and specially prepared (Youngjohn & Crook, 1996; Whitbourne, 2000).

Of course, one is still left with the issue of figuring out whether a person probably has Alzheimer disease while he or she is still alive. Although not definitive, the number and severity of behavioural changes lead clinicians to make fairly accurate diagnoses of *probable* Alzheimer disease (Qualls, 1999). But accuracy depends on a broad-based and thorough series of medical and psychological tests, including complete blood tests, metabolic and neurological tests, and neuropsychological tests (Youngjohn & Crook, 1996). Currently, researchers are working toward developing more sensitive and specific diagnostic procedures (Alzheimer Society, 2004). A great deal of diagnostic work goes into ruling out virtually all other possible causes of the observed symptoms. This effort is essential. Because Alzheimer disease is an incurable and fatal disease, every treatable cause of the symptoms must be explored first. In essence, Alzheimer disease is diagnosed by excluding all other possible explanations. A model plan for making sure the diagnosis is correct is shown in Figure 15.12.

FIGURE 15.12   Diagnosing Alzheimer Disease

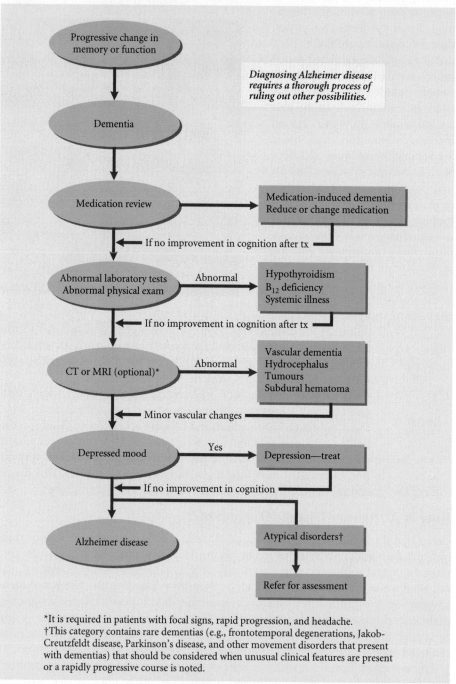

*It is required in patients with focal signs, rapid progression, and headache.
†This category contains rare dementias (e.g., frontotemporal degenerations, Jakob-Creutzfeldt disease, Parkinson's disease, and other movement disorders that present with dementias) that should be considered when unusual clinical features are present or a rapidly progressive course is noted.

SOURCE: Alzheimer Association online document. Developed and endorsed by the TriAD Advisory Board. Copyright 1996 Pfizer Inc. and Esai Inc. with special thanks to J. L. Cummings. Algorithm reprinted from TriAD, *Three for the Management of Alzheimer Disease*, with permission.

In an attempt to be as thorough as possible, clinicians usually interview family members about their perceptions of the observed behavioural symptoms. Most clinicians view this information as essential to understanding the history of the difficulties the person is experiencing. However, research indicates that spouses are often inaccurate in their assessments of the level of their partner's impairment (McGuire & Cavanaugh, 1992). In part, this inaccuracy is due to lack of knowledge about the disease. Also, spouses wish to portray themselves as in control, either by denying that the symptoms are in fact severe or by exaggerating the severity in order to give the appearance that they are coping well in a very difficult situation. Some spouses describe their partner's symptoms accurately, but family reports should not be the only source of information about the person's ability to function.

A great deal of attention has been given to the development of more definitive tests for Alzheimer disease while the person is still alive. *Much of this work has focused on amyloid, a protein that is produced in abnormally high levels in Alzheimer patients, perhaps causing the neurofibrillary tangles and neuritic plaques described earlier.* Research is progressing toward developing a way to measure amyloid concentrations in cerebrospinal fluid and blood. Additional work focuses on testing for the presence or absence of specific genes, a topic to which we now turn.

What Causes Alzheimer Disease?

We do not know for sure what causes Alzheimer disease (Qualls, 1999; Whitbourne, 2000). Over the years, several hypotheses have been offered, such as aluminum deposits in the brain and a slow-acting virus, but none have explained more than a few cases.

Currently, most research is concentrating on identifying genetic links (Gatz & Smyer, 2001). The evidence is growing that at least some forms of Alzheimer disease are inherited, based on studies of family trees, relatives, and identical twins. Indeed, several sites on various chromosomes have been tentatively identified as being involved in the transmission of Alzheimer disease, including chromosomes 12, 14, 19, and 21. The most promising work has noted links between the genetic markers and the production of amyloid protein, the major component of neuritic plaques (Raeburn, 1995). Much of this research focuses on apolipoprotein E4 (apo E4), associated with chromosome 19, which may play a central role in creating neuritic plaques. Interestingly, another version, apo E2, seems to have the reverse effect: It decreases the risk of Alzheimer disease (Gatz et al., 1997). Researchers are also looking for relationships between apolipoprotein E and cognitive functioning (Riley et al., 2000). And researchers have established a link between the cystatin C gene (CST3) and late-onset Alzheimer disease (Finckh et al., 2000).

Researchers can already identify genetic markers responsible for certain forms of early-onset Alzheimer disease, and they have developed a test to see whether people have the inheritance pattern (Steinbart et al., 2001). The development of genetic tests for Alzheimer disease not only provides a potential way to diagnose it but also presents some difficult personal choices for people. For example, individuals who know they have the genes responsible for the disease may be faced with difficult decisions about having children and how to live out their lives. Genetic counselling programs, which currently focus mostly on diseases of childhood, would need to be expanded to help individuals face decisions about diseases occurring later in life.

Estrogen level is being examined as a factor in women's increased risk of Alzheimer disease (Henderson, 1997; Simpkins et al., 1997). It is known that loss of estrogen after menopause is related to memory loss (see Chapter 14) and that this loss may be a source of the increased risk for Alzheimer disease. Currently the role of estrogen in Alzheimer disease is inconclusive (Alzheimer Society, 2004).

What Can Be Done for Victims of Alzheimer Disease?

Even though Alzheimer disease is incurable, much can be done to alleviate its symptoms. Most of the research has been focused on drugs aimed at improving cognitive functioning. Despite much research with numerous types of drugs, none currently available permanently reverses the memory symptoms (Brioni & Decker, 1997). However, a group of medications that inhibit acetylcholinesterase has produced promising results; galantamine appears to be the most effective of these agents (Tariot, 2001; Winblad, 2001). Ongoing research is attempting to determine the effectiveness of a number of drugs to treat Alzheimer disease, including anti-oxidants such as Vitamin E, selenium supplements, the omega-3 fatty acid docosahexaenoic acid (DHA), and the plant extract *Ginkgo biloba* (Alzheimer Society, 2004).

Other researchers have emphasized the importance of other criteria for therapeutic success besides cognitive function, such as functional abilities, behaviour, quality of life, resource utilization, and caregiver burden (Winblad et al., 2001). Medications such as *thioridazine* and *haloperidol* are used to treat severe psychotic symptoms. Antidepressants are effective in alleviating the depression that often accompanies Alzheimer disease. All these medications must be used carefully, as older adults have a high risk of side effects such as severe motor impairment and increased cognitive impairment (Brioni & Decker, 1997).

Numerous effective behavioural and educational interventions have also been developed. *One behavioural intervention, based on the E-I-E-I-O approach to memory intervention discussed earlier in this chapter, involves using the implicit-internal memory intervention called* **spaced retrieval.** Adapted by Camp and colleagues (Camp, 2001; Camp & McKitrick, 1991), spaced retrieval involves teaching individuals with Alzheimer disease to remember new information by gradually increasing the time between retrieval attempts. How this is done is explained in the Spotlight on Research feature. This easy, almost magical technique has been used to teach names of staff members and other information; it holds considerable potential for broad application.

SPOTLIGHT ON RESEARCH

What's Her Name? Memory Training in Alzheimer Disease

Who were the investigators and what was the aim of the study? Alzheimer disease is marked by progressive and severe memory loss. But can memory problems be remediated using implicit-internal memory strategies? Cameron Camp (2001) and Leslie McKitrick decided to find out by training a technique called *spaced retrieval.*

How did the investigators measure the topic of interest? The secret to spaced retrieval is progressively increasing the amount of time between the recall of the target information (e.g., a person's name). For example, the instructor shows the client a picture of a person and says the person's name. After an initial recall interval of five seconds, the instructor asks the client to remember the name. As long as the client remembers correctly, recall intervals are increased to 10, 20, 40, 60, 90, 120, 150 seconds, and so on. If the client forgets the target information, the correct answer is provided and the next recall interval is decreased to the length of the last correct trial. During the interval, the instructor

engages the client in conversation to prevent active rehearsal of the information.

Who were the participants in the study? Camp and McKitrick tested people who had been diagnosed as probably having Alzheimer disease who were also in an adult day-care centre.

What was the design of the study? The study used a longitudinal design so that Camp and McKitrick could track participants' performance over several weeks.

Were there ethical concerns with the study? Having persons with Alzheimer disease as research participants raises important issues with informed consent. Because of their serious cognitive impairments, these individuals may not fully understand the procedures. Thus, family members such as a spouse or adult child caregiver are also asked to give informed consent. Additionally, researchers must pay careful attention to participants' emotions; if participants become agitated or frustrated, the training or testing session must be stopped. Camp and McKitrick took all these precautions.

What were the results? Spaced retrieval worked like magic; even people who earlier could not retain information for more than 60 seconds could remember names taught through this technique for very long periods (e.g., five weeks or more). Learning the staff names usually involved a few failures, but with additional practice success occurred. For example, one participant looked sternly at the researchers who had come to her day-care centre. "I know you're going to ask me for Jane's name." Yet only a month before, Iris could not remember Jane's name; in fact, she seemed incapable of learning it at all using rote rehearsal. Most important, the new learning did not interfere with other information in long-term memory.

What did the investigators conclude? It appears that many types of information can be taught, making spaced retrieval a flexible intervention. Spaced retrieval can be used in virtually any setting, such as playing games or normal conversation, making it comfortable and nonthreatening to the client. Although more work is needed to continue refining the technique, spaced retrieval is one of the most promising nondrug memory interventions for people with cognitive impairments.

What converging evidence would strengthen these conclusions? Although spaced retrieval is effective for persons with Alzheimer disease, it has not yet been demonstrated to be effective with all other diseases that cause serious memory loss. We also do not know whether the information people learn through spaced retrieval lasts a very long time (e.g., several months); thus, long-term retention needs to be tested.

In designing interventions for persons with Alzheimer disease, the guiding principle should be optimizing the person's functioning. Regardless of the level of impairment, attempts should be made to help the person cope as well as possible with the symptoms. The key is helping all persons maintain their dignity as human beings. This can be achieved in some very creative ways, such as adapting the principles of Montessori methods of education to bring older adults with Alzheimer disease together with preschool children so that they can perform tasks together (Camp et al., 1997).

One of the best ways to find out about the latest medical and behavioural research, as well as about the educational and support programs available in your area, is to call the Canadian Alzheimer Society. The chapter in your area will be happy to supply a range of educational material and information about local programs.

FIGURE 15.13   Alzheimer Society of Canada

Brochure produced by Alzheimer Society of Canada.

TEST YOURSELF

1. Compared to younger adults, older adults are less likely to label their feelings of sadness as _____.

2. A form of psychotherapy that focuses on people's beliefs about the self, the world, and the future is called _____.

3. Relaxation techniques are an effective therapy for _____.

4. The only way to definitively diagnose Alzheimer disease is through a _____.

5. Twisted fibres called _____ occur in the axon of neurons in persons with Alzheimer disease.

After reading about the symptoms of Alzheimer disease, what do you think would be the most stressful aspects of caring for a parent who has the disease? (You may want to refer to the section on caring for aging parents in Chapter 14.)

Answers: (1) depression, (2) cognitive therapy, (3) anxiety disorders, (4) brain autopsy, (5) neurofibrillary tangles

PUTTING IT ALL TOGETHER

Someone once observed that, all things considered, growing old is much better than the alternative. Based on what we have seen concerning the personal contexts of aging, it is indeed much better in many respects (though not totally rosy, to be sure) than what our cultural conditioning expects it to be. We began by wondering why people like Justine live a long time and others do not, and we learned that many factors influence longevity. We saw how genetic and environmental factors interact (the biopsychosocial model strikes again!). We encountered Frank, the active 80-year-old, who exemplifies how maintaining fitness throughout life has an important influence on health in the later years. We also discovered how physical changes that began in midlife continue to affect functioning as a person keeps growing older.

Anne experiences the kinds of changes in recent memory ability common in older adults. Some older people gain wisdom through their experience in living. Thus, cognitive changes in later life are not all a matter of decline. Finally, we saw that psychopathologies can

exact a terrible toll among older adults; they must be properly diagnosed to separate treatable from untreatable conditions. People like Nora, who had depression, must be examined carefully to identify the most likely cause of the problems.

Many of the stereotypes society holds about older adults are simply untrue. For one thing, only a minority of people over age 65 ever get Alzheimer disease, whereas the clear majority continue to demonstrate improvement in some cognitive functions such as wisdom. Old age does not imply the across-the-board decline that is often portrayed. Indeed, some segments of society are beginning to understand the beauty and importance of older adults.

Our initial foray into later life reveals the complexity of older adults. Just as it is impossible to characterize all children, adolescents, or young adults as being all alike, older adults are also a very diverse group of people. This diversity will continue to be in evidence in the next chapter.

SUMMARY

15.1 What Are Older Adults Like?

The Demographics of Aging

■ The number of older adults is growing rapidly, especially the number of people over age 85. In the future, older adults will be more ethnically diverse and better educated than they are now.

How Long Will You Live?

■ *Average life expectancy* increased dramatically in the last century, due mainly to improvements in health

care. *Useful life expectancy* refers to the number of years that a person is free from debilitating disease. *Maximum life expectancy* is the longest time any human can live.

■ Genetic factors that can influence longevity include familial longevity and a family history of certain diseases. Environmental factors include acquired diseases, toxins, pollutants, and lifestyle.

■ Due to technological advances, there is controversy regarding the quantity of life as against the quality.

Women have a longer average life expectancy at birth than men. Ethnic group differences are complex; depending on how old people are, the patterns of differences change.

The Third-Fourth Age Distinction

- The Third Age refers to changes in research that led to cultural, medical, and economic advances for older adults (e.g., longer average longevity, increased quality of life). In contrast, the Fourth Age reflects the fact that the oldest-old are at the limits of their functional capacity, the rates of diseases such as cancer and dementia increase dramatically, and other aspects of psychological functioning (e.g., memory) also undergo significant and fairly rapid decline.

15.2 Physical Changes and Health

Biological Theories of Aging

- There are four main biological theories of aging. Wear-and-tear theory postulates that aging is caused by body systems simply wearing out. Cellular theories focus on reactions within cells, involving telomeres, free radicals, and cross-linking. Metabolic theories focus on changes in cell metabolism. Programmed cell death theories propose that aging is genetically programmed. No single theory is sufficient to explain aging.

Physiological Changes

- Three important structural changes in the neurons are neurofibrillary tangles, dendritic changes, and neuritic plaques. These have important consequences for functioning because they reduce the effectiveness with which neurons transmit information.
- The risk of cardiovascular disease increases with age. Normal changes in the cardiovascular system include buildup of fat deposits in the heart and arteries, a decrease in the amount of blood the heart can pump, a decline in heart muscle tissue, and stiffening of the arteries. Most of these changes are affected by lifestyle. Stroke and vascular dementia cause significant cognitive impairment, depending on the location of the brain damage.
- Strictly age-related changes in the respiratory system are hard to identify due to the lifetime effects of pollution. However, older adults suffer shortness of breath, and the risk of chronic obstructive pulmonary disorder increases.
- Parkinson's disease is caused by insufficient levels of dopamine, and it can be effectively managed with L-dopa. In a minority of cases, dementia develops.
- Age-related declines in vision and hearing are well documented. The main changes in vision concern the structure of the eye and the retina. Changes in hearing mainly involve presbycusis. However, similar changes in taste, smell, touch, pain, and temperature are not as clear.

Health Issues

- Older adults have more sleep disturbances than younger adults. Nutritionally, most older adults do not need vitamin or mineral supplements. Cancer risk increases sharply with age. Being an immigrant is related to having poorer health status due to communication problems and barriers to care.

15.3 Cognitive Processes

Information Processing

- Older adults are much slower than younger adults at visual search unless there is an advance signal.
- Age differences in attention tasks are complex and depend on the level of difficulty; on easy tasks, there are few differences, but on more difficult tasks, younger adults do better.
- Older adults' psychomotor speed is slower than younger adults'. However, the amount of slowing is lessened if older adults have practice or expertise in the task.
- Sensory and information-processing changes create problems for older drivers. Working memory is another powerful explanatory concept for changes in information processing with age.

Memory

- Older adults typically do worse on tests of episodic recall; age differences are less on recognition tasks. Semantic memory is largely unaffected by aging, as is implicit memory. People tend to remember best those events that occurred to them between ages 10 and 30.
- What people believe to be true about their memory is related to their performance. Beliefs about whether cognitive abilities are supposed to change may be most important.
- Differentiating memory changes associated with aging from memory changes due to disease should be accomplished through comprehensive evaluations.
- Memory training can be achieved in many ways. A useful framework is to combine explicit-implicit memory distinctions with external-internal types of memory aids.

Creativity and Wisdom

- Research indicates that creative output peaks in late young adulthood or early middle age and declines thereafter but that the point of peak activity varies across disciplines and occupations.
- Wisdom has more to do with being an expert in living than with age per se. Three factors that help people become wise are general personal conditions, specific expertise conditions, and facilitative life contexts.

15.4 Mental Health and Intervention

Depression

▨ The key symptom of depression is persistent sadness. Other psychological and physical symptoms also occur, but the importance of these depends on the age of the person reporting them.

▨ Major causes of depression include imbalances in neurotransmitters and psychosocial forces such as loss and internal belief systems.

▨ Depression can be treated with medications, such as heterocyclic antidepressants, MAO inhibitors, and selective serotonin reuptake inhibitors, and through psychotherapy, such as behavioural or cognitive therapy.

Anxiety Disorders

▨ A variety of anxiety disorders afflict many older adults. All of them can be effectively treated with either medications or psychotherapy.

Dementia: Alzheimer Disease

▨ Dementia is a family of diseases that cause severe cognitive impairment. Alzheimer disease is the most common form of irreversible dementia.

▨ Symptoms of Alzheimer disease include memory impairment, personality changes, and behavioural changes. These symptoms usually worsen gradually, with rates varying considerably among individuals.

▨ Definitive diagnosis of Alzheimer disease can only be made following a brain autopsy. Diagnosis of probable Alzheimer disease in a living person involves a thorough process through which other potential causes are eliminated.

▨ Most researchers are focusing on a probable genetic cause of Alzheimer disease.

▨ Although Alzheimer disease is incurable, various therapeutic interventions can improve the quality of the patient's life.

KEY TERMS

demographers (530)
population pyramid (530)
longevity (532)
average life expectancy (532)
useful life expectancy (532)
maximum life expectancy (532)
wear-and-tear theory (537)
cellular theories (537)
telomeres (537)
free radicals (538)
cross-linking (538)
metabolic theories (538)
programmed cell death theories (538)
neurofibrillary tangles (539)
neuritic plaques (539)
strokes (540)
cerebral vascular accidents (540)

hemorrhage (540)
transient ischemic attacks (TIAs) (540)
vascular dementia (541)
chronic obstructive pulmonary disease (COPD) (541)
Parkinson's disease (541)
presbyopia (542)
presbycusis (542)
circadian rhythm (546)
selective attention (548)
vigilance (548)
attentional control (548)
psychomotor speed (548)
explicit memory (550)
implicit memory (550)
episodic memory (550)
semantic memory (550)

external aids (552)
internal aids (552)
dysphoria (558)
internal belief systems (558)
heterocyclic antidepressants (HCAs) (559)
monoamine oxidase (MAO) inhibitors (559)
selective serotonin reuptake inhibitors (SSRIs) (559)
behaviour therapy (559)
cognitive therapy (559)
anxiety disorders (560)
dementia (560)
Alzheimer disease (561)
incontinence (561)
amyloid (563)
spaced retrieval (564)

SEE FOR YOURSELF: APPLYING WHAT YOU'VE LEARNED

The text lists several different ways in which people's memory can be helped. Perhaps you never thought about how many memory aids you use in your everyday life, such as notebooks, calendars, lists, setting things by the door, asking your friends, rereading things, and so forth.

This real-world exercise has two parts. First, using the E-I-E-I-O framework, analyze your own daily routine and list all the ways you help yourself remember. (You may be surprised at how many different ways you do this!) Next, do the same for a few of your friends and relatives. Try to talk with people of different ages. Tabulate your results and share them with your classmates. Which category in the table contains the aids that people use the most? See for yourself!

LEARN MORE ABOUT IT

Readings

ALBOM, M. (1997). *Tuesdays with Morrie.* New York: Doubleday. The true story of a journalist who reconnected with his former teacher who passed on wisdom.

CRAIK, F. I. M., & SALTHOUSE, T. A. (Eds.). (2000). *Handbook of aging and cognition* (2nd ed.). Mahwah, NJ: Erlbaum. Although difficult reading at times, this is the best single-volume coverage of cognitive aging available.

HAYFLICK, L. (1996). *How and why we age* (2nd ed.). New York: Ballantine. This summary of the biology of aging is presented in a very readable and easy-to-understand format. It is probably the best comprehensive summary available at the introductory level.

KOTRE, J. (1996). *White gloves: How we create ourselves through memory.* New York: Norton. This is the autobiographical story of a man who explores the meaning of memory after he finds his grandfather's white gloves. Interesting weaving of basic research on memory with everyday experience.

MARTZ, S. H. (Ed.). (1987). *When I am an old woman, I shall wear purple* and (1992) *If I had my life to live over, I would pick more daisies.* Watsonville, CA: Papier-Mache Press. Both of these books are anthologies of poems and short stories about the personal meanings of aging to women.

WHITBOURNE, S. K. (2000). *Psychopathology in later adulthood.* New York: Wiley. A good and very readable overview of the many types of psychopathology experienced by older adults.

 For additional readings, explore InfoTrac® College Edition, your online library. Go to http://www.infotrac.thomsonlearning.com.

Websites

http://aging.ufl.edu/apadiv20/apadiv20.htm

One of the very best sites for starting a search about any aspect of aging is kept by the Adult Development and Aging Division (Division 20) of the American Psychological Association.

http://www.cagp.ca

The Canadian Academy of Geriatrics, a branch of the Canadian Psychiatric Association, is a national organization of psychiatrists dedicated to promoting mental health in the Canadian elderly population. The website is easy to use and includes an up-to-date resource centre.

http://www.hc-sc.gc.ca/seniors-aines

The website of Health Canada's Division of Aging and Seniors provides federal leadership in areas pertaining to seniors and aging. There is a variety of information on many aspects of aging in Canada.

http://www.alzheimer.ca

The Alzheimer Society maintains an excellent database on the latest research advances about the causes and treatment of Alzheimer disease as well as the best information for caregivers.

http://www.memory-key.com

The Memory Key is a site devoted to research and practical advice about memory and how to improve it. It is one of the few sites dedicated to memory that has trustworthy information.

Website addresses are subject to change. The *Human Development* book companion website can be accessed for updated links.

The Human Development Book Companion Website

See http://www.humandevelopment.com for practice quiz questions, Internet links, updates, critical thinking exercises, discussion forums, and more.

Life-Span CD-ROM

For more information on the concepts covered in this chapter, go to

Module 6: Late Adulthood
- Physical Development
- Cognitive Development

Module 7: Death, Dying, and Bereavement
- Theories of Aging
- Stages of Dying
- Bereavement

Getty Images

CHAPTER 16

Social Aspects of Later Life

PSYCHOSOCIAL, RETIREMENT, RELATIONSHIP, AND SOCIETAL ISSUES

What's it really like to be an older adult? As we saw in Chapter 15, aging brings with it both physical limits (such as declines in vision and hearing) and psychological gains (such as increased expertise). Old age also brings social challenges. Older adults are sometimes stereotyped as marginal and powerless in society, much like children. Psychosocial issues confront older adults as well. How do people think about their lives and bring meaning and closure to them as they approach death? What constitutes well-being for older people? How do they use their time once they are no longer working full-time? Do they like being retired? What roles do relationships with friends and family play in their lives? How do older people cope if their partners are ill and require care? What if their partner should die? Where do older people live who need assistance?

These are a few of the issues we will examine in this chapter. As in Chapter 15, our main focus will be on the majority of older adults who are healthy and live in the community. The distinction made in Chapter 1 between young-old (60- to 80-year-olds) and old-old (80-year-olds and up) adults is important. We know the most about young-old people, even though the old-old reflect the majority of frail elderly and those who live in nursing homes.

Just as at other times in life, getting along in the environment is a complicated issue. We begin by considering a few ideas about how to optimize our fit with the environment. Next, we examine how we bring the story of our lives to a culmination. After that, we will consider how interpersonal relationships and retirement provide contexts for life satisfaction. We conclude with an examination of the social contexts of aging.

16.1

Theories of Psychosocial Aging

LEARNING OBJECTIVES

What is continuity theory? What is the competence and environmental press model, and how do docility and proactivity relate to the model?

Since Sandy retired from her job as secretary at the local library, she has hardly slowed down. She sings in the church choir, is involved in the local multicultural centre, and volunteers one day per week at a local nursery school. Sandy's friends say that she has to stay involved as that's the only way she's ever known. They claim that you'd never know Sandy is 71 years old.

Understanding how people grow old is not as simple as asking someone how old he or she is, as Sandy shows. As we saw in Chapter 15, aging is an individual process involving many variations in physical changes, cognitive functioning, and mental health. However, older adults are often marginalized in society. Psychosocial approaches to aging recognize these issues.

Sandy's life reflects several key points. Her level of activity has remained constant across her adult life. This consistency fits well in continuity theory, the first framework considered in this section. Her ability to maintain this level of commitment indicates that the match between her abilities and her environment is just about right, as discussed in competence–environmental press theory a bit later in this section.

CONTINUITY THEORY

People tend to keep doing whatever works for them (Atchley, 1989). *According to continuity theory, people tend to cope with daily life in later adulthood by applying familiar strategies based on past experience to maintain and preserve both internal and external structures.* That is, aging successfully involves maintaining a connection between the past and the present. By building on and linking to one's past life, change becomes part of continuity. Thus, Sandy's new activities represent both change (because they are new) and continuity (because she has always been engaged in her community). In this sense, continuity represents an evolution, not a complete break with the past (Atchley, 1989).

> **THINK ABOUT IT**
>
> How do the five-factor theory of personality and the life story approach to personality fit with continuity theory?

The degree of continuity in life falls into one of three general categories: too little, too much, and optimal (Atchley, 1989). Too little continuity results in feeling that life is too unpredictable. Too much continuity can create utter boredom or a rut of predictability; there is simply not enough change to make life interesting. Optimal continuity provides just enough change to be challenging and provide interest but not so much as to overly tax one's resources.

Continuity can be either internal or external (Atchley, 1989). Internal continuity refers to a remembered inner past, such as temperament, experiences, emotions, and skills; in brief, it is one's personal identity. Internal continuity allows you to see that how you are now is connected with your past, even if your current behaviour looks different. Internal continuity provides feelings of competence, mastery, ego integrity (discussed later in the chapter), and self-esteem. External continuity concerns remembered physical and social environments, role relationships, and activities. A person feels external continuity from being in familiar environments or with familiar people. For example, continuity theory provides a framework for understanding how friendships in late life provide a way for older adults to maintain connections with people, sometimes over many years (Finchum & Weber, 2000). Similarly, phasing from full-time employment to retirement offers some people (e.g., university faculty) a way to maintain connections with their professional life and facilitate the adjustment to retirement (Kim & Feldman, 2000).

Maintaining both internal and external continuity is very important for adaptation in later life (Atchley, 1989). For example, internal discontinuity, if severe enough, can seriously affect mental health. Indeed, one of the most pernicious aspects of Alzheimer disease is that it destroys internal continuity as it strips away one's identity. Similarly, external discontinuity can have serious consequences for adaptation. For example, if your physical environment becomes much more difficult to negotiate, the resulting problems can eat away at your identity as well.

Clearly, monitoring whether a person is maintaining internal and external continuity matters. Exactly how changes in either affect adaptation is the focus of the competence–environmental press framework, to which we now turn.

COMPETENCE AND ENVIRONMENTAL PRESS

Understanding psychosocial aging requires attention to individuals' needs rather than treating all older adults alike. One way of doing this is to focus on the relation between the person and the environment (Wahl, 2001). As discussed in Chapter 1, the competence–environmental press approach is a good example of a theory that incorporates elements of the biopsychosocial model into the person–environment relation (Lawton & Nahemow, 1973; Nahemow, 2000; Wahl, 2001).

Competence is defined as the upper limit of a person's ability to function in five domains: physical health, sensory-perceptual skills, motor skills, cognitive skills, and ego strength. We discussed most of these domains in Chapter 15; ego strength, which is related to Erikson's concept of integrity, is discussed later in this chapter. These domains are viewed as underlying all other abilities and reflecting the biological and psychological forces. *Environmental press refers to the physical, interpersonal, or social demands that environments put on people.* Physical demands might include having to walk up three flights of stairs to your apartment. Interpersonal demands include having to adjust your behaviour patterns to different types of people. Social demands include dealing with laws or customs that place certain expectations on people. These aspects of the theory reflect biological, psychological, and social forces. Both competence and environmental press change as people move through the life span; what you are capable of doing as a 5-year-old differs from what you are capable of doing as a 25-, 45-, 65-, or 85-year-old. Similarly, the demands put on you by the environment change as you age. Thus, the competence–environmental press framework reflects life-cycle factors as well.

The competence and environmental press model, depicted in Figure 16.1, shows how the two are related. Low to high competence is represented on the vertical axis, and weak to strong environmental press is represented on the horizontal axis. Points in the figure represent various combinations of the two. Most important, the shaded areas show that adaptive behaviour and positive affect can result from many different combinations of competence and press levels. *Adaptation level is the area where press level is average for a particular level of competence; this is where behaviour and affect are normal. Slight increases in press tend to improve performance; this area on the figure is labelled the* **zone of maximum performance potential.** *Slight decreases in press create the* **zone of maximum comfort,** *in which people are able to live happily without worrying about environmental demands.* Combinations of competence and environmental press that fall within either of these two zones result in adaptive behaviour and positive affect, which translate into a high quality of life.

As one moves away from these areas, behaviour becomes increasingly maladaptive and affect becomes negative. Notice that these outcomes, too, can result from several different combinations, and for different reasons. For example, too many environmental demands on a person with low competence and too few demands on a person with high competence both result in maladaptive behaviours and negative affect.

FIGURE 16.1   The Competence and Environmental Press Model

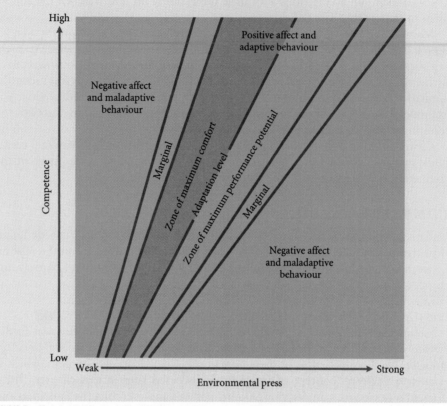

SOURCE: From "Ecology of the Aging Process," by M. P. Lawton and L. Nahemow. In C. Eisdorfer and M. P. Lawton (Eds.), *The Psychology of Adult Development and Aging*, pp. 619–674. Copyright © 1973 American Psychological Association. Reprinted with permission of the authors.

What does this figure mean with regard to late life? Is aging merely an equation relating certain variables? The important thing to realize about the competence–environmental press model is that each person has the potential of being happily adapted to some living situations, but not to all. Whether people are functioning well depends on whether what they are able to do fits what the environment forces them to do. When the abilities match the demands, people adapt; when there is a mismatch, they don't. In this view, aging is more than an equation, as the best fit must be determined on an individual basis.

How do people deal with changes in their particular combination of environmental press (such as adjusting to a new living situation) and competence (perhaps due to illness)? People respond in two basic ways (Lawton, 1989; Nahemow, 2000). *When people choose new behaviours to meet new desires or needs, they exhibit **proactivity** and exert control over their lives. In contrast, when people allow the situation to dictate the options they have, they demonstrate **docility** and have little control.* Lawton (1989) argues that proactivity is more likely to occur in people with relatively high competence and docility in people with relatively low competence.

The model has considerable research support. For example, the model accounts for why people choose the activities they do (Lawton, 1982), move to particular kinds of housing (Lawton, 1982), and need to exert some degree of control over their lives (Langer & Rodin, 1976). In short, there is considerable merit to the view that aging is a complex interaction between a person's competence level and environmental press, mediated by choice. This model can be applied in many different settings.

THINK ABOUT IT

How does the competence–environmental press approach help explain which coping strategies might work best in a particular situation?

Understanding how people age usually entails taking a broader perspective than just one theory. The Real People feature about Roman Jezek, an 89-year-old triathlete, shows that both continuity theory and competence–environmental press theory are important.

REAL PEOPLE: APPLYING HUMAN DEVELOPMENT

Still Competing at 88

Roman Jezek, a retired engineer from Beaconsfield, Quebec, is the world's oldest competitive triathlete and already a four-time world champion. Roman was born in 1914 in what is now Ukraine. He was a boxer in his teens, fought with the Polish army during World War II, and then completed a degree in engineering. He and his wife, Irene, emigrated to Canada in 1950 and he became chief engineer for the Port of Montreal. At the age of 55 Roman decided to become more active by joining the local cycling and recreation centre, and he quickly became interested in the competitive aspects. However, his work responsibilities made it difficult to find time for training, although he was able to cross-country ski during the winter and participated competitively in Europe and Canada.

He retired in August 1979, when he ran his first Montreal Marathon in 4 hours, 45 minutes, and 13 seconds. In 1993, at the age of 79, he completed his first triathlon and was part of the Canadian national team in the World Triathlon Championships in Manchester, England. He won a silver medal in the 75-to-79 category. He has continued competing and has subsequently competed in triathlons in Canada, the United States, England, New Zealand, Australia, and Mexico.

Roman has won two world titles in the 80-to-85 age group and two in the over-85 category, most recently at age 88 in 2002, despite having triple-bypass heart surgery a few months previously. ⏵

TEST YOURSELF

1. A central premise of _____ theory is that people make adaptive choices to maintain and preserve existing internal and external structures.

2. A person's ability to function in several key domains is termed _____,

whereas demands put on a person from external sources are termed _____.

How does continuity theory incorporate aspects of the biopsychosocial model?

Answers: (1) continuity, (2) competence, environmental press

16.2

Personality, Social Cognition, and Spirituality

LEARNING OBJECTIVES

⏵ What is integrity in late life? How do people achieve it?

⏵ How is well-being defined in adulthood? How do people view themselves differently as they age?

⏵ What role does religion play in late life?

> **Personality, Social Cognition, and Spirituality**
>
> Integrity Versus Despair
> Well-Being and Social Cognition
> Religiosity and Spiritual Support

Olive is a spry 88-year-old who spends more time thinking and reflecting about her past than she used to. She also tends to be much less critical now of decisions made years ago than she was at the time. Olive remembers her visions of the woman she wanted to become and concludes that she's come pretty close. Olive wonders if this process of reflection is something that most older adults go through.

Think for a minute about the older adults you know well. Perhaps they are your grandparents, co-workers, or neighbourhood acquaintances. What are they really like? How do they see themselves today? How do they visualize their lives a few years from now? How do they see themselves in the past?

These questions have intrigued authors for many years. In the late 19th century, William James (1890), one of the early pioneers in psychology, wrote that a person's personality traits are set by young adulthood. Some researchers agree; as we saw in Chapter 14, some aspects of personality remain relatively stable through adulthood. But people also change in important ways, as Carl Jung (1960/1933) argued, by integrating opposite tendencies, such as masculine and feminine traits. As we have seen, Erik Erikson (1982) was convinced that personality development takes a lifetime, unfolding over a series of stages.

In this section, we explore how people like Olive assemble the final pieces in the personality puzzle and see how important aspects of personality continue to evolve in later life. We first consider the issue of integrity, the process by which people try to make sense of their life. Next, we see how well-being is achieved, and how personal aspirations play themselves out. Finally, we will examine how religiosity is an important aspect of many older adults' lives.

INTEGRITY VERSUS DESPAIR

*As people enter late life, they begin the struggle of **integrity versus despair,** which involves the process by which people try to make sense of their lives.* According to Erikson (1982), this struggle comes about as older adults like Olive try to understand their life against the backdrop of the future of their family and community. Thoughts of a person's own death are balanced by the realization that the individual will live on through children, grandchildren, great-grandchildren, and the community as a whole. This realization produces what Erikson calls a "life-affirming involvement" in the present.

*The struggle of integrity versus despair requires people to engage in a **life review,** the process by which people reflect on the events and experiences they have had over their lifetime.* To achieve integrity, a person must come to terms with the choices and events that have made his or her life unique. There must also be acceptance of the fact that one's life is drawing to a close. Looking back on one's life may resolve some of the second-guessing of decisions that may have occurred earlier in adulthood (Erikson, Erikson, & Kivnick, 1986). People who were unsure whether they made the right choices concerning their children, for example, now feel satisfied that things eventually worked out well. In contrast, others feel bitter about their choices, blame themselves or others for their misfortunes, see their lives as meaningless, and greatly fear death. These people end up in despair rather than integrity.

Research shows a connection between engaging in a life review and achieving integrity. In one study, homebound older adults who were part of a program that assisted people in remembering and reviewing their lives showed significant improvements in life satisfaction, positive feelings, and depressive symptoms, compared to homebound older adults who did not participate (Haight, 1992). These improvements were still evident two months after the program ended. A study in Australia showed a connection between "accepting the past" and symptoms of depression (Rylands & Rickwood, 2001). Older women who accepted the past were less likely to show symptoms of depression than older women who did not.

Who reaches integrity? Erikson (1982) emphasizes that there is no one path. They come from many backgrounds and cultures. Such people have made many different choices and followed many different lifestyles; everyone has this opportunity. Those who reach integrity become self-affirming and self-accepting; they judge their lives to have been worthwhile and good. They are glad to have lived the lives they did.

WELL-BEING AND SOCIAL COGNITION

What do you think about your life? Are you reasonably content, or do you think you could be doing better? Answers to these questions provide insight into your subjective well-being. *Subjective well-being is a positive evaluation of one's life associated with positive feelings.* In life-span developmental psychology, subjective well-being is usually assessed with measures of life satisfaction, happiness, and self-esteem (Pinquart & Sörensen, 2001).

Whether older adults have high subjective well-being depends on several factors, but chronic illness, marital status, social network, and stress are especially important (Krause, 2001; Marshall, 2001; Martin, Grünendahl, & Martin, 2001; Pinquart & Sörensen, 2001). The role of these factors is explored in more detail in the Spotlight on Research feature. Although some gender differences increase with age, these are most likely due to the fact that older women are particularly disadvantaged compared with older men with regard to chronic illness, everyday competence, socioeconomic status, and widowhood (Pinquart & Sörensen, 2001). Such gender differences are also smaller in more recent cohorts, indicating that societal changes have influenced how people feel about themselves.

SPOTLIGHT ON RESEARCH
Understanding the Influences on Subjective Well-Being

Who were the investigators and what was the aim of the study? Research on subjective well-being has suggested that having a good social support system of friends can help improve well-being even when one experiences stress. Martin and colleagues (2001) decided to test this idea by examining the role of social support and stress as influences on people's subjective well-being. Because of conflicting data on the independent roles of social support and stress on well-being, it was unclear what would happen when both of these factors were examined simultaneously.

How did the investigators measure the topic of interest? The main data collection tool was an extensive semistructured interview used in previous longitudinal studies of aging. The interview was conducted and scored by five different interviewers who were highly trained. In the social support section of the interview, participants were asked to rate several components about each of eight social roles: partnership, parent, grandparent, child, relative, friends, acquaintance, and neighbour. The stress section asked about subjectively experienced level of stress in three domains: health, finances, and housing conditions. Subjective

well-being was assessed with the revised and standardized Philadelphia Geriatric Center Morale Scale, which has three parts: agitation, attitude toward one's own aging, and lonely dissatisfaction.

Who were the participants in the study? The data analyses were based on a random, representative sample of 938 middle-aged and older German-speaking residents of German nationality in Germany.

What was the design of the study? The data analyses conducted here were based on a cross-sectional design. However, the overall study from which these analyses come is a longitudinal study.

Were there ethical concerns with the study? No, because the researchers obtained permission from the participants.

What were the results? The researchers compared four models for each of the two age groups (middle-aged and older adults). Figures 16.2 and 16.3 show the best models for each age group. As you can see, in both models social resources has a direct negative effect on stress, stress has a direct negative effect on well-being, and social resources has a direct effect on well-being. Social resources

FIGURE 16.2

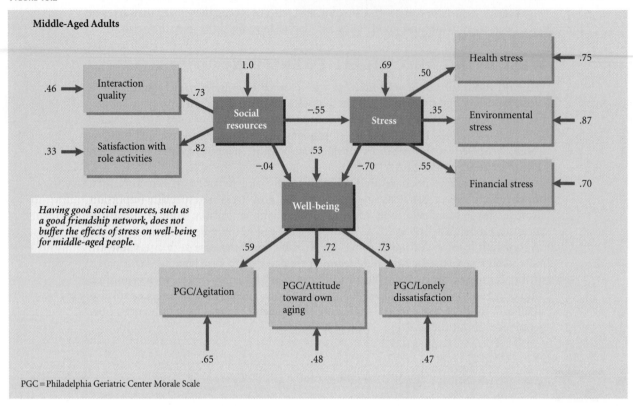

Middle-Aged Adults

Having good social resources, such as a good friendship network, does not buffer the effects of stress on well-being for middle-aged people.

PGC = Philadelphia Geriatric Center Morale Scale

FIGURE 16.3

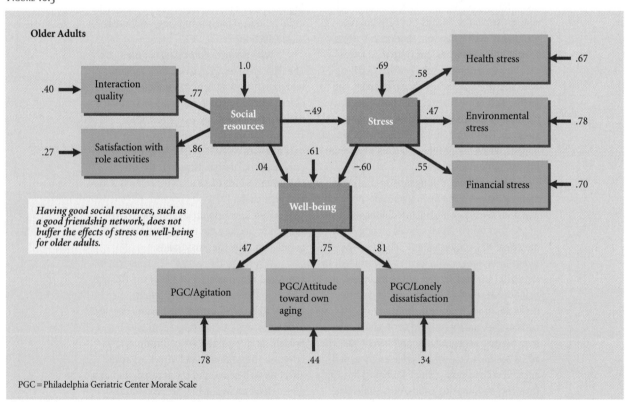

Older Adults

Having good social resources, such as a good friendship network, does not buffer the effects of stress on well-being for older adults.

PGC = Philadelphia Geriatric Center Morale Scale

does not mediate the effects of stress because stress has no direct effect on social resources, meaning that social resources does not directly counteract the effects of stress on well-being. However, stress does mediate the effects of social resources on well-being because it sits between social resources and well-being. Finally, there was no age difference in the models; the same basic model works for middle-aged and older adults.

What did the investigators conclude? The results raise three important points about the role of social resources for well-being. First, there are no age differences in perceived quality of social resources or in satisfaction with social activities. However, significant age differences in stress were found; older adults reported higher stress regarding health and lower stress regarding finances and housing conditions. Second, both social resources and stress affect well-being, with stress having a strong negative relation to both. Third, the lack of age differences in the final models indicates stability from middle age to old age in the relations among social resources, stress, and well-being.

What converging evidence would strengthen these conclusions? Because these analyses were conducted on cross-sectional data, they would be strengthened by longitudinal data. The investigators are gathering these data and will be able to reexamine the findings in the future. Additionally, because the study was conducted only in Germany, samples from other countries would be necessary to generalize the findings to other groups. ▨

How people experience their lives also reflects the ways in which they analyze the cause of events with regard to who or what is in control in a specific situation, a concept discussed in Chapter 11. Recall that personal control is the degree to which individuals believe that their performance in a situation depends on something that they personally do.

Brandtstädter and Greve (1994) propose that control beliefs in later life involve three interdependent processes. First, people engage in activities that prevent or alleviate losses in domains that are important for self-esteem and identity. Second, people readjust their goals as a way to lessen negative self-evaluations in key domains. Third, people guard against the effects of self-discrepant evidence through denial or by looking for another explanation. This approach, though, has been criticized on the grounds that the losses people experience may not actually threaten the self and that changes in goals could simply represent normative developmental processes (Carstensen & Freund, 1994).

These interdependent processes mean that the development of personal control into late life is complex, largely because it varies across domains. For example, Soederberg Miller and Lachman (1999) found lower levels of personal control with increasing age in the intellectual domain, whereas Brandstädter (1999) found increased personal control with age in the perceived marital support domain. Moreover, the shape of the developmental function in personal control varies across domain, as shown in Figure 16.4 (Grob, Little, & Wanner, 1999). As you can see, Grob and colleagues found an increase in perceived control for social (harmony within a close relationship) and personal (personal appearance) domains up to early middle age followed by a general decline. In contrast, perceived control over societal issues (such as pollution) was low across adulthood, with a slow, steady decline.

THINK ABOUT IT ⚲

How are the descriptions of personal control related to theories of cognitive development?

Why are there different trajectories depending on domain? It may be that people view control differently. For example, Brandstädter (1999) proposes that personal control involves the preservation of a positive view of the self. Similarly, Heckhausen and Schulz (1999) view personal control as a motivational system that regulates behaviour over the life span. These views agree that personal control has two parts: *assimilative activities* or *primary control* (bringing the environment into line

FIGURE 16.4   **Perceptions of Control**

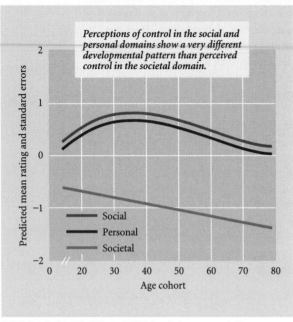

Perceptions of control in the social and personal domains show a very different developmental pattern than perceived control in the societal domain.

SOURCE: Grob, A., Little, T. D., & Wanner, B. (1999). Control judgements across the lifespan. *International Journal of Behavioural Decisions, 23*, 844.

with one's desires and goals) and *accommodative activities* or *secondary control* (bringing oneself into line with the environment). Both views have important implications for aging. Assimilative activities (primary control) increase during childhood as we develop our sense of independence and then plateau across adulthood. However, accommodative activities (secondary control) increase with age across adulthood as we deal with limits imposed on us as our functional competence declines.

Whether this explanation holds across cultures remains to be seen. As Gould (1999) points out, cultures that do not emphasize individualism, such as collectivist societies in Asia, may always place more emphasis on accommodative activities. Clearly, the development of personal control is complex and depends on one's cultural experiences in different domains.

RELIGIOSITY AND SPIRITUAL SUPPORT

When faced with the daily problems of living, what do most older adults do to help themselves cope? According to research, older adults use their religious faith and spirituality more than anything else, including family or friends (Koenig, 1999; Krause, 2001; McFadden, 1996). Evidence shows that older adults who are more involved and committed to their faith have better physical and mental health than older adults who are not religious (Blazer, 2000; Krause, 2001). When asked to describe ways of dealing with problems in life that affect mental health, many people list coping strategies associated with spirituality (Blazer, 2000; Gatz & Smyer, 2001). These strategies can also be used to augment other ways of coping. Caregivers for people with Alzheimer disease also report using religion and spiritual practices as primary coping mechanisms (Ishler et al., 1998; Stuckey, 2001).

*Researchers are increasingly focusing on **spiritual support**, which includes seeking pastoral care and participation in organized and nonorganized religious activities.* McFadden (1996) points out that even when under high levels of stress, people like the Buddhist monks in the photograph on page 581 who rely on spiritual support report better personal well-being. Krause (1995) reports that feelings of self-worth are lowest in older adults who have very little religious commitment, a finding supported by cross-cultural research with Muslims, Hindus, and Sikhs (Mehta, 1997). However, Pargament (1997) also notes the importance of individual differences in the effectiveness of spiritual support, because some people are helped more than others, some problems are more amenable to religious coping, and certain types of religious coping may be more effective than others.

Service providers would be well advised to keep in mind the self-reported importance of religion in the lives of many older adults when designing interventions to help them adapt to life stressors. For example, older adults may be more willing to talk with their minister about a personal problem than they would be to talk with a psychotherapist. Overall, many organized religious groups offer a wide range of programs to assist poor or homebound older adults in the community. Such programs may be

THINK ABOUT IT

What psychological and sociocultural factors make religion and spiritual support important for many different ethnic groups?

© Fotos and Photos/Index Stock Imagery

more palatable to the people served than programs based in social service agencies. To be successful, service providers should try to view life as their clients see it.

TEST YOURSELF

1. The Eriksonian struggle that older adults face is termed _____.

2. Personal control has been described as having two components, assimilative activities and _____.

3. The most commonly reported method for coping with life stress among older adults is_____.

Based on research on personal control discussed in this section, what do you think would be good areas to target for interventions designed to improve older adults' well-being?

Answers: (1) integrity versus despair, (2) accommodative activities, (3) religion or spiritual support

16.3

I Used to Work at . . . : Living in Retirement

LEARNING OBJECTIVES

☑ What does being retired mean?

☑ Why do people retire?

☑ How satisfied are retired people?

☑ How do retirees keep busy?

I Used to Work at . . . : Living in Retirement

What Does Being Retired Mean?

Why Do People Retire?

Adjustment to Retirement

Keeping Busy in Retirement

Mike is a 77-year-old retired construction worker who laboured hard all of his life. He managed to save a little money, but he and his wife live primarily off his monthly pension cheques. Though not rich, they have enough to pay the bills. Mike is largely happy with retirement, and he stays in touch with his friends. He thinks maybe he's a little strange, though—he has heard that retirees are supposed to be isolated and lonely.

You probably take it for granted that some day, after working for many productive years, you will retire. But until the early 20th century, Canada was largely an agricultural society and most people lived and worked on farms into their old age. When they were physically unable to work they were supported by their families or turned to local charities or public "relief" funds. Following World War I survivor and disability pensions were established, and with increasing industrialization and increased urban populations the need for a national pension program grew. The first Canadian Old Age Pension Act was passed in 1927, and although eligibility was limited, it was the beginning of the more inclusive system we have today, with most people expecting, planning, and experiencing retirement. Today, the number is increasing rapidly, and the notion that people work a specified time and then retire is built into our expectations about work. As we noted in Chapter 13, an increasing number of middle-aged workers either retire prior to age 65 or are planning for retirement.

In this section, we consider what retirement is like for older adults. We consider people like Mike as we examine how retirement is defined, why people retire, how people adjust to being retired, and how retirement affects interpersonal relationships.

WHAT DOES BEING RETIRED MEAN?

Take a moment to look at the photographs. Can you pick out which of the people would claim that he or she is "retired"? It turns out that retirement is more difficult to define than just guessing from someone's age (Henretta, 1997, 2001). One way is to equate retirement with complete withdrawal from the workforce. But this definition is inadequate; many retired people continue to work part-time (Mutchler et al., 1997). Another possibility would be to define retirement as a self-described state.

Part of the reason it is difficult to define retirement precisely is that the decision to retire involves the loss of occupational identity (see Chapter 13). What people do for a living is a major part of their identity; we introduce ourselves as postal workers, teachers, builders, or nurses as a way to tell people something about ourselves. Not doing those jobs anymore means that we either put that aspect of our lives in the past tense—"I used to work as a manager at The Bay"—or say nothing at all. Loss of this aspect of ourselves can be difficult to face, so some look for a label other than "retired" to describe themselves.

Photodisc

A useful way to view retirement is as a complex process by which people withdraw from full-time participation in an occupation (Henretta, 2001; Mutchler et al., 1997; Sterns & Gray, 1999). This withdrawal process can be described as either "crisp" (making a clean break from employment by stopping work entirely) or "blurred" (repeatedly leaving and returning to work, with some unemployment periods) (Mutchler et al., 1997). Bob is a good example of a "crisp" retirement. He retired from Air Canada at age 65; now in his late 80s, he has done nothing work-related in the interim.

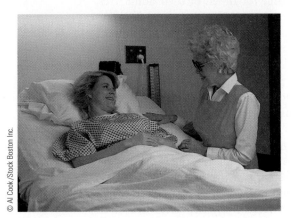

Whereas many people think of retirement as a crisp transition, the evidence shows that less than half of older men who retire fit this pattern (Mutchler et al., 1997). Most men adopt a more gradual or "blurred" process involving part-time work in an effort to maintain economic status. Jack is one of these men. When he retired from Safeway at age 62, he and a friend began a small consulting company. For about five years, Jack worked when he wanted, gradually cutting back over time.

The lack of crisp retirement creates another complicating factor—the idea of a "normal" retirement age such as age 65 may no longer be appropriate (Cornman & Kingson, 1996; Mutchler et al., 1997). Instead, the notion of a typical retirement age changes to a range of ages, further blurring the meaning of "early" or "late" retirement (Cornman & Kingson, 1996). *To reflect these changes, researchers describe a transition phase from career job, the career one has throughout most of adulthood, and* **bridge job,** *the job one holds between one's exit from the career job and final retirement.* Considerable research shows that an increasing number of workers hold bridge jobs for 10 or fewer years (Quinn, 1999), but it remains to be seen whether this indicates a change in the meaning of retirement to workers (Henretta, 2001). For some workers, these jobs are a continuation of a work history characterized by short-term employment. For others, they reflect a desire to continue working even if it is not financially necessary. Bridge jobs have been shown to be strongly related to both retirement satisfaction and overall life satisfaction (Kim & Feldman, 2000).

THINK ABOUT IT

In the absence of mandatory retirement, what does the term "early retirement" really mean?

WHY DO PEOPLE RETIRE?

More workers retire by choice than for any other reason (Hayward, Friedman, & Chen, 1998; Henretta, Chan, & O'Rand, 1992). Individuals usually retire when they feel financially secure, considering projected income from Old Age Security, Canadian and Quebec Pension Plans, and personal savings such as Registered Retirement Savings Plans (RRSP). Of course, some people are forced to retire because they lose their jobs. As corporations downsized in 2000 and 2001, some older workers were offered buyout packages involving supplemental payments if they retired. Others were permanently furloughed, laid off, or dismissed.

The decision to retire is complex and is influenced by one's occupational history (Hayward et al., 1998). The longest occupation held in the middle of one's career combines with occupational roles held in the last stages of the career to influence the decision to retire and the connection with health and disability. For example, self-employed people have few retirement options, often retiring only when health problems intervene. Additionally, health problems that cause functional impairment, such as serious cardiovascular disease or cancer, are a main reason many retire early (Stanford et al., 1991). People in physically demanding jobs also tend to retire earlier

(Ucello, 1998). Feeling that retirement is a choice rather than a requirement is associated with an earlier planned retirement age, as well as adjustment to retirement (Sterns & Gray, 1999).

Gender and Ethnic Differences

Most of what we know about retirement decisions is based on research on men (Sterns & Gray, 1999). However, women may enter the workforce later, have more discontinuous work histories, and spend less time in the workforce, and their financial resources may differ from men's, which may affect women's decisions to retire (Calasanti, 1996; Sterns & Gray, 1999). In fact, research indicates that men's and women's decisions to retire may be based on different factors. Talaga and Beehr (1995) found that women whose husbands were in poor health or who had more dependents were more likely to retire; the opposite was true for men. However, there were some similarities; having a retired spouse increased the likelihood that spouses would also retire. As more women remain in the workforce for much of their adult lives, more research will be necessary to understand the extent to which gender differences matter in the decision to retire. At this point, though, it appears that the male model of retirement is insufficient to account for women's experiences (Sterns & Gray, 1999).

Very little research has been conducted on retirement decisions as a function of ethnicity. However, a few investigators in the United States have examined the characteristics of retired African Americans (e.g., Gibson, 1986, 1987; Jackson & Gibson, 1985). These studies show that African Americans tend to label themselves as retired or not, based on subjective disability, work history, and source of income rather than simply on whether they are currently employed. An important finding is that gender differences appear to be absent among African Americans; men and women base their self-labels on the same variables. Thus, findings based on European-American samples must not be generalized to African Americans, and separate theoretical models for African Americans may be needed (Gibson, 1987). The same may be true for other ethnic groups as well.

ADJUSTMENT TO RETIREMENT

Researchers agree on one point: Retirement is an important life transition. New patterns of involvement must be developed in the context of changing roles and lifestyles (Antonovsky & Sagy, 1990). Until the early 1990s, research focused on what was thought to be a sequence of predictable phases of retirement, such as honeymoon, disenchantment, reorientation, acceptance, and termination (Atchley, 1982). Because retirement is now viewed as a process, the "typical" age of retirement has lost its meaning, and gender differences are evident in the decision to retire, the idea that retirement proceeds in an orderly stagelike sequence has been abandoned (Sterns & Gray, 1999). Instead, researchers support the idea that people's adjustment to retirement evolves over time as a result of complex interrelations with physical health, financial status, voluntary retirement status, and feelings of personal control (Gall, Evans, & Howard, 1997).

How do most people fare? As long as people have financial security, health, and a supportive network of relatives and friends, they report feeling very good about being retired (Gall et al., 1997; Matthews & Brown, 1987). For men, being in good health, having enough income, and having retired voluntarily is associated with relatively high satisfaction early in retirement; having an internal sense of personal control is correlated with well-being over the long run (Gall et al., 1997). For men, personal priorities are also important. Men who place more emphasis on family roles (e.g., as husband or grandfather) report being happier retirees. Interestingly, women's morale in retirement does not appear to be related to an emphasis on any specific roles (Matthews & Brown, 1987). For both men and women, high personal competence is associated with higher retirement satisfaction, probably because competent people are able to optimize their level of environmental press (discussed in Section 16.1).

One stereotype of retirement is that health begins to decline as soon as people stop working. Research findings do not support this belief; in fact, there is no evidence that retirement has any immediate negative effects on health (Ekerdt, 1987). Moreover, well-being typically increases for men during the first year of retirement (Gall et al., 1997).

A second stereotype is that retirement dramatically reduces the number and quality of personal friendships. Again, there is no research support for this belief. In fact, several studies have shown that men like Mike, from the vignette, are typical; neither the number nor the quality of friendships declines as a result of retiring (Bossé et al., 1993). When friendships change during retirement, it is usually due to other factors, such as very serious health problems, that interfere with people's ability to maintain friendships.

Finally, some people believe that retired people become much less active overall. This stereotype is also not supported by research. Although the number of hours in paid work decreases on average with age, older adults are still engaged for hundreds of hours per year in productive activities such as unpaid volunteer work and helping others (Herzog et al., 1989). We will specifically consider volunteer activities in the next section.

KEEPING BUSY IN RETIREMENT

Retirement is an important life transition, one that is best understood through a life course perspective (see Chapter 1) (Moen et al., 2000b). This life change means that retirees must look for ways to maintain social integration by being active in various ways.

The past few decades have witnessed the rapid growth of organizations devoted to providing such opportunities to retirees. National groups such as CARP (Canada's Association for the Fifty-Plus, formerly called the Canadian Association for Retired Persons) provide the chance to learn about other retirees' activities and about services such as insurance and discounts. Many smaller groups exist at the local community level, including seniors' centres and clubs. These organizations promote the notion of lifelong learning and help keep older adults cognitively active. Many also offer travel opportunities specifically designed for active older adults.

> **THINK ABOUT IT**
>
> What might the opportunity for more older adults to volunteer for organizations mean politically? Check your answer with research data later in the chapter.

Healthy, active retired adults also maintain community ties by volunteering (Moen et al., 2000a). Older adults report that they volunteer to help themselves deal with life transitions (Adlersberg & Thorne, 1990), to provide service to others (Hudson, 1996), and to maintain social interactions and improve their communities (Morrow-Howell & Mui, 1989). There are many opportunities for retirees to help others. A national agency called Volunteer Canada includes a resource for seniors to find volunteer activities. Why do so many people volunteer?

Several factors are responsible (Moen et al., 2000a, 2000b): developing a new aspect of the self, finding a personal sense of purpose, desire to share one's skills and expertise, a redefinition of the nature and merits of volunteer work, a more highly educated and healthy population of older adults, and greatly expanded opportunities for people to become involved in volunteer work that they enjoy. Given the demographic trends of increased numbers and educational levels of older adults (discussed in Chapter 15), even higher rates of voluntarism are expected during the next few decades. Moen and colleagues (2000a) argue that volunteerism offers a way for society to tap into the vast resources that older adults offer.

TEST YOURSELF

1. One useful way to view retirement is as a
   _____.

2. The most common reason people retire is
   _____.

3. Overall, most retirees are _____
   with retirement.

4. Many retirees keep contacts in their communities by _____.

Using the information from Chapter 13 on occupational development, create a developmental description of occupations that incorporates retirement.

Answers: (1) complex process by which people gradually withdraw from employment, (2) by choice, (3) satisfied, (4) volunteering

16.4

Friends and Family in Late Life

LEARNING OBJECTIVES

- What role do friends and family play in late life?
- What are older adults' marriages like?
- What is it like to provide basic care for one's partner?
- How do people cope with widowhood? How do men and women differ?
- What special issues are involved in being a great-grandparent?

Friends and Family in Late Life

Friends and Siblings

Marriage and Gay and Lesbian Partnerships

Caring for a Partner

Widowhood

Great-Grandparenthood

Alma was married to Charles for 46 years. Even though he died 20 years ago, Alma still speaks about him as if he had only recently passed away. Alma still gets sad on special dates, such as their anniversary, or Charles's birthday, or the date on which he died. Alma tells everyone that she and Chuck, as she called him, had a wonderful marriage and that she still misses him terribly even after all these years.

To older adults like Alma, the most important thing in life is relationships. In this section, we consider many of the relationships older adults have. Whether it is friendship or family ties, having relationships with others is what keeps us connected. Thus, when one's spouse is in need of care, it is not surprising to find wives and husbands devoting themselves to caregiving. Widows like Alma also feel close to departed spouses. For a growing number of older adults, becoming a great-grandparent is an exciting time.

We have seen throughout this text how our lives are shaped and shared by the company of others. *The term* **social convoy** *is used to suggest how a group of people journeys with us throughout our lives, providing us support in good and bad times.* People form the convoy, and under ideal conditions the convoy provides a protective, secure cushion that permits the person to explore and learn about the world (Antonucci, 2001). Especially for older adults, the social convoy also provides a source of affirmation of who they are and what they mean to others and leads to better mental health and well-being.

Several studies have shown that the size of the social convoy and the amount of support it provides do not differ across generations, a result that generalizes to many ethnicities (Levitt, Weber, & Guacci, 1993). The lack of differences by age strongly supports the conclusion that friends and family are essential aspects of all adults' lives. In U.S. studies, social support was found to be especially important in the

African-American community (Ajrouch, Antonucci, & Janevic, 2000; Taylor, Hardison, & Chatters, 1996). Although their networks are smaller, they have more family members who have more contact with each other. In general, there were more similarities than differences in the social networks of European Americans, African Americans, Latinos, and Asian Americans (Kim & McKenry, 1998).

FRIENDS AND SIBLINGS

By late life, some members of a person's social network have been friends for several decades. Research consistently finds that older adults' life satisfaction is hardly related at all to the number or quality of relationships with younger family members, but it is strongly correlated with the number and quality of their friendships (Essex & Nam, 1987; Fehr, 1996). Why? As will become clear, friends serve as confidants and sources of support in ways that children and nieces and nephews, for example, typically do not.

Friendships

The quality of late-life friendships is particularly important (Matthews, 1996). Having at least one very close friend or confidant provides a buffer against the losses of roles and status that accompany old age, such as retirement or the death of a loved one, and can increase people's happiness and self-esteem (Matthews, 1996; Sherman et al., 2000). Patterns of friendship among older adults tend to mirror those in young adulthood described in Chapter 12 (Fehr, 1996; Sherman et al., 2000). That is, older women have more numerous and more intimate friendships than older men do. As noted previously, these differences help explain why women are in a better position to deal with the stresses of life. Widows, especially, take advantage of their friendship networks; they are more involved with their friends than are married women, never-married women, or men (Hatch & Bulcroft, 1992).

In general, older adults have fewer relationships and develop fewer new relationships than younger or middle-aged adults (Carstensen, 1995). This decline in numbers does not merely reflect the loss of relationships to death or other means. Rather, the changes reflect a more complicated process (Carstensen, 1993, 1995). *This process, termed **socioemotional selectivity**, implies that social contact is motivated by many goals, including information seeking, self-concept, and emotional regulation.* Each of these goals is differentially relevant at different times, and results in different social behaviours. For example, information seeking tends to lead to meeting more people, whereas emotional regulation results in being very picky in the choice of social partners, with a strong preference for people who are familiar.

With time, older adults begin to lose members of their friendship network, usually through death. Rook (2000) proposes that older adults compensate for this loss by forming new ties, redefining the need for friends, or developing alternative nonsocial activities. Although not always successful, these strategies reflect the need to address an important loss in people's lives.

One very interesting aspect of friendship in older adults is the role of culture in determining how people define friendship. As discussed in the Forces in Action feature, older Canadian adults in Vancouver and older American adults in Greensboro, North Carolina, use different indicators (Adams, Blieszner, & de Vries, 2000). Although people around the world all have friends, the way they define "friend" is likely to differ.

Sibling Relationships

For many older adults like those in the photograph on page 588, the preference for long-term friendships may explain older adults' desire to keep in touch with their siblings. As we saw in Chapter 12, maintaining connections with a sibling is important for

FORCES IN ACTION

Who Is Your Friend?

Perceptions of friendship vary. What it takes for one person to call someone a "friend" may not be what it takes for another. We know that friendship in part is based on needs people have, some of which may be the result of biological forces such as disease. But psychological, sociocultural, and life-cycle factors may play more important roles.

Surprisingly little research has examined the role of these factors in people's definitions of friendship, especially in comparing definitions across cultures. Adams and colleagues' (2000) study comparing older adults' definitions of friendship in Vancouver, British Columbia, and in Greensboro, North Carolina, is one of the best. They found that psychological and sociocultural forces result in marked differences in how people define friendship. In

Vancouver, people based their definitions mostly on the affective (feeling) and cognitive processes of friendship, whereas in Greensboro people relied more on behavioural, relational quality, and being like themselves (solidarity and homogeneity) aspects. Additionally, life-cycle forces played a role in that middle-aged and young-old participants in both cities were less likely than middle-old and old-old participants to use relational quality and solidarity and homogeneity as part of their definitions.

These findings clearly show the need to examine how the basic developmental forces influence whom we choose to be our friend, and why we do so. Such differences are important if we are to better understand the role of social support. ▥

---

most adults (Connidis, 2001). Five types of relationships among older adult siblings have been identified (Gold, Woodbury, & George, 1990):

James R. Holland/Stock Boston Inc.

- ▥ *Intimate sibling relationships,* characterized by high levels of closeness and involvement but low levels of envy and resentment.
- ▥ *Congenial sibling relationships,* characterized by high levels of closeness and involvement, average levels of contact, and relatively low levels of envy and resentment.
- ▥ *Loyal sibling relationships,* characterized by average levels of closeness, involvement, and contact and relatively low levels of envy and resentment.
- ▥ *Apathetic sibling relationships,* characterized by low levels on all dimensions.
- ▥ *Hostile sibling relationships,* characterized by relatively high levels of involvement and resentment and relatively low levels on all other dimensions.

The relative frequencies of these five types of sibling relationships are shown in Figure 16.5. As you can see, loyal and congenial relationships characterize nearly two-thirds of all older sibling pairs. When different combinations of siblings are considered separately, ties between sisters are typically the strongest, most frequent, and most intimate (Schmeeckle et al., 1998). In contrast, brothers tend to maintain less fre-

FIGURE 16.5   Relationships Between Older Siblings

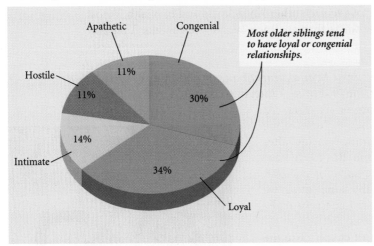

SOURCE: From "Relationship Classification Using Grade of Membership Analysis: A Typology of Sibling Relationships in Later Life," by D. T. Gold, M. A. Woodbury, and L. K. George, 1990, *Journal of Gerontology: Social Sciences, 45*, pp. 43–51. Copyright © 1990 The Gerontological Society of America. Reproduced by permission of the publisher.

quent contact (Connidis, 2001). Little is known about brother-sister relationships. Even though many older adults end up providing care for or living with one of their siblings, we know virtually nothing about how well this works.

Clearly, there are major gaps in our understanding of sibling relationships. This is truly unfortunate as brothers and sisters play an important and meaningful role throughout life.

MARRIAGE AND GAY AND LESBIAN PARTNERSHIPS

"It's great to be 72 and still married," said Lucia. "Yeah, it's great to have Juan around to share old times with and have him know how I feel even before I tell him." Lucia and Juan are typical of most older married couples. Marital satisfaction improves once the children leave home and remains fairly high in older couples (Connidis, 2001). Whether this is due to renewed commitment to the marriage, the fact that couples who were very unhappy have already broken up, or to cohort effects is unclear (Glenn, 1998).

Older married couples show several specific differences from their middle-aged counterparts (Levenson, Carstensen, & Gottman, 1993). Older couples have a reduced potential for marital conflict and greater potential for pleasure, are more likely to be similar in mental and physical health, and show fewer gender differences in sources of pleasure. In short, most older married couples have developed adaptive ways to avoid conflict and have grown more alike. In general, marital satisfaction among older couples remains high until health problems begin to interfere with the relationship (Connidis, 2001; Pearson, 1996).

Being married in late life has several benefits. An American study of 9,333 European Americans, African Americans, and Latino Americans showed that marriage helps people deal better with chronic illness, functional problems, and disabilities (Pienta, Hayward, & Jenkins, 2000). The division of household chores becomes more egalitarian after the husband retires than it was when the husband was employed (Kulik, 2001b, 2000c).

Very little research on long-term gay and lesbian partnerships has been conducted. Based on the available data, it appears that long-term relationships between gay and lesbian partners do not differ in quality from long-term heterosexual marriages (Connidis, 2001; O'Brien & Goldberg, 2000). As is true for heterosexual married couples, relationship satisfaction is better when partners communicate well and are basically happy themselves. Some researchers argue that occupying two stigmatizing statuses—being gay or lesbian and being old—may make aging especially challenging for these couples (Grossman, 1997). For example, age-related declines in health may force individuals to disclose their sexual orientation much more publicly.

CARING FOR A PARTNER

When most couples pledge their love to each other "in sickness and in health," most envision the sickness part to be no worse than an illness lasting a few weeks. That may be the case for many couples, but for some the illness they experience severely tests their pledge.

Francine and Ron are such a couple. After 42 years of mainly good times together, Ron was diagnosed as having Alzheimer disease. When first contacted by researchers, Francine had been caring for Ron for six years. "At times it's very hard, especially when he looks at me and doesn't have any idea who I am. Imagine, after all these years, not to recognize me. But I love him, and I know that he would do the same for me. But, to be perfectly honest, we're not the same couple we once were. We're just not as close; I guess we really can't be."

Francine and Ron are typical of couples like the one in the photograph in which one spouse cares for the other. Caring for a chronically ill partner presents different challenges than caring for a chronically ill parent (see Chapter 14). The partner caregiver assumes the new role after decades of shared responsibilities. Often without warning, the division of labour that had worked for years must be readjusted. Such change inevitably puts stress on the relationship (Cavanaugh & Kinney, 1994). This is especially true in cases involving Alzheimer disease or other dementias because of the cognitive and behavioural consequences of the disease (see Chapter 15), but it is also the case in diseases such as AIDS. Caregiving challenges are felt by partner caregivers in any type of long-term, committed relationship.

Studies of spousal caregivers of persons with Alzheimer disease show that marital satisfaction is much lower than for healthy couples (Cavanaugh & Kinney, 1994; Kinney et al., 1993). Spousal caregivers report a loss of companionship and intimacy over the course of caregiving (Williamson & Schulz, 1990; Wright, 1991). Marital satisfaction is also an important predictor of spousal caregivers' reports of depressive symptoms; the better the perceived quality of the marriage, the fewer symptoms caregivers report (Kinney et al., 1993). Sadly, caring for a spouse often leads the caregiver to question the meaningfulness of life (Wells & Kendig, 1997).

Most partner caregivers are forced to respond to an environmental challenge that they did not choose—their partner's illness. They adopt the caregiver role out of necessity. Once they adopt the role, caregivers assess their ability to carry out the duties required. Longitudinal research indicates that how caregivers perceive their ability to provide care at the outset of caregiving may be all-important (Kinney & Cavanaugh, 1993). Caregivers who perceive themselves as competent try to rise to the occasion. For example, data indicate that spousal caregivers who perceive themselves as highly competent report fewer and less intense caregiving hassles than spousal caregivers who see themselves as less competent (Kinney & Cavanaugh, 1993). However, spousal caregivers do not always remember their major hassles accurately over time; in one study, caregivers remembered only about two-thirds of their major hassles after a one-month delay (Cavanaugh & Kinney, 1998). This finding points out that health care professionals should not rely exclusively on partner caregivers' reports about the caregiving situation in making diagnostic judgments.

The importance of feeling competent as a partner caregiver fits with the docility component of the competence–environmental press model presented earlier in this chapter. Caregivers attempt to balance their perceived competence with the environmental demands of caregiving. Perceived competence allows them to be proactive rather than merely reactive (and docile), which gives them a better chance to optimize their situation.

Even in the best of committed relationships, providing full-time care for a partner is very stressful (Kinney & Cavanaugh, 1993). Coping with a wife, for example, who may not remember her husband's name, who may act strangely, and who has a chronic and fatal disease presents serious challenges even to the happiest of couples.

WIDOWHOOD

Alma, the woman we met in the vignette, still feels the loss of her husband, Chuck. "There are lots of times when I feel him around. We were together for so long that you take it for granted that your husband is just there. And there are times when I just don't want to go on without him. But I suppose I'll get through it."

Traditional marriage vows proclaim that the union will last "'til death do us part." Like Alma and Chuck, virtually all older married couples will see their marriages end because one partner dies. For most people, the death of a spouse follows a period of caregiving (Martin-Matthews, 1999) and is one of the most traumatic events they will ever experience (Pearson, 1996). Although widowhood may occur at any age, it is much more likely to occur in old age—and to women (Martin-Matthews, 1999). In Canada, nearly half of all women over age 65 are widows, but only 13% of men the same age are widowers (Statistics Canada, 2001e). The reasons for this discrepancy are related to biological and social forces. As we saw in Chapter 15, women have longer life expectancies, and women typically marry men older than themselves, as discussed in Chapter 12. Consequently, the average married woman can expect to live a number of years as a widow.

The impact of widowhood goes well beyond the ending of a long-term partnership (Martin-Matthews, 1999; Pearson, 1996). Widowed people may be left alone by family and friends who do not know how to deal with a bereaved person (see Chapter 17). As a result, widows and widowers may lose not only a spouse but also those friends and family who feel uncomfortable including a single person rather than a couple in social functions (Matthews, 1996). Because women tend to have more friends than men and keep stronger family ties, widows typically get more help than widowers from siblings and friends (Barrett & Lynch, 1999; Martin-Matthews, 2000). But feelings of loss do not dissipate quickly, as the case of Alma shows clearly. As we will see in Chapter 17, feeling sad on important dates is a common experience, even many years after a loved one has died.

Men and women react differently to widowhood. Widowers are at higher risk of dying themselves soon after their spouse, either by suicide or natural causes (Osgood, 1992; Smith & Zick, 1996), and are at higher risk for depression (Lee et al., 2001). Some people believe that the loss of a wife presents a more serious problem for a man than the loss of a husband for a woman. Perhaps this is because a wife is often a man's only close friend and confidant, or because men are usually unprepared to live out their lives alone (Martin-Matthews, 1999; see Chapter 12). Older men are often ill equipped to handle such routine and necessary tasks as cooking, shopping, and keeping house, and they become emotionally isolated from family members.

Although both widows and widowers suffer financial loss, widows often suffer more because survivor's benefits are usually much less than their husband's pensions (Martin-Matthews, 1999; Smith & Zick, 1996).

An important factor to keep in mind about gender differences in widowhood is that men are usually older than women when they are widowed. To some extent, the difficulties reported by widowers may be partly due to this age difference. Regardless of age, men have a clear advantage over women in the opportunity to form new heterosexual relationships, as there are fewer social restrictions on relationships between older men and younger women (Matthews, 1996). However, older widowers are actually less likely to form new, close friendships than are widows. Perhaps this is simply a continuation of men's lifelong tendency to have few close friendships (see Chapter 12).

For many reasons, including the need for companionship and financial security, some widowed people remarry. Widowers are much more likely than widows to remarry (Lee, Willetts, & Seccombe, 1998). However, remarriage after being widowed is still less likely than after divorce (Connidis, 2001). Most likely this is because there are objective limitations (decreased mobility, poorer health, poorer finances), absence of incentives common to younger ages (desire for children), and social pressures to protect one's estate (Talbott, 1998).

GREAT-GRANDPARENTHOOD

As discussed in Chapter 13, grandparenting is an important and enjoyable role for many adults. With increasing numbers of people, especially women, living to very old age, more people are experiencing great-grandparenthood. Age at first marriage and age at parenthood also play a critical role; people who reach these milestones at relatively younger ages are more likely to become great-grandparents. Most current great-grandparents, like the woman in the photograph, are women who married relatively young and had children and grandchildren who also married and had children relatively early in adulthood.

© Myrleen Ferguson Cate/PhotoEdit

Although little research has been conducted on great-grandparents, their sources of satisfaction and meaning apparently differ from those of grandparents (Doka & Mertz, 1988; Wentkowski, 1985).

Compared to grandparents, great-grandparents are much more similar as a group in what they derive from the role, largely because they are less involved with the children than grandparents are. Three aspects of great-grandparenthood appear to be most important (Doka & Mertz, 1988).

First, being a great-grandparent provides a sense of personal and family renewal—important components for achieving integrity. Their grandchildren have produced new life, renewing their own excitement for life and reaffirming the continuance of their lineage. Seeing their families stretch across four generations may also provide psychological support, through feelings of symbolic immortality, to help them face death. They take pride and comfort in knowing that their families will live many years beyond their own lifetime.

Second, great-grandchildren provide new diversions in great-grandparents' lives. There are now new people with whom they can share their experiences. Third, becoming a great-grandparent is a major milestone, a mark of longevity that most people never achieve. The sense that one has lived long enough to see the fourth generation is perceived very positively.

As you might expect, people with at least one living grandparent and great-grandparent interact more with their grandparent, who is also perceived as more influential (Roberto & Skoglund, 1996). Unfortunately, some great-grandparents must assume the role of primary caregiver to their great-grandchildren, a role that few great-grandparents are prepared for (Bengtson, Mills, & Parrott, 1995; Burton, 1992). As more people live longer, it will be interesting to see whether the role of great-grandparents changes and becomes more prominent.

TEST YOURSELF

1. The two most common forms of sibling relationships in old age are loyal and _____.

2. In general, marital satisfaction in older couples is high until _____.

3. A key predictor of stress among spousal caregivers is _____.

4. _____ are at a higher risk of dying themselves soon after they lose their spouses.

5. Three aspects of being a great-grandparent that are especially important are personal and family renewal, diversion, and _____.

How do the descriptions of marital satisfaction and spousal caregiving presented here fit with the descriptions of marital satisfaction in Chapter 12 and caring for aging parents in Chapter 14? What similarities and differences are there?

Answers: (1) congenial, (2) health problems arise, (3) marital satisfaction, (4) Widowers, (5) the fact that it is a milestone

16.5

Social Issues and Aging

LEARNING OBJECTIVES

▨ Who are frail older adults? How common is frailty?

▨ Who are the most likely people to live in nursing homes? What are the characteristics of good nursing homes?

▨ How do you know whether an older adult is abused or neglected? Which people are most likely to be abused and to be abusers?

▨ What are the key social policy issues?

Social Issues and Aging
Frail Older Adults
Living in Nursing Homes
Elder Abuse and Neglect
Politics, Social Security, and Medicare

Rose is an 82-year-old woman who still lives in the neighbourhood where she grew up. She has been in relatively good health for most of her life, but in the last year she has needed help with tasks such as preparing meals and shopping for personal items. Rose wants very much to continue living in her own home. She dreads being placed in a nursing home, but her family wonders whether that might be the best option.

Our consideration of late life thus far has focused on the experiences of most people. In this final section, we consider people like Rose, who represent a substantial number, but still a minority, of all older adults. Like Rose, some older adults experience problems completing such common tasks as taking care of themselves. We consider the prevalence and kinds of problems such people face. Although most older adults live in the community, some reside in nursing homes; we consider the kinds of people most likely to live in institutional settings. Unfortunately, some older adults are the victims of abuse or neglect; we will examine some of the key issues relating to how elder abuse happens. Finally, we conclude with an overview of the most important emerging social policy issues.

All these issues are critical when viewed from Baltes and Smith's (2002) Fourth Age perspective, described in Chapter 15. We will see that it is the oldest old who make up most of the frail and who live in nursing homes. With the very rapid increase in the number of oldest old on the horizon with the baby boom generation, finding ways to deal with these issues is essential.

FRAIL OLDER ADULTS

In our discussion about aging to this point, we have focused on the majority of older adults who are healthy, cognitively competent, and financially secure, and have secure family relationships. Some older adults, like the woman in the photograph, are not as fortunate. *They are frail older adults who have physical disabilities, are very ill, and may have cognitive or psychological disorders.* These frail older adults constitute a minority of the population over age 65, but a proportion that increases with age.

Frail older adults are people whose competence (defined by the competence–environmental press model presented earlier) is declining. However, they do not have one specific problem that differentiates them from their active, healthy counterparts (Guralnick & Simonsick, 1993; Strawbridge et al., 1998).

Assessing everyday competence consists of examining how well people can complete activities of daily living and instrumental activities of daily living (Diehl, 1998). *Activities of daily living (ADLs) are basic self-care tasks such as eating, bathing, toileting, walking, or dressing.* A person could be considered frail if

Photodisc

he or she needs help with one of these tasks. Other tasks are also considered important for living independently. *These instrumental activities of daily living (IADLs) are actions that require some intellectual competence and planning.* Which actions constitute IADLs vary considerably from one culture to another (Katz, 1983). For example, for most older adults in Western culture, IADLs would include shopping for personal items, paying bills, making telephone calls, taking medications appropriately, and keeping appointments. In other cultures, IADLs might include caring for animal herds, making bread, threshing grain, and tending crops.

Prevalence of Frailty

How common are people like Rose, the 82-year-old woman in the vignette who still lives in the neighbourhood in which she grew up? Not surprisingly, the number of older people needing help with ADLs increases dramatically with age. In a representative sample of elderly Canadians, 8% of females and 4.6% of males aged 65 to 74 need assistance with ADLs compared to 21.6% of females and 12.9% of males over the age of 85 who need assistance with ADLs (The Canadian Study of Health and Aging Working Group, 2001). As you can also see in Table 16.1, the number of adults requiring assistance with IADLs also increases drastically after age 85.

In addition to basic assistance with ADLs and IADLs, frail older adults have other needs. Research shows that these individuals are also prone to higher rates of anxiety disorders and depression (Solano, 2001).

Although frailty becomes more likely with increasing age, especially during the last year of life, there are many ways to provide a supportive environment for frail older adults. We have already seen how many family members provide care. Exercise can also help improve the quality of life of some frail older adults (Schechtman & Ory, 2001). Next, we will consider the role that nursing homes play. The key to providing

TABLE 16.1	Percentage of the Canadian Population Aged 65 or Over Classified as Frail by Differing Definitions, by Age and Sex			
	Age Group			
	65–74	75–84	85+	Total
ADL definition				
Males	4.6	12.9	25.3	8.0
Females	8.0	21.6	43.4	14.8
ADL or IADL definition				
Males	16.1	37.7	63.6	24.7
Females	26.7	53.3	82.5	39.1
ADL + Cognitive definition				
Males	22.9	40.3	62.6	29.9
Females	24.0	43.9	65.4	33.3
Balance definition				
Males	18.4	36.5	65.8	26.0
Females	26.6	51.0	75.7	37.9

SOURCE: The Canadian Study of Health and Aging Working Group, 2001

a supportive context for frail older adults is to create an optimal match between the person's competence and the environmental demands.

LIVING IN NURSING HOMES

The last place that Bessie thought she would ever end up was in a bed in a local nursing home. "That's a place where old people go to die," she would tell her friends. "It's not gonna be for me." But here she is. Bessie fell a few weeks ago and broke her hip. Because she lives alone, she needs to stay in the nursing home until she recovers. She detests the food; "tasteless" she calls it. Her roommate, Doris, refers to her room as "jail" to her daughter. Doris, age 78, has dementia.

Bessie and Doris represent many of the people who live in nursing homes, some temporarily, some permanently. If given the choice, the vast majority of older adults do not want to live in nursing homes; their families would also prefer some other solution. Sometimes, though, placement in a nursing home is necessary because of the older person's needs or the family's circumstances.

Misconceptions about nursing homes are common. Contrary to what some people believe, in Canada only about 7.5% of older adults live in institutional care. And, although living in health care institutions was most common for elderly aged 85 and over, the vast majority of this age group continue to live in the community (Statistics Canada, 2003c).

The decreasing numbers of elderly who receive institutional care are due to a shift away from these institutions resulting in most of the care being done by family and friends (Statistics Canada, 2003c). *Assisted-living facilities provide a supportive living arrangement for people who need assistance with ADLs or IADLs but who are not so impaired physically or cognitively that they need 24-hour care.* Such assisted-living services, for which a fee is paid, would generally include room, board, and assistance as needed with bathing, shopping, laundry, and transportation. This may occur in a multi-level centre or within institution facilities. The National Advisory Council on Aging, which was formed in 1980 to assist and advise the Minister of Health on matters related to aging and quality of life issues of Canadian seniors, believes that Canada's housing policies and practices need to change with the needs of Canadian seniors, both those who are independent and semi-independent, two groups that make up the majority (2003). The type of housing the council is recommending would be barrier-free, and be designed to meet both physiological and psychological needs, as well as social and cultural needs.

Because there is generally a high level of impairment among nursing home residents, frail older people and their relatives do not see nursing homes as an option until other avenues have been explored. This may account for the numbers of truly impaired people who live in nursing homes; the kinds and amount of problems make life outside the nursing home very difficult for them and their families and beyond the level of assistance provided by assisted-living facilities. For these reasons, the decision to enter a nursing home often is made quickly in reaction to a crisis, such as a person's impending discharge from a hospital or other health emergency (Hooyman & Kiyak, 1999).

What Characterizes a Good Nursing Home?

Nursing homes vary a great deal in the amount and quality of care they provide. One useful way of evaluating them is by applying the competence–environmental press model. When applied to nursing homes, the goal is to find the optimal level of environmental support for people who have relatively low levels of competence.

Selecting a nursing home should be done carefully to ensure that the institution is prepared to meet the needs of individuals. Based on the various theories of person-environment interaction discussed earlier in this chapter and in Chapter 1, researchers recommend a "person-centred planning" approach to nursing home policies (Reese, 2001). This approach is based on promoting residents' well-being through increasing their perceived level of personal control and treating them with respect. Taking this approach means such things as residents getting to decorate their own rooms, choosing what they want to eat from a buffet, and deciding whether they want to take a shower or a bath. Such policies are grounded in classic research showing that residents who have higher perceived personal control show significant improvement in well-being and activity level, and actually live longer (Langer & Rodin, 1976; Rodin & Langer, 1977).

Nursing homes that use the person-centred planning approach also note major decreases in the need for certain medications (e.g., sleep and anti-anxiety drugs) and soft restraints, as well as substantial declines in the number of residents who are incontinent (Reese, 2001). Feelings of self-efficacy are crucial to doing well and have a profound impact on nursing home residents' functional abilities (Johnson et al., 1998; Reese, 2001).

Equally important, people interacting with nursing home residents must avoid **patronizing speech,** *which is marked by slower speech, exaggerated intonation, higher pitch, increased volume, repetitions, closed-ended questions, and simplified vocabulary and grammar. A related form of demeaning speech, called* **infantilization,** *involves the use of a person's first name when it is not appropriate, terms of endearment, simplified expressions, short imperatives, assumptions that the resident has no memory, and manipulation to get compliance.* Several studies document that the use of patronizing speech and infantilization result in negative feelings on the part of residents and may lower self-esteem among those who perceive such speech negatively (Ryan et al., 2000; Whitmer & Whitbourne, 1997).

The first time most people visit a nursing home, they are ill prepared to talk to family members who are frail, have trouble remembering, and cannot get around very well. The hardest part is trying to figure out what to say to avoid patronizing speech. However, visiting residents of nursing homes like those in the photograph on page 597 is a way to maintain social contacts and provide a meaningful activity. Even if the person you are visiting is frail or has a sensory impairment or some other type

© Jeff Greenberg/PhotoEdit

of disability, visits can be uplifting. As noted earlier in the chapter, high-quality social contacts help older adults maintain their life satisfaction. Here are several suggestions for making visits more pleasant (Papalia & Olds, 1995; adapted from Davis, 1985):

- Concentrate on the older adult's expertise and wisdom, as discussed in Chapter 15, by asking for advice on a life problem that he or she knows a lot about, such as dealing with friends, cooking, or crafts.
- Allow the older person to exert control over the visit: where to go (even inside the facility), what to wear, what to eat (if choices are possible).
- Listen attentively, even if the older person is repetitive. Avoid being judgmental, be sympathetic to complaints, and acknowledge feelings.
- Talk about things the person likes to remember, such as raising children, military service, growing up, work, courtship, and so on.
- Do a joint activity, such as putting a jigsaw puzzle together, arranging a photograph album, or doing arts and crafts.
- Record your visit on audiotape or videotape. This is valuable for creating a family history that you will be able to keep. The activity may facilitate a life review as well as provide an opportunity for the older person to leave something of value for future generations by describing important personal events and philosophies.
- Bring children when you visit if possible. Grandchildren are especially important, and most older adults are very happy to include them in conversations. Such visits also give children the opportunity to see their grandparents and learn about the diversity of older adults.
- Stimulate as many senses as possible. Wearing bright clothes, singing songs, reading books, and sharing foods (as long as they have been checked with the staff) help keep residents involved with their environment. Above all, though, hold the resident's hands. There's nothing like a friendly touch.

Always remember that your visits may be the only way that the residents have of maintaining social contacts with friends and family. By following these guidelines, you will be able to avoid difficulties and make your visits more pleasurable.

ELDER ABUSE AND NEGLECT

Arletta, an 82-year-old woman in relatively poor health, has been living with her 60-year-old daughter Sally for the past two years. Recently, neighbours became concerned because they had not seen Arletta very much for several months. When they did, she looked rather worn and extremely thin, and as if she had not bathed in weeks. Finally, the neighbours decided that they should do something, so they called a senior abuse phone line. Upon hearing the details of the situation, a provincial caseworker was sent and immediately investigated. The caseworker found that Arletta was severely malnourished, had not bathed in weeks, and appeared disoriented. Based on these findings, the agency concluded that Arletta was a victim of neglect. She was moved to a nursing home temporarily.

Unfortunately, some older adults who need quality caregiving by family members or in nursing homes do not receive it. In some cases, older adults, like Arletta, are treated inappropriately. Arletta's case is representative of this sad but increasing problem: elder abuse and neglect. In this section, we consider what elder abuse and neglect are, how often they happen, and what victims and abusers are like.

Defining Elder Abuse and Neglect

Like child abuse (see Chapter 8) and partner abuse (see Chapter 12), elder abuse is difficult to define precisely in practice (Wilber & McNeilly, 2001). A summary definition is the *"mistreatment of older people by those in a position of trust, power or responsibility for their care"* (Swanson, 1998). Researchers and public policy advocates describe several different categories of elder abuse (Tatara, Thomas, & Cyphers, 1998):

- *Physical abuse:* the use of physical force that may result in bodily injury, physical pain, or impairment.
- *Sexual abuse:* nonconsensual sexual contact of any kind.
- *Emotional or psychological abuse:* infliction of anguish, pain, or distress.
- *Financial or material exploitation:* the illegal or improper use of an older adult's funds, property, or assets.
- *Abandonment:* the desertion of an older adult by an individual who had physical custody or otherwise had assumed responsibility for providing care for the older adult.
- *Neglect:* refusal or failure to fulfil any part of a person's obligation or duties to an older adult.

Prevalence

It is difficult to determine the actual numbers of abused elderly due to inconsistencies in definitions and behaviours, and there are no recent statistics. In addition, the numbers of reported cases are believed to be merely the "tip of the iceberg" (Hawranik and McKean, 2004). A 1990 Canadian survey of 2,000 older adults found that approximately 4% reported experiencing abuse or neglect. The most common form of abuse identified was financial or material abuse, followed by verbal (considered a component of psychological abuse), and third by physical abuse, most commonly by the victims' spouse (Podnieks et al., 1990).

Characteristics of Elder Abuse Victims

There are not clear differences in characteristics between abused and non-abused seniors with regard to age, gender, marital status, ethnicity, or income level.

However, abused seniors are more likely to be living with someone else rather than living alone, and living with grown offspring or other caregivers rather than a spouse (Health Canada, 1999a).

The abusers are most likely to be family members and male in cases of physical abuse, and female in cases of neglect and financial abuse (Health Canada, 1999a). People in positions of trust, such as bankers, accountants, attorneys, and clergy, are also in a position to take advantage of an older client (Kapp, 1999; Quinn, 1998). Telemarketing fraud against older adults, including fraudulent investment schemes and sweepstakes, is a growing problem (Gross, 1999; Schuett & Burke, 2000). Perpetrators of telemarketing fraud prey on the fears and needs of their targets by focusing on older adults' loneliness, desire to please, need to help, and other weaknesses.

Causes of Elder Abuse

Why elder abuse occurs is a matter of debate (Wilber & McNeilly, 2001). Several explanations have been offered that reflect the multidimensional and multidisciplinary approaches researchers have taken (Harbison, 1999).

One of the most popular theories, which has its roots in the child abuse literature, states that elder abuse occurs when caregivers who are under great stress take out their frustrations on the person requiring care (Quinn & Tomita, 1997). However, research evidence fails to support the idea that caregiver stress alone is the primary cause (Wilber & McNeilly, 2001). Similarly, the theory that patterns of abuse are transmitted across generations, shown to be a factor in other forms of family violence, also has little research support as a major cause of elder abuse (Wilber & McNeilly, 2001).

Research findings support a more complex set of causes. Based on two decades of research, Reis and Nahmiash (1998) showed that characteristics of both the caregiver and the care recipient must be considered. They found that abuse cases could be discriminated from non-abuse cases up to 84% of the time by considering several things: (a) intrapersonal problems of the caregiver, such as substance abuse, mental disorder, and behaviour problems; (b) interpersonal problems of the caregiver, such as family or marital conflict, a poor relationship with the care recipient, and financial dependence on the care recipient; and (c) social characteristics of the care recipient, such as lack of social support and past abuse.

Clearly, elder abuse is an important social problem that has had insufficient attention from researchers and policymakers. Increased educational efforts, better reporting and investigation, more options for placement of victims, and better mental health treatment for victims are all needed for the problem to be adequately addressed (Wilber & McNeilly, 2001).

POLITICS, SOCIAL SECURITY, AND MEDICARE

Without doubt, the 20th century saw a dramatic improvement in the everyday lives of older adults in industrialized countries. The increase in the number of older adults and their subsequent gain in political power, coupled with increased numbers of social programs addressing issues specific to older adults, created unprecedented gains for the average older person (Crown, 2001).

Canada's social security system has been changing gradually in response to the political and social issues that affect older adults. The system developed from modest beginnings early in the 20th century to one with universal benefits, social insurance plans, social assistance programs, and various health and social services. The Canadian Constitution ensures that both federal and provincial governments share responsibility for social security and thus both are involved in all aspects of planning, administration, and delivery of these services (Social Development Canada, 2004).

Human Resources Development Canada (HRDC) administers the federal government programs that provide financial benefits to individuals. These programs are the Old Age Security (OAS) Program and the Canada Pension Plan (CPP). Although

Canada's first Old Age Pensions Act was passed in 1927, it had a number of restrictions, including income levels. The OAS, introduced in 1952, was the first universal pension for Canadians. However, even with the OAS benefits retirement still meant a significant decrease in the standard of living for many people. Therefore in 1966 the CPP and Quebec Pension Plan (QPP) were established so that recipients would receive benefits at retirement based on the amount they contributed throughout their working lives. The federally administered CPP is responsible for all provinces and territories except Quebec, which has established the QPP to operate in place of the CPP (Social Development Canada, 2004).

Over the years a number of changes to CPP came into effect such as flexible retirement benefits payable as early as age 60, increased disability benefits, continuation of survivor benefits if the survivor remarries, sharing of retirement benefits between spouses or common-law partners, and an increase in contribution rates. However, due to uncertainty about the sustainability of Canada's public pensions because of increasing numbers of seniors compared to number of workers contributing, many people were concerned that there would not be sufficient funds when they retired.

Therefore in 1998 a number of changes were made to CPP that included increased CPP rates, the establishment of the CPP Investment Board to invest funds not being used, and changes to the administration and calculation of benefits. The government is confident that the CPP will continue for future generations. No group in Canada has experienced the same level of improvement in relative incomes as senior citizens. In 2000 all OAS and CPP benefits and obligations were extended to same-sex, common-law couples.

Health Care

A national medicare program has been in place across the country since the 1960s. Currently, the Canada Health Act is the federal health legislation. This legislation "affirms the federal government's commitment to a universal, accessible, comprehensive, portable and publicly administered health insurance system" (Health Canada, 2004b). The aim of this act is to ensure that all residents of Canada have prepaid access to necessary hospital and physician services. The federal government provides the provinces and territories with transfer payments to administer funds for health care. In turn, the provinces and territories must satisfy a number of criteria in order to receive these payments. These five criteria of the Canada Health Act (Health Canada, 2004b) are summarized below.

1. *Public Administration.* The provincial and territorial health care insurance plans must be administered on a non-profit basis by a public authority that is accountable to the province or territory.

2. *Comprehensiveness.* The provincial or health care insurance plan must insure all insured health services that are provided by hospitals and appropriate health care practitioners.

3. *Universality.* All insured residents must be entitled to the insured health services provided by that province or territory. Newcomers to Canada may be subject to a (maximum) three-month waiting period.

4. *Portability.* Residents moving from one province or territory to another must be covered by their former province or territory during any waiting time imposed.

5. *Accessibility.* Residents of a province or territory must have reasonable access to medically necessary services.

Under the Canada Health Act, hospitals or other health providers cannot charge extra billing or user charges for insurable services. This stipulation has become controversial as a number of jurisdictions have expressed interest in and/or intent to introduce private for-profit health services to decrease the waiting list times and increase accessibility to services. Critics are concerned that the medical care system will become a two-tiered system in which those with the financial resources can access specific services more readily. Others argue that this would not necessarily be a change for the worse since it would take pressure off the current system, possibly allowing increased accessibility for those who cannot afford the private clinics. The debate continues.

For seniors in Canada, the Canada Health Act ensures that their insurable medical costs continue to be covered after retirement. However, some aspects of the Canada Health Act may pose problems for some senior citizens, particularly in relation to covering all the costs of medications and community care. Coverage for these services varies among the provinces and territories. For example, many advocacy groups for seniors have advocated for the inclusion of a pharmacare program under the Health Care Act.

Despite a number of flaws and shortcomings, Canada's health care system is viewed overall very positively. People in Canada from every background and age do not have to be fearful about their access to care or that the costs of surgery or illness will have devastating financial implications for their family (Storch, 2003).

TEST YOURSELF

1. Activities of daily living (ADLs) include functioning in the areas of bathing, toileting, walking, dressing, and _____.

2. Most people who live in nursing homes are aged _____.

3. The group that most often abuses older adults is _____.

How would the competence–environmental press framework, presented earlier in this chapter, apply specifically to the various types of housing and nursing homes discussed in this section?

Answers: (1) eating, (2) 85 years and older, (3) their adult children

---

PUTTING IT ALL TOGETHER

We are involved in human relationships throughout our lives. In a very real sense, people grow old within the broader social context of their environment and social network.

The match between people's competence and the environmental demands they face sets the stage for how well they adapt. How older people cope with daily life is typically a continuation of the ways they coped throughout their lives. We encountered people who, like Olive, spend time reflecting on their past to determine whether their lives have been well spent. We saw that the view of retirement as detrimental to health and as a cause of isolation is wrong; most people are like Marcus, who greatly enjoys retirement. Many older women, like Alma, are widows; such women are especially vulnerable to financial pressures. Also, like Rosa, many people over 80 need assistance with their daily activities.

The general picture of older adults is characterized by continued activity for most. Still, we need to recog-

nize that, especially among the oldest old, physical limitations are an important aspect of living. Although only a very small proportion of older adults are in nursing homes, many people over 80 need varying degrees of help to continue living independently. The rapid increase in the number of older people that Canada will experience over the next few decades will seriously affect traditional public policies toward older adults.

Combined with Chapter 15, this chapter provides insight into the complexities of old age. So what is known about a person if we know she is 85 years old? Not much more than the fact that she has celebrated 85 birthdays. That's not bad either—it means that if you want to know something more than that, you'll need to get to know her.

We can now take a broader view of the biopsychosocial model as it relates to aging. In this chapter, we focused mainly on how sociocultural forces shape people's lives by setting the context for retirement and interpersonal relationships, as well as setting the agenda for social and public policy issues. How well people are able to face sociocultural forces (as exemplified by environmental press) is a function of their bio-logical and psychological competence. Of course, this function is a dynamic one that changes as people grow older.

SUMMARY

16.1 Theories of Psychosocial Aging

Continuity Theory

- Continuity theory is based on the view that people tend to cope with daily life in later adulthood by applying familiar strategies based on past experience to maintain and preserve both internal and external structures.

Competence and Environmental Press

- According to competence–environmental press theory, people's optimal adaptation occurs when there is a balance between their ability to cope and the level of environmental demands placed on them. When balance is not achieved, behaviour becomes maladaptive. Several studies indicate that competence–environmental press theory can be applied to a variety of real-world situations.

16.2 Personality, Social Cognition, and Spirituality

Integrity Versus Despair

- Older adults face the Eriksonian struggle of integrity versus despair, primarily through a life review. Integrity involves accepting one's life for what it is; despair involves bitterness about one's past. People who reach integrity become self-affirming and self-accepting, and they judge their lives to have been worthwhile and good.

Well-Being and Social Cognition

- Subjective well-being is positive evaluation of one's life associated with positive feelings. Personal control beliefs also play a major role in behaviour and thought through two processes: assimilative processes or primary control and accommodative processes or secondary control.

Religiosity and Spiritual Support

- Older adults use religion and spiritual support more often than any other strategy to help them cope with problems of life.

16.3 I Used to Work at . . . : Living in Retirement

What Does Being Retired Mean?

- Retirement is a complex process by which people withdraw from full-time employment. No single definition is adequate for all ethnic groups; self-definition involves several factors, including eligibility for certain social programs.

Why Do People Retire?

- People generally retire because they choose to, although some people are forced to retire or do so because of serious health problems such as cardio-vascular disease or cancer. However, there are important gender and ethnic differences in why people retire and how they label themselves after retirement.

Adjustment to Retirement

- Retirement is an important life transition. Most people are satisfied with retirement. Most retired people maintain their health, friendship networks, and activity levels, at least in the years immediately following retirement. For men, personal life priorities are all-important; little is known about women's retirement satisfaction. Most retired people stay busy in activities such as volunteer work and helping others.

Keeping Busy in Retirement

- From a life course perspective, it is important to maintain social integration in retirement. Participation in community organizations and volunteering are primary ways of achieving this.

16.4 Friends and Family in Late Life

Friends and Siblings

- A person's social convoy is an important source of satisfaction in late life. Patterns of friendships among older adults are very similar to those among young adults, but older adults are more selective. Sibling relationships are especially important in old age. Five types of sibling relationships have been identified: intimate, congenial, loyal, apathetic, and hostile. The loyal and congenial types are the most common. Ties between sisters are the strongest.

Marriage and Gay and Lesbian Partnerships

- Long-term marriages tend to be happy until one partner develops serious health problems. Older married couples show a lower potential for marital conflict and greater potential for pleasure. Long-term gay and lesbian relationships tend to be very similar in characteristics to long-term heterosexual marriages.

Caring for a Partner

- Caring for a spouse puts considerable strain on the relationship. The degree of marital satisfaction strongly affects how spousal caregivers perceive stress. Although caught off guard initially, most spousal caregivers are able to provide adequate care. Perceptions of competence among spousal caregivers at the outset of caregiving may be especially important.

Widowhood

- Widowhood is a difficult transition for most people. Feelings of loneliness are hard to cope with, especially during the first few months following bereavement. Men generally have problems in social relationships and in household tasks; women tend to have more severe financial problems. Some widowed people remarry, partly to solve loneliness and financial problems.

Great-Grandparenthood

- Becoming a great-grandparent is an important source of personal satisfaction for many older adults. Great-grandparents as a group are more similar to each other than grandparents are. Three aspects of great-grandparenthood are most important: sense of personal and family renewal, new diversions in life, and a major life milestone.

16.5 Social Issues and Aging

Frail Older Adults

- The number of frail older adults is growing. Frailty is defined by the impairment in activities of daily living (basic self-care skills) and instrumental activities of daily living (actions that require intellectual competence or planning). Many women over age 85 may need assistance with ADLs or IADLs. Supportive environments are useful in optimizing the balance between competence and environmental press.

Living in Nursing Homes

- Two levels of care are provided in nursing homes: intermediate care and skilled nursing care. Maintaining a resident's sense of control is an important component of good nursing homes. Communications with residents must avoid patronizing speech and infantilization.

Elder Abuse and Neglect

- Abuse and neglect of older adults is an increasing problem. However, abuse and neglect are difficult to define precisely. Several categories are used, including physical abuse, sexual abuse, emotional or psychological abuse, financial or material exploitation, abandonment, and neglect. Most perpetrators are family members, usually spouses or adult children of the victims. Research indicates that abuse results from a complex interaction of characteristics of the caregiver and care recipient.

Politics, Social Security, and Medicare

- The Old Age Security Program, Canada Pension Plan, and Quebec Pension Plan were developed to provide adequate incomes for senior citizens.
- The Canada Health Act was developed to ensure that all Canadians have reasonable access to medical services without direct charges at point of service.

KEY TERMS

continuity theory (572)
competence (573)
environmental press (573)
adaptation level (573)
zone of maximum performance potential (573)
zone of maximum comfort (573)
proactivity (574)

docility (574)
integrity versus despair (576)
life review (576)
subjective well-being (577)
spiritual support (580)
bridge job (583)
social convoy (586)
socioemotional selectivity (587)

frail older adults (594)
activities of daily living (ADLs) (594)
instrumental activities of daily living (IADLs) (594)
assisted-living facilities (595)
patronizing speech (596)
infantilization (596)

SEE FOR YOURSELF: APPLYING WHAT YOU'VE LEARNED

As mentioned in the text, people who no longer work full-time may or may not label themselves as retired. To find out firsthand how people label themselves and how they occupy their time, try the following exercise. Interview several older adults who you believe do not work full-time anymore. Don't interview only your relatives; make sure you have a diverse sample of older adults.

Begin your interview by asking them about the kinds of work (for pay or as a volunteer) they do now and the kinds they did in the past. Ask them if they call themselves retired. If so, why do they? If not, why not? How much do they miss not working in their old jobs? Ask also about how they keep themselves occupied now.

Gather the results of your interviews and see whether you can draw any general conclusions. Are there certain characteristics common to people who call themselves retired? Or to those who do not? Are there similarities in how people keep themselves occupied? Bring the data to class and compare your results with other students' findings. See for yourself how people view retirement.

LEARN MORE ABOUT IT

Books

CONNIDIS, I. A. (2001). *Family ties and aging.* Thousand Oaks, CA: Sage. This easy-to-read book covers many topics in family life and aging, including types of relationships, intimacy, singlehood, widowhood, and various types of intergenerational relations.

ERIKSON, E. H. (1982). *The life cycle completed: Review.* New York: Norton. By Erikson's own account, this short book represents a summary of his theory. It is moderately difficult reading.

GUBRIUM, J. F. (1994). *Speaking of life: Horizons of meaning for nursing home residents.* Hawthorne, NY: Aldine de Gruyter. This easy-to-read book provides a wealth of information about what life is like in nursing homes.

KIDDER, T. (1993). *Old friends.* Boston: Houghton Mifflin. This engaging book tells the story of two male residents of a nursing home and how they and others deal with everyday life.

KINNON, D. (2002). *Community awareness and response: Abuse and neglect of older adults.* Ottawa: Family Violence Prevention Unit. This document provides a discussion of current knowledge, emerging trends and issues, and up-to-date resources and research from across Canada.

MACE, N. L., & RABINS, P. V. (2001). The 36-hour day: A family guide to caring for persons with Alzheimer disease, related dementing illnesses, and memory loss in later life (rev. ed.). Baltimore: Johns Hopkins University Press. This is still the best available overall guide to family caregiving for dementia patients.

MACNAB, F. (1994). *The 30 vital years.* New York: Wiley. This easy-to-read book discusses psychosocial aging and includes many anecdotes and case studies.

MARTIN-MATTHEWS, A. (2001). *The ties that bind aging families.* Ottawa: The Vanier Institute of the Family. This publication provides an overview of the changing character and nature of aging families in Canada.

 For additional readings, explore InfoTrac® College Edition, your online library. Go to http://www.infotrac.thomsonlearning.com.

Websites

http://www.medicare.gov/Publications/Pubs/pdf/nhguide.pdf

The American government's Centers for Medicare and Medicaid Services provides an excellent publication describing in detail the key factors one should use in choosing a nursing home. Although not all aspects are relevant due to the differences in the Canadian and American health care systems, the booklet gives step-by-step guides for what type of facility to consider, important selection factors, nursing home resident rights, information to collect, and sources of help and other information.

http://www.hc-sc.gc.ca/seniors-aines/

The website for Health Canada's Division of Aging and Seniors provides an excellent source of current information on health and the psychological aspects of aging. It also includes a seniors' guide to federal programs and services such as pensions and benefits.

http://www.50plus.com

This website of the Canadian Association for Fifty-Plus (CARP, formerly known as the Canadian Association for Retired Persons) is for seniors and professionals to learn more about health, travel, home, family, and community aspects of aging. It provides a number of links to related sources of information.

http://www.civilization.ca

The Government of Canada has developed the Canadian Museum of Civilization website, which includes a Social Progress Gallery that provides links to information on social issues such as the history of public pensions.

http://www.coag.uvic.ca

The website for the Centre on Aging at the University of Victoria includes access to current multidisciplinary research on aging.

Website addresses are subject to change. The *Human Development* book companion website can be accessed for updated links.

The Human Development Book Companion Website

See http://www.humandevelopment.nelson.com for practice quiz questions, Internet links, updates, critical thinking exercises, discussion forums, and more.

 ### *Life-Span CD-ROM*

For more information on the concepts covered in this chapter, go to

Module 6: Late Adulthood

• Emotional and Social Development

© Royalty Free Corbis

CHAPTER 17

The Final Passage

DYING AND BEREAVEMENT

We have a paradoxical relationship with death. Sometimes we are fascinated by it. As tourists, we visit places where famous people died or are buried. We watch as television newscasts show people who have been killed in war. But when it comes to pondering our own death or that of someone close to us, we have many problems. As La Rochefoucauld, a French writer and reformer, wrote more than 300 years ago: Looking into the sun is easier than contemplating our death. When death is personal, we become uneasy. Looking at the sun is hard indeed.

In this chapter, we first consider definitional and ethical issues surrounding death. Next, we examine how people view death at different points in the life span, and we look specifically at the process of dying. Dealing with grief is important for survivors, so we will consider this topic in the third section. In the fourth section, we see how people cope with different types of loss.

17.1

Definitions and Ethical Issues

LEARNING OBJECTIVES

▨ How is death defined?

▨ What legal and medical criteria are used to determine when death occurs?

▨ What are the ethical dilemmas surrounding euthanasia?

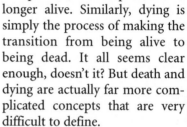

Definitions and Ethical Issues

Sociocultural Definitions of Death

Legal and Medical Definitions

Ethical Issues

Greta, a second-year university student, was very upset when she learned that her room-mate's mother had died suddenly. Her roommate is Jewish, and Greta had no idea what customs would be followed during the funeral. When Greta arrived at her roommate's house, she was surprised to find all of the mirrors in the house covered. Greta realized for the first time that death rituals vary in different religious traditions.

Take a look at the deceased person in the photograph. When one first thinks about it, death seems a very simple concept to define: It is the point at which a person is no longer alive. Similarly, dying is simply the process of making the transition from being alive to being dead. It all seems clear enough, doesn't it? But death and dying are actually far more complicated concepts that are very difficult to define.

As we will see, Greta's experience reflects the many cultural and religious differences in the definition of death and the customs surrounding it. The meaning of death depends on the observer's perspective as well as on the specific medical and biological criteria one uses.

SOCIOCULTURAL DEFINITIONS OF DEATH

What comes to mind when you hear the word *death*? A driver killed in a traffic accident? A transition to an eternal reward? Flags at half-staff? A cemetery? A car battery that doesn't work anymore? Each of these possibilities represents a way in which death can be considered in Western culture (Kalish, 1987; Kastenbaum, 1999). All cultures have their own views. Among the Melanesians, the term *mate* includes the very sick, the very old, and the dead; the term *toa* refers to all other living people (Counts & Counts, 1985). Other South Pacific cultures believe the life force leaves the body during sleep or illness; sleep, illness, and death are considered together. Thus, people "die" several times before experiencing "final death" (Counts & Counts, 1985). The Kwanga of Papua New Guinea believe most deaths are caused by sorcery (Brison, 1995).

Mourning rituals and states of bereavement also vary in different cultures (Rosenblatt, 2001). There is great variability across cultures in the meaning of death and whether there are rituals or other behaviours to express grief. Some cultures have formalized periods of time during which certain prayers or rituals are performed. For example, after the death of a close relative, Orthodox Jews recite ritual prayers and cover all the mirrors in the house. The men slash their ties as a symbol of loss. These are the customs that Greta, the university student in the vignette, experienced. Ancestor worship, a deep respectful feeling toward individuals from whom a family is descended or who are important to them, is an important part of Japanese culture and of Buddhism in Japan (Klass, 1996b). Some cultures, such as the Toraja of Indonesia, do not encourage people to dwell on the dead or memories of them; nevertheless, they still maintain contact with the deceased through dreams (Hollan, 1995). Thus, we must keep in mind that the experiences of our culture or particular group may not generalize to other cultures or groups.

Death can be a truly cross-cultural experience. The international outpouring of grief over the death of Princess Diana in 1997, whose funeral procession is shown in the photograph, and the tributes across Canada when former Prime Minister Pierre Elliott Trudeau died in 2000 drew much attention to the ways the death of people we do not know personally can still affect us. We realize at these times that death happens to us all and that death can simultaneously be personal and public.

CP Picture Archive /AP/ Barry Batchelor

Just as there are different mourning rituals, there are various customs involving funerals. Perhaps you have experienced a range of different types of funeral customs, from small, private services to very elaborate rituals. Variations in the customs surrounding death are reflected in some of the oldest monuments on earth, such as the pyramids in Egypt, and in some of the most beautiful, such as the Taj Mahal in India.

LEGAL AND MEDICAL DEFINITIONS

Sociocultural approaches help us understand the different ways people view death. But they do not address a very fundamental question: How do we determine that someone has died? The medical and legal communities have grappled with this question for centuries and continue to do so today. Let's see what the current answers are.

Determining when death occurs has always been subjective. *Traditionally, people accepted and applied the criteria that now define* **clinical death**: *lack of heartbeat and respiration. Today, however, the most widely accepted criteria are those that characterize* **brain death**. The Parliament of Canada Standing Committee on Health (1999) has established several criteria that must be met for the determination of brain death:

1. The patient must be unconscious.

2. The patient must be unable to breathe spontaneously.

3. There must be no response to external stimuli (i.e., verbal, pain).

4. There must be no response (eye movement) to passive head movements or to ice water syringed into the ears.

5. There must be no blinking in response to touching the cornea.

6. There must be no pupil response to a bright light shone into the eyes.

7. The patient must be unable to maintain blood pressure or control fluids and electrolytes or body temperature.

8. The physician must also consider the body temperature when consciousness was lost and whether there are any drugs in the system that could mimic death.

In all the provinces and territories, brain death is legally defined as "according to accepted medical practice," yet there is some variability in these practices since in Canada procedures associated with brain death are determined by individual hospitals (Canadian Medical Association, 2003).

Because of conditions like persistent vegetative state, which occurs when cortical functioning ceases but brainstem activity continues, family members sometimes face difficult ethical decisions concerning care for the individual. These issues are the focus of the next section.

ETHICAL ISSUES

An ambulance screeches to a halt, and emergency personnel rush a woman into the emergency room. As a result of an accident at a swimming pool, she has no pulse and no respiration. Working rapidly, the trauma team re-establishes a heartbeat through electric shock. A respirator is connected. An EEG and other tests reveal extensive and irreversible brain damage. What should be done?

*This is an example of the kinds of problems faced in the field of **bioethics**, the study of the interface between human values and technological advances in health and life sciences.* Bioethics grew from two bases: respect for individual freedom and the impossibility of establishing any single version of morality by rational argument or common sense (Cole & Holstein, 1996). In practice, bioethics emphasizes the minimization of harm over the maximization of good, and the importance of individual choice.

*In the arena of death and dying, the most important bioethical issue is **euthanasia**— the practice of ending life for reasons of mercy.* The moral dilemma posed by euthanasia becomes apparent when we try to decide the circumstances under which a person's life should be ended. In our society this dilemma occurs most often when a person is being kept alive by machines or when someone is suffering from a terminal illness.

Active Euthanasia

Euthanasia can be carried out in two different ways: active and passive. *Active euthanasia involves the deliberate ending of someone's life, which may be based on a clear statement of the person's wishes or a decision made by someone else who has the legal authority to do so.* Usually, this involves situations in which people are in a persistent vegetative state or suffer from the end stages of a terminal disease. Examples of active euthanasia would be administering a drug overdose, disconnecting a life-support system, or ending a person's life through so-called mercy killing.

Canadians' attitudes toward euthanasia have been shifting over the years. In 1992, 77% of those surveyed favoured voluntary euthanasia for terminally ill patients, compared to 45% who were in favour in 1968 (Health Canada, 2002c). Most Americans favour such actions as disconnecting life support in situations involving patients in a persistent vegetative state, but feelings also run strongly against it due to religious or other reasons (Benson, 1999). Similarly, Israelis hold a range of opinions (Leichtentritt & Rettig, 2000), as do Germans (Oehmichen & Meissner, 2000). A Swedish study showed that better education about palliative care options reduced the number of requests for active euthanasia (Valverius, Nilstun, & Nilsson, 2000).

The most controversial version of active euthanasia involves physician-assisted suicide. Dr. Jack Kevorkian (shown in the photograph), a physician in Michigan who was convicted of murder in 1999 for assisting in a patient's suicide broadcast on the TV news show *60 Minutes,* is a strong proponent of the right to die. He created a suicide machine to help people end their lives. Although Dr. Kevorkian's actions do not reflect mainstream thought on the subject, he has brought attention to the issue.

Although attitudes toward euthanasia have been changing in Canada, it is not known if they are related to a growing tolerance of this subject, an increased value of self-determination, a growing concern with the quality versus quantity of life, or an increased fear of losing control at the end of one's life (Health Canada, 2002c). However, physician-assisted euthanasia remains prohibited by current law so information on its prevalence is difficult to obtain. In 1993 a survey of Canadian Medical Association (CMA) members showed that 60% of them indicated they were in favour of amending the Canadian Criminal Code, which currently prohibits physician-assisted suicide. However, the following year, in 1994, CMA members voted to ban physician participation in euthanasia. This lack of consensus among the medical profession seems to reflect that of Canadian society in general (Health Canada, 2002c).

The Current Controversies feature outlines the rules governing physician-assisted suicides that are debated publicly and in the courts.

CURRENT CONTROVERSIES

Physician-Assisted Suicide

Should individuals have the right to obtain information that will help them end their lives before enduring horrible pain that will ultimately end in death anyway? Should physicians be permitted to give that information and provide assistance if the patient asks? What do you think?

Taking one's own life has never been popular in North America due to religious and other prohibitions. In other cultures, such as Japan, suicide is viewed as an honourable way to die under certain circumstances. Asian Americans have the highest suicide rate in the United States, and their suicide notes are more likely to reveal that they felt that they were a burden on their families (Pascual, 2000).

Several countries—including Switzerland, Belgium, and Colombia—tolerate physician-assisted suicide but do not have official policies about it. In 1984, the Dutch Supreme Court eliminated prosecution of physicians who assist in suicide if these five criteria are met:

1. The patient's condition is intolerable with no hope for improvement.

2. No relief is available.
3. The patient is competent.
4. The patient makes a request repeatedly over time.
5. Two physicians agree with the patient's request.

The Dutch Parliament approved the policy in April 2001, making the Netherlands the first country to have an official policy legalizing physician-assisted suicide (Deutsch, 2001).

Canadian law currently prohibits such acts. However, the well-known case of a British Columbian woman demonstrates the human face of the issue. Sue Rodriguez suffered from a terminal disease and lost her will to live due to her extreme pain and debilitation. She tried, unsuccessfully, to challenge the constitutionality of the Canadian Criminal Code, which deems that anyone who helps or counsels a person to commit suicide could go to jail. She took her case all the way to the Supreme Court, losing her legal fight by a 5–4 margin, demonstrating the close division on the issue. She died in 1994 of a drug overdose, reportedly with a physician present and then Member of Parliament Svend Robinson. The physician was not identified, and no charges were laid. Later, Robinson further pursued the issue in Parliament to change the law to allow for physician-assisted suicide in Canada but was unsuccessful.

In the United States the first physician-assisted suicide law was passed in Oregon in 1994, allowing a terminally ill person to obtain a prescription for medication for the purpose of ending his or her life. The Oregon law is more restrictive than the law in the Netherlands (Deutsch, 2001). The Oregon law requires that physicians inform the person that he or she is terminally ill, and of alternative options (e.g., hospice care, pain control); the person must be mentally competent and make two oral requests and a written one, with at least 15 days between each oral request. Such provisions are included to ensure that people making the request fully understand the issues and that the request is not made hastily.

Although many people support a person's right to decide when to die, many people do not. These differences of opinions have resulted in several court challenges to the right to die. Bioethicists must make the dilemmas clear, and we must make ourselves aware of the issues. What is at stake is literally a matter of life and death. What do you think? ■

Several studies have examined the impact of the Oregon law in the United States. In a direct comparison between the 69 Kevorkian cases and the first 43 Oregon cases, a key difference emerged: Only 25% of the Kevorkian cases were terminal, whereas all Oregon cases were (Roscoe et al., 2001). Other comprehensive reviews of the implementation of the Oregon law conclude that all safeguards appear to be working and that such things as depression, coercion, and misunderstanding of the law are carefully screened (Orentlicher, 2000). Available data also indicate that Oregon's law has psychological benefits for patients (Cerminara & Perez, 2000).

There is no question that the debate over physician-assisted suicide has only begun. As the technology to keep people alive continues to improve, the ethical issues about active euthanasia in general and physician-assisted suicide in particular will continue to get more complex.

Passive Euthanasia

A second form of euthanasia, **passive euthanasia,** *involves allowing a person to die by withholding available treatment.* For example, chemotherapy might be withheld from a cancer patient; a surgical procedure might not be performed; or food not given. Again, these approaches are controversial. On the one hand, few would argue with a decision not to treat a newly discovered cancer in a person in the late stages of Alzheimer disease, if treatment would do nothing but prolong and make even more agonizing an already certain death. Indeed, a survey in England revealed that caregivers agreed that treatments could and should be withheld from dementia patients in the case of a critical physical condition (Tadros & Salib, 2001). On the other hand, many people might argue against withholding nourishment from a terminally ill person; indeed, such cases often end up in court.

THINK ABOUT IT 💡

How do sociocultural forces shape attitudes about euthanasia?

Making Your Intentions Known

Euthanasia is a complex legal and ethical issue. In most jurisdictions, euthanasia is legal only when a person has made known his or her wishes concerning medical intervention. Unfortunately, many people fail to take this step, perhaps because it is difficult to think about such situations or because they do not know the options available to them. But without clear directions, medical personnel may be unable to take a patient's preferences into account.

There are two ways to make one's intentions known: living wills or health care directorate, in which a person simply states his or her wishes about life support and other treatments, and power of attorney, like the one shown in Figure 17.1. The

FIGURE 17.1   Health Care Directive

Health Care Directive

Manitoba

Please type or print legibly

This is the Health Care Directive of:

Name _____

Address _____ City _____

Province _____ Postal Code _____ Telephone ( ) _____

Part 1 – Designation of a Health Care Proxy

You may name one or more persons who will have the power to make decisions about your medical treatment when you lack the ability to make those decisions yourself. If you do not wish to name a proxy, you may skip this part.

I hereby designate the following person(s) as my Health Care Proxy:

Proxy 1

Name _____

Address _____

_____

City _____

Province _____ Postal Code _____

Telephone ( ) _____

Proxy 2

Name _____

Address _____

_____

City _____

Province _____ Postal Code _____

Telephone ( ) _____

(Check ✔ one choice only.) For an explanation of "consecutively" and "jointly" please see the reverse side of this form).

If I have named more than one proxy,
I wish them to act:
❑ **consecutively**   OR   ❑ **jointly**

My Health Care Proxy may make medical decisions on my behalf when I lack the capacity to do so for myself *(check ✔ one choice only):*

❑ With **no restrictions**

❑ With **restrictions as follows:**

_____
_____
_____
_____
_____

Part 2 – Treatment Instructions

In this part, you may set out your instructions concerning medical treatment that you do or do not wish to receive and the circumstances in which you do or do not wish to receive that treatment. REMEMBER – your instructions can only be carried out if they are set out clearly and precisely. If you do not wish to provide any treatment instructions, you may skip this part.

_____
_____
_____
_____
_____

Part 3 – Signature and Date

You must sign and date this Health Care Directive. No witness is required.

Signature _____

Date _____

If you are unable to sign yourself, a substitute may sign on your behalf. The substitute must sign in your presence and in the presence of a witness. The proxy or the proxy's spouse cannot be the substitute or witness.

Name of substitute: _____

Address _____
_____

Signature _____

Date _____

Name of witness: _____

Address _____
_____

Signature _____

Date _____

MG-3598 (Rev. 05/04)

Province of Manitoba.

purpose of both is to make known people's wishes about the use of life support in the event they are unconscious or otherwise incapable of expressing them (Freer & Clark, 1994). A power of attorney has an additional advantage; it names an individual who has the legal authority to speak for the person if necessary. Although there is considerable support for both mechanisms, there are several problems as well. Many people fail to inform their relatives and physicians about their health care decisions. Others do not tell the person named in a power of attorney where the document is kept. Obviously, this puts relatives at a serious disadvantage if decisions concerning the use of life-support systems need to be made.

A living will, health care directive, or a power of attorney can be the basis for a "Do Not Resuscitate" (DNR) medical order. A DNR order applies only to cardiopulmonary resuscitation should one's heart and breathing stop. In the normal course of events, a medical team will immediately try to restore normal heartbeat and respiration. With a DNR order, this treatment is not done. As with living wills, health care directives, and powers of attorney, it is very important to let all appropriate medical personnel know that a DNR order is desired.

TEST YOURSELF

1. The difference between brain death and a persistent vegetative state is

   _____.

2. Withholding an antibiotic from a person who dies as a result is an example of

   _____.

Describe how people at each level of Kohlberg's theory of moral reasoning (described in Chapter 10) would deal with the issue of euthanasia.

Answers: (1) the brainstem still functions in a persistent vegetative state, (2) passive euthanasia

17.2

Thinking About Death: Personal Aspects

LEARNING OBJECTIVES

- How do feelings about death change over adulthood?
- How do people deal with their own death?
- What is death anxiety, and how do people show it?
- How do people deal with end-of-life issues and create a final scenario?
- What is hospice?

Thinking About Death: Personal Aspects

A Life Course Approach to Dying

Dealing with One's Own Death

Death Anxiety

Creating a Final Scenario

The Hospice Option

Jean is a 72-year-old woman who was diagnosed with advanced colon cancer recently. She has vivid memories of her father dying a long, protracted death in great pain. Jean is very afraid that she will suffer the same fate. She has heard that the hospice in town emphasizes pain management and provides a lot of support for families. Jean wonders whether that is something she should explore in the time she has left.

Like Jean, most people are uncomfortable thinking about their own death, especially if they think it will be unpleasant. As one research participant put it, "You are nuts if you aren't afraid of death" (Kalish & Reynolds, 1976). Still, death is a paradox, as we noted at the beginning of the chapter. That is, we are afraid of or anxious about death, but we are drawn to it, sometimes in very public ways. We examine this paradox at the personal level in this section. Specifically, we focus on two questions: How do people's feelings about death differ with age? What is it about death that we fear or that makes us anxious?

Before proceeding, however, take a few minutes to complete this exercise.

A Self-reflective Exercise on Death

1. In 200 words or less, write your own obituary. Be sure to include your age and cause of death. List your lifetime accomplishments. Don't forget to list your survivors.

2. Think about all the things you will have done that are not listed in your obituary. List some of them.

3. Think of all the friends you will have made and how you will have affected them.

4. Would you make any changes in your obituary now?

A LIFE COURSE APPROACH TO DYING

How do you feel about dying? Do you think people of different ages feel the same way? It probably doesn't surprise you to learn that feelings about dying vary across adulthood.

Because young adults are just beginning to pursue the family, career, and personal goals they have set, they tend to be more intense in their feelings toward death. If you were to ask the young adults in the photograph who are at a funeral how they feel about death, they would be likely to report a strong sense that those who die at this point in their lives would be cheated out of their future (Attig, 1996).

Understanding how young adults deal with death is best explained from the perspective of attachment theory (Balk, 1996; Jacobs, 1993). In this view, a person's reactions are a natural consequence of forming attachments and then losing them. We consider adult grief a bit later in the chapter.

© David Young-Wolff/PhotoEdit

Although not specifically addressed in research, the shift from formal operational to postformal thinking (see Chapter 11) could be important in young adults' contemplation of death. Presumably, this shift in cognitive development is accompanied by a lessening of the feeling of immortality as young adults begin to integrate personal feelings and emotions with their thinking.

Midlife is the time when most people confront the death of their parents. Up until that point, people tend not to think much about their own death; the fact that their parents are still alive buffers them from reality. After all, in the normal course of events, our parents are supposed to die before we do.

Once their parents have died, people realize that they are now the oldest generation of their family—the next in line to die. Reading the obituary pages, they are reminded of this, as the ages of many of the people who have died get closer and closer to their own.

Probably as a result of this growing realization of their own mortality, middle-aged adults' sense of time undergoes a subtle yet profound change. It changes from an emphasis on how long they have already lived to how long they have left to live

(Attig, 1996; Neugarten, 1969). This may lead to occupational change or other redirection such as improving relationships that had deteriorated over the years.

In general, older adults are less anxious about death and more accepting of it than any other age group (Kastenbaum, 1999; Keller, Sherry, & Piotrowski, 1984). In part, this results from the achievement of ego integrity, as described in Chapter 11. For many older adults, the joy of living is diminishing (Kalish, 1987). More than any other group, they have experienced loss of family and friends and have come to terms with their own mortality. Older adults have more chronic diseases, which are not likely to go away. They may feel that their most important life tasks have been completed (Kastenbaum, 1999).

DEALING WITH ONE'S OWN DEATH

Thinking about death from an observer's perspective is one thing. Thinking about one's own, like Jean is doing, is quite another. The reactions people have to their own impending death, long thought to be the purview of religion and philosophy, were not researched until well into the 20th century.

Many authors have tried to describe the dying process, often using the metaphor of a trajectory that captures both the duration of time between the onset of dying (e.g., from the diagnosis of a fatal disease) and death, and the course of the dying process (Wilkinson & Lynn, 2001). These dying trajectories vary a great deal across diseases, as illustrated in Figure 17.2. Some diseases, such as lung cancer, have a clear and rapid period of decline; this "terminal phase" is often used to determine eligibility for certain services (e.g., hospice, discussed later). Other diseases, such as congestive heart failure, have no clear terminal phase; any significant health event could cause death. The two approaches of describing the dying process that we will consider try to account for both types of trajectories.

Kübler-Ross's Theory

Elisabeth Kübler-Ross became interested in the experience of dying as an instructor in psychiatry at the University of Chicago in the early 1960s. When she began her investigations into the dying process, such research was controversial; her physician

FIGURE 17.2   Dying Trajectories

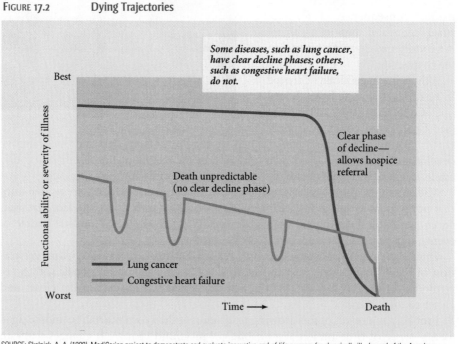

SOURCE: Skolnick, A. A. (1998). MediCaring project to demonstrate and evaluate innovative end-of-life program for chronically ill. *Journal of the American Medical Association, 279,* 1511–1512. Reprinted by permission of the American Medical Association.

colleagues initially were outraged, and some even denied that their patients were terminally ill. Still, she persisted. More than 200 interviews with terminally ill people convinced her that most people experienced several emotional reactions. Using her experiences, she described five emotional states that represented the ways in which people dealt with death: denial, anger, bargaining, depression, and acceptance (Kübler-Ross, 1969). Although they were first presented as a sequence, it was subsequently realized that the emotions can overlap and can be experienced in different orders. Kübler-Ross, who died in 2004, had a monumental influence on how we perceive and care for patients during the dying process.

When people are told that they have a terminal disease, their first reaction is likely to be shock and disbelief. Denial is a normal part of getting ready to die. Some want to shop around for a more favourable diagnosis, and most feel that a mistake has been made. Others try to find assurance in religion. Eventually, though, reality sets in for most people.

At some point, people express anger as hostility, resentment, and envy toward health care workers, family, and friends. People ask, "Why me?" and express a great deal of frustration. The fact that they are going to die when so many others will live seems so unfair. With time and work, most people confront their anger and resolve it.

In the bargaining phase, people look for a way out. Maybe a deal can be struck with someone, perhaps God, that would allow survival. For example, a woman might promise to be a better mother if only she could live. Or a person sets a timetable: "Just let me live until my daughter graduates from university." Eventually, the person becomes aware that these deals will not work.

When one can no longer deny the illness, perhaps because of surgery or pain, feelings of depression are very common. People report feeling deep loss, sorrow, guilt, and shame over their illness and its consequences. Kübler-Ross believed that allowing people to discuss their feelings with others helps move them to an acceptance of death. In the acceptance stage, the person accepts the inevitability of death and often seems detached from the world and at peace. "It is as if the pain is gone, the struggle is over, and there comes a time for the 'final rest before the journey' as one patient phrased it" (Kübler-Ross, 1969, p. 100).

Although she believed that these five stages represented the typical range of emotional development in the dying, Kübler-Ross (1974) cautioned that not everyone experiences all of them or progresses through them at the same rate or in the same order. Research supports the view that her "stages" should not be viewed as a sequence (Neimeyer, 1997). In fact, we could actually harm dying people by considering these stages as fixed and universal. Individual differences are great, as Kübler-Ross pointed out. Emotional responses may vary in intensity throughout the dying process. Thus, the goal in applying Kübler-Ross's theory to real-world settings would be to help people achieve an appropriate death. An appropriate death is one that meets the needs of the dying person, allowing him or her to work out each problem as it comes.

A Contextual Theory of Dying

One of the difficulties with most theories of dying is a general lack of research evaluating them in a wide variety of contexts (Kastenbaum & Thuell, 1995). By their very nature, stages or sequences imply a particular directionality. Stage theories, in particular, emphasize qualitative differences between the various stages. However, the duration of a particular stage, or a specific phase, varies widely from person to person. Such theories assume some sort of underlying process for moving through the stages or phases but do not clearly state what causes a person to move from one to another.

One reason for these problems is the realization that there is no one right way to die, although there may be better or worse ways of coping (Corr, 1991–1992). A perspective that recognizes this realization would approach the issue from the perspective of the dying person and the issues or tasks he or she must face. Corr (1991–1992) identified four dimensions of such tasks: bodily needs, psychological security, interpersonal attachments, and spiritual energy and hope. This holistic approach acknowledges individual differences and rejects broad generalizations. Corr's task work approach also recognizes the importance of the coping efforts of family members, friends, and caregivers as well as those of the dying person.

© Michael Newman/PhotoEdit

Kastenbaum and Thuell (1995) argue that what is needed is an even broader contextual approach that takes a more inclusive view of the dying process. They point out that theories must be able to handle people who have a wide variety of terminal illnesses and be sensitive to dying people's own perspectives and values related to death. The socioenvironmental context within which dying occurs, which often changes over time, must be recognized. For example, a person may begin the dying process living independently but end up in a long-term care facility. Such moves may have profound implications for how the person copes with dying. A contextual approach would provide guidance for health care professionals and families, like the ones in the photograph, for discussing how to protect the quality of life, provide better care, and prepare caregivers for dealing with the end of life. Such an approach would also provide research questions.

We do not yet have such a comprehensive theory of dying. But as Kastenbaum and Thuell point out, we can move in that direction by rejecting a reductionistic approach for a truly holistic one. One way to accomplish this is to examine people's experiences as a narrative that can be written from many points of view (e.g., the patient, family members, caregivers). What would emerge would be a rich description of a dynamically changing process.

DEATH ANXIETY

We have seen that how people view death varies with age. In the process, we encountered the notion of feeling anxious about death. Death anxiety is tough to pin down; indeed, it is the ethereal nature of death, rather than something about it in particular, that usually makes us feel so uncomfortable. We cannot put our finger on something specific about death that is causing us to feel uneasy. Because of this, we must look for indirect behavioural evidence to document death anxiety. Research findings suggest that death anxiety is a complex, multidimensional construct.

In the late 1990s, researchers began using terror management theory (Pyszczynski, Greenberg, & Solomon, 1997, 1999) as a framework to study death anxiety. Terror management theory addresses the issue of why people engage in certain behaviours to achieve particular psychological states (Strachan et al., 2001). The theory proposes that ensuring that one's life continues is the primary motive underlying behaviour; all other motives can be traced to this basic one. Thus, death anxiety is a reflection of one's concern over dying, an outcome that would violate the prime motive.

On the basis of several diverse studies using many different measures, researchers conclude that death anxiety consists of several components. Each of these components is most easily described with terms that resemble examples of fear but cannot be tied to anything specific. Early research indicated that components of death anxiety included pain, body malfunction, humiliation, rejection, nonbeing, punishment, interruption of goals, and negative impact on survivors (Fortner & Neimeyer, 1999). To complicate matters further, any of these components can be assessed at any of three levels: public, private, and nonconscious. That is, what we admit feeling about death in public may differ greatly from what we feel when we are alone with our own thoughts. In short, the measurement of death anxiety is complex, and researchers need to specify which aspects they are assessing.

THINK ABOUT IT
Why does death anxiety have so many components?

Much research has been conducted to learn what demographic and personality variables are related to death anxiety. Although the results often are ambiguous, some patterns have emerged. For example, older adults tend to have lower death anxiety than younger adults, perhaps because of their tendency to engage in life review and their higher level of religious motivation (Thorson & Powell, 2000a, 2000b). Lower ego integrity, more physical problems, and more psychological problems are predictive of higher levels of death anxiety in older adults (Fortner & Neimeyer, 1999). Men show greater fear of the unknown than women, who fear the dying process more (Cicirelli, 2001). And few differences have been reported in death anxiety levels across ethnic groups (Cicirelli, 2000).

Strange as it may seem, death anxiety may have a beneficial side. For one thing, being afraid to die means that we often go to great lengths to make sure we stay alive, as argued by terror management theory (Pyszczynski et al., 1997, 1999). Because staying alive helps to ensure the continuation and socialization of the species, fear of death serves as a motivation to have children and raise them properly.

Learning to Deal with Death Anxiety

Although some degree of death anxiety may be appropriate, we must guard against letting it become powerful enough to interfere with our normal daily routines. Several ways exist to help us in this endeavour. Perhaps the one most often used is to live life to the fullest. Kalish (1984, 1987) argues that people who do this enjoy what they have; although they may still fear death and feel cheated, they have few regrets. Adolescents are particularly likely to do this; research shows that teenagers, especially males, engage in risky behaviour like rock climbing, shown in the photograph, that is correlated with low death anxiety (Cotter, 2001).

Koestenbaum (1976) proposes several exercises and questions to increase one's death awareness. Some of these are to write your own obituary and plan your own death and funeral services, as you did in the self-reflective exercise. You can also ask yourself, "What circumstances would help make my death acceptable?" "Is death the sort of thing that could happen to me right now?"

These questions serve as a basis for an increasingly popular way to reduce anxiety: death education. Most death education programs combine factual information about death with issues aimed at reducing anxiety and fear to increase sensitivity to others' feelings. These programs vary widely in orientation; they can include such topics as philosophy, ethics, psychology, drama, religion, medicine, art, and many others. Additionally, they can focus on death, the process of dying, grief and bereavement, or any combination of them. In general, death education programs help primarily by increasing our awareness of the complex emotions felt and expressed by dying people and their families. Research shows that participating in experiential workshops about death significantly lowers death anxiety in younger, middle-aged, and older adults (Abengozar, Bueno, & Vega, 1999).

CREATING A FINAL SCENARIO

When given the chance, many adults would like to discuss a variety of issues, collectively called end-of-life issues: management of the final phase of life, after-death disposition of their body and memorial services, and distribution of assets (Kastenbaum, 1999). People want to manage the final part of their lives by thinking through the choices between traditional care (e.g., provided by hospitals and nursing homes) and alternatives (such as hospices), completing advance directives (e.g., power of attorney, living will), resolving key personal relationships, and perhaps choosing the alternative of ending one's life prematurely.

What happens to one's body and how one is memorialized is very important to most people. Is a traditional burial preferred over cremation? A traditional funeral over a memorial service? Such choices often are based in people's religious beliefs and their desire for privacy for their families after they have died.

Making sure that one's estate and personal effects are passed on appropriately often is overlooked. Making a will is especially important in ensuring that one's wishes are carried out. Providing for the informal distribution of personal effects also helps prevent disputes between family members.

Whether people choose to address these issues formally or informally, it is important that they be given the opportunity to do so. In many cases, family members are reluctant to discuss these matters with the dying relative because of their own anxiety about death. *Making such choices known about how they do and do not want their lives to end constitutes a final scenario.*

One of the crucial parts of a final scenario for most people is the process of separation from family and friends (Kastenbaum, 1999). The final days, weeks, and months of life provide opportunities to affirm love, resolve conflicts, and provide peace to dying people. The failure to complete this process often leaves survivors feeling that they did not achieve closure in the relationship, which can result in bitterness toward the deceased.

Health care workers realize the importance of giving dying patients the chance to create a final scenario and recognize the uniqueness of each person's final passage. Any given final scenario reflects the person's personal past, which is the unique combination of the development forces the person experienced. Primary attention is paid to how people's total life experiences have prepared them to face end-of-life issues (Neimeyer, 1997).

One's final scenario helps family and friends interpret one's death (Byock, 1997; Kastenbaum, 1992). When completing a living will, as in the photograph on page 621, it is important to remember that the different perspectives of everyone involved are unlikely to converge without clear communication and discussion. Respecting each person's perspective is key and greatly helps in creating a good final scenario.

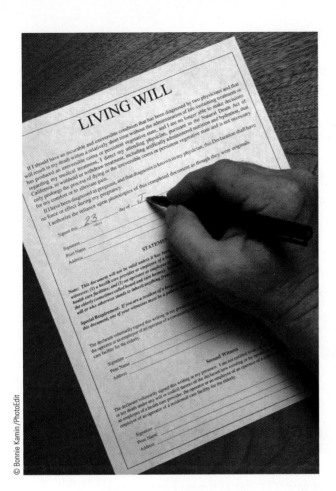

© Bonnie Kamin /PhotoEdit

Encouraging people to decide for themselves how the end of their lives should be handled has helped people take control of their dying (Wass, 2001). Taking personal control over one's dying process is a trend that is occurring even in countries like Japan, where individuals traditionally defer to physicians' opinions (Hayashi et al., 2000). The emergence of final scenarios as an important consideration fits well with the emphasis on addressing pain through palliative care, an approach underlying hospice.

THE HOSPICE OPTION

As we have seen, most people would like to die at home among family and friends. An important barrier to this choice is the availability of support systems when the person has a terminal disease. In this case most people believe they have no choice but to go to a hospital or nursing home. However, another alternative exists. *Hospice or palliative care "aims to relieve suffering and improve the quality of living and dying"* (Canadian Hospice Palliative Care Association, 2004). The emphasis is on the quality of life. This approach grows out of an important distinction between the prolongation of life and the prolongation of death, a distinction that is important to Jean, the woman we met in the vignette. In a hospice the concern is to make the person as peaceful and comfortable as possible, not to delay an inevitable death. Although medical care is available with hospice or palliative care, it is aimed primarily at controlling pain and restoring normal functioning. This orientation places hospice care between hospitals and homes in the contexts for dying.

Modern hospices are modelled after St. Christopher's Hospice in England, founded in 1967 by Dr. Cicely Saunders. Hospice services are requested only after the person or physician believes that no treatment or cure is possible, making the hospice program markedly different from hospital or home care. The differences are evident in the principles that underlie hospice care: Clients and their families are viewed as a unit, clients should be kept free of pain, emotional and social impoverishment must be minimal, clients must be encouraged to maintain competencies, conflict resolution and fulfilment of realistic desires must be assisted, clients must be free to begin or end relationships, and staff members must seek to alleviate pain and fear (Saunders, 1997).

Two types of hospices exist: inpatient and outpatient. Inpatient hospices provide all care for clients; outpatient hospices provide services to clients who remain in their own homes. Palliative care is increasingly recognized as a specialty in the nursing profession and has a growing influence on end-of-life care in many settings (Dean & McClement, 2002). The first hospice care program in Canada was established in 1974 at the St. Boniface General Hospital in Winnipeg. The outpatient variation, in which a hospice nurse like the one shown in the photograph on page 622 visits clients in their home, is becoming increasingly popular, because patients can remain in their own familiar surroundings and as well more clients can be served at a lower cost.

Having hospice services available to people at home is a viable option for many more people (Appleton & Henschell, 1995).

In a Canadian study examining the perspectives of family members as caregivers when palliative care is given at home, Stajduhar (2003) found that the palliative caregiving resulted in life-enriching experiences for a number of the caregivers. However, many of the family caregivers identified the need for improved support and improved communication between the health care providers and family members.

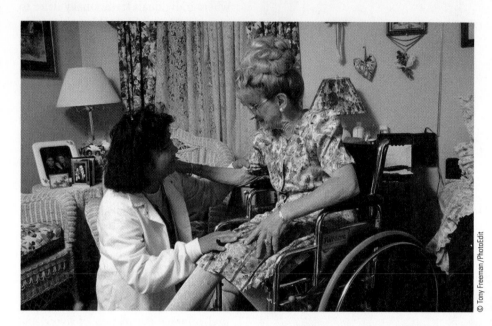

© Tony Freeman /PhotoEdit

Hospices do not follow a hospital model of care. The role of the staff in a hospice is not so much to treat the client as it is just to be with the client. A client's dignity is always maintained; often more attention is paid to appearance and personal grooming than to medical tests. Hospice staff members also provide a great deal of support to the client's family. At inpatient hospices visiting hours are unrestricted, and families are strongly encouraged to take part in the client's care (VandenBos, DeLeon, & Pallack, 1982).

Researchers have documented important differences between inpatient hospices and hospitals (Kastenbaum, 1999). Hospice clients are more mobile, less anxious, and less depressed; spouses visit hospice clients more often and participate more in their care; and hospice staff members are perceived as more accessible. In addition, Walsh and Cavanaugh (1984) showed that most hospice clients who were in hospitals before coming to a hospice strongly preferred the care at the hospice. In a Canadian study on hospice palliative care, significant improvements in clients' quality of life were documented after hospice placement (Cohen et al., 2001). These researchers found that within a week of admission, patients showed improvements in both their physical and psychological well-being, and that even though patients were approaching death, they experienced an improved quality of life.

Although the hospice is a valuable alternative for many people, it may not be appropriate for everyone. Most people who select hospice care are suffering from cancer, AIDS, or a progressive neurological condition (most often amyotrophic lateral sclerosis, also known as Lou Gehrig's disease; Kastenbaum, 1999). Other disorders may necessitate treatments or equipment not available at hospices, and some people may find that a hospice does not meet their needs or fit with their personal beliefs. Walsh and Cavanaugh (1984) found that the perceived needs of hospice clients, their families, and the staff did not always coincide. In particular, the staff and family members emphasized pain management, whereas many clients wanted more attention paid to personal issues. The important point from this study is that the staff and family members may need to ask clients what they need more often rather than making assumptions about what they need.

How do people decide to explore the hospice option? Kastenbaum (1999) lists six key considerations:

- *Is the person completely informed about the nature and prognosis of his or her condition?* Full knowledge and the ability to communicate with health care personnel are essential to understand what hospice has to offer.
- *What options are available at this point in the progress of the person's disease?* Knowing about all available treatment options is essential. Exploring treatment options also requires health care professionals to be aware of the latest approaches and willing to disclose them.
- *What are the person's expectations, fears, and hopes?* Some older adults, like Jean, remember or have heard stories about people who suffered greatly at the end of their lives. This can produce anxiety about one's own death. Similarly, fears of becoming dependent play an important role in a person's decision-making. Discovering and discussing these anxieties helps clarify options.
- *How well do the people in the person's social network communicate with each other?* Talking about death in many families is still taboo (Book, 1996). In others, intergenerational communication is difficult or impossible. Even in families with good communication, the pending death of a loved relative is difficult. As a result, the dying person may have difficulty expressing his or her wishes. The decision to explore the hospice option is best made when it is discussed openly.
- *Are family members available to participate actively in terminal care?* Hospice relies on family members to provide much of the care, which is supplemented by professionals and volunteers. We saw in Chapter 12 that being a primary caregiver can be highly stressful. Having a family member who is willing to accept this responsibility is essential for the hospice option to work.
- *Is a high-quality hospice care program available?* Hospice programs are not uniformly good. As with any health care provider, patients and family members must investigate the quality of local hospice programs before making a choice.

Hospice provides an important end-of-life option for many terminally ill people and their families. Moreover, the supportive follow-up services they provide are used by many surviving family and friends. Most important, the success of the hospice option has influenced progress toward a national strategy for end-of-life care in Canada by emphasizing quality of life at the end of life. For example, in 2000 a meeting of 24 national stakeholders met in Toronto to set the groundwork of a national strategy for end-of-life care. This meeting resulted in the Quality End-of-Life Care Coalition (QELCC) and Blueprint for Action. The role of the QELCC is to advocate for improvements in clients' ability to access hospice palliative care services since there are differences in both quality and access to hospice palliative care across Canada (QELCC, 2000).

THINK ABOUT IT

How might the availability of hospices relate to physician-assisted suicide?

Despite the importance of the hospice option for end-of-life decisions, terminally ill older adults cannot benefit from it unless two barriers are overcome (Kastenbaum, 1999): family reluctance to face the reality of terminal illness and participate in the decision-making process; and physician reluctance to approve hospice care for patients until very late in the terminal process, thereby depriving them of the supportive benefits they may have otherwise received.

As the end of life approaches, the most important thing to keep in mind is that the dying person has the right to state-of-the-art approaches to treatment and pain management. Irrespective of the choice of traditional health care or hospice, the wishes of the dying person should be honoured, and family members must participate.

In 2004 Health Canada launched the web-based Canadian Virtual Hospice (CVH) to help support patients, their families, health care providers, and volunteers. It was created in recognition of the fact that Canadians dealing with life-threatening illness often need more resources than they are able to easily access. The website offers information and resources that may help people better understand the physical, emotional, and spiritual aspects of their experiences, but does not offer any medical advice. The CVH is designed to be interactive in order to facilitate information exchange, communication, and mutual support between and among patients, their friends and family, and others associated with their care.

TEST YOURSELF

1. _____ are most likely to face the death of their parents.

2. A _____ approach to dying acknowledges individual differences and rejects broad generalizations.

3. The primary framework for studying death anxiety is _____

4. Making choices known about how people do and do not want their lives to end constitutes a _____.

5. _____ is an approach to assisting dying people that emphasizes pain management and death with dignity.

Using Erikson's theory as a framework, explain how death anxiety changes from adolescence to late life.

Answers: (1) Middle-aged adults, (2) holistic, (3) terror management theory, (4) final scenario, (5) Hospice or palliative care

17.3

Surviving the Loss: The Grieving Process

LEARNING OBJECTIVES

▶ How do people experience the grief process?

▶ What feelings do grieving people have?

▶ What is the difference between normal and abnormal grief?

> **Surviving the Loss: The Grieving Process**
> The Grief Process
> Normal Grief Reactions
> Coping with Grief
> Traumatic Grief Reactions

After 67 years of marriage, Bertha recently lost her husband. At 90, Bertha knew that neither she nor her husband was likely to live much longer, but the death was a shock just the same. Bertha thinks about him much of the time and often finds herself making decisions on the basis of "what John would have done" in the same situation.

Each of us suffers many losses over a lifetime. Whenever we lose someone close to us through death or other separation, like Bertha we experience bereavement, grief, and mourning. *Bereavement is the state or condition caused by loss through death. Grief is the sorrow, hurt, anger, guilt, confusion, and other feelings that arise after suffering a loss. Mourning concerns the ways in which we express our grief.* For example, you can tell that the woman in the photograph on page 625 is bereaved and in mourning because of her black dress and the veil covering her face. Mourning is highly influenced by culture. For some, mourning may involve wearing black, attending funerals, and observing an official period of grief; for others, it means drinking, wearing white, and marrying the deceased spouse's sibling. Grief corresponds to the emotional reactions following loss, whereas mourning is the culturally approved behavioural manifestations of those feelings. Even though mourning rituals may be fairly standard within a culture, how people grieve varies, as we see next. We will also see how Bertha's reactions are fairly typical of most people.

THE GRIEF PROCESS

How do people grieve? What do they experience? Perhaps you already have a good idea about the answers to these questions from your own experience. If so, you already know that the process of grieving is a complicated and personal one. Just as there is no right way to die, there is no right way to grieve. Recognizing that there are plenty of individual differences, we consider these patterns in this section.

© Amy Etra/PhotoEdit

The grieving process is often described as reflecting many themes and issues that people confront (Attig, 1996; Stroebe et al., 1996). Like the process of dying, grieving does not have clearly demarcated stages through which we pass in a neat sequence. When someone close to us dies, we must reorganize our lives, establish new patterns of behaviour, and redefine relationships with family and friends. Indeed, Attig (1996) considers grief to be the process by which we relearn the world.

Unlike bereavement, over which we have no control, grief is a process that involves choices in coping (Attig, 1996). From this perspective, grief is an active process in which a person must do several things (Worden, 1991):

- *Acknowledge the reality of the loss.* We must overcome the temptation to deny the reality of our loss, fully and openly acknowledge it, and realize that it affects every aspect of our life.
- *Work through the emotional turmoil.* We must find effective ways to confront and express the complete range of emotions we feel after the loss, and we must not avoid or repress them.
- *Adjust to the environment where the deceased is absent.* We must define new patterns of living that adjust appropriately and meaningfully to the fact that the deceased is not present.
- *Loosen ties to the deceased.* We must free ourselves from the bonds of the deceased in order to re-engage with our social network. This means finding effective ways to say goodbye.

© Bob Daemmrich /Stock Boston Inc.

The notion that grief is an active coping process emphasizes that survivors must come to terms with the physical world of things, places, and events, as well as our spiritual place in the world; the interpersonal world of interactions with family and friends, the dead, and, in some cases, God; and aspects of our inner selves and our personal experiences (Attig, 1996). Bertha, the woman in the vignette, is in the middle of this process. Like the woman in the photograph, even the matter of deciding what to do with the deceased's personal effects can be part of this active coping process (Attig, 1996).

In considering the grief process, we must avoid making several mistakes. First, grieving is a highly individual experience. The process that works well for one person may not be the best for someone else. Second, we must not underestimate the amount of time people need to deal with the various issues. To a casual observer, it may appear that a survivor is "back to normal" after a few weeks. Actually, it takes much longer to resolve the complex emotional issues that are faced during bereavement (Attig, 1996; Stroebe et al., 1996). Researchers and therapists alike agree that a person needs at least one year following the loss to begin recovery, and two years is not uncommon. Finally, *recovery* may be a misleading term. It is probably more accurate to say that we learn to live with our loss rather than that we recover from it (Attig, 1996). The impact of the loss of a loved one lasts a very long time, perhaps for the rest of one's life. Recognizing these aspects of grief makes it easier to know what to say and do for bereaved people. Among the most useful things are to simply let the person know that you are sorry for his or her loss, that you are there for support, and mean what you say.

Risk Factors in Grief

Bereavement is a life experience that most people have many times, and most people eventually handle. However, there are some risk factors that may make bereavement much more difficult. Several of the more important are the mode of death, personal factors (e.g., personality, religiosity, age, gender), and interpersonal context (social support, kinship relationship) (W. Stroebe & Schut, 2001).

Most people believe that the circumstances or mode of death affects the grief process. A person whose family member was killed in an automobile accident has a different situation to deal with than a person whose family member died after a long period with Alzheimer disease. When death is anticipated, it is believed that people go through a period of anticipatory grief before the death that supposedly serves to buffer the impact of the loss when it does come, as well as facilitating recovery (Attig, 1996). However, the research evidence for this is mixed. Some studies find that sudden loss increases the likelihood of problems, whereas other studies have found that anticipating the death of someone close produces considerable stress in itself (Attig, 1996; W. Stroebe & Schut, 2001). Other research reveals a more complex outcome. Caregivers of Alzheimer patients, for example, show a decline in feelings of anticipatory grief during the middle stages of caregiving, only to have these feelings increase in intensity later (Ponder & Pomeroy, 1996).

The strength of attachment to the deceased person does make a difference. When the deceased person was one with whom the survivor had a strong and close attachment, and the loss was sudden, greater grief is experienced (Wayment & Vierthaler, 2002). However, such secure attachment styles tend to result in less depression after the loss.

Few studies of personal risk factors have been done, and few firm conclusions can be drawn. To date there are no consistent findings regarding personality traits that either help buffer people from the effects of bereavement or exacerbate them (W. Stroebe & Schut, 2001). There is some evidence to suggest that church attendance helps people deal with bereavement 13 to 18 months after the loss (Nolen-Hoeksema & Larson, 1999), but this effect may be due more to the social support such people receive than from religion per se (W. Stroebe & Schut, 2001). There are, however, consistent findings regarding gender. Men have higher mortality rates following bereavement than women, who have higher rates of depression than men, but the reasons for these differences are unclear (W. Stroebe & Schut, 2001). Research also consistently shows that younger people suffer more health consequences following bereavement than older people, with the impact perhaps being strongest for middle-aged adults (Nolen-Hoeksema & Larson, 1999; W. Stroebe & Schut, 2001).

Two interpersonal risk factors have been examined: lack of social support and kinship. Studies indicate that social support helps buffer the effects of bereavement more for older adults than for middle-aged adults (Stroebe & Schut, 1999; W. Stroebe &

Schut, 2001). The type of kinship relationship involved in the loss matters a great deal. Research consistently shows that the loss of a child is the most difficult, followed by loss of a spouse or partner and parent (Leahy, 1993; Nolen-Hoeksema & Larson, 1999).

THINK ABOUT IT

How are risk factors in grief influenced by sociocultural factors?

NORMAL GRIEF REACTIONS

The feelings experienced during grieving are intense, which not only makes it difficult to cope but can also make a person question her or his own reactions. The feelings involved usually include sadness, denial, anger, loneliness, and guilt. A summary of these feelings is presented in the following list (Vickio, Cavanaugh, & Attig, 1990). Take a minute to read through them to see whether they agree with what you expected.

Disbelief	Denial	Shock
Sadness	Anger	Hatred
Guilt	Fear	Anxiety
Confusion	Helplessness	Emptiness
Loneliness	Acceptance	Relief
Happiness	Lack of enthusiasm	Absence of emotion

Many authors refer to the psychological side of coming to terms with bereavement as grief work. This notion fits well with the earlier discussion of grief as active coping (Attig, 1996). Even without personal experience of the death of close family members, people recognize the need to give survivors time to deal with their many feelings. One study asked post-secondary students to describe the feelings they thought were typically experienced by a person who had lost particular loved ones (such as a parent, child, sibling, friend). The students were well aware of the need for grief work, recognized the need for at least a year to do it, and were very sensitive to the range of emotions and behaviours demonstrated by the bereaved (Vickio et al., 1990).

Muller (2002) examined people's experience of grief in a detailed interview study and found five themes. *Coping* relates to what people do to deal with their loss in terms of what helps them. *Affect* refers to people's emotional reactions to the death of their loved one; for example, most people have certain topics that serve as emotional triggers for memories of their loved one. *Change* involves the ways in which survivors' lives change as a result of the loss; personal growth (e.g., "I didn't think I could deal with something that painful, but I did.") is a common experience. *Narrative* relates to the stories survivors tell about their deceased loved one, which sometimes include details about the process of the death. Finally, *relationship* reflects who the deceased person was and the nature of the ties between that person and the survivor. Collectively, these themes indicate that the experience of grief is complex and involves dealing with one's feelings as a survivor and the memories of the deceased person.

How people show their feelings of grief varies across ethnic groups. For example, American research demonstrates that Latino-American men show more of their grief behaviourally than do European-American men (Sera, 2001). Such differences also are found across cultures. For example, in many cultures the bereaved construct a relationship with the person who died, but how this happens differs widely, from "ghosts" to appearances in dreams to connection through prayer (Rosenblatt, 2001).

In the time following the death of a loved one, dates that have personal significance may reintroduce feelings of grief. For example, holidays such as Thanksgiving or birthdays that were spent with the deceased person may be difficult times. The actual anniversary of the death can be especially troublesome. *The term anniversary reaction refers to changes in behaviour related to feelings of sadness on this date.* Personal experience and research show that recurring feelings of sadness or other examples of the anniversary reaction are very common in normal grief (Attig, 1996; Rosenblatt, 1996).

Grief over Time

Most research on how people react to the death of a loved one is cross-sectional. However, some work has been done to examine how people continue grieving many years after the loss. Rosenblatt (1996) reported that people still felt the effects of the deaths of family members 50 years after the event. The depth of the emotions over the loss of loved ones never totally went away, as people still cried and felt sad when discussing the loss despite the length of time that had passed.

Norris and Murrell (1987) conducted a longitudinal study of older adults' grief work; three interviews were conducted before the death and one after. The fascinating results of their research are described in more detail in the Spotlight on Research feature. The results of this study fit nicely with the earlier discussion on expected versus unexpected death. They also have important implications for interventions. That is, interventions aimed at reducing stress or promoting health may be more effective if performed before the death. Additionally, because health problems increased only among those in the bereaved group who felt no stress before the death, it may be that the stress felt before the death is a product of anticipating it. Lundin (1984) also found it to be the case that health problems increased only for those experiencing sudden death.

SPOTLIGHT ON RESEARCH

Family Stress and Adaptation Before and After Bereavement

Who were the investigators and what was the aim of the study? What happens to a family that experiences the death of a loved one? Fran Norris and Stanley Murrell (1987) sought to answer this question by tracking families before and after bereavement.

How did the investigators measure the topic of interest? As part of a very large normative longitudinal study, they conducted detailed interviews approximately every six months. The researchers used a variety of instruments to obtain extensive information on physical health, including functional abilities and specific ailments, psychological distress, and family stress. The psychological distress measure tapped symptoms of depression. The family stress measure assessed such things as new serious illness of a family member, having a family member move in, additional family responsibilities, new family conflict, or new marital conflict.

Who were the participants in the study? In all, 63 older adults in families experiencing the death of an immediate family member were compared to 387 older adults in families who had not experienced such a death in order to document the extra stress people feel due to grief.

What was the design of the study? Norris and Murrell used a longitudinal design and assessed people every 6 months from 18 months before bereavement to 12 months after bereavement.

Were there ethical concerns in the study? Like all researchers who study bereavement, Norris and Murrell needed to be sensitive to people's feelings and monitor their participants for signs of abnormal reactions.

What were the results? Among bereaved families, overall family stress increased before the death and then decreased. The level of stress experienced by these families was highest in the period right around the death. Moreover, bereavement was the only significant predictor of family stress, meaning that the anticipation and experience of bereavement caused stress.

Even more interesting were the findings concerning the relationship between health and stress. As shown in Figure 17.3, bereaved individuals who reported stress before the death were in poorer health before the death than were bereaved persons who were not experiencing stress. However, as shown in Figure 17.4, bereaved individuals reporting prior stress showed a significant drop in physical symptoms six months after the death; bereaved persons reporting no prior stress reported a slight increase. The net result was that both groups ended up with about the same level of physical symptoms six months after bereavement.

What did the investigators conclude? Norris and Murrell described two major implications. First, bereavement does not appear to

FIGURE 17.3

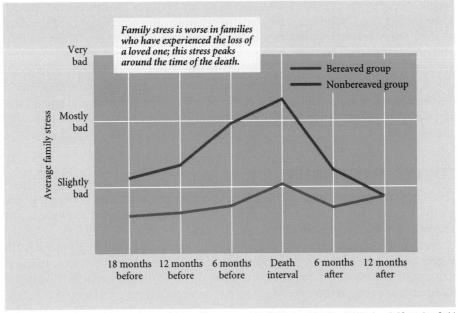

Family stress is worse in families who have experienced the loss of a loved one; this stress peaks around the time of the death.

SOURCE: From "Older Adult Family Stress and Adaptation Before and After Bereavement," by F. N. Norris and S. A. Murrell, 1987, *Journal of Gerontology: Social Sciences, 42,* pp. 606–612. Copyright © 1990 Gerontological Society of America. Reprinted with permission.

FIGURE 17.4

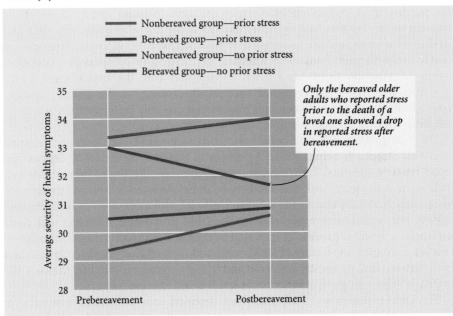

Only the bereaved older adults who reported stress prior to the death of a loved one showed a drop in reported stress after bereavement.

SOURCE: From "Older Adult Family Stress and Adaptation Before and After Bereavement," by F. N. Norris and S. A. Murrell, 1987, *Journal of Gerontology: Social Sciences, 42,* pp. 606–612. Copyright © 1990 Gerontological Society of America. Reprinted with permission.

cause poor health; the bereaved groups were not much different from the group of nonbereaved people in nonstressful families. Second, bereavement appears to increase psychological distress substantially. In sum, marked changes in psychological distress following bereavement are normal, but marked changes in physical health are not.

What converging evidence would strengthen these conclusions? This study only focused on older adults, and the sample was not very diverse. Additional research is necessary to know whether the findings regarding stress and health would also hold for people of other ages, or for people from other cultures.

Religiosity and/or spirituality are thought to provide a support mechanism for people following the loss of a loved one. Research evidence for this belief is mixed. Some studies (e.g., Nelson, 2001) show that religiosity has no effect on the duration of grief. Other research points to a different conclusion. For example, Latino men who practise their religion openly show lower levels of grief than Latino men who are not openly religious and than majority culture men (Sera, 2001). Bereavement counsellors also report better outcomes when religious or spiritual issues are included in the therapeutic process (Golsworthy & Coyle, 2001). Clearly, more and more carefully designed research is needed to understand the role that survivors' spirituality plays in grief.

COPING WITH GRIEF

Thus far, we have considered the behaviours people show when they are dealing with grief. We have also seen that these behaviours change over time. How does this happen? How can we explain the grieving process?

Numerous theories have been proposed to account for the grieving process, such as general life event theories, psychodynamic theories, attachment theories, and cognitive process theories (M. Stroebe & Schut, 2001). All of these approaches to grief are based on more general theories, which results in none of them providing an adequate explanation of the grieving process. Two integrative approaches have been proposed that are specific to the grief process: the four-component model and the dual-process model of coping with bereavement.

The four-component model proposes that (1) *the context of the loss*, referring to the risk factors discussed earlier, (2) *the continuation of subjective meaning associated with loss*, ranging from evaluations of everyday concerns to major questions about the meaning of life, (3) *the changing representations of the lost relationship over time*, and (4) *the role of coping and emotion-regulation processes* that cover all coping strategies are used to deal with grief (Bonanno & Kaltman, 1999). The four-component model relies heavily on emotion theory, has much in common with the transactional model of stress, and has some empirical support. According to the four-component model, dealing with grief is a complex process that can only be understood as a complex outcome that unfolds over time.

The dual-process model of coping with bereavement (DPM) integrates existing ideas (M. Stroebe & Schut, 2001). As shown in Figure 17.5, the DPM defines two broad types of stressors. *Loss-oriented stressors* are those having to do with the loss itself, such as the grief work that needs to be done. *Restoration-oriented stressors* are those relating to adapting to the survivor's new life situation, such as building new relationships and finding new activities. The DPM proposes that dealing with these stressors is a dynamic process, as indicated by the lines connecting them in the figure. This is a distinguishing feature of DPM. It shows how bereaved people cycle back and forth between dealing mostly with grief and trying to move on with life. At times, the emphasis will be on grief; at other times it will be on moving forward.

The DPM captures well the process that bereaved people themselves report—at times they are nearly overcome with grief, while at other times they handle life well. The DPM also helps us understand how, over time, people come to a balance between the long-term effects of bereavement and the need to live life.

TRAUMATIC GRIEF REACTIONS

Not everyone is able to cope with grief well and begin rebuilding a life. Sometimes the feelings of hurt, loneliness, and guilt are so overwhelming that they become the focus of the survivor's life to such an extent that there is never any closure and the grief continues to interfere indefinitely with one's ability to function. Thus, what distinguishes normal from traumatic grief is that traumatic grief involves (a) symptoms of *separation distress* such as preoccupation with the deceased to the point that it interferes

FIGURE 17.5   The Dual Process Model of Coping with Bereavement

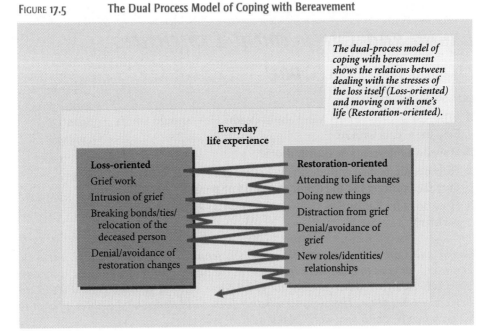

The dual-process model of coping with bereavement shows the relations between dealing with the stresses of the loss itself (Loss-oriented) and moving on with one's life (Restoration-oriented).

Everyday life experience

Loss-oriented
Grief work
Intrusion of grief
Breaking bonds/ties/ relocation of the deceased person
Denial/avoidance of restoration changes

Restoration-oriented
Attending to life changes
Doing new things
Distraction from grief
Denial/avoidance of grief
New roles/identities/ relationships

SOURCE: M. Stroebe & Schut, 2001.

with everyday functioning, upsetting memories of the deceased, longing and searching for the deceased, loneliness following the loss, and (b) symptoms of *traumatic distress* such as feeling disbelief about the death, mistrust, anger, and detachment from others as a result of the death, feeling shocked by the death, and the experience of somatic symptoms of the deceased (Prigerson & Jacobs, 2001).

Two common manifestations of traumatic grief are excessive guilt and self-blame (Anderson, 1997). In some people, guilt results in a disruption of everyday routines and a diminished ability to function. People begin to make judgment errors, may reach a state of agitated depression, may experience problems sleeping or eating, and may have intense recurring thoughts about the deceased person. Many of these individuals either seek professional help voluntarily or are referred by concerned family members or friends.

How to identify traumatic grief is not always easy because there are cultural variations in the process of grief that must be respected (Anderson, 1997). Length of time after the loss is not a good indicator, as grief can still be quite strong 10 years after a loss (Derman, 2000). Prigerson and Jacobs (2001) report that the criteria listed earlier for traumatic grief can be used successfully to differentiate the typical grief of bereaved people, even when they are depressed, and traumatic grief.

TEST YOURSELF

1. Feeling sad on the date when your grandmother died the previous year is an example of _____.

2. Compared to other age groups, _____ show the most negative effects following bereavement.

3. Two common manifestations of traumatic grief are guilt and _____.

If you were to create a brochure listing the five most important things to do and not to do in reacting to someone who just lost a close family member or friend through death, what would you include? Why?

Answers: (1) anniversary reaction, (2) middle-aged adults, (3) self-blame

17.4

Dying and Bereavement Experiences Across the Life Span

LEARNING OBJECTIVES

▥ What do children understand about death? How should adults help them deal with it?

▥ How do adolescents deal with death?

▥ How do adults deal with death? What are the special issues they face concerning the death of a child or parent?

▥ How do older adults face the loss of a child, grandchild, or partner?

Dying and Bereavement Experiences Across the Life Span

Childhood

Adolescence

Adulthood

Late Adulthood

Donna and Carl have a 6-year-old daughter, Jennie, whose grandmother just died. Jennie and her grandmother were very close, as the two saw each other almost every day. Other adults have told her parents not to take Jennie to the funeral. Donna and Carl aren't sure what to do. They wonder whether Jennie will understand what happened to her grandmother, and they worry about how she will react.

Coming to grips with the reality of death is probably one of the hardest things we have to do in life. North American society does not help much either, as it tends to distance itself from death through euphemisms, such as "passed away" or "dearly departed," and by eliminating many rituals from the home.

These trends make it difficult for people like Donna, Carl, and Jennie to learn about death in its natural context. Dying itself occurs primarily in hospitals and other institutions such as nursing homes. The closest most people get to death is a quick glance inside a nicely lined casket at a corpse that has been made to look as if the person were still alive.

What do people, especially children like Jennie, understand about death? How do Donna and Carl feel? How do the friends of Jennie's grandmother feel? In this section, we consider how our understanding of death changes throughout the life span.

CHILDHOOD

Parents often take their children to funerals of relatives and close friends. But many adults, like Donna and Carl in the vignette, wonder whether young children really know what death means. Young preschool-age children tend to believe that death is temporary and magical. They think it is something dramatic that comes to get you in the middle of the night like a burglar or a ghost (Dickinson, 1992). Not until 5 to 7 years of age do children realize that death is permanent, that it eventually happens to everyone, and that dead people no longer have any biological functions (Silverman & Nickman, 1996).

Why does this shift occur? Three major areas of developmental change in children affect their understanding of death and grief (Oltjenbruns, 2001): cognitive-language ability, psychosocial development, and coping skills. With regard to cognitive-language ability, think back to Chapters 5 and 7, especially to the discussion of Piaget's theory of cognitive development. Where would Jennie, the 6-year-old daughter of Donna and Carl in the vignette, be in Piaget's terms? In this perspective, the ages 5 to 7 include the transition from preoperational to concrete-operational thinking. Concrete-operational thinking permits children to know that death is final and permanent. Therefore, Jennie is likely to understand what happened to her grandmother.

Children's feelings at the loss of a loved one vary according to Erikson's theory of psychosocial development. For example, in the middle childhood stage of initiative versus guilt, the child may feel responsible and guilty for the loved one's death. Sensitivity to these feelings is essential for the child to understand that he or she did not cause the death.

The ability to cope is more limited in children than in adults. Several common manifestations of grief among children are shown in Figure 17.6. Typical reactions in early childhood include regression, guilt for causing the death, denial, displacement, repression, and wishful thinking that the deceased will return. In later childhood, common behaviours include problems at school, anger, and physical ailments. As children mature, they acquire more coping skills that permit a shift to problem-focused coping, which provides a better sense of personal control. Children will often flip between grief and normal activity, a pattern they may learn from adults (Stroebe & Schut, 1999).

Figure 17.6   Common Manifestations of Grief Among Children

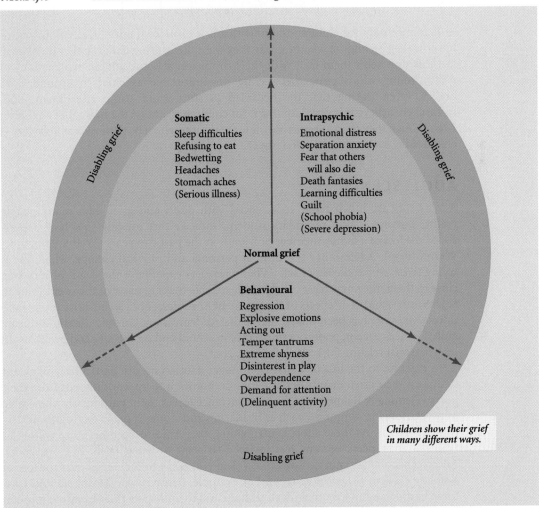

SOURCE: Oltjenbruns, K. A. (2001). Developmental Context of Childhood: Grief and Regrief Phenomena. *Handbook of Bereavement Research: Consequences, Coping, and Care.* Edited by M. S. Stroebe, R. O. Hansson, W. Stroebe, & H. Schut. Fig. 8.1, p. 177. Copyright © 2001 by the American Psychological Association. Reprinted with permission.

Research shows that bereavement per se during childhood typically does not have long-lasting effects, such as depression (Oltjenbruns, 2001). Problems are more likely to occur if the child does not get adequate care following the death.

Understanding death can be particularly difficult for children when adults are not open and honest with them, especially about the meaning of death (Buchsbaum, 1996). The use of euphemisms, such as "Grandma has gone away" or "Mommy is only sleeping," is unwise. Young children do not understand the deeper level of meaning in such statements; they are likely to take them literally (Attig, 1996; Silverman & Nickman, 1996).

When explaining death to children, it is best to deal with them on their terms. Keep explanations simple, at a level they can understand. Try to allay their fears and reassure them that whatever reaction they have is okay. Providing loving support for the child will maximize the potential for a successful (albeit painful) introduction to one of life's realities. One male college student recalled how, when he was 9, his father helped him deal with his feelings after his grandfather's death:

> The day of my grandfather's death my dad came over to my aunt and uncle's house where my brother and I were staying. He took us into one of the bedrooms and sat us down. He told us Grandaddy Doc had died. He explained to us that it was okay if we needed to cry. He told us that he had cried, and that if we did cry we wouldn't be babies, but would just be men showing our emotions. (Dickinson, 1992, pp. 175–176)

It is important for children to know that it is okay for them to feel sad, to cry, or to show their feelings in whatever way they want. Reassuring children that it's okay to feel this way helps them deal with their confusion at some adults' explanations of death. Young adults remember feeling uncomfortable as children around dead bodies, often fearing that the deceased person would come after them. Still, researchers believe it is very important for children to attend the funeral of a relative. Even though they tend to remember few details immediately, their overall recovery is enhanced (Silverman & Worden, 1992).

ADOLESCENCE

Adolescents are much more experienced with death and grief than many people realize. Surveys of post-secondary students indicate that roughly 50% have experienced the loss of a family member or friends in the past two years (Wettemann, 1999; Wrenn, 1999). Adolescence is a time of personal and physical change, when one is trying to develop a theory of self. When teenagers experience the death of someone close to them, they may have considerable trouble making sense of the event (Hogan & DeSantis, 1996). The effects of bereavement in adolescence can be quite severe, and unresolved grief has been linked with agitated depression, chronic illness, enduring guilt, low self-esteem, poorer performance in school and on the job, and problems in interpersonal relationships (Balk & Corr, 2001).

In reaction to the loss of a sibling, younger adolescents are particularly reluctant to discuss their grief, mainly because they do not want to appear different from their peers (Fleming & Balmer, 1996). This reluctance leaves them particularly vulnerable to psychosomatic symptoms such as headaches and stomach pains that signal underlying problems. As these adolescents mature, they tend to become more willing to talk, but their peers become less inclined to want to listen (Balk & Corr, 2001). Adolescents often do not demonstrate a clear end point to their grief over the loss of a sibling (Hogan & DeSantis, 1996). For example, bereaved adolescent siblings continue to miss and to love their dead siblings and to anticipate their eventual reunion in the afterlife. However, grief does not interfere with normative developmental processes. Bereaved adolescent siblings experience continued personal growth following the death of a sibling, in much the same way as adolescents who did not experience such a loss (Hogan & DeSantis, 1996).

Adolescents who experience the loss of a parent show many similar behaviours to those who have lost a sibling. Tyson-Rawson (1996) reports that women college students whose fathers had died reported maintaining a continuing presence of the deceased parent in their lives. However, few nonbereaved peers were willing to talk with the bereaved students about their experience or even felt comfortable being with them. Wrenn (1999) relates that one of the challenges faced by bereaved college students is learning "how to respond to people who ignore their grief, or who tell them that they need to get on with life, that it's not good for them to continue to grieve" (p. 134). Adolescents who lose a parent also get involved in the family dynamics of reallocating roles within the family, finding a way to refer to the deceased parent, and dealing with different ways of expressing grief among different family members (Tyson-Rawson, 1996).

Little research has examined adolescents' reactions to the death of a friend. Oltjenbruns (1996) reports that grief following the death of a peer is often accompanied by survivor guilt. Such feelings may result in the ending of relationships with other mutual friends and an increase in grief. However, these adolescents also report some positive outcomes, such as gaining a deeper appreciation of life as a result of their friend's death. The complexity of these feelings is a major reason schools offer grief counselling, shown in the photograph, following tragedies at schools.

© Dennis MacDonald/PhotoEdit

ADULTHOOD

Because young adults are just beginning to pursue the family, career, and personal goals they have set, they tend to be more intense in their feelings toward death. When asked how they feel about death, young adults report a strong sense that those who die at this point in their lives would be cheated out of their future (Attig, 1996).

Understanding how young adults deal with death is best understood from the perspective of attachment theory (Balk, 1996; Jacobs, 1993). In this view, a person's reactions are a natural consequence of forming attachments and then losing them. We will consider adult grief a bit later in the chapter.

Although not specifically addressed in research, the shift from formal-operational to postformal thinking could be an important one in young adults' contemplation of death. Presumably, this shift in cognitive development is accompanied by a lessening of the feeling of immortality, as young adults begin to integrate personal feelings and emotions with their thinking.

Experiencing the loss of one's partner in young adulthood can be very traumatic, not only because of the loss itself but also because such loss is unexpected. As Trish Straine, a 32-year-old widow whose husband was killed in the World Trade Center attack, put it, "I suddenly thought, 'I'm a widow.' Then I said to myself, 'A widow? That's an older woman, who's dressed in black. It's certainly not a 32-year-old

THINK ABOUT IT

How might young adults' thoughts about death change with each different level of reflective judgment?

like me'" (Lieber, 2001). One of the most difficult aspects for young widows and widowers is that they must deal with both their own and their young children's grief, and provide the support their children need. Additional research on young adult widows shows that the level of grief does not typically diminish significantly until 5 to 10 years after the loss and that these widows maintain strong attachments to their deceased husbands for as long (Derman, 2000).

Midlife is the time when most people confront the death of their parents. Until that point, people tend not to think much about their own death (see Chapter 14); the fact that their parents are still alive buffers them from this issue. After all, in the normal course of events, our parents are supposed to die before we do. Once their parents have died, people realize that they are now the oldest generation of their family—the next in line to die. Reading the obituary pages, they are reminded of this as the ages of many of the people who have died get closer and closer to their own.

Losing one's spouse in midlife often results in the survivor challenging basic assumptions about self, relationships, and life options (Danforth & Glass, 2001). By the first-year anniversary of the loss, the surviving spouse has usually begun transforming his or her perspective on these issues.

Probably as a result of this growing realization of their own mortality, middle-aged adults' sense of time undergoes a subtle yet profound change. It changes from an emphasis on how long they have already lived to how long they have left to live (Attig, 1996). This may lead to occupational change or other redirection such as improving relationships that had deteriorated over the years (see Chapter 12).

Death of One's Child in Young and Middle Adulthood

AP/World Wide Photos

The Van Damms, shown in the photograph, experienced what many people believe is the worst type of loss: the death of their daughter Danielle in 2002 (Klass, 1996a). Because children are not supposed to die before their parents, it is as if the natural order of things has been violated, shaking parents to their core (Rubin & Malkinson, 2001). Mourning is always intense, and some parents never recover or reconcile themselves to the death of their child (Klass, 1996a). The intensity of feelings is due to the strong parent-child bond that begins before birth and that lasts a lifetime (Bornstein, 1995).

Young parents who lose a child due to Sudden Infant Death Syndrome (SIDS) report high anxiety, a more negative view of the world, and much guilt, resulting in a devastating experience (Rubin & Malkinson, 2001). One of the most overlooked losses of a child are those that happen through stillbirth, miscarriage, abortion, or neonatal death (Klass, 1996a; McCarthy, 2002; Rubin & Malkinson, 2001). Attachment to the child begins before birth, especially for mothers, so the loss hurts very deeply. Yet parents who experience this type of loss are expected to recover very quickly. The experience of parents in support groups, such as Compassionate Friends, tells a very different story though (Klass, 1996a). These parents report a deep sense of loss and hurt, especially when others do not understand their feelings. Worst of all, if societal expectations for quick recovery are not met, the parents may be subjected to unfeeling comments. As one mother notes, parents often just wish somebody would acknowledge the loss (Okonski, 1996). The Real People feature tells the personal story of one couple's experience of miscarriage.

 REAL PEOPLE: APPLYING HUMAN DEVELOPMENT

The Grief of Miscarriage

One of the most overlooked types of loss is through miscarriage. Unfortunately, many people react to miscarriages by telling the grieving couple that they "can have more children," "It's not that bad, because you really didn't know the baby," "It probably would have been deformed anyway, so it's good that it happened this way," and similar insensitive statements.

One of the authors personally experienced this type of loss. He and his wife had undergone extensive treatment for infertility, and they were elated at the news of the pregnancy. When they lost their baby, they were devastated. All the statements noted above were actually said to them. Their grief was worse because they knew that it would be difficult to get pregnant again. This poem was written the night the miscarriage happened and is testimony to the grief couples in this situation experience.

Last night
as I sat holding your hand
in the emergency room,
watching helplessly as the life we had
    created
came to an end,
I felt more alone and powerless
than in my whole life.
Your look of fear, your trembling, the
lack of control over events, my own
ocean of grief
All swept over me like a tidal wave.
I became too intimately familiar with
the deepest pit of my stomach,
too closely acquainted with utter
    helplessness.
Intellectually, the event is over now.
Gone. In the past. Life goes on.
But I know that from time to time
for the rest of my life
I'll see him or her in every child I'll
ever meet.
I'll never really forget.
How could I?

The loss of a young adult child for a middle-aged parent is experienced differently but is equally devastating (Rubin & Malkinson, 2001). For example, parents who lost sons in wars (Rubin, 1996) and in traffic accidents (Shalev, 1999) still report strong feelings of anxiety, problems in functioning, and difficulties in relationships with both surviving siblings and the deceased as long as 13 years after the loss.

Death of One's Parent

Most parents die after their children are grown. But whenever parental death occurs, it hurts. We lose not only a key relationship but also an important psychological buffer between ourselves and death (Anderson, 1997; Attig, 1996). We, the children, are now next in line. Indeed, the death of a parent often leads the surviving children to redefine the meaning of their relationships with their siblings, children, and other family members (Moss, Moss, & Hansson, 2001).

As it did for the woman in the photograph, the death of a parent deprives people of a source of guidance and advice, a source of love, and a model for their own par-

enting style (Buchsbaum, 1996). It also cuts off the opportunity to improve aspects of their relationship with the parent. Expressing feelings toward a parent before he or she dies is important.

The loss of a parent is perceived as a very significant one; no matter how old we are, society allows us to grieve for a reasonable length of time. Middle-aged women who lost a parent report feeling a complex set of emotions (Westbrook, 2002). For example, they report having intense emotional feelings of loss and freedom, they remember both positive and negative aspects of their parent, and they experience shifts in their own sense of self.

The feelings accompanying the loss of an older parent reflect a sense of letting go, loss of a buffer against death, better acceptance of one's own eventual death, and a sense of relief that the parent's suffering is over (Moss et al., 2001). Whether the adult child now tries to separate from the deceased parent's expectations or finds comfort in the memories, the impact of the loss is great.

LATE ADULTHOOD

In general, older adults are less anxious about death and more accepting of it than any other age group (Kastenbaum, 1999). In part, this is due to the achievement of ego integrity, as described in Chapter 16. More than any other group, they have experienced loss of family and friends and have come to terms with their own mortality. Older adults have more chronic diseases, which are not likely to just go away. They may feel that their most important life tasks have been completed (Kastenbaum, 1999).

Death of One's Child or Grandchild in Late Life

Many older adults experience the loss of one or more of their children, who are typically middle-aged or older (Moss & Moss, 1996), and others continue to feel the loss of a child from many years before (Ben-Israel Reuveni, 1999). Older bereaved parents tend to re-evaluate their grief as experienced shortly after the loss and years and decades later. Even after the passage of more than 30 years after the death of a child, older adults still feel a keen sense of loss and continued difficulty coming to terms with it (Malkinson & Bar-Tur, 2000). The long-lasting effects of the loss of a child are often accompanied by a sense of guilt that the pain affected the parents' relationships with the surviving children.

Clearly, the loss of a child has profound, lifelong effects. The meaning of the loss changes somewhat over time (Neimeyer, Keese, & Fortner, 2000), but the feelings of distress may never go away. Indeed, many parents view the relationship to the deceased child as either the closest or one of the closest relationships they ever had (Ben-Israel Reuveni, 1999).

The loss of a grandchild results in similar feelings: intense emotional upset, survivor guilt, regrets about the relationship with the deceased grandchild, and a need to restructure relationships with the surviving family (Fry, 1997). However, bereaved grandparents tend to control and hide their grief behaviour in an attempt to shield their child (the bereaved parent) from the level of pain being felt.

Death of One's Partner

Experiencing the loss of one's partner is the type of loss in late life we know most about. The death of a partner differs from other losses. It clearly represents a deep personal loss, especially when the couple has had a long and close relationship (Moss et al., 2001). In a very real way, when our partner dies, a part of our self dies too.

There is pressure from society to mourn the loss of one's partner for a period of time (Lopata, 1996; Moss & Moss, 1996). Typically, this pressure is manifested if the survivor begins to show interest in finding another partner before an "acceptable" period of mourning has passed. Although North Americans no longer specify the length of the period, many feel that about a year is appropriate. The fact that such pressure and negative commentary usually do not accompany other losses is another indication of the seriousness with which most people take the death of a partner.

Older bereaved spouses may grieve for a long time; in one study grief lasted for at least 30 months (Thompson et al., 1991). Social support plays a significant role in the outcome of the grieving process during the first two years after the death of a partner. Particularly important is the quality of the support system for the grieving partner rather than simply the number of friends. Survivors who have a few friends or relatives with whom they have strong, close relationships are better off than survivors who have many acquaintances (Dimond, Lund, & Caserta, 1987).

One study of spousal bereavement measured how the surviving spouse rated the marriage. Bereaved older adults rated their relationships at 2, 12, and 30 months after the death of their spouse. Nonbereaved older adults served as a comparison group. The results are summarized in Figure 17.7. Bereaved widows and widowers gave their marriages more positive ratings than nonbereaved older adults. A marriage lost through death left a positive bias in memory. However, bereaved spouses' ratings were related to depression in an interesting way. The more depressed the bereaved spouse, the more positive the marriage's rating. In contrast, depressed nonbereaved spouses gave their marriages negative ratings. This result suggests that depression following bereavement signifies positive aspects of a relationship; whereas depression

FIGURE 17.7   Spousal Bereavement

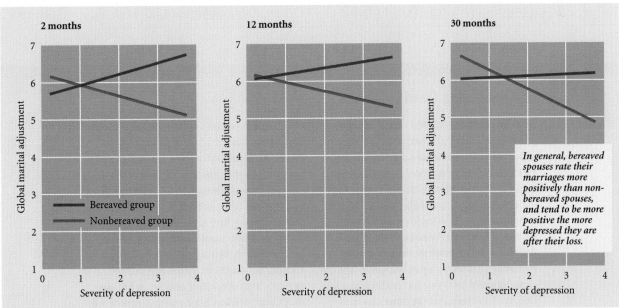

SOURCE: From "Retrospective Assessment of Marital Adjustment and Depression During the First Two Years of Spousal Bereavement," by A. Futterman, D. Gallagher, L. W. Thompson, S. Lovett, and M. Gilewski, 1990, *Psychology and Aging, 5,* 277–283. Copyright © 1990 American Psychological Association. Reprinted with permission of the author.

not connected with bereavement indicates a troubled relationship (Futterman et al., 1990).

Several studies of widows document a tendency for some women to "sanctify" their husbands (Lopata, 1996). Sanctification involves describing deceased husbands in idealized terms, and it serves several functions: validating that the widow had a strong marriage, is a good and worthy person, and is capable of rebuilding her life.

Getting older bereaved spouses to talk about their feelings concerning their loss reduces feelings of hopelessness, intrusive thoughts, and obsessive-compulsive behaviours (Segal et al., 1999). Cognitive-behavioural therapy is one especially effective intervention to help bereaved people make sense of the loss and deal with their other feelings and thoughts (Fleming & Robinson, 2001).

Unmarried heterosexual couples and gay and lesbian couples may experience other feelings and reactions on top of typical feelings of grief. For example, family members of the deceased may not make the partner feel welcome at the funeral, making it hard for the partner to bring closure to the relationship. Gays whose partner died of AIDS may experience increased personal concern and have difficulty dealing with feelings (Goodkin et al., 1997).

Learning about and dealing with death is clearly a developmental process across the life span. As noted in the Forces in Action feature, it reflects the integration of biological, psychological, and sociocultural forces.

TEST YOURSELF

1. In general, adults should be _____ when discussing death with children.

2. Adolescents are usually _____ to talk about their grief experiences.

3. The most devastating type of loss for an adult is the loss of a _____.

4. In general, a marriage ended by death is rated _____ than a marriage ended in some other way.

How do the different ways adults view death relate to the stages of Erikson's theory discussed in Chapters 11, 13, 14, and 16?

Answers: (1) honest, (2) reluctant, (3) child, (4) more positively

---

FORCES IN ACTION

Understanding Death

Understanding death is not a topic in which you expect to see the developmental forces in action. Actually, the framework provides an excellent way to tie together several different threads. Most apparent is that biological forces are essential to understanding death. The very definition of death is based on whether certain biological functions are present; these same definitions create numerous ethical dilemmas that must be dealt with psychologically and socioculturally. Life-cycle forces also play a key role. We have seen that the same concept—death—has varied meanings beyond the mere cessation of life depending on people's age.

How a person's understanding of death develops is also the result of psychological forces. As the ability to think and reflect undergoes fundamental change, the view of death changes from a mostly magical approach to one that can be transcendent and transforming. As we have seen, people who are facing their own imminent death experience certain feelings. Having gained experience through the deaths of friends and relatives, a person's level of comfort with his or her own death may increase. Such personal experience may also come about by sharing rituals, defined through sociocultural forces. People observe how others deal with death and how the culture sets the tone and prescribes behaviour for survivors. The combined action of forces also determines how they cope with the grief that accompanies the loss of someone close. Psychologically, confronting grief depends on many things, including the quality of the support system we have.

Thus, just as the beginning of life represents a complex interaction of biological, psychological, sociocultural, and life-cycle factors, so does death. What people believe about what happens after death is also an interaction of these factors. So, as we bring the study of human development to a close, we end where we began—what we experience in our lives cannot be understood if one uses only a single perspective. ▨

PUTTING IT ALL TOGETHER

As we've discovered in this chapter, thinking about death isn't easy. We aren't taught how to deal with it very well. Like Greta, we encounter different rituals and customs concerning funerals and mourning and we do not fully understand them. You may have been in a situation like that of Donna and Carl, facing the dilemma of whether to bring young children to a funeral. You may know someone like Betty who has just been diagnosed with a terminal disease, or someone like Bertha who just lost a spouse. Like Clare and Alex, you may have experienced the loss of a close relative or friend.

Death is not as pleasant a topic as children's play or occupational development. It's not something we can go to college to master. What it represents to many people is the end of their existence, and that is a very scary prospect. But because we all share in this fear at some level, each of us is equipped to provide support and comfort for grieving survivors.

Death is the last life-cycle force we encounter, the ultimate triumph of biological forces that limit the length of life. Yet the same psychological and social forces that are so influential throughout life help us deal with death, either our own or someone else's. As we come to the end of our life journey, we understand death through an interaction of psychological forces, such as coping skills and intellectual and emotional understanding of death, and the sociocultural forces expressed in a particular society's traditions and rituals.

SUMMARY

17.1 Definitions and Ethical Issues

Sociocultural Definitions of Death

▨ Death is a difficult concept to define precisely. There is great variability across cultures in the meaning of death and behaviours to express grief.

Legal and Medical Definitions

▨ For many centuries, a clinical definition of death was used: the absence of a heartbeat and respiration. Currently, brain death is the most widely used definition. It is based on several highly specific criteria, including brain activity and responses to specific stimuli.

Ethical Issues

▨ Two types of euthanasia are distinguished. Active euthanasia consists of deliberately ending someone's life, such as turning off a life-support system. Physician-assisted suicide is a controversial issue and a form of active euthanasia. Passive euthanasia is ending someone's life by withholding some type of intervention or treatment (e.g., by not providing nutrition). It is essential that people make their wishes known, either through a durable power of attorney or a living will.

17.2 Thinking About Death: Personal Aspects

A Life Course Approach to Dying

▨ Young adults report a sense of being cheated by death. Cognitive developmental level is important for understanding how young adults view death.

▨ Middle-aged adults begin to confront their own mortality and undergo a change in their sense of time lived and time until death.

▨ Older adults are more accepting of death.

Dealing with One's Own Death

▨ Kübler-Ross's theory includes five stages: denial, anger, bargaining, depression, and acceptance. Some people do not progress through all these stages, and some people move through them at different rates. People may be in more than one stage at a time and do not necessarily go through them in order.

▨ A contextual theory of dying emphasizes the tasks a dying person must face. Four dimensions of these tasks have been identified: bodily needs, psychological security, interpersonal attachments, and spiritual energy and hope. A contextual theory would be able to incorporate differences in reasons people die and the places people die.

Death Anxiety

▨ Most people exhibit some degree of anxiety about death, even though it is difficult to define and measure. Individual difference variables include gender, religiosity, age, ethnicity, and occupation. Death anxiety may have some benefits.

▨ The main ways death anxiety is shown are by avoiding death (e.g., refusing to go to funerals) and deliberately challenging it (e.g., engaging in dangerous sports). Other ways of showing it include changing lifestyles, dreaming and fantasizing, using humour, displacing fears, and becoming a death professional.

▨ Several ways to deal with anxiety exist: living life to the fullest, personal reflection, and education. Death education has been shown to be extremely effective.

Creating a Final Scenario

▨ Managing the final aspects of life, after-death disposition of the body and memorial services, and distribution of assets are important end-of-life issues. Making choices about what people do and do not want done constitutes making a final scenario.

The Hospice Option

▨ The goal of a hospice or palliative care is to maintain the quality of life and to manage the pain of terminally ill patients. Hospice clients typically have cancer, AIDS, or a progressive neurological disorder. Family members tend to stay involved in the care of hospice clients.

17.3 Surviving the Loss: The Grieving Process

The Grief Process

▨ Grief is an active process of coping with loss. Four aspects of grieving must be confronted: the reality of the loss, the emotional turmoil, adjusting to the environment, and loosening the ties with the deceased. When death is expected, survivors go through anticipatory grief; unexpected death is usually more difficult for people to handle.

Normal Grief Reactions

▨ Dealing with grief, called *grief work,* usually takes at least one to two years. Grief is equally intense for both expected and unexpected death, but it may begin before the actual death when the patient has a terminal illness. Normal grief reactions include sorrow, sadness, denial, disbelief, guilt, and anniversary reactions.

▨ With regard to dealing with normal grief, middle-aged adults have the most difficult time. Poor copers tend to have low self-esteem before losing a loved one.

Coping with Grief

▨ The four-component model proposes that the context of the loss, continuation of subjective meaning associated with the loss, changing representations of the lost relationship over time, and the role of coping and emotion-regulation processes describe the grief process.

▨ The dual-process model of coping with bereavement focuses on loss-oriented stressors and restoration-oriented stressors.

Traumatic Grief Reactions

▨ Traumatic grief involves symptoms of separation distress and symptoms of traumatic distress. Excessive guilt and self-blame are common manifestations of traumatic grief.

17.4 Dying and Bereavement Experiences Across the Life Span

Childhood

▨ The cognitive and psychosocial developmental levels of children determine their understanding of and ability to cope with death. This is especially evident in the behaviours children use to display their grief.

▨ Research indicates that there are few long-lasting effects of bereavement in childhood.

Adolescence

▨ Adolescents may have difficulty making sense of death, and they are often severely affected by bereavement. Adolescents may be reluctant to discuss their feelings of loss, and peers often provide little support.

Adulthood

▨ Young and middle-aged adults usually have intense feelings about death. Attachment theory provides a useful framework to understand these feelings.

▨ Midlife is a time when people usually deal with the death of their parents and confront their own mortality.

- The death of one's child is especially difficult to cope with.
- The death of one's parent deprives an adult of many important things, and the feelings accompanying it are often complex.

Late Adulthood
- Older adults are usually less anxious about death and deal with it better than any other age group.

- The death of a grandchild can be very traumatic for older adults, and the feelings of loss may never go away.
- The death of one's partner represents a deep personal loss, especially when the couple had a long and close relationship. Older widowers often have a difficult time coping, whereas older widows often have a difficult time financially.

KEY TERMS

clinical death (609)
brain death (609)
bioethics (610)
euthanasia (610)
active euthanasia (610)

passive euthanasia (612)
end-of-life issues (620)
final scenario (620)
hospice care (621)
palliative care (621)

bereavement (624)
grief (624)
mourning (624)
grief work (627)
anniversary reaction (627)

SEE FOR YOURSELF: APPLYING WHAT YOU'VE LEARNED

To gain firsthand knowledge of how the rituals and customs surrounding death vary across cultures, gather the following information from your local community. Visit a funeral home and learn about the different options for burial or cremation. Find out the costs associated with each option and the range of prices and services that are available. Talk with members of various religious and cultural groups about the different types of funeral services that each uses. Bring your information to class and discuss the wide variations you have discovered.

LEARN MORE ABOUT IT

Books

JAFFE, C. (1997). *All kinds of love: Experiencing hospice.* Amityville, NY: Baywood. An excellent source of information about the philosophy and role of hospice.

KUHL, D. (2002). *What dying people want.* Toronto: Anchor Canada. This book is written by a Canadian physician who worked with the dying for many years. The purpose is to provide people who have a terminal illness, or know someone who does, with an enhanced understanding of the dying process. It is based on stories of people who knew they were dying.

KUNG, H., & JENS, W. (1995). *Dying with dignity: A plea for personal responsibility.* New York: Continuum. A superb, easy-to-read book that discusses death with dignity. This book will make you think.

KUSHNER, H. S. (1981). *When bad things happen to good people.* New York: Schocken. This is easy reading but contains very thought-provoking material. The book was written by a rabbi after the death of his son.

NULAND, S. B. (1994). *How we die: Reflections on life's final chapter.* New York: Knopf. This is a good discussion of the actual things that happen when people die. It is excellent for countering myths about death.

ROSENBLATT, P. C. (2000). *Parent grief: Narratives of loss and relationship.* Philadelphia: Brunner/Mazel. This book is a compilation of interviews of 29 couples who lost at least one child (age newborn to mid-30s). It is an excellent source for understanding the nature of parental grief.

TAYLOR, N. (1993). *A necessary end.* New York: Nan A. Talese. The author tells how he dealt with the death of his parents and found meaning in it.

 For additional readings, explore InfoTrac® College Edition, your online library. Go to http://www.infotrac.thomsonlearning.com.

Websites

http://www.chpca.net/home.htm

The Canadian Hospice Palliative Care website provides general information about end-of-life issues and information on national and public policy initiatives and provides a link to the Canadian Directory of Hospice Palliative Care Services.

http://www.virtualhospice.ca

Launched in 1994, the Canadian Virtual Hospice is an interactive network for people such as patients, their families and health care workers dealing with life-threatening illness and loss.

http://www.tcfcanada.net/

The Compassionate Friends of Canada is a chapter of the original organization in the United States dedicated to helping parents deal with the grief of the loss of a child.

http://www.hc-sc.gc.ca/seniors-aines/

Health Canada's website for seniors provides information on a wide variety of topics including loss and grief.

Website addresses are subject to change. The *Human Development* book companion website can be accessed for updated links.

The Human Development Book Companion Website

See http://www.humandevelopment.nelson.com for practice quiz questions, Internet links, updates, critical thinking exercises, discussion forums, and more.

GLOSSARY

abusive relationship when one partner in a relationship becomes violent or aggressive toward the other

accommodation according to Piaget, changing existing knowledge based on new knowledge

achievement identity status in which adolescents have explored alternative identities and are now secure in their chosen identities

active euthanasia deliberate ending of someone's life

active gene-environment interaction phenomenon in which individuals actively seek an environment conducive to their heredity

activities of daily living (ADLs) self-care tasks such as eating, bathing, toileting, walking, or dressing

activity dimension of temperament defined by the tempo and vigour of a child's activity

adaptation level area where environmental press is average for a particular level of competence

addiction physical dependence on a particular substance, such as alcohol

adolescent egocentrism self-absorption that is characteristic of teenagers as they search for identity

adolescent-limited antisocial behaviour the behaviour of youths who engage in relatively minor criminal acts yet aren't consistently antisocial

aerobic exercise exercise that places a moderate stress on the heart by maintaining a pulse rate between 60 and 90% of the maximum heart rate

age discrimination denying a job or promotion to someone solely on the basis of age

age of viability age at which a fetus can survive because most of its bodily systems function adequately; typically at 7 months after conception

agreeableness dimension of personality associated with being accepting, willing to work with others, and caring

alert inactivity state in which a baby is calm with eyes open and attentive, and the baby seems to be deliberately inspecting the environment

alienation when workers feel that what they are doing is meaningless, that their efforts are devalued, or when they do not see the connection between what they do and the final product

alleles variations of genes

altruism prosocial behaviour such as helping and sharing in which the individual does not benefit directly from his or her behaviour

Alzheimer disease disease associated with aging characterized by gradual declines in memory, learning, attention, and judgment; confusion as to time and where one is; difficulties in communicating and finding the words one wants to use; declines in personal hygiene and self-care skills; inappropriate social behaviour; and changes in personality

amniocentesis prenatal diagnostic technique that involves withdrawing a sample of amniotic fluid through the abdomen using a syringe

amnion inner sac in which the developing child rests

amniotic fluid fluid that surrounds the fetus

amyloid protein that is produced in abnormally high levels in Alzheimer disease and that may be responsible for the neurofibrillary tangles and neuritic plaques

angry cry more intense version of a basic cry

animism crediting inanimate objects with life and lifelike properties such as feelings

anniversary reaction changes in behaviour related to feelings of sadness on the actual anniversary of a death

anorexia nervosa persistent refusal to eat, accompanied by an irrational fear of being overweight

anxiety disorders problems such as feelings of severe anxiety for no apparent reason, phobias to specific things or places, and obsessive-compulsive disorders in which thoughts or actions are repeatedly performed

appraise to evaluate a situation to determine whether it exceeds a person's resources and is, therefore, stressful

approval-focused orientation behaving as one thinks society expects "good people" to behave

assimilation according to Piaget, taking in information that is compatible with what one already knows

assisted-living facilities a supportive living arrangement for people who need assistance with ADLs or IADLs but who are not so impaired physically or cognitively that they need 24-hour care

assortative mating theory of mating that states that people find partners based on their similarity to each other

attachment enduring social-emotional relationship between infants and their caregivers

attention processes that determine which information will be processed further by an individual

attentional control the abilities to focus, switch, and divide attention

authoritarian parenting parents who show high levels of control and low levels of warmth toward their children

authoritative parenting parents who use a moderate amount of control and are warm and responsive to their children

autobiographical memory memories of the significant events and experiences of one's own life

autosomes first 22 pairs of chromosomes

average life expectancy age at which half of the people born in a particular year will have died

avoidant attachment relationship in which infants turn away from their mothers when they are reunited following a brief separation

axon tubelike structure that emerges from the cell body and transmits information to other neurons

babbling speechlike sounds that consist of vowel-consonant combinations

basal metabolism rate the speed at which the body consumes calories

basic cry cry that starts softly and gradually becomes more intense; often heard when babies are hungry or tired

basic emotions emotions experienced by humankind and that consist of three elements: a subjective feeling, a physiological change, and an overt behaviour

battered woman syndrome situation in which a woman believes that she cannot leave an abusive situation

behaviour therapy approach to treating depression based on increasing the number of rewards or reinforcements in the environment

behavioural genetics the branch of genetics that studies the inheritance of behavioural and psychological traits

bereavement state or condition caused by loss through death

binge drinking consuming five or more drinks in a row for men or four or more drinks in a row for women within the past two weeks

bioethics study of the interface between human values and technological advances in health and life sciences

biological forces all genetic and health-related factors that affect development

biopsychosocial framework view that integrates biological, psychological, sociocultural, and life-cycle forces on development

blended family family consisting of a biological parent, a stepparent, and children

body mass index (BMI) an adjusted ratio of weight to height; used to define overweight

brain death most widely accepted definition of death, including no heartbeat, respiration, responsiveness, reflexes, or brain activity

bridge job the job one holds between one's exit from the career job and final retirement

bulimia nervosa disease in which people alternate between binge eating— periods when they eat uncontrollably— and purging through self-induced vomiting or with laxatives

burnout depletion of a person's energy and motivation

caesarean section (C-section) surgical removal of infant from the uterus through an incision made in the mother's abdomen

cardinality principle counting principle that the last number name denotes the number of objects being counted

career plateauing either a lack of promotional opportunity from the organization or a person's decision not to seek advancement

cell body centre of the neuron that keeps the neuron alive

cellular theories theories of aging that focus on processes that occur within individual cells, which cause the buildup of harmful substances over one's lifetime

centrality meaning derived when grandparenting is the most important thing in grandparents' lives

centration according to Piaget, narrowly focused type of thought characteristic of preoperational children

cephalocaudal sequence of growth occurring from the head downward (head to caudal or tail region)

cerebral cortex wrinkled surface of the brain that regulates many functions that are distinctly human

cerebral vascular accidents *See* strokes

chorionic villus sampling prenatal diagnostic technique that involves taking a sample of tissue from the chorion

chromosomes threadlike structures in the nuclei of cells that contain genetic material

chronic obstructive pulmonary disease (COPD) most common form of incapacitating respiratory disease among older adults; examples are asthma and emphysema

circadian rhythm sleep-wake cycle

classical conditioning a form of learning that involves pairing a neutral stimulus and a response originally produced by another

climacteric loss of ability to bear children, which usually begins in the 40s and is complete by age 50 or 55

clinical death death defined by a lack of heartbeat and respiration

clique small group of friends who are similar in age, sex, and race

cognitive therapy approach to depression based on the idea that maladaptive beliefs or cognitions about oneself are responsible for depression

cohabitation two or more unrelated adults living together

cohort effects differences between individuals that result from experiences and circumstances unique to a person's particular generation

common couple violence violence that occurs occasionally within a relationship that is instigated by either partner

comparable worth equating pay in occupations that are determined to be equivalent in importance but differ in the gender distribution of the people in them

competence upper limit of a person's ability to function in five domains: physical health, sensory-perceptual skills, motor skills, cognitive skills, and ego strength

componential subtheory idea that intelligent behaviour involves skilfully adapting to an environment

components basic cognitive processes

comprehension the process of extracting meaning from a sequence of words

cones specialized neurons in the back of the eye that sense colour

conscientiousness dimension of personality associated with being hard-working, ambitious, energetic, scrupulous, and persevering

contextual subtheory idea that intelligent behaviour involves skilfully adapting to an environment

continuity theory view that people tend to cope with daily life in late adulthood in essentially the same ways they coped in earlier periods of life

continuity-discontinuity issue issue concerned with whether a developmental phenomenon follows a smooth progression throughout the life span or a series of abrupt shifts

conventional level second level of reasoning in Kohlberg's theory, where moral reasoning is based on society's norms

convergent thinking using information to arrive at one standard and correct answer

cooing early vowel-like sounds that babies produce

cooperative play play that is organized around a theme, with each child taking on a different role; begins at about 2 years of age

coping attempts to deal with stress

core knowledge hypothesis infants are born with rudimentary knowledge of the world, which is elaborated based on experiences

corpus callosum thick bundle of neurons that connects the two hemispheres

correlation coefficient statistic that reveals the strength and direction of the relation between two variables

correlational study investigation looking at relations between variables as they exist naturally in the world

counterimitation learning what should not be done by observing the behaviour

cross-linking theory of aging in which some proteins interact randomly with certain body tissues, such as muscles and arteries

cross-sectional study research design in which people of different ages are compared at one point in time

crowd large group including many cliques that have similar attitudes and values

crowning appearance of the top of the baby's head during labour

crying state in which a baby cries vigorously, usually accompanied by agitated but uncoordinated movement

crystallization first phase in Super's theory of career development, in which adolescents use their emerging identities for ideas about careers

crystallized intelligence knowledge acquired through experience and education in a particular culture

culture-fair intelligence tests intelligence tests devised using items common to many cultures

date (acquaintance) rape when someone is forced to have sexual intercourse with someone they know

deductive reasoning drawing conclusions from facts; characteristic of formal operational thought

dementia family of diseases involving serious impairment of behavioural and cognitive functioning

demographers people who study population trends

dendrite end of the neuron that receives information; it looks like a tree with many branches

deoxyribonucleic acid (DNA) molecule composed of four nucleotide bases that is the biochemical basis of heredity

dependent variable behaviour that is observed after other variables are manipulated

depression disorder characterized by pervasive feelings of sadness, irritability, and low self-esteem

differentiation distinguishing and mastering individual motions

diffusion identity status in which adolescents do not have an identity and are doing nothing to achieve one

direct instruction telling a child what to do, when, and why

disorganized (disoriented) attachment relationship in which infants don't seem to understand what's happening when they are separated and later reunited with their mothers

dispositional praise praise that links a child's altruistic behaviour to an underlying altruistic disposition

divergent thinking thinking in novel and unusual directions

dizygotic twins result of the fertilization of two separate eggs by two sperm; also called fraternal twins

docility when people allow the situation to dictate the options they have

dominance hierarchy ordering of individuals within a group in which group members with lower status defer to those with greater status

dominant form of an allele whose chemical instructions are followed

dream as related to vocational development, a vision of one's career

dynamic systems theory theory that views motor development as involving

many distinct skills organized and reorganized over time to meet specific needs

dynamic testing measures learning potential by having a child learn something new in the presence of the examiner and with the examiner's help

dysphoria feeling sad or down; the most prominent symptom of depression

ecological theory view that human development cannot be separated from the environmental contexts in which development occurs

ectoderm outer layer of the embryo that will become the hair, outer layer of skin, and the nervous system

ego resilience powerful personality resource that enables people to handle midlife

egocentrism difficulty in seeing the world from another's point of view; typical of children in the preoperational period

electroencephalogram (EEG) pattern of brain waves recorded from electrodes that are placed on the scalp

embryo term given to the zygote once it is completely embedded in the uterine wall

emotionality aspect of temperament that refers to the strength of the infant's emotional response to a situation, the ease with which that response is triggered, and the ease with which the infant can be returned to a nonemotional state

empathic orientation according to Eisenberg, a level of prosocial reasoning common in some children and many adolescents in which their thinking considers the injured child's perspective and how their own actions would make the child feel

empathy experiencing another person's feelings

encapsulated result of the processes of thinking becoming connected with the products of thinking

endoderm inner layer of the embryo, which will become the lungs and the digestive system

end-of-life issues includes management of final phase of life, disposition of body and memorial services, and distribution of assets

environmental press number and types of physical, interpersonal, or social demands that environments make on people

epigenetic principle view in Erikson's theory that each psychosocial stage has its own period of importance

episodic memory the general class of memory having to do with the conscious recollection of information from a specific time or event

equilibration according to Piaget, a process by which children reorganize their schemes to return to a state of equilibrium when disequilibrium occurs

estrogen-related symptoms symptoms associated with the climacteric and menopause, including hot flashes, night sweats, vaginal dryness, and urine leakage that are due to the drop in estrogen

ethnic identity feeling of belonging to a specific ethnic group

ethology branch of biology concerned with adaptive behaviours that are characteristic of different species

eugenics effort to improve the human species by letting only people whose characteristics are valued by a society mate and pass along their genes

euthanasia practice of ending a life for reasons of mercy

evocative gene-environment interaction phenomenon in which different genotypes provoke different reactions from the environment

exchange theory view that a relationship is based on each partner contributing something to the relationship that the other would be hard-pressed to provide

exosystem according to Bronfenbrenner, social settings that influence one's development even though one does not experience them firsthand

experiential subtheory idea that intelligence is revealed in both novel and familiar tasks

experiment systematic way of manipulating factors that a researcher thinks cause a particular behaviour

explicit memory conscious and intentional recollection of information

extended family family in which grandparents and other relatives live with parents and children

external aids memory aids that rely on environmental resources, such as notebooks or calendars

extraversion dimension of personality in which an individual thrives on social interaction, likes to talk, takes charge easily, readily expresses opinions and feelings, likes to keep busy, has seemingly unending energy, and prefers stimulating and challenging environments

extremely low birth weight newborns who weigh less than 1,000 grams (2 pounds)

familial intellectual impairment form of mental retardation that does not involve biological damage but represents the low end of the normal distribution of intelligence

fast mapping fact that children make connections between new words and referents so quickly that they can't be considering all possible meanings

fetal alcohol spectrum disorder (FASD) group of conditions that include fetal alcohol syndrome

fetal alcohol syndrome (FAS) disorder affecting babies whose mothers consumed large amounts of alcohol while they were pregnant

fetal medicine field of medicine concerned with treating prenatal problems before birth

filial obligation sense of responsibility to care for a parent if necessary

final scenario making choices known to others about how a person wants his or her life to end

fine motor skills motor skills associated with grasping, holding, and manipulating objects

fluid intelligence abilities such as thinking in a flexible, adaptive manner, drawing inferences, and understanding relations between concepts

foreclosure identity status in which adolescents have an identity that was chosen based on advice from adults rather than one that resulted from personal exploration of alternatives

frail older adults older adults who have physical disabilities, are very ill, and may have cognitive or psychological disorders

free radicals chemicals produced randomly during normal cell metabolism that bond easily to other substances

inside cells; may cause cellular damage associated with aging

frontal cortex brain region that regulates personality and goal-directed behaviour

functional magnetic resonance imaging (F-MRI) method of studying brain activity by using magnetic fields to track blood flow in the brain

gender constancy understanding that maleness and femaleness do not change over situations or personal wishes

gender identity sense of oneself as male or female

gender labelling young children's understanding that they are either boys or girls and naming themselves accordingly

gender stability understanding in preschool children that boys become men and girls become women

gender stereotype beliefs and images about males and females that are not necessarily true

gender-schema theory theory that states that children first decide whether an object, activity, or behaviour is female or male, then use this information to decide whether they should learn more about the object, activity, or behaviour

gene group of nucleotide bases that provide a specific set of biochemical instructions

generativity according to Erikson, being productive by helping others to ensure the continuation of society by guiding the next generation

generic memory starts at about age 2 that results in the production of a script, which is an outline of a repeated event, such as nap time at day care, and helps in the recall of what to expect

genotype person's hereditary makeup

germ disc small cluster of cells near the centre of the zygote that will eventually develop into a baby

glass ceiling level to which women and minorities may rise in a company but beyond which they may not go

grammatical morphemes words or endings of words that make a sentence grammatical

grief sorrow, hurt, anger, guilt, confusion, and other feelings that arise after suffering a loss

grief work psychological side of coming to terms with bereavement

habituation becoming unresponsive to a stimulus that is presented repeatedly

hassles day-to-day events that upset and annoy people

hedonistic orientation according to Eisenberg, a level of prosocial reasoning common in preschool and elementary school children in which they emphasize pursuing their own pleasure

hemispheres right and left halves of the cortex

hemorrhage break in any blood vessel that leads to loss of blood

heterocyclic antidepressants (HCAs) type of medication used to treat depression

heterozygous when the alleles differ from each other

high-density lipoproteins (HDLs) lipoproteins that help clear arteries

homogamy similarity of values and interests

homozygous when the chromosomes in a pair are the same

hope according to Erikson, an openness to new experience tempered by wariness that occurs when trust and mistrust are in balance

hormone replacement theory treatment for symptoms accompanying the climacteric in which women take low doses of estrogen and progesterone

hospice care movement that provides a supportive environment for dying people by keeping families engaged in caregiving and by providing professional assistance during this very stressful time

human development multidisciplinary scientific study of how people change and how they stay the same

Huntington's disease progressive and fatal type of dementia

hypoxia a birth complication in which umbilical blood flow is disrupted and the infant does not receive adequate oxygen

illusion of invulnerability adolescents' belief that misfortunes cannot happen to them

imaginary audience adolescents' feeling that their behaviour is constantly being watched by their peers

imitation (observational learning) learning that happens by watching those around us

immortality through clan meaning derived from grandparenting when grandparents take pride in the fact that they will be followed by not one but two generations

implantation step in which the zygote burrows into the uterine wall and establishes connections with a woman's blood vessels

implementation third phase in Super's theory of career development, in which individuals now enter the workforce

implicit memory effortless recollection of information

implicit stereotyping the automatic and nonconscious activation of strong stereotypes

in vitro fertilization process by which sperm and an egg are mixed in a petri dish to create a zygote, which is then placed in a woman's uterus

incomplete dominance situation in which one allele does not dominate another completely

incontinence loss of bladder or bowel control

independent variable factor that researchers manipulate in an experiment

indifferent-uninvolved parenting parents who are neither warm nor controlling and who try to minimize the amount of time spent with their children

indulgence meaning derived when grandparents spoil their grandchildren

indulgent-permissive parents parents who are warm and caring but exert little control over their children

infant mortality the number of infants out of 1,000 births who die before their first birthday

infant-directed speech way of speaking in which adults speak slowly and with exaggerated changes in pitch and loudness

infantilization way of speaking to a nursing home resident based on using a person's first name when it is not appropriate, terms of endearment, simplified expressions, short imperatives, assumptions that a nursing home resident has no memory, and manipulation to get compliance

information-processing theory view that human cognition consists of mental hardware and software

instrumental activities of daily living (IADLs) acts that require some intellectual competence and planning, such as cooking and doing the laundry

instrumental orientation characteristic of Kohlberg's Stage 2, in which moral reasoning is based on the aim of looking out for one's own needs

integration linking individual motions into a coherent, coordinated whole

integrity versus despair according to Erikson, a struggle that comes about as older adults try to integrate their lives with a view of their family's and community's futures

intellectual impairment the preferred term for a condition sometimes referred to as mental retardation in which the level of intellectual functioning is considered to be low

intelligence quotient (IQ) mathematical representation of how a person scores on an intelligence test in relation to how other people of the same age score

interindividual variability patterns of change in a domain (e.g., intelligence) are different for different people

internal aids memory aids that rely on mental processes, such as imagery

internal belief systems what one tells oneself about why certain things are happening

internal working model infant's understanding of how responsive and dependable the mother is; thought to influence close relationships throughout the child's life

interpersonal norms characteristic of Kohlberg's Stage 3, in which moral reasoning is based on winning the approval of others

intersensory redundancy infants' sensory systems are attuned to information presented simultaneously to different sensory modes

intimacy versus isolation according to Erikson, the psychosocial conflict of young adulthood

intonation pattern of rising and falling pitch that appears around the age of 7 months in infants' babbling

job satisfaction   good feeling that results from a positive appraisal of one's work

joint custody   when, following divorce, both parents retain legal custody of their children

juvenile delinquency   when adolescents commit illegal acts that are destructive toward themselves or others

kinkeepers   people who gather their family together for celebrations and keep family members in touch with each other

knowledge telling strategy   writing down information as it is retrieved from memory, a common practice for young writers

knowledge transforming strategy   deciding what information to include and how best to organize it to convey a point

lateralization   certain cognitive functions are located on one side of the brain more than the other

learned helplessness   feeling that one is always at the mercy of external events and that one does not have any control over one's own destiny

learning disability   when a child with normal intelligence has difficulty mastering at least one academic subject

leisure   discretionary activity that includes simple relaxation, activities for enjoyment, creative pursuits, and sensual transcendence

life-course persistent antisocial behaviour   antisocial behaviour that emerges at an early age and continues throughout life

life course perspective   describes the ways in which various generations experience the biological, psychological, and sociocultural forces of development in their respective historical context

life review   process of reviewing one's life

life story   second manifestation of the life-span construct, a personal narrative that organizes past events into a coherent sequence

life-cycle forces   differences in how the same event may affect people of different ages

life-span construct   unified sense of the past, present, and future that is based on one's experiences and input from others

life-span perspective   view that development is determined by many biological, psychological, and social factors and that all parts of the life span are interrelated

locomote   to move around in the world

longevity   number of years a person will live

longitudinal study   research design in which a single cohort is studied over multiple measurements

long-term memory   permanent storehouse for memories that has unlimited capacity

low birth weight   weight of less than 2,500 grams (5 pounds) in a newborn

low-density lipoproteins (LDLs)   lipoproteins that cause fatty acids to accumulate in arteries, which impedes the flow of blood

macrosystem   according to Bronfenbrenner, the cultural and subcultural settings in which the microsystems, mesosystems, and exosystems are embedded

malnourished   being small for one's age because of inadequate nutrition

maximum life expectancy   oldest age to which any person lives

menarche   onset of menstruation

menopause   cessation of menstruation

mental age (MA)   in intelligence testing, a measure of children's performance corresponding to the chronological age of those whose performance equals the child's

mental hardware   mental and neural structures that are built in and that allow the mind to operate

mental operations   cognitive actions that can be performed on objects or ideas

mental software   mental "programs" that are the basis for performing particular tasks

mesoderm   middle layer of the embryo; becomes the muscles, bones, and circulatory system

mesosystem   according to Bronfenbrenner, the interrelations between different microsystems

metabolic theories   theories of aging that focus on aspects of the body's metabolism as a reason people age

metabolism   energy required for bodily functions

microsystem   according to Bronfenbrenner, the people and objects that are present in one's immediate environment

midlife crisis   time of psychological questioning during which people reevaluate their lives

monoamine oxidase (MAO) inhibitors   type of medication used to treat depression

monozygotic twins   result when a single fertilized egg splits to form two new individuals; also called identical twins

moratorium   identity status in which adolescents are still examining different alternatives and have yet to find a satisfactory identity

motor skills   coordinated movements of the muscles and limbs

mourning   culturally approved ways in which people express their grief

multidimensional   approaches to intelligence that identify different areas of intellectual abilities

multidirectionality   refers to the fact that some aspects of intelligence improve and other aspects decline across adulthood

myelin   fatty sheath that wraps around neurons to permit them to transmit information more rapidly

naturalistic observation   form of systematic observation in which people are observed as they behave spontaneously in some real-life situation

nature-nurture issue   issue concerning the manner in which genetic and environmental factors influence development

needs-oriented orientation   according to Eisenberg, a level of prosocial reasoning common in some preschool and many elementary school children in which they are concerned about others' needs and want to help

negative reinforcement trap   unwittingly reinforcing a behaviour you want to discourage

neural plate   flat group of cells present in prenatal development that becomes the brain and spinal cord

neuritic plaques   damaged and dying neurons that collect around a core of protein

neurofibrillary tangles abnormal filaments found in large numbers of neurons in persons with Alzheimer disease

neuron basic cellular unit of the brain and nervous system that specializes in receiving and transmitting information

neuroplasticity extent to which brain organization is flexible

neuroticism dimension of personality that refers to the extent that individuals tend to be anxious, hostile, self-conscious, depressed, impulsive, and vulnerable

neurotransmitters chemicals released by the terminal buttons that allow neurons to communicate with each other

niche-picking process of deliberately seeking environments that are compatible with one's genetic makeup

nonshared environmental influences forces within a family that make siblings different from one another

norepinephrine neurotransmitter that helps control arousal; low levels are related to depression

nuclear family family consisting of parent(s) and child(ren)

obedience orientation characteristic of Kohlberg's Stage 1, in which moral reasoning is based on the belief that adults know what is right and wrong

one-to-one principle counting principle that states that there must be one and only one number name for each object counted

openness to experience dimension of personality that displays a vivid imagination and dream life, appreciation of art, and a strong desire to try anything once

operant conditioning view of learning, proposed by B. F. Skinner, that emphasizes reward and punishment

optimal level of development the highest level of information-processing capacity that a person is capable of doing

optimally exercised ability level of performance a normal, healthy adult demonstrates under the best conditions of training or practice

ordinality numbers that differ in magnitude with some values greater than others

organic intellectual impairment intellectual impairment that can be traced to a specific biological or physical problem

orienting response individual fixes eyes on a strong or unfamiliar stimulus and changes in heart rate and brainwave activity occur

osteoarthritis a bone disease marked by gradual onset and progression of joint pain and disability with minor signs of inflammation

osteoporosis disease in which bones become porous like honeycombs and extremely easy to break

overextension when children define words more broadly than adults do

overregularization grammatical usage that results from applying rules to words that are exceptions to the rule

pain cry cry that begins with a sudden long burst, followed by a long pause and gasping

palliative care a type of care that aims to relieve suffering and improve the quality of life for individuals with terminal illness or conditions

parallel play when children play alone but are aware of and interested in what another child is doing

Parkinson's disease common disease among older adults that results in motor problems, including slow walking, difficulty getting into and out of chairs, and hand tremors

passive euthanasia allowing a person to die by withholding an available treatment

passive gene-environment relation phenomenon in which parents pass on both genes and an environment that supports the expression of those genes

patriarchal terrorism systematic violence within a relationship that is directed to a woman from a man

patronizing speech way of speaking to older adults that is marked by slower rate, exaggerated intonation, higher pitch, increased volume, repetitions, closed-end questions, and simplified vocabulary and grammar

perception processes by which the brain receives, selects, modifies, and organizes incoming nerve impulses that are the result of physical stimulation

perimenopause the time from when the first symptoms of menopause start until menopause occurs

period of the fetus longest period of prenatal development, extending from the 9th until the 38th week after conception

personal control beliefs beliefs about the degree to which one's performance in a situation is within one's control

personal fable attitude of many adolescents that their feelings and experiences are unique and have never been experienced by anyone else before

personality-type theory view proposed by Holland that people find their work fulfilling when the important features of a job or profession fit the workers' personalities

phenotype physical, behavioural, and psychological features that result from the interaction between one's genes and the environment

phenylketonuria (PKU) inherited disorder in which the infant lacks a liver enzyme

phonemes unique speech sounds that can be used to create words

pincer grasp occurs when the thumb is used in opposition to the fingers

placenta structure through which nutrients and wastes are exchanged between the mother and the developing child

plasticity the fact that abilities can be modified by certain conditions or experiences

polygenic inheritance when phenotypes are the result of the combined activity of many separate genes

population broad group of people that are the focus of research (we refer to the study population)

population pyramid graphic technique used by demographers to illustrate population trends

positron emission tomography (PET-scan) procedure that shows the amount of activity in various regions of the brain by monitoring levels of radioactive glucose

possible selves projecting what we could become, what we would like to become, and what we are afraid of becoming

postconventional level third level of reasoning in Kohlberg's theory, in which morality is based on a personal moral code

postformal thought   thought characterized by the realization that the correct answer may vary from situation to situation, that problem solutions must be realistic, that most situations are ambiguous, and that emotion and other subjective factors are an important part of thought

postmenopause   the time following completion of menopause

practical intelligence   skills and knowledge necessary for people to function in everyday life

preconventional level   first level of reasoning in Kohlberg's theory, where moral reasoning is based on external forces

prejudice   a view of other people, usually negative, that is based on their membership in a specific group

prenatal development   the many changes that turn a fertilized egg into a newborn human

presbycusis   loss in the ability to hear high-pitched tones

presbyopia   difficulty in seeing close objects clearly, caused by the inability of the lens to focus as the muscles around it stiffen

preterm (premature)   babies born before the 36th week after conception

primary circular reaction   according to Piaget, when infants accidentally produce pleasant events that are centred on the body and then try to re-create the events

primary mental abilities   groups of related intellectual skills, such as spatial skill and mathematical skill

primary sex characteristics   physical signs of maturity directly linked to the reproductive organs

primitive reflexes   a newborn's involuntary, automatic reflexes that disappear in the first few weeks

private speech   comments that are not intended for others but serve the purpose of helping children regulate their behaviour

proactivity   when people choose new behaviours to meet new desires or needs

processes of thinking   information processing, memory, fluid intelligence

products of thinking   products applied to thinking, expertise

programmed cell death theories   theories that suggest that aging is genetically programmed

propositions   ideas derived by combining words

prosocial behaviour   any behaviour that benefits another person

proximodistal   a pattern of growth from inward to outward

psychodynamic theories   theories in which human behaviour is said to be guided by motives and drives that are internal and often unconscious

psychological forces   all internal perceptual, cognitive, emotional, and personality factors that affect development

psychometricians   psychologists who specialize in measuring psychological traits such as intelligence and personality

psychomotor speed   speed with which a person makes a particular response

psychosocial theory   theory proposed by Erik Erikson in which personality development results from the interaction of maturation and societal demands

puberty   collection of physical changes that marks the onset of adolescence, such as growth of breasts or testes and the growth spurt

punishment   applying an aversive stimulus (e.g., a time-out) or removing an attractive stimulus (e.g., TV viewing)

purpose   according to Erikson, balance between individual initiative and the willingness to cooperate with others

qualitative study   a study in which researchers look in-depth at experiences and processes, usually of a relatively small group of subjects about which very little is known

rapid eye movement (REM) sleep   sleep in which a person's eyes dart rapidly beneath the eyelids

reaction range   a genotype is manifested in reaction to the environment where development takes place, so a single genotype can lead to a range of phenotypes

recall   the ability to replicate something from one's memory

recessive   allele whose instructions are ignored when it is combined with a dominant allele

recognition   the ability to recognize something previously encountered

reflective judgment   reasoning about dilemmas that is characterized by the realization that the search for truth is an ongoing, never-ending journey

reflexes   unlearned responses triggered by specific stimulation

regular (nonREM) sleep   sleep in which heart rate, breathing, and brain activity are steady

reinforcement   consequence that increases the likelihood that a behaviour will be repeated in the future

reinvolvement with personal past   meaning grandparents derive from recalling the relationship they had with their own grandparents

relational aggression   aggression used to hurt others by undermining their social relationships

reliability   as applied to tests, when test scores are consistent from one testing time to another

resistant attachment   relationship in which, after a brief separation, infants want to be held but are difficult to console

retinal disparity   way to infer depth based on differences in the retinal images in the left and right eyes

reversibility   point at which children realize that important characteristics of objects (or sets of objects) stay the same despite changes in their physical appearance

rheumatoid arthritis   a more destructive joint disease than osteoarthritis that develops slowly and affects joints, causing stiffness and pain

rites of passage   initiation rituals that mark the onset of a new phase of development, such as adulthood

role transitions   assuming new responsibilities and duties when a person moves from one phase of development (e.g., adolescence) to another (e.g., adulthood)

sample   subset of a population

sandwich generation   middle-aged adults between two generations (their parents and children) that put demands and pressures on them

savants individuals with intellectual impairment who are extremely talented in one domain

scaffolding teaching style in which adults adjust the amount of assistance that they offer, based on the learner's needs

scenario life-span construct that consists of expectations about the future

scheme according to Piaget, a mental structure that organizes information and regulates behaviour

secondary circular reaction according to Piaget, when infants accidentally produce interesting events with objects and then try to repeat those events

secondary mental abilities broad categories of related primary mental abilities

secondary sex characteristics physical signs of maturity not directly linked to reproductive organs

secure attachment relationship in which infants have come to trust and depend on their mothers

selective attention the selection of relevant information for further processing and inhibition of irrelevant information

selective optimization with compensation (SOC) a model of successful adaptation to aging that emphasizes selection of goals, followed by efforts to maintain or enhance those chosen goals

selective serotonin reuptake inhibitors (SSRIs) type of medication used to treat depression that alters the balance of serotonin in the brain

self-efficacy belief that one is capable of performing a certain task

self-reports people's answers to questions about the topic of interest

semantic memory the general class of memory concerning the remembering of meanings of words or concepts

sensorimotor period first of Piaget's four stages of cognitive development, which lasts from birth to approximately 2 years

sequential design complex research design consisting of multiple cross-sectional or longitudinal designs

serotonin neurotransmitter that regulates brain centres to allow people to experience pleasure

sex chromosomes 23rd pair of chromosomes; these determine the sex of the child

sex discrimination denying a job to someone solely on the basis of whether the person is a man or woman

sickle-cell trait disorder in which individuals only show signs of mild anemia when they are seriously deprived of oxygen; occurs in individuals who have one dominant allele for normal blood cells and one recessive sickle-cell allele

simple social play occurs when toddlers engage in similar activities and talk or smile at one another

skill acquisition the gradual, somewhat haphazard process by which people learn new abilities

sleeping state in which a baby alternates from being still and breathing regularly to moving gently and breathing irregularly and in which the eyes are closed throughout

sociability dimension of temperament defined by preference for being with other people

social clock when adults associate future events with a time or age by which they expect to complete them

social cognitive flexibility a person's skill in solving social problems with relevant social knowledge

social cognitive theory view that thinking, as well as direct reinforcement and punishment, plays an important part in shaping behaviour

social contract characteristic of Kohlberg's Stage 5, in which moral reasoning is based on the belief that laws are for the good of all members of society

social convoy group of people who journey together throughout their lives and provide each other support in good and bad times

social referencing behaviour in which infants in unfamiliar or ambiguous environments often look at their mother or father, as if searching for cues to help them interpret the situation

social role set of cultural guidelines about how one should behave, especially with other people

social smiles smile that infants produce when they see a human face

social system morality characteristic of Kohlberg's Stage 4, in which moral reasoning is based on maintenance of order in society

socialization teaching children the values, roles, and behaviours of their culture

sociocultural forces all interpersonal, societal, cultural, and ethnic factors that influence development

socioemotional selectivity way of maintaining social contact that is motivated by many goals, including information seeking, self-concept, and emotional regulation

somatic symptoms changes related to the climacteric and menopause unrelated to changes in estrogen, such as difficulties sleeping, headaches, rapid heartbeat, and stiffness or soreness in the joints, neck, or shoulders

spaced retrieval memory intervention that involves teaching persons with Alzheimer disease to remember new information by gradually increasing the time between retrieval attempts

specification second phase in Super's theory of career development, in which adolescents learn more about specific lines of work and begin training

spermarche first spontaneous ejaculation of sperm

spina bifida disorder in which the embryo's neural tube does not close properly

spiritual support type of coping in which people seek pastoral care, participate in organized and nonorganized religious activities, and express faith in a God who cares for people

stable-order principle counting principle that states that number names must always be counted in the same order

stagnation according to Erikson, a state in which people are not able to deal with the needs of their children or are unable to provide mentoring to younger adults

stereotypes a special type of social knowledge structure or social belief representing organized prior knowledge about a group of people that affects how we interpret new information

stranger wariness first distinct signs of fear that emerge around 6 months of age when infants become wary in the presence of unfamiliar adults

stress and coping paradigm dominant framework used to study stress

stress physical and psychological responses to threatening or challenging conditions

strokes interruption in the flow of blood in the brain due to a blockage in a cerebral artery

structured observations setting created by a researcher that is particularly likely to elicit the behaviour of interest so that it can be observed

subjective well-being a positive evaluation of one's life associated with positive feelings

sudden infant death syndrome (SIDS) situation in which a healthy baby dies suddenly, for no apparent reason

survival reflexes reflexes, such as coughing, that are present in newborns and are important for survival

synaptic pruning gradual reduction in the number of synapses, beginning in infancy and continuing until early adolescence

systematic observation involves watching people and carefully recording what they say or do

telegraphic speech speech used by young children that contains only the words that are necessary to get a message across

telomeres tips of the chromosomes, which apparently play a major role in limiting the number of times a cell can divide before dying

temperament consistent style or pattern of behaviour

teratogen agent that causes abnormal prenatal development

terminal buttons small knobs at the end of the axon that release neurotransmitters

tertiary circular reaction according to Piaget, repeating old schemes with new objects

theory organized set of ideas that explains development

theory of mind ideas about connections between thoughts, beliefs, intentions, and behaviour

toddlers young children who have learned to walk

toddling early, unsteady form of walking done by infants

transient ischemic attacks (TIAs) an interruption of blood flow to the brain that often is an early warning sign of stroke

triarchic theory Sternberg's three-part theory of the different elements of intelligence

Type A behaviour pattern ongoing displays of intense competitiveness, anger, hostility, restlessness, aggression, and impatience

Type B behaviour pattern ongoing displays of noncompetitiveness, calm, lack of aggression, and patience

ulnar grasp an almost clawlike grasp that permits very little manipulation

ultrasound prenatal diagnostic technique that bounces sound waves off the fetus to generate an image of the fetus

umbilical cord structure containing veins and arteries that connects the developing child to the placenta

underextension when children define words more narrowly than adults do

unexercised ability level of performance a person exhibits without practice or training

universal ethical principles characteristic of Kohlberg's Stage 6, in which moral reasoning is based on moral principles that apply to all

universal versus context-specific development issue issue of whether there is one path of development or several

useful life expectancy number of years a person has that are free from debilitating chronic disease and impairment

validity as applied to tests, the extent to which the test measures what it is supposed to measure

valued elder status grandparents derive from being seen as wise

vascular dementia disease caused by numerous small cerebrovascular accidents

vernix substance that protects the fetus's skin during development

very low birth weight weight of less than 1,500 grams (3 pounds) in a newborn

vigilance the maintenance of attention over time; also called sustained attention

visual acuity smallest pattern that one can distinguish reliably

visual cliff glass-covered platform that appears to have a "shallow" side and "deep" side; used to study infants' depth perception

vocational maturity degree of congruity between a person's age and occupational behaviours

waking activity state in which a baby's eyes are open but seem unfocused and the arms or legs move in bursts of uncoordinated motion

wear-and-tear theory theory of aging that suggests that the body, much like a machine, gradually deteriorates over time and finally wears out

will according to Erikson, a young child's understanding that he or she can act on the world intentionally, which occurs when autonomy, shame, and doubt are in balance

word recognition the process of identifying a unique pattern of letters

work-family conflict feeling of being pulled in multiple directions by incompatible demands from one's job and one's family

working memory type of memory in which a small number of items can be stored briefly

zone of maximum comfort in environmental press theory, the area where slight decreases in press allow people to live happily without worrying about environmental demands

zone of maximum performance potential in environmental press theory, the area in which slight increases in press tend to improve performance

zone of proximal development difference between what children can do with assistance and what they can do alone

zygote fertilized egg

REFERENCES

AARP. (1999). AARP/Modern Maturity sexuality survey: Summary of findings [Online]. Available: http://www.aarp.org/mmaturity/sept_oct99/greatsex.html.

Abengozar, M. C., Bueno, B., & Vega, J. L. (1999). Intervention on attitudes toward death along the life span. *Educational Gerontology, 25,* 435–447.

Aboud, F. E. (1993). The developmental psychology of racial prejudice. *Transcultural Psychiatric Research Review, 30,* 229–242.

Abraham, M. (2000). Isolation as a form of marital violence: The South Asian immigrant experience. *Journal of Social Distress and the Homeless, 9,* 221–236.

Abraham, R. (2000). Organizational cynicism: Bases and consequences. *Genetic, Social, and General Psychology Monographs, 126,* 269–292.

Ackerman, B. P. (1993). Children's understanding of the speaker's meaning in referential communication. *Journal of Experimental Child Psychology, 55,* 56–86.

Acock, A. C., & Demo, D. H. (1994). *Family diversity and well-being.* Thousand Oaks, CA: Sage.

Adamczyk-Robinette, S. L., Fletcher, A. C., & Wright, K. (2002). Understand-ing the authoritative parenting–early adolescent tobacco use link: The mediating role of peer tobacco use. *Journal of Youth & Adolescence, 31,* 311–318.

Adams, J. (1999). On neurodevelopmental disorders: Perspectives from neurobehavioral teratology. In H. Tager-Flusberg (Ed.), *Neurodevelopmental disorders* (pp. 451–468). Cambridge, MA: MIT.

Adams, M. J., Treiman, R., & Pressley, M. (1998). Reading, writing, and literacy. In W. Damon (Ed.), *Handbook of child psychology* (Vol. 4). New York: Wiley.

Adams, R. G., Blieszner, R., & de Vries, B. (2000). Definitions of friendship in the third age: Age, gender, and study location effects. *Journal of Aging Studies, 14,* 117–133.

Adams, R. J. (1995). Further exploration of human neonatal chromatic-achromatic discrimination. *Journal of Experimental Child Psychology, 60,* 344–360.

Adams, R. J., & Courage, M. L. (1995). Development of chromatic discrimination in early infancy. *Behavioural Brain Research, 67,* 99–101.

Adler, L. L. (2001). Women and gender roles. In L. L. Adler & U. P. Gielen (Eds.), *Cross-cultural topics on psychology* (2nd ed.; pp. 103–114). Westport, CT: Praeger/Greenwood.

Adler, N. (1994). *Adolescent sexual behavior looks irrational—But looks are deceiving.* Washington, DC: Federation of Behavioral, Psychological, and Cognitive Sciences.

Adlersberg, M., & Thorne, S. (1990). Emerging from the chrysalis: Older women in transition. *Journal of Gerontological Social Work, 16,* 4–8.

Adolph, K. E. (1997). Learning in the development of infant locomotion. *Monographs of the Society for Research in Child Development, 62,* 1–140.

Adolph, K. E. (2000). Specificity of learning: Why infants fall over a veritable cliff. *Psychological Science, 11,* 290–295.

Adolph, K. E. (2002). Learning to keep balance. In R. V. Kail (Ed.), *Advances in child development and behavior* (Vol. 30). Orlando, FL: Academic Press.

Adolph, K. E., Eppler, M. A., & Gibson, E. J. (1993). Crawling versus walking infants' perception of affordances for locomotion over sloping surfaces. *Child Development, 64,* 1158–1174.

Adolph, K. E., Vereijken, B., & Denny, M. A. (1998). Learning to crawl. *Child Development, 69,* 1299–1312.

Ainsworth, M. D. S. (1978). The development of infant-mother attachment. In B. M. Caldwell & H. N. Ricciuti (Eds.), *Review of child development research* (Vol. 3). Chicago: University of Chicago Press.

Ainsworth, M. S. (1993). Attachment as related to mother-infant interaction. *Advances in Infancy Research, 8,* 1–50.

Ajrouch, K. J., Antonucci, T. C., & Janevic, M. (2000). Social networks among blacks and whites: The interaction between race and age. *Journal of Gerontology: Social Sciences, 56B,* S112–S118.

Akhtar, N., Jipson, J., & Callanan, M. (2001). Learning words through overhearing. *Child Development, 72,* 416–430.

Albeck, S., & Kaydar, D. (2002). Divorced mothers: Their network of friends pre- and post-divorce. *Journal of Divorce and Remarriage, 36,* 111–118.

Albert, M. S., & Killiany, R. J. (2001). Age-related cognitive change and brain-behavior relationships. In J. E. Birren & K. W. Schaie (Eds.), *Handbook of the psychology of aging* (5th ed., pp. 161–185). San Diego, CA: Academic Press.

Aldwin, C. M., & Gilmer, D. F. (1999). Immunity, disease processes, and optimal aging. In J. C. Cavanaugh & S. K. Whitbourne (Eds.), *Gerontology: Interdisciplinary perspectives* (pp. 123–154). New York: Oxford University Press.

Alexander, J. F., Waldron, H. B., Barton, C., & Mas, C. H. (1989). The minimizing of blaming attributes and behaviors in delinquent families. *Journal of Consulting and Clinical Psychology, 57,* 19–24.

Allaire, J. C., & Marsiske, M. (1999). Everyday cognition: Age and intellectual ability correlates. *Psychology and Aging, 14,* 627–644.

Allen, K. R., & Chin-sang, V. (1990). A lifetime of work: The context and meanings of leisure for aging black women. *The Gerontologist, 30,* 734–740.

Allen, M. C. (1984). Developmental outcome and follow-up of the small for gestational age infant. *Seminars in Perinatology, 8,* 123–156.

Allen, T. D. (2001). Family-supportive work environments: The role of organizational perceptions. *Journal of Vocational Behavior, 58,* 414–435.

Allgeier, A. R., & Allgeier, E. R. (1995). *Sexual interactions* (4th ed.). Lexington, MA: Heath.

Alwin, D. F. (1994). Aging, personality, and social change: The stability of individual differences over the adult life span. In D. L. Featherman, R. M. Lerner, & M. Perlmutter (Eds.), *Life-span development and behavior* (Vol. 12, pp. 135–185). Hillsdale, NJ: Erlbaum.

Alzheimer Society of Canada. (2004). *Research update.* [Online]. Available: http://www.Alzheimer.ca/english/research/update04.htm. (Retrieved April 25, 2004.)

Aman, C. J., Roberts, R. J., & Pennington, B. F. (1998). A neuropsychological examination of the underlying deficit in attention deficit hyperactivity disorder: Frontal lobe versus right parietal lobe theories. *Developmental Psychology, 34,* 956–969.

Amato, P. R. (2001). Children of divorce in the 1990s: An update of the Amato and Keith (1991) meta-analysis. *Journal of Family Psychology, 15,* 355–370.

Amato, P. R., & Keith, B. (1991). Parental divorce and the well-being of children: A meta-analysis. *Psychological Bulletin, 110,* 26–46.

Ambert, A. (2002). Divorce: Facts, causes and consequences. In The Vanier Institute of the Family, *Contemporary family trends.* Ottawa, ON: Author.

Anand, K. J., & Hickey, P. R. (1987). Pain and its effect in the human neonate and fetus. *New England Journal of Medicine, 31,* 1321–1329.

Anastasi, A. (1988). *Psychological testing* (6th ed.). New York: Macmillan.

Andersen, A. M. N., Wohlfahrt, J., Christens, P., Olsen, J., & Melbye, M. (2000). Maternal age and fetal loss: Population based register linkage study. *British Medical Journal, 320,* 1708–1712.

Anderson, C. A., & Bushman, B. J. (2001). Effects of violent video games on aggressive behavior, aggressive cognition, aggressive affect, physiological arousal, and prosocial behavior: A meta-analytic review of the scientific literature. *Psychological Science, 12,* 353–359.

Anderson, D. R., Huston, A. C., Schmitt, K. L., Linebarger, D. L., & Wright, J. C. (2001). Early childhood television viewing and adolescent behavior. *Monographs of the Society for Research in Child Development, 66.*

Anderson, E. R., Greene, S. M., Hetherington, E. M., & Clingempeel, W. G. (1999). The dynamics of parental remarriage: Adolescent, parent, and sibling. In E. M. Hetherington (Ed.). *Coping with divorce, single parenting, and remarriage: A risk and resiliency perspective.* Mahwah, NJ: Erlbaum.

Anderson, S. W., Damasio, H., Tranel, D., & Damasio, A. R. (2001). Long-term sequelae of prefrontal cortex damage acquired in early childhood. *Developmental Neuropsychology, 18,* 281–296.

Anderson, W. T. (1997). Dying and death in aging intergenerational families. In T. D. Hargrave & S. M. Hanna (Eds.), *The aging family* (pp. 270–291). New York: Brunner/Mazel.

Andrews, J. A., Hops, H., & Duncan, S. C. (1997). Adolescent modeling of parent substance abuse: The moderating effect of the relationship with the parent. *Journal of Family Psychology, 11,* 259–270.

Anglin, J. M. (1993). Vocabulary development: A morphological analysis. *Monographs of the Society for Research in Child Development, 58* (10, Serial No. 238).

Anisfeld, M. (1991). Neonatal imitation. *Developmental Review, 11,* 60–97.

Anisfeld, M. (1996). Only tongue protrusion modeling is matched by neonates. *Developmental Review, 16,* 149–161.

Antonarakis, S. E., & The Down Syndrome Collaborative Group. (1991). Parental origin of the extra chromosome in trisomy 21 as indicated by analysis of DNA polymorphisms. *New England Journal of Medicine, 324,* 872–876.

Antonovsky, A., & Sagy, S. (1990). Confronting developmental tasks in the retirement transition. *The Gerontologist, 30,* 362–368.

Antonucci, T. (2001). Social relations: An examination of social networks, social support, and sense of control. In J. E. Birren & K. W. Schaie (Eds.), *Handbook of the psychology of aging* (5th ed., pp. 427–453). San Diego: Academic Press.

Antonucci, T. C., Akiyama, H., & Lansford, J. E. (1998). Negative effects of close social relations. *Family Relations, 47,* 379–384.

Apgar, V. (1953). A proposal for a new method of evaluation of the newborn infant. *Current Researches in Anesthesia and Analgesia, 32,* 260–267.

Appleton, M., & Henschell, T. (1995). *At home with terminal illness: A family guide to hospice in the home.* Englewood Cliffs, NJ: Prentice Hall.

Apter, T. (2001). *The myth of maturity: What teenagers need from parents to become adults.* New York: Norton.

Archer, N., & Bryant, P. (2001). Investigating the role of context in learning to read: A direct test of Goodman's model. *British Journal of Psychology, 92,* 579–591.

Arcus, D., & Kagan, J. (1995). Temperament and craniofacial variation in the first two years. *Child Development, 66,* 1529–1540.

Arellano, L. M. (2001). The psychological experiences of Latina professionals. *Dissertation Abstracts International Section B: The Sciences and Engineering, 62(1-B),* 534.

Arendell, T. (1995). *Fathers and divorce.* Thousand Oaks, CA: Sage.

Arenofsky, J. (1993, February 8). Childless and proud of it. *Newsweek,* 12.

Arnett, J., & Taber, S. (1994). Adolescence terminable and interminable: When does adolescence end? *Journal of Youth and Adolescence, 23*, 517–537.

Arseneault, L., Tremblay, R. E., Boulerice, B., & Saucier, J. F. (2002). Obstetrical complications and violent delinquency: Testing two developmental pathways. *Child Development, 73*, 496–508.

Aryee, S. (1993). Dual-earner couples in Singapore: An examination of work and nonwork sources of their experienced burnout. *Human Relations, 46*, 1441–1468.

Aryee, S., & Luk, V. (1996). Work and nonwork influences on the career satisfaction of dual-earner couples. *Journal of Vocational Behavior, 49*, 38–52.

Aseltine, R. H., Jr., & Gore, S. L. (2000). The variable effects of stress on alcohol use from adolescence to early adulthood. *Substance Use and Misuse, 35*, 643–668.

Ashcraft, M. H. (1982). The development of mental arithmetic: A chronometric approach. *Developmental Review, 2*, 212–236.

Aslin, R. N., Jusczyk, P. W., & Pisoni, D. B. (1998). Speech and auditory processing during infancy: Constraints on and precursors to language. In W. Damon (Ed.), *Handbook of child psychology* (Vol. 2). New York: Wiley.

Aslin, R. N., Saffran, J. R., & Newport, W. L. (1998). Computation of conditional probability statistics by 8-month-old infants. *Psychological Science, 9*, 321–324.

Atchley, R. C. (1982). Retirement as a social institution. *American Review of Sociology, 8*, 263–287.

Atchley, R. C. (1989). A continuity theory of normal aging. *The Gerontologist, 29*, 183–190.

Ateah, C., & Durrant, J. E. (in press). Maternal use of physical punishment in response to child misbehavior: Implications for child abuse prevention. *International Journal of Child Abuse and Neglect.*

Ateah, C. A., Durrant, J. E., & Mirwaldt, J. (2004). Physical punishment and physical abuse of children: Strategies for prevention. In C. A. Ateah & J. Mirwaldt (Eds.), *Within our reach: Preventing abuse across the lifespan.* Halifax, NS: Fernwood Publishing and RESOLVE (Research and Education for Solutions to Violence and Abuse).

Atkinson, M. (1992). *Children's syntax.* Cambridge, MA: Blackwell.

Attig, T. (1996). *How we grieve: Relearning the world.* New York: Oxford University Press.

Atwater, E. (1992). *Adolescence.* Englewood Cliffs, NJ: Prentice Hall.

Au, T. K., & Glusman, M. (1990). The principle of mutual exclusivity in word learning: To honor or not to honor? *Child Development, 61*, 1474–1490.

Bachman, J. (1983, Summer). Premature affluence: Do high school students earn too much? *Economic Outlook USA*, 64–67.

Bachman, J. G., & Schulenberg, J. (1993). How part-time work intensity relates to drug use, problem behavior, time use, and satisfaction among high school seniors: Are these consequences or merely correlates? *Developmental Psychology, 29*, 229–230.

Bäckman, L., Small, B. J., & Wahlin, Å. (2001). Aging and memory: Cognitive and biological processes. In J. E. Birren & K. W. Schaie (Eds.), *Handbook of the psychology of aging* (5th ed., pp. 349–377).

Backscheider, A. G., Shatz, M., & Gelman, S. A. (1993). Preschoolers' ability to distinguish living kinds as a function of regrowth. *Child Development, 64*, 1242–1257.

Baer, D. M., & Wolf, M. M. (1968). The reinforcement contingency in preschool and remedial education. In R. D. Hess & R. M. Baer (Eds.), *Early education.* Chicago: Aldine.

Bagwell, C. L., Newcomb, A. F., & Bukowski, W. M. (1998). Preadolescent friendship and peer rejection as predictors of adult adjustment. *Child Development, 69*, 140–153.

Bahrick, L. E., & Lickliter, R. (2000). Intersensory redundancy guides attentional selectivity and perceptual learning in infancy. *Developmental Psychology, 36*, 190–201.

Bahrick, L. E., & Lickliter, R. (2002). Intersensory redundancy guides early perceptual and cognitive development. In R. V. Kail (Ed.), *Advances in child development and behavior* (Vol. 30). Orlando, FL: Academic Press.

Bailey, J. M., Bobrow, D., Wolfe, M., & Mikach, S. (1995). Sexual orientation of adult sons of gay fathers. *Developmental Psychology, 31*, 124–129.

Bailey, J. M., Dunne, M. P., & Martin, N. G. (2000). Genetic and environmental influences on sexual orientation and its correlates in an Austrian twin sample. *Journal of Personality and Social Psychology, 78*, 524–436.

Baillargeon, R. (1987). Object permanence in 3 1/2- and 4 1/2-month-old infants. *Developmental Psychology, 23*, 655–664.

Baillargeon, R. (1994). How do infants learn about the physical world? *Current Directions in Psychological Science, 3*, 133–140.

Baillargeon, R. (1998). Infants' understanding of the physical world. *Advances in Psychological Science, 2*, 503–529.

Baker, L. (1994). Fostering metacognitive development. In H. W. Reese (Ed.), *Advances in child development and behavior* (Vol. 25). San Diego, CA: Academic Press.

Baker, L., & Brown, A. L. (1984). Metacognitive skills and reading. In P. D. Pearson (Ed.), *Handbook of reading research* (Part 2). New York: Longman.

Baker, T. B. (1988). Models of addiction. *Journal of Abnormal Psychology, 97*, 115–117.

Baldwin, D. A., Markman, E. M., Bill, B., Desjardins, R. N., & Irwin, J. M. (1996). Infants' reliance on a social criterion for establishing word-object relations. *Child Development, 67*, 3135–3153.

Balk, D. E. (1996). Attachment and the reactions of bereaved college students: A longitudinal study. In D. Klass, P. R. Silverman, & S. L. Nickman (Eds.), *Continuing bonds: New understandings of grief* (pp. 311–328). Washington, DC: Taylor & Francis.

Balk, D. E., & Corr, C. A. (2001). Bereavement during adolescence: A review of research. In M. S. Stroebe, R. O. Hansson, W. Stroebe, & H. Schut (Eds.), *Handbook of bereavement research: Consequences, coping, and care* (pp. 169–197). Washington, DC: American Psychological Association.

Ball, K. (1997). Enhancing mobility in the elderly: Attentional interventions for driving. In S. M. C. Dollinger & L. F. Dilalla (Eds.), *Assessment and intervention issues across the lifespan* (pp. 267–292). Mahwah, NJ: Erlbaum.

Ball, K., & Owsley, C. (1993). The Useful Field of View Test: A new technique for evaluating age-related declines in visual function. *Journal of the American Optometric Association, 64,* 71–79.

Ball, K., Owsley, C., Sloane, M. E., Roenker, D. L., & Bruni, J. R. (1993). Visual attention problems as a predictor of vehicle accidents among older drivers. *Investigative Ophthalmology and Visual Science, 34*(11), 3110–3123.

Baltes, M. M., & Carstensen, L. L. (1999). Social-psychological theories and their applications to aging: From individual to collective. In V. L. Bengtson & K. W. Schaie (Eds.), *Handbook of theories of aging* (pp. 209–226). New York: Springer.

Baltes, P. B. (1987). Theoretical propositions of life-span developmental psychology: On the dynamics between growth and decline. *Developmental Psychology, 23,* 611–626.

Baltes, P. B. (1993). The aging mind: Potential and limits. *The Gerontologist, 33,* 580–594.

Baltes, P. B. (1997). On the incomplete architecture of human ontogeny: Selection, optimization, and compensation as foundation of developmental theory. *American Psychologist, 52,* 366–380.

Baltes, P. B., Lindenberger, U., & Staudinger, U. M. (1998). Lifespan theory in developmental psychology. In R. M. Lerner (Ed.), *Handbook of child psychology, Vol. 1. Theoretical models of human development* (5th ed., pp. 1029–1143). New York: Wiley.

Baltes, P. B., & Smith, J. (2002, April). *New frontiers in the future of aging: From successful aging of the young old to the dilemmas of the fourth age.* Paper presented at the Valencia Forum: An International Scientific Congress, Valencia, Spain.

Baltes, P. B., & Staudinger, U. M. (1993). The search for a psychology of wisdom. *Current Directions in Psychological Science, 2,* 75–80.

Baltes, P. B., & Staudinger, U. M. (2000). Wisdom: A meta-heuristic (pragmatic) to orchestrate mind and virtue toward excellence. *American Psychologist, 55,* 122–136.

Baltes, P. B., Staudinger, U. M., & Lindenberger, U. (1999). Lifespan psychology: Theory and application to intellectual functioning. *Annual Review of Psychology, 50,* 471–507.

Bandura, A. (1977). *Social learning theory.* Englewood Cliffs, NJ: Prentice Hall.

Bandura, A. (1986). *Social foundations of thought and action: A social-cognitive theory.* Englewood Cliffs, NJ: Prentice Hall.

Bandura, A., Ross, D., & Ross, S. A. (1963). Imitation of film-mediated aggressive models. *Journal of Abnormal and Social Psychology, 66,* 3–11.

Barenboim, C. (1981). The development of person perception in childhood and adolescence: From behavioral comparisons to psychological constructs to psychological comparisons. *Child Development, 52,* 129–144.

Bargh, J. A., Chaiken, S., Raymond, P., & Hymes, C. (1996). The automatic evaluation effect: Unconditional automatic attitude activation with a pronunciation task. *Journal of Experimental Psychology, 32,* 104–128.

Barinaga, M. (1997). Researchers find signals that guide young brain neurons. *Science, 278,* 385–386.

Barkley, R. A. (1990). Attention deficit disorders: History, definition, and diagnosis. In M. Lewis & S. M. Miller (Eds.), *Handbook of developmental psychopathology.* New York: Plenum.

Barkley, R. A. (1994). Impaired delayed responding: A unified theory of attention-deficit hyperactivity disorder. In R. A. Barkley (Ed.), *Disruptive behavior disorders in childhood.* New York: Plenum.

Barkley, R. A. (1996). Attention-deficit hyperactivity disorder. In E. J. Mash & R. A. Barkley (Eds.), *Child psychopathology.* New York: Guilford Press.

Barr, R., & Hayne, H. (1999). Developmental changes in imitation from television during infancy. *Child Development, 70,* 1067–1081.

Barrett, A. E., & Lynch, S. M. (1999). Caregiving networks of elderly persons: Variation by marital status. *The Gerontologist, 39,* 695–704.

Bartsch, K., & Wellman, H. M. (1995). *Children talk about the mind.* New York: Oxford University Press.

Baskett, L. M. (1985). Sibling status effects: Adult expectations. *Developmental Psychology, 21,* 441–445.

Basso, K. H. (1970). *The Cibecue Apache.* New York: Holt, Rinehart, & Winston.

Bates, J. E., Pettie, G. S., Dodge, K. A., & Ridge, B. (1998). Interaction of temperamental resistance to control and restrictive parenting in the development of externalizing behavior. *Developmental Psychology, 34,* 982–995.

Bauer, P. J., Burch, M. M., & Kleinknecht, E. F. (2002). Developments in early recall memory: Normative trends and individual differences. In R. V. Kail (Ed.), *Advances in child development and behavior* (Vol. 30). San Diego, CA: Academic Press.

Baugh, S. G., Lankau, M. J., & Scandura, T. A. (1996). An investment of the effects of protégé gender on responses to mentoring. *Journal of Vocational Behavior, 49,* 309–323.

Baumeister, A. A., & Baumeister, A. A. (1995). Mental retardation. In M. Hersen & R. T. Ammerman (Eds.), *Advanced abnormal child psychology.* Hillsdale, NJ: Erlbaum.

Baumrind, D. (1975). *Early socialization and the discipline controversy.* Morristown, NJ: General Learning Press.

Baumrind, D. (1991). Parenting styles and adolescent development. In R. M. Lerner, A. C. Petersen, & J. Brooks-Gunn (Eds.), *Encyclopedia of adolescence.* New York: Garland.

Bauserman, R. (2002). Child adjustment in joint-custody versus sole-custody arrangements: A meta-analytic review. *Journal of Family Psychology, 16,* 91–102.

Beal, C. R. (1996). The role of comprehension monitoring in children's revision. *Educational Psychology Review, 8,* 219–238.

Beal, C. R., & Belgrad, S. L. (1990). The development of message evaluation skills in young children. *Child Development, 61,* 705–712.

Beck, A. T. (1967). *Depression: Clinical, experimental, and theoretical aspects.* New York: Harper & Row.

Beck, A. T., Rush, J., Shaw, B., & Emery, G. (1979). *Cognitive therapy of depression.* New York: Guilford Press.

Becker, B. J. (1986). Influence again: An examination of reviews and studies of gender differences in social influence. In J. S. Hyde & M. C. Linn (Eds.), *The psychology of gender differences. Advances through meta-analysis.* Baltimore, MD: Johns Hopkins University Press.

Behnke, M., & Eyler, F. D. (1993). The consequences of prenatal substance use for the developing fetus, newborn, and young child. *International Journal of the Addictions, 28,* 1341–1391.

Behrend, D. A., Rosengren, K. S., & Perlmutter, M. S. (1992). The relation between private speech and parental interactive style. In R. M. Diaz & L. E. Berk (Eds.), *Private speech: From social interaction to self-regulation* (pp. 85–100). Hillsdale, NJ: Erlbaum.

Bell, A. P., Weinberg, M. S., & Hammersmith, S. K. (1981). *Sexual preference: Its development in men and women.* New York: Simon & Schuster.

Beller, M., & Gafni, N. (1996). The 1991 international assessment of educational progress in mathematics and sciences: The gender differences perspective. *Journal of Educational Psychology, 88,* 365–377.

Belsky, J. (1993). Etiology of child maltreatment: A developmental-ecological analysis. *Psychological Bulletin, 114,* 413–434.

Belsky, J. (1996). Parent, infant, and social-contextual antecedents of father-son attachment security. *Developmental Psychology, 32,* 905–913.

Belsky, J., Fish, M., & Isabella, R. A. (1991). Continuity and discontinuity in infant negative and positive emotionality: Family antecedents and attachment consequences. *Developmental Psychology, 27,* 421–431.

Belsky, J., Steinberg, L., & Draper, P. (1991). Childhood experience, interpersonal development, and reproductive strategy: An evolutionary theory of socialization. *Child Development, 62,* 647–670.

Belsky, J., Woodworth, S., & Crnic, K. (1996). Trouble in the second year: Three questions about family interaction. *Child Development, 67,* 556–578.

Bem, D. J. (1996). Exotic becomes erotic: A developmental theory of sexual orientation. *Psychological Review, 103,* 320–335.

Bengtson, V. L., Mills, T. L., & Parrott, T. M. (1995). Ageing in the United States at the end of the century. *Korea Journal of Population and Development, 24,* 215–244.

Benin, M. H., & Agostinelli, J. (1988). Husbands' and wives' satisfaction with the division of labor. *Journal of Marriage and the Family, 50,* 349–361.

Ben-Israel Reuveni, O. (1999). *The effects of time on the adjustment of war bereaved parents: Functioning, relationship and marital adjustment.* Unpublished master's thesis, University of Haifa.

Benokraitis, N. V. (1999). *Marriages and families: Changes, choices, and constraints.* Upper Saddle River, NJ: Prentice Hall.

Benson, J. M. (1999). The polls-trends: End of life issues. *Public Opinion Quarterly, 63,* 263–277.

Benton, S. L., Corkill, A. J., Sharp, J. M., Downey, R. G., et al. (1995). Knowledge, interest, and narrative writing. *Journal of Educational Psychology, 87,* 66–79.

Berdahl, J. L., Magley, V. J., & Waldo, C. R. (1996). The sexual harassment of men? *Psychology of Women Quarterly, 20,* 527–547.

Bereiter, C., & Scardamalia, M. (1987). *The psychology of written composition.* Hillsdale, NJ: Erlbaum.

Bergeman, C. S. (1997). *Aging: Genetic and environmental influences.* Thousand Oaks: Sage.

Berk, L. E. (1992). Children's private speech: An overview of theory and the status of research. In R. M. Diaz & L. E. Berk (Eds.), *Private speech: From social interaction to self-regulation.* Hillsdale, NJ: Erlbaum.

Berk, L. E. (1994). Vygotsky's theory: The importance of make believe play. *Young Children, 50,* 30–38.

Berko, J. (1958). The child's learning of English morphology. *Word, 14,* 150–177.

Berkowitz, M. W., & Gibbs, J. C. (1985). The process of moral conflict resolution and moral development. In M. W. Berkowitz (Ed.), *Peer conflict and psychological growth* (pp. 71–84). San Francisco: Jossey-Bass.

Berliner, A. J. (2000). Re-visiting Erikson's developmental model: The impact of identity crisis resolution on intimacy motive, generativity formation, and psychological adaptation in never-married, middle-aged adults. *Dissertation Abstracts International: Section B: The Sciences and Engineering, 61,* 560.

Berndt, T. J., & Keefe, K. (1995). Friends' influence on adolescents' adjustment to school. *Child Development, 66,* 1312–1329.

Berndt, T. J., & Murphy, L. M. (2002). Influences of friends and friendships: Myths, truths, and research recommendations. *Advances in Child Development and Behavior, 30,* 275–310.

Berndt, T. J., & Perry, T. B. (1990). Distinctive features and effects of adolescent friendships. In R. Montemeyer, G. R. Adams, & T. P. Gullotta (Eds.), *From childhood to adolescence: A transition period?* London: Sage.

Berry, J. W. (1993). Ethnic identities in plural societies. In M. E. Bernal & G. P. Knight (Eds.), *Ethnic identity: Formation and transmission among Hispanics and other minorities.* New York: State University of New York Press.

Bertenthal, B. H., & Clifton, R. K. (1998). Perception and action. In W. Damon (Ed.), *Handbook of child psychology* (Vol. 2). New York: Wiley.

Berthier, N. E. (1996). Learning to reach: A mathematical model. *Developmental Psychology, 32,* 811–823.

Bertrand, R. M., Lachman, M. E., & Tun, P. A. (2000, August). *The effects of menopausal status on cognitive performance.*

Paper presented at the annual meeting of the American Psychological Association, Washington, DC.

Besharov, D. J., & Gardiner, K. N. (1997). Trends in teen sexual behavior. *Children and Youth Services Review, 19,* 341–367.

Bess, I. (1999). Seniors behind the wheel. *Canadian Social Trends.* Autumn, 2–7.

Best, C. T. (1995). Learning to perceive the sound pattern of English. In C. Rovee-Collier (Ed.), Advances in infancy research. Norwood, NJ: Ablex.

Best, D. L. (2001). Gender concepts: Convergence in cross-cultural research and methodologies. *Cross-Cultural Research: The Journal of Comparative Social Science, 35,* 23–43.

Best, D. L., Williams, J. E., Cloud, J. M., Davis, S. W., Robertson, L. S., Edwards, J. R., Giles, H., & Fowles, J. (1977). Development of sex-trait stereotypes among young children in the United States, England, and Ireland. *Child Development, 48,* 1375–1384.

Bettencourt, B. A., & Miller, N. (1996). Gender differences in aggression as a function of provocation: A meta-analysis. *Psychological Bulletin, 119,* 422–447.

Bialystok, E., Majumder, S., & Martin, M. (2003). Developing phonological awareness: Is there a bilingual advantage? *Applied Psycholinguistics, 24,* 27–44.

Bigler, R. S., Jones, L. C., & Lobliner, D. B. (1997). Social categorization and the formation of intergroup attitudes in children. *Child Development, 68,* 530–543.

Bigler, R., Brown, C., & Markell, M. (2001). When groups are not created equal: Effects of group status on the formation of intergroup attitudes in children. *Child Development, 72,* 1151–1162.

Birch, L. L. (1991). Obesity and eating disorders: A developmental perspective. *Bulletin of the Psychonomic Society, 29,* 265–272.

Birch, L. L., & Fisher, J. A. (1995). Appetite and eating behavior in children. *Pediatric Clinics of North America, 42,* 931–953.

Birch, S. A. J., & Bloom, P. (2002). Preschoolers are sensitive to the speaker's knowledge when learning proper names. *Child Development, 73,* 434–444.

Bird, D. J. (2001). The influences and impact of burnout on occupational therapists. *Dissertation Abstracts International Section B: The Sciences and Engineering, 62(1-B),* 204.

Birman, D., & Trickett, E. J. (2001). Cultural transitions in first-generation immigrants: Acculturation of Soviet Jewish refugee adolescents and parents. *Journal of Cross-Cultural Psychology, 32,* 456–477.

Birnholz, J. C., & Benacerraf, B. R. (1983). The development of human fetal hearing. *Science, 222,* 516–518.

Black, S. A., Markides, K. S., & Miller, T. Q. (1998). Correlates of depressive symptomatology among older community-dwelling Mexican Americans: The Hispanic EPESE. *Journal of Gerontology: Social Sciences, 53B,* S198–S208.

Black-Gutman, D., & Hickson, F. (1996). The relationship between racial attitudes and social-cognitive development in children: An Australian study. *Developmental Psychology, 32,* 448–456.

Blake-Beard, S. D. (2001). Taking a hard look at formal mentoring programs: A consideration of potential challenges facing women. *Journal of Management Development, 20,* 331–345.

Blanchard, R. (1997). Birth order and sibling sex ratio in homosexual versus heterosexual males and females. *Annual Review of Sex Research, 8,* 27–67.

Blanchard, R., Zucker, K. J., Siegelman, M., Dickey, R., & Klassen, P. (1998). The relation of birth order to sexual orientation in men and women. *Journal of Biosocial Science, 30,* 511–519.

Blanchard-Fields, F. (1986). Reasoning on social dilemmas varying in emotional saliency: An adult developmental study. *Psychology and Aging, 1,* 325–333.

Blanchard-Fields, F. (1996). Causal attributions across the adult life span: The influence of social schemas, life context, and domain specificity. *Applied Cognitive Psychology, 10* (Spec. Issue) 5137–5146.

Blanchard-Fields, F. (1999). Social schematicity and causal attributions. In T. M. Hess & F. Blanchard-Fields (Eds.), *Social cognition and aging* (pp. 219–236). San Diego, CA: Academic Press.

Blanchard-Fields, F., Baldi, R., & Constantin, L. P. (in preparation). *Interrole conflict across the adult life-span: The role of parenting stage, career stages, and quality of experiences.* School of Psychology, Georgia Institute of Technology.

Blanchard-Fields, F., Chen, Y., & Norris, L. (1997). Everyday problem solving across the adult life span: Influence of domain specificity and cognitive appraisal. *Psychology and Aging, 12,* 684–693.

Blanchard-Fields, F., & Hertzog, C. (2000). Age differences in schematicity. In U. von Hecker, S. Dutke, & G. Sedek (Eds.), *Processes of generative mental representation and psychological adaptation.* Dordrecht, The Netherlands: Kluwer.

Blanchard-Fields, F., Janke, H. C., & Camp, C. J. (1995). Age differences in problem-solving style: The role of emotional salience. *Psychology and Aging, 10,* 173–180.

Blazer, D. G. (2000). Spirituality, aging, and depression. In J. A. Thorson (Ed.), *Perspectives on spiritual well-being and aging* (pp. 161–169). Springfield, IL: Charles C. Thomas.

Block, J. (1995). A contrarian view of the five-factor approach to personality description. *Psychological Bulletin, 117,* 187–215.

Bloom, L. (1991). *Language development from two to three.* Cambridge, UK: Cambridge University Press.

Bloom, L., & Tinker, E. (2001). The intentionality model and language acquisition. *Monographs of the Society for Research in Child Development, 66,* Serial No. 267.

Bogatz, G. A., & Ball, S. (1972). *The second year of "Sesame Street": A continuing evaluation.* Princeton, NJ: Educational Testing Service.

Bohannon, J. N., Padgett, R. J., Nelson, K. E., & Mark, M. (1996). Useful evidence on negative evidence. *Developmental Psychology, 32,* 551–555.

Boivin, M., Vitaro, F., & Gagnon, C. (1992). A reassessment of the self-perception profile for children: Factor structure, reliability, and convergent validity of a French version among second through sixth grade children. *International Journal of Behavioral Development, 15,* 275–290.

Bolger, K. E., & Patterson, C. J. (2001). Developmental pathways from child maltreatment to peer rejection. *Child Development, 72,* 549–568.

Bonanno, G., & Kaltman, S. (1999). Toward an integrative perspective on bereavement. *Psychological Bulletin, 125,* 760–776.

Bond, T. G. (1995). Piaget and measurement II: Empirical validation of the Piagetian model. *Archives de Psychologie, 63,* 155–185.

Book, P. L. (1996). How does the family narrative influence the individual's ability to communicate about death? *Omega: Journal of Death and Dying, 33,* 323–342.

Boone, R. T., & Cunningham, J. G. (1998). Children's decoding of emotion in expressive body movement: The development of cue attention. *Developmental Psychology, 34,* 1007–1016.

Booth, J. R., Perfetti, C. A., & MacWhinney, B. (1999). Quick, automatic, and general activation of orthographic and phonological representations in young readers. *Developmental Psychology, 35,* 3–19.

Bootzin, R. R., Epstein, D., Engle-Friedman, M., & Salvio, M. A. (1996). Sleep disturbances. In L. L. Carstensen, B. A. Edelstein, & L. Dornbrand (Eds.), *The practical handbook of clinical gerontology* (pp. 398–420). Thousand Oaks, CA: Sage.

Bornstein, M. C. (Ed.). (1995). *Handbook of parenting* (Vols. 1–3). Mahweh, NJ: Erlbaum.

Bornstein, M. H., Haynes, O. M., O'Reilly, A. W., & Painter, K. M. (1996). Solitary and collaborative pretense play in early childhood: Sources of individual variations in the development of representation competence. *Child Development, 67,* 2910–2929.

Bortz, W. M., II, & Bortz, S. S. (1996). Prevention, nutrition, and exercise in the aged. In L. L. Carstensen, B. A. Edelstein, & L. Dornbrand (Eds.), *The practical handbook of clinical gerontology* (pp. 36–53). Thousand Oaks, CA: Sage.

Bossé, R., Aldwin, C. M., Levenson, M. R., Spiro, A., III, & Mroczek, D. K. (1993). Change in social support after retirement: Longitudinal findings from the Normative Aging Study. *Journal of Gerontology: Psychological Sciences, 48,* P210–P217.

Bouchard, T. J., Jr. (1997). The genetics of personality. In K. Noble (Ed.), *Handbook of psychiatric genetics* (pp. 273–296). Boca Raton, FL: CRC Press.

Bowlby, J. (1969). *Attachment and loss* (Vol. 1). New York: Basic Books.

Bowles, S. (2001, May 1). Elderly drivers die at record pace. *USA Today,* pp. A1–2.

Bozikas, V., Kioseoglou, V., Palialia, M., Nimatoudis, I., Iakovides, A., Karavatos, A., & Kaprinis, G. (2000). Burnout among hospital workers and community-based mental health staff. *Psychiatriki, 11,* 204–211.

Brabeck, M. M., & Weisgerber, K. (1989). College students' perceptions of men and women choosing teaching and management: The effects of gender and sex role egalitarianism. *Sex Roles, 21,* 841.

Bradley, E. A., Thompson, A., & Bryson, S. E. (2002). Mental retardation in teenagers: Prevalence data from the Niagara Region, Ontario. *Canadian Journal of Psychiatry, 47,* 652–659.

Bradley, R. H., Caldwell, B. M., Rock, S. L., Ramey, C. T., Barnard, K. E., Gray, C., Hammond, M. A., Mitchell, S., Gottfried, A. W., Siegel, L., & Johnson, D. L. (1989). Home environment and cognitive development in the first 3 years of life: A collaborative study involving six sites and three ethnic groups in North America. *Developmental Psychology, 25,* 217–235.

Brady, J. E., Newcomb, A. F., & Hartup, W. W. (1983). Context and companion's behavior as determinants of cooperation and competition in school-age children. *Journal of Experimental Child Psychology, 36,* 396–412.

Braet, C., Mervielde, I., & Vandereycken, W. (1997). Psychological aspects of childhood obesity: A controlled study in a clinical and nonclinical sample. *Journal of Pediatric Psychology, 22,* 59–71.

Braine, M. D. S. (1976). Children's first word combinations. *Monographs of the Society for Research in Child Development, 41* (Serial No. 164).

Braine, M. D. S. (1992). What sort of innate structure is needed to "bootstrap" into syntax? *Cognition, 45,* 77–100.

Brainerd, C. J. (1996). Piaget: A centennial celebration. *Psychological Science, 7,* 191–203.

Brandtstädter, J. (1989). Personal self-regulation of development: Cross-sequential analyses of development-related control beliefs and emotions. *Developmental Psychology, 25,* 96–108.

Brandtstädter, J. (1999). Sources of resilience in the aging self. In T. M. Hess & F. Blanchard-Fields (Eds.), *Social cognition and aging* (pp. 123–141). San Diego, CA: Academic Press.

Brandtstädter, J., & Greve, W. (1994). The aging self: Stabilizing and protective processes. *Developmental Review, 14,* 52–80.

Braungart, J. M., Plomin, R., DeFries, J. C., & Fulker, D. W. (1992). Genetic influence on tester-rated infant temperament as assessed by Bayley's Infant Behavior Record: Nonadoptive and adoptive siblings and twins. *Developmental Psychology, 28,* 40–47.

Brazelton, T. B. (1984). *Brazelton Behavior Assessment Scale* (Rev. ed.). Philadelphia: Lippincott.

Brazelton, T. B., Nugent, J. K., & Lester, B. M. (1987). Neonatal behavioral assessment scale. In J. D. Osofsky (Ed.), *Handbook of infant development* (2nd ed.). New York: Wiley.

Brennan, P. A., Grekin, E. R., Mortensen, E. L., & Mednick, S. A. (2002). Relationship of maternal smoking during pregnancy with criminal arrest and hospitalization for substance abuse in male and female adult offspring. *American Journal of Psychiatry, 159,* 48–54.

Bretherton, I. (1992). The origins of attachment theory: John Bowlby and Mary Ainsworth. *Developmental Psychology, 28,* 759–775.

Bretherton, I. (1995). A communication perspective on attachment relationships and internal working models. *Monographs of the Society for Research in Child Development, 60,* 310–329.

Brioni, J. D., & Decker, M. W. (Eds.). (1997). *Pharmacological treatment of Alzheimer's disease.* New York: Wiley.

Brison, K. J. (1995). You will never forget: Narrative, bereavement, and worldview among Kwanga women. *Ethos, 23,* 474–488.

Brissette, I., Scheier, M. F., & Carver, C. S. (2002). The role of optimism in social network development, coping, and psychological adjustment during a life transition. *Journal of Personality and Social Psychology, 82,* 102–111.

Brodie, D. (1999). *Untying the knot: Ex-husbands, ex-wives, and other experts on the passage of divorce.* New York: St. Martin's Griffin.

Brody, G. H. (1998). Sibling relationship quality: Its causes and consequences. *Annual Review of Psychology, 49,* 1–24.

Brody, G. H., Stoneman, A., & McCoy, J. K. (1994). Forecasting sibling relationships in early adolescence from child temperaments and family processes in middle childhood. *Child Development, 65,* 771–784.

Brodzinsky, D. M., & Pinderhughes, E. (2002). Parenting and child development in adoptive families. In M. H. Bornstein (Ed.), *Handbook of parenting, vol. 1: Children and parenting* (pp. 279–311). Mahwah, NJ: Erlbaum.

Brodzinsky, D. M., & Rightmyer, J. (1980). Individual differences in children's humor development. In P. McGhee & A. Chapman (Eds.), *Children's humour.* Chichester, UK: Wiley.

Bronfenbrenner, U. (1979). Contexts of child rearing: Problems and prospects. *American Psychologist, 34,* 844–850.

Bronfenbrenner, U. (1989). Ecological systems theory. In R. Vasta (Ed.), *Annals of child development: Vol. 6. Theories of child development: Revised formulations and current issues.* Greenwich, CT: JAI Press.

Bronfenbrenner, U. (1995). Developmental ecology through space and time: A future perspective. In P. Moen, G. H. Elder, Jr., & K. Luscher (Eds.), *Examining lives in context: Perspectives on the ecology of human development* (pp. 619–647). Washington, DC: American Psychological Association.

Brooks, L., & Betz, N. E. (1990). Utility of expectancy theory in predicting occupational choices in college students. *Journal of Counseling Psychology, 37,* 57–64.

Brooks-Gunn, J., Klebanov, P. K., & Duncan, G. J. (1996). Ethnic differences in children's intelligence test scores: Role of economic deprivation, home environment, and maternal characteristics. *Child Development, 67,* 396–408.

Brooks-Gunn, J., & Paikoff, R. (1993). "Sex is a gamble, kissing is a game": Adolescent sexuality, contraception, and sexuality. In S. P. Millstein, A. C. Petersen, & E. O. Nightingale (Eds.), *Promoting the health behavior of adolescents.* New York: Oxford University Press.

Brooks-Gunn, J., & Ruble, D. N. (1982). The development of menstrual-related beliefs and behaviors during early adolescence. *Child Development, 53,* 1567–1577.

Brown, B. B., & Lohr, M. J. (1987). Peer-group affiliation and adolescent self-esteem: An integration of ego-identity and symbolic-interaction theories. *Journal of Personality and Social Psychology, 52,* 47–55.

Brown, B. B., Lohr, M. J., & McClenahan, E. L. (1986). Early adolescents' perceptions of peer pressure. *Journal of Early Adolescence, 6,* 139–154.

Brown, B. B., Mounts, N., Lamborn, S. D., & Steinberg, L. (1993). Parenting practices and peer group affiliation in adolescence. *Developmental Psychology, 64,* 467–482.

Brown, B. B., & Theobald, W. (1999). How peers matter: A research synthesis of peer influences on adolescent pregnancy. In P. Bearman, H. Bruckner, B. B. Brown, W. Theobald, & S. Philliber (Eds.), *Peer potential: Making the most of how teens influence each other.* Washington, DC: National Campaign to Prevent Teen Pregnancy.

Brown, C. S., & Bigler, R. S. (2002). Effects of minority status in the classroom on children's intergroup attitudes. *Journal of Experimental Child Psychology, 83,* 77–110.

Brown, J. R., & Dunn, J. (1992). Talk with your mother or your sibling? Developmental changes in early family conversations about feelings. *Child Development, 63,* 336–349.

Brown, R., Pressley, M., Van Meter, P., & Schuder, T. (1996). A quasi-experimental validation of transactional strategies instruction with low-achieving second-grade readers. *Journal of Educational Psychology, 88,* 18–37.

Bryant, B. K., & Crockenberg, S. B. (1980). Correlates and dimensions of prosocial behavior: A study of female siblings with their mothers. *Child Development, 51,* 529–554.

Bryce, J. (2001). The technological transformation of leisure. *Social Science Computer Review, 19,* 7–16.

Buchanan, C. M., Eccles, J. S., & Becker, J. B. (1992). Are adolescents the victims of raging hormones? Evidence for activational effects of hormones on moods and behavior at adolescence. *Psychological Bulletin, 111,* 62–107.

Buchholz, M., Karl, H. W., Pomietto, M., & Lynn, A. (1998). Pain scores in infants: A modified infant pain scale versus visual analogue. *Journal of Pain & Symptom Management, 15,* 117–124.

Buchsbaum, B. C. (1996). Remembering a parent who has died: A developmental perspective. In D. Klass, P. R. Silverman, & S. L. Nickman (Eds.), *Continuing bonds: New understandings of grief* (pp. 113–124). Washington, DC: Taylor & Francis.

Buckle, L., Gallup, G. G., Jr., & Rodd, Z. A. (1996). Marriage as a reproductive contract: Patterns of marriage, divorce, and remarriage. *Ethology and Sociobiology, 17,* 363–377.

Buehler, J. W., Kleinman, J. C., Hogue, C. J., Strauss, L. T., & Smith, J. C. (1987). Birth weight-specific infant mortality, United States, 1960 and 1980. *Public Health Reports Washington, D.C., 102,* 151–61.

Buhrmester, D., & Furman, W. (1987). The development of companionship and intimacy. *Child Development, 58,* 1101–1113.

Buhrmester, D., & Furman, W. (1990). Perceptions of sibling relationships during middle childhood and adolescence. *Child Development, 61,* 1387–1398.

Bullock, M., & Lütkenhaus, P. (1990). Who am I? The development of self-understanding in toddlers. *Merrill-Palmer Quarterly, 36,* 217–238.

Bullock, W. A., & Dunn, N. J. (1988, August). *Aging, sex, and marital satisfaction.* Paper presented at the meeting of the American Psychological Association, Atlanta.

Bumpass, L. L., & Aquilino, W. S. (1995). *A social map of midlife: Family and work over the middle years.* Madison, WI: University of Wisconsin-Madison, Center for Demography and Ecology.

Bunce, D. (2001). The locus of age 3 health-related physical fitness interactions in serial choice responding as a function of task complexity: Central processing or motor function? *Experimental Aging Research, 27,* 103–122.

Burchinal, M. R., Roberts, J. E., Riggins, R., Zeisel, S. A., Neebe, E., & Bryant, D. (2000). Relating quality of center-based child care to early cognitive and language development longitudinally. *Child Development, 71,* 338–357.

Burgess, D., & Borgida, E. (1997). Sexual harassment: An experimental test of sex-role spillover theory. *Personality and Social Psychology Bulletin, 23,* 63–75.

Burton, L. M. (1992). Black grandparents rearing children of drug-addicted parents: Stressors, outcomes, and social service needs. *The Gerontologist, 32,* 744–751.

Bush, T. L., Whiteman, M., & Flaws, J. A. (2001). Hormone replacement therapy and breast cancer: A qualitative review. *Obstetrics and Gynecology, 98,* 498–508.

Buss, A. H., & Plomin, R. (1984). *Temperament: Early developing personality traits.* Hillsdale, NJ: Lawrence Erlbaum.

Buss, D. M., Abbott, M., Angeleitner, A., Asherian, A., Biaggio, A., Blanco Villasenor, A. et al. (1990). International preferences in selecting mates: A study of 37 cultures. *Journal of Cross-Cultural Psychology, 21,* 5–47.

Buss, K. A., & Goldsmith, H. H. (1998). Fear and anger regulation in infancy: Effects on the temporal dynamics of affective expression. *Child Development, 69,* 359–374.

Byock, I. (1997). *Dying well.* New York: Riverhead.

Byrne, B. M., & Gavin, D. A. W. (1996). The Shavelson model revisited: Testing for the structure of academic self-concept across pre-, early, and late adolescents. *Journal of Educational Psychology, 88,* 215–228.

Cain, K. (1999). Ways of reading: How knowledge and use of strategies are related to reading comprehension. *British Journal of Developmental Psychology, 17,* 293–312.

Calasanti, T. M. (1996). Gender and life satisfaction in retirement: An assessment of the male model. *Journal of Gerontology: Social Sciences, 51B,* S18–S29.

Calciano, R., Chodak, G. W., Garnick, M. B., Kuban, D. A., & Resnick, M. I. (1995, April 15). The prostate cancer conundrum. *Patient Care, 29,* 84–88, 91–95, 99–102, 104.

Callahan, C. M. (2000). Intelligence and giftedness. In R. J. Sternberg (Ed.), *Handbook of intelligence* (pp. 159–175). Cambridge, England: Cambridge University Press.

Camlibel, A. R. (2000). Affectivity and attachment: A comparison of binge drinking and non-binge drinking first-year college students. *Dissertation Abstracts International: Section B: The Sciences and Engineering, 60,* 5757.

Camp, C. J. (2001). From efficacy to effectiveness to diffusion: Making the transitions in dementia intervention research. *Neuropsychological Rehabilitation, 11,* 495–517.

Camp, C. J., Foss, J. W., Stevens, A. B., Reichard, C. C., McKitrick, L. A., & O'Hanlon, A. M. (1993). Memory training in normal and demented elderly populations: The E-I-E-I-O model. *Experimental Aging Research, 19,* 277–290.

Camp, C. J., Judge, K. S., Bye, C. A., Fox, K. M., Bowden, J., Bell, M., Valencic, K., & Mattern, J. M. (1997). An intergenerational program for persons with dementia using Montessori methods. *The Gerontologist, 37,* 688–692.

Camp, C. J., & McKitrick, L. A. (1991). Memory interventions in Alzheimer's-type dementia populations: Methodological and theoretical issues. In R. L. West & J. D. Sinnott (Eds.), *Everyday memory and aging: Current research and methodology* (pp. 155–172). New York: Springer-Verlag.

Campbell, F. A., Pungello, E. P., Miller-Johnson, S., Burchinal, M., & Ramey, C. T. (2001). The development of cognitive and academic abilities: Growth curves from an early childhood educational experiment. *Developmental Psychology, 37,* 231–242.

Campbell, F. A., & Ramey, C. T. (1994). Effects of early intervention on intellectual and academic achievement: A follow-up study of children from low-income families. *Child Development, 65,* 684–698.

Campos, J. J., Hiatt, S., Ramsay, D., Henderson, C., & Svejda, M. (1978). The emergence of fear on the visual cliff. In M. Lewis & L. Rosenblum (Eds.), *The origins of affect.* New York: Plenum.

Campos, R. G. (1989). Soothing pain-elicited distress in infants with swaddling and pacifiers. *Child Development, 60,* 781–792.

Camras, L. A., Oster, H., Campos, J., Campos, R., Ujiie, T., Miyake, K., Wang, L., & Meng, Z. (1998). Production of emotional facial expressions in European, American, Japanese, and Chinese infants. *Developmental Psychology, 34,* 616–628.

Canadian Cancer Society. (2004). *Early detection and screening for prostate cancer* [Online]. Available: http://www.cancer.ca. (Retrieved October 4, 2004.)

Canadian Centre on Substance Abuse (1999). *Canadian profile* [Online]. Available: http://www.ccsa.ca/index.asp. (Retrieved March 18, 2004.)

Canadian Heritage Multiculturalism. (1998). *Multicultural Canada: A demographic overview 1996.* Ottawa, ON: Minister of Public Works and Government Services Canada.

Canadian Hospice Palliative Care Association. (2004). [Online]. Available: http://www.chpca.net/home.htm. (Retrieved May 15, 2004.)

Canadian Hospitals Injury Reporting and Prevention Program. (1994). *The CHIRPP sampler: Sports and recreational injuries among 5-19 year olds for 1993 from the CHIRPP database*

[Online]. Available: http://www.hc-sc.gc.ca/pphb-dgspsp/publicat/chirpp-schirpt/02jul94/iss2h_e.html. (Retrieved April 13, 2004.)

Canadian Medical Association. (2003). Advancing toward a modern death: The path from severe brain injury to neurological determination of death. *Canadian Medical Association Journal, 168.*

Canadian Paediatric Society. (2001). *Joint statement on Shaken Baby Syndrome. Pediatrics and Child Health, 6,* 663–667.

Canadian Paediatric Society. (2004). Effective discipline for children. *Paediatric & Child Health, 9,* 37–44.

Canadian Paediatric Society. (2004, September). *Healthy eating* [Online]. Available: http://www.caringforkids.cps.ca/eating/index.htm. (Retrieved September 19, 2004.)

Canadian Perinatal Surveillance System. (1999). Sudden Infant Death Syndrome. Ottawa: Health Canada.

The Canadian Study of Health and Aging Working Group (Canada). (2001). Disability and frailty among elderly Canadians: A comparison of six surveys. *International Psychogeriatrics, 10* (Supplement 1), 169–176.

Canfield, R. L., & Smith, E. G. (1996). Number-based expectations and sequential enumeration by 5-month-old infants. *Developmental Psychology, 32,* 269–279.

Capaldi, D. M., & Patterson, G. R. (1991). Relation of parental transitions to boys' adjustment problems: I. A linear hypothesis. II. Mothers at risk for transitions and unskilled parenting. *Developmental Psychology, 27,* 489–504.

Carey, G. (1996). Family and genetic epidemiology of aggressive and antisocial behavior. In D. M. Stoff & R. B. Cairns (Eds.), *Aggression and violence: Genetic, neurobiological, and biosocial perspectives.* Mahwah, NJ: Erlbaum.

Carey, S., & Spelke, E. S. (1994). Domain-specific knowledge and conceptual change. In L. A. Hirschfeld & S. A. Gelman (Eds.), *Mapping the mind* (pp. 169–200). Cambridge, UK: Cambridge University Press.

Carlo, G., Koller, S. H., Eisenberg, N., Da Silva, M. S., & Frohlich, C. B. (1996). A cross-national study on the relations among prosocial moral reasoning, gender role orientations, and prosocial behaviors. *Developmental Psychology, 32,* 231–240.

Carlson, C. L., Pelham, W. E., Milich, R., & Dixon, J. (1992). Single and combined effects of methylphenidate and behavior therapy on the classroom performance of children with attention-deficit hyperactivity disorder. *Journal of Abnormal Child Psychology, 20,* 213–232.

Carlson, E. A. (1998). A prospective longitudinal study of attachment disorganization/disorientation. *Child Development, 69,* 1107–1128.

Carnelley, K., & Ruscher, J. B. (2000). Adult attachment and exploratory behavior in leisure. *Journal of Social Behavior and Personality, 15,* 153–165.

Carpenter, P. A., & Daneman, M. (1981). Lexical retrieval and error recovery in reading: A model based on eye fixations. *Journal of Verbal Learning and Verbal Behavior, 20,* 137–160.

Carrere, S., & Gottman, J. M. (1999). Predicting the future of marriages. In E. M. Hetherington (Ed.), *Coping with divorce,*

single parenting, and remarriage: A risk and resiliency perspective. Mahwah, NJ: Erlbaum.

Carroll, J. B. (1993). *Human cognitive abilities: A survey of factor-analytic studies.* New York: Cambridge University Press.

Carstensen, L. L. (1993). Motivation for social contact across the life span: A theory of socioemotional selectivity. In J. E. Jacobs (Ed.), *Nebraska symposium on motivation: Vol. 40. Developmental perspectives on motivation* (pp. 209–254). Lincoln: University of Nebraska Press.

Carstensen, L. L. (1995). Evidence for a life-span theory of socioemotional selectivity. *Current Directions in Psychological Science, 4,* 151–156.

Carstensen, L. L., & Freund, A. M. (1994). The resilience of the aging self. *Developmental Review, 14,* 81–92.

Carstensen, L. L., Graff, J., Levenson, R. W., & Gottmann, J. M. (1996). Affect in intimate relationships: The developmental course of marriage. In C. Magai & S. H. McFadden (Eds.), *Handbook of emotion, adult development, and aging* (pp. 227–247). San Diego, CA: Academic Press.

Carver, L. J., & Bauer, P. J. (2001). The dawning of a past: The emergence of long-term explicit memory in infancy. *Journal of Experimental Psychology: General, 130,* 726–745.

Casaer, P. (1993). Old and new facts about perinatal brain development. *Journal of Child Psychology and Psychiatry, 34,* 101–109.

Cascio, W. F. (1995). Whither industrial and organizational psychology in a changing world of work? *American Psychologist, 50,* 928–939.

Caselli, M. C., Bates. E., Casadio, P., Fenson, J., Fenson, L., Sanderl, L., & Weir, J. (1995). Cross-linguistic lexical development. *Cognitive Development, 10,* 159–199.

Casey, B. J., Giedd, J. N., & Thomas, K. M. (2000). Structural and functional brain development and its relation to cognitive development. *Biological Psychology, 54,* 241–257.

Casey, M. B. (1996). Understanding individual differences in spatial ability within females: A nature/nurture interactionist framework. *Developmental Review, 16,* 241–260.

Casper, W. J. (2000). The effects of work-life benefits and perceived organizational support on organizational attractiveness and employment desirability. *Dissertation Abstract International Section B: The Sciences and Engineering, 61(5-B),* 2803.

Cassidy, L., & Hurrell, R. M. (1995). The influence of victim's attire on adolescents' judgments of date rape. *Adolescence, 30,* 319–323.

Castro, I. L. (1997). Worth more than we earn: Fair pay as a step toward gender equity. *National Forum, 77(2),* 17–21.

Cattell, R. B. (1965). *The scientific analysis of personality.* Baltimore: Penguin.

Cavanaugh, J. C. (1981). Early developmental theories: A brief review of attempts to organize developmental data prior to 1925. *Journal of the History of the Behavioral Sciences, 17,* 38–47.

Cavanaugh, J. C. (1996). Memory self-efficacy as a key to understanding cognitive aging. In F. Blanchard-Fields &

T. M. Hess (Eds.), *Perspectives on cognitive changes in adulthood and aging* (pp. 488–507) New York: McGraw-Hill.

Cavanaugh, J. C. (2000). Metamemory from a social-cognitive perspective. In D. Park & N. Schwarz (Eds.), *Cognitive aging: A primer* (pp. 115–130). Philadelphia: Psychology Press.

Cavanaugh, J. C., Feldman, J. M., & Hertzog, C. (1998). Metamemory as social cognition: A reconceptualization of what memory questionnaires assess. *Review of General Psychology, 2,* 48–65.

Cavanaugh, J. C., & Kinney, J. M. (1994, July). *Marital satisfaction as an important contextual factor in spousal caregiving.* Paper presented at the 7th International Conference on Personal Relationships, Groningen, The Netherlands.

Cavanaugh, J. C., & Kinney, J. M. (1998). Accuracy of caregivers' recollections of caregiving hassles. *Journal of Gerontology: Psychological Sciences, 53B,* P40–P42.

Cavanaugh, J. C., & Nocera, R. (1994). Cognitive aspects and interventions in Alzheimer's disease. In J. D. Sinnott (Ed.), *Interdisciplinary handbook of adult lifespan learning* (pp. 389–407). New York: Greenwood Press.

Ceci, S. J., & Bruck, M. (1995). *Jeopardy in the courtroom: A scientific analysis of children's testimony.* Washington, DC: American Psychological Association.

Ceci, S. J., & Bruck, M. (1998). Children's testimony: Applied and basic issues. In W. Damon (Ed.), *Handbook of child psychology* (Vol. 4). New York: Wiley.

Cerminara, K. L., & Perez, A. (2000). Therapeutic death: A look at Oregon's law. *Psychology, Public Policy, and Law, 6,* 503–525.

Cervantes, C. A., & Callanan, M. A. (1998). Labels and explanations in mother-child emotion talk: Age and gender differentiation. *Developmental Psychology, 34,* 88–98.

Chandler, M., & Moran, T. (1990). Psychopathy and moral development: A comparative study of delinquent and non-delinquent youth. *Development and Psychopathology, 2,* 227–246.

Chanquoy, L. (2001). How to make it easier for children to revise their writing: A study of text revision from 3rd to 5th grades. *British Journal of Educational Psychology, 71,* 15–41.

Chao, G. T. (1997). Mentoring phases and outcomes. *Journal of Vocational Behavior, 51,* 15–28.

Chao, R. K. (1994). Beyond parental control and authoritarian parenting style: Understanding Chinese parenting through the cultural notion of training. *Child Development, 65,* 1111–1119.

Chapman, P. D. (1988). *Schools as sorters: Lewis M. Terman, applied psychology, and the intelligence testing movement, 1890–1930.* New York: New York University Press.

Charles, S. T. (1998). Genetic and environmental influences on osteoarthritis. *Dissertation Abstracts International: Section B: The Sciences and Engineering, 58(11B),* 6272.

Charness, N., & Bosman, E. A. (1990). Expertise and aging: Life in the lab. In T. M. Hess (Ed.), *Aging and cognition: Knowledge organization and utilization* (pp. 343–385). Amsterdam, The Netherlands: North-Holland.

Chase-Lansdale, P. L., Cherlin, A. J., & Kiernan, K. E. (1995). The long-term effects of parental divorce on the mental health of young adults: A developmental perspective. *Child Development, 66,* 1614–1634.

Chase-Lansdale, P. L., & Hetherington, E. M. (1990). The impact of divorce on life-span development: Short and long term effects. In P. B. Baltes, B. L. Featherman, & R. M. Lerner, (Eds.), *Life-span development and behavior* (Vol. 10). Hillsdale, NJ: Erlbaum.

Chassin, L., Presson, C. C., Pitts, S. C., & Sherman, S. J. (2000). The natural history of cigarette smoking from adolescence to adulthood in a Midwestern community sample: Multiple trajectories and their psychological correlates. *Health Psychology, 19,* 223–231.

Chasteen, A. L. (1994). "The world around me": The environment and single women. *Sex Roles, 31,* 309–328.

Chen, X., Rubin, K. H., & Li, Z. (1995). Social functioning and adjustment in Chinese children. *Developmental Psychology, 31,* 531–539.

Chen, X., Unger, J. B., Palmer, P., Weiner, M. D., Johnson, C. A., Wong, M. M., & Austin, G. (2002). Prior cigarette smoking initiation predicting current alcohol use: Evidence for a gateway drug effect among California adolescents from eleven ethnic groups. *Addictive Behaviors, 27,* 799–817.

Cherlin, A. J., & Furstenberg, F. F., Jr. (1986). *The new American grandparent: A place in the family, a life apart.* New York: Basic Books.

Cherlin, A. J., & Furstenberg, F. F., Jr. (1994). Stepfamilies in the United States: A reconsideration. *Annual Review of Sociology, 20,* 359–381.

Chetro-Szivos, J. (2001). Exploring the meaning of work: A CMM analysis of the grammar of working Acadian-Americans. *Dissertation Abstracts International Section A: Humanities and Social Sciences, 62(1-A),* 14.

Chilman, C. S. (1983). *Adolescent sexuality in a changing American society* (2nd ed.). New York: Wiley.

Chinen, A. B. (1989). *In the ever after.* Willmette, IL: Chiron.

Chiu, W. C. K., Chan, A. W., Snape, E., & Redman, T. (2001). Age stereotypes and discriminatory attitudes towards older workers: An East-West comparison. *Human Relations, 54,* 629–661.

Chorpita, B. F., & Barlow, D. H. (1998). The development of anxiety: The role of control in the early environment. *Psychological Bulletin, 124,* 3–21.

Christensen, A., & Heavey, C. L. (1999). Intervention for couples. *Annual Review of Psychology, 50,* 165–190.

Cicchetti, D., Toth, S. L., & Maughan, A. (2000). An ecological-transactional model of child maltreatment. In A. J. Sameroff, M. Lewis, & S. M. Miller (Eds.), *Handbook of developmental psychopathology, second edition* (pp. 689–722). New York: Kluwer Academic/Plenum Publishers.

Cicirelli, V. G. (2000). Older adults' ethnicity, fear of death, and end-of-life decisions. In A. Tomer (Ed.), *Death attitudes and the older adult: Theories, concepts, and applications* (pp. 175–191). Philadelphia: Brunner-Routledge.

Cicirelli, V. G. (2001). Personal meaning of death in older adults and young adults in relation to their fears of death. *Death Studies, 25,* 663–683.

Cielinski, K. L., Vaughan, B. E., Seifer, R., & Contreras, J. (1995). Relations among sustained engagement during play, quality of play, and mother-child interaction in samples of children with Down syndrome and normally developing toddlers. *Infant Behavior and Development, 18,* 163–176.

Cleek, M. B., & Pearson, T. A. (1985). Perceived causes of divorce: An analysis of interrelationships. *Journal of Marriage and the Family, 47,* 179–191.

Clements, M., & Markman, H. J. (1996). The transition to parenthood: Is having children hazardous to marriage? In N. Vanzetti & S. Duck (Eds.), *A lifetime of relationships* (pp. 290–310). Pacific Grove, CA: Brooks/Cole.

Clifton, R., Perris, E., & Bullinger, A. (1991). Infants' perception of auditory space. *Developmental Psychology, 27,* 187–197.

Cohen, G. D. (1990). Psychopathology and mental health in the mature and elderly adult. In J. E. Birren & K. W. Schaie (Eds.), *Handbook of the psychology of aging* (3rd ed., pp. 359–371). San Diego, CA: Academic Press.

Cohen, R. R., Boston, P., Mount, B. M., & Porterfield, P. (2001). Changes in quality of life following admission to palliative care units. *Palliative Medicine, 15,* 363–371.

Cohen, S., & Hebert, T. B. (1996). Psychological factors and physical disease from the perspective of human psychoneuroimmunology. *Annual Review of Psychology, 47,* 113–142.

Cohen, S., Lichtenstein, E., Prochaska, J. O., Rossi, J. S., Gutz, E. R., Carr, C. R., et al. (1989). Debunking myths about self-quitting: Evidence from 10 prospective studies of persons who attempt to quit smoking by themselves. *American Psychologist, 44,* 1355–1365.

Cohen, S., & Williamson, G. M. (1991). Stress and infectious disease in humans. *Psychological Bulletin, 109,* 5–24.

Colby, A., Kohlberg, L., Gibbs, J., & Lieberman, M. (1983). A longitudinal study of moral judgment. *Monographs of the Society for Research in Child Development, 48* (Serial No. 200).

Cole, D. A., & Jordan, A. E. (1995). Competence and memory: Integrating psychosocial and cognitive correlates of child depression. *Child Development, 66,* 459–473.

Cole, D. A., Maxwell, S. E., Martin, J. M., Peeke, L. G., Seroczynski, A. D., Tram, J. M., Hoffman, K. B., Ruiz, M. D., Jacquez, F., & Maschman, T. (2001). The development of multiple domains of child and adolescent self-concept: A cohort sequential longitudinal design. *Child Development, 72,* 1723–1746.

Cole, M. L. (2000). The experience of never-married women in their thirties who desire marriage and children. *Dissertation Abstracts International Section A: Humanities and Social Sciences, 60*(9-A), 3526.

Cole, T. R., & Holstein, M. (1996). Ethics and aging. In R. H. Binstock & L. K. George (Eds.), *Handbook of aging and the social sciences* (4th ed., pp. 480–497). San Diego, CA: Academic Press.

Collins, J. F. (2000). Biracial Japanese American identity: An evolving process. *Cultural Diversity and Ethnic Minority Psychology, 6,* 115–133.

Collins, N. L., & Read, S. J. (1990). Adult attachment, working models, and relationship quality in dating couples. *Journal of Personality and Social Psychology, 58,* 644–663.

Coltheart, M., Curtis, B., Atkins, P., & Haller, M. (1993). Models of reading aloud: Dual-route and parallel-distributed-processing approaches. *Psychological Review, 100,* 589–608.

Conger, R. D., Patterson, G. R., & Ge, X. (1995). It takes two to replicate: A mediational model for the impact of parents' stress on adolescent adjustment. *Child Development, 66,* 80–97.

Connidis, I. A. (2001). *Family ties and aging.* Thousand Oaks, CA: Sage.

Conway, M. A., & Pleydell-Pearce, C. W. (2000). The construction of autobiographical memories in the self-memory system. *Psychological Review, 107,* 261–288.

Cooney, T. M., Pedersen, F. A., Indelicato, S., & Palkovitz, R. (1993). Timing of fatherhood: Is "on time" optimal? *Journal of Marriage and the Family, 55,* 205–215.

Cooney, T. M., Smyer, M. A., Hagestad, G. O., & Klock, R. (1986). Parental divorce in young adulthood: Some preliminary findings. *American Journal of Orthopsychiatry, 56,* 470–477.

Cooney, T. M., & Uhlenberg, P. (1990). The role of divorce in men's relations with their adult children after mid-life. *Journal of Marriage and the Family, 52,* 677–688.

Coopersmith, S. (1967). *The antecedents of self-esteem.* San Francisco: W. H. Freeman.

Coplan, R. J., Rubin, K. H., Fox, N. A., Calkins, S. D., et al. (1994). Being alone, playing alone, and acting alone: Distinguishing among reticence and passive and active solitude in young children. *Child Development, 65,* 129–137.

Copper, R. L., Goldenberg, R. L., Das, A., Elder, N., Swain, M., Norman, G., Ramsey, R., Cotroneo, P., Collins, B. A., Johnson, F., Jones, P., & Meier, A. M. (1996). The preterm prediction study: Maternal stress is associated with spontaneous preterm birth at less than thirty-five weeks' gestation. National Institute of Child Health and Human Development Maternal-Fetal Medicine Units Network. *American Journal of Obstetrics and Gynecology, 175,* 1286–92.

Corballis, M. C. (1997). The genetics and evolution of handedness. *Psychological Review, 104,* 714–727.

Cordes, C. L., & Doughtery, T. W. (1993). A review and integration of research on job burnout. *Academy of Management Review, 18,* 621–656.

Cornelius, M., Taylor, P., Geva, D., & Day, N. (1995). Prenatal tobacco exposure and marijuana use among adolescents: Effects on offpsring gestational age, growth, and morphology. *Pediatrics, 95,* 738–743.

Cornman, J. M., & Kingson, E. R. (1996). Trends, issues, perspectives, and values for the aging of the baby boom cohorts. *The Gerontologist, 36,* 15–26.

Cornwell, K. S., Harris, L. J., & Fitzgerald, H. E. (1991). Task effects in the development of hand preference in 9-, 13-, and

20-month-old infant girls. *Developmental Neuropsychology, 7,* 19–34.

Corr, C. A. (1991–1992). A task-based approach to coping with dying. *Omega: Journal of Death and Dying, 24,* 81–94.

Corrigan, P. W., Holmes, E. P., Luchins, D., Buichan, B., et al. (1994). Staff burnout in a psychiatric hospital: A cross-lagged panel design. *Journal of Organizational Behavior, 15,* 65–74.

Costa, P. T., Jr., & McCrae, R. R. (1988). Personality in adulthood: A six-year longitudinal study of self-reports and spouse ratings on the NEO Personality Inventory. *Journal of Personality and Social Psychology, 54,* 853–863.

Costa, P. T., Jr., & McCrae, R. R. (1997). Longitudinal stability of adult personality. In R. Hogan, J. Johnson, & S. Briggs (Eds.), *Handbook of personality psychology* (pp. 269–292). San Diego, CA: Academic Press.

Costa, P. T., Jr., McCrae, R. R., & Arenberg, D. (1980). Enduring dispositions in adult males. *Journal of Personality and Social Psychology, 38,* 793–800.

Costin, S. E., & Jones, D. C. (1992). Friendship as a facilitator of emotional responsiveness and prosocial interventions among young children. *Developmental Psychology, 28,* 941–947.

Cotter, R. P. (2001). High-risk behaviors in adolescence and their relationship to death anxiety and death personification. *Dissertation Abstracts International Section B: The Sciences and Engineering, 61*(8-B), 4446.

Cotton, S., Anthill, J. K., & Cunningham, J. D. (1989). The work motivations of mothers with preschool children. *Journal of Family Issues, 10,* 189–210.

Coulton, C. J., Korbin, J. E., Su, M., & Chow, J. (1995). Community level factors and child maltreatment rates. *Child Development, 66,* 1262–1276.

Counts, D., & Counts, D. (Eds.). (1985). *Aging and its transformations: Moving toward death in Pacific societies.* Lanham, MD: University Press of America.

Cox, C. B. (2000). Why grandchildren are going to and staying at grandmother's house and what happens when they get there. In C. B. Cox (Ed.), *To grandmother's house we go and stay: Perspectives on custodial grandparents* (pp. 3–19). New York: Springer.

Craig, K. D., Whitfield, M. F., Grunau, R. V. E., Linton, J., & Hadjistavropoulos, H. D. (1993). Pain in the preterm neonate: Behavioural and physiological indices. *Pain, 52,* 238–299.

Craton, L. G., & Yonas, A. (1988). Infants' sensitivity to boundary flow information for depth at an edge. *Child Development, 59,* 1522–1529.

Creed, P. A., Bloxsome, T. D., & Johnston, K. (2001). Self-esteem and self-efficacy outcomes for unemployed individuals attending occupational skills training programs. *Community, Work and Family, 4,* 285–303.

Crick, N. R., & Dodge, K. A. (1994). A review and reformulation of social information-processing mechanisms in children's social adjustment. *Psychological Bulletin, 115,* 74–101.

Crick, N. R., & Grotpeter, J. K. (1995). Relational aggression, gender, and social-psychological adjustment. *Child Development, 66,* 710–722.

Crispi, E. L., Schiaffino, K., & Berman, W. H. (1997). The contribution of attachment to burden in adult children of institutionalized parents with dementia. *The Gerontologist, 37,* 52–60.

Cristofalo, V. J., Tresini, M., Francis, M. K., & Volker, C. (1999). Biological theories of senescence. In V. L. Bengtson & K. W. Schaie (Eds.), *Handbook of theories of aging* (pp. 98–112). New York: Springer.

Crocker, D., & Kalemba, V. (1999). The incidence and impact of women's experiences of sexual harassment in Canadian workplaces. *Canadian Review of Sociology and Anthropology, 36,* 541-558.

Cross, S., & Markus, H. (1991). Possible selves across the lifespan. *Human Development, 34,* 230–255.

Crowder, R. G., & Wagner, R. K. (1992). *The psychology of reading: An introduction* (2nd ed.). New York: Oxford University Press.

Crown, W. (2001). Economic status of the elderly. In R. H. Binstock & L. K. George (Eds.), *Handbook of aging and the social sciences* (5th ed., pp. 352–368). San Diego, CA: Academic Press.

Csikszentmihalyi, M., & Larson, R. (1984). *Being adolescent: Conflict and growth in the teenage years.* New York: Basic Books.

Cuellar, I., Nyberg, B., Maldonado, R. E., & Roberts, R. E. (1997). Ethnic identity and acculturation in a young adult Mexican-origin population. *Journal of Community Psychology, 25,* 535–549.

Cunningham, A. E., Perry, K. E., Stanovich, K. E., & Share, D. L. (2002). Orthographic learning during reading: Examining the role of self-teaching. *Journal of Experimental Child Psychology, 85,* 185–199.

Curcio, C. A., Buell, S. J., & Coleman, P. D. (1982). Morphology of the aging central nervous system: Not all downhill. In J. A. Mortimer, F. J. Pirozzola, & G. I. Maletta (Eds.), *Advances in neurogerontology: Vol. 3. The aging motor system* (pp. 7–35). New York: Praeger.

Cutler, S. J., & Hendricks, J. (1990). Leisure and time use across the life course. In R. H. Binstock & L. K. George (Eds.), *Handbook of aging and the social sciences* (3rd ed., pp. 169–185). San Diego, CA: Academic Press.

Cutrona, C. E. (1996). *Social support in couples.* Thousand Oaks, CA: Sage.

Dalton, S. T. (1992). Lived experience of never-married women. *Issues in Mental Health Nursing, 13,* 69–80.

Damon, W., & Hart, D. (1988). *Self-understanding in childhood and adolescence.* New York: Cambridge University Press.

Danforth, M. M., & Glass, J. C., Jr. (2001). Listen to my words, give meaning to my sorrow: A study in cognitive constructs in middle-age bereaved widows. *Death Studies, 25,* 513–529.

Dannemiller, J. L. (1998). Color constancy and color vision during infancy: Methodological and empirical issues. In V. Walsh & J. Kulikowski (Eds.), *Perceptual constancy: Why things look as they do.* New York: Cambridge University Press.

D'Augelli, A. R. (1996). Lesbian, gay, and bisexual development during adolescence and young adulthood. In R. P. Cabaj & T. S. Stein (Eds.), *Textbook of homosexuality and mental health.* Washington, DC: American Psychiatric Press.

Davidson, K. M., Richards, D. S., Schatz, D. A., & Fisher, D. A. (1991). Successful in utero treatment of fetal goiter and hypothyroidism. *New England Journal of Medicine, 324,* 543–546.

Davies, L. (2000). *Transitions and singlehood: The forgotten life course.* Unpublished manuscript.

Davies, P. T., & Cummings, E. M. (1998). Exploring children's emotional security as a mediator of the link between marital relations and child adjustment. *Child Development, 69,* 124–139.

Davis, B. L., MacNeilage, P. F., Matyear, C. L., & Powell, J. K. (2000). Prosodic correlates of stress in babbling: An acoustical study. *Child Development, 71,* 1258–1270.

Davis, B. W. (1985). *Visits to remember: A handbook for visitors of nursing home residents.* University Park: Pennsylvania State University Cooperative Extension Service.

Davis, M., McKay, M., & Eshelman, E. R. (2000). *The relaxation and stress reduction workbook.* Oakland, CA: New Harbinger.

Dawson Hughes, B. (1996). Calcium and vitamin D nutritional needs of elderly women. *Journal of Nutrition, 126,* 1165s–1167s.

Day, D.M. (1998). Risk for court contact and predictors of an early age for a first court contact among a sample of high risk youths: A survival analysis approach. *Canadian Journal of Criminology, 40,* 421–446.

Day, J. D., Engelhardt, S. E., Maxwell, S. E., & Bolig, E. E. (1997). Comparison of static and dynamic assessment procedures and their relation to independent performance. *Journal of Educational Psychology, 89,* 358–368.

Day, S. X., Rounds, J., & Swaney, K. (1998). The structure of vocational interests for diverse racial-ethnic groups. *Psychological Science, 9,* 40–44.

De Andrade, C. E. (2000). Becoming the wise woman: A study of women's journeys through midlife transformation. *Dissertation Abstracts International Section B: The Sciences and Engineering, 61(2-B),* 1109.

De Beni, R., & Palladino, P. (2000). Intrusion errors in working memory tasks: Are they related to reading comprehension ability? *Learning & Individual Differences, 12,* 131–143.

de St. Aubin, E., & McAdams, D. P. (1995). The relations of generative concern and generative action to personality traits, satisfaction/happiness with life, and ego development. *Journal of Adult Development, 2,* 99–112.

de Vries, B. (1996). The understanding of friendship: An adult life course perspective. In C. Magai & S. H. McFadden (Eds.), *Handbook of emotion, adult development, and aging* (pp. 249–268). San Diego, CA: Academic Press.

Dean, R.A., & McClement, S.E. (2002). Palliative care research: Methodological and ethical challenges. *International Journal of Palliative Nursing, 8,* 376–380.

DeAngelis, T. (1997). Menopause symptoms vary among ethnic groups. *APA Monitor, 28*(11), 16–17.

Deater-Deckard, K. (2000). Parenting and child behavioral adjustment in early childhood: A quantitative approach to studying family processes. *Child Development, 71,* 468–484.

DeCasper, A. J., & Spence, M. J. (1986). Prenatal maternal speech influences newborn's perception of speech sounds. *Infant Behavior and Development, 9,* 133–150.

Dekovic, M., & Janssens, J. M. (1992). Parents' child-rearing style and child's sociometric status. *Developmental Psychology, 28,* 925–932.

Dellas, M., & Jernigan, L. P. (1990). Affective personality characteristics associated with undergraduate ego identity formation. *Journal of Adolescent Research, 5,* 306–324.

DeLoache, J. S. (1995). Early understanding and use of models: The model model. *Current Directions in Psychological Science, 4,* 109–113.

DeLoache, J. S. (2000). Dual representation and young children's use of scale models. *Child Development, 71,* 329–338.

DeLoache, J. S., Miller, K. F., & Rosengren, K. S. (1997). The credible shrinking room: Very young children's performance with symbolic and nonsymbolic relations. *Psychological Science, 8,* 308–313.

DeMaris, A., & Rao, K. V. (1992). Premarital cohabitation and subsequent marital stability in the United States: A reassessment. *Journal of Marriage and the Family, 54,* 178–190.

Denney, N. W. (1982). Aging and cognitive changes. In B. B. Wolman (Ed.), *Handbook of developmental psychology* (pp. 807–827). Englewood Cliffs, NJ: Prentice-Hall.

Denney, N. W. (1989). Everyday problem solving: Methodological issues, research findings, and a model. In L. W. Poon, D. C. Rubin, & B. A. Wilson (Eds.), *Everyday cognition in adulthood and late life* (pp. 330–351). Cambridge, UK: Cambridge University Press.

Denney, N. W. (1990). Adult age differences in traditional and practical problem solving. In E. A. Lovelace (Ed.), *Aging and cognition: Mental processes, self-awareness, and interventions* (pp. 329–349). Amsterdam, The Netherlands: North-Holland.

Denney, N. W., Pearce, K. A., & Palmer, A. M. (1982). A developmental study of adults' performance on traditional and practical problem-solving tasks. *Experimental Aging Research, 8,* 115–118.

Denton, K., & Zarbatany, L. (1996). Age differences in support processes in conversations between friends. *Child Development, 67,* 1360–1373.

Department of Justice Canada. (2004). *Civil marriage and the legal recognition of same-sex unions* [Online]. Available: http://www.canada.justice.gc.ca/en/news/fs/2004doc_3. (Retrieved June 1, 2004.)

Derman, D. S. (2000). Grief and attachment in young widowhood. *Dissertation Abstracts International Section A: Humanities and Social Sciences, 60*(7-A), 2383.

Deutsch, A. (2001, April 11). Dutch parliament oks strict euthanasia bill. *Wilmington (NC) Morning Star,* p. 2A.

Devine, M. A., & Lashua, B. (2002). Constructing social acceptance in inclusive leisure contexts: The role of individuals with disabilities. *Therapeutic Recreation Journal, 36,* 65–83.

Devine, P. G. (1989). Stereotypes and prejudice: Their automatic and controlled components. *Journal of Personality and Social Psychology, 56*, 5–18.

DeWolff, M. S., & van IJzendoorn, M. H. (1997). Sensitivity and attachment: A meta-analysis on parental antecedents of infant attachment. *Child Development, 68*, 571–591.

Diamond, A., Prevor, M. B., Callender, G., & Druin, D. P. (1997). Prefontal cortex deficits in children treated early and continuously for PKU. *Monographs of the Society for Research in Child Development, 62* (4, Serial No. 252).

Dick, D. M., & Rose, R. J. (2002). Behavior genetics: What's new? What's next? *Current Directions in Psychological Science, 11*, 70–74.

Dick, D. M., Rose, R. J., Viken, R. J., & Kaprio, J. (2000). Pubertal timing and substance abuse: Associations between and within families across late adolescence. *Developmental Psychology, 36*, 180–189.

Dickens, W. T., & Flynn, J. R. (2001). Heritability estimates versus large environmental effects: The IQ paradox resolved. *Psychological Review, 108*, 346–369.

Dickinson, G. E. (1992). First childhood death experiences. *Omega, 25*, 169–182.

Diehl, M. (1998). Everyday competence in later life: Current status and future directions. *The Gerontologist, 4*, 422–433.

Diehl, M., Willis, S. L., & Schaie, K. W. (1995). Everyday problem solving in older adults: Observational assessment and cognitive correlates. *Psychology and Aging, 10*, 478–491.

Dielman, T., Schulenberg, J., Leech, S., & Shope, J. T. (1992, March). *Reduction of susceptibility to peer pressure and alcohol use/misuse through a school-based prevention program.* Paper presented at the meeting of the Society for Research on Adolescence, Washington, DC.

Dietitians of Canada. (2004). *Caloric needs of adolescents* [Online]. Available: http://www.dietitians.ca/update 2004. (Retrieved April 4, 2004.)

DiGrande, L., Perrier, M. P., Lauro, M. G., & Contu, P. (2000). Alcohol correlates of binge drinking among university students on the Island of Sardinia. *Substance Use and Misuse, 35*, 1471–1483.

Dimond, M., Lund, D. A., & Caserta, M. S. (1987). The role of social support in the first two years of bereavement in an elderly sample. *The Gerontologist, 27*, 599–604.

DiPietro, J. A., Bornstein, M. H., Costigan, K. A., Pressman, E. K., Hahn, C-S., Painter, K., Smith, B. A., & Yi, L. J. (2002). What does fetal movement predict about behavior during the first two years of life? *Developmental Psychobiology, 40*, 358–371.

Dixon, R. A., & Hultsch, D. F. (1999). Intelligence and cognitive potential in late life. In J. C. Cavanaugh & S. K. Whitbourne (Eds.), *Gerontology: An interdisciplinary perspective* (pp. 213–237). New York: Oxford University Press.

Dixon, R. A., Kramer, D. A., & Baltes, P. B. (1985). Intelligence: A life-span developmental perspective. In B. B. Wolman (Ed.), *Handbook of intelligence: Theories, measurements, and application* (pp. 301–350). New York: Wiley.

Doka, K. J., & Mertz, M. E. (1988). The meaning and significance of great-grandparenthood. *The Gerontologist, 28*, 192–197.

Domino, G. (1992). Cooperation and competition in Chinese and American children. *Journal of Cross Cultural Psychology, 23*, 456–467.

Donatelle, R. J., & Davis, L. G. (1997). *Health: The basics* (2nd ed.). Englewood Cliffs, NJ: Prentice Hall.

Dorgan, J. F., Stanczyk, F. A., Longcope, C., Stephenson, H. E., Jr., Chang, L., Miller, R., Franz, C., Falk, R. T., & Kahle, L. (1997). Relationship of serum dehydroepiandrosterone (DHEA), DHEA sulfate, and 5-androstene-3 beta, 17 beta-diol to risk of breast cancer in postmenopausal women. *Cancer Epidemiology, Biomarkers and Prevention, 6*, 177–181.

Dorton, H. E., Jr. (2001). Job exit and the meaning of work in declining industries: Comparing retirement, displacement by retirement, and displacement by layoff at Weirton Steel Corporation. *Dissertation Abstracts International Section A: Humanities and Social Sciences, 61*(12-A), 4952.

Downey, J., Elkin, E. J., Ehrhardt, A. A., Meyer-Bahlburg, H. F. L., Bell, J. J., & Morishima, A. (1991). Cognitive ability and everyday functioning in women with Turner's Syndrome. *Journal of Learning Disabilities, 24*, 32–39.

Draghi-Lorenz, R., Reddy, V., & Costall, A. (2001). Rethinking the development of "nonbasic" emotions: A critical review of existing theories. *Developmental Review, 21*, 263–304.

Dryfoos, J. G. (1990). *Adolescents at risk: Prevalence and prevention.* New York: Oxford University Press.

Dumas, J. E., LaFreniere, P. J., & Serketich, W. J. (1995). "Balance of power": A transactional analysis of control in mother-child dyads involving socially competent, aggressive, and anxious children. *Journal of Abnormal Psychology, 104*, 104–113.

Dunham, P. J., Dunham, F., & Curwin, A. (1993). Joint-attentional states and lexical acquisition at 18 months. *Developmental Psychology, 29*, 827–831.

Dunlosky, J., & Hertzog, C. (2001). Measuring strategy production during associative learning: The relative utility of concurrent versus retrospective reports. *Memory & Cognition, 29*, 247–253.

Dunn, J., Brown, J. R., & Maguire, M. (1995). The development of children's moral sensibility: Individual differences and emotion understanding. *Developmental Psychology, 31*, 649–659.

Dunn, J., & Kendrick, C. (1981). Social behavior of young siblings in the family context: Differences between same-sex and different-sex dyads. *Child Development, 52*, 1265–1273.

Dunn, J., & Plomin, R. (1990). *Separate lives: Why siblings are so different.* New York: Basic Books.

Dunn, J., Slomkowski, C., & Beardsall, L. (1994). Sibling relationships from the preschool period through middle childhood and early adolescence. *Developmental Psychology, 30*, 315–324.

Dunson, D. B., Colombo, B., & Baird, D. D. (2002). Changes in age in the level and duration of fertility in the menstrual cycle. *Human Reproduction, 17*, 1399–1403.

Durik, A. M., Hyde, J. S., & Clark, R. (2000). Sequelae of cesarean and vaginal deliveries: Psychosocial outcomes for mothers and infants. *Developmental Psychology, 36,* 251–260.

Durrant, J.E. (1993–94). Sparing the rod: Manitobans' attitudes toward the abolition of physical discipline and implications for policy change. *Canada's Mental Health,* Winter, 2–6.

Durrant, J. E., Rose-Krasnor, L., Broberg, A. G., (1999). Predicting mothers' use of physical punishment during mother-child conflicts in Sweden and Canada. In P. D. Hastings & C. C. Piotrowski (Eds.), *New directions for child and adolescent development, Vol. 86: Conflict as a context for understanding maternal beliefs about child rearing and children's misbehavior* (p. 25–41). San Francisco: Jossey-Bass.

Duxbury, L. E., Higgins, C., & Coghill, D. (2003). *Voices of Canadians: Seeking work-life balance.* Hull, Quebec: Human Resources Development Canada, Labour Program.

Dworet, D., & Bennett, S. (2002). A view from the North: Special education in Canada. *Teaching Exceptional Children, 34,* 22–27.

Dyk, P. H., & Adams, G. R. (1990). Identity and intimacy: An initial investigation of three theoretical models using cross-lag panel correlations. *Journal of Youth and Adolescence, 19,* 91–110.

Eagly, A. H., Karau, S. J., & Makhijani, M. G. (1995). Gender and the effectiveness of leaders: A meta-analysis. *Psychological Bulletin, 117,* 125–145.

Eaton, W. O., Chipperfield, J. G., & Singbeil, C. E. (1989). Birth order and activity level in children. *Developmental Psychology, 25,* 668–672.

Eaton, W. O., & Enns, L. R. (1986). Sex differences in human motor activity level. *Psychological Bulletin, 100,* 19–28.

Ebberwein, C. A. (2001). Adaptability and the characteristics necessary for managing adult career transition: A qualitative investigation. *Dissertation Abstracts International Section B: The Sciences and Engineering, 62*(1-B), 545.

Ebersole, P., & Hess, P. (1998). *Toward healthy aging: Human needs and nursing response* (5th ed.). St. Louis: Mosby.

Edelbrock, C., Rende, R., Plomin, R., & Thompson, L. A. (1995). A twin study of competence and problem behavior in childhood and early adolescence. *Journal of Child Psychology & Psychiatry & Allied Principles, 36,* 775–785.

Edelstein, B., & Kalish, K. (1999). Clinical assessment of older adults. In J. C. Cavanaugh & S. K. Whitbourne (Eds.), *Gerontology: An interdisciplinary perspective* (pp. 269–304). New York: Oxford University Press.

Edwards, C. A. (1994). Leadership in groups of school-age girls. *Developmental Psychology, 30,* 920–927.

Eisenberg, N. (1982). The development of reasoning regarding prosocial behavior. In N. Eisenberg (Ed.), *The development of prosocial behavior.* New York: Academic Press.

Eisenberg, N. (1986). *Altruistic emotion, cognition, and behavior.* Hillsdale, NJ: Erlbaum.

Eisenberg, N., Carlo, G., Murphy, B., & Van Court, P. (1995). Prosocial development in late adolescence: A longitudinal study. *Child Development, 66,* 1179–1197.

Eisenberg, N., Cumberland, A., Spinrad, T. L., Fabes, R. A., Shepard, S. A., Reiser, M., Murphy, B. C., Losoya, S. H., & Guthrie, I. K. (2001). The relations of regulation and emotionality to children's externalizing and internalizing problem behavior. *Child Development, 72,* 1112–1134.

Eisenberg, N., Fabes, R. A., Schaller, M., Carlo, G., & Miller, P. A. (1991). The relations of parental characteristics and practices to children's vicarious emotional responding. *Child Development, 62,* 1393–1408.

Eisenberg, N., & Morris, A. S. (2002). Children's emotion-related regulation. *Advances in Child Development and Behavior, 30,* 189–229.

Eisenberg, N., & Shell, R. (1986). Prosocial moral judgment and behavior in children: The mediating role of cost. *Personality and Social Psychology Bulletin, 12,* 426–433.

Eizenman, D. R., & Bertenthal, B. I. (1998). Infants' perception of object unity in translating and rotating displays. *Developmental Psychology, 34,* 426–434.

Ekerdt, D. J. (1987). Why the notion persists that retirement harms health. *The Gerontologist, 27,* 454–457.

Elkind, D. (1978). *The child's reality: Three developmental themes.* Hillsdale, NJ: Erlbaum.

Elkind, D., & Bowen, R. (1979). Imaginary audience behavior in children and adolescents. *Developmental Psychology, 15,* 38–44.

Ellen, T. R. (2000). The expression of generativity and the relationship among generativity, life satisfaction, and self-esteem in black American males between ages 37 and 55. *Dissertation Abstracts International Section A: Humanities and Social Sciences, 60*(8-A), 3136.

Ellis, B. J., & Garber, J. (2000). Psychosocial antecedents of variation in girls' pubertal timing: Maternal depression, stepfather presence, and marital and family stress. *Child Development, 71,* 485–501.

Elmer-DeWitt, P. (1994, January 17). The genetic revolution. *Time,* pp. 46–53.

Emick, M. A., & Hayslip, B., Jr. (1999). Custodial grandparenting: Stresses, coping skills, and relationships with grandchildren. *International Journal of Aging and Human Development, 48,* 35–61.

Engle, E., Miguel, R., Steelman, L., & McDaniel, M. A. (1994, April). *The relationship between age and work needs: A comprehensive research integration.* Paper presented at the annual meeting of the Society for Industrial and Organizational Psychology, Nashville, TN.

Enright, R. D., Gassin, E. A., & Wu, C. (1992). Forgiveness: A developmental view. *Journal of Moral Education, 21,* 99–114.

Epstein, L. H., & Cluss, P. A. (1986). Behavioral genetics of childhood obesity. *Behavior Therapy, 17,* 324–334.

Epstein, L. H., Valoski, A. M., Vara, L. S., McCurley, J., et al. (1995). Effects of decreasing sedentary behavior and increasing activity on weight change in obese children. *Health Psychology, 14,* 109–115.

Erel, O., & Burman, B. (1995). Interrelatedness of marital relations and parent-child relations: A meta-analytic review. *Psychological Bulletin, 118,* 108–132.

Erel, O., Margolin, G., & John, R. S. (1998). Observed sibling interaction: Links with the marital and the mother-child relationship. *Developmental Psychology, 34,* 288–298.

Erera-Weatherley, P. I. (1996). On becoming a stepparent: Factors associated with the adoption of alternative stepparenting styles. *Journal of Divorce and Remarriage, 25,* 155–174.

Ericsson, K. A., & Smith, J. (Eds.). (1991). *Toward a general theory of expertise: Prospects and limits.* New York: Cambridge University Press.

Erikson, E. H. (1968). *Identity: Youth and crisis.* New York: Norton.

Erikson, E. H. (1982). *The life cycle completed: Review.* New York: Norton.

Erikson, E. H., Erikson, J. M., & Kivnick, H. Q. (1986). *Vital involvement in old age.* New York: Norton.

Ernst, M., Moolchan, E. T., & Robinson, M. L. (2001). Behavioral and neural consequences of prenatal exposure to nicotine. *Journal of the American Academy of Child & Adolescent Psychiatry, 40,* 630–641.

Essex, M. J., & Nam, S. (1987). Marital status and loneliness among older women. *Journal of Marriage and the Family, 49,* 93–106.

Etaugh, C., & Liss, M. B. (1992). Home, school, and playroom: Training grounds for adult gender roles. *Sex Roles, 26,* 129–147.

Ettinger, W. H. (1995). Bone, joint, and rheumatic disorders. In W. B. Abrams, M. H. Beers, & R. Berkow (Eds.), *The Merck manual of geriatrics* (2nd ed., pp. 925–945). Whitehouse Station, NJ: Merck Research Laboratories.

Eyler, A. E., Wilcox, S., Matson-Koffman, D., Evenson, K. R., Sanderson, B., Thompson, J., Wilbur, J., & Rohm-Young, D. (2002). Correlates of physical activity among women from diverse racial/ethnic groups. *Journal of Women's Health and Gender Based Medicine, 11,* 239–253.

Fabes, R. A., Eisenberg, N., Jones, S., Smith, M., Guthrie, I., Poulin, R., Shepard, S., & Friedman, J. (1999). Regulation, emotionality, and preschoolers' socially competent peer interactions. *Child Development, 70,* 432–442.

Fagot, B. I. (1985). Changes in thinking about early sex role development. *Developmental Review, 5,* 83–98.

Falbo, T., & Polit, E. F. (1986). Quantitative review of the only child literature: Research evidence and theory development. *Psychological Bulletin, 100,* 176–186.

Farrant, K., & Reese, E. (2000). Maternal style and children's participation in reminiscing: Stepping stones in children's autobiographical memory development. *Journal of Cognition & Development, 1,* 193–225.

Farver, J. M., & Branstetter, W. H. (1994). Preschoolers' prosocial responses to their peers' distress. *Developmental Psychology, 30,* 334–341.

Farver, J. M., & Shin, Y. L. (1997). Social pretend play in Korean- and Anglo-American preschoolers. *Child Development, 68,* 544–556.

Fehr, B. (1996). *Friendship processes.* Thousand Oaks, CA: Sage.

Feigenson, L., Carey, S., & Hauser, M. (2002). The representations underlying infants' choice of more: Object files versus analog magnitudes. *Psychological Science, 13,* 150–156.

Feldhusen, J. F. (1996). Motivating academically able youth with enriched and accelerated learning experiences. In C. P. Benbow & D. J. Lubinski (Eds.), *Intellectual talent: Psychometric and social issues.* Baltimore, MD: Johns Hopkins Press.

Feldman, D. H., & Goldsmith, L. T. (1991). *Nature's gambit.* New York: Teachers College Press.

Feldman, H. M., Dollaghan, C. A., Campbell, T. F., Kurs-Lasky, M., Janosky, J. E., & Paradise, J. L. (2000). Measurement properties of the MacArthur Communicative Development Inventories at ages one and two years. *Child Development, 71,* 310–322.

Feltey, K. M., Ainslie, J. J., & Geib, A. (1991). Sexual coercion attitudes among high school students: The influence of gender and rape education. *Youth and Society, 23,* 229–250.

Fenson, L., Dale, P. S., Reznick, J. S., Bates, E., Thal, D. J., & Pethick, S. J. (1994). Variability in early communicative development. *Monographs of the Society for Research in Child Development, 59* (5, Serial No. 242).

Fergusson, D. M., Horwood, L. J., & Shannon, F. T. (1987). Breastfeeding and subsequent social adjustment in six- to eight-year-old children. *Journal of Child Psychology and Psychiatry and Allied Disciplines, 28,* 379–386.

Fergusson, D. M., & Woodward, L. J. (2000). Teenage pregnancy and female educational underachievement: A prospective study of a New Zealand birth cohort. *Journal of Marriage & the Family, 62,* 147–161.

Ferreol-Barbey, M., Piolat, A., & Roussey, J. (2000). Text recomposition by eleven-year-old children: Effects of text length, level of reading comprehension, and mastery of prototypical schema. *Archives de Psychologie, 68,* 213–232.

Field, T. M. (1990). *Infancy.* Cambridge, MA: Harvard University Press.

Fields, R. (1992). *Drugs and alcohol in perspective.* Dubuque, IA: William C. Brown.

Finch, C. E., & Seeman, T. E. (1999). Stress theories of aging. In V. L. Bengtson & K. W. Schaie (Eds.), *Handbook of theories of aging* (pp. 81–97). New York: Springer.

Fincham, F. (1998). Child development and marital relations. *Child Development, 69,* 543–574.

Finchum, T., & Weber, J. A. (2000). Applying continuity theory to elder adult friendships. *Journal of Aging and Identity, 5,* 159–168.

Finckh, U., von der Kammer, H., Velden, J., Michel, T., Andersen, B., Deng, A., Zhang, J., Mueller, T. T., Zuchowski, K., Menzer, G., Mann, U., Papassotiropoulos, A., Jeun, R., Zurdel, J., Holst, F., Benussi, L., Stoppe, G., Reiss, J., Miserez, A. R., Staehelin, H. B., Rebeck, G. W., Hyman, B. T., Binetti, G., Hock, C., Growdon, J. H., & Nitsch, R. M. (2000). Genetic association of a cystatin C gene polumorphism with late-onset Alzheimer disease. *Archives of Neurology, 57,* 1579–1583.

Fingerman, K. L. (1996). Sources of tension in the aging mother and adult daughter relationship. *Psychology and Aging, 11,* 591–606.

Fischer, M., Barkley, R. A., Fletcher, K. E., & Smallish, L. (1993). The adolescent outcome of hyperactive children: Predictors of psychiatric, academic, social, and emotional adjustment. *Journal of the American Academy of Child and Adolescent Psychiatry, 32,* 324–332.

Fischhoff, B., & Quadrel, M. J. (1995). Adolescent alcohol decisions. In G. M. Boyd, J. Howard, & R. A. Zucker (Eds.), *Alcohol problems among adolescents: Current directions in prevention research.* Hillsdale, NJ: Erlbaum.

Fisher, C. (1996). Structural limits on verb mapping: The role of analogy in children's interpretations of sentences. *Cognitive Psychology, 31,* 41–81.

Fisher, H. E. (1994). The nature of romantic love. *Journal of NIH Research, 6,* 59–64.

Fisher, J. E., & Noll, J. P. (1996). Anxiety disorders. In L. L. Carstensen, B. A. Edelstein, & L. Dornbrand (Eds.), *The practical handbook of clinical gerontology* (pp. 304–323). Thousand Oaks, CA: Sage.

Fiske, S. (1993). Social cognition and social perception. *Annual Review of Psychology, 50,* 229–238.

Fitzgerald, H. E., & Brackbill, Y. (1976). Classical conditioning in infancy: Development and constraints. *Psychological Bulletin, 83,* 353–375.

Fitzgerald, J. (1987). Research on revision in writing. *Review of Educational Research, 57,* 481–506.

Fitzgerald, J. M. (1999). Autobiographical memory and social cognition: Development of the remembered self in adulthood. In T. M. Hess & F. Blanchard-Fields (Eds.), *Social cognition and aging* (pp. 143–171). San Diego, CA: Academic Press.

Fitzgerald, L., Hulin, C. L., Drasgow, F., Gelfand, M., & Magley, V. J. (1997). Antecedents and consequences of sexual harassment in organizations: A test of an integrated model. *Journal of Applied Psychology, 82,* 578–589.

Flaks, D. K., Filcher, I., Masterpasqua, F., & Joseph, G. (1995). Lesbians choosing motherhood: A comparative study of lesbian and heterosexual parents and their children. *Developmental Psychology, 31,* 105–114.

Flavell, J. H. (1985). *Cognitive development* (2nd ed.). Englewood Cliffs, NJ: Prentice Hall.

Flavell, J. H. (1996). Piaget's legacy. *Psychological Science, 7,* 200–203.

Fleischman, D. A., & Gabrieli, J. D. E. (1998). Repetition priming in normal aging and Alzheimer's disease: A review of findings and theories. *Psychology and Aging, 13,* 88–119.

Fleming, S. J., & Balmer, L. E. (1996). Bereavement in adolescence. In C. A. Coor & D. E. Balk (Eds.), *Handbook of adolescent death and bereavement* (pp. 139–154). New York: Springer.

Fleming, S., & Robinson, P. (2001). Grief and cognitive-behavioral therapy: The reconstruction of meaning. In M. S. Stroebe, R. O. Hansson, W. Stroebe, & H. Schut (Eds.), *Handbook of bereavement research: Consequences, coping, and care* (pp. 647–669). Washington, DC: American Psychological Association.

Flynn, J. R. (1998). IQ gains over time: Toward finding the causes. In U. Neisser (Ed.), *The rising curve: Long-term gains in IQ and related measures* (pp. 25–66). Washington, DC: American Psychological Association.

Flynn, J. R. (1999). Searching for justice: The discovery of IQ gains over time. *American Psychologist, 54,* 5–20.

Fonzi, A., Schneider, B. H., Tani, F., & Tomada, G. (1997). Predicting children's friendship status from their dynamic interaction in structured situations of potential conflict. *Child Development, 68,* 496–506.

Foreyt, J. P., & Goodrick, G. K. (1995). Obesity. In R. T. Ammerman & M. Hersen (Eds.), *Handbook of child behavior therapy in the psychiatric setting.* New York: Wiley.

Fortner, B. V., & Neimeyer, R. A. (1999). Death anxiety in older adults: A quantitative review. *Death Studies, 23,* 387–411.

Fox, N. A., Kimmerly, N. L., & Schafer, W. D. (1991). Attachment to mother/attachment to father: A meta-analysis. *Child Development, 62,* 210–225.

Fozard, J. L., & Gordon-Salant, S. (2001). Changes in vision and hearing with aging. In J. E. Birren & K. W. Schaie (Eds.), *Handbook of the psychology of aging* (5th ed., pp. 241–266). San Diego, CA: Academic Press.

Frazer, D. W., Leicht, M. L., & Baker, M. D. (1996). Psychological manifestations of physical disease in the elderly. In L. L. Carstensen, B. Edelstein, & L. Dornbrand (Eds.), *The practical handbook of clinical gerontology* (pp. 217–235). Thousand Oaks, CA: Sage.

Freer, J. P., & Clark, E. G. (1994). *The living will: A guide to health care decision making* [Online]. Available: http://freenet.buffalo.edu/%7Ebioethic/lwill.html.

Frerichs, F., & Naegele, G. (1997). Discrimination of older workers in Germany: Obstacles and options for the integration into employment. *Journal of Aging and Social Policy, 9,* 89–101.

Fretz, B. R. (2001). Coping with licensing, credentialing, and lifelong learning. In S. Walfish & A. K. Hess (Eds.), *Succeeding in graduate school: The career guide for psychology students* (pp. 353–367). Mahwah, NJ: Erlbaum.

Fried, P. A., O'Connell, C. M., & Watkinson, B. (1992). 60- and 72-month follow-up of children prenatally exposed to marijuana, cigarettes, and alcohol: Cognitive and language assessment. *Journal of Developmental & Behavioral Pediatrics, 13,* 383–391.

Friedman, J. M., & Polifka, J. E. (1996). *The effects of drugs on the fetus and nursing infant: A handbook for health care professionals.* Baltimore: Johns Hopkins University Press.

Friedman, M., & Rosenman, R. H. (1974). *Type A behavior and your heart.* New York: Random House.

Froman, L. (1994). Adult learning in the workplace. In J. D. Sinnott (Ed.), *Interdisciplinary handbook of adult lifespan learning* (pp. 203–217). Westport, CT: Greenwood Press.

Frone, M. R., Russell, M., & Barnes, G. M. (1996). Work-family conflict, gender, and health-related outcomes: A study of employed parents in two community samples. *Journal of Occupational Health Psychology, 1,* 57–69.

Frone, M. R., & Yardley, J. K. (1996). Workplace family-supportive programmes: Predictors of employed parents' importance ratings. *Journal of Occupational and Organizational Psychology, 69,* 351–366.

Fry, P. S. (1997). Grandparents' reactions to death of a grandchild: An exploratory factor analytic study. *Omega: Journal of Death and Dying, 35,* 119–140.

Frye, D. (1993). Causes and precursors of children's theories of mind. In D. F. Hay & A. Angold (Eds.), *Precursors and causes in development and psychopathology.* Chichester, England: Wiley.

Furman, W. (1995). Parenting siblings. In M. H. Bornstein (Ed.), *Handbook of parenting* (Vol. 1). Mahwah, NJ: Erlbaum.

Furman, W. (2002). The emerging field of adolescent romantic relationships. *Current Directions in Psychological Science, 11,* 177–180.

Furstenberg, F. F., Brooks-Gunn, J., & Morgan, S. P. (1987). *Adolescent mothers in later life.* New York: Cambridge University Press.

Furstenberg, F. F., & Teitler, J. O. (1994). Reconsidering the effects of marital disruption: What happens to children of divorce in early adulthood? *Journal of Family Issues, 15,* 173–190.

Futterman, A., Gallagher, D., Thompson, L. W., Lovett, S., & Gilewski, M. (1990). Retrospective assessment of marital adjustment and depression during the first two years of spousal bereavement. *Psychology and Aging, 5,* 277–283.

Gable, S., & Isabella, R. A. (1992). Maternal contributions to infant regulation of arousal. *Infant Behavior and Development, 15,* 95–107.

Gaddis, A., & Brooks-Gunn, J. (1985). The male experience of pubertal change. *Journal of Youth and Adolescence, 14,* 61–69.

Galinsky, E., Bond, J. T., & Friedman, D. E. (1996). The role of employers in addressing the needs of employed parents. *Journal of Social Issues, 52,* 111–136.

Gall, T. L., Evans, D. R., & Howard, J. (1997). The retirement adjustment process: Changes in the well-being of male retirees across time. *Journal of Gerontology: Psychological Sciences, 52B,* P110–P117.

Gallagher, M. (1996). Re-creating marriage. In D. Popenoe, J. B. Elshtain, & D. Blankenhorn (Eds.), *Promises to keep: Decline and renewal of marriage in America* (pp. 233–246). Lanham, MD: Rowman & Littlefield.

Galler, J. R., & Ramsey, F. (1989). A follow-up study of the influence of early malnutrition on development: Behavior at home and at school. *Journal of the American Academy of Child and Adolescent Psychiatry, 28,* 254–261.

Galler, J. R., Ramsey, F., & Forde, V. (1986). A follow-up study of the influence of early malnutrition on subsequent development: IV. Intellectual performance during adolescence. *Nutrition and Behavior, 3,* 211–222.

Ganong, L. M., & Coleman, M. (1994). *Remarried family relationships.* Thousand Oaks, CA: Sage.

Garbarino, J., & Kostelny, K. (1992). Child maltreatment as a community problem. *Child Abuse and Neglect, 16,* 455–464.

Gardner, H. (1983). *Frames of mind: The theory of multiple intelligences.* New York: Basic Books.

Gardner, H. (1993). *Multiple intelligences: The theory in practice.* New York: Basic Books.

Gardner, H. (1995). Reflections on multiple intelligences: Myths and messages. *Phi Delta Kappan, 77,* 200–203, 206–209.

Gardner, H. (1999). *Intelligence reframed: Multiple intelligences for the 21st century.* New York: Basic Books.

Gardner, H. (2002). *MI millennium: Multiple intelligences for the new millennium* [video recording]. Los Angeles: Into the Classroom Media.

Garland, A. F., & Zigler, E. (1993). Adolescent suicide prevention: Current research and social policy implications. *American Psychologist, 48,* 169–182.

Garner, P. W., Jones, D. C., & Palmer, D. J. (1994). Social cognitive correlates of preschool children's sibling caregiving behavior. *Developmental Psychology, 30,* 905–911.

Garvey, C., & Berninger, G. (1981). Timing and turn taking in children's conversations. *Discourse Processes, 4,* 27–59.

Gatz, M. (2000). Variations on depression in later life. In S. H. Qualls & N. Abeles (Eds.), *Psychology and the aging revolution* (pp. 239–254). Washington, DC: American Psychological Association.

Gatz, M., Pedersen, N. L., Berg, S., Johansson, B., Johansson, K., Mortimer, J. A., Posner, S. F., Viitanen, M., Winblad, B., & Ahlbom, A. (1997). Heritability for Alzheimer's disease: The study of dementia in Swedish twins. *Journal of Gerontology: Medical Sciences, 52A,* M117–M125.

Gatz, M., & Smyer, M. A. (2001). Mental health and aging at the outset of the twenty-first century. In J. E. Birren & K. W. Schaie (Eds.), *Handbook of the psychology of aging* (5th ed., pp. 523–544). San Diego, CA: Academic Press.

Gavin, L. A., & Furman, W. (1996). Adolescent girls' relationships with mothers and best friends. *Child Development, 67,* 375–386.

Gaylord, S. A., & Zung, W. W. K. (1987). Affective disorders among the aging. In L. L. Carstensen & B. A. Edelstein (Eds.), *Handbook of clinical gerontology* (pp. 76–95). New York: Pergamon Press.

Ge, X., Conger, R. D., & Elder, G. H. (1996). Coming of age too early: Pubertal influences on girls' vulnerability to psychological distress. *Child Development, 67,* 3386–3400.

Ge, X., Conger, R. D., & Elder, G. H. (2001). Pubertal transition, stressful life events, and the emergence of gender differences in adolescent depressive symptoms. *Developmental Psychology, 37,* 404–417.

Gelman, R., & Meck, E. (1986). The notion of principle: The case of counting. In J. Hiebert (Ed.), *Conceptual and procedural knowledge: The case of mathematics.* Hillside, NJ: Erlbaum.

Gelman, S. A., & Gottfried, G. M. (1996). Children's casual explanations of animate and inanimate motion. *Child Development, 67,* 1970–1987.

Genome Programs of the U.S. Department of Energy Office of Science. (2003). www.doegenomes.org, accessed on June 23, 2004.

Gerbner, G. (1993). *Women and minorities on television (a report to the Screen Actors Guild)*. Philadelphia: University of Pennsylvania, Annenberg School for Communication.

Gershoff, E. T. (2002). Corporal punishment by parents and associated child behaviors and experiences: A meta-analytic and theoretical review. *Psychological Bulletin, 128,* 539–579.

Giarusso, R., Feng, D., Silverstein, M., & Marenco, A. (2000). Primary and secondary stressors of grandparents raising grandchildren: Evidence from a national survey. *Journal of Mental Health and Aging, 6,* 291–310.

Gibbs, J. C., Clark, P. M., Joseph, J. A., Green, J. L., Goodrick, T. S., & Makowski, D. (1986). Relations between moral judgment, moral courage, and field independence. *Child Development, 57,* 185–193.

Giberson, P. K., & Weinberg, J. (1992). Fetal alcohol syndrome and functioning of the immune system. *Alcohol Health and Research World, 16,* 29–38.

Gibran, K. (1923). *The prophet.* New York: Knopf.

Gibson, E. J., Riccio, G., Schmuckler, M. A., Stoffregen, T. A., Rosenberg, D., & Taormina, J. (1987). Detection of the traversability of surfaces by crawling and walking infants. *Journal of Experimental Psychology: Human Perception & Performance, 13,* 533–544.

Gibson, E. J., & Walk, R. D. (1960). The "visual cliff." *Scientific American, 202,* 64–71.

Gibson, R. C. (1986). *Blacks in an aging society.* New York: Carnegie.

Gibson, R. C. (1987). Reconceptualizing retirement for black Americans. *The Gerontologist, 27,* 691–698.

Gignac, M. A. M., Kelloway, E. K., & Gottlieb, B. H. (1996). The impact of caregiving on employment: A mediational model of work-family conflict. *Canadian Journal on Aging, 15,* 525–542.

Gilligan, C. (1982). *In a different voice: Psychological theory and women's development.* Cambridge, MA: Harvard University Press.

Gilligan, C., & Attanucci, J. (1988). Two moral orientations: Gender differences and similarities. *Merrill-Palmer Quarterly, 34,* 223–237.

Gilmore, D. (1990). *Manhood in the making: Cultural components of masculinity.* New Haven, CT: Yale University Press.

Ginn, J., & Arber, S. (1996). Gender, age, and attitudes toward retirement in midlife. *Aging and Society, 16,* 27–55.

Gjerdingen, D., McGovern, P., Bekker, M., Lundberg, U., & Willemsen, T. (2000). Women's work roles and their impact on health, well-being and career: Comparisons between the United States, Sweden, and The Netherlands. *Women and Health, 31,* 1–20.

Glamser, F., & Hayslip, B., Jr. (1985). The impact of retirement on participation in leisure activities. *Therapeutic Recreation Journal, 19,* 28–38.

Glenn, N. D. (1998). The course of marital success and failure in five American 10-year marriage cohorts. *Journal of Marriage and the Family, 60,* 569–576.

Glickman, H. M. (2001). The relationship between person-organization value congruence and global job satisfaction. *Dissertation Abstracts International Section B: The Sciences and Engineering, 61*(12-B), 6745.

Gliksman, L., Adlaf, E. M., Demers, A., Newton-Taylor, B. (2003). Heavy drinking on Canadian campuses. *Canadian Journal of Public Health, 94,* 17–21.

Goff, S. J., Fick, D. S., & Opplinger, R. A. (1997). The moderating effect of spouse support on the relation between serious leisure and spouses' perceived leisure-family conflict. *Journal of Leisure Research, 29,* 47–60.

Goff, S. J., Mount, M. K., & Jamison, R. L. (1990). Employer supported child care, work/family conflict, and absenteeism: A field study. *Personnel Psychology, 43,* 793–809.

Gold, D. T., Woodbury, M. A., & George, L. K. (1990). Relationship classification using grade of membership analysis: A typology of sibling relationships in later life. *Journal of Gerontology: Social Sciences, 45,* S43–S51.

Goldsmith, H. H., Buss, A. H., Plomin, R., & Rothbart, M. K. (1987). What is temperament? Four approaches. *Child Development, 58,* 505–529.

Goldsmith, H. H., Buss, K. A., & Lemery, K. S. (1997). Toddler and childhood temperament: Expanded content, stronger genetic evidence, new evidence for the importance of environment. *Developmental Psychology, 33,* 891–905.

Goldsmith, H. H., & Harman, C. (1994). Temperament and attachment: Individuals and relationships. *Current Directions in Psychological Science, 3,* 53–57.

Golombok, S., & Tasker, F. (1996). Do parents influence the sexual orientation of their children? Findings from a longitudinal study of lesbian families. *Developmental Psychology, 32,* 3–11.

Golsworthy, R., & Coyle, A. (2001). Practitioners' accounts of religious and spiritual dimension in bereavement therapy. *Counselling Psychology Quarterly, 14,* 183–202.

Gomez, T. R. A. (2000). College undergraduate binge drinking: A reconceptualization of the problem and an examination of socialization contexts. *Dissertation Abstracts International: Section A: Humanities and Social Sciences, 60,* 4621.

Good, T. L., & Brophy, J. E. (1994). *Looking in classrooms* (6th ed.). New York: HarperCollins.

Goodkin, K., Burkhalter, J. E., Blaney, N. T., Leeds, B., Tuttle, R. S., & Feaster, D. J. (1997). A research derived bereavement support group technique for the HIV-1 infected. *Omega: Journal of Death and Dying, 34,* 279–300.

Goodman, G. S., Emery, R. E., & Haugaard, J. J. (1998). Developmental psychology and law: Divorce, child maltreatment, foster care, and adoption. In W. Damon (Ed.), *Handbook of child psychology* (Vol. 4). New York: Wiley.

Goodnow, J. J. (1992). *Parental belief systems: The psychological consequences for children.* Hillsdale, NJ: Erlbaum.

Gordon, B. N., Baker-Ward, L., & Ornstein, P. A. (2001). Children's testimony: A review of research on memory for past experiences. *Clinical Child & Family Psychology Review, 4,* 157–181.

Gordon, C. P. (1996). Adolescent decision making: A broadly based theory and its application to the prevention of early pregnancy. *Adolescence, 31,* 561–584.

Gordon, C., Gaitz, C. M., & Scott, J. (1976). Leisure and lives: Personal expressivity across the life span. In R. H. Binstock & E. Shanas (Eds.), *Handbook of aging and the social sciences* (2nd ed., pp. 310–341). New York: Van Nostrand Reinhold.

Gottesman, I. I. (1963). Genetic aspects of intelligent behavior. In N. R. Ellis (Ed.), *Handbook of mental deficiency.* New York: McGraw-Hill.

Gottfredson, L. S. (1997). Why g matters: The complexity of everyday life. *Intelligence, 24,* 79–132.

Gottlieb, L. N., & Mendelson, M. J. (1990). Parental support and firstborn girls' adaptation to the birth of a sibling. *Journal of Applied Developmental Psychology, 11,* 29–48.

Gottman, J. M. (1986). The world of coordinated play: Same- and cross-sex friendships in children. In J. M. Gottman & J. G. Parker (Eds.), *Conversations of friends.* New York: Cambridge University Press.

Gottman, J. M., Katz, L. F., & Hooven, C. (1996). Parental meta-emotion philosophy and the emotional life of families: Theoretical models and preliminary data. *Journal of Family Psychology, 10,* 243–268.

Goubet, N., & Clifton, R. K. (1998). Object and event representation in 6 ½-month-old infants. *Developmental Psychology, 34,* 63–76.

Goubet, N., Clifton, R. K., & Shah, B. (2001). Learning about pain in preterm newborns. *Journal of Developmental and Behavioral Pediatrics, 22,* 418–424.

Gould, R. L. (1978). *Transformation: Growth and change in adult life.* New York: Simon & Schuster.

Gould, S. J. (1999). A critique of Heckhausen and Schulz's (1995) life-span theory of control from a cross-cultural perspective. *Psychological Review, 106,* 597–604.

Government of Canada. (2000). Bill C-23 Modernization of benefits and obligations. Available: http://canada.justice.gc.ca/en/news/nr/2000/doc_25021.html. (Retrieved April 21, 2004).

Government of Canada. (2002). *Children come first: A report to parliament reviewing the provisions and operation of the federal child support guidelines (vol 2)* [Online]. Available: http://www.justice.gc.ca/en/ps/sup/pub/rp/volume_2.pdf. (Retrieved October 2, 2004.)

Govier, E., & Salisbury, G. (2000). Age-related sex differences in performance on a side-naming spatial task. *Psychology, Evolution, & Gender, 2,* 209–222.

Graber, J. A., Brooks-Gunn, J., & Warren, M. P. (1995). The antecedents of menarcheal age: Heredity, family environment, and stressful life events. *Child Development, 66,* 346–359.

Graesser, A. C., Singer, M., & Trabasso, T. (1994). Constructing inferences during narrative text comprehension. *Psychological Review, 101,* 371–395.

Graham, S., Berninger, V. W., Abbott, R. D., Abbott, S. P., & Whitaker, D. (1997). Role of mechanics in composing of elementary school students: A new methodological approach. *Journal of Educational Psychology, 89,* 170–182.

Graham, S., Harris, K. R., & Fink, B. (2000). Is handwriting causally related to learning to write? Treatment of handwriting problems in beginning writers. *Journal of Educational Psychology, 92,* 620–633.

Grandey, A. A. (2001). Family friendly policies: Organizational justice perceptions of need-based allocations. In R. Cropanzano (Ed.), *Justice in the workplace: From theory to practice* (pp. 145–173). Mahwah, NJ: Erlbaum.

Grantham-McGregor, S., Ani, C., & Fernald, L. (2001). The role of nutrition in intellectual development. In R. J. Sternberg & E. L. Grigorenko (Eds.), *Environmental effects on cognitive abilities* (pp. 119–155). Mahwah, NJ: Erlbaum.

Greenberg, B. S., Fazel, S., & Weber, M. (1986). *Children's view on advertising.* New York: Independent Broadcasting Authority Research Report.

Greenberg, M. T., & Crnic, K. A. (1988). Longitudinal predictors of developmental status and social interaction in premature and full-term infants at age two. *Child Development, 59,* 554–570.

Greenfield, P. M. (1998). The cultural evolution of IQ. In U. Neisser (Ed.), *The rising curve: Long-term gains in IQ and related measures* (pp. 81–123). Washington, DC: American Psychological Association.

Greenglass, E. R., Burke, R. J., & Konarski, R. (1998). Components of burnout, resources, and gender-related differences. *Journal of Applied Social Psychology, 28,* 1088–1106.

Greenwald, A. G., McGhee, D. E., & Schwaartz, J. L. K. (1998). Measuring individual differences in implicit cognition: The implicit association test. *Journal of Personality and Social Psychology, 74,* 1464–1480.

Grice, H. P. (1975). Logic and conversation. In P. Cole & J. Morgan (Eds.), *Speech acts: Syntax and semantics.* (Vol. 3, pp. 41–58). New York: Academic Press.

Grigorenko, E. L., & Sternberg, R. J. (1998). Dynamic testing. *Psychological Bulletin, 124,* 75–111.

Grigorenko, E. L., & Sternberg, R. J. (2001). Analytical, creative, and practical intelligence as predictors of self-reported adaptive functioning: A case study in Russia. *Intelligence, 29,* 57–73.

Grob, A., Little, T. D., & Wanner, B. (1999). Control judgements across the lifespan. *International Journal of Behavioral Decisions, 23,* 833–854.

Groen, G. J., & Resnick, L. B. (1977). Can preschool children invent addition algorithms? *Journal of Educational Psychology, 69,* 645–652.

Gross, A. M., Bennet, T., Sloan, L., Marx, B. P., & Juergens, J. (2001). The impact of alcohol and alcohol expectancies on male perception of female sexual arousal in a date rape analog. *Experimental and Clinical Psychopharmacology, 9,* 380–388.

Gross, E. A. (1999). *Telemarketing fraud.* Unpublished doctoral dissertation, Department of Educational Counseling, University of Southern California, Los Angeles.

Gross, R. T. (1984). Patterns of maturation: Their effects on behavior and development. In M. D. Levine & P. Satz (Eds.), *Middle childhood: Development and dysfunction.* Baltimore: University Park Press.

Grossman, A. H. (1997). The virtual and actual identities of older lesbians and gay men. In M. Duberman (Ed.), *A queer world: The Center for Lesbian and Gay Studies reader* (pp. 615–626). New York: New York University Press.

Guelzow, M. G., Bird, G. W., & Koball, E. H. (1991). An exploratory path analysis of the stress process for dual-career men and women. *Journal of Marriage and the Family, 53,* 151–164.

Guillemin, J. (1993). Cesarean birth: Social and political aspects. In B. K. Rothman (Ed.), *Encyclopedia of childbearing.* Phoenix, AZ: Oryx Press.

Gunnar, M. R., Bruce, J., & Grotevant, H. D. (2000). International adoption of institutionally reared children: Research and policy. *Development and Psychopathology, 12,* 677–693.

Gunter, N. C., & Gunter, B. G. (1990). Domestic division of labor among working couples: Does androgyny make a difference? *Psychology of Women Quarterly, 14,* 355–370.

Guralnick, J. M., & Simonsick, E. M. (1993). Physical disability in older Americans. *The Journals of Gerontology, 48* (Special Issue), 3–10.

Gurucharri, C., & Selman, R. L. (1982). The development of interpersonal understanding during childhood, preadolescence, and adolescence: A longitudinal follow-up study. *Child Development, 53,* 924–927.

Gutek, B. A., Searle, S., & Klepa, L. (1991). Rational versus gender role explanations for work-family conflict. *Journal of Applied Psychology, 76,* 560–568.

Gutmann, D. L. (1987). *Reclaimed powers: Toward a new psychology of men and women in later life.* New York: Basic Books.

Guttmacher, A. F., & Kaiser, I. H. (1986). *Pregnancy, birth, and family planning.* New York: New American Library.

Haas, L. (1990). Gender equality and social policy: Implications of a study of parental leave in Sweden. *Journal of Family Issues, 11,* 401–423.

Hagestad, G. O., & Dannefer, D. (2001). Concepts and theories of aging: Beyond microfication in social science approaches. In R. H. Binstock & L. K. George (Eds.), *Handbook of aging and the social sciences* (5th ed., pp. 3–21). San Diego, CA: Academic Press.

Hagestad, G. O., & Neugarten, B. L. (1985). Age and the life course. In R. H. Binstock & E. Shanas (Eds.), *Handbook of aging and the social sciences* (2nd ed., pp. 35–61). New York: Van Nostrand Reinhold.

Haight, B. K. (1992). Long-term effects of a structured life review process. *Journal of Gerontology: Psychological Sciences, 47,* P312–P315.

Hall, D. G., Lee, S. C., & Belanger, J. (2001). Young children's use of syntactic cues to learn proper names and count nouns. *Developmental Psychology, 37,* 298–307.

Hall, D. R., & Zhao, J. Z. (1995). Cohabitation and divorce in Canada: Testing the selectivity hypothesis. *Journal of Marriage and the Family, 57,* 421–427.

Hall, J. A., & Halberstadt, A. G. (1981). Sex roles and nonverbal communication skills. *Sex Roles, 7,* 273–287.

Halpern, D. F. (2000). *Sex differences in cognitive abilities* (3rd ed.). Mahwah, NJ: Erlbaum.

Halpern, J. (1987). *Helping your aging parents.* New York: McGraw-Hill.

Halpern L. F., MacLean, W. E., & Baumeister, A. A. (1995). Infant sleep-wake characteristics: Relation to neurological status and the prediction of developmental outcome. *Developmental Review, 15,* 255–291.

Hamill, S. B., & Goldberg, W. A. (1997). Between adolescents and aging grandparents: Midlife concerns of adults in the sandwich generation. *Journal of Adult Development, 4,* 135–147.

Hamon, R. R., & Blieszner, R. (1990). Filial responsibility expectations among adult child–older parent pairs. *Journal of Gerontology: Psychological Sciences, 45,* P110–P112.

Hance, V. M. (2000). An existential perspective describing undergraduate students' ideas about meaning in work: A q-method study. *Dissertation Abstracts International Section A: Humanities and Social Sciences, 61*(3-A), 878.

Harbison, J. (1999). Models of intervention for "elder abuse and neglect": A Canadian perspective on ageism, participation, and empowerment. *Journal of Elder Abuse and Neglect, 10,* 1–17.

Hareven, T. K. (1995). Introduction: Aging and generational relations over the life course. In T. K. Hareven (Ed.), *Aging and generational relations over the life course: A historical and cross-cultural perspective* (pp. 1–12). Berlin: de Gruyter.

Hareven, T. K., & Adams, K. (1996). The generation in the middle: Cohort comparisons in assistance to aging parents in an American community. In T. K. Hareven (Ed.), *Aging and generational relations: Life course and cross-cultural perspectives* (pp. 3–29). New York: Aldine de Gruyter.

Harringer, C. (1994). Adults in college. In J. D. Sinnott (Ed.), *Interdisciplinary handbook of adult lifespan learning* (pp. 171–185). Westport, CT: Greenwood Press.

Harrington, D., Bean, N., Pintello, D., & Mathews, D. (2001). Job satisfaction and burnout: Predictors of intentions to leave a job in a military setting. *Administration in Social Work, 25,* 1–16.

Harris, L. J. (1983). Laterality of function in the infant: Historical and contemporary trends in theory and research. In G. Young, S. J. Segalowitz, C. M. Corter, & S. E. Trehub (Eds.), *Manual specialization and the developing brain.* New York: Academic Press.

Harris, P. L., Brown, E., Marriot, C., Whithall, S., & Harmer, S. (1991). Monsters, ghosts, and witches: Testing the limits of the fantasy-reality distinction in young children. *British Journal of Developmental Psychology, 9*, 105–123.

Harris, P. L., & Kavanaugh, R. D. (1993). Young children's understanding of pretense. *Monographs of the Society for Research in Child Development, 58*, Serial No. 231.

Harrist, A. W., Zaia, A. F., Bates, J. E., Dodge, K. A., & Pettit, G. S. (1997). Subtypes of social withdrawal in early childhood: Sociometric status and social-cognitive differences across four years. *Child Development, 68*, 278–294.

Hart, D. A. (1992). *Becoming men: The development of aspirations, values, and adaptational styles.* New York: Plenum.

Harter, S. (1990). Self and identity development. In S. S. Feldman & G. R. Elliott (Eds.), *At the threshold: The developing adolescent.* Cambridge, MA: Harvard University Press.

Harter, S. (1994). Developmental changes in self-understanding across the 5 to 7 shift. In A. Sameroff & M. M. Haith (Eds.), *Reason and responsibility: The passage through childhood.* Chicago: University of Chicago Press.

Harter, S. (1999). *The construction of the self: A developmental perspective.* New York: Guilford.

Harter, S., Waters, P., & Whitesell, N. R. (1998). Relational self-worth: Differences in perceived worth as a person across interpersonal contexts among adolescents. *Child Development, 69*, 756–766.

Harter, S., Whitesell, N. R., & Kowalski, P. S. (1992). Individual differences in the effects of educational transitions on young adolescents' perceptions of competence and motivational orientation. *American Educational Research Journal, 29*, 777–807.

Hartman, P. S. (2001). Women developing wisdom: Antecedents and correlates in a longitudinal sample. *Dissertation Abstracts International Section B: The Sciences and Engineering, 62*(1-B), 591.

Hartup, W. W. (1983). Peer relations. In P. H. Mussen (Ed.), *Handbook of child psychology* (Vol. 4). New York: Wiley.

Hartup, W. W. (1992a). Friendships and their developmental significance. In H. McGurk (Ed.), *Contemporary issues in childhood social development.* London: Routledge.

Hartup, W. W. (1992b). Peer relations in early and middle childhood. In V. B. Van Hasselt & M. Hersen (Eds.), *Handbook of social development: A lifespan perspective.* New York: Plenum.

Hartup, W. W., & Stevens, N. (1999). Friendships and adaptation across the life span. *Current Directions in Psychological Science, 8*, 76–79.

Haselager, G. J. T., Hartup, W. W., van Lieshout, C. F. M., & Riksen-Walraven, J. M. A. (1998). Similarities between friends and nonfriends in middle childhood. *Child Development, 69*, 1198–1208.

Hastings, P. D., & Rubin, K. H. (1999). Predicting mothers' beliefs about preschool-aged children's social behavior: Evidence for maternal attitudes moderating child effects. *Child Development, 70*, 722–741.

Hatch, L. R., & Bulcroft, C. (1992). Contact with friends in later life: Disentangling the effects of gender and marital stability. *Journal of Marriage and the Family, 54*, 222–232.

Havighurst, R. J. (1982). The world of work. In B. B. Wolman (Ed.), *Handbook of developmental psychology* (pp. 771–787). Englewood Cliffs, NJ: Prentice Hall.

Haviland, J. M., & Lelwica, M. (1987). The induced affect response: 10-week-old infants' responses to three emotion expressions. *Developmental Psychology, 23*, 97–104.

Hawranik, P., & McKean, E. (2004). Elder abuse. In C. A. Ateah & J. Mirwaldt (Eds.), *Within our reach: Preventing abuse across the lifespan.* Halifax, NS: Fernwood Publishing and RESOLVE (Research and Education for Solutions to Violence and Abuse).

Hayashi, M., Hasui, C., Kitamura, F., Murakami, M., Takeuchi, M., Katoh, H., & Kitamura, T. (2000). Respecting autonomy in difficult medical settings: A questionnaire study in Japan. *Ethics and Behavior, 10*, 51–63.

Hayflick, L. (1996). *How and why we age* (2nd ed.). New York: Ballantine.

Hayflick, L. (1998). How and why we age. *Experimental Gerontology, 33*, 639–653.

Hayslip, B., Jr., & Goldberg-Glen, R. (2000). *Grandparents raising grandchildren: Theoretical, empirical, and clinical perspectives.* New York: Springer.

Hayslip, B., Jr., Shore, R. J., Henderson, C. E., & Lambert, P. L. (1998). Custodial grandparenting and the impact of grandchildren with problems on role satisfaction and role meaning. *Journal of Gerontology: Social Sciences, 53B*, S164–S173.

Hayward, M. D., Friedman, S., & Chen, H. (1998). Career trajectories and older men's retirement. *Journal of Gerontology: Social Sciences, 53B*, S91–S103.

Hazan, C., & Shaver, P. (1987). Romantic love conceptualized as an attachment process. *Journal of Personality and Social Psychology, 52*, 511–524.

Hazan, C., & Shaver, P. (1990). Love and work: An attachment-theoretical perspective. *Journal of Personality and Social Psychology, 59*, 270–280.

Hazan, C., & Shaver, P. (1994). Attachment as an organizational framework for research on close relationships. *Psychological Inquiry, 5*, 1–22.

Health Canada. (1998). *Reaching out: A guide to communicating with Aboriginal Seniors* [Online]. Available: http://www.hc-sc.ca/seniors-aines/. (Retrieved October 4, 2004.)

Health Canada. (1999a). *Abuse and neglect of older adults* [Online]. Available: http://www.hc-sc.gc.ca/hppb/familyviolence/html/agenegl_e.html. (Retrieved May 15, 2004.)

Health Canada. (1999b). *A diagnostic on the health of First Nations and Inuit people of Canada.* Ottawa: Author.

Health Canada. (1999c). *Nutrition for a healthy pregnancy: National guidelines for the childbearing years.* Ottawa: Author.

Health Canada. (1999d). *A second diagnostic on the health of First Nations and Inuit people in Canada.* [Online]. Available:

http://www.hc-sc.gc.ca/fnihb/cp/publications/second_diagnostic_fni.pdf. (Retrieved March 14, 2004.)

Health Canada. (2000/2001). *Canadian community health survey.* Ottawa: Author.

Health Canada. (2000a). *Acting on what we know: Preventing youth suicide in First Nations* [Online]. Available: http://www.hc-sc.gc.ca/fnihb-dgspni/fnihb/cp/publications/preventing_youth_suicide.pdf. (Retrieved March 13, 2004.)

Health Canada. (2000b). *Chronic diseases in Canada – Mortality attributed to tobacco use in Canada and its regions, 1994 and 1996.* [Online]. Available: http://www.hc-sc.gc.ca/pphb-dgspsp/publicat/cdic-mcc/20-3/b_e.html. (Retrieved March 20, 2004.)

Health Canada. (2000c). *Fetal Alcohol Syndrome/Fetal Alcohol Effects* [Online]. Available: http://www.hc-sc.gc.ca. (Retrieved January 16, 2004.)

Health Canada. (2002a). *Canadian youth sexual health and the AIDS study* [Online]. Available: http://cmec.ca/publications/aids/CYSHHAS_2002_EN.pdf. (Retrieved March 12, 2004.)

Health Canada. (2002b). Children making a community whole: A review of Aboriginal Head Start in urban and Northern communities. Ottawa: Author.

Health Canada. (2002c). Updated. *Choosing when and how to die* [Online]. Available: http://www.hc-sc.gc.ca/seniors-aines/naca/expression/10-1-exp_10_1_e.htm. (Retrieved May 15, 2004.)

Health Canada. (2002d). *Report on smoking.* Available: http://www.statcan.ca/Daily/English/021216/d021216g.htm. (Retrieved March 15, 2004.)

Health Canada. (2002e). *Trends in the health of Canadian youth – coping with life* [Online]. Available: http://www.hc-sc.gc.ca/dca-dea/publications/hbsc_05_e.html. (Retrieved April 19, 2004.)

Health Canada. (2003a). *Canadian guidelines for body weight classification in adults* [Online]. Available: http://www.hc-sc.gc.ca/hpfb-dgpsa/onpp-bppn/weight_book_e.pdf. (Retrieved March 23, 2004.)

Health Canada. (2003b). *Canadian perinatal health report.* Ottawa: Author.

Health Canada. (2003c). *Canadian youth sexual health and the AIDS study* [Online]. Available: http://cmec.ca/publications/aids/CYSHHAS_2002_EN.pdf. (Retrieved March 12, 2004.)

Health Canada. (2003d). *Canada's oldest seniors* [Online]. Available: http://www.hc-sc.gc.ca/seniors-aines/pubs/factoids/2001/no02_e.htm. (Retrieved May 1, 2004.)

Health Canada. (2003e). *Canada's physical activity guide to healthy active living* [Online]. Available: http://www.hc-sc.gc.ca/hppb/fitness/index.html. (Retrieved April 25, 2004.)

Health Canada. (2003f). *The growing burden of heart disease and stroke in Canada 2003* [Online]. Available: http://www.cvinfobase.ca/cvdbook/En/Index.htm. (Retrieved May 10, 2004.)

Health Canada. (2003g). *An integrated Pan-Canadian healthy living strategy: A discussion document* [Online]. Available: http://www.hc-sc.gc.ca/english/lifestyles/healthy living/symposium/.

Health Canada. (2003h). *Statistical profile on the health of First Nation Canadians* [Online]. Available: http://www.hc-sc.ca/fnihb-dgspni/fnihb/sppa/hia/publications/statistical_profile.pdf. (Retrieved May 1, 2004.)

Health Canada. (2003i). *Women's health surveillance report: Perimenopausal and postmenopausal health* [Online]. Available: http://www.hc-sc.gc.ca/pphb-dgspsp/publicat/whsr-rssf/chap_22_e.html. (Retrieved April 22, 2004.)

Health Canada. (2004a). *Benefits and risks of combined (Estrogen and Progestin) hormone replacement therapy* [Online]. Available: http://www.hc-sc.gc.ca/english/iyh/medical/estrogen.html. (Retrieved April 23, 2004.)

Health Canada. (2004b). Updated. *Canada Health Act: Overview* [Online]. Available: http://www.hc-sc.gc.ca/medicare/home.htm. (Retrieved May 15, 2004.)

Health Canada. (2004c). *The facts about tobacco – What is second-hand smoke?* [Online]. Available: http://www.hc-sc.gc.ca/hecs-sesc/tobacco/facts/health_facts/second_hand.html. (Retrieved March 20, 2004.)

Health Canada. (2004d). *Go smoke free* [Online]. Available: http://www.hc-sc.gc.ca/hecs-sesc/tobacco/index/html. (Retrieved March 18, 2004.)

Health Canada. (2004e). *On the road to quitting—benefits of quitting* [Online]. Avaialble: http://www.hc-sc.gc.ca/hecs-sesc/tobacco/quitting/ontheroad/self_diagnosis/unit2/10.html. (Retrieved April 20, 2004.)

Health Canada - National Advisory Council on Aging. (2003). *Dementia in Canada* [Online]. Available: http://www.hc-sc.gc.ca/seniors/aines/pubs/vignette/pdf/vig34-50_e.pdf. (Retrieved May 1, 2004.)

Hearold, S. (1986). A synthesis of 1,043 effects of television on social behavior. In G. Comstock (Ed.), *Public communications and behavior* (Vol. 1, pp. 65–133). New York: Academic Press.

Heckhausen, J., & Schulz, R. (1999). Selectivity in lifespan development: Biological and societal canalizations and individuals developmental goals. In J. Brandtstädter, B. M. Lerner, et al. (Eds.), *Action and self development: Theory and research through the lifespan* (pp. 67–130). Thousand Oaks, CA: Sage.

Heidrich, S. M., & Denney, N. W. (1994). Does social problem solving differ from other types of problem solving during the adult years? *Experimental Aging Research, 20,* 105–126.

Heimann, B., & Pittenger, K. K. S. (1996). The impact of formal mentorship on socialization and commitment of newcomers. *Journal of Managerial Issues, 8,* 108–117.

Henderson, B. N., Davison, K. P., Pennebaker, J. W., Gatchel, R. J., & Baum, A. (2002). Disease disclosure patterns among breast cancer patients. *Psychology and Health, 17,* 51–62.

Henderson, K. A. (1990). The meaning of leisure for women: An integrative review of the research. *Journal of Leisure Research, 22,* 228–243.

Henderson, V. W. (1997). Estrogen, cognition, and a woman's risk of Alzheimer's disease. *American Journal of Medicine, 103*(3A), 11S–18S.

Henkel, J. (1998). Parkinson's disease: New treatments slow onslaught of symptoms. *FDA Consumer, 32*(4), 13–18.

Henretta, J. C. (1997). Changing perspectives on retirement. *Journal of Gerontology: Social Sciences, 52B*, S1–S3.

Henretta, J. C. (2001). Work and retirement. In R. H. Binstock & L. K. George, (Eds.), *Handbook of aging and the social sciences* (pp. 255–271). San Diego, CA: Academic Press.

Henretta, J. C., Chan, C. G., & O'Rand, A. M. (1992). Retirement reason versus retirement process: Examining the reasons for retirement typology. *Journal of Gerontology: Social Sciences, 47*, S1–S7.

Herrnstein, R. J., & Murray, C. (1994). *The bell curve: Intelligence and class structure in American life.* New York: Free Press.

Hershberger, S. L., & D'Augelli, A. R. (1995). The impact of victimization on the mental health and suicidality of lesbian, gay, and bisexual youths. *Developmental Psychology, 31*, 65–74.

Hertz, R. (1997). A typology of approaches to child care: The centerpiece of organizing family life for dual-earner couples. *Journal of Family Issues, 18*, 355–385.

Herzog, A. R., Kahn, R. L., Morgan, J. N., Jackson, J. S., & Antonucci, T. C. (1989). Age differences in productive activities. *Journal of Gerontology: Social Sciences, 44*, S129–S138.

Hertzog, C., & Hultsch, D. F. (2000). Metacognition in adulthood and old age. In F. I. M. Craik & T. A. Salthouse (Eds.), *The handbook of aging and cognition* (2nd ed., pp. 417–466). Mahwah, NJ: Erlbaum.

Hespos, S. J., & Baillargeon, R. (2001). Infants' knowledge about occlusion and containment events: A surprising discrepancy. *Psychological Science, 121*, 141–147.

Hess, U., & Kirouac, G. (2000). Emotion expression in groups. In M. Lewis & J. Haviland-Jones (Eds.), *Handbook of emotions* (2nd ed.). New York: Guilford Press.

Hetherington, E. M. (1988). Family relations six years after divorce. In K. Pasley & M. Ihinger-Tallman (Eds.), *Remarriage and stepparenting: Current research and theory.* New York: Guilford Press.

Hetherington, E. M. (1989). Coping with family transitions: Winners, losers and survivors. *Child Development, 60*, 1–14.

Hetherington, E. M. (1993). An overview of the Virginia Longitudinal Study of Divorce and Remarriage with a focus on early adolescence. *Journal of Family Psychology, 7*, 39–56.

Hetherington, E. M., & Kelly, J. (2002). *For better or for worse: Divorce reconsidered.* New York: W. W. Norton.

Hetherington, S. E. (1990). A controlled study of the effect of prepared childbirth classes on obstetric outcomes. *Birth, 17*, 86–90.

Heyman, G. D., & Gelman, S. A. (1999). The use of trait labels in making psychological inferences. *Child Development, 70*, 604–619.

Higgins, A. (1991). The Just Community approach to moral education: Evolution of the idea and recent findings. In W. M.

Kurtines & J. L. Gewirtz (Eds.), *Handbook of moral behavior and development* (Vol. 3). Hillsdale, NJ: Erlbaum.

Hilton, J. L., & von Hippel, W. (1996). Stereotypes. *Annual Review of Psychology, 47*, 237–271.

Himsel, A. J., Hart, H., Diamond, A., & McAdams, D. P. (1997). Personality characteristics of highly generative adults as assessed in Q-sort ratings of life stories. *Journal of Adult Development, 4*, 149–161.

Hobart, C. (1988). The family system in remarriage: An exploratory study. *Journal of Marriage and the Family, 50*, 649–661.

Hobdy, J. (2000). The role of individuation processes in the launching of children into adulthood. *Dissertation Abstracts International Section B: The Sciences and Engineering, 60*(9-B), 4929.

Hodges, E. V. E., Boivin, M., Vitaro, F., & Bukowski, W. M. (1999). The power of friendship: Protection against an escalating cycle of peer victimization. *Developmental Psychology, 35*, 94–101.

Hoff, E. (2001). *Language development* (2nd ed.). Belmont, CA: Wadsworth.

Hoff, E., & Naigles, L. (2002). How children use input to acquire a lexicon. *Child Development, 73*, 418–433.

Hoff-Ginsberg, E. (1990). Maternal speech and the child's development of syntax: A further look. *Journal of Child Language, 17*, 85–99.

Hoff-Ginsberg, E. (1997). *Language development.* Pacific Grove, CA: Brooks/Cole.

Hoffman, M. L. (1988). Moral development. In M. H. Bornstein & M. E. Lamb (Eds.), *Developmental psychology: An advanced textbook* (2nd ed.). Hillsdale, NJ: Erlbaum.

Hoffman, M. L. (1994). Discipline and internalization. *Developmental Psychology, 30*, 26–28.

Hogan, D. P., & Astone, N. M. (1986). The transition to adulthood. *Annual Review of Sociology, 12*, 109–130.

Hogan, N., & DeSantis, L. (1996). Basic constructs of a theory of adolescent sibling bereavement. In D. Klass, P. R. Silverman, & S. L. Nickman (Eds.), *Continuing bonds: New understandings of grief* (pp. 235–254). Washington, DC: Taylor & Francis.

Hoge, D. D., Smit, E. K., & Hanson, S. L. (1990). School experiences predicting changes in self-esteem of sixth- and seventh-grade students. *Journal of Educational Psychology, 82*, 117–127.

Hogge, W. A. (1990). Teratology. In I. R. Merkatz & J. E. Thompson (Eds.), *New perspectives on prenatal care.* New York: Elsevier.

Holcomb, D. R., Savage, M. P., Seehager, R., & Waalkes, D. M. (2002). A mixed-gender date rape prevention intervention targeting freshman college athletes. *College Student Journal, 36*, 165–179.

Holden, G. W. (1988). Adults' thinking about a child-rearing problem: Effects of experience, parental status and gender. *Child Development, 59*, 1623–1632.

Holden, G. W., & Miller, P. C. (1999). Enduring and different: A meta-analysis of the similarity in parents' child rearing. *Psychological Bulletin, 125,* 223–254.

Hollan, D. (1995). To the afterworld and back: Mourning and dreams of the dead among the Toranja. *Ethos, 23,* 424–436.

Holland, J. L. (1985). *Making vocational choices: A theory of vocational personalities and work environments* (2nd ed.). Englewood Cliffs, NJ: Prentice Hall.

Holland, J. L. (1987). Current status of Holland's theory of careers: Another perspective. *Career Development Quarterly, 36,* 24–30.

Holland, J. L. (1996). Exploring careers with a typology: What we have learned and some new directions. *American Psychologist, 51,* 397–406.

Hollich, G. J., Hirsh-Pasek, K., & Golinkoff, R. M. (2000). Breaking the language barrier: An emergentist coalition model for the origins of word learning. *Monographs of the Society for Research in Child Development, 65* (Serial No. 262).

Hollon, S. D., Thase, M. E., & Markowitz, J. C. (2002). Treatment and prevention of depression. *Psychological Science in the Public Interest, 3,* 39–77.

Hom, P. W., & Kinicki, A. J. (2001). Toward a greater understanding of how dissatisfaction drives employee turnover. *Academy of Management Journal, 44,* 975–987.

Honda-Howard, M., & Homma, M. (2001). Job satisfaction of Japanese career women and its influence on turnover intention. *Asian Journal of Social Psychology, 4,* 23–38.

Hood, B., Carey, S., & Prasada, S. (2000). Predicting the outcomes of physical events: Two-year-olds fail to reveal knowledge of solidity and support. *Child Development, 71,* 1540–1554.

Hooker, K. (1999). Possible selves in adulthood: Incorporating teleonomic relevance into studies of the self. In T. M. Hess & F. Blanchard-Fields (Eds.), *Social cognition and aging* (pp. 97–122). San Diego, CA: Academic Press.

Hooyman, N., & Kiyak, H. A. (1999). *Social gerontology: A multidisciplinary perspective* (5th ed.). Boston: Allyn & Bacon.

Horn, J. L. (1982). The aging of human abilities. In B. B. Wolman (Ed.), *Handbook of developmental psychology* (pp. 847–870). Englewood Cliffs, NJ: Prentice Hall.

Horn, J. L., & Hofer, S. M. (1992). Major abilities and development in the adult period. In R. J. Sternberg & C. A. Berg (Eds.), *Intellectual development* (pp. 44–99). Cambridge, UK: Cambridge University Press.

Hovey, J. D., & Magana, C. (2000). Acculturative stress, anxiety, and depression among Mexican farmworkers in the Midwest United States. *Journal of Immigrant Health, 2,* 119–131.

Howe, N., Petrakos, H., & Rinaldi, C. M. (1998). "All the sheeps are dead. He murdered them": Sibling pretense, negotiation, internal state language, and relationship quality. *Child Development, 69,* 182–191.

Howe, N., & Ross, H. S. (1990). Socialization perspective taking and the sibling relationship. *Developmental Psychology, 26,* 160–165.

Howes, C., & Matheson, C. C. (1992). Sequences in the development of competent play with peers: Social and social pretend play. *Developmental Psychology, 28,* 961–974.

Howes, C., Unger, O., & Seidner, L. B. (1990). Social pretend play in toddlers: Parallels with social play and with solitary pretend. *Child Development, 60,* 77–84.

Hoyer, W. J., & Rybash, J. M. (1994). Characterizing adult cognitive development. *Journal of Adult Development, 1,* 7–12.

Hudson, J. A. (2001). The anticipated self: Mother-child talk about future events. In C. Moore & K. Lemmon (Eds.), *The self in time: Developmental perspectives* (pp. 53–74). Mahwah, NJ: Erlbaum.

Hudson, R. B. (1996). Social protection and services. In R. H. Binstock & L. K. George (Eds.), *Handbook of aging and the social sciences* (4th ed., pp. 446–466). San Diego, CA: Academic Press.

Huesmann, L. R., & Miller, L. S. (1994). Long-term effects of repeated exposure to media violence in childhood. In L. R. Huesmann (Ed.), *Aggressive behavior: Current perspectives.* New York: Plenum.

Hulme, C., Hatcher, P. J., Nation, K., Brown, A., Adams, J., & Stuart, G. (2002). Phoneme awareness is a better predictor of early reading skill than onset-rime awareness. *Journal of Experimental Child Psychology, 82,* 2–28.

Huston, A. C., & Wright, J. C. (1998). Mass media and children's development. In W. Damon (Ed.), *Handbook of child psychology* (Vol. 4). New York: Wiley.

Huston, M., & Schwartz, P. (1995). The relationships of lesbians and of gay men. In J. T. Wood & S. Duck (Eds.), *Understudied relationships: Off the beaten track* (pp. 89–121). Thousand Oaks, CA: Sage.

Huston, T. L., Caughlin, J. P., Houts, R. M., Smith, S. E., & George, L. J. (2001). The connubial crucible: Newlywed years as a predictors of marital delight, distress, and divorce. *Journal of Personality and Social Psychology, 80,* 237–252.

Huttenlocher, J., Haight, W., Bryk, A., Seltzer, M., & Lyons, T. (1991). Early vocabulary growth: Relation to language input and gender. *Developmental Psychology, 27,* 236–248.

Huyck, M. H. (1990). Gender differences in aging. In J. E. Birren & K. W. Schaie (Eds.), *Handbook of the psychology of aging* (3rd ed., pp. 124–132). San Diego, CA: Academic Press.

Inhelder, B., & Piaget, J. (1958). *The growth of logical thinking from childhood to adolescence.* New York: Basic Books.

Interagency Advisory Panel on Research Ethics. (1998). *The Tri-Council policy statement: Ethical conduct for research involving humans.* Ottawa: Government of Canada.

Inwood, S. (2001). Grandparents raising grandchildren. *Canadian Nurse, 98,* 21–25.

Isaksen, J. (2000). Constructing meaning despite drudgery of repetitive work. *Journal of Humanistic Psychology, 40,* 84–107.

Ishler, K., Pargament, K. I., Kinney, J. M., & Cavanaugh, J. C. (1998). *Religious coping, general coping, and controllability: Testing the hypothesis of fit.* Unpublished manuscript, Bowling Green State University.

Iskra, G. I., Folkard, S., Marek, T., & Noworol, C. (1996). Health, well-being and burnout of ICU nurses on 12- and 8-hour shifts. *Work and Stress, 10,* 251–256.

Isley, S. L., O'Neil, R., Clatfelter, D., & Parke, R. D. (1999). Parent and child expressed affect and children's social competence: Modeling direct and indirect pathways. *Developmental Psychology, 35,* 547–560.

Israel, A. C., Guile, C. A., Baker, J. E., & Silverman, W. K. (1994). An evaluation of enhanced self-regulation training in the treatment of childhood obesity. *Journal of Pediatric Psychology, 19,* 737–749.

Ivancevich, J. M., & Matteson, M. T. (1988). Type A behavior and the healthy individual. *British Journal of Medical Psychology, 61,* 37–56.

Ivy, D. K., & Hamlet, S. (1996). College students and sexual dynamics: Two studies of peer sexual harassment. *Communication Education, 45,* 149–166.

Iwasaki, Y., & Mannell, R. C. (2000). Hierarchical dimensions of leisure-stress coping. *Leisure Sciences, 22,* 163–181.

Izard, C. E. (1991). *The psychology of emotions.* New York: Plenum Press.

Izard, C. E., Fantauzzo, C. A., Castle, J. M., Haynes, O. M., Rayias, M. F., & Putnam, P. H. (1995). The ontogeny and significance of infants' facial expressions in the first 9 months of life. *Developmental Psychology, 31,* 997–1013.

Jackson, J. S., & Gibson, R. C. (1985). Work and retirement among the black elderly. In Z. Blau (Ed.), *Current perspectives on aging and the life cycle* (pp. 193–222). Greenwich, CT: JAI.

Jacobs, J. A., & Gerson, K. (2001). Overworked individuals or overworked families? Explaining trends in work, leisure, and family time. *Work and Occupations, 28,* 40–63.

Jacobs, J. E., & Eccles, J. S. (1992). The impact of mothers' gender-role stereotypic beliefs on mothers' and children's ability perceptions. *Journal of Personality and Social Psychology, 63,* 932–944.

Jacobs, S. (1993). *Pathologic grief: Maladaptation to loss.* Washington, DC: American Psychological Association.

Jacobson, J. L., & Jacobson, S. W. (1996). Intellectual impairment in children exposed to polychlorinated biphenyls in utero. *The New England Journal of Medicine, 335,* 783–789.

Jacobson, S. W., & Jacobson, J. L. (2000). Teratogenic insult and neurobehavioral function in infancy and childhood. In C. A. Nelson (Ed.), *The Minnesota symposium on child psychology, Vol. 31: The effects of early adversity on neurobehavioral development* (pp. 61–112). Mahwah, NJ: Erlbaum.

Jaffe, J., Beatrice, B., Stanley, F., Crown, C. L., & Jasnow, M. D. (2001). Rhythms of dialogue in infancy: Coordinated timing in development. *Monographs of the Society for Research in Child Development, 66* (Serial No. 265).

Jaffee, S., & Hyde, J. S. (2000). Gender differences in moral orientation: A meta-analysis. *Psychological Bulletin, 126,* 703–726.

James, W. (1890). *The principles of psychology.* New York: Holt.

Janoff-Bulman, R., & Berger, A. R. (2000). The other side of trauma: Toward a psychology of appreciation. In J. H. Harvey & E. D. Miller (Eds.), *Loss and trauma: General and close relationship perspectives* (pp. 29–44). Philadelphia: Brunner-Routledge.

Jenkins, C. L. (1997). Women, work, and caregiving: How do these roles affect women's well-being? *Journal of Women and Aging, 9,* 27–45.

Jensen, P. S., Hinshaw, S. P., Swanson, J. M., Greenhill, L. L., Conners, C. K., Arnold, L. E., et al. (2001). Findings from the NIMH Multimodal Treatment Study of ADHD (MTA): Implications and applications for primary care providers. *Journal of Developmental and Behavioral Pediatrics, 22,* 60–73.

Jiao, S., Ji, G., & Jing, Q. (1996). Cognitive development of Chinese urban only children and children with siblings. *Child Development, 67,* 387–395.

Jiao, Z. (1999, April). *Which students keep old friends and which become new friends across school transition?* Paper presented at the 1999 meeting of the Society for Research in Child Development, Albuquerque, NM.

Johanson, R. B., Rice, C., Coyle, M., Arthur, J., Anyanwu, L., Ibrahim, J., Warwick, A., Redman, C. W. E., & O'Brien, P. M. S. (1993). A randomized prospective study comparing the new vacuum extractor policy with forceps delivery. *British Journal of Obstetrics and Gynecology, 100,* 524–530.

Johansson, B., Whitfield, K., Pedersen, N. L., Hofer, S. M., Ahern, F., & McClearn, G. E. (1999). Origins of individual differences in episodic memory in the oldest-old: A population-based study of identical and same-sex fraternal twins aged 80 and older. *Journal of Gerontology: Psychological Sciences, 54B,* P173–P179.

Johnson, B. D., Stone, G. L., Altmaier, E. M., & Berdahl, L. D. (1998). The relationship of demographic factors, locus of control and self-efficacy to successful nursing home adjustment. *The Gerontologist, 38,* 209–216.

Johnson, J. G., Cohen, P., Smailes, E. M., Kasen, S., & Brook, J. S. (2002). Television viewing and aggressive behavior during adolescence and adulthood. *Science, 295,* 2468–2471.

Johnson, M. H. (2000). Functional brain development in infants: Elements of an interactive specialization framework. *Child Development, 71,* 75–81.

Johnson, M. P. (1995). Patriarchal terrorism and common couple violence: Two forms of violence against women. *Journal of Marriage and the Family, 57,* 283–294.

Johnson, M. P. (2001). Conflict and control: Symmetry and asymmetry in domestic violence. In A. Booth, A. C. Crouter, & M. Clements (Eds.), *Couples in conflict* (pp. 95–104). Mahwah, NJ: Erlbaum.

Johnson, M. P., & Ferraro, K. J. (2000). Research on domestic violence in the 1990s: Making distinctions. *Journal of Marriage and the Family, 62,* 948–963.

Johnson, S. P. (2001). Visual development in human infants: Binding features, surfaces, and objects. *Visual Cognition, 8,* 565–578.

Johnson, S. P., & Aslin, R. N. (1995). Perception of object unity in 2-month-old infants. *Developmental Psychology, 31,* 739–745.

Johnson-Laird, P. N. (1988). *The computer and the mind: An introduction to cognitive science.* London, UK: Fontana.

Johnston, L. D., O'Malley, P. M., & Bachman, J. G. (2002). *Monitoring the future national survey results on drug use, 1975–2001, volume 1: Secondary school students* (NIH publication No. 02–5106). Bethesda, MD: National Institute on Drug Abuse.

Johnstone, B., Frame, C. L., & Bouman, D. (1992). Physical attractiveness and athletic and academic ability in controversial-aggressive and rejected-aggressive children. *Journal of Social and Clinical Psychology, 11,* 71–79.

Jones, C. J., & Meredith, W. (1996). Patterns of personality change across the life span. *Psychology and Aging, 11,* 57–65.

Jones, D. C., Abbey, B. B., & Cumberland, A. (1998). The development of display rule knowledge: Linkages with family expressiveness and social competence. *Child Development, 69,* 1209–1222.

Jones, D., & Christensen, C. A. (1999). Relationship between automaticity in handwriting and students' ability to generate written text. *Journal of Educational Psychology, 91,* 44–49.

Jones, K., & Day, J. D. (1997). Discrimination of two aspects of cognitive-social intelligence from academic intelligence. *Journal of Educational Psychology, 89,* 486–497.

Joseph, R. (2000). Fetal brain behavior and cognitive development. *Developmental Review, 20,* 81–98.

Josephson, W.L. (1995). *Television violence: A review of the effects on children of different ages.* Ottawa: National Clearinghouse on Family Violence.

Jung, C. G. (1960). The stages of life. In G. Adler, M. Fordham, & H. Read (Eds.), *The collected works of C. G. Jung: Vol. 8. The structure and dynamics of the psyche.* London, UK: Routledge & Kegan Paul. [Original work published 1933]

Jusczyk, P. W. (1995). Language acquisition: Speech sounds and phonological development. In J. L. Miller & P. D. Eimas (Eds.), *Handbook of perception and cognition: Vol. 11. Speech, language, and communication.* Orlando, FL: Academic Press.

Jusczyk, P. W. (2002). How infants adapt speech-processing capacities to native-language structure. *Current Directions in Psychological Science, 11,* 15–18.

Jusczyk, P. W., & Aslin, R. N. (1995). Infants' detection of the sound patterns of words in fluent speech. *Cognitive Psychology, 29,* 1–23.

Kadushin, A., & Martin, J.A. (1981). *Child abuse: An interactional event.* New York: Columbia University Press.

Kagan, J. (1989). Temperamental contributions to social behavior. *American Psychologist, 44,* 668–674.

Kagan, J., Arcus, D., Snidman, N., Feng, W. Y., Hendler, J., & Greene, S. (1994). Reactivity in infants: A cross-national comparison. *Developmental Psychology, 30,* 342–345.

Kagan, J., & Moss, H. A. (1962). *Birth to maturity: A study in psychological development.* New York: Wiley.

Kagan, J., Snidman, N., & Arcus, D. (1998). Childhood derivatives of high and low reactivity in infancy. *Child Development, 69,* 1483–1493.

Kager, M. B. (2000). Factors that affect hiring: A study of age discrimination and hiring. *Dissertation Abstracts International Section A: Humanities and Social Sciences, 60*(11-A), 4201.

Kaijura, H., Cowart, B. J., & Beauchamp, G. K. (1992). Early developmental change in bitter taste responses in human infants. *Developmental Psychobiology, 25,* 375–386.

Kail, R. (1990). *The development of memory in children* (3rd ed.). New York: Freeman.

Kail, R. (1991). Processing time declines exponentially during childhood and adolescence. *Developmental Psychology, 27,* 259–266.

Kail, R., & Bisanz, J. (1992). The information-processing perspective on cognitive development in childhood and adolescence. In R. J. Sternberg & C. A. Berg (Eds.), *Intellectual development.* New York: Cambridge University Press.

Kail, R. V., & Salthouse, T. A. (1994). Processing speed as a mental capacity. *Acta Psychologica, 86,* 199–225.

Kalish, R. A. (1984). *Death, grief, and caring relationships* (2nd ed.). Pacific Grove, CA: Brooks/Cole.

Kalish, R. A. (1987). Death and dying. In P. Silverman (Ed.), *The elderly as modern pioneers* (pp. 320–334). Bloomington: Indiana University Press.

Kalish, R. A., & Reynolds, D. (1976). *Death and ethnicity: A psychocultural study.* Los Angeles: University of Southern California Press.

Kalmijn, M., & Flap, H. (2001). Assortative meeting and mating: Unintended consequences of organized settings for partner choices. *Social Forces, 79,* 1289–1312.

Kalnins, D., & Saab, J. (2001). *Better baby food: Your essential guide to nutrition, feeding and cooking for all babies and toddlers.* Toronto: Robert Rose.

Kandel, D. B. (1978). Homophily, selection, and socialization in adolescent friendships. *American Journal of Sociology, 84,* 427–436.

Kandel, E., & Mednick, S. A. (1991). Perinatal complications predict violent offending. *Criminology, 29,* 519–529.

Kanekar, S., Kolsawalla, M. B., & Nazareth, T. (1989). Occupational prestige as a function of occupant's gender. *Journal of Applied Social Psychology, 19,* 681–688.

Kann, L., Collins, J. L., Pateman, B. C., Small, M. L., Ross, J. G., & Kolbe, L. J. (1995). The School Health Policies and Programs Study (SHPPS): Rationale for a nationwide status report on school health programs. *Journal of School Health, 65*(8), 291–294.

Kaplan, P. S., Goldstein, M. H., Huckeby, E. R., & Cooper, R. P. (1995). Habituation, sensitization, and infants' responses to motherese speech. *Developmental Psychobiology, 28,* 45–57.

Kapp, M. B. (1999). *Geriatrics and the law: Patient rights and professional responsibilities* (3rd ed.). New York: Springer.

Karney, B. R., & Bradbury, T. N. (1995). The longitudinal course of marital quality and stability: A review of theory, method, and research. *Psychological Bulletin, 118,* 3–34.

Karniol, R. (1989). The role of manual manipulative states in the infant's acquisition of perceived control over objects. *Developmental Review, 9,* 205–233.

Kaslow, F. W., Hansson, K., & Lundblad, A. (1994). Long-term marriages in Sweden: And some comparisons with similar couples in the United States. *Contemporary Family Therapy, 16*, 521–537.

Kastenbaum, R. (1992). *The psychology of death* (Rev. ed.). New York: Springer.

Kastenbaum, R. (1999). Dying and bereavement. In J. C. Cavanaugh & S. K. Whitbourne (Eds.), *Gerontology: An interdisciplinary perspective* (pp. 155–185). New York: Oxford University Press.

Kastenbaum, R., & Thuell, S. (1995). Cookies baking, coffee brewing: Toward a contextual theory of dying. *Omega, 31*, 175–187.

Katz, L. F., & Woodin, E. M. (2002). Hostility, hostile detachment, and conflict engagement in marriages: Effects on child and family functioning. *Child Development, 73*, 636–652.

Katz, S. (1983). Assessing self-maintenance: Activities of daily living, mobility, and instrumental activities of daily living. *Journal of the American Geriatrics Society, 31*, 721–727.

Kawas, C., Resnick, S., Morrison, A., Brookmeyer, R., Corrada, M., Zonderman, A., Bacal, C., Lingle, D. C., & Metter, E. (1997). A prospective study of estrogen replacement therapy and the risk of developing Alzheimer's disease: The Baltimore Longitudinal Study of Aging, *Neurology, 48*, 1517–1521.

Kazdin, A. E. (1990). Childhood depression. *Journal of Child Psychology and Psychiatry and Allied Disciplines, 31*, 121–160.

Keane, S. P., Brown, K. P., & Crenshaw, T. M. (1990). Children's intention-cue detection as a function of maternal social behavior: Pathways to social rejection. *Developmental Psychology, 26*, 1004–1009.

Kegan, R. (1982). *The evolving self*. Cambridge, MA: Harvard University Press.

Keith, J. (1990). Age in social and cultural context: Anthropological perspectives. In R. H. Binstock & L. K. George (Eds.), *Handbook of aging and the social sciences* (3rd ed., pp. 91–111). San Diego, CA: Academic Press.

Keller, J. W., Sherry, D., & Piotrowski, C. (1984). Perspectives on death: A developmental study. *Journal of Psychology, 116*, 137–142.

Keller, M., Edelstein, W., Schmid, S., Fang, F., & Fang, G. (1998). Reasoning about responsibilities and obligations in close relationships: A comparison across two cultures. *Developmental Psychology, 34*, 731–741.

Kellman, P. J., & Banks, M. S. (1998). Infant visual perception. In W. Damon (Ed.), *Handbook of child psychology* (Vol. 2). New York: Wiley.

Kelly, J. R., Steinkamp, M. W., & Kelly, J. R. (1987). Later-life satisfaction: Does leisure contribute? *Leisure Sciences, 9*, 189–200.

Kennedy, G. E. (1991). Grandchildren's reasons for closeness with grandparents. *Journal of Social Behavior and Personality, 6*, 697–712.

Kenney, R. A. (1982). *Physiology of aging: A synopsis*. Chicago: Yearbook Medical.

Kenrick, D. T. (1987). Gender, genes, and the social environment. In P. C. Shaver & C. Hendrick (Eds.), *Review of Personality and Social Psychology: Vol. 7. Sex and gender* (pp. 14–43). Newbury Park, CA: Sage.

Kim, H. K., & McKenry, P. C. (1998). Social networks and support: A comparison of African Americans, Asian Americans, Caucasians, and Hispanics. *Journal of Comparative Family Studies, 29*, 313–334.

Kim, S. S. (2000). Gradual return to work: The antecedents and consequences of switching to part-time work after first childbirth. *Dissertation Abstract International Section A: Humanities and Social Sciences, 61*(3-A), 1182.

Kim, S., & Feldman, D. C. (2000). Working in retirement: The antecedents of bridge employment and its consequences for quality of life in retirement. *Academy of Management Journal, 43*, 1195–1210.

Kim, Y. H., & Goetz, E. T. (1994). Context effects on word recognition and reading comprehension of good and poor readers: A test of the interactive compensatory hypothesis. *Reading Research Quarterly, 29*, 178–188.

Kimball, M. M. (1986). Television and sex-role attitudes. In T. M. Williams (Ed.), *The impact of television* (pp. 265–301). New York: Academic Press.

Kimball, M. M. (1989). A new perspective on women's math achievement. *Psychological Bulletin, 105*, 198–214.

King, P. M., & Kitchener, K. S. (1994). *Developing reflective judgment: Understanding and promoting intellectual growth and critical thinking in adolescents and adults.* San Francisco: Jossey-Bass.

King, V., Elder, G. H., & Whitbeck, L. B. (1997). Religious involvement among rural youth: An ecological and life-course perspective. *Journal of Research on Adolescence, 7*, 431–456.

Kinney, J. M., & Cavanaugh, J. C. (1993, November). *Until death do us part: Striving to find meaning while caring for a spouse with dementia.* Paper presented at the annual meeting of the Gerontological Society of America, New Orleans.

Kinney, J. M., Haff, M., Isacson, A., Nocera, R., Cavanaugh, J. C., & Dunn, N. J. (1993, November). *Marital satisfaction and caregiving hassles among caregivers to spouses with dementia.* Paper presented at the annual meeting of the Gerontological Society of America, New Orleans.

Kirby, D. (2002a). *Do abstinence-only programs delay the initiation of sex among young people and reduce teen pregnancy?* Washington, DC: National Campaign to Prevent Teen Pregnancy.

Kirby, D. (2002b). *Emerging answers: Research findings on programs to reduce teen pregnancy (summary).* Washington, DC: National Campaign to Prevent Teen Pregnancy.

Kisilevsky, B. S., & Low, J. A. (1998). Human fetal behavior: 100 years of study. *Developmental Review, 18*, 1–29.

Kitchener, K. S., & Fischer, K. W. (1990). A skill approach to the development of reflective thinking. In D. Kuhn (Ed.), *Contributions to human development: Developmental perspectives on teaching and learning* (Vol. 21, pp. 48–62). Basel, Switzerland: Karger.

Kitchener, K. S., & King, P. M. (1989). The reflective judgment model: Ten years of research. In M. L. Commons, C. Armon, L. Kohlberg, F. A. Richards, T. A. Grotzer, & J. D. Sinnott (Eds.), *Adult development: Vol. 2. Models and methods in the study of adolescent and adult thought* (pp. 63–78). New York: Praeger.

Kittrell, D. (1998). A comparison of the evolution of men's and women's dreams in Daniel Levinson's theory of adult development. *Journal of Adult Development, 5,* 105–115.

Kivnick, H. Q. (1982). *The meaning of grandparenthood.* Ann Arbor, MI: UMI Research.

Kivnick, H. Q. (1985). Grandparenthood and mental health: Meaning, behavior, and satisfaction. In V. L. Bengtson & J. F. Robertson (Eds.), *Grandparenthood* (pp. 151–158). Beverly Hills, CA: Sage.

Klaczynski, P. A., & Narasimham, G. (1998). Development of scientific reasoning biases: Cognitive versus ego-protective explanations. *Developmental Psychology, 34,* 175–187.

Klapper, J. T. (1968). The impact of viewing "aggression": Studies and problems of extrapolation. In O. N. Larsen (Ed.), *Violence and the mass media.* New York: Harper & Row.

Klass, D. (1996a). The deceased child in the psychic and social worlds of bereaved parents during the resolution of grief. In D. Klass, P. R. Silverman, & S. L. Nickman (Eds.), *Continuing bonds: New understandings of grief* (pp. 199–215). Washington, DC: Taylor & Francis.

Klass, D. (1996b). Grief in Eastern culture: Japanese ancestor worship. In D. Klass, P. R. Silverman, & S. L. Nickman (Eds.), *Continuing bonds: New understandings of grief* (pp. 59–70). Washington, DC: Taylor & Francis.

Kleiber, D. A., Hutchinson, S. L., & Williams, R. (2002). Leisure as a resource in transcending negative life events: Self-protection, self-restoration, and personal transformation. *Leisure Sciences, 24,* 219–235.

Kline, R. B., Canter, W. A., & Robin, A. (1987). Parameters of teenage alcohol use: A path analytic conceptual model. *Journal of Consulting and Clinical Psychology, 55,* 521–528.

Klohnen, E. C., Vandewater, E. A., & Young, A. (1996). Negotiating the middle years: Ego-resiliency and successful midlife adjustment in women. *Psychology and Aging, 11,* 431–442.

Knapp, M. L., & Taylor, E. H. (1994). Commitment and its communication in romantic relationships. In A. L. Weber & J. H. Harvey (Eds.), *Perspectives on close relationships* (pp. 153–175). Boston: Allyn & Bacon.

Knight, G. P., Fabes, R. A., & Higgins, D. A. (1996). Concerns about drawing causal inferences from meta-analyses: An example in the study of gender differences in aggression. *Psychological Bulletin, 119,* 410–421.

Knowles, M. (1984). *The adult learner: A neglected species.* Houston, TX: Gulf.

Knox, D., Custis, L. L., & Zusman, M. E. (2000). Abuse in dating relationships among college students. *College Student Journal, 34,* 505–508.

Kobak, R. (1994). Adult attachment: A personality or relationship construct? *Psychological Inquiry, 5,* 42–44.

Kochanska, G. (1993). Toward a synthesis of parental socialization and child temperament in early development of conscience. *Child Development, 64,* 325–347.

Kochanska, G. (1997). Multiple pathways to conscience for children with different temperaments: From toddlerhood to age 5. *Developmental Psychology, 33,* 228–240.

Koenig, H. G. (1999). *The healing power of faith: Science explores medicine's last great frontier.* New York: Simon & Schuster.

Koestenbaum, P. (1976). *Is there an answer to death?* Englewood Cliffs, NJ: Prentice Hall.

Kogan, N. (1983). Stylistic variation in childhood and adolescence: Creativity, metaphor, and cognitive style. In P. H. Mussen (Ed.), *Handbook of child psychology* (Vol. 3, pp. 630–706). New York: Wiley.

Kohlberg, L. (1966). A cognitive-developmental analysis of children's sex-role concepts and attitudes. In. E. E. Maccoby (Ed.), *The development of sex differences.* Stanford: Stanford University Press.

Kohlberg, L. (1969). Stage and sequence: The cognitive-development approach to socialization. In D. Goslinan (Ed.), *Handbook of socialization theory and research* (pp. 347–480). Chicago: Rand McNally.

Kohlberg, L., & Ullian, D. Z. (1974). Stages in the development of psychosexual concepts and attitudes. In R. C. Friedman, R. M. Richart, & R. L. Van Wiele (Eds.), *Sex differences in behavior.* New York: Wiley.

Kolata, G. (1990, February 6). Rush is on to capitalize on test for gene causing cystic fibrosis. *New York Times,* p. C3.

Kolb, B. (1989). Brain development, plasticity, and behavior. *American Psychologist, 44,* 1203–1212.

Kolberg, K. J. S. (1999). Environmental influences on prenatal development and health. In T. L. Whitman & T. V. Merluzzi (Eds.), *Life-span perspectives on health and illness* (pp. 87–103). Mahwah, NJ: Erlbaum.

Kopp, C. B., & Krakow, J. B. (1982). *The child: Development in a social context.* Reading, MA: Addison-Wesley.

Kotovsky, L., & Baillargeon, R. (1998).The development of calibration-based reasoning about collision events in young infants. *Cognition, 67,* 311–351.

Kovacs, D. M., Parker, J. G., & Hoffman, L. W. (1996). Behavioral, affective, and social correlates of involvement in cross-sex friendship in elementary school. *Child Development, 67,* 2269–2286.

Kowal, A., & Kramer, L. (1997). Children's understanding of parental differential treatment. *Child Development, 68,* 113–126.

Kowalski, R. M. (1992). Nonverbal behaviors and perceptions of sexual intentions: Effects of sexual connotativeness, verbal response, and rape outcome. *Basic and Applied Social Psychology, 13,* 427–445.

Kram, K. E. (1980). *Mentoring processes at work: Developmental relationships in managerial careers.* Unpublished doctoral dissertation, Yale University, New Haven, CT.

Kram, K. E. (1985). *Mentoring at work: Developmental relationships in organizational life.* Glenview, IL: Scott, Foresman.

Kramer, A. F., Hahn, S., McAuley, E., Cohen, N. J., Banich, M. T., Harrison, C., Chason, J., Boileau, R. A., Bardell, L., Colcombe, A., & Vakil, E. (2001). Exercise, aging, and cognition: Healthy body, healthy mind? In W. A. Rogers & A. D. Fisk (Eds.), *Human factors interventions for the health care of older adults* (pp. 91–120). Mahwah, NJ: Erlbaum.

Kramer, D. A. (1989). A developmental framework for understanding conflict resolution processes. In J. D. Sinnott (Ed.), *Everyday problem solving: Theory and applications* (pp. 138–152). New York: Praeger.

Kramer, D. A. (1990). Conceptualizing wisdom: The primacy of affect-cognition relations. In R. J. Sternberg (Ed.), *Wisdom: Its nature, origins, and development* (pp. 279–313). Cambridge, UK: Cambridge University Press.

Kramer, D. A., Angiuld, N., Crisafi, L., & Levine, C. (1991, August). *Cognitive processes in real-life conflict resolution.* Paper presented at the annual meeting of the American Psychological Association, San Francisco.

Kramer, D. A., & Kahlbaugh, P. E. (1994). Memory for a dialectical and nondialectical prose passage in younger and older adults. *Journal of Adult Development, 1,* 13–26.

Krause, N. (1991). Stress and inoculation from close ties in later life. *Journal of Gerontology: Social Sciences, 46,* S183–S194.

Krause, N. (1995). Religiosity and self-esteem among older adults. *Journal of Gerontology: Psychological Sciences, 50B,* P236–P246.

Krause, N. (2001). Social support. In R. H. Binstock & L. K. George (Eds.), *Handbook of aging and the social sciences* (pp. 273–294). San Diego, CA: Academic Press.

Krauss, R. M. (2002). Individualized hormone-replacement therapy? *New England Journal of Medicine, 346,* 1017–1018.

Krebs, D., & Gillmore, J. (1982). The relationship among the first stages of cognitive development, role-taking abilities, and moral development. *Child Development, 53,* 877–886.

Krevans, J., & Gibbs, J. C. (1996). Parents' use of inductive discipline: Relations to children's empathy and prosocial behavior. *Child Development, 67,* 3263–3277.

Krispin, O., Sternberg, K. J., & Lamb, M. E. (1992). The dimensions of peer evaluation in Israel: A cross-cultural perspective. *International Journal of Behavioral Development, 15,* 299–314.

Kroger, J., & Green, K. E. (1996). Events associated with identity status change. *Journal of Adolescence, 19,* 477–490.

Kübler-Ross, E. (1969). *On death and dying.* New York: Macmillan.

Kübler-Ross, E. (1974). *Questions and answers on death and dying.* New York: Macmillan.

Kuhl, P. K., Andruski, J. E., Chistovich, I. A., Chistovich, L. A., Kozhevnikova, E. V., Ryskina, V. L., Stolyarova, E. I., Sundberg, U., & Lacerda, F. (1997). Cross-language analysis of phonetic units in language addressed to infants. *Science, 277,* 684–686.

Kuhn, D. (2000). Metacognitive development. *Current Directions in Psychological Science, 9,* 178–181.

Kulik, L. (2001a). Impact of length of unemployment and age on jobless men and women: A comparative analysis. *Journal of Employment Counseling, 38,* 15–27.

Kulik, L. (2001b). The impact of men's and women's retirement on marital relations: A comparative analysis. *Journal of Women and Aging, 13,* 21–37.

Kulik, L. (2001c). Marital relationships in late adulthood: Synchronous versus asynchronous couples. *International Journal of Aging and Human Development, 52,* 323–339.

Kulwicki, A. D. (2002). The practice of honor crimes: A glimpse of domestic violence in the Arab world. *Issues in Mental Health Nursing, 23,* 77–87.

Kumar, R., O'Malley, P. M., Johnston, L. D., Schulenberg, J. E., & Bachman, J. G. (2002). Effects of school-level norms on student substance use. *Prevention Science, 3,* 105–124.

Kunzig, R. (1998). Climbing through the brain. *Discover, 19,* 60–69.

Kurdek, L. A. (1991a). Predictors of increases in marital distress in newlywed couples: A 3-year prospective longitudinal study. *Developmental Psychology, 27,* 627–636.

Kurdek, L. A. (1991b). The relations between reported well-being and divorce history, availability of a proximate adult, and gender. *Journal of Marriage and the Family, 53,* 71–78.

Kurdek, L. A. (1995a). Developmental changes in relationship quality in gay male and lesbian cohabiting couples. *Developmental Psychology, 31,* 86–94.

Kurdek, L. A. (1995b). Lesbian and gay couples. In A. R. D'Augelli & C. J. Patterson (Eds.), *Lesbian, gay, and bisexual identities over the lifespan* (pp. 243–261). New York: Oxford University Press.

Kurz, D. (1995). *For richer, for poorer: Mothers confront divorce.* Philadelphia: Women's Studies Program, University of Pennsylvania.

Labouvie-Vief, G. (1997). Cognitive–emotional integration in adulthood. In K. W. Schaie & M. P. Lawton (Eds.), *Annual review of gerontology and geriatrics* (Vol. 17, pp. 206–237). New York: Springer.

Labouvie-Vief, G., & Diehl, M. (1999). Self and personality development. In J. C. Cavanaugh & S. K. Whitbourne (Eds.), *Gerontology: Interdisciplinary perspectives* (pp. 238–268). New York: Oxford University Press.

Labouvie-Vief, G., & Diehl, M. (2000). Cognitive complexity and cognitive-affective integration: Related or separate domains of adult development? *Psychology and Aging, 15,* 490–504.

Lachman, M. E. (1985). Personal efficacy in middle and old age: Differential and normative patterns of change. In G. H. Elder, Jr. (Ed.), *Life-course dynamics: Trajectories and transitions, 1968–1980* (pp. 188–213). Ithaca, NY: Cornell University Press.

Lachman, M. E., Howland, J., Tennstedt, S., Jette, A., Assmann, S., & Peterson, E. W. (1998). Fear of falling and activity restriction: The survey of activities and fear of falling in the elderly (SAFE). *Journal of Gerontology, 53B,* P43–P50.

Ladd, G. W. (1998). Peer relationships and social competence during early and middle childhood. *Annual Review of Psychology, 50,* 333–359.

Ladd, G. W., & Le Sieur, K. D. (1995). Parents and children's peer relationships. In M. H. Bornstein (Ed.), *Handbook of parenting. Vol. 4. Applied and practical parenting* (pp. 377–410). Mahwah, NJ: Erlbaum.

LaGreca, A. M. (1993). Social skills training with children: Where do we go from here? *Journal of Clinical Child Psychology, 22,* 288–298.

Laible, D. J., & Thompson, R. A. (1998). Attachment and emotional understanding in preschool children. *Developmental Psychology, 34,* 1038–1045.

Lakshmanan, I. A. R. (1997, September 22). Marriage? Think logic, not love. *Baltimore Sun,* A2.

Lalumière, M. L., Blanchard, R., & Zucker, K. J. (2000). Sexual orientation and handedness in men and women: A meta-analysis. *Psychological Bulletin, 126,* 575–592.

Lamanna, M. A., & Riedmann, A. (2003). *Marriages and families: Making choices in a diverse society* (8th ed.). Belmont, CA: Wadsworth.

Lamb, M. E. (1999). Nonparental child care. In M. E. Lamb (Ed.), *Parenting and child development in "nontraditional" families.* Mahwah, NJ: Erlbaum.

Lamb, M. E., & Oppenheim, D. (1989). Fatherhood and father-child relationships: Five years of research. In S. H. Cath, A. Gurwitt, & L. Gunsberg (Eds.), *Fathers and their families.* Hillsdale, NJ: Erlbaum.

Lamb, M. E., Sternberg, K. J., & Esplin, P. W. (2000). Effects of age and delay on the amount of information provided by alleged sex abuse victims in investigative interviews. *Child Development, 71,* 1586–1596.

Lampinen, J. M., & Smith, V. L. (1995). The incredible (and sometimes incredulous) child witness: Child eyewitnesses' sensitivity to source credibility cues. *Journal of Applied Psychology, 80,* 621–627.

Lampman, C., & Dowling-Guyer, S. (1995). Attitudes toward voluntary and involuntary childlessness. *Basic and Applied Social Psychology, 17,* 213–222.

Landy, S., & Tam, K. K. (1998). *Understanding the contributions of multiple risk factors in child development at various ages.* Ottawa: Applied Research Branch Strategic Policy, Human Resources Development Canada.

Lang, F. R., & Heckhausen, J. (2001). Perceived control over development and subjective well-being: Differential benefits across adulthood. *Journal of Personality and Social Psychology, 81,* 509–523.

Langer, E. J., & Rodin, J. (1976). The effects of choice and enhanced personal responsibility for the aged: A field experiment in an institutional setting. *Journal of Personality and Social Psychology, 34,* 191–198.

Langlois, J. H., & Downs, A. C. (1980). Mothers, fathers, and peers as socialization agents of sex-typed play behaviors in young children. *Child Development, 51,* 1237–1247.

Larson, R. W. (1997). The emergence of solitude as a constructive domain of experience in early adolescence. *Child Development, 68,* 80–93.

Larson, R.W. (2000). Toward a psychology of positive youth development. *American Psychologist, 55,* 170–183.

Larson, R. W., Gillman, S. A., & Richards, M. H. (1997). Divergent experiences of family leisure: Fathers, mothers, and young adolescents. *Journal of Leisure Research, 29,* 78–97.

Larson, R. W., Raffaelli, M., Richards, M. H., Ham, M., & Jewell, L. (1990). Ecology of depression in late childhood and early adolescence: A profile of daily states and activities. *Journal of Abnormal Psychology, 99,* 92–102.

Laungani, P. (2001). The influence of culture on stress: India and England. In L. L. Adler & U. P. Gielen (Eds.), *Cross-cultural topics in psychology* (2nd ed., pp. 149–169). Westport, CT: Praeger.

Laursen, B., & Collins, W. A. (1994). Interpersonal conflict during adolescence. *Psychological Bulletin, 115,* 197–209.

Lawrence, J., Alcock, D., McGrath, P. et al. (1993). The development of a tool to assess neonatal pain. *Neonatal Network, 12,* 59–66.

Lawton, M. P. (1982). Competence, environmental press, and the adaptation of old people. In M. P. Lawton, P. G. Windley, & T. O. Byerts (Eds.), *Aging and the environment: Theoretical approaches* (pp. 33–59). New York: Springer-Verlag.

Lawton, M. P. (1989). Environmental proactivity in older people. In V. L. Bengtson & K. W. Schaie (Eds.), *The course of later life: Research and reflections* (pp. 15–23). New York: Springer.

Lawton, M. P., & Nahemow, L. (1973). Ecology of the aging process. In C. Eisdorfer & M. P. Lawton (Eds.), *The psychology of adult development and aging* (pp. 619–674). Washington, DC: American Psychological Association.

Lazarus, R. S., & Folkman, S. (1984). *Stress, appraisal, and coping.* New York: Springer.

Leach, P. (1991). *Your baby and child: From birth to age five* (2nd ed.). New York: Knopf.

Leahy, J. M. (1993). A comparison of depression in women bereaved of a spouse, a child, or a parent. *Omega, 26,* 207–217.

Leana, C. R., & Feldman, D. C. (1992). *Coping with job loss.* New York: Lexington Books.

Leaper, C., Anderson, K. J., & Sanders, P. (1998). Moderators of gender effects on parents' talk to their children: A meta-analysis. *Developmental Psychology, 34,* 3–27.

Learning Disabilities Association of Canada. (2001). *Fact sheet: Statistics on learning disabilities.* Ottawa: Author.

Learning Disabilities Association of Canada. (2002). *Official definition of learning disabilities.* Ottawa: Author.

LeDoux, J. E., & Gorman, J. M. (2001). A call to action: Overcoming anxiety through active coping. *American Journal of Psychiatry, 158,* 1953–1955.

Lee, G. R., Demaris, A., Bavin, S., & Sullivan, R. (2001). Gender differences in the depressive effect of widowhood in later life. *Journal of Gerontology: Social Sciences, 56B,* S56–S61.

Lee, G. R., Seccombe, K., & Shehan, C. L. (1991). Marital status and personal happiness: An analysis of trend data. *Journal of Marriage and the Family, 53,* 839–844.

Lee, G. R., Willetts, M. C., & Seccombe, K. (1998). Widowhood and depression: Gender differences. *Research on Aging, 20,* 611–630.

Lee, J. W., & Guerrero, L. K. (2001). Types of touch in cross-sex relationships between coworkers: Perceptions of relational and emotional messages, inappropriateness, and sexual harassment. *Journal of Applied Communication Research, 29,* 197–220.

Legge, R., Josephson, W., Hicks, C., & Kepron, L. (2004). Dating violence: "What's Love Got to Do With It" program evaluation. In C. A. Ateah & J. Mirwaldt. (Eds.), *Within our reach: Preventing abuse across the lifespan.* Halifax, NS: Fernwood Publishing and RESOLVE (Research and Education for Solutions to Violence and Abuse).

Leichtentritt, R. D., & Rettig, K. D. (2000). Elderly Israelis and their family members' meanings towards euthanasia. *Families, Systems, and Health, 18,* 61–78.

LeMare, L. J., & Rubin, K. H. (1987). Perspective taking and peer interaction: Structural and developmental analyses. *Child Development, 58,* 306–315.

Lemery, K. S., Goldsmith, H. H., Klinnert, M. D., & Mrazek, D. A. (1999). Developmental models of infant and childhood temperament. *Developmental Psychology, 35,* 189–204.

Lemire, L., Saba, T., & Gagnon, Y. C. (1999). Managing career plateauing in the Quebec public sector. *Public Personnel Management, 28,* 375–391.

Lengua, L. J. (2002). The contribution of emotionality and self-regulation to the understanding of children's response to multiple risk. *Child Development, 73,* 144–161.

Lengua, L. J., Sandler, I. N., West, S. G., Wolchik, S. A., & Curran, P. J. (1999). Emotionality and self-regulation, threat appraisal, and coping in children of divorce. *Development & Psychopathology, 11,* 15–37.

Leon, G. R., Gillum, B., Gillum, R., & Gouze, M. (1979). Personality stability and change over a 30-year period: Middle to old age. *Journal of Consulting and Clinical Psychology, 47,* 517–524.

Lepper, M. R., & Gurtner, J. (1989). Children and computers. *American Psychologist, 44,* 170–178.

Lester, D. (1996). Trends in divorce and marriage around the world. *Journal of Divorce and Remarriage, 25,* 169–171.

Levenson, R. W., Carstensen, L. L., & Gottman, J. M. (1993). Long-term marriage: Age, gender, and satisfaction. *Psychology and Aging, 8,* 301–313.

Leventhal, H., Rabin, C., Leventhal, E. A., & Burns, E. (2002). Health risk behaviors and aging. In J. E. Birren & K. W. Schaie (Eds.), *Handbook of the psychology of aging* (5th ed., pp. 186–214). San Diego, CA: Academic Press.

Levine, L. E. (1983). *Mine:* Self-definition in 2-year-old boys. *Developmental Psychology, 19,* 544–549.

Levinger, G. (1980). Toward the analysis of close relationships. *Journal of Experimental Social Psychology, 16,* 510–544.

Levinger, G. (1983). Development and change. In H. H. Kelley, E. Berscheid, A. Christensen, J. H. Harvey, T. L. Hutson, G. Levinger, E. McClintock, L. A. Peplau, & D. R. Peterson (Eds.), *Close relationships* (pp. 315–359). New York: Freeman.

Levinson, D. J., Darrow, C., Kline, E., Levinson, M., & McKee, B. (1978). *The seasons of a man's life.* New York: Knopf.

Levinson, D., & Levinson, J. D. (1996). *The seasons of a woman's life.* New York: Knopf.

Levitt, A. G., & Utman, J. A. (1992). From babbling towards the sound systems of English and French: A longitudinal two-case study. *Journal of Child Language, 19,* 19–49.

Levitt, M. J., Guacci-Franco, N., & Levitt, J. L. (1993). Convoys of social support in childhood and early adolescence: Structure and function. *Developmental Psychology, 29,* 811–818.

Levitt, M. J., Weber, R. A., & Guacci, N. (1993). Convoys of social support: An intergenerational analysis. *Psychology and Aging, 8,* 323–326.

Levy, G. D., Taylor, M. G., & Gelman, S. A. (1995). Traditional and evaluative aspects of flexibility in gender roles, social conventions, moral rules, and physical laws. *Child Development, 66,* 515–531.

Levy, J. (1976). A review of evidence for a genetic component in the determination of handedness. *Behavior Genetics, 6,* 429–453.

Lewinsohn, P. M. (1975). The behavioral study and treatment of depression. In M. Hersen, R. M. Eisler, & P. M. Miller (Eds.), *Progress in behavior modification* (Vol. 1, pp. 19–64). New York: Academic Press.

Lewinsohn, P. M., & Gotlib, I. H. (1995). Behavioral theory and treatment of depression. In E. E. Beckham & W. R. Leber (Eds.), *Handbook of depression* (2nd ed., pp. 352–375). New York: Guilford Press.

Lewis, K. G., & Moon, S. (1997). Always single and single again women: A qualitative study. *Journal of Marital and Family Therapy, 23,* 115–134.

Lewis, M. (1987). Social development in infancy and early childhood. In J. D. Osofsky (Ed.), *Handbook of infant development.* New York: Wiley.

Lewis, M. I. (1995). Sexuality. In W. B. Abrams, M. H. Beers, & R. Berkow (Eds.), *The Merck manual of geriatrics* (2nd ed., pp. 827–838). Whitehouse Station, NJ: Merck Research Laboratories.

Lewis, M. (2000). The emergence of human emotions. In M. Lewis & J. Haviland-Jones (Eds.), *Handbook of emotions* (2nd ed.). New York: Guilford Press.

Lewis, M., & Brooks-Gunn, J. (1979). *Social cognition and the acquisition of self.* New York: Plenum.

Lewis, M., Ramsay, D. S., & Kawakami, K. (1993). Differences between Japanese infants and Caucasian American infants in behavioral and cortisol response to inoculation. *Child Development, 64,* 1722–1731.

Lewis, R. A., & Lin, L-W. (1996). Adults and their midlife parents. In N. Vanzetti & S. Duck (Eds.), *A lifetime of relationships* (pp. 364–382). Pacific Grove, CA: Brooks Cole.

Lewkowicz, D. J. (2000). Infants' perception of the audible, visible, and bimodal attributes of multimodal syllables. *Child Development, 71*, 1241–1257.

Lewontin, R. (1976). Race and intelligence. In N. J. Block & G. Dworkin (Eds.), *The IQ controversy* (pp. 78–92). New York: Pantheon Books.

Liben, L. S., & Signorella, M. L. (1993). Gender-schematic processing in children: The role of initial interpretations of stimuli. *Developmental Psychology, 29*, 141–149.

Lichtman, R. (1996). Perimenopausal and postmenopausal hormone replacement therapy. Part 1. An update of the literature on benefits and risks. *Journal of Nurse Midwifery, 41*, 3–28.

Lieber, J. (2001, October 10). Widows of towers disaster cope, but with quiet fury. *USA Today*, pp. A1–A2.

Lieberman, M., Doyle, A., & Markiewicz, D. (1999). Developmental patterns in security of attachment to mother and father in late childhood and early adolescence: Associations with peer relations. *Child Development, 70*, 202–213.

Liebert, R. M., & Sprafkin, J. (1988). *The early window: Effects of television on children and youth*. New York: Pergamon.

Liebert, R. M., Sprafkin, J. N., & Poulos, R. W. (1975). Selling cooperation to children. In W. S. Hale (Ed.), *Proceedings of the 20th annual conference of the Advertising Research Foundation* (pp. 54–57). New York: Advertising Research Foundation.

Liebowitz, M. (1983). *The chemistry of love*. Boston: Little, Brown.

Lin, C. C., & Fu, V. R. (1990). A comparison of childrearing practices among Chinese, immigrant Chinese, and Caucasian-American parents. *Child Development, 61*, 429–433.

Linden, M. G., Bender, B. G., Harmon, R. J., Mrzek, D. A., & Robinson, A. (1988). 47, XXX: What is the prognosis? *Pediatrics, 82*, 619–630.

Lindlaw, S. (1997, April 25). Ethical issues surround oldest new mom. *News Journal* (Wilmington, DE), p. A13.

Lipsitt, L. P. (1990). Learning and memory in infants. *Merrill-Palmer Quarterly, 36*, 53–66.

Lips-Wiersma, M. S. (2000). The influence of "spiritual meaning making" on career choice, transition and experience. *Dissertation Abstracts International Section A: Humanities and Social Sciences, 61*(4-A), 1374.

Livesley, W. J., & Bromley, D. B. (1973). *Person perception in childhood and adolescence*. New York: Wiley.

Logan, R. D. (1986). A reconceptualization of Erikson's theory: The repetition of existential and instrumental themes. *Human Development, 29*, 125–136.

Lopata, H. Z. (1996). Widowhood and husband sanctification. In D. Klass, P. R. Silverman, & S. L. Nickman (Eds.), *Continuing bonds: New understandings of grief* (pp. 149–162). Washington, DC: Taylor & Francis.

Lord, S. E., Eccles, J. S., & McCarthy, K. A. (1994). Surviving the junior high transition: Family processes and self-perception as protective and risk factors. *Journal of Early Adolescence, 14*, 162–199.

Lourenco, O. M. (1993). Toward a Piagetian explanation of the development of prosocial behaviour in children: The force of negational thinking. *British Journal of Developmental Psychology, 11*, 91–106.

Lovett, S. B., & Pillow, B. H. (1996). Development of the ability to distinguish between comprehension and memory: Evidence from goal-state evaluation tasks. *Journal of Educational Psychology, 88*, 546–562.

Lovoy, L. (2001). A historical survey of the glass ceiling and the double bind faced by women in the workplace: Options for avoidance. *Law and Psychology Review, 25*, 179–203.

Löwik, M. R. H., Wedel, M., Kok, F. J., Odink, J., Westenbrink, S., & Meulmeester, J. F. (1991). Nutrition and serum cholesterol levels among elderly men and women (Dutch nutrition surveillance system). *Journal of Gerontology: Medical Sciences, 46*, M23–M28.

Lozoff, B., Klein, N. K., Nelson, E. C., McClish, D. K., Manuel, M., & Chacon, M. E. (1998). Behavior of infants with iron-deficiency anemia. *Child Development, 69*, 24–36.

Lozoff, B., Wolf, A. W., & Davis, N. S. (1985). Sleep problems seen in pediatric practice. *Pediatrics, 75*, 477–483.

Lucas, J. L. (2000). Mentoring as a manifestation of generativity among university faculty. *Dissertation Abstracts International Section A: Humanities and Social Sciences, 61*(3-A), 881.

Ludemann, P. M. (1991). Generalized discrimination of positive facial expressions by seven- and ten-month-old infants. *Child Development, 62*, 55–67.

Luecke-Aleksa, D., Anderson, D. R., Collins, P. A., & Schmitt, K. L. (1995). Gender constancy and television viewing. *Developmental Psychology, 31*, 773–780.

Lueptow, L. B., Garovich-Szabo, L., & Lueptow, M. B. (2001). Social change and the persistence of sex typing: 1974–1997. *Social Forces, 80*, 1–36.

Lundin, T. (1984). Morbidity following sudden and unexpected bereavement. *British Journal of Psychiatry, 144*, 84–88.

Luo, T. Y. (1996). Sexual harassment in the Chinese workplace: Attitudes toward and experiences of sexual harassment among workers in Taiwan. *Violence Against Women, 2*, 284–301.

Luthar, S. S., Zigler, E., & Goldstein, D. (1992). Psychosocial adjustment among intellectually gifted adolescents: The role of cognitive-developmental and experiential factors. *Journal of Child Psychology and Psychiatry and Allied Disciplines, 33*, 361–373.

Lutz, S. E., & Ruble, D. N. (1995). Children and gender prejudice: Context, motivation, and the development of gender conceptions. In R. Vasta (Ed.), *Annals of child development: A research annual* (Vol. 10). London, UK: Jessica Kingsley.

Lyness, K. S., & Thompson, D. E. (1997). Above the glass ceiling? A comparison of matched samples of female and male executives. *Journal of Applied Psychology, 82*, 359–375.

Lyon, G. R. (1996). Learning disabilities. In E. J. Mash & R. A. Barkley (Eds.), *Child psychopathology*. New York: Guilford Press.

Lytton, H. (2000). Toward a model of family-environmental and child-biological influences on development. *Developmental Review, 20,* 150–179.

Lytton, H., & Romney, D. M. (1991). Parents' differential socialization of boys and girls: A meta-analysis. *Psychological Bulletin, 109,* 267–296.

Maccoby, E. E. (1988). Gender as a social category. *Developmental Psychology, 24,* 755–765.

Maccoby, E. E. (1990). Gender and relationships: A developmental account. *American Psychologist, 45,* 513–520.

Maccoby, E. E., & Jacklin, C. N. (1974). *The psychology of sex differences.* Palo Alto, CA: Stanford University Press.

Maccoby, E. E., & Martin, J. A. (1983). Socialization in the context of the family: Parent-child interaction. In P. H. Mussen (Ed.), *Handbook of child psychology* (Vol. 4). New York: Wiley.

MacDermid, S. M., De Haan, L. G., & Heilbrun, G. (1996). Generativity in multiple roles. *Journal of Adult Development, 3,* 145–158.

Madden, D. J. (2001). Speed and timing of behavioral processes. In J. E. Birren & K. W. Schaie (Eds.), *Handbook of the psychology of aging* (5th ed., pp. 288–312). San Diego, CA: Academic Press.

Magai, C. (2001). Emotions over the life span. In J. E. Birren & K. W. Schaie (Eds.), *Handbook of the psychology of aging* (5th ed., pp. 399–426). San Diego, CA: Academic Press.

Mahvani, V., & Sood, A. K. (2001). Hormone replacement therapy and cancer risk. *Current Opinion in Oncology, 13,* 384–389.

Main, M. (1996). Introduction to the special section on attachment and psychopathology: 2. Overview of the field of attachment. *Journal of Consulting and Clinical Psychology, 64,* 237–243.

Main, M., & Cassidy, J. (1988). Categories of response to reunion with the parent at age 6: Predictable from infant attachment classifications and stable over a 1-month period. *Developmental Psychology, 24,* 415–426.

Malinosky-Rummell, R., & Hansen, D. J. (1993). Long-term consequences of childhood physical abuse. *Psychological Bulletin, 114,* 68–79.

Malkinson, R., & Bar-Tur, L. (2000). The aging of grief: Parental grief of Israeli soldiers. In J. H. Harvey & B. G. Pauwels (Eds.), *Post-traumatic stress theory: Research and application* (pp. 147–162). Philadelphia: Brunner/Mazel.

Mandel, D. R., Jusczyk, P. W., & Pisoni, D. B. (1995). Infants' recognition of the sound patterns of their own names. *Psychological Science, 6,* 314–317.

Mange, A. P., & Mange, E. J. (1990). *Genetics: Human aspects* (2nd ed.). Sunderland, MA: Sinhauer Associates.

Mangelsdorf, S. C. (1992). Developmental changes in infant-stranger interaction. *Infant Behavior and Development, 15,* 191–208.

Mangelsdorf, S., Gunnar, M., Kestenbaum, R., Lang, S., & Andreas, D. (1990). Infant proneness-to-distress temperament, maternal personality, and mother-infant attachment: Associations and goodness of fit. *Child Development, 61,* 820–831.

Mangelsdorf, S. C., Shapiro, J. R., & Marzolf, D. (1995). Developmental and temperamental differences in emotional regulation in infancy. *Child Development, 66,* 1817–1828.

Manitoba Agriculture, Food and Rural Initiatives. (2004). *The cost of raising a child: 2004* [Online]. Available http://www.gov.mb.ca/agriculture/homeec/coc2004/cba28s02.html. (Retrieved October 3, 2004.)

Manitoba Education, Training and Youth. (2002). *French Immersion in Manitoba.* Winnipeg, MB: Author.

Marcia, J. E. (1980). Identity in adolescence. In J. Adelson (Ed.), *Handbook of adolescent psychology.* New York: Wiley.

Marcia, J. E. (1991). Identity and self-development. In R. M. Lerner, A. C. Petersen, & J. Brooks-Gunn (Eds.), *Encyclopedia of adolescence* (Vol. 1). New York: Garland.

Marcovitch, S., & Zelazo, P.D. (1999). The A-not-B error: Results from a logistic meta-analysis. *Child Development, 70,* 1297–1313.

Marcus, G. F., Pinker, S., Ullman, M., Hollander, M., Rosen, T. J., & Xu, F. (1992). Overregularization in language acquisition. *Monographs of the Society for Research in Child Development, 58* (4, Serial No. 228).

Marcussen, K. A. (2001). Marital status and psychological well-being: A comparison of married and cohabiting individuals. *Dissertation Abstracts International Section A: Humanities and Social Sciences, 61*(8-A), 3372.

Margolin, L., & White, J. (1987). The continuing role of physical attractiveness in marriage. *Journal of Marriage and the Family, 49,* 21–27.

Markovits, H., & Vachon, R. (1989). Reasoning with contrary-to-fact propositions. *Journal of Experimental Child Psychology, 47,* 398–412.

Markus, H., & Nurius, P. (1986). Possible selves. *American Psychologist, 41,* 954–969.

Marsh, H. W. (1991). Employment during high school: Character building or a subversion of academic goals? *Sociology of Education, 64,* 172–189.

Marsh, H. W., & Yeung, A. S. (1997). Causal effects of academic self-concept on academic achievement: Structural equation models of longitudinal data. *Journal of Educational Psychology, 89,* 41–54.

Marshall, E. O. (2001). The influence of marital satisfaction on the cognitive component of subjective well-being among the elderly. *Dissertation Abstracts International Section B: The Sciences and Engineering, 61B*(7-B), 3850.

Marsiglio, W. (1993). Attitudes toward homosexual activity and gays as friends: A national survey of heterosexual 15- to 19-year-old males. *Journal of Sex Research, 30,* 12–17.

Martin, C. L., Eisenbud, L., & Rose, H. (1995). Children's gender-based reasoning about toys. *Child Development, 66,* 1453–1471.

Martin, C. L., & Fabes, R. A. (2001). The stability and consequences of young children's same-sex peer interactions. *Developmental Psychology, 37,* 431–446.

Martin, C. L., & Halverson, C. F. (1987). The roles of cognition in sex roles and sex typing. In D. B. Carter (Ed.), *Current conceptions of sex roles and sex typing: Theory and research.* New York: Praeger.

Martin, C. L., & Little, J. K. (1990). The relation of gender understandings to children's sex-typed preferences and gender stereotypes. *Child Development, 61,* 1427–1439.

Martin, G. M. (1998). Toward a genetic analysis of unusually successful neural aging. In E. Wang & D. Snyder (Eds.), *Handbook of the aging brain* (pp. 125–142). San Diego, CA: Academic Press.

Martin, M., Grünendahl, M., & Martin, P. (2001). Age differences in stress, social resources, and well-being in middle and older age. *Journal of Gerontology: Psychological Sciences, 56B,* P214–P222.

Martin-Matthews, A. (1999). Widowhood: Dominant renditions, changing demographics, and variable meaning. In S. M. Neysmith (Ed.), *Critical issues for future social work practice with aging persons* (pp. 27–46). New York: Columbia University Press.

Martin-Matthews, A. (2000). Change and diversity in aging families and intergenerational relations. In N. Mandell & A. Duffy (Eds.), *Canadian families: Diversity, conflict, and change* (2nd ed., pp. 323–359). Toronto: Harcourt Brace.

Masheter, C. (1991). Postdivorce relationships between ex-spouses: The role of attachment and interpersonal conflict. *Journal of Marriage and the Family, 53,* 103–110.

Masheter, C. (1997). Healthy and unhealthy friendship and hostility between ex-spouses. *Journal of Marriage and the Family, 59,* 463–475.

Masi, L., & Bilezikian, J. P. (1997). Osteoporosis: New hope for the future. *International Journal of Fertility and Women's Medicine, 42,* 245–254.

Matthews, A. M., & Brown, K. H. (1987). Retirement as a critical life event: The differential experiences of men and women. *Research on Aging, 9,* 548–571.

Matthews, L. S., Conger, R. D., & Wickrama, K. A. S. (1996). Work-family conflict and marital quality: Mediating processes. *Social Psychology Quarterly, 59,* 62–79.

Matthews, R., & Matthews, A. M. (1986). Infertility and involuntary childlessness: The transition to nonparenthood. *Journal of Marriage and the Family, 48,* 641–649.

Matthews, S. H. (1996). Friendships in old age. In N. Vanzetti & S. Duck (Eds.), *A lifetime of relationships* (pp. 406–430). Pacific Grove, CA: Brooks/Cole.

Mattys, S. L., & Jusczyk, P. W. (2001). Phonotactic cues for segmentation of fluent speech by infants. *Cognition, 78,* 91–121.

Mattys, S. L., Jusczyk, P. W., Luce, P. A., & Morgan, J. L. (1999). Phonotactic and prosodic effects on word segmentation in infants. *Cognitive Psychology, 38,* 465–494.

Matula, K. E., Huston, T. L., Grotevant, H. D., & Zamutt, A. (1992). Identity and dating commitment among women and men in college. *Journal of Youth and Adolescence, 21,* 339–356.

Maughan, A., & Cicchetti, D. (2002). Impact of child maltreatment and interadult violence on children's emotion regulation abilities and socioemotional adjustment. *Child Development, 73,* 1525–1542.

Maurer, D., & Adams, R. J. (1987). Emergence of the ability to discriminate blue from gray at one month of age. *Journal of Experimental Child Psychology, 44,* 147–156.

Maynard, A. E. (2002). Cultural teaching: The development of teaching skills in Maya sibling interactions. *Child Development, 73,* 969–982.

Mayo Clinic. (2000a). *Hormonal conditions. Male menopause: Does it exist?* [Online]. Available: http://www.mayoclinic.com.

Mayo Clinic. (2000b). *Menopause. What is menopause?* [Online]. Available: http://www.mayoclinic.com.

Mayo Clinic. (2001). *Alcohol addiction* [Online]. Available: http://www.mayoclinic.com.

Mazur, E., Wolchik, S. A., Virdin, L., Sandler, I. N., & West, S. G. (1999). Cognitive moderators of children's adjustment to stressful divorce events: The role of negative cognitive errors and positive illusions. *Child Development, 70,* 231–245.

McAdams, D. P. (1992). The five-factor model in personality: A critical appraisal. *Journal of Personality, 60,* 329–361.

McAdams, D. P. (2001). Generativity at midlife. In M. E. Lachman (Ed.), *Handbook of midlife development* (pp. 395–443). New York: Wiley.

McAdams, D. P., Hart, H. M., & Maruna, S. (1998). The anatomy of generativity. In D. P. McAdams & E. de St. Aubin (Eds.), *Generativity and adult development: How and why do we care for the next generation* (pp. 7–43). Washington, DC: American Psychological Association.

McBride-Chang, C., & Kail, R. V. (2002). Cross-cultural similarities in the predictors of reading acquisition. *Child Development, 73,* 1392–1407.

McCall, R. B. (1979). *Infants.* Cambridge, MA: Harvard University Press.

McCarthy, M. R. (2002). Gender differences in reactions to perinatal loss: A qualitative study of couples. *Dissertation Abstracts International Section B: The Sciences and Engineering, 62*(8B), 3809.

McCarty, M. E., & Ashmead, D. H. (1999). Visual control of reaching and grasping in infants. *Developmental Psychology, 35,* 620–631.

McCarty, M. E., Clifton, R. K., Ashmead, D. H., Lee, P., & Goubet, N. (2001). How infants use vision for grasping objects. *Child Development, 72,* 973–987.

McClure, E. B. (2000). A meta-analytic review of sex differences in facial expression processing and their development in infants, children, and adolescents. *Psychological Bulletin, 126,* 424–453.

McConaghy, T. (1998). Canada's participation in TIMSS. *Phi Delta Kappan, 79,* 793, 2p, 1c.

McCormick, C. (2000, August 26). Twin miracles: Mashpee mother has groundbreaking surgery to save her two fetuses. *Cape Code Times* [Online]. Available: http://www.capecodonline.com/cctimes/archives/2000/aug/26/twinmiracles2.

McCrae, S. (1997). Cohabitation: A trial run for marriage? *Sexual and Marital Therapy, 12*, 259–273.

McCutchen, D., Covill, A., Hoyne, S. H., & Mildes, K. (1994). Individual differences in writing: Implications of translating fluency. *Journal of Educational Psychology, 86*, 256–266.

McCutchen, D., Francis, M., & Kerr, S. (1997). Revising for meaning: Effects of knowledge and strategy. *Journal of Educational Psychology, 89*, 667–676.

McDowd, J. M., & Shaw, R. J. (2000). Attention and aging: A functional perspective. In F. I. M. Craik & T. A. Salthouse (Eds.), *Handbook of aging and cognition* (2nd ed., pp. 221–292). Mahwah, NJ: Erlbaum.

McEwen, B. S. (1998). Protective and damaging effects of stress mediators. *New England Journal of Medicine, 338*, 171–179.

McFadden, S. H. (1996). Religion, spirituality, and aging. In J. E. Birren & K. W. Schaie (Eds.), *Handbook of the psychology of aging* (4th ed., pp. 162–177). San Diego, CA: Academic Press.

McGhee, P. E. (1976). Children's appreciation of humor: A test of the cognitive congruency principle. *Child Development, 47*, 420–426.

McGee, R., Williams, S., & Feehan, M. (1992). Attention deficit disorder and age of onset of problem behaviors. *Journal of Abnormal Child Psychology, 20*, 487–502.

McGilly, K., & Siegler, R. S. (1990). The influence of encoding and strategic knowledge on children's choices among serial recall strategies. *Developmental Psychology, 26*, 931–941.

McGivern, J. E., Levin, J. R., Pressley, M., & Ghatala, E. S. (1990). A developmental study of memory monitoring and strategy selection. *Contemporary Educational Psychology, 15*, 103–115.

McGraw, M. B. (1935). *Growth: A study of Johnny and Jimmy.* East Norwalk, CT: Appleton-Century-Crofts.

McGuire, L. C., & Cavanaugh, J. C. (1992, April). *Objective measures versus spouses' perceptions of cognitive status in dementia patients.* Paper presented at the biennial Cognitive Aging Conference, Atlanta.

McGuire, L. C., & Codding, R. (1998, August). *Improving older adults' memory for medical information: The efficacy of note taking and elder speak.* Paper presented at the annual meeting of the American Psychological Association, San Francisco.

McHale, S. M., Bartko, W. T., Crouter, A. C., & Perry-Jenkins, M. (1990). Children's housework and psychosocial functioning: The mediating effects of parents' sex-role behaviors and attitudes. *Child Development, 61*, 1413–1426.

McManus, I. C., Sik, G., Cole, D. R., Kloss, J., Mellon, A. F., & Wong, J. (1988). The development of handedness in children. *British Journal of Developmental Psychology, 6*, 257–273.

Mehta, K. K. (1997). The impact of religious beliefs and practices on aging: A cross-cultural comparison. *Journal of Aging Studies, 11*, 101–114.

Meilman, P. W. (1979). Cross-sectional age changes in ego identity status during adolescence. *Developmental Psychology, 15*, 230–231.

Meltzoff, A. N., & Moore, M. K. (1989). Imitation in newborn infants: Exploring the range of gestures imitated and the underlying mechanisms. *Developmental Psychology, 25*, 954–962.

Meltzoff, A. N., & Moore, M. K. (1994). Imitation, memory, and the representation of persons. *Infant Behavior and Development, 17*, 83–99.

Mennella, J. A., & Beauchamp, G. K. (1996). The human infant's response to vanilla flavors in mother's milk and formula. *Infant Behavior and Development, 19*, 13–19.

Mennella, J., & Beauchamp, G. K. (1997). The ontogeny of human flavor perception. In G. K. Beauchamp & L. Bartoshuk (Eds.), *Tasting and smelling. Handbook of perception and cognition.* San Diego, CA: Academic Press.

Mera, S. L. (1998). The role of telomeres in ageing and cancer. *British Journal of Biomedical Science, 55*, 221–225.

Mervis, C. B., & Johnson, K. E. (1991). Acquisition of the plural morpheme: A case study. *Developmental Psychology, 27*, 222–235.

Messinger, D. S. (2002). Positive and negative: Infant facial expressions and emotions. *Current Directions in Psychological Science, 11*, 1–6.

Metropolitan Area Agency on Aging. (1998). *Checklist on adult day care* [Online]. Available: http://www.tcaging.org/com_adck.htm.

Michael, R. T., Gagnon, J. H., Lauman, E. O., & Kolata, G. (1994). *Sex in America: A definitive survey.* Boston: Little, Brown.

Migliardi, P., Blum, E., & Heinomen, T. (2004). Immigrant women abuse. In C. A. Ateah & J. Mirwaldt (Eds.), *Within our reach: Preventing abuse across the lifespan.* Halifax, NS: Fernwood Publishing and RESOLVE (Research and Education for Solutions to Violence and Abuse).

Milford, M. (1997, November 9). Making a tough transition. *Sunday News Journal* (Wilmington, DE), pp. G1, G6.

Miller, B. C., Benson, B., & Galbraith, K. A. (2001). Family relationships and adolescent pregnancy risk: A research synthesis. *Developmental Review, 21*, 1–38.

Miller, J. G., & Bersoff, D. M. (1992). Culture and moral judgment: How are conflicts between justice and interpersonal responsibilities resolved? *Journal of Personality and Social Psychology, 62*, 541–554.

Miller, K. F., Smith, C. M., Zhu, J., & Zhang, H. (1995). Preschool origins of cross-national differences in mathematical competence: The role of number-naming systems. *Psychological Science, 6*, 56–60.

Miller, L. K. (1999). The Savant Syndrome: Intellectual impairment and exceptional skill. *Psychological Bulletin, 125*, 31–46.

Miller, P. A., Eisenberg, N., Fabes, R. A., & Shell, R. (1996). Relations of moral reasoning and vicarious emotion to young children's prosocial behavior toward peers and adults. *Developmental Psychology, 32*, 210–219.

Miller, P. M., Danaher, D. L., & Forbes, D. (1986). Sex-related strategies of coping with interpersonal conflict in children aged five to seven. *Developmental Psychology, 22*, 543–548.

Miller, R. B., Hemesath, K., & Nelson, B. (1997). Marriage in middle and later life. In T. D. Hargrave & S. M. Hanna

(Eds.), *The aging family: New visions in theory, practice, and reality* (pp. 178–198). New York: Brunner/Mazel.

Miller, S. S., & Cavanaugh, J. C. (1990). The meaning of grandparenthood and its relationship to demographic, relationship, and social participation variables. *Journals of Gerontology: Psychological Sciences, 45,* 244–246.

Mills, R. S. L., & Grusec, J. E. (1989). Cognitive, affective, and behavioral consequences of praising altruism. *Merrill-Palmer Quarterly, 35,* 299–326.

Mirabella, R. L. (2001). Determinants of job satisfaction in psychologists. *Dissertation Abstracts International Section B: The Sciences and Engineering, 61*(12-B), 6714.

Mischel, W. (1970). Sex-typing and socialization. In P. H. Mussen, (Ed.), *Carmichaels' manual of child psychology* (Vol. 2). New York: Wiley.

Mischel, W., & Shoda, Y. (1995). A cognitive–affective system theory of personality: Reconceptualizing situations, dispositions, dynamics, and invariance in personality structure. *Psychological Review, 102,* 246–268.

Mitchell, C. V. (2000). Managing gender expectations: A competency model for women in leadership. *Dissertation Abstracts International Section B: The Sciences and Engineering, 61*(3-B), 1682.

Miura, I. T., Kim, C. C., Chang, C. M., & Okamoto, Y. (1988). Effects of language characteristics on children's cognitive representation of number: Cross-national comparisons. *Child Development, 59,* 1445–1450.

Mize, J., & Ladd, G. W. (1990). A cognitive social-learning approach to social skill training with low-status preschool children. *Developmental Psychology, 26,* 388–397.

Mize, J., & Pettit, G. S. (1997). Mothers' social coaching, mother-child relationship style, and children's peer competence: Is the medium the message? *Child Development, 68,* 312–332.

Mize, J., Pettit, G. S., & Brown, E. G. (1995). Mothers' supervision of their children's peer play: Relations with beliefs, perceptions, and knowledge. *Developmental Psychology, 31,* 311–321.

Mizes, J. S. (1995). Eating disorders. In M. Hersen, R. T. Ammerman, et al. (Eds.), *Advanced abnormal child psychology* (pp. 375–391). Hillsdale, NJ: Erlbaum.

Moats, L. C., & Lyon, G. R. (1993). Learning disabilities in the United States: Advocacy, science, and the future of the field. *Journal of Learning Disabilities, 26,* 282–294.

Mobily, K. E., Lemke, J. H., & Gisin, G. J. (1991). The idea of leisure repertoire. *Journal of Applied Gerontology, 10,* 208–223.

Moen, P., Fields, V., Meador, R., & Rosenblatt, H. (2000a). Fostering integration: A case study of the Cornell Retirees Volunteering in Service (CRVIS) program. In K. Pillemer & P. Moen (Eds.), *Social integration in the second half of life* (pp. 247–264). Baltimore: Johns Hopkins University Press.

Moen, P., Fields, V., Quick, H. E., & Hofmeister, H. (2000b). A life course approach to retirement and social integration. In K. Pillemer & P. Moen (Eds.), *Social integration in the second half of life* (pp. 75–107). Baltimore: Johns Hopkins University Press.

Moen, P. J., Robinson, J., & Fields, V. (1994). Women's work and caregiving roles: A life course approach. *Journal of Gerontology: Social Sciences, 49,* S176–S186.

Moffitt, T. E. (1993). Adolescence-limited and life-course-persistent antisocial behavior: A developmental taxonomy. *Psychological Review, 100,* 674–701.

Moffitt, T. E., Caspi, A., Belsky, J., & Silva, P. A. (1992). Childhood experience and the onset of menarche: A test of a sociobiological model. *Child Development, 63,* 47–58.

Molfese, D. L., & Burger-Judisch, L. M. (1991). Dynamic temporal-spatial allocation of resources in the human brain: An alternative to the static view of hemisphere differences. In F. L. Ketterle (Ed.), *Cerebral laterality: Theory and research. The Toledo symposium.* Hillsdale, NJ: Erlbaum.

Moller, L. C., Hymel, S., & Rubin, K. H. (1992). Sex typing in play and popularity in middle childhood. *Sex Roles, 26,* 331–353.

Monczunski, J. (1991). That incurable disease. *Notre Dame Magazine, 20(1),* 37.

Monk, C., Fifer, W. P., Myers, M. M., Sloan, R. P., Trien, L., & Hurtado, A. (2000). Maternal stress responses and anxiety during pregnancy: Effects on fetal heart rate. *Developmental Psychobiology, 36,* 67–77.

Montague, D. P., & Walker-Andrews, A. S. (2001). Peekabo: A new look at infants' perception of emotion expressions. *Developmental Psychology, 37,* 826–838.

Montgomery, M. J., Anderson, E. R., Hetherington, E. M., & Clingempeel, W. G. (1992). Patterns of courtship for remarriage: Implications for child adjustment and parent-child relationships. *Journal of Marriage and the Family, 54,* 686–698.

Moore, B. S., Underwood, B., & Rosenhan, D. L. (1973). Affect and altruism. *Developmental Psychology, 8,* 99–104.

Moore, K. L., & Persaud, T. V. N. (1993). *Before we are born* (4th ed.). Philadelphia: Saunders.

Morgan, B., & Gibson, K. R. (1991). Nutritional and environmental interactions in brain development. In K. R. Gibson & A. C. Peterson (Eds.), *Brain maturation and cognitive development: Comparative and cross-cultural perspectives.* New York: Aldine de Gruyter.

Morgane, P. J., Austin-Lafrance, R., Bronzino, J. D., Tonkiss, J., Diaz-Cintra, S., Cintra, L., Kemper, T., & Galler, J. R. (1993). Prenatal malnutrition and development of the brain. *Neuroscience and Biobehavioral Reviews, 17,* 91–128.

Morioka, K. (1998). Comment 1: Toward a paradigm shift in family sociology. *Japanese Journal of Family Sociology, 10,* 139–144.

Morison, P., & Masten, A. S. (1991). Peer reputation in middle childhood as a predictor of adaptation in adolescence: A seven-year follow-up. *Child Development, 62,* 991–1007.

Morrison, A. M., White, R. P., Van Velsor, E., & the Center for Creative Leadership. (1992). *Breaking the glass ceiling: Can women reach the top of America's largest corporations?* (Updated ed.). Reading, MA: Addison-Wesley.

Morrongiello, B. A., Fenwick, K. D., & Chance, G. (1990). Sound localization acuity in very young infants: An observer-based testing procedure. *Developmental Psychology, 26,* 75–84.

Morrow, D. G., Hier, C. M., Menard, W. E., & Von Leirer, O. (1998). Icons improve older and younger adults' comprehension of medication information. *Journal of Gerontology: Psychological Sciences, 53B,* P240–P254.

Morrow-Howell, N., & Mui, A. (1989). Elderly volunteers: Reasons for initiating and terminating service. *Journal of Gerontological Social Work, 13,* 21–34.

Mortimer, J. T., Finch, M. D., & Kumka, D. (1982). Persistence and change in development: The multidimensional self-concept. In P. B. Baltes & O. G. Brim, Jr. (Eds.), *Life-span development and behavior* (Vol. 4, pp. 263–313). New York: Academic Press.

Mortimer, J. T., Finch, M. D., Rye, S., Shanahan, M. J., & Call, K. T. (1996). The effects of work intensity on adolescent mental health, achievement, and behavioral adjustment: New evidence from a prospective study. *Child Development, 67,* 1243–1261.

Mortimer, J. T., Harley, C., & Staff, J. (2002). The quality of work and youth mental health. *Work & Occupations, 29,* 166–197.

Moses, L. J., Baldwin, D. A., Rosicky, J. G., & Tidball, G. (2001). Evidence for referential understanding in the emotions domain at twelve and eighteen months. *Child Development, 72,* 718–735.

Moshman, D. (1998). Cognitive development beyond childhood. In W. Damon (Ed.), *Handbook of child psychology* (5th ed.). New York: Wiley.

Moss, E., Rousseau, D., Parent, S., St-Laurent, D., & Saintonge, J. (1998). Correlates of attachment at school age: Maternal reported stress, mother-child interaction, and behavior problems. *Child Development, 69,* 1390–1405.

Moss, M. S., & Moss, S. Z. (1996). Remarriage of widowed persons: A triadic relationship. In D. Klass, P. R. Silverman, & S. L. Nickman (Eds.), *Continuing bonds: New understandings of grief* (pp. 163–178). Washington, DC: Taylor & Francis.

Moss, M. S., Moss, S. Z., & Hansson, R. O. (2001). Bereavement and old age. In M. S. Stroebe, R. O. Hansson, W. Stroebe, & H. Schut (Eds.), *Handbook of bereavement research: Consequences, coping, and care* (pp. 241–260). Washington, DC: American Psychological Association.

Mounts, N. S., & Steinberg, L. (1995). An ecological analysis of peer influence on adolescent grade point average and drug use. *Developmental Psychology, 31,* 915–922.

Muehlenhard, C. L. (1988). "Nice women" don't say yes and "real men" don't say no: How miscommunication and the double standard can cause sexual problems. *Women & Therapy, 7*(2–3), 95–108.

Mueller, J. H., Grove, T. R., & Thompson, W. B. (1993). Test anxiety and handedness. *Bulletin of the Psychonomic society, 31,* 461–464.

Muller, E. D. (2002). The experience of grief after bereavement: A phenomenological investigation. *Dissertation Abstracts International Section B: The Sciences and Engineering, 62*(8B), 3810.

Mumme, D. L., Fernald, A., & Herrera, C. (1996). Infants' responses to facial and vocal emotional signals in a social referencing paradigm. *Child Development, 67,* 3219–3237.

Munakata, Y., McClelland, J. L., Johnson, M. H., & Siegler, R. S. (1997). Rethinking infant knowledge: Toward an adaptive process account of successes and failures in object permanence tasks. *Psychological Review, 104,* 686–713.

Murphy, C. (1986). Taste and smell in the elderly. In H. L. Meiselman & R. S. Rivlin (Eds.), *Clinical measurement of taste and smell* (pp. 343–371). New York: Macmillan.

Murphy, N., & Messer, D. (2000). Differential benefits from scaffolding and children working alone. *Educational Psychology, 20,* 17–31.

Murray, B. (1998). Workplace harassment hurts everyone on the job. *APA Monitor, 29*(7), 36.

Murrell, A. J., Frieze, I. H., & Frost, J. L. (1991). Aspiring to careers in male- and female-dominated professions: A study of black and white college women. *Psychology of Women Quarterly, 15,* 103–126.

Murstein, B. I. (1987). A clarification and extension of the SVR theory of dyadic pairing. *Journal of Marriage and the Family, 49,* 929–933.

Mutchler, J. E., Burr, J. A., Pienta, A. M., & Massagli, M. P. (1997). Pathways to labor force exit: Work transitions and work instability. *Journal of Gerontology: Social Sciences, 52B,* S4–S12.

Myers, E. G., & Cavanaugh, J. C. (1995). Filial anxiety in mothers and daughters: Cross-validation of the Filial Anxiety Scale. *Journal of Adult Development, 2,* 137–145.

Nadig, A. S., & Sedivy, J. C. (2002). Evidence of perspective-taking constraints in children's on-line reference resolution. *Psychological Science, 13,* 329–336.

Nahemow, L. (2000). The ecological theory of aging: Powell Lawton's legacy. In R. L. Rubinstein & M. Moss (Eds.), *The many dimensions of aging* (pp. 22–40). New York: Springer.

Naigles, L. G., & Gelman, S. A. (1995). Overextensions in comprehension and production revisited: Preferential-looking in a study of dog, cat, and cow. *Journal of Child Language, 22,* 19–46.

Nation, K., Adams, J. W., Bowyer-Crane, C. A., & Snowling, M. J. (1999). Working memory deficits in poor comprehenders reflect underlying language impairments. *Journal of Experimental Child Psychology, 73,* 139–158.

National Advisory Council on Aging. (2003). A choice of housing lifestyle. *Newsletter of the National Advisory Council on Aging, 10* (4).

National Center for Education Statistics. (1997). *Pursuing excellence: A study of U.S. fourth-grade mathematics and science achievement in an international context.* Washington, DC: U.S. Government Printing Office.

National Center for Health Statistics. (2001). *Health, United States, 2001 with urban and rural health chartbook* [Online]. Available: http://www.cdc.gov/nchs/products/pubs/pubd/hus/hus.htm.

Neft, N., & Levine, A. D. (1997). *Where women stand: An international report on the status of women in over 140 countries, 1997–1998*. New York: Random House.

Neimeyer, R. (1997). Knowledge at the margins. *The Forum Newsletter* (Association for Death Education and Counseling), *23*(2), 2, 10.

Neimeyer, R., Keese, B. V., & Fortner, M. (2000). Commemoration and bereavement: Cultural aspects of collective myth and the creation of national identity. In R. Malkinson, S. Rubin, & E. Witztum (Eds.), *Traumatic and non-traumatic loss and bereavement: Clinical theory and practice* (pp. 295–320). Madison, CT: Psychosocial Press/International Universities Press.

Neisser, U., Boodoo, G., Bouchard, T. J., Boykin, A. W., Brody, N., Ceci, S. J., Halpern, D. F., Loehlin, J. C., Perloff, R., Sternberg, R. J., & Urbina, S. (1996). Intelligence: Knowns and unknowns. *American Psychologist, 51*, 77–101.

Nell, V. (2002). Why young men drive dangerously: Implications for injury prevention. *Current Directions in Psychological Science, 11*, 75–79.

Nelson, C. A. (1997). The neurobiological basis of early memory development. In N. Cowan (Ed.), *The development of memory in childhood: Studies in developmental psychology* (pp. 41–82). Hove, UK: Psychology Press/ Erlbaum (UK) Taylor & Francis.

Nelson, C. A. (1999). Neural plasticity and human development. *Current Directions in Psychological Science, 8*, 42–45.

Nelson, C. H. (2001). Determinants of grief duration: An exploratory model and multivariate analysis. *Dissertation Abstracts International Section A: Humanities and Social Sciences, 61*(12A), 4963.

Nelson, K. (1973). Structure and strategy in learning to talk. *Monographs of the Society for Research in Child Development, 38* (Serial No. 149).

Nelson, K. (1993). Explaining the emergence of autobiographical memory in early childhood. A. F. Collins & S. E. Gathercole (Eds.), *Theories of memory*. Hove, UK: Erlbaum.

Nesdale, D., & Flesser, D. (2001). Social identity and the development of children's group attitudes. *Child Development, 72*, 506–517.

Neugarten, B. L. (1969). Continuities and discontinuities of psychological issues into adult life. *Human Development, 12*, 121–130.

Neugarten, B. L., & Weinstein, K. K. (1964). The changing American grandparent. *Journal of Marriage and the Family, 26*, 299–304.

Newcomb, A. F., & Bagwell, C. L. (1995). Children's friendship relations: A meta-analytic review. *Psychological Bulletin, 117*, 306–347.

Newman, B. S., & Muzzonigro, P. G. (1993). The effects of traditional family values on the coming out process of gay male adolescents. *Adolescence, 28*, 213–226.

Newman, L. S., Cooper, J., & Ruble, D. N. (1995). Gender and computers: II. Interactive effects of knowledge and constancy on gender-stereotyped attitudes. *Sex Roles, 33*, 325–351.

Newsom, J. T. (1999). Another side to caregiving: Negative reactions to being helped. *Current Directions in Psychological Science, 8*, 183–187.

NICHD Early Child Care Research Network. (1997). The effects of infant child care on infant-mother attachment security: Results of the NICHD Study of Early Child Care. *Child Development, 68*, 860–879.

NICHD Early Child Care Research Network. (2001). Child-care and family predictors of preschool attachment and stability from infancy. *Developmental Psychology, 37*, 847–862.

Nicholls, W. J., & Pike, L. T. (2002). Contact fathers' experience of family life. *Journal of Family Studies, 8*, 74–90.

Nielson, A. C. (1990). *Annual Nielsen report on television: 1990*. New York: Nielson Media Research.

Nolen-Hoeksema, S., & Larson, J. (1999). *Coping with loss*. Mahwah, NJ: Erlbaum.

Noller, P., & Fitzpatrick, M. A. (1993). *Communication in family relationships*. Upper Saddle River, NJ: Prentice-Hall.

Norris, F. N., & Murrell, S. A. (1987). Older adult family stress and adaptation before and after bereavement. *Journal of Gerontology, 42*, 606–612.

Notarius, C. I. (1996). Marriage: Will I be happy or will I be sad? In N. Vanzetti & S. Duck (Eds.), *A lifetime of relationships* (pp. 265–289). Pacific Grove, CA: Brooks/Cole.

Nurmi, J., Poole, M. E., & Kalakoski, V. (1996). Age differences in adolescent identity exploration and commitment in urban and rural environments. *Journal of Adolescence, 19*, 443–452.

Nwokah, E., & Fogel, A. (1993). Laughter in mother-infant emotional communication. *Humor: International Journal of Humor Research, 6*, 137–161.

O'Brien, C.-A., & Goldberg, A. (2000). Lesbians and gay men inside and outside families. In N. Mandell & A. Duffy (Eds.), *Canadian families: Diversity, conflict, and change* (2nd ed., pp. 115–145). Toronto: Harcourt Brace.

O'Connell, P., Sedighdeilami, F., Peplar, D. J., Craig, W., Connolly, J., Atlas, R., Smith, C., & Charach, A. (1997). *Prevalence of bullying and victimization among Canadian elementary and middle school children*. Report.

Oehmichen, M., & Meissner, C. (2000). Life shortening and physician assistance in dying: Euthanasia from the viewpoint of German legal medicine. *Gerontology, 46*, 212–218.

Offermann, L. R., & Growing, M. K. (1990). Organizations of the future: Changes and challenges. *American Psychologist, 45*, 95–108.

Offord, D.R., Boyle, M.H., Szatmari, P., et al. (1987). Ontario child health study, II: Six month prevalence of disorders and rates of service utilization. *Archives of General Psychiatry, 44*, 832-836.

Ogletree, R. J. (1993). Sexual coercion experience and help-seeking behavior of college women. *Journal of American College Health, 41*, 149–153.

Okagaki, L., & Sternberg, R. J. (1993). Parental beliefs and children's school performance. *Child Development, 64*, 36–56.

Okie, S. (2000, April 12). Over the tiniest patients, big ethical questions: Fetal surgery's growing reach raises issues of need and risks. *Washington Post*, pp. A1, A16.

Okonski, B. (1996, May 6). Just say something. *Newsweek*, p. 14.

O'Leary, K. D. (1993). Through a psychological lens: Personality traits, personality disorders, and levels of violence. In R. J. Gelles & D. R. Loseke (Eds.), *Current controversies on family violence* (pp. 7–30). Newbury Park, CA: Sage.

Olian, J. D., Carroll, S. J., Giannantonia, C. M., & Feren, D. B. (1988). What do proteges look for in a mentor? Results from three experimental studies. *Journal of Vocational Behavior, 33,* 15–37.

Olsen, O. (1997). Meta-analysis of the safety of home birth. *Birth-Issues in Perinatal Care, 24,* 4–13.

Olson, D. H., & McCubbin, H. (1983). *Families: What makes them work.* Newbury Park, CA: Sage.

Olson, L. N. (2000). Power, control, and communication: An analysis of aggressive, violent, and abusive couples. *Dissertation Abstracts International Section A: Humanities and Social Sciences, 61*(2-A), 427.

Oltjenbruns, K. A. (1996). Death of a friend during adolescence: Issues and impacts. In C. A. Coor & D. E. Balk (Eds.), *Handbook of adolescent death and bereavement* (pp. 196–215). New York: Springer.

Oltjenbruns, K. A. (2001). Developmental context of childhood: Grief and regrief phenomena. In M. S. Stroebe, R. O. Hansson, W. Stroebe, & H. Schut (Eds.), *Handbook of bereavement research: Consequences, coping, and care* (pp. 169–197). Washington, DC: American Psychological Association.

O'Neill, D. K. (1996). Two-year-old children's sensitivity to a parent's knowledge state when making requests. *Child Development, 67,* 659–677.

O'Rand, A. M., & Campbell, R. T. (1999). On reestablishing the phenomenon and specifying ignorance: Theory development and research design in aging. In V. L. Bengtson & K. W. Schaie (Eds.), *Handbook of theories of aging* (pp. 59–78). New York: Springer.

Orentlicher, D. (2000). The implementation of Oregon's death with dignity act: Reassuring, but more data are needed. *Psychology, Public Policy, and Law, 6,* 489–502.

Organization for Economic Cooperation and Development. (2002). *OECD health data 2001: Infant mortality, Deaths per 1000 live births* [Online]. Available: http://www.oecd.org/document. (Retrieved March 4, 2004.)

Orlick, T., Zhou, Q. Y., & Partington, J. (1990). Co-operation and conflict within Chinese and Canadian kindergarten settings. *Canadian Journal of Behavioural Science, 22,* 20–25.

Orwoll, L., & Perlmutter, M. (1990). The study of wise persons: Integrating a personality perspective. In R. J. Sternberg (Ed.), *Wisdom: Its nature, origins, and development* (pp. 160–177). Cambridge, UK: Cambridge University Press.

Osgood, N. J. (1992). *Suicide in later life.* Lexington, MA: Lexington Books.

Oygard, L., & Hardeng, S. (2001). Divorce support groups: How do group characteristics influence adjustment to divorce? *Social Work with Groups, 24,* 69–87.

Ozawa, M. N., & Yoon, H. S. (2002). The economic benefit of remarriage: Gender and class income. *Journal of Divorce and Remarriage, 36,* 21–39.

Paarlberg, K. M., Vingerhoets, A. J. J. M., Passchier, J., Dekker, G. A., et al. (1995). Psychosocial factors and pregnancy outcome: A review with emphasis on methodological issues. *Journal of Psychosomatic Research, 39,* 563–595.

Palacio-Quentin, E. (2000). The impact of day care on child development. *isuma, 1* (2) [Online]. Available: http://www.isuma.net/v01n02/palacio/palacio_e.shtml. (Retrieved February 9, 2004.)

Papalia, D. E., & Olds, S. W. (1995). *Human development* (6th ed.). New York: McGraw-Hill.

Parasuraman, R. (1998). The attentive brain: Issues and prospects. In R. Parasuraman (Ed.), *The attentive brain* (pp. 3–15). Cambridge, MA: MIT Press.

Parazzini, F., Luchini, L., La Vecchia, C., & Crosignani, P. G. (1993). Video display terminal use during pregnancy and reproductive outcome: A meta-analysis. *Journal of Epidemiology and Community Health, 47,* 265–268.

Pargament, K. I. (1997). *The psychology of religion and coping: Theory, research, and practice.* New York: Guilford Press.

Park, D. C., Lautenschlager, G., Hedden, T., Davidson, N., Smith, A. D., & Smith, P. K. (2002). Models of visuospatial and verbal memory across the adult lifespan. *Psychology and Aging, 17,* 299–320.

Park, D. C., Morrell, R. W., & Shifrin, K. (Eds.). (1999). *Processing of medical information in aging patients: Cognitive and human factors perspectives.* Mahwah, NJ: Erlbaum.

Park, D. C., Smith, A. D., Lautenschlager, G., Earles, J. L., Frieski, D., Zwahr, M., & Gaines, C. L. (1996). Mediators of long-term memory performance across the life span. *Psychology and Aging, 11,* 621–637.

Parke, R. D. (1977). Punishment in children: Effects, side effects and alternative strategies. In H. L. Hom, Jr., & A. Robinson (Eds.), *Psychological processes in early education.* New York: Academic Press.

Parke, R. D. (1990). In search of fathers: A narrative of an empirical journey. In I. Sigel & G. Brody (Eds.), *Methods of family research.* Hillsdale, NJ: Erlbaum.

Parke, R. D. (1995). Fathers and families. In M. H. Bornstein (Ed.), *Handbook of parenting* (Vol. 3). Mahwah, NJ: Erlbaum.

Parke, R. D., & Bahvnagri, N. P. (1989). Parents as managers of children's peer relationships. In D. Belle (Ed.), *Children's social networks and social supports.* New York: Wiley.

Parke, R. D., & Buriel, R. (1998). Socialization in the family: Ethnic and ecological perspectives. In W. Damon (Ed.), *Handbook of child psychology* (Vol. 3). New York: Wiley.

Parker, J. G., & Seal, J. (1996). Forming, losing, renewing, and replacing friendships: Applying temporal parameters to the assessment of children's friendship experiences. *Child Development, 67,* 2248–2268.

Parker, R. A., & Aldwin, C. M. (1997). Do aspects of gender identity change from early to middle adulthood? Disentangling age, cohort, and period effects. In M. E. Lachman & J. B. James (Eds.), *Multiple paths of midlife development* (pp. 67–107). Chicago: University of Chicago Press.

Parliament of Canada Standing Committee on Health. (1999). *Organ and tissue donation and transplantation: A Canadian approach* [Online]. Available: http://www.parl.gc.ca/InfoComDoc/36/1/HEAL/Studies/Reports/healrp05-e.htm#toc. (Retrieved May 1, 2004.)

Parritz, R. H. (1996). A descriptive analysis of toddler coping in challenging circumstances. *Infant Behavior and Development, 19,* 171–180.

Parten, M. (1932). Social participation among preschool children. *Journal of Abnormal and Social Psychology, 27,* 243–269.

Pascual, C. (2000, October 3). Asians have highest elderly suicide rate. *Wilmington (NC) Morning Star,* p. 5D.

Pascual-Leone, J. (1990). An essay on wisdom: Toward organismic processes that make it possible. In R. J. Sternberg (Ed.), *Wisdom: Its nature, origins, and development* (pp. 244–278). Cambridge, UK: Cambridge University Press.

Patterson, C. J. (1992). Children of lesbian and gay parents. *Child Development, 63,* 1025–1042.

Patterson, G. R. (1980). Mothers: The unacknowledged victims. *Monographs of the Society for Research in Child Development, 45* (5, Serial No. 186).

Patterson, G. R. (1995). Coercion as a basis for early age of onset for arrest. In J. McCord (Ed.), *Coercion and punishment in long-term perspectives.* New York: Cambridge University Press.

Patterson, G. R., DeVaryshe, B. D., & Ramsey, E. (1989). A developmental perspective on antisocial behavior. *American Psychologist, 44,* 329–335.

Patterson, S. J., Sochting, I., & Marcia, J. E. (1992). The inner space and beyond: Women and identity. In G. R. Adams, T. P. Gullotta, & R. Montemayor (Eds.), *Adolescent identity formation: Vol. 4. Advances in adolescent development.* Newbury Park, CA: Sage.

Pavalko, E. K., & Artis, J. E. (1997). Women's caregiving and paid work: Causal relationships in late midlife. *Journals of Gerontology: Social Sciences, 52B,* S170–S179.

Pearlin, L. I., Mullan, J. T., Semple, S. J., & Skaff, M. M. (1990). Caregiving and the stress process: An overview of concepts and their measures. *The Gerontologist, 30,* 583–594.

Pearson, J. C. (1996). Forty-forever years? Primary relationships and senior citizens. In N. Vanzetti & S. Duck (Eds.), *A lifetime of relationships* (pp. 383–405). Pacific Grove, CA: Brooks/Cole.

Pearson, J. D., Morrell, C. H., Brant, L. J., Landis, P. K., & Fleg, J. L. (1997). Age-associated changes in blood pressure in a longitudinal study of healthy men and women. *Journal of Gerontology: Medical Sciences, 52A,* M177–M183.

Pederson, D. R., Gleason, K. E., Moran, G., & Bento, S. (1998). Maternal attachment representations, maternal sensitivity, and the infant-mother attachment relationship. *Developmental Psychology, 34,* 925–933.

Pennebaker, J. W. (1999). Psychological factors influencing the reporting of physical symptoms. In A. A. Stone, J. S. Turkkan, & C. Bachrach (Eds.), *The science of self report: Implications for research and practice* (pp. 299–315). Mahwah, NJ: Erlbaum.

Pennebaker, J. W., & Graybeal, A. (2001). Patterns of natural language use: Disclosure, personality, and social integration. *Current Directions in Psychological Science, 10,* 90–93.

Pennington, B. F., Groisser, D., & Welsh, M. C. (1993). Contrasting cognitive deficits in attention deficit hyperactivity disorder versus reading disability. *Developmental Psychology, 29,* 511–523.

Peplau, L., & Gordon, S. L. (1985). Women and men in love: Sex differences in close heterosexual relationships. In V. O'Leary, R. K. Unger, & B. S. Wallston (Eds.), *Women, gender, and social psychology* (pp. 257–292). Hillsdale, NJ: Erlbaum.

Pepler, D. J., Craig, E., Ziegler, S., & Charach, A. (1993). A school-based anti-bullying intervention: Preliminary evaluation. In D. Tattum (Ed.), *Understanding and managing bullying* (pp. 76-91). London: Heinemann Books.

Perdue, C. W., & Gurtman, M. B. (1990). Evidence for the automaticity of ageism. *Journal of Experimental Social Psychology, 26,* 199–216.

Perfetti, C. A., & Curtis, M. E. (1986). Reading. In R. F. Dillon & R. J. Sternberg (Eds.), *Cognition and instruction.* Orlando, FL: Academic Press.

Perls, T. T. (1995). The oldest old. *Scientific American,* 70–75.

Perry, W. I. (1970). *Forms of intellectual and ethical development in the college years.* New York: Holt, Rinehart & Winston.

Peters, A. M. (1995). Strategies in the acquisition of syntax. In P. Fletcher & B. MacWhinney (Eds.), *The handbook of child language* (pp. 462–483). Oxford, UK: Blackwell.

Peterson, B. E., & Klohnen, E. C. (1995). Realization of generativity in two samples of women at midlife. *Psychology and Aging, 10,* 20–29.

Peterson, C. (1996). *The psychology of abnormality.* Fort Worth, TX: Harcourt Brace.

Peterson, C., Maier, S. F., & Seligman, M. E. P. (1993). *Learned helplessness: A theory for the age of personal control.* New York: Oxford University Press.

Peterson, L. (1983). Role of donor competence, donor age, and peer presence on helping in an emergency. *Developmental Psychology, 19,* 873–880.

Petraitis, J., Flay, B. R., & Miller, T. Q. (1995). Reviewing theories of adolescent substance use: Organizing pieces in the puzzle. *Psychological Bulletin, 117,* 67–86.

Pettit, G. S., Bakshi, A., Dodge, K. A., & Coie, J. D. (1990). The emergence of social dominance in young boys' play groups: Developmental differences and behavioral correlates. *Developmental Psychology, 26,* 1017–1025.

Pettit, G. S., Bates, J. E., & Dodge, K. A. (1997). Supportive parenting, ecological context, and children's adjustment: A seven-year longitudinal study. *Child Development, 68,* 908–923.

Pettit, G. S., & Mize, J. (1993). Substance and style: Understanding the ways in which parents teach children about social relationships. In S. Duck (Ed.), *Learning about relationships*. Newbury Park, CA: Sage.

Pfost, K. S., & Fiore, M. (1990). Pursuit of nontraditional occupations: Fear of success or fear of not being chosen? *Sex Roles, 23*, 15–24.

Phelps, J. A., Davis, J. O., & Schartz, K. M. (1997). Nature, nurture, and twin research strategies. *Current Directions in Psychological Science, 6*, 117–121.

Phinney, J. (1990). Ethnic identity in adolescents and adults. *Psychological Bulletin, 108*, 499–514.

Phinney, J. S. (1996). When we talk about American ethnic groups, what do we mean? *American Psychologist, 51*, 918–927.

Phinney, J. S., & Chavira, V. (1992). Ethnic identity and self-esteem: An exploratory longitudinal study. *Journal of Adolescence, 15*, 271–281.

Phinney, J. S., Ong, A., & Madden, T. (2000). Cultural values and intergenerational value discrepancies in immigrant and non-immigrant families. *Child Development, 71*, 528–539.

Piaget, J. (1929). *The child's conception of the world*. New York: Harcourt, Brace.

Piaget, J. (1951). *Plays, dreams, and imitation in childhood*. New York: Norton.

Piaget, J. (1952). *The origins of intelligence in children*. New York: International Universities Press.

Piaget, J. (1954). *The construction of reality in the child*. New York: Basic Books.

Piaget, J., & Inhelder, B. (1956). *The child's conception of space*. Boston: Routledge & Kegan Paul.

Pickard, M., Bates, L., Dorian, M., Greig, H., & Saint, D. (2000). Alcohol and drug use in second-year medical students at the University of Leeds. *Medical Education, 34*, 148–150.

Pienta, A. M., Hayward, M. D., & Jenkins, K. R. (2000). Health consequences of marriage for the retirement years. *Journal of Family Issues, 21*, 559–586.

Pierce, C. A., & Aguinis, H. (1997). Bridging the gap between romantic relationships and sexual harassment in organizations. *Journal of Organizational Behavior, 18*, 197–200.

Pierce, S. H., & Lange, G. (2000). Relationships among metamemory, motivation, and memory performance in young school-age children. *British Journal of Developmental Psychology, 18*, 121–135.

Pillemer, D. B., Picariello, M. L., Law, A. B., & Reichman, J. S. (1996). In D. C. Rubin (Ed.), *Remembering our past: Studies in autobiographical memory* (pp. 318–337). New York: Cambridge University Press.

Pinquart, M., & Sörensen, S. (2001). Gender differences in self-concept and psychological well-being in old age: A meta-analysis. *Journal of Gerontology: Psychological Sciences, 56B*, P195–P213.

Piotrkowski, C. (1998). Gender harassment, job satisfaction, and distress among employed white and minority women. *Journal of Occupational Health Psychology, 3*, 33–43.

Pleck, J. H. (1997). Paternal involvement: Levels, sources, and consequences. In M. E. Lamb (Ed.), *The role of the father in child development* (pp. 66–103). New York: Wiley.

Plomin, R. (1990). *Nature and nurture*. Pacific Grove, CA: Brooks/Cole.

Plomin, R., & Crabbe, J. (2000). DNA. *Psychological Bulletin, 126*, 806–828.

Plomin, R., Fulker, D. W., Corley, R., & DeFries, J. C. (1997). Nature, nurture, and cognitive development from 1 to 16 years: A parent-offspring adoption study. *Psychological Science, 8*, 442–447.

Plomin, R., & Petrill, S. A. (1997). Genetics and intelligence: What's new? *Intelligence, 24*, 53–77.

Plosker, G. L., & McTavish, D. (1996). Intranasal salcatonin (salmon calcitonin). A review of its pharmacological properties and role in the management of postmenopausal osteoporosis. *Drugs and Aging, 8*, 378–400.

Plumert, J. M., & Nichols-Whitehead, P. (1996). Parental scaffolding of young children's spatial communication. *Developmental Psychology, 32*, 523–532.

Plunkett, K. (1996). *Connectionism and development: Neural networks and the study of change*. New York: Oxford University Press.

Podnieks, E., Pillemer, K., Nicholson, J., Shillington, T., and Frizell, A. (1990). *National survey on abuse of the elderly in Canada*. Toronto: Ryerson Polytechnical Institute.

Ponde, M. P., & Santana, V. S. (2000). Participation in leisure activities: Is it a protective factor for women's mental health? *Journal of Leisure Research, 32*, 457–472.

Ponder, R. J., & Pomeroy, E. C. (1996). The grief of caregivers: How pervasive is it? *Journal of Gerontological Social Work, 27*, 3–21.

Porter, R. H., & Winberg, J. (1999). Unique salience of maternal breast odors for newborn infants. *Neuroscience & Biobehavioral Reviews, 23*, 439–449.

Poulin-Dubois, D., & Forbes, J. N. (2002). Toddlers' attention to intentions-in-action in learning novel action words. *Developmental Psychology, 38*, 104–114.

Poulson, C. L., Kymissis, E., Reeve, K. F., Andreatos, M., & Reeve, L. (1991). Generalized vocal imitation in infants. *Journal of Experimental Child Psychology, 51*, 267–279.

Power, F. C., Higgins, A., & Kohlberg, L. (1989). *Lawrence Kohlberg's approach to moral education*. New York: Columbia University Press.

Powers, S. W., & Roberts, M. W. (1995). Simulation training with parents of oppositional children: Preliminary findings. *Journal of Clinical Child Psychology, 24*, 89–97.

Powlishta, K., Serbin, L. A., Doyle, A., & White, D. R. (1994). Gender, ethnic, and body type biases: The generality of prejudice in childhood. *Developmental Psychology, 30*, 526–536.

Pozzi, S., Healy, L., & Hoyles, C. (1993). Learning and interaction in groups with computers: When do ability and gender matter? *Social Development, 2*, 222–241.

Pratt, M. W., Danso, H. A., Arnold, M. L., Norris, J. E., & Filyer, R. (2001). Adult generativity and the socialization of adolescents: Relations to mothers' and fathers' parenting beliefs, styles, and practices. *Journal of Personality, 69,* 89–120.

Prigerson, H. G., & Jacobs, S. C. (2001). Traumatic grief as a distinct disorder: A rationale, consensus criteria, and a preliminary empirical test. In M. S. Stroebe, R. O. Hansson, W. Stroebe, & H. Schut (Eds.), *Handbook of bereavement research: Consequences, coping, and care* (pp. 613–637). Washington, DC: American Psychological Association.

Principe, G. F., & Ceci, S. J. (2002). I saw it with my own ears: The effects of peer conversations on preschoolers' reports of nonexperienced events. *Journal of Experimental Child Psychology, 83,* 1–25.

Project Zero. (1999). *Project SUMIT: Schools Using Multiple Intelligence Theory* [Online]. Available: http://pzweb.harvard.edu/SUMIT/OUTCOMES.HTM.

Pruchno, R. (1999). Raising grandchildren: The experiences of black and white grandmothers. *The Gerontologist, 39,* 209–221.

Pyszczynski, T., Greenberg, J., & Solomon, S. (1997). Why do we need what we need? A terror management perspective on the roots of human social motivation. *Psychological Inquiry, 8,* 1–20.

Pyszczynski, T., Greenberg, J., & Solomon, S. (1999). A dual-process model of defense against conscious and unconscious death-related thoughts: An extension of terror management theory. *Psychological Review, 106,* 835–845.

Quality End-of-Life Care Coalition. (2000). [Online]. Available: http://www.chpca.net.quality_end-of-life_care_coalition.htm. (Retrieved May 12 2004.)

Qualls, S. H. (1999). Mental health and mental disorders in older adults. In J. C. Cavanaugh & S. K. Whitbourne (Eds.), *Gerontology: An interdisciplinary perspective* (pp. 305–328). New York: Oxford University Press.

Quinn, J. F. (1999). *Retirement patterns and bridge jobs in the 1990s* (Issue Brief 206). Washington, DC: Employee Benefit Research Institute.

Quinn, M. J. (1998). Undue influence: An emotional con game. *Aging Today, 9,* 11.

Quinn, M. J., & Tomita, S. K. (1997). *Elder abuse and neglect: Causes, diagnosis, and intervention strategies* (2nd ed.). New York: Springer.

Radford, A. (1995). Phrase structure and functional categories. In P. Fletcher & B. MacWhinney (Eds.), *The handbook of child language* (pp. 483–507). Oxford, UK: Blackwell.

Raeburn, P. (1995, November 7). Genetic trait may delay Alzheimer's. *News Journal* (Wilmington, DE), p. A3.

Ragins, B. R., Cotton, J. L., & Miller, J. S. (2000). Marginal mentoring: The effects of type of mentor, quality of relationship, and program design on work and career attitudes. *Academy of Management Journal, 43,* 117–1194.

Ragland, O. R., & Brand, R. J. (1988). Type A behavior and mortality from coronary heart disease. *New England Journal of Medicine, 318,* 65–69.

Ragozin, A. S., Basham, R. B., Crnic, K. A., Greenberg, M. T., & Robinson, N. M. (1982). Effects of maternal age on parenting role. *Developmental Psychology, 18,* 627–634.

Rakic, P. (1995). Corticogenesis in human and nonhuman primates. In M. S. Gazzaniga (Ed.), *The cognitive neurosciences.* Cambridge, MA: MIT Press.

Rakison, D. H., & Poulin-Dubois, D. (2001). Developmental origin of the animate-inanimate distinction. *Psychological Bulletin, 127,* 209–228.

Ramey, C. T., & Campbell, F. A. (1991). Poverty, early childhood education, and academic competence: The Abecedarian experiment. In A. Huston (Ed.), *Children reared in poverty.* New York: Cambridge University Press.

Ramsey, P. G. (1995). Growing up with the contradictions of race and class. *Young Children, 50,* 18–22.

Ransjoe-Arvidson, A. B., Matthiesen, A. S., Lilja, G., Nissen, E., Widstroem, A. M., & Uvnaes-Moberg, K. (2001). Maternal analgesia during labor disturbs newborn behavior: Effects on breastfeeding, temperature, and crying. *Birth-Issues in Perinatal Care, 28,* 5–12.

Ranwez, S., Leidig, T., & Crampes, M. (2000). Formalization to improve lifelong learning. *Journal of Interactive Learning Research, 11,* 389–409.

Rapaport, J. L., & Ismond, D. R. (1990). *DSM-III-R training guide for diagnosis of childhood disorders.* New York: Brunner/Mazel.

Rapoport, R., & Rapoport, R. N. (1975). *Leisure and the family life cycle.* London, UK: Routledge & Kegan Paul.

Rapport, M. D. (1995). Attention-deficit hyperactivity disorder. In M. Hersen & R. T. Ammerman (Eds.), *Advanced abnormal child psychology.* Hillsdale, NJ: Erlbaum.

Rast, M., & Meltzoff, A. N. (1995). Memory and representation in young children with Down syndrome: Exploring deferred imitation and object permanence. *Development and Psychopathology, 7,* 393–407.

Rathunde, K. R., & Csikszentmihalyi, M. (1993). Undivided interest and the growth of talent: A longitudinal study of adolescents. *Journal of Youth and Adolescence, 22,* 385–405.

Rawlins, W. K. (1992). *Friendship matters.* Hawthorne, NY: Aldine de Gruyter.

Read, J. P., Wood, M. D., Davidoff, O. J., McLacken, J., & Campbell, J. F. (2002). Making the transition from high school to college: The role of alcohol-related social influence factors in students' drinking. *Substance Abuse, 23,* 53–65.

Reese, D. (2001, May). Putting the resident first. *Contemporary Long Term Care,* pp. 24–28.

Reese, E., & Cox, A. (1999). Quality of adult book reading affects children's emergent literacy. *Developmental Psychology, 35,* 20–28.

Reid, J., & Hardy, M. (1999). Multiple roles and well-being among midlife women: Testing role strain and role enhancement theories. *Journal of Gerontology: Social Sciences, 54B,* S329–S338.

Reimer, M. S. (1996). "Sinking into the ground": The development and consequences of shame in adolescence. *Developmental Review, 16,* 321–363.

Reis, M., & Nahmiash, D. (1998). Validation of the Indicators of Abuse (IOA) screen. *The Gerontologist, 38,* 471–480.

Repacholi, B. M. (1998). Infants' use of attentional cues to identify the referent of another person's emotional expression. *Developmental Psychology, 34,* 1017–1025.

Reynolds, A. J., & Robertson, D. L. (2003). School-based intervention and later child maltreatment in the Chicago Longitudinal Study. *Child Development, 73,* 3–26.

Rhodes, J. E., & Jason, L. A. (1990). A social stress model of substance abuse. *Journal of Consulting and Clinical Psychology, 58,* 395–401.

Ricciuti, H. N. (1993). Nutrition and mental development. *Current Directions in Psychological Science, 2,* 43–46.

Rice, M. L., Huston, A. C., Truglio, R., & Wright, J. (1990). Words from "Sesame Street": Learning vocabulary while viewing. *Developmental Psychology, 26,* 421–428.

Rich, C. L., Sherman, M., & Fowler, R. C. (1990, Winter). San Diego suicide study: The adolescents. *Adolescence,* pp. 855–865.

Richardson, G. A. (1998). Prenatal cocaine exposure. A longitudinal study of development. *Annals of the New York Academy of Sciences, 846,* 144–152.

Richters, J. E., Arnold, L. E., Jensen, P. S., Abikoff, H., Conners, C. K., Greenhill, L. L., et al. (1995). NIMH collaborative multisite multimodal treatment study of children with ADHD: I. Background and rationale. *Journal of the American Academy of Child and Adolescent Psychiatry, 34,* 987–1000.

Riley, K. P., Snowden, D. A., Saunders, A. M., Roses, A. D., Mortimer, J. A., & Nanayakkara, N. (2000). Cognitive function and apolipoprotein E in very old adults: Findings from the nun study. *Journal of Gerontology: Social Sciences, 55B,* S69–S75.

Riley, M. W. (1979). Introduction. In M. W. Riley (Ed.), *Aging from birth to death: Interdisciplinary perspectives* (pp. 3–14). Boulder, CO: Westview Press.

Rindfuss, R. R., Cooksey, E. C., & Sutterlin, R. L. (1999). Young adult occupational achievement: Early expectations versus behavioral reality. *Work and Organizations, 26,* 220–263.

Ritchie, K. L. (1999). Maternal behaviors and cognitions during discipline episodes: A comparison of power bouts and single acts of noncompliance. *Developmental Psychology, 35,* 580–589.

Roberto, K. A., & Skoglund, R. R. (1996). Interactions with grandparents and great-grandparents: A comparison of activities, influences, and relationships. *International Journal of Aging and Human Development, 43,* 107–117.

Roberts, J. E., Burchinal, M., & Durham, M. (1999). Parents' report of vocabulary and grammatical development of African American preschoolers: Child and environmental associations. *Child Development, 70,* 92–106.

Roberts, R. E., Phinney, J. S., Masse, L. C., Chen, Y. R., Roberts, C. R., & Romero, A. (1999). The structure of ethnic identity of young adolescents from diverse ethnocultural groups. *Journal of Early Adolescence, 19,* 301–322.

Roberts, W., & Strayer, J. (1996). Empathy, emotional expressiveness, and prosocial behavior. *Child Development, 67,* 449–470.

Robinson, A., & Clinkenbeard, P. R. (1998). Giftedness: An exceptionality examined. *Annual Review of Psychology, 49,* 117–139.

Rodin, J., & Langer, E. J. (1977). Long-term effects of a control relevant intervention with the institutionalized aged. *Journal of Personality and Social Psychology, 35,* 897–902.

Roffwarg, H. P., Muzio, J. N., & Dement, W. C. (1966). Ontogenetic development of the human sleep-dream cycle. *Science, 152,* 604–619.

Rogers, S. J., & Amato, P. R. (1997). Is marital quality declining? The evidence from two generations. *Social Forces, 75,* 1089–1100.

Rogers, W. A., & Fisk, A. D. (2001). Understanding the role of attention in cognitive aging research. In J. E. Birren & K. W. Schaie (Eds.), *Handbook of the psychology of aging* (5th ed., pp. 267–287). San Diego, CA: Academic Press.

Rogoff, B., Mistry, J., Goncu, A., & Mosier, C. (1993). Guided participation in cultural activity by toddlers and caregivers. *Monographs of the Society for Research in Child Development, 58* (Serial No. 236).

Romney, J. C., Romney, D. M., & Menzies, H. M. (1995). Reading for pleasure in French: A study of the reading habits and the interests of French immersion children. *The Canadian Modern Language Review, 51,* 474-493.

Rook, K. S. (2000). The evolution of social relationships in later adulthood. In S. H. Qualls & N. Abeles (Eds.), *Psychology and the aging revolution* (pp. 173–191). Washington, DC: American Psychological Association.

Roopnarine, J. (1992). Father-child play in India. In K. MacDonald (Ed.), *Parent-child play.* Albany: State University of New York Press.

Roscoe, L. A., Malphurs, J. E., Dragovic, L. J., & Cohen, D. (2001). A comparison of characteristics of Kevorkian euthanasia cases and physician-assisted suicides in Oregon. *The Gerontologist, 41,* 439–446.

Rose, A. J., & Asher, S. R. (1999). Children's goals and strategies in response to conflicts within a friendship. *Developmental Psychology, 35,* 69–79.

Rose, J. S., Chassin, L., Presson, C. C., & Sherman, S. J. (1999). Peer influence on adolescent cigarette smoking: A prospective sibling analysis. *Merrill-Palmer Quarterly, 45,* 62–84.

Rose, S. A., Feldman, J. F., & Jankowski, J. J. (2001). Visual short-term memory in the first year of life: Capacity and recency effects. *Developmental Psychology, 37,* 539–549.

Rose, S., & Zand, D. (2000). Lesbian dating and courtship from young adulthood to midlife. *Journal of Gay and Lesbian Social Services, 11,* 77–104.

Rosenberg, E. B. (1992). *The adoption life cycle.* Lexington, MA: Lexington Books.

Rosenberg, J. (1993). Just the two of us. In L. Abraham, L. Green, M. Krance, J. Rosenberg, J. Somerville, & C. Stoner (Eds.), *Reinventing love: Six women talk about lust, sex, and romance* (pp. 301–307). New York: Plume.

Rosenberg, S. D., Rosenberg, H. J., & Farrell, M. P. (1999). Midlife crisis revisited. In S. L. Willis & J. D. Reid (Eds.), *Life in the middle: Psychological and social development in middle age* (pp. 47–70). San Diego, CA: Academic Press.

Rosenblatt, P. C. (1996). Grief that does not end. In D. Klass, P. R. Silverman, & S. L. Nickman (Eds.), *Continuing bonds: New understandings of grief* (pp. 45–58). Washington, DC: Taylor & Francis.

Rosenblatt, P. C. (2001). A social constructivist perspective on cultural differences in grief. In M. S. Stroebe, R. O. Hansson, W. Stroebe, & H. Schut (Eds.), *Handbook of bereavement research: Consequences, coping, and care* (pp. 285–300). Washington, DC: American Psychological Association.

Rosengren, K. S., Gelman, S. A., Kalish, C., & McCormick, M. (1991). As time goes by: Children's early understanding of growth in animals. *Child Development, 62,* 1302–1320.

Rosenthal, D. A., & Feldman, S. S. (1992). The relationship between parenting behaviour and ethnic identity in Chinese-American and Chinese-Australian adolescents. *International Journal of Psychology, 27,* 19–31.

Rosenthal, R., & Vandell, D. L. (1996). Quality of care at school-aged child-care programs: Regulatable features, observed experiences, child perspectives, and parent perspectives. *Child Development, 67,* 2434–2445.

Rosin, H. M., & Korabik, K. (1990). Marital and family correlates of women managers' attrition from organizations. *Journal of Vocational Behavior, 37,* 104–120.

Rosin, H. M., & Korabik, K. (1991). Workplace variables, affective responses, and intention to leave among women managers. *Journal of Occupational Psychology, 64,* 317–330.

Roskies, E., & Louis-Guerin, C. (1990). Job insecurity in managers: Antecedents and consequences. *Journal of Organizational Behavior, 11,* 345–359.

Ross, C. E. (1995). Reconceptualizing marital status as a continuum of social attachment. *Journal of Marriage and the Family, 57,* 129–140.

Rostenstein, D., & Oster, H. (1997). Differential facial responses to four basic tastes in newborns. In P. Ekman & E. L. Rosenberg (Eds.), *What the face reveals: Basic and applied studies of spontaneous expression using the Facial Action Coding System (FACS). Series in affective science.* New York: Oxford University Press.

Rotenberg, K. J., & Mayer, E. V. (1990). Delay of gratification in native and white children: A cross-cultural comparison. *International Journal of Behavioral Development, 13,* 23–30.

Roth, W. F. (1991). *Work and rewards: Redefining our work-life reality.* New York: Praeger.

Rothbaum, F., & Weisz, J. R. (1994). Parental caregiving and child externalizing behavior in nonclinical samples: A meta-analysis. *Psychological Bulletin, 116,* 55–74.

Rothbaum, F., Weisz, J., Pott, M., Miyake, K., & Morelli, G. (2000). Attachment and culture: Security in the United States and Japan. *American Psychologist, 55,* 1093–1104.

Rotheram-Borus, M. J., Rosario, M., Van Rossem, R., & Reid, H. (1995). Prevalence, course, and predictors of multiple problem behaviors among gay and bisexual male adolescents. *Developmental Psychology, 31,* 75–85.

Rotondo, D. M., & Perrewe, P. L. (2000). Coping with a career plateau: An empirical examination of what works and what doesn't. *Journal of Applied Social Psychology, 30,* 2622–2646.

Rotto, P. C., & Kratochwill, T. R. (1994). Behavioral consultation with parents: Using competency-based training to modify child noncompliance. *School Psychology Review, 23,* 669–693.

Rotundo, M., Nguyen, D. H., & Sackett, P. R. (2001). A meta-analytic review of gender differences in perceptions of sexual harassment. *Journal of Applied Psychology, 86,* 914–922.

Rovee-Collier, C. (1987). Learning and memory in infancy. In J. D. Osofsky (Ed.), *Handbook of infant development* (2nd ed.). New York: Wiley.

Rovee-Collier, C. (1997). Dissociations in infant memory: Rethinking the development of implicit and explicit memory. *Psychological Review, 104,* 467–498.

Rovee-Collier, C. (1999). The development of infant memory. *Current Directions in Psychological Science, 8,* 80–85.

Rowe, J. W., & Kahn, R. I. (1998). *Successful aging.* New York: Pantheon.

Roxburgh, S. (1997). The effect of children on the mental health of women in the paid labor force. *Journal of Family Issues, 18,* 270–289.

Rubenfeld, M. I., & Gilroy, F. D. (1991). Relationship between college women's occupational interests and a single-sex environment. *Career Development Quarterly, 40,* 64–70.

Rubin, D. C., Rahhal, T., & Poon, L. W. (1998). Things learned in early adulthood are remembered best: Effects of a major transition on memory. *Memory & Cognition, 26,* 3–19.

Rubin, K. H., Bukowski, W., & Parker, J. G. (1998). Peer interactions, relationships, and groups. In W. Damon (Ed.), *Handbook of child psychology* (Vol. 3). New York: Wiley.

Rubin, K. H., Chen, X., & Hymel, S. (1993). Socioemotional characteristics of withdrawn and aggressive children. *Merrill-Palmer Quarterly, 39,* 518–534.

Rubin, K. H., Stewart, S., & Chen, X. (1995). Parents of aggressive and withdrawn children. In M. Bornstein (Ed.), *Handbook of parenting* (Vol. 1). Hillsdale, NJ: Erlbaum.

Rubin, R. S. (1996). The wounded family: Bereaved parents and the impact of adult child loss. In D. Klass, P. R. Silverman, & S. L. Nickman (Eds.), *Continuing bonds: New understandings of grief* (pp. 217–232). Philadelphia: Taylor & Francis.

Rubin, S. S., & Malkinson, R. (2001). Parental response to child loss across the life cycle: Clinical and research perspectives. In M. S. Stroebe, R. O. Hansson, W. Stroebe, & H. Schut (Eds.), *Handbook of bereavement research: Consequences, coping, and care* (pp. 169–197). Washington, DC: American Psychological Association.

Ruff, H. A., Capozzoli, M., & Weissberg, R. (1998). Age, individuality, and context as factors in sustained visual attention during the preschool years. *Developmental Psychology, 34,* 454–464.

Ruffman, T., Perner, J., Naito, M., Parkin, L., & Clements, W. A. (1998). Older (but not younger) siblings facilitate false belief understanding. *Developmental Psychology, 34,* 161–174.

Russell, J. A., & Paris, F. A. (1994). Do children acquire concepts for complex emotions abruptly? *International Journal of Behavioral Development, 17,* 349–365.

Rwampororo, R. K. (2001). Social support: Its mediation of gendered patterns in work-family stress and health for dual-earner couples. *Dissertation Abstract International Section A: Humanities and Social Sciences, 61*(9-A), 3792.

Ryan, E. B., Kennaley, D. E., Pratt, M. W., & Shumovich, M. A. (2000). Evaluations by staff, residents, and community seniors of patronizing speech in the nursing home: Impact of passive, assertive, or humorous responses. *Psychology and Aging, 15,* 272–285.

Rybash, J. M., Hoyer, W. J., & Roodin, P. A. (1986). *Adult cognition and aging.* New York: Pergamon Press.

Ryff, C. D., Lee, Y. H., Essex, M. J., & Schmutte, P. S. (1994). My children and me: Mid-life evaluations of grown children and of self. *Psychology and Aging, 9,* 195–205.

Rylands, K., & Rickwood, D. J. (2001). Ego integrity versus despair: The effect of "accepting the past" on depression in older women. *International Journal of Aging and Human Development, 53,* 75–89.

Sabbagh, M. A., & Baldwin, D. A. (2001). Learning words from knowledgeable versus ignorant speakers: Links between preschoolers' theory of mind and semantic development. *Child Development, 72,* 1054–1070.

Sacco, W. P., & Beck, A. T. (1995). *Cognitive theory and therapy.* In E. E. Beckham & W. R. Leber (Eds.), *Handbook of depression* (2nd ed.). New York: Guilford Press.

Saffran, J. R., Aslin, R. N., & Newport, E. L. (1996). Statistical learning by 8-month-old infants. *Science, 274,* 1926–1928.

Sagi, A., Koren-Karie, N., Gini, M., Ziv, Y., & Joels, T. (2002). Shedding further light on the effects of various types and quality of early child care on infant-mother attachment relationship: The Haifa study of early child care. *Child Development, 73,* 1166–1186.

Sagi, A., van IJzendoorn, M. H., Aviezer, O., Donnell, F., & Mayseless, O. (1994). Sleeping out of home in a kibbutz communal arrangement: It makes a difference for infant-mother attachment. *Child Development, 65,* 992–1004.

Sagraves, R. (2001). New views on hormone replacement therapy. *Drug Topics, 145,* 59–68.

Salomone, P. R. (1996). Tracing Super's theory of vocational development: A 40-year retrospective. *Journal of Career Development, 22,* 167–184.

Salthouse, T. A. (1984). Effects of age and skill in typing. *Journal of Experimental Psychology: General, 113,* 345–371.

Salthouse, T. A. (2000). Steps toward the explanation of adult age differences in cognition. In T. Perfect & E. Maylor (Eds.), *Theoretical debate in cognitive aging* (pp. 19–49). Oxford, UK: Oxford University Press.

Sandler, I. N., Tein, J., Mehta, P., Wolchik, S., & Ayers, T. (2000). Coping efficacy and psychological problems of children of divorce. *Child Development, 71,* 1099–1118.

Sangrador, J. L., & Yela, C. (2000). "What is beautiful is loved": Physical attractiveness in love relationships in a representative sample. *Social Behavior and Personality, 28,* 207–218.

Sanson, A., Prior, M., Smart, D., & Oberklaid, F. (1993). Gender differences in aggression in childhood: Implications for a peaceful world. *Australian Psychologist, 28,* 86–92.

Saunders, S. (1997). Hospices worldwide: A mission statement. In C. Saunders & R. Kastenbaum (Eds.), *Hospice care on the international scene* (pp. 3–12). New York: Springer.

Saxe, G. B. (1988). The mathematics of child street vendors. *Child Development, 59,* 1415–1425.

Saxon, S. V., & Etten, M. J. (1994). *Physical changes and aging* (3rd ed.). New York: Tiresias.

Sbraga, T. P., & O'Donohue, W. (2000). Sexual harassment. *Annual Review of Sex Research, 11,* 258–285.

Scahill, L. (2000). Epidemiology of ADHD in school-age children. *Child and Adolescent Psychiatry Clinics of North America, 9,* 541–555.

Scarr, S. (1992). Developmental theories for the 1990s: Development and individual differences. *Child Development, 63,* 1–19.

Scarr, S. (1993). Genes, experience, and development. In D. Magnusson & P. J. M. Casaer (Eds.), *Longitudinal research on individual development: Present status and future perspectives. European network on longitudinal studies on individual development, 8.* (pp. 26–50). Cambridge, UK: Cambridge University Press.

Scarr, S., & McCartney, K. (1983). How people make their own environments: A theory of genotype environment effects. *Child Development, 54,* 424–435.

Schaal, B., Marlier, L., & Soussignan, R. (1998). Olfactory function in the human fetus: Evidence from selective neonatal responsiveness to the odor of amniotic fluid. *Behavioral Neuroscience, 112,* 1438–1449.

Schaffer, H. R., & Emerson, P. E. (1964). The development of social attachments in infancy. *Monographs of the Society for Research in Child Development, 29* (Serial No. 3).

Schaie, K. W. (1994). The course of adult intellectual development. *American Psychologist, 49,* 304–313.

Schaie, K. W. (1995). *Intellectual development in adulthood: The Seattle longitudinal study.* New York: Cambridge University Press.

Schaie, K. W., Maitland, S. B., Willis, S. L., & Intrieri, R. L. (1998). Longitudinal invariance of adult psychometric ability factor structures across seven years. *Psychology and Aging, 13,* 8–20.

Schechtman, K. B., & Ory, M. G. (2001). The effects of exercise on the quality of life of frail older adults: A preplanned meta-analysis of the FICSIT trials. *Annals of Behavioral Medicine, 23,* 186–197.

Schlegel, A., & Barry, H. (1991). *Adolescence: An anthropological inquiry.* New York: Free Press.

Schmeeckle, M., Giarusso, R., & Wang, Q. (1998, November). *When being a brother or sister is important to one's identity: Life stage and gender differences.* Paper presented at the annual meeting of the Gerontological Society, Philadelphia.

Schmidt, F. L., & Hunter, J. E. (1998). The validity and utility of selection methods in personnel psychology: Practical and theoretical implications of 85 years of research findings. *Psychological Bulletin, 124,* 262–274.

Schmiege, C. J., Richards, L. N., & Zvonkovic, A. M. (2001). Remarriage: For love or money? *Journal of Divorce and Remarriage, 36,* 123–140.

Schneider, B. H., Atkinson, L., & Tardif, C. (2001). Child-parent attachment and children's peer relations: A quantitative review. *Developmental Psychology, 37,* 86–100.

Schneider, K. T., Swan, S., & Fitzgerald, L. F. (1997). Job-related and psychological effects of sexual harassment in the workplace: Empirical evidence from two organizations. *Journal of Applied Psychology, 82,* 401–415.

Schneider, M. L. (1992). The effect of mild stress during pregnancy on birthweight and neuromotor maturation in rhesus monkey infants (Macaca mulatta). *Infant Behavior and Development, 15,* 389–403.

Schneider, M. L., Roughton, E. C., Koehler, A. J., & Lubach, G. R. (1999). Growth and development following prenatal stress exposure in primates: An examination of ontogenetic vulnerability. *Child Development, 70,* 253–274.

Schneider, W., & Bjorklund, D. F. (1998). Memory. In W. Damon (Ed.), *Handbook of child psychology* (Vol. 2). New York: Wiley.

Schneider, W., & Pressley, M. (1997). *Memory development between 2 and 20* (2nd ed.). Mahwah, NJ: Erlbaum.

Schnorr, T. M., Grajewski, B. A., Hornung, R. W., Thun, M. J., Egeland, G. M., Murray, W. E., Conover, D. L., & Halperin, W. E. (1991). Video display terminals and the risk of spontaneous abortion. *The New England Journal of Medicine, 324,* 727–733.

Schoon, I. (2001). Teenage job aspirations and career attainment in adulthood: A 17-year follow-up study of teenagers who aspired to become scientists, health professionals, or engineers. *International Journal of Behavioral Development, 25,* 124–132.

Schuett, A., & Burke, W. J. (2000). *The hazards of participating in sweepstakes games by the elderly* [Unpublished manuscript cited in Wilber & McNeilly, 2001].

Schulz, R., & Heckhausen, J. (1999). Aging, culture, and control: Setting a new research agenda. *Journal of Gerontology: Psychological Sciences, 54B,* P139–P145.

Schwartz, F., with J. Zimmerman. (1992). *Breaking with tradition: Women and work, the new facts of life.* New York: Warner Books.

Scott, W. A., Scott, R., & McCabe, M. (1991). Family relationships and children's personality: A cross-cultural, cross-source comparison. *British Journal of Social Psychology, 30,* 1–20.

Scozzaro, P. P., & Subich, L. M. (1990). Gender and occupational sex-type differences in job outcome factor perceptions. *Journal of Vocational Behavior, 36,* 109–119.

Sears, P. S., & Barbee, A. H. (1978). Career and life satisfaction among Terman's gifted women. In J. C. Stanley, W. C. George, & C. H. Solano (Eds.), *The gifted and the creative: Fifty year perspective* (pp. 28–66). Baltimore, MD: Johns Hopkins University Press.

Segal, D. L., Bogaards, J. A., Becker, L. A., & Chatman, C. (1999). Effects of emotional expression on adjustment to spousal loss among older adults. *Journal of Mental Health and Aging, 5,* 297–310.

Segal, E. S. (1996). Common medical problems in geriatric patients. In L. L. Carstensen, B. A. Edelstein, & L. Dornbrand (Eds.), *The practical handbook of clinical gerontology* (pp. 451–467). Thousand Oaks, CA: Sage.

Segal, H. G., DeMeis, D. K., Wood, G. A., & Smith, H. L. (2001). Assessing future possible selves by gender and socioeconomic status using the Anticipated Life History measure. *Journal of Personality, 69,* 57–87.

Seidenberg, M. S., & McClelland, J. L. (1989). A distributed, developmental model of word recognition and naming. *Psychological Review, 96,* 523–568.

Seifer, R., Schiller, M., Sameroff, A. J., Resnick, S., & Riordan, K. (1996). Attachment, maternal sensitivity, and infant temperament during the first year of life. *Developmental Psychology, 32,* 12–25.

Selman, R. L. (1980). *The growth of interpersonal understanding: Developmental and clinical analyses.* New York: Academic Press.

Selman, R. L. (1981). The child as a friendship philosopher: A case study in the growth of interpersonal understanding. In S. R. Asher & J. M. Gottman (Eds.), The development of children's friendships. Cambridge, UK: Cambridge University Press.

Selman, R. L., & Byrne, D. F. (1974). A structural-developmental analysis of levels of role-taking in middle childhood. *Child Development, 45,* 803–806.

Seltzer, J. A. (1991). Relationships between fathers and children who live apart: The father's role after separation. *Journal of Marriage and the Family, 53,* 79–102.

Sénéchal, M., & LeFevre, J. (2002). Parental involvement in the development of children's reading skill: A five-year longitudinal study. *Child Development, 73,* 445–460.

Sénéchal, M., Thomas, E., & Monker, J. (1995). Individual differences in 4-year-old children's acquisition of vocabulary during storybook reading. *Journal of Educational Psychology, 87,* 218–229.

Sera, E. J. (2001). Men and spousal bereavement: A cross-cultural study of majority-culture and Hispanic men and the role of religiosity and acculturation on grief. *Dissertation Abstracts International Section B: The Sciences and Engineering, 61(11-B),* 6149.

Serbin, L. A., Powlishta, K. K., & Gulko, J. (1993). The development of sex typing in middle childhood. Monographs of the Society for Research in Child Development, 58 (Serial No. 232).

Serdula, M. K., Ivery, D., Coates, R. J., Freedman, D. S., Williamson, D. F., & Byers, T. (1993). Do obese children become obese adults? A review of the literature. *Preventive Medicine, 22,* 167–177.

Sevy, S., Mendlewicz, J., & Mendelbaum, K. (1995). Genetic research in bipolar illness. In E. E. Beckham & W. R. Leber (Eds.), *Handbook of depression* (2nd ed.). New York: Guilford Press.

Shaiko, R. G. (1996). Female participation in public interest nonprofit governance: Yet another glass ceiling? *Nonprofit and Voluntary Sector Quarterly, 25,* 302–320.

Shainess, N. (1984). *Sweet suffering: Woman as victim.* Indianapolis, IN: Bobbs-Merrill.

Shalev, R. (1999). Comparison of war-bereaved and motor vehicle accident-bereaved parents. Unpublished master's thesis, University of Haifa.

Shanahan, M. J., Elder, G. H., Burchinal, M., & Conger, R. D. (1996a). Adolescent paid labor and relationships with parents: Early work-family linkages. *Child Development, 67,* 2183–2200.

Shanahan, M. J., Elder, G. H., Burchinal, M., & Conger, R. D. (1996b). Adolescent earnings and relationships with parents: The work-family nexus in urban and rural ecologies. In J. T. Mortimer & M. D. Finch (Eds.), *Adolescents, work, and family: An intergenerational developmental analysis.* Thousand Oaks CA: Sage.

Share, D. L. (1999). Phonological recoding and orthographic learning: A direct test of the self-teaching hypothesis. *Journal of Experimental Child Psychology, 72,* 95–129.

Sharpe, R. M., & Skakkebaek, N. E. (1993). Are oestrogens involved in falling sperm counts and disorders of the male reproductive tract? *Lancet, 341,* 1392–1395.

Shaw, D. S., Winslow, E. B., & Flanagan, C. (1999). A prospective study of the effects of marital status and family relations on young children's adjustment among African American and European American families. *Child Development, 70,* 742–755.

Shaw, G. M. (2001). Adverse human reproductive outcomes and electromagnetic fields: A brief summary of the epidemiologic literature. *Bioelectromagnetics, 5,* S5–18.

Shaw, G. M., Schaffer, D., Velie, E. M., Morland, K., & Harris, J. A. (1995). Periconceptional vitamin use, dietary folate, and the occurrence of neural tube defects. *Epidemiology, 6,* 219–226.

Shebilske, L. J. (2000). Affective quality, leisure time, and marital satisfaction: A 13-year longitudinal study. *Dissertation Abstracts International Section A: Humanities and Social Sciences, 60(9-A),* 3545.

Shelov, S. P. (1993). *Caring for your baby and young child: Birth to age 5.* New York: Bantam Books.

Sher, T. G. (1996). Courtship and marriage: Choosing a primary relationship. In N. Vanzetti & S. Duck (Eds.), *A lifetime of relationships* (pp. 243–264). Pacific Grove, CA: Brooks/Cole.

Sherman, A. M., de Vries, B., & Lansford, J. E. (2000). Friendship in childhood and adulthood: Lessons across the life span. *International Journal of Aging and Human Development, 51,* 31–51.

Sherwin, B. B. (1997). Estrogen effects on cognition in menopausal women. *Neurology, 48*(5 Suppl. 7), S21–S26.

Shi, R., & Werker, J. F. (2001). Six-month-old infants' preference for lexical words. *Psychological Science, 12,* 70–75.

Shirom, A., & Mazeh, T. (1988). Periodicity in seniority-job satisfaction relationship. *Journal of Vocational Behavior, 33,* 38–49.

Shiwach, R. (1994). Psychopathology in Huntington's disease patients. *Acta Psychiatrica Scandinavica, 90,* 241–246.

Shonk, S. M., & Cicchetti, D. (2001). Maltreatment, competency deficits, and risk for academic and behavioral maladjustment. *Developmental Psychology, 37,* 3–17.

Shotland, R. L., & Goodstein, L. (1992). Sexual precedence reduces the perceived legitimacy of sexual refusal: An examination of attribution concerning date rape and consensual sex. *Personality and Social Psychology Bulletin, 18,* 756–764.

Shulman, S., & Kipnis, O. (2001). Adolescent romantic relationships: A look from the *future. Journal of Adolescence, 24,* 337–351.

Shultz, S. K., Scherman, A., & Marshall, L. J. (2000). Evaluation of a university-based date rape prevention program: Effects on attitudes and behavior related to rape. *Journal of College Student Development, 41,* 193–201.

Shuter-Dyson, R. (1982). Musical ability. In D. Deutsch (Ed.), *The psychology of music.* New York: Academic Press.

Shwe, H. I., & Markman, E. M. (1997). Young children's appreciation of the mental impact of their communicative signals. *Developmental Psychology, 33,* 630–636.

Siddiqui, A. (1995). Object size as a determinant of grasping in infancy. *Journal of Genetic Psychology, 156,* 345–358.

Siegler, I. C., George, L. K., & Okun, M. A. (1979). A crosssequential analysis of adult personality. *Developmental Psychology, 15,* 350–351.

Siegler, R. S. (1981). Developmental sequences within and between concepts. *Monographs of the Society for Research in Child Development, 46* (Serial No. 189).

Siegler, R. S. (1986). Unities in strategy choices across domains. In M. Perlmutter (Ed.), *Minnesota symposia on child development* (Vol. 19). Hillsdale, NJ: Erlbaum.

Siegler, R. S. (1988). Strategy choice procedures and the development of multiplication skill. *Journal of Experimental Psychology: General, 117,* 258–278.

Siegler, R. S. (1998). *Children's thinking* (3rd ed). Upper Saddle River, NJ: Prentice Hall.

Siegler, R. S., & Jenkins, E. (1989). *How children discover new strategies.* Hillsdale, NJ: Erlbaum.

Siegler, R. S., & Robinson, M. (1982). The development of numerical understandings. In H. W. Reese & L. P. Lipsitt (Eds.), *Advances in child development and behavior* (Vol. 16). New York: Academic Press.

Siegler, R. S., & Shrager, J. (1984). Strategy choices in addition and subtraction: How do children know what to do? In C. Sophian (Ed.), *Origins of cognitive skills.* Hillsdale, NJ: Erlbaum.

Signorielli, N., & Lears, M. (1992). Children, television, and conceptions about chores: Attitudes and behaviors. *Sex Roles, 27,* 157–170.

Silverman, P. R., & Nickman, S. L. (1996). Children's construction of their dead parents. In D. Klass, P. R. Silverman, & S. L. Nickman (Eds.), *Continuing bonds: New understandings of grief* (pp. 73–86). Washington, DC: Taylor & Francis.

Silverman, P. R., & Worden, J. W. (1992). Children's understanding of funeral ritual. *Omega, 25,* 319–331.

Silverman, W. K., La Greca, A. M., & Wasserstein, S. (1995). What do children worry about? Worries and their relations to anxiety. *Child Development, 66,* 671–686.

Silverstein, J. S. (2001). Connections and disconnections: Towards an understanding of reasons mid-career professional women leave large corporations. *Dissertation Abstracts International Section B: The Sciences and Engineering, 62*(1-B), 581.

Simmons, R., & Blyth, D. (1987). *Moving into adolescence.* New York: Aldine de Gruyter.

Simons, D. J., & Keil, F. C. (1995). An abstract to concrete shift in the development of biological thought: The inside story. *Cognition, 56,* 129–163.

Simonton, D. K. (1997). Creative productivity: A predictive and explanatory model of career trajectories and landmarks. *Psychological Review, 104,* 66–89.

Simpkins, J. W., Green, P. S., Gridley, K. E., Singh, M., De Fiebre, N. C., & Rajakumar, G. (1997). Role of estrogen replacement therapy in memory enhancement and the prevention of neuronal loss associated with Alzheimer's disease. *American Journal of Medicine, 103*(3A), 19S–25S.

Simpson, E. L. (1974). Moral development research: A case study of scientific cultural bias. *Human Development, 17,* 81–106.

Sinnott, J. D. (1986). Sex roles and aging: Theory and research from a systems perspective. *Contributions to human development* (Vol. 15). New York: Karger.

Sinnott, J. D. (1994a). New science models for teaching adults: Teaching as a dialogue with reality. In J. D. Sinnott (Ed.), *Interdisciplinary handbook of adult lifespan learning* (pp. 90–104). Westport, CT: Greenwood Press.

Sinnott, J. D. (1994b). The relationship of postformal thought, adult learning, and lifespan development. In J. D. Sinnott (Ed.), *Interdisciplinary handbook of adult lifespan learning* (pp. 105–119). Westport, CT: Greenwood Press.

Sinnott, J. D. (1998). *The development of logic in adulthood: Postformal thought and its applications.* New York: Plenum.

Siu, O-L., Spector, P. E., Cooper, C. L., & Donald, I. (2001). Age differences in coping and locus of control: A study of managerial stress in Hong Kong. *Psychology and Aging, 16,* 707–710.

Skegg, D. C. G. (2001). Hormone therapy and heart disease after the menopause. *Lancet, 358,* 1196–1197.

Smith, C. J., Beltran, A., Butts, D. M., & Kingson, E. R. (2000). Grandparents raising grandchildren: Emerging program and policy issues for the 21st century. *Journal of Gerontological Social Work, 34,* 81–94.

Smith, E. R., & Mackie, D. M. (2000). *Social psychology* (2nd ed.). Philadelphia: Psychology Press.

Smith, K. R., & Zick, C. D. (1996). Risk of mortality following widowhood: Age and sex differences by mode of death. *Social Biology, 43,* 59–71.

Smith, L. B., Thelen, E., Titzer, R., & McLin, D. (1999). Knowing in the context of acting: The task dynamics of the A-not-B error. *Psychological Review, 106,* 235–260.

Smith, L. L. (2001). On the relationship between goals and possible selves. *Dissertation Abstracts International: Section B: The Sciences and Engineering, 61,* 4465.

Smith, M., Colligan, M., Horning, R. W., & Hurrell, J. (1978). *Occupational comparisons of stress-related disease incidence.* Cincinnati, OH: National Institute for Occupational Safety and Health.

Smoll, F. L., & Schutz, R.W. (1990). Quantifying gender differences in physical performance: A developmental perspective. *Developmental Psychology, 26,* 360–369.

Snedeker, B. (1992). *Hard knocks: Preparing youth for work.* Baltimore, MD: Johns Hopkins University Press.

Snow, C. W. (1998). *Infant development* (2nd ed.). Upper Saddle River, NJ: Prentice Hall.

Snow, M. E., Jacklin, C. N., & Maccoby, E. E. (1983). Sex-of-child differences in father-child interaction at one year of age. *Child Development, 54,* 227–232.

Social Development Canada (2004). *Overview: Old age security and Canada Pension Plan* [Online]. Available: http://www.sdc.gc.ca/asp/gateway. (Retrieved May 15, 2004.)

Soederberg Miller, L. M., & Lachman, M. (1999, August). *Stress reactivity and cognitive performance in adulthood.* Paper presented at the annual meeting of the American Psychological Association, Boston.

Soffa, V. M. (1996). Alternatives to hormone replacement therapy. *Alternative Therapy, 2,* 34–39.

Solano, N. H. (2001). Anxiety, depression, and older veterans: Implications for functional status. *Dissertation Abstract International Section B: The Sciences and Engineering, 61*(7-B), 3862.

Solomon, G. E. A., Johnson, S. C., Zaitchik, D., & Carey, S. (1996). Like father, like son: Young children's understanding of how and why offspring resemble their parents. *Child Development, 67,* 151–171.

Soulsman, G. (1999, March 15). Understanding hearing loss. *The News Journal* (Wilmington, DE), pp. E1–2.

Spector, A., Orrell, M., Davies, S., & Woods, B. (2004). *Reality orientation for dementia.* The Cochrane Library: Oxford. CD-ROM, CD001119.

Spelke, E. S. (1994). Initial knowledge: Six suggestions. *Cognition, 50,* 431–445.

Spence, J. T. (1985). Achievement American style: The rewards and costs of individualism. *American Psychologist, 40,* 1285–1295.

Spetner, N. B., & Olsho, L. W. (1990). Auditory frequency resolution in human infancy. *Child Development, 61,* 632–652.

Springer, K., & Keil, F. C. (1991). Early differentiation of causal mechanisms appropriate to biological and nonbiological kinds. *Child Development, 62,* 767–781.

Square, D. (1997). Fetal alcohol syndrome epidemic on Manitoba reserve. *Canadian Medical Association Journal, 157,* 59–60.

Sroufe, L. A., & Waters, E. (1976). The ontogenesis of smiling and laughter: A perspective on the organization of development in infancy. *Psychological Review, 83,* 173–189.

St. George, I. M., Williams, S., & Silva, P. A. (1994). Body size and the menarche: The Dunedin study. *Journal of Adolescent Health, 15,* 573–576.

St. James-Roberts, I., & Plewis, I. (1996). Individual differences, daily fluctuations, and developmental changes in amounts of infant waking, fussing, crying, feeding, and sleeping. *Child Development, 67,* 2527–2450.

Stafford, J. (2002). *A profile of the childcare services industry* [Online]. Available: http://www.statcan.ca/english/research/63F0002XIE/63F0002XIB2002040.pdf. (Retrieved March 22, 2004.)

Stajduhar, K.I. (2003). Examining the perspectives of family members involved in the delivery of palliative care at home. *Journal of Palliative Care, 19,* 27–35.

Stalikas, A., & Gavaki, E. (1995). The importance of ethnic identity: Self-esteem and academic achievement of second-generation Greeks in secondary school. *Canadian Journal of School Psychology, 11,* 1–9.

Stanford, E. P., Happersett, C. J., Morton, D. J., Molgaard, C. A., & Peddecord, K. M. (1991). Early retirement and functional impairment from a multi-ethnic perspective. *Research on Aging, 13,* 5–38.

Stanton-Rich, H. M., Iso-Ahola, S. E., & Seppo, E. (1998). Burnout and leisure. *Journal of Applied Social Psychology, 28,* 1931–1950.

Starko, A. J. (1988). Effects of the Revolving Door Identification Model on creative productivity and self-efficacy. *Gifted Child Quarterly, 32,* 291–297.

Statistics Canada. (1996a). *Labour force status of couple with children.* 1996 Census: The Nation Series tables. CD-ROM, 93F0020XCB96004.

Statistics Canada. (1996b). [Online]. Available: http://www.statcan.ca.

Statistics Canada. (1998a). *Average time spent on activities, by sex* [Online]. Available: http://www.statcan.ca/english/Pgdb/famil36b.htm. (Retrieved April 21, 2004.)

Statistics Canada. (1998b). *International adult literacy survey—at risk: Socio-economic analysis of health and literacy among seniors.* [Online]. Available: http://www.statcan.ca/english/freepub/89-552-MIE/89-552-MIE5.pdf. (Retrieved April 5, 2004.)

Statistics Canada. (1999a). *The crowded nest: Young adults at home* [Online]. Available: http://www.statcan.ca/english/kits/pdf/social/nest2.pdf. (Retrieved April 21, 2004.)

Statistics Canada. (1999b). *Statistical report on health of Canadians* [Online]. Available: http://www.statcan.ca/english/freepub/82-570-XIE/free.htm. (Retrieved April 3, 2004.)

Statistics Canada. (2000a). *Family violence in Canada: A statistical profile 2000.* Ottawa, ON: Author.

Statistics Canada. (2000b). *Teen pregnancy, by outcome of pregnancy and age group, count and rate per 1000 women aged 15 to 19, Canada* [Online]. Available: http://www.statcan.ca/english/freepub/82-221-XIE/01103/tables/html/411.htm. (Retrieved March 12, 2004.)

Statistics Canada. (2001a). *Aboriginal peoples survey 2001 – Initial findings: Well-being of the non-reserve Aboriginal population* [Online]. Available: http://www.statcan.ca/english/freepub/89-589-XIE/index.htm. (Retrieved March 14, 2004.)

Statistics Canada. (2001b). [Online]. Available: http://www.statcan.ca. (Retrieved March 18, 2004.)

Statistics Canada. (2001c). *Causes of death, 2001* [Online]. Available: http://www.statcan.ca/english/freepub/84-208-XIE/2001/pdf/20540_01.pdf. (Retrieved February 29, 2004.)

Statistics Canada. (2001d). *Causes of death* [Online]. Available: http://www.statcan.ca/english/freepub/84-208-XIE/2001/index.htm. (Retrieved March 30, 2004.)

Statistics Canada. (2001e). *Legal marital status* [Online]. Available: http://www.statcan.ca/english/census01. (Retrieved May 1, 2004.)

Statistics Canada. (2001f). *Marital status of Canadians* [Online]. Available: http://www.statcan.ca/english/census01/products/standards/thems/ListProducts.cfm. (Retrieved April 4, 2004.)

Statistics Canada. (2001g). *Marriages* [Online]. Available: http://www.statcan.ca/Daily/English/031120/d031120c.htm. (Retrieved April 5, 2004.)

Statistics Canada. (2001h). *The persistent gap: New evidence on the Canadian gender wage gap.* [Online]. Available: http://www.statcan.ca/english/research/11F0019MIE/11F0019MIE2001157.pdf. (Retrieved April 21, 2004.)

Statistics Canada. (2001i). *Postsecondary education participation survey* [Online]. Available: http://2www.statcan.ca/Daily/English/030910/d030910b.htm. (Retrieved April 20, 2004.)

Statistics Canada. (2001j). *Preventing substance use problems among young people* [Online]. Available: http://www.hc-sc.gc.ca/hecs-sesc/cds/pdf/substanceyoungpeople.pdf. (Retrieved March 13, 2004.)

Statistics Canada. (2001/2002). *Maintenance enforcement survey: child and spousal support* [Online]. Available: http://www.statcan.ca/Daily/English/030617/d030617b.htm. (Retrieved April 21, 2004.)

Statistics Canada. (2002a). *Aboriginal peoples of Canada: Definitions* [Online]. Available: http://www12.statcan.ca/English/census01/. (Retrieved December 10, 2003.)

Statistics Canada. (2002b). *Canadian community health survey: Mental health and well-being* [Online]. Available: http://www.statcan.ca/Daily/English/030903/d030903a.htm. (Retrieved April 5, 2004.)

Statistics Canada. (2002c). *Depression* [Online]. Available: http://www.statcan.ca/english/freepub/82-221-XIE/01002/high/region/hdepres.htm. (Retrieved May 11, 2004.)

Statistics Canada. (2002d). *Divorces* [Online]. Available: http://www.statcan.ca/Daily/English/021202/d021202f.htm. (Retrieved February 23, 2004.)

Statistics Canada. (2002e). *Postsecondary education participation survey* [Online]. Available: http://www.statcan.ca/Daily/English/030910/d03910b.htm. (Retrieved March 17, 2004.)

Statistics Canada. (2003a). *Across the generations: Grandparents and grandchildren* [Online]. Available: http://www.statcan.ca/english/kits/pdf/social/generations/pdf. (Retrieved April 30, 2004.)

Statistics Canada. (2003b). *Canada's e-book: The people; employers* [Online]. Available: http://www.statcan.ca/142.206.72.67/02/02e/02e_002_e.htm#t01. (Retrieved March 13, 2004.)

Statistics Canada. (2003c). *Caring for an aging society* [Online]. Available: http://www.statcan.ca/english/freepub/89-852-XIE/index.htm. (Retrieved May 5, 2004.)

Statistics Canada. (2003d). *Deaths* [Online]. Available: http://www.statcan.ca/Daily/English/030402/d030402b.htm. (Retrieved May 1, 2004.)

Statistics Canada. (2003e). *The evolving workplace series – new evidence on the determinants of training in Canadian business locations* [Online]. Available: http://www.statcan.ca/english/freepub/71-584-MIE/71-584-MIE03005.pdf. (Retrieved April 21, 2004.)

Statistics Canada. (2003f). *An examination of sex differences in delinquency* [Online]. Available: http://www.statcan.ca/english/research/85-51-MIE/001/findings.htm#1. (Retrieved March 13, 2004.)

Statistics Canada. (2003g). *Factors related to adolescents' self-perceived health* [Online]. Available: http://www.statcan.ca/Daily/Engish/031031/d031031b.htm. (Retrieved March 13, 2004.)

Statistics Canada. (2003h). *Health Indicators* [Online]. Available: http://www.statcan.ca/english/freepub/82-221-XIE/01103/high/region/hdrink.htm. (Retrieved April 4, 2004.)

Statistics Canada. (2003i). *Labour force, employed and unemployed, numbers and rates* [Online]. Available: http://www.statcan.ca/english/Pgdb/labor07a.htm. (Retrieved April 21, 2004.)

Statistics Canada. (2003j). *Women in Canada: Work chapter updates* [Online]. Available: http://www.statcan.ca/english/freepub/89F0133XIE/89F01XIE2003000.pdf. (Retrieved April 21, 2004.)

Statistics Canada. (2003, May). *Canada e-book: The people* [Online]. Available: http://142.206.72.67/02/02d/02d_001b_e.htm. (Retrieved October 2, 2004.)

Statistics Canada. (2004). *Health reports: Stress, health and the benefit of social support* [Online]. Available: http://www.statcan.ca/cgi-bin/downpub/pickpub. (Retrieved April 21, 2004.)

Staudinger, U. M. (1999). Social cognition and a psychological approach to the act of life. In T. M. Hess, F. Blanchard-Fields, et al. (Eds.), *Social cognition and aging* (pp. 343–375). San Diego, CA: Academic Press.

Steelman, J. D. (1994). Revision strategies employed by middle level students using computers. *Journal of Educational Computing Research, 11*, 141–152.

Stein, J. H., & Reiser, L. W. (1994). A study of white middle-class adolescent boys' responses to "semenarche" (the first ejaculation). *Journal of Youth and Adolescence, 23*, 373–384.

Steinbart, E. J., Smith, C. O., Poorkaj, P., & Bird, T. D. (2001). Impact of DNA testing for early-onset familial Alzheimer disease and frontotemporal dementia. *Archives of Neurology, 58*, 1828–1831.

Steinberg, L. (1990). Autonomy, conflict, and harmony in the family relationship. In S. S. Feldman & G. R. Elliott (Eds.), *At the threshold: The developing adolescent.* Cambridge, MA: Harvard University Press.

Steinberg, L., & Cauffman, E. (2001). Adolescents as adults in court: A developmental perspective on the transfer of juveniles to criminal court. *Social Policy Report, 15*(4), 3–13.

Steinberg, L., & Dornbusch, S. M. (1991). Negative correlates of part-time employment during adolescence: Replication and elaboration. *Developmental Psychology, 27*, 304–313.

Steinberg, L., Fegley, S., & Dornbusch, S. M. (1993). Negative impact of part-time work on adolescent adjustment: Evidence from a longitudinal study. *Developmental Psychology, 29*, 171–180.

Steinberg, L. D. (1999). *Adolescence* (5th ed.). Boston, MA: McGraw-Hill.

Stephens, G. K., & Sommer, S. M. (1996). The measurement of work to family conflict. *Educational and Psychological Measurement, 56*, 475–486.

Stephens, M. A. P., & Clark, S. L. (1996). Interpersonal relationships in multi-generational families. In N. Vanzetti & S. Duck (Eds.), *A lifetime of relationships* (pp. 431–454). Pacific Grove, CA: Brooks/Cole.

Stephens, M. A. P., & Franks, M. M. (1999). Intergenerational relationships in later-life families: Adult daughters and sons as caregivers to aging parents. In J. C. Cavanaugh & S. K. Whitbourne (Eds.), *Gerontology: An interdisciplinary perspective* (pp. 329–354). New York: Oxford University Press.

Stephens, M. A. P., & Townsend, A. L. (1997). Stress of parent care: Positive and negative effects of women's other roles. *Psychology and Aging, 12*, 376–386.

Stephens, M. A. P., Townsend, A. L., Martire, L. M., & Druley, J. A. (2001). Balancing parent care with other roles: Interrole conflict of adult daughter caregivers. *Journal of Gerontology: Psychological Sciences, 56B*, P24–P34.

Stern, M., & Karraker, K. H. (1989). Sex stereotyping of infants: A review of gender labeling studies. *Sex Roles, 20*, 501–522.

Sternberg, C. R., & Campos, J. (1990). The development of anger expressions in infancy. In N. Stein, B. Leventhal, & T. Trabasso (Eds.), *Psychological and biological approaches to emotion.* Hillsdale NJ: Erlbaum.

Sternberg, R. J. (1977). *Intelligence, information processing, and analogical reasoning.* Hillsdale, NJ: Erlbaum.

Sternberg, R. J. (1985). *Beyond IQ: A triarchic theory of human intelligence.* Cambridge, UK: Cambridge University Press.

Sternberg, R. J. (1986). A triangular theory of love. *Psychological Review, 93*, 119–135.

Sternberg, R. J. (2002). Successful intelligence: A new approach to leadership. In R. E. Riggio & S. E. Murphy (Eds.), *Multiple intelligences and leadership* (pp. 9–28). Mahwah, NJ: Erlbaum.

Sternberg, R. J., & Grigorenko, E. L. (2002a). *Dynamic testing: The nature and measurement of learning potential.* New York: Cambridge University Press.

Sternberg, R. J., & Grigorenko, E. L. (2000b). Practical intelligence and its development. In R. Bar-On & D. A. Parker (Eds.), *The handbook of emotional intelligence: Theory, development, assessment, and application at home, school, and in the workplace* (pp. 215–243). San Francisco: Jossey-Bass.

Sternberg, R. J., & Kaufman, J. C., (1998). Human abilities. *Annual Review of Psychology, 49,* 479–502.

Sternberg, R. J., & Lubart, T. I. (2001). Wisdom and creativity. In J. E. Birren & K. W. Schaie (Eds.), *Handbook of the psychology of aging* (5th ed., pp. 500–522). San Diego, CA: Academic Press.

Sterns, A. A., Marsh, B. A., & McDaniel, M. A. (1994). *Age and job satisfaction; A comprehensive review and meta-analysis.* Unpublished manuscript, University of Akron.

Sterns, H. L., & Gray, J. H. (1999). Work, leisure, and retirement. In J. C. Cavanaugh & S. K. Whitbourne (Eds.), *Gerontology: Interdisciplinary perspectives* (pp. 355–390). New York: Oxford University Press.

Stevens, B., Johnston, C., Petryshen, P., & Taddio, A. (1996). Premature infant pain profile: Development and initial validation. *Clinical Journal of Pain, 12* (1), 13–22.

Stevens, J. C., & Choo, K. K. (1998). Temperature sensitivity of the body surface over the life span. *Somatosensory & Motor Research, 15* (1), 13–28.

Stevenson, H. W., & Lee, S. (1990). Contexts of achievement. *Monographs of the Society for Research in Child Development, 55* (Serial No. 221).

Stevenson, H. W., & Stigler, J. W. (1992). *The learning gap.* New York: Summit Books.

Steward, R. J., & Krieshok, T. S. (1991). A cross-cultural study of vocational identity: Does a college education mean the same for all persisters? *Journal of College Student Development, 32,* 562–563.

Stewart, A. J., Ostrove, J. M., & Helson, R. (2001). Middle aging in women: Patterns of personality change from the 30s to the 50s. *Journal of Adult Development, 8,* 23–37.

Stewart, L., & Pascual-Leone, J. (1992). Mental capacity constraints and the development of moral reasoning. *Journal of Experimental Child Psychology, 54,* 251–287.

Stewart, R. B., Mobley, L. A., Van Tuyl, S. S., & Salvador, W. A. (1987). The firstborns' adjustment to the birth of a sibling: A longitudinal assessment. *Child Development, 58,* 341–355.

Stice, E. (2001). Risk factors for eating pathology: Recent advances and future directions. In R. H. Striegel-Moore & L. Smolak (Eds.), *Eating disorders: Innovative directions in research and practice* (pp. 51–73). Washington, DC: American Psychological Association.

Stice, E., & Barrera, M., Jr. (1995). A longitudinal examination of the reciprocal relations between perceived parenting and adolescents' substance use and externalizing behaviors. *Developmental Psychology, 31,* 322–334.

Stice, E., Presnell, K., & Bearman, S. K. (2001). Relation of early menarche to depression, eating disorders, substance abuse, and comorbid psychopathology among adolescent girls. *Developmental Psychology, 37,* 608–619.

Stier, H., & Lewin-Epstein, N. (2000). Women's part-time employment and gender inequality in the family. *Journal of Family Issues, 21,* 390–410.

Stifter, C. A., & Fox, N. A. (1990). Infant reactivity: Physiological correlates of newborn and 5-month temperament. *Developmental Psychology, 26,* 582–588.

Stiles, J. (2000). Spatial cognitive development following prenatal or perinatal focal brain injury. In H. S. Harvey & J. Grafman (Eds.), *Cerebral reorganization of function after brain damage* (pp. 201–217). New York: Oxford University Press.

Stiles, J. (2001). Neural plasticity and cognitive development. *Developmental Neuropsychology, 18,* 237–272.

Stine-Morrow, E. A. L., & Soederberg Miller, L. M. (1999). Basic cognitive processes. In J. C. Cavanaugh & S. K. Whitbourne (Eds.), *Gerontology: An interdisciplinary perspective* (pp. 186–212). New York: Oxford University Press.

Stone, A. A., Neale, J. M., Cox, D. S., Napoli, A., Valdimarsdottir, H., & Kennedy-Moore, E. (1994). Daily events are associated with a secretory immune response to an oral antigen in men. *Health Psychology, 13,* 440–446.

Storch, J. (2003). The Canadian health care system and Canadian nurses. In M. McIntyre & E. Thomlinson (Eds.), *Realities of Canadian nursing* (pp. 35–59). Philadelphia: Lippincott.

Strachan, E., Pyszczynski, T., Greenberg, J., & Solomon, S. (2001). Coping with the inevitability of death: Terror management and mismanagement. In C. R. Snyder (Ed.), *Coping with stress: Effective people and processes* (pp. 114–136). New York: Oxford University Press.

Strauss-Blasche, G., Ekmekcioglu, C., & Marktl, W. (2002). Moderating effects of vacation on reactions to work and domestic stress. *Leisure Sciences, 24,* 237–249.

Strawbridge, W. J., Shema, S. J., Balfour, J. L., Higby, H. R., & Kaplan, G. A. (1998). Antecedents of frailty over three decades in an older cohort. *Journal of Gerontology: Social Sciences, 53B,* S9–S16.

Strober, M. (1995). Family-genetic perspectives on anorexia nervosa and bulimia nervosa. In K. Brownell & C. G. Fairburn (Eds.), *Eating disorders and obesity: A comprehensive handbook.* New York: Guilford Press.

Stroebe, M. S., Gergen, M., Gergen, K., & Stroebe, W. (1996). Broken hearts or broken bonds? In D. Klass, P. R. Silverman, & S. L. Nickman (Eds.), *Continuing bonds: New understandings of grief* (pp. 31–44). Washington, DC: Taylor & Francis.

Stroebe, M. S., & Schut, H. (1999). The dual process model of bereavement: Rationale and description. *Death Studies, 23,* 197–224.

Stroebe, M. S., & Schut, H. (2001). Models of coping with bereavement: A review. In M. S. Stroebe, R. O. Hansson,

W. Stroebe, & H. Schut (Eds.), *Handbook of bereavement research: Consequences, coping, and care* (pp. 375–403). Washington, DC: American Psychological Association.

Stroebe, W., & Schut, H. (2001). Risk factors in bereavement outcome: A methodological and empirical review. In M. S. Stroebe, R. O. Hansson, W. Stroebe, & H. Schut (Eds.), *Handbook of bereavement research: Consequences, coping, and care* (pp. 349–371). Washington, DC: American Psychological Association.

Strough, J., & Berg, C. A. (2000). Goals as a mediator of gender differences in high-affiliation dyadic conversations. *Developmental Psychology, 36,* 117–125.

Stuckey, J. C. (2001). Blessed assurance: The role of religion and spirituality in Alzheimer's disease caregiving and other significant life events. *Journal of Aging Studies, 15,* 69–84.

Stunkard, A. J., Sorensen, T. I. A., Hanis, C., Teasdale, T. W., Chakraborty, R., Schull, W. J., & Schulsinger, F. (1986). An adoption study of human obesity. *New England Journal of Medicine, 314,* 193–198.

Sullivan, H. S. (1953). *The interpersonal theory of psychiatry.* New York: Norton.

Sullivan, L. W. (1987). The risks of the sickle-cell trait: Caution and common sense. *New England Journal of Medicine, 317,* 830–831.

Sullivan, S. A., & Birch, L. L. (1990). Pass the sugar, pass the salt: Experience dictates preference. *Developmental Psychology, 26,* 546–551.

Suls, J., & Wills, T. A. (1991). *Social comparison: Contemporary theory and research.* Hillsdale, NJ: Erlbaum.

Summerville, M. B., Kaslow, N. J., & Doepke, K. J. (1996). Psychopathology and cognitive and family functioning in suicidal African-American adolescents. *Current Directions in Psychological Science, 5,* 7–11.

Super, C. M. (1981). Cross-cultural research on infancy. In H. C. Triandis & A. Heron (Eds.), *Handbook of cross-cultural psychology, Vol. 4: Developmental psychology.* Boston: Allyn & Bacon.

Super, C. M., Herrera, M. G., & Mora, J. O. (1990). Long-term effects of food supplementation and psychosocial intervention on the physical growth of Colombian infants at risk of malnutrition. *Child Development, 61,* 29–49.

Super, D. E. (1957). *The psychology of careers.* New York: Harper & Row.

Super, D. E. (1976). *Career education and the meanings of work.* Washington, DC: U.S. Offices of Education.

Super, D. E. (1980). A life span, life space approach to career development. *Journal of Vocational Behavior, 16,* 282–298.

Swanson, J. L. (1992). Vocational behavior, 1989–1991: Life-span career development and reciprocal interaction of work and nonwork. *Journal of Vocational Behavior, 41,* 101–161.

Swanson, S.M. (1998). *Abuse and neglect of older adults: Information from the National Clearinghouse on Family Violence.* Ottawa: Health Canada.

Swarr, A. E., & Richards, M. H. (1996). Longitudinal effects of adolescent girls' pubertal development, perceptions of pubertal timing, and parental relations in eating problems. *Developmental Psychology, 32,* 636–646.

Swenson, C. H., Eskew, R. W., & Kohlhepp, K. A. (1981). Stages of the family life cycle, ego development, and the marriage relationship. *Journal of Gerontology, 43,* 841–853.

Sykes, D. H., Hoy, E. A., Bill, J. M., McClure, B. G., et al. (1997). Behavioral adjustment in school of very low birthweight children. *Journal of Child Psychology and Psychiatry and Allied Disciplines, 38,* 315–325.

Taaffe, D. R., Jin, I. H., Vu, T. H., Hoffman, A. R., & Marcus, R. (1996). Lack of effect of recombinant human growth hormone (GH) on muscle morphology and GH-insulin-like growth factor expression in resistance-trained elderly men. *Journal of Clinical Endocrinology and Metabolism, 81,* 421–425.

Tadros, G., & Salib, E. (2001). Carer's views on passive euthanasia. *International Journal of Geriatric Psychiatry, 16,* 230–231.

Talaga, J. A., & Beehr, T. A. (1995). Are there gender differences in predicting retirement decisions? *Journal of Applied Psychology, 80,* 16–28.

Talbott, M. M. (1998). Older widows' attitudes towards men and remarriage. *Journal of Aging Studies, 12,* 429–449.

Tamis-Lemonda, C. S., & Bornstein, M. H. (1996). Variation in children's exploratory, nonsymbolic, and symbolic play: An explanatory multidimensional framework. In C. Rovee-Collier & L. P. Lipsitt (Eds.), *Advances in infancy research* (Vol. 10). Norwood, NJ: Ablex.

Tamis-Lemonda, C. S., & Bornstein, M. H. (2002). Maternal responsiveness and early language acquisition. In R. V. Kail & H. W. Reese (Eds.), *Advances in child development and behavior* (Vol. 29, pp. 90–127). San Diego, CA: Academic Press.

Tang, T. L. P., & McCollum, S. L. (1996). Sexual harassment in the workplace. *Public Personnel Management, 25,* 53–58.

Tanner, J. M. (1970). Physical growth. In P. H. Mussen (Ed.), *Carmichael's manual of child psychology* (3rd ed.). New York: Wiley.

Tanner, J. M. (1990). *Fetus into man: Physical growth from conception to maturity* (2nd ed.). Cambridge, MA: Harvard University Press.

Tariot, P. N. (2001). Maintaining cognitive function in Alzheimer disease: How effective are current treatments? *Alzheimer Disease and Related Disorders, 15*(Suppl. 1), S26–S33.

Tatara, T., Thomas, C., & Cyphers, G. (1998). *The National Elder Abuse Incidence Study: Final Report.* Washington, DC: National Center on Elder Abuse.

Taub, G. E., Hayes, B. G., Cunningham, W. R., & Sivo, S. A. (2001). Relative roles of cognitive ability and practical intelligence in the prediction of success. *Psychological Reports, 88,* 931–942.

Taylor, M., Cartwright, B. S., & Carlson, S. M. (1993). A developmental investigation of children's imaginary companions. *Developmental Psychology, 29,* 276–285.

Taylor, R., Casten, R., Flickinger, S. M., Roberts, D., & Fulmore, C. D. (1994). Explaining the school performance of African-American adolescents. *Journal of Research on Adolescence, 4,* 21–44.

Taylor, R. J., Hardison, C. B., & Chatters, L. M. (1996). Kin and nonkin as sources of informal assistance. In H. W. Neighbors & J. S. Jackson (Eds.), *Mental health in black America* (pp. 130–145). Thousand Oaks, CA: Sage.

Teichman, Y. (2001). The development of Israeli children's images of Jews and Arabs and their expression in human figure drawings. *Developmental Psychology, 37,* 749–761.

Terkel, S. (1974). *Working.* New York: Pantheon Books.

Terman, M. (1994). Light therapy. In M. H. Kryger, T. Roth, & W. C. Dement (Eds.), *Principles and practice of sleep medicine* (2nd ed., pp. 1012–1029). Philadelphia: Saunders.

Tesch-Römer, C. (1997). Psychological effects of hearing aid use in older adults. *Journal of Gerontology: Psychological Sciences, 52B,* P127–P138.

Thelen, E., & Smith, L. B. (1998). Dynamic systems theories. In W. Damon (Ed.), *Handbook of child psychology* (Vol. 1). New York: Wiley.

Thelen, E., & Ulrich, B. D. (1991). Hidden skills. *Monographs of the Society for Research in Child Development, 56* (Serial No. 223).

Thelen, E., Ulrich, B. D., & Jensen, J. L. (1989). The developmental origins of locomotion. In M. H. Woollacott & A. Shumway-Cook (Eds.), *Development of posture and gait across the life span.* Columbia, SC: University of South Carolina Press.

Thomas, A., & Chess, S. (1984). Genesis and evolution of behavioral disorders: From infancy to early life. *American Journal of Orthopsychiatry, 14,* 1–9.

Thomas, J. L. (1992). *Adult development and aging.* Boston: Allyn & Bacon.

Thomas, J. L., Bence, S. L., & Meyer, S. M. (1988, August). *Grandparenting satisfaction: The roles of relationship meaning and perceived responsibility.* Paper presented at the meeting of the American Psychological Association, Atlanta.

Thomas, J. W., Bol, L., Warkentin, R. W., Wilson, M., Strage, A., & Rohwer, W. D. (1993). Interrelationships among students' study activities, self-concept of academic ability, and achievement as a function of characteristics of high-school biology courses. *Applied Cognitive Psychology, 7,* 499–532.

Thomas, N. G., & Berk, L. E. (1981). Effects of school environments on the development of young children's creativity. *Child Development, 52,* 1152–1162.

Thompson, L. W., Gallagher-Thompson, D., Futterman, A., Gilewski, M. J., & Peterson, J. (1991). The effects of late-life spousal bereavement over a 30-month interval. *Psychology and Aging, 6,* 434–441.

Thompson, R. A. (1998). Early socio-personality development. In N. Eisenberg (Ed.), *Handbook of child psychology, Vol. 3: Social, emotional, and personality development* (5th ed., pp. 25–104). New York: Wiley.

Thompson, R. A. (2000). The legacy of early attachments. *Child Development, 71,* 145–152.

Thompson, R. A., & Limber, S. (1991). "Social anxiety" in infancy: Stranger wariness and separation distress. In H. Leitenberg (Ed.), *Handbook of social and evaluation anxiety.* New York: Plenum.

Thomson, E., & Colella, U. (1992). Cohabitation and marital stability: Quality or commitment? *Journal of Marriage and the Family, 54,* 259–267.

Thorson, J. A., & Powell, F. C. (2000a). Death anxiety in younger and older adults. In A. Tomer (Ed.), *Death attitudes and the older adult: Theories, concepts, and applications* (pp. 123–136). Philadelphia: Brunner-Routledge.

Thorson, J. A., & Powell, F. C. (2000b). Developmental aspects of death anxiety and religion. In J. A. Thorson (Ed.), *Perspectives on spiritual well-being and aging* (pp. 142–158). Springfield, IL: Charles C. Thomas.

Thurstone, L. L., & Thurstone, T. G. (1941). Factorial studies of intelligence. *Psychometric Monograph,* No. 2.

Tiffany, D. W., & Tiffany, P. G. (1996). Control across the life span: A model for understanding self-direction. *Journal of Adult Development, 3,* 93–108.

Tincoff, R., & Jusczyk, P. W. (1999). Some beginnings of word comprehension in 6-month-olds. *Psychological Science, 10,* 172–175.

Tobler, N.S ., & Stratton, H. H. (1997). Effectiveness of school-based drug prevention programs: A meta-analysis of the research. *Journal of Primary Prevention, 18,* 71–128.

Toda, S., & Fogel, A. (1993). Infant response to the still-face situation at 3 and 6 months. *Developmental Psychology, 29,* 532–538.

Toffler, A. (1970). *Future shock.* New York: Random House.

Trainor, L. J., Austin, C. M., & Desjardins, R. N. (2000). Is infant-directed speech prosody a result of the vocal expression of emotion? *Psychological Science, 11,* 188–195.

Transport Canada. (2001). *Mature drivers in casualty motor vehicle collisions, 1988-1998* [Online]. Available: http://www.tc.gc.ca/roadsafety/tp2436/rs200104/pdf/rs200104e.pdf. (Retrieved May 10, 2004.)

Treiman, R. (2000). The foundations of literacy. *Current Directions in Psychological Science, 9,* 89–92.

Trocmé, N., MacLaurin, B., Fallon, B., Daciuk, J., Billingsley, D., Tourigny, M., Mayer, M., Wright, J., Barter, K., Burford, G., Hornick, J., Sullivan, R., & McKenzie, B. (2001). *Canadian Incidence Study of Reported Child Abuse and Neglect: Final Report.* Ottawa: Minister of Public Works and Government Services of Canada.

Troll, L. E., & Bengtson, V. (1982). Intergenerational relations throughout the life span. In B. B. Wolman (Ed.), *Handbook of developmental psychology* (pp. 890–911). Englewood Cliffs, NJ: Prentice Hall.

Troll, L. E., & Fingerman, K. L. (1996). Connections between parents and their adult children. In C. Magai & S. H. McFadden (Eds.), *Handbook of emotion, adult development, and aging* (pp. 185–205). San Diego, CA: Academic Press.

Trujillo, K. M., Walsh, D. M., & Brougham, R. R. (1991, June). *Age differences in exercise motivation.* Paper presented at the annual meeting of the American Psychological Society, Washington, DC.

Tsang, A. K. T., Irving, H., Alaggia, R., Chau, S. B. Y., & Benjamin, M. (2003). Negotiating ethnic identity in Canada: The case of the "Satellite Children." *Youth & Society, 34* (3), 359–384.

Turiel, E., & Neff, K. (2000). Religion, culture, and beliefs about reality in moral reasoning. In K. S. Rosengren, C. N. Johnson, & P. L. Harris (Eds.), *Imagining the impossible: Magical, scientific, and religious thinking in children* (pp. 269–304). New York: Cambridge University Press.

Turkheimer, E., & Waldron, M. (2000). Nonshared environment: A theoretical, methodological, and quantitative review. *Psychological Bulletin, 126,* 78–108.

Turner, B. F. (1982). Sex-related differences in aging. In B. B. Wolman (Ed.), *Handbook of developmental psychology* (pp. 912–936). Englewood Cliffs, NJ: Prentice Hall.

Tutty, L. M., & Rothery, M. A. (2002). How well do emergency shelters assist abused women and their children? In L. M. Tutty & C. G. Goard (Eds.), *Reclaiming self: Issues and resources for women abused by intimate partners* (pp. 25-42). Halifax, NS: Fernwood.

Twenge, J. M., & Campbell, W. K. (2001). Age and birth cohort differences in self-esteem: A cross-temporal meta-analysis. *Personality & Social Psychology Review, 5,* 321–344.

Tyrka, A. R., Graber, J. A., & Brooks-Gunn, J. (2000). The development of disordered eating: Correlates and predictors of eating problems in the context of adolescence. In A. J. Sameroff, M. Lewis, & S. M. Miller (Eds.), *Handbook of developmental psychopathology* (2nd ed., pp. 607–624). New York: Kluwer Academic/Plenum.

Tyson-Rawson, K. J. (1996). Adolescent responses to the death of a parent. In C. A. Coor & D. E. Balk (Eds.), *Handbook of adolescent death and bereavement* (pp. 155–172). New York: Springer.

U. S. Census Bureau. (2001). Statistical abstract of the United States. Washington, DC: Government Printing Office.

U. S. Department of Health and Human Services. (2000). *Reducing tobacco use: A report of the Surgeon General— executive summary.* Atlanta, GA: U. S. Department of Health and Human Services, Centers for Disease Control and Prevention, National Center for Chronic Disease Prevention and Health Promotion, Office on Smoking and Health.

Ucello, C. E. (1998). *Factors influencing retirement: Their implications for raising retirement age.* Washington, DC: Washington Public Policy Institute.

Uhlenberg, P., Cooney, T. M., & Boyd, R. (1990). Divorce for women after midlife. *Journal of Gerontology: Social Sciences, 45,* S3–S11.

Unger, R., & Crawford, M. (1996). *Women and gender: A feminist psychology* (2nd ed.). New York: McGraw-Hill.

Urberg, K. A., Değirmencioğlu, S. M., & Pilgrim, C. (1997). Close friend and group influence on adolescent cigarette smoking and alcohol use. *Developmental Psychology, 33,* 834–844.

Vaillant, G. E. (1977). *Adaptation to life.* Boston: Little, Brown.

Valkenburg, P. M., & van der Voort, T. H. A. (1994). Influence of TV on daydreaming and creative imagination: A review of research. *Psychological Bulletin, 116,* 316–339.

Valkenburg, P. M., & van der Voort, T. H. A. (1995). The influence of television on children's daydreaming styles: A 1-year-panel study. *Communication Research, 22,* 267–287.

Valois, R. F., Dunham, A. C. A., Jackson, K. L., & Waller, J. (1999). Association between employment and substance abuse behaviors among public high school adolescents. *Journal of Adolescent Health, 25,* 256–263.

Valverius, E., Nilstun, T., & Nilsson, B. (2000). Palliative care, assisted suicide and euthanasia: Nationwide questionnaire to Swedish physicians. *Palliative Medicine, 14,* 141–148.

van den Boom, D. C. (1994). The influence of temperament and mothering on attachment and exploration: An experimental manipulation of sensitive responsiveness among lower-class mothers with irritable infants. *Child Development, 65,* 1457–1477.

van den Boom, D. C. (1995). Do first-year intervention effects endure? Follow-up during toddlerhood of a sample of Dutch irritable infants. *Child Development, 66,* 1798–1816.

Van IJzendoorn, M. H., Goldberg, S., Kroonenberg, P. M., & Frenkel, O. J. (1992). The relative effects of maternal and child problems on the quality of attachment: A meta-analysis of attachment in clinical samples. *Child Development, 63,* 840–858.

van IJzendoorn, M. H., & Kroonenberg, P. M. (1988). Cross-cultural patterns of attachment: A meta-analysis of the Strange Situation. *Child Development, 59,* 147–156.

van IJzendoorn, M. H., Moran, G., Belsky, J., Pederson, D., Bakermans-Kranenburg, M. J., & Kneppers, K. (2000). The similarity of siblings' attachments to their mother. *Child Development, 71,* 1086–1098.

van IJzendoorn, M. H., & Sagi, A. (1998). Cross-cultural patterns of attachment. In J. Cassidy & P. R. Shaver (Eds.), *Handbook of attachment: Theory, research, and clinical applications* (pp. 713–734). New York: Guilford Press.

Van Manen, K., & Whitbourne, S. K. (1997). Psychosocial development and life experience. *Psychology and Aging, 12,* 239–246.

Vandell, D. L., Pierce, K., & Stright, A. (1997). Childcare. In G. Bear, K. Minke, & A. Thomas (Eds.), *Children's needs II: Development, problems, and alternatives* (pp. 575–584). Washington, DC: National Association of School Psychologists.

Vandello, J. A. (2000). Domestic violence in cultural context: Male honor, female fidelity, and loyalty. *Dissertation Abstracts International: Section B: The Sciences and Engineering, 61*(5-B), 2821.

VandenBos, G. R., DeLeon, P. H., & Pallack, M. S. (1982). An alternative to traditional medical care for the terminally ill. *American Psychologist, 37,* 1245–1248.

The Vanier Institute of the Family (2000). *Profiling Canada's families II.* Ottawa: Author.

Ventura, S. J., Martin, J. A., Hartin, A., Taffell, S. M., Mathews, T. J., & Clarke, S. C. (1994). Advance report of final natality statistics, 1992. *National Center for Health Statistics, Monthly Vital Statistics Report, 43.*

Verhaeghen, P., & Salthouse, T. A. (1997). Meta-analysis of age–cognition relations in adulthood: Establishment of linear and non-linear age effects and structural models. *Psychological Bulletin, 122,* 231–249.

Vicary, J. R., & Karshin, C. M. (2002). College alcohol abuse: A review of the problems, issues, and prevention approaches. *Journal of Primary Prevention, 22,* 299–331.

Vickio, C. J., Cavanaugh, J. C., & Attig, T. (1990). Perceptions of grief among university students. *Death Studies, 14,* 231–240.

Viinamaki, H., Koskela, K., & Niskanen, L. (1996). Rapidly declining mental well-being during unemployment. *European Journal of Psychiatry, 10,* 215–221.

Vinters, H. V. (2001). Aging and the human nervous system. In J. E. Birren & K. W. Schaie (Eds.), *Handbook of the psychology of aging* (5th ed., pp. 135–160). San Diego, CA: Academic Press.

Vitaro, F., Tremblay, R. E., Kerr, M., Pagani, L., & Bukowski, W. M. (1997). Disruptiveness, friends' characteristics, and delinquency in early adolescence: A test of two competing models of development. *Child Development, 68,* 676–689.

Volling, B. L., & Belsky, J. (1992). The contribution of mother-child and father-child relationships to the quality of sibling interaction: A longitudinal study. *Child Development, 63,* 1209–1222.

Volling, B. L., MacKinnon-Lewis, C., Rabiner, D., & Baradaran, L. P. (1993). Children's social competence and sociometric status: Further exploration of aggression, social withdrawal, and peer rejection. *Development and Psychopathology, 5,* 459–483.

Von Hofsten, C., Vishton, P., Spelke, E. S., Feng, Q., & Rosander, K. (1998). Predictive action in infancy: Tracking and reaching for moving objects. *Cognition, 67,* 255–285.

Vorhees, C. V., & Mollnow, E. (1987). Behavior teratogenesis: Long-term influences on behavior. In J. D. Osofsky (Ed.), *Handbook of infant development* (2nd ed.). New York: Wiley.

Vosler, N. R., & Page-Adams, D. (1996). Predictors of depression among workers at the time of a plant closing. *Journal of Sociology and Social Welfare, 23*(4), 25–42.

Voyer, D., Voyer, S., & Bryden, M. P. (1995). Magnitude of sex differences in spatial abilities: A meta-analysis and consideration of critical variables. *Psychological Bulletin, 117,* 250–270.

Vygotsky, L. S. (1986). *Thought and language* (A. Kozulin, Trans.). Cambridge, MA: MIT Press. (Original work published in 1934)

Wachs, T. D. (1983). The use and abuse of environment in behavior-genetic research. *Child Development, 54,* 396–407.

Wagner, R. K., Torgesen, J. K., Rashotte, C. A., Hecht, S. A., Barker, T. A., Burgess, S. R., Donahue, J., & Garon, T. (1999). Changing relations between phonological processing abilities and word-level reading as children develop from beginning to skilled readers: A 5-year longitudinal study. *Developmental Psychology, 33,* 468–479.

Wahl, H.-W. (2001). Environmental influences on aging and behavior. In J. E. Birren & K. W. Schaie (Eds.), *Handbook of the psychology of aging* (5th ed., pp. 215–237). San Diego, CA: Academic Press.

Walberg, H. J. (1995). General practices. In G. Cawelti (Ed.), *Handbook of research on improving student achievement.* Arlington, VA: Educational Research Service.

Waldrop, D. P., & Weber, J. A. (2001). From grandparent to caregiver: The stress and satisfaction of raising grandchildren. *Families in Society, 82,* 461–472.

Walker, L. E. A. (1984). *The battered woman syndrome.* New York: Springer.

Walker, L. J. (1980). Cognitive and perspective-taking prerequisites for moral development. *Child Development, 51,* 131–139.

Walker, L. J. (1995). Sexism in Kohlberg's moral psychology? In W. M. Kurtines & J. L. Gewirtz (Eds.), *Moral development: An introduction.* Boston: Allyn & Bacon.

Walker, L. J., Hennig, K. H., & Krettenauer, T. (2000). Parent and peer contexts for children's moral reasoning development. *Child Development, 71,* 1033–1048.

Walker, L. J., & Taylor, J. H. (1991). Family interactions and the development of moral reasoning. *Child Development, 62,* 264–283.

Wallace, J. E. (2001). The benefits of mentoring for female lawyers. *Journal of Vocational Behavior, 58,* 366–391.

Wallace, J. I., & Schwartz, R. S. (1994). Involuntary weight loss in the elderly. In R. R. Watson (Ed.), *Handbook of nutrition in the aged* (pp. 99–111). Boca Raton, FL: CRC Press.

Wallerstein, J. S., & Blakeslee, S. (1989). *Second chances: Men, women, and children a decade after divorce.* New York: Ticknor & Fields.

Walsh, E. K., & Cavanaugh, J. C. (1984, November). *Does hospice meet the needs of dying clients?* Paper presented at the annual meeting of the Gerontological Society of America, San Antonio.

Walther, A. N. (1991). *Divorce hangover.* New York: Pocket Books.

Ward, S. L., & Overton, W. F. (1990). Semantic familiarity, relevance, and the development of deductive reasoning. *Developmental Psychology, 26,* 288–493.

Washko, M. (2001). *An examination of generativity: Past, present, and future research directions.* Unpublished master's thesis, University of Delaware.

Wass, H. (2001). Past, present, and future of dying. *Illness, Crisis, and Loss, 9,* 90–110.

Waters, E., & Cummings, E. M. (2000). A secure base from which to explore close relationships. *Child Development, 71,* 164–172.

Waters, H. F. (1993, July 12). Networks under the gun. *Newsweek,* pp. 64–66.

Waters, H. S. (1980). "Class news": A single-subject longitudinal study of prose production and schema formation during childhood. *Journal of Verbal Learning and Verbal Behavior, 19,* 152–167.

Waters, L., & Moore, K. A. (2001). Coping with economic deprivation during unemployment. *Journal of Economic Psychology, 22,* 461–482.

Watson, J. B. (1925). *Behaviorism.* New York: Norton.

Wayment, H. A., & Vierthaler, J. (2002). Attachment style and bereavement reactions. *Journal of Loss and Trauma, 7,* 129–149.

Webb, S. J., Monk, C. S., & Nelson, C. A. (2001). Mechanisms of postnatal neurobiological development: Implications for human development. *Developmental Neuropsychology, 19,* 147–171.

WebMD. (2000). *What are the negative effects of stress?* [Online]. Available: http://www.webmd.com/content/article/1680. 51974.

Wechsler, D. (1991). *Manual for Wechsler Intelligence Test for Children-III.* New York: The Psychological Corporation.

Weinberg, M. K., & Tronick, E. Z. (1994). Beyond the face: An empirical study of infant affective configurations of facial, vocal, gestural, and regulatory behaviors. *Child Development, 65,* 1503–1515.

Weinberg, M. K., Tronick, E. Z., Cohn, J. F., & Olson, K. L. (1999). Gender differences in emotional expressivity and self-regulation during early infancy. *Developmental Psychology, 35,* 175–188.

Weishaus, S., & Field, D. (1988). A half century of marriage: Continuity or change? *Journal of Marriage and the Family, 50,* 763–774.

Weisner, T. S., & Wilson-Mitchell, J. E. (1990). Nonconventional family lifestyles and sex typing in six-year-olds. *Child Development, 61,* 1915–1933.

Weissman, M. D., & Kalish, C. W. (1999). The inheritance of desired characteristics: Children's view of the role of intention in parent-offspring resemblance. *Journal of Experimental Child Psychology, 73,* 245–265.

Weldon, B. (1997). *Arthritis and osteoporosis: Women's health seminar* [Online]. Available: http://www.nih.gov/niams/healthinfo/orwhseminar.htm (National Institute of Arthritis and Musculoskeletal and Skin Diseases).

Welle, S., Thompson, C., Statt, M., & McHenry, B. (1996). Growth hormone increases muscle mass and strength but does not rejuvenate myofibrillar protein synthesis in healthy subjects over 60 years old. *Journal of Clinical Endocrinology and Metabolism, 81,* 3239–3243.

Wellman, H. M. (1992). *The child's theory of mind.* Cambridge, MA: MIT Press.

Wellman, H. M. (1993). Early understanding of mind: The normal case. In S. Baron-Cohen, H. Tager-Flusberg, & D. J. Cohen (Eds.), *Understanding other minds: Perspectives from autism.* Oxford, UK: Oxford University Press.

Wellman, H. M., Cross, D., & Bartsch, K. (1986). Infant search and object permanence: A meta-analysis of the A not B error. *Monographs of the Society for Research in Child Development, 51* (Serial No. 214).

Wellman, H. M., Cross, D., & Watson, J. (2001). Meta-analysis of theory-of-mind development: The truth about false belief. *Child Development, 72,* 655–684.

Wellman, H. M., & Gelman, S. A. (1998). Knowledge acquisition in foundational domains. In W. Damon (Ed.), *Handbook of child psychology* (Vol. 2). New York: Wiley.

Wells, Y. D., & Kendig, H. L. (1997). Health and well-being of spouse caregivers and the widowed. *The Gerontologist, 37,* 666–674.

Welty, F. K. (2001). Women and cardiovascular risk. *The American Journal of Cardiology, 88*(7, Supplement 2), 48–52.

Wen, S. W., Liu, S., Joseph, K. S., Rouleau, J., & Allan, A. (2000). Patterns of infant mortality caused by major congenital anomalies. *Teratology, 61,* 342–346.

Wendland-Carro, J., Piccinini, C. A., & Millar, W. S. (1999). The role of an early intervention on enhancing the quality of mother-infant interaction. *Child Development, 70,* 713–721.

Wentkowski, G. (1985). Older women's perceptions of great-grandparenthood: A research note. *The Gerontologist, 25,* 593–596.

Wentworth, N., Benson, J. B., & Haith, M. M. (2000). The development of infants' reaches for stationary and moving targets. *Child Development, 71,* 576–601.

Wentzel, K. R., & Asher, S. R. (1995). The academic lives of neglected, rejected, popular, and controversial children. *Child Development, 66,* 754–763.

Wentzel, K. R., & Erdley, C. A. (1993). Strategies for making friends: Relations to social behavior and peer acceptance. *Developmental Psychology, 29,* 819–826.

Werker, J. F., & Tees, R. C. (1999). Influences on infant speech processing: Toward a new synthesis. *Annual Review of Psychology, 50,* 509–535.

Werner, E. (1994). Overcoming the odds. *Journal of Developmental and Behavioral Pediatrics, 15,* 131–136.

Werner, E. E. (1989). Children of Garden Island. *Scientific American, 260,* 106–111.

Werner, E. E. (1995). Resilience in development. *Current Directions in Psychological Science, 4,* 81–85.

Werner, E. E., & Smith, R. S. (1992). *Overcoming the odds: High risk children from birth to adulthood.* Ithaca, NY: Cornell University Press.

Werner, H. (1948). *Comparative psychology of mental development.* Chicago: Follet.

Wertsch, J. V., & Tulviste, P. (1992). L. S. Vygotsky and contemporary developmental psychology. *Developmental Psychology, 28,* 548–557.

Westbrook, L. A. (2002). The experience of mid-life women in the years after the deaths of their parents. *Dissertation Abstracts International Section A: Humanities and Social Sciences, 62*(8A), 2884.

Wettemann, B. A. (1999). *Bereavement and college students.* Unpublished manuscript, Oklahoma State University, Stillwater.

Whitbourne, S. K. (1986). *The me I know: A study of adult identity.* New York: Springer-Verlag.

Whitbourne, S. K. (1987). Personality development in adulthood and old age: Relationships among identity style, health, and well-being. In K. W. Schaie (Ed.), *Annual review of gerontology and geriatrics* (Vol. 7, pp. 189–216). New York: Springer.

Whitbourne, S. K. (1996). *The aging individual.* New York: Springer.

Whitbourne, S. K. (1999). Physical changes. In J. C. Cavanaugh & S. K. Whitbourne (Eds.), *Gerontology: An interdisciplinary perspective* (pp. 91–122). New York: Oxford University Press.

Whitbourne, S. K. (2000). *Psychopathology in later adulthood.* New York: Wiley.

Whitbourne, S. K., & Tesch, S. A. (1985). A comparison of identity and intimacy statuses in college students and alumni. *Developmental Psychology, 21*, 1039–1044.

Whitbourne, S. K., & VanManen, K. W. (1996). Age differences in and correlates of identity status from college through middle adulthood. *Journal of Adult Development, 3*, 59–70.

Whitehead, J. R., & Corbin, C. B. (1997). Self-esteem in children and youth: The role of sport and physical education. In K. R. Fox, et al. (Eds.), *The physical self: From motivation to well-being.* Champaign, IL: Human Kinetics.

Whitehurst, G. J., & Vasta, R. (1977). *Child behavior.* Boston: Houghton Mifflin.

Whiting, B. B., & Edwards, P. E. (1988). *Children of different worlds.* Cambridge, MA: Harvard University Press.

Whitmer, R. A., & Whitbourne, S. K. (1997). Evaluation of infantilizing speech in a rehabilitation setting: Relation to age. *International Journal of Aging and Human Development, 44*, 129–136.

Whitney, E. N., & Hamilton, E. M. N. (1987). *Understanding nutrition* (4th ed). St. Paul, MN: West.

Wickrama, K. A. S., Lorenz, F. O., Conger, R. D., & Elder, G. H., Jr. (1997). Marital quality and physical illness: A latent growth curve analysis. *Journal of Marriage and the Family, 59*, 143–155.

Wicks-Nelson, R., & Israel, A. C. (1991). *Behavior disorders of childhood* (2nd ed.). Englewood Cliffs, NJ: Prentice Hall.

Wiegers, T. A., van der Zee, J., & Keirse, M. J. (1998). Maternity care in the Netherlands: The changing home birth rate. *Birth-Issues in Perinatal Care, 24*, 4–13.

Wilber, K. H., & McNeilly, D. P. (2001). Elder abuse and victimization. In J. E. Birren & K. W. Schaie (Eds.), *Handbook of the psychology of aging* (5th ed., pp. 569–591). San Diego, CA: Academic Press.

Wilk, C. (1986). *Career, women, and childbearing: A psychological analysis of the decision process.* New York: Van Nostrand Reinhold.

Wilkinson, A. M., & Lynn, J. (2001). The end of life. In R. H. Binstock & L. K. George (Eds.), *Handbook of aging and the social sciences* (5th ed., pp. 444–461). San Diego, CA: Academic Press.

Williams, J. E., & Best, D. L. (1990). *Measuring sex stereotypes: A thirty-nation study* (Rev. ed.). Newbury Park: Sage.

Williams, J. M. (1997). *Style: Ten lessons in clarity and grace* (5th ed.). New York: Longman.

Williams, T. M., & Cox, R. (1995, April). *Informative versus other children's TV programs: Portrayals of ethnic diversity, gender, and aggression.* Paper presented at the meeting of the Society for Research in Child Development, Indianapolis, IN.

Williamson, G. M., & Schulz, R. (1990). Relationship orientation, quality of prior relationship, and distress among caregivers of Alzheimer's patients. *Psychology and Aging, 5*, 502–509.

Wilson, G. T., Hefferman, K., & Black, C. M. D. (1996). Eating disorders. In E. J. Mash & R. A. Barkley (Eds.), *Child psychopathology.* New York: Guilford Press.

Wilson, R. D. (2000). Amniocentesis and chorionic villus sampling. *Current Opinion in Obstetrics & Gynecology, 12*, 81–86.

Wilson, R. S. (1983). The Louisville Twin Study: Developmental synchronies in behavior. *Child Development, 54*, 298–316.

Wilson, R. S., Gilley, D. W., Bennett, D. A., Beckett, L. A., & Evans, D. A. (2000). Person-specific paths of cognitive decline in Alzheimer's disease and their relation to age. *Psychology and Aging, 15*, 18–28.

Winblad, B. (2001). Maintaining functional and behavioral abilities in Alzheimer disease. *Alzheimer Disease and Related Disorders, 15*(Suppl. 1), S34–S40.

Winblad, B., Brodaty, H., Gauthier, S., Morris, J. C., Orgogozo, J. M., Rockwood, K., Schneider, L., Takeda, M., Tariot, P., & Wilkinson, D. (2001). Pharmacotherapy of Alzheimer's disease: Is there a need to redefine treatment success? *International Journal of Geriatric Psychiatry, 16*, 653–666.

Windle, M., & Windle, R. C. (1996). Coping strategies, drinking motives, and stressful life events among middle adolescents: Associations with emotional and behavioral problems and with academic functioning. *Journal of Abnormal Psychology, 105*, 551–560.

Winer, G. A., Craig, R. K., & Weinbaum, E. (1992). Adults' failure on misleading weight-conservation tests: A developmental analysis. *Developmental Psychology, 28*, 109–120.

Winick, M.P., & Winick, C. (1979). *The television experience: What children see.* Beverly Hills, CA: Sage.

Wink, P., & Helson, R. (1997). Practical and transcendent wisdom: Their nature and some longitudinal findings. *Journal of Adult Development, 4*, 1–15.

Winner, E. (2000). Giftedness: Current theory and research. *Current Directions in Psychological Science, 9*, 153–156.

Winner, K. (1996). *Divorced from justice: The abuse of women and children by divorce lawyers and judges.* New York: Regan Books.

Wirth, L. (2001). *Breaking through the glass ceiling: Women in management.* Geneva: International Labour Office.

Wise, B. W., Ring, J., & Olson, R. K. (1999). Training phonological awareness with and without explicit attention to articulation. *Journal of Experimental Child Psychology, 72*, 271–304.

Wolfe, D. A. (1985). Child-abusive parents: An empirical review and analysis. *Psychological Bulletin, 97*, 462–482.

Wolfe, R., Morrow, J., & Fredrickson, B. L. (1996). Mood disorders in older adults. In L. L. Carstensen, B. A. Edelstein, & L. Dornbrand (Eds.), *The practical handbook of clinical gerontology* (pp. 274–303). Thousand Oaks, CA: Sage.

Wolff, P. H. (1987). *The development of behavioral states and the expression of emotions in early infancy.* Chicago: University of Chicago Press.

Wolfson, A. R., & Carskadon, M. A. (1998). Sleep schedules and daytime functioning in adolescents. *Child Development, 69,* 875–887.

Wolfson, C., Handfield-Jones, R., Glass, K. C., McClaran, J., & Keyserlingk, E. (1993). Adult children's perceptions of their responsibility to provide care for dependent elderly parents. *The Gerontologist, 33,* 315–323.

Wolraich, M. L., Lindgren, S. D., Stumbo, P. J., Stegink, L. D., Appelbaum, M. I., & Kiritsy, M. C. (1994). Effects of diets high in sucrose or aspartame on the behavior and cognitive performance of children. *New England Journal of Medicine, 330,* 301–307.

Woodruff-Pak, D., & Papka, M. (1999). Theories of neuropsychology and aging. In V. L. Bengtson & K. W. Schaie (Eds.), *Handbook of theories of aging* (pp. 113–132). New York: Springer.

Woodward, A. L., & Markman, E. M. (1998). Early word learning. In W. Damon (Ed.), *Handbook of child psychology* (Vol, 2). New York: Wiley.

Woollacott, M. H., Shumway-Cook, A., & Williams, H. (1989). The development of balance and locomotion in children. In M. H. Woollacott & A. Shumway-Cook (Eds.), *Development of posture and gait across the life span.* Columbia, SC: University of South Carolina Press.

Worden, W. (1991). *Grief counseling and grief therapy: A handbook for the mental health practitioner* (2nd ed.). New York: Springer.

Wrenn, R. L. (1999). The grieving college student. In J. D. Davidson & K. J. Doka (Eds.), *Living with grief: At work, at school, at worship* (pp. 131–141). Levittown, PA: Brunner/Mazel.

Wright, J. C., & Huston, A. C. (1995). *Effects of educational TV viewing of lower income preschoolers on academic skills, school readiness, and school adjustment one to three years later.* Lawrence, KS: Center for Research on the Influences of Television on Children.

Wright, L. K. (1991). The impact of Alzheimer's disease on the marital relationship. *The Gerontologist, 31,* 224–237.

Wu, Z. (1994). Remarriage in Canada: A social exchange perspective. *Journal of Divorce and Remarriage, 21,* 191–224.

WuDunn, S. (1997, September 2). The face of the future in Japan. *New York Times,* pp. D1, D14.

Wynn, K. (1996). Infants' individuation and enumeration of actions. *Psychological Science, 7,* 164–169.

Xiaohe, X., & Whyte, M. K. (1990). Love matches and arranged marriages: A Chinese replication. *Journal of Marriage and the Family, 52,* 709–722.

Xu, X., Ji, J., & Tung, Y. Y. (2000). Social and political assortative mating in urban China. *Journal of Family Issues, 21,* 47–77.

Yamagata, H. Yeh, K., Stewman, S., & Dodge, H. (1997, August). *Sex segregation and glass ceilings: A comparative statistics model of women's career opportunities in the federal government over a quarter of a century.* Paper presented at the annual meeting of the American Sociological Association, Toronto.

Yang, B., Ollendick, T. H., Dong, Q., Xia, Y., & Lin, L. (1995). Only children and children with siblings in the People's Republic of China: Levels of fear, anxiety, and depression. *Child Development, 66,* 1301–1311.

Yang, N., Chen, C. C., Choi, J., & Zou, Y. (2000). Sources of work-family conflict: A Sino-U.S. comparison of the effects of work and family. *Academy of Management Journal, 43,* 113–123.

Yates, M., & Youniss, J. (1996). Community service and political-moral identity in adolescents. *Journal of Research on Adolescence, 6,* 271–284.

Yick, A. G. (2000). Domestic violence beliefs and attitudes in the Chinese American community. *Journal of Social Service Research, 27,* 29–51.

Yonas, A., & Owsley, C. (1987). Development of visual space perception. In P. Salapatek & L. Cohen (Eds.), *Handbook of infant perception* (Vol. 2). Orlando, FL: Academic Press.

Youngblade, L. M., & Dunn, J. (1995). Individual differences in young children's pretend play with mother and sibling: Links to relationships and understanding of other people's feelings and beliefs. *Child Development, 66,* 1472–1492.

Youngjohn, J. R., Beck, J., Jogerst, G., & Caine, C. (1992). Neuropsychological impairment, depression, and Parkinson's disease. *Neuropsychology, 6,* 149–158.

Youngjohn, J. R., & Crook, T. H., III. (1996). Dementia. In L. L. Carstensen, B. Edelstein, & L. Dornbrand (Eds.), *The practical handbook of clinical gerontology* (pp. 239–254). Thousand Oaks, CA: Sage.

Yuill, N., & Pearson, A. (1998). The development of bases for trait attribution: Children's understanding of traits as causal mechanisms based on desire. *Developmental Psychology, 34,* 574–586.

Zacks, R. T., Hasher, L., & Li, K. Z. H. (2000). Human memory. In F. I. M. Craik & T. A. Salthouse (Eds.), *Handbook of aging and cognition* (2nd ed., pp. 293–357). Mahwah, NJ: Erlbaum.

Zahn-Waxler, C., Friedman, R. J., Cole, P. M., Mizuta, I., & Hiruma, N. (1996). Japanese and United States preschool children's responses to conflict and distress. *Child Development, 67,* 2462–2477.

Zahn-Waxler, C., Radke-Yarrow, M., Wagner, E., & Chapman, M. (1992). Development of concern for others. *Developmental Psychology, 28,* 126–136.

Zappert, L. T. (1996). Psychological aspects of sexual harassment in the academic workplace: Considerations for forensic psychologists. *American Journal of Forensic Psychology, 14,* 5–17.

Zaslow, M. J., & Hayes, C. D. (1986). Sex differences in children's responses to psychosocial stress: Toward a cross-context analysis. In M. E. Lamb, A. L. Brown, & B. Rogoff (Eds.), *Advances in developmental psychology* (Vol. 4). Hillsdale, NJ: Erlbaum.

Zelazo, N. A., Zelazo, P. R., Cohen, K. M., & Zelazo, P. D. (1993). Specificity of practice effects on elementary neuro-motor patterns. *Developmental Psychology, 29,* 686–691.

Zelazo, P. R. (1993). The development of walking: New findings and old assumptions. *Journal of Motor Behavior, 15,* 99–137.

Zick, C. D., & McCullough, J. L. (1991). Trends in married couples' time use: Evidence from 1977/78 and 1987/88. *Sex Roles, 24,* 459–488.

Zigler, E., & Finn-Stevenson, M. (1992). Applied developmental psychology. In M. H. Bornstein & M. E. Lamb (Eds.), *Developmental psychology: An advanced textbook.* Hillsdale, NJ: Erlbaum.

Zimiles, H., & Lee, V. E. (1991). Adolescent family structure and educational progress. *Developmental Psychology, 27,* 314–320.

Zisk, R.Y. (2003). Our youngest patients' pain – from disbelief to belief? *Pain Management Nursing, 4* (1), 40–51.

Zmuda, J. M., Cauley, J. A., Kriska, A., Glynn, N. W., Gutai, J. P., & Kuller, L. H. (1997). Longitudinal relation between endogenous testosterone and cardiovascular disease risk factors in middle-aged men: A 13-year follow-up of former Multiple Risk Factors Intervention Trial participants. *American Journal of Epidemiology, 146,* 609–617.

Zukow-Goldring, P. (2002). Sibling caregiving. In M. H. Bornstein (Ed.), *Handbook of parenting: Vol. 3. Status and social conditions of parenting* (2nd ed., pp. 253–286). Mahwah, NJ: Erlbaum.

NAME INDEX

Webb, S. J., 98, 101
Weber, J. A., 521, 572
Weber, M., 297
Weber, R. A., 586
WebMD, 497
Wechsler, D., 247
Weinbaum, E., 175
Weinberg, J., 70
Weinberg, M. K., 150
Weinberg, M. S., 358
Weinstein, K. K., 520
Weisgerber, K., 462
Weishaus, S., 436
Weisner, T. S., 227
Weissberg, R., 177
Weissman, M. D., 176
Weisz, J. R., 198
Weldon, B., 489
Welle, S., 491
Wellman, H. M., 122, 123, 137, 175, 210, 211
Wells, Y. D., 590
Welsh, M. C., 258
Welty, F. K., 494
Wendland-Carro, J., 146
Wentkowski, G., 592
Wentworth, N., 106
Wentzel, K. R., 291
Werker, J. F., 129, 130
Werner, E. E., 77
Werner, H., 104
Wertsch, J. V., 182
Westbrook, L. A., 638
Westheimer, R., 525
Wettemann, B. A., 634
Whitbeck, L. B., 346
Whitbourne, S. K., 385, 387, 408, 409, 431, 453, 489, 492, 493, 494, 495, 499, 509, 510, 538, 539, 540, 541, 542, 543, 544, 545, 558, 561, 563, 569, 596
White, J., 436
Whitehead, J. R., 323
Whitehurst, G. J., 202
Whiteman, M., 494
Whitesell, N. R., 351, 353
Whiting, B. B., 222
Whitmer, R. A., 596
Whyte, M. K., 356
Wickrama, K. A. S., 436, 477

Wicks-Nelson, R., 206, 321
Wiegers, T. A., 75
Wilber, K. H., 598
Wilkinson, A. M., 616
Willetts, M. C., 592
Williams, H., 102, 481
Williams, J. E., 511
Williams, J. M., 263
Williams, M. E., 485
Williams, S., 258, 314
Williams, T. M., 296
Williamson, G. M., 64, 590
Willis, S. L., 503
Wills, T. A., 516
Wilner, A., 415–416
Wilson, G. T., 321
Wilson, R. S., 248, 561
Wilson-Mitchell, J. E., 227
Winberg, J., 108
Winblad, B., 564
Windle, M., 368
Windle, R. C., 368
Winer, G. A., 175
Winick, C., 296
Winick, M. P., 296
Wink, P., 556
Winner, E., 253
Winner, K., 444
Winslow, E. B., 284
Wise, Barbara, 256
Wolf, A. W., 165
Wolf, M. M., 14
Wolfe, D. A., 204
Wolfe, R., 558, 559
Wolff, P. H., 88
Wolfson, A. R., 354
Wolfson, C., 518
Wolraich, M. L., 258
Woodbury, M. A., 588
Woodin, E. M., 284
Woodruff-Pak, D., 538
Woods, B., 553
Woodward, A. L., 185
Woodward, L. J., 64
Woodworth, S., 203
Woollacott, M. H., 102
Worden, J. W., 634
Worden, W., 625
World Health Organization, 94

Wrenn, R. L., 634–635
Wright, J. C., 294, 295, 296, 298, 299
Wright, K., 368
Wright, L. K., 590
Wu, C., 436
Wu, Z., 446
WuDunn, S., 532
Wynn, K., 127

Xiaohe, X., 356
Xu, X., 426

Yamagata, H. Yeh, 465
Yang, B., 281
Yang, N., 478
Yardley, J. K., 476
Yates, M., 346
Yela, C., 423
Yeung, A. S., 353, 354
Yick, A. G., 428
Yonas, A., 112
Yoon, H. S., 446
Young, A., 513
Youngblade, L. M., 213
Youngjohn, J. R., 541, 542, 545, 560, 561, 562
Youniss, J., 346
Yuill, N., 302

Zacks, R. T., 550
Zahn-Waxler, C., 152, 159
Zand, D., 420
Zappert, L. T., 466
Zarbatany, L., 287
Zaslow, M. J., 222
Zelazo, N. A., 104
Zelazo, P. D., 122
Zelazo, P. R., 86
Zhao, J. Z., 431
Zhou, Q. Y., 217
Zick, C. D., 477, 591
Zigler, E., 252, 254, 371
Zimiles, H., 283
Zisk, C. D., 109
Zmuda, J. M., 498
Zucker, K. J., 358
Zukow-Goldring, P., 279
Zung, W. W. K., 558
Zvonkovic, A. M., 446

SUBJECT INDEX